Human Development

Fourth Edition

Human Development
A Life-Span Approach

F. Philip Rice
UNIVERSITY OF MAINE

Prentice
Hall

Upper Saddle River, New Jersey 07458

Library of Congress Cataloging-in-Publication Data

Rice, F. Philip.
    Human development : a life-span approach / F. Philip Rice.—4th ed.
        p.   cm.
    Includes bibliographical references and index.
    ISBN 0–13–018565–5
        1. Developmental psychology.   2. Life cycle, Human.
    3. Developmental psychobiology.   I. Title.
    BF713.R52 2001
    305.2—dc21

                                                    00-27448
                                                    CIP

VP/Editorial Director: Laura Pearson
Senior Acquisitions Editor: Jennifer Gilliland
Assistant Editor: Allison Westlake
Production Liaison: Fran Russello
Production Editor: Bruce Hobart (Pine Tree Composition)
AVP/Director of Production and Manufacturing: Barbara Kittle
Managing Editor: Mary Rottino
Manufacturing Manager: Nick Sklitsis
Prepress and Manufacturing Buyer: Tricia Kenny

Creative Design Director: Carole Anson
Art Director: Kathryn Foot
Cover Designer: Tom White
Cover Art: Tom White
Photo Researcher: Kathy Ringrose
Line Art Coordinator: Guy Ruggiero
Director, Image Resource Center: Melinda Reo
Manager, Photo Rights and Permissions: Kay Dellosa
Image Specialist: Beth Boyd

This book was set in 10/11 Janson by Pine Tree Composition, Inc.
and was printed and bound by World Color. The cover
was printed by Phoenix Color Group.

For permission to use copyrighted material, grateful
acknowledgment is made to the copyright holders on p. 643,
which is hereby made part of this copyright page.

© 2001, 1998, 1995, 1992 by Prentice-Hall, Inc.
A Division of Pearson Education
Upper Saddle River, New Jersey 07458

Printed in the United States of America.

10   9   8   7   6   5   4   3   2

ISBN: 0-13-018565-5

Prentice-Hall International (UK) Limited, *London*
Prentice-Hall of Australia Pty. Limited, *Sydney*
Prentice-Hall Canada Inc., *Toronto*
Prentice-Hall Hispanoamericana, S.A., *Mexico*
Prentice-Hall of India Private Limited, *New Delhi*
Prentice-Hall of Japan, Inc., *Tokyo*
Pearson Education Asia Pte. Ltd., *Singapore*
Editora Prentice-Hall do Brasil, Ltda., *Rio de Janeiro*

To Irma Ann Rice
with Deepest Love

Brief Contents

Contents

Part *Four* *Adolescent Development*

Box Features

Parenting Issues

Living Issues

Focus

Preface

The story of human development is an exciting portrayal of life in the process of becoming. From conception to death, the drama unfolds, revealing an ever more complex being in the making. This story is about you, me, and everyone around us: how we began, how we grew and how we changed before we were born, during our infancy, childhood, adolescence, and adult years. As you read this story, examine your own life. Learn as much as possible about the various influences that have fashioned you into the person you are today. In doing so, you will acquire a keen understanding of the development of others. You will gain an appreciation for the factors that have influenced your friends and family, and learn how those factors have shaped their identities. By looking back and thinking about who you are and how you became you, you will be well equipped to set new sights for the future, and to adjust your own life course so that your development proceeds in the new directions that you chart for yourself.

Organization and Divisions

There are two basic ways to write about and teach the subject of human development. One method is the chronological approach, which presents all aspects of development during each separate stage of life. The other is the topical approach, which discusses each aspect of development through the entire life span. This text combines the best features of both approaches.

This life span development text is organized into five major parts. Part I provides an introduction to a life-span development perspective. It outlines the periods and theories of development, as well as the research methods used in studying this subject. Part II discusses heredity and environmental influences on development, prenatal development, childbirth, and the characteristics of the neonate. Parts III, IV, and V divide the life span into broad chronological age divisions: childhood, adolescence, and adulthood, respectively. Five topics are discussed within each of these age categories: perspectives, and physical, cognitive, emotional, and social development. While each of these dimensions emphasizes a particular aspect of development, there is a considerable interdependency among them all. Equal attention is given to these three major age groups, reflecting an emphasis on development throughout the life span. This is important because many development books will devote a majority of space to the discussion of the child at the expense of the adolescent and adult. The topical presentation within each of these age groups makes this text ideal for use in courses emphasizing either a topical or chronological approach to life span development.

Developmental Theory

The aim of this text is not to adopt and present one theory of development. Rather, it is to reflect an eclectic point of view that recognizes the wide variety of theories that can contribute to the total picture of human development, and select the most important ideas from those numerous theoretical positions. The result is a modern philosophy of human development that provides a comprehensive understanding of the theories of developmental psychology.

Development is explored as a life-span process, influenced by the interaction of heredity and the environment, beginning with conception and continuing until death (or after death, as some believe). This text examines how development can be seen as simultaneously continuous and discontinuous, controllable and beyond our control, stable and changing. There are many different theories that can tell the story of human development across the life span, and it is the similarities we find in these theories that teach us about ourselves and each other.

Features of the Text

What is studied must be relevant. This text deftly applies academic and scholarly principles to our everyday lives, personalizing discussions through the use of many *real-life examples, case studies, anecdotal stories and quotations* gathered from the author's extensive experience as a Marriage, Family and Child Counselor.

RESEARCH

In addition to the flexible organization of this book, the eclectic theoretical approach, and the application of principles to our everyday experiences, a solid research base offers an authoritative introduction to the field of developmental psychology. Over 2,000 references are included, with over 500 from research completed within the last three years. Background information on the studies is provided, but the findings are incorporated into the body of the text so that the emphasis is on the subject rather than the details of the studies.

BOXES

Special boxed features, entitled *Parenting Issues, Living Issues,* and *Focus* are integrated within each chapter to highlight contemporary issues and concerns.

- *Parenting Issues* presents practical solutions to problems in raising children and adolescents.
- *Living Issues* highlights everyday problems and issues faced by adolescents and adults, and enables students to see the relevance of the topics to their own lives.
- *Focus* discusses research findings, opinions, and viewpoints about interesting and timely developmental issues. Professors can highlight individual topics of special interest to enliven classroom discussion.

The boxes illuminate a wide range of issues and topics that are also explored throughout the text. These issues include Human Sexuality, Marriage and Emotional Development, Issues of the Handicapped, and Television and Computers in Our Lives, just to name a few. Women's Issues such as feminist methodology in research, female empowerment, self-esteem, and the changing role of women are explored. Adolescent Issues such as sex education, contraceptives, unwanted sexual aggression and teen violence are also discussed.

New to this Edition

Careful attention has been given to the task of editing, correcting and updating the material in this edition. Material deemed no longer relevant has been replaced or updated in order to provide current and relevant information.

NEW TOPICS

There are a number of new topics that are addressed in this edition, some of which are listed below:

Maternity leaves and childbirth	Sexual abuse of children
Children's inner speech	Writing
Magic and the supernatural	Child-care arrangements
Critique of attachment theory	Expression and control of anger
Foster care, adoption reunion	Adolescent physical development
Revision of SAT	
Antibiotic steroids	Correlates of juvenile violence
Relationship between physiological functioning and emotions	

UPDATED TOPICS

The following topics have been updated to include more current information:

Masturbation	Adult differences in intelligence
Population trends	
Changes in late adulthood	Adult emotional development
Sleep	
Information processing	Pregnancy
Premarital sexual intercourse	Height/weight
Middle age	Cholesterol
Adult physical development	Expression Control

LEARNING AIDS

Each chapter contains a detailed outline at its beginning. At the end of each chapter you will find a summary, a list of key terms, questions for discussions, and suggested readings. Within each chapter, the key terms are printed in boldfaced type; they are defined next to the text as well as in the glossary at the end of the book. Key thoughts and phrases in selected paragraphs are italicized throughout. The text includes a full bibliography of references as well as author and subject indexes. A listing of internet resources has also been added.

TOOLS FOR THE INSTRUCTOR

- An *Instructor's Manual with Tests* is provided to the teacher. This manual includes learning objectives, extended lecture outlines, teaching strategies, individual and classroom activities, suggested test questions, and suggested video tapes for each chapter. (ISBN 0-13-018566-3)

- *Prentice Hall Custom Tests* are available in two platforms, Windows and Macintosh, to allow instructors complete flexibility in building and editing their own customized tests. (Windows ISBN 0-13-018567-1; Macintosh ISBN 0-13-018568-X)

- *Prentice Hall Color Overhead Transparencies for Human Development* are also available and can be used to add visual appeal to your discussion of key concepts in Developmental Psychology. (ISBN 0-13-233131-4)

- *Psychology on the Internet 1999–2000* is designed to enhance the effectiveness of the textbook by helping students capitalize on all the resources that the Internet and World Wide Web have to offer. (ISBN 0-13-022074-4)

- *ABC News/Prentice Hall Video Libraries*: Consisting of brief segments from award-winning programs such as "Nightline," "20/20," "Prime Time Live," and "The Health Show," these videos discuss current issues and are a great way to launch your lectures. The following three videos are ideal for adopters of this text:
  Human Development 1998 (ISBN 0-13-888272-X)
  Child Development 1995 (ISBN 0-13-367327-8)

TOOLS FOR THE STUDENT

- A *Study Guide* provides students with chapter outlines, learning objectives, key terms, applications exercises, and self-test questions. (ISBN 0-13-018569-8)

- *New York Times Supplement for Human Development* is a complimentary newspaper supplement produced through a joint venture between Prentice Hall and the *New York Times* containing recent articles discussing issues and research. (ISBN 0-13-013998-X)

- *The Human Development Companion Website* is an online study guide providing unique tools and support to integrate the World Wide Web into your course. It can be found at **www.prenhall.com/rice**.

Acknowledgments

I would particularly like to thank the following reviewers of the first edition for their helpful suggestions and comments: David S. Dungan, Emporia State University; Kathleen V. Fox, Salisbury State University; Carole A. Martin, Rutgers University; Dr. Edward A. Nicholas, University of Iowa; Joe M. Tinnin, Richland College of the Dallas County Community College District; Karen K. Colbert, Iowa State University; Elaine Purcell, Midwestern State University; Philip Mohan, University of Iowa; Karen Caplovitz Barrett, Colorado State University; Sally Carr, Lakeland Community College; William S. Gnagey, Illinois State University; Donald H. Wycoff, Slippery Rock

University; James A. Blackburn, University of Wisconsin-Milwaukee; and Nancy Snyder, Northeastern University.

I would also like to thank the following reviewers for their helpful suggestions for the second edition: Nancy Hamblen Acuff, East Tennessee State University; Patricia Guth RN, MS, CS, Westmoreland Co. Community College; Traci Haynes, Columbus State Community College; Harry W. Hoeman, Bowling Green State University; Janet Kalinowski, Ithaca College; Paul S. Silverman, University of Montana; and Frederick Sweitzer, University of Hartford.

My heartfelt thanks to the following reviewers for their suggestions for the third edition: Harry W. Hoeman, Bowling Green State University; Paul S. Silverman, University of Montana; Cindy Miller-Perrin, Pepperdine University; Andrew Kinney, Mohawk Valley Community College; and Patricia Jarvis, Illinois State University.

Acknowledgment is also given to my children Richard Nopper, Ellen Nopper, Elise Sola, Marie Crocker, Ann Place, and my secretary, Glenda MacLachlan for their help in preparing the manuscript

Finally, my sincerest thanks to the following people for their comments and suggestions for this fourth edition: Michele J. Eliason, University of Iowa; Stewart Pisecco, University of Houston; Anne Watson, West Virginia University; Jean Peterson, Truman State University; Russell A. Isabella, University of Utah; Lauren Shapiro, Emporia State University; K. Laurie Dickson, Northern Arizona University; and Robert Bryson Lowe, Angelo State University.

My appreciation is also extended to the staff who helped me on this project: Laura Pearson, Editorial Director; Jennifer Gilliland, Senior Acquisitions Editor; Allison Westlake, Assistant Editor; Fran Russello, Production Liaison; Bruce Hobart, Production Editor; Barbara Kittle, Director of Production and Manufacturing; and Mary Rottino, Managing Editor.

F. PHILIP RICE

Human Development

A Life-Span Development Perspective

Chapter 1

INTRODUCTION TO THE STUDY OF HUMAN DEVELOPMENT

Scope

Congratulations on enrolling in this course in human development! You should find it a fascinating and intriguing subject, primarily because it is about people: ourselves and others. *This course is about the changes that take place in our lives:* in our bodies, our personalities, our ways of thinking, our feelings, our behavior, our relationships, and in the roles that we play during different periods of our lives.

In this course, we seek to *describe* the changes that take place from conception through adulthood. Information about these changes comes primarily from scientific research that accurately observes, measures, records, and interprets so that objective data are obtained. For example, one researcher may want to understand better the changes that take place in sexual behavior during childhood, adolescence, and adulthood. Another researcher may want to trace physical growth and development; another may want to measure changes in cognitive thinking.

In addition to describing the changes, we will seek to *explain* the changes insofar as possible. Why have they occurred? What roles do heredity and environment play in causing these changes?

Explaining the reasons for changes is vitally important. A parent may ask: "Why has my preschool child developed so many fears?" An adolescent may wonder: "Why have I become so self-conscious?" The wife of a 40-year-old man may complain:

> I don't understand what's happening to my husband. He used to be so dependable and conservative. He'd come home for supper every night. We spent most evenings together at home. Now, he dresses in loud clothes, bought a sports car, and has been arrested twice for speeding. He stops off at a lounge after work, and sometimes doesn't get home until 9 or 10 o'clock. He's even talking about what it would be like not to be married, and to be free again. (Author's counseling notes)

This woman needs some explanation of her husband's changed behavior.

Human developmental psychology also seeks to *predict* changes that may occur. What types of parent–child relationships are most conducive to the development of emotional security or positive self-esteem in children? What health habits are more conducive to lowering the probability of heart attacks? If an adolescent achieves a particular score on an SAT, what is the statistical probability of academic success in college?

Each of these questions seeks to predict future behavior. We need to remember, however, that general research evaluates statistical probability of something happening under a given set of conditions. The findings do not suggest that every individual is affected in the same way or to the same extent. No research predicts with 100% accuracy what happens to every individual in a group.

Once we are able to describe, explain, and pre-

One of the purposes of therapy is to help people make changes in themselves.

The goal of life-span developmental psychology is to help people live meaningful, productive lives.

dict changes, the last step is to be able to *influence* changes. If we know, for example, that we have been raised in an alcoholic family, what can we do to overcome possible negative effects? We may decide to go for therapy or join an Al-Anon group for adult children of alcoholics. Our goal is to try to initiate positive changes that would be helpful in our lives. Thus, the personal goal of the study of life-span development is *self-assessment* for the purpose of *self-improvement* and *self-enhancement* (Heckhausen & Krueger, 1993).

Similarly, the more we know about human development, especially the development of children at very young ages, the more likely we will be able to identify those children who may be at cognitive or behavioral risk while they are young enough to be able to do something about the problem to affect changes (Auerbach, Lerner, Barasch, Tepper, & Palti, 1995).

PERIODS OF DEVELOPMENT

For ease of discussion, the life span is usually divided into three major developmental periods: child development, adolescent development, and adult development. The first and last of these two are divided into subdivisions. Child development includes the prenatal period, infancy, early childhood, and middle childhood. Adolescence includes early and late adolescence. Adult development in-

Prenatal period—the period from conception to birth

Infancy—the first two years of life

Early childhood—the preschool period of development from 3 to 5 years

Middle childhood—the elementary school years, from 6 to 11 years

cludes early adulthood, middle adulthood, and late adulthood. The age ranges within specific periods differ slightly, particularly during adulthood, depending on the preferences of the individual psychologist.

Prenatal Period

The **prenatal period** includes the developmental process from conception through birth, during which time the human organism grows from a fertilized cell to billions of cells. During this period, the basic body structure and organs are formed. Both heredity and environment influence development. During the early months, the organism is more vulnerable to negative environmental influences than during any other period of growth.

Infancy

Infancy, which extends from childbirth through toddlerhood—usually the second year of life—is a period of tremendous changes. Infants grow in motor ability and coordination, and develop sensory skills and an ability to use language. They form attachments to family members and other caregivers, learn to trust or distrust, and to express or withhold love and affection. They learn to express basic feelings and emotions and develop some sense of self and independence. Already, they evidence considerable differences in personality and temperament.

Childhood

During the **early childhood** preschool years (from ages 3 to 5), children continue their rapid physical, cognitive, and linguistic growth. They are better able to care for themselves, begin to develop a concept of self and of gender identities and roles, and become very interested in play with other children. The quality of parent–child relationships is important in the socialization process that is taking place.

During **middle childhood,** (6 to 11 years), children make significant advances in their ability to read, write, and do arithmetic; to understand their world; and to think logically. Achievement becomes vitally important, as does successful adjustment with parents. Both psychosocial and moral development proceed at a rapid rate. The quality of family relationships continues to exert a major influence on emotional and social adjustments.

During early childhood, children begin to develop a concept of self.

During middle age, adults begin to feel a time squeeze as their social and biological clocks continue ticking away.

Adolescence

Adolescence is the period of transition between childhood and adulthood. During early adolescence (12 to 14 years), sexual maturation takes place, and formal operational thinking begins. As adolescents seek greater independence from parents, they also want increased contact and a closer sense of belonging and companionship with peers.

The formation of a positive identity is an important psychosocial task. The late adolescent (15 to 19 years) begins to make career choices, to seek to complete his or her education, and to enter the world of work. Heterosexual relationships are developed, along with the ability to relate in friendly and intimate ways to others.

Adulthood

Achieving intimacy, making career choices, and attaining vocational success are important challenges of **early adulthood.** Young adults face other decisions, such as whether to marry, the selection of a mate, and whether to become parents. Some face the prospects of divorce and remarriage, which can result in a reconstituted family. Many of the decisions made during this period set the stage for later life.

During **middle adulthood,** many people begin to feel a time squeeze as their social and biological clocks tick away. This stimulates a midlife crisis in some, during which

they reexamine many facets of their lives. For those parents who have launched their children, the middle years may be a time of increased freedom, because the parents can now pursue their own interests. This is a period during which many people achieve maximum personal and social responsibility and vocational success. However, adjustments need to be made to changing bodies and changing emotional, social, and job situations.

Late adulthood is a time of adjustment, particularly to changing physical capacities, personal and social situations, and relationships. Increasing attention to health care is needed to maintain physical vigor and well-being. The persistence of verbal abilities allows some to continue to grow in knowledge and cognitive skills. Relationships with adult children, grandchildren, and other relatives take on a new meaning, especially for the widowed. Maintaining and establishing meaningful friendships with peers is especially important to well-being. Many people in this stage of life report a high degree of happiness and life satisfaction, and little fear of death.

Adolescents turn to their peers to find belonging and companionship.

Adolescence—the period of transition from childhood to young adulthood, from about 12 to 19 years of age

Early adulthood—the young adult years, including the 20s and 30s

Middle adulthood—middle age, including the 40s and 50s

Late adulthood—age 60 and over

Late adulthood requires increasing attention to health care to maintain vigor and well-being.

A PHILOSOPHY OF LIFE-SPAN DEVELOPMENT

Some Important Questions

Since the study of human development covers the entire life span, the subject is very involved. Because of this complexity and of the importance of the subject, a large number of questions are asked in understanding the whole process. Some of these questions are as follows: What factors influence human development? How do these factors exert themselves, and can development be stopped, retarded, speeded up, or terminated? Do we have any control over either our own development or that of others? What aspects of control might we reasonably expect to exert, and what other factors might we expect not to have control over? Do we have any control over particular characteristics? For example, if parents hope to have a blonde daughter, what can they do to influence this process other than to get the right hair color? What can we do to avoid the development of traits or characteristics; how is development influenced by particular cultural, ethnic, or racial

characteristics; and why do some persons develop faster than others? Are all aspects of development taking place at the same time, or is there a differential time table so that some aspects of development take place before others? When certain characteristics develop, are these stable, or do they change sometime during the life span itself? Is there a relationship between various aspects of development? For example, how is physical development influenced by emotional development, or how might cognitive development be influenced by social development?

The science of life-span development has slowly evolved over the years as longevity has increased and people begin to realize the importance of every age period of life. A large body of research has also evolved that sheds increasing light on the developmental process. Gradually, there has emerged a philosophy of life-span development that reflects this increasing knowledge (Baltes, 1987). The most important elements of this philosophy are discussed here.

Development Is Multidimensional and Interdisciplinary

Human development is a complex process that may be divided into four basic dimensions: **physical, cognitive, emotional,** and **social development.** These four dimensions are discussed in this book under each of the major age periods. Though each dimension emphasizes a particular aspect of development, there is considerable interdependency among the areas. Cognitive skills, for example, may depend on physical and emotional health and social experience. The child who is in good physical and emotional health and exposed to a variety of social experiences learns more than does the child who is in the opposite situation.

Social development is influenced by biological maturation, cognitive understanding, and emotional reactions. In effect, each dimension reflects the others. Figure 1.1 outlines the four dimensions.

In describing all four of these areas, life-span development has become a multidisciplinary science, borrowing from biology, physiology, medicine, education, psychology, sociology, and anthropology (Baltes, 1987; McCall, Groark, Strauss, & Johnson, 1995). The most up-to-date knowledge available is taken from each of these disciplines and used in the study of human development (Hinde, 1992).

Physical development

Cognitive development

Emotional development

Social development

Human Development

Physical Development	Cognitive Development	Emotional Development	Social Development
Physical development includes genetic foundations for development; the physical growth of all the components of the body; changes in motor development, the senses, and bodily systems; plus related subjects such as health care, nutrition, sleep, drug abuse, and sexual functioning.	Cognitive development includes all changes in the intellectual processes of thinking, learning, remembering, judging, problem solving, and communicating. It includes both heredity and environmental influences in the developmental process.	Emotional development refers to the development of attachment, trust, security, love, and affection; and a variety of emotions, feelings, and temperaments. It includes development of concepts of self and autonomy, and a discussion of stress, emotional disturbances, and acting out behavior.	Social development emphasizes the socialization process, moral development, and relationships with peers and family members. It discusses marriage, parenthood, work, and vocational roles and employment.

FIGURE 1.1   The dimensions of human development.

Development Continues Through the Life Span

For years, psychologists accepted what now seems an incredible notion: that development starts prenatally and stops with adolescence. In the past, it was assumed that most aspects of development (physical, cognitive, emotional, and social) reached their zenith in late adolescence and somehow magically stopped after that point. Although some aspects of physical growth stop, development in terms of change and adaptation continues throughout life (Datan, Rodeheaver, & Hughes, 1987). Even in the physical sense, persons who were sickly during childhood and adolescence may become healthy adults. Emotional maturation continues, as does the socialization process. Some measures of intelligence indicate that cognitive development continues past age 60. Some findings suggest that even scores on tests of performance-type tasks requiring speed and motor coordination can be improved with practice during late adulthood. The notion that adults cannot or will not learn is a fallacy. As the life span increases, it becomes more important that adults continue learning for years to prepare themselves for new and changing challenges.

Both Heredity and Environment Influence Development

For years, psychologists have tried to sort out the influences of heredity and environment on development (Himelstein, Graham, &

Weinter, 1991). Actually, both **nature** (heredity) and **nurture** (environment) exert important influences. Some aspects of development seem to be influenced more by heredity, others by environment (Coll, 1990). Most are influenced by both. Children inherit their physical constitutions that enable them to stand, walk, and play as maturation proceeds. Poor diet, illness, drugs, and physical restriction can retard the process. Because some children are not very strong or well-coordinated, they have poor athletic ability, but practice may overcome these deficiencies. Children are born with the capacity to love but must learn how to express it.

The critical question is not *which* factor— heredity or environment—is responsible for our behavior, but how these two factors interact and how they may be controlled so that optimum development takes place. *Both nature and nurture are essential to development.*

Development Reflects Both Continuity and Discontinuity

Some developmental psychologists emphasize that development is a gradual, continuous process of growth and change. Physical growth and language development, or other aspects of development, show smooth, incremental changes. Other developmental psychologists describe development as a series of distinct stages, each preceded by abrupt changes that occur from one phase to another.

Psychologists who emphasize continuous development tend to emphasize the impor-

Nature—biological and genetic factors that influence development

Nurture—the influence of environment and experience on development

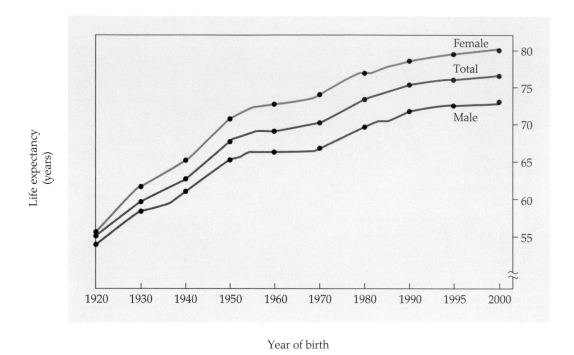

FIGURE 1.2   Expectation of life at birth, United States: 1920–2000.

From *Statistical Abstract of the United States, 1997* (p. 88) by U.S. Bureau of the Census, 1997, Washington, D.C.: U.S. Government Printing Office.

tance of environmental influences and social learning in the growth process. Psychologists who emphasize discontinuous development or stage theories of development tend to stress the role of heredity (nature) and maturation in the growth sequence.

Today, many psychologists do not ally themselves with either extreme point of view. They recognize that some aspects of development are continuous, whereas others show stagelike characteristics. Environment continuously affects people, but because people grow and develop from within, in stages, they can in turn influence their environment. (The nurture–nature issue is discussed later.) Several psychologists have combined the two points of view by emphasizing the way that individuals experience and negotiate the various stages (Neugarten & Neugarten, 1987; Rosenfeld & Stark, 1987).

Much attention has also been given in developmental theory to the problem of how continuities arise across generations. One research study compared the social and cognitive development of young mothers when they were children with the social and cognitive development of their offspring (Cairns, Cairns, Xie, Leung, & Hearne, 1998). Intergenerational development was investigated over a 17-year-period for fifty-seven women

who had been studied longitudinally from childhood to adulthood and who became mothers. The children of these women, in turn, were followed prospectively from 1 to 2 years old through the early school years. The research found that the academic competence of mothers when they were children was significantly linked to the academic competence of their children at school age. In

Some psychologists emphasize that development is a continuous process of growth and change.

other words, there was competence across generations. However, this same study, found few direct links between the aggressive patterns of the mothers and aggressive patterns of their sons and daughters. There was scant support for the widely accepted position that an intergenerational "cycle of violence" is inevitable. In other words, there was discontinuity between generations. We must be careful in drawing conclusions on the basis of one or two studies, however. The predominant explanation for spousal violence for almost twenty years has been when both husbands and wives witness violence in their own families of origin (Capaldi & Clark, 1998). Mixed findings sometimes suggest that there is often continuity between generations and that at other times, there is discontinuity in generations when certain traits or characteristics are measured.

Development Is Cumulative

We all recognize that our lives today are affected by what has happened before. Psychoanalysts especially emphasize the influence of early childhood experiences on later adjustment. Block, Block, and Keyes (1988) were able to show that girls who were undercontrolled by parents during their nursery school years—that is, raised in unstructured, laissez-faire homes—were more likely to use drugs during adolescence than those whose parents exerted more control. Such studies emphasized the influence of early childhood experiences on later life.

Other studies propose a link between early family experiences and depression or other psychological problems in adulthood (Amato, 1991). Depressed individuals typically recall more rejecting and coercive behavior on the part of parents than do nondepressed individuals. Those who recall their parents' marriage as unhappy report lower life satisfaction and more psychological distress than those who remember their parents' marriage as happy. One interview survey conducted with a representative sample of 367 elderly community residents, ages 65 to 74, showed that early experiences with parents had an impact on the well-being of these elderly persons (Andersson and Stevens, 1993).

One longitudinal study of 75 white, middle-class children from infancy to adolescence revealed that children who were excessively aggressive and hostile and who showed negative emotional states (anxiety, depression, or rejection) in early childhood showed poorer emotional and social adjustment as

adolescents (Lerner, Hertzog, Hooker, Hassibi, & Thomas, 1988). The researchers were able to predict adolescent adjustment through emotional behavior in early childhood. They also suggested that early intervention might ameliorate later behavior and adjustment problems. This study is consistent with others that show that early temperamental patterns are predictive of later social behavior (Calkins & Fox, 1992).

Does this finding mean that if we have an unhappy childhood, we are condemned to maladjustment and unhappiness as adults? A traumatic incident or abusive childhood may have serious consequences, but neither is 100% predictive of later adjustment. Countless people have emerged from dysfunctional family backgrounds and found nurturing environments that enable them to lead productive, meaningful lives.

Development Is Both Controllable and beyond Our Control

Heckhausen (1997) makes the distinction between primary and secondary control over our lives. Primary control pertains to attempts to change the external world so that it fits the needs and desires of the individual. Secondary control, by contrast, targets the internal world of the individual in efforts to "fit in with the world." The theory of secondary control would say, "If you don't like the way the world looks, change the way you look at the world." Primary control would say, however, "If you don't like your job, change jobs," or, "If you don't like the community you live in, move." On the other hand, secondary control would say, "You don't need to change your job, you simply need to change how you adjust to the job that you're doing, or you need to learn to fit into the community in which you are residing; moving won't necessarily solve all your problems."

Development Reflects Both Stability and Change

We have already suggested that the study of human development investigates the changes that occur over the life span (Sroufe, Egeland, & Kruetzer, 1990). The question arises: "Are there elements of personality that remain stable? If a person manifests certain personality characteristics during childhood, will these persist into adolescence or adulthood?"

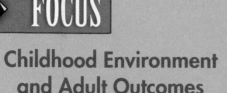

FOCUS

Childhood Environment and Adult Outcomes

George Vaillant (1977a, 1977b), a psychiatrist teaching at Harvard Medical School, made a longitudinal study of 94 males who were among 268 college sophomores carefully selected for the Grant Study begun in 1938. The average age in 1969 was 47. Childhood histories were obtained from parental interviews. Physical, physiological, and psychological examinations were conducted each year until 1955, and every two years after that. A social anthropologist conducted in-depth home interviews with each subject between 1950 and 1952. Vaillant interviewed each man in 1967, usually at home, using identical interview questionnaires.

One of the study's most interesting aspects was the comparison of the childhoods, family backgrounds, and earlier years of the men who, in their 50s, were labeled *Best Outcomes* and *Worst Outcomes*. One-half of the men who had experienced unsatisfactory (poor) childhood environments were among the 30 *Worst Outcomes*. Twenty-three of these men whose childhoods had been bleak and loveless showed four characteristics: (1) they were unable to have fun, (2) they were dependent and lacking in trust, (3) they were more likely to have become mentally ill, and (4) they were lacking in friends. However, 17% with poor childhood environments were among the 30 *Best Outcomes*, indicating that childhood environment was not the sole determinant of adult success.

Psychologists are not in agreement as to how much personality change can take place and how much remains stable. Will the child who is shy and quiet ever become an outgoing, extroverted adult? Sometimes this transformation happens. Will the child who is a mediocre student become a brilliant scholar in college? Sometimes this outcome happens. The adolescent who earns a reputation for being wild and irresponsible can sometimes settle down to become a responsible, productive adult. Not all students who are voted "most likely to succeed" actually make it. Some who are overlooked capture top honors later in life. All we can say for certain is that there is evidence for personality stability in some people, and change of personality in others. Sometimes external events of a traumatic nature completely change the course of a person's life. For this reason, developmental trajectories are not always predictable.

One longitudinal study (a study of the same group over a period of years) of IQ scores of children from 4 to 13 years of age showed that high risk factors such as stressful life events, disadvantaged minority status, mother's poor mental health, low educational attainment, or little family support in the lives of some children explained one-third to one-half of the variance in IQ at 4 and 13 years of age (Sameroff, Seifer, Baldwin, & Baldwin, 1993).

Results obtained from two longitudinal studies of adults (referred to as the JESMA studies), ages 46 to 83 at the time of data collection, conducted over a period of 17 years, revealed considerable consistency of personality traits over that period of time. There were, however, wide individual differences and unaccounted-for variances indicating changes in some persons (Shanan, 1991).

Another longitudinal study, a 22-year sequential study of psychosocial development of adults, ages 20 to 42, revealed increasing ability of these adults to solve the psychosocial tasks of each stage of life. The authors concluded that culturally based environmental effects could have a marked effect on the development of some adults (Whitbourne, Elliot, Zuschlag, & Waterman, 1992). It appears the stability-versus-change controversy is far from settled. There are many variables affecting both.

One of the reasons for these inconsistencies is the fact that early childhood experiences have declining effects as people get older. For example, family disruption, mental conflicts, and disengaged child relations increase antisocial behavior in childhood. But these effects do not generally persist into early adulthood. The results of research indicate that the decline in family effects are due to adaptation and maturational processes, so that people are able to adjust better as they get older (Sim & Buchinich, 1996).

Development Is Variable

Growth is uneven. Not all dimensions of the personality grow at the same rate. A child may be exceptionally bright, but lags in physical growth and development. Most adolescents become physically mature before they are emotionally mature or socially responsible. An adolescent boy who is physically mature with the body of a man, may be childish and immature in behavior and actions, leading his parents to ask: "When is he going to grow up?" Similarly, an adolescent girl who develops early may have the body of a woman, the social interests of an adult, but the emotions of a child. Her parents may feel very confused about her behavior because she acts childish in some ways and adultlike in other ways.

Development Is Sometimes Cyclical and Repetitive

There may be some repetition during anyone's life. A person may face an identity crisis during adolescence, and another at middle age. Adolescents may go through a period of value conflict, and as adults, may go through another years later. Entering the 30s may involve reevaluating one's life, but so does entering the 40s (Levinson, 1977). Likewise, vocational adjustments are necessary when one enters or retires from employment.

In addition to repetition in an individual life, there may be a repetition of similar phases occurring at different times in the life cycle of other individuals. Different persons may experience similar stages of life, but with individual and cultural differences. Different influences shape each life, producing alternate routes (one may marry, and another may remain single). A variety of factors speed up and slow down the timetable, or even stop the development process altogether. But where similarities in developmental phases do exist, we can learn from the experiences of others. This fact makes a life-span approach meaningful.

Development Reflects Individual Differences

Whereas there is some repetition of developmental sequences from one person to another, *there is also a wide range of individual differences.* Many of these differences are present at birth. Different infants show different amounts of time spent asleep, awake, feeding, fussing, and crying. Also, day-to-day fluctuations are found in the same infant. Developmental changes also affect infant waking, fussing, crying, feeding, and sleeping. (St. James-Roberts & Plewis, 1996). Individuals differ in timing and rates of development; in such factors as height, weight, body build, physical abilities, and health; and in cognitive characteristics, emotional reactions, and personality characteristics. They differ in social abilities, leisure-time preferences, relationships with friends, vocational interests, job competence, marriage and family situations, and lifestyles.

There are also inconsistencies within individuals. Developmental psychologists measure consistencies or homogeneity across individuals. However, they must also try to account for heterogeneity or inconsistencies within individuals (Bibace, Sagarin, & Dyl, 1998).

Development Reflects Gender Differences

There are obviously a good number of differences due to gender. Physical differences between boys and girls are most evident. If and when differences in temperament and personality exist, are these due to inherited genetic differences, or are they due to other factors in relation to the way boys and girls are raised or in the attitudes of society towards boys and girls? The development of temperament may be a function of both sex-differentiated maternal child-raising attitudes as well as constitutional behavior factors.

A random sample of 386 6-year-old children were studied over a 9-year period (Katainen, Raikkonen, & Keltikangas-Jarbinen, 1998). Childhood temperament dimensions (activity, sociability, and negative emotionality) and the mother's child-rearing attitudes were measured at age 6 and at age 9 on the basis of the mother's report. Self-reports of adolescent temperament were attained at age 15. There were some gender differences in maternal disciplinary style, and these, in turn, had a differential effect on children, depending on whether the child was a girl or boy. A mother's low level of strict disciplinary style at childhood predicted a low level of negative emotionality in girls, and a high level of strict disciplinary style predicted low sociability and a high negative emotionality in boys. This study reflects the fact that parents often raise boys and girls differently. In general, parents are less strict in the discipline of girls than of boys, and girls seem to maintain a lower level of negative emotionality than boys. Since parents are more strict with their sons, the sons are more likely to have lower sociability and higher negative emotionality as a consequence.

We must be very careful, however, in ascribing differences to gender. Many differences that were formerly thought to be a result of inheritance and of gender have been found to be a result of the differential treatment that boys and girls receive.

Development Reflects Cultural and Class Differences

Cultural and class differences also exert a profound influence on human development. (Julian, McKenry, & McKelvey, 1994). This is the case because both culture and socioeconomic status influence parental beliefs regarding desirable and undesirable long-term socialization goals and child behavior (Stevenson-Hinde, 1998). The society and the class in which mother and father are brought up influence their values, and these parental belief systems, in turn, are taught to subsequent generations and influence social development (Harwood, Schoelmerich, Ventura-Cook, Schultz, & Wilson, 1996).

Numerous researchers have broadly characterized the United States culture as "individualistic." In particular, Anglo-American culture generally stresses values associated with individualism, such as self-confidence, individual achievement, and independence. The individualism of American culture has been contrasted to a cultural perspective variously termed "sociocentric," "interdependent," "holistic," and "collective." In this perspective, the self is assumed to be an integral part of the social context rather than an autonomous unit moving within it. This sociocentrism emphasizes the interdependence between people whose aim is to belong and to maintain harmony. Both this individualism and sociocentricism will have different expressions in different sociocultural groups (Markus and Kitayama, 1991).

One comparison of Anglo mothers compared with Puerto Rican mothers found that Anglo mothers evaluated their child's behavior in terms of the construct of self-maximization, whereas Puerto Rican mothers were more likely to hold socialization goals and to evaluate child behavior in terms of the construct of proper demeanor (Harwood, Schoelmerich, Ventura-Cook, Schulze, & Wilson, 1996). The Anglo and the Puerto Rican mothers evaluated their toddler's behavior as desirable or undesirable according to their different cultural belief systems and reacted differently to specific behaviors that were viewed as consonant or not with these goals and values. Thus, Anglo mothers used active play as a sign of qualities that were contained within the self-maximization construct (independence, boldness, curiosity) but also perceived such behaviors to be relatively more desirable than did the Puerto Rican mothers. In contrast, the Puerto Rican mothers not only viewed waiting for permission before playing with toys in a public setting as a sign of qualities that were contained within the proper demeanor construct (respectfulness, quietness, attentiveness) but also perceived such behavior to be relatively more desirable than did the Anglo mothers.

A common cause of sociocultural differences in parental beliefs is socioeconomic status. Typically, studies have found middle-class parents to be more likely to view their children as active processors of information rather than as passive recipients of direct instruction and to emphasize self-direction and initiative over conformity to authority. These class differences are generally held to facilitate greater social competence among middle-class compared with lower-class children. In this case, it is differences in socioeconomic status that account for differences in social development and social competence.

Comparisons of Asian cultures with Western cultures also emphasize some of the same differences in values. Asian cultures often reflect traditions that emphasize the group over the individual, and cooperation over competition and dominance. Western cultures place greater emphasis on attending to the self. A comparison of Japanese and United States preschool students' responses to conflict and distress highlighted these differences. U.S. children showed more anger, more aggressive behavior and language, and underregulation of emotion than did Japanese children. U.S. mothers were more likely to encourage children's emotional expression, whereas Japanese mothers emphasized psychological discipline, through reasoning and guilt and anxiety induction. These findings suggest that at a very early age, children from Japanese and U.S. cultures have different scripts for responding to interpersonal dilemmas (Zahn-Waxler, Friedman, Cole, Mizuta, & Hiruma, 1996).

Cross-cultural differences exist also in social time clocks. A girl may be betrothed at age 13 in a primitive society, be a mother at 14, and be a widow at 30 or 35, whereas these events usually come at later ages in industrial societies. Each society prescribes an ideal time for assuming various responsibilities and for the bestowal of privileges, but these ages differ from one culture to another. During adulthood, age has become a poor predictor of the timing of life events: pregnancy, family status, health, work status, interests, and activities. Cultural variations are more determinative than chronological age (Neugarten & Neugarten, 1987).

Developmental Influences Are Reciprocal

Psychologists used to emphasize the influence of adults and environment on children. Now the emphasis is also on how the differ-

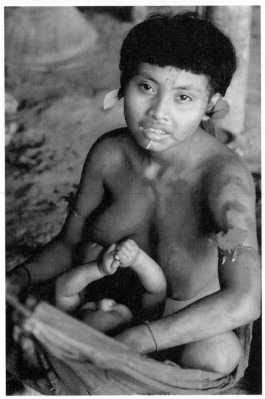

Cultural differences exert a profound influence on how parents and children relate to one another.

ence in children can influence caregivers (Scarr, 1992). Rather than being passive recipients of care, infants and children are active, influential partners in their interactions with the people around them. A placid, pleasant, easy-to-care-for child may have a very positive influence on parents, encouraging them to act in a friendly, warm, and loving manner; but an overactive, temperamental, hard-to-care-for child who is easily upset may stimulate parents to be hostile, short-tempered, and rejecting. From this point of view, children—however involuntarily—are partly responsible for creating their own environments. And because of individual differences, different people, at different developmental stages, interpret and act on their environments in differing ways that create different experiences for each person.

RESEARCH IN HUMAN DEVELOPMENT: THE SCIENTIFIC METHOD

Psychologists use scientific methods to obtain information on human development. The **scientific method** involves four major steps:

1. Formulate the problem to be solved or the question to be answered.
2. Develop a hypothesis in the form of a proposition to be tested.
3. Test the hypothesis through research to determine the truth or fallacy of the proposition.
4. Draw conclusions and state them in the form of a theory that explains the data or facts observed.

The conclusions of the study are usually published in scientific journals. Other scientists may seek to replicate the findings of the study, or to clarify the conclusions further to increase their knowledge about the subject.

DATA COLLECTION METHODS

Before a hypothesis can be tested, the researcher must gather as much data about it as possible. The primary data-gathering techniques are naturalistic observation, interviews, questionnaires, case studies, and standardized testing.

Scientific method—series of steps used to obtain accurate data; these include formulating the problem, developing a hypothesis, testing the hypothesis, and drawing conclusions that are stated in the form of a theory

Naturalistic Observation

Yogi Berra, the famous New York Yankee catcher, captured the sentiments of observational researchers when he said, "You can see a lot just by watching" (Markman, Leber, Cordova, & St. Peters, 1995).

Naturalistic observation involves watching people in natural environments (such as at home, in school, in a neighborhood, in a park, in a shopping center, or at a party), and then recording their behavior without making any effort to manipulate the situation. This approach provides information about what is happening, but not why or how it is happening, or how the behavior might change under a different set of circumstances. Because observers make no effort to influence what is happening, they are limited to recording what they see.

Interviews

Because **interviews** are conducted face-to-face, much detailed and personal information can be obtained with probing follow-up questions to clarify responses. Interviews review feelings, emotions, and attitudes, all of which are sometimes more important than factual information. Another advantage is that it is a flexible method so that a broad range of subjects may be explored, depending on the needs of the interviewer. Questions may be predetermined and the same ones asked of everyone to be certain to obtain information on the same topic from each person.

This technique has some disadvantages. Interviews are time-consuming and expensive, and usually involve only a limited number of subjects. The success of the interview depends on the ability of the interviewer to establish a rapport with the subject and to encourage self-disclosure.

Some subjects are less verbal than others, making it difficult for the interviewer to obtain information. Sometimes subjects give false data, simply because they don't remember accurately. Interviewers need training in how to be both objective and professional. Because of biases, an interviewer might distort or misunderstand a subject's responses. In spite of this disadvantage, the technique continues to be a rich source of information for researchers.

Questionnaires and Checklists

One frequently used method in human development research is the survey method, by which one gathers information through **questionnaires.** They may be used to obtain relevant information from older children and adolescents. Subjects may be asked to fill out a written questionnaire. At other times, an interviewer asks questions verbally and then records the responses. One advantage of questionnaires is that large numbers of people may be surveyed fairly easily through the mail or in large groups, with a minimum expense, and data are standardized and easy to summarize. Because questionnaires are given anonymously, people usually respond honestly. However, questions can be misunderstood, and wrong answers can be obtained. If the researchers omit significant questions, they may not receive some important information. Checklists provide a short form of questionnaires that obtain data easily and quickly.

Case Studies

Case studies are a means of summarizing data rather than a technique for obtaining information. They involve longitudinal investigations of individuals rather than groups of subjects. Counseling, school, and clinical psychologists use case studies frequently in summarizing data as a foundation for treatment in emotionally disturbed individuals. However, the method is used also to do in-depth studies of normal individuals. The primary drawback of this approach is that data obtained about individuals may not be applicable to other persons. Conclusions about groups of people cannot be made from a sample size of one person.

Standardized Testing

Psychologists have developed a wide variety of **tests** to measure specific characteristics. Tests include those for intelligence, aptitude, achievement, vocational interests, and personality; there are also diagnostic tests, and a wide variety of others. Tests have a high **validity** if they measure what they claim to measure. If a test is supposed to measure intelligence, it has a high validity if it predicts performance on tasks that most people agree require intelligence. A test has high **reliability** if the same scores are obtained when the test is administered on two or more occasions, or by two or more examiners. If the scores change from one testing to the next, the test may not be a reliable means of evaluation.

Tests are usually used in addition to other means of obtaining data. Tests can be a valuable source of information, but are most

Naturalistic observation—research conducted in a natural setting by watching and recording behavior

Interviews—research method conducted face-to-face between an interviewer and subject where information is obtained through recorded responses to questions

Questionnaires—research method whereby the subject writes out answers to written questions

Case studies—research method involving in-depth, longitudinal investigations and records of individuals

Tests—research instruments used to measure specific characteristics such as intelligence, aptitude, achievement, vocational interests, personality traits, and so forth

Validity

Reliability

helpful when supplemented by data from other sources. Many colleges require scores on SATs as a basis for admission, but they also evaluate high school grades, class standings, letters of recommendation, interviews, and essays.

SAMPLING

The **sample** (the group of subjects chosen) is an important consideration in research. **Random samples** are often taken from groups enlisted for study. A truly **representative sample** of a population includes the same percentages of people from the different cultural, ethnic, socioeconomic, and educational backgrounds as contained in the population. In addition, sufficient numbers are necessary to be representative of a much larger group. Practical considerations often prohibit such a sampling. However, researchers have to be careful not to generalize to apply their findings to groups that are different from those studied.

EXPERIMENTAL METHODS

Procedure

Experimental methods are closely controlled procedures whereby the experimenter manipulates variables to determine how they affect one another. Changes are compared with those in control groups that have not been exposed to the variables. Because the experimenter changes the variables, a link between cause and effect is more easily established than by other methods. Experiments can be conducted in a laboratory, in the field, or as part of a subject's everyday experience. Laboratory experiments are usually easiest to conduct because they permit a high degree of control over the situation.

Suppose, for example, we wanted to observe attachment behavior and separation anxiety in three different ages of children attending nursery school for the first time. The population of 15 children is divided into three age groups—2-year-olds, 3-year-olds, and 4-year-olds—and each separate group of 5 children is brought into the nursery room along with their parents. We might want to keep changing the situation, or altering the variables, as follows:

- Observe the children with both parents present.

- Observe the children when the mother leaves the room.
- Observe the children when the father leaves the room.
- Observe the children when both parents leave the room, but with a teacher present.

We might compare the behavior of these children with a control group that had attended the nursery school continuously for one month. We might want to compare the behavior of the boys and girls. And we certainly would want to compare the behavior of the children of different age groups. A number of variables might be introduced. For example, would there be any difference in the reaction of the children whose parents sneaked out without telling them, compared with children whose parents explained that they were going to leave?

Independent and Dependent Variables

Note that in the previous example, both independent and dependent variables are used. The **independent variable** is the variable over which the experimenter has direct control. The **dependent variable** is so named because it changes as a result of changes in the independent variable. In this case, the independent variable is the changing situation under which the children are observed—both parents present, only the mother present, and so forth. The dependent variable in the example is the behavior and separation anxiety experienced by the children. The purpose of the experiment is to change the independent variable to determine how that change affects the dependent variable (the behavior and separation anxiety of the children).

In another example, suppose that an experimenter wants to sort out social and demographic factors that increase or decrease the probability of divorce. The experimenter decides to test a selected number of independent variables: age, religion, race, socioeconomic status, geographic area of residence, and parental divorce. By looking at one independent variable at a time, and establishing correlations with the dependent variable, the researcher is able to show the relationship of each independent variable to the dependent variable (the probability of divorce). By changing one variable at a time while holding the others constant, the researcher can sort out the variables that exert the most influence.

Sample

Random sample

Representative sample

Experimental methods—methods of gathering scientific data, in which procedures are closely controlled and the experimenter manipulates variables to determine how one affects the other

Independent variable—in an experiment, a factor that is manipulated or controlled by the experimenter to determine its effect on the subjects' behavior

Dependent variable—in an experiment, a factor that is influenced by the independent or manipulated variable

FOCUS

Feminist Methodology

One of the criticisms of human development research has been the lack of emphasis on women's lives. Linda Thompson of the University of Wisconsin–Madison addresses the concerns in a revealing article emphasizing the importance of conducting research *on* women and research *for* women (Thompson, 1992). She writes as follows:

Research *on* women aims to document and correct for sexism. Feminists compile evidence to show what is amiss in the way women are treated in various social institutions, including marriage and family. Beside documenting sexual inequality, research *on* women fills in the gaps in our knowledge about women. . . . Feminists who do research *on* women hope to sensitize people to the reality of women's lives, including sexism and social injustice (p. 4).

Research *for* women is consciously aimed at emancipating women and enhancing their lives (p. 4).

Feminists believe that social justice should characterize the process of doing research. . . . Everyone is treated of equal worth, and differences are respected. . . . People have the right to define their selves and their situations apart from the standards, constraints, demands, and agendas of others. . . . An ethic of compassion and care should also characterize our research. We should be attentive and actively promote the well-being of participants (p. 16).

Establishing Relationships: Correlational Studies

One way of evaluating data, once obtained, is to establish the degree of **correlation** between variables (Green, 1992). When a correlation exists, there is a relationship, or association, between the variables. Correlation is indicated statistically from −1.0 to +1.0. Minus 1 indicates a completely negative association: When one variable increases, the other decreases. Plus 1 indicates a completely positive association: When one variable increases, the other also increases. Zero means there is no correlation or relationship at all. Correlation coefficients are expressed in r values from −1 to +1. A correlation of +.8 is not twice the correlation of +.4 (because the relationships are not linear), but it would indicate a high degree of positive association.

Researchers have established a great number of correlations relating to human development. There is a positive correlation between children's exposure to violence on television and showing aggression themselves (Tooth,

1985). There is a negative correlation between the degree of religiousness of adolescents and premarital sexual permissiveness (Fisher & Hall, 1988). There is a positive correlation between education and income of adults (U.S. Bureau of the Census, 1998).

Correlation is an important concept, but it does not indicate causation. A relationship between A and B does not mean that A causes B, or B causes A. Both A and B may be caused by other factors. For years, for example, psychologists showed a relationship between broken homes and delinquency. But does this mean that divorce causes delinquency? Not necessarily. There may be other variables that need to be taken into consideration. For example, divorce may follow family conflict. And there has been research indicating that family conflict contributes to delinquency, whether divorce has occurred or not (Demo & Acock, 1988). In addition, there are many other factors that may accompany divorce. After divorce, some mothers with custody of their children may be forced to live in poverty, in poor sections of town with high crime rates. The mothers have to go out to work and leave their children unsupervised. Their children are not as likely to complete their education as they would be in intact families. Any one of these factors, and not the divorce alone, may have some relationship to delinquency. We need to be careful, therefore, not to assume that because there are correlations, causes are also established.

RESEARCH DESIGNS

Age, Cohort, and Time of Testing

Researchers seek to design their studies very carefully to provide the information that is wanted. One common goal is to discover changes that take place. If changes are noted as people age, is age responsible, or are there other causes? One cause may relate to a cohort. A **cohort** consists of a group of people born during the same time period, for example, during 1960–1965. There may be significant differences among people born at different time periods, not because of differences in their ages, but because of the different economic and social conditions under which they grew up. Similarly, time of testing may influence results. If we were to measure life satisfaction of an older group of adults during a recession, and later were to measure life satisfaction of a younger group of adults during an economic boom, and found that the younger group reported higher life satisfac-

Correlation—the extent to which two factors are associated or related to one another

Cohort—group of subjects born during the same time period

tion than the older group, is this finding a result of the younger age or of the differences in time of testing? Researchers seek to sort out exact causes.

The three basic research designs are (1) cross-sectional studies, (2) longitudinal studies, and (3) sequential studies. Each design has its own characteristics.

Cross-Sectional Studies

A **cross-sectional study** compares one age group, or cohort, with another age group at one time of testing. For example a cross-sectional study conducted in 2000 might compare four groups of cohorts: those born in 1940, with those born in 1945, 1950, and 1955. As illustrated in Figure 1.3, group D (45-year-olds born in 1955) would be compared with group G (50-year-olds born in 1950) with group I (55-year-olds born in 1945) with group J (60-year-olds born in 1940). This method measures the different age groups during one testing period and compares these groups to determine differences. As shown, comparisons of groups C, F, and H during 1995, or groups B and E during 1990, would also represent cross-sectional studies.

The chief advantage of the cross-sectional approach is that data for different age groups can be obtained over the same time period, usually a brief one. Therefore, it is easier to obtain information and conclude the study fairly quickly. But this method makes it difficult to determine the exact cause of any detected age differences. For example, if intellectual decline is found, is it due to physical and mental deterioration with age, or to the life situation of the older groups? Up to now, older adults generally have less education and also perform less effectively on intellectual tests than do younger adults. Because of this difference in education between the two groups, cross-sectional studies exaggerate intellectual decline with age. What cross-sectional studies often attribute to age may in fact be due to cohort effects. Furthermore, comparing a sampling of 20-year-olds with a sampling of persons over 40 fails to show changes occurring in the intervening years. Are those changes gradual, sudden, or concentrated at specific ages?

Longitudinal Studies

Longitudinal research studies one group of people repeatedly over a period of years. For example, a select group might be studied at

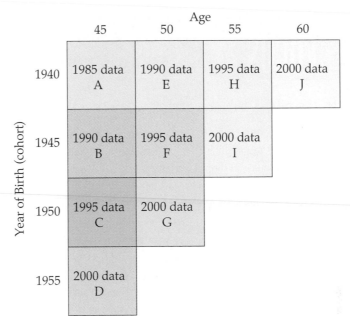

FIGURE 1.3   Research designs.

Within the figure:

Age: 45, 50, 55, 60

Year of Birth (cohort):

1940 — 1985 data A | 1990 data E | 1995 data H | 2000 data J
1945 — 1990 data B | 1995 data F | 2000 data I
1950 — 1995 data C | 2000 data G
1955 — 2000 data D

Cross-Sectional Studies
   2000 Study: DGIJ
   1995 Study: CFH
   1990 Study: BE

Longitudinal Studies
   Groups AEHJ in 1985, 1990, 1995, and 2000
   Groups BFI in 1990, 1995, and 2000
   Groups CG in 1995 and 2000

ages 45, 50, 55, and 60. Referring to Figure 1.3, if the group of adults born in 1940 were studied during 1985, 1990, 1995, and 2000 (those groups labeled A, E, H, J), the study would be longitudinal. Similarly, a study of the 1945 cohort during 1990, 1995, and 2000 (groups B, F, I), at ages 45, 50, and 55, or of the 1950 cohort during 1995 and 2000 (groups C, G), would be longitudinal as well.

A *longitudinal study* periodically compares the same group of people over the years. Obvious difficulties are the amount of time and money necessary to complete the study. In addition, researchers might die or lose interest. And subjects might move, leaving no address, or otherwise become unavailable. Some might even die before the study is completed. There is therefore a selective subject dropout and availability factor: Subjects who tend to perform poorly become less available over time than those who perform well. As time passes, the most competent subjects remain, tending to minimize any effect of age on intellectual decline.

Cross-sectional study—comparing one age group with others at one time of testing

Longitudinal research—the repeated measurement of a group of subjects over a period of years

FOCUS

Research with Children

The *Society for Research in Child Development* has issued a set of guidelines for research with children (Cooke, 1982). Research on children raises sensitive issues, since minor children have a limited ability to give informed consent. *The Belmont Report* of the Department of Health and Human Services (1979) identifies three elements of adequate informed consent: *information, comprehension,* and *voluntariness.* Children of very young ages cannot meet the criteria of informed consent. One ethics panel has stated that children age 7 or over should be asked for their consent and should be overruled only if the research promises direct benefit to the child (National Commission for the Protection of Human Biomedical and Behavioral Research, 1978). One research study found that, in general, children of ages 5 to 12 have the capacity to assent meaningfully to participation in research, but that there are substantial problems in guaranteeing that they are able to make this decision freely (Abramovitch, Freedman, Thoden, & Nikolich, 1991). When parents and guardians are empowered to decide whether minors will be used as research subjects, they must decide what is in the best interests of the children. Researchers, too, have a responsibility to proceed objectively and as humanely as possible. They have a responsibility for the welfare of the children (Heatherington, Friendlander, & Johnson, 1989).

an 11-year period (ages 10 to 21) achieved in only five years of research.

Cross-Cultural Research

In recent years, interest in cross-cultural research has continued to grow. There are many benefits from this growing interest. One important contribution is the documentation of the diverse culturally structured environments in which people develop. Such documentation gives us insight into larger patterns of cultural organization and captures the diversity of human experience. Knowledge of the spectrum of environments for healthy development provides reconsideration of developmental theories that reflect only a middle-class Western way of life (Harkness, 1992).

Ethical Issues in Research

A number of ethical issues are important in human development research. The ethical standards of the *American Psychological Association (APA)* and the *American Sociological Association (ASA)* insist on two fundamental principles: *informed consent* and *protection from harm* (American Psychological Association, 1982). Informed consent entitles subjects to a complete explanation of the nature, purpose, and methods of the research before the study begins. Subjects also must be told exactly what will happen and what they agree to do if they participate. They must be informed of their right to choose not to participate and of their freedom to withdraw from the research at any time.

Researchers must be careful to minimize physical and psychological stress during the procedures in order to protect their subjects from harm. If subjects are to suffer electrical shock, for example, it should be moderate and necessary. If subjects are to be asked certain questions that will cause emotional stress, questions must be carefully selected and worded, and must be asked in ways to minimize the upset. For example, if abused wives are being interviewed, this may be an extremely stressful experience for them. In any case, interviewers need to take the subjects' stress into account, to ask questions tactfully, and to provide therapeutic help if required.

Protection from harm includes keeping the confidentiality of subjects. Exposure might result in embarrassment, ridicule, or conflict within relationships. Thus, data on individuals may be assigned code numbers as well as be

Thus, the combination of random and selective availability factors can easily lead to invalid conclusions (Tennstedt, Dettling, & McKinley, 1992).

The primary advantage of a longitudinal study is that it eliminates cohort effects. Because the same people are studied, change with age or time is really due to these factors.

Sequential Studies

Because of the problems in both cross-sectional and longitudinal studies, researchers have designed another approach that combines the best features of both. This pattern is called the **sequential study.** Using this approach, researchers do not have to follow a group of children over many years' time; instead, they study children at different ages for shorter periods. For example, they might study one group of 10-year-olds, another of 12-year-olds, a third of 14-year-olds, and a fourth of 16-year-olds. If the researchers follow these children for five years, they would see changes from 10 to 15, 12 to 17, 14 to 19, and 16 to 21. The result would be a view of

Sequential study—combination of cross-sectional and longitudinal research designs that attempts to sort out age, cohort, and time effects; age changes are not measured.

Cross-cultural research gives us knowledge of the diverse environments in which people develop.

restricted and kept in locked places. All possible means of identifying individuals with the findings of a study should be eliminated.

Universities have special committees to review planned research projects before they are begun. If particular ethical questions arise, the committee may ask the researchers to withdraw their proposal or to modify it to meet required standards.

Summary

1. Life-span human development seeks to describe, explain, predict, and influence the changes that take place from conception through adulthood. The ultimate goal of life-span developmental psychology is to help people live meaningful, productive lives.

2. Human development over the life span is divided into three major periods of development: child development, adolescent development, and adult development.

3. Child development may be subdivided into the prenatal period (from conception to birth), infancy (the first 2 years), early childhood (3 to 5 years), and middle childhood (6 to 11 years).

4. Adolescent development extends from approximately 12 to 19 years of age. Early adolescence is 12 to 14; late adolescence is 15 to 19 years of age.

5. Adult development may be divided into early adulthood (20s and 30s), middle adulthood (40s and 50s), and late adulthood (60 and over).

6. A philosophy of life-span development includes the following important elements:

   • Development is multidimensional and interdisciplinary and includes four dimensions: physical, cognitive, emotional, and social development.
   • Development continues through the life span; it does not stop at adolescence.
   • Both heredity and environment influence development.

- Development reflects both continuity and discontinuity.
- Development is cumulative, although what happens early is not 100% predictive of what happens later.
- Development is both controllable and beyond our control.
- Development reflects both stability and change.
- Development is variable, so that not all dimensions of the personality grow at the same rate.
- Development is sometimes cyclical and repetitive.
- Development reflects individual differences.
- Development reflects gender differences.
- Development reflects cultural differences.
- Developmental influences are reciprocal. Children not only influence caregivers and their environment but also are influenced by them.

7. Research in human development utilizes scientific methods to obtain information. Both nonexperimental and experimental research methods are used.

8. Data collection methods include naturalistic observation, interviews, questionnaires and checklists, case studies, and standardized testing. The selection of a subject sample who are representative of the group studied is important in obtaining accurate results.

9. Experimental methods manipulate variables to see how one affects the others. By changing variables, a link between cause and effect is more easily established than in nonexperimental methods. An independent variable is one over which the experimenter has control. A dependent variable is dependent on the independent variable. Correlational studies show the relationship between the independent variables and the dependent variables.

10. In developmental research, experimenters seek to sort out the relative influences of age, cohorts, and time of testing.

11. Research designs are of three basic types: cross-sectional studies, longitudinal studies, and sequential studies. Each has advantages and disadvantages.

12. Ethical standards governing research insist on two fundamental principles: informed consent and protection from harm.

13. Research with children raises sensitive issues. For example, to what extent can minor children give informed consent? If they cannot, parents, guardians, and researchers must decide issues according to what is in the best interests of children.

Key Terms

Adolescence   *p. 5*
Case studies   *p. 14*
Cognitive development   *p. 6*
Cohort   *p. 16*
Correlation   *p. 16*
Cross-sectional study   *p. 17*
Dependent variable   *p. 15*
Early adulthood   *p. 5*
Early childhood   *p. 4*
Emotional development   *p. 6*
Experimental methods   *p. 15*
Independent variable   *p. 15*
Infancy   *p. 4*
Interviews   *p. 14*
Late adulthood   *p. 5*
Longitudinal research   *p. 17*
Middle adulthood   *p. 5*

Middle childhood   *p. 4*
Naturalistic observation   *p. 14*
Nature   *p. 7*
Nurture   *p. 7*
Physical development   *p. 6*
Prenatal period   *p. 4*
Questionnaires   *p. 14*
Random sample   *p. 15*
Reliability   *p. 14*
Representative sample   *p. 15*
Sample   *p. 15*
Scientific method   *p. 13*
Sequential study   *p. 18*
Social development   *p. 6*
Tests   *p. 14*
Validity   *p. 14*

Discussion Questions

1. Have you noticed any particular changes that have taken place in your life in the past few years? Describe these changes. Are the changes for the better or for the worse? What are the causes of these changes? How much control did you have over these changes? Did they take place in opposition to your will, or were you glad that they took place?

2. How much control do you have over your life and the changes that take place? Would you like to have more control?

3. Can people continue to develop physically, cognitively, emotionally, and socially during their entire lifetime? Why or why not? What factors may prevent continued development in any of these areas?

4. Do you believe that development is continuous or that it occurs in stages? Give examples.

5. To what extent is your life now partially a product of what has happened to you before? Explain. Have you faced any traumatic or unusual incidents that have changed the course of your life? Describe.

6. In what ways have early childhood experiences had an influence on your life? Describe some of the most important influences.

7. The text says that development is variable, that not all aspects of our lives develop at the same rate. Can you describe a person whom you know whose personality structure shows uneven development?

8. What aspects of development do you believe are more controlled by heredity, and which are more controlled by environment?

9. If you had to select a subject for a research study, what would it be? What method or methods would you use to obtain information? Who would your subjects be, and how would you select them? Would you prefer a cross-sectional or longitudinal study? Why?

10. Give some examples of how environmental influences mold gender differences.

Suggested Readings

AMBERT, A. (1992). *The effect of children on parents.* New York: Haworth Press. Children have significant positive and negative effects on parents.

American Psychological Association. (1982). *Ethical principles in the conduct of research with human participants.* Washington, D.C.: American Psychological Association. A basic guidebook.

AUHAGEN, A. E., & SALISCH, M. (Eds.). (1996). *The diversity of human relationships.* New York: Cambridge University Press. Discusses the broad range of interpersonal relationships experienced by people in daily life.

DAMON, W., & EISENBERG, M. (Eds.). (1998). *Handbook of child psychology, social, emotional, and personality development* (Vol. 3, 5th ed.). New York: John Wiley & Sons, Inc. This is one of three references by Damon et al. that are part of a series covering all aspects of child psychology, which are suggested as basic reference works.

DAMON, W., KUHN, D., & SIEGLER, R. S. (Eds.). (1998). *Handbook of child psychology, cognition, perception, and language* (Vol. 2, 5th ed.). New York: John Wiley & Sons, Inc. Basic handbook.

DAMON, W., & LERNER, R. M. (Eds.). (1998). *Handbook of child psychology, theoretical models of human development* (Vol. 1, 5th ed.). New York: John Wiley & Sons, Inc. Basic handbook.

GARBARINO, J. (1992). *Children and families in the social environment.* New York: Aldine deGruyter.

Emphasizes the development of healthy, normal children and families in social context, utilizing Bronfenbrenner's ecological model.

KAGAN, J. (1994). *The nature of the child.* New York: Basic Books. Argues against the irreversibility of early experience and emphasizes the capacity to change throughout life.

KEGAN, R. (1982). *The evolving self: Problems and process in human development.* Cambridge, MA: Harvard University Press. Humans organize their world in meaningful ways so that their lives make sense to themselves and others.

MAGNUSSON, D. (Eds.) (First published in 1996, paperback, 1997). *The lifespan development of individuals: Behavioral, neurobiological, and psychosocial perspectives: A synthesis.* Cambridge: Cambridge University Press. Comprehensive text.

RAY, W. J., & RAVIZZA, R. (1997). *Methods toward a science of behavior and experience* (3rd ed.). Belmont, CA: Wadsworth. Scientific methods in conducting experimental research and in writing research articles.

YOUNG, G. (1997). *Adult development, therapy, and cultures: A postmodern synthesis.* New York: Plenum. Therapeutic applications as related to theories of adult development in our culture.

Web Resources

http://www.nih./gov   National Institute of Health. Scientific sources for research, health information, and library services.

Theories
of Development

Chapter 2

THE ROLES OF THEORIES

One of our human characteristics is that we seek logical explanations of things that happen. We ask "What happened?" or "How did it happen?" or "Why did it happen?" Last summer a house in our neighborhood caught fire. The owner, an elderly gentleman who lived alone, was found dead in his chair in the living room. Apparently he had been asleep and had been overcome by smoke inhalation before he could wake up and get out of the house. Everyone in our neighborhood sought an explanation of what happened, and how and why it did happen. Investigators were called in to make an official report.

We all seem to have been born with a natural curiosity and with logical minds that seek to make sense out of events. Most of us have said at one time or another, "I have a theory about that"—meaning, "I think I have a logical explanation." Human development theories are really one expression of the human tendency to want to explain things. As we've seen, the scientific method involves formulating a problem, developing a hypothesis, testing it, and then drawing conclusions that are stated in the form of a **theory.** *A theory organizes the data, ideas, and hypotheses, and states them in coherent, interrelated, general propositions, principles, or laws.* These propositions, principles, or laws are useful in explaining and predicting phenomena, now and in the future. Theories are particularly useful because they look beyond detailed data and give broad, comprehensive views of things.

A human development theory may focus on only one aspect of development, such as cognitive development, or may emphasize development of the total self. A theory may focus on only one time period: adolescence, for example; or it may cover the entire life span.

In this chapter, we will examine some of the major theories that researchers have developed to explain human development. The theories may be arranged into five categories: *psychoanalytic theories, learning theories, humanistic theories, cognitive theories,* and *ethological theories.*

PSYCHOANALYTIC THEORIES

Freud: Psychoanalytical Theory

Sigmund Freud (1856–1939) was the originator of **psychoanalytical theory** (Freud, 1917). *This theory emphasizes the importance of early childhood experiences and unconscious motivations in influencing behavior.* Many instinctual urges and memories of traumatic experiences are repressed early in life. They are driven out of conscious awareness into the unconscious mind, where they continue to cause anxiety and conflict and to influence behavior.

Freud was a Viennese physician in the Victorian era. He became interested in neurology, the study of the brain, and nervous disorders. At first, he used *hypnosis* in treating these nervous disorders, but later he became interested in delving further into his patients' thoughts to uncover the causes of emotional disturbances. In a method he called **free association,** he asked patients to lie down on a couch and talk about anything that came to mind. Freud sat behind his patients so that they couldn't see his facial reactions. His patients would gradually reveal repressed thoughts and urges that were the causes of their conflicts. Freud also used *dream interpretation* to delve into the unconscious.

Freud felt that sexual urges and aggressive instincts and drives were the primary determinants of behavior. The individual was motivated by the **pleasure principle,** the desire to achieve maximum pleasure and to avoid pain. However, sexual and aggressive instincts put people in direct conflict with social mores, especially during the Victorian era, when prudishness and social convention were emphasized. The conflict within

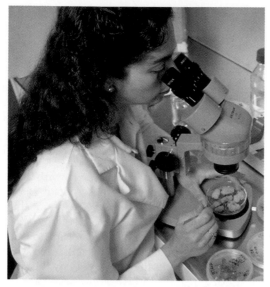

The scientific method involves formulating a problem, developing a hypothesis, testing it, and then drawing conclusions in the form of a theory.

Theory—a tentative explanation of facts and data that have been observed

Psychoanalytical theory—Freud's theory that the structure of personality is composed of the id, ego, and superego, and that mental health depends on keeping the balance among them

Free association—a method of treatment of Freud in which the patient is encouraged to say anything that comes to mind, allowing unconscious thoughts to slip out

Pleasure principle—the motivation of the id to seek pleasure and avoid pain, regardless of the consequences

Id—according to Freud, the inborn instinctual urges that a person seeks to satisfy

Ego—according to Freud, the rational part of the mind, which uses the reality principle to satisfy the id

Superego—according to Freud, the socially induced moral restrictions that strive to keep the id in check and help the individual attain perfection

Defense mechanisms—according to Freud, unconscious strategies used by the ego to protect itself from disturbance and to discharge tension

the individual between these instinctual urges and societal expectations was the primary cause of emotional disturbances and illnesses.

In outlining his theory, Freud developed an explanation of the basic structure of personality. His theory states that *personality is composed of three components: the id, ego, and superego.* The **id** is present from birth and consists of the basic instincts and urges that seek immediate gratification, regardless of the consequences. Left unchecked, the id places the individual in deep conflict with other people and society.

The second element of personality structure is the **ego,** which begins to develop during the first year of life. The ego consists of mental processes, the powers of reasoning and common sense, that seek to help the id find expression without getting into trouble. The ego operates according to a *reality principle.*

The third element of personality structure is the **superego,** which develops from a culmination of maturation, parental identification and modeling, and societal teaching. It represents those social values that are incorporated into the personality structure of the child. It becomes the conscience that seeks to influence behavior to conform to social expectations. The id and superego are often in conflict, causing guilt, anxiety, and disturbances. The ego strives to minimize the conflict by keeping the instinctual urges and societal prohibitions in balance.

According to Freud, one of the ways in which people relieve anxiety and conflict is by employing **defense mechanisms,** which are mental devices that distort reality to minimize psychic pain. Defense mechanisms are employed unconsciously and become pathological only when used in excess to impair effective functioning. The defense mechanisms include the following (Clark, 1991):

- **Repression**—dealing with unacceptable impulses by pushing them down into the unconscious mind, where they continue to cause conflict and exert powerful influences over our behavior.

- **Regression**—reverting to earlier, childish forms of behavior when confronted with anxiety. For example, an older child reverts to bed-wetting or to thumbsucking.

- **Sublimation**—replacing distasteful, unacceptable behavior with behavior that is socially acceptable. For example, a man filled with anger and hostility and aggression participates in competitive sports, lest he explode into violence (Kohn, 1988).

- **Displacement**—transferring strong emotions from a source of frustration and venting them on another object or person who becomes the scapegoat. An example would be a child who becomes angry at her parents and takes out her hostile feelings on a pet dog.

- **Reaction formation**—acting completely opposite of the way that one feels to hide unacceptable feelings or tendencies. A person might crusade against child sexual abuse (pedophilia) because he or she has such tendencies.

Sigmund Freud is the originator of psychoanalytical theory.

- **Denial**—protecting oneself from anxiety by refusing to acknowledge that a situation exists. One example might be to refuse to acknowledge that a child is mentally retarded.
- **Rationalization**—making up excuses for behavior that would otherwise be unacceptable.

Not only did Freud develop a theory of personality structure, but he outlined a **psychosexual theory** of development as well. According to Freud, the center of sensual sensitivity, or *erogenous zones*, shifts from one body zone to another as children mature. The stages of psychosexual development according to Freud are as follows:

- **Oral stage**—first year of life, during which the child's chief source of sensual gratification centers around the mouth. The infant's chief source of pleasure and gratification is through sucking, chewing, and biting. Such activity increases security and relieves tension.
- **Anal stage**—ages 2 to 3, during which the child's principal source of greatest pleasure is through anal activity. This is the age when the child becomes very interested in eliminative functions, toileting activities, and training.
- **Phallic stage**—ages 4 to 5, during which the center of pleasure shifts to the genitals as children explore their bodies through self-manipulation.
- **Latency stage**—age 6 to puberty, during which time the child represses sexual urges and devotes time and energy to learning and physical and social activities. The source of pleasure shifts from self to other persons as the child becomes interested in cultivating the friendship of others.
- **Genital stage**—beginning with sexual maturation, after which the young person seeks sexual stimulation and satisfaction from a member of the opposite sex. This stage continues through adulthood.

Freud also taught that boys experience *castration anxiety* and that girls develop *penis envy* because of the lack of a phallus. Freud said that penis envy in girls becomes a major source of what he termed women's sense of inferiority. Also, during this period, boys develop an **Oedipal complex** and fall in love with their mother, becoming jealous of their father as they compete for their mother's love and affection (Thomas, 1991).

Parenting Issues

The Overly Developed Superego

Five-year-old Stephen was a very quiet, shy, inhibited child. In kindergarten he usually sat in a chair, watching the other children play. When given finger paint, the typical five-year-old will put the fingers into the paint, then the whole hand, then the other hand, then smear it all over the paper, and if not supervised, may smear it over the table, wipe it on the clothes, or on the clothes of another child nearby.

In one-half hour, Stephen had barely put the end of one finger in the paint and had quickly withdrawn it. Stephen was obviously a very inhibited child.

The teacher discussed the situation with the parents. The parents admitted that Stephen had always been a very inhibited child from the time of birth, but they also mentioned that they had been very strict and that they were pleased to see such a "good boy." They were willing to admit that perhaps they had been too strict in disciplining him. At the teacher's suggestion, both the parents and the teacher agreed to encourage more initiative and spontaneity.

A year later Stephen was more relaxed and far happier, willing to try new things and to enter into all activities along with the other children.

Keeping the id and superego in balance is not always easy. Some children are undercontrolled; others, like Stephen, are overcontrolled with a too highly developed superego. Either extreme can cause problems for individuals who need to learn to consider both their own desires and needs and those of other individuals as well. (Author's counseling notes)

Gradually, they repress their incestuous feelings and begin to identify with their father during the next stage of development. Meanwhile, during this period, girls develop an **Electra complex** and fall in love with their father, becoming jealous of their mother as they compete for their father's love and affection. They also blame their mother for the fact that they have no penis. They are ready for the next stage when they are able to repress their incestuous feelings for their father and identify with their mother.

Freud said that if children receive too much or too little gratification at any given stage, they become **fixated** at that stage, so that their psychosexual development is incomplete. Thus, if children receive too little oral gratification during that stage, they may continue to try to find oral gratification later in life through smoking, eating, kissing, drinking, or chewing. Children who become fixated at the latency stage seek to repress sexual feelings and continue to identify with the same-sex parent, never moving on to make mature heterosexual adjustments (Emde, 1992).

Psychosexual theory—Freud's theory in which the center of sensual sensitivity shifts from one body zone to another in stages as children mature

Oedipal complex—according to Freud, the unconscious love and sexual desire of male children for their mother

Electra complex—according to Freud, the unconscious love and sexual desire of female children for their father

Fixated—according to Freud, remaining at a particular psychosexual stage because of too much or too little gratification

Erikson: Pscyhosocial Theory

Erik Erikson (1902–1994) studied under a Freudian group in Germany before coming to the United States in 1933. He became a U.S. citizen and taught at Harvard University. While leaving Freud's theory intact, Erikson disagreed with Freud on several points. For example, he felt that Freud placed too much emphasis on the sexual basis for behavior. In contrast to Freud, Erikson concluded in his **psychosocial theory** that there are other psychosocial motivations and needs that become the driving forces in human development and behavior. Erikson accepted Freud's emphasis on early experiences and the importance of unconscious motivation, but he rejected Freud's neglect of the adult years (Erikson, 1982). Also, Erikson rejected Freud's cynical view of human nature and his belief that humans are unable to deal with their problems. Erikson said that humans can resolve their difficulties and conflicts as they arise.

Erikson divided human development into eight stages and said that the individual has a psychosocial task to master during each stage. The confrontation with each task produces conflict with two possible outcomes. If the task during each stage is mastered, a positive quality is built into the personality and further development takes place. If the task is not mastered and the conflict is unsatisfactorily resolved, the ego is damaged because a negative quality is incorporated in it. The overall task of the individual is to acquire a positive identity as he or she moves from one stage to the next.

The positive solution of each task and its negative counterpart are shown in Figure 2.1 for each period. The stages are as follows:

- **Trust versus distrust** (0 to 1 year). Infants learn that they can trust caregivers for sustenance, protection, comfort, and affection, or they develop a distrust because their needs are not met.

- **Autonomy versus shame and doubt** (1 to 2 years). Children gain control over eliminative functions, learn to feed themselves, are allowed to play alone and to explore the world (within safe limits), and develop some degree of independence, or if too restricted by caregivers, they develop a sense of shame and doubt about their own abilities.

- **Initiative versus guilt** (3 to 5 years). Children's motor and intellectual abilities continue to increase; they continue to explore the environment and to experience many new things, assuming more responsibility for initiating and carrying out plans. Caregivers who cannot accept children's developing initiative instill a feeling of guilt over misbehavior.

- **Industry versus inferiority** (6 to 11 years). Children learn to meet the demands of home and school, and develop a feeling of self-worth through accomplishment and interaction with others, or they come to feel inferior in relation to others.

- **Identity versus role confusion** (12 years to 19 years). Adolescents develop a strong sense of self, or they become confused about their identity and their roles in life.

- **Intimacy versus isolation** (young adulthood: 20s and 30s). Young adults develop close relationships with others, or they remain isolated from meaningful relationships with others.

- **Generativity versus stagnation** (middle adulthood: 40s and 50s). Middle adults assume responsible, adult roles in the community, at work, and in teaching and guiding the next generation, or they become personally impoverished, self-centered, and stagnant (McAdams & St. Aubin, 1992).

- **Integrity versus despair** (late adulthood: 60 and over). Late adults evaluate their lives, and accept them for what they are, or they despair because they cannot find meaning in their lives.

Psychosocial theory—the term used to describe Erikson's stage theory of development in which there are psychosocial tasks to master at each level of development

Erik Erikson developed a psychosocial theory that divided the developmental process into eight stages.

Table 2.1 shows a comparison between Freud's and Erikson's stages of development.

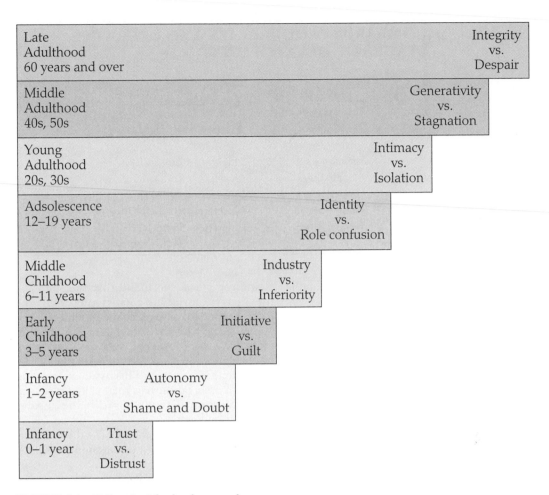

FIGURE 2.1   Erikson's eight developmental stages.

Evaluation of Psychoanalytical Theories

Freud's psychoanalytical theory is an influential one. His emphasis on unconscious motivations and ego defense mechanisms has been particularly valuable for psychotherapists in gaining insight into either the mental health or the illnesses of their clients. Freud's method of treatment, which was unique, became the foundation for subsequent development of a variety of treatment techniques. Freud also made parents and professionals realize how important the experiences of the early years can be. His emphasis on environmental influences placed the responsibility for development directly into the hands of all caregivers of children.

Freud's psychosexual theory of development is limited in scope, with an overemphasis (according to some) on sexual motivations as the basis of behavior, and the resolution of psychosexual conflict as the key to healthy behavior. Because Freud developed his theory on

the basis of treatment of adult patients, the theory was not tested on children. In fact, much of Freud's ideas are not easily tested by research. Freud also had a very cynical view of human nature that certainly does not explain the motivations of countless millions who act out of genuine care and concern.

Erikson's theory is much broader than Freud's, focusing on the importance of both maturational and environmental factors in development and on the importance of a variety of psychological motivations for behavior. In addition, Erikson's theory encompasses the entire life span, outlining the stages that occur. Erikson also emphasized individual responsibility during each stage of development and the opportunity to achieve a positive and healthy resolution of the identity crisis. In Erikson's view, it is the ego and not the id that is the life force of human development (Hamachek, 1988). Erikson has also been criticized for his antifemale bias and his failure to take into account different social and cultural influences in the lives of men and women. Erikson's descriptions of

TABLE 2.1	COMPARISON OF FREUD'S AND ERIKSON'S STAGES OF DEVELOPMENT	
Approximate Age	*Freud*	*Erikson*
Birth–1 year	Oral Stage	Trust vs. Distrust
1–2 years	Anal Stage	Autonomy vs. Shame and Doubt
3–5 years	Phallic Stage	Initiative vs. Guilt
6–11 years	Latency Stage	Industry vs. Inferiority
12–Young Adulthood	Genital Stage	Identity vs. Role Confusion
Early Adulthood	Genital Stage	Intimacy vs. Isolation
Middle Adulthood	Genital Stage	Generativity vs. Stagnation
Late Adulthood	Genital Stage	Industry vs. Despair

development are validated by a considerable body of research findings.

Learning Theories

Behaviorism

The theory of development known as **behaviorism** emphasizes the role of environmental influences in molding behavior. For the behaviorist, *behavior becomes the sum total of learned or conditioned responses to stimuli.* Such a view is labeled **mechanistic** or **deterministic.** Behaviorism is partially a reaction to psychoanalytical thought.

Behaviorists are not interested in unconscious motives for behavior. Furthermore, they see learning as progressing in a continuous manner, rather than in a sequence of stages, as in psychoanalytical theory. The process of learning, according to behaviorist theory, is called **conditioning.** There are two types of conditioning: classical conditioning and operant conditioning.

Pavlov: Classical Conditioning

The Russian physiologist Ivan Pavlov (1849–1936) first discovered the link between stimulus and response. He was doing research on salivation in dogs and noticed that a dog would begin to salivate not only at the sight of food, but also at the sound of the approaching attendant. The dog began to associate the sound of the approaching attendant with being fed.

Pavlov then began a series of experiments to test what was happening. He presented a clicking metronome to the dog, then blew a small amount of meat powder into the dog's mouth to elicit salivation. Eventually, after some repetition, he found that the sound of the metronome alone elicited salivation. The dog began to associate the sound of the metronome with the subsequent presentation of food. The best results were obtained when the metronome preceded the food powder by about half a second. This type of learning through association has been called **classical conditioning.** Figure 2.2 shows the apparatus used by Pavlov.

Learning through classical conditioning always involves a series of stimuli and responses: an unconditioned stimulus (UCS), an unconditioned response (UCR), a conditioned stimulus (CS), and a conditioned response (CR). In the case of Pavlov and his dogs, the stimuli and responses were as follows:

- *Unconditioned stimulus* (UCS)—was the meat powder in the dog's mouth that elicited the response of salivation without any learning.

Pavlov discovered how learning takes place through classical conditioning.

Behaviorism—the school of psychology that emphasizes that behavior is modified through conditioning

Mechanistic or deterministic—as applied to behaviorism, a criticism that behavior is a result of mindless reactions to stimuli

Conditioning—simple process of learning

Classical conditioning—form of learning through association, in which a previously neutral stimulus is paired with an unconditioned stimulus to stimulate a conditioned response that is similar to the unconditioned response

- *Unconditioned response* (UCR)—was salivation in response to meat powder in the mouth, an inborn reaction.
- *Conditioned stimulus* (CS)—was the metronome, which, when associated with the meat powder, acquired the ability to elicit a response.
- *Conditioned response* (CR)—was salivation in response to the metronome alone.

Classical conditioning is a form of learning because an old behavior can be elicited by a new stimulus.

Some years later in the United States, John Watson (1878–1958) and his associate Rosalie Rayner tested this idea by teaching fear to a young child named Albert. Albert was first allowed to play with a white laboratory rat and was not in the least afraid of it. Then Watson began striking a steel bar with a hammer just behind Albert's head as he played with the rat. The loud noise made Albert cry. After seven such pairings, Albert showed fear of the rat when it was placed near him. He had been conditioned to fear it. Furthermore, his fear responses became generalized; that is, Albert became afraid of other white, furry objects as well. The conduct of this experiment raises some serious ethical issues about research with children, and such an experiment would not be permitted today (Watson & Raynor, 1920). Watson made no effort to extinguish Albert's fears after the experiment was over. Nevertheless, this example illustrates how a series of responses may be conditioned in children.

As a result of his experiments, Watson came to feel that conditioning was the sole process responsible for development. He felt that experience and the environment were the factors that shaped the human behavioral repertoire (Horowitz, 1992). Human behavior was a result of learning.

Skinner: Operant Conditioning

The second type of conditioning is **operant conditioning,** which is learning from the consequences of behavior. According to B. F. Skinner (1904–1990), who originated the term, our behavior operates on the environment to produce consequences: either desirable or undesirable. The nature of the consequences determines the probability of the behavior's reoccurrence. Put very simply, if our behavior results in something positive (a **positive reinforcement**), the probability that the behavior will reoccur is increased. If our behavior results in undesirable happenings, the consequence decreases the probabil-

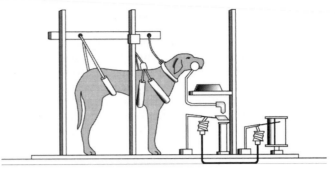

FIGURE 2.2   Apparatus used by Pavlov in his studies of conditioning.

ity that the behavior will reoccur. In summary, *operant conditioning is learning in which the consequences of behavior lead to changes in the probability of that behavior's occurrence.* This principle has numerous applications in child-rearing and in adult learning (Skinner, 1953).

In a classic study in the 1960s, a group of preschool teachers decided to help a young girl overcome her shyness with other children (Allen, Hart, Buell, Harris, & Wolf, 1964). The teachers were concerned that the girl spent too little time playing with other children and too much time with adults, so they decided to give her praise only when she was playing with another child. When she was doing anything else, they paid very little attention to her. As a result of the positive reinforcement of the praise and attention, the little girl's frequency of playing with other children increased considerably.

Many kinds of behavior can be encouraged with positive reinforcement. Even pain can be a learned response. After minor

B. F. Skinner originated the concept of operant conditioning.

Operant conditioning— learning from the consequences of behavior so that the consequences change the probability of the behavior's reoccurrence

Positive reinforcement—a consequence of behavior that leads to an increase in the probability of its occurrence

surgery at the Johns Hopkins Children's Center, 2-year-old Adam was woozy but ready to go home. The surgeon told his mother, "Be cheerful and optimistic, compliment him when he moves around without whimpering or crying. Don't ask him if it hurts. Give him a baby aspirin only if he really complains about pain. But he won't."

After a full night's sleep Adam toddled downstairs for breakfast—slowly, but without complaints of pain (Rodgers, 1988, p. 26).

Bandura: Social Cognitive and Learning Theory

Social learning theorists accept the view of behaviorists that behavior is learned and that development is influenced by the environment, but they reject the mechanistic view that altered behavior is a mindless response to stimuli. **Social cognitive and learning theory** emphasizes the role of both cognition and environmental influences in development. We are all thinking creatures with some powers of self-determination, not just robots that show B response when A stimulus is introduced. We can think about what is happening, evaluate it, and alter our responses accordingly.

Albert Bandura (1977, 1986), Stanford University psychologist, is one of the most important contemporary exponents of social learning theory. Bandura says that children learn by observing the behavior of others and imitating and **modeling** their behavior (Grusec, 1992). Thus, a child may watch another play baseball: how to hold the bat and swing it, how to run the bases, how to catch and throw a ball. The child learns the fundamentals of the game through watching others. When given the opportunity, he or she then tries to imitate, or model, what was seen. Children are great imitators: They imitate parents caring for the baby; imitate them mowing the lawn; or imitate them in learning how to eat, talk, walk, or dress.

In his classic study, Bandura let children observe a film in which an adult kicked, hit, and sat on a blow-up Bobo doll (Bandura, Ross, & Ross, 1963). When the children were placed in a playroom with a Bobo doll, they were significantly more aggressive toward the Bobo doll than a group of children who had not seen the film. They learned to act more aggressively through modeling.

Once modeled, behavior can be strengthened through reinforcement. Behavior can also be influenced by seeing others rewarded or punished. Suppose, for example, the chil-

Albert Bandura developed social learning theory.

dren had seen the adult rewarded for hitting the Bobo doll. Their own aggressive behavior would be increased through **vicarious reinforcement.** Thus, children learn to behave both by modeling and by observing the consequences of their own behavior and the behavior of others.

In recent years, Bandura has expanded his social learning theory to include the role of cognition (Bandura, 1989). Rather than describing individuals as determined strictly by environmental influences, Bandura emphasized that they influence their own destiny by choosing their future environments as well as other goals they wish to pursue. Social-cognitive theorists emphasize that individuals, rather than accepting passively whatever the environment provides, partially control the environment by the way they react to it. For example, a placid, pleasant, easy-to-care-for adolescent may have a very positive influence on parents, encouraging them to act in a warm, friendly, and loving manner. However, an overactive, temperamental, hard-to-care-for adolescent who is easily upset may stimulate parents to be hostile, short-tempered, and rejecting. From this point of view, children, however consciously, are partly responsible for creating their own environment. Because of individual differences, different people at different developmental stages, interpret and act on their environment in different ways that create different experiences for each person (Bandura, 1989).

Evaluation of Learning Theories

Learning theorists have contributed much to the understanding of human development. Their emphasis on the role of environmental influences in shaping behavior patterns has

Social cognitive and learning theory—view of learning that emphasizes that behavior is learned through social interaction with other persons

Modeling—learning through observing and imitating the behavior of others

Vicarious reinforcement—observing that the positive consequences of another's behavior increases the probability of the behavior in the observer

put the responsibility for creating positive environments for child development directly in the hands of parents, teachers, and other caregivers. The principles of social learning through modeling and reinforcement have also made adults very aware of the example that they set in teaching children and youth. When psychologists concluded that much behavior is caused and learned, they began to develop many *behavioral modification* programs to eliminate problem behaviors such as phobias, explosive tempers, compulsions, or drug addiction. Behaviorist approaches to treating problem behaviors are among the most successful of the treatment approaches. They are based on a very optimistic view of the ability to control and change behavior.

Social learning theories have been criticized for leaving out the role of unconscious, psychodynamic factors and of underlying feelings in influencing behavior. They also neglect the role of biology and maturation in development. In spite of these criticisms, learning theories have contributed much to the overall understanding of human development.

HUMANISTIC THEORIES

Humanistic theory has been described as the third force in modern psychology. It rejects both the Freudian determinism of instincts and the environmental determinism of learning theory. Humanists have a very positive, optimistic view of human nature. The humanistic view states that *humans are free agents with superior ability to use symbols and to think in abstract terms.* Thus, people are able to make intelligent choices, to be responsible for their actions, and to realize their full potential as self-actualized persons. Humanists hold a **holistic view** of human development, which sees each person as a whole and unique being of independent worth. In the holistic view, a person is more than a collection of drives, instincts, and learned experiences. Three of the most famous leaders of humanistic psychology were Charlotte Buhler (1893–1974), Abraham Maslow (1908–1970), and Carl Rogers (1902–1987).

Buhler: Developmental Phase Theory

Charlotte Buhler, a Viennese psychologist, was the first president of the Association of Humanistic Psychology. Buhler rejected the contention of psychoanalysts that restoring psychological *homeostasis* (equilibrium)

through release of tensions is the goal of human beings. According to Buhler's theory, *the real goal of human beings is the fulfillment they can attain by accomplishment in themselves and in the world* (Buhler, 1935). The basic human tendency is **self-actualization,** or self-realization, so that the peak experiences of life come through creativity. Buhler emphasized the active role that humans play through their own initiative in fulfilling goals. Table 2.2 illustrates the phases outlined by Buhler (1935). In the last phase of life, most human beings evaluate their total existence in terms of fulfillment or failure.

Maslow: Hierarchy of Needs Theory

Abraham Maslow was one of the most influential leaders in humanistic psychology. Born into an Orthodox Jewish family in New York, he earned his Ph.D. in psychology from Columbia University in 1934. According to him, human behavior can be explained as motivation to satisfy needs. Maslow arranged human needs into five categories: *physiological needs, safety needs, love and belongingness needs, esteem needs,* and *self-actualization needs* (Maslow, 1970). Figure 2.3 shows the hierarchy of needs as arranged by Maslow.

In Maslow's view, our first concern as human beings is to satisfy basic needs for survival: food, water, protection from harm. Only when these needs are satisfied can we direct our energy to more exclusively human needs: for love, acceptance, and belonging. The satisfaction of these needs makes possible our concern about self-esteem: We need to gain recognition, approval, and competence. And finally, if we grow up well-fed, safe, loved, and respected, we are more likely to become self-actualized persons who have fulfilled our potential. According to Maslow, *self-actualization is the highest need, and the culmination of life.*

Like other humanists, Maslow was very optimistic about human potential: "Healthy children enjoy growing up and moving forward, gaining new skills, capacities, and powers. . . . In the normal development of the healthy child . . . if he is given a full choice, he will choose what is good for his growth" (Maslow, 1968).

Rogers: Personal Growth Theory

Carl Rogers was raised in a very religious family in the midwest and became a Protestant minister, graduating from Union Theological Seminary in New York (Rogers,

Humanistic theory—psychological theory that emphasizes the ability of individuals to make the right choices and to reach their full potential

Holistic view—emphasizes the functioning of the total individual to try to grow, improve, and reach his or her full potential

Self-actualization—according to Buhler, the drive of individuals to try to grow, improve, and reach their full potential

Living Issues

Racial Prejudice

One good example of social learning through observation, imitation, and modeling is the development of racial prejudice. Children are not born prejudiced against those of other races. They do begin to be aware of racial differences at a young age. Some 3-year-olds and the majority of 5-year-olds can identify racial differences between blacks and whites. By 8 years of age, they can label themselves as a member of a particular ethnic group (Spencer & Markstrom-Adams, 1990). But becoming aware of one's ethnic identity and that of others doesn't lead to racial prejudice and discrimination unless the child is exposed to prejudice as modeled by other people. If a young boy hears his father ridicule blacks, his exposure to his father's attitude is likely to affect his attitude toward blacks. If the boy then goes to school and hears disparaging remarks about blacks made by his peers, prejudicial attitudes will be strengthened. This attitude creates problems for minority children who must reconcile their own self-image with the unpleasant stereotypes and prejudices that they encounter. They learn that their differences make them unwelcome and are held against them.

Because racial prejudices permeate our whole society, children gradually absorb the cultural attitudes of those around them as they get older. One study in California found that children in older grades were less likely to have a friend of a different race than were younger children. The reason is that children exert pressure on one another to avoid friendships with those of other groups. Prejudices can be partly minimized by promoting positive interracial contacts and by desegregation in schools at early ages and in neighborhoods (Howes & Wu, 1990).

1961). During his career as a minister, Rogers became more and more interested in counseling and therapy as a means of ministering to people with problems, for whom he developed a specialized form of therapy called **client-centered therapy** (Rogers, 1951). His theory is based on the humanistic principle that if people are given freedom and emotional support to grow, they can develop into fully functioning human beings. Without criticism or direction, but encouraged by the accepting and understanding environment of the therapeutic situation, people will solve their own problems and develop into the kind of individuals they wish to become.

Rogers said that each of us has two selves: the self that we perceive ourselves to be (the "I" or "me" that is our perception of our *real self*), and our *ideal self* (which we would like to be). Rogers (1961) taught that each of us is a victim of **conditional positive regard** that others show us. We can't have the love and approval of parents or others unless we conform to rigid parental and social standards. We are told what we must do and think. We are criticized, called names, rejected, or punished when we don't live up to the standards of others. Too often we fail, with the result that we develop low self-esteem, devalue our true self, and lose sight of who we really are.

Rogers said that when we have a very poor self-image or are behaving badly, we need the love, approval, companionship, and support of others even more. We need

Client-centered therapy—
Rogers's approach to humanistic therapy, in which the discussion focuses on the client's thoughts and feelings and the therapist creates an atmosphere of acceptance

Conditional positive regard—giving love, praise, and acceptance only if the individual conforms to parental or social standards

TABLE 2.2	BUHLER'S PHASES OF LIFE
Phase	*Development*
Phase One: 0 to 15 Years	Progressive biological growth; child at home; life centers around narrow interest, school, family
Phase Two: 16 to 27 Years	Continued biological growth, sexual maturity; expansion of activities, self-determination; leaves family, enters into independent activities and personal relations
Phase Three: 28 to 47 Years	Biological stability; culmination period; most fruitful period of professional and creative work; most personal and social relationships
Phase Four: 48 to 62 Years	Loss of reproductive functions, decline in abilities; decrease in activities; personal, family, economic losses; transition to this phase marked by psychological crises; period of introspection
Phase Five: 63 Years and Over	Biological decline, increased sickness; retirement from profession; decrease in socialization, but increase in hobbies, individual pursuits; period of retrospection; feeling of fulfillment or failure

Adapted from "The Curve of Life as Studied in Biographies," by C. Buhler, 1935, *Journal of Applied Psychology, 19,* pp. 405–409.

Abraham Maslow said that human behavior can be explained as motivation to satisfy needs.

The humanist Carl Rogers developed client-centered therapy.

unconditional positive regard, not because we deserve it, but because we are human beings of worth and dignity. With it, we can find self-worth and the ability to achieve our ideal self. Without unconditional positive regard, we cannot overcome our faults and become fully functioning persons (Rogers, 1980).

Rogers taught that the healthy individual, the fully functioning person, is one who has achieved a congruence between the real self and ideal self, a situation that results in freedom from internal conflict and anxiety. When there is a merger between what people perceive themselves to be and what they want to be, they are able to accept themselves, be themselves, and live as themselves without conflict.

Evaluation of Humanistic Theories

Humanists teach people to believe in themselves and to assume responsibility for developing their full potential. They also emphasize that people have very real human needs that must be met for growth and

Unconditional positive regard—giving acceptance and appreciation of the individual regardless of socially unacceptable behavior

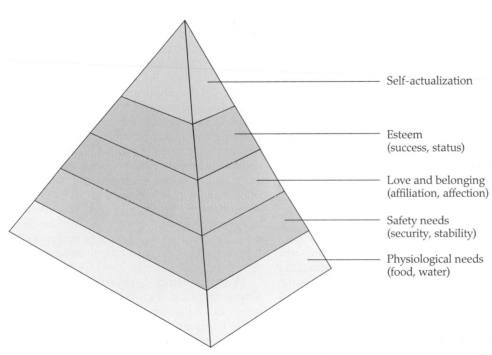

FIGURE 2.3   Maslow's hierarchy of needs.

- Self-actualization
- Esteem (success, status)
- Love and belonging (affiliation, affection)
- Safety needs (security, stability)
- Physiological needs (food, water)

Living Issues

Female Empowerment

The feminist movement has been concerned with the struggle of women to free themselves from male domination, to win equal rights and recognition as persons in their own right (McWhirter, 1991). The traditional concept of power describes the effort to gain control over others, so that the increase in power for one leads to a decrease in power for the other. This usually leads to inequality, in dominance and submission, in the stronger prevailing over the weaker. The newest concept of female empowerment involves the process of gaining control over one's own life, not by seeking to dominate males, but through the development of one's capacities, skills, and abilities (Lips, 1991). Through such development, women use professional training to free themselves of any feelings of inferiority or submissive behavior. Along with assertiveness training, they develop concrete skills to use in the workforce.

Just as important, this newer concept means recognizing that the feminine qualities of sensitivity and understanding that caused women to be labeled as the weaker sex, are really strengths that enable them to relate to others and to solve problems in relationships. Women's power rests partly in their ability to be nurturers, to support the growth of others by promoting family cohesion and stability. Women's care of children and the elderly and their emotional support of the entire family is being increasingly recognized as the cement that holds the fabric of our society together.

Cognition—the act of knowing

Schema—According to Piaget, the original patterns of thinking that people use for dealing with specific situations in their environment

Adaptation—According to Piaget, the process by which individuals adjust their thinking to new conditions or situations

Assimilation

Accommodation

Equilibrium

---

development. Adults are also taught to respect the uniqueness of each child. This places an obligation to meet these needs on those who are responsible for directing the development of growing children.

Humanists are sometimes criticized for having a view of human nature that is too optimistic. Children don't always choose what is best for them. They need some direction and guidance. Nevertheless, humanism has exerted a very positive influence on the whole mental health movement, especially in relation to counseling and therapy.

COGNITIVE THEORIES

Cognition is the act or process of knowing. There are three basic approaches to understanding cognition. One is the *psychometric approach*, which measures quantitative changes in intelligence as people mature. The second approach is the *Piagetian approach*, which emphasizes the qualitative changes in the way people think as they develop. The third approach is the *information-processing view*, which examines the progressive steps, actions, and operations that

take place when people receive, perceive, remember, think about, and use information. The Piagetian and information-processing approaches are discussed here in relation to developmental theory. The psychometric approach is discussed in Chapters 7, 12, and 17.

Piaget: Cognitive Development

Jean Piaget (1896–1980) was a Swiss developmental psychologist who became interested in the growth of human cognitive capacities. He began working in Alfred Binet's Paris laboratory, where modern intelligence testing originated. Piaget began to explore how children grow and develop in their thinking abilities. He became more interested in how children reach conclusions than in whether their answers were correct. Instead of asking questions and scoring them right or wrong, Piaget questioned children to find the logic behind their answers. Through painstaking observation of his own and other children, he constructed his theory of cognitive development (Piaget, 1950; Piaget & Inhelder, 1969).

Piaget taught that cognitive development is the combined result of maturation of the brain and nervous system and adaptation to our environment. He used five terms to describe the dynamics of development. A **schema** represents a mental structure, the pattern of thinking that a person uses for dealing with a specific situation in the environment. For example, infants see an object they want, so they learn to grasp what they see. They form a schema that is appropriate to the situation. **Adaptation** is the process by which children adjust their thinking to include new information that furthers their understanding. Piaget (1954) said that children adapt in two ways: assimilation and accommodation. **Assimilation** means acquiring new information and incorporating it into current schemas in response to new environmental stimuli. **Accommodation** involves adjusting to new information by creating new schemas when the old ones won't do. Children may see dogs for the first time (assimilation), but then learn that some dogs are safe to pet and others aren't (accommodation). As children acquire more and more information, they construct their understanding of the world differently.

When a balance between assimilation and accommodation has been accomplished, a state of equilibrium exists. **Equilibrium** is the harmony between sensory information and accumulated knowledge. As new sensory information—in the form of questions, problems, and ideas—disturbs existing,

Jean Piaget studied how children's thinking changes as they develop.

incomplete, or incorrect knowledge, the equilibrium is thrown into a new disequilibrium, and a new assimilation-accommodation process begins. As these questions, problems, or ideas are taken into the existing mental structure (assimilation) and the existing structure grows, changes, and expands in the process (accommodation), a new, higher-level equilibrium is attained. The accommodation of new experiences produces modifications in the structure and the schema, which means that the child has gained something that allows him or her to make more sophisticated observations, to solve more difficult problems, or to advance higher-level conceptions. Thus, the theory allows for continuous progressive cognitive development. Assimilating and accommodating environmental experiences lead slowly but steadily to cognitive growth. Piaget views children as active participants in their own development.

The concept of equilibrium is essential in Piaget's definition of intelligence as a "form of equilibration . . . toward which all functions lead" (Piaget, 1962: 120). **Equilibration** is defined as a compensation for an external disturbance. Intellectual development becomes a continuous progression moving from one structural disequilibrium to a new, higher, structural equilibrium.

Piaget outlined four stages of cognitive development (Beilin, 1992).

During the **sensorimotor stage** (birth to 2 years), children learn to coordinate sensory experiences with physical, motor actions. Infants' senses of vision, touch, taste, hearing,

and smell bring them into contact with things with various properties. They learn how far to reach to touch a ball, to move their eyes and head to follow a moving object, to move their hand and arm to pick up an object. Elkind (1970) labels the principal cognitive task during this period the *conquest of the object*.

Through the **preoperational stage** (2 to 7 years), children acquire language, and learn that they can manipulate these symbols that represent the environment. Preoperational children can deal with the world symbolically but still cannot perform mental operations that are reversible. That is why Piaget (1967a) called this stage the preoperational stage of thought. Elkind (1970) labels the principal cognitive task during this period the *conquest of the symbol*.

Children in the **concrete operational stage** (7 to 11 years) show a greater capacity for logical reasoning, though this is limited to things actually experienced. They can perform a number of mental operations. They can arrange objects into *hierarchical classifications*; they can understand *class inclusion relationships*, *serialization* (grouping objects by size or alphabetical order), and the principles of *symmetry* and *reciprocity* (two brothers are brothers to each other). They understand the principle of *conservation*, that you can pour a liquid from a tall to a flat dish without altering the total quantity of the liquid. Elkind (1970) calls the major cognitive task of this period *mastering classes, relations, and quantities*.

In the **formal operational stage** (11 years and up), adolescents move beyond concrete, actual experiences to think in more abstract, logical terms. They are able to use systematic, *propositional logic* in solving hypothetical problems and drawing conclusions. They are able to use *inductive reasoning* to systemize their ideas and to construct theories about them. They are able to use *deductive reasoning* to play the role of scientist in constructing and testing theories. They can use *metaphorical speech* and *algebraic symbols* as symbols for symbols. They can move from what is real to what is possible, and they can think about what might be, projecting themselves into the future and planning for it.

Information Processing

The **information-processing approach** to cognition emphasizes the progressive steps, actions, and operations that take place when the person receives, perceives, remembers, thinks about, and uses information. The steps in information processing are illustrated in Figure 2.4. The diagram shows the informa-

Equilibration

Sensorimotor stage

Preoperational stage

Concrete operational stage

Formal operational stage

Information-processing approach—approach to cognition that emphasizes the steps, actions, and operations by which persons receive, perceive, remember, think about, and utilize information

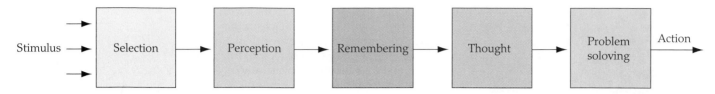

FIGURE 2.4 Steps in information processing.

tion flowing in one direction, but there also may be some flow backward. A person may take information in and out of memory to think about it for a time before making a decision. Nevertheless, the steps shown help us to understand the total process.

The process begins with our being bombarded with stimuli that are received through our senses. Because we are interested in some happenings more than others, we select that which is of value to us. However, the information is not just photocopied by our mind; it is interpreted and evaluated according to our perception of it, which, in turn, depends partly on our past experience. If information seems of value, it is then stored in our memory for future use. When needed, the information is retrieved from memory stores. We think about it, seek to relate it to our own present situation, and use it as a basis for solving our problems. In subsequent discussions in this book, we talk about the development of information-processing skills during various phases of the life span (Rice, 1990).

Evaluation of Cognitive Theories

Piaget has exerted more influence on cognitive theory and applications than any other person. He has revolutionized developmental psychology by focusing attention on mental processes and their role in behavior. He has made us aware that children think differently than adults and that children can do only what they can understand at different stages. Piaget has helped educators, parents, and researchers understand the capabilities of children at different stages. Many school curricula have been redesigned on the basis of Piagetian findings.

Piaget has been criticized for several points. He underestimated the role of the school and home in fostering cognitive development, because he stressed biological maturation rather than environmental influences. However, he did teach that children influence the course of their development through their exploratory activities and that

they should be given learning materials appropriate to each stage of growth. A major criticism of Piaget is the lack of evidence for comprehensive stages across domains. Piaget's depiction of stages as universal is not always true. Many persons never reach the higher stages of development. In fact, formal operational thinking may have limited usefulness in adult life. For example, a carpenter needs the ability to do concrete operational thinking, whereas an architect needs formal operational abilities. Furthermore, people may advance to a certain cognitive level in one aspect of their lives, but not in others. The separation of stages is not always distinct. Growth, then, is uneven.

The information-processing approach has stimulated much research on learning, memory, and problem solving. It is a useful concept in describing mental processes. However, both the Piagetian and information-processing approaches ignore the role of unconscious emotions and emotional conflict as causes of behavior.

ETHOLOGICAL THEORIES

Lorenz: Imprinting

Ethology emphasizes that behavior is a product of evolution and is biologically determined. Each species learns what adaptations are necessary for survival, and through the process of natural selection, the fittest live to pass on their traits to their offspring.

Konrad Lorenz (1903–1989), a Nobel-Prize-winning ethologist, studied the behavior patterns of graylag geese and found that goslings were born with an instinct to follow their mothers (Lorenz, 1965). This behavior was present from birth and was part of their instinct for survival. Lorenz also found that if goslings were hatched in an incubator, they would follow the first moving object that they saw, believing that object to be their mother. Lorenz stood by when the lid of one incubator was lifted. He was the first person whom the goslings saw, so from that point

Ethology—the view that behavior is a product of evolution and biology

on, they followed Lorenz as they would their mother. The goslings would even follow him when he went swimming.

Lorenz called this process **imprinting**, which involved rapidly developing an attachment for the first object seen. Lorenz found that there was a critical period, shortly after hatching, during which imprinting would take place.

Bonding and Attachment Theories

Efforts have been made to apply the principles of ethology to human beings. Although there is no human equivalent to imprinting, bonding shows some similarities. There is some evidence to show that parent-infant contacts during the early hours and days of life are important to later parent-child relationships (Klaus & Kennel, 1982). Studies at Case-Western Reserve University in Cleveland confirmed the maternal feeling that the emotional bonds between mother and infant are strengthened by intimate contact during the first hours of life (Klaus & Kennel, 1982). One group of mothers was allowed sixteen extra hours of intimacy during the first three days of life—an hour after birth and five hours each afternoon. When the babies were one month of age and when they were a year old, these mothers were compared with a control group that had gone through the usual hospital

Konrad Lorenz's goslings developed an attachment to him, a process that he called imprinting.

FOCUS

King, the Guard Duck

A number of years ago I raised Labrador retrievers for hunting and field trial work. Part of the training procedure was to teach the dogs to retrieve live birds. I was able to find two white ducks, newly hatched, at a nearby farm. Apparently, the ducks thought I was their mother because they developed a very special attachment to me. The male, whom we named King, would follow me around the yard of our camp. He became very protective of me and would attack any person who tried to come into the yard. If someone tried to come too close to me when I was swimming, King would dive underwater, swim to the outsider, and bite the person's legs and toes. King became the terror of the neighborhood. Even the Labrador retrievers were afraid of him. So King lived in style, king of our castle, until he died. (From the author's experience)

routine. The mothers who had had more time with their babies fondled them more, sought close eye contact, and responded to their cries. The researchers concluded that keeping the mother and baby together during the first hours after birth strengthened a mother's "maternal sensitivities" and that prolonged infant-mother separation during the first few days would have negative effects.

Although early parent-infant contact is important, other studies fail to confirm Klaus and Kennel's finding that there is a critical period during which **bonding** must take place, and that if it does not, harmful effects will be felt and lasting. In contrast, Egeland and Vaughn (1981) found no greater incidence of neglect, abuse, illness, or adjustment problems among infants who had been separated from their mothers for a time after birth. The point is that the importance of a few crucial hours immediately after birth has not yet been conclusively established.

It is evident, however, that there must be a powerful genetic predisposition in the child that encourages the formation of a relationship. However, no emotional bond ties the infant to its mother immediately at birth. Infants taken from their mother can form a bond with another person. However, Schaffer (1984) pointed out that the infant has certain biological biases and tendencies that facilitate the development of a bond with someone.

John Bowlby (1969) shed a great deal of light on the subject in his discussion of **attachment theory** (Bretherton, 1992). Infants are not born with attachment to anyone: mother,

Imprinting—a biological ability to establish an attachment on first exposure to an object or a person

Bonding—the formation of a close relationship between a person and a child through early and frequent association

Attachment theory—the description of the process by which infants develop close emotional dependence on one or more adult caregivers

FOCUS

Mother's Recognition of Newborn

The mother's recognition of her newborn is a milestone in the unique relationship between the mother and her infant. An integral component of attachment, it promotes and fosters care. During their earliest contacts, a mother is exposed to her infant's visual and olfactory characteristics. She is able to recognize her infant by odor and sight after an exposure of less than one hour. Even more amazing, 36% of nursing mothers were able to recognize their newborns by stroking their hand after an average exposure of less than one hour, 65% after a mean exposure of 6.7 hours.

(Kaitz, Lapidot, Bronner, & Eidelman, (1992).

Evaluation of Ethological Theories

Ethological theories have emphasized the role of evolution and biology in human development and behavior, an emphasis that deserves serious attention. Although ethological emphasis on critical periods of development is too rigid and narrow, the principle of sensitive periods of development is a helpful one. Even then, the theories overlook the importance of positive environmental influences in overcoming the deficits of early deprivation. Biology has a marked influence on behavior, but it is not destiny. People are more than a combination of genes and chromosomes; they are developing human beings, influenced by a wide variety of environmental experiences over many years.

father, or others. However, since the infant's survival depends on a loving caregiver, the infant needs to develop attachments. Bowlby suggested that during the first six months, infants' attachments are quite broad. Infants become attached to people in general, so they seem to have no particular preference for who cares for them. However, from six months on, attachments become more specific. The child may develop multiple attachments, but these are with individuals—the mother, the father, a baby-sitter—so that the child is upset when left with an unfamiliar caregiver.

Hinde: Sensitive Periods of Development

Ethologist Robert Hinde (1983), professor of psychology at Cambridge University, England, prefers the term **sensitive period** to "critical period" in reference to certain times of life when the organism is more affected by particular kinds of experiences. The term *sensitive period*, which was originally used by Maria Montessori, seems broader and is a more flexible concept than the narrow concept of critical period. With human children, there seem to be particularly sensitive periods for development of language, emotional attachments, or social relationships (Bornstein, 1987). When deficits occur during these sensitive periods, the question remains whether they can be made up during subsequent periods of development. Much depends on the extent of the early deprivation and the degree to which later environmental influences meet important needs (Werner & Smith, 1982).

AN ECLECTIC THEORETICAL ORIENTATION

The point of view of this book is that no one theory completely explains human developmental processes or behavior. The theories represent different and enlightened perceptions, all of which are worthy of consideration. For this reason, the book presents an *eclectic* theoretical

Whether the mother and infant need to be together during the first crucial hours after birth for bonding to take place is a matter of dispute.

Sensitive period—period during which a given effect can be produced more readily than at other times

orientation. This presentation means that no one point of view has a monopoly on the truth, and that each theory has contributed an element of understanding to the total, complex process of human development over the life span.

Summary

1. The scientific method involves formulating a problem, developing a hypothesis, testing it, and drawing conclusions that are stated in the form of a theory. A theory organizes the data, ideas, and hypotheses, and states them in coherent, interrelated, general propositions, principles, or laws.

2. Freud's psychoanalytical theory emphasizes the importance of early childhood experiences and unconscious motivations in influencing behavior. Freud thought that sexual urges and aggressive instincts and drives were the primary determinants of behavior, or that people operated according to the pleasure principle.

3. Freud said that the basic structure of the personality consists of the id, ego, and superego, and that the ego strives to minimize the conflict within by keeping the instinctual urges (the id) and societal prohibitions (the superego) in balance.

4. According to Freud, one of the ways in which people relieve anxiety and conflict is by employing defense mechanisms: repression, regression, sublimation, displacement, reaction formation, denial, and rationalization.

5. According to Freud's psychosexual theory, the center of sensual sensitivity shifts from one part of the body to another as development proceeds through the following series of stages: oral stage (to age 1); anal stage (ages 2, 3); phallic stage (ages 4, 5); latency stage (age 6 to puberty); and genital stage (puberty on).

6. Erikson thought that Freud placed too much emphasis on the sexual basis for behavior and that his view of human nature was too cynical. Erikson divided human development into eight stages and said that the individual has a psychosocial task to master during each stage.

7. The eight stages, according to Erikson, are trust versus distrust (0 to 1 year); autonomy versus shame and doubt (1 to 2 years); initiative versus guilt (3 to 5 years); industry versus inferiority (6 to 11 years); identity versus role confusion (12 to 19 years); intimacy versus isolation (young adulthood: 20s and 30s); generativity versus stagnation (middle adulthood: 40s and 50s); and integrity versus despair (late adulthood: 60 and over).

8. Freud's psychoanalytical theory is an influential one. His emphases on unconscious motivations and defense mechanisms, as well as on environmental influences, and his treatment methods have made a real contribution to psychological theory and practice. Some feel his psychosexual theory of development is limited in scope, with overemphasis on sexual motivations and aggressive instincts as the basis of behavior. He has also done a disservice to women by blaming the survivors—the female victims themselves—for incest.

9. Erikson's theory is much broader than Freud's and encompasses the entire life span, with emphasis on a greater variety of motivational and environmental factors.

10. Behaviorism emphasizes the role of environmental influences in molding behavior. Behavior becomes the sum total of learned or conditioned responses to stimuli, a view that is somewhat mechanistic.

11. According to behaviorists, learning takes place through conditioning. There are two types of conditioning: classical conditioning, which is learning through association, and operant conditioning, which is learning from the consequences of behavior.

12. Social learning theory says that children learn by observing the behavior of others and by modeling their behavior after them.

13. Learning theorists have contributed much to the understanding of human development by emphasizing the role of environmental influences in shaping behavior. However, learning theories have been criticized for being too mechanistic and for neglecting the role of biology and maturation in development.

14. Humanism takes a very positive view of human nature and says that people are free to use their superior abilities to make intelligent choices and to realize their full potential as self-actualized persons.

15. Buhler said that the real goal of humans is fulfillment through accomplishment.

16. Maslow said that human behavior can be explained as motivation to satisfy needs, which can be classified into five categories: physiological needs, safety needs, love and belongingness needs, esteem needs, and self-actualization needs. Self-actualization is the highest need and the culmination of life.

17. Carl Rogers reflected the humanistic philosophy that if people are given both freedom to grow and emotional support (which he called unconditional positive regard), they can develop into fully functioning human beings.

18. Humanists have taught people to believe in themselves and in human nature, but are sometimes criticized for having a too optimistic view of human nature.

19. Cognition is the act or process of knowing. The Piagetian approach to cognitive development emphasizes the qualitative changes in the way people think as they develop.

20. Piaget divided the process of cognitive development into four stages: sensori-motor stage (birth to 2 years), preoperational stage (2 to 7 years), concrete operational stage (7 to 11 years), and formal operational stage (11 years and up).

21. The information-processing approach to cognition emphasizes the progressive steps, actions, and operations that take place when a person receives, perceives, remembers, thinks about, and utilizes information.

22. The cognitive theorists have made a real contribution by focusing attention on mental processes and their role in behavior. Piaget has been criticized for stressing biological maturation and minimizing the importance of environmental influences. Both Piagetian and information-processing approaches emphasize mental processes at a conscious level, ignoring any unconscious, psychodynamic causes of behavior.

23. Ethology emphasizes that behavior is a product of evolution and is biologically determined. Imprinting, bonding, and attachment theory are examples of this emphasis. Ethologist Robert Hinde prefers the term *sensitive period*, referring to certain times of life when the organism is more affected by particular kinds of experiences.

24. This book presents an eclectic theoretical orientation.

Key Terms

Accommodation   *p. 34*
Adaptation   *p. 34*
Anal stage   *p. 25*
Assimilation   *p. 34*
Attachment theory   *p. 37*
Autonomy vs. shame and doubt   *p. 36*
Behaviorism   *p. 28*
Bonding   *p. 37*
Classical conditioning   *p. 28*
Client-centered therapy   *p. 32*
Cognition   *p. 34*
Concrete operational stage   *p. 35*
Conditional positive regard   *p. 32*
Conditioning   *p. 28*
Defense mechanisms   *p. 24*
Denial   *p. 25*
Displacement   *p. 24*
Ego   *p. 24*
Electra complex   *p. 25*
Equilibration   *p. 35*
Equilibrium   *p. 34*
Ethology   *p. 36*
Fixated   *p. 25*
Formal operational stage   *p. 35*

Free association   *p. 24*
Generativity vs. stagnation   *p. 26*
Genital stage   *p. 25*
Holistic view   *p. 31*
Humanistic theory   *p. 31*
Id   *p. 24*
Identity vs. role confusion   *p. 26*
Imprinting   *p. 37*
Industry vs. inferiority   *p. 26*
Information-processing approach   *p. 35*
Initiative vs. guilt   *p. 26*
Integrity vs. despair   *p. 26*
Intimacy vs. isolation   *p. 26*
Latency stage   *p. 25*
Mechanistic or deterministic   *p. 28*
Modeling   *p. 30*
Oedipal complex   *p. 25*
Operant conditioning   *p. 29*
Oral stage   *p. 25*
Phallic stage   *p. 25*
Pleasure principle   *p. 24*
Positive reinforcement   *p. 29*
Preoperational stage   *p. 35*
Psychoanalytical theory   *p. 24*

Discussion Questions

1. Give examples of human behavior that support Freud's view of human nature and motivations. Give examples that do not support Freud's view of human nature and motivations.

2. What do you think of Freud's theory of psychosexual development? Which points do you agree with? Which do you disagree with? Give examples.

3. If you have children of your own, or if you teach children or care for them, give examples of their behavior that support Erikson's descriptions of one or more stages of psychosocial development.

4. Describe and give examples of learning through the following:

   a. Classical conditioning
   b. Operant conditioning
   c. Modeling
   d. Vicarious reinforcement

5. Do you agree or disagree with Buhler that the real goal of humans is fulfillment that is attained through accomplishment? Explain your views.

6. Is it possible to find self-actualization without first having the needs for love and belonging and esteem met? Explain.

7. According to humanistic theory, if children are given freedom and emotional support, they will make right choices and develop into fully functioning people. According to this view, do children need parental guidance? Why or why not? What are your views?

8. Compare formal operational thinking with the scientific methods of discovering truth.

9. Do you believe that bonding between a mother and her baby shortly after birth is a prerequisite for a satisfying parent-child relationship later in life? Explain.

10. Give examples of sensitive periods for optimum development of particular characteristics, skills, habits, or relationships in the lives of children. Describe.

Suggested Readings

BANDURA, A. (1986).   *Social foundations of thought and action.* Englewood Cliffs, NJ: Prentice-Hall. Bandura's social learning view of development.

CUMMINGS, M. R. (1998).   *Human heredity, principles and issues* (5th ed.). New York: Wadsworth.

ERIKSON, E. H. (1994).   *Identity and the life cycle.* New York: W. W. Norton. Erikson's basic views on identity development.

FLAVELL, J. H. (1992).   *Cognitive development* (2nd ed.). Englewood Cliffs, NJ: Prentice-Hall. A helpful summary.

KEGAN, O. (1997).   *The evolving self: Problem and process in human development.* Cambridge, MA: Harvard University Press. An integration of a number of theories to explain personality during adolescence and adulthood.

LOEVINGER, J. (1995).   *Paradigms of personality.* New York: W. H. Freeman. General summary and comparison of major theories.

MISHELL, D. R. (1999).   *Atlas of reproductive endocrinology.* New York: Appleton & Lange.

ROGOFF, B. (1990).   *Apprenticeship in thinking: Cognitive development in social context.* New York: Oxford University Press. Cross-cultural theory and research on children's thinking.

SPENCE, D. P. (1994).   *The rhetorical voice of psychoanalysis: Development of evidence by theory.* Cambridge, MA: Harvard University Press.

THOMAS, R. M. (1996).   *Comparing theories of child development* (4th ed.). Belmont, CA: Wadsworth.

Web Resources

http://mentalhelp.net Mental Health Net. Comprehensive listing of websites and health resources.

http://funderstanding.com/theories Funderstanding. All about learning theories.

Heredity, Environmental Influences, and Prenatal Development

The development of a human being from a fertilized egg to full-term baby is a fascinating process. This chapter covers the periods of prenatal development, with an emphasis on the kind of environment and prenatal care essential to the birth of a healthy baby. The roles of heredity and environmental influences in development are highlighted. Some hereditary defects and environmentally caused disorders are discussed, together with ways and means to avoid them.

REPRODUCTION

Two kinds of sex cells, or **gametes,** are involved in human reproduction: the male gamete, or sperm cell, and the female gamete, or ovum. Reproduction begins when a sperm cell fuses with an ovum to form a single new cell called a **zygote.** But let's begin at the beginning.

Spermatogenesis

Spermatogenesis refers to the process of sperm production that takes place in the *testes* of the male after he reaches puberty. Through a repeated cell division called **meiosis,** about 300 million sperm are produced daily and then stored in the *epididymis,* a system of ducts located at the back of the *testis.* Ordinarily, 200 million to 500 million sperm are released at each ejaculation. Some of these sperm are abnormal or dead, but for the sperm count to be normal, a minimum of 20 million healthy sperm per milliliter of *semen* needs to be present. Sperm are microscopic in size—only about one-five-hundredth of an inch long. About 10 to 20 ejaculations contain as many sperm as there are people on the planet. The sperm has a *head,* containing the cell nucleus that houses the chromosomes; a *midpiece;* and a *tail.* The midpiece produces chemical reactions that provide energy for the tail to lash back and forth, to propel the sperm along.

During intercourse, millions of sperm are ejaculated into the *vagina* during male orgasm, and begin a fantastic journey up the *vagina,* into the *uterus,* and up the *fallopian tubes.* When fertilization occurs, only a single sperm gains entrance to each available ovum.

Oogenesis

Oogenesis is the process by which female gametes, or egg cells called **ova,** are ripened in the *ovaries.* All of the egg cells that will ever be in the ovaries are present at birth, though undeveloped. Beginning at puberty, ordinarily one ovum ripens and is released every 28 days or so (depending on the length of the menstrual cycle).

The ovum is the largest cell of the body, about one-two-hundredth of an inch in diameter, large enough to be visible. In this cell, a clear thin shell encloses a liquid composed of hundreds of fat droplets and proteins in which a nucleus containing the chromosomes is found.

Conception

After the ovum is released (a process called **ovulation**), fingerlike projections of the fallopian tube sweep the egg into it. Inside the tube, hairlike projections called *cilia* propel the ovum toward the uterus. The journey from the ovary to the uterus usually takes about 3 to 4 days, but fertilization must take place within 48 hours after ovulation. **Fertilization,** or **conception,** normally takes place in the third of the fallopian tube nearest the ovary. Eventually, a few sperm reach the egg, but a sperm cannot penetrate the egg's outer wall without the help of chemical *enzymes* released from the head of the sperm. The enzymes

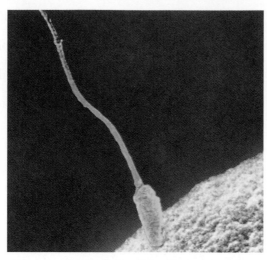

At each ejaculation, 200 to 500 million sperm are released.

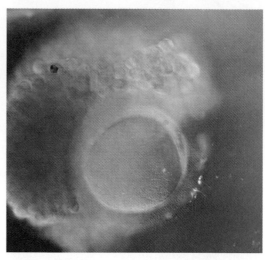

Millions of sperm attempt to fertilize the ovum, but only one will be able to penetrate the wall.

dissolve the wall of the ovum, allowing one sperm to penetrate. Immediately, the outer layer of the egg hardens so that the other sperm cannot enter. The tail of the sperm drops off, and its nucleus unites with the nucleus of the ovum so that the first single new cell is formed (Grobstein, 1989).

FAMILY PLANNING

Family planning means having children by choice and not by chance. Its goal is to enable people to have the number of children they want, when they want to have them. This objective covers prevention of unintended pregnancy as well as pursuit of infertility

treatment by couples having difficulty conceiving. Another important goal of certain family planning methods is to prevent the spread of sexually transmitted disease (Cates & Stone, 1992b; Williams, 1991).

Benefits

There are many benefits of family planning. The most urgent need is to protect the health of the mother and her children. Births spaced too close together pose an added health risk for both the mother and the baby (Bresler, 1998). A study in Hungary, Sweden, and the United States found that birth intervals of less than two years posed a 5 to 10% increased risk of low birth weight, preterm

Gametes—sex cells

Zygote—fertilized ovum

Spermatogenesis—process by which sperm are produced

Meiosis—process of cell division by which gametes reproduce

Oogenesis—process by which ova mature

Ova—female egg cells

Ovulation—process by which the mature ovum separates from the ovarian wall and is released from the ovary

Fertilization or conception—union of sperm and ovum

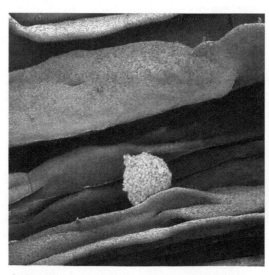

Ordinarily, at the time of ovulation, only one ovum ripens and is released during each menstrual cycle.

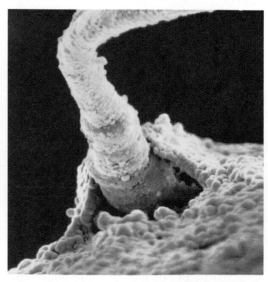

This sperm is penetrating the ovum.

birth, and neonatal death (Miller, 1991). The mother who bears one child this soon after the other is also at risk.

The timing of childbirth is a crucial factor. The psychological impact of parenthood is lessened if the parents are ready for parenthood and the birth is welcomed. Unfortunately, unintended pregnancy rates are high, among both married and unmarried women. Babies born to women who have not intended to conceive when they did have an elevated risk of adverse health outcomes, such as premature births, low birth rate, and intrauterine growth retardation (Kost, Landry, & Darroch, 1998).

Excluding miscarriages, 49% of the pregnancies concluding in 1994 were unintended; 54% of these ended in abortion. Forty-eight percent of women aged 15 to 44 in 1994 had at least one unplanned pregnancy sometime in their lives; 29% had had one or more unplanned births. 30% had had one or more abortions, and 11% had both. Rates of unintended pregnancy have declined, probably as a result of higher contraceptive prevalence and use of more effective methods (Henshaw, 1998).

Family planning is also necessary for the good of marriage. Couples who marry because of pregnancies have reduced chances of marital success. Both premarital pregnancies and early postmarital pregnancies are followed by higher-than-average divorce rates. Adolescent mothers are more likely to be unemployed, out of school, and on welfare. Many live with their parents after the baby is born. Older couples with large families often experience financial and management problems that often put a great strain on their relationship. Parents who have small families are able to offer their children intellectual and educational advantages (Blake, 1991).

Contraceptive Use

Data from the 1995 *National Survey of Family Growth* (NSFG) reveal the percentage distribution of contraceptive users aged 15 to 44, by current methods (Piccinino & Mosher, 1998). According to the NSFG, the most commonly reported methods were female sterilization and oral contraceptives. The male condom and male sterilization were the next most widely used methods. The implant, the IUD, the diaphragm, foam, periodic abstinence, and "other" methods were each used by fewer than one million women in 1995. The principle changes from 1995 to 1988 were the continued increase in condom use and the sharp decline in the use of the IUD and diaphragm. Two new methods—the implant and the

Living Issues

AIDS and the Use of Condoms

Since the advent of AIDS, the use of condoms has increased significantly (Sonenstein, Pleck, & Ku, 1989). The reason is that, except for abstinence, condoms are the best method of preventing the spread of sexually transmitted diseases. When used in addition to spermicides, which are detrimental to the HIV virus, they provide even better protection.

Condom failure is due to one or more reasons. Natural lambskin condoms are permeable to the AIDS, herpes, and hepatitis B viruses. Intact latex condoms do not allow the viruses to pass through, but some latex condoms leak. One government study found that 11 of 106 batches of American-made condoms and 30 of 98 imported condoms flunked a leak test (Parachini, 1987). These figures indicate that condoms should be blown up and submerged in water to test for leaks before usage.

The most common reasons for condom failure are breakage or slipping off (Trussell, Warner, & Hatcher, 1992). The end of the condom should protrude over the end of the penis to minimize strain on the material during intercourse. Slippage can occur during intercourse or withdrawal, even if the penis remains erect. Holding onto the condom during withdrawal minimizes slippage during that time (Cates & Stone, 1992a).

Certainly condoms provide *safer*, but not completely safe, sex.

TABLE 3.1	PERCENTAGE DISTRIBUTION OF CONTRACEPTIVE USERS AGED 15 TO 44 BY CURRENT METHODS, 1995

Method	Percentage
Sterilization	38.6
Female	27.7
Male	10.9
Pill	26.9
Implant	1.3
Injectible	3.0
IUD	0.8
Diaphragm	1.9
Male condoms	20.4
Foam	0.4
Periodic abstinence	2.3
Withdrawal	3.0
Other*	1.3
Total	100.0

*Other consists of douche, sponge, jelly or cream alone, and other methods.

Reproduced with the permission of The Alan Guttmacher Institute. From Piccinino, L.J. and Mosher, W.D. Trends in contraceptive use in the United States: 1982–1995, *Family Planning Perspectives*, 1998, 30(1):5, table 2.

injectible, were used by small numbers of women in 1995 (Piccinino & Mosher, 1998).

Prenatal Development

Periods of Development

Prenatal development takes place during three periods (Rice, 1989b):

1. the **germinal period**—from conception to implantation (attachment to the uterine wall)—about 14 days;
2. the **embryonic period**—from 2 weeks to 8 weeks after conception; and
3. the **fetal period**—from 8 weeks through the remainder of the pregnancy.

Figure 3.1 shows the early stages of the germinal period.

Germinal Period

The fertilized ovum is called a **zygote** (see Figure 3.2), which continues to be propelled through the fallopian tube by the cilia. About 30 hours after fertilization, the process of cell division begins. One cell divides into two, two into four, four into eight, and so on, the collection forming a **morula** (from the Latin word meaning "mulberry"). Every time the cells divide, they become smaller, allowing the total mass, called the **blastula,** to pass through the fallopian tube. The result of the repeated cell dividing is the formation of a hollow inner portion containing fluid.

Three to 4 days after fertilization, the newly formed blastula enters the uterus and floats around for another 3 to 4 days before the inner layer, called the **blastocyst,** begins to attach itself to the inner lining of the uterus (the *endometrium*) in a process called **implantation.** The implanting blastocyst releases an enzyme that literally eats a hole in the soft, spongy tissue of the endometrium until it completely buries itself in the uterine wall. By about 10 days after the blastula enters the uterus, implantation of the blastocyst is complete.

Embryonic Period

As stated previously, *about 14 days after conception, the blastocyst implants itself in the uterine wall.* The embryonic period begins at the end of the second week. The embryo develops from a round layer of cells across the center of the blastocyst. At 18 days, the **embryo** is about 0.0625 (1⁄16) of an inch long. During its

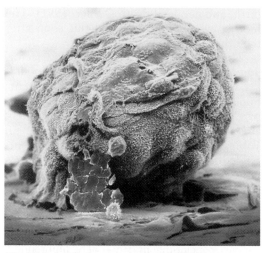

The blastocyst facilitates its landing on the uterine wall with leglike structures composed of sugar molecules.

early weeks, human embryos closely resemble those of other vertebrate animals, as Figure 3.3 illustrates. The embryo has a tail and traces of gills, both of which soon disappear. The head develops before the rest of the body. Eyes, nose, and ears are not yet visible at one month, but a backbone and vertebral canal have formed. Small buds that will develop into arms and legs appear. The heart forms and starts beating; other body systems begin to take shape.

Fetal Period

By the end of the embryonic period (2 months) the **fetus** has developed the first bone structure and distinct limbs and digits

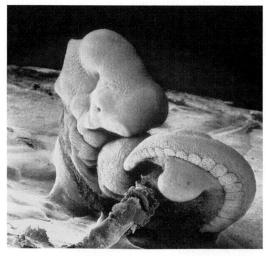

By 4½ weeks a rudimentary heart and an early eye have formed. The tail will disappear, leaving behind shrunk vertebrae that remain.

Germinal period

Embryonic period

Fetal period

Morula

Blastula

Blastocyst

Implantation

Embryo—growing baby from the end of the second week to the end of the eighth week after conception

Fetus—growing baby from the beginning of the third month of development to birth

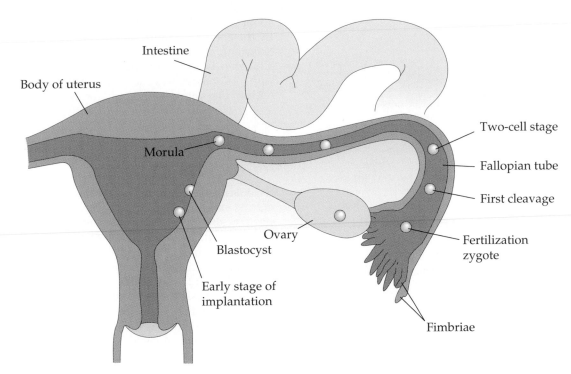

FIGURE 3.1   From zygote to implanted blastocyst. From the time of ovulation, it takes about two weeks before the fertilized egg is completely implanted in the wall of the uterus. In the meantime, the ovum divides and subdivides, forming the *morula* and then the *blastocyst*.

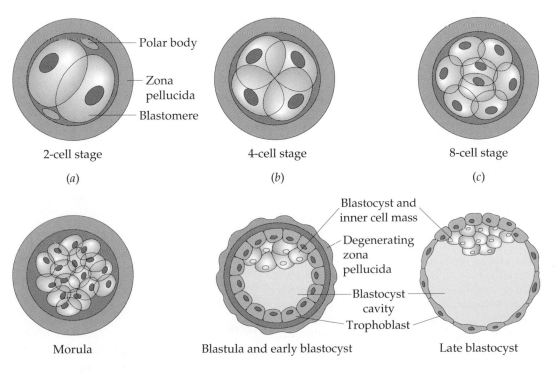

FIGURE 3.2   Early development from zygote to blastocyst.

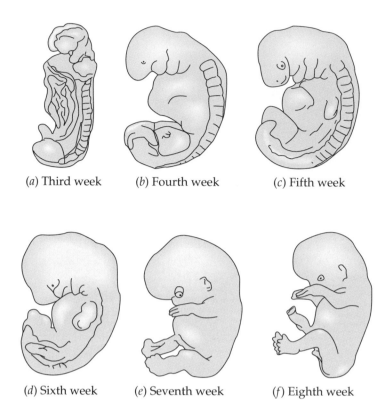

(a) Third week   (b) Fourth week   (c) Fifth week

(d) Sixth week   (e) Seventh week   (f) Eighth week

FIGURE 3.3   Development of human embryo from the third week to the eighth week after conception. The embryo grows from about 1 inch in length after the third week to 1¼ inches at the end of the eighth week.

that take on human form. Major blood vessels form, and internal organs continue to develop. By the end of the first **trimester** (one-third the length of pregnancy, or 12.7 weeks), the fetus is about 3 inches long; most major organs are present, a large head and face are well formed, and a heartbeat can be detected with a stethoscope. Figure 3.4 shows embryonic and fetal sizes from 2 to 15 weeks following conception.

By the end of the fourth or fifth month, the mother can usually feel fetal movement. The skin of the fetus is covered with a fine hair, usually shed before birth. At the end of the fifth month, the fetus weighs about 1 pound and is about 12 inches long. It sleeps and wakes, sucks, and moves its position. At the end of the sixth month, eyes, eyelids, and eyelashes form. The fetus's eyes are light sensitive, and he or she can hear uterine sounds and respond to vibrations and acoustical stimulation (Kisilevsky, Muir, & Low, 1992).

The head and body of the fetus become more proportionate during the third trimester. Fat layers form under the skin. By the end of the eighth month, the fetus weighs

Trimester—one-third of the gestation period, or about 12.7 weeks

about 5 pounds and is about 18 inches long. By the end of the ninth month, the nails have grown to the ends of the fingers and toes. The skin becomes smoother and is covered with a protective waxy substance called *vernix caseosa*. The baby is now ready for delivery.

PRENATAL CARE

Medical and Health Care

Ordinarily the fetus is well protected in its uterine environment, but as soon as a woman suspects she is pregnant, she needs to receive good prenatal care. Time is of the essence because the first 3 months of fetal development are crucial to the optimum health of the child. Initial prenatal visits include a complete physical examination. Because the prospective father is involved and concerned as well, it is helpful for him to accompany his partner on prenatal visits. The examiner will take a complete medical history of the mother, and the father if necessary, perform various tests, and make recommendations regarding health care during pregnancy. Sexual relations, minor complications of pregnancy, and danger signs to watch for in avoiding major complications will be discussed to allay the couple's fear and anxieties (Rice, 1989b).

Minor Side Effects

No pregnancy is without some discomfort. Expectant mothers may experience one or several of the following to varying degrees: nausea (morning sickness), heartburn, flatus (gas), hemorrhoids, constipation, shortness of breath, backache, leg cramps, uterine contractions, insomnia, minor vaginal discharge, and varicose veins. The caregiver, or examiner, will suggest the best ways in which each woman can minimize her discomforts (Rice, 1989b).

Major Complications of Pregnancy

Major complications of pregnancy arise infrequently; however, when they do, they more seriously threaten the health and life of the woman and the developing embryo or fetus than do the usual minor discomforts of pregnancy.

Pernicious Vomiting

This condition is prolonged and persistent vomiting, which may dehydrate the woman and rob her of adequate nutrients for proper fetal growth. One woman in several hundred suffers from vomiting to the extent that she requires hospitalization.

Toxemia

This condition is characterized by high blood pressure; waterlogging of the tissues (edema), indicated by swollen face and limbs or rapid weight gain; albumin in the urine; headaches; blurring of vision; and eclampsia (convulsions). If not treated, toxemia can be fatal to mother and embryo or fetus. Most commonly it is a disease of neglect because proper prenatal care is lacking. Toxemia during pregnancy ranks as one of three chief causes of maternal mortality (Guttmacher, 1983).

Threatened Abortion

The first symptom of this condition is usually vaginal bleeding. Studies reveal that about one in six pregnancies is spontaneously aborted before the fetus is of sufficient size to survive. Most spontaneous abortions occur early in pregnancy. Three out of four happen before the twelfth week, and only one in four occurs between 12 and 28 weeks (Guttmacher, 1983).

Placenta Abrupto and Placenta Praevia

Placenta abrupto refers to the premature separation of the placenta from the uterine wall. In *placenta praevia*, the placenta grows partially or entirely over the cervical opening. One in 200 pregnant women suffers from this problem, which usually occurs in the third trimester. If they are given proper treatment, 80% to 85% of the babies will survive. About 60% are delivered by cesarean section.

Ectopic Pregnancy

Ectopic pregnancy occurs when the fertilized ovum attaches and grows in an area other than within the uterus. Sometimes the pregnancy is in the fallopian tubes; at other times, it is situated in the ovary, abdomen, or cervix. Such pregnancies have to be terminated by surgery. Surveys indicate that the number of ectopic pregnancies has been climbing steadily. Possible causes may be the postponement of childbearing, during which time the fallopian tubes age; previous abortion; pelvic inflammatory disease (PID); sexually transmitted diseases (STDs); frequent douching with commercial preparations; and previous surgery (Althaus, 1991b). Any condition that affects the fallopian tubes can impede transport of the fertilized

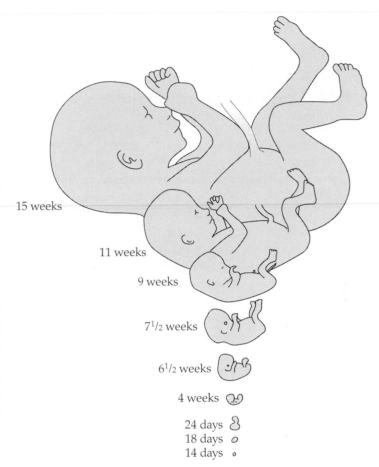

15 weeks

11 weeks

9 weeks

7½ weeks

6½ weeks

4 weeks

24 days

18 days

14 days

FIGURE 3.4   Embryonic and fetal development from 2 to 15 weeks following conception.

ovum, thus contributing to an ectopic pregnancy. Despite the increase in ectopic pregnancies, which must always be terminated, fetal mortality rates have fallen because women are getting prompter and better treatment (Rice, 1989b).

RH Incompatibility

This condition involves an expectant mother with Rh negative blood who carries a fetus with Rh positive blood (Rice, 1989b). Rh incompatibility is determined during an initial prenatal exam. The Rh factor is a protein found in the blood. Because some of a baby's red blood cells cross the placenta and enter the mother's bloodstream during pregnancy and delivery, an Rh-negative mother will develop antibodies to the blood cells of an Rh-positive baby. If she has another Rh-positive baby, the antibodies in her blood will pass through the placenta and destroy the baby's red blood cells, possibly causing jaundice, anemia, mental retardation, and even death. Fortunately, a

Ectopic pregnancy—attachment and growth of the embryo in any location other than inside the uterus

Living Issues

Ethnicity, Race, and Infant Mortality

Infant mortality refers to the number of infants dying per 1,000 population during the first year of life. Overall, the rate among whites was 6.0 in 1996 (U.S. Bureau of the Census, 1998). This is in sharp contrast to the rates among minority races or ethnic groups. The rate of infant mortality is highest among Native Americans. One study of infant mortality on an Oregon Indian reservation showed a rate almost three times higher than the overall U.S. rate (Remez, May/June, 1992). The rate among blacks is 15.8, over two times greater than for whites (U.S. Bureau of the Census, 1998). Infants born to poor, young, undereducated, or unmarried black women are at special risk (Jamieson & Buescher, 1992). However, the rates among poor women of all races, including whites, are high, although not as high as among blacks (Turner, 1992). Infant mortality among Hispanics is lower than among blacks, but still higher than among whites (Klitsch, 1991). The rate is especially high among Puerto Ricans as compared with Mexican Americans and Cuban Americans.

The most significant factor in relation to these figures is the lack of proper prenatal care from the beginning of pregnancy. Nationally, 16% of all pregnant women receive inadequate prenatal care. Either they don't go to the doctor at all, go late in pregnancy, or make fewer visits than recommended (Harvey & Faber, 1993). Nationally almost 7% of mothers are pregnant for five months or more before they receive any prenatal care (National Survey on Family Growth, 1997, p. 93). Yet, early and regular prenatal care is associated with reduced infant mortality and favorable outcomes on key measures of child health, such as birth weight. The primary reason for lack of care is financial. Medicaid coverage for pregnant women with family incomes below 133% of the poverty level has been expanded. This increase has helped considerably. Nonetheless, there are still many women not eligible for Medicaid who lack the resources to get insurance coverage and, as a result, go without care (Althaus, 1991a). Only some of these women are able to obtain help through local public health departments, community hospitals, or other maternity care providers. Providing adequate prenatal care is actually cost-effective. Every dollar spent on pre-natal care for high-risk women saves an average of over $3 in the care of low-birth-weight infants (Harvey & Faber, 1993).

serum called anti-Rh gamma-globulin was developed in the 1960s. When administered to a previously unsensitized Rh-negative mother within a few hours of giving birth to an Rh-positive baby, the serum prevents the development of antibodies; or it may be given at about 28 weeks of pregnancy. The antibodies are gradually destroyed, and the mother remains unsensitized (Berkow, 1997). If tests of the amniotic fluid (amniocentesis) reveal that the fetus may already be affected, intrauterine blood transfusions may be given into the fetal abdominal cavity.

Infertile—unable to conceive or to effect pregnancy

INFERTILITY

In 1995, the NSFG provided new information on impaired fertility in the United States over the past decade. The proportion of U.S. women aged 15 to 44 who report some form of fertility impairment grew from 8% in 1982 to 10% in 1995, an increase in absolute numbers from 4.6 million to 6.2 million women. This substantial change in **infertility** was not in age-specific infertility rates but in the numbers of women who reported infertility problems and sought medical help to have a baby. The dramatic increase in the numbers of U.S. women with impaired fertility occurred because the large baby-boom cohort, many of whom delayed childbearing, had reached their later and less fertile reproductive years. This increase in both rates and numbers occurred across almost all age parity, marital status, education, income, racial, and ethnic subgroups (Chandra & Stephen, 1998).

Causes

About 20% of infertility cases involve both partners. Both are "subfertile": they have too frequent or too infrequent intercourse; they have intercourse only during those times of the month when the woman is least likely to get pregnant; they use Vaseline or some other vaginal lubricant that injures sperm cells or acts as a barrier preventing the sperm from entering the *cervix*; or they are too old or in poor health.

About 40% of infertility cases involve the man. To impregnate a woman, a man must meet four biological requirements. He must

1. produce healthy live sperm in sufficient numbers;
2. secrete seminal fluid in proper amounts and with the right composition to transport sperm;
3. have an unobstructed throughway from the testicle to the end of the penis, allowing the sperm to pass; and
4. be able to achieve and sustain an erection in order to ejaculate sperm within the vagina.

A number of physical and psychological factors may cause male infertility.

About 40% of infertility cases involve the woman. To be capable of pregnancy, a woman also must meet several basic biological requirements. She needs to be ovulating, the passage through the fallopian tubes needs to be clear, and the cervical mucus must allow passage of the sperm (Ansbacher & Adler, 1988). Several additional factors may affect female fertility: Abnormalities of the uterus sometimes prevent conception or full-term pregnancy; the climate of the vagina may be too acid, thus immobilizing the sperm; and the age of the mother may also be a factor. Fertility decreases gradually after age 35 and ceases completely after menopause.

Impact

Involuntary childlessness due to infertility can cause significant emotional and psychological distress for some persons (Daniluk, 1991). A lack of self-esteem, a sense of loss of internal control of one's life, and depression may result from infertility (Abbey, Andrews, & Halman, 1992). Grief, anger, and guilt reactions are common (Higgins, 1990). Stress is often higher among wives than among husbands, if the women are less willing than their husbands to forgo parenthood, or if they see infertility as role failure on their part (Benazon, Wright, & Sabourin, 1992; Ulbrich, Coyle, & Llabre, 1990). Also, if a couple seeks treatment, the majority of tests and treatments focus on the woman's body, regardless of whether it is the man or the woman whose physical problems are causing the infertility. Other people may assume that infertility is the wife's fault and treat her as a second-class citizen. She may feel out of place around other women who are mothers.

Continued infertility may have an effect on marital and sexual satisfaction (Pepe & Byrne, 1991). If treatment does not seem to be working, couples show greater dissatisfaction with their sexual relationship as time goes on (Benazon, Wright, & Sabourin, 1992). Social changes may also occur, as infertile couples alter their network interactions in an attempt to avoid painful reminders of their childlessness (Higgins, 1990).

In contrast to these unhappy couples, some couples report that their problems brought them closer together, that they were more affectionate and had higher levels of communication. They became even more committed to their marriage and to share their lives together (Ulbrich, Coyle, & Llabre, 1990). Much depends on the attitudes of the couple. The longer they are married and childless, the less trouble they have adjusting to involuntary childlessness as a permanent state. Two-career couples usually have less trouble adjusting

Living Issues

Abortion and the Question of Viability

On January 22, 1973, the United States Supreme Court ruled that a state could not inhibit or restrict a woman's right to obtain an abortion during the first trimester of pregnancy (12.7 weeks) and that the decision to have an abortion was the woman's own in consultation with her doctor (*Roe* v. *Wade*, 1973). In a 5 to 4 decision announced on July 3, 1989, the court overthrew the trimester provisions of *Roe* v. *Wade*, and said that a doctor, before aborting a fetus believed to be at least 20 weeks gestation, will determine if the fetus is **viable** and perform tests that establish the fetus's gestational age, weight, and lung maturity. The court reaffirmed that states may pass laws regulating abortion after viability "except where it is necessary . . . for the preservation of the life or health of the mother" (*Webster* v. *Reproductive Health Services, Inc.*, 1988). The majority opinion in this decision said that the statement was interpreted to mean that only those tests that are necessary to determine viability be performed. If viability is determined, the mother and doctor are subject to any special laws passed by the particular state.

Several comments need to be made.

1. Determination of viability through tests is expensive and, because of their costs, women who cannot afford the tests are prevented from having an abortion.

2. The tests sometimes impose health risks for both the pregnant woman and the fetus.

3. The tests are sometimes unreliable and inaccurate.

4. At 20 weeks of age, no fetus is viable or can be made viable by any foreseeable new scientific techniques (Rosoff, 1989).

5. Tests of lung maturity cannot provide the necessary information until the fetus is at least 28 to 30 weeks gestation. Any tests before these ages are imprecise ("The Court Edges Away from Roe v. Wade," 1989).

6. Using viability tests as a basis for decision eliminates the woman's right to choose whether she will have an abortion or not.

7. There is confusion over calculating the weeks of gestation. Physicians and a number of health agencies calculate the period of gestation from the first day of the woman's last menstrual period instead of from the day of fertilization, which comes two weeks later (DiPietro & Allen, 1991). Because the law does not specify how the period of gestation should be calculated, there is confusion as to when a viability test is necessary (Santee & Henshaw, 1992). For these reasons, many thoughtful persons are opposed to viability tests as one determinant of whether a woman can have an abortion.

to the situation than those where the wife does not work. Some research suggests that couples usually divorce if the husband wants a child and the wife does not, but they tend to stay together if the wife wants a child and the husband does not. The couple's attitude toward a childless lifestyle has a significant effect on

Viable—able to live

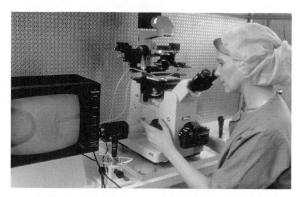

In in vitro fertilization, scratching the surface of the ovum allows the sperm to penetrate more easily.

Artificial insemination—injection of sperm cells into the vagina or uterus for the purpose of inducing pregnancy

Homologous insemination (AIH)—artificial insemination with the husband's sperm

Heterologous insemination (AID)—artificial insemination using the sperm from a donor

Surrogate mother

In vitro fertilization—removal of the ovum from the mother and fertilizing it in the laboratory, then implanting the zygote within the uterine wall

their marital adjustment (Ulbrich, Coyle, & Llabre, 1990).

Alternate Means of Conception

Artificial Insemination

If other medical treatments for infertility don't succeed, several techniques may permit couples to have children. One technique is **artificial insemination.** In this procedure, the sperm are injected into the woman's vagina or uterus for the purpose of inducing pregnancy. If the husband's sperm are used, the process is called **homologous insemination,** or **AIH** (artificial insemination husband). If the husband's sperm count is low, the sperm may be collected, frozen, and stored until a sufficient quantity is available, then thawed and injected. Generally, AIH is effective in only 5% of the cases, because the sperm were incapable of effecting pregnancy in the first place. Using sperm from a donor

is called **heterologous insemination,** or **AID** (artificial insemination donor). Increasingly, lesbian as well as heterosexual women have been utilizing donor insemination and other reproductive technologies to conceive children (Chan, Raboy, & Patterson, 1998).

Surrogate Mother

Sometimes a woman not able to bear a child still wants to have one by her partner, so together they find a consenting woman who acts as a **surrogate mother.** The surrogate mother agrees to be inseminated with the semen of the male member of the couple, to carry the fetus to term, and then to give the child (and all rights to it) to the couple. When 70 women were questioned regarding their motives for serving as surrogate mothers, they gave the following reasons: money, compassion for the childless couple and desire to help them, or enjoyment of pregnancy (Sobel, 1981). Half the surrogate mothers were married and already had children of their own. There are many unsettled legal questions relating to the rights to the child and to the legitimacy of surrogate agreements.

In Vitro Fertilization

The **in vitro fertilization** procedure is used when the fallopian tubes are blocked so that the sperm never reaches the ovum. One or more eggs are removed from the mother, fertilized in the laboratory with the partner's sperm, grown for 3 or 4 days until the uterus is hormonally ready, and then one or more are implanted in the uterine wall. Up to four blastocysts may be returned to the womb, since using multiple blastocysts increases the chance of pregnancy. With in vitro fertilization, there is about a 25% pregnancy rate. IVF offers the reward of a biological child, but it entails extremely high financial, emotional, and physical costs (L. S. Williams, 1992). The procedure is opposed by those who feel it is immoral and tampering with nature. Since the success rate of IVF is low, some couples simultaneously apply for adoption (Williams, 1992).

Cryopreservation, or the freezing of blastocysts (preembryos), is fast becoming commonplace as a way of augmenting in vitro fertilization. Cryopreservation makes it possible to store the extra blastocysts for later use in the event that earlier attempts at implantation are unsuccessful. Cryopreservation further allows for the possibility of blastocyst adoption. It is estimated that frozen blasto-

FOCUS

Treatments for Infertility

Generally speaking, if couples are younger than 35 years of age, they should wait for a full year of attempting pregnancy before consulting a physician. This waiting period gives enough time for conception to take place if the couple are fertile. If they are older than 35, they should see a doctor after 6 months of unsuccessful attempts. Older couples should get help sooner because psychological and physical factors that work against conception grow stronger with time. For the younger couple, waiting for a reasonable period of time (1 year) improves the chances of fertility.

cysts may be kept potentially viable for 600 years and perhaps up to 10,000 years.

Gamete Intrafallopian Transfer (GIFT)

The **gamete intrafallopian transfer (GIFT)** procedure involves inserting a thin, plastic tube carrying the sperm and egg directly into the fallopian tube, where the gametes unite just as they would in normal conception. "GIFT is what nature really does, with a little help from us," says Dr. Ricardo Asch, professor of obstetrics and gynecology at the University of California at Irwin (Ubell, 1990). The success rate is 40%—double that of in vitro fertilization.

Embryo Transplant

Embryo transplant is even more controversial (Dunn, Ryan, & O'Brien, 1988). In this procedure, a volunteer female donor is artificially inseminated with the sperm of the infertile woman's partner. After about 5 days, the zygote is removed from the donor and transferred into the uterus of the mother-to-be, who carries the child during pregnancy. Embryos may even be frozen and stored prior to implantation in a uterus. At present, the procedure is experimental and costly, and has a low success rate.

HEREDITY

Chromosomes, Genes, and DNA

Chromosomes are rodlike structures in the nucleus of each cell. The chromosomes carry the hereditary material called **genes,** which control physical characteristics that are inherited. The genes do this by directing the physical changes in the body throughout its development. Each body cell, except the sex cells, or gametes, contains 23 pairs of chromosomes, and each chromosome has between 20,000 and 100,000 genes. The gametes contain only half the number of chromosomes present in other body cells. Instead of 23 pairs, each sperm or ovum has 23 single chromosomes. *When the sperm and ovum unite, the 23 single chromosomes within the nucleus of each gamete combine in pairs with those in the other gamete to produce 46 chromosomes in the resulting zygote.* Figure 3.5 shows the process. After fertilization takes place and the one-celled zygote begins to divide and subdivide, the 46 chromosomes each split in half with each cell division, so that each daughter cell contains the same 23 pairs of chromosomes. This process means that each

Body cells of men and women contain 23 pairs of chromosomes.

Man   Woman

At maturity, each sex cell has only 23 single chromosomes. Through meiosis, a member is taken randomly from each original pair of chromosomes.

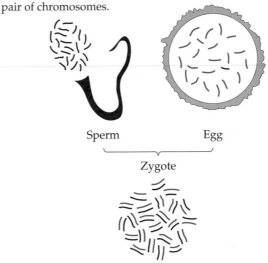

Sperm   Egg

Zygote

At fertilization, the chromosomes from each parent pair up so that the zygote contains 23 pairs of chromosomes—half from the mother and half from the father.

FIGURE 3.5   Hereditary composition of the zygote.

new cell produced contains the same 23 pairs of chromosomes with their genes.

Genes are made up of numerous molecules called deoxyribonucleic acid, or **DNA.** The DNA molecule looks like a double helix, or a spiral staircase, with a phosphate-sugar structure on the outside framework and with four *base* molecules (*adenine, thymine, guanine,* and *cytosine*) occurring in pairs that form the steps of the staircase on the inside. The bases are labeled A, T, G, and C, as shown in Figure 3.6. One strand of DNA may continue for thousands of base pairs, and the number of different strands that can be made is almost infinite. Each section of DNA is a separate gene, and the vertical sequence of the base pairs acts as a code to direct the cells as they reproduce and manufacture proteins that maintain life. Each cell of the body has the same DNA code and the same genes that direct growth. The particular code that we inherit from our parents directs our growth as humans rather than as other creatures, and is responsible for all the physical characteristics we develop.

Gamete intrafallopian transfer (GIFT)—inserting sperm cells and an egg cell directly into the fallopian tube, where fertilization is expected to occur

Embryo transplant—insemination of a volunteer female with the sperm of an infertile woman's partner; the resulting zygote is transferred, about 5 days later, into the uterus of the mother-to-be

Chromosomes—rodlike structures in each cell, occurring in pairs, that carry the hereditary material

Genes—the hereditary material of the chromosomes

DNA—complex molecules in genes that form the basis for the genetic structure, deoxyribonucleic acid

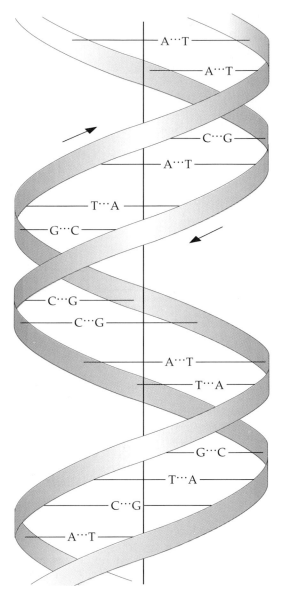

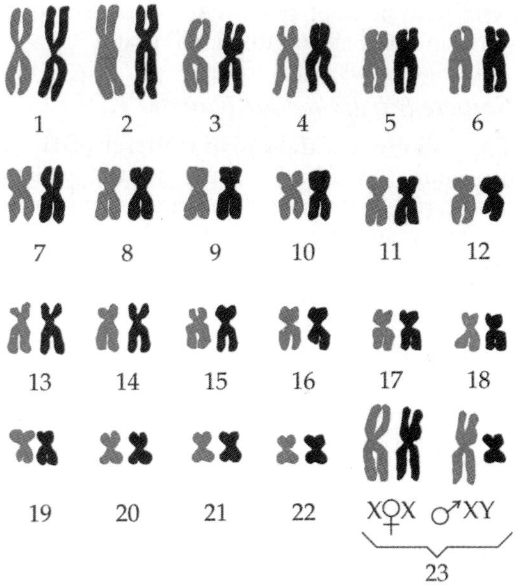

FIGURE 3.7   The twenty-third pair of chromosomes.

FIGURE 3.6   DNA molecule.

somes. If a sperm containing an X chromosome unites with the ovum (producing an XX combination), a girl is conceived. If a sperm containing a Y chromosome unites with the ovum (producing an XY combination), a boy is conceived. Because the Y-carrying sperm have a longer tail and a lighter head, they swim faster and may reach the egg cell sooner. For this reason, there is a conception ratio of 160 males to 100 females. However, because the male zygote is more vulnerable, the ratio is reduced to 120 males to 100 females by the time of implantation; to 110 males to 100 females by full term; and to 105 to 100 females born live.

Multiple Births

Twins may be of the same sex or of both sexes, depending on whether they start from one egg, as **monozygotic (identical) twins,** or from two eggs, as **dizygotic (fraternal) twins.** *Identical twins result when an ovum fertilized by one sperm divides during development to produce two embryos.* The embryos have the same heredity, are always of the same sex, and usually share a common *placenta.* If the two developing embryos do not completely separate, **Siamese twins** (conjoined twins) result. *Fraternal twins result when two ova are fertilized by two separate sperm.* They may be of the same sex or of different sexes and will be as different in heredity as are any other siblings. They develop with separate placentas. Triplets, quadruplets, and so forth may

Autosomes—twenty-two pairs of chromosomes that are responsible for most aspects of the individual's development

Sex chromosomes—twenty-third pair of chromosomes that determines the gender of the offspring

Monozygotic (identical) twins—one-egg, or identical, twins

Dizygotic (fraternal) twins—two-egg, or fraternal, twins

Siamese twins—monozygotic twins where complete separation did not occur during development

The Twenty-Third Pair and Sex Determination

Each sperm cell and each ovum contains 23 chromosomes. Twenty-two of these are labeled **autosomes** and are responsible for most aspects of the individual's development. Figure 3.7 illustrates the twenty-third pair, the **sex chromosomes,** which determine whether the offspring will be male or female. As shown in Figure 3.8, the man produces two types of sperm: one type with an X chromosome, having a larger head and shorter tail; another type with a Y chromosome, having a smaller head and longer tail. The woman produces ova with only X chromo-

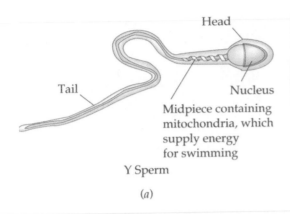

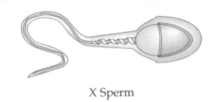

Head

Tail

Nucleus

Midpiece containing
mitochondria, which
supply energy
for swimming

Y Sperm

(a)

X Sperm

FIGURE 3.8 Two types of sperm.

*Identical twins are called monozygotic twins because
they develop from one egg.*

be all identical (from one ova), all fraternal (from separately fertilized ova), or a combination. Two of three triplets may be identical, for example, with the third fraternal. In this case, two ova are fertilized by two sperm, and one of the resulting zygotes divides after fertilization to produce two embryos.

Simple Inheritance and Dominant–Recessive Inheritance

An Austrian monk named Gregor Mendel (1822–1884) first discovered the laws that govern inheritance. He experimented by crossing garden pea plants with one another, and noticed that various traits such as yellow or green color, wrinkled or smooth seeds, tall or short height appeared or disappeared from one generation to the next.

The peas that Mendel used for his experiments came in two colors: yellow or green. When Mendel crossed purebred plants producing yellow peas with other purebreds containing yellow peas, he noticed that all the resulting offspring plants produced yellow peas. When he crossed two purebred plants producing green peas, the result was always plants with green peas. However, when he crossed purebred plants producing yellow peas with those producing purebred green peas, all the offspring plants produced yellow peas. If he then bred these hybrids, 75% of the offspring had yellow peas and the remaining 25% had green peas. Mendel explained this result by formulating the **law of dominant inheritance.** The law says that when an organism inherits competing traits (such as green and yellow colors), only one trait will be expressed. The trait that is expressed is *dominant* over the other, which is recessive. The dominant trait is written with a capital letter, the *recessive* with a lowercase letter.

The diagrams in Figure 3.9 illustrate possible results when peas are crossed.

Let's see how **dominant genes** and **recessive genes** work. Genes that govern alternate expressions of a particular characteristic (such as skin color) are called **alleles.** An organism receives a pair of alleles for a given characteristic, one from each parent. When both alleles are the same, the organism is **homozygous** for

Law of dominant inheritance

Dominant gene

Recessive gene

Alleles

Homozygous

Parenting Issues

Selecting the Sex of Your Child

Various techniques have been used to try to control the sex of the child that is conceived. Sperm carrying Y chromosomes are more fragile than X-carrying sperm, and all sperm are more viable in an alkaline environment. Therefore, if a male baby is desired, one theory suggests that everything possible be done to keep the Y-carrying sperm alive and healthy: use an alkaline douche; have intercourse two days or so after ovulation (so the sperm can reach the egg easily); use deep penetration during intercourse; and have the female orgasm precede male ejaculation (so the sperm are not squirted out during female orgasm). The opposite measures would be taken if a female baby is desired. Some researchers have found this total approach to sex selection reliable (Simcock, 1985).

A more promising technique is to separate the Y and X sperm, and through artificial insemination, to inject the type needed, depending on the sex desired.

Gregor Mendel discovered the laws that govern inheritance by crossing garden pea plants with one another.

the trait; when the alleles are different, the organism is **heterozygous** for the characteristic. When the alleles are heterozygous, the dominant allele is expressed. Thus, in Figure 3.9, YY or gg alleles are *homozygous*, and gY or Yg are *heterozygous*. Only when there is a pairing of recessive alleles (gg) can the recessive trait be expressed.

An observable trait (like seed color) is called a **phenotype**, while the underlying genetic pattern is called a **genotype.** Organisms may have identical phenotypes but different genotypes. For example, the plants that produce yellow peas (the phenotype) may have different genotypes (YY, Yg, or gY).

The same principle holds true in humans. Brown eyes, for example, are dominant over blue eyes. If we let B = brown eyes, and b = blue eyes, and pair a brown-eyed man with heterozygous alleles with a blue-eyed woman with homozygous alleles, we get the possible results shown in Figure 3.10. In this case, half the offspring would have brown eyes (bB and bB), and half would have blue eyes (bb and bb), because two recessive genes would have to be paired to produce blue eyes.

Table 3.2 shows a variety of dominant and recessive human characteristics.

Incomplete Dominance

Sometimes one allele is not completely dominant over the other. This phenomenon is known as **incomplete dominance.** An example is *sickle-cell anemia*, a condition common among blacks. In this condition, the red blood cells of a person are sickle-shaped or crescent-shaped instead of circular, and they tend to clog the blood vessels, restricting blood circulation, causing tissue damage and even death. Also, the spleen tries to destroy the blood cells, causing anemia. Sickle-cell anemia occurs only in persons who carry homozygous genes for that trait. The result for these people is that both sickle-cell genes direct the body to manufacture the abnormal blood cells. Other people are heterozygous with respect to the sickle-cell trait, having one sickle-cell gene and one normal one. The result is that neither gene is dominant or recessive, so the person has a mixture of two types of blood cells: part normal and part sickle-cell. Such a person functions all right except at high altitudes, where oxygen is scarce. Interestingly, people with sickle-cells are protected against malaria because the malaria parasite apparently doesn't thrive in blood containing these cells.

Polygenic Inheritance

In many instances, traits do not result from a single gene pair, but from a combination of many gene pairs. For example, numerous genes or gene pairs are involved in body height, weight, and shape. When gene pairs interact, one gene pair may inhibit or allow the expression of the other gene pair. A system of interacting gene pairs is called a **polygenic system of inheritance.** Such systems produce a wide variety of phenotypes that may differ from those of either parent.

Heterozygous

Phenotype

Genotype

Incomplete dominance—where neither gene is dominant over the other

Polygenic system of inheritance—number of interacting genes that produce a phenotype

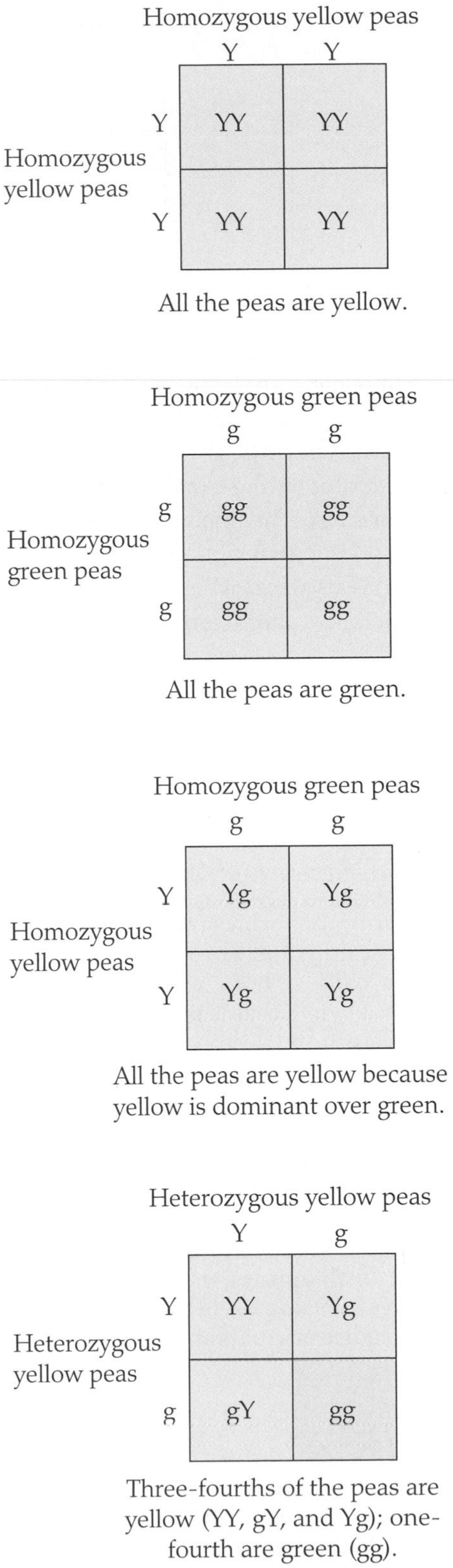
Homozygous yellow peas
Y Y
Y YY YY
Homozygous yellow peas
Y YY YY
All the peas are yellow.
Homozygous green peas
g g
g gg gg
Homozygous green peas
g gg gg
All the peas are green.
Homozygous green peas
g g
Y Yg Yg
Homozygous yellow peas
Y Yg Yg
All the peas are yellow because yellow is dominant over green.
Heterozygous yellow peas
Y g
Y YY Yg
Heterozygous yellow peas
g gY gg
Three-fourths of the peas are yellow (YY, gY, and Yg); one-fourth are green (gg).

FIGURE 3.9 Mendelian inheritance in peas.

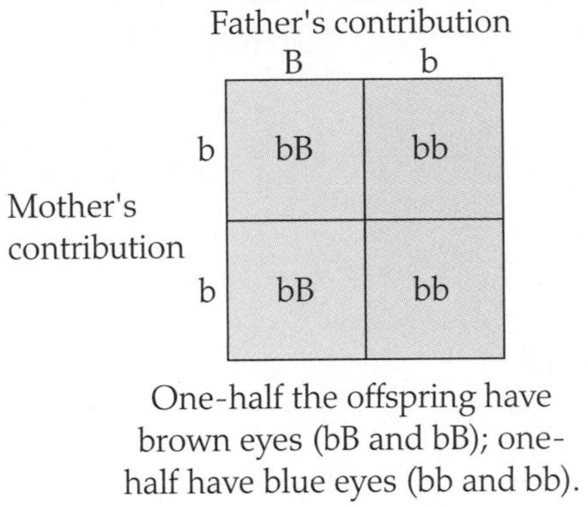
Father's contribution
B b
b bB bb
Mother's contribution
b bB bb
One-half the offspring have brown eyes (bB and bB); one-half have blue eyes (bb and bb).

FIGURE 3.10 Inheritance for eye color.

One example is skin color, which is the result of the action of a number of genes. A light-skinned person and a dark-skinned person usually have children with skin tone between their own because half the genes come from each parent. However, the child may also have a lighter or darker skin than either parent, with the child inheriting only the light- or dark-skin genes from the parents.

Many other characteristics, including personality traits such as intelligence, sociability, and temperament, are a result of polygenic inheritance. Even then, inheritance only predisposes us toward certain traits. We inherit a range of possibilities called the **reaction range,** which is the range of phenotypes for each genotype (Scarr, 1984). Environmental influences may enhance or detract from the inherited possibilities.

Some genotypes seem to produce characteristics that persist regardless of environmental influences. A child who seems to have a predisposition toward superior intelligence, for example, may evidence this characteristic in spite of adverse environmental circumstances. This tendency for a trait to persist is called **canalization.**

Reaction range—range of possible phenotypes given a particular genotype and environmental influences

Canalization—tendency for inherited characteristics to persist along a certain path regardless of environmental conditions

Sex-Linked Traits

Some defective, recessive genes are carried on only the twenty-third pair of chromosomes, the sex chromosomes, to produce what are called **sex-linked disorders.** One example is *hemophilia*, a disorder characterized by inability of the blood to clot. If a woman inherits a defective, recessive, hemophilic gene on the X chromosome that she receives from her mother, and a second, normal, dominant gene on the X chromosome

Sex-linked disorders—disorders carried only by the mother, through defective, recessive genes on the X chromosome

TABLE 3.2 DOMINANT AND RECESSIVE TRAITS IN HUMANS

Dominant	*Recessive*
Brown eyes	Blue or hazel eyes
Long eyelashes	Short eyelashes
Near- or farsightedness	Normal vision
Dark hair	Light or red hair
Curly hair	Straight hair
Cataract	Normal vision
Skin pigmentation	Albinism
Glaucoma	Normal eyes
Color vision	Color blindness
Free earlobes	Attached earlobes
Normal metabolism	Phenylketonuria
Broad lips	Thin lips
Scaly skin Ichthyosis)	Normal skin
Polydactylism (extra fingers and toes)	Normal
Dwarfism (Achondroplasia)	Normal
Huntington's disease	Normal
Normal hearing or deafness	Deafness

Adapted from "The Curve of Life as Studied in Biographies" by C. Buhler, 1935, *Journal of Applied Psychology, 19*, pp. 406–409.

that she receives from her father, she will not be a hemophiliac but will be a carrier (because she has one defective gene). However, if she has a son, and passes the defective, recessive gene on the X chromosome to him, there is no corresponding dominant, healthy X chromosome to counterbalance the defective gene, so the son inherits hemophilia. Figure 3.11 shows the possible combinations and results when a woman who is a carrier has children. *Color blindness, baldness,* some *allergies, Duchenne's muscular dystrophy,* and other diseases are examples of sex-linked traits that are inherited. A woman cannot inherit such a trait unless she receives two defective genes, one from her mother who is a carrier, and one from her father who manifests the defect.

Congenital deformity—defect present at birth, which may be the result of hereditary factors, conditions during pregnancy, or damage occurring at the time of birth.

Mother's contribution	Father's contribution X	Father's contribution Y
X.	X. X Girl (carrier)	X. Y Boy (hemophiliac)
X	XX Girl (normal)	XY Boy (normal)

The odds for a male child being a hemophiliac are 50%; the odds for a female child being a carrier are 50%.
The odds for having a male child who is also a hemophiliac are 25%; the odds for having a female child who is also a carrier are 25%.
X. = defective chromosome.

FIGURE 3.11 Sex-linked inheritance.

HEREDITARY DEFECTS

Causes of Birth Defects

The majority of babies coming into the world are healthy and normal. Occasionally, however, a child is born with a **congenital deformity:** a defect that is present at the time of birth. Currently, 1 in 16 infants is born with some sort of serious defect (National Foundation for the March of Dimes, 1997).

Birth defects result from three causes: (1) hereditary factors, (2) faulty environments that prevent the child from developing normally, and (3) birth injuries. Only 20% of birth defects are inherited. The other 80% are caused by a faulty environment, birth injuries, or a combination of causes. Let's concentrate here on defects that are inherited because of faulty genes.

Genetic Defects

Some defects are inherited via a single, dominant, defective gene. Scientists are in the process of identifying which gene is responsible for each inherited disorder. McKusick's catalogue of genetic diseases lists 1,172 dominant gene disorders, 618 recessive gene disorders, and 124 sex-linked disorders (McKusick, 1986). *Huntington's disease* is a common example of a dominant gene

Skin color is an example of polygenetic inheritance since it is controlled by a number of genes.

disorder. The disease causes a gradual deterioration of the nervous system, physical weakness, emotional disturbance, mental retardation, and eventually, death. The symptoms do not appear until after 30 years of age (Pines, 1984).

Large numbers of diseases are caused by pairs of recessive genes. These include *cystic fibrosis, phenylketonuria (PKU), Tay-Sachs disease*, and many others (Welsh, Pennington, Ozonoff, Rouse, & McCabe, 1990). Babies born with cystic fibrosis lack an enzyme. This lack causes mucous obstructions in the body, especially in the lungs and digestive organs. Treatments have improved, but death is still inevitable. PKU is caused by an excess of *phenylalanine*, an amino acid, which causes mental retardation and neurological disturbances. The disease is treatable with diet regulation. Tay-Sachs disease is caused by an enzyme deficiency. It is characterized by progressive retardation of development, paralysis, dementia, blindness, and death by age 3 or 4. It is most common in families of Eastern European Jewish origin (Berkow, 1997). Carriers of both cystic fibrosis and Tay-Sachs disease can be detected through genetic counseling. All three diseases can usually be detected through prenatal examinations.

A large number of defects have multiple factors as causes. The defects do not become apparent until a faulty prenatal or postnatal environment triggers their onset. *Cleft palate* or *cleft lip* is one example. It may be related to hereditary factors, to the position of the embryo in the uterus, to the blood supply, or to some drugs taken during pregnancy. *Spina bifida* is another example, characterized by incomplete closure of the lower spine. Both hereditary defects and environmental factors play a causative role. Recent data point to a vitamin deficiency (folic acid) as a contributing factor (Berkow, 1997).

Chromosomal Abnormalities

Chromosomal abnormalities are of two types: sex chromosomal abnormalities and autosomal chromosomal abnormalities. Five of the most common sex-linked chromosomal abnormalities are summarized in Table 3.3

Down's syndrome is the most common chromosomal disorder resulting in physical and mental retardation.

| | Chromosome | | |
Name	Combination	Characteristics	Incidence
None	XYY	Tall stature; subnormal intelligence; severe acne; impulsive and aggressive behavior, which may stem from psychosocial problems.	1 in 1,000 males
Kleinfelter's Syndrome	XXY	Feminine appearance; small penis and testicles; infertile; low sexual drive; decreased body hair; prominent breasts; tendency toward mental impairment.	1 in 1,000 males
Fragile X	Usually XY	X chromosome not influential; some persons normal, others retarded; males may have enlarged testicles.	1 in 1,000 males; 1 in 5,000 females
Turner's Syndrome	XO	Lack of functioning ovaries; incompletely developed internal and external sex organs; loose skin; webbed neck; widely spaced nipples; short stature; deafness and mental deficiency are common (McCauley, Kay, Ito, & Treder, 1987).	1 in 10,000 females
None	XXX	Characteristics vary; some women are normal, fertile; others are sterile, suffer mental retardation.	1 in 1,000 females

TABLE 3.3   COMMON SEX-LINKED CHROMOSOMAL ABNORMALITIES

(Berch & Bender, 1987). These abnormalities arise during meiosis. When an ova or sperm is formed, the 46 chromosomes divide unevenly, producing a gamete that has too few or too many chromosomes.

Sometimes problems result from abnormalities in the autosomes rather than the sex chromosomes. One of the most common of these is *Down's syndrome*. Down's children have an extra chromosome: 47 instead of 46. The overall incidence is about 1:700 live births, but the rate rises to about 1:40 live births in mothers over age 40. There is also a greater risk when the father is over age 45. Characteristics include a flattened skull; folds of skin over the eyes; a flattened bridge of the nose; protruding tongue; short, broad hands and fingers; and short stature. Congenital heart disease is common. Both physical and mental development are retarded; mean IQ is about 50. Most individuals without a major heart disease survive to adulthood.

Genetic Counseling

Couples who have inherited disabilities themselves, or who have a family history of some types of disability, should get genetic counseling to *discover the possibility of passing on the defect to a child yet to be conceived.* Once the couple know the odds of passing on a defect, they are faced with making a decision regarding whether or not to risk having children. After pregnancy occurs, there are various procedures for discovering defects.

Amniocentesis

Amniocentesis can be performed between the fifteenth and sixteenth weeks of gestation. It involves inserting a hollow needle into the abdomen to obtain a sample of *amniotic fluid* containing fetal cells. The cells are cultured for genetic and chemical studies. One disadvantage of this procedure is that it can be performed only in the second trimester of pregnancy, after the fetus is fairly well developed. Another disadvantage is that it results in fetal loss in 1 in 200 amniocenteses. Some of these fetuses are normal and would have survived if the test had not been done. The risk of amniocentesis is that it may cause spontaneous abortion and limb abnormality (Turner, 1992). Women who obtain an amniocentesis before the thirteenth week of pregnancy face a higher risk

Amniocentesis—removal of cells from the amniotic fluid to test for abnormalities

The Process of Decision Making in Cases of Possible Defect

Genetic counseling provides information with which couples can make informed decisions in cases of possible defects. Couples can find out before pregnancy the risk of having a baby with a genetic defect, so that they can decide whether to take the risk of having a child at all. After pregnancy has occurred, couples can find out whether a defect is present, and—if it is—make a decision regarding the course of action to take. The flow chart shown in Figure 3.12 traces the decision-making process involved.

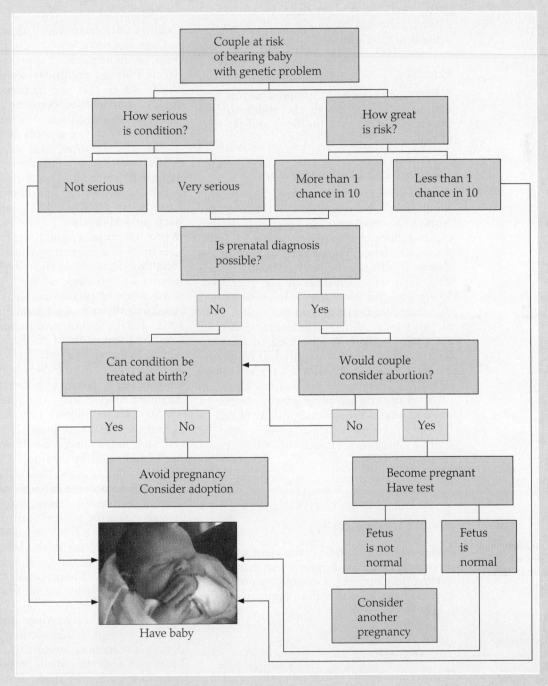

FIGURE 3.12 The process of decision making in case of a possible defect.

From *The Developing Person Through the Life Span*, 2e by Berger © 1988. Worth Publishers, Inc. Used with permission.

of experiencing a fetal loss or of bearing an infant with a club foot (Schreck, 1998).

Sonogram

A **sonogram** uses high-frequency sound waves to obtain a visual image of the fetus's body structure, to see whether growth is normal or whether there are any malformations (Hill, Breckle, & Gehrking, 1983). It is often used to confirm or deny the presence of fetal defects indicated by an elevation of a-Feto-protein in the amniotic fluid (Berkow, 1997).

Fetoscope

A **fetoscope** is passed through a narrow tube that is inserted through the abdomen into the uterus to observe the fetus and placenta directly.

Chorionic Villi Sampling (CVS)

The **chorionic villi** are threadlike protrusions from the membrane enclosing the fetus. The test involves inserting a thin catheter through the vagina and cervix into the uterus, from which a small sample of the chorionic villi is removed for analysis (Cadkin, Ginsberg, Pergament, & Verlinski, 1984). The real advantage of the procedure is that it can be performed in the eighth week of pregnancy. With earlier results, simpler and safer methods can be used to treat the fetus or the mother, if required. If no abnormality is detected, the couple's anxiety can be relieved earlier in the pregnancy. The risks of chorionic villi sampling are comparable to those of amniocentesis except that the risk of injuring the fetus's hands or feet may be slightly increased (1 out of 3,000 cases) (Berkow, 1997).

PRENATAL ENVIRONMENT AND INFLUENCES

Following conception, the environment in which the fetus grows is crucial to healthy development. Let's focus now on the environment to which the pregnant mother is exposed.

Teratogens

Teratogens are any substances that cross the placental barrier, harm the embryo or fetus, and cause birth defects. The timing of exposure to teratogens is particularly important because there is a critical period during which organs and body parts develop, and during which exposure to teratogens is most damaging. Figure 3.13 shows the most sensitive periods. As can be seen, the first 8 weeks of development are most critical, but damage to the central nervous system (including the brain), the eyes, and the genitals may occur during the last weeks of pregnancy as well.

Drugs

Doctors now recommend that the pregnant mother not take any medication, even aspirin, without medical approval. The list of harmful drugs continues to grow and includes drugs that are commonly used and abused. This section contains a brief discussion of the effects on offspring associated with some of the most-used drugs.

Narcotics, sedatives, and *analgesics* are all central nervous system depressants. These include heroin and other forms of narcotics, barbiturates, aspirin, and other substances. If a mother is a heroin addict, the baby will be born an addict also. Large doses of aspirin may cause prepartal and postpartal bleeding.

Alcohol is a particular cause for concern. Drinking alcohol during pregnancy is the leading known cause of birth defects. Consuming one or two drinks a day substantially heightens the risk of physical and mental defects. Fetal alcohol syndrome, one of the major consequences of drinking during pregnancy, if found in about 2 out of 1,000 live births and is seen in babies born to mothers who are heavy drinkers (National Institute on Alcohol Abuse and Alcoholism, NIAAA, 1986). This condition includes retardation before or after birth; joint abnormalities; facial defects; a small head (microcephaly), probably caused by subnormal brain growth; and abnormal behavioral development. Mental retardation more often results from fetal alcohol syndrome than from any other known cause. In addition, alcohol can cause problems ranging from miscarriage to severe behavioral problems in the baby or developing child, such as antisocial behavior and attention deficit. These problems can occur even when the baby has no obvious physical birth defects.

The risk of miscarriage almost doubles when a woman drinks alcohol in any form during pregnancy, especially if she drinks heavily. Often the birth weight of babies born to women who drink during pregnancy is below normal. The average birth weight is about four pounds for babies exposed to alcohol, compared with seven pounds for all babies (Berkow, 1997).

Sonogram—visual image of the fetus, produced from sound waves, used to detect fetal abnormalities

Fetoscope

Chorionic villi sampling (CVS)

Teratogen—harmful substance that crosses the placental barrier and harms the embryo or fetus and causes birth defects

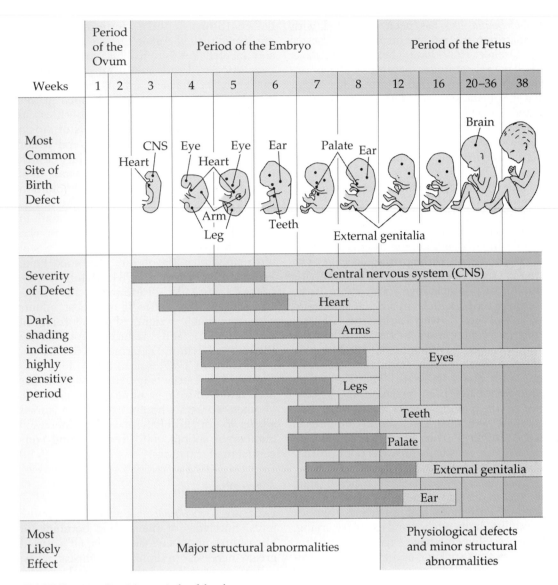

FIGURE 3.13   Sensitive periods of development.

Tranquilizers and *antidepressants* have been associated with congenital malformation.

Nicotine is clearly a factor in low birth weight. The mean birth weight of infants of mothers who smoke during pregnancy is 6 ounces less than that of infants born to non-smoking mothers. Growth retardation occurs when mothers smoke five or more cigarettes a day. The incidence of spontaneous abortion, premature birth, stillbirth, and neonatal death is increased, as is the risk of placenta abrupto (Edwards, 1992; Rind, 1992b). Also, children of mothers who smoke 10 or more cigarettes per day run 50% greater risk of developing cancer during childhood (Stjernfeldt, Berglund, Lindsten, & Ludvigsson, 1986).

Birth defects of the heart, brain, and face are more common in babies of smokers than in those of nonsmokers. Smoking by the mother may increase the risk of sudden infant death syndrome. In addition, children of smoking mothers have slight but measurable deficiencies in physical growth, intellectual development, and behavior. These effects are thought to be caused by carbon monoxide, which may reduce the oxygen supplied to the body's tissues, and by nicotine, which stimulates the release of hormones that constrict the vessels supplying blood to the placenta and uterus. A pregnant woman who doesn't smoke should avoid exposure to secondhand smoke because it may similarly harm the fetus (Berkow, 1997). According to the NSFG, about 18% of pregnant or postpartum women were currently smoking in 1995 (National Survey of Family Growth, 1997).

Marijuana use has been associated with premature birth and low birth weight. Lester and Dreher (1989) have labeled marijuana as a behavioral teratogen because it affects the functioning of infants after birth. They found that marijuana smoking during pregnancy affected a newborn infant's cry, suggesting respiratory involvement. Other studies have shown a relationship between prenatal risk factors and various developmental outcomes (Lester, 1987).

The alarming rise in the use of *cocaine* by pregnant women has led to increased concern about the potential deleterious effects of in utero cocaine exposure on the infant. If the mother ingests cocaine, the drug is transmitted to the infant through the placenta. The drug causes vasoconstriction of the mother's blood vessels—including constriction of the uterine arteries, which impairs the blood supply and oxygen delivery to the fetus. This results in reduction in infant birth weight, length, and head circumference (Lester et al., 1991). Together with an increase in heart rate and blood pressure, vasoconstriction often stimulates preterm labor, the separation of the placenta from the uterine wall, followed by hemorrhage, shock, and anemia in the mother. Furthermore, the mother who ingests cocaine usually provides poor postnatal care of the infant.

Cocaine exposure also has a direct effect on the neonates. Some are born very excitable. Neurological findings include tremors, irritability, high-pitched and excessive crying, jitteriness, hyperactivity, rigidity, hypertension, vigorous sucking, and abnormal neuromuscular signs. The infant may have feeding difficulties and poor sleep-wake schedules. Other infants are born depressed or underaroused, have fleeting attention, and are difficult to wake (Lester et al., 1991). Early intervention after birth may reduce some of the harmful effects of prenatal exposure.

Delivery and neonatal hospital costs are much greater when a cocaine baby is delivered. According to one Oregon study, costs for neonatal care averaged about $12,000 more (Klitsch, 1992). It is estimated that at least 5% of babies born in the United States are exposed to cocaine use during gestation, adding about $500 million to the cost of neonatal medical services each year (Klitsch, 1992).

Chemicals, Heavy Metals, and Environmental Pollutants

In recent years, authorities have become concerned about chemicals, heavy metals, and environmental pollutants as a source of birth defects (Stokols, 1992). Herbicides containing *dioxin*, called Agent Orange in Vietnam and labeled 2,4,5-T in this country, have been associated with an alarming rate of miscarriages, malformed infants, and cancer. The herbicide has now been banned in this country. However, health authorities in Maine recently found unsafe levels of dioxin in the flesh of fish found in several major Maine rivers. These are rivers into which paper companies discharge their wastes.

Industry is still a major source of pollution in many states (Miller, 1985). *PCB* (an industrial chemical, now banned) was found in Lake Michigan fish. Infants of mothers who ate the fish showed developmental deficits at birth and after (Jacobson, Jacobson, Fein, Schwartz, & Dowler, 1984; Raloff, 1986). *Lead* is a particularly toxic metal, and mothers who are exposed to it may bear infants with low birth weight, slow neurological development, and reduced intelligence (Bellinger, Leviton, Watermaux, Needleman, & Rabinowitz, 1987; Raloff, 1986). This toxicity is one reason why tetraethyl lead has been removed from gasoline for automobiles. Women workers who are exposed to *gaseous anesthetics* in hospitals have an increased number of spontaneous abortions and congenital malformations.

Radiation

Exposure to *radiation* may also endanger the fetus. Survivors of the atomic bombing of Hiroshima and Nagasaki in Japan showed great increases in stillbirths, miscarriages, and birth of babies with congenital malformations. Researchers found prenatal chromosome malformations in children in West Germany, which they believed were associated with the nuclear power plant disaster at Chernobyl in Russia (West Berlin Human Genetics Institute, 1987). The whole area around Chernobyl is now deserted because of the continued hazard of radiation. Prenatal exposure to *X rays*, especially in the first 3 months of pregnancy, has the potential of harming the fetus if the level of radiation is too high. Even radiation from video display terminals (VDTs) used in industry may be a factor in high miscarriage rates of pregnant women working on them (Meier, 1987).

Heat

Too much heat can also harm a fetus. If a pregnant woman immerses herself in very hot water, the temperature of the fetus may be raised enough to damage its central nervous system. As little as 15 minutes in a hot tub at 102°F or 10 minutes at 106°F may cause fetal damage. Studies have shown that some women gave birth to malformed babies after spending 45 minutes to 1 hour in hot tubs (Harvey, McRorie, & Smith, 1981).

Maternal Diseases

Many bacteria and viruses cross the placental barrier, so if a pregnant woman is infected, her baby becomes infected also. A variety of maternal illnesses during pregnancy cause birth defects. The extent of the damage depends on the nature and timing of the illness.

Rubella

In the case of rubella, or German measles, if the mother is infected with the virus before the eleventh week of pregnancy, the baby is almost certain to be deaf and to have heart defects and visual and intellectual deficiencies. The chance of defects is 1 in 3 for cases occurring between 13 and 16 weeks, and almost none after 16 weeks. For these reasons, immunization against rubella is recommended for all children (age 15 months and older) and for adults who show no evidence of rubella immunity. Pregnant women should not receive the vaccine; adult women should not become pregnant for 3 months after immunization (Berkow, 1997).

Toxoplasmosis

Toxoplasmosis is a parasite found in uncooked meat and in fecal matter of cats and other animals. The pregnant mother should not change the cat's litter if blood tests reveal that she is not immune. The parasite affects the nervous system of the fetus, resulting in retardation, deafness, and blindness (Larsen, 1986).

Sexually Transmitted Diseases: AIDS

One of the most serious of the sexually transmitted diseases is *acquired immuno-deficiency syndrome (AIDS)*. A person who has been exposed to the virus may become a carrier prior to actually having the disease. The AIDS virus can cross the placental barrier, so that if the mother is a carrier, there is a substantial risk she will give birth to children with the disease (Iosub et al., 1987; Koop, 1986; Marion, Wiznia, Hutcheon, & Rubinstein, 1986; Rogers, 1985). About one-fourth of pregnant women who have the infection transmit it to the fetus. Still, more than two-thirds of chil-

Parenting Issues

Prenatal Exposure to Drugs in California Newborns

A recent survey found that more than one in ten pregnant women in California use drugs, smoke cigarettes, or drink alcohol shortly before giving birth (Klitsch, 1994). Using the results of this survey, the researchers estimated that in California in 1992, more than 67,000 newborns had been exposed to one or more drugs in utero. Overall, levels of substance use were generally lowest among women who began prenatal care in the first trimester, and the highest among those who received late or no prenatal care. Public-care officials recommended that extensive clinical and educational interventions be introduced. This program should include prenatal counseling and residential treatment programs especially designed for pregnant women.

dren born to women with HIV infections will not become infected. Because the virus can be transmitted in breast milk, breast-fed infants may acquire the infection from their mother after birth. Infection before, during, or shortly after birth isn't immediately apparent. For about 10% to 20% of children, problems start during the first or second year of life; for the remaining 80% to 90% of children, problems may not appear until years later. About half of the children infected with HIV are diagnosed with AIDS by their third birthday. If the disease begins after infancy, periods of illness may alternate with periods of relatively normal health. A variety of symptoms and complications can appear as the child's immune system deteriorates. About a third of the HIV-infected children develop lung inflammation. Coughing and swelling at the ends of the fingers may result. More than half of the children infected with HIV develop pneumonia at some time. A great number of HIV-infected children show progressive brain damage that interferes with walking and talking and that causes impaired intelligence. The head may be small in relation to body size; up to 20% of infected children progressively lose social and language skills and muscle control. They become partially paralyzed or unsteady on their feet, or their muscles may become somewhat rigid. Some children develop inflammation of the liver (hepatitis) and damage to the heart (heart failure) or to the kidneys (kidney failure). Cancer is uncommon in children with AIDS.

An increasing number of drugs are being used to treat HIV infection in adults and adolescents, but not all of these drugs have been tested in children. Many experts believe that combinations of drugs may be more useful than single doses. With current drug therapy, 75% of children with HIV infection born today are alive at five years, and 50% are alive at eight years. The average age of death is about 10 years for HIV-infected children, and more and more children are surviving well into adolescence. HIV-infected children need close medical supervision or their condition worsens, but treatment is best given in the least restrictive environment, such as at home rather than at a hospital.

One of the most significant advances in HIV research is the prevention in many cases of HIV transmission from mothers to babies by using anti-HIV drugs. Pregnant women known to be infected with HIV are given drugs during their second and third trimesters of pregnancy and during labor and delivery. These measures have reduced the transmission from the mother to the child by more than two-thirds (from 25% to 80%) (Berkow, 1997).

Other Sexually Transmitted Diseases

These diseases are a major cause of birth defects. *Congenital syphilis* is contracted by the fetus of the pregnant woman when the spirochete crosses the placental barrier. If the disease is diagnosed and treated before the fourth month of pregnancy, the fetus will not develop syphilis. Later in pregnancy the fetus may suffer bone, liver, or brain damage (Grossman, 1986). If a woman is not treated in the primary or secondary stage of the disease, her child is likely to die before or shortly after birth.

Genital herpes, gonorrhea, and *chlamydial infections* are sexually transmitted diseases (STDs) transmitted to infants when they pass through the birth canal, so doctors recommend a cesarean section if the woman has an infection. Between 50% and 60% of newborns who contract *herpes* die, and half of the survivors suffer brain damage or blindness (Subak-Sharpe, 1984). Infants of infected mothers may get *gonorrhea* of the eyes when passing through the birth canal and, if not treated with silver nitrate or antibiotics, can become blind. Some babies born to infected mothers contract the *chlamydia bacterium* when passing through the birth canal and become subject to eye infections, pneu-

monia, and sudden infant death syndrome (Faro, 1985). Chlamydia is the greatest single cause of preventable blindness (Crum & Ellner, 1985). The best precaution against birth defects caused by STDs is to make sure the woman is not exposed before or during pregnancy.

Other Diseases

Large numbers of other diseases may cause birth defects. *Poliomyelitis, diabetes, tuberculosis,* and *thyroid disease* have all been implicated in problems of fetal development.

Other Maternal Factors

Maternal Age

At first glance, maternal age seems to be associated with the well-being of the fetus. *Younger teenage mothers are more likely to have miscarriages, premature birth, and stillbirths than are mothers in their twenties.* The infants are more likely to be of low birth weight, to have physical and neurological defects, and to be retarded than are babies born to women over 20 (Reichman & Pagnini, 1997). However, it is not necessarily the mother's age that is the problem, but the fact that many of

More and more women in their late thirties and early forties are having babies.

these babies are born out of wedlock to low socioeconomic status mothers who do not receive adequate nutrition and prenatal health care. Black children born to very young adolescent mothers are more likely to be born prematurely and to have low birth weights than are white children, primarily because of poor prenatal care of black children (Ketterlinus, Henderson, & Lamb, 1991).

The most recent findings indicate that births to women in their middle and late thirties have risen among both the black and white population since 1980. *The statistics indicate that women over 35 run progressively greater risks during pregnancy.* These include greater risks of miscarriages, of complications during pregnancy and delivery, a greater chance of having twins and of developmental abnormalities than for women under 35. Here again, however, it may not be that age is the causative factor but the fact that the older mother may not be in as good health as the younger. She is more likely to be obese, have high blood pressure, or have diabetes than is the younger woman. *Modern health care has made it possible for older women to deliver healthy full-term babies.* The risks of pregnancy for women over 40 have not been found to be greater than those for women 20 to 30, particularly when such factors as maternal weight, health condition, and cigarette smoking are taken into account (Kopp & Kaler, 1989). However, if any woman has health problems, she is certainly at greater risk.

Nutrition

Lack of vitamins, minerals, and protein in the diet of the expectant mother may affect the embryo adversely. Nutritional deficiencies

Twin studies help psychologists examine the influences of heredity and environment.

Parenting Issues

Maternal Stress and Infant Hyperactivity

Most expectant mothers experience some stress during pregnancy. A moderate amount of stress probably has no harmful effects on the fetus, but persistent, excessive stress does. When the mother is anxious, afraid, or upset, adrenaline is pumped into the bloodstream, which increases heart rate, blood pressure, respiration, and levels of blood sugar, and diverts blood away from digestion to the skeletal muscles to prepare the body for emergency action. The emergency mobilization leaves the body exhausted afterward, severely disrupting bodily functioning.

The physical changes that occur in the mother's body take place in the fetus as well, since *adrenaline* passes through the placenta and enters the blood of the fetus. The fetus becomes hyperactive for as long as the mother is stressed. Furthermore, the stress is associated with low birth weight, infant hyperactivity, feeding problems, irritability, and digestive disturbances. Furthermore, the overly stressed mother is more likely to have complications during pregnancy and labor (Istvan, 1986).

have been associated with stillbirths, miscarriages, and major deformities. The extent of damage depends on the time during the pregnancy and on the duration and severity of the deficiencies. A lack of vitamin A or calcium in the mother may result in improperly developed teeth in the infant. A serious protein deficiency may cause mental retardation, premature birth, low resistance to infections, or low fetal birth weight (Guttmacher, 1983).

HEREDITY-ENVIRONMENT INTERACTION

Studying Heredity and Environment

For years, psychologists have been trying to sort out the relative influences of heredity and environment on development and behavior. There are two principal methods for sorting out these influences: the study of twins and the study of adopted children.

Twin Studies

Identical twins share the same heredity, but if they are reared apart, they would be subject to different environmental influences. Any shared traits that are still similar, therefore, would be caused by heredity and not by environment. Fraternal twins are as different in heredity as are any other brothers or sisters. Comparisons are sometimes made between fraternal twins and identical twins, or between fraternal twins or other siblings and adopted children raised in the same family. Such comparisons help to sort out environmental versus hereditary influences. Table 3.4 gives a summary of correlation coefficients between monozygotic twins, dizygotic twins, and siblings on measures of intelligence (comparisons of twins and of siblings are of children raised in the same home). The findings are summaries of a number of studies (Bouchard & McGue, 1981).

Investigation of children's observed prosocial and antisocial behavior toward their caregiver found correlations of approximately .45 for monozygotic twins and .25 for dizygotic twins (O'Connor, Hetherington, Reiss, & Polomin, 1995). The same study by O'Connor and colleagues found that genetic variations counted for an average of 55% of the reliable variance in children's observed behavior toward their parents. Dozens of other studies attempt to disentangle the effects of "nurture" from "nature" on the behavior of children (Leve, Winebarger, Fagot, Reid, & Goldsmith, 1998).

Adoption Studies

Studies of adopted children enable researchers to try to disentangle the relative contributions of heredity and environment. In the Texas Adoption Project, researchers have found that the influence of heredity on intelligence is a strong one (Horn, 1983; Loehlin, 1985). *Children reared away from their biological parents are still more similar in IQ to their biological mother than to their adoptive parents.* As seen in Table 3.5, the strongest correlations of intelligence were between natural children and their father or between natural siblings. The weakest correlations were between adopted children and their adopted parents, indicating that the influence of environment alone was not high.

In one longitudinal Minnesota adoption study, black children adopted into white homes were still more closely related in intelligence to their biological parents than to their adoptive parents, indicating that genetics had more influence than environment (Scarr & Weinberg, 1983). However, these adopted black children had higher average intelligence test scores than their biological parents, indicating that performance had been improved by environmental influences. Other studies show a striking diversity of genetic and environmental influences that

TABLE 3.4	CORRELATIONS BETWEEN MONOZYGOTIC TWINS, DIZYGOTIC TWINS, SIBLINGS, AND UNRELATED CHILDREN ON MEASURES OF INTELLIGENCE

Relationship	Correlation Coefficient
Monozygotic twins	.86
Same-sex dizygotic twins	.60
Siblings	.47
Unrelated children (raised in different homes)	00

Adapted from "Family Studies of Intelligence: A Review," by T. J. Bouchard and M. McGue, 1981, *Science, 212,* pp. 1055–1059. © 1981 by AAAS.

determine continuity and change in individual differences in general cognitive ability during the period of development from infancy to middle adulthood (Cardon et al., 1992).

The *Colorado Adoption Project* (CAP) is an ongoing, prospective, longitudinal study of behavioral development that assesses adoptive and matched nonadoptive children with a multitude of developmental measures. When each of these children was seven years old, ratings on the *Colorado Childhood Temperament Inventory* were obtained from the teacher and the tester for more than 50 pairs each of adoptive and nonadoptive siblings. Significant genetic influence on temperament emerged for both teacher and tester ratings of activity, for tester ratings for sociability, and for teacher ratings of emotionality. Both teacher and tester ratings for temperament yielded evidence for genetic influence in this first sibling adoption study in middle childhood (Schmetz, Saudino, Plomin, Fulker, & DeFries, 1996).

Influences on Personality and Temperament

Heredity not only has an important influence on intelligence, but it also exerts a strong influence on personality and temperament (Chipuer et al.,

TABLE 3.5	IQ CORRELATIONS IN THE TEXAS ADOPTION PROJECT		
Pairing		*Number of Pairs*	*Observed Correlations*
Share Genes Only			
Adopted child and biological mother		297	0.28
Share Environment Only			
Adopted child and adoptive mother		401	0.15
Adopted child and adoptive father		405	0.12
All unrelated children		266	0.18
Share Genes and Environment			
Natural child and mother		143	0.21
Natural child and father		144	0.29
Natural child and natural child		40	0.33

From "The Texas Adoption Project," by J. M. Horn, 1983, *Child Development, 54,* pp. 268–275. © 1983 The Society for Research in Child Development.

1993; Emde et al., 1992; Heath, Kessler, Neale, Eaves, & Kendler, 1992). Intensive studies of 348 pairs of identical twins at the University of Minnesota, including 44 pairs who were reared apart, revealed that heredity was a stronger influence than environment on a number of key personality traits (Goleman, 1986; Leo, 1987). Figure 3.14 shows the extent to which selected personality traits were found to be inherited. A 60% figure would mean that 60% of the trait is due to heredity, and 40% to environmental influences.

The influence of heredity can be seen in identifiable characteristics that seem to be present in very young infants (Braungart, Plomin, DeFries, & Fulker, 1992). One study showed some heritability of empathy in both monozygotic and dizygotic twin pairs between 14 and 20 months of age (Zahn-Waxler, Robinson, & Emde, 1992). These twins showed emotional concern, reaction to the distress of others, and some ability to engage in prosocial acts. Infants' temperament is also strongly influenced by genetics, as indicated by their level of activity, irritability, sociability, and sleep patterns (Wilson & Matheny, 1983). Goldsmith (1983) found that identical twins were more similar than fraternal twins in personality traits such as emotionality: in the expression of anger and aggressive feelings, in activity level and sociability, and in work habits in school, such as task persistence.

Goldsmith and Gottesman (1981) found that, as infants got older, the relative influence of heredity on temperament usually declined, whereas environmental influences became more important (Riese, 1990). Kagan and his associates studied the development of inhibited and uninhibited 2- to 3-year-old children for 6 years to discover the relative stability of the tendency to be shy or not shy (Kagan, Reznick, Clarke, Snidman, & Garcia-Coll, 1984; Reznick, Kagan, Snidman, Gersten, Baak, & Rosenberg, 1986; Robinson et al., 1992). About 5% to 10% of the children seemed to be born with a biological predisposition to be fearful of unfamiliar people, events, or objects. After 5½ years,

FOCUS

Twins Reared Apart

Jack Yufe and Oskar Stohr are identical twins. They were separated at 6 months of age from their parents and reared apart. Jack was raised in Israel as a Jew, and he spent time in an Israeli kibbutz and in the navy. Oskar was brought up in Germany as a Catholic and was involved in Hitler's youth movement. When they were brought together at age 47 by University of Minnesota researchers, they had similar personality profiles, and they both did well in sports, had trouble with math, had mustaches, wore wire-rimmed glasses, and read magazines from back to front (Bouchard, 1984). The researchers concluded that at least half the similarities in a wide range of personality characteristics were caused by heredity.

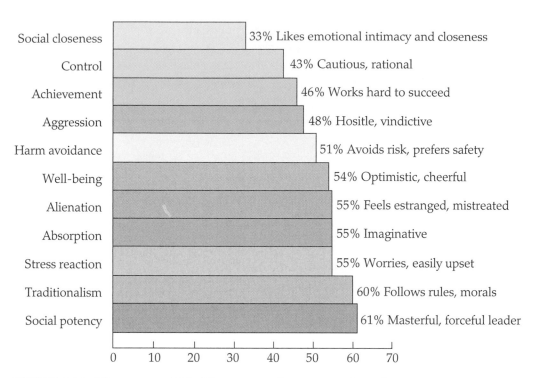

FIGURE 3.14   The extent to which different personality traits are inherited.

From "Major Personality Study Finds That Traits Are Mostly Inherited," by D. Goleman. December 2, 1986. *The New York Times*, pp. 17, 18. Copyright © 1986 by The New York Times Co. Reprinted by permission.

40% of the originally inhibited children—usually boys—had become much less inhibited. However, 10% had become more timid. Some parents had helped their shy children overcome timidity by bringing playmates into the home, offering encouragement and support, and through other means. Other parents made matters worse by undermining their children's confidence. Certainly then, the quality of nurturing experiences exerted strong modifying influences on children's temperament and behavior. Of course, children also exerted strong influences on parents. Children who are different tax the patience of parents, but if parents start to become rejecting, critical, and punishing, they may make matters worse. The children who are hardest to love are the ones who need love, acceptance, and encouragement the most.

Some Disorders Influenced by Heredity and Environment

Not only are some superior traits inherited and then enhanced or minimized through environmental influences, but also various disorders with genetic origins can either be promoted or counteracted to some degree by environment. Several of these disorders are the focus in this section.

Alcoholism

Alcoholism runs in families and develops because of a combination of genetic and environmental factors (Berkow, 1997). The evidence for genetic factors in alcoholism is convincing: (1) the concordance rate for alcoholism between identical twins is twice that between fraternal twins; (2) sons of alcoholics are four times as likely as sons of nonalcoholics to become alcoholics themselves, even if they are adopted at birth, and regardless of whether the adoptive parents are alcoholics; and, (3) children whose natural parents are nonalcoholics, but whose adoptive parents are, do not appear to have an unusually high risk themselves (Schuckit, 1985, 1987). Alcoholics tend to inherit an ability to metabolize alcohol differently, and thus to find drinking more pleasurable, than nonalcoholics do. In contrast to alcoholics, some people can't drink because their bodies can't tolerate alcohol (Zucker & Gomberg, 1986). There is some evidence, also, that male alcoholics exhibit different brain wave patterns than nonalcoholics prior to exposure to alcohol (Porjesz & Begleitner, 1985).

Alcoholism runs in families because of a combination of genetic and environmental factors.

Environmental influences are also a factor in alcoholism. In families where there is a lack of closeness, love, and recognition or trust; where there is parental rejection, hostility, conflict, inadequate role models or discipline; or where children do not learn coping skills from parents, the children are more prone to become alcoholics or abusers of other drugs than are those brought up in a more positive home environment (Jurich, Polson, Jurich, & Bates, 1985).

Schizophrenia

Schizophrenia is another disorder that has both hereditary and environmental causes. The incidence of schizophrenia in the general population is about 1%, but if one parent has it, about 12% of their offspring will be affected. If both parents are schizophrenic, 39% of their children will be afflicted (Kinney & Matthysse, 1978). One study found that 48% of the monozygotic twins of schizophrenic individuals also had schizophrenia, whereas only 10% of the dizygotic twins of a schizophrenic parent had the disease (Farmer, McGuffin, & Gottesman, 1987). However, the fact that the majority of children were not affected indicates that children do not inherit the disease, per se. Rather, some inherit a predisposition toward it. Schizophrenia seems to be particularly sensitive to the action of *dopamine*, which is a neurochemical transmitter that speeds nerve transmission. In schizophrenia, the rapid speed of transmission between neurons or nerve cells causes incoherent, bizarre behav-

ior. Administering the drugs called *phenothiazines* inhibits the effect of dopamine on nerve transmission and is an effective treatment (Uhr, Stahl, & Berger, 1984). Environmental influences, such as coming from a dysfunctional family situation, tend to increase the chances of developing the illness.

Depression

Depression is another disorder that may be caused by biological factors including a genetic predisposition. Identical twins have a 70% concordance rate; fraternal twins, other siblings, and parents and their children have about a 15% concordance rate, indicating a genetic influence (U.S. Department of Health and Human Services, 1981). Depression seems to be accompanied by an excess of *acetylcholine*, a chemical that inhibits the transmission of messages between nerve cells. Here again, depression may be triggered by stressful life events, such as the sudden loss of love. However, some people apparently have a predisposition to the illness.

Infantile Autism

Infantile autism is first noticed in early infancy, with a diagnosis confirmed by age 2 or 3 (Rutter & Schopher, 1987). The word *autism* comes from *auto*, meaning "self." Autistic children are self-involved, oblivious to other people; they don't cuddle, smile, or make eye contact when greeted (Kasari, Sigman, Mundy, & Yirmiya, 1988). Autistic children may spend hours performing repetitive motions such as clapping their hands or turning a ball over and over. They may scream in terror when something in the environment is changed. They are often mute but may echo, word for word, things that they hear, such as a television ad. About one-third have IQs of 70 or more. One in six makes fair adjustment and is able to work as an adult.

Autism is very rare (about 3 cases per 10,000 people). One study found a concordance of 96% among identical twins and 23% among fraternal twins; the evidence suggested that autism is an inherited neurobiological disorder passed on through recessive genes, and that environmental influences as causes are minimal (Dawson, Meltzoff, Osterling, & Rinaldi, 1998; Ritvo, Freeman, Mason-Brothers, Mo, & Ritvo, 1985).

Paternal Factors in Defects

Advanced *paternal age* is also associated with reduced fertility and several hereditary defects. Negative environmental influences in the life of the father also contribute to birth defects. *Chronic marijuana use* suppresses the production of the male hormone testosterone, reduces sexual desire, interferes with erectile responses, and inhibits sperm production and motility. Sperm from *alcoholic men* have been found to be highly abnormal. Exposure to *radiation, lead, tobacco, arsenic, mercury, some solvents*, and *various pesticides* may contribute to male infertility, to lower sperm count, or genetic abnormalities in sperm cells (Meier, 1987). Even passive exposure of the fetus to *tobacco smoking* by the father reduces fetal birth weight and interferes with lung development of the fetus (Rubin et al., 1986). Another study at a University of North Carolina hospital revealed a twofold increase in risk for developing cancer during their lifetime among children of men who smoked (Sandler, Everson, Wilcox, & Browder, 1985). This risk factor may have been due to prenatal or postnatal exposure or both.

We do know that excessive heat is detrimental to sperm production and viability. Sperm are most effectively produced and most healthy when the temperature in the testes is 5.6°F below body temperature. This lower temperature is achieved because the testes hang outside the body cavity in the scrotum. But when sperm are exposed to sources of artificial heat, there is a rise in their temperature, which is very detrimental.

As can be seen, the great majority of birth defects are preventable. Every effort needs to be made to keep them from happening.

Summary

1. Reproduction begins when the male gamete, or sperm cell, fuses with the female gamete, or ovum.

2. Spermatogenesis refers to the process of sperm production; oogenesis is the process by which ova are ripened in the ovary.

3. Conception, or fertilization, normally takes place in the upper third of the fallopian tube.

4. Family planning means having children by choice and not by chance. It is necessary to protect the health of the mother and baby, to reduce the psychological impact of unintended pregnancy, and to promote the good of the marriage.

5. Contraceptive failure is a serious problem, resulting in a high rate of unintended pregnancy. Since the advent of AIDs, condom use has increased. Unfortunately, some condoms are defective and leak, or they tear and come off. The most commonly reported methods used by women are female sterilization and oral contraceptives; the male condom and sterilization are the methods most commonly used by men.

6. Prenatal development may be divided into three periods: (1) the germinal period—from conception to completion of implantation, about 14 days; (2) the embryonic period—from 2 weeks to 8 weeks after conception; and (3) the fetal period—from 8 weeks through the remainder of pregnancy.

7. Infant mortality in the United States is high among minority groups, primarily because of a lack of proper prenatal care from the beginning of pregnancy.

8. Minor side effects may cause varying degrees of discomfort during pregnancy. Major complications of pregnancy include pernicious vomiting, toxemia, threatened abortion, placenta abrupto and placenta praevia, ectopic pregnancy, and Rh incompatibility.

9. Many thoughtful people object to viability tests as determinants of whether a woman can have an abortion, because the tests are expensive, impose health risks for the mother and fetus, and are sometimes unreliable and inaccurate, especially if performed between 20 and 30 weeks.

10. About 10% of U.S. women aged 15 to 44 have impaired fertility. About 20% of infertility cases involve the couple, about 40% the man, and about 40% the woman.

11. Involuntary childlessness can cause significant emotional and psychological distress for some persons.

12. Alternate means of conception include artificial insemination (both homologous insemination and heterologous insemination), use of a surrogate mother, in vitro fertilization, gamete intrafallopian transfer (GIFT), and embryo transplant.

13. Chromosomes carry the hereditary material called genes that direct the physi-

cal changes in the body throughout development. When the sperm and ovum unite, the 23 single chromosomes within the nucleus of each gamete combine in pairs with those in the other gamete to produce 46 chromosomes in the resulting zygote.

14. Genes are made up of molecules called DNA. Each cell of the body has the same DNA code and the same genes that direct growth.

15. In the zygote, twenty-two of the chromosomes from each gamete are labeled autosomes; the twenty-third pair are sex chromosomes, which determine whether the offspring will be male or female. An XY chromosome pairing produces a male; an XX combination produces a female.

16. Twins may be identical (monozygotic, or one-egg) twins, or fraternal (dizygotic, or two-egg) twins.

17. Mendel formulated the law of dominant inheritance, which says that when an organism inherits competing traits, the trait that is expressed is dominant over the other, which is recessive. An organism may be homozygous or heterozygous for a trait.

18. A trait that is observable in an organism is called a phenotype, while the underlying genetic pattern is called a genotype.

19. When one allele is not completely dominant over the other, the phenomenon is known as incomplete dominance. Polygenic inheritance occurs when numerous interacting genes produce a trait.

20. We inherit a range of possibilities for many traits, known as the reaction range. Canalization is the tendency for a trait to persist regardless of environment.

21. Sex-linked disorders are inherited by being passed on through defective recessive genes on the X chromosome.

22. Birth defects result from three causes: (1) hereditary factors, (2) faulty environments, and (3) birth injuries. Some genetic diseases are inherited through dominant genes, others through recessive genes.

23. Chromosomal abnormalities are of two types: sex chromosomal abnormalities and autosomal chromosomal abnormalities.

24. Couples who have inherited disabilities themselves or who have a family history of such disabilities, should get genetic counseling to discover the possibility of passing on a defect.

25. Adverse prenatal environmental influences include various teratogens, drugs, chemicals, heavy metals, environmental pollutants, radiation, and excessive heat. The earlier in development that the embryo or fetus is exposed, the greater the possibility of harm. Thus, there are sensitive periods when exposure is most harmful.

26. Drinking alcohol and/or smoking during pregnancy are among the leading causes of birth defects and developmental problems.

27. There are also many maternal diseases that can affect the development of the unborn child. Sexually transmitted diseases, especially AIDS, present serious threats to the baby's health and life.

28. Other maternal factors that need to be taken into account are maternal age, nutrition, and stress.

Key Terms

Alleles   *p. 55*
Amniocentesis   *p. 60*
Artificial insemination   *p. 52*
Autosomes   *p. 54*
Blastocyst   *p. 46*
Blastula   *p. 46*
Canalization   *p. 57*
Chorionic villi sampling (CVS)   *p. 62*
Chromosomes   *p. 53*
Congenital deformity   *p. 58*
Dizygotic (fraternal) twins   *p. 54*
DNA   *p. 53*
Dominant gene   *p. 55*
Ectopic pregnancy   *p. 49*

Embryo   *p. 46*
Embryonic period   *p. 46*
Embryo transplant   *p. 53*
Fertilization or conception   *p. 44*
Fetal period   *p. 46*
Fetoscope   *p. 62*
Fetus   *p. 46*
Gamete intrafallopian transfer
   (GIFT)   *p. 53*
Gametes   *p. 44*
Genes   *p. 53*
Genotype   *p. 56*
Germinal period   *p. 46*
Heterologous insemination (AID)   *p. 52*

Discussion Questions

1. What do you think about each of the following alternate means of conception?

   Artificial insemination: AIH, AID
   Using a surrogate mother
   Gamete intrafallopian transfer (GIFT)
   In vitro fertilization
   Embryo transplant

2. If you wanted a child of a particular sex, would you try to employ means to determine your child's sex? Explain.

3. Do any members of either side of your family have inherited defects, or might they be carriers of defects? Has any member of your family received genetic counseling? With what results?

4. Do you know of anyone who has borne defective children because of exposure to teratogens, radiation, heat, or maternal diseases?

5. Regardless of whether you are now a parent, would you want to consider having children when you are over 35 years of age? Why or why not?

6. Do you know any mothers who are nervous, hyperactive people? Were they that way during pregnancy? Compare their children with children of mothers who are calm, easygoing persons who do not get upset easily. Do you notice any difference in the temperament of the children? Is a nervous temperament inherited or due to environmental influence?

7. To women who are mothers: Did you have any minor discomforts during your pregnancy? What bothered you the most? What did you do about it? Did you have any of the major complications of pregnancy that are mentioned in the text? Explain.

8. To men who are fathers: How did you feel about your wife's becoming pregnant? In what ways were you able to assist her? What bothered you the most during her pregnancy?

9. Do you know anyone who tests HIV positive for AIDS? How was the virus contracted? Do you know anyone who is sexually active with different persons who is not using protection against AIDS? Describe.

10. Do you know anyone who has a problem with infertility? Is the person seeking treatment? What has been the person's reaction to unwanted childlessness?

11. Do you know a woman who took drugs during her pregnancy? With what result?

Suggested Readings

The American College of Obstetricians and Gynecologists. (1996). *Planning for pregnancy, birth, and beyond* (2nd. ed.). New York: Dutton. Published by the American College of Obstetricians and Gynecologists. America's leading authority on women's health care.

ANDERSON, G. R. (1986). *Children and AIDS: The challenge for child welfare.* Washington, DC:

Child Welfare League of America. Implications of AIDS for social workers.

ANTHONY, E. J., & COHLER, B. J. (Eds.). (1987). *The invulnerable child.* New York: Guilford Press. A book of readings on how children are resistant to unfortunate environments.

BERKOW, R. (Ed.) (1997). *The Merck manual of medical information* (Home editon). Whitehouse

Station, NJ: Merck and Co. A comprehensive medical guide.

CUMMINGS, M. R. (1998). *Human heredity, principles and issues* (5th ed.). New York: Wadsworth. A college textbook.

ENKIN, M. (Ed.). (1995). *A guide to effective care in pregnancy and childbirth* (2nd ed.). Oxford University Press. A must for expectant parents.

FARBER, S. (1981). *Identical twins reared apart: A re-analysis.* New York: Basic Books. Summary of findings of studies.

GALLAGHER, W. (1997). *Just the way you are: How heredity and the environment create the individual.* Random House. Answers the central questions of human individuality: Who am I? How did I get that way?

KEVLES, D. J. (1985). *In the name of eugenics.* New York: Knopf. A thought-provoking discussion.

LASKER, J. N., & BORG, S. (1994). *In search of parenthood: Coping with infertility and high-tech conception* (Revised). Philadelphia, PA: Temple University Press. The new reproductive options available to infertile couples.

NILSSON, L. (1990). *A child is born.* New York: Delacorte Press. Full-color photos and helpful text on the psychological and medical facts of prenatal development.

PLOMIN, R. (1990). *Nature and nurture: An introduction to human behavioral genetics.* Pacific Grove, CA: Brooks/Cole. For the lay reader.

STERNBERG, R. J. (Ed.). (1997). *Intelligence, heredity, and the environment.* New York, Cambridge University Press. The nature-nurture issue on intelligence.

http://cerhr.niehs.nih.gov   Center for the Evaluation of Risks to Human Reproduction (CERHR) Assessment of Environmental risks on pregnancies.

http://humrep.oupjournals.com   Human Reproduction. Oxford Journals on-line.

Web Resources

Childbirth and the Neonate

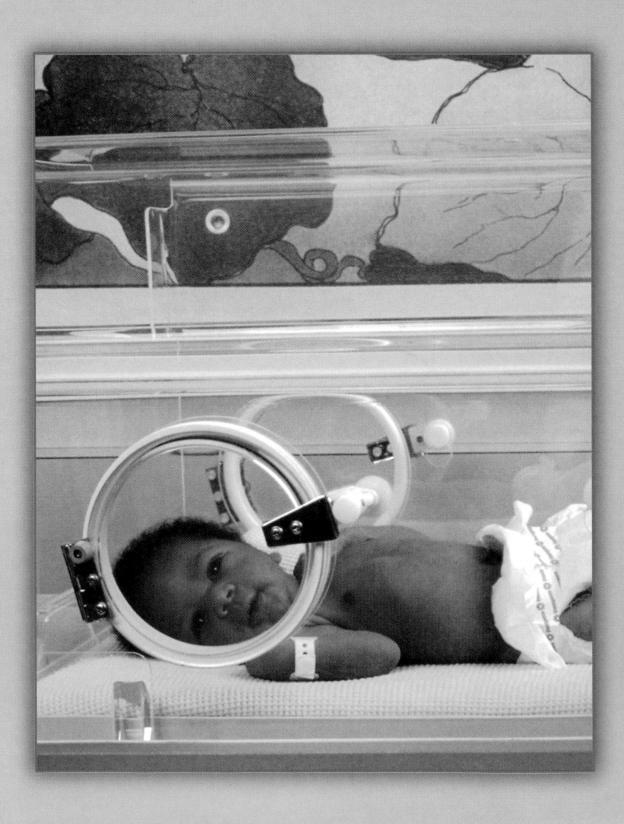

Chapter 4

Having a baby is a normal occurrence, happening millions of times every year. But it is an experience that requires considerable knowledge and preparation if the maximum health of baby and mother are to be assured. This chapter describes the process of childbirth from the beginning of labor to postpartum care, emphasizing the importance of preparation ahead of time.

Some babies are born prematurely or are small for their gestational age. These require special care and modifications of the parental roles.

Once born, the neonate is a miraculous creature. This chapter describes the physical appearance and characteristics, physiological functioning, senses and perception, reflexes, brain and nervous system, and individual differences in neonates that enable them to survive and to adjust to the new world into which they are born.

CHILDBIRTH

Prepared Childbirth

The term **prepared childbirth** here refers to the physical, social, intellectual, and emotional preparation for the birth of a baby. Good physical care of the body provides a favorable environment for the growing fetus, and physical conditioning readies the body for labor and childbirth. Social preparation of the home and family provides a secure environment in which the child can grow. Intellectual preparation ensures adequate instruction in and understanding of the birth process, prenatal and postnatal hospitalization, and infant and child care. Emotional preparation minimizes fear and tension so that childbirth can be as pleasant and painless as possible.

Prepared childbirth, as used in this context, does not necessarily mean labor and delivery without medication, although these may be drug free if the mother so desires. Emphasis is not just on natural childbirth (in a sense all childbirth is natural), but on the overall preparations a woman and her partner can make for the experience of becoming parents.

The Lamaze Method of Natural Childbirth

The **Lamaze method,** which originated in Russia, was introduced to the Western World in 1951 by Dr. Fernand Lamaze (1970), a French obstetrician. The following are important elements of the Lamaze method:

1. Education about birth, including the ability to relax muscles not involved in the labor and delivery process
2. Physical conditioning through exercises
3. Controlled breathing, providing the psychological technique for pain prevention and the ability to release muscular tension by "letting go"
4. Emotional support during labor and delivery, primarily through instruction of the partner in coaching and supportive techniques

The Lamaze method emphasizes the man-woman relationship and communication. In this method, as well as in the Dick-Read method, attendance of the partner or another support person in childbirth education classes is essential. The underlying feature of the Lamaze method is its focus on teaching the woman that she can be in control during the experience.

Critique

Prepared childbirth, by whatever method, is not without its critics, especially if a particular advocate emphasizes a drug-free labor and delivery. Medical opinion has changed gradually in relation to the role of the father. Fathers are encouraged to attend classes with their partners and to

Couples need to be prepared for childbirth and the experience of becoming parents.

act as coaches during labor and delivery. Certainly, a partner's willingness to participate in childbirth can be critical to the physical comfort and satisfaction of his mate's experience. To avoid misunderstanding, the issue of the father's presence during delivery needs to be worked out between the couple and the physician beforehand. In some cultures, fathers are not allowed to attend the birth of their child. Other fathers just don't want to be present.

A majority of obstetricians accept most concepts of prepared childbirth and think they are advantageous. The combined benefits of psychological suggestion and physical conditioning can enhance the woman's comfort and happiness throughout the labor and delivery process.

Birthing Rooms and Family-Centered Care

Birthing rooms are lounge-type, informal, pleasantly decorated rooms with homelike settings within the hospital itself. Medical equipment is present but unobtrusive. Both labor and delivery take place in the birthing room, attended by the father and a nurse-midwife or obstetrician. The woman can be moved into another room if complications arise. The mother is encouraged to keep her baby with her after delivery to encourage bonding.

Birthing centers are another alternative to the standard hospital setting. They are separated from, but near, a hospital. They seek to combine the advantages of delivery in a home-like environment with the medical backup of a hospital. Birthing centers provide complete prenatal and delivery services to families. They emphasize childbirth as a family-centered event, giving both parents maximum involvement (Eakins, 1986). One big advantage of birthing centers is that new parents learn about infant care while still at the center.

LABOR

Beginning

Real **labor** is rhythmic in nature, recurring at fixed intervals, with uterine contractions usually beginning about 15 to 20 minutes apart and then decreasing to 3- to 4-minute intervals when labor is well under way. In addition, the total length of each contraction increases from less than ½ minute to more than 1 minute. The **show,** or discharge of a blood-tinged mucus plug sealing the neck of the uterus, may precede the onset of labor by as much as 72 hours. At other times, it is an indication that labor has begun (Berkow, 1997).

Sometimes the first sign of impending labor is rupture of the **amniotic sac** (bag of waters), followed by a gush or leakage of watery fluid from the vagina. In one-eighth of all pregnancies, especially in first pregnancies, the amniotic membranes rupture *before* labor begins. When this happens, labor will commence 6 to 24 hours later if the woman is within a few days of term. If she is not near

Prepared childbirth—the physical, social, intellectual, and emotional preparation for the birth of a baby

Lamaze method—natural childbirth method emphasizing education, physical conditioning, controlled breathing, and emotional support

Labor—rhythmic contractions of the uterus that expel the baby through the birth canal

Show—blood-tinged mucus expelled from the cervix

Amniotic sac (bag of waters)—sac containing the liquid in which the fetus is suspended during pregnancy

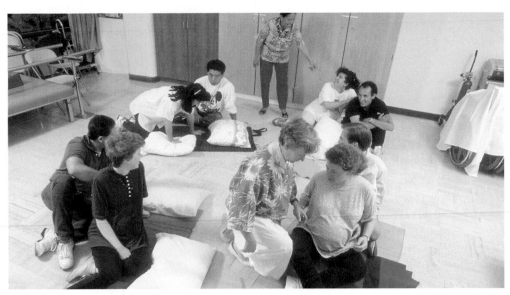

Both prospective fathers and mothers attend childbirth education classes.

term, doctors try to delay labor until the fetal lungs are mature. Bed rest in the hospital is usually prescribed, or medication is necessary. The real problem is the risk of infection. If infection is suspected or fatal maturity is reached, delivery is accomplished (Berkow 1997). About half the time, however, the bag of waters does not rupture until the last hours of labor.

Duration

Labor usually lasts no more than 12 to 14 hours in a woman's first pregnancy and tends to be shorter, averaging 6 to 8 hours, in subsequent pregnancies (Berkow, 1997).

Birthing centers are an alternative to the standard hospital setting.

Stages

The actual process of labor can be divided into three stages. The first and longest is the *dilation stage*, during which the force of the uterine muscles pushing on the baby gradually opens the mouth of the cervix. The cervix increases from less than 0.8 (⅘) inch in diameter to 4 inches. The woman can do nothing to help except relax as completely as possible, allowing the involuntary muscles to do their work. Dilation progresses faster if the mother is not tense. Dilation is complete when the baby's head can start to pass through the cervix.

Upon complete dilation of the cervix, the second stage of labor begins, during which *the baby passes through the birth canal*. When hard contractions come, the woman alternatively pushes and relaxes to help force the baby through the vagina. After the baby is born and tended to, the obstetrician again turns his or her attention to the mother to assist in the third stage of labor.

Passage of the placenta, or afterbirth, occurs during the third stage.

Use of Anesthesia

To alleviate pain in childbirth, **general anesthesia** or **local or regional anesthesia** may be used. General anesthesia affects the body by acting on the whole nervous system; it can slow or stop labor and lower the mother's blood pressure. It crosses the placental barrier and affects the fetus as well, decreasing the responses of the newborn infant. Local or regional anesthesia blocks pain in specific

General anesthesia

Local or regional anesthesia

Parenting Issues

Home Versus Hospital Delivery

Around 1900, about 95% of all babies were born at home. Birthing was a family event. Today about 99% are born in the hospital and only 1% at home (U.S. Bureau of the Census, 1997; Stewart, 1998). The switch has been at the urging of physicians who prefer delivery in sterile, well-equipped, more convenient hospital settings.

Some expectant parents are concerned about hospital practices being too rigid, impersonal, and expensive. They object to the separation of family members and want more control over the childbirth process. Some parents seek midwives to perform home deliveries. Midwives should be certified nurse-midwives (CNMs) who practice in conjunction with physicians, referring problem pregnancies to them and calling on them as needed.

Many physicians will not deliver babies at home. Even those who approve may lose hospital privileges or insurance coverage. Many couples also find that their health insurance policies will not cover home deliveries.

Even with careful screening, there are risks and disadvantages to home births. The couple must weigh the benefits against the risks.

areas; some types have a minimal effect on the baby. Table 4.1 describes various types of anesthesia under each category.

Fetal Monitoring

Electronic fetal monitoring, with external devices applied to the woman's abdomen, detects and records fetal heart tones and uterine contractions. Internal leads may also be used, with an electrode attached to the fetal scalp and a catheter through the cervix into the uterus to measure amniotic fluid pressure. The external devices are generally employed

Episiotomy—surgical incision of the perineum to allow for passage of the baby from the birth canal without tearing the mother's tissue

Perineum—area of skin between the vagina and anus

Cesarean section—removal of the fetus through a surgical incision of the abdominal and uterine walls

Coaching the mother during labor helps her to relax and speeds the birth process.

for normal pregnancies, and the internal methods for high-risk or problem pregnancies. External fetal monitoring is routinely used in all labors by many obstetricians. Other obstetricians feel that it is not always necessary and that it restricts the mother's movement. If a problem occurs or has been previously identified, internal monitoring is used to provide more reliable information about fetal heart patterns and uterine contraction patterns (Berkow, 1997). There is some disagreement among physicians over when to use fetal monitoring.

DELIVERY

Normal Delivery

In normal delivery, the baby's head is delivered first, the baby's body then rotates so that one shoulder and then the other is delivered and finally the rest of the baby's body is delivered without difficulty. The baby's nose, mouth, and pharynx are aspirated with a bulb syringe to remove mucus and fluid and help establish breathing. The umbilical cord is double clamped, cut between the clamps, and tied. Normally, obstetricians recommend that an **episiotomy** be performed on almost all patients having their first baby, or on those who have had a previous episiotomy (Berkow, 1997). An episiotomy involves a surgical incision to prevent excessive stretching or tearing of the tissues of the **perineum.** It is easily stitched up after birth and heals more easily than a tear.

Stress on the Infant

Giving birth produces stress on the baby as well as on the mother. The powerful muscles of the uterus squeeze the baby, usually head first, through the birth canal. Contractions may compress the *placenta* and *umbilical cord* periodically, causing some oxygen deprivation during those times. Furthermore, the infant passes from its dark, warm, secure environment into the outside world with bright lights, cool temperatures, and noises.

Research has revealed that the stress of birth produces large amounts of *adrenaline* and *noradrenaline* in the baby's blood. These are the same hormones that prepare the adult to flee or fight in situations of danger or emergency. The hormones in the infant have a stimulating affect on breathing, heart action, and all organs and cells of the body. As a consequence, the baby is usually born alert. Babies delivered by **cesarean section** before

TABLE 4.1   TYPES OF ANESTHESIA USED IN CHILDBIRTH

General Anesthesia	*Effects*

Inhalation anesthesia
  nitrous oxide
  ether
  halothane
  thiopental
	In sufficient quantities, renders women unconscious. Used only in advanced stages of labor. May cause vomiting and other complications; leading cause of maternal death. Depresses infant's nervous system and respiration. Nitrous oxide may delay infant motor skill development.

Barbiturates
  Nembutal
  Seconal
  Amytal
  Sodium Pentothal
	Usually taken orally, except for Sodium Pentothal. Reduce anxiety and cause drowsiness. Pentothal is injected intravenously to induce sleep. All types may slow labor and depress infant's nervous system and respiration.

Narcotics
  Demerol
  Dolophine
  Nisentil
	Reduce pain, elevate mood; may inhibit uterine contractions; may cause nausea and vomiting; depress infant's nervous system and respiration.

Tranquilizers
  Valium
  Vistaril
  Sparine
  promethazine
	Induce physical relaxation, relieve anxiety, may reduce pain. Have minimal effect on infant.

Amnesics
  scopolamine
  atropine
	Do not reduce pain, but induce "twilight sleep" or forgetfulness. May cause physical excitation. Have minimal effect on infant.

Local or Regional Anesthesia	*Effects*
Pudendal: local injection of novocaine in vulval-perineal area	Blocks pain in vulva and perineum in 50% of cases. Has minimal effect on infant.
Paracervical: local injection of novocaine into cervix and uterus	Blocks pain in cervix and uterus for short duration; not effective late in labor. Can lower mother's blood pressure, cause complications, slow fetal heartbeat, precipitate fetal death.
Spinal: regional injection into space around spinal column	Used during delivery to anesthetize entire birth area from abdomen to toes. Stops labor, motor functions. Requires forceps delivery. Generally does not affect infant unless misadministered; then can cause heart and respiratory failure and death.
Epidural: regional injection administered continuously through a tiny catheter and a needle in the back	Effectively numbs area around perineum, lower uterus, and belly to knees. Can cause serious drop in mother's blood pressure and seizures. May require forceps delivery. Used frequently for cesarean sections.
Caudal: regional injection administered continuously through a catheter and needle in the back	Requires larger doses than epidural. Carries greater risk to infant and mother. May cause sudden drop in mother's blood pressure and lack of oxygen to infant.

labor has begun lack these high levels of hormones, which is one reason why these babies may have problems breathing right after birth (1968).

Delivery Complications

Complications during delivery may include vaginal bleeding during the first stage of labor, abnormal fetal heart rate, breathing problems of the baby after birth, a disproportion in size between the fetus and the pelvic opening, or abnormal fetal presentations and positions. Abnormal presentations include a *face presentation*, *brow presentation*, *shoulder presentation*, or *breech presentation* (when the buttocks present rather than the head). Sometimes feet are presented before the buttocks. All of these abnormal presentations require expert attention. Sometimes delivery by cesarean section is essential to protect the infant.

Anoxia—oxygen deprivation to the brain

Prolapsed umbilical cord—squeezing of the umbilical cord between the baby's body and the wall of the birth canal during childbirth, causing oxygen deprivation to the fetus

Apgar score—method of evaluating the physical condition of the neonate

Brazelton Neonatal Behavior Assessment Scale—method of evaluating the neurological condition of the neonate

Anoxia and Brain Injury

Two of the most serious delivery complications are **anoxia** (oxygen deprivation to the brain) and *brain injury*. Anoxia may result from a **prolapsed umbilical cord** (the cord is squeezed between the baby's body and the birth canal). It also may result from placental insufficiency, premature labor, severe maternal bleeding, maternal hypotension, toxemia, neonatal pulmonary dysfunction, placental passage of maternal analgesics or anesthetics, or because of malformations (Berkow, 1997). The result of anoxia may be permanent damage to the infant's brain cells or even death. The brain can also be injured during difficult deliveries, especially when forceps are used improperly during the procedure.

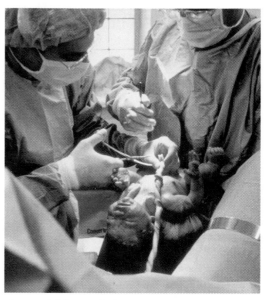

A normal delivery of a healthy baby boy.

FOCUS

Too Many Cesareans?

As discussed, a cesarean can be a life-saving procedure in many emergency situations. Cesarean sections now account for up to 22% of all births in the United States. The rapid increase in their use has led some to cry out that too many cesareans are being performed without sufficient cause, although numerous reasons account for the increase.

1. Obstetrician anxiety, the doctor's fear of being sued if a baby is born less than perfect. Physicians think that cesarean procedures cover them legally.
2. Once a cesarean, always a cesarean. However, in 1982 the American College of Obstetricians and Gynecologists reversed its 75-year-old policy and said that some women who had previously had a cesarean could have a vaginal delivery (Gellman et al., 1983; Lavin, Stephens, Miodovnik, & Barden, 1982; Porreco & Meier, 1983).
3. Obstetrician unwillingness or inability to perform difficult deliveries.
4. Improved obstetrical technology, which detects fetal distress that requires cesarean intervention.
5. Improved training, which reduces the surgical risks.
6. Obstetrical practices making cesarean intervention more necessary, for example, a complication arising from labor induction.
7. Belief that cesareans mean better babies.
8. Patient pressure: Some women want to avoid labor.
9. Medical enthusiasm for cesareans: "What's so great about delivery from below? . . . You don't want the baby squeezed out like toothpaste in a tube. . . . You might say we're helping women to do what nature hasn't evolved to do for herself" (Boston Women's Health Book Collective, 1984, p. 386).
10. Financial incentives: Physicians and hospitals make more money, and many insurance companies reimburse most of the cost of cesareans, though they cover only a small portion of the cost of vaginal delivery (Remez 1991).

POSTPARTUM

Evaluating Neonatal Health and Behavior

Apgar Score

After delivery, the physician will evaluate the health status of the neonate. The most common method is a widely used system developed by Virginia Apgar in 1952 called the **Apgar score.** The system has designated values for various neonatal signs and permits a tentative and rapid diagnosis of major problems (Apgar, 1953). The neonate is evaluated at 1 minute and again at 5 minutes after birth.

There are five signs of the baby's physical condition that compose the Apgar Score: *heart rate, respiratory effort, muscle tone, reflex response* (response to breath test and to skin stimulation of the feet), and *color.* Each sign is given a value of 0, 1, or 2, as shown in Table 4.2 (Greenberg, Bruess, & Sands, 1986). The maximum score on all five scales is 10, and it is rare. A score of 0 may indicate neonatal death; a score of 1 to 3 indicates the infant is very weak; 4 to 6, moderately weak, and 7 to 10, in good condition.

Brazelton Assessment

Dr. T. Berry Brazelton (1984) developed the **Brazelton Neonatal Behavior Assessment Scale,** which is used to evaluate both the neurological condition and the behavior of the neonate (Brazelton, 1990). The scale is a useful indicator of central nervous system maturity and of social behavior and is helpful in predicting subsequent developmental problems (Behrman & Vaughan, 1983). The scale assesses four areas of infant behavior:

1. Motor behaviors (reflexes, hand-to-mouth coordination, and muscle tone)
2. Interactive, adaptive behavior (alertness, cuddliness)
3. Response to stress (startle reaction)
4. Physiological control (ability to calm down after being upset)

Altogether, the scale looks at 26 specific behaviors as well as the strength of various reflexes (Brazelton, 1984).

Postpartal Depression

The period following childbirth is one in which conflicting feelings may surface. The long pregnancy is over, thus bringing a feeling of relief. If the baby is wanted and healthy, the family experiences considerable happiness and elation. Usually within three days of delivery, however, the mother may suffer varying degrees of "baby blues," or

postpartal depression, characterized by feelings of sadness, periods of crying, depressed mood, insomnia, irritability, and fatigue, usually lasting less than two weeks. Often, family support is the best treatment. Depression that is combined with lack of interest in the baby, suicidal or violent thoughts, hallucinations, or bizarre behavior is considered abnormal. Treatment usually is needed. Serious depression is more likely to occur in a woman who had a mental illness before the pregnancy (Berkow, 1997).

Numerous causes precipitate postpartal depression. The mother may have been under emotional strain while she anxiously awaited her baby. Once the baby comes, feelings of exhaustion and depression may result from a letdown of tension. Childbirth itself may impose considerable physical strain on a woman's body, which requires a period of rest and recovery. Estrogen and progesterone levels decline rapidly following delivery, which may have an upsetting, depressive effect on her. Other reports have suggested that diminished thyroid activity following delivery is associated with postpartum depression (Albright, 1993).

Postpartal depression— feelings of sadness, crying, depression, insomnia, irritability, and fatigue commonly experienced by the mother several days after her baby is born

---

TABLE 4.2   APGAR SCORE

The Apgar scoring, developed in 1952 by Dr. Virginia Apgar, is an index to the health status of the newborn infant. The scoring system was developed to predict survival, to compare various methods of resuscitation, to evaluate certain obstetrical practices (such as inducing labor, maternal anesthesia, cesarean section), and to ensure closer observation of the infant during the first minutes of life.

Five signs of a baby's physical condition at birth were chosen for measurement: heart rate, respiratory effort, muscle tone, reflex response (response to breath test and to skin stimulation of the feet), and color. Each sign is given a score of 0, 1, or 2, as shown in the table.

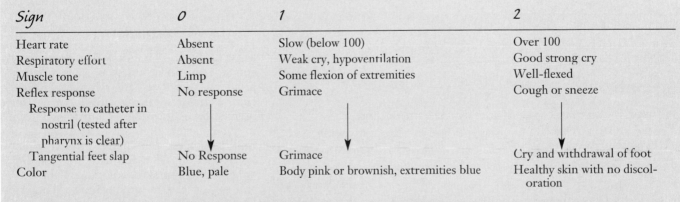

Sign	0	1	2
Heart rate	Absent	Slow (below 100)	Over 100
Respiratory effort	Absent	Weak cry, hypoventilation	Good strong cry
Muscle tone	Limp	Some flexion of extremities	Well-flexed
Reflex response	No response	Grimace	Cough or sneeze
Response to catheter in nostril (tested after pharynx is clear)	↓	↓	↓
Tangential feet slap	No Response	Grimace	Cry and withdrawal of foot
Color	Blue, pale	Body pink or brownish, extremities blue	Healthy skin with no discoloration

The Apgar Score is the sum of the five values and ranges from 0 to 10, with 10 being the optimum. A score of 0 may indicate neonatal death; a score of 1–3 indicates that the infant is very weak; 4–6, moderately weak; and 7–10, in good to excellent condition. One-minute and five-minute scoring are done. The one-minute score indicates the condition at birth; the five-minute score combines the condition at birth and the results of care given during the first five minutes.

On returning home, the mother may feel the strain of "trying to do everything right" in caring for the baby. One young mother remarked, "I never imagined that one small baby would require so much extra work. I'm exhausted" (Author's counseling notes). If the baby is colicky and fussy, even the most patient and experienced mother can become tense and exhausted.

If the woman does not have much help from her partner, or if the baby or other children in the household continue to make personal demands on her, she may become exhausted from the lack of sleep, and from the physical and emotional strain. Some women even return to their jobs outside the home very soon after having a baby. Clearly, the mother needs help and understanding. A conscientious partner will do everything he can to be a full partner in the process and to assume maximum responsibility in caring for her. He will share the responsibility of caring for the baby and will take full or increased responsibility in the care of other children and in managing the household during at least the first several months with a new baby. The father is more likely to do this if he is included in prebirth planning and if the total procreative experience is shared with him from the beginning of the pregnancy. Marsiglio (1991) suggests that the male's procreative consciousness and responsibility must be encouraged.

Of course, some women don't have partners at all to help them. Compared with women in biological families, women in single-parent families and stepfamilies report significantly elevated rates of depression (O'Connor, Hawkins, Dunn, Thorpe, Golding, & the ALSPAC Study Team, 1998). This elevated depression is due to several factors. Women in stepfamilies are more likely to be cohabiting and to have had several previous broken relationships. Women in stepfamilies and single women are more likely to have insufficient social support. Crowded housing conditions, which are more frequent in single-parent families and stepfamilies than in biological families, together with restricted financial resources add to life stresses.

Cultural Factors in Postpartum Care

Cultural factors influence the postpartum care that the new mother receives. That care is often very different in the United States from that in other countries. In the United States, women without physical complications may be sent home from the hospital within 6 hours after giving birth. Once out of the hospital, the focus of care shifts from the mother to the baby. The mother often feels inadequate, with lowered self-esteem. This practice is in sharp contrast to the expectations of the mother in China or Japan. The behavioral restrictions on the Chinese mother promote rest and award her special attention during the first postnatal month. The traditional Japanese mother is expected to go to her parents' home for a month to be cared for with her baby and to have generally more support from multigenerational living arrangements (Albright, 1993).

Sexual Relationships

Most authorities indicate that sexual intercourse may be resumed as soon as desired provided that it is comfortable. However, contraceptive measures are required since pregnancy is possible. Contraceptive pills may be started after the first menstrual period regardless of whether the mother is breast-feeding. A diaphragm may be fitted only after complete involution of the uterus at 6 to 8 weeks. In the meantime, foams, jellies, or condoms may be used. Conception has been reported as early as 2 weeks postpartum, so that caution must be exercised to prevent pregnancy. Nursing mothers tend to ovulate usually at 10 to 12 weeks postpartum, but an occasional nursing mother will ovulate and menstruate as quickly as nonlactating women (Berkow, 1997).

Parenting Issues

Returning Home

In an effort to save on medical expenses, some medical insurance companies insist on early discharge following childbirth. Many family-centered obstetrical units discharge as early as 6 hours postpartum if the patient does not have major complications. For many mothers, early discharge may be unwise because of medical complications or for personal and family reasons. There is always a possibility of maternal infection, hemorrhage, pain, urine retention and bladder overdistention, and constipation. Some of these medical administrations require hospitalization; in addition, all require careful instruction to the new mother and her partner. If the mother is rushed out of the hospital before instruction and care can be given, she may face some of the problems at home where it is not easy to take care of them.

Returning to Work

One of the considerations following childbirth is whether or not a mother returns to work and what should be the timing of such return. One study of 597 women was used to analyze when women start paid work following a birth (Joesch, 1994). This study investigated which month after the birth of the child women started to work outside the home, as well as the factors related to timing of reentering the workforce. Timing of paid work was hypothesized to depend on a woman's financial benefits from working for pay relative to the benefit of staying home. Findings showed that close to one in five women interrupted paid work for 1 month or less after giving birth, 53% had begun to work by month 6, and 61% by the beginning of month 12.

The question arises as to what entices women to stay home longer. According to the financial benefit argument, the more a woman gives up by staying at home, the more likely she is to work for pay. Thus, financial considerations seem to play an important role in the timing of women's employment after childbirth. In particular, women from families that own a home requiring mortgage payments, those with higher income tax rates, and those working during pregnancy were all found to start to work sooner. Higher family income from sources other than women's earnings had the opposite effect: Women were more likely to stay home longer.

Could maternity leave entice women to stay home longer (Joesch, 1997)? In 1993, the *Family and Medical Leave Act* enabled women to take time off from work without pay without being penalized by losing their job. Also, they are entitled to return to work without penalty. The act lengthens the time out of employment to some degree, since health benefits are covered by the employer during the leave. More importantly, the law guarantees either the same or a comparable position on the woman's return from leave, reducing the cost associated with finding a new job, which lowers the cost of staying at home. However, relinquished earnings during the absence and consequences for future earnings, child security, and promotions are likely to be more important considerations than the relatively minor aspect of health insurance. These findings underlie the importance of access to quality nonparental child care, if children's welfare is not to be compromised. Apparently, the desire for paid work is stronger than the desire to stay home with one's children while the children are young, but such a decision requires adequate care of the children while the mother is at work. Surprisingly, additional child-care costs are not substantial enough to influence the timing of the mother's return (Joesch, 1994).

There are significant benefits to both mother and child from having a long enough maternity leave. An investigation of 198 employed mothers of 4-month-old infants were interviewed and videotaped in their homes during feeding time. The analysis indicated a direct association between a shorter length of leave and more negative affect behavior in maternal interactions with their infants. Mothers who reported more depressive symptoms or who perceived their infant as having a more difficult temperament and who had shorter leaves compared with mothers who had longer leaves, were observed to express less positive affect, sensitivity, and responsiveness in their interactions with their infants (Clark, Hyde, Essex, & Klein, 1997).

PREMATURE AND SMALL-FOR-GESTATIONAL-AGE (SGA) INFANTS

Classifications

Each newborn may be classified as full-term, premature, or postmature. A **full-term infant** is one whose gestational age is 37 to 42 weeks. A **premature infant** is one whose gestational age is less than 37 weeks (Duffy, Als, & McAnulty, 1990). A **postmature infant** has a gestational age of over 42 weeks. The neonate may also be classified as of appropriate size and weight for gestational age, small for gestational age, or large for gestational age. Figure 4.1 represents intrauterine growth based on birth weight and gestational age of live-born, single, white infants (Sweet, 1979).

Premature Infants

A premature infant is one who is born before 37 weeks gestation. Previously, any infant weighting less than 2.5 kg (5.5 lb) was termed premature, but this definition was inappropriate because many newborns weighing less than 2.5 kg are actually mature or postmature but small for gestational age (SGA) and have different appearance and problems than premature infants (Berkow, 1997). However, most premature infants are also small, weighing less than 2.5 kg, and have thin, shiny, pink or brownish skin with underlying veins that are

Full-term infant

Premature infant

Postmature infant

easily seen. They have little fat, hair, or external ear cartilage. Spontaneous activity and tone are at a minimum, and their extremities are not held in a fixed position. The testes are undescended in males; the labia majora do not cover the labia minora in females.

Problems with premature infants relate to immaturity of the organs. The infants may have immature development of the brain (Doussard-Roosevelt, Porges, Scanlon, Alemi, & Scanlon, 1997). They may have various kinds of respiratory difficulties. They may have inadequate sucking and swallowing reflexes; they may have a small stomach capacity and may have to be tube fed or fed intravenously. They often suffer from colitis and other gastrointestinal problems. They have lower immunity and are more subject to various infections than full-term infants. They exhibit various signs of metabolic difficulties: hypothermia (below normal body temperature); hypoglycemia (low blood glucose levels);

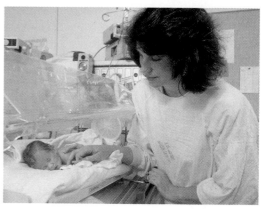

A premature infant is one whose gestational age is less than 37 weeks.

hypocalcemia (low calcium levels); and hypernatremia (high sodium concentrations) are common. Renal function is immature, so that the kidneys are less able to excrete fluids. Premature infants are also more prone to cerebral hemorrhage and injury (Ross, Testmand, Auld, & Nass, 1992; Sostek, Smith, Katz, & Grant, 1987).

The survival rate of premature infants closely correlates with their birth weight. Low-birth-weight infants have been divided into three subgroups: *Low birth weight* (LBW, less than 2,500 grams), *very low birth weight* (VLBW, less than 1,500 grams), and *extremely low birth weight* (ELBW, less than 1,000 grams). This categorization reflects the importance attributed to birth weight in the consideration of risk level. It is assumed that ELBW will have poorer outcomes than VLBW infants, and that LBW infants will have better outcomes than either subgroup, although not as good as those of full-term infants. Birth weight and gestational age, along with specific medical risk factors, have been used with some success in predicting developmental outcomes in LBW infants (Doussard-Roosevelt, Porges, Scanlon, Alemi, & Scanlon, 1997).

Birth weight and gestational age are highly correlated. Infants of VLBW have a mortality rate of approximately 10%, whereas infants of ELBW have a mortality rate of approximately 50%. Twenty-seven percent of all LBW children will die prior to discharge. Sixteen percent will exhibit moderate or severe disability, and 59% will be categorized as normal but may exhibit mild forms of disability. Although they often score in the normal range on standardized tests, both VLBW and ELBW children exhibit scores lower than those of their full-term peers (Hack, Taylor, Klein, Eiben, Schatschneider, & Mercuri-Minich, 1994).

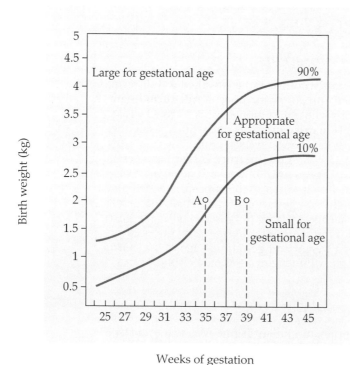

FIGURE 4.1 Intrauterine growth of live-born, white infants. Baby A is premature, whereas baby B is mature but small for gestational age. Curves show growth of infants in 10th and 90th percentiles.

Adapted from "Classification of the Low-Birth-Weight Infant," by A. Y. Sweet, in *Care of the High-Risk Neonate*, 2nd ed., 1979 by M. H. Klaus and A. A. Fanaroff. Copyright 1979 by W. B. Saunders Co.

Advances made in intensive-care, preterm infants have led to dramatic increases in survival rates. However, studies show that those born at very low birth weight continue to manifest poor cognitive performance, relative to their normal birth rate peers. There have been repeated reports of poor performance in infant developmental tests and in various assessments of early language, even when infants with serious sensory or mental impairments are excluded. The poor performance of preterms persists into early and middle childhood, where they continue to be at a disadvantage when compared with normal children. Relative deficits on tests of intelligence, language, and academic development are common. Three relatively large studies assess the 8-year outcome of infants born weighing less than 1,500 grams (Hack et al., 1992; Rickards et al., 1993; Ross, Lipper, & Auld, 1991). Although the mean IQ of preterms in these studies was generally in the normal range, the scores tended to average as much as ten points lower than those of their lower birth rate controls. Moreover, 6 to 8 percent of the preterms had scores indicating mental deficiency (IQ of less than 70). The preterms had poorer scores on language measures, visual-motor integration, and all measures of academic achievement, including reading, arithmetic, and spelling, even among those with normal intelligence. About 20% displayed learning disabilities. As a result, school-aged preterms often require more remedial and/or special education then their full-term peers (Rose & Feldman, 1996). Another study examined the effects of prematurity on 11-year-olds' performance on two specific batteries of cognition—memory and processing speed. Preterms performed more poorly than their full-term controls on all memory tasks; this relative deficit was associated with the presence and severity of neonatal *Respiratory Distress Syndrome* (RDS).

Low-birth-weight infants are at elevated risk for adverse developmental outcomes, including impaired cognition, but the outcome depends partly on the home environment in which the child is raised and the IQ of the mother. Maternal IQ has been found to have a major direct effect on consequences, whereas indirect effects are also influenced by income and home environment. Taken together with results of other studies, these findings suggest that standard family interventions to improve cognitive outcome for children of poor and intellectually deficient women are not likely to produce impressive results (Bacharach & Baumeister, 1998).

Assuming that there have been no significant abnormalities, and assuming that proper medical, emotional, and social care and attention have been provided, preterm infants can sometimes make up deficits in cognitive, language, and social development during the first 3 years of life.

The *Neurobehavioral Assessment of the Preterm Infant (NAPI)* scale was developed to assess neurological development (Korner, Constantinou, Dimiceli, & Brown, 1991). Behavioral problems of both preterm and small-for-gestational-age (SGA) infants are assessed with various instruments (Spiker, Kraemer, Constantine, & Bryant, 1992).

Small-for-Gestational-Age (SGA) Infants

An *SGA infant* is one whose weight is below the 10th percentile for gestational age, whether premature, full-term, or postmature (Achenbach, Phares, & Howell, 1990). Despite their small size, SGA infants have physical characteristics and behavior similar to normal-size infants of the same gestational age. An infant weighing less than 2.5 kilograms, but born between 37 and 42 weeks gestation, may have the same skin, ear, genital, and neurologic development as any other full-term infant. If low birth weight is due to prenatal malnutrition, such infants catch up quickly when given an adequate caloric intake (Berkow, 1997).

Perinatal (near the time of birth) *asphyxia* (lack of oxygen) is the greatest problem of these infants. If intrauterine growth retardation is due to placental insufficiency, asphyxia during labor is common, so that a rapid delivery, sometimes by cesarean section, is needed. An infant who does not breathe spontaneously requires immediate resuscitation to sustain life and avoid brain damage. If asphyxia can be avoided, the neurologic prognosis is good. *Hypoglycemia* (low blood sugar) is also common because of inadequate glycogen storage (Berkow, 1997). Throughout childhood, but especially during the first 6 years, children who have been of low birth weight have a greater number of chronic conditions, are hospitalized more often, and generally exhibit a pattern of poorer health than do children who are of normal birth weight. The most common chronic condition was *respiratory illness*. The lower the birth weight, the greater likelihood a child will have physical, health, intellectual, and behavioral problems at school age (Turner, November/December, 1992).

FOCUS

Kilogram Kids and Intensive Neonatal Care

Remarkable advances have been made in caring for preterm infants. Highly specialized neonatal intensive-care units (NICUs) have been developed to take over various functions of organ systems of the body that are not sufficiently mature to sustain life on their own. The NICU is a series of blinking lights, numbers, monitors, and alarms, all of which are connected by tubes, catheters, and electrodes to the tiny infant. The NICU monitors brain waves, heartbeat, respiration, and other vital signs, and provides food, oxygen, and medicines. The infant lies on an undulating water bed in an incubator that carefully controls temperature and humidity.

Researchers have found that, even when confined to incubators, these tiny infants need normal skin contacts, handling, cuddling, talking, singing, and rocking from caregivers and parents. Such contacts facilitate development (Scafidi, 1986).

The survival rate of premature infants closely correlates with their birth weight. Kilogram infants weigh 1,000 grams (2.2 lb). Intensive care of these smallest infants poses a real dilemma, however. They may survive, but some are neurologically impaired. Costs for intensive care in the hospital may run from $100,000 to $200,000, leaving a family poverty-stricken. The question remains: How much care is too much? At what point should infants be allowed to die, rather than be saved to live with such severe impairments that they can never have a chance for a normal life?

Parental Roles and Reactions

Ordinarily, the birth of a full-term infant is a positive event bringing happiness and closeness to family members. The birth of a preterm infant is a stressful event, leaving family members unsure what their roles are and how to respond. Grandparents, for example, may need to grieve over the loss of their idealized grandchild. Rituals such as showers and birth announcements may be eliminated or postponed, leaving other family members in the dark. The anxiety and stress of the parents is increased when they don't find positive social supports (Coffman, Levit, Deets, & Quigley, 1991).

One study investigated maternal psychological distress, in relationship to perceptions of social support, and parenting strain after the birth of a very-low-birth-weight infant. Compared with mothers of full-term infants, mothers of very-low-birth-weight infants had significantly higher incidents of psychological distress during the neonatal period. Lower general social support predicted high

distress levels. Mothers with a low sense of parenting competence but with support from spouse/partners reported lower maternal distress (Singer, Davillier, Bruening, Hawkins, & Yamashita, 1996).

Furthermore, parents often find preterm infants less attractive, more irritating, and less likable (Easterbrooks, 1989). Mothers of preterm infants have been found to have lower maternal sensitivity to their infants than do mothers of full-term babies (Zarling, Hirsch, & Landry, 1988). The mother's reduced sensitivity interferes with the infant's total development because preterm infants are critically dependent on parents to provide an adequate caregiving environment, social enrichment, and encouragement (Levy-Shiff, Sharir, & Mogilner, 1989).

Intervention programs for parents of low-birth-weight, preterm infants are needed to help parents gain more self-confidence and satisfaction with parenting and to develop more positive perceptions of their infants (Affleck, Tennen, Rowe, Roscher, & Walker, 1989). Such programs usually consist of a series of teaching sessions in the hospital and follow-ups in the parents' home after the infant is discharged (Rauh, Achenbach, Nurcombe, Howell, & Teti, 1988).

Prevention

The risk of low birth weight is reduced when pregnant women receive more complete prenatal care. Care that is recommended includes such components as conducting appropriate physical examinations and appropriate laboratory tests for high-risk patients, taking a health

Preterm infants are critically dependent on parents to provide an adequate caregiving environment. A newborn's skin is covered with a protective cheeselike substance: vernix caseosa.

history, and advising women on behavior such as drug or alcohol use (Turner, 1994). In one experimental prenatal care program conducted in Los Angeles, preterm deliveries were reduced by 20%. The prenatal care program included increased prenatal visits combined with instruction on how to prevent a preterm birth (Donovan, 1994).

The Neonate

Physical Appearance and Characteristics

At birth, the average full-term baby in the United States is about 20 inches long (50.8 cm) and weighs about 7 pounds (3.2 kg). Males tend to be larger and heavier than females, and size at birth bears a relationship to size during childhood. Most newborns lose 5% to 10% of their birth weight in the first few days of life because of fluid loss, until they take in and digest enough food to begin gaining weight (Berkow, 1997).

Some newborns are not very attractive (Ritter, Casey, & Longlois, 1991). The *head* may be long-pointed or misshapen from being squeezed through the birth canal. The ears and nose may be flattened for the same reason. The head is disproportionately large in relation to the rest of the body, and too heavy for the neck muscles to support it. The *legs and buttocks* are small in proportion of the rest of the body. The face, especially the flesh around the eyes, is usually puffy; the brow is wrinkled. The skin of the baby is covered with a protective cheeselike substance: **vernix caseosa.** Some babies have fuzzy body hair that drops off in a short time. Underweight babies look like wrinkled old people.

Physiological Functioning

Although most neonates will not win any beauty contests, they are remarkable creatures with their own independently functioning systems. They must *breathe* on their own as soon as they emerge into the air. In the beginning, breathing may be rapid, shallow, and irregular, but it gradually settles into a more regular rhythm. The infant can cough and sneeze to clear mucus from air passages.

The baby has had an *independent circulatory system*, with a heart pumping blood to the embryo, since the end of the sixth week of gestation (Berkow, 1997). At birth, the heartbeat is still accelerated at about 120 to 150 beats per minute. Blood pressure begins to stabilize in about 10 days.

The baby has a strong *sucking reflex* to be able to take in milk. However, the mother's breasts don't begin secreting milk for 2 to 3 days after birth. In the meantime, a thin, watery, high-protein liquid called **colostrum** is produced, which is nutritionally rich and contains antibodies that enable the baby to fight infections. Some babies develop *physiological jaundice* for a while because of the immaturity of the liver. The condition is characterized by a yellowish tinge to the skin and eyeballs. The condition is not serious and is treated by exposure to fluorescent light, which helps the action of the liver.

Because newborns lack fat layers under their skin, they lose heat very quickly, so that they have difficulty maintaining stable body temperature. Crying and physical activity help them control the temperature.

The Senses and Perception

Infants cannot gain information, learn about the world, or interact socially unless they actively attend to relevant features of their environment (Gardner, Zarmel, & Magnano, 1992). At one time it was thought that newborns' senses were not very well developed. Now it is recognized that *neonates are seeing, hearing, feeling, smelling, touching, tasting creatures who respond to a variety of stimuli, including pain.* There are, however, wide individual differences in infants' reactivity to environmental stimuli (DiPietro, Porges, & Uhly, 1992).

Vision

Vision is the least developed of the senses. Newborns can see clearly objects between 7 and 15 inches away. Their eyes cannot focus properly at closer or farther distances. They have poor *visual acuity:* the ability to distinguish details of objects. Their visual acuity at distances has been estimated to be between 20/150 and 20/800. (Normal vision is 20/20.) Therefore, the neonate can see details of objects at 20 feet no more clearly than adults with normal vision would see them at 150 to 800 feet. However, at close distances, newborns can discriminate among circles, crosses, squares, and rectangles (Bronson, 1991). They prefer looking at faces to looking at objects, and by 1 month of age can distinguish their mother's face from those of others (Ludemann, 1991). They can tell the difference between different facial expressions and even imitate some of them.

By 6 months of age, visual acuity is about normal (Banks & Salapatek, 1983). The irises of babies' eyes open and close as lights go

Vernix caseosa—waxy substance covering the skin of the neonate

Colostrum—a thin, watery, high-protein liquid produced by the breast before the milk comes in

from dim to bright. Some infants have *binocular vision* at birth; that is, they use both eyes to focus on an object. It is not known whether they can see colors immediately, although this ability can be demonstrated by a few months of age (Bornstein, 1985b).

Hearing

Infants can hear sounds while still in the uterus. They respond to various loud noises such as cars honking (Birnholz & Benacerraf, 1983). In fact, they can probably distinguish between their mother's voice and the voices of others. On the basis of a method called discriminative sucking, infants less than 3 days old showed that they could tell their mother's voice from that of a stranger (DeCasper & Fifer, 1980). When given a choice, infants sucked more on a nipple that activated a tape of their mother's voice rather than a nipple that produced the voice of a strange woman. As young as they were, babies sucked about 25% more when they heard their own mother's voice. Apparently, they recognized their mother's voice and took an interest in producing it.

After birth, infants' hearing is only slightly less sensitive than that of adults. They seem to be able to discriminate among sounds of different intensity, pitch, and duration; are more sensitive to higher-pitched than lower-pitched sounds; and are most sensitive to human voices (Spetner & Olsho, 1990). They can also detect the direction from which sound comes and will turn their head toward it (Brody, Zelago, & Chaik, 1984). Like adults, neonates can get bored with the continuous presentation of a sound, but when presented with a new sound, such as a bell ringing, they will pay attention or even show a startle response to it (Madison, Madison, & Adubato, 1986; Weiss, Zelazo, & Swain, 1988). They apparently are able to retain memory for a specific sound over a 24-hour period when presented with the same sound over both days (Swain, Zelazo, & Clifton, 1993).

Smell

Human neonates are responsive to various odors, including odors from their mother's breast. Within several days after birth, breast-feeding infants respond preferentially either to breast or axillary odors from their own mother when paired with comparable stimuli from an unfamiliar lactating female (Marlier, Schaal, & Soussignan, 1998). In another experiment, 2-week-old bottle-feeding girls with no prior breast-feeding experience found the breast odors of lactating females especially attractive (Makin & Porter, 1989).

Taste

Newborns can also discriminate among various taste stimuli. Rosenstein and Oster (1988) demonstrated that within 2 hours of birth, infants with no prior taste experience differentiated sour and bitter stimuli as well as sweet versus nonsweet taste stimuli. The responses to the sour, salty, and bitter stimuli were all characterized by negative facial actions in the brow and midface regions. This study and others showed clearly that newborns also have an innate preference for sweet solutions (Beauchamp & Cowart, 1985) and that sucrose can have a calming effect and relieve pain in the newborn infant (Blass & Smith, 1992; Smith et al., 1992).

Touch and Pain

There is strong evidence of touch sensitivity in neonates, with no discernible differences between the sexes. If you stroke the cheeks of newborns, they will turn their head in that direction. If you stimulate the soles of infants' feet, they will flex their toes. Every parent knows that one way to soothe infants is to hold and stroke them. Recent studies indicate that infants are also sensitive to pain and that this sensitivity increases during the first 5 days of life (Haith, 1986).

Reflexes

Reflexes are unlearned behavioral responses to particular stimuli in the environment. Table 4.3 describes some of the reflexes of the neonate. Some of these reflexes, such as

Human neonates are responsive to various odors, including odors from the mother's breast.

Reflexes—unlearned behavioral responses to particular stimuli in the environment

the *rooting and sucking reflex*, are critical to the infants' survival. Others evolved during evolutionary development. For example, *Palmar's grasp* was necessary to keep babies from falling when their mothers carried them around all the time. The *Moro reflex* could help infants to grasp something when in danger of falling. Other reflexes, such as blinking or the rage reflex, help protect the baby from physical discomfort. Only the *blinking, knee jerk,* and *sneezing reflexes* are permanent for a lifetime. The rest of the reflexes gradually disappear and are replaced by more deliberate, voluntary movements, as development proceeds. The majority of newborn infants show stronger and more coordinated movements on the right side of the body that on the left, which forms the basis for right-handedness and right-biased movements in adulthood (Gratten et al., 1992).

Motor Activity

Although newborns have a variety of reflexes, they don't have much control over voluntary movements. Their arms and legs jerk and flail, and they have trouble getting their fingers or hands to their mouths. When awake and in a supine position, neonates make general movements such as whole-body flexes or more localized movements of the limbs. As they gain control over their muscle activity, they become more successful at accomplishing their goals with less excess motion. Studies of the development of hand-mouth coordination in newborn infants suggest that the relationship between the hand and mouth is not random but that it is far from skilled. However, considerable development does occur in hand-mouth coordination after the newborn period (Lew & Butterworth, 1995). Training can influence early motor development. One research study shows that practice facilitated stepping in 8-week-old infants and led to an earlier onset of unaided walking. Similarly, infants who received sitting exercises were able to sit upright longer than infants who received no exercise (Zelazo, Zelazo, Cohen, & Zelazo, 1993).

Brain and Nervous System

The nervous systems are composed of **neurons,** or nerve cells, which transmit messages. A neuron contains a *cell body*; *dendrites*, which receive neural messages; and an *axon*, which passes along the neural messages, in the form of electrical impulses, to the dendrites of the next neuron. The axon is insu-

FOCUS

Learning Before Birth

In one study, pregnant women tape-recorded three different readings—two from the book *The Cat in the Hat,* by Dr. Seuss, and the third from the story *The King, the Mice, and the Cheese* (Decasper & Spence, 1996). During the last 6 weeks of pregnancy, women recited just one of the readings an average of 67 times. On the third day after birth, the babies who had heard one of the readings prenatally sucked more on the nipples that activated the recordings of the story that they had heard in the womb, showing that they recognized the story. On the other hand, babies in a controlled group, who had not heard a reading before birth, responded equally to all three recordings, suggesting that the babies learned even before birth.

lated with the *myelin sheath*, which prevents the electrical impulses from leaking out. Figure 4.2 shows a typical neuron.

There are several differences between the brain and neurons of a neonate and those of a mature adult. (1) The neonate continues to form new nerve cells, a process that continues until about the second month after birth (Lipsitt, 1986). (2) The billions of nerve cells that are present continue to mature. Especially the dendrites grow and develop, increasing their

Neurons—nerve cells

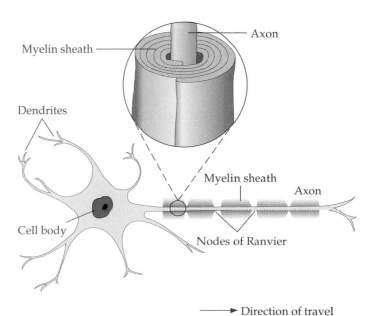

FIGURE 4.2 Neuron. The neurons are wrapped in an insulation substance called myelin. The myelin sheath also speeds transmission though the neuron by preventing the electrical charge from escaping.

TABLE 4.3   REFLEXES OF THE NEONATE

Reflex	Stimulus and Responses
Babinski	Stimulate the sole of the foot; the infant's toes fan out and upward.
Babkin	Apply pressure to both palms of the infant's hands; the infant's eyes close, the mouth opens, and the infant turns its head.
Blinking	Flash on a light, or move an object toward the infant's eyes; the infant blinks.
Knee jerk	Tap on the kneecap; the foot kicks upward.
Moro	Make sudden loud noise or suddenly remove body support; the infant's arms and legs fling outward and toward the body as if to hold onto something.
Palmar grasp	Place an object or finger in the infant's palm; the infant grasps tightly and may even be lifted to a standing position.
Rage	Restrain the infant's movements or put a cloth over its mouth; the baby cries and struggles.
Rooting	Touch the infant's cheek; the baby turns toward the touch and attempts to suck.
Sneezing	Stimulate or tickle the nasal passages; the infant sneezes to clear the passages.
Stepping	Hold the infant upright with feet on the ground; the baby attempts to step as in walking.
Sucking	Put an object in the infant's mouth; the infant begins rhythmic sucking.
Swallowing	Put food in the mouth; the neonate swallows it.
Swimming	Place the infant on its stomach; its arms and legs fan out and move as in swimming.

efficiency in receiving messages. (3) Many of the neurons in the newborn are not yet *myelinated*, or enclosed in a sheath, which allows electrical impulses to escape and result in inefficient nerve transmission, jerky responses, and lack of coordination. Myelination continues until adolescence. (4) The brain of the newborn is noticeably immature, with large areas dysfunctional. Brain activity is concentrated in the *brain stem*, which controls automatic physiological functions such as breathing, digestion, and a variety of reflexes. The *cerebral cortex*, or upper levels of the brain that control more complex functions, is quite immature in newborns. Growth of the cortex as the infant matures allows more flexible, complex motor and intellectual functioning as time goes by (Bell & Fox, 1992; Chugani & Phelps, 1986).

FOCUS

Sudden Infant Death Syndrome (SIDS)

SIDS is the sudden death of any infant or young child which is unexpected according to the health history and for which an adequate cause of death cannot be demonstrated. It is the most common cause of death between 2 weeks and 1 year of age, amounting to 30% of all deaths in this age group. Peak incidence is between the second and fourth month of life. The incidence is greater among lower socioeconomic groups, in premature infants, during the cold months, in siblings of SIDS victims, and in infants born to mothers who smoke during pregnancy or who are narcotic addicts.

Almost all the deaths occur while the infant is sleeping: He or she just stops breathing. Parents are usually grief-stricken, and because no definite cause of the death can be found, usually have excessive guilt feelings. These feelings are increased if social workers or the police become involved in investigating the death. To deal with the grief and guilt, family members will need a great deal of support for several months (Berkow, 1997).

Individual Differences

It must be emphasized that babies show distinct individuality in temperament from the first weeks of life. There are differences in activity level, as well. Some babies are very alert, responsive, and active; others are lethargic and quiet. Some are very happy and cheerful, always smiling and pleasant. Others are irritable, cry a lot, or express frequent frustration and anger. Some babies are very sociable and outgoing; others are shy and withdrawn. Some show regular patterns of eating and sleeping and are easy to care for on a routine basis. Others do not show regular cycles. Some babies want to be held and cuddled; others seldom do. These differences in temperament mean that parents have to be flexible in the care they give. Not all babies can be cared for alike, since not all infants are the same (Thomas and Chess, 1987).

Stress Reactions

Infants show physiological reactions to stress. Stress produces an elevation of cortisol from the adrenal cortex. Epinephrine is secreted and travels in the bloodstream to every cell of the body. Cardiovascular function increases, including an increase of heart rate, blood pressure, and a constriction of blood vessels. Respiration increases as does muscular tension and strength. Infants show differences in stress reactions during labor itself. These reactions reflect differences in temperament. Uterine contractions are an example of intermittent stress and suggest that stress responses may be individually specific at birth and may influence behavioral style throughout infancy. In one study, 40% of infants whose heart rates during labor were characterized by either acceleration or deceleration were rated by their mothers as being temperamentally difficult at 4 months and 1 year of age. Infants who showed variable and mixed heart rate reactions to labor were always rated as easy or agreeable.

Literature indicates that responsiveness to stress, particularly intermediate stress early in life, can have a permanent physiological effect on brain tissue. The effect on brain tissue produces adaptive and maladaptive temperamental characteristics. This mechanism implies the existence of physiological basis of stress responses that may predispose individuals to unique behavioral characteristics. Thus some forms of stress reactivity have biological underpinnings, and the data support the hypothesis that stress reactivity is the characteristic of temperament (Davis & Emory, 1995).

Summary

1. Prepared childbirth refers to the physical, social, intellectual, and emotional preparation for the birth of a baby. In this context, it does not necessarily refer to labor and delivery without medication.

2. One of the most popular methods of natural childbirth is the Lamaze method.

3. Birthing rooms and centers provide homelike settings where birth takes place and where the mother, and sometimes the whole family, may take care of the infant afterward. These settings seek to combine the advantages of delivery in a homelike environment with the medical backup of a hospital.

4. About 99% of babies are delivered in the hospital. If couples consider a home delivery, they ought to follow certain standards as outlined by the NAPSAC (The National Association of Parents and Professionals for Safe Alternatives in Childbirth). Even with careful screening, home delivery has risks and disadvantages.

5. Real labor is rhythmic in nature and may be divided into three phases: the dilation phase; the childbirth phase; and passage of the placenta, or afterbirth, during the third phase.

6. General anesthesia or local or regional anesthesia may be used to alleviate pain during childbirth. General anesthesia affects the body by acting on the whole nervous system. It crosses the placental barrier and affects the fetus as well. Local anesthesia blocks pain in specific areas; some types have minimal effect on the baby.

7. In normal delivery the baby's head is delivered first. Complications during delivery may include vaginal bleeding, abnormal fetal heart rate, a disproportion in size between the fetus and pelvic opening, or abnormal fetal presentations and positions.

8. Birth is a stress on the baby, but the infant produces large amounts of adrenaline and noradrenaline, which have a stimulating effect on the infant and help it to breathe immediately after birth.

9. One of the most serious delivery complications is anoxia (oxygen deprivation to the brain) from a prolapsed umbilical cord or other causes. The result may be permanent damage to the infant's brain cells or even death. Brain injury can also occur during difficult deliveries, especially when forceps are used improperly.

10. A cesarean section can be a life-saving procedure when rapid delivery is needed, but some authorities complain that cesareans are being performed unnecessarily.

11. After delivery, the physician evaluates the health status of the neonate and gives it an Apgar Score. The Brazelton Neonatal Behavior Assessment Scale is also used to

evaluate both the neurological condition and the behavior of the neonate.

12. Postpartal depression is common following childbirth. The mother needs help and understanding. Cultural factors influence the care that the new mother receives.

13. In an effort to save on medical expenses, some medical insurance companies insist on early discharge following childbirth. This early discharge may be unwise if there are medical complications or if the mother has little help at home when she returns.

14. Most authorities indicate that sexual intercourse may be resumed as soon as desired provided that it is comfortable and that there are no medical reasons why it shouldn't be resumed.

15. One of the considerations following childbirth is whether or not the mother returns to work and what is the timing of such return. Timing of paid work depends on a woman's financial benefits from working for pay relative to the benefits of staying home. Women from families that depend on her income and that have a great number of ongoing expenses are more likely to return to work sooner than those who have fewer obligations. The Family and Medical Leave Act enables women to take time off from work without losing their job; they are entitled to return to work without penalty. One of the important factors is the access to quality, nonparental child care when the mother returns to work.

16. Newborns may be classified as full-term (37 to 42 weeks gestation), premature (less than 37 weeks gestation), and postmature (over 42 weeks gestation). Premature infants may have problems because of the immaturity of their organs.

17. Small-for-gestational-age (SGA) infants weigh below the 10th percentile for gestational age, whether premature, full-term, or postmature. They have physical characteristics and behavior similar to normal-size infants of the same gestational age. Perinatal asphyxia (lack of oxygen) is the greatest problem for these infants. However, throughout childhood, especially the first 6 years, they have poorer health than normal-size infants.

18. Remarkable advances have been made in intensive neonatal care for preterm infants. However, intensive care of the very smallest infants, especially those less than 1.6 pounds (750 grams), poses a special dilemma. These infants may survive, but up to 100% are neurologically impaired. How much intensive care is too much? Costs may run from $100,000 to $200,000.

19. The average full-term neonate is about 20 inches long and weighs about 7 pounds. Some are not very attractive.

20. However, the neonate is a remarkable creature. It must breathe on its own; it has had an independent circulatory system operating since the sixth week of gestation. It has a strong sucking reflex to take in milk. It may have problems for a few days with physiological jaundice and may have some trouble regulating body temperature.

21. Neonates possess all the senses, though not all of these are well-developed. Vision is the least developed. Newborns can see clearly objects between 7 and 15 inches away, but they have difficulty at closer or farther distances. By 6 months of age, visual acuity is about normal.

22. Infants can hear sounds while still in the uterus. After birth, their hearing is only slightly less sensitive than that of adults.

23. Human neonates are responsive to various odors, including odors from their mother's breast. They can also discriminate among various taste stimuli. There is strong evidence of touch sensitivity.

24. Reflexes are unlearned behavioral responses to particular stimuli in the environment. Reflexes help the infant to survive, to protect itself from harm and from physical discomfort. Only the blinking, knee jerk, and sneezing reflexes are permanent. The rest of the reflexes gradually disappear and are replaced by more deliberate, voluntary movements.

   Newborns don't have much control over voluntary movements. The development of hand-mouth coordination occurs slowly.

25. The nervous systems are composed of neurons, or nerve cells. The cells in neonates continue to multiply for about the first 2 months. The existing cells become more mature and more capable of transmitting messages. The brain also continues to develop, especially in the cerebral cortex, or higher levels. Growth of the cortex allows more flexible, complex motor and intellectual functioning as time goes by.

26. Sudden Infant Death Syndrome (SIDS) is a frequent cause of death between 2 weeks and 1 year of age, amounting to 30% of all deaths in this age group. The

incidence is greater among some groups of mothers than others. Parents are usually grief-stricken and often feel guilty.

27. Babies show distinct individuality of temperament from the first weeks of life.

28. Infants show physiological reactions to stress that are similar to those found in adults. They may show differences in stress reactions during labor itself, which reflect differences in temperament. Stress reactions may be individually specific at birth and may influence behavioral style throughout infancy.

Key Terms

Amniotic sac (bag of waters)   *p. 78*
Anoxia   *p. 82*
Apgar score   *p. 82*
Brazelton Neonatal Behavior Assessment Scale   *p. 82*
Cesarean section   *p. 80*
Colostrum   *p. 89*
Episiotomy   *p. 80*
Full-term infant   *p. 85*
General anesthesia   *p. 79*
Labor   *p. 78*
Lamaze method   *p. 78*

Local or regional anesthesia   *p. 79*
Neurons   *p. 91*
Perineum   *p. 80*
Postmature infant   *p. 85*
Postpartal depression   *p. 83*
Premature infant   *p. 85*
Prepared childbirth   *p. 78*
Prolapsed umbilical cord   *p. 82*
Reflexes   *p. 90*
Show   *p. 78*
Vernix caseosa   *p. 89*

Discussion Questions

1. What do you think of the Lamaze method of natural childbirth? What are some advantages and disadvantages? Have you known any parents who used the Lamaze method or a similar method for having their baby? How did it work out?

2. For yourself, what do you think about having both parents participate actively in the labor and delivery process? About both parents being present in the delivery room when the baby is born? Explain your answers.

3. Do you know anyone who had induced labor? Delivery by cesarean section? With what results?

4. Do you know any couple who had a premature baby? What were some of their reactions? What problems did they encounter?

5. Assume you had a 750-gram baby that was premature. Would you want the doctor to try to save the life of your baby if the infant would be severely mentally retarded afterward?

6. To you who have had a child: What was your first feeling and reaction when you saw your baby? What pleased you the most? What troubled you the most? Explain.

Suggested Readings

BEAN, C. A. (1990). *Methods of Childbirth*. New York: William Morrow. All aspects of childbirth from late pregnancy to postpartum considerations.

BERGER, G. S., GOLDSTEIN, M., & FUERST, M. (1995). *The couple's guide to fertility*. New York: Doubleday. A guide for infertile couples.

EISENBERG, A., HATHAWAY, S., & MERKOFF, H. E. (1991). *What to expect while you're expecting* (rev. ed.). New York: Workman Publishing. An encyclopedia for expectant and new parents.

ENKIN, M. (Ed.). (1995). A guide to effective care in pregnancy and childbirth (2nd ed.). Oxford University Press. A must for parents.

MARZOLLO, J. (1993). *Fathers and babies*. New York: Harper-Collins. A guide for fathers of infants from birth to the first 18 months.

NILSSON, L., & HAMBERGER, L. (1993). *A child is born*. New York: DPT/Seymour Lawrance. From fertilization to birth; with exceptional photographs.

PROFET, M. (1995). *Protecting your baby to be: Preventing birth defects in the first trimester*. Reading, MA: Addison-Wesley. A guide to prenatal care.

SIMKIN, P., WHALLEY, J., & KAPLIN, A. (1991). Pregnancy, childbirth, and the newborn. (rev. ed.). Paperback. An up-to-date and complete guide.

Web Resources

http://www.obgyn.net OBGYN.Net. A physician reviewed service for accessing information and global interaction.

Perspectives
on Child Development

Chapter 5

CHILD DEVELOPMENT AS A SUBJECT OF STUDY

Child development is a specialized discipline devoted to the understanding of all aspects of human development from birth to adolescence. It is a relatively new field of study. Sara Wiltse (1894), the first secretary to the child study section of the National Education Association, remarked that child study really began in America and that "previous to 1888, practically no scientific observations of child life had been done. . . . One searched libraries in vain to find what the average child could either know or do at a given age" (p. 191). Child development leader Margaret Schallenberger (1894) of Stanford University wrote that children were "among the last of nature's productions to become the privileged subjects of scientific study" (p. 87).

HISTORICAL PERSPECTIVES

Children as Miniature Adults

One reason that interest in child development was so long in happening is that, *during the Middle Ages and until several hundred years later, childhood was not considered a separate stage of life.* Children were permitted a few short years of dependence, then expected to be little adults. As soon as children outgrew their swaddling clothes (which were wrapped around their bodies), they were dressed like adult men and women. They played adult games, drank with adults, and worked beside them in fields and shops. Children could be married, crowned as monarchs, or hanged as criminals. Medieval law made no distinction between childhood crimes and adult crimes (Borstelmann, 1983). No effort was made to protect their innocence in sexual matters. For example, Louis XIV of France became king at age 5 and played sexual games with his nursemaids. Because childhood was not considered a special stage, and because children were treated as little adults, no effort was made to consider them special in any way.

Children as Burdens

Before modern birth control was available, many of the children brought into the world were really not wanted. Children were considered a burden rather than a blessing. Each child born meant one more body to clothe and look after, and one more mouth to feed. While infanticide was a crime during the Middle Ages and after, it was probably the most frequent crime in all of Europe until 1800 (Piers, 1978). Unwanted babies were sometimes abandoned or drowned. In the 1300s, Pope Innocent III established the first foundling home in Italy when he became upset at the sight of so many infants' bodies floating down the Tiber River. Some parents, not wanting to kill their infants, sent them to the country to be wet-nursed, or they put them in foundling homes or orphanages where they most likely died. As late as the nineteenth century, one Irish orphanage had admitted 10,272 children, of which only 45 survived (Thompson & Grusec, 1970, p. 603). Conditions were not any better in the United States. One 1915 study in Baltimore, Maryland, revealed that 90% of children admitted to foundling homes and orphanages in the city died within one year of admission (Gardner, 1972).

Child development is a specialized discipline devoted to understanding all aspects of human development from birth to adolescence.

Utilitarian Value of Children

Until the twentieth century, child labor was an accepted practice. Like animals and slaves, children were forced to work at a variety of arduous tasks for the economic benefit of the family. During the Middle Ages, children were farmed out as apprentices to tradespeople and farmers. With the beginning of the industrial revolution in the eighteenth century, children were employed in textile mills, mines, and other industries for 12 hours a day, 6 days a week. The work was dangerous, dirty, exhausting, and unhealthy. Children as young as 5 or 6 crawled into the narrow, dark passages of mines to sit alone for 12 hours a day while they tended the doors that sealed off the shafts. Older children were "hurriers," whose job was to haul coal out of the narrow tunnels. They were harnessed to sleds that they pulled like draft animals. One child recalls:

Child development—all aspects of human growth from birth to adolescence; the study of this growth

I went into a pit at seven years of age. When I drew with the girdle and chain the skin was broken and blood ran down. . . . If we said anything, they would beat us. I have seen many draw at six [years]. They must do it or be beat. They cannot straighten their backs during the day. I

Paintings during the Middle Ages portrayed children as miniature adults.

FOCUS

Paintings of Children

Art before recent times portrayed children as little adults. Their bodily proportions and appearances were shown to resemble those of grown-ups, and certainly the clothing they wore would not permit them to run and play as today's children do.

In the early 1900s, most children admitted to orphanages died within a year after admission.

have sometimes pulled till my hips have hurt me so that I have not known what to do with myself. (Bready, 1926, p. 273)

Children working in textile mills fared only a little better. Small children 5 years old had to crawl into the looms to retie threads. Older children were loom operators, exposed to turning spindles and whirling machinery.

The accompanying photo gives some idea of the dangers involved.

England passed the first child labor laws in 1832. Ten years later, laws to regulate the use of children in mines were passed. Girls

During the Industrial Revolution in the eighteenth century, children as young as 5 to 6 years of age were employed to work in mines for 12 hours a day.

These spindle boys in a Georgia cotton mill were exposed to the dangers of turning spindles and whirling machinery.

were not allowed to work underground, and boys had to be at least 10 years of age. However, the widespread use of child labor continued abroad and in the United States. Not until the twentieth century were laws passed to really regulate child labor, require children to get an education, and prosecute parents for child abuse. Gradually, societies for prevention of cruelty to children, children's aid societies, and various social programs were established to further the welfare of children (Siegel & White, 1982). In addition, machines were used increasingly to replace people, and the first to be freed were the children who worked in factories and mills.

EARLY PHILOSOPHIES REGARDING THE MORAL NATURE OF CHILDREN

Original Sin

Historically, there were three major philosophies regarding the moral nature and development of children. One view was the Christian doctrine of **original sin.** According to this view, children were born sinful and rebellious, depraved in nature and spirit, and were in desperate need of redemption. They were unable to save themselves; their only hope lay in conversion and surrender to God, who would save them from eternal damnation. In the meantime, the role of parents and teachers was to break the rebellious spirit of children, to employ strict punishment and discipline, and to guide them toward virtue and salvation. *The New England Primer*, originally published in puritan America in 1687, began:

Original sin—the Christian doctrine that, because of Adam's sin, a sinful nature has been passed on to succeeding generations

Tabula rasa—literally, a blank slate; refers to John Locke's view that children are born morally neutral

In the late 1800s, Horace Bushnell said that God's love and grace are mediated through caring parents.

"A—In Adam's fall we sinned all." This was the child's first reader. In school, the three Rs—reading, 'riting, and 'rithmetic—were taught to the tune of the hickory stick, which was routinely used to beat disobedient pupils.

Not all adults agreed with this philosophy. Many were reluctant to use harsh measures and sought to achieve a balance between discipline and kindness (Moran & Vinovskis, 1986). Horace Bushnell (1888) in his book *Christian Nurture*, first published in 1861, objected to raising children in an atmosphere of unchristian love, in which parents did nothing positive while they prayed for their children's salvation. *Bushnell said that the family as a social group influences the life and character of children, and that God's love and grace are mediated through caring parents.* "The child must not only be touched with some gentle emotions toward what is right, but he must love it [what is good] with a fixed love, love it for the sake of its principle, receive it as a vital and formative power" (Bushnell, 1888). Bushnell further observed that "infancy and childhood are the ages most pliant to good" (p. 14). Bushnell's view was certainly the forerunner of modern concepts of child development and of the family's role in the socialization of children.

Tabula Rasa: John Locke

Regarding the moral nature and development of children, *the second major philosophy was that of John Locke (1632–1704), who said that children are morally neutral.* Locke said that children are a **tabula rasa,** a "blank slate" in the literal translation. According to this view, children have no inborn tenden-

Schoolmasters often employed strict punishment and discipline to break the rebellious spirit of children.

cies. They are neither good nor bad, and how they turn out depends on what they experience while growing up. Locke said that parents could mold their children in any way they wished through the use of associations, repetitions, imitations, rewards, and punishments (Locke, 1892). Locke suggested that parents reward their children with praise and approval. He objected to physical punishment because he said it does not foster self-control and only teaches fear and anger. Locke was a forerunner of modern behaviorism and encouraged treating children with kindness and love.

Noble Savages: Jean-Jacques Rousseau

The third major philosophy reflecting the moral nature and development of children was espoused by Jean-Jacques Rousseau (1712–1778). *Rousseau said that children are* **noble savages,** *endowed with a sense of right and wrong.* They will develop positively according to nature's plan because they have an innate moral sense. Rousseau felt that any attempt by adults to provide indoctrination and training would only interfere with children's development and corrupt them. Rousseau outlined four stages of development: *infancy, childhood, late childhood,* and *adolescence,* and said that adults should be responsive to the child's needs at each stage of development. Rousseau was the first to emphasize **maturation**—the unfolding of the genetically determined patterns of growth and development, which reflect unique patterns of thought and behavior at each stage of growth.

EVOLUTIONARY BIOLOGY

Origin of the Species: Charles Darwin

Charles Darwin (1809–1882) published *On the Origin of Species* in 1859 (Darwin, 1936). He emphasized that the human species had evolved over millions of years through the process of **natural selection** and the **survival of the fittest.** Natural selection means that certain species were selected to survive because they had characteristics that helped them adapt to their environment (implying that the human species has evolved from lower life forms). Survival of the fittest means that only the fittest live to pass on their superior traits to future generations. Gradually,

Charles Darwin emphasized natural selection and the survival of the fittest.

higher and more adaptable forms of life evolved. Darwin also observed that the embryos of many species were very much alike during certain stages of their development, indicating that they had evolved from common ancestors. (See Figure 5.1 on p. 102.)

Modern theorists emphasize that human behavior is still adaptive (Hinde, 1991). For example, children develop different personality characteristics in an insecure family environment than in a secure one. Fears of falling, darkness, or being left alone were formerly called irrational fears of childhood, but they make good sense in an environment where proximity to the mother is essential to survival. Many aspects of infant behavior such as the rooting reflex and bonding are also necessary for the infant's survival. Anthropologists suggest that society-specific cultural practices produce personalities conducive to the maintenance of the society.

There are at least four major contributions that Darwin made to developmental psychology. One, humans are kin to all living things by virtue of sharing a common origin. There is a recognition that there is a substantial continuity in mental functioning between animals and humans. Two, Darwin emphasized individual differences. Three, Darwin focused on human behavior as an adaptation to the environment. Four, Darwin emphasized the importance of scientific observation

Noble savages—beings endowed with a sense of right and wrong; a term used by Jean-Jacques Rousseau to describe his view of children

Maturation—the unfolding of the genetically determined patterns of growth and development

Natural selection

Survival of the fittest

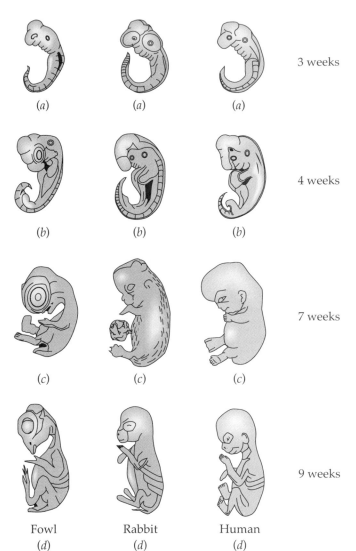

(a) (a) (a)	3 weeks
(b) (b) (b)	4 weeks
(c) (c) (c)	7 weeks
Fowl (d) Rabbit (d) Human (d)	9 weeks

FIGURE 5.1 Embryonic development of a fowl, rabbit, and human shown in four parallel stages.

in gathering data. Thus, he broadened psychological methodology and extended it beyond the introspection of the day (Charlesworth, 1992).

Elements of Darwin's theory are also evident in Piaget's ideas. Piaget said that children's development is an effort to adjust their behavior to societal demands. Ethologists also compare animal and human behavior. For example, they compare imprinting and bonding behavior to better understand how human children develop.

BABY BIOGRAPHIES

During the late nineteenth and early twentieth centuries, attempts were made to study children by keeping biographical records of

their behavior. Darwin (1877) himself kept an account of the development of his young son. Milicent Shinn (1900) published *The Biography of a Baby*, which recorded the growth of her young niece during her first year of life. The baby biographies did not yield very much objective, scientific information about child development, but they were the forerunners of later observations that tried to describe normal growth patterns during various stages of development.

NORMATIVE STUDIES

The Contents of Children's Minds: G. Stanley Hall

G. Stanley Hall attempted to record facts concerning children's development during different stages. His approach launched the movement to make normative studies of children, to find out what to expect during each age regarding their growth and behavior. Hall made up elaborate questionnaires that were distributed to schoolchildren. The questionnaires asked the children to describe almost everything in their lives: their interests, play, friendships, fears, and so forth. Hall's stated purpose was to "discover the contents

G. Stanley Hall made the first normative study of children's development during different stages.

of children's minds" (Hall, 1891). The casual data-collecting procedures left sample characteristics undetermined. The results were difficult to summarize, and the usefulness of the data was doubtful, but this approach spawned several decades of more sophisticated normative research.

Growth Patterns: Arnold Gesell

Arnold Gesell (1880–1961) was one of Hall's pupils. He devoted a major part of his career to observing infants and children and to collecting normative information on them. He wrote volumes describing typical motor skills, social behavior, and personality traits to help parents and professionals know what to expect at each stage (Gesell & Ilg, 1943; Gesell & Ilg, 1946; Gesell & Ames, 1956). Gesell's books became the bibles of child development during the 1940s and 1950s. Actually, Gesell drew his conclusions from samples of boys and girls of favorable socioeconomic status in school populations in New Haven, Connecticut, where the Gesell Institute of Child Development is located. Gesell contended that such a homogeneous sample would not lead to false generalizations. However, to try to correct the deficiencies of the earlier studies, the Gesell Institute has since conducted new normative studies of diverse samples of preschool children from differ-

ent socioeconomic groups (Ames, Gillespie, Haines, & Ilg, 1978).

Gesell's theory is a biologically oriented one, in which maturation is mediated by genes and biology that determine behavioral traits and developmental trends. Since development is biologically determined, there is very little that parents and teachers can do to alter its progress. Gesell felt that acculturation can never transcend the primary importance of maturation. In spite of genetically determined individual differences, Gesell considered many of the principles, trends, and sequences to be universal among humans.

Although it is interesting, Gesell's normative theory has generally been discounted today by behaviorists and social learning theorists, who tend to emphasize the importance of experience and environmental influences on children's development. (See the "Focus" box on p. 104.)

Intelligence Testing: Lewis Terman

Lewis Terman (1877–1956) was another student of Hall's. A professor at Stanford University, he published in 1916 the first widely used intelligence test for children in the United States. He called it the *Stanford-Binet Intelligence Scale*, which was a revision of Binet's test that had been developed earlier in Paris. Binet's test had been used to identify retarded children in the Paris school system and to sort out children of varying scholastic

Arnold Gesell, founder of the Gesell Institute of Child Development in New Haven, Connecticut.

Lewis Terman published the first widely used intelligence test for children in the United States.

FOCUS

Gesell's Behavior Profile of the 2-Year-Old

At 2 years the child cuts his last milk teeth. He is no longer an infant, though compared with a 3-year-old child he is still very immature. There is danger of overestimating his capacities, simply because he is sturdy on his feet and is beginning to put words together. . . .

He does not yet walk erect. There remains a little of the angularity of the ancient man in his posture. . . . When he picks up something from the floor, he half bends at the waist as well as at the knees; whereas at 18 months he squatted. Stooping is more advanced behavior than squatting. But the 2-year-old still leans forward as he runs. . . .

To get up from a sitting position on the floor, he leans forward, pushes up buttocks first, and head second, instead of raising an erect trunk as he will later. He goes up and down stairs mark-time fashion, without alternating his feet. . . .

His is still geared to gross motor activity, and likes to run and romp, lug, push and pull, but with better coordination than at 18 months. His fine motor control also has advanced. . . . He also likes to take things apart and fit them together again.

The muscles of eyes and face are more adept. He moves his eyes more freely and is sensitive to marginal fields, whereas at 18 months he ran headlong as though he had blinders on. He stops and engages in long periods of looking. . . .

The whole linguistic apparatus, mouth, lips, tongue, larynx and thorax is undergoing rapid organization. Jargon is dropping out, sentences are coming in. Soliloquy is taking the place of the babbling of the 6-month-old child, as though on an advanced level the 2-year-old is under a similar compulsion to exercise his vocal abilities, to repeat words, to name things, to suit words to action and action to words. Vocabularies vary enormously in size from a half dozen to a thousand words. . . .

The third year is also the year when the sphincter muscles of bladder and bowel are coming under voluntary control. . . .

The action system of the 2-year-old is not yet sufficiently advanced to effect delicate and long sustained interpersonal relations. He still prefers solitary play to parallel play and seldom plays cooperatively. He is in the pre-coopera-

tive stage; watching what others are doing rather than participating. He cannot share; he cannot as a rule let someone else play with what is his own. He must learn "It's mine" first. He does so by holding on and by hoarding. . . . The hitting, patting, poking, biting, hairpulling, and tug of war over materials so characteristic of Two need to be handled with understanding and sensible techniques on the part of parent and guidance teacher. . . .

So to sum him up, what are his dominating interests? He loves to romp, flee, and pursue. He likes to fill and empty, to put and to pull out, to tear apart, and to fit together, to taste (even clay and wood), to touch and rub. He prefers action toys such as trains, cars, telephones. He is intrigued by water and washing. Although he is not yet an humanitarian, he likes to watch the human scene. He imitates the domesticities of feminine laundry work and doll play. He has a genuine interest in the mother–baby relationship. (Gesell & Ilg, 1943, pp. 159–161)

---

abilities. Terman also conducted the first longitudinal study of children of superior intelligence. Terman followed more than 1,500 children with IQs averaging 150 and above from 1921 into mature adulthood to determine the relationship between intelligence and social adjustment, emotional stability, professional and marital success, health, and other characteristics. Generally, *he found intellectually gifted children to be superior in other ways as well* (Terman, 1925; Terman & Oden, 1959). Daniel Goleman (1980) has since reported on follow-up studies of Terman's subjects, now in their 60s and 70s. Terman's work produced a useful instrument for measuring intelligence and launched the whole intelligence test movement. Contemporary studies focus on the relative roles of genetics

versus environmental influences on intellectual abilities, as was discussed in Chapter 3.

MODERN CONTRIBUTIONS TO CHILD DEVELOPMENT

Research Centers

By the beginning of the twentieth century, thousands of adults working with children began to demand public and government intervention to help protect children who were under their care. The first White House Conference on Child Health and Protection was held in 1909. The conferences became yearly events and led to the establishment of

FOCUS

John Dewey

John Dewey (1859–1952) was an American psychologist-philosopher-educator of international acclaim. In Dewey's day, psychology was becoming a laboratory-based enterprise devoted to the search for empirical knowledge. Dewey warned of the limits to the knowledge that could be gathered in those laboratories and therefore established a small primary school at the University of Colorado. He called his school a "laboratory school" and used it for his scientific experimentation in education. He felt that by controlling the school environment, he could foster the natural growth of children. The school was an experiment in the possibilities of human development in arranged environments. By varying the school's social environment, child development could be directed toward desired ends. The classroom became the context in which Dewey's ideals for society were expressed as desirable norms of growth for the individual child.

Dewey felt that education should be in accordance with nature, that educational procedures should encourage the unfolding of the physical, mental, and moral nature of children. The immediate goals and objectives of education are set by the interests and capabilities of the child and are not imposed by adults as fixed ends. Dewey placed a great deal of emphasis on learning through experiences and on self-directed activities. The school was a laboratory of life and not just a preparation for life. The school reproduces within itself the typical conditions of social life. The school is structured as a small society unto itself. Direct experience enables the child to develop intellectual and moral virtues that enable him or her to develop a better society (Cahan, 1992).

John Dewey said that the school classroom ought to be a laboratory for living.

---

the U.S. Children's Bureau in 1912 (McCullers & Love, 1976).

Interest in research in child development blossomed during the years following World War I. In 1917, the Iowa legislature allocated $50,000 for an Iowa Child Welfare Research Station. This effort, which was the first of its kind, was followed by the establishment of the Teachers College Child Development Institute (at Columbia University), the Yale University Psycho-Clinic (later called the Yale Clinic of Child Development and still later the Gesell Institute of Child Development), the University of Minnesota Institute of Child Welfare, and the University of California Institute of Child Welfare (at Berkeley). In the early period, most of the money for the child-research institutes was provided by the Laura Spellman Rockefeller Memorial Fund. Federal funds became available after World War II. Today, there are hundreds of universities and organizations involved in child development research. One of the most prestigious organizations is the Society for Research in Child Development located in Chicago.

Medical and Mental Health Practitioners

Substantial information on child development has also been provided by medical and child guidance practitioners. *Pediatrics* was developed as a medical specialty, and pediatricians have made tremendous strides in treating acute illnesses and diseases of children. Pediatricians have also been called on by concerned parents to answer their questions about normal development as well as about behavior problems. Benjamin Spock's *Commonsense Book of Baby and Child Care*, first published in 1946, has sold millions of copies and has become many modern parents' bible of child-rearing (Spock, 1946; Spock & Rothenberg, 1992). Dr. T. Berry Brazelton's (1974, 1983) books for parents of infants and toddlers are also popular. Numerous child psychologists, one of whom is Dr. Lee Salk (1974), have published popular guidebooks for parents.

Recently, child development specialists and pediatricians have collaborated to share their knowledge, which has resulted in the emergence of a new field, **developmental pediatrics,** which integrates medical and psychological understanding, health care, and parental guidance.

Child guidance professionals who are psychiatrists, social workers, clinical and/or child psychologists, or child development specialists have always been concerned especially with the mental health and the intellectual, emotional, and social development of children. Behavioral misconduct, school failure, social maladjustments, or problems in parent or peer relationships are better understood than ever before. Hundreds of child guidance clinics now provide assessment of children's problems and guidance for parents, teachers, and other concerned adults.

Today

Interest in child development continues. Research studies by the thousands pour out of universities and child development centers. These studies provide a wealth of information on all aspects of child care, growth, and development. Countless organizations seek to apply this knowledge in ways that will benefit the children they serve. Medical and psychological help for children with problems is more accurate than ever before but is often unavailable to those who need it the most.

Developmental pediatrics—new field of study that integrates medical knowledge, psychological understanding, health care, and parental guidance in relation to children

FULLY REVISED
AND UPDATED FOR THE 1990s
THE CENTURY'S GREATEST BESTSELLER
THE ONE ESSENTIAL PARENTING BOOK

DR. SPOCK'S BABY AND CHILD CARE

BENJAMIN SPOCK, M.D., and
MICHAEL B. ROTHENBERG, M.D.

Dr. Spock's book has been a best-seller for 50 years.

Today, there are child-development research centers scattered throughout the United States.

Conscientious parents seek to improve their parenting skills whenever possible.

Numerous problems remain. There is still tremendous need for adequate child care for working parents. Public attention continues to be focused on physical and sexual abuse of children. All too many children, born in and out of wedlock, do not receive the necessary physical and emotional care to grow into healthy, happy individuals. Infant mortality in the United States is one of the highest in the Western world, reflecting the lack of prenatal and postnatal care of mothers and their infants. Too many children suffer the consequences of their parents' drug abuse, or of the growing incidence of AIDS and other sexually transmitted diseases. Thousands of children are born unplanned and unwanted—and thus suffer the lack of proper care. It is vital that all caring people join in the effort to provide the kind of environment in which children can be cared for and loved, and to deliver necessary services to those needing extra care.

Parenting Issues

Changing Child-Rearing Philosophies in the Government's Bulletin on Infant Care

One thing that has been evident throughout the study of child development is how much the philosophies and emphases in child-rearing have changed over the years (Young, 1990). This change is especially evident in the government's bulletin *Infant Care* (Arkin, 1989). This booklet was first published in 1914, has gone through many editions, and has been completely rewritten numerous times. Between 1914 and 1921, the dangers of thumb sucking and masturbation were emphasized: Parents were advised to bind their children to the bed, hand and foot, so that they would not suck their thumbs, touch their genitals, or rub their thighs together. Between 1929 and 1938, autoerotic impulses were not considered dangerous, but lack of proper bowel training and improper feeding habits were. The emphasis was on rigid schedules, strictly according to the clock. Bowel training was to be pursued with great determination. Weaning and the introduction of solid foods were to be accomplished with firmness, never yielding to the baby's protests for one instant, for fear the infant would dominate the parents.

Between 1942 and 1945, the views expressed in the bulletin changed drastically. The child was then thought to be devoid of dominating impulses. Mildness was advocated in all areas. Thumb sucking and masturbation were not to be discouraged. Weaning and toilet training were to be put off until later and to be accomplished more gently.

At the present time, *Infant Care* has a fairly permissive attitude toward thumb sucking, weaning, discipline, and bowel and bladder training. It is evident that child-rearing philosophies change from one generation to the next, so that parents often have to sort out conflicting advice.

Summary

1. Child development is a specialized discipline devoted to the understanding of all aspects of human development from birth to adolescence. It is a relatively new field of study.

2. One reason that interest in studying child development was so long in happening is that, during the Middle Ages and until several hundred years later, childhood was not regarded as a separate stage of life. Children were expected to be little adults.

3. Before modern birth control, many children were unwanted and were considered a burden rather than a blessing. Unwanted children were killed, abandoned, or put in foundling homes or orphanages, where most of them died.

4. Until the twentieth century, the use of child labor was an accepted practice. Children had to work in shops, fields, mines, and mills for 12 hours a day, 6 days a week.

5. Historically, there were three major philosophies regarding the moral nature and development of children. The first of these, the Christian doctrine of original sin, held that children were born sinful and rebellious. The role of parents was to break the rebellious spirit of children and to pray for their salvation. Opposing this philosophy, Horace Bushnell held that God's love and grace are mediated through caring parents, who should raise their children in an atmosphere of Christian love.

6. Representing the second major philosophy of child development, John Locke said that children are a tabula rasa, a blank slate; that they are morally neutral, and how they turn out depends on how they are raised. In effect, parents can mold their children in any way they wish.

7. In the third major philosophy concerning children, Jean-Jacques Rousseau said that they are noble savages, endowed with a sense of right and wrong, and that they will develop positively according to nature's plan if parents don't interfere with their development and corrupt them.

8. Charles Darwin was the first of the evolutionary biologists. He taught that the human species evolved over millions of years through the process of natural selection and the survival of the fittest.

9. During the late nineteenth and early twentieth centuries, attempts were made to study children by keeping biographical records of their behavior.

10. G. Stanley Hall made the first attempt to study children's behavior during different stages. His effort launched the movement to make normative studies of children.

11. Arnold Gesell of Yale University devoted a major part of his career to observing infants and children and collecting normative information on them. Gesell's theory, which is biologically oriented, states that maturation is mediated by genes and biology, which determine behavioral traits and developmental trends. Gesell felt that acculturation can never transcend maturation.

12. Lewis Terman of Stanford University published the Stanford-Binet Intelligence Scale, the first widely used intelligence test for children in the United States. He also conducted the first longitudinal studies of intellectually gifted individuals.

13. Early in the twentieth century, numerous organizations and research centers were established to study child development and to discover how best to protect and guide children.

14. John Dewey said the school classroom should be a laboratory of life and should offer children the kinds of experiences that enable them to grow physically, mentally, and morally so that they can develop a better society.

15. Substantial contributions to understanding child development have also been made by pediatric and child guidance practitioners. Developmental pediatrics integrates medical and psychological understanding, health care, and parental guidance. Hundreds of child guidance clinics now provide assessment of children's problems and guidance for parents, teachers, and other concerned adults.

Key Terms

Child development   *p. 98*
Developmental pediatrics   *p. 106*
Maturation   *p. 101*
Natural selection   *p. 101*

Noble savages   *p. 101*
Original sin   *p. 100*
Survival of the fittest   *p. 101*
Tabula rasa   *p. 100*

Discussion Questions

1. Historically, children were considered miniature adults. Can you give any evidence or examples of this view still being held today? Explain.

2. Unwanted children were considered burdens and were killed, abandoned, or given to orphanages. What do you think should be done about the problem of unwanted children today?

3. It is hard for us to imagine the extent to which child labor was exploited before laws were passed that outlawed it. Do you think that children today are exploited, *or* not given enough work to do? Explain your views.

4. Of the three philosophies—that children are born sinful and rebellious, that they are born neutral, that they are born with an innate sense of right and wrong—with which do you most agree? Why? Are there elements of truth in all three views? Explain.

5. What might be some of the values of Gesell's normative studies? What might be some disadvantages? Why are his findings discounted by behaviorists and social learning theorists? From a cognitive point of view, how would you evaluate Gesell's findings?

6. According to Terman, is intelligence innate? What are some advantages and disadvantages of IQ tests? Would you want your children to know their IQ scores? Explain.

7. Have you had any contacts with child guidance clinics, child development specialists, or child psychologists? Under what circumstances? With what results?

8. In what ways do modern schools resemble John Dewey's concept of laboratories of living? What type of teaching methods reflect John Dewey's philosophy?

9. To parents: What do you like about your child's pediatrician, and what don't you

like? Should pediatricians give advice to parents about child-rearing?

10. In what ways are your views of child-rearing similar to and different from those of your parents? What do you like about your parents' views, and what do you disagree with?

BENSON, P., & GLICKSON, C. (1997). *All kids are our kids: What communities must do to raise caring and responsible children and adolescents.* Jossey-Bass: San Francisco. For responsible citizens.

BOWLBY, J. (1992). *Charles Darwin: A new life.* New York: Norton. Darwin's internal struggles, family life, and achievements.

COLES, R. (1991). *The spiritual life of children.* Boston: Houghton Mifflin. Children's understandings of the meaning of life.

ECKARDT, G., BRINGMAN, W. G., & SPRING, L. (Eds.). (1985). *Contributions to a history of development psychology.* Berlin: Morton. The status of children throughout history.

HERTZIG, M. (Ed.). (1998). *Annual progress in child psychology and child development.* London: Brunner/Mazel. Annual publication. Research Studies

HEWLETT, S. (1991). *When the bough breaks: The cost of neglecting our children.* New York: Basic Books. The plight of children in our society.

KESSEN, W. (1965). *The child.* New York: Wiley. The child is viewed by Rousseau, Darwin, Baldwin, Freud, Piaget, and others.

SOMMERVILLE, J. (1990). *The rise and fall of childhood.* New York: Vantage Books. The status of children at different times in history.

STRAUS, M. M. (1994). *Beating the devil out of them: Corporal punishment in American families.* New York: Lexington Books. The long-term consequences of all forms of corporal punishment.

http://www.srcd.org Society for Research and Child Development. Information about the society, job listings, announcements, publications, and resources.

Suggested Readings

Web Resources

Physical Development

Chapter 6

*I*n this chapter we are concerned with the physical development of children: with growth in height, weight, body proportion, and organ systems including the brain and nervous system. We are concerned with the development of fine-motor and gross-motor skills, with handedness, physical fitness, and perceptual abilities. We emphasize also the development and maintenance of good health through proper nutrition, adequate sleep, and good health care. And, finally we turn our attention to sexual development and behavior of children, and to an ever-increasing problem: the sexual abuse of children.

PHYSICAL GROWTH

Body Height and Weight

Growth from birth to adolescence occurs in two different patterns. The first pattern (from birth to age 1) is one of very rapid but decelerating growth; the second (from age 1 to before the onset of puberty) shows a more linear and steadier annual increment. Typically, the infant's increase in length is approximately 30% up to 5 months of age and greater than 50% by 1 year of age. Height doubles by age 5. Figure 6.1 shows median heights by age of boys and girls. Boys and girls have little difference in size and growth rates during infancy and childhood. Note the very rapid increase in height from birth to age 1, followed by a gradual slowing of increase until about age 10 for girls and age 12 for boys.

Figure 6.2 shows the rates of increase in height in boys and girls. Ages 10 to 12 represent the onset of puberty in girls; ages 12 to 14, the onset of puberty in boys. The growth spurts are evident during these periods. If puberty is delayed, growth in height may virtually cease.

Infants' increases in weight are even more dramatic than their early growth in length. The infant doubles in weight by 5 months of age, triples in 1 year, and almost quadruples by age 2. Annual increases are fairly constant from ages 2 to 6, and then are slower until the onset of puberty. (See Figure 6.3.)

Individual Differences

There are wide individual differences in growth patterns. At 36 months, boys in the 5th to the 95th percentiles may be 36 to 41 inches in length and weigh between 27 and 38 pounds. At the same age, girls in the 5th to the 95th percentiles may be 35½ to 40 inches in length and weigh between 25½ and 36½ pounds. Growth differentials depend on heredity (tall parents bear tall children), nutrition and eating habits, and

Physical growth after the first year shows a fairly linear and steady annual increment.

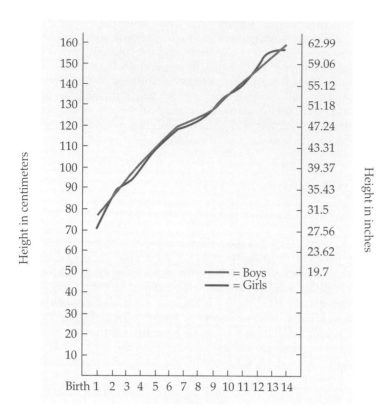

FIGURE 6.1   Median heights (by age) of boys and girls.

Adapted from *The Merck Manual of Diagnosis and Therapy*, 17th edition (p. 2093), by M. H. Beers and R. Berkow, Eds., 1999. Copyright 1999 by Merck & Co., Inc., Whitehouse Station, NJ. Used with permission.

Cephalocaudal principle— downward distribution of physical growth, starting in the head and proceeding, by stages, down the body to the feet

Proximodistal principle— outward distribution of physical growth, starting in the center of the body and proceeding out to the extremities

total health care. Children from upper-class, better-educated families are taller than lower-class children, primarily because of superior nutrition and health care that allows them to grow as tall as their genes permit.

Cultural and ethnic differences also influence growth (Widmayer et al., 1990). In the United States, black children tend to have longer legs and be taller than white children who, in turn, are taller than Asian-American children. In Canada, English-speaking children tend to be taller than French-speaking children.

Children with slower physical maturation suffer social disadvantages. They may be the last ones selected on teams for games and sports, may have some difficulty in establishing friendships, and may be lonely and unhappy because they are "different."

Body Proportions

Not all parts of the body grow at the same rate. Development follows the **cephalocaudal principle;** that is, it proceeds downward from the head to the feet. Growth comes first in the head region, then in the trunk, and finally in the leg region. From birth to adulthood, the head doubles in size, the trunk trebles, the arms and hands quadruple in length, and the legs and feet grow five-fold. At birth, the newborn's head is about one-fourth of the total body length, compared with one-eighth of the body length in adults. The legs of the newborn are one-quarter of the total body length, but about one-half of the body length in adults. (See Figure 6.4.)

Development also follows the **proximodistal principle;** that is, it proceeds from the center of the body outward to the extremities. This is why large-muscle development in the trunk, arms, and legs precede small-muscle development in the hands and fingers. Infants are able to run and jump before they can perform detailed manual and grasping movements.

Organ Systems

Three organ systems do not follow the general pattern of growth of the rest of the body and organs. The *lymphoid system* grows fairly constantly and rapidly during childhood, so that at puberty the adolescent has almost twice the lymphoid tissue of the adult. After puberty, the lymphoid size recedes. The *reproductive system* shows little growth until puberty. Most of the growth of the *central nervous system* occurs during the early years of life. At birth, the brain is 25% of adult size; at 1 year it is 75% of adult size. Growth gradually slows down, but the brain has reached 80% of adult size by 3 years, and 90% by age 7 (Berkow, 1987). Figure 6.5 shows the growth patterns of the different systems.

There are wide individual differences in growth patterns.

Brain Growth and Nerve Maturation

Not only does the brain grow in size, but also increasingly complex nerve pathways and connections among nerve cells develop so that the central nervous system is able to perform more complex functions. Figure 6.6 shows the development of nerve-cell connections from birth to 15 months.

Myelinization

Another important change is the increase in **myelinization** of individual neurons (discussed in Chapter 4). Myelinization is the process by which neurons become coated with a fatty insulating substance called myelin, which helps to transmit nerve impulses faster and more efficiently. The myelinization process parallels the maturation of the nervous system. The pathways between the brain and sense organs are partly myelinated at birth, so that the neonate's senses are in fairly good working order. As neural pathways between the brain and skeletal muscles myelinate, the child becomes capable of more complex motor activities. Though myelinization proceeds rapidly for the first few years of life, some areas of the brain are not completely myelinated until the late teens or early adulthood.

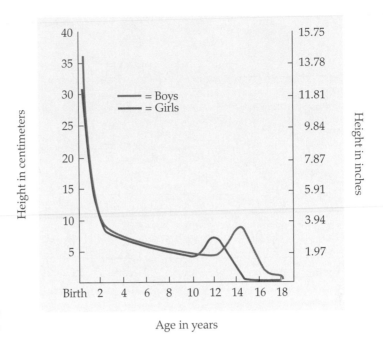

FIGURE 6.2   Rates of increase in height in boys and girls.

Adapted from *The Merck Manual of Diagnosis and Therapy*, 17th ed. (p. 2094), by M. H. Beers and R. Berkow, Eds., 1999. Copyright 1999 by Merck & Co., Inc., Whitehouse Station, NJ. Used with permission.

Myelinization—the process by which neurons become coated with an insulating, fatty substance called myelin

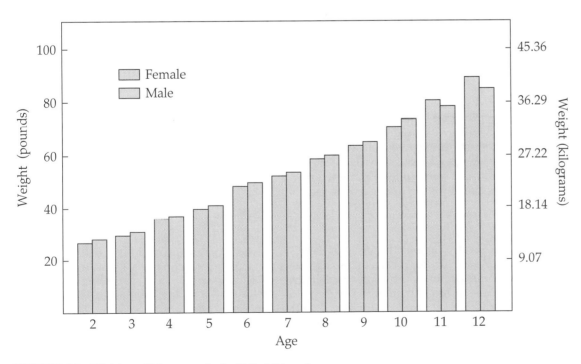

FIGURE 6.3   Weight at 50th percentile for U.S. children, by age.

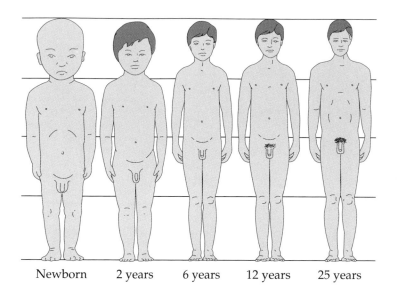

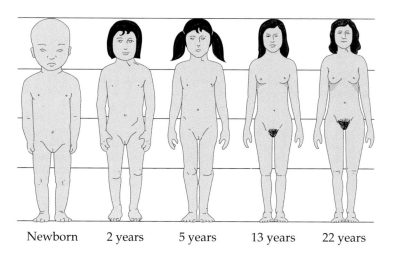

FIGURE 6.4 Bodily proportions at different ages.

Multiple sclerosis results when the myelin sheaths begin to disintegrate. As the condition worsens, the person loses muscular control and may become paralyzed or die. Myelinization is very important, therefore, in the development of the total nervous system.

Cerebral Cortex

The **cerebral cortex**, that is the largest structure of the forebrain, contains the higher brain centers controlling intellectual, sensory, and motor functions. The cerebral cortex is larger in proportion to total body weight and is more highly developed in humans than in any other animals. In humans, the cerebral cortex accounts for 70% of the neurons in the central nervous system.

Cerebral cortex—two large hemispheres of the forebrain, which control intellectual, motor, and sensory functions

It is divided into two hemispheres, with the left side of the brain mainly controlling the right side of the body and the right side of the brain controlling the left side of the body. The two hemispheres are connected by a band of fibers called the corpus callosum.

The two sides of the brain each perform specialized functions. The *right hemisphere* is superior in music, drama, fantasy, intuition, and art. It is superior in recognizing patterns, faces, and melodies, and in visualizing spatial relationships. Thus, it is better in arranging blocks in a pattern, completing a puzzle, or drawing a picture. The *left hemisphere* is superior in logic, mathematics, language, writing, and judging time. About 95% of all adults use

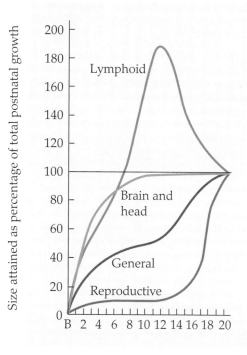

FIGURE 6.5 Growth patterns of different organ systems. These curves are based on the percentage of a person's total growth attained by age 20. Thus, size at age 20 is 100 on the vertical scale. The lymphoid system includes the thymus and lymph nodes. The curve labeled "Brain and head" includes the brain, the skull, and the spinal cord. The curve labeled "General" covers the skeletal system, lungs, kidneys, and digestive organs. The reproductive system covers testes, ovaries, prostate, seminal vesicles, and Fallopian tubes.

From "The Measurement of the Body in Childhood," by Richard E. Scammon, 1930, in *The Measurement of Man* (Figure 73, p. 193) by J. A. Harris, C. M. Jackson, D. G. Paterson, and R. E. Scammon, Eds., Minneapolis: University of Minnesota Press. Reprinted by permission.

the left hemisphere in speaking, writing, and understanding language (Levy, 1985). In addition, 97% of right-handed people use the left hemisphere more than the right. They are said to be left-hemisphere dominant. About 60% of left-handed people are right-hemisphere dominant. Dyslexic children have difficulty learning to read and show a type of abnormal lateralization, with spatial functions being directed from both hemispheres (Tan, 1985).

Lateralization is the preference for using one side of the body more than the other in performing special tasks. Lateralization may be biologically programmed from the day a baby is born. It is a tendency that occurs throughout childhood, becoming stronger over time, and is not complete until puberty. Recognizing shapes by touch is a spatial ability controlled by the right hemisphere, and is most easily accomplished with the left hand. One-year-olds are not especially proficient at recognizing shapes with either hand, but 3-year-olds are already better at recognizing shapes with their left than with their right hand.

Cortical Functions

The control of particular functions is located in various areas of the cerebral cortex. Figure 6.7 shows the location of several major func-

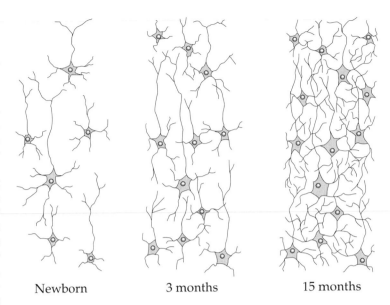

Newborn   3 months   15 months

FIGURE 6.6   The development of nerve cell connections.

tions in the left cerebral hemisphere. The development of these functions results from brain and nervous system maturation combined with experience and practice. Neurons that are stimulated continue to grow new dendrite branches and myelin sheaths, increasing synaptic connections and the efficiency of nerve transmission. Thus, the

Lateralization—the preference for using one side of the body more than the other in performing special tasks, depending on which hemisphere is dominant for the task

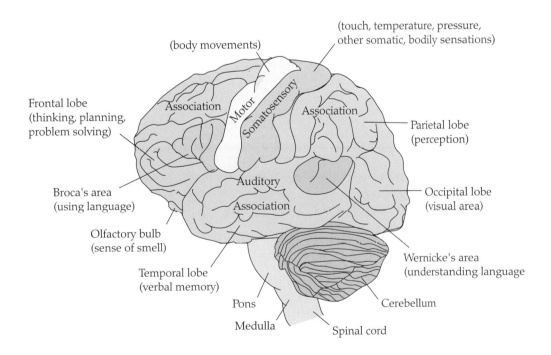

Association regions process and combine information from different senses.

FIGURE 6.7   Location of major functions in the left cerebral hemisphere.

growth of the brain and nervous system is influenced by both heredity and environment.

Different regions of the cortex mature at different rates. The first area to mature is the *motor area*, followed by the *sensory area*. The *association areas* are the last to mature, continuing their growth into the twenties or thirties. The higher functions of thinking, planning, and problem solving, performed by the frontal lobes, take years to develop. Adults with frontal lobe damage show decreased emotionality, altered personalities, and an inability to reason or to plan. They repeat the same wrong answers over and over. Injury to the left hemisphere of the frontal lobe of adults may produce either depression or increased aggression (Miller, 1988). When brain damage occurs during childhood, lost abilities are sometimes regained, depending on the extent of the damage.

Two areas of the cortex are related to language. The *Broca's area* is involved in using language, the *Wernicke's area* in understanding it. Injury to either area can cause *aphasia*, an impaired ability to use language.

Growth of cortical structures depends partly on environmental influences (Greenough, Black, & Wallace, 1987). Particularly during the third trimester of pregnancy, during which development of the central nervous system is proceeding at an astounding pace, malnutrition can lead to a permanent loss in brain weight, a reduction in the number of brain cells, and serious mental retardation. Sensory deprivation in the early years of life can lead to degenerative changes in the cortex. Light deprivation for a brief period of 3 or 4 days can cause degenerative changes in the visual cortex of a 4-week-old kitten.

Teeth Eruption Times

The timing of teeth eruption is somewhat variable, depending on family factors (both heredity and nutrition). Occasionally, teeth eruption is significantly delayed because of *hypothyroidism*. *Deciduous teeth* (baby teeth) eruption is similar in both sexes; *permanent teeth* tend to appear earlier in girls. Deciduous teeth are smaller than their permanent counterparts. Table 6.1 shows average teeth eruption times.

The first permanent molars (so-called 6-year molars, which erupt between the ages of 5 and 7 years) come in farther back than the baby molars. The first baby teeth to be lost are the *incisors*, followed by the *molars*, and *canines (cuspids)*. The permanent teeth that take the place of the baby molars are

---

TABLE 6.1   TEETH ERUPTION TIMES

Deciduous Teeth[1] (20 in number)	Number	Time of Eruption[2] (in months)	Permanent Teeth (32 in number)	Number	Time of Eruption[2] (in years)
Lower central incisors	2	5–9	First molars[3]	4	5–7
Upper central incisors	2	8–12	Incisors	8	6–8
Upper lateral incisors	2	10–12	Bicuspids	8	9–12
Lower lateral incisors	2	12–15	Canines (cuspids)	4	10–13
First molars[3]	4	10–16	Second molars[3]	4	11–13
Canines (cuspids)	4	16–20	Third molars[3]	4	17–25
Second molars[3]	4	20–30			

[1]The average child should have 6 teeth at age 1 year, 12 teeth at 1½ years, 16 teeth at 2 years, 20 teeth at 2½ years.
[2]Varies greatly.
[3]Molars are numbered from the front to the back of the mouth.
From *The Merck Manual of Diagnosis and Therapy* (17th ed., p. 2095), by M. H. Beers and R. Berkow (Eds.), 1999. Copyright 1999 by Merck & Co., Inc., Whitehouse Station, NJ. Used with permission.

called *bicuspids*. The 2nd molars (or 12-year molars, which erupt between the ages of 11 and 13 years) come in behind the 6-year molars, with the 3rd molars (18-year molars, also called wisdom teeth) coming behind the 12-year molars. Figure 6.9 identifies the location of different teeth.

MOTOR DEVELOPMENT

Gross-Motor Skills and Locomotion During Infancy

Children's motor development is dependent primarily on overall physical maturation, especially on skeletal and neuromuscular development. To a lesser extent, motor development is also influenced by the opportunities children have for exercise and practice (Sporns & Edelman, 1993). Infants spend a great deal of time in rhythmic motor activity—kicking, waving, bouncing, rocking, banging, rubbing, swinging, twisting, thrusting, and scratching. These rhythmic activities are an important transition between uncoordinated activity and more coordinated, complex motor behavior.

Independent locomotion is a dramatic event in the acquisition of new motor skills. Some infants crawl on their bellies prior to crawling on hands and knees, whereas others skip the belly-crawling period and proceed directly to crawling on hands and knees. Duration of experience with earlier forms of crawling predicts the speed and efficiency of later, quite different forms of crawling. Most important, infants who had formerly belly-crawled are more proficient crawling on hands and knees than infants who skip the belly-crawling period. The entire course of crawling is characterized by continuous improvement in crawling speed and efficiency (Adolph, Vereijken, & Denny, 1998).

Figure 6.10 shows the sequence of motor development in average infants as they finally develop the ability to walk alone. Note that they can raise their chin up by 1 month, sit with support at 3 months, sit alone at 6 months, creep at 8 months, pull to a standing position holding onto furniture by 10 months, climb stairs at 11 months, and walk alone at 13 months. However, there are variations in abilities with different individuals. Table 6.2 shows age norms for motor skills according to the Denver Developmental Screening Test (Frankenburg, Frandal, Sciarillo, & Burgess, 1981). According to the table, by 20 months of

Parenting Issues

Maturation and Toilet Training

The importance of both maturation and learning in development can be illustrated by discussing the task of toilet training. Experience plays an important role in toilet training—children must be taught to use the toilet. However, maturation also plays an important part. In a classic study, McGraw (1940) began training one identical twin, Hugh, when he was only 50 days old. No progress was achieved until Hugh was about 650 days (21 months) of age. Training of the other twin, Hilton, began at 700 days (23 months) of age. Hilton's progress was rapid from the beginning. Both children learned, but only when they reached a particular level of maturation. Figure 6.8 illustrates the progress of the twins.

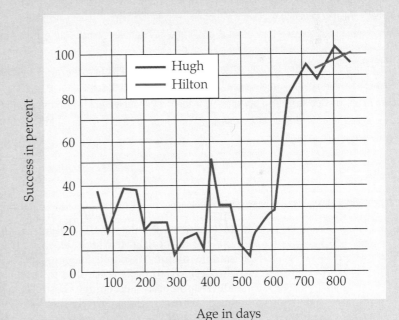

FIGURE 6.8 Maturation and achievement of bladder control.

Adapted from "Neural Maturation as Exemplified in Achievement of Bladder Control," by M. B. McGraw, 1940, *Journal of Pediatrics, 16*, pp. 580–590.

age, half the infants could kick a ball forward, but not until 24 months had 90% of them mastered this skill (Beringen, Ende, Campos, & Applebaum, 1995).

Fine-Motor Skills During Infancy

Fine-motor skills involve the smaller muscles of the body used in reaching, grasping, manipulating, pincering, clapping, turning,

Parenting Issues

Dental Care for Children

Parents sometimes think they don't have to take a small child to a dentist because all the baby teeth are going to fall out anyway. This is unwise thinking. Decayed teeth may cause pain to the child or may lead to a jaw infection. If a baby tooth is so painful it has to be pulled, nearby teeth tend to grow into the space and out of position, so that there isn't enough room for the permanent tooth when it's ready to come through. The last baby teeth are not lost until around 12 years of age. This is a long time to go without dental care.

Children should be given a toothbrush and be taught to brush their teeth beginning at about age 2. They aren't very efficient brushers at first, but they enjoy imitating parents, and early training in dental hygiene is important. Ordinarily, regular trips to the dentist—every 6 months to a year—may begin at about age 3. Tooth decay may start early, and the time to fill cavities is when they are small. Even if the child has no cavities, getting used to going to the dentist without fear is important. Dentists need to be consulted about jaw malformations or malaligned teeth. However, teeth that come through crooked or out of place often straighten out later. Permanent teeth often erupt behind baby teeth and later move forward. A dentist will help to determine whether any special treatments are needed for these conditions.

TABLE 6.2	AGE NORMS FOR MOTOR SKILLS (IN MONTHS)	
Skill	When 50% Master the Skill	When 90% Master the Skill
Lifts head 90% when lying on stomach	2.2	3.2
Rolls over	2.8	4.7
Sits propped up (head steady)	2.9	4.2
Sits without support	5.5	7.8
Stands holding on	5.8	10.0
Walks holding on	9.2	12.7
Stands momentarily	9.8	13.0
Stands alone well	11.5	13.9
Walks well	12.1	14.3
Walks backward	14.3	21.5
Walks up steps	17.0	22.0
Kicks ball forward	20.0	24.0

From "The Newly Abbreviated and Revised Denver Developmental Screening Test," by W. K. Frankenburg, A. Frandal, W. Sciarillo, and D. Burgess, 1981, *Journal of Pediatrics, 99,* pp. 995–999.

opening, twisting, pulling, or scribbling (Mathew & Cook, 1990). Table 6.3 shows the age in months at which 90% of a normal sample of infants could accomplish each of the designated tasks according to the Denver Developmental Screening Test (Frankenburg, Frandal, Sciarillo, & Burgess, 1981). Note that 90% of the infants were 4 months old before they could grasp a rattle, 15 months before they could grasp a raisin with a neat pincer grasp, and 25 months before they could scribble spontaneously.

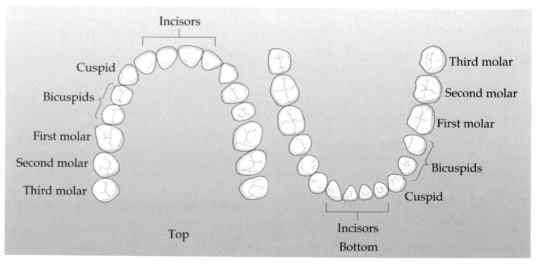

FIGURE 6.9   Permanent teeth.

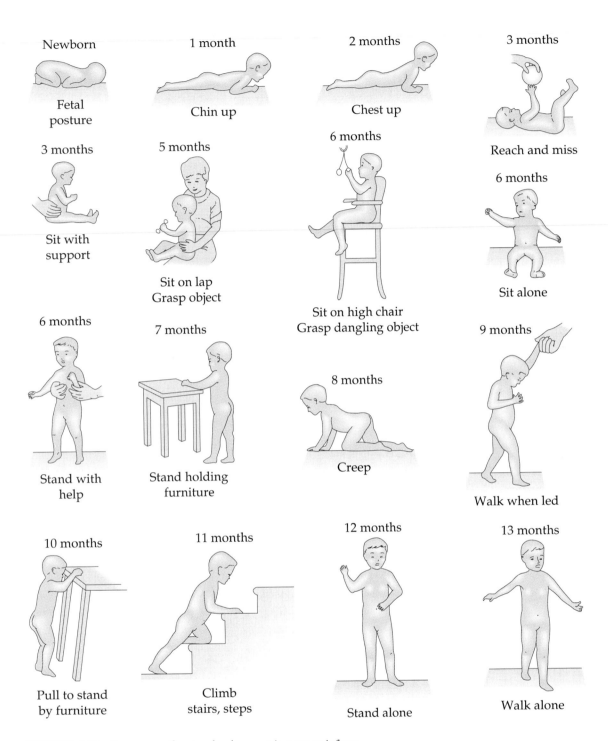

Newborn

Fetal posture

1 month

Chin up

2 months

Chest up

3 months

Reach and miss

3 months

Sit with support

5 months

Sit on lap
Grasp object

6 months

Sit on high chair
Grasp dangling object

6 months

Sit alone

6 months

Stand with help

7 months

Stand holding furniture

8 months

Creep

9 months

Walk when led

10 months

Pull to stand by furniture

11 months

Climb stairs, steps

12 months

Stand alone

13 months

Walk alone

FIGURE 6.10   Sequences of motor development in average infants.

Gross-Motor Skills of Preschool Children

Preschool children between 2 and 5 years of age make important advances in motor development. With stronger bones, muscles, lung power, and neuromuscular coordination between the arms, legs, senses, and central nervous system, these children show increased skill and mastery of their bodies in performing physical feats that would have been impossible before. Table 6.4 shows some gross-motor skills of preschool children of different ages. Notice the skills of 5-year-olds. They can skip smoothly; broad jump up to 3 feet; jump 1 foot high; hop on one foot a distance of 16 feet; start, turn, and stop effectively in

TABLE 6.3	AGE NORMS FOR FINE-MOTOR SKILLS WHEN 90% OF INFANTS COULD ACCOMPLISH A TASK

Fine-Motor Task	Months
Hands together	3.7
Grasps rattle	4.2
Reaches for objects	5.0
Sits, takes 2 cubes	7.5
Transfers cube hand to hand	7.5
Thumb-finger grasp	10.6
Neat pincer grasp of raisin	14.7
Scribbles spontaneously	25.0

From "The Newly Abbreviated and Revised Denver Developmental Screening Test," by W. K. Frankenburg, A. Frandal, W. Sciarillo, and D. Burgess, 1981, *Journal of Pediatrics, 99,* pp. 995–999.

Fine-motor skills involve a high degree of small-muscle and eye-hand coordination.

playing games; descend a long stairway unaided, alternating the feet; walk a balance beam; throw a ball with one leg stepping forward on the same side as the throwing arm; and catch a ball using their hands only.

Fine-Motor Skills of Preschool Children

Fine-motor skills involve a high degree of small-muscle and eye-hand coordination. With small muscles under control, children

TABLE 6.4	LARGE-MUSCLE MOTOR SKILLS OF AVERAGE PRESCHOOL CHILDREN

2-Year-Olds	3-Year-Olds	4-Year-Olds	5-Year-Olds
Jump 12 inches	Broad jump 15 to 24 inches	Broad jump 24 to 34 inches	Broad jump 28 to 36 inches
Throw ball overhand, body stationary	Balance on 1 foot, 1 second	Can gallop	Can skip smoothly
Cannot turn or stop smoothly or quickly	Hop up to three times	Hop up to 6 steps on one foot	Hop on one foot a distance of 16 feet
Kick a large ball forward	Can propel a wagon with one foot	Catch a bounced ball	Can catch small ball using hands only
	Ascend a stairway unaided, alternating the feet		Descend a long stairway unaided, alternating feet
	Pedal a tricycle		Jump 1 foot high
	Basket catch of ball using body		Can start, turn, and stop effectively in games
			Can walk a balance beam

gain a sense of competence and independence because they can do a lot of things, such as eating or dressing, for themselves. Table 6.5 shows some small-muscle motor skills of average preschool children of different ages. For eating, note that 2-year-olds can hold a glass with one hand, and 3-year-olds can eat with a spoon and pour from a pitcher. For dressing, 2-year-olds can put on simple clothing, 4-year-olds can dress themselves, and 5-year-olds may be able to manage a zipper, fasten buttons, or even tie shoelaces. For other small-muscle activities, 2-year-olds will scribble; 3-year-olds can copy a circle or draw a straight line; 4-year-olds can draw simple figures, cut on a line with scissors, and make crude letters; and 5-year-olds can copy squares, a task that takes considerably more manipulative skill and eye-hand coordination than drawing a circle.

Handedness

Handedness is the preference for using one hand rather than another in the performance of a variety of motor functions. Approximately 90 to 93% of the population eventually develop a preference for use of the right hand as the left hemisphere of the brain assumes dominance and control over motor functions (Searleman, Porac, & Coren, 1989). The remainder of the population either develop left-handedness, become hand-specific, in which they prefer one hand for one activity and another hand for another, or ambidextrous, possessing equal skill with both hands.

Handedness develops slowly in children, but, by first grade, shifts from one hand to the other are fairly infrequent.

Handedness develops slowly in children and is not always consistent in the early years (Ramsey, 1985; Ramsey & Webber, 1986). One study found that 7- to 9-month-olds used their right hands to reach for a toy but often used either hand when manipulating an object (Michel, Harkins, and Ovrut, 1986). Before 2 years of age, most children show considerable flexibility in shifting from one hand to another (McCormick and Maurer, 1988). By age 4, most children show a preference for

Handedness—preference for using one hand rather than another

Table 6.5	Small-Muscle Motor Skills of Average Preschool Children		
2-Year-Olds	**3-Year-Olds**	**4-Year-Olds**	**5-Year-Olds**
Scribble spontaneously	Copy a circle	Draw shapes, simple figures	Copy squares
Imitate vertical line within 30%	Draw a straight line	Draw man, 3 parts	String beads
Put on simple clothing	Can eat with a spoon	Can dress self	Can fasten buttons that are visible to the eye
Construct tower of 6 to 8 blocks	Smear and daub paint	Make crude letters	
Hold a glass with one hand	Pour from a pitcher	Use blocks to build buildings	Can manage zipper
Turn pages of a book singly		Cut on a line with scissors	May tie shoelaces

Parenting Issues

Rough-and-Tumble Play

Rough-and-tumble play is a part of the motor activities of many preschool children, especially after they have been sitting for a period of time. It's a way of releasing excess energy, of enjoying social contact, and of having fun. All children need frequent periods of physical activity.

Rough-and-tumble play is not the same as aggression, but it sometimes gets out of hand, especially among children who are used to roughhousing at home. Hank, a big 5-year-old in our preschool class, was used to roughhousing with his dad. He and his father seldom played without vigorous, but playful, physical contact. As a result, Hank was usually too rough when he played with smaller children in his class. He was not a bully, but he often hurt other children only because he had learned to be so rough. (Author's teaching experience)

use of the right hand. By first grade, shifts from one hand to the other become relatively infrequent. Some specialists feel that forcing a left-handed child to become right-handed may cause stuttering, reading problems, or emotional problems, so parents and teachers would be wise not to confuse a possible left-hander (Spock & Rothenberg, 1992).

There are both advantages and disadvantages to being left-handed. Southpaws have some advantages in sports. The left-handed batter is harder to pitch to. The curve ball of the left-handed pitcher swerves the opposite way from expectation. The serve of the left-handed tennis player spins in the opposite direction. Left-handed people are right-hemisphere dominant: the side of the brain that controls such skills as art, drama, sculpture, and spatial relations. Michelangelo, Leonardo da Vinci, and Pablo Picasso were all left-handed. However, left-handed people suffer more from environmental risk so that their accident-related injuries are 5 times those of right-handed persons (Coren & Halpern, 1991). They are 12 times more likely than right-handers to have learning and reading disabilities. It is most likely that handedness is caused by a combination of genetic, prenatal, and learning factors.

Changes During the School Years

Elementary-school-age children gradually increase in motor ability as their bodies continue to grow. Muscles increase in size and coordination continues to improve, so that most children can run, hop, skip, and jump with agility. Most 6-year-olds can ride a bicycle, jump rope, skate, climb trees, and scale fences if given the opportunity to learn.

Fine-motor skills also increase. Most 8- or 9-year-olds can learn to hammer, saw, use garden tools, sew, knit, draw in proportion, write, print, and cut fingernails.

There are inconsistent gender differences in motor development between boys and girls during middle childhood. Girls are more physically mature than same-age boys; that is, girls have reached a greater percentage of their adult height than same-age boys (Eaton & Yu, 1989). For that reason, in comparing boys and girls of the same chronological age, developmental studies often compare developmentally more mature girls with less mature boys. Doing so ignores substantial sex differences in maturational tempo.

In general, older children are less active than younger ones, with activity level decreasing with maturational age. Boys are thought to be superior in physical skills requiring strength and gross-motor performance, such as football. Girls are considered superior in physical skills requiring grace, flexibility, and agility, such as gymnastics. However, prior to puberty, many of these differences are due to differential expectations and experiences of boys and girls. A group of third-, fourth-, and fifth-grade boys and girls who had been in co-educational physical education classes for at least a year were compared on scores on sit-ups, shuttle run, 50-yard dash, broad jump, and 600-yard walk-run. The girls scored as well as the boys on most measures. In the third year of the program, the girls performed better than the boys on a number of tests (Hall & Lee, 1984). *The American Academy of Pediatrics has said that there is no reason to separate prepubertal boys and girls for physical activities.* After puberty, girls are lighter, and their smaller frames make them more subject to injury in heavy collision sports (American Academy of Pediatrics Committee on Pediatric Aspects, 1981).

One important factor in motor skills is reaction time, which depends partly on brain maturation. One study of reaction time of children aged 5 through 14 found that older children were almost twice as fast as younger ones (Southard, 1985). In another study, none of the children who were 7, 9, or 11 years old did as well as any adults, even 75-year-olds, in pressing a button in response to a flash of light (Stern, Oster, & Newport, 1980). Seven-year-olds took twice as long as the typical adult to react to the flash of light.

Adults have a decided advantage over younger children in sports that require quick reactions.

Nine-year-olds were better than 7-year-olds, and 11-year-olds were even better. Thus, *older children have a decided advantage over younger children in sports that require quick reactions. Adults are better still.* This is one reason why so many children have trouble in catching balls. By the time they close arms, hands, or mitts, the ball has fallen through or bounced out. Also, throwing or batting balls efficiently requires distance judgment, eye-hand coordination, and quick reaction times—all skills that young, elementary school children may not possess. Many sports that adults play are not ideal for children.

Physical Fitness

Today's schoolchildren are less physically fit than were children in the 1960s (National Children and Youth Fitness Study, 1984). They have more body fat. They are less fit in terms of heart rate, muscle strength, lung capacity, and physical endurance. Many have high levels of cholesterol or high blood pressure.

The reason is that they are not active enough. Only about half of all children are involved in physical education classes twice a week. Generally, children spend too much time watching television. One survey indicated that the average American child aged 2 to 11 views television 27.5 hours per week (Tooth, 1985). Or, physical activities in or out of school emphasize competitive sports or games rather than teaching lifetime fitness activities such as walking, running, bicycling, skating, swimming, golf, tennis, or bowling, which children can continue to enjoy in the adult years.

One health education and fitness program involving 24,000 children in Michigan schools taught children what foods to eat; how to measure their own blood pressure, heart rate, and body fat; and how to resist unhealthy foods and drugs. The program also encouraged them to participate in activities and games that build fitness. An analysis of the effects of the program on 360 second-, fifth-, and seventh-graders revealed that the children had lowered their cholesterol levels, blood pressure, and body fat, and had improved their time for running a mile (Fitness Finders, 1984). Children's fitness can be improved through carefully designed programs.

PHYSICALLY HANDICAPPED CHILDREN

Physical handicaps in children may be divided into at least four basic categories: *speech disorders; hearing impairments; visual impairments;* and various types of *skeletal, orthopedic, or motor skills handicaps.* Mental retardation and learning disabilities will be discussed in Chapter 7 on cognitive development of children.

Speech-Handicapped Children

Speech handicaps are among the most common of all physical handicaps in children. They may be due to congenital malformations, such as cleft palate, or arise as a consequence of hearing, neurological, or developmental problems. *Infantile autism* appears in the first two years of life and is characterized by language disorder with impaired understanding

If hearing problems are suspected, tests should be given.

as well as abnormal social relationships, rituals and compulsive activities, and uneven intellectual development. Other children with *developmental expressive language disorder* have trouble expressing themselves. Other children with *developmental articulation disorder* have trouble making themselves understood. The basic task is to get a correct diagnosis to discover the cause of the difficulty to see what can be done to improve the situation (Berkow, 1997).

Hearing-Handicapped Children

Hearing problems in children may not be discovered until the child is 1 or 2 years old. Young infants are visually responsive, but after 6 months or so the parent-child communication starts to break down. The child seems to ignore what the parents say and is not responsive enough for their satisfaction. The child seems to be disobedient and is startled by persons approaching whom he or she does not hear. Two-year-olds may either withdraw or manifest behavioral problems with frequent anger and temper tantrums. If hearing deficits are suspected, the child is given a complete examination, including various types of hearing tests. Children from birth to 6 months of age are exposed to relatively intense levels of sound and their reflexes recorded. In the child from 6 months to 2 years of age, localized responses to tones and speech are evaluated. If a child is 12 months of age or more, the *speech reception threshold (SRT)* is determined by having the child point to body parts or identify common objects in response to speech of controlled intensity. In the child above 3 years of age, play audiometry is used by conditioning the child to perform a task in response to a tone. Once the level of hearing is established, the next task is to diagnose the cause and establish treatment if possible. *Hearing aids* can be given to children as young as 6 months of age if sound amplification will correct the problem. *Surgical remedies* are sometimes possible. If the child suffers chronic and irremedial loss of hearing, special education is needed and should be started as soon as possible, since there is an optimum time for the acquisition of language. Children are able to learn American Sign Language (ASL) readily if given an opportunity.

Congenital hearing loss (present from birth) is commonly caused by *rubella* during the first trimester of pregnancy. Other causes are *anoxia* (lack of oxygen) during birth, *bleeding* into the inner ear because of birth trauma, *ototoxic drugs* (for ear infections) given to the mother, or *hereditary conditions* (Berkow, 1997).

Visually Handicapped Children

Blindness in children may be congenital or may develop gradually or suddenly from a wide variety of causes. Ordinarily, visual communication between caregivers and the child is basic to the establishment of an attachment relationship. Babies look at and follow everything new going on around them. They follow movements and especially like to look at human faces. In turn, caregivers rely heavily on subtle responses of the infant—smiling, babbling, moving, laughing—to maintain and support their own behavior. However, visually handicapped infants may not develop their signals for "I want you to do something" or "pick me up" until near the end of the first year. This lack of communication can be very frustrating to both the caregiver

FOCUS

Otitis Media

Otitis media (middle-ear disease) is the most frequently diagnosed childhood disease except for upper respiratory infections. Although the disease may be mild, it is usually associated with a mild to moderate hearing loss that may affect the short-term language and speech of young children and has been associated with long-term effects on language, behavioral problems, and school achievement in older children. Children with infrequent episodes of *otitis media* (OM) do not show a hearing loss ordinarily, whereas chronic OM may have adverse effects when there's a hearing loss associated with it and when children are in a suboptimal environment, like low-quality child care (Vernon-Feagans, Emanuel, & Blood, 1997). Findings suggest that day-care children with chronic otitis media in the first three years of life play more often alone and have fewer positive and fewer negative interactions with peers than nonchronic children in day care (Vernon-Feagans, Manlove, & Volling, 1996).

Some infants and children develop symptoms associated with otitis media, including fussiness, pulling of the ear, and fever. However, many children do not have any symptoms at all, thus making it difficult to diagnose. Children in the first few years of life are most likely to have otitis media, but certain groups are more at risk than others. These groups include children who are in day care, or children who live in large families or in crowded conditions. Children who are in close contact with many other children and adults have more otitis media. Some treatments like antibiotic and tube placement can be effective in reducing the accompanying fluid in the middle ear. Up to one-third of young children have chronic middle-ear disease (Feagans, Kipp, & Blood, 1994).

Visual handicaps in children may be congenital or may develop gradually from a wide variety of causes.

and the infant. *The baby's lack of responsiveness* can be emotionally upsetting to the caregiver, who cherishes some response. Visually handicapped babies may not develop smile language as do sighted children and may have very few facial expressions. However, they rapidly develop a wide variety of hand signals and body language to direct and relate these signals to their caregivers. Parents and caregivers need training to learn how to interpret signals and to react to the blind child so that attachment and socialization can take place.

Communicative strategies for accommodating new experiences and regulating responses to novelty and potential threats are important to the development of all toddlers, but they may have an even greater impact on the development of toddlers with severe visual impairment. In the absence of quick visual input to facilitate exploration, children with visual impairment may rely more heavily on mothers for communication about environmental events. Children with severe visual impairments have to engage in more active communication with their parents. The mothers help them to make appraisals of strange or threatening stimuli (Recchia, 1997).

Visually handicapped infants usually lag behind normal infants in mobility and locomotion, usually taking longer to crawl and to walk. They lag behind in fine-motor coordination and in developing basic manual skills. Postural motor skills such as sitting and standing become more difficult without the ability to see. In general, lack of sight contributes to developmental delays (Troster and Brambring, 1993). When measured with the *Battelle Developmental Inventory* (BDI), vision-impaired preschool children show lower developmental age scores overall and slower rates of growth. The domains measured by the BDI are personal-social, adaptive, motor,

cognition, and communication, with slower rates of growth indicated in the personal-social and motor domains (Hatton, Bailey, Jr., Burchinal, & Ferrell, 1997).

If the child is not totally blind and corrective lenses will help, glasses should be prescribed and worn as soon as feasible, which for some children is by 3 years of age. *Cross-eyes* (eyes turned in), *walleyes* (eyes turned out), or *near-sightedness* are common difficulties in children. Near-sightedness, which commonly develops in children between 6 and 10 years of age, can come on quite rapidly (Spock & Rothenberg, 1992).

Children with Skeletal, Orthopedic, or Motor-Skills Handicaps

These types of handicaps range all the way from almost complete disability, such as the *quadraplegic* with paralysis of all four limbs, to minor orthopedic or motor-skills dysfunctions. Some handicaps, such as handicaps from *spina bifida*, are congenital. Others, such as *Duchenne muscular dystrophy*, are also hereditary but not evident in children until later in childhood. In the case of MD, the disease typically appears in boys from 3 to 7 years old. Most are confined to a wheelchair by age 10 or 12, with most dying by age 20. Some less serious defects, such as *clubfoot*, are caused by a combination of hereditary and prenatal environmental factors and are amenable to treatment. Other defects are caused by injuries during childhood.

Tennis is one of many sports that physically challenged children can play. This child is sponsored by The National Foundation for Wheelchair Tennis.

Adjustments

Handicapped children may be subject to cruel remarks and teasing by other children. They may feel stigmatized and rejected, and are likely to be denied opportunities and activities open to the nonhandicapped. Physical appearance has been found to be important in influencing children's desire to socially interact with others (Zebrowitz & Montepare, 1992). Life is not always fair for the handicapped, but many children are able to overcome discrimination and to make very happy social adjustments. In fact, some nonhandicapped children compete to be their friends and become very protective of those less fortunate. Just as important, large numbers of the physically handicapped lead productive lives, accomplishing amazing things. Some of the blind and physically disabled students in the author's classes have done superior work in relation to other students.

Family Coping

Raising children with disabilities places a great deal of stress on the family. All such families have to learn to cope the best way they can. Coping may be defined as constantly changing cognitive and behavioral efforts to manage specific external and/or internal demands that are appraised as taxing or exceeding the resources of the person (Judge, 1998). According to this definition, coping includes any attempt or effort to manage stress regardless of how well it works. Coping strategies may involve two basic types: (1) *problem-focused coping* and (2) *emotion-focused* coping. Problem-focused forms of coping include active problem-solving and seeking social support as well as aggressive interpersonal efforts to alter the situation. One example might be to find the ways and means for the physically handicapped child to attend public school. This undertaking involves arranging for equipment that the child needs to get around and to adjust to the classroom; it is also necessary to find a way to get back and forth to school and to meet the child's needs while in the school situation. In contrast, emotion-focused forms of coping includes detaching from the situation, controlling one's feelings, wishing the problem would go away, and blaming one's self for the situation. Obviously, problem solving is the preferred style of coping with a disability-related difficulty. Research indicates that emotion-focused coping that involves wishful thinking, denial, or avoidance is positively related to reports of depressed moods. Professionals who offer family-centered services for young children and their parents emphasize an approach that promotes positive family functioning. This approach assumes that all families have strengths that they can build on and that the family's strength, including the social networks and informal supports already available to and within the family should be the foundation on which new supports are designed or provided. By using family strengths as building blocks and tools, the family becomes even stronger and more capable of supporting the well-being of both individual family members and the family unit (Judge, 1998).

Education

In 1975, federal law in the United States mandated that all children, regardless of their handicap, receive public education in the least restrictive environment that is educationally sound. This means that handicapped children should be mainstreamed (put in schools with normal children) unless mainstreaming is deleterious to them. The purpose of mainstreaming is to try to avoid stigmatizing handicapped children as being different and to give them the same educational and social advantages as others.

Some schools adopted the idea of resource rooms where specially trained persons could assist handicapped pupils for part of the day.

Parenting Issues

Rearing a Handicapped Child

Rearing a child with a physical handicap is particularly stressful. Children with physical handicaps require extra physical care at home and more visits to doctors and other professionals. Parents must make decisions about a child's school, medical treatment, and other aspects of the care. They must also cope with the stigma of having a child with a disability and with the long-term uncertainty regarding the child's future functioning. Of more importance is that parents must come to terms with the loss of the "perfect" child.

Paradoxically, the demands of rearing a child with physical handicaps make it more difficult for social networks to be established. Parents of children with handicaps have less energy and time available for network associations. Mothers who have satisfying social networks are able to depend on other people and to have more of their own emotional needs met and, consequently, are better able to meet the needs of their children (Jennings, Stagg, Connors, & Ross, 1995).

In spite of some advantages, mainstreaming has not always met the needs of handicapped children. When school budgets are cut, it is frequently the special education programs that suffer. Moreover, handicapped children are different to some extent. Putting them in regular classrooms to be taught by an already overworked teacher who may not have special training is not necessarily the wisest decision. The children may be left on their own to sink or swim. Certainly, blind children, deaf children, and children who are severely handicapped in other ways can profit more by being sent to special schools just for them where they receive total assistance, training, and education to develop their capacities to the fullest.

PERCEPTUAL DEVELOPMENT

Depth Perception

The ability to see things in three dimensions—to distinguish things that are closer from those that are farther away—is an ability that develops very early in infancy. Infants as young as 6 weeks of age will blink or show other avoidance reactions when objects approach their face (Dod-well, Humphrey, & Muir, 1987). However, it takes about 4 months for full binocular vision to develop (Aslin & Smith, 1988). Five-month-old infants will try to grasp a closer object rather than a more distant one.

One well-known test of depth perception involves a special box on legs, 2 to 3 feet long. One-half of the box has a shallow side, with a heavy piece of glass over a checkered floor, which is about 10 inches below the sides. The other half of the box provides an illusion of a cliff by the placement of the checkered material on the floor of the room several feet below the glass. The infant's mother stands first on the shallow side and then on the deep side, coaxing her infant to crawl toward her. Most of the infants 6 to 14 months of age who were old enough to crawl would not crawl to the deep side, indicating that they perceived depth. Those not old enough to crawl showed heart-rate changes when they were placed on the cliff side. Some cried, others crawled away from their mothers when coaxed to crawl over the cliff (Reed, 1988).

Not only do children develop the perception of depth, but they also develop the ability to portray depth and distance in the drawings they make. Preschool children represent front or behind by placing objects side by side. As they get

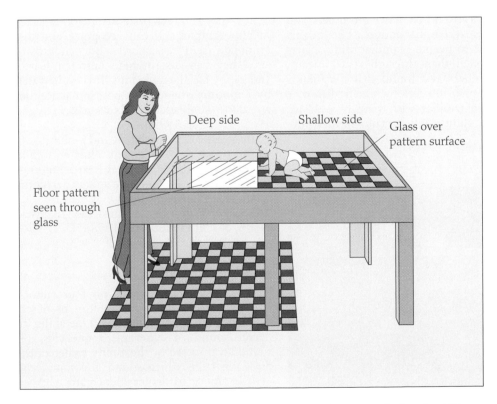

FIGURE 6.11   The mother calls her infant to the deep side to determine whether the child perceives depth.

older, children draw diagonal alignments to represent depth. Still older children use vertical arrangements more frequently, with the objects at the top of a picture being smaller and looking farther away (Braine et al., 1993).

Perception of Form and Motion

During the first two years of life, the way that infants perceive the form of objects changes. Two-month-old infants notice patterns that have a high degree of contrast and that move (Bertenthal & Bradbury, 1992). Before 4 months of age, infants will notice the corners of black triangles that are mounted on white paper. They perceive parts of figures, rather than whole representations. Thus, infants see a square and a circle, rather than a square within a circle. By 4 or 5 months of age, and as they mature, they increasingly see a whole figure rather than just its parts. By 3 to 12 months of age, children notice figures that are familiar enough to be recognized, but different enough to be novel. Figures that are too novel do not receive as much attention. Fourteen-week-old infants will pay attention to an object that moves and is of a significantly different color than is the color of the background behind it (Nagata & Dannemiller, 1996).

In one study, 12-month-olds were tested for object recognition through touch and through visual familiarization. The infants took longer to become familiar with objects through touch than through visual means. The researchers also found that the infants could recognize objects by touch that they had become familiar with visually and vice versa. This ability, called **cross-modal per-ception,** shows that infants have the ability to recognize the visual equivalent of objects that previously have only been touched (Rose & Orlian, 1991). They have somewhat less ability to recognize tactically objects that previously have only been seen.

Research has also shown that there are wide individual differences in the speed at which infants process visual information. When presented with visual stimuli, some infants, called *long-lookers*, focus on the stimuli for relatively long periods of time, while others, called *short-lookers*, focus their attention for short intervals. Short-lookers are superior at perceptual-cognitive tasks because they are speedier and more efficient at stimulus-interpretation processing. In one study, these differences were found in infants who were only 4 months of age (Colombo, Mitchell, Coldren, & Freesemen, 1991).

Perception of the Human Face

Infants prefer to look at human faces rather than at inert objects. This preference is characteristic of infants only 5 days old. By one month of age, babies can discriminate the faces of their mothers from the faces of strangers. Under certain circumstances, infants are able to recognize their mother's face shortly after birth (deHaan & Nelson, 1997). By 3 months of age, they can recognize their mother's face in photographs and can recognize and discriminate faces of strangers. By 7 months of age, they can discriminate between fearful and happy facial expressions. It is evident that by 7 months of age their perceptual abilities are quite sophisticated (Nelson & Dolgin, 1985; Younger, 1992).

In another experiment, 4- and 7-month-old infants were able to match adult and child faces with the voices that they heard. Findings suggest that the infants were able to detect the relationship between the age of maturity of a person's face and the person's voice (Bahrick, Netto, & Hernandez-Reif, 1998).

Auditory Perception

Auditory perception depends on four factors: (1) auditory acuity or the ability to detect sound of minimum loudness, (2) the ability to detect sound of different frequencies, (3) sound localization or the ability to detect the direction from which sound is coming, and (4) the ability to detect silent gaps between words—also called auditory temporal acuity. Only the last two factors will be discussed in this section.

Cross-modal perception— the ability to perceive objects with more than one sense

By one month of age, babies can distinguish the face of their mother from the face of a stranger.

Sound Localization

Sound localization is possible because the ears are placed on the opposite side of the head. This placement means that the sound from one side arrives sooner and with a higher sound level than from the other side. These interaural time and level differences enable the listener to detect the direction from which the sound is coming. Research has shown that sound localization improves substantially during the first year after birth, with an especially high rate of change during the first half-year (Ashmead et al., 1991). The auditory system apparently has a very precise mechanism for registering interaural time differences, and this mechanism is in operation from the first few months of life.

Gap Detection

The ability to understand human speech depends partly on the ability to detect the spaces or gaps between words. If we did not detect these gaps or silent intervals, the words would seem to run together, so that speech would sound garbled. Gap detection, in turn, depends on a high degree of auditory temporal acuity. The minimum detectable gap, called the **gap threshold**, is considerably worse for 3- and 6-month-olds than for adults, indicating that gap-detection abilities are quite poor in infants. Gap detection is better for low-frequency sounds than for those of higher pitch. Tests of 12-month-olds indicate a wide variation in gap detection. Some perform no better than 3- to 6-month olds, whereas others attain thresholds close to those of adults (Werner et al., 1992). This finding means that adults need to speak more slowly to young children than to adults in order to make themselves understood.

NUTRITION

Breast-Feeding Versus Bottle-Feeding

Another way to improve physical health is through good nutrition. The question arises whether children are healthier being breast- or bottle-fed. Breast-feeding declined rapidly in popularity during the early years of this century and up until about 1970. This decline occurred not only in the United States but also in countries all over the world. Whenever this occurred in developing countries, infant mortality rates increased because commercial formula was diluted with conta-

Intestinal diseases increased in developing countries when mothers mixed formula with contaminated water.

minated water that transmitted intestinal diseases to infants (Hinds, 1982). As a consequence, the World Health Organization is urging women in these countries to return to breast-feeding and is discouraging the distribution of formula.

The downward trend in the popularity of breast-feeding has been reversed, so that today more than half of all mothers in the United States breast-feed their babies, and this proportion is steadily increasing (Berkow, 1997).

Advantages

Breast-feeding has some distinct advantages. Breast milk is the *best food* available for infants and is nutritionally superior to formulas and to cow's milk. It contains the right proportion of fats, calories, proteins, vitamins, and minerals. In relation to cow's milk, it contains several additional amino acids necessary for neural development. It also contains more iron and vitamins A and C. Moreover, it is more digestible than cow's milk. Breast-fed babies have fewer cases of digestive up-sets, allergies, coughs, respiratory difficulties, gastrointestinal infections, and diarrhea. Breast milk is clean and always at body temperature.

Gap threshold—the minimum detectable gap between sounds

Breast-fed babies gain weight more rapidly than bottle-fed babies, yet breast-fed babies are less prone to subsequent obesity. One big advantage is that breast milk *contains antibodies* derived from the mother's body that immunize the infant from disease and infection. Another advantage is that nursing *helps shrink the uterus* back to normal size more quickly.

The mother needs extra nourishment, especially calcium, while breast-feeding. Dairy products are an excellent source of calcium, but nuts and green, leafy vegetables may be substituted if she can't tolerate milk products. Vitamin supplements aren't necessary if the diet is well balanced, especially if it includes enough vitamin C, B6, and 12. However, the average American diet is low in vitamin B6, and vegetarian diets are typically low in vitamin B12.

In some respects, breast-feeding is also *convenient and practical.* There are no bottles to sterilize, no formulas to mix, no refrigeration required, no bottles to warm. In those ways, it saves time and money. And parents don't have to bring along as much equipment when they go on a trip.

There are also some *psychological advantages.* Many nursing mothers gain a great deal of satisfaction from breast-feeding: from giving good nutrition to their baby, from seeing their devotion, and from the feeling of closeness.

Infants also gain emotional satisfaction and security from the closeness of breast-feeding, from feeling the mother's warmth, and from the experience of sucking. All infants need to suck. Usually, they have to suck harder and longer during breastfeeding than during bottle-feeding to get enough milk. This sucking fulfills their psychological needs and provides nutrition. Parents need to recognize, however, that babies can achieve the same emotional security from bottle-feeding as from breast-feeding, provided that they are held and cuddled during feeding. All infants need physical contact and warmth, the sound of a pleasant voice, and the sight of a happy face. A warm, accepting parent who is bottle-feeding the baby can help the infant feel more secure and loved. The important consideration is the total parent-infant relationship, not just the method of feeding.

Disadvantages

There are also some disadvantages to breast-feeding. One of the most-frequent criticisms is that *it is too confining, that it limits the mother's physical freedom, and that it is inconvenient,* especially for the mother who works outside the home. This latter obstacle can be overcome if the working mother can take time off during the day to nurse the baby, especially if the infant is being cared for nearby in a child-care center at the place of business or if the business allows time during the day for the mother to nurse. Mothers who do not work but must occasionally go out of the house either have to find at time and place to nurse their baby or have to hurry home in time for feeding.

Before bottle-feeding was widespread, nursing mothers used to feel free to nurse in public—while shopping, on buses, even in church—but as nursing became less acceptable, the practice gradually declined. One answer, of course, is to use a breast pump and keep the milk in a relief bottle for the caregiver to feed the baby when the mother is out of the house. Formula may also be used in a relief bottle. Spock and Rothenberg (1985) suggest that the baby be introduced to the bottle at about 6 weeks of age, only after the flow of milk has become well established.

One disadvantage of breast-feeding is that *some drugs and chemicals are passed to the baby through the breast milk.* Some drugs are not passed in large enough quantities to affect the baby. Other drugs, such as alcohol and narcotics, come through in sufficient amounts to cause addiction. The mother needs to check with her doctor to determine what medication she is allowed to take. Some diseases, such as AIDS, may also be transmitted through the mother's milk (Rogers, 1985).

Personal Choice

One of the most important considerations is the mother's attitude toward nursing itself. Breast-feeding requires a personal choice. Some women find breast-feeding to be a challenge, and they become very upset if they can't manage it. Others really want to breast-feed but let other people dissuade them. In these cases, the father's support can be a crucial positive contribution. Individual mothers can follow their best instincts and do what they really want to do and what seems to be best for the baby. If needed, they can receive support and consultation from La Leche League, an organization that promotes breast-feeding and offers help to nursing mothers; the League has chapters all over the world.

When to stop breast-feeding depends on the needs and desires of both mother and baby. Breast-feeding for at least 6 months is considered desirable. Gradual weaning over weeks or months is easier for both the baby and the mother than is stopping suddenly.

Dietary Requirements

As children get older, a balanced diet is vitally important for their good health and vigor. Their bodies need protein, minerals, vitamins, carbohydrates, fats, roughage, and water. These nutrients are derived from four basic food groups: *milk and dairy products, meat, fruits and vegetables,* and *breads and cereals.* Children can be taught to eat foods from the four basic food groups every day as the best way of assuring good nutrition.

Breakfast

Parents are told by nutritionists that children should get a good breakfast before going off to school. It is suggested that children do better in school—that they behave better, are not as restless, are more attentive, learn more, and have better adjustments—if they have food in their stomachs before they attend classes. One study in Peru showed that breakfast increases attention span and memory functions among nutritional at-risk boys (Cueto, Jacoby, & Pollitt, 1998). The at-risk boys were those who were below average height and weight, indicating that they had some nutritional deficiencies. They were enrolled in the fourth or fifth grade of a public elementary school. Breakfast distributed by the Peruvian government and used in this study consisted of a small cake (80 grams) and a protein beverage similar in taste and color to milk (50 grams). All children consumed the entire meal. A diet soda without caffeine was used as a placebo. The children were asked to stay overnight at the research center on two occasions with a one-week interval. They were then given breakfast the following morning at about 11 A.M. Overall, 16 hours went by before the children had breakfast.

The results of this study showed that the performance of the at-risk children declined in the discrimination of visual stimuli and in standing recall from working memory. No such decline was observed in the healthy and tall comparison groups that were not at risk. The researchers concluded that among nutritionally at-risk boys, some cognitive functions were sensitive to short-term changes in the availability of nutrient supply.

There have been observations made on cognitive performance among middle-class, well-nourished children in high-income countries on the effect of skipping breakfast.

Parenting Issues

When Are Solid Foods Introduced?

Sometimes conflict develops between the mother and the pediatrician over the age at which solid foods are to be introduced to the child. Some pediatricians insist that infants do not need solid foods before 6 months of age. Some mothers prefer to give solid foods after several months of age because they say "it helps the baby sleep through the night."

There are several important considerations. Infants must develop a new movement of the tongue and mouth to swallow solid foods. Neurologic development has progressed sufficiently for this process to happen at about 3 to 4 months of age. Infants can swallow foods at a younger age only if the food is placed on the back of the tongue, but this represents a kind of force-feeding. Some infants rebel and develop feeding problems later.

The time to start solid foods depends partially on the infant's needs and readiness. An infant who has loose bowels may not tolerate solid foods as easily. Certainly, babies do best with breast milk or formula, rather than cow's milk, until at least 6 months of age (American Academy of Pediatrics, Committee on Nutrition, 1986). If there are no other problems, infants can benefit from beginning to eat cereal at about 4 months of age. Cereal has a high iron content that babies need. Fruit is usually started after babies have become used to cereal, followed by vegetables, then strained meat at about 6 months of age. Parents need to avoid too many "dinners" (combination foods) with large amounts of starch, cellulose, and sodium. Puddings and other desserts contain large quantities of cornstarch and sugar that are not advisable for children, especially for obese children or for those not getting enough other nutrients. By 6 months of age most babies are eating cereal and a variety of fruits, vegetables, and meats (Spock & Rothenberg, 1997). Wheat, eggs, and chocolate should be avoided until the child is 1 year of age to prevent unnecessary food sensitivities (Berkow, 1997).

Most babies are very messy when they first start feeding themselves.

An overnight and morning fast caused comparative poor performance in a visual discrimination test among children in Cambridge, Massachusetts, and Houston, Texas. However, the middle-class children sampled in Cambridge and Houston were of average weight and height among their peers and were not as used to skipping breakfast as were the exceptionally healthy and tall boys among the low-income population in Peru (Pollitt, 1995).

There is enough evidence to show that consuming breakfast generally has a short-term positive effect on basic cognitive processes. This finding suggests that there could be more profound long-term effects. Besides the effect directly on brain functions, consuming a daily balanced breakfast at school could help school performance first by lowering morbidity and improving the overall physical condition. The consumption of a balanced breakfast could benefit children by making them more active in exploring their environment and more attentive in the classroom.

Obesity

Body weight that is 20% over what is shown in standard height-weight tables is considered obesity. Obesity may be a health problem as children get older, and it is a distinct disadvantage to children in a society that places a social stigma on being fat (Kolata, 1986). Because fat children tend to become fat adults, obesity presents a future health hazard to them.

There is increasing and widespread concern about body size, eating disorders, and dieting. Newspapers, magazines, videos, and TV bombard young people with exercise and diet regimes. These concerns were previously more prevalent among adolescent and young adults, but now they have become increasingly common among younger children. Results of studies lead to the conclusion that motivation to diet has little to do with actual weight. Rather, it is the perception of body shape and the negative attitudes towards certain body builds that are critical in the decision to reduce food intake (Cramer & Steinwert, 1998). The importance of perceived body self, as compared with actual body size, has been clearly demonstrated in studies of children's self-esteem. Over the age range from 3 to 12 years old, it has been found that actual body weight is not related to self-esteem. Indeed, it is the perception of self as fat, the presence of negative feelings about appearance, or the belief that parents have

negative feelings about their body size that predicts lower self-esteem in children. The cultural stereotype that "fat is bad" is pervasive across gender regardless of the child's own body build (Mendelson and Mendelson, White, 1996; Pierce & Wardle, 1993).

Several factors influence obesity. One is *heredity*. If parents are obese, children tend to be obese also, and not just because the parents teach their children to overeat (Stunkard, Foch, & Hrubec, 1986). Obese children tend to be born with more and larger fat cells than slim children, and the number of fat cells increases even more if there is excess weight gain before the age of 12 (Krieshok & Karpowitz, 1988). Another finding is that obese people have longer intestines than slim people, allowing more calories to be absorbed (Powers, 1980). Of course, appetite is partly inherited. From birth, some children seem to have voracious appetites. Others appear less interested in food.

Another factor in obesity is *eating habits* (Olvera-Ezzell, Power, & Cousins, 1990). Obese children do not necessarily eat more food, but they prefer calorific foods high in fats, starches, and sugars. When they eat such foods, their level of insulin increases, which, in turn, further increases hunger and food consumption. It's a vicious circle.

One major problem that contributes to obesity is the habit of eating junk food—potato chips, sweets, and sodas—which are high in calories from fats and sugars, but low in nutritional value. The fat content and calorie ratings of foods from various fast-food restaurants is shown in Table 6.6 (CSPI, 1990). The American Heart Association recommends that the percentage of calories from fat should be no more than one-third. This recommendation means no more than 15 teaspoons of fat per day for women and 20 teaspoons of fat per day for men. As seen in Table 6.6, most of the foods from fast-food restaurants are high in fat.

Activity level also affects obesity. Obese children tend to be less active, which reduces metabolism and the amount of food burned up, thus increasing fat accumulation. There is a similar link between television watching and obesity. A study of 7,000 children between the ages of 6 and 11 and of 6,500 adolescents found that every hour per day spent watching television increases the prevalence of obesity by 2% (Dietz & Gortmacher, 1985). The reason is that television watching reduces physical activity and increases snack consumption. *Psychological factors* may also be a cause of obesity. Children may eat as a

One major problem that contributes to becoming over-weight is the habit of eating junk food.

means of relieving tension or gaining security when they are tense, unhappy, or lonely.

The important question is what to do about obesity. Parents must try to prevent it in the first place by regulating the diet and eating habits of children while they are young. They should serve nutritious foods, low in calories from fat, starches, and sugars. As infants, fat children may look cute, but they will feel bad about themselves when they are older.

Parents should not put their obese children on crash diets. Children may lose weight, but not permanently. *There are two principal ways to help children reduce their weight.* The first way is gradually to help them change their eating habits. Avoid keeping junk foods in the house, for example, and serve only healthy foods. The second way is to increase children's physical activity so they will use up more calories—for example, enroll children in groups emphasizing physical activities. Parents also can exercise with their children, acting as good role models and having fun as well. And they can encourage their children to cut down on TV.

Malnutrition

Malnutrition results from inadequate intake of all nutrients: proteins, calories, vitamins, and minerals, which the child needs to grow and to maintain health. Children from any country in the world may be malnourished.

Inanition, or starvation, also called **marasmus** in young children, results from the inadequate intake of all nutrients: proteins, calories, vitamins, and minerals. Marasmus is common in developing countries, such

Inanition—starvation

Marasmus—starvation in young children

TABLE 6.6	FAT, CALORIE, AND SODIUM CONTENT OF SELECTED FAST-FOOD MEALS			
Selected Meal	Calories	Fat (tsp.)	Sodium Content
Burger King Whopper, medium fries, chocolate shake	1,312	15	1,301
McDonald's Big Mac, medium fries, iced cheese danish	1,070	16	1,520
Kentucky Fried Chicken, original recipe, two-piece dinner	1,002	12	2,362
Arby's regular roast beef sandwich, two potato cakes, side salad with light Italian dressing	607	6	1,270
Wendy's bacon swiss burger, small fries, medium Frosty	1,470	17	1,771
Dairy Queen double hamburger, onion rings, chocolate-dipped large cone	1,320	15	1,045
Hardee's big country breakfast with sausage, juice, milk	1,050	14	2,110
Burger King Croissan'wich (sausage, egg, cheese), milk	665	10	1,107

FOCUS

Sugar Consumption and Children's Behavior

Not only is excessive sugar consumption unhealthy, but it also may be associated with behavior problems. Many parents feel that candy, cookies, and other sweets transform children into overactive and irrational hellions, furniture-destroying versions of their former selves (Chollar, 1988b). There is evidence to show that high sugar consumption increases aggression, hyperactivity, and inattentiveness, especially in unstructured situations when children are bored (Goldman, Lerman, Contois, & Udall, 1986). One of the problems is that many processed foods have large amounts of sugar, so that there is much hidden sugar in children's diets. The negative effects can be greater when snacks or meals already consumed have been very high in carbohydrates. When the child's basic diet contains high amounts of carbohydrates, sugar consumption increases inappropriate behavior; but if balanced with necessary proteins, the added sugar has less effect. If a child's blood sugar is low, as when he or she has not had breakfast, additional carbohydrates may have a calming effect (Chollar, 1988b).

Kwashiorkor, characterized by a protruding belly, results from a protein deficiency even though the calorie intake is sufficient.

as Somalia, where warfare among competing factions has destroyed the government and agricultural production of the land. It is also common in countries without famine where it is associated with the early abandonment or failure of breast-feeding, with consequent *gastroenteritis infections.* In marasmus, because the energy intake is insufficient to match requirements, the body draws on its own stores. Marasmic infants show gross *weight loss, growth retardation,* and *wasting of subcutaneous fat and muscle. Vital organs* lose weight and function. The *heart, liver, kidney,* and *intestines* are affected. *Heart* and *lung capacity* and output are reduced. *Blood pressure* drops. The *endocrine system* is disturbed. Energy capacity is diminished because of *muscle destruction* and *anemia. Hypothermia* may contribute to death (Berkow, 1997).

Emaciation is obvious. The *bones* protrude; the *skin* becomes thin, dry, inelastic, and cold. A patchy, brown pigmentation may occur. The *hair* is sparse and falls out easily.

Research reveals that an inadequate diet prenatally and after birth may result in retarded brain development and mental retardation. Malnourished children do not perform well on intelligence and cognitive tasks (Rose, 1994). The degree of mental impairment is related to the duration of malnutrition and to the age of onset. The infant with marasmus is more

severely affected than the older child (Rizzo, Metzger, Dooley, & Cho, 1997).

Kwashiorkor results when children have a protein deficiency even though the calorie intake is sufficient. Kwashiorkor is characterized by generalized edema, flaky dermatosis, thinning and decoloration of the hair, enlarged fatty liver, a protruding belly due to the liver enlargement and water retention, and general apathy and retarded growth. In addition to famine-stricken countries, kwashiorkor is found in parts of the world, such as the Caribbean and the Pacific islands, where staples and weaning foods, such as yams, cassava, or green bananas are protein-deficient (Berkow, 1997).

What Is Safe to Eat?

Health and injury statistics indicate that children, especially preschool children, do not always understand what objects are appropriate to eat. Poisoning and choking result. Krause & Saarnio presented 3- to 5-year-olds with nondeceptive common food and nonfood objects and with deceptive objects (e.g., a magnet that looks like candy). The researchers found that 3-year-olds did not understand

Kwashiorkor—protein deficiency

the edibleness of nondeceptive objects although 4- and 5-year-olds clearly did. Examples of nondeceptive food objects included a cookie, a peanut, a carrot, a lollipop, and an apple. Nondeceptive nonfood items included a key chain, a magnet, an eraser, a rock, a pen, and a candle. Children of all ages had trouble distinguishing the edibleness of deceptive objects, that is, clearly distinguishing between appearance and reality of objects. Some deceptive nonfood items included a key chain that looks like a cookie, a magnet that looks like a piece of candy, an eraser that looks like a peanut, a pencil sharpener that looks like an ice-cream cone, a pen that looks like a lollipop, and a candle that looks like an apple.

This resemblance to foods means that young children's safety may be at risk when they encounter deceptive objects. For example, play foods made of plastic may also be mistaken as edible, as may objects such as wax food. Similarly, various poisons, such as rodenticides, may mislead or confuse children because of their similarity in appearance to common foods (Krause & Saarnio, 1993).

SLEEP

Needs

If they are made comfortable, get enough food to eat, and have plenty of fresh, cool air, most infants will get the amount of sleep they need. In the early months, most infants sleep from feeding to feeding, although, from the beginning, some are wakeful during certain times of the day. By the end of the first year, most infants take only two naps a day, after the breakfast and lunch feedings. Between 1 and 1½ years they usually give up one of these (Spock & Rothenberg, 1992). If naps

Parenting Issues

How Not to Create Eating Problems

Feeding problems most often develop because overly zealous parents try to make their children eat well, because careless parents don't feed them properly, or because overindulgent parents give children anything they want, including too many sweets. The following suggestions will help to avoid eating problems:

1. Avoid force-feeding children, or use of excessive urging to get them to eat. And avoid fighting with them over food. When pushed too hard, children will rebel and refuse to eat.

2. Recognize that children's appetites vary. Sometimes they eat a lot, sometimes a little. The amount usually evens out over time. Serve small portions—less than they will eat, not more—giving seconds as needed. This way, you can avoid hostility about their finishing their meals.

3. Use a gradual introduction to new foods, giving only small amounts at first and allowing the child time to learn to like them. Sometimes children will never accept a particular food, but as long as other foods provide the basic nutrients, there is no problem. Most adults admit that there are foods they now eat that they didn't like as children.

4. Keep mealtimes happy and pleasant, avoiding arguments, controversy, and threats.

5. Serve balanced meals, avoiding excess sweets and fats. Some parents complain that their children will not eat vegetables. These parents may dislike vegetables and seldom serve them.

6. When children are old enough to eat adult table food, serve the same food to the whole family; don't cook separately for the children. It's certainly all right to serve children's favorites now and then, but not in addition to or as a substitute for food eaten by the rest of the family.

7. Generally avoid asking children what they want to eat. It may be all right now and then or for special occasions, but if you do it on a regular basis, you'll be forever catering to their whims. Some children ask for one food, then when given it, don't want it and prefer something else. Letting children dictate their diets is really asking for trouble.

8. Don't bribe children to eat by promising a reward of any kind, whether it is a piece of candy, a gold star, or any other prize. The less fuss about eating, the better.

Children go to bed more willingly if parents follow the same routine each night.

are too long in the afternoon, children don't want to go to bed at night.

Infants will take the sleep they need. Two-year-olds won't. They may be kept awake by overexcitement, conflicts, tenseness, or fears of various kinds. Resistance to going to bed generally peaks between 1 and 2 years of age. Children cry when left alone in the crib, or they climb out and seek their parents. The cause is usually **separation anxiety,** or an effort to control their environment. When children get out of bed, the best way for parents to handle

Separation anxiety—anxiety experienced by children when they are separated from caregivers to whom they are emotionally attached

the situation is to put them back in the bed, and then to wait in the hallway to make sure the children stay in bed. Parents need to avoid (1) letting the children stay up; (2) lying down in bed with them; (3) reading more stories and allowing more play; or (4) taking children into bed with them. Once children learn that they will not be allowed out of their own bed and cannot entice parents for some stories or play, they will usually settle down and go to sleep (Berkow, 1997).

It is up to parents to see that children get the sleep they need. The average 2-year-old child needs 12 hours of sleep at night plus 1 to 2 hours of nap. Naps are gradually discontinued over several years. From age 6 to 9, children need about 11 hours sleep; 10- to 12-year-olds need about 10 hours. Some children need either more or less than these averages.

Habits

There are several things that parents can do to develop regular sleeping habits for their children.

1. Put children to bed at the same time every night.
2. Develop a relaxed bedtime routine. Get washed and undressed, put pajamas on, have a snack, put the doll to bed, read a story, get tucked in, give a good-night kiss. Children thrive on routine and are upset by variations. Routines help to give them security and condition them to settle down to sleep. Also, it's easier to put them to sleep in their own bed than in strange places, which requires extra effort and attention.
3. Avoid excessive stimulation before bedtime. Rough play, disturbances in the parent-child relationship, or tension in the home cause wakefulness. Parents can't let children roughhouse and then expect them to settle down and go to sleep immediately.
4. Keep bedtime relaxed and happy. It's far more pleasant to carry children to bed lovingly than angrily to order them to bed, or to spank them for not obeying instantly.
5. Avoid sending children to bed as a means of discipline. They will come to associate going to bed with punishment, which makes it harder to get them to bed at other times.
6. Avoid frightening stories or television programs, which may precipitate **night-**

mares, especially in 3- to 4-year-olds, who cannot distinguish fantasy from reality. **Night terrors** are characterized by sudden awakening, panic, and screaming. They are most common between ages 3 to 8 years. **Sleepwalking** is estimated to occur in 15% of children between 5 and 12 years of age. Stressful events may trigger an episode of sleepwalking. If these difficulties persist, psychological help may be necessary.

HEALTH CARE

Health Supervision of the Well Child

Proper health supervision of the well child will help to promote optimum development of infants and children. Such supervision by medical personnel ought to include (1) instruction of parents in child-rearing, health maintenance, accident prevention, and nutrition; (2) routine immunizations for the prevention of disease; (3) early detection of disease through interview and examination; and (4) early treatment of disease. To meet these objectives, parents and children should be seen by their doctor at regular intervals throughout the early years of life. The frequency of subsequent visits will vary, depending on children's age and condition and the population served.

The American Academy of Pediatrics has recommended the preventive health-care schedule that is found in Table 6.7. This schedule is for children who have not manifested any important health problems and who are growing and developing satisfactorily. More frequent and sophisticated visits are necessary for children with special problems. (See Table 6.8 on p. 140 for an immunization schedule for infants and children.)

Health Education

Beginning at an early age, children ought to be taught responsibility for their own health. This undertaking means instruction in good health habits, proper nutrition, and daily hygiene, as well as the importance of adequate sleep and exercise (Blecke, 1990). Children's health attitudes and behavior are influenced by the family, their peers, the school, and the media (Tinsley, 1992). Free or reduced-price lunches at school can help make up for nutritional deficiencies (Glovinsky-Fahsholtz, 1992).

Nightmares

Night terrors

Sleepwalking

SEXUAL DEVELOPMENT

Infancy

The infant's capacity for sexual response begins early. Ultrasound pictures reveal that erections occur in developing male fetuses several months before birth (Calderone, 1983). Many male babies have erections even before the umbilical cord is cut or in the first few months after birth. Erections can occur with or without penile stimulation, and they often occur during feeding and sleep. Apparently, the warmth and softness of the mother's body, along with the stimulation of sucking, are pleasurable sensations that stimulate sexual reflexes.

Female infants also exhibit sexual response, evidenced by the presence of vaginal lubrication and clitoral erection during the first 24 hours of life. Vaginal lubrication can also occur during nursing. Although their sexual reflexes respond to emotional and physical stimuli, both male and female infants are too young to be aware consciously of the encounters; therefore, they cannot be considered sexually awakened.

Infants begin to discover their bodies during the first year of life. During their exploration, they randomly touch their genitals. Later, as their motor abilities develop, children deliberately touch and rub their genitals. In the process, they discover that such touching brings pleasant sensations.

Early Childhood

Preschool children are curious about everything. This curiosity extends to their own bodies, which they continue to explore. Most masturbate at some time or another. Both boys and girls are fascinated with toileting procedures. They also develop curiosity about other children's bodies and about boy-girl differences. As a result, they peek at one another's bodies to see what they look like. "Doctor" games are one method of body exploration.

Parents need to recognize that some exploration, peeking, and touching represent fairly common behavior that results from children's curiosity. If sexual exploration during play becomes too frequent, however, children may require greater supervision. In addition, parents need to be concerned about protecting younger children from advances of those who are older. They should teach children to report sexual requests from older children or adults, such as solicitations to

Children should learn the basic facts about human reproduction at an early age.

take off their clothes or to touch their genitals (Geasler, Dannison, & Edlund, 1995).

Middle Childhood

Because society becomes less accepting of children's sexual interests during middle childhood, sexual activities take place more covertly than during the preschool years. Sexual experimentation does not cease or decrease. In fact, it may become more frequent. In one survey, parents of 6- and 7-year-old children reported that 83% of their sons and 76% of their daughters had participated in sexual play with siblings or friends of the same sex (Kolodny, 1980). Hunt (1974) found that one-third of females and two-thirds of males who responded to a questionnaire reported that they had masturbated by age 13.

Children remain fascinated with sex and with facts concerning sexual development, human reproduction, and sexual intercourse. The delightful thing about children of school age is that they are not embarrassed to ask detailed questions, given the opportunity. An ideal time to teach children all the basic facts about sex is before they reach puberty and

TABLE 6.7   RECOMMENDATIONS FOR PREVENTIVE PEDIATRIC HEALTH CARE COMMITTEE ON PRACTICE AND AMBULATORY MEDICINE (RE 9535)

Each child and family is unique; therefore, these **Recommendations for Preventive Pediatric Health Care** are designed for the care of children who are receiving competent parenting, have no manifestations of any important health problems, and are growing and developing in satisfactory fashion. Additional visits may become necessary if circumstances suggest variations from normal. These guidelines represent a consensus by the Committee on Practice and Ambulatory Medicine in consultation with national committees and sections of the American Academy of Pediatrics. The Committee emphasizes the great importance of continuity of care in comprehensive health supervision and the need to avoid fragmentation of care.

		Infancy[3]								Early Childhood[3]				
Age[4]	Newborn[1]	2–4d[2]	By 1mo	2mo	4mo	6mo	9mo	12mo	15mo	18mo	24mo	3y	4y
HISTORY													
Initial/Interval	•	•	•	•	•	•	•	•	•	•	•	•	•
MEASUREMENTS													
Height and Weight	•	•	•	•	•	•	•	•	•	•	•	•	•
Head Circumference	•	•	•	•	•	•	•	•	•	•	•	•	
Blood Pressure												•	•
SENSORY SCREENING													
Vision	S	S	S	S	S	S	S	S	S	S	S	O[5]	O
Hearing[6]	S/O	S	S	S	S	S	S	S	S	S	S	O	O
DEVELOPMENTAL/ BEHAVIORAL ASSESSMENT[7]	•	•	•	•	•	•	•	•	•	•	•	•	•
PHYSICAL EXAMINATION[8]	•	•	•	•	•	•	•	•	•	•	•	•	•
PROCEDURES–GENERAL[9]													
Hereditary/Metabolic Screening[10]	←	—	•										
Immunization[11]	•	—	→	•	•	•		←	—	→			←
Lead Screening[12]							→				•		
Hematocrit or Hemoglobin			←	—	—	—	—	→					
Urinalysis													
PROCEDURES-PATIENTS AT RISK													
Tuberculin Test[15]								*	*	*	*	*	
Cholesterol Screening[16]											*	*	
STD Screening[17]													
Pelvic Exam[18]													
ANTICIPATORY GUIDANCE[19]	•	•	•	•	•	•	•	•	•	•	•	•	•
Injury Prevention[20]	•	•	•	•	•	•	•	•	•	•	•	•	•
INITIAL DENTAL REFERRAL[21]								←	—	—	→		

*To be performed by patients at home.

[1]Breastfeeding encouraged and instruction and support offered.

[2]For newborns discharged in less than 48 hours after delivery.

[3]Developmental, psychosocial, and chronic disease issues for children and adolescents may require frequent counseling and treatment visits separate from preventive care visits.

[4]If a child comes under care for the first time at any point on the schedule, or if any items are not accomplished at the suggested age, the schedule should be brought up to date at the earliest possible time.

[5]If the patient is uncooperative, rescreen within six months.

[6]Some experts recommend objective appraisal of hearing in the newborn period. The Joint Committee on Infant Hearing has identified patients at significant risk for hearing loss. All children meeting these criteria should be objectively screened. See the Joint Committee on Infant Hearing 1994 Position Statement.

[7]By history and appropriate physical examination: if suspicious, by specific objective developmental testing.

[8]At each visit, a complete physical examination is essential, with infant totally unclothed, older child undressed and suitably draped.

[9]These may be modified, depending upon entry point into schedule and individual need.

[10]Metabolic screening (eg, thyroid, hemoglobinopathies, PKU, galactosemia) should be done according to state law.

[11]Schedule(s) per the Committee on Infectious Diseases, published periodically in *Pediatrics*. Every visit should be an opportunity to update and complete a child's immunizations.

[12]Blood lead screen per AAP statement "Lead Poisoning: From Screening to Primary Prevention" (1993).

[13]All menstruating adolescents should be screened.

A prenatal visit is recommended for parents who are at high risk, for first-time parents, and for those who request a conference. The prenatal visit should include anticipatory guidance and pertinent medical history. Every infant should have a newborn evaluation after birth.

Middle Childhood[3]   *Adolescence*[3]

5y	6y	8y	10y	11y	12y	13y	14y	15y	16y	17y	18y	19y	20y	21y
•	•	•	•	•	•	•	•	•	•	•	•	•	•	•
•	•	•	•	•	•	•	•	•	•	•	•	•	•	•
•	•	•	•	•	•	•	•	•	•	•	•	•	•	•
O	S	S	O	S	O	S	S	O	S	S	O	S	S	S
O	S	S	O	S	O	S	S	O	S	S	O	S	S	S
•	•	•	•	•	•	•	•	•	•	•	•	•	•	•
•	•	•	•	•	•	•	•	•	•	•	•	•	•	•

5y	6y	8y	10y	11y	12y	13y	14y	15y	16y	17y	18y	19y	20y	21y
←•——→				←•—————————————→										
•				←—————•13—————————————————→										
•				←—————•14—————————————————→										
*	*	*	*	*	*	*	*	*	*	*	*	*	*	*
*	*	*	*	*	*	*	*	*	*	*	*	*	*	*
		*	*	*	*	*	*	*	*	*	*	*	*	*
		*	*	*	*	*	*	←—*——*——18——*——→*						
•	•	•	•	•	•	•	•	•	•	•	•	•	•	•
•	•	•	•	•	•	•	•	•	•	•	•	•	•	•

[14]Conduct dipstick urinalysis for leukocytes for male and female adolescents.

[15]TB testing per AAP statement "Screening for Tuberculosis in Infants and Children" (1994). Testing should be done upon recognition of high risk factors. If results are negative but high risk situation continues, testing should be repeated on an annual basis.

[16]Cholesterol screening for high risk patients per AAP "Statement on Cholesterol" (1992). If family history cannot be ascertained and other risk factors are present, screening should be at the discretion of the physician.

[17]All sexually active patients should be screened for sexually transmitted diseases (STDs).

[18]All sexually active females should have a pelvic examination. A pelvic examination and routine pap smear should be offered as part of preventive health maintenance between the ages of 18 and 21 years.

[19]Appropriate discussion and counseling should be an integral part of each visit for care.

[20]From birth to age 12, refer to AAP's injury prevention program (TIPP®) as described in "A Guide to Safety Counseling in Office Practice" (1994).

[21]Earlier initial dental evaluations may be appropriate for some children. Subsequent examinations as prescribed by dentist.

Key: • = to be performed * = to be performed for patients at risk,   S = subjective, by history   O = objective, by a standard testing method ←•→ = the range during which a service may be provided, with the dot indicating the preferred age.

NB: Special chemical, immunologic, and endocrine testing is usually carried out upon specific indications. Testing other than newborn (eg, inborn errors of metabolism, sickle disease, etc.) is discretionary with the physician.

The recommendations in this publication do not indicate an exclusive course of treatment or serve as a standard of medical care. Variations, taking into account individual circumstances, may be appropriate.

TABLE 6.8	IMMUNIZATION SCHDULE FOR INFANTS AND CHILDREN

Immunization plays an important role in keeping infants and children healthy. Shown are the routinely recommended ages for having an infant or child immunized with specific vaccines. The recommended age for immunization may vary depending on the circumstances. For example, if an infant is born to a woman with the hepatitis B surface antigen in her blood, a doctor will likely recommend immunization with hepatitis B vaccine within 12 hours of birth. However, other infants may receive their first dose of hepatitis B vaccine at age 1 or 2 months. A range of acceptable ages exists for many vaccines, and a child's own doctor will provide specific recommendations. Often, combination vaccines are used, which lessens the number of shots a child will recieve.

Key

◯ Single dose of vaccine

△ "Catch-up" vaccination for those children not previously immunized (or, in the case of varicella-zoster virus, for those who have not had chicken-pox)

▭ Range of acceptable ages for a single dose of vaccine

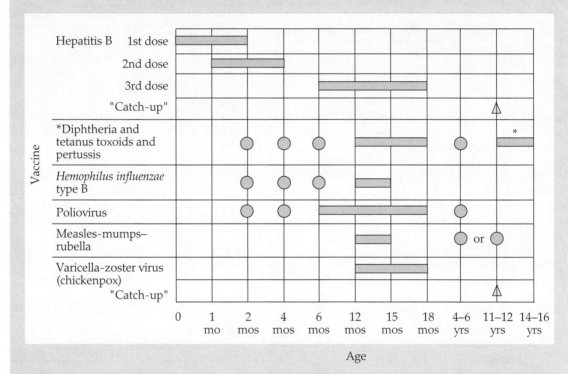

*A booster dose containing just diphtheria and tetanus toxoids (without pertussis vaccine) is recommended between the ages of 11 and 16 if at least 5 years have elapsed since the last dose.

Adapted from R. Berkow (Ed.), (1997). *The Merck Manual of Medical Information* (Home ed.). Whitehouse Station, NJ: Merck Research Laboratories.

---

become self-conscious about discussing the subject openly.

Parents as Sex Educators

Transmission of values and attitudes about sexuality from parents to children is inevitable; values and attitudes are transmitted whether parents choose to participate actively in the sex education of their children or to neglect it completely. Empirical evidence indicates that adolescents whose parents communicated openly with them about sexuality when they were young feel much more comfortable discussing sexual topics with their parents and are more likely to make

Parents can use good books to help with sex education at home.

personal decisions about sexual behavior that reflect parental values and morals.

Goals of Sex Education

Sex education can help children to understand the process of the physical development of their own bodies and to prepare for the bodily changes at puberty. Parents need to explain such things as nocturnal emissions and menstruation. Sex education also seeks to help children accept their own sexuality: their understanding of their gender and their coming to terms with the prescribed sex roles in the society in which they are growing up.

One customary purpose of sex education is to help children understand the great wonders of life, such as where babies come from; how they are conceived, grow, and are born; and how life is passed on from generation to generation (Johnson & Solomon, 1997). Another major role of sex education is to encourage mature, responsible, and knowledgeable sexual conduct. Parents need to discuss morals and behavior, along with the facts of life. The day has passed when parental silence, which tries to keep children ignorant, is perceived as the way to keep children from sexual experimentation. Children are already taught through movies, magazines, television, books, street corners, and public rest rooms. Not all such information is factual, and much is associated with negative feelings and attitudes that demonstrate sexual irresponsibility. There is need, therefore, for parents to present a more mature point of view to help their children not only to grow to be sexually responsive but also to be sexually responsible. Such things as venereal disease and teen pregnancies are preventable—

with the right sex education and with parental and medical help.

SEXUAL ABUSE OF CHILDREN

Patterns of Activity

Sexual abuse and *sexual molestation* may be considered synonymous, since they include unwanted sexual advances and activities. They may involve a variety of activities. Exhibitionism, suggestive language or looks, and passive and active petting and fondling are the most common abusive activities. Sexual encounters are usually quite brief, involving fondling of nongenital and genital areas. The offender may achieve orgasm during the episode, or through fantasy about the incident, accompanied by masturbation, at a later time. Anal and/or vaginal intercourse is infrequent. The older the child, the more likely coitus will occur.

Molestation is most likely to take place in the child's own home or in that of the molester. Only a small percent of molesters are complete strangers to the child. Usually the molester is a family member or a friend of the family. A stranger may have to spend days or hours winning the child's trust. The molester may seduce by offering candy, toys, trips to parks or movies, but first must find situations in which children are available. Volunteering for service in organizations, schools, sports groups, boys' or girls' clubs, nursery schools, church choirs, or children's theater groups is a way of establishing contact with children.

As the child begins to feel comfortable, "Mr. Nice Guy" tries some wrestling, tickling, or fondling. The child may be shown child pornography or pictures of other children touching and playing. The perpetrator tries to convince the child that these are ways to have a good time, and may ask the child to disrobe or may force the child to undress.

Abused children may get involved in frequent sexual activity such as oral sex. The more involved the children become, the more they feel trapped. They are threatened with blackmail or with the murder of their parents if they tell anyone. One question frequently asked is "How come they never said anything?" The reasons are complex; often the child believes that threats against his or her parents will be carried out if he or she reveals the sexual abuse. Plus, the children feel guilty and are afraid that they will get into trouble, so they keep quiet.

Parenting Issues

Easy Victims and Bad Witnesses

Two sets of parents—of a 3-year-old boy and a 4-year-old girl—believed that their children were among several toddlers who were forced into sexual acts by three counselors at a summer day camp.

Authorities investigated the incident, but also warned parents of a frequently insurmountable problem involving such cases: small children make easy victims and bad witnesses. The parents, in separate interviews, told similar stories about what had happened involving three unnamed counselors. The 3-year-old described bizarre games involving anal and oral sex. The 4-year-old described a lot of sex play in the camp, initiated by the counselors.

All four parents felt that their children would be able to testify. The 3-year-old told his mother that the perpetrators had threatened to kill his mother if he told and that he would go to jail and be molested there also. He first spoke of the incidents to his grandmother, since he was fearful for his mother's life. The toddler was put under a therapist's care. The toddler said he thought that people who did this should get a spanking. Every day he asked whether the counselors were in jail. He felt he'd like to testify to help put them in jail. However, the boy became suicidal and deliberately ran out into a busy street to try to get run over. "I should be dead now," he said.

The mother of the 4-year-old girl felt that she would be a good witness. The caseworker was surprised at how astute she was. However, the girl was very troubled. She became convinced that she would have to go to jail because she had done the same thing that the counselors had done. She had also been warned that if she told anyone, her parents would die. She began bedwetting and passing stools in inappropriate places. She received therapy but told her therapist that she would go to jail for what was done to her (Lovell, 1984).*

*Subsequent investigation revealed that this case was dropped for lack of evidence.

Effects

Victims describe feelings of powerlessness, anger, depression, and anxiety. Low self-esteem is expressed through self-blame, shame, and guilt. Sexual abuse may be a causative factor in some of the most severe mental disorders. Sexual abuse survivors have high levels of anxiety, depression, self-destructive suicidal tendencies, and difficulty with intimate relationships. Depression is the most common symptom. Victims can suffer from anxiety attacks and phobias; in addition, depression and anxiety may cause sleep and appetite disturbances. Providers may suffer from all kinds of somatic disorders, including gastrointestinal problems, and may have significantly more medical complaints than nonabused persons. In the case of female victims, long-term effects on the individual include having shattered trust in men in general; never marrying or making poor choices in marriage; having a poor self-concept; being sexually promiscuous and using sex as the only way to relate to men; taking part in substance abuse; being confused about the difference between intimacy and sexuality; and having a lack of support from family and society (Canavan, Meyer, & Higgs, 1992; Haverkamp & Daniluk, 1993; Luster & Small, 1997). It is estimated that approximately 500,000 children are sexually abused each year. Although estimates of the prevalence of sexual abuse vary from study to study. Finkelhor (1994) concluded that approximately 20% of females and from 5% to 10% of males are sexually abused in childhood or adolescence.

Summary

1. Physical growth from birth to adolescence manifests two different patterns: (a) very rapid but decelerating growth from birth to age 1, and (b) linear and steady annual increments after age 1. Increases in both height and weight are dramatic during the first year of life.

2. There are wide individual, cultural, ethnic, and socioeconomic class differences in growth patterns.

3. Body parts grow at different rates. They grow according to the cephalocaudal principle, from the head to the feet, and according to the proximodistal principle, from the center of the body outward.

4. Three organ systems—the lymphoid system, the reproductive system, and the central nervous system—do not follow the general patterns of growth of the rest of the body and organs.

5. Brain growth and nerve maturation include increased myelinization and the development of increasingly complex nerve pathways.

6. The cerebral cortex, which is the largest structure of the forebrain, contains the higher brain centers controlling intellectual, sensory, and motor functions.

7. The cerebral cortex is larger in proportion to total body weight and is more highly developed in humans than in any other animals.

8. The cerebral cortex is divided into two hemispheres; the left side of the brain controls mainly the right side of the body, and the right side of the brain controls mainly the left side of the body.

9. Right- or left-handedness is reasonably well established by age 2. Lateralization is the preference for using one side of the body more than the other in performing specific tasks.

10. The right hemisphere specializes in music, drama, fantasy, intuition, and art; in recognizing patterns, faces, and melodies; and in visualizing spatial relationships. The left hemisphere specializes in logic, mathematics, language, writing, and judging time.

11. The motor, sensory, and association areas of the cortex each control particular functions.

12. The Broca's area of the cortex is involved in using language, the Wernicke's area in understanding language.

13. Both maturation and learning are important in the development of cortical structures and in learning such functions as toilet training.

14. The eruption of deciduous teeth (baby teeth) begins at about 5 months and is completed by 30 months of age. The eruption of permanent teeth begins at 5 years of age and is completed by age 25. Children need dental care of baby teeth as well as of permanent teeth.

15. Gross-motor skills develop in infancy before fine-motor skills. The average infant can walk alone by 15 months of age and can scribble spontaneously by 25 months.

16. Five-year-olds can perform a variety of physical feats, involving both gross-motor skills and fine-motor skills, that would have been impossible several years earlier.

17. Handedness develops slowly in young children and is not always consistent in the early years. There are both advantages and disadvantages to being left-handed.

18. Most differences between elementary school boys and girls in motor abilities are due to differential expectations and experiences. Children exposed to the same physical education classes show few gender differences in abilities.

19. Reaction time of children decreases with age. This is an important factor in many games children play.

20. Physical handicaps discussed here include speech handicaps, hearing handicaps, visual handicaps, and skeletal, orthopedic, and motor skills handicaps. Otitis media is a middle-ear disease in children, often causing partial hearing loss.

21. Handicapped children may be subject to cruel remarks and teasing by other children, but many are able to overcome these things and live happy, productive lives.

22. Rearing a child with a physical handicap is particularly stressful. Parents must meet the child's special needs as well as the normal developmental needs that all children require. Parents who have satisfying social networks are able to depend on other people and to have more of their own emotional needs met; consequently, they are better able to meet the needs of children.

23. Coping strategies involve two major types: problem-focused coping and emotion-focused coping.

24. Federal law mandates that all children, regardless of their handicap, receive public education in the least restrictive environment that is educationally sound.

25. Perceptual developments discussed in this chapter include depth perception, perception of form and motion, perception of the human face, and auditory perception.

26. Breast-feeding and bottle-feeding both have advantages and disadvantages, but most authorities would say that breast-feeding is superior from a health standpoint alone. The chief disadvantage of breast-feeding is that it is hard to manage for mothers who work.

27. Eating a good breakfast before going to school has a positive effective on cognitive processes.

28. Generally speaking, solid foods are introduced about 4 months of age, so that by the sixth month, babies are eating cereal, fruits, vegetables, and meat.

29. It is vitally important for children to eat a balanced diet derived from four basic food groups daily: milk and dairy products; meat; fruits and vegetables; and breads and cereals.

30. Obesity is a distinct disadvantage to children and has multiple causes: heredity; eating habits that involve eating a lot of high-calorie food; low activity level; and using eating to ease tension or gain security.

31. Excessive sugar consumption makes children hyperactive if the basic diet is unbalanced or if the sugar is not combined with sufficient protein.

32. Inanition, or starvation, also called marasmus in young children, is all too common in many parts of the world. Kwashiorkor results from a deficiency of protein even though calorie intake is sufficient.

33. Young preschool children do not always understand what objects are appropriate to eat. Some objects are deceptive, such as play foods that are made of plastic that are mistaken as edible. Consequently, young children's safety may be at risk when they encounter deceptive objects.

34. Most infants will take the amount of sleep that they need; 2-year-olds won't. It is up to parents to see that children get the required sleep.

35. Health supervision of the well child ought to include (a) instruction of parents in child-rearing, health maintenance, accident prevention, and nutrition; (b) routine immunizations; (c) early detection of disease through interview and examination; and (d) early treatment of disease.

36. The American Academy of Pediatrics has a recommended schedule for child health supervision and a recommended schedule for immunizations.

37. Children's capacity for sexual responses begins in infancy.

38. Both preschool and grade-school children engage in body exploration and masturbation, and are interested in matters pertaining to sex.

39. Parents have an important role to play in the sex education of their children. Not only should parents seek to develop mature attitudes and to impart factual information to their children, but also they should present a mature point of view to help their children to grow to be both sexually responsive and sexually responsible.

40. Sexual abuse of children is most commonly perpetrated by members of the child's own family or by a family friend. Sexual abuse can have a devastating effect, depending on the nature and extent of the abuse and on the age of the child. Because children usually make easy victims and bad witnesses, it is difficult to convict offenders.

Key Terms

Cephalocaudal principle *p. 112*	Marasmus *p. 133*
Cerebral cortex *p. 114*	Myelinization *p. 113*
Cross-modal perception *p. 128*	Nightmares *p. 136*
Gap threshold *p. 129*	Night terrors *p. 136*
Handedness *p. 121*	Otitis media *p. 124*
Inanition *p. 133*	Proximodistal principle *p. 112*
Kwashiorkor *p. 134*	Separation anxiety *p. 135*
Lateralization *p. 115*	Sleepwalking *p. 136*

Discussion Questions

1. Do you know any children who are smaller or larger than average for their age group? Describe them. What are some of the social and psychological consequences for them?

2. Should parents play an active role in helping children develop gross-motor skills and fine-motor skills? Explain. Does doing so help? What might be some of the possible negative results? Should parents help children to learn sports?

3. What do you think of having boys and girls in the same physical education classes at school? Explain.

4. Are any of you left-handed? Do you experience any particular difficulty as a result? Explain.

5. Do you know anyone personally who has a physical handicap? Tell about that person.

6. Do you have children of toddler age? What particular perceptual abilities does your child have? Describe.

7. Have you breast-fed, or have you been the father of a breast-fed baby? How did you get along? What do you think of breast-feeding? What are your attitudes toward breast-feeding versus bottle-feeding?

8. Have you bottle-fed a baby, or do you know someone who has? What were the results?

9. What should parents do about children who are obese? Were you obese as a child? If so, how did obesity affect you and your relationships with others? If not, what were your experiences or friendships with children who were obese? How did obesity affect their behavior and attitudes as you saw them?

10. Do you know any children who have a very inadequate diet? Why is their diet inadequate? What is the effect?

11. Do you know any person who was sexually abused as a child? Describe. What has been the effect on that person?

12. What do you or would you do about children who won't go to bed at night? Explain your choices.

13. Did you sleep with your parents while you were growing up? How do you feel now about children's sleeping with their parents? How did it affect you? Do you think it encourages sexual stimulation, guilt, and anxiety? Why or why not?

14. What do you think of the recommended health-care schedule for well children that is found in the book? Are there any aspects you object to? What do you think of taking a child who is not sick to the doctor? Why do some people never want to take their children to the doctor, whereas others run to the doctor at every little illness?

15. Did your parents provide you with any sex education at home while you were growing up? What was the effect? Did the school play a role in your own sex education? Was it helpful? Why, or why not?

Suggested Readings

BASS, E., & DAVIS, L. (1994). *The courage to heal* (3rd. ed.). New York: Harper & Collins. A guide for women survivors of child sexual abuse.

BATSHAW, M. L., & PETTET, Y. M. (1997). *Children with handicaps*. Baltimore: Paul H. Brooks. Dental care, vision, hearing, attention-deficit disorder, and cerebral palsy.

BROWN, E. W., & BRANTA, C. F. (Eds.). (1987). *Competitive sports for children and youth*. Champaign, IL: Human Kinetics. A series of articles summarizing research and issues.

CAPLAN, T. (1993). *The first twelve months of life*. New York. Perigee. A summary, easily read.

CAPLAN, T., & CAPLAN, F. (1984). *The early childhood years: The 2- to 6-year-old*. New York: Putnam. Physical, cognitive, social, and emotional growth during the years 2 to 6.

FELDMAN, R. S. (1998). *Child development: A topical approach*. Prentice-Hall. A comparative textbook on the subject.

FIELD, T. (1990). *Infancy*. Cambridge, MA: Harvard University Press. The latest on infant research, plus current practical concerns.

HAYWOOD, K. M. (1993). *Life span motor development*. (2nd ed.). Champaign, IL: Human Kinetics. Summary of development over the life span.

LAMB, M. E., & Bornstein, M. C. (1987). *Development in infancy*. New York: Random House. Description by two leading researchers.

OSOFSKY, J. D. (1987). *Handbook of infant development* (2nd ed.). New York: Wiley. Numerous topics about infants.

SHELOV, S. P., & HANNEMANN, R. E. (Eds.). (1993). *Caring for your baby and young child, birth to age five*. New York: Bantam Books. The official guide of the American Academy of Pediatrics.

SPOCK, B., & ROTHENBERG, M. B. (1992). *Dr. Spock's baby and child care*. New York: Pocket Books. Updated revision of this best-seller.

Web Resources

http://kidsource.com KidSource—in depth and timely education and healthcare information.

Cognitive Development

Chapter 7

The word *cognition* means, literally, "the act of knowing or perceiving." So in discussing the cognitive development of children, we seek to inquire into the process by which children grow in knowledge and in the ability to perceive, think, and understand, and then utilize these abilities to solve the practical problems of everyday living.

We begin the chapter with a discussion of the development of language, which is so important to all communication, learning, and problem solving. We then discuss the three basic approaches to the study of cognition. The first is the Piagetian approach, which emphasizes the qualitative changes in the way children think. The second is the information-processing approach, which examines the progressive steps, actions, and operations that take place when the child receives, perceives, remembers, thinks about, and utilizes information. The third approach is the psychometric approach, which measures quantitative changes in children's intelligence.

The chapter ends with a discussion of school, education, and achievement.

LANGUAGE

Language and Communication

Long before they can use spoken words, human infants can communicate. The *rooting reflex* indicates an ability to suck and to eat. Various types of cries indicate upset, pain, or tiredness. *Nonverbal body language* includes such things as posture, facial expressions, still or tense muscles, movement, tears, sweating, shivering, or quivering. Alert parents learn to interpret these body signs and to give correct meaning to their expression (Goodwyn & Acredolo, 1993).

Language, therefore, represents only one method of communication. It is certainly the most important, however. With it, humans are able to transmit information, ideas, attitudes, and emotions to one another. Without it, what we think of as meaningful human relationships would be impossible. Language enables humans to transcend space or time, to pass on the knowledge of millions of years gone by to future generations. Language has a *generative function* also. It can be used to originate new ideas and thoughts by reordering words and phrases in combinations that have not been expressed before (Baldwin, 1993). Language goes beyond concrete experiences by using symbols to represent reality, to refer to objects, actions, and events in the world (Namay & Waxman, 1998), yet in such a way that reality is understood. Above all, through thousands of words, language is an efficient way of communicating unlimited pieces of information, thoughts, ideas, and feelings from one person to others (Teasley, 1995).

Elements and Rules of Language

In accurately fulfilling its functions, language contains a finite set of elements that are used according to set rules. The basic elements of language include *phonemes, morphemes, syntax and grammar, semantics,* and *pragmatics* (Bialystok, 1992).

Phonemes

A **phoneme,** derived from the Greek word meaning "sound," is the smallest unit of sound in a language. There may be 20 to 60 phonemes, depending on the language. In English, everything we say is made up of only 44 phonemes; that is, our language is generated from only 44 basic sound distinctions. There are more phonemes than letters of the alphabet,

Infants communicate with body language long before they can speak.

Phoneme—the smallest unit of sound in a language

Morpheme—the smallest unit of meaning in a language

Syntax—the grammatical rules of a language

Semantics—the meaning of words and sentences

Pragmatics—the practical use of language to communicate with others in a variety of social contexts

Nativist view—says that children have a predisposition to learn language at a certain age

Language acquisition device—the inherited characteristics that enable children to listen to and imitate speech sounds and patterns

because some letter combinations, such as *ch* and *th*, stand for different phonemes.

Morphemes

Morphemes are the smallest units of meaning in a language. They may be single words, such as *word* or *help*, or they may exist in combination with other morphemes, such as *anti-biotic* or *push-ed*. Combinations of morphemes always occur in particular sequences according to set rules. We wouldn't say *biotic-anti*, for example. We know too that the article "the" occurs at the beginning of noun phrases and that the auxiliary verb "was" occurs at the beginning of verb phrases (Gerken and McIntosh, 1993). In developing language, children come to know thousands of morphemes.

Syntax

Syntax is the system of rules by which phonemes are combined in morphemes, and morphemes are combined in words, and words are combined in phrases and sentences, to form acceptable utterances. In English, we would say, "Mr. Jones went to town." We would not say, "Mr. Jones gone to town" or "Mr. Jones to town went." The formal description of syntactical rules comprises the grammar of the language.

Semantics

Semantics deals with the meanings of words and sentences. It assures proper word usage. Thus, a child learns that a pair of puppies is "two puppies," not "too puppies," or that *mother* is not synonymous with *woman*.

Pragmatics

Pragmatics refers to the practical use of language to communicate with others in a variety of social contexts (Capelli, Nakagawa, & Madden, 1990). Children learn appropriate choices of words and intensity of tone of voice when talking with their parents. They may use other words or vocal expressions when talking to their peers. These are practical applications of language. Pragmatics also refers to the ability to engage in meaningful conversation, to describe an event, or to explain something to a teacher. It's not enough to be able to know the correct usage of words and sentences. Children must be able to apply this knowledge in specific situations. This application is the science of pragmatics.

Theories of Language Development

One of the most amazing aspects of human development is how quickly children learn language. Infants progress from simple cooing and babbling of sounds to the acquisition of a vocabulary of thousands of words, plus an understanding of the basic rules of syntax and grammar. How can we explain this very rapid development of language? Basically there are four different theories of language development: *biological theory*, *learning theory*, *cognitive theory*, and *interactionist theory*.

Biological Theory

Biological theory (called the **nativist view**) says that children inherit a predisposition to learn language at a certain age (Chomsky, 1968). Chomsky (1980) and McNeill (1970) maintained that infants are born into the world with a **language acquisition device** (LAD) that enables them to listen to speech and to imitate sounds and sound patterns. The LAD enables them to produce phonemes at about 6 months, the first word at about 1 year, and the first sentences at about 2 years, regardless of the child's language, race, ethnic origin, or nationality. The development of language parallels neurological changes that occur as a result of maturation. In a sense, this biological view does not explain the origins of language. All it says is that children learn language

The biological theory of language development says that children inherit a predisposition to learn language at a certain age.

because they have the neurological structure and biological equipment to learn it. If children are not exposed to a particular language, they don't learn it.

Learning Theory

Learning theory suggests that language is learned just as other behavior is learned: through *imitation, conditioning, association,* and *reinforcement* (Skinner, 1957; 1983). Children hear others talk, and then they imitate the sounds. Parents point to objects and name them, and then children repeat the words. Examples would be naming articles of clothing: "shoes," "shirts," "pants," and "socks" as each is put on. At other times when children repeat words, their behavior is reinforced with a positive response. If when children say "mama" or "dada," they are greeted with smiles, appreciation, and laughter, they are thereby encouraged to repeat the word again. Not only do they learn to associate "mama" or "dada" with their parent, but also calling mama or dada may bring food, a clean diaper, or cuddling. Their use of the word is *positively reinforced* because the repetition of it attracts their parents' attention and care. Similarly, they learn to say "bottle" when they want their milk, or they learn that saying "cookie" may bring a sweet.

Learning theory goes a long way in explaining the acquisition of language, but it does not explain everything. Children create sounds, words, phrases: "Mr. Fester, Dester,

Mester, Pester." Children seem to like the sounds they create. Or they make up words for things if they don't know the correct names. A pacifier becomes a "gully." They can compose sentences that they have never heard before: "Daddy, bye bye, big truck."

Cognitive Theory

Cognitive theory emphasizes that language develops out of mental images, that it is a direct result of cognitive development. Piaget (1926) said that children form a mental scheme and then apply linguistic labels to it. For example, the Inuit have several different words for snow. It seems plausible that they first learned to perceive different consistencies among types of snow, and then invented a vocabulary for talking about them to others. Children do the same thing. They begin to form concepts of things and actively construct their own grammar to express their thoughts. Children begin to master language near the end of the sensorimotor stage and near the beginning of the preoperational stage of cognitive development, when they use symbols to represent the environment.

Interactionist Theory

Interactionist theory emphasizes the equal importance of both biological maturation and the role of environmental influences and experiences in language development.

Clearly the role of biology is important, but developing structures must have an environment in which they can be expressed.

Influences on Language Development

It seems clear that no one theory alone explains language development. As a result, this book tends to reflect an interactionist perspective in which both biological maturation and environmental influences play important roles. A large body of research supports this point of view. It has been found, for example, that differences in children's temperament (which is partly inherited) exerts a major influence on language development from toddlerhood to middle childhood (Slomkowski et al., 1992). Extraversion or sociability increases language susceptibility and thus may be important for the development of language abilities. Phonological memory skills are also partly inherited and appear to exert a direct causal influence on language acquisition (Gathercole et al., 1992).

Environmental influences on language development are well known (Peterson & McCabe, 1994). Parental influences are especially important.

Child language measures are associated with the mother's socioeconomic status, edu-

Cooing—the initial vowel-like utterances by young infants

Babbling—one-syllable utterances containing vowels and consonants in combination

cation, and verbal intelligence (Bornstein & Haynes, 1998). Frequent dyadic interactions between infants and responsive adults are conducive to early language learning, as are mother-infant-sibling interactions (Barton & Tomasello, 1991). One study found that the time mothers spent interacting with 18- to 29-month-old children in different settings was an important influence on children's linguistic experience (Hoff-Ginsberg, 1991). The quality of parental speech also affects the quality of infants' vocalizations (Masataka, 1992). Hart and Risley (1992) divide group parenting variables that influence language development into three major categories: (1) the absolute amount of parenting per hour, (2) parents' social interaction with their children, and (3) the content quality of what parents say to their children. These factors were found to be related to the social and economic status of the family, and the subsequent IQ of the child (Hart & Risley, 1992). Another important factor is the interest that parents show in their children's language development. One study showed that when parents correct the morpheme usage of their children, the children were 2 to 3 times more likely to use correct grammar (Farrar, 1992).

Sequence of Language Development

Prelinguistic Period

Children the world over seem to follow the same timetable and sequence of language development. Table 7.1 shows the sequence through 48 months of age. During the prelinguistic period, before children actually verbalize, they seem to understand far more than they can express (Kuczaj, 1986). Even newborns come to recognize their mother's voice. Moreover, even very young infants can perceive the sounds of human speech phonetically. They demonstrate categorical perception of consonants and can perceive different vowels (Marean, Werner, & Kuhl, 1992). Crying is the first major sound uttered by the newborn. **Cooing** begins at about 2 months of age. It consists of squeals, gurgles, or vowel-like sounds of short duration such as "ahhh." Babbling begins at about 6 months of age. **Babbling** is one-syllable utterances, usually containing vowels and consonants in combinations, for example, "ma-ma-ma-ma." Most babbling is of sounds without meaning. Even deaf infants babble, so they are not imitating sounds they hear.

FOCUS

Accelerating Language Development of Mexican Day-Care Children Through Picture-Book Reading

A research study was carried out with 20 Mexican 2-year-olds (from low-income backgrounds who were attending day care) to determine the effect that reading children's books had on their language development. The children were monolingual (Spanish speaking) from Tepic, Mexico. They were read to (in Spanish), one-on-one, for 10 to 12 minutes on 30 consecutive school days, becoming very involved in discussing the stories with their teacher. The children were asked many questions and encouraged to help the teacher tell the story. Subsequent evaluations of the children's language development revealed large and enduring improvement, indicating that a dialogue-reading program is an important intervention technique in improving the language abilities of culturally deprived children (Valdez-Menchaca & Whitehurst, 1992).

Table 7.1	SEQUENCE OF LANGUAGE DEVELOPMENT

Age in Months	Language
2	Begins making vowel-like cooing sounds
4	Smiles, coos pitch-modulated, makes vowel-like sounds interspersed with consonant sounds
6	Begins babbling (one-syllable utterances), vowels interspersed with consonants
8	Often uses two-syllable utterances such as "mama" or "baba," imitates sounds
10	Understands some words, gestures (may say "no" and shake head); uses holophrases (single words with different meanings)
12	Understands some simple commands; uses more holophrases such as "baby," "bye-bye," and "hi"; may imitate sounds of dog: "bow-wow"; some control over intonation
18	Vocabulary of 3 to 50 words; may use 2-word utterances; still babbles; uses words with several syllables with intricate intonation pattern
24	Vocabulary over 50 words; 2-word phrases; interested in verbal communication
30	Rapid increase in vocabulary; uses 3- to 5-word phrases; many grammatical errors; some children hard to understand; excellent comprehension
36	Vocabulary of 1,000 words, of which 80% intelligible; colloquial grammar; fewer syntactic errors
48	Well-established language; style may differ some from adult speech

Adapted from *The First Twelve Months of Life*, by F. Caplan, 1973, New York: Grosset and Dunlap, and *Biological Foundations of Language* (pp. 128–130), by E. H. Lenneberg, 1973, New York: Wiley.

Inner Speech

Children learn to talk because they must communicate with others, make social contact, and influence surrounding individuals. Infants begin the process of developing language. At first they engage in an internal dialogue in which they talk to themselves. In adults, private speech is usually silent, but in children, especially in preschoolers, it is more likely to be uttered out loud. With time, this self-taught speech becomes a whisper and then becomes inner, private speech. Private speech helps preschoolers to think. They review what they know, decide what to do, and explain things to themselves. Some children who have learning disabilities seem to be slower to develop private speech or to use it as a guide to their behavior. An important way that language develops is this inner or private speech that takes place first. During the transitional period to external speech, the utterances referred to as ego-centric speech. Its purpose is partly to make social contact and partly to express inner thoughts. The function of language, according to Bygotsky, is to provide a bridge from the child's current understanding to a higher level of understanding.

First Spoken Words

At about 10 months of age, infants use **holophrases,** which are single words that convey different meanings, depending on the context in which they are used. Only the parents may understand what the child is saying. By 12 months of age, most infants are speaking 1 or 2 words that are recognizable language. "Mama" or "dada" may be the first words spoken. By 18 months, the average toddler knows 3 to 50 words, usually naming objects—"car"; animals—"doggie"; items of clothing—"shoes"; a part of the body—"eye"; or an important person—"mama" (Waxman & Hall, 1993). Action words such as "bye-bye," adjectives such as "hot," or adverbs such as "no" may also be included (Barrett, 1986). The number of new words that children learn depends a lot on the extent of parent-child interaction. Some parents talk to their infants all the time. They name objects (Baldwin, 1991), repeat single words and phrases, ask questions, speak in short sentences, and converse with their children whenever they are together (Hall & Waxman, 1993). Word production and comprehension increase dramatically during the second year of life (Reznick and Goldfield, 1992).

Holophrases—single words that infants use to convey different meanings

Adults tend to speak at a slower rate and with correct grammar, when talking to young children.

TABLE 7.2	MEANINGS CONVEYED IN TWO-WORD UTTERANCES

Meaning	Utterances
Identification	"See kittie"
Location	"Table there"
Repetition	"More juice"
Nonexistence	"Allgone milk"
Negation	"Not doggie"
Possession	"Katy dress"
Attribution	"Big house"
Agent action	"Baby eat"
Action object	"Hurt daddy"
Action location	"Sit potty"
Question	"Where car?"

This tendency of adults to adjust their speech when talking to children is called **parentese** (D'Odorico & Franco, 1985). When speaking to young children, adults usually use a slower rate of speech, try to speak correct grammar, usually use a higher and more varied pitch, and use more present-tense words (Cooper & Aslin, 1990). When parents say "tum-tum" for stomach, or "choo-choo" for train, they are speaking parentese. Such interaction facilitates the development of understanding and the ability to communicate. It encourages children to talk about things that they are experiencing (Cooper & Aslin, 1994).

Two-Word Utterances

Two word utterances (**duos**) usually begin when children are from 18 to 24 months of age. Children begin to combine words to express ideas that they want to communicate with others: "Amanda cry," "milk gone," "mama bye-bye." These expressions indicate knowledge of subject-predicate order. Other constructions are not acceptable English sentences: "More-water," "noup," "mamahat," "allgone soup." Two-word utterances represent attempts of children to express themselves through their own unique language (Clark, Gelman, & Lane, 1985).

Children begin to use literally hundreds of two-word utterances, expressing many different meanings. Table 7.2 shows some of the meanings possible with two-word utterances.

Telegraphic Speech

Telegraphic speech consists of two-, three-, or several-word utterances that convey meaning but exclude any unnecessary words such as articles, auxiliary verbs, conjunctions, prepositions, or other connectives. The speech is telegraphic, like a telegram that omits any unnecessary words, but still conveys meaning. "Daddy give Billy money" is an example of telegraphic speech. By 30 months of age, children are using three- to five-word phrases. Vocabulary may have grown to 1,000 words by age 3.

Sentences

From 2½ to 4 years of age, children are using multiple-word sentences (three to five words are common), each with a subject and predicate and with fewer grammatical errors. The syntax may still differ from adult speech, but improvement continues. The following are examples:

1. "She's a pretty baby."
2. "Read it, my book."
3. "Where is daddy?"
4. "I can't play."
5. "I would like some milk."
6. "Take me to the store."
7. "Ask what time it is."

Between the ages of 4 and 5, children's sentences average four to five words. They can use locative words like *over, under, in, on, up, down, here,* and *behind,* and they use more verbs than nouns (Stockman & Cooke-Vaughn, 1992). Between ages 5 and 6, sentences consist of six to eight words, including some conjunc-

Parentese—baby talk that adults use in speaking to infants

Duos—two-word utterances

Telegraphic speech—several-word utterances that convey meaning

tions, prepositions, and articles. The first interrogatives are usually "where?" and "what?", followed by "who?", "how?", and "why?" By ages 6 and 7, children's speech resembles that of adults. They can use both correct grammar and all parts of speech, and can construct compound and complex sentences.

Vocabulary and Semantics

Preschool and early-school-age children seem to soak up new words like a sponge. At about 18 months, infants are at the age of the "vocabulary spurt" or "naming explosion," a developmental milestone at which they begin to show a marked increase in the rate of addition to their productive vocabularies (Schafer & Plunkett, 1998). Their vocabulary grows from over 50 words at age 2 to between 8,000 and 14,000 words at age 6 (Smith, Jones, & Landau, 1992). Estimates of the size of children's vocabulary vary widely. We do know that vocabulary growth continues at a high rate well through adolescence and adulthood. Children learn nouns before verbs, followed by adjectives, adverbs, conjunctions, and interrogatives (Waxman & Kosowski, 1990). Basic nouns such as *cars* are learned before specific nouns such as *Porsches* or more inclusive nouns such as *vehicles* (Waxman & Senghas, 1992). On hearing a new word for an object, children have to learn whether it is a proper noun that refers to an individual (e.g., "Garfield") or a regular noun that refers to a kind of object of which the individual is a member (e.g., "cat") (Hall, 1991; Hall, 1994). By about 1 year of age, children begin to group objects from a single category: for example, they place all balls in a single pile. By 18 months of age, children begin to form multicategory groupings of all objects in an array. For example, they will place all boxes in one pile and all balls in another. This ability to categorize objects bears a close relation to naming in young children (Gopnik & Meltzoff, 1992).

One of the difficulties in obtaining an accurate assessment of the size of vocabulary is in finding an acceptable definition of what it means to "know a word." Does it mean being able to comprehend the word, to define it, or to use it in a sentence? Usually children comprehend a word before they can define it or speak it. However, their knowledge may be only partial or incorrect. Because some words have several meanings, comprehension of meanings is built slowly, usually through repeated exposure. Children learn new words by noticing how they are used, the context in

Reading to children is one of the best ways to accelerate language development.

which they are found, and their relationships to other words (Golinkoff et al., 1992). A single exposure teaches little about a word's many meanings and the subtleties of its use. Children learn new words through conversation and through reading. The more others talk and read to children, and the more children read themselves, the more opportunities they have of learning new vocabulary (Wilson, 1985). Children who are early talkers do not necessarily become early readers, but parents' reading to children contributes to the development of their reading skills (Crain-Thoreson & Dale, 1992). Children who have superior phonological skills do have an advantage in learning about spelling sequences in reading (Goswami, 1991).

Grammar

Grammar is the formal description of structure and rules that a language uses to communicate meaning. Grammar defines word form (such as singular or plural of nouns or verbs); word order in sentences; the relationship of words to one another; the use of modifiers; the use of clauses and phrases; tenses of verbs; the use of suffixes and prefixes; the subjective, objective, and possessive forms of pronouns; and the use of interrogatives and

Grammar—the formal description of structure and rules that a language uses to communicate meaning

FOCUS

Is There a Critical Period for Learning Language?

One major question in language development research is whether there is a critical period during which human beings are especially receptive to acquiring language. As we have seen in Chapter 6, brain lateralization (or localization) of language functions takes place in the left hemisphere of the brain (Kee, Gottfried, Bathurst, & Brown, 1987). One point of view is that because language lateralization in the left hemisphere begins during the early years of life, language itself must also be acquired early or it becomes impossible or difficult to learn (Witelson, 1987).

Studies of severely abused and neglected children who are not exposed to language early in childhood lend some support for this hypothesis. Historically, there have been about 60 recorded cases of children who were abandoned in the wild at an early age, but who survived and were eventually returned to human society. Among the 60 cases, 11 children (ranging in age between 4 and 18) acquired some but very immature language ability. The rest of the children never learned any language (Reich, 1986).

The most famous modern case was *Genie*, who was a normal, alert, responsive baby until 20 months of age. At that time she was kept isolated and naked in the back room of her parents' home, harnessed to a potty-chair, and able only to move her hands and feet. At night, she was laced in a kind of straitjacket and enclosed in a wire cage. She was fed sparingly by her brother, who was not permitted to talk to her. She heard only her father's doglike barking when he beat her for crying or making noise.

When she was discovered at age 13 in 1970, she had no bowel or bladder control, could not stand erect, could not chew solid food, and could neither speak nor understand language. After her release, doctors at Los Angeles Children's Hospital took care of her bodily needs and nursed her back to health. Psychologists were called in to evaluate her mental and emotional state and begin socialization, including teaching language.

Genie made some limited progress in language development. After 7 years, she learned as much language as a normal child learns in 2 to 3 years. By age 24, she lacked some of the language skills of 5-year-olds. She developed a fairly large vocabulary, could comprehend everyday conversation, but had limited knowledge of grammar, could not use some syntactic forms such as pronouns, showed poor pitch control, and was not able to use intonation to express meaning. Neurolinguistic assessments revealed that Genie used the right hemisphere of her brain to process linguistic information. Apparently, the developmental period had passed during which specialized language areas in the left hemisphere could facilitate language learning (Curtis, 1977). Nonlanguage areas in the right hemisphere were forced to take over language functioning, but never efficiently, particularly with grammar. The case of Genie gives some support to the critical period hypothesis, although it is impossible to determine the extent to which malnutrition, physical and mental abuse, and social isolation affected her language retardation (Pines, 1981).

---

negatives. Grammar includes both the correct pronunciation of words and proper intonations. Grammar is all-important in understanding language. It makes a difference whether we are told "Billy hit Johnny" or "Johnny hit Billy." Our knowledge of grammar enables us to understand who hit whom.

Children do not use adult syntactic structures immediately, but they do start showing some knowledge from the time they begin to combine words into sentences. They learn to put the subject before the verb and the verb before the object (Ferreira & Morrison, 1994). They learn singular and plural forms, verb tenses, and interrogatives such as "Where are you going?" Their understanding of negatives progresses from "no nap" to "I don't want to go to sleep because I am not tired." They learn which words can modify nouns and in what order. They will make in-

creasing use of adjectives to describe nouns, and adverbs to modify verbs, adjectives, or other adverbs. They will say, "That's a very beautiful bicycle," for example. School-age children continue to learn increasingly complex structures, such as those with conjunctions and difficult clauses: "Although Wednesday was a school day, George did not go because he was sick." They learn to sort out ideas in clauses that are embedded in sentences: "The man who is 75 years old finished painting the house."

Children younger than school age have difficulty in understanding the use of verbs in the passive voice. They are used to the subject of the sentence acting on an object, and not the subject being acted on. During the elementary school years, they learn the difference between saying "The ball was hit by the boy" and "The boy hit the ball." They learn that the ball didn't do the hitting. Romaine (1984) found that compared with 6-year-olds, 8-year-olds used the passive voice 2½ times more frequently, and 10-year-olds 3½ times more frequently.

Pragmatics

Pragmatics, the practical ability to use language to communicate with others in a variety of social contexts, is an aspect of language use that develops during the elementary school years (Ebeling & Gelman, 1994). Preschool and young school-age children may talk a lot, but they sometimes have difficulty in making themselves understood. They often begin by getting attention: "Guess what?" They may stop to see whether others are listening or whether they are understood. "Are you listening?" They may pause, start again, repeat themselves, correct themselves, or change subjects. However, they do learn to take turns in talking and to show by various means that they are listening. Parents try hard to teach them to say "please" and "thank you," not to interrupt others, and to speak respectfully to adults. The following is a conversation among second-graders (Dorval & Eckerman, 1984):

1. Well, we . . . uh . . . have paper plates . . . with turkey on it and lots of (unintelligible). You know.
2. Doo-doo-doo-doo-doo (singing).
3. I don't know what you're talking about.
4. You know what? My uncle killed a turkey.
5. Not frying pan?

Parenting Issues

When Your Child Uses Bad Language

By the age of 2 to 4, most children have picked up a number of words that their parents prefer they not use in polite company. Children seem to delight in bathroom language: "poo-poo," "ca-ca," and "wee-wee" (and large numbers of other words). They enjoy repeating them at the most inappropriate times, and soon learn that such words bring giggles from other children and that they can be used to shock parents and get their immediate attention. If parents use swear words, children pick up this language also.

With young children (preschool age), the less fuss made about such words, the better. If parents pay too much attention and act shocked, the attention that children receive acts as positive reinforcement and only encourages their using the language even more.

As children get older, they will hear a variety of sexual words and swear words from other children and adults. Four-letter slang words for sexual parts or functions sound indecent when repeated by 10-year-olds.

There are several things parents can do.

1. They need to avoid using the language themselves. If parents say it, children will say it.
2. They need to avoid being shocked. If children can shock parents, they may try to do it even more.
3. They can use correct language for sexual parts and functions. Certainly, *penis, vagina, anus,* or *urinate* don't have the negative connotations of their slang counterparts.
4. Parents need to let children know that they and other parents disapprove of the language. Parents don't need to accept "dirty talk" from children. Sometimes children use words but don't know the real meaning. Parents need to explain the meaning and why they disapprove. Usually, by discussing the issues of language with their children and setting up a few guidelines, the cooperation of children can be obtained.

Pragmatics is the practical ability to use language to communicate with others.

6. No.
7. I seen a frying pan at Hulen's store!

Children's conversation can be quite disjointed, shifting off topic and often containing many false starts ("The car . . . it was . . . uh . . . the door . . . the kid he pushed on the door. . . . They . . . uh . . . he pushed . . . he closed it hard.").

Contrast this conversation with that of fifth-graders (Dorval & Eckerman, 1984, p. 22):

1. Be quiet! Start off, Billy, what if you was the teacher?
2. OK. If I was the teacher, I'd give us less work and more time to play . . . and I'd be mean to y'all, too.

3. OK. Ann (meaning that it is her turn).
4. If I was the teacher, I'd do work . . . um. I'd sit around and watch TV. I wouldn't assign no papers . . . umm. . . .
5. I'd let y'all watch TV stories.
6. I'd turn the TV on Channel 4 at 9:30 to watch "Popeye"!

One characteristic of children's conversation at this age is that it stays with a topic.

Gender and Communication Patterns

Peer interactions are influential contexts for modeling and enforcing gender norms for social relationships and roles. Boys' interactions are often oriented around independence, competition, and dominance. In contrast, girls' interactions are generally based on cooperation, closeness, and interpersonal harmony. Girls are more likely than boys to deploy language strategies that demonstrate support, responsivity, and attentiveness. In contrast, boys use more strategies that establish dominance, give orders, and demand attention.

Gender differences in interpersonal style have been observed in children as young as 3 years of age. Preschool boys tend to use more demanding and more direct communicative strategies with their peers; preschool girls typically use more cooperative and polite strategies.

There are some gender differences in communication style.

These trends continue in children between the ages of 3 and 7 years. By age 7, children have acquired gender constancy (knowledge that one will remain a particular gender) and learned gender stereotypes. During the shift to middle childhood, interaction strategies become even more gender-differentiated. Girls become more competent in their collaborative strategies; boys remain relatively unchanged in their domineering influence patterns. Girls' use of language that emphasizes mutual cooperation and boys' use of language that emphasizes dominance reflect these learned gender stereotypes (Leaper, 1991).

Bilingualism

One half of the world's population is *bilingual*. In North America, millions of children grow up in bilingual families or in families where English is not the dominant or preferred language. Many questions arise regarding bilingualism. What effect does a second language have on the first? When should a second language be taught?

For some children in groups where their first language is a minority language, a second language may be a subtractive influence. That is, the minority children become less fluent in their first language as their language skills improve in the second. Because the second language is the dominant language, the one others speak and the one used in the community and the media, the children come to prefer it. The first language receives little support and attention outside the home; it is not taught in school, so that the children have little opportunity to read or write it (Landry, 1987). As a result, competence in the minority language suffers.

For children whose first language is the majority language, learning a second language is largely an additive experience (Cummins & Swain, 1986). Thus, English-speaking children enrolled in French- or Spanish-language programs can develop linguistic skills in the second language without interfering with their competence in English (Genesee, 1985). Good bilingual programs not only develop proficiency in a second language but also can strengthen the first language (Umbel et al., 1992).

Research indicates, however, that *instruction for minority group children should be primarily in the minority language*, with English learned as the second language. One study showed that when French minority group children were taught in French, with English taught as the second language, not only did their French become better than that of French children who were taught primarily in English, but their English became better as well (Cummins, 1986). When a person learns two languages, the process does not involve competition for mental resources (Hakuta & Garcia, 1989). Research has also shown that formal instruction in the second language can be introduced in the early elementary grades, provided that the children are already proficient in their majority language, that the teachers are bilingual and trained and skilled in language teaching, that the language to be learned and the native language are both of relatively high status in the culture, and that parents and the community are supportive of the program (McLaughlin, 1985). Unfortunately, there are parents and communities that object to the public schools' teaching a second language. Recently, a judge in Texas charged a woman with child abuse for speaking Spanish to her daughter at home. Such actions reveal deep-seated prejudices and actually work to the detriment of the children.

Some children are taught to suppress their emotions and feelings.

Parenting Issues

Talking About Feelings

The ability to talk about feelings—to communicate when distressed or happy—has major implications for children's social relationships. Language studies have revealed substantial increases in the frequency of children's references to feelings in the third and fourth years. During this period, children develop increasing ability to use their knowledge of others' thoughts, desires, and intentions to explain observed behavior and to infer how others feel in emotion-provoking situations.

In the emotionally charged atmosphere of daily family life, talk about feelings is important in children's efforts to influence their own and others' emotions. Studies of family conversations about feelings offer a unique opportunity to examine quantitative and qualitative developments in children's social interactions in the preschool period. To whom does the child relate and talk as she grows up and becomes a more capable participant in family conversations?

One longitudinal study examined the developmental changes in early conversations about feelings. Some 50 families with second-born children were observed at home when the younger siblings were 33 months old and again at 47 months of age. The mean age gap between the siblings was 43 months (range 16 to 73 months) (Brown & Dunn, 1992). The patterns of interactions between preschool children and their parents changed a great deal over the 14 months. As the siblings aged, they directed more conversation to each other and discussed feelings more often. However, when talking about feelings, each sibling usually tried to draw the other's attention to his or her own feelings. The conversation tended to be self-centered. In contrast, mother-child talk was "caretaking" in which the mother tried to comfort, acknowledging the child's hurts or fears, and referring to the child's reactions in an effort to influence the child's behavior.

Learning to Read

Learning to read is an important milestone in the total development of children. Educators are not in complete agreement as to the best ways to teach children to read. In this section, we are concerned with the total process, with various methods that are used, and with those factors that contribute to the development of this skill.

Approaches to Teaching Reading

There are essentially two different approaches to teaching reading, the **skills approach** and the **whole-language approach.**

The skills approach may include either the **phonics approach** or the **word recognition approach.** As explained earlier in this chapter, a phoneme is the smallest unit of sound in the language. In English, everything we say is

Skills approach—method of teaching reading that involves either a phonics approach or a word recognition approach

Whole-language approach—method of teaching reading that presents reading materials as a whole so the child learns the meaning of the passage before learning individual words

Phonics approach—method of teaching reading by teaching the child to sound out the various phonemes of the word

Word recognition approach—method of teaching reading by teaching the child to recognize the whole word

made up of 44 phonemes; that is, our language is generated from only 44 basic sound distinctions. There are more phonemes than letters of the alphabet because some letter combinations, such as *ch* and *th* stand for different phonemes. The phonics approach to teaching reading involves learning what sounds different letters make. Children learn that letters of the alphabet represent phonemes and that each phoneme has a particular sound. By sounding out the phonemes in a word and then combining these together, the words are distinguished. The child has learned to read a word when he or she has correctly sounded out all the letters of that word.

There is now a massive body of evidence to link the development of reading skills in children to their underlying phonological skills (Hatcher, Hulmer, & Ellis, 1994). Children who are good at phonological analysis have early reading success. Thus, the ability to learn to read suggests ability to detect phonemes (Hansen & Bowey, 1994). Phonological awareness tasks are among the best predictors

The phonics approach to learning to read teaches children to sound out the letters of words.

of reading skill and, typically, these relationships can be shown to account for significant amounts of variance in reading skill, even after the effects of intelligence have been sorted out. The relationship between phonological skill and reading skill is reciprocal. Phonological sensitivity facilitates early reading acquisition, and learning to read facilitates subsequent psychological awareness (Wagner, Torgesen, & Rashotte, 1994). One disadvantage of using the phonological approach exclusively is that children who speak dialects may make spelling errors reflecting the characteristics of their dialect, for example, the child who adds an *r* to such a word as *idea* (Treiman, Goswami, Tincoff, & Leevers, 1997).

Another skill approach in teaching reading is to teach word recognition. In this approach, which is sometimes called the "look-say" approach, the child starts with whole words and eventually begins to think about them in terms of their parts, that is, letters and sounds. By looking at the word while it is repeated, the child learns to make the same sound when he or she is looking at the word. Or sometimes a word is a description of a picture, so that the teacher can point to the picture and say, "What picture is this?" and the child then repeats the whole word. To be able to recognize words, children have attained some word-decoding skills. In recognizing the word *house*, they perhaps have used the *ou*, as well as the *h* and the *se*, in order to avoid confusing *house* with similarly spelled words. Word recognition sets the stage for increasing reading comprehension because children can now devote their mental resources to understanding the meaning of the text rather than recognizing words.

There is no question about it, the more capable children become in phonological processing, the better they are able to read. In

Parenting Issues

Stuttering

In the past, stuttering was considered a symptom of disturbed interpersonal relationships and emotional maladjustment. As a consequence, parents bore a burden of guilt for their child's problem. Currently, except in cases of a traumatic event or illness, stuttering appears to have a genetic base with environmental factors either aggravating the predisposition to stutter or helping children to overcome it. If one identical twin stutters, there is a 77% chance that the other will too. Only 1 out of 3 fraternal twins of stutterers also stutter. Stuttering seems to result from difficulty in coordinating respiration, larynx functioning, and articulation.

There are several ways parents can help.

1. Speak slowly and simply, giving children the feeling that they have more time to talk.
2. Before responding to the child's speech, allow more time after he or she talks, so that the child feels more relaxed and less hurried.
3. Minimize stress in the home, because anxiety and stress can trigger stuttering.
4. Find a quiet time during the day to talk with the children.
5. Don't overreact to early speech problems or temporary lapses in fluency. Many young children stutter over words or repeat phrases, particularly when tired or excited.
6. If the problem persists, seek professional help during the period of most rapid speech development, between ages 2 and 7. It's better to correct the problem before children become neurotic about their speech (Chollar, 1988c).

turn, early reading experience teaches phonological analysis. Here again, the relationships are reciprocal. Phonological sensitivity facilitates early reading acquisition, and learning to read facilitates subsequent phonological awareness. For this reason, many teachers teach phonics as well as word recognition because each skill enhances the abilities of the other (Wagner, Torgesen, & Rashotte, 1994).

The second major approach to teaching reading is the whole-language approach, which stresses that reading instruction should parallel children's natural language learning. Reading materials are presented as a whole. That is, in early reading instruction, children are presented with materials in their complete form, such as entire stories and poems. The whole-language approach helps children appreciate language's communicative function. Thus, children first learn the meaning of a text and then begin to abstract and arrive at word-attack skills.

From one point of view, this approach is very natural to children. They learn a story before they learn the words that comprise that story and before they learn the phonetic pronunciation of those words. This process is like leaning to play music by ear before one learns to read the notes. Proponents of the whole-language approach emphasize that it engages children in actual reading while they are acquiring basic decoding skills and not after they have undergone a long initial period of skills instruction. Critics of the whole-language approach comment that teachers sometimes underplay the need for some explicit skills instruction, certainly some instruction in phonics.

It must be stressed that the whole-language approach does not emphasize memorizing complete sentences or whole utterances. The number of permissible English sentences of 20 words or less is in the order of 10^{20}. It would take about one hundred billion centuries simply to utter these, let alone learn them by rote. What is stored, therefore, cannot be whole sentences; instead, it must be the discreet units—words—of which utterances are composed (Jusezyk, Cutler, & Redanz, 1993). Most experts agree that a balance between explicit skills instruction and experience in authentic reading offers the best approach to beginning reading.

Writing

One important advance in cognitive and motor skills in the preschool years is the development of handwriting. Children progress from producing seemingly random scribbles on a page to producing meaningful and organized forms. Mastering handwriting is so commonplace, however, that one can easily underestimate the complicated interrelationship of the cognitive, perceptual, and motor processes that underlie this skill. In the development of handwriting, one goal has been to describe the motor aspects of early writing by focusing on the grip patterns that children use. Researchers carefully chart month-by-month the changes in children's grip patterns, describing how preschool children progress from employing the Palmer grip to one characterized by finger-thumb opposition. Through a combination of physical growth and exploration of different forms of an action, children eventually settle on more stable forms or grips. Research indicates that there's a reduction in the number of grips that individual children routinely use as they get older. Of interest is that Martlew (1992) found little relation between young elementary schoolchildren's type of pen grip

FOCUS

Functional Illiteracy

Literacy is essential for functioning in industrial societies. Reading and writing skills are keys to a lifetime learning process in our society where job requirements change continuously. Moreover, literacy enables active participation in society, because many of the political and economic transactions are based on written documents. However, there are significant literacy problems in the United States. The United States ranks 49 among 159 members of the United Nations in its average level of literacy. The number of adults who are not functionally literate in the United States is estimated to be between 54 to 64 million. About one-fifth of all young adults and about one-half to one-third of minority young adults in the United States read under the eighth-grade level. The number of individuals who have levels of literacy that are not adequate for active participation in advanced society is a serious problem.

There are all degrees of functional illiteracy. Some individuals may have the ability to sign documents even though they cannot read them very well. They may be able to recognize traffic signs or extract information from television program listings. Others have skills that are insufficient for daily tasks, such as making out a check, locating dosage information on a medicine label, filling in a school registration form, or using classified advertisements. Because of the historical trend in the job market, which requires increasing proportions of jobs with higher levels of skill and literacy, functionally illiterate adults or semi-illiterate adults are ill-equipped to enter today's workforce (Baydar, Brooks-Gunn, & Furstenberg, 1993).

and how legibly they wrote letters. Clearly, the act of early writing entails more than holding a pen in an adultlike fashion. Nevertheless, by the end of the preschool period, children have begun to achieve some notable forms of relative invariance in their handwriting behavior (Greer & Lockman, 1998).

APPROACHES TO THE STUDY OF COGNITION

There are three basic approaches to the study of cognition during childhood. One is the **Piagetian approach,** which emphasizes the qualitative changes in the ways children think. A second is the **information-processing approach,** which examines the progressive steps, actions, and operations that take place when the child receives, perceives, remembers, thinks about, and utilizes information. The third approach is the **psychometric approach,** which measures quantitative changes in children's intelligence. Each of these approaches is discussed in this chapter.

A PIAGETIAN PERSPECTIVE

As discussed in Chapter 2, the Swiss developmental psychologist Jean Piaget outlined four stages of cognitive development: the *sensorimotor stage* (birth to 2 years), the *preoperational stage* (2 to 7 years), the *concrete operational stage* (7 to 11 years), and the *formal operational stage* (11 years and up). The formal operational stage is discussed in the sections of this book on adolescence.

Sensorimotor Stage (Birth to 2 Years)

Piaget (1954; 1963) labeled the first stage of cognitive development the sensorimotor period because it involves learning to respond through motor activity to the various stimuli that are presented to the senses. The child not only hears and sees a rattle but also learns how to grasp it, shake it, or suck on it (Ruff, Saltarelli, Capozzoli, & Dubiner, 1992). *The task is learning to coordinate sensorimotor sequences to solve simple problems.* Piaget has subdivided the sensorimotor period into six substages.

1. *Stage one (0 to 1 month)—exercising reflexes.* Infants use their inborn reflexes and gain some control over them. For example, they suck whatever is near their mouth or grasp

Piagetian approach

Information-processing approach

Psychometric approach

The sensorimotor period of cognitive development involves learning to respond to various stimuli through motor activity.

whatever touches their palm. They practice these and other reflexes repeatedly and become more proficient, but they can't reach out deliberately to suck or grasp the object.

2. *Stage two (1 month to 4 months)—primary circular reactions.* Infants repeat pleasurable behavior that occurs by chance (such as thumb sucking). By chance, a child's thumb touches the mouth, triggering the sucking reflex, which results in a pleasurable sensation, which leads to a repetition of the response. This circular reaction is called *primary* because it involves the child's own body.

3. *Stage three (4 to 8 months)—secondary circular reactions.* The child accidentally does something interesting or pleasing, like moving an overhead mobile. The action is then deliberately repeated to obtain the same result. (The action-reaction is circular.) It is called *secondary* because it happens outside the child's own body.

4. *Stage four (8 to 12 months)—purposeful coordination of secondary schemes.* Behavior is more deliberate and purposeful as infants coordinate motor activities with sensory input. Thus, infants will look at and grasp a rattle, or see a toy across the room and crawl to it. They begin to anticipate events and to try out previous schemes to solve problems in present situations. They will, for example, lean toward an object when trying to grasp it when their arm is too short (McKenzie et al., 1993). If they feel the distance is too great to reach across even when leaning, some children by 5 months of age will not attempt the reach (Yonas & Hartman, 1993).

5. *Stage five (12 to 18 months)—tertiary circular reactions.* In this stage, babies begin to experiment with novel actions to see what will happen rather than merely repeating behavior patterns that they have already learned. They use trial and error to find the most efficient way of reaching new goals. The stage is called *tertiary reactions* because their purpose is to explore. For example, a child will crawl into a box, then lie down in the box, and then put it on his or her head, or try to put the cat into the box.

6. *Stage six (18 to 24 months)—mental solutions.* Children begin to think about problems to find mental solutions; that is, they begin to internalize actions and their consequences, no longer relying exclusively on trial and error. Thus, they begin to develop insight into how to solve simple problems. This development is accompanied by a growing ability to use word symbols (language) in dealing with people and situations.

Object Permanence

One of the accomplishments during the sensorimotor stage is the development of a concept of **object permanence**—the knowledge that an object continues to exist independently of our seeing, hearing, touching, tasting, or smelling it (Piaget, 1954). According to Piaget, during stage three (4 to 8 months), infants will search for a partially hidden object that is already present (Baillargeon & DeVos, 1991). During stage four (8 to 12 months), infants will search for objects that have disappeared, but only in the place previously found, even if they saw it moved to a new place. During stage five (12 to 18 months), toddlers will follow a series of object displacements and will search for the object, but only where they have observed its being hidden. They can't imagine its being moved without their seeing it. And finally, during stage six, object permanence is fully developed. Toddlers can figure out where an object might be, and will look for it, though

Object permanence—the concept that an object continues to exist independently of our perceiving it

Parenting Issues

Offering Environmental Stimulation

One important requirement for mental growth is that children be reared in an intellectually stimulating environment (Pellegrini, Perlmutter, Galda, & Brody, 1990). Infants begin to get acquainted with their world from the moment of birth. If they have a variety of objects to see, touch, or taste; different sounds to hear; or different odors to smell, they learn more than if their exposure is quite limited. Sensory stimulation encourages motor learning and coordination as infants reach out to grasp or as they toddle forward. Auditory stimulation, especially exposure to words, encourages language development and speech.

But what children learn, and how much, depends not only on the amount of stimulation but also on its type, variety, intensity, regularity, duration, and timing. Children who are regularly given appropriate materials are going to learn more from their play activities over periods of time than children whose exposure is more lim-

ited. Children who are encouraged to explore the environment around them will learn faster than those who are not given much opportunity to move about. Children whose parents handle them, talk to them, and play with them will learn more than children who are left alone for long periods of time without social contacts. Parents who take their children out with them are going to increase their children's knowledge and understanding of the world to a greater extent than parents who never permit their children out of their own yard.

Maximum mental growth takes place when children are stimulated mentally from infancy on, year after year. No one year, experience, or situation is as important as what happens over several years of growth. Mental growth may accelerate when children are exposed to an enriching environment, such as that provided by a superior teacher, but growth then stops or even

reverses when children are economically and intellectually deprived for a period of time.

Of course, it is entirely possible to expose children to excessive stimulation or to experiences inappropriate to their age level. In face-to-face interactions with their infants, some parents try too hard to get their attention, resulting in an information overload that causes infants to avert their gaze and turn away. Children can tolerate only a certain amount of stimulation, after which they want to escape and not respond. The same principle holds true in the classroom. The teacher who tries to expose the students to too much material in too short a time causes them to become uninterested in further learning. The maximum learning takes place when teachers or parents take their cues from their children and expose them to as much as they can assimilate at a time and no more.

they didn't see it placed there (Bai & Bertenthal, 1992).

According to some modern researchers using different and more refined techniques, the acquisition of object permanence comes at younger ages than Piaget claimed. Baillargeon (1987) found that infants as young as 3½ months seemed to hold some primitive and short-lived memories of absent objects. But this possibility does not mean that the infants would search for objects that had not been present recently, so that there was no real sense of object permanence.

Imitation

Another characteristic of the sensorimotor stage is **imitation,** or copying the behavior of another. Reissland (1988), in an experiment with 12 neonates in the first hour after birth, found that when adults bent over the infants and either widened their lips or pursed them, the neonates moved their lips in a similar manner. Kaitz, Meschaulach-Sarfaty, Auerbach, and Eidelman (1988) found that infants 10 to 51 hours old demonstrated modeling of tongue protrusion but not of facial expressions (Jones, 1996).

Piaget (1962) maintained that imitation is not likely to occur before 9 to 12 months of age, but he was talking about **deferred imitation**—imitating someone or something no longer present. A 2-year-old who diapers her dolly in the absence of her mother is exhibiting deferred imitation. Meltzoff (1988) had a model perform 6 different actions with 6 different objects in the presence of a group of 14-month-old infants. The infants were not allowed to interact with the model and objects. One full week later, when showed the same objects, the infants showed a tendency to imitate the behavior of the model. This activity means that the infants had the ability to make mental images of the behavior, to remember it, and to do it 1 week later. This ability is important to language development and to many aspects of learned behavior.

Preoperational Stage (2 to 7 Years)

Piaget called the second stage preoperational thinking because a mental operation involves logical thought, and children at this stage do not yet have this ability to think logically. Instead, children develop the ability to deal with the world *symbolically*, or *representationally*. That is, they develop the ability to imagine doing something, rather than actually

doing it. For example, a child in the sensorimotor stage of development learns how to pull a toy along the floor. A child reaching the preoperational stage of development develops a mental representation of the toy and a mental picture of pulling the toy. If the child can use words to describe the action, the action is accomplished mentally and symbolically through the use of words. One of the major accomplishments during this period is the development of language, the ability to think and communicate by using words that represent objects and events.

Symbolic Play

Symbolic, or pretend, **play** also becomes more frequent each year of the preoperational period. A 2-year-old child may use one object (such as a teddy bear) to symbolize another (such as mommy). As children get older, they will pretend a series of events: going shopping, cooking dinner, playing house; or they will play doctor and have mommy or daddy go off to the hospital. Much of the symbolic play of 5- or 6-year-olds involves other children: playing store or army, for example (Harris, Kadanaugh, & Meredith, 1994). Pretend play peaks during the preschool years and decreases in frequency between the ages of 5 and 8. A somewhat less well-documented phenomenon is that of children's imaginary companions. Recent estimates of the frequency of children's having imaginary companions range between 25% and 65%. Here, too, the highest incidence is between 3 and 8 years of age, with most children's abandoning their

Children in the preoperational stage engage in frequent pretend play.

Imitation—copying the behavior of another

Deferred imitation—imitating someone or something no longer present

Symbolic play—using one object to represent another in play imaginary companions by the age of 10 (Woolley, 1997).

Magic and the Supernatural

Children's beliefs and fantasy figures appear to be strongest between the ages of 3 and 8. The boundary between reality and fantasy may still not be clearly drawn. Children live in their own world, in which fantasy and reality are more intertwined than they are for adults. Three-year-olds may not be sure about whether simply imagining something can cause it to come into existence. Young 3-year-olds tend to believe that imagination reflects or creates reality. In one experiment, after imagining an object to be inside an empty box, 3-year-old children claimed that the object would then appear inside the box. The researchers found that 4- to 6-year olds, when asked to pretend that a monster or a bunny was inside a box, would act as if they believed the creatures to be inside. When left alone in a room with boxes, children often peaked inside and acted afraid of the monster. In contrast to these findings, other researchers presented children with a similar situation, but they gave the children a clear message that the pretend game was over before observing their behavior and asking questions. The researchers submitted that when they made it clear to children that the pretense mode had come to an end, the children did not behave as if they believed imagination created reality (Golomb & Galasso, 1995; Harris, Brown, Marriot, Whittall, & Harmer, 1991). Children are fully able to reason rationally in a situation that appears to have practical consequences. If a child wants a cookie, it seems more likely that the child will ask for one rather than trying to get a cookie through imagining.

In one survey, parents reported that their preschool children believed that Santa Claus, the Easter Bunny, and the Tooth Fairy were real figures. Many parents feel that children should come to learn the distinction between fantasy and reality by age 5 or 6. This finding implies that parents may shift from actively encouraging the belief in certain supernatural figures to allowing children to figure things out on their own. Preschoolers also label magic tricks and extraordinary events as magic. Magic involves special powers that an individual is either born with or has bestowed on him or her by someone vested with these powers. However, by 5 years of age, children view magic as involving tricks and deception. These children view magic as a skill that can be learned through reading, from other magicians, or in special "magic" school (Rosengren & Hickling, 1994).

Transductive Reasoning

Transductive reasoning occurs when the child proceeds from particular to particular, without generalization, rather than from the particular to the general (**inductive reasoning**) or from the general to the particular (**deductive reasoning**). For example, the dog Sport jumps on you because he has done so before, and Blackie will jump on you because he is frisky like Sport, but Rex will not jump on you because he is too big (when in fact he may). An error in judgment is made because the general concept that dogs jump on you is never developed (Rice, 1990).

Syncretism

Syncretism involves making errors of reasoning by trying to link ideas that are not always related. Mother had a baby last time she went to the hospital, so the next time she goes to the hospital, she is mistakenly expected to bring home another baby (Rice, 1990).

Egocentrism

Egocentrism is the inability to take the perspective of another, to imagine the other person's point of view. Children get upset, for example, when they cannot convince their mother not to wash their dirty rag doll. They gain security from it, and that is the important thing to them, whereas to their mother the important thing is that the doll is dirty. Children are also egocentric in their attitudes about other things. Space and time are focused on them: When they walk, the moon follows them. Gradually, however, children learn to conceive of a world in time and space existing independently of themselves and, through social interaction, they learn to take into account the viewpoints of others (Rice, 1990).

Animism

Animism is ascribing lifelike qualities to inanimate objects. Children will usually ascribe life to objects that represent figures that are alive in real life: stuffed animals, toy people, and so on. They may be confused about things in nature—flowers, trees, the wind, or the moon—and talk to them or about them as though they could hear. Animism probably reveals incomplete knowledge and understanding of the world, but it is also

Transductive reasoning— proceeding from particular to particular in thought, without making generalizations

Inductive reasoning—gathering individual items of information and putting them together to form a hypothesis or conclusions

Deductive reasoning—beginning with a hypothesis or premise and breaking it down to see whether it is true

Syncretism—trying to link ideas together that are not always related

Egocentrism—the inability to take the perspective of another, to imagine the other person's point of view

Animism—ascribing lifelike qualities to inanimate objects

Planting seeds helps children see how plants grow.

a reflection of children's vivid imagination (Bullock, 1985).

Living Kinds

Early research has shown that children under 10 may not understand what it means to be a living thing. Piaget claims that young children do not understand the word *alive*; instead, children progress from having no concept of what it means to be alive to using movement as a criterion. Thus, he found that young children do not believe that plants are alive, but they do believe that the sun is alive. Preschool children either draw the living kind boundary too widely or too narrowly. Some children say that plants are alive, but those who attribute life to plants may also attribute life to inanimate objects.

Children have knowledge about some of the properties that separate living things from nonliving things. First, children know something about animal growth and plant growth. Children realize that living things grow because they take in food, not because they want to, and they realize that an animal's change in weight is affected by food intake, not by intention and desire (Backscheider, Shatz, & Gelman, 1993; Hickling & Gelman, 1995). One of the characteristics of children's increasing biological knowledge is the development of an understanding that biological processes are autonomous; that is, that they take place whether we want them to or not. In other words, children recognize that the growth of living things is beyond intentional control. Along with this, children recognize that illness is caused not by moral but by medical factors. They develop substantial knowledge of contagion and contamination as causes of illness (Blewitt, 1994; Inagaki & Hatano, 1993).

Centration

Part of the reason that preoperational children can't think logically is that they focus attention either on one aspect of a situation or on one detail, and are unable to take into account other details. This tendency is called **centration**—meaning to center on one idea at a time. For example, our 6-year-old grandson knew that his mother was coming home this morning, so he woke us up an hour earlier than usual. When told it was too early to get up, he replied, "But mommy is coming home." Or, the other day he wanted to go to the beach. When told it was cloudy, wet, and misty, he insisted that it was not and that we should go to the beach. Children of this age will get an idea in their head and completely ignore other thoughts. They fail to understand that beliefs sometimes do not match reality (Lilliard & Flavell, 1992).

Conservation

The tendency to practice centration is revealed in tasks of **conservation.** For example, children may conclude that there is more water in a shallow dish than in a glass because the dish is wider, even though they have already seen all the water poured from the glass into the dish. Figure 7.1 shows that the child has ignored the greater height of the glass and the demonstration of pouring. As a result of their inability to maintain more than one relationship in their thinking at a time, children make errors of judgment, give inadequate or inconsistent explanations, and show a lack of logical sequence in their

Centration—focusing attention on only one aspect or one detail of a situation

Conservation—the idea that properties of objects such as weight and mass stay the same regardless of how the shape or arrangement changes

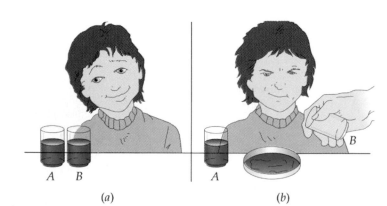

(a)   (b)

FIGURE 7.1 Understanding the principle of conservation of liquid. (a) The child agrees that glasses A and B have the same amount of water. (b) The water from B is poured into the dish. The child is unable to understand that glass A and the dish still have the same amount of water, because the dish appears broader even though it is shallower. The child is unable to retain one aspect (the amount) when another aspect changes (the height of the water column and the width of the column).

arguments and a lack of comprehension of constants. Similarly, other tests of conservation of numbers, volume, length, or area are beyond the cognitive ability of preschoolers (Rice, 1999).

However, by the age of 3, children can understand that matter can be decomposed into tiny pieces by being dissolved in liquid, and that this matter still exists even though it cannot be seen with the naked eye. This concept is important in understanding things like germs that are too small to be seen (Kit-fong Au, Sidle, & Rollins, 1993; Rosen & Rozin, 1993).

Classification

Classification means that objects can be thought of in terms of categories or classes (Jones, Smith, & Landau, 1991). Preoperational children are somewhat limited in their ability to classify objects according to categories (Waxman, Shipley, & Shepperson, 1991). Suppose that children are shown 7 cats of different breeds: 4 Siamese, 1 Persian, 1 tiger, and 1 Maine coon. The examiner makes certain that the children know the animals are all cats and that the children can name each

Classification—arranging objects into categories or classes

FOCUS

Research on Abilities During the Preoperational Stage

A vast amount of research has been conducted to determine children's cognitive abilities during the preoperational stage. Some of these findings are summarized here.

Two-and-one-half-year-old children have difficulty appreciating the relation between a scale model and the larger figure that it represents, although they understand the relation between a picture and its referent (DeLoache, 1991).

Knowing the location of things, such as the location of food, shelter, or danger, is necessary for survival. Three-, four-, and five-year-olds can code spatial locations in terms of a frame of spatial reference and can use these codings to answer questions about occupied points and locations stored in memory. They can clearly indicate locations relative to another position (Newcombe and Huttenlocher, 1992).

The concept of the distance between two points is fundamental to mature notions of space. Only about 40% of 4-year-olds are able to say that a direct route between two points is shorter than an indirect route because it is straight and the indirect route is not (Fabricius & Wellman, 1993).

Children as young as age 6 can make some proportional judgments. They can discriminate between less than half and more than half.

Their recognition of "half" may eventually lead them to the understanding of part-whole relations (Spinillo & Bryant, 1991).

From ages 3 and older, children understand that animals grow larger over time. They are able to think beyond present appearances and make judgments about transformations caused by growth (Rosengren et al., 1991).

What a person believes has a causal impact on his or her actions, statements, and emotions. The ability to recognize false beliefs, to recognize those perspectives that run counter to reality, is important in avoiding unreasonable actions. Children's understanding of false beliefs and deceptive ploys emerges at about 4 years of age. Two- and three-year-olds will participate in removing true trails and laying false ones to mislead someone about the location of a hidden object, but they show no clear understanding of the effect of their deception on others (Sodian et al., 1991).

Adults recognize that other people can have beliefs different from their own and that these mental representations of things can be different from the things themselves. Not so with 3-year-olds. When children of ages 3, 4, and 5 were told or shown that characters in children's stories held different beliefs from their own or from one another, the 3-year-olds had difficulty in attribut-

ing to others deviant beliefs of all types (Flavell et al., 1992). Beginning about age 6, children understand that even though different people all hear the same message, individuals may perceive it differently (Montgomery, 1993).

By 4 or 5 years of age, children begin to develop a crude understanding of the biological implications of kinship, that family members share more biological properties than unrelated members of the same species, even though the latter look alike or have social ties (Springer, 1992).

In one study, four 7-year-old children were told a story in which a boy was born to one man and adopted by another. The biological father was described as having one set of features (e.g., green eyes) and the adoptive father as having another (e.g., brown eyes). Subjects were asked which man the boy would resemble when he grew up. It was not until age 7 that children substantially associated the boy with his biological father on physical features and his adoptive father on beliefs. That is, it was not until age 7 that children demonstrated that they understood birth as part of a process selectively mediating the acquisition of physical traits and learning or nurturance as mediating the acquisition of beliefs (Solomon, Johnson, Zaitchik, & Carey, 1996).

breed. The children are then asked, "Are there more Siamese or more cats?" Until about 7 or 8 years of age, most children will reply, "More Siamese." They cannot segregate the concept of cats from the subclassification "Siamese." They do, however, have some ability to categorize according to different properties (Kalish and Gelman, 1992). Even 3-year-olds will categorize a given object, depending on the property in question.

Irreversibility

Preoperational children also make errors in their thinking because of **irreversibility,** that is, their inability to recognize that an operation can go both ways. For example, they do not understand that if water is poured from a tall container into a flat container, it can also be poured back again, keeping the same amount of water. Preoperational children cannot mentally accept that the original state can be regained (Rice, 1990).

Concrete Operational Stage (7 to 11 Years)

During the concrete operational stage, children show a greater capacity for logical reasoning, though still at a very concrete level (Jacobs & Potenza, 1991). The child's thinking is still linked to empirical reality (Piaget, 1967a). Inhelder and Piaget (1958) wrote: "Concrete thought remains essentially attached to empirical reality. . . . Therefore, it attains no more than a concept of 'what is possible,' which is a simple (and not very great) extension of the empirical situation" (p. 250). Children have made some progress toward extending their thoughts from the actual toward the potential (Elkind, 1970), but the starting point must still be what is real because concrete operational children can reason only about those things with which they have had direct, personal experience. When children have to start with any hypothetical or contrary-to-fact proposition, they have difficulty. They can distinguish between hypothetical belief and evidence, but they fail to test hypotheses in a systematic, scientific way (Sodian, Zaitchik, & Carey, 1991).

Elkind (1967) also pointed out that one of the difficulties at this stage is that the child can deal with only two classes, relations, or quantitative dimensions at the same time. When more variables are present, the child flounders.

However, concrete operational children are able to arrange objects into **hierarchical classifications** and comprehend **class inclu-**sion relationships** (the inclusion of objects in different levels of the hierarchy at the same time). This comprehension gives children the ability to understand the relations of the parts to the whole, the whole to the parts, and the parts to the parts. Suppose children are given a randomly organized array of yellow and red squares and black and white circles. If they understand inclusion relationships, they discover that there are two major collections (squares and circles) and two subtypes of each (yellow versus red squares and black versus white circles). There is a hierarchy whose higher level is defined by shape and whose lower level is defined by color. This enables the children to say that all the squares are either yellow or red, that there are more squares than just yellow squares, that there are more squares then just red squares, and that if you take away the red squares, the yellow ones are left, and so on.

The ability to group things into categories enables children to expand their scope of knowledge through category-based inductions. They are able to conclude that a property that is true of some category members may also be true of other category members. For example, humans have tonsils, therefore gorillas probably have tonsils. Without categories, children would have to learn about each instance anew, being unable to benefit from past instances. Inductive inferences allow them to set forth assumptions, make predictions, and generalize from the known to the unknown, extending knowledge beyond the range of direct experience (Farrar, Raney, & Boyer, 1992; Lopez et al., 1992).

Concrete operational children are capable also of **serialization,** serial ordering. They learn that different objects may be grouped by size, or by alphabetical order.

Conservation refers to the recognition that properties of things such as weight or volume are not altered by changing their container or shape. Conservation tasks involve some manipulation of the shape of matter without altering its mass or volume (Pieget & Inhelder, 1969). A typical conservation problem is represented by the ball of clay in Figure 7.2.

Muuss (1988b) summarizes four concrete operations the child is able to perform:

1. **Combinativity.** This represents the ability to combine two or more classes into one larger, more comprehensive class. For example, all men and all women equal all adults; A is larger than B and B is larger than C can be combined into a new statement that A is larger than C.

Irreversibility—failure to recognize that an operation can go both ways

Hierarchical classification—arranging objects into categories according to level

Class inclusion relationships—the inclusion of objects in different levels of hierarchy at the same time

Serialization—arranging objects into a hierarchy of classes

Combinativity—ability to combine two or more classes into one larger class

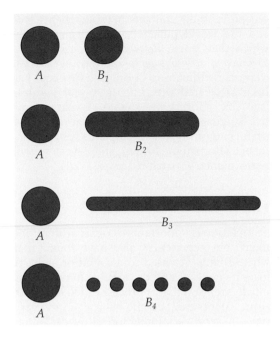

FIGURE 7.2 Conservation of mass. In this example, the child is asked to confirm that A and B$_1$ are the same size. Then B$_1$ is changed to B$_2$, then to B$_3$, then to B$_4$. The child is asked to compare A with B$_2$, then with B$_3$, and with B$_4$, each time stating whether A and B are still the same. Children in the preoperational stage are guided by the shapes they see. Children in the concrete operational stage preserve recognition of the equal quantity between A and B that transcends their physical shape.

2. **Reversibility.** This is the concept that every operation has an opposite operation that reverses it. Supraclasses can be taken apart, reversing the effect of combining subclasses. All adults except all women equal all men.

3. **Associativity.** The child whose operations have become associative can reach a goal in various ways . . . but the results obtained . . . remain the same. For example, (3 plus 6) plus 4 equals 13, and 6 plus (3 plus 4) equals 13.

4. **Identity or nullifiability.** This is the understanding that an operation that is combined with its opposite becomes nullified, resulting in no change. An example is that to give 3 and take away 3 results in null (Muuss, 1988b, p. 185).

Vygotsky's Theory of Cognitive and Language Development

Over the past decade there has been a major upsurge of interest in the ideas of the Russian psychologist L. S. Vygotsky (1896–1934).

Perhaps the major reason for Vygotsky's current appeal in the West is his analysis of the social origins of mental processes (Wertsch and Tulviste, 1992). *In Vygotsky's views, mental functioning primarily is derived, not from maturation, but from social and cultural influences.* To Vygotsky, the social dimensions of consciousness are primary; the individual dimensions are derivative and secondary. Instead of beginning with the assumption that mental functioning occurs first and foremost within the individual (intramentally), Vygotsky emphasizes that mental processes occur between people on an intermental plane. Intramental functioning is a derivative, emerging through the mastery and internalization of social processes. As a result of Vygotsky's influence, psychologists now speak of *socially shared cognition* (Resnick, Levine, & Behrend, 1991), *socially distributed cognition* (Hutchins, 1991), and *collective memory* (Middleton, 1987). Mental functioning is viewed as a kind of action carried out by dyads or larger groups.

This concept is basic to Vygotsky's idea of the **"zone of proximal development"** (ZPD). The ZPD is Vygotsky's term for tasks too difficult for children to master alone that need to be mastered with the guidance and assistance of others. The zone is the distance between the child's actual development level reached through individual problem solving, and the higher level of potential development as determined through problem solving under adult guidance or in collaboration with more capable peers (Vygotsky, 1978). Vygotsky argued that measuring the child's potential level of development is just as important as measuring the actual level, since instruction needs to be tied closely to the level of potential development. To Vygotsky, the actual level of functioning corresponds to intramental processes; the potential level of functioning derives from intermental processes. The goal is to improve and change intramental functioning through reciprocal teaching.

Vygotsky also had important things to say about language development. Vygotsky said that *language and thought initially develop independently of each other, but eventually merge.* Children learn to talk because they must communicate with others, make social contact, and influence surrounding individuals. Gradually, beginning in the preschool years, children make a transition from *external speech* to *inner speech.* Inner speech is the child talking to himself or herself and becomes the child's thoughts. Children seem to acquire the knowledge and awareness of their own inner speech (Flavell, Green, Flavell, & Grossman, 1997). Speech during

Reversibility—the concept that every operation has an opposite operation that reverses it

Associativity—the understanding that operations can reach a goal in various ways

Identity or nullifiability—the understanding that an operation that is combined with its opposite becomes nullified

Zone of proximal development—the distance between a child's actual development level reached through individual problem solving, and a higher level of potential development

the transitional period is referred to as *egocentric speech*. Its purpose is partly to make social contact and partly to express inner thoughts. The more the child engages in self-talk, the more the ideas become a part of himself or herself that can be acted on without further verbalizing. Eventually, egocentric speech is internalized and becomes the inner speech or the thoughts of the child. Vygotsky claimed that inner speech enables humans to plan and regulate their action and derives from previous participation in verbal social interaction (Wertsch and Tulviste, 1992).

INFORMATION PROCESSING

The *Piagetian approach* to cognition describes the stages involved in the development of logical thinking. The *information-processing approach* describes the way that children obtain information, remember it, retrieve it, and use it in solving problems. These abilities during the first year of life have been found to be predictive of both specific cognitive abilities and IQ at 6 years of age (Rose, Feldman, & Wallace, 1992).

Information processing has often been compared with the actions of a computer. Information is coded and fed into a computer in an organized way, and then it is stored in the memory banks. When any of that information is required, the computer is asked to produce it. The machine searches for the relevant information and reproduces or prints out the items requested.

Information processing by children is basically similar but far more sophisticated. The child receives information, organizes it, stores it, retrieves it, thinks about it, and combines it to answer questions, solve problems, and make decisions. The most elaborate computer used in creating *artificial intelligence* cannot match the capacity of the human mind and nervous system in the input and output of information. Each new generation of computers is more advanced than the last. Similarly, as each year passes, the child's ability to process information increases, partly because of the continued development of the brain and nervous system, and partly because of the learning experience and practice that improve mental abilities and strategies (Goodman & Haith, 1987; Teyler & Fountain, 1987).

Stimuli

Before information can be processed, it must be received. Children are constantly bombarded with stimuli. Their senses are their receptors, their contacts between themselves and the world outside, and the method by which they learn. *Research has shown the importance of stimulation in the learning process.* Maternal stimulation during the first year has been associated with infants' 1-year vocabulary size (Bornstein, 1985a), 2-year cognitive/language competence, 3-year language performance, 4-year intelligence test performance (Bornstein, 1985a), and 6-year school performance (Coates & Lewis, 1984).

Habituation

Stimulation is important to cognitive development, but researchers also have found that when infants get used to a sound or sight, it loses its novelty, and the infants do not pay as much attention to it, a process called **habituation.** Infants can become habituated to every type of sensory stimulation (Rovee-Collier, 1987b). Furthermore, this tendency becomes increasingly developed during the first 3 months of life (Lipsitt, 1986). It is important in parent-infant interaction that parents repeat stimuli to facilitate learning, but once children stop responding, the parents need to stop or change the type of stimulation.

Habituation is important because it has been used to measure infants' sensory perception, memory, and neurological health. It can have important implications for a child's present and future cognitive, emotional, and social development (Dunham, Dunham, Hurshman, & Alexander, 1989). Habituation assessments during the first year are predictive of later IQ (McCall & Carriger, 1993). For example, habituation in the first 6 months of life has been reported to explain 59% of the variance in indexes of childhood intelligence between 2 and 8 years (Bornstein & Sigman, 1986; Tamis-LeMonda & Bornstein, 1986). Babies with low Apgar scores, brain damage, or Down's syndrome show impaired habituation.

Selective Attention

Another important factor in learning is that children don't pay equal amounts of attention to everything. *They attend selectively to stimuli, with dramatic increases in selectivity with age.* One study showed that when 5- to 6-year-old children were shown a videotape of a routine medical exam, they showed reduced memory for events witnessed in the tape when it showed children in distress. The children witnessing the distress became upset themselves and did not pay attention to other

Habituation—the tendency to adapt to a repeated stimulus and to lose interest in it

events that were happening (Bugental et al., 1992). The older the children, the more they develop a selective strategy, that is, they are better able to sort out relevant from nonrelevant information, and to learn more efficiently (DeMarie-Dreblow & Miller, 1988; Woody-Ramsey & Miller, 1988).

Memory

The ability to remember is basic to all learning. Without memory, we would never be able to recall or recognize what we have already experienced. We would not be able to accumulate a body of useful knowledge, to learn from past mistakes, or to think and reason intelligently. Memory is a central part of information processing. Although memory depends partly on knowledge (something can't really be remembered unless it is first known), the process is more complicated, because it also involves the capacity to recall (DeMarie-Dreblow, 1991). Memory ability also is related to IQ (Schneider & Bjorklund, 1992).

Infant Memory

Studies of infants reveal some memory ability from the early weeks of life (Borovsky & Rovee-Collier, 1990; Perris, Myers, &

FOCUS

Distractibility

Every parent knows that young children are easily distracted by competing stimuli (Pillow, 1988). Toddlers may start to do one thing, be attracted to something else, and then turn their attention to the second thing. As a result, it is hard to get them to focus their attention on any one activity for very long (Ruff, Lawson, Parrinello, & Weissberg, 1990). In contrast, preschool children may be able to focus their attention for much longer periods. In one experiment, 3- and 5-year-old children were observed as they watched a 58-minute "Sesame Street" program on television. They were distracted during the program by the presentation of attractive pictures projected through colored slides. Altogether, the children watched the television during 43% of the program, with older children paying more visual attention (47%) than younger children (35%) (Anderson, Choi, & Lorch, 1987). The attention span of children increases even more dramatically with age between early preschool and early elementary school age.

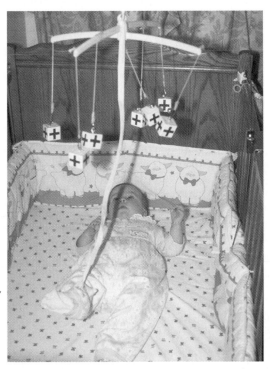

The infant quickly learned which leg kicked the mobile and two weeks later remembered how to make the mobile move.

Clifton, 1990). Newborns can distinguish different speech sounds and odors, and by one month of age they can distinguish their mother's face from other faces. These abilities are evidence of memory (Cernoch & Porter, 1985; Rovee-Collier, 1987a). Rovee-Collier (1987a) hung a mobile over an infant's crib and attached a ribbon from the mobile to one of the baby's legs. The 6-week-old infant quickly learned which leg would move the mobile. Two weeks later the child was put into the crib and, as a "reminder," was allowed to look at the mobile without having the ribbon attached. The next day, with the ribbon reconnected, the infant kicked to move the mobile as it had learned to do two weeks before. Obviously, it had remembered the behavior previously taught (Hayne & Rovee-Collier, 1995; Linde, Morrongiello, & Rovee-Collier, 1985).

Infants are also able to remember objects that they have seen and touched previously. Haptic processing, which involves the use of touch to convey information about the features and identity of objects, relies principally on input from kinesthetic receptors in the hands and fingers. Infants can retain haptic information at least for a brief period beyond initial exposure (Catherwood, 1993).

The ability to remember is facilitated if infants are tested in the same context in which they first learned. For example, the same context might mean the same room or the same crib (Amabile & Rovee-Collier, 1991), or use of the same test equipment (Rovee-Collier et al., 1992; Shields & Rovee-Collier, 1992; Singer & Fagen, 1992). Other research has shown that by late in the first year of life, children are able to remember the sequence of specific events (Bauer & Hertsgaard, 1993; Bauer & Mandler, 1992).

The memory of infants is fairly short-lived, however. Without a repetition of the stimuli, the memory trace fades fairly quickly (Hayne, Rovee-Collier, & Perris, 1987). Reenacting events or parts of events can remind very young children of past experiences and inoculate against forgetting over very long periods of time (Hudson & Sheffield, 1998). Infants have to be over 7 months of age before they will search for objects that have disappeared. One mother reported that her 9-month-old daughter was looking for ribbons. She looked first in the old drawer from which they had been removed. She then looked in other drawers until she found them. The next day she went directly to the new drawer to find the ribbons.

The duration of a memory of a stimulus is affected by the amount of attention allocated to it during encoding. Deeper processing is thought to be associated with stronger encoding, which thereby increases the duration of retention of the memory, whereas shallow processing is thought to be associated with weaker encoding, which thereby decreases the duration of retention of the memory. Deeper encoding or processing is accomplished by repeated exposure to stimuli or by increasing the length of time of exposure to stimuli (Adler, Gerhardstein, & Rovee-Collier, 1998).

These early memories are not permanent, however. *Only a few people can recall events that happened prior to 3 years of age.* We don't remember being born; we don't remember nursing, crawling, starting to walk, or the birth of a sibling 2 or 3 years younger than

we are. I have a sister who is 4 years younger than I am. I can remember my mother's nursing her. I can remember my first day in kindergarten at age 5, but very little before that. This phenomenon is known as **infantile amnesia,** the essential lack of memory of events experienced before 3 years of age.

One study of 9- and 10-year-old children measures their ability to remember the faces of former preschool classmates. Recognition of faces was at a low level but significantly above chance. This study shows that infantile amnesia may not always involve complete loss of encoded information (Newcombe & Fox, 1994).

Memory Capacity and Storage

The process of remembering involves a series of steps. The most widely accepted model is a three-stage one: **sensory storage, short-term storage,** and **long-term storage.** Information is seen as passing from one compartment to another, with decreasing amounts passed on at any one time to the next stage (Rice, 1990). Figure 7.3 illustrates the three-stage model of memory. Information is held only briefly (as little as a fraction of a second) in sensory storage before the image begins to decay or is blocked out by other incoming sensory information. Information that has not already faded from the sensory storage is read out to the short-term storage, where it may be held for up to 30 seconds. Because of the limited capacity of the short-term storage, information to be held longer must be rehearsed and transferred to the relatively permanent long-term storage. For all practical purposes, long-term storage capacity is infinite. In the process of retrieval, stored information is obtained by searching, finding, and remembering, either through **recall** (remembering without cues) or **recognition** (remembering with cues). Memory efficiency depends on all three of these processes.

Sensory Storage

In sensory storage, no cognitive processing takes place. Our senses of vision, hearing, taste, smell, or touch are momentarily stimulated. We pay attention to some of the stimuli, then the sensation fades. Some significant information is passed on to the short-term storage.

Short-Term Storage

Short-term storage involves very little processing of information. As a result, it is not remembered for longer than about 30 seconds.

Infantile amnesia—the lack of memory of events experienced before age 3

Sensory storage—the process by which information is received and transduced by the senses, usually in a fraction of a second

Short-term storage—the process by which information is still in the conscious mind and being rehearsed and focused on

Long-term storage—the process by which information is perceived and processed deeply so that it passes into the layers of memory below the conscious level

Recall—remembering without cues

Recognition—remembering after cues have been given

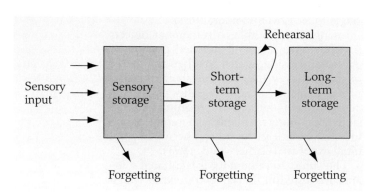

FIGURE 7.3   Three-stage model of memory.

Furthermore, it involves the equivalent of only about 7 digits—the same amount of data as in a local telephone number. Siegler (1989) suggests that children are often unable to solve certain problems because they can't keep all the relevant information in mind long enough. Obviously, they have not rehearsed it long enough to put it in long-term storage.

Short-term memory ability increases during childhood (Raine, Hulme, Chadderton, & Bailey, 1991). One way to measure short-term memory is to ask subjects to repeat a series of digits that they have heard repeated at a fairly rapid rate. In one study, 2- to 3-year-old children were able to remember 2 digits. By 9 years of age, the children were able to repeat 6 digits. After that, the number remembered continued to increase, but at a much slower rate, so that 12-year-olds could repeat 6½ digits and adults could repeat about 7 (Dempster, 1981). As mentioned, short-term memory capacity is usually about 7 digits. *The short-term memory span is fairly constant throughout adolescence and adulthood.*

Long-Term Storage

Long-term memory contains information that is processed deeply (for example, it is rehearsed and repeated until it is thoroughly familiar) and stored on a fairly permanent basis. Unlike short-term memory, *long-term memory increases fairly rapidly with age during middle and late childhood; it continues to increase until young adulthood* (Price & Goodman, 1990). Research has shown that children as young as 3 years of age have well-organized memories of events and that they remember the events over a long period of time (Bauer & Hertsgaard, 1993).

A life-span study of memory for pictures was conducted for 7-year-olds, 9-year-olds, young adults, and older adults over 68 (Pezdek, 1987). Subjects were presented simple and complex line drawings and then tested with the same and changed forms of these pictures, at both 5-second and 15-second presentation rates. For each test picture, the experimenter asked, "Is this picture the same as a picture you saw before, or are there some changes in the picture?" The questions were asked long enough after the picture was presented (3 minutes) to ensure that the test measured long-term memory. Figure 7.4 shows examples of pictures in both simple and complex forms. Figure 7.5 shows the percentage correct, by age group, when the test pictures presented were complex forms of simple pictures. The graph shows the results of both 5-second and 15-second presen-

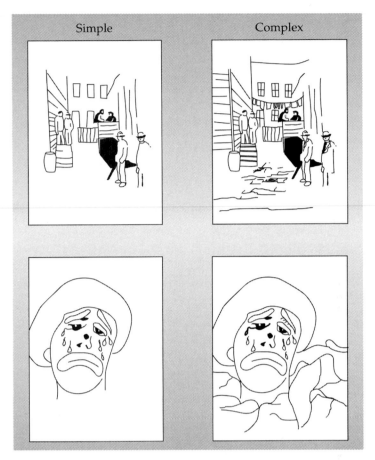

| Simple | Complex |

FIGURE 7.4   Examples of pictures in both simple and complex forms.

Data from "Memory for Pictures: A Life-Span Study of the Role of Visual Detail," by K. Pezdek, 1987, *Child Development, 58,* pp. 807–815.

tation rates. As can be seen, the ability of subjects to remember the pictures increased from age 7 to college age, then declined in older adults over 68 years of age. For all age groups, pictures presented in their simple form were recognized more accurately than pictures presented in their complex form. Also, memory for pictures increased as the exposure duration per picture increased. Longer study intervals allowed for greater efficiency in encoding and storing the information on picture details. Other research shows that with increasing age, up to young adulthood, individuals execute cognitive processes more rapidly (Kail, 1992). This research indicates that memory ability increases from early childhood to young adulthood (Brainerd & Reyna, 1995).

Investigations of children's and adults' memory for television stories indicate that the overall number of events that are recalled increases with age but, of more importance, that the age groups differ in their patterns of recall as well. Older participants more strongly

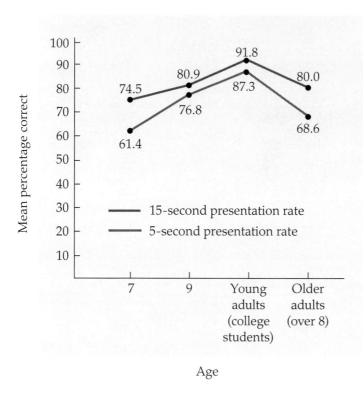

FIGURE 7.5   Memory for pictures by age of subject.

Data from "Memory for Pictures: A Life-Span Study of the Role of Visual Detail," by K. Pezdek, 1987, *Child Development, 58*, pp. 807–815.

emphasize idea units that are part of the story from beginning to end. Children may focus more on certain events, especially action events that are part of the story, rather than on the ideas themselves. As children grow older, they become more attuned to the importance of the goals and intentions of the actors and the events that set the entire train of action in the story in motion (van den Broek, Lorch, & Thurlow, 1996). Memory for specific events increases if there is a repetition of the experience (Powell & Thomson, 1996).

Other research shows that levels of memory performance are overall greater for high-IQ than for low-IQ children but that the levels of performances can be enhanced as a result of training. Individual differences in knowledge base can compensate for some differences in memory ability. For example, third-grade soccer experts had higher levels of recall from a soccer story than did fifth- and seventh-grade soccer novices (Bjorklund, Schneider, Cassel, & Ashley, 1994).

Metamemory

Metamemory consists of knowledge of memory strategies that people employ to learn and remember information. There are

a number of **mnemonic,** or memory-aiding, strategies that are useful (Best, 1993). One is *rehearsal,* the repetition of information to be remembered. This helps to process information deeply and to store it in long-term memory. Another way to aid memory is through *organization.* Material can be arranged by categories (for example, animals), alphabetically, or in some other logical order. **Chunking** consists of dividing material into meaningful parts. Thus, it is easier to remember the telephone number 1-516-799-4362 than it is to remember 15167994362. Material can also be *coded:* for example, by color. A map with its symbols is a good illustration of visual representation of roads, cities, railroads, rivers, highways, and so forth. Children often use codes to make maps or posters. A code may also be audible, such as the ringing of a timer bell to remind a child that it's bedtime.

Another mnemonic device is to provide children with *memory cues:* for example, the letters representing notes on a music staff, shown in Figure 7.6. The letters F A C E refer to the notes between the lines. The letters E G B D F are the first letters of the words in the phrase "Every Good Boy Does Fine." These letters represent the notes on the lines.

Another way to remember material is by *visualizing position or place:* the so-called **method of loci.** Children often remember material they have read by visualizing its position on a page of their textbook. Children are also better able to remember material or events that are *meaningful and familiar* (Farrar & Goodman, 1992; Fivush, Kuebli, & Clubb, 1992). They would have more trouble remembering the letters NOTGNIHSAW than they would the letters WASHINGTON, unless they were able to recognize that NOTGNIHSAW is WASHINGTON backwards. If children are motivated to learn

Metamemory—knowledge of memory strategies that people employ to learn and remember information

Mnemonic—memory-aiding

Chunking—dividing material into meaningful parts to remember it

Method of loci—remembering by visualizing the position of something

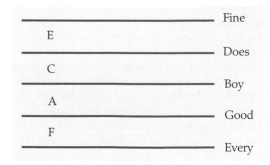

FIGURE 7.6   Cues to remember notes on a music staff.

When rooms are well-organized, children are better able to remember where things go and to put them away.

material because it is either *interesting* or *important*, it's surprising how much they can learn and remember (Lorch, Bellack, & Augsbach, 1987). They may never learn material that they are not interested in. In support of this assertion, it has been found that preschool children have extremely good memories for stories or for social or family events. In one study, children were told a detailed story about two boys who had lunch at McDonald's. The children were later asked to identify which words from a list were in the story. The memory of these children was extremely accurate (Mistry & Lange, 1985). Researchers have found that the use of *mnemonic devices* increases from preschool years through adolescence (Brown, Bransford, Ferrara, & Champione, 1983). Teachers can play an important role in teaching memory strategies to children in their classrooms (Lange & Pierce, 1992; Moely et al., 1992).

INTELLIGENCE

So far we have discussed two approaches to the study of cognition: the *Piagetian approach* and the *information-processing approach*. The third approach, discussed here, is the *psychometric approach*. This is a quantitative approach, which is concerned with the level of intelligence as measured by test scores, with those changes that take place in the level of intelligence, and with the factors that influence that level over a lifetime.

Views of Intelligence

To measure successfully the quantity or level of intelligence, it is necessary to know what intelligence is. Unfortunately, psychologists are not in complete agreement as to what constitutes intelligence.

Binet

One of the first persons to address the problem was *Alfred Binet* (1857–1911), a professor of psychology at the Sorbonne, the University of Paris. In the 1890s, he was asked by the Paris Ministry of Education to develop a test to sort out those children who were slow learners and who could not benefit from regular classroom instruction. The result was the creation of an intelligence test that was later revised and translated in America to become the current, widely used *Stanford-Binet Intelligence Scale*. To Binet, intelligence was a general capacity for comprehension, reasoning, judgment, and memory (Binet & Simon, 1916). Binet described this capacity as **mental age (MA):** the level of development in relation to **chronological age (CA).** The higher MA is in relation to CA, the brighter the child. The German psychologist *William Stern* originated the term **IQ, intelligence quotient,** which is calculated as follows:

$$IQ = \frac{MA}{CA} \times 100$$

Mental age (MA)—measure that expresses the intellectual level of a person

Chronological age (CA)—age in years

Intelligence quotient (IQ)—MA divided by CA × 100

Parenting Issues

Children's Memory for Spatial Locations in Organized and Unorganized Rooms

Every parent is faced with the task of teaching children orderliness by putting things back where they belong and then remembering where they are (Plumert, Pick, Marks, Kintsch, & Wegesin, 1994). One study of children from 3 years of age through the second grade showed that children remembered the spatial location of an object if they had seen the item in a logically organized room, as opposed to an unorganized one (Golbeck, 1992). Logical organization meant clustering together in space those objects sharing functional or abstract properties. Even 3- and 4-year-olds remembered where an object could be found if they had previously seen that object in an organized arrangement. *Moral:* If parents want to teach children to put things away and to remember where to put them, they first need to organize those things in the room (Bushnell, McKenzie, Lawrence, & Connell, 1995; Plumert, Ewert, & Spear, 1995).

If *MA* is equal to *CA*, *IQ* is 100. If *MA* is greater than *CA*, then *IQ* is over 100. If *MA* is less than *CA*, the *IQ* is under 100.

Spearman

In England, *Charles Spearman* (1863–1945) advanced a **two-factor theory of intelligence** (Spearman, 1927). He concluded that there is a *general intellectual factor* that he labeled *g*, and a number of *specific abilities—s* factors—that are useful for different tasks: for example, arithmetic or spatial relations.

Thurstone

This concept of many kinds of intelligence was expanded by *Louis Thurstone* (1887–1955), a mathematician who worked in Thomas Edison's laboratory. Thurstone believed that even though persons were intelligent in one area, they were not necessarily intelligent in other areas (Thurstone, 1938). Thurstone's research enabled him to identify seven distinct **primary mental abilities:**

1. verbal meaning
2. perceptual speed
3. logical reasoning
4. number
5. rote memory
6. word fluency
7. a spatial or visualization factor

These factors were tested separately in the *Primary Mental Abilities Test.* A version was eventually developed for young schoolchildren (Thurstone & Thurstone, 1953). After additional research, Thurstone found that his primary mental abilities correlated moderately with one another, so he eventually acknowledged a *g* factor as well as the individual primary factors.

Guilford

More recently, *J. P. Guilford* (1967) expanded the idea of specific abilities by identifying 120 factors in intelligence. Although other psychologists agree that there are different kinds of intelligence, they disagree as to the number.

Gardner

Howard Gardner (1983) divides intelligence into seven dimensions:

1. Linguistic intelligence—verbal abilities.
2. Logical mathematical intelligence—ability to reason logically and to use mathematical symbols.
3. Spatial intelligence—ability to form spatial images and to find one's way around in an environment. The sailors in the Caroline Islands of Micronesia navigate among hundreds of islands using only the stars and their bodily feelings.
4. Musical intelligence—ability to perceive and create pitch and rhythmic patterns. There are individuals who are otherwise mentally retarded who can play a song on the piano after hearing it once.
5. Body-kinesthetic intelligence—the gift of graceful motor movement as seen in a surgeon or dancer.
6. Interpersonal intelligence—understanding of others, how they feel, what motivates them, and how they interact.
7. Intrapersonal intelligence—individual's ability to know himself or herself and to develop a sense of identity.

Gardner's concept is unique because he claims independent existences for different intelligences in the human neural system. He would like to stop measuring people according to some unitary dimension called intelligence. Instead, he would like to think in terms of different intellectual strengths.

Sternberg

Robert Sternberg (1985) and his colleagues at Yale University arranged abilities into the following three major groupings in describing intelligence. His theory is called the **triarchic theory of intelligence.**

Componential intelligence includes the ability to acquire and store information; general learning and comprehension abilities such as good vocabulary and high reading comprehension; ability to do test items such as analogies, syllogisms, and series; and ability to think critically. This is the traditional concept of intelligence as measured on tests.

Experiential intelligence (intelligence based on experience) includes the ability to select, encode, compare, and combine information in meaningful ways to create new insights, theories, and ideas.

Contextual intelligence includes adaptive behavior in the real world, such as the ability to get along with other people, size up situations, achieve goals, and solve practical problems (Sternberg & Wagner, 1986).

Cattell

In an effort to include the influence of both heredity and environment in the development of intelligent, *Raymond Cattell* (1963)

Two-factor theory of intelligence—concept that intelligence consists of a general factor—"g"—and a number of specific abilities—"s" factors

Primary mental abilities—seven basic abilities described by Thurstone

Triarchic theory of intelligence—three components of intelligence described by Sternberg

described two dimensions of intelligence: *crystallized* and *fluid*. **Crystallized intelligence** includes knowledge and skills measured by tests of vocabulary, general information, and reading comprehension. It arises out of experience and represents the extent of acculturation and education. **Fluid intelligence** is a person's ability to think and reason abstractly as measured by reasoning tests, such as figural analogies and figural classifications. It involves the processes of perceiving relationships, deducing correlates, reasoning inductively, abstracting, forming concepts, and solving problems as measured by tasks with figural, symbolic, and semantic content. Fluid intelligence has a hereditary base in neurophysiological structures; therefore, it is not influenced as much as crystallized intelligence by intensive education and acculturation.

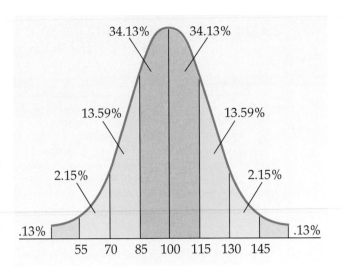

FIGURE 7.7 Normal distribution of IQ scores.

Intelligence Tests

Stanford-Binet

Revisions of Binet's tests were made by *Lewis Terman* (1877–1956) of Stanford University and became the Stanford-Binet test. It is used with individuals from age 2 through adulthood. The fourth edition of the Stanford-Binet was published in 1985 (Thorndike, Hagan, & Sattler, 1985) and yields scores in four areas: *verbal reasoning, quantitative reasoning, abstract/visual reasoning,* and *short-term memory*. It also provides a composite score that can be interpreted as an *Intelligence Quotient (IQ)* that reflects overall intelligence. Figure 7.7 shows a normal distribution of intelligence test scores on the Stanford-Binet. Note that 68.26% of individuals have scores between 85 and 115. Only 2.28% score above 130 or below 70.

The Wechsler Scales

The Wechsler Scales, developed by *David Wechsler*, are also widely used. There are three scales: the *Wechsler Adult Intelligence Scale—Revised (WAIS-III, 1991);* the *Wechsler Intelligence Scale for Children—Revised (WISC-III, 1991)* for use with children ages 6 to 16; and the *Wechsler Preschool and Primary Scale of Intelligence—Revised (WPPSI-R)* for use with children ages 4 to 7½ (Wechsler, 1981, 1991, 1989). The Wechsler Scales yield a composite IQ score, plus a verbal IQ from the six verbal subscales, and a performance IQ from the six performance subscales. Table 7.3 describes the various subtests in the WISC-R.

Critique of IQ and IQ Tests

IQ, School Performance, Job and Personal Success

IQ tests were designed initially to predict school performance. They do a pretty good job of this. Correlations between measured IQ and grades in school usually average about + .65. This accounts for about 45% of the variance in school grades. Still, over one-half of the variance in school grades is not predicted by IQ. Future school success is better predicted by past and present school success than by IQ. IQ tests are more predictive of job success in some occupations (for example, stockbroker) than they are in others, such as police officer. If a job requires academic skills, an IQ test will be a fairly good predictor of success on that kind of job. However, IQ scores tell us nothing about the ability to get along with other people; flexibility and the ability to adapt to different situations; work habits, motivation, interest, and effort; or emotional factors such as self-esteem, emotional security, or emotional stability. Yet, these are all important factors in job success or in interpersonal relationships.

Stability of IQ

As is covered in a subsequent discussion of infant intelligence testing, tests given in infancy (at about age 2) are almost worthless in predicting later IQ scores. By age 5, future IQ scores are more predictable. By age 10, scores

Crystallized intelligence— Cattell's concept that knowledge and skills arise out of acculturation and education

Fluid intelligence—Cattell's concept of inherited ability to think and reason abstractly

TABLE 7.3   THE WECHSLER INTELLIGENCE SCALE
                 FOR CHILDREN REVISED (WISC-III, 1991)

Verbal Scale	*Performance Scale*
1. *General information.* Questions relating to information most children in our society have the opportunity to acquire	1. *Picture completion.* Child indicates what is missing in pictures; measures visual alertness and ability to organize visually.
2. *General comprehension.* Questions designed to assess child's judgment and common sense.	2. *Picture arrangement.* Series of pictures must be arranged to tell a story; ability to think logically and meaningfully.
3. *Arithmetic.* Oral arithmetic problems: addition, subtraction, multiplication, division.	3. *Block design.* Child is required to copy exactly a design with colored blocks; visual-motor coordination, perceptual organization, spatial visualization.
4. *Similarities.* Child thinks logically and abstractly to determine how certain things are alike.	4. *Object assembly.* Puzzles to be assembled by the child; visual-motor coordination and spatial visualization.
5. *Vocabulary.* Child gives meanings of words of increasing difficulty.	5. *Coding.* Child pairs symbols with digits following a key; visual-motor coordination and speed of thought.
6. *Digit span.* Child repeats orally presented sequence of numbers forward and backward; measures short-term memory.	6. *Mazes.* Child traces way out of mazes with pencil; an optional scale.

Subtest scores may be regrouped into the following factors or individual scores:

1. Verbal comprehension
2. Freedom from distraction
3. Perceptual organization
4. Processing speed

are even more stable. However, there are wide individual variations in patterns even after this age. For some children, IQ may remain fairly constant. Correlations between tests in middle childhood and later scores are generally quite high (about + .7 or more). In other children, IQ scores may increase, decrease, or go up and down like a bouncing ball (François, 1990). Pinneau (1961) reanalyzed the data from the *Berkeley Growth Study* and converted all the scores to deviation IQs. He found that children tested at 5 years and at subsequent ages up to 17 years showed median changes from 6 to 12 points, with the range of individual changes from 0 to 40 points. Eichorn, Hunt, and Honzik (1981) found a correlation of + .80 between IQ in adolescence and IQ in middle age. However, 11% of the persons showed IQ gains of 13 points or more between adolescence and middle age. Another 11% showed IQ drops of 6 points or more. Overall, there was a 4-point gain in IQ between adolescence and middle age. IQ scores, therefore, are not fixed norms. They can vary, depending on many factors. Even Binet emphasized frequent retesting. He explained that intellectual development is uneven, reflecting both different rates of maturation and different educational experiences (Siegler, 1992).

Personal Factors Influencing Test Results

Test results may be influenced by such personal factors as *test anxiety, motivation* and *interest* in the tasks, or *rapport* with the *test giver.* A prime example is that of a 10-year-old in the Boston school system who would not answer test questions and whose record subsequently contained this entry: "The child's IQ is so low, she is not testable." After a young psychologist talked with the child and established rapport with her, he tested her and found that she achieved an IQ score of 115 ("Aptitude Test Scores," 1979).

Cultural Bias

The chief criticism of intelligence tests is that they are biased in favor of white, middle-class children. Tests to measure IQ were originally designed to measure "innate" general intelligence apart from environment influences. But research over a long period has shown that sociocultural factors play a significant role in the outcome of the tests (Carmines & Baxter, 1986). Children reared in stimulus-rich environments may show superiority in intelligence, whereas those reared under intellectually sterile conditions may not reach their full intelligence capacities. Furthermore, the test language, illustrations, examples, and abstractions are middle-class, and thus are designed to measure intelligence according to middle-class standards. Many children from low socioeconomic backgrounds grow up in a nonverbal world or a world where words used are so different, that to understand middle-class expressions on an intelligence test is difficult. These children do poorly not because they are less intelligent but because they do not comprehend language foreign to their backgrounds and experiences. Children from minority groups who are also from lower socioeconomic families experience greater difficulties. Native American children and others from rural areas who have been raised in an environment free from considerations of time do poorly on tests with a time limit. When allowed to do the test at their own rate, they score much higher.

Efforts to develop culturally unbiased tests have been very frustrating. The general approach has been to use language familiar to the particular minorities for which the test is designed. But the major problem is how to evaluate their accuracy. Most have been measured against IQ scores, which continue to reflect a cultural bias.

A more promising approach is known as *SOMPA (System of Multicultural Pluralistic*

FOCUS

Terman's Study of Gifted Men*

A follow-up of 52 superintelligent men from a study begun by Lewis Terman in 1921 at Stanford University revealed some interesting results (Hagan, 1983). Sixty years after the initial study began, the men with the highest IQs could scarcely be distinguished from the general population in relation to marriage, family, and domestic relations. However, the majority had received advanced degrees and were successful and superior achievers in their professions, though those with IQs of 150 were as successful as those with IQs of 180. IQ at best taps only a few facets of intelligence and prerequisites for success in life (Trotter, 1986).

*One of the criticisms of Terman's research is that it did not include women.

Assessment), which consists of the Wechsler IQ test; an interview in which the examiner learns the child's health history; a "sociocultural inventory" of the family's background; and an "adaptive-behavior inventory" of the child, which evaluates the child's nonacademic performance in school, at home, and in the neighborhood. A complete medical exam evaluates the child's physical condition, manual dexterity, motor skills, and visual and auditory ability. The final score on the SOMPA is obtained not only from the IQ test but also from the other inventories. Thus, a child who receives 68 on the Wechsler may earn an *adjusted IQ* of 89 when scores on the sociocultural and the adaptive-behavior inventories are taken into account. Thus, SOMPA tries to measure potential rather than current ability.

IQ and Race

Although the full range of IQ scores is found in all ethnic groups, the average IQ difference for blacks is about 15 points lower than for whites. The question is this: "Why the difference?"

In 1969, Arthur Jensen sparked a heated debate by claiming that IQ differences were hereditary. He said that because intelligence is 80% genetic in origin, differences between blacks and white are largely due to inheritance.

There are several weaknesses in this argument. Jensen's estimate of the percent by

Intelligence tests may discriminate against culturally and economically deprived children living in urban areas.

FOCUS

The Kaufman Assessment Battery for Children (K-ABC)

This test was developed by Alan and Nadeen Kaufman in the early 1980s, in part to reduce racial differences. The test cuts the IQ differences between blacks and whites by 50% (to about 7 points) and eliminates the differences between Hispanic and white children, thus reducing cultural bias.

The K-ABC has been found to correlate well with achievement tests (Childers, Durham, Bolen, & Taylor, 1985; Valencia, 1985). This finding means that the K-ABC distinguishes between those who have acquired knowledge and those who haven't, without reflecting as much racial or ethnic bias.

which intelligence is inherited is too high. A maximum figure is closer to 60% due to hereditary and the rest due to environmental influences. The same differences in IQ scores exist among those of all races if scores of those from lower classes are compared with those of higher classes. Ethnic differences in intelligence are really social class differences in disguise. When blacks from poor socioeconomic backgrounds are adopted into more well-to-do white families, the blacks score as high as or higher than the whites, indicating that social environment plays an important role in determining the average IQ level of black children. Furthermore, IQ tests are culturally biased, so that the scores of blacks are lower, not because of lower intelligence,

Development quotient (DQ)—score developed by Gesell to evaluate an infant's behavioral level in four categories: motor, language, adaptive, and personal-social

It is difficult to test the intelligence of infants because they are easily distracted.

but because the tests are not valid when used with blacks; the tests measure the mastery of white middle-class values and language skills rather than innate intelligence. The gap in IQ scores is gradually closing, however, as educational opportunities for blacks improve (Mackenzie, 1984).

Infant Intelligence and Measurement

For a number of years, psychologists have been interested in testing the intelligence of infants. If measurements could be made accurately, this undertaking would be of considerable help in matching adoptive parents and children, or in planning educational activities. The problem is that because infants are less verbal than older children, they are tested on the basis of what they do, not what they say. However, infants are distractible; it's hard to get their attention to test them. If they don't do something, is it because they don't know how to do it, don't feel like doing it, or don't know what is expected?

Developmental Quotient (DQ)

Arnold Gesell (1934) developed a measure that was used to sort out babies for adoption. The Gesell test divided behavior into four categories: *motor, language, adaptive,* and *personal-social.* The scores in these four areas could be combined into a **developmental quotient (DQ).** The problem is that DQs during infancy do not correlate highly with IQs in later childhood, so that any efforts to predict IQs of normal children before age 2 are practically worthless.

Bayley's Scales of Infant Development

The *Bayley Scales of Infant Development* were developed by Nancy Bayley (1969). The three scales assess the developmental status of children from 2 months to 2½ years of age in three areas: *mental abilities* such as memory, learning, perception, and verbal communication (for example, infants are asked to imitate simple actions or words); *motor abilities,* including both gross- and fine-motor skills; and *infant behavior record* (during mental and motor assessments). Separate scores are given for each scale. Unfortunately, the scores for infants are highly unreliable in predicting later IQ in childhood and adolescence. However, the closer children are to their 5th birthday when tested, the higher the correlation between their intelligence scores and those in later childhood (Bornstein &

Sigman, 1986). It's easier to predict the future IQ of a handicapped infant than of one with normal intelligence, but some of those who are handicapped as infants improve greatly as they get older.

Parental IQ and educational level is a much more reliable predictor of childhood IQ. Also, measures of *habituation or dishabituation* in infancy have been found to be a much better predictor of intelligence in childhood than the developmental scales (Bornstein & Sigman, 1986), as was discussed previously in this chapter in the section on habituation.

Recent Studies

The classical longitudinal studies of mental development found little stability in performance from infancy to later childhood. However, the most recent studies indicate there is more stability in early intelligence than previously thought. Using newly developed indices of infant mental functioning, researchers have found significant relations between infant cognition and later intelligence. The new infant measures include visual recognition memory, habituation, cross-modal transfer (both visual and tactual recognition memory), object permanence, and various qualitative and quantitative aspects of attention. These measures appear to involve some of the same basic cognitive abilities that characterize later intelligence (Rose & Feldman, 1995).

These findings support the speculation that speed of processing is an important factor underlying individual and developmental differences in many aspects of cognition, both in infancy and older children (Rose & Feldman, 1995).

Early Intervention

Can early intervention through remedial programs increase the intelligence of young children (Seitz & Apfel, 1994; Wasik, Ramey, Bryant, & Sparling, 1990)? The general consensus seems to be that *high-quality programs for economically deprived children can have lasting and valuable effects* (Campbell & Ramey, 1994). The best example comes from research on *Head Start* programs, which were designed to help disadvantaged preschool children do better in school as they grow older (Lee, Brooks-Gunn, Schnur, & Liaw, 1990). An 18-year study of the progress of 123 children, beginning when they were 3- and 4-year-olds, at Perry Elementary School in Ypsilanti, Michigan, showed that those who had been in the Head Start program scored higher on reading, math, and language achievement tests than children in a control group. The Head Start children also showed fewer antisocial and delinquent tendencies as they grew up.

If programs are well funded and teachers are competent, Head Start children show "improved intellectual performance during early childhood, better scholastic placement and improved scholastic achievement during elementary school years, and, during adolescence, a lower rate of delinquency and higher rates of both graduation from high school and employment at age 19" (Schweinhart & Weikert, 1985, p. 547). These are significant findings.

An important part of Head Start is the involvement of parents: giving them information and training in child development and care, home management, family relationships, nutrition, health, and other topics. Parents are involved in planning their own programs. In one study, trained mothers gave their children more instruction, information, and praise; gave them more encouragement to think and talk; were more emotionally responsive, sensitive, and accepting of their children; and were less critical than mothers in a control group (Andrews et al., 1982). Overall, parent-child relationships are important factors in cognitive development.

Environmental Input and Cognitive Growth

Overall, the environmental influence from parents and school significantly affect cognitive growth. Children from homes providing more influence do better on tests of ability and tests of achievement. Language development is significantly related to the amount of vocal stimulation at home. Children from schools providing more input attain higher skill levels than children from schools providing less input. Chinese children who receive more massive instruction at school than American children attain higher levels of mathematical skill than American children. And most studies also show that variations in environment input is related to brain development as indicated by measurement of the cerebral cortex (Huttenlocher, Levine, & Vevea, 1998).

Mental Retardation

Mental retardation may be genetically or environmentally determined. The incidence of familial retardation in the offspring of two

Mental retardation—below normal intelligence

Parenting Issues

Pushing Preschoolers

Programs like Head Start have been found to help children from economically disadvantaged homes overcome disparity in their backgrounds. But what is the effect of providing accelerated, academically enriched programs for preschool children from middle-class families? Two psychologists, Dr. Marion Hyson at the University of Delaware and Dr. Leslie Rescoria at Bryn Mawr College, compared 85 children who had gone to academically enriched preschools with those who went to preschools where they simply played. Accelerated activities included learning numbers, letters, computer instruction, social studies, and foreign languages. When tested at age 4, in comparison to those in other preschools, those children in the accelerated program tended to share the following characteristics:

1. They showed a slight advantage on ability tests, but the advantage disappeared a year later when the children went on to kindergarten.

2. They knew their numbers and letters better, but there was no difference in other cognitive skills that contributed to academic success.

3. Their parents tended to push them and to have higher academic expectations. These parents tended to be more controlling, critical, and emotionally negative.

4. The net result emotionally was that the children tended to be more anxious, more critical, and less positive toward school (Goleman, 1989).

retarded persons is 40%; of one, 20%. About 1.5% of the total U.S. population has been identified as mentally retarded. The total group may be classified into categories as follows (Berkow, 1997).

1. *Borderline.* This category includes slow learners with IQs of about 69 to 84, but they are not mentally retarded. They are rarely identified before they begin school, at which time educational and behavioral problems become evident. When they leave school, they generally blend in with the rest of the population. They usually can support themselves as long as they can find employment.

   Mildly Retarded. These are educable children with IQs of 52 to 68 and various degrees of educational achievement. They can learn up to about the sixth-grade level, can usually achieve enough social and vocational skills for self-support, but may need guidance and assistance during times of stress.

2. *Moderately Retarded.* These are trainable children with IQs of 36 to 51, with language and motor problems. They can learn some social and occupational skills, but progression beyond second-grade level in schoolwork is unlikely. They achieve self-support by performing unskilled or semi-skilled work under sheltered conditions but need supervision and guidance when under stress.

3. *Severely Retarded.* These children have IQs of 20 to 35. They can say a few words, are able to learn some self-help skills, can talk or learn to communicate. They can learn simple health habits, and can benefit from habit-training. They contribute partially to self-care under complete supervision. They need a completely controlled environment.

4. *Profoundly Retarded.* These children have IQs of 19 or below and are extremely retarded, and they have little muscle coordination so that they need nursing care. They are most unlikely to walk or talk. Although they may achieve very limited self-care, they need nursing care (Kenny & Clemmens, 1997).

High Cognitive Ability

Many theorists have been attempted to describe the causal origins of high cognitive ability (designate high *g*). These theories can be grouped into three schools of thought (Ericsson, Krampe, & Heizmann, 1993). The first theory, the *talent view*, holds that genetically mediated abilities determine ultimate performance. Genetic influences are partly responsible for high cognitive ability. In contrast, the *character ethic* view holds that high cognitive ability is not simply a matter of genetically endowed individuals' rising to

Whether mentally retarded children should be mainstreamed in regular classes or put in special classes of their own is a common question among educators.

high levels of cognitive performance. Instead, this view holds that innate talent must also be nurtured by environments that foster perseverance, hard work, single-mindedness, and goal orientation. Finally, the *skill acquisition* view holds that genetic influence is immaterial to the development of high cognitive ability, which is due to environmental influences. Instead, perseverance, hard work, and single-mindedness enable a person to reach high levels of performance regardless of genetic factors. According to this view, genetic factors have no bearing on the development of cognitive abilities other than severe forms of mental retardation caused by major gene or chromosomal abnormalities.

One report gives the results of a twin study of 600 children of high cognitive ability at 14, 20, 24, and 36 months of age. The high *g* groups were formed from the 90th percentile and above at each age, with high IQ equivalent means at or above 126 across the ages. The results suggest increasing genetic influence and increasing genetic stability from 14 to 36 months of age. Genetic influences were substantial when examining individuals who possess high *g* scores averaged across all four ages. The results suggest that although high cognitive ability may be genetically influenced in early childhood, these influences differ in magnitude from 14 to 36 months. In contrast, shared environmental influences appeared less important at 36 months. Genetic influences were primarily responsible for persistently high *g* across infancy and early childhood (Petrill et al., 1998).

SCHOOL

Early Childhood Education

The numbers of children in some kind of early childhood education program have grown tremendously. There are several reasons for this trend. In 1997, 32% of all families with children at home were maintained by one parent. The comparable figures for black families were 64% (U.S. Bureau of the Census, 1998). Furthermore, in 1994, 64% of married women with the youngest child under age 6 were employed outside the home (U.S. Bureau of the Census, 1998). These circumstances necessitated parents' placing their children in some kind of child-care arrangement. In addition, many parents, whether they work or not, have come to recognize the benefits of preschool education for their children. Table 7.4 shows the primary child-care arrangements used by employed mothers for children under 5 (U.S.

Bureau of the Census, 1998). Note that 23% of these children were cared for in organized child-care facilities: a day-care center, group-care home, nursery school, or other preschool.

Nursery Schools

Nursery schools are usually for children after age 2½ to 3, after they have been toilet trained. They typically operate 3 to 5 half-days a week, so do not meet the needs of parents working full-time. The best schools offer college-trained teachers, as well as enriched intellectual and social experiences in informal settings.

Montessori Schools

These schools for children 3 to 7 are named after their founder, Dr. Maria Montessori, an Italian physician. They are expensive private schools featuring a prepared environment and carefully designed, individually paced, self-taught, self-correcting materials. The teacher arranges the environment but otherwise does not interfere with the learning process.

Group-Care Home

The best group-care homes are licensed by the state to accommodate a small number of children—usually in the home of the teacher. Teachers are not usually as well trained as those in larger day-care centers, but if they are warm, caring persons who love children, the effect on the children may be quite positive.

Day-Care Centers

Day-care centers, which are licensed by the state, are open year round, all day, five or more days a week. They are deliberately planned to meet the needs of children of working parents. Day-care centers vary tremendously in quality. The best centers are characterized by the following (American Academy of Pediatrics, 1986; Bredekamp, 1987; Howes & Rubenstein, 1985):

1. Have a low child-to-adult ratio: 3 to 4 infants and toddlers per adult, or 7 to 9 3- to 5-year-olds per adult.
2. Have workers who are trained in early childhood education and who are affectionate, sensitive, and responsive to the needs of children.
3. Have teachers who encourage self-control, set clear limits, reward expected behavior,

TABLE 7.4	PRIMARY CHILD-CARE ARRANGEMENTS USED BY EMPLOYED MOTHERS

For Children Under Five	Precentage of Mothers Making Arrangements
Other parent or stepparent	13.5
Grandparent or other relative	32.0
Nonrelative	30.5
Day-care center or preschool	28.7
Other arrangement[1]	4.7

For Children 5–12 years of age	
Other parent or stepparent	16.5
Grandparent or other relative	22.4
Nonrelative	13.3
Day-care center or preschool	14.8
Brother or sister	13.6
Child cares for self	5.9
School (regular hours)	14.2
Other arrangement[2]	9.1

Amount Paid per Week for Child Care with at Least One Child in the Family Under 13 Years of Age	
Percentage with no payment for child care	50.7
One child	58.0
Two children	80.0
Three or more children	82.0

[1]Other arrangements include child's siblings; child cares for self; school (regular hours); before-school or after-school care/program; respondent while she was working; and other arrangements at home.
[2]Other arrangements include before-school or after-school care/program; respondent while she was working; and other arrangements not shown separately.
From U.S. Department of Health and Human Services, data from the National Survey of Family Growth, 1995.

and redirect troublesome children to more acceptable activities.

4. Provide a safe, clean, and healthy environment both indoors and outdoors that affords optimum physical development.

5. Offer an environment that encourages children to select from a variety of activities, to master cognitive and language skills, to learn to think and to do, and to solve problems.

6. Encourage children's curiosity, creativity, and self-development at their own pace.

7. Foster children's social skills, respect for others, and ability to get along with others.

8. Foster children's self-esteem, emotional development, and security.

9. Promote cooperation and communication with parents and assist them in parenting skills.

A good day-care program helps parents meet the needs of children, helps enrich children's lives, and can strengthen the family rather than simply separate parent and child. The key lies in the quality of service that is provided. A growing number of businesses are offering in-house child care for children of employees.

Instructional Approaches

Developmental psychologists and educators have, for many years, debated the effects of different instructional approaches on young children's learning and social-motivational development. There is an increasing interest in early childhood education and an apparent trend toward early introduction of basic skills, using the teacher-directed approach to instruction. Practices that were previously not usually encountered until the first grade or later—such as whole-class, teacher-directed instruction, formal reading instruction, written assignments out of workbooks, and frequent grading—are now common in kindergarten.

Many child-development experts fear that a proliferation of early childhood programs that focus on basic skills may have more negative than positive effects on children. For example, experts have argued that didactic, teacher-controlled instruction that emphasizes performance, undermines young children's intrinsic interest in learning, their perceptions of competence, and their willingness to take academic risks. Experts also fear that didactic instruction fosters dependency in young children on adult authority for defining tasks and evaluating outcomes and engenders anxiety about achievement.

One study of 227 poor, minority, and middle-class children between the ages of 4 and 6 years, sought to evaluate the effects of different instructional approaches in young children's achievement and motivation. Children in didactic programs that stress basic skills had significantly higher scores on letters/reading achievement tests and not on a numbers achievement test. Being enrolled in a didactic early-childhood education program was associated with relatively negative outcomes in most of the motivation measures. Compared with children in child-centered programs, children in didactic programs rated their abilities significantly lower, had lower expectations for success on academic tasks, showed more dependency on adults for permission and approval, showed less pride in their accomplishments, and claimed that they worried more about school. Program effects were the same for economically disadvantaged and middle-class children, and for preschoolers and kindergartners (Stipek, Feiler, Daniels, & Milburn, 1995).

American Education

We periodically hear outcries that American education is in trouble. The reports pointed to poor achievement test scores; the long-term decrease in SAT scores for college admission; declining enrollments and achievement in science and math; poor abilities in communication, writing, and thinking skills; and the need for remedial education and training to prepare students for jobs.

Successful Schools

Before we condemn all U.S. schools as inferior, we need to point out that there are tremendous differences among schools in this country. There are schools that are vastly superior. Our task here, then, is to delineate some of the factors that make schools great.

One of the most important characteristics of successful schools is that *they emphasize academic excellence.* They have high expectations of their students, give regularly assigned and graded homework (Rutter, 1983), and devote a high proportion of classroom time to active teaching. Teachers are expected to plan lessons carefully, and they are adequately supervised to see that this is done. The administration supplies the equipment and materials so that teachers can do a good job. Students are encouraged to have pride in their work and their school.

Successful schools *pay attention to the needs of individual students.* Students who have low reading scores, or who are below level in other subjects, are given individual help to bring their achievement up. Staff and teaching personnel are encouraged to build good relations with students and to be alert to provide assistance with personal problems. Teachers are expected to respect their students and to help them have pride in themselves.

Another characteristic of successful schools is *the emphasis on no-nonsense discipline.* Teachers are not left to their own devices to discipline students. They receive the guidance and support that they need from the administration, so it is easier for them to keep order, and they therefore have more time to devote to teaching (Jensen, 1986).

Great teachers are also important in building great schools. Great teachers are well-trained, intelligent persons who know the subjects they are teaching. They have superior understanding of instructional knowledge and skills. They keep up-to-date in their field and are willing to spend time in preparation for class. They are also personable, mature adults who like the students whom they teach and have a genuine interest in their welfare. The best teachers have a real understanding of children, their developmental needs, interests, problems, and adjustments. They show genuine concern, tolerance, and friendliness, and tremendous

Great teachers are intelligent and well-trained, and have an understanding of the needs, interests, problems, and adjustments of children.

respect and love for their pupils (Howes, Hamilton, & Matheson, 1994).

Achievement

Heredity

Educators have spent a lot of time and energy sorting out the reasons why some pupils achieve in school and others do not. As discussed in Chapter 3, one most important factor is heredity. Success is not inherited, but heredity is an important factor in intelligence, and intelligence is an important factor in achievement.

Learning Disabilities

Some of the reasons for underachievement are physical: *poor hearing, poor eyesight,* and *various physical illnesses* or *handicaps.* One child did poorly in school for 3 years before the parents found out that she was seeing images upside down. Another was found to be so *deaf* that he could not hear most of what the teacher was saying. Some children suffer from brain impairments, such as *dyslexia,* which causes reading problems. Others are *hyperkinetic* because of brain injuries. Is the child doing poorly in school because of mental retardation or because of other physical impairments? Parents and teachers need to seek expert advice to see whether there are physical causes for problems before they assume that the child is "just lazy" or "not trying."

Children with **learning disabilities** have average or above average general intelligence but manifest specific problems with reading, arithmetic, spelling, and written expression. Nelson Rockefeller, governor of New York

Learning disabilities— problems with reading, arithmetic, spelling, and written expression even in a person with normal intelligence

Dyslexia—developmental language disorder in which the person reads from right to left, reverses letters and words, omits words, or loses his or her place

and vice president of the United States, had so much trouble reading that he would ad-lib his speeches. Thomas Edison never learned how to write or spell grammatically. Gen. George Patton read very poorly and depended on his memory to get through West Point (Schulman, 1986).

Each of these men suffered from **dyslexia,** a developmental language disorder in which the person reads from right to left, reverses letters and words ("saw" becomes "was"; "p" is substituted for "g"), omits words entirely, or loses the place on a page. Children may make up stories when they can't read them; or they may read, but without comprehension. Symptoms of frustration become evident; deficits in learning and school performance may lead to behavioral problems, aggression, delinquency, withdrawal, and alienation from teachers, parents, and other children.

Treatment is multidimensional, by means of corrective, remedial, and compensatory education, since perceptual deficits cannot be corrected. By age 7 or 8, the intelligent child may be able to cope with the problem by developing compensatory techniques. For other children, dyslexia remains a lifelong problem, preventing them from reaching their full potential. Dyslexia is only one of a number of learning disabilities.

Achievement Motivation

Another important factor is achievement motivation, or the desire to succeed. Individuals vary in the strength of this desire. Studies of 348 pairs of identical twins at the University of Minnesota showed that heredity accounted for 46% of the variance (or differences) in the motivation to work hard to succeed (Goleman, 1986). Some children seem to be born with the desire to succeed; others are more laid back and seem not to care (Smiley & Dweck, 1994). However, part of achievement motivation is instilled in children by parents, teachers, or other influential persons. In contrast, the parents of other students actively discouraged achievement motivation. These parents take very little interest in their children's progress in school during the grade-school years. They cannot wait until their children are old enough to leave school and go to work. These parents actively discourage their children from going to college.

One study examined the relationship of family factors to children's intrinsic/extrinsic motivational orientation and academic performance. The study examined three family factors: parental surveillance of homework,

Parental encouragement stimulates children to get better grades.

parental reactions to grades, and general family style. The subjects were 93 fifth-graders and their parents. Results of the study showed that higher parental surveillance of homework, parental reaction to grades that included negative control, uninvolvement, or extrinsic reward, and over- and under-controlling family styles were found to be related to an extrinsic motivational orientation, and to lower academic performance. However, parental encouragement in response to grades that children received was associated with an intrinsic motivational orientation, and autonomy-supporting family styles were associated with intrinsic motivation and higher academic performance. In addition, socioeconomic level was a significant predictor of motivational orientation and academic performance (Ginsburg & Bronstein, 1993).

Dysfunctional Family Relationships and Divorce

Dysfunctional family relationships have a negative effect on school achievement. Family conflict and tension, physical or emotional abuse, parental rejection and neglect, criticism, or hostility undermine children's sense of security and self-esteem, creating anxi-

eties, tensions, and fears that interfere with school achievement. Divorce itself is perceived as a negative event that can stimulate painful emotions, confusion, and uncertainty in children (Kalter, 1983). Many children regain their psychological equilibrium in a year or so and resume normal intellectual growth and development, but the initial upset may create substantial emotional and social upheaval that affects schoolwork (Wallerstein & Kelly, 1980). The long-term effects on social, emotional, and cognitive growth are variable (Kalter, 1983).

One-Parent Families

At the present time, 32% of families with children living at home are maintained by one parent (U.S. Bureau of the Census, 1998). However, this is the percentage of one-parent families at the time of the survey. Projections show that nearly 60% of all children born in 1986 may be expected to spend a large part of a year or longer in a one-parent family before reaching the age of 18.

Overall, the quality of parenting and family relationships strongly affects children's social, psychological, and academic adjustments, in both traditional and nontraditional families. In comparison with children in families with two biological parents, single-parent children in divorced families score higher on measures of problem behavior and lower on social competence, academic achievement, and self-concepts. Children who grow up in single-parent households, especially if their mothers never marry, are significantly more likely to live below the poverty line than are children who live with two parents. They are more likely to perform poorly in school, to have repeated a grade, and to have been expelled from school (Downey, 1994). They also demonstrate a higher incidence of emotional or behavioral problems and of health problems due to accidents, injuries, or poisonings (Remez, 1992).

Stressful life events and their influence on maternal psychological well-being affect the single-parent child in ways that may not affect children from two-parent homes. The combination of single-parent family status and frequent stressful events appears to have a special effect on child behavior. Children from single-parent, high-stress-level families demonstrate the highest incidence of behavior problems, the lowest social competency ratings, and the lowest evaluations of academic performance. However, single-parent children are rated no differently than two-parent families when maternal stress does not differ (Gringlas &

Weintraub, 1995). It must be emphasized that because children, parents, and circumstances all differ, the effects of a one-parent family structure of children are not always the same. A study of a random sample of Baltimore schoolchildren during the first two years of school found no effect of parental configuration on marks or test-score gains in reading and math, with one exception: African-American children in single-mother families where other adults were present had higher marks in reading at the beginning of the first grade than did their counterparts of mother-only or mother-father families. Children whose families had more economic resources and whose parents had higher expectations for their school performance consistently outperformed other children in reading and math (Entwisle & Alexander, 1996).

One other factor ought to be mentioned here. Studies of children's academic performances may be based on teacher evaluations and ratings, which reflect prejudices against those from one-parent families: "He comes from a broken home." Teachers' ratings do not always agree with objective evaluations.

Sociocultural Influences

Many of the studies of achievement of minority groups indicate lower achievement levels of blacks, Hispanics, and others (Stevenson, Chen, & Uttal, 1990). Table 7.5 shows the percentage of people age 25 or older with designated years of schooling, by race and ethnic origin for 1997 (U.S. Bureau of the Census, 1998). As can be seen, 48.6% of Mexican Americans age 25 or older had at least a high school education. This contrasts with 75% of blacks and 83% of whites. However, there are many reasons for this lower

---

Parenting Issues

Report Cards

Bringing home report cards is one of the most upsetting events in the lives of some children. Children who fear that they have done poorly, or those who have not lived up to parental expectations, think up every scheme in the world to keep parents from finding out. They "forget to bring it home"; they "lost it." They are sick, and so they don't go to school that day. They try to erase and change marks. I know one child who didn't come home until midnight because of fear of parental punishment. Another told me that he stole a blank card from the school office, put his own grades on it for each semester (all A's), and brought only that card to his parents. It was the only report card that his parents saw for one whole year.

Report cards should be of help to parents and their children, not a major source of family disaster. But how? First, parents should be very cautious about how they react to a poor report. Some parents become violently upset and resort to severe punishments, physical or verbal

thrashings, or threats of disciplinary measures that are excessive or unwise. "Grounding" children every night and weekend for a whole semester, for example—not letting them have any social life at all—may create a lot of resentment and may not accomplish the purpose of stimulating better study habits or grades. No child can study all the time. Nervous, upset children may do far better when they are studying if they have a chance to relax and have fun in between study times. I've known parents to try to force an overactive child to remain inactive and study for long hours at a time. It just doesn't improve grades sometimes. Other parents may try to push a child of average ability to do better than he or she is capable of doing. I know one family in which the parents won't let their 10-year-old son watch television until he makes the honor roll. It's been two years and the boy hasn't made it yet—and he may never make it. In fact, such achievement may be beyond his capabilities.

Second, parents should interpret a report card as an evaluating of achievement and progress and as an indication of strengths and weaknesses. They should give praise and recognition for strengths as well as thoughtful consideration for weaknesses. Do parents compliment their children on the good marks and evaluations? Or do they notice only the low ones? Most children need encouragement, morale building, and emotional support in overcoming problems. Poor marks may indicate the need for tutoring, counseling, or remedial attention of some kind.

Third, report cards are more helpful if followed up by parent–teacher conferences to discuss the reasons for the marks and the child's individual needs, and to decide on a course of remedial action, if needed. If children are having trouble, what will help the most? What should the parent's role be? (Author's counseling notes)

| TABLE 7.5 | PERCENTAGE OF PEOPLE AGE 25 OR OLDER WITH DESIGNATED YEARS OF SCHOOLING, BY RACE AND ETHNIC ORIGIN, 1997 |

Number of Years of Schooling	White	Black	Mexican
Elementary: 0–8	7.5	8.8	N/A
Four years of high school or more	83	75.0	48.6
Four years or more of college	24.6	13.3	7.4

Adapted from U.S. Bureau of the Census. (1998), *Statistical Abstract of the United States, 1998* (118th ed.). Washington, DC: U.S. Government Printing Office, 51.

achievement of Mexican Americans. There is often a language problem if parents do not speak English at home. Teachers may be poorly trained, may not speak Spanish, or may be prejudiced against Hispanics. The schools they attend are more often poorly funded, and educational programs are inferior (Casas & Ponterotto, 1984). Many parents are not able to give their children the support that they need for academic success. Under these circumstances, it is not suprising that scholastic performance is poor.

However, many of the studies of minority groups do not take into account socioeconomic status (which is determined by the combination of education, occupation, and income). In many instances, socioeconomic status is a better predictor of achievement than race (Graham, 1986). For example, middle-class blacks have an achievement orientation similar to that of middle-class whites. Many times, as blacks grow up, their overall achievement is lower than that of whites, but this is because of prejudices that prevent them from getting ahead, not a lack of motivation to succeed. Middle- and upper-class blacks—like comparable classes of whites—have high expectations of success.

Summary

1. Language is only one of many methods of communication.

2. The basic elements of language include phonemes, morphemes, syntax and grammar, semantics, and pragmatics.

3. Theories of language development include biological theory, learning theory, cognitive theory, and interactionist theory.

4. Parental influences on language development are especially important.

5. The sequences of language development are prelinguistic period, first spoken words, two-word utterances, telegraphic speech, and sentences.

6. The vocabulary of preschool and early-school-age children grows from over 50 words at age 2 to 8,000 to 14,000 words at age 6.

7. There is considerable support for the theory that there is a critical period for language development.

8. Grammar is the formal description of structure and rules that a language uses in order to communicate meaning.

9. Pragmatics is the practical ability to use language to communicate with others in a variety of social contexts.

10. Studies of gender differences in communication patterns in children reveal that boys use more demanding, domineering patterns; girls use cooperative, polite, and collaborative strategies.

11. For children in groups where their first language is a minority language, a second language may be a subtractive influence. For children whose first language is the majority language, learning

a second language is largely an additive experience.

12. Learning to read is an important milestone in the total development of children. There are two different approaches to teaching reading, the skills approach and the whole-language approach. The skills approach may include either the phonics approach or the word-recognition approach.

    Many teachers teach phonics as well as word recognition because each skill enhances the abilities of the other. In the whole-language approach to teaching reading, children learn a story before they learn the words that comprise the story and before they learn the phonetic pronunciation of the words. Most experts agree that balance between explicit skills instruction and experience in authentic reading offers the best approach to beginning reading.

13. Stuttering appears to have both a genetic base and to be influenced by environment.

14. One important advance in cognitive and motor skills in the preschool years is the development of handwriting. Children progress from producing seemingly random scribbles on a page to producing meaningful and organized forms. There is little relation between elementary schoolchildren's type of pen grip and how legibly they wrote letters.

15. The United States ranks 49 among 159 members of the United Nations in its average level of literacy. About one-fifth of all young adults and about one-half to one-third of minority young adults in the United States read under the eighth-grade level. There are all degrees of functional illiteracy.

16. There are three approaches to the study of cognition: the Piagetian approach, the information-processing approach, and the psychometric approach.

17. Piaget divided the stages of cognitive development into four stages: the sensorimotor stage (birth to 2 years), the preoperational stage (2 to 7 years), the concrete operational stage (7 to 11 years), and the formal operational stage (11 years and up).

18. During the sensorimotor stage, children learn to respond through motor activity to stimuli.

19. During the sensorimotor stage, children develop the concept of object permanence. They also develop the ability to imitate.

20. The parental role is to offer a stimulating intellectual environment so that children can grow cognitively.

21. During the preoperational stage, children develop the ability to deal with the word symbolically and representationally. Symbolic or pretend play peaks during the preschool period.

22. Four- and five-year-old children have some trouble distinguishing fantasy from reality. They tend to believe that Santa Claus, the Easter Bunny, and the Tooth Fairy are real figures. Preschoolers tend to label magic tricks and extraordinary events as magic. Magic involves special powers that an individual is born with that are bestowed on him or her by someone vested with these powers. However, by 5 years of age, children view magic as involving tricks and deception or as a skill that can be learned through reading, other magicians, or a special "magic" school.

23. Children acquire language, reason transductively, make errors of reasoning because of syncretism, and may be characterized as exhibiting egocentrism, animism, centration, and lack of comprehension of conservation. They are limited in their classification ability and make errors because their thinking is irreversible.

24. Early research has shown that children under age 10 may not understand what it means to be a living thing. Piaget claims that young children do not understand the word *alive*. Preschool children may either draw the living-kind boundary too widely or too narrowly. Some children say that plants are alive, but they also attribute life to inanimate objects. Children know something about plant and animal growth and realize that certain things are needed for growth.

25. Research on cognitive abilities during the preoperational stage indicates that children understand the relation between a picture and its referent, remember the location of things in rooms, can make proportional judgments in relation to half, understand that animals grow larger, can recognize false beliefs, and begin to understand kinship. They have trouble understanding the relation between a scale model and the larger figure it represents, that a straight line is the shortest distance between points, and that other beliefs may be different from their own.

26. During the concrete operational stage, children show some ability to do logical thinking, but only at a concrete level. They are capable of classification and serialization, understand conservation, and can perform tasks involving combinativity, reversibility, associativity, and identity or nullifiability.

27. Vygotsky's theory of cognitive and language development emphasizes that both are derived from social and cultural influences. He introduced the concepts of zone of proximal development, inner speech, egocentric speech, and external speech.

28. The information-processing approach to cognition describes the way children obtain, remember, retrieve, and utilize information in solving problems.

29. Stimulation is important to the learning process; when infants get used to a particular stimulation, they don't pay any attention to it, a process called habituation. Children are very distractible and attend selectively to stimuli.

30. The ability to remember, which begins in infancy, is basic to all learning. However, few people can remember events that happened before they were 3 years old.

31. The process of remembering involves three stages: sensory storage, short-term storage, and long-term storage. Short-term memory ability increases during childhood. Long-term memory increases fairly rapidly to young adulthood.

32. Metamemory consists of knowledge of memory strategies that people employ to learn and remember information. Mnemonic, or memory-aiding, strategies include rehearsal, organization, chunking, using memory cues, using the method of loci, and being motivated to learn material because it is interesting and important.

33. Children are better able to remember the spatial locations of things in an organized room than in an unorganized room.

34. The psychometric approach to the study of cognition is concerned with the level of intelligence as measured by test scores.

35. Different psychologists discuss differing views of intelligence. Some of the more important views were those introduced by Binet (mental age versus chronological age), Spearman (two-factor theory of intelligence), Guilford (120 factors), Gardner (seven frames of mind), Sternberg (triarchic theory of intelligence), and Cattell (crystallized and fluid intelligence).

36. The two most important intelligence tests used with children are the Stanford-Binet and the Wechsler Scales.

37. IQ is correlated with school grades, but still only accounts for 45% of the variance in grades. Present school success is a better predictor of future school grades than is IQ. IQ is more predictive of job success in some occupations than in others.

38. By age 10, IQ scores are fairly stable, but there are still wide individual variations in patterns even after this age.

39. There are many personal factors influencing test results: text anxiety, motivation and interest, and rapport with the test giver.

40. The chief criticism of intelligence tests is that they are culturally biased in favor of white, middle-class families.

41. Differences in IQ between blacks and whites are due to social and environmental influences and not to heredity.

42. SOMPA is a more promising approach in eliminating cultural bias in measuring IQ. The Kaufman Assessment Battery for Children (K-ABC) also was developed to eliminate racial differences.

43. Trying to predict the intelligence of infants by testing before 2 years of age is practically worthless in predicting later IQ. The closer the child is to age 5, the more valid a test becomes. The two principal tests used with the infant are Gesell's Developmental Quotient (DQ) and Bayley's Scales of Infant Development.

44. Parental IQ and educational level and habituation are more reliable predictors of childhood IQ than the developmental tests.

45. More recent studies indicate that there is more stability in early intelligence than previously thought. Using newly developed indices of infant mental functioning, researchers have found significant relations between infant cognition and later intelligence. These findings support the speculation that speed of processing is an important factor underlying individual and developmental differences in many aspects of cognition, both in infancy and in older children.

46. High-quality programs for economically deprived children can have lasting and valuable effects.

47. The environmental influence from parents and school significantly influence cognitive growth.

48. Mental retardation may be genetically or environmentally determined and may be classified as borderline, mild, moderate, severe, or profound.

49. Three theories to describe the casual origins of high cognitive ability are the talent view, the character ethic view, and the skill acquisition view.

50. The numbers of children in some kind of early childhood education program continue to rise. The principal programs are nursery schools, Montesorri schools, group-care homes, and day-care centers. Programs differ tremendously in quality.

51. Periodically, reports emphasize that American education is in trouble. When our children are compared with Asians in science and math, our children score considerably lower.

52. Not all American schools are mediocre, however. Successful schools emphasize academic excellence, pay attention to the needs of individual children, emphasize no-nonsense discipline, and have great teachers.

53. Learning disabilities involve problems with reading, arithmetic, spelling, and written expression. One common problem is dyslexia.

54. There are a number of factors that influence achievement: heredity, physical factors, achievement motivation, family background and relations, and sociocultural influences. However, many of the studies of minority groups don't take into account socioeconomic status.

55. High parental surveillance of homework, negative control, uninvolvement, or extrinsic reward, and over- and under-controlling family styles are found to be related to lower academic performance. Parental encouragement and autonomy-supporting family styles are associated with intrinsic motivation and higher academic performance.

56. The quality of parenting and family relationships strongly affects children's social, psychological, and academic adjustments in both traditional and nontraditional families. The effects of growing up in a one-parent family are not always the same for every child.

57. Since sociocultural influences on children are important, they must be taken into consideration in evaluating cognitive growth.

58. Report cards should be a stimulus to parents to find out how their children are doing, what the reasons are for their marks, and whether remedial action is needed.

Key Terms

Animism *p. 163*
Associativity *p. 167*
Babbling *p. 150*
Centration *p. 164*
Chronological age (CA) *p. 173*
Chunking *p. 172*
Classification *p. 165*
Class inclusion relationships *p. 166*
Combinativity *p. 166*
Conservation *p. 164*
Cooing *p. 150*
Crystallized intelligence *p. 175*
Deductive reasoning *p. 163*
Deferred imitation *p. 162*
Developmental quotient (DQ) *p. 178*
Duos *p. 152*
Dyslexia *p. 184*
Egocentrism *p. 163*
Fluid intelligence *p. 175*
Grammar *p. 153*
Habituation *p. 168*
Hierarchical classification *p. 166*
Holophrases *p. 151*
Identity or nullifiability *p. 167*

Imitation *p. 162*
Inductive reasoning *p. 163*
Infantile amnesia *p. 170*
Information-processing approach *p. 160*
Intelligence quotient (IQ) *p. 173*
Irreversibility *p. 166*
Language acquisition device *p. 148*
Learning disabilities *p. 184*
Long-term storage *p. 170*
Mental age (MA) *p. 173*
Mental retardation *p. 179*
Metamemory *p. 172*
Method of loci *p. 172*
Mnemonic *p. 172*
Morpheme *p. 148*
Nativist view *p. 148*
Object permanence *p. 161*
Parentese *p. 152*
Phoneme *p. 148*
Phonics approach *p. 157*
Piagetian approach *p. 160*
Pragmatics *p. 148*
Primary mental abilities *p. 174*
Psychometric approach *p. 160*

Discussion Questions

1. Have you ever known a young preschool child who did not talk? What were the reasons?

2. Have you ever known a child who seemed to be advanced in language development? Describe. What were the reasons for this advanced development?

3. When you were growing up, were family members encouraged or discouraged from talking about feelings? With what result?

4. What can parents do to stimulate the cognitive development of their children?

5. Why has the influence of Piaget been so felt in the psychological world? What are some of the charactcristics of his theories that you like? What are some of your major criticisms of his viewpoints?

6. In what ways is the distractibility of young children a handicap to parents? In what ways is it a help?

7. Can you give examples of the memory ability of children you know?

8. What are the advantages and disadvantages for parents and teachers of knowing the IQ scores of children? In what ways are IQ test results misused?

9. Do you know anyone who is mentally retarded? Tell about that person.

10. Do you know any children who go to nursery school, Montessori school, a group-care home, or a day-care center? What are some of the benefits? What are some of the negative effects or problems?

11. Do you know anyone who has dyslexia? Tell about that person.

12. Describe your experiences as a child when you brought your report card home. What do you think of parents giving the child money for good grades? What should parents do and not do when their child brings home a poor report card?

Suggested Readings

ANASTASI, A. (1997). *Psychological testing* (7th ed.). Prentice Hall. The science of assessment.

DOUVILLE-WATSON, L., WATSON, M. A., WILSON, L. C., & WATSON, L. D. (1998). *Infants and Toddlers: Curriculum and Teaching*. Albany, NY: Delman. Designed for teachers and caregivers.

FLAVELL, J. H. (1992). *Cognitive development* (3rd ed.). Englewood Cliffs, NJ: Prentice-Hall. Esteemed introductory book.

GINSBURG, H., & OPPER, S. (1989). *Piaget's theory of intellectual development* (3rd ed.). Englewood Cliffs, NJ: Prentice-Hall. Good explanation of Piaget.

KAIL, R. (1990). *The development of memory in children*. San Francisco: W. H. Freeman. Changes in children's memory.

McLANE, J. B., & McNAMEE, G. D. (1990). *Early literacy*. Cambridge, MA: Harvard University Press. Pros and cons of early reading for young children.

PORTER, R. P. (1994). *Forked tongue: The politics of bilingual education*. New York: Basic Books. Successes and failures of bilingual education in the United States.

SIEGLER, R. (1997). *Children's thinking* (3rd ed.). Englewood Cliffs, NJ: Prentice-Hall. Cognitive development from infancy to adolescence.

WILSON, L. C. (1990). *Infants and toddlers: Curriculum and teaching*. Albany, NY: Delman. Designed for teachers and caregivers.

Web Resources

http://www.puckett.org/childlearn/index.html
Early Childhood Learning. Opportunities Research Institute. Case studies, research, and links to other resources put together by the institute which is funded by the U.S. Department of Education. Particular attention paid to young children with or at-risk for disabilities.

http://matia.stanford.edu/cogsci/   Cognitive and Psychological Sciences on the Internet. An index of internet resources relevant to research in cognitive sciences and psychology.

Emotional Development

Chapter 8

The emotional development of children is concerned with the development of their feelings and the expression of them in relation to themselves, their parents, peers, other people, and, literally, everything in the world. Emotional development is extremely important because emotions play an adaptive function to ensure survival (for example, feeling fear may save a child's life). Emotions are also a means of communication, important factors in social relationships, and powerful motivators of behavior. And, as a source of pleasure or pain, they also play an important role in moral development.

The chapter begins with a discussion of the development of attachments or emotional bonds with caregivers, and the development of trust and security. The discussion then turns to the development of basic emotions: to a developmental timetable and to both biological and environmental influences. Attention is then focused on the development of temperament: its components, patterns, and relationship to personality.

The chapter concludes with a discussion of the development of self-awareness, autonomy, separation-individuation, self-definition, self-concept, self-reference, self-efficacy, and self-esteem.

ATTACHMENT

Meaning and Importance

The development of attachment theory is the joint work of John Bowlby and Mary Ainsworth (Ainsworth and Bowlby, 1991; Bretherton, 1992). **Attachment** means the feeling that binds a person and a child together. It is the emotional link between them, the desire to maintain contact through physical closeness, touching, looking, smiling, listening, or talking (Pipp & Harmon, 1987). Young children who have developed a positive and helpful attachment to their parents run to them when frightened, seek the comfort of their arms when upset, and otherwise derive pleasure and security from just being near them or from being able to see or communicate with them.

Infants benefit from a secure emotional attachment to someone: a mother, father, other family member, or a substitute caregiver (Bowlby, 1982). To feel emotionally secure, children need warm, loving, stable relationships with a responsive adult on whom they can depend (Kochanska, 1991). If for some reason parents can't be close, the child needs to form a similar attachment to whoever is the primary caregiver. Children's attachment patterns are related to later personal and interpersonal competencies (Jacobsen & Hofmann, 1997).

The formation of such attachments is vitally important to children's total development (Main & Cassidy, 1988; Sroufe, 1985). It gives them security, a developing sense of self, and makes their socialization possible (Pipp, Easterbrooks, & Harmon, 1992). They are less shy and uninhibited in their relationships with others (Calkins & Fox,

Securely attached infants have affectionate, loving, attentive, and responsive caregivers.

Parenting Issues

Intergenerational Influences on Attachment

The desire and ability of parents to form close attachments with their children depend partly on the way the parents were brought up. Psychoanalysts have long emphasized that there is an intergenerational concordance in relationship patterns. Parents who were closely attached to their parents in close, affectionate relationships, are more likely to establish such relationships with their own children (Fonagy, Steele, & Steele, 1991). Parents' own emotional experiences, expressive behavior, and personality traits are significant predictors of the level of security of their infant–parent attachment, but these, in turn, are partly the result of the kind of relationships their parents developed with them (Izard et al., 1991).

1992). They are better able to get along with other children, both siblings and those outside the family (Jacobson & Willie, 1986; Park & Waters, 1989; Teti & Ablard, 1989). Children begin to identify with, imitate, and learn from the person(s) to whom they feel closest. And it is through these contacts that children learn what society expects of them. Such relationships become the basis for personality and character formation. We know, too, that mental growth is accelerated if children have secure relationships from which to reach out to explore and learn (Bus & Ijzendoorn, 1988; Frankel & Bates, 1990).

Multiple Attachments

Children can develop close attachments to more than one person (Fox, Kimmerly, & Schafer, 1991; Goossens & van Ijzendoorn, 1990). Most studies show that young children can and often do become equally attached to both their mother and their father (Dickstein & Parke, 1988; La Rossa, 1988). This represents two significant attachments. Then, if there are other relatives, such as a grandparent or older children in the home, strong attachments may also be developed with these persons. Anthropologists have emphasized that in some societies, children are regularly cared for by a number of persons and that these children enjoy healthy interpersonal relations with all the family members. In fact, in such families, the loss of the mother is not completely disastrous because the child has already become closely attached to other

Attachment—the feeling that binds a child to a parent or caregiver

adults. The same thing holds true in our own society in extended families. One woman said that when her father deserted the family, she was not very upset because she had her grandmother, grandfather, aunt, mother, and older sisters and brothers in the household, all of whom were very close to her (Author's counseling notes).

Because children can form multiple attachments does not mean that caregivers can be constantly changed. Stability of care, whether by a parent, relative, or babysitter, is one element in the maintenance of emotional security. It *is* upsetting to a child who has formed a close attachment to one person to have that person leave and be replaced by another person and then by another. One of the hardest problems that working parents face is to get dependable substitute care that will not be changing continually, yet this is one factor that determines the overall effect of substitute care on children. It is important that the child who is separated from a primary attachment figure, have a chance to form a close attachment with a substitute (Tompson, 1997).

The important factor in attachment development is the total dialogue that goes on between parent and child (Isabella & Belsky, 1991). Some parents are supersensitive to their children's needs (Smith & Pederson, 1988). They seem tuned to their children's signals and respond fairly promptly and appropriately to their babies' cries (Pederson, Moran, Sitko, Campbell, Ghesquire, & Acton, 1990; van den Boom, 1997). They are able to interpret behavioral cues to discover what their infants are trying to communicate. They like their babies, are interested in them, spend time interacting with them, and are understanding in their responses to them. As a result, their babies often smile, bounce, and vocalize in interaction with their parents, and show in other ways that they enjoy the social contacts with them (Lewis & Feiring, 1989).

Children can form attachments to multiple caregivers.

Specific Attachments

On the average, attachments to specific persons do not develop until about 6 or 7 months of age. Before this age, we find little upset at separation, such as the mother's leaving the room. It is true that babies left alone in a room may begin to fret, but they may be comforted by anyone. They seek attention in general rather than the attention of a specific person. Consider the following two observations.

> A 10-week-old baby is lying in her crib. Her mother, tidying the blankets, leans over her, talking and smiling, while the baby coos and "talks" back. The mother leaves the room to greet a visitor. The baby cries. The visitor, who has not seen the baby before, comes over, leans down, smiles, and talks to the baby. The baby stops crying and smiles as the visitor picks her up.
>
> An 8-month-old baby is playing on his mother's knee, when his mother puts him down and leaves the room to answer the door. As the visitor enters, the baby cries. When the visitor attempts to comfort him by picking him up, the baby cries more frantically until the mother returns and holds him. Then the baby calms down. From his mother's lap he first stares and later smiles at the visitor (Dunn, 1977, p. 29).

The two situations demonstrate a crucial change. Both the 10-week-old and the 8-month-old babies protested at being left, but the older child protested at his *mother's* departure. The visitor seems to upset him more. He no longer treats people as interchangeable companions; separation from his mother has taken on new meaning because he is now attached to *her.*

Decreases in Attachment Behavior

From 12 to 18 months of age is probably the most vulnerable time, when specific attachments are at their maximum (Vaughn & Waters, 1990). Generally, we see a change in the attachment behavior of children over the course of the second year, indicating increasing independence and maturity. Also, the need for contact, which is sought through physical closeness and touching at 1 year of age, gradually expands to the social realm.

Children want contact by looking and talking, by verbal soothing, and by reinforcement. The older that children get, the more they seek such contact. Also, as their social contacts expand, so do the number of attachments they form.

Nonattached Children and Insecure Attachment

Some young children whose parents reject them are distant and unemotional, and they don't even seem to notice when their parents come home in the evening or have taken a trip. Of course, sometimes children don't notice because they are preoccupied with their own activities, but if this behavior happens frequently, it may indicate a lack of attachment to the parents. Young children may show marked differences in the degree of attachment. **Nonattached children,** or those whose attachment development is delayed, continue to make no distinctions between their own parents and other members of the household or the caretaker. They reject the attention of most people, including that of their own parents. These children do not cry when their parents leave the room, nor do they attempt to follow them. They are sometime precociously independent. This is not normal behavior for children who are old enough to have developed attachments to their parents.

At the other extreme are **insecurely attached children,** who are so dependent on their parents that they won't let them out of their sight at all (Lieberman, Weston, & Pawl, 1991). Insecurely attached children experience care that is insensitive, inconsistently responsive, or rejecting (Booth, Rubin, & Rose-Krasnor, 1998). If parents have to leave, the children scream. The clinging, dependent behaviors of these children are symptoms of their insecurities. Insecurely attached infants are fussy babies. They cry not only when they are parted from their parents, but also when they are in close proximity. They cry to be picked up, or they cry when their parents put them down (Belsky & Braungart, 1991). They seek almost continuous physical contact and are unable to tolerate even a little distance from their parents.

Turner (1991) found some differences in attachment behavior according to gender of insecurely attached children in preschool. Insecure boys showed more aggressive, disruptive, assertive, controlling, and attention-seeking behavior than secure boys. Insecure girls showed more dependent behavior and were less assertive and controlling than secure girls.

There are various reasons for overdependent behavior (Egeland & Farber, 1984).

Nonattached children— children who have not developed a close emotional relationship with parents or caregivers

Insecurely attached children— children who are overly dependent on parents or caregivers because of insufficient attachment

Children who receive insufficient food and who are chronically hungry may develop these symptoms. Children who are chronically ill may become overly dependent. Children who are rejected and neglected may develop an excessive need for attachment. If parents are highly anxious, nervous, or neurotic persons, this anxiety is felt by their children, who seek reassurance as a result. Also, parents who become depressed, mentally ill (van Ijzendoorn, 1992) or preoccupied with their own personal problems are not able to give their children the attention and assurance they need. Any one or a combination of these conditions may result in children who are overly dependent and insecurely attached (Lyons-Ruth, Connell & Grunelbaum, 1990). Parents need to be sensitive, to have a lot of social support, and be secure persons themselves in order to provide their children what they need (Jacobson & Freye, 1991). *One study showed that parent-infant attachment at 12 months of age could be predicted from the qualities of interaction at 3 months and from the amount of time parents spent with their infant* (Cox et al., 1992; Pederson, Gleason, Moran, & Bento, 1998).

We must be careful, however, in attributing all differences in attachment behavior to the quality of parenting that children receive. Cause and effect relationships are hard to establish. Sometimes there seem to be inconsistent and weak associations between parental behavior and attachment security (Rosen & Rothbaum, 1993). This condition means that hereditary factors and natural differences in temperament also play important roles in attachment behavior. Some children seem to be born needing closeness; others seem more independent from the beginning of life. There does seem to be a relationship between temperament and attachment behavior, but this relationship is often variable and inconsistent, varying from child to child (Vaughn et al., 1992). Because of this finding, Erikson has suggested that the basic psychosocial task of the child during the elementary school years is to evidence industry and to learn to meet the demands of home and school, as well as to develop the feeling of self-worth through accomplishment and interaction with others. Failure to do so leads to feelings of inferiority in relationships with others.

Critique of Attachment Theory

Much of the early literature on attachment theory is based on the underlying belief that it is mothers who should or will take primary responsibility for the raising of the children. Attachment theory focuses on maternal rather than on parental attachment. Researchers tell us that they have studied mothers rather than fathers because the available data on fathers are insufficient. A view of egalitarian parenting assumes that there is more than one single primary caregiver who cares for the child. Parental attachment is important because the fathers have a key role to play in this whole relationship. Actually, attachment theory should take into account that it is not only the parents who are caregivers but also relatives, friends, and other persons (Dendoorn & DeWolff, 1997).

The implicit gendering of parental attachment is only one of the problematic assumptions of research. Equally disturbing is the actual prescription for healthy caregiver-to-child attachment. There has been a long history of attacks on mothers whom our culture has described as neurotically and sadistically attached to their children. These mothers are charged with damaging their children by keeping them perpetually tied to invisible

Parenting Issues

Response to Crying

One mother asked this: "If I go in to see what is the matter as soon as the baby cries, isn't he more likely to cry even more the next time? Shouldn't I let him cry it out to show him that he can't get my attention any time he wants?" (Frodi & Senchak, 1990). Generally speaking, a sensitive and prompt response by the parent to the baby promotes a harmonious relationship with a child who is secure and content. Parents who respond promptly to distress tend to have children who are among the least fretful (Donovan, Levitt, & Walsh, 1997).

Babies whose crying is ignored early in life tend to cry more persistently thereafter. Furthermore, this persistent crying aggravates the parents and discourages response (Bisping, Steingrueber, Oltmann, & Wenk, 1990; Donovan & Leavitt, 1989).

However, overanxious parents who respond unnecessarily when the baby really doesn't need them are encouraging excessive crying and demands. In other words, some of the most fretful babies may have parents who are overly anxious about responding. This view supports the social-learning theorists.

As in many other instances, avoiding extremes in raising children is often the wisest thing. If a parent never responds to the baby's cries of distress, one reaction is for the child to give up crying entirely and become withdrawn, but no one would say such a quiet child is well adjusted. The other extreme is for the parent to respond anxiously to every whimper (Zeskind, Klein, & Marshall, 1992).

Some children are overly dependent on parents.

apron strings. For these attachment theorists, almost no level of attachment is too strong.

For other theorists, it is clear that the mother or caregiver who receives the highest marks is the one who is constantly, completely, and totally devoted to the child. According to this view, the good, child-centered caregiver will happily bury her own interests and desires in order to focus on those of the child. She will be perfectly content with the fact that the demands of parenting have caused her to give up things that she once enjoyed, just as she is pleased that people are less interested in her than they are in her child and just as she is happy that her child is the center of every social interaction.

Obviously, the caregiver does not completely have to lose her sense of self to be meeting the child's emotional needs. There is a happy medium. Attachment that is carried to extremes retards emotional development and the development of autonomy. Attachment theory properly implies that many children suffer from some level of maternal deprivation. But it should also imply that there is an optimal level of care for children in our society. The all-consuming, intensive, permissive mother care is not necessarily the best form of care for children. Attachment theorists need to take a more balanced approach toward both the needs of children and the needs of caregivers (Hays, 1998).

Separation Anxiety

Symptoms

Signs of separation anxiety vary somewhat according to individual children, their ages, and the frequency and length of time they are separated from the attachment figure (Field, 1991b; Lollis, 1990). After infants develop attachments to specific persons, they begin to show signs of distress when these persons leave them (Bridges, Connell, & Belsky, 1988). The simplest manifestations is a baby's crying when a parent leaves the room (Vaughn, Lefever, Seifer, & Barglow, 1989). Observers have found that some babies as young as 15 weeks will cry when parents leave. Most babies certainly will by 30 weeks.

The most common separation is a parent leaving a child alone in a room and closing the door. Infants may cry, and their play may cease soon after the parent leaves. If they are old enough to creep or walk, they may try to follow. If the parent leaves the room but the child can observe the parent in the adjacent room, anxiety is minimized. One observer discovered that young children in a park commonly "froze" when their mothers kept in sight while walking away from them, but they did not cry or attempt to follow. However, a group of infants in a laboratory experiment played contentedly for several minutes and then tried to follow their mothers, who had walked out of sight (Corter, 1976).

In the movie Home Alone, *the parents mistakenly left on vacation without their child.*

Effects of Repeated or Long-Term Separation

If separation is repeated or continues for very long, usually over a period of days, symptoms become more serious. The initial phase of protest and searching is followed by a period of despair, during which children become quiet, apathetic, listless, unhappy, and unresponsive to a smile or coo. Finally, if separation continues, the children enter a period of detachment and withdrawal when they seek to sever the emotional ties with the attachment figure. They appear to have lost all interest in the person to whom they were formerly attached. In extreme cases, they seem to lose interest in almost everything going on around them. There is no attempt to contact a stranger and no brightening if strangers contact them. Their activities are retarded. They often sit or lie in a dazed stupor. They lose weight and catch infections easily. There is a sharp decline in general development (Bowlby, 1980).

The trauma of long-term separations without an adequate substitute attachment figure is best illustrated by the following description of a 2-year-old child who had a good relationship with his parents at the time he was hospitalized. He was looked after by the same mother substitute and visited daily by his parents during the first week. However, his behavior deteriorated when the parents reduced their visits to twice a week and then gave up visiting him.

> He became listless, often sat in a corner sucking and dreaming; at other times he was very aggressive. He almost completely stopped talking. . . . He sat in front of his plate eating very little, without pleasure, and started smearing his food over the table. At this time, the nurse who had been looking after him fell ill, and Bobby did not make friends with anyone else, but let himself be handled by everyone without opposition. A few days later he had tonsillitis and went to the sickroom. In the quiet atmosphere there he seemed not quite so unhappy, played quietly but generally gave the impression of a baby. He hardly ever said a word, had entirely lost his bladder and bowel control, sucked a great deal. On his return to the nursery he looked very pale and tired. He was very unhappy after rejoining the group, always in trouble and in need of help and comfort. He did not seem to recognize the nurse who had looked after him at first (Bowlby, 1973).

The trauma of extensive separation without an adequate substitute can be quite severe.

Age Factors

Generally speaking, distress over separation is greatest after 6 months and until about 3 years of age. It is most evident in young children who

---

Parenting Issues

When a Child Goes to the Hospital

One parent asks the following: "My 4-year-old may have to go to the hospital for a major operation, and he will probably have to stay a week. What should I do to minimize the emotional upset?" It is helpful if one parent can stay with the child, making arrangements to sleep in the same room, if possible. If one parent can't stay all the time, the other parent, older relatives, and/or teenagers can rotate so that a family member is present all the time. Such arrangements can be made in many hospitals and are vitally important to the child's emotional health. Going to the hospital is frightening enough, but having to stay there for a week is far more upsetting than most children, even the best-adjusted ones, can handle. All of the symptoms of separation anxiety are frequently seen after a few days of hospitalization. In addition, children fear being hurt or mutilated or being left alone. Also, they may interpret being sent to the hospital as punishment for wrongdoing. "I will be good, don't make me go" is the way some children feel. One 7½-year-old boy who had been in the hospital three times since the age of 3 recalled: "I thought I was never coming home again because I was only 6 years old. I heard my sister say they were going to dump me and that I'd never come home again" (Bowlby, 1982).

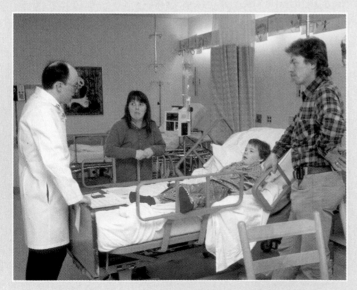

Familial comfort, attention, and support diminish a child's fears of staying in a hospital.

have had a close relationship with their parents and who are separated suddenly without an adequate substitute caregiver provided to whom the child has already become attached. Protest over temporary separation begins to decline most sharply around age 3. The decline in anxiety accompanies the increase in the power of recall: Children are able to remember their parents and a promise that they will return; also, increasing autonomy and mobility make them less dependent.

Preschool children from 3 to 5 years of age can still experience a great deal of separation anxiety, however, as every nursery schoolteacher knows. The older that children become, the less they are upset at separation, partially because they are more independent and partially because they will take more readily to mother substitutes. Between the ages of 5 and 8, the risks of upset decrease even further. Contrary to what we find in younger ages, the children of this age who have the happiest relationships with their parents are better able to tolerate separations than those who are only insecurely attached. A happy child, secure in parental love, is not made unbearably anxious. The insecure child, already anxious in his or her attachments, may become even more troubled by forced separation (Ainsworth, 1988).

School-age children or even adolescents are not untouched by separations. Surveys of children between the ages of 5 and 16 who were evacuated from the city of London during World War II confirm the finding that children are not yet emotionally self-supporting. Teachers reported that homesickness was prevalent; that the power of concentration on schoolwork declined; and that bedwetting, nervous symptoms, and delinquency increased. In most cases, there were no serious aftereffects following the children's return home, but in others, the problems persisted for a while afterward (Bowlby, 1982). Young people as old as college age may go through a period of extreme homesickness when first away from home. They get over it, but it's very upsetting for a while.

Homesickness

Homesickness is one manifestation of separation anxiety. Homesickness is experienced by millions of the children who spend time away from home. Some children experience high levels of homesickness associated with severe depressive and anxious symptoms. Homesickness has been documented in children at boarding schools, residential summer camps, and hospitals, as well as in refugee children living with host families. One study found that homesick first-year college students were three times more likely to drop out of school than their nonhomesick peers (Burt, 1993). An investigation of over a thousand boys and girls spending two weeks at a summer residential camp found that the most frequent and effective way of coping with homesickness was to exert control by engaging in a distracting physical activity (Thurber & Weisz, 1997).

In one longitudinal and clinical investigation of homesickness in children, the moods of 329 boys ages 8 to 16 were assessed on a daily basis during either a 2- or 4-week period of separation from primary caregivers. The subjects were all campers at a residential boys' sports camp. The study confirmed four major hypotheses. Homesickness was quite prevalent, varied in intensity, and, for some boys, reached levels associated with severe depression and anxiety. Younger boys were at greater risk for homesickness than older boys (Thurber, 1995).

Reunion Behavior

Investigations of reunion behavior of children reveal various reactions (Bowlby, 1982). Some children become very dependent and possessive, clinging, whining, crying for attention, and placing great demands on their parents. In such cases, it is helpful if the parents can devote themselves exclusively to their children after they get home; otherwise, their attachment behavior may increase.

Some children are quite angry at their parents and resist (at least initially) their efforts to hug them and to pay attention to them. It is evident that they have ambivalent feelings toward their parents. On the one hand, they want their love and attention. On the other hand, they resist because they are angry and fearful. If a separation has been long and upsetting, any withdrawal behavior of children is their effort to keep from being rejected or deserted again.

Sometimes, on reunion, children are emotionally cold and unable to speak or express their feelings until tearful sobs finally burst forth, accompanied by accusing questions: "Why did you leave me?" The worse that children behave, the more evident it is that they have been upset by the parent's being away.

Strangers

Fear of strangers, when it develops, ordinarily begins at about 6 or 7 months of age, and increases to about 2 years, after which it declines (Fagot &

Kavanagh, 1990). Usually, this fear begins after the onset of specific attachments. Children who are very frightened may cry or cling to their parents. Less upsetting reactions include general wariness or active turning away and avoidance (refusing to be picked up, refusing to speak, or running away).

Children differ considerably in their reactions to strangers (Thompson, Connell, & Bridges, 1988). Some children never seem to show much fear at all. They smile readily, seldom turn away from being approached, and may even approach the strangers after only a few minutes of contact. Individual differences relate to how secure children are and to what their background of social experiences are. Some children are more accustomed to having pleasant experiences with a variety of persons. However, children who have suffered repeated and upsetting exposures to strangers become even more wary and frightened the next time they are approached.

If children are with their parents at the same time that they are in the presence of strangers, they are less frightened than when they are alone with strangers. Children are less frightened of strangers in familiar surroundings. This fact means that parents who invite friends over to their own home and let the children stay around during the socializing are helping the children get used to other people in an environment that is not stressful. Or, if parents stay with their children when they go out among strangers, they are getting their children used to other persons at the same time that they are giving them the security of their presence. The most frightening situation is to leave the children with strangers in an unfamiliar setting. Also, it is wise to avoid separations and frightening experiences at a time when the fear of strangers is developing or is at its peak. From 1 to 2 years of age is an especially bad time. Either before fears develop or after children begin to lose their fear of strangers is a better time to expose children to new people.

Baby-Sitters and Substitute Caregivers

Leaving a child with a stranger can be a very upsetting experience, but it need not affect the child negatively at all if the proper arrangements are made. The arrangement considered the least upsetting is care by the other parent in the child's own home while the one parent is gone, or substitute care by a close, dependable relative in the child's own home (Darling-Fisher & Tiedje, 1990). If neither of these alternatives is possible, the next alternative is a dependable, capable baby-sitter in the child's own home, provided that the child has become acquainted with the sitter. It is perhaps a good idea to help children become attached to several substitute caregivers in case one cannot show up. It is often worse for the parents to surprise the child with a complete stranger and then leave for several days or longer without warning.

Another alternative is family day care in the home of the day-care provider. Usually, the provider is caring for several children at once. If the home is licensed, the state regulates the number of children per provider. The number of infants permitted is fewer per provider than the number of older children that may be cared for. The effect on children depends greatly on the quality of the care. Home environments that are free of tension and provide the requisite materials and interactions build security and stimulate the cognitive development of children (Goelman, Shapiro, & Pence, 1990).

Many children are being cared for in formalized child-care centers. Parents are usually more willing to place older preschool children in such centers than they are to place infants and toddlers. Day-care centers are the most costly type of child-care arrangement, and resources are limited. The odds that parents enroll their children in a center-based program are greatest when mothers are more highly educated, when the child is older, and when plenty of (nonpaternal) social support is available to the mother, such as from a resident grandparent (Fuller, Holloway, & Liang, 1996). These considerations, plus a general parental preference for other child-care arrangements, limit the numbers of children cared for in this manner (Camasso & Roche, 1991; Caruso, 1992; Kontos, Hsu, & Dunn, 1994).

The question of the long-term effects of substitute care on children is a very controversial one (Belsky, 1990; Rapp & Lloyd, 1989). Some studies find no association between a mother's work status and the quality of the infant's attachment to her (Chase-Lansdale & Owen, 1987). Belsky and Rovine (1988) have concluded that when infants were from intact families, 12 and 13 months of age, and exposed to 20 or more hours of substitute care per week, they were more likely to be insecurely attached than are infants cared for less than 20 hours per week. However, leaving a child daily in the care of a baby-sitter so that both parents can go to work, even over a period of years, is far different from leaving a child to be cared for by a procession of baby-sitters with whom the child has only superficial attachments. Also, leaving a child in a well-run, well-staffed infant-care center is far different from leaving a child in an overcrowded, understaffed nursery where care is inadequate, where the staff changes frequently (Howes & Hamilton, 1992b), and where the personnel cannot give sufficient attention to each child. The biggest problem is finding dependable, high-quality care (Meredith, 1986; Trotter, 1987b).

Evidence is accumulating that the effect of high-quality day care on children is very positive. One study examined the relationship between cognitive and socioemotional competence at ages 8 and 13 to children's earlier day-care experiences (Andersson, 1992). The results indicated long-lasting positive effects of early day-care experiences. At ages 8 and 13, school performance was rated highest among those children who had entered day care before the age of 1. At age 13, school performance was lowest among those without out-of-home care. Similar results were found for some socioemotional variables. School adjustment at age 8 was highest for children who entered day care before age 1, and lowest among those without out-of-home care. The same was true for social competence at age 13. No signs of negative effects of early entry into day care were found.

Another study, this of children 5 to 8 years of age, found that children who had spent time in quality infant day care appeared to be better off socially and emotionally during the early grade school period than those who had not been in day care. According to the parents, children who had experienced quality infant day care were more popular, had more friends, and engaged in more extracurricular activities

The effect of day care on children depends on the quality of the care.

than those who had had less or lower-quality care. They exhibited greater social skills, assertiveness, and leadership abilities (Field, 1991a). This same researcher found that sixth-graders who had experienced full-time stable infant care in a variety of centers starting at different ages in infancy were more physically affectionate and more assertive (not aggressive), were more attractive, showed superior emotional well-being, and received higher math grades than those not attending infant-care centers. Time spent in quality infant care was significantly related to being assigned to the gifted program in school (Field, 1991a).

DEVELOPMENT OF TRUST AND SECURITY

Theorectical Perspectives

Erik Erikson (1963, 1968) suggested that the "cornerstone of a vital personality" is formed in infancy as the child interacts with parents or other caregivers. This cornerstone is one of basic trust as infants learn that they can depend on the caregivers to meet their needs for sustenance, protection, comfort, and affection. If these needs are not met, the infants become mistrustful and insecure.

Margaret Mahler, a clinical psychologist, emphasizes the importance of the mother–child relationship (Mahler, Pine, & Bergman, 1975). From birth to 2 months, infants go through an **autistic phase** during which their only awareness of the mother is as an agent to meet their basic needs. Then from 2 to 5 months, they enter a second phase, **symbiosis,** during which they establish dependency on their mother, building a solid foundation for later growth and independence. Mothers who are sensitive and responsive encourage a symbiotic relationship with their infants. A less sensitive mother can frustrate the infant's need to fuse with her, causing the infant to be insecure. The basic psychosocial task, therefore, is to build trust and security through dependency and need fulfillment.

Requirements for the Development of Trust and Security in Infants

There are a number of requirements if trust and security are to be developed. One requirement is for children to receive regular and adequate feedings. The chronically hungry child becomes an anxious child (Valenzuela, 1990).

A second requirement for the development of trust and security is for babies to get

Autistic phase—age during which children are aware of their mother only as an agent to meet their basic needs

Symbiosis—period in which children establish a close dependency on their mothers, to the extent that there is almost a fusing of personalities

sufficient sucking. Most need several hours a day in addition to their nutritional requirements. Since sucking is a source of comfort and emotional security, feeding time needs to be a relaxed, unhurried experience, allowing the baby ample opportunity to suck. Most babies can empty the mother's breast in a short time, but they continue to suck for a period afterward.

Another important emotional need of children is for cuddling and physical contact (Anisfeld, Casper, Nozyce, & Cunnigham, 1990). Children have an emotional need for fondling, touching, stroking, warmth, the sound of a pleasant voice, and the image of a happy face (Herman & McHale, 1993; MacDonald, 1992; Pelaez-Nogueras, Field, Hossain, & Pickens, 1996). Studies involving tactile stimulation of neonates and infants have reported improvements in growth and in motor, cognitive, and social development following touch interventions. Touch intervention has shown

This Inuit mother in Canada demonstrates sensitivity to the needs of her child.

to be especially important to high-risk infants. Touch can regulate arousal, enhance proximity between mother and infant, and organize and sooth the infant. It is used to increase infants' social behavior such as attention (eye contact) and positive affect (smiles and vocalization) (Pelaez-Nogueras, Gewirtz, Field, Cigales, Malthurs, Clasky, & Sanchez, 1996).

The most important requirement for the development of trust and security in children is for parents to show them that they love them. Parents need to convey through attitude, word, and deed that they adore their children. It is also important that parents be sensitive and responsive to their children's needs (Bornstein et al., 1992).

Some Causes of Distrust and Insecurity

Parental Deprivation

As already discussed, once children have formed close emotional attachments to a parent or parent substitute, any extended separation has negative effects. The longer the deprivation continues, the more pronounced the effects. Such children are typically described as emotionally withdrawn and

Living Issues

Learning to Express Affection

A frequent complaint of both men and women is that their partner is not affectionate enough. By affection, they do not always mean sexual intercourse; instead, they mean touching, hugging, cuddling, holding, kissing. In a response to a challenge from one of her readers, Ann Landers (1985) asked women to reply to this question: "Would you be content to be held close and treated tenderly and forget about the act?" Over 100,000 replies poured in. Yes, answered 72% of the respondents. Of the total, 40% were under 40 years of age. Whatever else the replies indicated, they revealed that these women wanted to feel cared about, that they wanted tender words and loving embraces more than intercourse with an inexpressive partner. The fortunate women were those who received both emotional expressions of affection and complete physical satisfaction as well.

Shere Hite (1981), in her report on male sexuality, discovered that men wanted more than mechanical sex. They wanted physical affection—touching, hugging, kissing, back rubs, and stroking. They also wanted friendship, communication, emotional closeness, warmth, and genuine affection.

Although the need for affection is inborn, learning ways of expressing it is not (Money, 1980). Some children grow up in families in which hugging, kissing, and demonstrations of affection are a part of everyday life. The parents hold children on their laps, cuddle with them, hug and kiss them, tuck them in bed at night, tell them that they love them, and show their love in word and deed. Other children grow up in families that are not at all demonstrative. If they love one another, they never say or show it in intimate ways. Children from these families may grow up embarrassed to express affection and feelings. When they marry, they may have the same hesitancy in being demonstrative.

isolated, with an air of coldness and an inability to show warmth and sincere affection or to make friends in a caring way. One woman, who adopted a 5½-year-old girl who had been shifted from one relative to another, described her daughter as not being able to show affection. The mother complained that she "would kiss you, but it would mean nothing." The adoptive father explained that "you just can't get to her." A year and a half after the adoption, the mother remarked: "I have no more idea today what's going on in that child's mind than I knew the day she came" (Bowlby, 1971, p. 37).

What is significant is that some children can remain with parents and be similarly deprived if their parents are not able to fulfill their needs for affection, for loving care, for understanding and approval, or for protection from harm. Parents who have babies they don't want and who reject them or fail to care for them properly are exposing their children to parental deprivation just as surely as if they went away and left them.

Parents themselves need a lot of special support of their parenting task. This social support can come from family, friends, organizations, or the community at large. Adequate social support has been associated with parental satisfaction, personal well-being, maternal adjustment, increased verbal and emotional responsiveness on the part of parents, nurturance, mother-child communication, and with the child showing increased compliance with parental requests (Pianta & Ball, 1993). Social support moderates the negative impact of stresses such as poverty, child illness, or disability.

Tension

Another important cause of emotional insecurity is to be cared for by parents who are tense, nervous, anxious, and irritable (Crnic & Greenberg, 1990; Holden & Titchie, 1991; Sternberg et al., 1993). Parents need to be aware that quarreling between family members upsets children, especially if the quarrels are frequent and violent. A husband and wife start to shout at one another; the baby begins to cry. Even the dog hides under the table. Children who are forced to listen to repeated parental fights become more and more anxious themselves. The direct negative impact of marital conflict has been demonstrated in child research (Davies & Cummings, 1998). Also, when there is economic stress in the family, the children's emotional well-being and behavior are affected. The children often show more depressive symptoms and antiso-

Quarreling among family members upsets children.

cial and impulsive behavior (Takeuchi, Williams, & Adair, 1991). The prevalence of stressful events in a person's life is positively related to psychological symptoms in adults, adolescents, and school-aged children. Child behavior problems are correlated with parenting stress, both maternal and paternal (Creasey & Reese, 1996).

Exposure to Frightening Experiences

The effects of isolated exposure to frightening experiences are usually temporary, unless the experience is quite traumatic. Many adults can recall frightening experiences: being locked in a closet, being chased by a dog, getting lost on the way home from school. Sometimes such experiences are traumatic enough or repeated often enough to cause long-term upset. Children who are sexually molested may be deeply affected psychologically, depending on the situation.

Criticism

Frequent disapproval and criticism may make children unsure of themselves. Actually, some disapproving parents are showing their children that they resent them or even hate them. Two psychiatrists describe the life of a boy whose parents hate him:

From the time he awakens in the morning until he goes to bed at night he is nagged, scolded, and frequently slapped. His attempts at conversation are received with curt, cold silence or he is told to be quiet. If he attempts to show any demonstration of affection, he is pushed away and told not to bother his parents. He receives no praise for anything he does no matter how well he has done it. If he walks with his parents, and lags a little, his arm is seized and he is yanked forward. If he falls, he is yanked to his feet. . . . At meal times he is either

Parenting Issues

Child Abuse

Child abuse takes two main forms: neglect and attack (Gelles & Conte, 1990). The effects of parental neglect have been discussed. But the effects caused by parents who physically attack and hurt their children may be devastating—both emotionally and physically. The battered child may suffer burns, lacerations, fractures, hemorrhages, and bruises to the brain or the internal organs. A case in point is that of an 18-month-old infant whose father sat him on the red-hot burner of the stove because he wouldn't stop crying!

Battered children are often unplanned, premature, or sickly children who make extra demands on parents who are not able to cope (Zucavin, 1988). Parents who batter their children expect and demand behavior from them that is far beyond the children's ability. Such parents are immature themselves, with poor impulse control, and in great need of love (Kugler & Hansson, 1988). In some cases they are emotionally ill (Walker, Downey, & Bergman, 1989). Often they were neglected and abused while growing up. One such example is that of Kathy, the mother of a 3-week-old boy, Kenny: "I have never felt loved in all my life. When the baby was born, I thought he would love me, but when he cried all the time, it meant he didn't love me. So I hit him." Not only do battered children suffer the pains of physical abuse, but they are also deeply scarred emotionally by the rage and hatred directed at them. Pathological fear, deep-seated hostility or cold indifference, and an inability to love others are often the results.

The negative effects of child abuse are compounded because abuse has a detrimental effect on children's social relationships. Abused children exhibit a higher proportion of negative behavior, are behaviorally disturbed, are more aggressive and less cooperative, and so are less well liked by their peers (Haskett & Kistner, 1991; Salzinger et al., 1993). Teachers view them as disturbed. The children have more discipline referrals and suspensions and often show poor academic performance (Eckenrode, Laird, & Doris, 1993). One researcher even pointed out that adults who were abused as children show increased use of alcohol and drugs and a higher incidence of HIV infection than adults who were not abused. Evidently they are more willing to engage in self-destructive behavior that reflects very low self-esteem (Allers & Benjack, 1991). Other research indicates that not only is the child who is abused affected, but siblings in the same family are affected as well (Jean-Gilles & Crittenden, 1990). The possibility for success of emotional rehabilitation will depend on the damage done. There are cases of battered children blossoming into happy persons after being adopted by loving parents. Play therapy is widely used in treating abused children. It has become an important clinical technique (White & Allers, 1994).

Some parents who were abused while growing up resolve never to abuse their own children. Unfortunately, other parents who have been abused themselves as children are likely to abuse their own children. Therefore, it is vitally important to get help, so that the cycle of abuse can be broken. One study found that abused mothers who were able to break the cycle of abuse were likely to have received emotional support from a nonabusive adult during childhood; to have received therapy; and to have married a stable, emotionally supportive mate with whom they have a satisfying relationship (Egeland, Jacobovitz, & Sroufe, 1988).

Adolescents who become parents have a high rate of abuse of their children. One program was designed to lower that rate by teaching pregnant teenagers what they could expect during and after pregnancy and how to properly care for themselves and their children (Rind, 1992).

Not only is abuse perpetrated by parents, but nongenetic caregivers, such as stepparents, baby-sitters, or child-care workers, especially those in home-based child-care centers, may also be abusive. Small, fussy infants, especially those under the care of adolescents, are particularly subject to abuse (Gelles & Harrop, 1991; Margolin, 1991). Although females are more often accused of abuse, males are frequently guilty of abuse as well (Margolin, 1992).

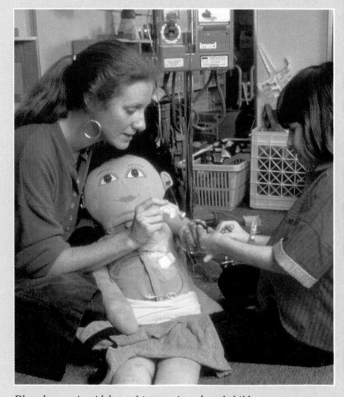

Play therapy is widely used in treating abused children.

FOCUS

Children of Alcoholics

In recent years, much attention has been focused on adult children of alcoholics (ACOAs) and the effects of having been brought up in an alcoholic family. In this section we are concerned with the effect on growing children. Approximately 7 million children under the age of 18 in the United States have an alcoholic parent (Noll et al., 1992). These children are at high risk for a host of emotional and behavioral difficulties during childhood, adolescence, and adulthood.

Children of alcoholics (COAs) are prone to becoming alcoholics themselves, because the vulnerability to alcoholism is inherited (Perkins & Berkowitz, 1991), especially between fathers and sons (Jacob, 1992). Sons of alcoholics are four times as likely as sons of nonalcoholics to become alcoholics themselves, even if they are adopted at birth, and regardless of whether the adoptive parents are alcoholics (Schuckit, 1987). Fetal alcohol syndrome is a well-known and disastrous result of mothers' drinking heavily during pregnancy.

There are, however, some other possible effects on the children of being raised by one or more alcoholic parents. These children are at high risk for mental health problems (Roosa et al., 1993). Depression, anxiety, and problem behavior are common among children of alcoholic parents (Tubman, 1993). Some findings suggest that parental alcoholism may affect a child's cognitive, fine-motor development (such as drawing and manipulative skills) and personal/social growth (such as ability to play cooperatively). The explanation is that alcoholic parents who manifest antisocial behavior themselves, or who suffer from depression, are not as attentive to their children's needs and are not able to provide the cognitive, social, and emotional experiences and stimulation necessary for their children's development (Noll et al., 1992).

Alcoholism affects parents and families in such a way that normal patterns of parent–child interaction and marital relationships are disturbed. In alcoholic families, parental depression, family stress and conflict, and marital discord create problems for the children (Tubman, 1993). Family cohesiveness, positive affect, and pleasant relationships are destroyed, creating stress and antisocial behavior in the children. Family rituals and get-togethers during holidays are disrupted because a parent is drunk, so that even happy times become occasions for stress and conflict (Jacob, 1992). Discipline in the alcoholic family is often inconsistent, and parental guidance and support are lacking (Roosa et al., 1993).

In spite of the negative effects just described, some children reared in alcoholic families become happy, well-adjusted adults (Easley and Epstein, 1991). Some children are remarkable survivors and learn how to cope. In many families where only one parent is an alcoholic, the other parent is able to provide for the children's needs. In one study of families in which the fathers were alcoholics, Hispanic mothers particularly were able to exert a strong, positive influence on their children's mental health (Roosa, et al., 1993).

Then, too, it often takes many years before negative effects become evident. One study of 3-year-old sons of alcoholics found no difference in development age, IQ, or behavior problems when compared with sons of nonalcoholic parents (Fitzgerald et al., 1993). The only apparent difference was that the sons of alcoholics were more impulsive, with less control over their actions than the other children in the study.

The whole family is involved in counseling when there is a problem with alcoholism of one family member.

ignored or his table manners and inconsequential food fads are criticized severely. He is made to finish whatever is on his plate. . . . The child soon realizes that he can expect nothing but a hurt body or hurt feelings from his parents, and instead of feeling love for them, he feels fear, loathing, and hatred (English & Pearson, 1945, p. 108).

Frequent criticism can be devastating, resulting in deep-seated insecurities and poor self-esteem.

Overprotection

Parents who are filled with anxieties themselves and who are fearful for the safety and well-being of their children, may not permit any activities in which there is an element of danger. One girl remarked: "My parents would never let me go to dances because they were afraid I'd get involved with boys." Overprotected children, whose parents never let them develop autonomy, may become so fearful of making decisions or of doing things on their own that they have difficulty establishing themselves as independent adults.

Overindulgence

One of the chief causes of insecurity in children is poor impulse control on their part, resulting in guilt and anxiety over their own behavior. Children who are permitted every satisfaction and liberty, whether these things are good for them or not, are inadequately prepared to face the frustrations and disappointments of life. Because such children are not disciplined or taught to consider others, they become selfish and demanding. Anxiety results when these persons get into the world and discover that other people resent them or dislike them because of their selfish behavior. They are puzzled that others don't indulge them as their parents have done, and they become more and more anxious that they won't be successful in their social relationships.

DEVELOPMENT OF EMOTIONS

Components

Psychologists have attempted to explain emotions in various ways. One book quotes over 30 different definitions of emotions (Strongman, 1987). Most of the descriptions include a sequence of four basic components of emotions:

1. Stimuli that provoke a reaction
2. Feelings—positive or negative conscious experiences of which we become aware
3. Physiological arousal produced by the hormonal secretions of the endocrine glands
4. Behavioral response to the emotions

To retrace the sequence, suppose that a child

1. is confronted by a growling dog and interprets this as danger;
2. reacts with fear;
3. experiences physiological arousal from the adrenal hormone secretion **epinephrine,** which produces an increase in heart rate, blood pressure, blood flow, sugar in the blood, respiration, and other changes; and
4. trembles and runs away (Tout, deHaan, Campbell, & Gunnar, 1998).

Psychologists are not in complete agreement as to whether the child (a) trembles and runs because of feeling afraid, or (b) becomes afraid only after experiencing the bodily reactions, or (c) experiences both the fear and the physiological arousal simultaneously. Cognitive theorists would disagree with all these explanations and say that emotional reactions depend on how the children would interpret the stimuli from the environment (the growling dog), and how they would interpret the internal bodily stimuli. Whatever the explanation, all emotions involve the same four basic components: stimuli (which are interpreted cognitively), feelings, physiological arousal, and behavioral response.

Functions

Emotions play a number of important functions in our lives (Barrett & Campos, 1987). They play *an adaptive function* to ensure survival. The fear that children may feel because of a growling dog motivates them to want to get away from the danger. Emotions are also *a means of communication* (Kochanska, Coy, Tjebkes, & Husarek, 1998; Russell, 1990). When children are sad or angry, they are transmitting the message that something is wrong. When they are happy, they are telling others that all is right with their world (Sullivan, Lewis, & Alessandri, 1993). Preschoolers 3 to 4 years of age are able to recognize their own internal emotional states or those of their younger siblings and to direct comments to their siblings about these feelings (Howe, 1991).

Emotions also are extremely *important in social relationships.* They are operative in forming social bonds and attachments, or in keeping other people at a distance. Emotions *are also powerful motivators* and have a

Epinephrine—hormone secreted by the adrenal glands that produces physiological arousal

Emotions are an important means of communication.

significant influence on behavior. Children tend to act out what they feel, be it love or anger. A boy may become hostile toward all women because he has an abusive, rejecting, cruel mother. His hostility influences his relationships with other women, especially with those who remind him of his mother. Or a girl may become hostile toward all men because of an abusive, rejecting, cruel father.

Emotions play an important role in *sociomoral development*, beginning with the awareness of "wrongness" and the feelings of guilt that are experienced when expectations of "rightness" are violated (Cole, Barrett, & Zahn-Waxler, 1992). Emotions are also *a source of pleasure or of pain.* Children who feel joyful and happy are able to enjoy the luxury of these positive feelings. In the same way, negative emotions of anger, disgust, fear, or sadness create disturbing feelings that can be very painful to endure. Yet, without feelings, either positive or negative, life would be colorless and dull.

There is considerable evidence that in our culture, boys are taught to inhibit their emotions, whereas girls are allowed to express them. This practice puts considerable burden on the boys to hide their feelings and makes communication more difficult between the sexes because boys have trouble expressing how they feel (Casey, 1993).

Basic Emotions

Psychologists have sought to identify and separate different emotions. Ekman (1972) and his colleagues found that people from all over the world were able to distinguish six basic emotions by distinctive facial expres-sions; *happiness, sadness, anger, surprise, disgust,* and *fear.* Carroll Izard (1977, 1980) has spe-cialized in studying the emotional develop-ment of children. Like Ekman, he says that each emotion has its own distinctive facial ex-pression. Four of Izard's basic emotions are shown by the facial expressions in the accom-panying photos.

Subsequent research has revealed that identification of infants' emotions from facial expressions is only partly successful. One study revealed that college graduate students were able to identify correctly the emotions of joy, interest, and surprise, but those de-picting fear, anger, sadness, and disgust were all labeled distress (Oster, Hegley, & Nagel, 1992). Other research has found some blend-ing of emotional expressions of infants. Some 23 facial expressions were classified as inter-est, according to one research study (Matias & Cohn, 1993). Some emotions are easier to recognize than others. Happiness, for exam-ple, is easier to recognize than fear and anger (Kestenbaum, 1992). Emotional expressions are easier to recognize when facial features show movement rather than being still-faced (Soken & Pick, 1992).

The ability to interpret correctly the emotions and feelings of others is important in interpersonal relationships. The fact that people are not al-ways able to identify emotions correctly means that what others say, think, and do may be sub-ject to misunderstanding. Studies do indicate that the ability to express and interpret re-sponses correctly improves during childhood, so that one would expect that empathy would increase (Strayer, 1993). Both children and adults tend to be overconfident in their ability to interpret how others feel, but there is an increase with age in children's tendency to

   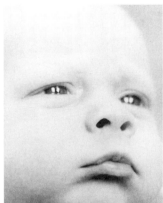

Infants' emotions (left to right): **Fear**—*brows level, drawn in and up, eyelids lifted, mouth retracted.* **Surprise**—*brows raised, eyes widened, mouth rounded in oval shape.* **Joy**—*mouth formed in smile, cheeks lifted, twinkle in eyes.* **Sadness**—*inner corners of brows raised, mouth corners drawn down. (From "The Young Infant's Ability to Produce Discreet Emotion Expressions," by Dr. Carroll E. Izard, 1980,* Developmental Psy-chology, 16, *132–140. Reprinted with permission.)*

consider more than one possible emotional reaction of others (Gnepp & Klayman, 1992).

Timetable of Development

Izard said that emotions develop according to a biological timetable. Interest, distress, and disgust are present from birth; joy (social smile) develops from 4 to 6 weeks; anger, surprise, and sadness are experienced at 3 to 4 months; and fear at 5 to 7 months. Shame and shyness (Broberg, Lamb, & Hwang, 1990) are experienced after the infant develops self-awareness at 6 to 8 months; contempt and guilt are felt during the second year of life (Lewis, Alessandri, & Sullivan, 1992). Table 8.1 shows the chronology.

Not all psychologists agree with this timetable. Campos, Barrett, Lamb, Goldsmith, & Stenberg (1983) believe that all emotions are experienced at birth but observers are not always aware that these various feelings are being expressed. Also, the feelings that are being expressed depend a lot on what is experienced and when. Abused children develop fear and sadness earlier than others (Gaensbauer & Hiatt, 1984).

Children's Fears

Children are not born afraid, except for two fears: fear of loud noises and fear of falling. Yet, beginning the first year or so of life, children may begin to develop many types of fears. The baby may become afraid of being bathed after getting soap in her eyes. She may become afraid of the noise made by the water going down the drain. Later, children may become afraid of the toilet flushing, the vacuum cleaner, thunderstorms, the dark, dogs, ghosts and monsters, Halloween masks, different-looking people, new situations, or being left alone. Night terrors in which the preschool child wakes up screaming, sometimes with no clear recollection of the frightening dream, are very upsetting experiences (Hartman et al., 1987).

Children's fears have many different origins. Some fears are learned behavior. They are *conditioned* by actual experiences. One of my clearest recollections of my preschool years was being chased and bitten by a dog that tore my new Easter suit to shreds. My subsequent fear of dogs took several years to overcome, but it was based on real experience. Unwittingly, parents sometimes instill fears in children because of the example they set. I had a sister-in-law who used to hide in the closet during a thunderstorm. Fortunately, she did not do so when children were around.

Children also have *vivid imaginations.* Because they have trouble separating fact from fantasy, they become afraid of the monster hiding under the bed. They have *limited experience and understanding,* so that if they experience something different, they may scream in terror because they haven't seen anything like that before (Harris et al., 1991). Today, young children are exposed to *scary stories* in books, in the movies, and on television. Even so-called children's stories can be quite scary. Older children may deliberately attend horror movies and then have nightmares that night.

Sometimes the security of children is threatened by adults who try to scare children into being good. "If you're not good, I'll call the police to come and get you and put you in jail." "If you're not good, I'm going to go away and never come back." One 2-year-old refused to lie down in his crib to fall asleep. Eventually, he fell asleep sitting up. It was found that his mother had punished him severely for wetting the bed while asleep; therefore, he was determined to keep himself awake so that he would not wet the bed and be punished. Sometimes older children scare younger ones by saying that the bogey man is going to get them.

The best way for parents to help is to accept the fact that children are afraid, offer them reassurance in cheerful, positive ways, and avoid ridiculing or punishing them. Parents who either ignore the fears or make too much fuss over them may make the fears worse (Spock & Rothenberg, 1992).

TABLE 8.1	TIMETABLE OF DEVELOPMENT OF INFANT EMOTIONS

Emotion	Time of Emergence
Interest	Present at birth
Distress	Present at birth
Disgust	Present at birth
Joy (social smile)	4–6 weeks
Anger	3–4 months
Surprise	3–4 months
Sadness	3–4 months
Fear	5–7 months
Shame, shyness	6–8 months
Contempt	Second year of life
Guilt	Second year of life

Children's Worries

Worry involves thoughts and images that relate to possible negative or threatening outcomes. Worry may serve an adaptive function and resemble problem solving, leading to effective preparation in coping for the future. At other times, however, when worry becomes excessive, it is as if the danger is constantly being rehearsed without a solution to it being found. Irrational or unrealistic threat scenarios predominate that are incompatible with successful problem solving. Indeed, recent research with adults demonstrates that individuals who worry excessively do not engage in adaptive problem solving at the same level as individuals who worry less. Most adults and children have to learn to attend selectively to threats and stimuli that cause anxiety. Low-anxious adults and children shift attention away from threatening stimuli, whereas those who are anxious attend to the stimuli and are more affected by them. The ability to attend selectively to some stimuli while ignoring others is essential for regulation of childhood anxiety (Vasey, El-Hag, & Daleiden, 1996).

One study of elementary-school-aged children examined worry and its relationship to anxiety. The children were from the second through the sixth grade (ages 7 to 12 years). The findings revealed few age-related differences but found that girls reported more worries than boys and that African Americans reported more worries than white or Hispanic children. The three most common areas of worry reported by children in this sample concerned *school*, *health*, and *personal harm*. Frequent concerns about school are consistent with previous findings. However, personal harm emerged as a central concern of children. In fact, worries about physical harm or attack by others was the single most frequent response reported by the children in the sample as one of their most intense worries. It is interesting that the school that participated in this project was not in a high-crime area. Moreover, children rated these events as low in their frequency of occurrence.

Concerns about classmates largely focused on rejection, exclusion from social activities, or being ignored by others, whereas friendship concerns predominantly reflected worries about betrayal (e.g., friends not keeping a secret). Health also emerged as a frequent area of worry among children. Specific health concerns were varied and included worries about their parents' health, operations, specific bodily functions (e.g., stomachaches), and contracting AIDS. It is possible that

Children worry about conflict in the family.

these health-related worries were a reflection of the substantial media attention devoted to health-care problems. Although the most intense worries pertained to personal safety, the areas that children worried about that occur frequently were predominantly social in nature (family, friends, and classmates). Children worried frequently about their families and reflected concerns about family or marital conflict. Overall, these findings provided an informative and interesting picture of the kinds of concerns that preoccupy children of elementary school age (Silverman, LaGreca, & Wasserstein, 1995).

Environmental and Biological Influences in Development

Hyson and Izard (1985) agree that emotional responses are partly learned; for example, infants are affected by their mother's moods and emotional expressions. Infants tend to model their mother's emotional expressions. One study found that 3- to 6-month-old infants of depressed mothers also showed depressed behavior and that this behavior carried over into their interactions with other adults who were nondepressed (Field, Healy, Goldstein, Perry, & Bendell, 1988). Another study showed that when 1½-year-old infants

Parenting Issues

When Your Child Is Angry

Anger is a basic human emotion. It arises out of frustration, when children find a discrepancy between what they believe ought to happen and what, in fact, is happening (Olthof, Ferguson, & Luiten, 1989). Typically, the causes of anger involve real or threatened physical or psychological pain, a violation of an expectation, and a perception that the situation is illegitimate or unfair. Responses include both physical and verbal aggression, outbursts, body tightness and rigidity, preoccupation with the situation, or withdrawal from social contact.

Anger can be a motivating force in overcoming obstacles, as a means of standing up for oneself or others. In these cases, anger can produce positive results. However, it can also lead to hurting others, to conflict, and to violence. Everyone gets angry sometimes. The real question is, is it controlled anger, and does it produce positive results? A central developmental task for children is learning to control the expression of anger and to direct it in harmless and positive ways. Self-control attempts are common and include suppressing anger and redefining the situation so as to make it less anger-provoking (Whitesell & Harter, 1996).

Parents have several important roles to play in this regard.

1. Parents can represent positive models for their children; that is, parents can show restraint in their own expressions of anger, so that children learn acceptable, helpful means of expression. Children who grow up in a house where there is a lot of anger are more likely to learn negative means of expression themselves (Cummings, 1987).

2. Parents can help children control anger by letting them know that certain expressions of anger such as temper tantrums, hitting, biting, or screaming are not acceptable. Children learn to control their emotions by parents' helping them to exercise control: "I know you're angry, but I can't let you bite your brother. You'll have to sit in the chair for a while."

3. Parents can help children to dissipate anger through physical activity, verbalization, and directed play. "Go out and play in the yard until you're not angry." "Let's talk about why you're mad." "Maybe if we played with the puppets it would help you with your anger." (Then have the child use various puppets that represent both the angry one and the one the child is expressing anger toward.)

4. Parents can tell children that they recognize their being angry, and that anger feelings are normal, but that children have to learn to control and redirect their reactions to their feelings. Spock and Rothenberg (1992) wrote the following:

> It helps children to realize that their parents know they have angry feelings, and that their parents are not enraged at them or alienated from them on account of them. This realization helps them get over their anger and keeps them from feeling too guilty or frightened because of it. (p. 402)

5. If anger becomes excessive and persistent, parents need to get at the root causes of the anger and to correct situations that cause it, if possible. If parents don't seem to make progress themselves, it is helpful for them to get counseling for themselves and their child.

Children need to learn how to express anger and direct it in positive ways.

smiled and when their mothers or mother substitutes were attentive and smiled back, the infants' frequency of smiling increased (Jones & Raag, 1989). Thus, open channels of social communication promote the outward expression of internal feelings.

Izard also emphasizes that emotional expressions have a biological component, because they seem to be fairly constant and stable (Trotter, 1987a). Kagan and colleagues found that behavioral inhibition in children may be due to the lower threshold of physical responsivity, so that some children don't react as readily to stimuli (Kagan, Rezneck, & Snidman, 1987). Kagan and colleagues also found that children who were inhibited or uninhibited at 21 months of age showed the same characteristics of inhibition and lack of inhibition at 4, 5½, and 7½ years of age (Kagan, Reznick, Snidman, Gibbons, & Johnson, 1988). Thus, *emotional expression and behavior in infancy tell us something about the personality of the child later in life* (Izard, Hembree, & Huebner, 1987). Biology defines the broad outlines and limits of emotional development; environmental influences stimulate and modify that evolution. Part of the task of being a parent or teacher is *socialization:* influencing the feelings and behavior of children so that they conform to societal expectations (Malatesta, Grigoryev, Lamb, Albin, & Culver, 1986). This goal would be impossible if feelings and behavior were only biologically determined.

Aggression

Aggression in children takes two forms: verbal aggression or physical aggression. The child who is verbally aggressive may be involved frequently in arguments, name calling, shouting matches, or in attempting to criticize other children, shame them, and make them feel guilty or inferior by the way in which they are spoken to. Physical aggression may manifest itself as hitting, wrestling, pushing, shoving, throwing things at each other, and getting into fistfights.

Naturalistic observations of children while playing at a playground revealed that aggression was not a rare event. Aggressive children were observed to be verbally and physically aggressive once every three and eight minutes respectively (Dolan et. al., 1993; Pepler & Craig, 1995). Prior studies demonstrate that as a group, boys exhibit significantly higher levels of aggression than do girls, a difference that persists throughout the life span (Hines & Kaufman, 1994). But this finding may reflect a lack of research on forms of aggression that are relevant to young females rather than an actual gender difference in levels of overall aggressiveness. Boys are more overtly aggressive (i.e., they manifest more physical and verbal aggression), whereas girls show more relational aggression, which focuses more on relationships between children. Girls seek to harm others through purposeful manipulation and by damaging peer relationships, whereas boys are more likely to harm peers through overt aggression, physical aggression, and verbal threats (Crick & Grotpeter, 1995).

Aggressive behavior in children often has its origins in the family situation. Children tend to model their behavior after that of their parents. This practice reveals why parents who use severe punishment, especially if it is cruel and abusive, stimulate resentment, rejection, and similar harsh, cruel behavior

on the part of children (MacKinnon-Lewis, Volling, Lamb, Dechman, Rabiner, & Curtner, 1994; Rohner, Kean, & Cournoyer, 1991; Simons, Beaman, Conger, & Chao, 1993; Weiss & Dodge, 1992).

Aggression in children must also be considered in a social context. The social characteristics of a group play an influential role in

FOCUS

Reducing Peer-Directed Aggression Among Boys

Childhood aggression is often predictive of low academic achievement, school dropout, juvenile delinquency, and even adult criminality and psychopathology. Therefore, any program that can reduce aggression ought to produce worthwhile, long-term benefits.

Hudley and Graham (1993) conducted an attributional intervention program to reduce peer-directed aggression among 101 elementary-school-age African American boys. Many fights among children are caused by their attributing hostile intent to the actions of others and then retaliating. However, excessively aggressive children often arrive at inappropriate, incorrect, and therefore maladaptive beliefs about the intent of others. As a result, their aggressive retaliation is unwarranted.

The researchers conducted a 12-session program to train males to infer nonhostile intent following ambiguous peer provocation, to train them to detect intentionality more accurately, and to practice making attributions and making decisions about how to respond, given attributional uncertainty. Role-playing and a variety of training methods were used.

At the end of the 4 months, the subjects showed a marked reduction in the presumption of hostile intent, a lowering in the preference for aggressive behavior, and a reduction in actual aggressive behavior.

Many fights among children are caused by their attributing hostile intent to others and then retaliating.

the expression of aggression within a group. When children associate with others who are aggressive, they themselves are stimulated to follow the aggressive patterns. Sometimes older children become members of violent gangs, in which aggression is considered a norm for the group (DeRosier, Cillessen, Coie, & Dodge, 1994). Children are also influenced by neighborhood environments. Those living in high-risk neighborhoods have more social and behavioral problems than children living in low-risk neighborhoods (Kupersmidt, Griesler, DeRosier, Patterson, & Davis, 1995).

Aggression puts children at risk for later problem behavior. The consequences of early aggression, which have been well documented, result in such negative outcomes as low academic achievement, early school dropout, heavy drug use, and juvenile delinquency (Graham, & Hoehn, 1995). Overaggression is frequently a cause of poor relationships with peers.

Aggressive children are also clearly at risk for negative interaction with adults at home and in the school setting. Teachers spend more time in negative interaction with aggressive children than with nonaggressive children, and they rate aggressive behavior as being more disturbing than other classroom problems. Aggressive behavior is also associated with increased school failure. Over time, aggressive children tend to expect more hostility from their teachers, just as they tend to expect more hostility from their peers (Trachtenberg & Biken, 1994).

Emotional Expression and Control

Peer groups can have a marked influence on children's emotional control. Children learn not to express their emotions. They act cool and unruffled as though things didn't bother them at all. Children who cry too easily or who get upset are picked on by other children of their age. This tendency is especially true among boys who generally discourage each other from expressing much negative emotion and feeling (Gottman, Katz, & Hooven, 1996).

Children report controlling their expression of emotion significantly more when in the presence of peers than when they are with their father or mother or when they are alone (Zeman & Garber, 1996).

Ideally, to be an emotionally mature individual means to develop proper balance between emotional expression and control. The ability to regulate emotions is a major goal of social development (Buss & Goldsmith, 1998). Children who can manage their emotions in emotion-related behavior are better able to behave in appropriate and socially competent ways at school (Eisenberg et al., 1997). The ability to control the expression of emotion is a positive predictor of the ability to focus on the needs of others and is an important determinant of prosocial behavior (Garner & Power, 1996). The socialization of the expression of emotion has been linked to children's sociocognitive development as well as to children's social and prosocial reactions and behavior (Cole, Zahn-Waxler, & Smith, 1994; Eisenberg, Fabes, & Murphy, 1996).

In some families, children are not permitted to express true feelings and emotions. They are not allowed to get angry, to argue with their parents, to express frustration, to be sad or to cry, to be exuberant, or to show pleasure and joy in living. Such parents try to inhibit the emotions of their children, somehow believing that emotions are a sign of weakness. Many men, in particular, grow up never being allowed to express feelings, with the result that it becomes very difficult to communicate with them and to establish what they are really thinking and feeling. It may take hours and hours of therapy to help these men unlock their feelings so that they can become genuine persons again.

The author had a woman student in class who was brought up by a very cruel father. The father would line up the children in the family and start to whip them with a belt. He told them that if they cried, they were being a sissy, but he continued to beat them until somebody cried, and then the child who cried would get beaten even more. Obviously, this was a no-win situation for the children. They learned that to express emotion was to face punishment.

Some children are not permitted to express true feelings.

Some parents tell their young sons, "Don't be a crybaby" if the children begin to cry. Other parents try to hide their feelings from their children, so that the children grow up believing that any expression of true feelings is somehow unacceptable. They learn to repress their feelings, just as their parents do. The extreme situation is the psychopath who grows up without any conscience or feelings at all. Such persons have arrived at a completely nonfeeling state, at least as far as outward manifestations are concerned.

At the other extreme are parents who do not try to help their children gain any control over their emotions at all. Their 2-year-old child has a temper tantrum, which frightens the parents, thus making them want to indulge the child to end the tantrum. Children learn that all they have to do is have temper tantrums in order to get their own way. Young children need external control in the beginning, but as they mature, the goal of discipline is to help the child to experience self-regulation, to move from external authority to internal control. The development of conscience and the internalization of values are the central goals of socialization (Kochanska, Murray, Jacques, Koenig, & Vandegeest, 1996).

Part of the problem that parents face is to maintain positive relationships with their children, to communicate positive feelings of love and affection at the same time that they communicate their displeasure at the children's antisocial or unsocial actions. Parents need to love their children at the same time that they hate what their children are doing. Children who are exposed to high levels of parental positive affect, that is, positive emotions, are the ones who become the most socialized and most cooperative human beings (Parker, 1995).

DIFFERENCES IN TEMPERAMENT

Personality and Temperament

Psychologists make a distinction between personality and temperament. **Personality** is the sum total of the physical, mental, emotional, and social characteristics of an individual. Personality is a global concept that includes all those characteristics that make every person an individual, different from every other person. Personality is not static; it is developed over the years and is always in the process of becoming.

Temperament refers to relatively consistent, basic dispositions inherent in people, which underlie and modulate much of their behavior (McCall, in Goldsmith et al., 1987). Rothbart defines temperament as "relatively stable, primarily biologically based individual differences in reactivity and self-regulation" (Rothbart in Goldsmith et al., 1987, p. 510). *Reactivity* means excitability or arousability. *Self-regulation* means inhibition (Rothbart, 1988). Thus, temperament involves differences in excitability and inhibition. Goldsmith identifies temperament as "individual differences in the probability of experiencing and expressing the primary emotions and arousal" (Goldsmith et al., 1987, p. 510).

Three aspects of temperament are emphasized: temperament (a) is objectively definable in individuals, (b) has a constitutional basis, and (c) is evident in infancy and shows some degree of stability (Braungart-Rieker & Stifter, 1996). Qualities of temperament are not a "flash in the pan" in the progression of children's behavioral development. Rather, individual differences appear in early behavioral styles and are thought to provide wide insight into an infant's future social identity. One study examined whether temperamental differences at age 3 were linked to interpersonal functioning in young adulthood. In a sample of over 900 children, researchers identified five distinct groups of children on the basis of behavioral observations: *well-adjusted, undercontrollable, reserved, confident,* and *inhibited children.* At age 21, the children's interpersonal functioning was assessed in four social contexts: *in the social network, at home, in romantic relationships,* and *at work.* Three patterns of relations were found: (a) *Well-adjusted, reserved,* and *confident children* defined a heterogeneous range of normative adult interpersonal behavior; (b) *inhibited children* had lower levels of social support with normative adjustment in romantic relationships and at work; and (c) *undercontrolled* children had lower levels of adjustments and greater interpersonal conflicts across adult social contexts. Inhibited children were characterized by overcontrolled, very cautious, and nonassertive personality styles, expressing little desire to take on leadership roles or to exert influence over others. Undercontrolled children were characterized by high levels of impulsivity, aggression, interpersonal alienation, and excitement and danger-seeking in adulthood (Newman, Caspi, & Moffitt, 1997).

Temperament is composed primarily of inherited biological factors, so that basic dispositions comprising temperament are

Personality—the sum total of the physical, mental, social, and emotional characteristics of an individual

Temperament—the relatively consistent, basic dispositions inherent in people that underlie and modulate much of their behavior

present early in life (Gunnar & Nelson, 1994). It has been found that preterm infants already demonstrate highly reliable individual differences in temperament. Full-term babies already showed high self-consistency over time in their availability to sensory stimulation, excitability, irritability, and activation. This finding illustrates heredity as an important component of temperament (Korner, 1996).

Children differ markedly in their reactions to stress. Some are called *stress reactive*, meaning that they react more sensitively to things that upset them, so that their hormonal systems are constantly being stimulated and their physiological reactions to being upset are greater than in other children. An active inhibition system reflects efforts at impulse control. This temperament system denotes more active processes of inhabition, effortful, or willful control of actions and of self-regulation (Nachmias, Gunnar, Magelsdorf, Parritz, & Buss, 1996).

As development proceeds, the *expression* of temperament becomes increasingly influenced by environmental factors (Goldsmith & Campos, 1990). (Hereditary factors in personality and temperament were discussed in Chapter 3.) A child's activity level, for example, is influenced by heredity, but the environment either permits or inhibits such a level of activity (Saudino & Eaton, 1991). Similarly, an infant's negative emotionality (crying, negative mood, emotional reactions, and social demandedness) is associated with less sensitive interaction on the part of the mother, even though basic emotionality is influenced by genetics (Fish, Stifler, & Belsky, 1991).

Components and Patterns of Temperament

Buss and Plomin (1984) specify three traits as constituting temperament. The first is *emotionality*, which is the intensity of emotional reactions. This dimension varies from an almost stoic lack of reaction to very intense, agitated reactions (Mangelsdorf, Gunnar, Kestenbaum, Lang, & Andreas, 1990). The second trait is *activity*, which has tempo and vigor as its two major components. Individuals vary from lethargy to almost mania. The third trait is *sociability*, which is the preference for being with others rather than being alone.

In the New York Longitudinal Study of 133 children discussed in Chapter 3, Thomas and Chess (1977) followed their subjects from infancy into early adulthood and identified these nine components of temperament:

1. *Rhythmicity*—regularity of biological cycles of eating, sleeping, and toileting
2. *Activity* level—energy level as expressed by the degree of movement
3. *Approach* or withdrawal from new stimuli—how a person reacts to new stimuli
4. *Adaptability*—ability to adjust to change
5. *Sensory threshold*—sensitivity to sensory stimuli
6. *Predominant quality of mood*—whether a person is predominantly happy or unhappy
7. *Intensity of mood expression*—the degree to which a person responds
8. *Distractibility*—how easily an added stimulus can capture a person's attention
9. *Persistency* and attention span—how long a person focuses on one activity and pursues it.

The researchers also grouped the children whom they studied into three categories, or temperament patterns: the *easy child*, the *difficult child*, and the *slow-to-warm-up child* (Chess & Thomas, 1986). Table 8.2 shows the temperament characteristics of each of these categories of children. Some of the components of temperament would not be identified with any one cluster. These are indicated by the dashes in some sections of the table.

Stability of Temperament

One study assessed the relationships between early temperament and behavioral problems across twelve years in an unselected sample of over 800 children. A battery of medical, psychological, and sociological measures were administered every two years since the children were age 3. They were assessed at age 3, 5, 7, 9, 11, and 15. Over the years, the sample remained representative of the full range of the general population on important variables such as socioeconomic status and IQ. Results from the study added to a growing body of research that is beginning to document connections between specific temperamental characteristics in early childhood and specific behavioral problems in later childhood and adolescence. Long-term continuity of individual differences was apparent for both sexes. Boys and girls who were characterized by lack of control in early childhood were more likely to experience behavioral problems a decade later (Caspi, Henry, McGee, Moffitt, & Silva, 1995).

TABLE 8.2 THREE TEMPERAMENT PATTERNS

Component of Temperament	Easy Child	Difficult Child	Slow-to-Warm-Up Child
Rhythmicity	Regular eating, sleeping, toileting schedules	Irregular schedules	—
Activity level	—	High activity level	Low activity level
Approach or withdrawal	Easily approaches new situations, people	Suspicion of new situations, strangers	Mildly negative initial response to new stimuli
Adaptability	Adjusts easily to newroutines, circumstances Accepts most frustrations without fuss	Adjusts slowly Temper tantrums when frustrated	Gradually likes new situations after unpressured repeated exposure
Sensory threshold	—	—	—
Quality of mood	Positive moods	Negative moods	—
Intensity of mood expression	Mild to moderate intensity of mood	High mood intensity. Loud laughter, crying	Low intensity of mood
Distractibility	—	—	—
Persistency, attention span	—	—	—

Adapted from "Genesis and Evolution of Behavioral Disorders: From Infancy to Early Adult Life," by A. Thomas and S. Chess, 1984, *American Journal of Psychiatry, 141*, pp. 1–9. Copyright 1984, the American Psychiatric Association. Reprinted by permission.

DEVELOPMENT OF SELF, AUTONOMY, SELF-CONCEPT, AND SELF-ESTEEM

Self-Awareness

The development of self-awareness means that children begin to understand their separateness from others and other things. In the first few months of life, babies discover their arms and hands appearing and disappearing. They see them move and are fascinated by what they see. Imagine coming into the world and never having seen an arm and hand before! At this time, however, infants are not aware that the hand is part of them. It comes in and out of view by accident. Sometime later, they also discover feet and toes. But they still don't associate them with themselves.

The sense of self emerges gradually. At about 1 year of age, infants become aware that other children are distinct persons whom they can see, hear, and touch, and who may take a toy. At about 18 months of age, infants are able to recognize their own reflection in a mirror and to develop a sense of *me* and *mine*.

As they become aware of themselves, they begin to develop a sense of possessiveness: "my hair," "my chair," "my bed," as distinct from "mama's hair," "mama's chair," or "daddy's bed." Feelings of jealousy, anger, or guilt are possible as a result of increased self-awareness and the need to protect the self from other selves (Campos et al., 1983). This new awareness of others also allows the development both of affection toward them and of rebellion against them.

Autonomy

Erikson (1950, 1959) said that the chief psychosocial task between 1 and 2 years of age is the development of autonomy. This desire for autonomy puts increasing demands on parents (Fagot & Kavanagh, 1993). As the self emerges, children also want some degree of independence: to feed themselves, to explore the world, to do what they want to do without being too restricted by caregivers. If they aren't permitted to do some things (within reasonable limits), they develop a sense of shame and doubt about their abilities. According to Freud, part of the conflict over autonomy centers around toilet

FOCUS

Attention-Deficit Hyperactive Disorder

Attention-deficit hyperactive disorder (ADHD), appears in about 3% of elementary school children (American Psychiatric Association, 1994). Boys are 3 times more likely to be diagnosed with the problem than girls (Moffitt, 1990). Those afflicted have 3 major symptoms: *excessive activity, inattentiveness,* and *impulsivity.* ADHD children engage in almost continuous talking, fidgeting, climbing, crawling, or running. They have difficulty remaining seated in the classroom or playing quietly, and they often engage in physically dangerous activities. They have difficulty in sustaining attention, do not seem to listen to what is being said, are easily distracted, shift from one uncompleted activity to another, have difficulty following through on instructions, and often lose clothes, school supplies, or notes from school. They have a low frustration tolerance, difficulty in taking turns, and poor peer adjustments; they blurt out answers to questions before they have been completed; and they interrupt or intrude on others, butting into conversations and groups (Clark et al., 1988; Landau & Milich, 1988). Age of onset must be before age 7 to differentiate ADHD from disorders that might arise because of stress. The American Psychiatric Association (1994) stipulates a duration of

at least one year to distinguish it from disorders due to stress.

There are many possible causes: *Genetic, neurological, biochemical,* or *environmental factors* are all possibilities. Birth injury, prenatal exposure to teratogens such as alcohol or other drugs, prematurity, infections that affect the brain, lead poisoning, vitamin deficiencies, food allergies, or reactions to food additives and colorings have all been suspected (Hartsough & Lambert, 1985; Jacobvitz & Sroufe, 1987). Of all the causes, heredity seems to have one of the most important influences. Children with this disorder don't outgrow the problems, which include academic failure, low self-esteem, anxiety, depression, and difficulty in learning, and which emerge or persist into adolescence and adulthood.

1. *Psychostimulant drugs* are the most effective treatment. Of the various drugs, *Ritalin* is the most commonly prescribed. This drug is a stimulant that has a reversal effect on hyperactive children, by increasing attention and decreasing restlessness. Its results are remarkable for some children (Sprague & Ullman, 1981; Whalen, Henker, Castro, & Granger, 1987). Sometimes, however, the drug produces adverse side effects such as

appetite loss, growth retardation, sleeping difficulties, and lethargy in the classroom (Nemeth, 1990). The drug should never be used as a one-step solution; rather, it should always be given in conjunction with other treatment programs.

2. *Psychotherapy* for families and children. This treatment is used to help parents and siblings deal with their resentment and anger. *Behavior-modification techniques* are used as teaching devices to help hyperactive children gain some control over their behavior (Ross & Ross, 1982). Parents need training in how to manage the hyperactive child (Dubey, O'Leary, & Kaufman, 1983).

3. *Educational planning.* Such planning is needed to offer ADHD children the optimum educational environment. Teachers need to be taught how *not* to make the problem worse. The best teachers are flexible in allowing minor disruptions and some physical activity in the classroom, while still providing some structure and guidance. Teachers can help children break up work into small, manageable units (Nemeth, 1990) and to channel excess activity into appropriate instrumental motor and attention responses (Zentall & Meyer, 1987).

Attention-deficit hyperactive disorder (ADHD)—a hyperactivity disorder characterized by excessive activity, inattentiveness, and impulsivity

training. Parents who are too strict during this anal stage of development create shame and doubt. Children's increasing mobility, however, gets them in trouble or can endanger lives, so reasonable controls are necessary to keep them safe and to help them manage their actions and emotions. How often parents exercise control is probably not as important in developing autonomy as *how* control is exercised. Control that is fair and reasonable and that shows respect for the child helps the child achieve disciplined autonomy.

Children react differently to two kinds of help—direct and indirect help. When ex-

tending indirect help, the helper guides the child towards a viable solution, frequently through suggestions or use of hints. Indirect help, therefore, enables the child to generate at least partially his or her own solution to a problem and affords the opportunity to master a difficult task or situation. When direct help is administered, the helper assumes primary responsibility for solving a child's problem. No process information such as hints, suggestions, or redefining the problem is offered to the child. Typically, direct help consists of simply giving answers or completing the difficult task for the child. Direct help is likely to elicit feelings of threat and incompetence rather than to engender a sense of personal control (Shell & Eisenberg, 1996).

To maintain a sense of individuality, children need discretionary control over personal areas of action. One study examined mothers' concepts of their young children's personal autonomy, including whether their children should be given behavioral discretion and what types of issues they viewed as their children's personal prerogative. The study was with 40 white, suburban, working-class mothers with children ages 5 and 7. The mothers were interviewed regarding their concepts of children's areas of personal discretion, autonomy, and individuality. In open-ended interviews, mothers reported that they set limits around issues of safety, family conventions, and daily routines but that they permitted children to make decisions about food, recreational activities, clothes, and playmates. Mothers viewed their roles as educators and nurturers, and valued the development of individuality in their children, which they thought was to emerge in infancy or toddlerhood. Other research has shown that mothers report giving their children choices with regard to clothing, food type and amount, play, and playmates; however, they report restricting their children with respect to actions tht would result in the harm of the child or of others (Nucci & Smetana, 1996).

FOCUS

Cross-Cultural Differences and Temperament

Most developmentalists agree that ease and intensity of behavioral arousal from external stimulation is an important temperamental quality of infants. This characteristic has been called *reactivity*, or ease of arousal. An important question is whether infants of different nationalities and of different genetic or cultural backgrounds or both, differ in ease of arousal. Research reports suggest that Asian infants have a lower level of arousal than Caucasian infants. Newborn Asian American infants, compared with European American infants, are calmer and are less likely to remove a cloth placed on their face, and more easily consoled when distressed. Chinese American infants living in Boston were less active, were less vocal, and smiled less often to the presentation of visual and auditory events during their first year than did European American infants. Other studies have shown that Japanese infants are reported to be less easily aroused and are less reactive than European American infants in the United States. A new study of four-month-old infants from Boston, Dublin, and Beijing administered the same battery of visual, auditory, and olfactory stimuli to evaluate differences in levels of reactivity. The Chinese infants were significantly less active, irritable, and vocal than the Boston and Dublin samples, with American infants showing the highest level of reactivity. The data suggest the possibility of temperamental differences between Caucasian infants and Asian infants in reactivity to stimulation (Kagan, Arcus, Snidman, YuFeng, Hendler, & Greene, 1994).

Separation-Individuation

In a previous section, we discussed Margaret Mahler's concept of the period of *symbiosis*, during which infants develop a strong dependency on the mother to such an extent that there is some fusing of personalities. However, at about 5 months of age, lasting until about age 3, Mahler says a new period begins: a period of **separation-individuation**, during which infants gradually develop a self apart from the mother (Mahler, Pine, & Bergman, 1975). Infants are still dependent on their mothers. But as they gradually develop greater physical and psychological separation, they need to achieve a balance in their dependent-independent conflict while developing a sense of self. They want to be independent, yet they are frightened of too great a separation. The development of autonomy is vital to their later development as an independent adult. However, too much autonomy may produce an inconsiderate, selfish person who has no regard for the rights and needs of others, or an insecure

person with excessive fears, anxieties, and doubts about self.

Self-Definition and Self-Concept

As children begin to develop real awareness, they also begin to define themselves, to develop a concept of self, to develop an identity (Spencer & Markstrom-Adams, 1990). For a full discussion of children from minority groups, see *Child Development* (April 1990) *61*, Number 2. *By 3 years of age, personal characteristics are defined in childlike terms, and are usually positive and exaggerated.* "I'm bigger, strong, the fastest runner; can jump high, can skip, can sing pretty songs." Two researchers found that even when preschool children have just scored low on a game, they predicted that they would do very well the next time (Stipek & Hoffman, 1980). Other research indicates that preschool children usually have a very high opinion of their physical and intellectual abilities (Harter & Pike, 1984; Stipek & MacIver, 1989). Children's

Separation-individuation— period during which the infant gradually develops a self apart from the mother

Parenting Issues

Freedom Versus Control

One of the questions that parents face, at all stages of their children's development, is how much autonomy and freedom to allow and still ensure the safety, well-being, and socialization of their children. I once heard a psychiatrist say in a speech to a group that he lived at the top of a steep cliff, but that he wouldn't think of fencing in his yard, because his 2-year-old son had learned to avoid the danger. Most of us would not be willing to go this far in allowing autonomy and in teaching responsibility. How controlling or permissive to be is one of the difficult dilemmas of parenting (Remley, 1988).

However, the degree of control is not the only important factor to consider. Another one is the attitude of parents toward their children, whether loving or hostile. In our culture, children seem to thrive best in a loving and democratic environment, where there are rules of conduct and social restrictions on behavior, but where the children are also held in high esteem and are encouraged to explore, to try new things, and to do things themselves (Denham, Renwick, & Holt, 1991). As they get older, they are given opportunities to participate in decision making. Children in this environment tend to be independent, self-confident, assertive, outgoing, and active. Children who are loved in a dominating way tend to be dependent, polite, submissive, and obedient, but they lack initiative and self-whose parents are overly permissive and hostile toward them tend to be rebellious, disobedient, angry, aggressive, and delinquent. Children reared by hostile but controlling parents tend to be sullen and socially withdrawn. Because they are not allowed to express their anger outwardly, it may erupt sometimes in violence or may turn inward, resulting in self-recrimination (Remley, 1988).

Parents often face the task of how much autonomy and freedom to allow their children.

self-perceptions become more realistic with age (Marsh, Craven, & Debus, 1998).

By the middle elementary grades, most children begin to develop a more realistic concept of self and admit that they are not as capable in some areas as in others (Butler, 1990). "I'm a good reader, but I don't like arithmetic"; "I'm good in baseball, but I can't run." Markus and Nurius (1984) emphasize that as children enter middle childhood, they begin to develop truer self-understanding; to become aware of their achieved characteristics and their own values, norms, and goals; and to develop standards for their own behavior (Eder, 1990). They begin to be more specific and realistic about themselves and to realize that they do sometimes try to fool themselves (Eder, 1989).

There are, however, children who are highly competent but who fail to acquire positive perceptions of their abilities. Phillips (1987) found that in these cases, children's self-perceptions of competence are influenced more by their parents' negative appraisals than by objective evidence of their achievements. There are also children with only average abilities who have an inflated perception of themselves because of exaggerated views instilled by parents. One study found that children's perceptions of their academic competence was influenced by the warmth of their relationship with their father (Wagner & Phillips, 1992). The positive father-child relationship gave the children more confidence in their academic abilities.

Self-Reference and Self-Efficacy

Self-reference has to do with ourselves, our estimates of our abilities, and how capable and effective we are in dealing with others and the world (Ruble & Flett, 1988). Estimates of our effectiveness have been termed

Babies start reaching toward their mirror image at about 4 months of age.

self-efficacy. Self-efficacy is not so much our actual skill and effectiveness in dealing with situations and with others. Rather, it is our *perceptions* of these things.

Self-efficacy is important because it influences children's relationships, their willingness to undertake difficult tasks, and their feelings about themselves: their self-worth and competence (Schunk, 1984). Some children have very high opinions of their competence, regardless of others' opinions to the contrary. The important consideration is how they perceive themselves. Those with low opinions of themselves are supersensitive, and they easily feel rejected because they believe that others don't like them or don't approve of them. Self-perceptions have a great influence on how children deal with others (Downey, Lebolt, Rincon, & Freitas, 1998).

Bandura (1986) suggests that children's judgment of personal efficacy stems from the following four main causes:

First, self-efficacy depends on personal accomplishments and children's judgments about these accomplishments. Children who do well in school or in sports are more likely to feel self-efficacious than those who fail. Bandura calls this sense of self-efficacy *enactive* because it is based on the outcome of actions. Erikson has said that the chief psychosocial task during the 3- to 5-year-old period is *initiative versus guilt.* Children seek to become more assertive and to pursue a variety of activities, yet in ways that bring praise rather than reprimand. If they fail, their efforts result in criticism or self-blame, so that they feel guilty. Similarly, the chief psychosocial task during the school years is *industry versus inferiority.* Children strive for competence and proficiency. Failure results in feelings of inferiority.

Second, self-efficacy is derived partly from children's comparison of themselves with others. Ten-year-olds may compare their skill in a game with the skills of others. If they discover that they do very well, they feel very good about themselves. Bandura calls this a *vicarious* source of self-efficacy (based on comparison of personal performance with that of others).

Third, self-efficacy is also influenced by persuasion. "You can do it, you're capable." Positive persuasion increases self-efficacy, whereas negative persuasion—"don't try it"—decreases self-efficacy. Bandura calls this the *persuasory* source of self-efficacy.

The fourth source of influence on judgments of self-efficacy is the person's arousal level: the level of physiological and emotional arousal. High arousal can affect judgments—either positively or negatively. For example, if a child is very aroused and excited before being in a school play, this emotional state may lead to a superior performance if it motivates effort, or to a poor performance if nervousness prevents the child from doing his or her best. Bandura calls this an *emotional* source of self-efficacy.

Self-Esteem

Self-esteem is closely related to self-concept and self-efficacy. When children perceive their worth, their abilities, their accomplishments, do they view themselves positively or negatively? Everyone needs to feel loved, liked, accepted, valued, capable, and competent. How children feel about themselves is their self-esteem (Damon, 1983). It is their liking and respect for themselves.

There is a significant and beneficial relationship between the positiveness of self with competence in social acceptance, with behavioral adjustment to school, and with behavioral manifestations of self-esteem. Children with a positive representation of themselves will eventually become more confident or better adjusted than children with a negative self-representation. There is also a positive and strong connection between the security of the child-mother attachment and the positiveness of self (Berschueren, Marcoen, & Schoefs, 1996).

There are four primary sources of self-esteem: children's emotional relationships with parents, their social competence with peers, their intellectual prowess at school, and the attitudes of society and community toward them. Children who are *loved and wanted,* whose parents are warm, supportive, concerned, interested, and active in their

Self-reference—estimates of our abilities and of how effectively we deal with others and the world

Self-efficacy—our perceptions of our actual skill and personal effectiveness

Self-esteem—our perception of our worth, abilities, and accomplishments; our view of ourselves, negative or positive

guidance, tend to develop positive self-esteem (Abraham & Christopherson, 1984; Felson & Zielinski, 1989). As children develop, *social competence* becomes an increasing component of self-esteem (Waters & Sroufe, 1983). *School success* is also related to high self-esteem (Entwisle, Alexander, Pallas, & Cadigan 1987). It's hard to feel good about oneself while doing poorly in school (Coopersmith & Gilberts, 1982). And finally, *the attitudes of society* influence self-esteem. Children of some minority groups have trouble in developing a positive self-image if they feel that others look down on them because of their racial or ethnic origin (Rotheram-Borus, 1990a,b). However, society's attitudes are not always enough to produce low self-esteem. Children brought up in families that teach pride in their race or background, where they develop a strong ethnic identity and social pride, are able to maintain high self-esteem despite some of the prejudices that they encounter from others (Miller & Davis, 1992).

Conclusions

Self-definition, self-concept, self-reference, self-efficacy, and self-esteem are all similar concepts. Self-definition and self-concept are our self-perceived identity. Self-reference and self-efficacy are our estimates and perceptions of our self-worth, abilities, and accomplishments. Self-esteem is our overall perception of our self-worth and abilities. How children feel about themselves is crucial to their mental health, as well as to their later relationships and successes in life.

Summary

1. Attachment is the feeling that binds a person and a child together. The formation of attachment is vitally important to children's total development.

2. Children can develop close attachments to more than one person. Attachments to specific persons do not develop until about 6 or 7 months of age, after infants can distinguish among different human beings. Specific attachments are at their maximum from 12 to 18 months of age.

3. Nonattached children are very unemotional and distant; insecurely, attached children are overly dependent.

4. Some attachment theorists emphasize extreme attachment, which is not healthy and interferes with the child's establishing autonomy.

5. Separation anxiety varies with individual children, depending on their age and the length of the separation. The effects of long-term separation can be serious.

6. Distress over separation is greatest after 6 months of age and until about 3 years of age.

7. If a child has to go to the hospital, one parent ought to stay and make arrangements to sleep in the same room.

8. Homesickness is a manifestation of separation anxiety.

9. Children show various forms of reunion behavior. Some children are very dependent; others are angry; others are emotionally cold.

10. Fear of strangers begins at about 6 or 7 months of age and increases until about 2 years, after which it declines.

11. Parents need to let the child develop attachment to baby-sitters or substitute caregivers before leaving the child alone with them. Much depends on the quality of the substitute care.

12. Family day-care and regular child-care centers are another solution to the child-care problem. The effect of high-quality day care on children can be quite positive. The quality of teachers is crucial.

13. Erikson has said that the basic psychosocial task of infancy is the development of trust. Mahler says that infants need to establish a symbiotic relationship with their mother.

14. Development of trust and security is aided by the following: regular and adequate feelings, sufficient sucking, and cuddling and physical contact. Their most important requirement is for parents to show children their love.

15. Children learn to express affection by having affection shown them.

16. There are a number of causes of distrust and insecurity: parental deprivation, tension in the home, exposure to frightening experiences, child abuse, criticism, overprotection, and overindulgence.

17. Child abuse takes two main forms: neglect and attack.

18. Being brought up in an alcoholic family can have a very negative effect on children's proneness to alcoholism, on their mental health and behavior, and on their physical, emotional, and social development. However, there are some COAs who become happy, well-adjusted adults.

19. There are four basic components of emotions: (a) stimuli, (b) feelings, (c) physiological arousal, and (d) behavioral response.

20. Emotions play a number of important functions in our lives: they play an adaptive function, are a means of communication, are important in social relationships, are powerful motivators, and are a source of pleasure or of pain.

21. Ekman and colleagues found six basic emotions: happiness, sadness, anger, surprise, disgust, and fear. Emotions develop according to a biological timetable. Some psychologists say that all emotions are present at birth.

22. Children's fears may be conditioned or taught by parents; or they may arise out of children's vivid imaginations and limited experience and understanding, from seeing and hearing scary stories, or out of the actions of other children.

23. The three most common worries reported by children relate to school, health, and personal harm.

24. Everyone gets angry; the real task for children is to learn to express and control anger in harmless and positive ways.

25. Aggression takes two forms: verbal aggression and physical aggression.

26. Overaggression is frequently a cause of poor relationships with peers. Aggressive children are at risk for negative interactions with adults at home and in school.

27. Aggression must be considered in social context, since peer groups and neighborhood environments have an influence over behavior.

28. Children need to achieve a balance between emotional expression and control.

29. Temperament refers to relatively consistent, basic dispositions inherent in people, which underlie and modulate much of their behavior. Because temperament is primarily inherited, basic dispositions are present early in life; expression of temperament is progressively affected by environment.

30. Different researchers have identified different components of temperament: emotionality, activity level, sociability, rhythmicity, approach or withdrawal from new stimuli, adaptability, sensory threshold, quality of mood, intensity of mood expression, distractibility, and persistency and attention span. Some children are easy to take care of, others difficult, and others in between, depending on temperament.

31. Hyperactive children, those with attention-deficit hyperactive disorder (ADHD), have 3 major symptoms: excessive activity, inattentiveness, and impulsivity.

32. There is some continuity between temperamental characteristics in childhood and behavioral characteristics later.

33. Children vary in temperament, partly because of cross-cultural influences.

34. The development of self-awareness means that children begin to understand their separateness from others and other things. The sense of self emerges gradually.

35. Erikson said that the chief psychosocial task between 1 and 2 years of age is the development of autonomy. One of the parenting tasks is to decide how much freedom to allow and how much control to exercise.

36. Mahler says that after 5 months and until age 3, children go through a period of separation-individuation during which they develop a self apart from the mother.

37. Children also begin to develop real awareness and definition of the self and a self-concept. Preschoolers describe themselves in exaggerated and positive terms. By the middle elementary grades, most children begin to develop a more realistic concept of self. Children's self-perceptions are influenced greatly by their parents' appraisals.

38. Self-reference has to do with our estimates of our abilities; self-efficacy is our perceptions of our effectiveness in dealing with situations and with others.

39. Bandura says that self-efficacy stems from four main causes: personal accomplishments and perceptions of them;

comparison of self with others; persuasion by others; and arousal level.

40. Self-esteem is the way in which children view themselves: positively or negatively. There are four primary sources of children's self-esteem: relationships with parents, social competence, intellectual prowess at school, and the attitudes of society and community toward them.

Key Terms

Attachment   *p. 194*
Attention-deficit hyperactive disorder (ADHD)   *p. 216*
Autistic phase   *p. 201*
Epinephrine   *p. 206*
Insecurely attached children   *p. 195*
Nonattached children   *p. 195*

Personality   *p. 213*
Self-efficacy   *p. 219*
Self-esteem   *p. 219*
Self-reference   *p. 219*
Separation-individuation   *p. 217*
Symbiosis   *p. 201*
Temperament   *p. 213*

Discussion Questions

1. Describe the attachment behavior of a child you know. Does this child manifest separation anxiety? What suggestions do you have for minimizing separation anxiety?

2. Do you know a child who had to go to the hospital? Describe the experience. How did it affect the child emotionally?

3. Describe the experience of a child you know who went to nursery school or kindergarten for the first time.

4. How can separation anxiety be minimized when employing a baby-sitter?

5. Do you know any parents who placed their child in a day-care center from infancy on? What were some of the effects on the child?

6. Can family arguments cause children to become distrustful and insecure? Explain.

7. Have you ever known a child who had been physically abused? Describe. What were the effects? Would you report parents who you knew were abusing their child? Why, or why not?

8. Were you a child of an alcoholic? If so, what effect did growing up in an alcoholic family have on you?

9. Can you experience emotion without physiological arousal? Explain.

10. Are emotions present from birth, or are they developed? Explain.

11. What would you do if your toddler was afraid of water? That is, how would you help the child overcome the fear?

12. What might parents do when their child has temper tantrums?

13. Psychologists feel that temperament is inherited. How do you feel about that statement? Compare your temperament now with your temperament when you were younger.

14. Have you ever known a child who was difficult to care for? Have you ever known a child who was easy to care for? Can two children in the same family be this different?

15. Have you ever known a child who was hyperactive? Describe. What were the causes? What did the parents do?

16. What might happen if children are not allowed to develop autonomy when young? Effects depend not only on the degree of control but also on whether parents are loving or hostile. Explain.

17. What are the most important factors in the development of self-esteem?

18. What helps the most in helping children to develop self-efficacy?

Suggested Readings

BOWLBY, J. (1983). *Attachment and loss* (Vol. 1) (2nd ed.). New York: Basic Books. Mother-infant interaction and attachment.

BOWLBY, J. A. (1990). *A secure base: Parent-child attachment and healthy human development.* New York: Basic Books. Bowlby's theory.

BRAZELTON, T. B. (1994). *Touchpoints: Your child's emotional and behavioral development.* New York: Addison-Wesley Publishing Company. Focuses primarily on preschool children. Questions that parents have.

CUMMINGS, E. M., & DAVIES, P. (1994). *Children and marital conflict: The impact of family dispute and resolution.* New York: Guilford. A compilation of research on the impact of interparental conflict on child development outcomes.

FINKELHOR, D., et al. (Eds.). (1986). *A sourcebook on child sexual abuse.* Beverly Hills, CA: Sage. A guide for parents and leaders of children.

IZARD, C. E. (1982). *Measuring emotion in infants and children.* New York: Cambridge University Press. Classic study on how to assess emotions of infants and children.

JOHNSON, J. H. (1986). *Life events as stressors in childhood and adolescence.* Beverly Hills, CA: Sage. Effects of major changes in the lives of children and adolescents.

KELLERMAN, J. (1981). *Helping the fearful child: A parents' guide.* New York: Warner Books.

LAMB, M. E. (1987). *The father's role: Cross-cultural perspectives.* Hillsdale, NJ: Erlbaum. Father's role in English, American, Israeli, Italian, Swedish, Chinese, and AKa pygmy families.

LEWIS, M. (1995). *Shame: The exposed self.* New York: Free Press. History, personal development of, reactions to, and how it is handled in the individual. Shame is normal, not pathological.

SROUFE, L. A., & FLEESON, J. (1986). *Attachment and the construction of relationships.* In W. Hartup and Z. Rubin (Eds.), *Relationships and development.* Hillsdale, NJ: Erlbaum. Attachment theory and applications.

WHITE, B. L. (1995). *The first three years of life.* (rev. ed.). New York: Prentice-Hall. Parent-toddler relationships.

WRIGLEY, J. (1995). *Other people's children: An intimate account of the dilemmas facing middle-class parents and the women they hire to raise their children.* New York: Basic Books. Hiring in-home caregivers to take care of children.

ZIGLER, E. F., & LANG, M. E. (1991). *Child-care choices: Balancing the needs of children, families, and society.* New York: Free Press. Child-care options in relation to children's needs.

Web Resources

http://ehsnrc.org Early Head Start National Resource Center Documents and annotations on early childhood development and health.

Social Development

Chapter 9

INTRODUCTION

This chapter discusses the influence of television and computers on children. No chapter on social development would be complete without a discussion of the development of those factors that influence gender roles and their relationship between age and gender role development, as well as the development of stereotypes in our society that affects gender role development. Lastly, the development of androgyny is summarized. Finally, this chapter discusses the process of development of moral judgment, of moral behavior, and the role of conscience development in morality.

SOCIOCULTURAL INFLUENCES

Children do not develop in a vacuum. They develop in the context of their family, neighborhood, community, country, and world. In this context, children are influenced by parents, siblings, other relatives, friends, and peers; other adults with whom they come in contact; and the school, the church, and the groups of which they are a part. They are influenced by the media: newspapers, magazines, radio, and TV. They are influenced by community and national leaders, by the culture in which they are growing up, and even by things going on in the world. They are partly a product of social influences.

Bronfenbrenner (1979, 1987) developed an ecological model for understanding social influences. As can be seen in Figure 9.1, social influences are perceived as a series of systems extending beyond the child. The child is at the center of the model. The most immediate influences are within the **microsystem** and include those with which the child has immediate contact. The **mesosystem** involves the reciprocal relationships among microsystem settings. For example, what happens at home influences what happens at school and vice versa. Thus, the child's social development is understood best when the influences from many sources are considered, and in relation to one another.

The **exosystem** includes those settings in which the child usually does not have an active role as a participant but that influence the child indirectly through their effects on the microsystem. For example, what happens to the parents at work influences them, and they in turn influence their child's development. Also, community organizations provide family support that affects child rearing.

The **macrosystem** includes the ideologies, values, attitudes, laws, mores, and customs of a particular culture. Cultures may differ among countries or among racial, ethnic, or socioeconomic groups. There are also differences within each group (Gutierrez, Sameroff, & Carrer, 1988). In Sweden, for example, it is against the law for parents to hit children, yet the practice is condoned by some groups in the United States. Middle-class parents in this country often have goals and philosophies of child-rearing different from those in low socioeconomic status groups (Gutierrez & Sameroff, 1990; Harrison, Wilson, Pine, Chan, & Buriel, 1990; McLoyd, 1990; Slaughter-Defoe, Nakagawa, Takanishi, & Johnson, 1990). Rural families may have parenting values different from those of urban families (Coleman, Ganong, Clark, & Madsen, 1989). All such value-related and setting-related elements have different effects on children. In talking about social development, therefore, we have to discuss issues and concerns in the contexts in which children are growing up.

THE FAMILY AND SOCIALIZATION

What is the family's role in socialization, and how has it changed? Of all of those sociocultural influences that play a part in children's development, the family is still the transmitter of values, morals, ideals, habits, and ways of thinking and acting.

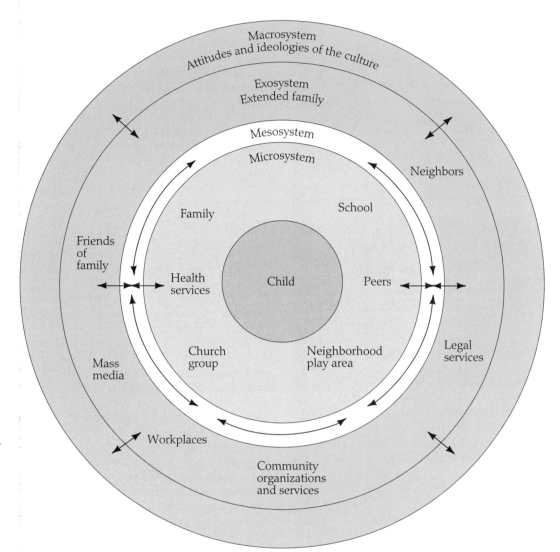

FIGURE 9.1   Bronfenbrenner's ecological model for understanding social influences.

Data from "Contexts of Child Rearing: Problems and Prospects," by U. Bronfenbrenner, 1979, *American Psychologist 34*, pp. 844–850.

Microsystem—the child's immediate contacts

Mesosystem—social influences involving reciprocal relationships

Exosystem—social settings in which the child usually is not an active participant, but that influence the child indirectly through their effects on the microsystem

Macrosystem—influences of a particular culture

Family—any group of persons united by the ties of marriage, blood, or adoption, or any sexually expressive relationship, in which (1) the people are committed to one another in an intimate, interpersonal relationship, (2) the members see their identity as importantly attached to the group, and (3) the group has an identity of its own

Single-parent family

Nuclear family

Extended family

Blended or reconstituted family

The Family's Role

In the discussion here, a **family** may be defined as "any group of persons united by the ties of marriage, blood, or adoption or any sexually expressive relationship, in which (1) the people are committed to one another in an intimate, interpersonal relationship, (2) the members see their identity as importantly attached to the group, and (3) the group has an identity of its own" (Rice, 1999, p. 4).

The following are some of the different types of families.

A **single-parent family** consists of a parent (who may or may not have been married) and one or more children.

A **nuclear family** consists of a father, a mother, and their children. This type of family as a proportion of all families has been declining in recent years.

The **extended family** consists of one person, a possible mate, any children they might have, and other relatives who live with them in their household. More broadly, the extended family can include relatives living in close proximity or those who are in frequent contact with a household's members.

The **blended or reconstituted family** is formed when a widowed or divorced person, with or without children, remarries another person who may or may not have been married before and who may or may not have children. If either the remarried husband or wife has children from the former marriage, a **stepfamily** is formed.

Numerous sociocultural influences play a part in children's development.

A **binuclear family** is an original family divided into two by divorce. It consists of two nuclear families, the maternal nuclear family headed by the mother, and the paternal nuclear family headed by the father. The families include whatever children have been in the original family. Each new family may be headed by a single parent or by two parents if former spouses remarry (Ahrons & Rodgers, 1987).

A **communal family** consists of a group of people who live together and share various aspects of their lives. They can be considered a family if the group falls within the preceding general definition. Some communal groups are not families in this sense.

A **gay or lesbian family** consists of adults of the same sex who live together, with their children, and who share sexual expression and commitment.

A **cohabiting family** consists of two people of the opposite sex who live together, with or without children, and who share sexual expression and commitment to their relationship without formal legal marriage.

When talking about the family, then, we need to specify which type we are referring to. With such a wide variety of family forms, we can no longer assume that the word *family* is synonymous with nuclear family (Cheal, 1993; Wisensale, 1992; Zimmerman, 1992). When families are so different in structure and composition, the influence of different family members is variable. Grandparents or great-grandparents may have considerable influence on children in an extended family, but very little in some nuclear families (Pearson, Hunter, Ensminger, & Kellam, 1990; Tolson & Wilson, 1990). Or, a noncustodial father may have a limited role in socializing his children in a single-parent family in which the children are living with the mother. *Total influence varies with family forms* (Stevens, 1988).

Overall, however, the family is the principal transmitter of knowledge, values, attitudes, roles, and habits that one generation passes on to the next (Thornton, Chatters, Taylor, & Allen, 1990). Through word and example, the family shapes children's personality and instills modes of thought and ways of acting that become habitual (Kochanska, 1990). Peterson and Rollins (1987) refer to this process as **generational transmission.**

Socialization is the process by which persons learn the ways of society or social groups so that they can function within it or them (Kalmuss & Seltzer, 1989). A dictionary says it is "to make fit for life in companionship with others." Children are taught the ways and values of their society through contact with already socialized individuals, initially the family (Maccoby, 1992).

Binuclear family

Communal family

Gay or lesbian family

Cohabiting family—a family formed by two people of the opposite sex who live together, with or without children; who are committed to the relationship, without formal legal marriage, within the general definition in this book.

Generational transmission—transmitting of knowledge, values, attitudes, roles, and habits from one generation to the next

Socialization—the process by which persons learn the ways of society or social groups so that they can function within them

The process takes place partly through *formal instruction* that parents provide their children and partly by the efforts of parents to control children through *rewards and punishments*. Learning also takes place through *reciprocal parent-child interaction* as each influences and modifies the behavior of the other in an intense social process. Learning also occurs through *observational modeling*, as children observe, imitate, and model the behavior that they find around them (Bandura, 1986). It is not only what parents say that is important but also what children actually perceive parents to believe and do that most influences them.

Not all children are influenced to the same degree by their families. The degree of parental influence depends partly on the frequency, duration, intensity, and priority of social contacts that parents have with their children. Parents who are emotionally close to their children, in loving relationships for long periods of time, exert more influence than do those not so close and who relate to their children less frequently (Russell & Russell, 1987).

Another factor in determining the influence of the family is the difference in individual children. Not all children react in the same way to the same family environment, because of

Parenting Issues

Low Socioeconomic Status and Parenting

The term **low socioeconomic status** (SES) refers to low social class and status, including educational deprivation and low income. In comparison with middle-class families, consider the possible effects of the following conditions under which low SES families bring up their children (Patterson, Kupersmidt, & Vaden, 1990; Wasserman, Raugh, Brunelli, Garcia-Castro, & Necos, 1990).

Low income means inadequate, crowded housing in poor neighborhoods, where crime rates and social and family problems are greater (Chilman, 1991). Low SES families often have poor medical care, higher mortality rates, and higher rates of physical and mental illnesses. The incidence of accidental death, suicide, and homicide is higher. Expectant mothers are more likely to be young and unmarried (Harris, 1991), to use alcohol and other drugs, and to receive inadequate prenatal care; therefore, they are more likely to deliver premature and difficult babies who are harder to care for and love. One consequence is that child abuse is higher (Young & Gately, 1988). Low SES families are at the mercy of life's unpredictable events: sickness, loss of work, injury, legal problems, and school and family difficulties. Low income means less likelihood of

having insurance to cover property, life, disability, or health. Low SES families strive for security to protect themselves and just to provide themselves with the basic necessities of life. The families more often are one-parent families, with fathers playing less of an active role in caring for their children (Paasch & Teachman, 1991).

As a result of life circumstances, low SES parents have more stresses, and stress affects the way parents carry out their functions. One study of 585 children from the lowest socioeconomic class found that low socioeconomic status was significantly correlated with eight factors in the child's socialization and social context, including harsh discipline, lack of maternal warmth, exposure to aggressive adult models, maternal aggressive values, family life stressors, mother's lack of social support, peer group instability, and lack of cognitive stimulation (Dodge, Pettit, & Bates, 1994).

We should keep in mind that these class-linked differences represent group averages that do not apply to all low SES families and individuals. One study of low-income, black, urban mothers indi-

cated a rather wide range of disciplinary practices. Mothers varied greatly in their attitude toward physical punishment. In general, the more religious mothers had more child-oriented disciplinary attitudes (Kelley, Power, & Wimbush, 1992).

Low socioeconomic status families are at the mercy of life's unpredictable events.

differences in heredity, temperament, cognitive perception, developmental characteristics, and maturational levels. Because A happens does not mean that B will inevitably result. When children are brought up in an unhappy, conflicting family, it is more difficult for them to establish happy marriages themselves. However, some do. Not all children are influenced by their families to the same degree.

Parental Competence and Family Environment

Not all parents have a positive influence on their children, nor are all parents able to create a positive and healthy family environment in which children can grow. *The parents' psychological adjustment, parenting style, and the quality of their marriage all have an effect on the children's emotional maturity, social competence, and cognitive development* (Miller et al., 1993). This process can be illustrated in a number of ways. Let's look first at the psychological adjustment of parents.

Parents' Psychological Adjustment

When parents expose children to high levels of parental anger, the result is heightened emotional and behavioral reactivity on the part of the children. One study showed that if parents suffer from hypertension (high blood pressure), the children show increased cardiovascular reactivity to the stress with consequent high blood pressure and more negative behavior (Ballard, Cummings, & Larkin, 1993). Another study showed the relationship between parent and grandparent drug use and maladjustment among children (Stein, Newcomb, & Bentler, 1993).

Parents who are psychologically healthy are more likely to have a positive effect on their children's development (Hock & Schirtzinger, 1992). For example, mothers who have high self-efficacy or who believe in their ability to be competent and effective parents, are more likely to have less difficulty in caring for their infants than mothers who do not have confidence (Teti & Gelfand, 1991). Mothers who are satisfied with the quality and quantity of their personal relationships and social networks are more likely to demonstrate optimal maternal behavior (Jennings, Stagg, & Connors, 1991). They praise their children more and are less intrusively controlling. Fathers, too, exert an important influence. Goodman and colleagues found that the father's psychiatric status and the marital status of the

couple, explain much of the variability in children's social and emotional competence (Goodman et al., 1993).

A number of studies have dealt with the relationship between parental depression, especially maternal depression, and the psychological health of children. One study of 6- to 12-year-old children found that maternal depression was associated with lower self-esteem, a reduced sense of personal control, lower cognitive ability, and poorer social-perspective-taking ability of boys (Kershner & Cohen, 1992). The boys of depressive mothers received higher ratings of problem behaviors. In another study, depressed mothers less often complied with the requests of their 5-year-olds (Kochanska & Kuczynski, 1991).

Figure 9.2 shows a path model to illustrate the effect of parents' depression on a child's overt behavior. The top path illustrates that the more the parents are depressed, the less positive affection they show one another, which in turn affects the warmth that they express to their child, which affects the child's external behavior (Miller et al., 1993). The bottom path shows that the more the parents are depressed, the greater the couple's conflict, which in turn affects the child's external behavior. When one parent or both parents have been diagnosed with a serious

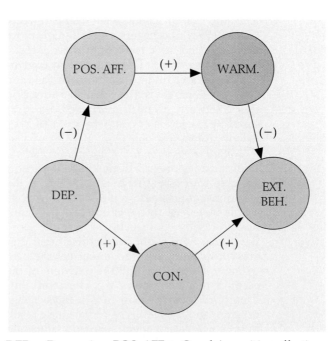

DEP. = Depression; POS. AFF. = Couple's positive affection; WARM. = Parenting warmth; CON. = Couple's conflict; EXT. BEH. = Child's externalized (overt) behavior.

FIGURE 9.2   Parents' depression and child's overt behavior.

disturbance (e.g., psychosis or depression), the children are at risk for cognitive, social, emotional, and school-related difficulties.

Marital Quality

The association between marital functioning and child adjustment has been well established (Floyd, Gilliom, & Costigan, 1998). There is a reciprocal relationship between marital happiness and parenting satisfaction, and parents who are most satisfied with their role have children who seem to be better adjusted (Rogers & White, 1998). *The quality of the marital relationship affects children's adjustments and development and influences children's behavior problems over a wide age span* (Jouriles et al., 1991). Harmonious marriages tend to be associated with sensitive parenting and warm parent-child relationships (Floyd & Zmich, 1991). When husbands and wives are satisfied with their marriage, the children tend to be more secure (Gable, Belsky, & Crnic, 1992). However, when there is marital discord, children tend to be more anxious and/or aggressive, to internalize and externalize behavior problems, and to manifest more insecurities. Parents with poor marital quality are more likely to engage in problematic parenting and socialization practices, such as increased hostility and punitiveness, decreased warmth and reasoning, and increased inconsistency and ineffective parenting, all of which adversely affect the parent-child relationship quality (Shek, 1998). Teenagers especially are more reactive to negative features of their parents' marital functioning. The simplest way to summarize research findings relating marriage and child development is to say that an association exists between troubled marriages—as measured by the levels of conflict—and child behavior problems (Gable et al., 1992).

   Not all marital conflict is harmful to children. If discussions are relatively calm, if parents are able to resolve disagreements, and if the emotional atmosphere is pleasant, the net effect is beneficial to the children: They learn how to resolve conflicts by the example set in the home. So it is not conflict itself that creates problems, it is the intensity, the frequency, the content, and the outcome of the conflict that determines the effect on children (Grych & Fineham, 1993). Physical aggression and high levels of verbal abuse result in greater levels of anger, fear, and sadness in children. The subject of the discussion makes a difference also. If the content relates to the children (for example, differences over child rearing), the children are more likely to be upset. Children are more likely to blame

themselves and be afraid of becoming involved in the argument. They become very fearful if the argument is likely to escalate and if they will be drawn in. How conflicts end also seems to matter. Unresolved conflicts result in the most negative response for the children. The children are left with a great deal of stress, along with bad feelings, **dysphoria,** fear, anger, and a sense of helplessness. After all, what can they do about it (Grych, Seid, & Fineham, 1992)?

Patterns of Parenting

Just as there are differences in families, there are also various patterns of parenting (McNally, Eisenberg, & Harris, 1991). These patterns partly reflect differences in parental values (Luster, Rhoades, & Haas, 1989; Simons et al., 1993). For example, some parents value conformity in children; others value self-direction (Mills & Rubin, 1990). One study compared the attitudes of Anglo and Puerto Rican mothers in relation to what they considered to be acceptable attachment behavior. The Anglo mothers focused on the degree of individual autonomy. The Puerto Rican mothers placed more emphasis on the child's ability to maintain proper demeanor in public (Harwood, 1992). Another study showed that parents with higher educational and occupational levels used more reasoning in directing their children. In turn, higher levels of reasoning were related to authoritative (not authoritarian) patterns of child-rearing, the use of indirect positive control, warmth, acceptance, and support (Dekovic & Gerris, 1992). Still another study showed that increased maternal responsiveness during infancy, particularly verbal responsiveness, was influenced by the mother's cultural background and school attendance (Richman, Miller, & Levine, 1992). Diana Baumrind (1978, 1980) examined the way that parenting styles affected the social characteristics of preschool children from 300 families. Baumrind was particularly concerned with the patterns of control that parents used, and she identified three general styles of parenting: authoritarian, permissive, and authoritative.

Authoritarian

Authoritarian parents emphasize obedience, using force to curb children's self-will, keeping children subordinate, restricting autonomy, and discouraging verbal give and take (Kochanska, Kuczynski, & Radke-Yarrow, 1989). These types of parents tend to use harsh discipline because that is the way they

Dysphoria—generalized unhappiness

themselves were brought up (Simons et al., 1992). This type of parenting tends to produce withdrawn, fearful children who exhibit little or no independence and are either generally irritable, unassertive, and moody, or hostile, angry, and overly aggressive.

Permissive

Permissive parents free children from restraint, accept their impulses and actions without trying to shape their behavior. Some of these parents are indulgent, whereas others are indifferent, letting children do what they want as a way of avoiding responsibility for them. These children tend to be rebellious, self-indulgent, aggressive, impulsive, and socially inept. Lack of discipline in the home is associated with social aggression, which, in turn, is associated with peer rejection (Travillion & Snyder, 1993).

Authoritative

Authoritative parents seek to direct their children's activities in a rational manner, encouraging discussion and also exerting firm control when children disobey, but without being overly restrictive. These parents recognize children's individual needs and interests, but set standards of conduct (Kochanska et al., 1989). These children are the best adjusted of the three groups; they are the most self-reliant, self-controlled, self-confident, and socially competent (Dekovic & Janssens, 1992).

On the basis of her research, Baumrind concluded that *authoritative parenting, which is firm but reasonable,* and *which is warm, nurturing, and loving, works best in the socialization of children* (Donovan, Leavitt, & Walsh, 1990).

Research by Schaefer (1959) emphasized both the pattern of control—the autonomy versus control dimension—and the degree of affection—the love versus hostility dimension (Amato, 1990). These dimensions interact to form four patterns: *love-autonomy, love-control, hostility-autonomy,* and *hostility-control.* Of course, there are degrees within each pattern. The four dimensions are shown in Figure 9.3. The secret of successful parenting seems to be to show the maximum amount of love (children are never spoiled by love) and the right balance between autonomy and control.

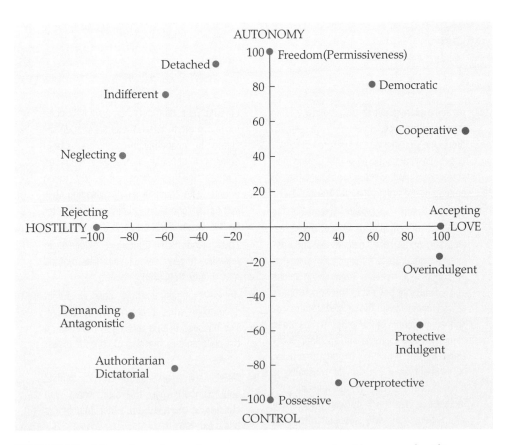

FIGURE 9.3   Dimensions of parenting: autonomy versus control and love versus hostility.

From "A Circumplex Model for Maternal Behavior," by E. S. Schaefer, 1959, *Journal of Abnormal and Social Psychology 59,* pp. 226–235.

Autonomy without any control is permissiveness and overindulgence. Hostility without any control results in a high rate of aggression. Hostility with a high degree of control may produce extreme hostility and anger that sometimes erupt in destructive ways. Of course, children are different and sometimes are affected differently by a specific pattern of parenting. Also, these findings were determined from the study of middle-class populations in the United States. Firm control patterns in some Asian countries are usual and therefore may produce less reactionary results.

Other research has attempted to relate specific child-care practices to children's socialization and personality development. Several studies have shown the relationship between parents' empathy and responsiveness to the children's growing ability to respond empathetically and sympathetically to others (Eisenberg et al., 1991, 1992). What researchers have found is that *the one parenting variable that was most related to adjustment was*

Discipline—a process of learning by which socialization takes place; its purpose is instruction in proper conduct

love. Parents who genuinely loved their children provided them with the most important requirement for successful socialization (Jakab, 1987).

Discipline

The word **discipline** comes from the same root as does the word *disciple*, which means "a learner." *Discipline, therefore, is a process of learning, of education, a means by which socialization takes place.* Its purpose is to instruct in proper conduct or action rather than to punish. The ultimate goal of discipline is to sensitize the conscience and to develop self-control, so that individuals live according to the standards of behavior and in accord with the rules and regulations established by the group.

In the beginning, control over the child is established by external authority; but gradually children are encouraged to develop internal controls so that the standards they strive

---

Parenting Issues

Parental Control Techniques

Smith (1988) has given a helpful summary of seven control techniques that are used by parents.

- *Power-assertive discipline*—physical punishment, deprivation, and threats. Harsh physical punishment especially has been associated with physical aggression in children who model their parent's behavior (Dishion, 1990; Hart, Ladd, & Burleson, 1990; Kandel, 1990; Vuchinich, Bank, & Patterson, 1992).

- *Command*—imperative statements not accompanied by punishment or overt threat of punishment. The success of this technique depends on the child's acceptance of parental authority (Kochanska, 1992). If the child does not accept parental authority and disobeys the parents' wishes, then noncompliance must be dealt with by some sort of reasonable punishment.

- *Soft-oriented induction*—reasoning in pointing out gains or costs that children might ex-

perience as a result of their behavior. This technique produces positive effects on children. One study found that children of inductive mothers were more popular among their peers and exhibited more prosocial behavior on the playground (Hart et al., 1992).

- *Other-oriented induction*—reasoning in pointing out religious or ethical principles, altruism, or personal obligations and reasons for children to change their behavior. This technique helps in internalizing values and acceptable behavior. The effectiveness of reasoning alone as a disciplinary response depends on whether it has been combined with punishment on other occasions. Research findings suggest that using punishment as a backup for reasoning is often crucial. Parents who use reasoning effectively by backing it up with punishment when necessary will subsequently have well-behaved children who pay attention to

parental reasoning and thus have little need for punishment. When these parents do respond to misbehavior, reasoning works quite well because it has been enforced through the preschool years. By being paired with punishment, reasoning becomes a condition punisher (Larzelere, Sather, Schneider, Larson, & Pike, 1998).

- *Love withdrawal*—temporary coldness or rejection to gain compliance. This method may threaten children's security.

- *Advice*—suggesting how children might accomplish what is desired by the parent. The success of this technique depends on the children's recognition of parents' expert power.

- *Relationship maintenance*—striving to build and maintain a positive relationship with children at the same time that influence is being exerted.

Everyday Rules of Behavior

One study examined how mothers socialized their young children towards behavior self-regulation. A group of mothers and their children were seen in home and laboratory visits at six-month intervals (i.e., at 13, 18, 24, and 30 months). Only the results at 13 and 30 months of age are reported here. The mothers were asked whether they had communicated particular prohibitions and requests to their children. In reporting this, they were asked to look at a list submitted to them and to check whether or not they had recently asked for each behavior. The list contained everyday rules of behavior divided into eight categories as follows:

- *Child safety* included not touching things that are dangerous, not climbing on the furniture, and not going into the street.

- *Protection of personal property* included keeping away from prohibited objects such as knives or stoves, not tearing up books, not getting into prohibited drawers or rooms, and not coloring on walls or furniture.

- *Respect for others* included not taking toys away from other children and not being too rough with other children.

- *Food and mealtime routines* included not playing with food, not leaving the table in the middle of the meal, and not spilling drinks or juice.

- *A delay category* included waiting while the mother was on the telephone, not interrupting others' conversations, and being willing to wait for a meal.

- *Manners* included saying "please" and "thank you."

- *Self-care* included dressing self, asking to use the toilet, washing up when requested, brushing teeth when requested, and going to bed when requested.

- *Family routines* included helping with chores when requested, putting toys away, and keeping their own room neat.

As seen in Figure 9.4, when the children were 13 months of age, the mothers were in-terested in the protection of personal property, respect for others, and child safety. Mothers were least interested in self-care, helping with family routines, and manners. However, when the children were 30 months of age, the mothers were interested in respect for others, manners, child safety, protection of personal property, and being willing to delay by waiting for the mother while she was on the telephone and not interrupting others' conversations. Mothers were least interested in children's helping with family routines, self-care, or mealtime and food routines. It was obvious that the frequency of the mothers' instructions had increased greatly between the time their children were 13 months of age and 30 months of age (Gralinski & Kopp, 1993).

to follow become a part of their own lives, not because they have to, but because they want to. When this process happens, these internalized truths become their own standards of conduct.

If discipline is to accomplish its goal of developing inner control, there are a number of principles that, if followed, enhance this development (Schneider-Rosen & Wenz-Gross, 1990). These are summarized here (Rice, 1990).

1.   Children respond more readily to parents within the context of a *loving, trusting relationship of mutual esteem*. Children who receive nurturance and emotional support from parents show lower levels of aggression than do those who do not receive this support (Zelkowitz, 1987).

2.   Discipline is more effective when it is *consistent rather than erratic*. It is helpful if

parents agree on discipline (Deal, Halverson, & Wampler, 1989; Vaughn, Block, & Block, 1988).

3.   Learning is enhanced if responses involve *rewards and punishments*. (Day, Peterson, & McCracken, 1998).

4.   Discipline is more effective when applied *as soon after the offense as possible*.

5.   *Discipline that inflicts pain should not be used*, including the avoidance of spanking. Severe punishment, especially if it is cruel and abusive, is counterproductive because it stimulates resentment, feelings of rejection, and similar harsh, cruel behavior on the part of children (Rohner, Kean, & Cournoyer, 1991; Weiss & Dodge, 1992). Sweden has laws making spanking of children a crime.

6.   *Discipline becomes less effective if it is too strict or too often applied*. A parent who

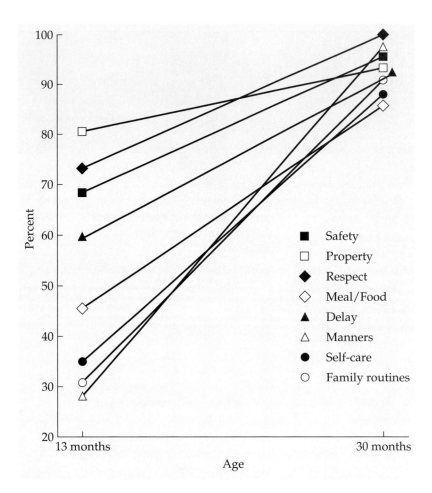

FIGURE 9.4   Developmental trends in proportions of rules requested, by rule category.

Statistics from "Everyday Rules for Behavior: Mothers' Requests to Young Children," J. H. Gralinski & C. B. Kopp, 1993, *Developmental Psychology 29*, pp. 573–584. Copyright 1993 by the American Psychological Association. Adapted with permission.

continually criticizes a child no matter what the child does is teaching the child that it is impossible to please the parents.

7.   In the beginning, most children want and need external controls because they are not yet mature enough to exert self-control over their own behavior. Appropriate methods of discipline will vary according to the child's age and level of understanding. However, *extremes of either permissiveness or authoritarianism are often counterproductive.* For children at very young ages, discipline may be accomplished through wise management: providing interesting toys and activities; equipping sections of the residence as a playroom, play yard, or play area; and childproofing the house by keeping dangerous things out of reach. Young children may be disciplined through distraction and offering substitute activities (Holden & West, 1989).

Sometimes the wisest discipline is achieved through environmental manipulation: removing the child from the situation or the situation from the child. Parents can discuss issues with older children and arrive at joint decisions, whereas instruction to preschoolers necessarily involves more imperatives. Even then, explanations and reasons are helpful, depending on the children's level of understanding.

8.   All children are different. There are cases in which highly resistant children in high-restrictive families turn out very well. This outcome assumes some degree of effectiveness in the parents' control. Considering the resistant child, if the parents' high level of control is consistent, over time it may reduce the impact of the child's early unmanageability. Highly controlling mothers may prevent highly resistant children's tempera-

mental resistance from leading to coercion training by bringing the child under control. In contrast, less controlling parents, perhaps because they feel more distress from perceived uncontrollability of the child, intend to participate in coercive processes, more often see their resistant children becoming behaviorally disruptive. In relation to low-resistant children, low parental control may be an optimal environment for the development of internalized self-control. Relatively low levels of control provide ample opportunities for developing autonomous functioning, thereby helping the child to internalize social limits. Low-resistant children experiencing high control, however, may have less involvement with autonomy and thus less practice in cognitively and emotionally internalizing social limits. This situation might facilitate the development of coercive, destructive behavior patterns. In addition, because these children lack a level of resistance to control, they suffer many interruptions without many successes, thus possibly leading to some level of frustration-based anger (Bates, Dodge, Pettit, & Ridge, 1998).

Parenting Issues

Maternal Responsiveness

Patterns of mother-child interaction from infancy to age 12 were investigated in a longitudinal study of 44 English-speaking mothers and their preterm children. Maternal responsiveness was evaluated by home observations during infancy and in two structured laboratory situations at age 12. Children of mothers who were consistently more responsive during infancy and early adolescence and those who became more responsive by the time their children were 12 achieved higher IQ and arithmetic scores, and they had more positive self-esteem and fewer behavioral and emotional problems, as reported by their teachers, than children of less responsive mothers (Beckwith, Rodning, & Cohen, 1992).

Parenting Issues

Children's Chores

A study of 790 Nebraska homes in which there were children revealed some interesting data on the extent to which children were regularly required to do chores around the house or yard. Apparently, assigning chores was a developmental process. In some households, chores were assigned to very young children (about a third of boys and girls 4 years of age or under were assigned work). The older that children became, the more work was assigned, so that by age 9 or 10, well over 90% of the children were involved in regular chores. The median number of hours spent on chores was 4 hours per week. Even among the older, hardest workers, only 6 hours per week were required (White & Brinkerhoff, 1981).

In the beginning, children were responsible for themselves, picking up their own toys, making beds, cleaning their rooms. By 10 years of age, children moved beyond self-centered chores and were now required to help the family.

Parents gave five types of reasons for assigning chores:

1. *Developmental*—doing chores builds character, develops responsibility, helps children learn.

2. *Reciprocal obligation*—it is children's duty to help the family.

3. *Extrinsic*—parents need help.

4. *Task learning*—children need to learn to do these tasks.

5. *Residual*—miscellaneous reasons, including earning an allowance or needing to keep busy (White & Brinkerhoff, 1981).

In many families, children help their parents with household chores.

9. *Discipline needs to take into account children's age.* One study found that discipline among preschoolers peaked between 30 and 36 months of age. That is, there were peaks in negative behavior during these ages. By 48 months, there was a decrease in the discipline problems caused by physical aggression and immaturity of the children (Larzelare, Amberson, & Martin, 1992).

10. *Methods of discipline to be avoided are those that threaten the child's security or development of self-esteem.* In some cases, parents threaten to give children away if they aren't good or to call the police to put them in jail. Similarly, threats to withdraw love if children aren't good are harmful means of disciplining, but they are often employed by middle-class parents to try to control their children's behavior. Such threats are devastating to children's security if regularly employed.

The Father's Role

With increasing numbers of married women employed outside the home, fairness would seem to demand that husbands take increased responsibility for housework and child care. This has happened to some extent, but *equality of roles has not been fully achieved* (Atkinson & Blackwelder, 1993). More educated fathers, especially those reared in homes where the father was expected to do housework and care for children, generally participate in these tasks; but study after study shows that in other homes, even those in which the mother works full-time, the mothers still take major responsibility, with the father occasionally

Many fathers play a vital role in the care of their infant children.

"helping" (Levant, Slattery, & Loiselle, 1987; Shelton, 1990). When fathers do participate in household tasks and child care, they usually do so in limited ways. They often "help" on tasks of their own choosing (Marsiglio, 1991b). Some fathers will spend time with their sons, especially when the sons are old enough to play games, but leave the rearing of their daughters to their wives. Cartoons and other media often picture fathers as too inept to change diapers or otherwise care for infants (LaRossa et al., 1991). Such images further discourage fathers who might otherwise want to take care of the baby.

Not only is paternal involvement fair, but it has other advantages. When both parents share responsibilities, the marital relationship improves, individual well-being of the wife increases, and the children benefit because the quality of parent-child relationships is enhanced. Men can have a positive impact on their children's development when men are actively engaged in direct child-rearing activities (McBride & Rane, 1998). Kaplan (1990) suggests that combining marriage, work, and motherhood forms an impossible triangle and that, as a result, the whole family suffers.

Research tends to indicate that many fathers have a closer relationship with their sons than with their daughters (Ishii-Kuntz, 1994; Mott, 1994; Smith & Morgan, 1994; Starrels, 1994). In spite of father-son closeness, most mothers are more involved in the day-to-day care of their children than are fathers. Interestingly enough, fathers are less likely to leave home if they have sons (Mott, 1994). If the father does leave home, the mother usually shows greater equalitarianism in child upbringing than if her husband is present.

Working Mothers

The past two decades have seen a remarkable rise in the number of two-earner and single-parent households in the United States, with corresponding increases in the labor force participation rates of women with young children. Today, fewer than one third of households fit the definition of the so-called traditional family. Psychologists, economists, sociologists, and other behavioral scientists have stormed into this politically charged arena with dozens of studies evaluating the potential effects of maternal employment and substitute child care on children's well-being. There is a considerable amount of disagreement among researchers. It has been suggested that full-time, nonparental care places infants at considerable risk. Other studies do not reach such a conclusion. Two decades of exhaustive research have failed to document consistent, meaningful negative findings of the effects of maternal employment and substitute child care on children's well-being. While the studies show that maternal employment is not uniformly detrimental to the child's well-being, neither is it likely that it is uniformly beneficial.

Many studies omit the influence of socioeconomic status when considering the effects of maternal employment. They also do not take into account the level of emotional support at home as contrasted to the level of emotional support provided by substitute child care. Greenstein (1993) reports on a study of 2,209 children who were between 4 years and 6 years of age. The sampling overrepresents children who have been born to young mothers, less educated mothers, and minority mothers. A number of the children are black, Hispanic, and economically disadvantaged. The average age of the mothers at the time of their child's birth was approximately 22 years. The results of the study showed that there was a stronger negative net effect of maternal employment on the child in high socioeconomic status families. The use of substitute child care resulted in less positive behavioral outcomes for children from high-income households than for children from low-income households. This finding is based on the assumption that when high-income households choose child care, they are not likely to obtain an environment for their children that is significantly better than that which they have at home. However, the additional experiences provided by the formal child-care arrangement to children from low-income households may well significantly expand the developmental opportunities available to such children.

Attention was also given to the level of emotional support in the home and its interaction with the type of substitute child care used during the child's infancy. In homes where children received high levels of emotional support, substitute care (unless it was of extremely high quality) did not adequately substitute for the affective process lost by the mother's absence from the home. In homes where children received relatively low levels of emotional support, the substitute care arrangements had positive effects on social behavior, for it provided a higher level of emotional support than the child would receive if cared for at home. The findings suggest that among middle- and upper-income families, maternal employment implies a significant loss of resources for their children that are not replaced

or compensated for by the child-care setting. However, the additional market goods of services made possible by maternal employment in low-income families may have a far more beneficial effect on child outcomes than negative effect of maternal absence from the home (Greenstein, 1993).

Other important research takes into account the interrelationship between maternal employment, the mother's mental health and emotional well-being, and her parenting style. Research suggests that employment has a positive effect on the mother's emotional well-being and that her emotional well-being enhances her parenting style. Thus, employment has an indirect effect on children's well-being in that it influences the mother's relationship with her children.

One study investigated the relationships that link the mother's employment status, emotional well-being, and parenting style, separately for each social class, in a socioeconomically diverse sample of urban families with a child in the third or fourth grade of the public schools. Results show that in the lower socioeconomic groups, employed mothers had lower scores on levels of depression than did full-time homemakers, and also indicated that those mothers had less authoritarian, more authoritative, and less permissive parenting styles. In the middle class, there was no significant relationship between employment status and depressive mood. It is in the working class, rather than the middle class, that maternal employment was found to be associated with emotional well-being. Moreover, well-being was found to mediate the relationship between the employment and both permissive and authoritative parenting (Hoffman & Youngblade, 1998).

Sibling Relationships

Not only are parents an important influence on the social development of children, but siblings also exert considerable influence. Researchers have tried to discover the importance of birth order and number of siblings in the family, the gender of those siblings, whether the siblings are older or younger, and how these factors influence the children themselves. Sibling relationships are unique because they are different from relationships with parents and peers. Siblings are closer, although usually not identical, in age. Their interests are often different from those of parents, and they have different outlooks and interests in life. Sometimes siblings exert important influences on one another well into

Parenting Issues

Sibling Rivalry

Sibling rivalry is a favorite expression in psychological textbooks. *It refers to the competition of brothers and sisters for the attention, approval, and affection of the parents.* The problem arises because of envy or jealousy and the fear that one brother or sister is receiving more physical or emotional care and benefits from parents than another. The problem is actually quite a common one but varies in degree of severity. Sometimes the problem is created by parents who show differential treatment of their children, even when they are well-intentioned and try to treat all the children the same. If one child is shown favoritism, the other children develop feelings of jealousy, anger, or inferiority (McHale & Pawletko, 1992). Because each child occupies a special place within the family, the home experiences of each child are quite different. Since children differ in personality, it is impossible for parents to treat them all the same. So no matter what parents do, sometimes their actions result in intensification of feelings of sibling rivalry. Other times, parents are certainly ideal parents and are not at fault. As an example, one child may become very jealous because he has been special for several years before a baby brother or sister has been born (Quittner & Opipari, 1994).

Siblings exert an important socializing influence on one another.

adulthood and maintain close relationships all their lives. At other times, the relationships are quite troubling from the beginning, and parents have difficulty in knowing how to manage two or more children in the same family. Of these topics, let's look first at birth order.

Birth Order

It does seem to make a difference whether a child is an only child, a first child, a middle child, or a youngest child in the family. *Research tends to indicate that firstborn children have some advantages over other children in the family.* For example, they are statistically overrepresented among students in graduate and professional schools (Goleman, 1985). Fifty-two percent of U.S. presidents are firstborn children.

There are some good reasons for such levels of attainment. Research reveals that parents usually attach greater importance to their first child. The first child is special because he or she is first; and because there are no competing children, parents are able to give their entire attention and energies to raising that child until the next one is born. For this reason, the oldest sibling usually experiences a richer intellectual environment than younger siblings do. The research indicates that older, first children are usually more social and affectionate, and achieve more in life than do others in the family.

The youngest in the family are also usually given special attention because they are the youngest. The youngest child gets special attention from older brothers and sisters. Because there are others to socialize with, researchers find that later-born children usually possess better social skills than do the firstborn.

Middle children tend to have lower self-esteem than do firstborn and last born, probably because they have a less well-defined function within the family. The middle children are somewhat overlooked. They are not special because of being the first, nor are they the last. They are there and accepted as they are, but usually do not receive as much special attention as the oldest or the youngest child.

Number of Siblings

The total number of children in a family makes a difference also. *In general terms, the greater the number of children, the less they will be able to complete their education.* Usually they have lower levels of schooling, because the parents are not able to offer great educational advantages to all the children in the family. Family size is linked to greater or lesser degrees of achievement (Blake, 1989).

Gender

The sex of a sibling may also be of some significance. Individuals with an older, opposite-sex sibling with whom they have a good relationship usually develop a very positive attitude towards those of the opposite sex. However, if the relationship with the opposite-sex sibling is very troublesome and quarrelsome, the child may develop very negative attitudes towards persons of the opposite sex and have difficulty relating to them later in life. For example, if girls in the family have brothers within the same family, they get acquainted with men by getting acquainted with their brothers. They feel more comfortable with men and learn how to relate to them if they have good relationships with their own masculine siblings.

Older Brothers and Sisters

Having older brothers and sisters in the same family can have a significant influence on younger children—either positively or negatively. The older siblings can serve as role models for the younger ones. Older siblings spend more time with their younger brothers and sisters than their parents do, and they have considerable influence in the children's socialization. Some older children are very good with younger brothers and sisters. Others have a very disturbing, negative influence. In the neighborhood in which I grew up, I lived next door to a boy whose older sister was left to care for him. The sister was ten years older than the boy. The boy used to cry almost constantly for hours while his mother was gone, primarily because the sister teased him unmercifully, probably because he was the only son and she was quite jealous of him. This boy grew up really hating girls, especially anyone who reminded him of his sister. My sister grew up in a family where she had three brothers. As a consequence, she became very much of a tomboy for a while because her role models were all masculine.

All we can say is that sometimes brothers or sisters are positive influences, sometimes negative. If mothers or fathers suspect that younger children are not being properly cared for, they need to give more guidance and supervision so that older brothers and sisters will not be a negative influence. I have counseled with clients who were given a very poor self-image because they were unmercifully teased and persecuted by older siblings within the same family. On the other hand, many people develop quite positive attitudes towards others by loving relationships with brothers and sisters.

Grandparents

The grandparent-grandchild relationship can be important in the lives of children (Barranti, 1985). Many times grandparents and grand-

Grandparent-grandchild relationships are important in the lives of children.

children adore one another. Emotional attachments develop, and the relationship becomes unique and important in the lives of both the older and the younger people (Cherlin & Furstenberg, 1986). It is an important relationship for children for a number of different reasons (Denham & Smith, 1989). Let's see what some of those reasons are.

1. *Grandparents can help children feel loved and secure.* Children can never have too much of the right kind of love. Love that adds security and trust, that accepts and understands, is always needed. The modern role of the grandparent is associated more with warmth and affection and less with authority and power than it used to be (Wilcoxon, 1987). Many grandparents continue to play an important role in the lives of their grandchildren even after the parents are divorced (Clingenpeel et al., 1992; Gladstone, 1988).

2. *Grandparents can help children to know, trust, and understand other people.* Children can learn that other members of the family can be just as comforting as their fathers and mothers. They discover that grandmother's house is a safe and happy home away from home. They learn how to adjust to the way the grandparents think and feel, and learn rules other than the ones that their mothers and fathers find important. This experience helps children to learn how to be flexible and adjust to the ways others act.

3. *Grandparents help children to bridge the gap between the past and the present*, to give children a sense of history. Many children enjoy hearing their grandparents tell about life when the grandparents were growing up. Grandchildren will ask to be told about when you were a little boy or when you were a little

girl. Hearing such anecdotes gives children a sense of history, of what has gone before and the way life was back in the old days. It helps them to have a broader foundation on which to base their lives and to build new knowledge (Martin, Hagestad, & Diedrich, 1988). This knowledge about their cultural and family heritage helps children develop an identity based on the experiences of their forebears as well as on the present.

4.   *Grandparents can provide children with experiences and supervision that their own parents do not have money or time to provide* (Presser, 1989). Most grandparents are called on to baby-sit and enjoy doing so. Some grandparents now help to take care of the home and children while the parents go to work. In this sense, the grandparent acts as a surrogate parent.

5.   *Grandparents—as a result of years of living—can give children a fine sense of values and a philosophy of life.* Not everything that is new is good nor everything that is old, bad. Sometimes the old values need to be reaffirmed. In this sense, grandparents play the traditional role of valued elders sharing the wisdom of the ages with their grandchildren.

6.   *Grandparents can give children a wholesome attitude toward old age.* In our culture in which youth is virtually worshipped, children need to know and to learn to respect their elders. Older people can give rich and fruitful meaning to the lives of their children. They provide a role model for the children's future role as grandparents and for family relationships. By getting to know their grandparents, children can learn what the aged are like and can love and respect them as part of the family.

Grandparents' Problems

Some people say that grandparents never discipline children, that they spoil and pamper them or give them too many gifts. Other people say that grandparents undermine parental authority, try to buy the children's affection, or try to possess children to satisfy their own personal needs. Such is true regarding some grandparents, who actually are problems. But others are not; when problems occur, they usually arise over one or more of the following situations.

1.   *Grandparents are often puzzled about the roles they're expected to play in relationship to their grandchildren.* If they take too much interest and assume too much responsibility, they are accused of taking over the relationship or of meddling. If they do not pay very much attention, they are accused of neglect. One grandmother said, "I don't know what kind of grandmother they really expect me to be." Such a remark points to the need for couples and grandparents to discuss feelings and expectations about the role the grandparents should assume in the family.

2.   *Grandparents may have different ideas about raising children.* They tend to base their philosophy on the way they were brought up themselves and on the way they raised their own children. If the grandmother interferes while the parent is disciplining the grandchildren, such interference causes rebellion and resentment and does much harm. Children get mixed up when they don't know what to expect, whether to follow grandmother's rules or the rules of their parents. It is necessary for grandparents to play a supportive role and not to undermine or contradict the parents (Sistler & Gottfried, 1990).

3.   *Grandparents have a tendency to give unsolicited advice to parents and grandchildren and to preach.* This tendency may cause rebellion, especially in young parents who need an opportunity to work out their own rules and their own procedures with their own children. It may cause resentment on the part of older grandchildren also, who do not like to be told what to do, or who feel it is their parents' prerogative—not that of their grandparents—to guide them and direct them (Oyserman et al., 1993).

4.   *Sometimes parents become jealous of the affection that the children develop for their grandparents.* An insecure parent, in particular, may develop deep-seated resentment at the fact that the children seem to love the grandparent more than they love their parent. Such a mother or father is not emotionally mature or secure in the child's love, and this insecurity poses a problem for the grandparent. Because of this situation, grandparents have to realize that the child belongs to the parent, not to the grandparent. The married parent has to realize also that children certainly will usually put their first loyalty with the parent.

5.   *Some grandparents become too possessive of their grandchildren.* Grandparents who are in need of love and affection and attention, or who are lonely, may use their grandchildren to fill their own empty life. When the grandparents start competing with a child's parents for affection and loyalty, friction and resentment develop. It is necessary for grandparents to accept the fact that the parents have the final

responsibility for the grandchildren. Grandparents also need to remember that being a grandparent is not a full-time career. They have to continue to live their own lives, not get so wrapped up in the lives of their grandchildren that they have nothing else left.

6. *In the case of disagreements, parents and grandparents need to talk things over.* They can learn from one another and can come to respect one another's point of view and feelings. Certainly there is room for compromise, and certainly children need all the love they can get from any member of the family who takes an interest in them.

NONNUCLEAR FAMILIES

The family of today is not necessarily the same as families of yesterday. In the past, we spoke of the nuclear family, which consisted of the husband and wife and children in a fairly limited household. Today, a large number of families are nonnuclear, in that they do not include the same persons as did the families of yesterday. One type of nonnuclear family is the one-parent family. Other types of nonnuclear families are gay and lesbian, divorced, stepfamily, foster-care, and adoptive. Some researchers would put the adolescent mother family in a separate category, especially if she is unmarried and has children.

One-Parent Families

Between 1970 and 1997, there was a 216% increase in the number of one-parent families in the United States (Demo, 1992; U.S. Bureau of Census, 1998). Of this total number, 83% were maintained by mothers, but only 17% were maintained by fathers. (See Figure 9.5 below.) High divorce and illegitimacy rates mean that both the number and total percentage of these families will con-

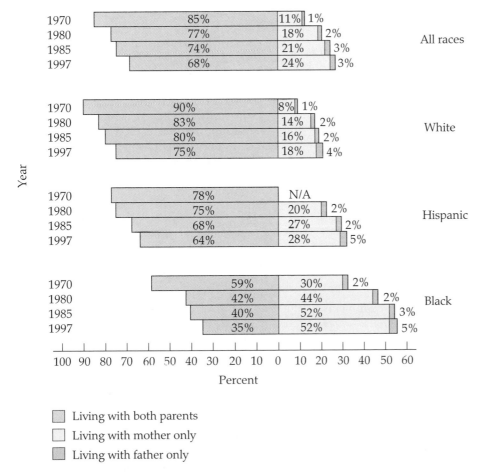

FIGURE 9.5   Percentage of children under 18 years old living with parents, 1970–1997.

From U.S. Bureau of the Census (1998), *Statistical Abstract of the United States, 1998.* Washington, DC: U.S. Government Printing Office, p. 68.

One-parent families with at least one child under 18 years of age represent one-fourth of all families with children.

tinue to increase. The one-parent family, therefore, represents a major segment of the population, especially among black families and especially among the poor. Among blacks, 52% of all children under 18 are currently living with a lone mother, as compared with 18% among whites and 28% among Hispanics (U.S. Bureau of the Census, 1998). Large numbers of these single mothers have never been married (Campbell, Breitmayer, & Ramey, 1986; Dawson, 1991).

Children who grow up in single-parent households, especially those whose mothers have never married, are significantly more likely to live below the poverty line. They are also more likely than children who live with both biological parents to perform poorly in school and to have repeated a grade or to have been expelled. They are also more likely to demonstrate emotional or behavior problems. The most common health problems are accidents, injuries, and poisonings. These conditions hold true after adjusting statistically for social and demographic characteristics (Remez, 1992).

The Female-Headed Family

One of the most important problems of the female-headed family is *limited income* (Pett & Vaughn-Cole, 1986). The median income of families headed by a woman is 63% of the income of families with a male head (U.S. Bureau of the Census, 1998). These women often have to cope with problems such as inadequate child care, thus placing their children at greater risk for depression, conduct problems, and lower self-esteem (Gomel, Tinsley, Parke, & Clark, 1998). Mothers who are left alone to bring up their children themselves may have *difficulty performing all family functions well* (Sanik & Mauldin, 1986). There may be little time or energy left to

perform household tasks, meaning that the house is less clean, less time is available for food preparation, or the physical and emotional care of the children is neglected (Quinn & Allen, 1989). Role strain is common among single mothers (Campbell & Moen, 1992; Goldberg et al., 1992). Low-income single mothers of young children are especially exposed to high levels of daily stress (Olson & Banyard, 1993).

Several studies have shown that after divorce, many custodial mothers have *more trouble communicating with their children, showing as much affection, controlling them,* and *spending as much time with them as previously* (Machida & Holloway, 1991). Because of demands on their time, mothers are often too absorbed with their own problems to help their children (McLanahan & Booth, 1989). Some of these problems in mother-child relationships improve and stabilize after the first year or two following separation (Wallerstein & Kelly, 1980).

We must be careful not to assume that all one-parent families are the same. A study of 156 6- to 9-year-old African American children living in single-mother-headed households in rural areas of the South, 82% of whom lived in poverty, revealed some distinct differences among mothers and their children. In this study, maternal education, paternal religiosity, and adequacy of financial resources were linked with "no nonsense" parenting, mother-child relationship quality, and maternal involvement in the child's school activities as well as with children's cognitive competence, social competence, and internalizing problems as children's development of self-regulation was speeded up. This study reinforces other studies that point to the fact that African Americans' religious involvement promotes supportive and responsive family relationships, no-nonsense parenting, and more maternal involvement in the child's school. No-nonsense parenting is a combination of high levels of control, including physical control, and of displays of warmth and affection. High levels of parental control and vigilance with modern family openness are positively associated with academic performance among African American students (Brody & Flor, 1998).

The Male-Headed Family

Solo fathers face many of the same problems as solo mothers do. However, they usually do not suffer poverty to the same extent as do solo mothers (Norton & Glick, 1986), although *financial pressure* is still one of the most common complaints. Also, most single fathers are concerned about not *spending enough time with their children* (Resman, 1986). If the children are of preschool age, fathers are faced with the same dilemmas as are solo mothers who must work: that of finding adequate child-care services. Part of their stress arises because they are often *forced to change their circle of friends* and to rebuild their social life (Greif, 1988).

Effects of Paternal Absence on Sons

The important question that plagues both parents and professionals is whether children grow up to be maladjusted because of the lack of two parents in the home. The findings reveal that *the earlier a boy is separated from his father and the longer the separation is, the more affected the boy will be in his early years* (Stanley, Weikel, & Wilson, 1986). One study of fifth-grade boys who were father-absent before age 2 found them to be less trusting, less industrious, and having more feelings of inferiority than did boys who became father-absent between the age of 3 and 5 (Santrock, 1970a). *Father absence may also affect the development of masculinity.* As boys grow older, however, the earlier effects of father absence decrease. By late childhood, lower-class father-absent boys appear to score as high as their father-present counterparts on certain measures of sex role preference and sex role adoption.

There is one fairly certain difference between boys raised in single-parent and dual-parent families. Those in single-parent families have a *lower level of educational attainment and consequent lower income as adults* (Krein & Beller, 1988; Mueller & Cooper, 1986; Nock, 1988).

The effect of father absence is dependent partially on whether boys have surrogate male models (Hawkins & Eggebeen, 1991). The quality of a boy's relationship with a male role model is as important as whether he lives in a single-mother or a two-parent household (Florsheim, Tolan, & Gorman-Smith, 1998). Father-absent boys with a father substitute such as an older male sibling are less affected than those without a father substitute (Santrock, 1970b). Young father-absent male children seek the attention of older males and are strongly motivated to imitate and please potential father figures.

Effects of Paternal Absence on Daughters

Some researchers contend that the effect of paternal absence on daughters is not as great as on sons (Stevenson & Black, 1988). The reasoning has been that children make a same-sex identification, and so daughters would be affected less by the father's absence than would sons. Some girls aren't affected as much when they are young, but they may be affected more during adolescence. *Lack of meaningful male-female relationships in childhood can make it more difficult to relate to the opposite sex.* In one study of a group of girls who grew up without fathers, Eberhardt and Schill (1984) found few effects during preadolescence; but during adolescence, the girls of divorced parents who had lived with their mothers were inappropriately assertive, seductive, and sometimes sexually promiscuous. Having ambivalent feelings about men because of their negative memories of their fathers, they pursued men in inept and inappropriate ways. They began dating early and were likely to engage in sexual intercourse at an early age. Hepworth, Ryder, and Dreyer (1984) reported two major effects of parental loss on the formation of intimate relationships: avoidance of intimacy and accelerated courtship. In summary, therefore, fathers appear to play a significant role in encouraging their daughters' feminine development (Heilbrun, 1984). The father's acceptance and reinforcement of his daughter's femininity greatly facilitates the development of her self-concept. Interaction with a competent father also provides the girl with basic experiences that help in her relationships with other males.

Nevertheless, *a father-present home is not necessarily always better for the children than a father-absent home.* Some fathers, though home, spend little time in caring for their children or relating to them (Levant, Slattery, & Loisell, 1987). In such families, father absence would not have as much effect as in homes where the father spent more time with his children. Some fathers are also inappropriate models. If there is a father at home who is rejecting, paternal deprivation may be a significant cause of emotional problems and/or antisocial behavior.

The effect of paternal absence on the mother is crucial in determinig the influence on the children. Many father-absence studies have failed to take into account the mother's changed position following a divorce, separation, or the death of her husband. If the mother is quite upset, if her income is severely reduced, if she must be away from home frequently because she has to work, or if she has inadequate care for her children when she is gone, the children are going to be affected—not because of the father's absence, as such, but because of the subsequent effect on their mother and their relationship with her. Furthermore, the presence of surrogate father figures exerts a modifying influence on both boys and girls.

Gay and Lesbian Families

An increasing number of gay couples and lesbian couples are raising children and seek to live together as a family. There is a wide diversity of gay and lesbian lifestyles. Many same-sex couple relationships are of short duration, and a pattern of serial monogamy is common.

FOCUS

Same-Sex Parent

The belief that children fare better living with the same-sex parent has been widely accepted among certain academic and legal circles. The argument is that the child will have a same-sex parent with whom to identify. Indeed, several social and behavioral scientific frameworks offer convincing reasons to accept the same-sex pattern. Despite the appeal of this argument, the empirical basis for it is limited to scattered, small-scale projects. Downey and Powell (1993) explored a wide array of outcomes by using a nationally representative data set of cases of children living in father-only households. After the result of exhaustive study, they found that they could not find even one case in which either males or females significantly benefited from living with their same-sex parent, as contrasted to their opposite-sex parent.

Do children fare better living with the same-sex parent?

However, a large number of gay males and lesbian females have made long-term commitments in stable couple relationships. Only a few states have legitimized same-sex marriage; however, marriage liaisons are increasing. Many of these gay and lesbian couples are raising children. Between 1 and 5 million lesbians are biological or adoptive mothers. Between 6 and 14 million children are conceived by gays or lesbians (Allen & Demo, 1995). Both figures probably underestimate the actual numbers because of the threat of discrimination and of homophobia.

Most children in families headed by lesbian mothers were born into the context of a heterosexual relationship between the biological parents. After leaving the heterosexual relationship, some mothers enter a relationship with another woman, who may or may not act as a stepparent. Some lesbians conceive children through alternative insemination, selecting a friend, relative, acquaintance, or unknown donor.

The involvement of biological fathers ranges from low to moderate and tends to vary over time (Hare & Richards, 1993). Most lesbian mothers are supportive of the father's involvement. In families where only one of the women is the birth mother, the partner tends to assume the role of friend. However, a clear distinction is made between partner and mother in terms of parental authority. Overall, the relationships are very positive; however, some strain is reported. Families formed by lesbian mothers closely resemble heterosexual stepfamilies: All relationships require adjustment in terms of new responsibilities and roles (Hare & Richards, 1993).

Divorce and Children

Parental divorce involves a series of stressful interactions between children and their environment as the family restructures following parental separation. Many of these interactions, such as interparental quarrels, badmouthing, and missed visits by the noncustodial parent, present serious adaptation challenges for children. Children's success in coping with these negative interactions has important implications for their mental health. In fact, postdivorce stressors may have a more important impact on children's mental health than does the occurrence of the divorce per se. However, not everyone is affected equally by these stresses (Sandler, Tein, & West, 1994).

A growing number of clinicians emphasize that children perceive divorce as a major, negative event that stimulates painful emotions, confusion, and uncertainty (Kalter, 1983). Some clinicians feel that the majority of children regain psychological equilibrium in a year or so and resume a normal curve of growth and development. Others feel that for a substantial portion of children, the upheaval in their lives will result in interferences in wholesome, social-emotional growth (Amato, 1991a; Giudubaldi & Perry, 1985; Wallerstein & Kelly, 1980).

Wallerstein and Blakeslee (1990) found that 10 years after divorce, half the women and one-third of the men were still so angry at their former spouses that their anger colored their relationships with their children. The children felt they had been abandoned by the father, that they were denied basic security with which to grow, and that they had been compelled to assume adult responsibilities for their parents' well-being. Half the children entered adulthood as self-deprecating, underachieving young women and men. High levels of alcohol abuse, delinquency, and promiscuity showed up 10 to 15 years after the divorce.

Researchers have found a larger number of variables—individual, family, and environmental—that affect the quality of adjustment to divorce. These variables include the child's gender and age at the time of separation or divorce; the child's temperament, interpersonal knowledge, and level of coping resources; the amount of interparental conflict prior to, during, and following the divorce; the quality of parent-child relationships; the parents' mental and physical health; the type of custody arrangement; parental remarriage; the number of major life experiences following divorce, including the amount of financial decline experienced by the postdivorce family; and the social support available to both the parents and the children (Gately & Schwebel, 1991).

However, children are individuals and react differently to the same experience (Hetherington, 1989; Monahan et al., 1993). We do know that children of divorced parents are more likely to marry at an early age and to get divorced themselves (Amato, 1988b; Amato & Booth, 1991; Glenn & Kramer, 1987). Overall, the long-term impact on social, emotional, and cognitive growth is not clear and continues to be studied and debated.

Short-term reactions have been fairly well described. Children go through a period of *mourning and grief*, and the mood and feeling may be one of sadness, depression, and dejection. One 7-year-old described divorce as "when people go away" (Rice, 1999, p. 613). Other common reactions are a *heightened*

There are many variables that influence the effect of divorce on children.

sense of insecurity and anxiety about their future. Children feel that "if you really loved me, you wouldn't go away and leave me." Some become very possessive with the parent. One mother remarked: "Since the divorce, Tommy has been very upset when I go to work or when he goes to school. I think he's afraid that he'll come home and not find me there" (Rice, 1999).

Another common reaction is for children to *blame themselves*. If one major source of couple conflict is over the children, the children feel that the departing parent is abandoning them because they haven't been "good boys or girls." Another common reaction is *preoccupation with reconciliation*, to try to bring their parents together. They "wish that everyone could live together and be

FOCUS

Sequence of Adjustments of Children to Divorce

According to Wallerstein, the sequence of adjustments that children have to make to divorce are the following: (1) Acknowledge the marital disruption, (2) regain a sense of direction and freedom to pursue customary activities, (3) deal with loss and feelings of rejection, (4) forgive the parents, (5) accept the permanence of divorce and relinquish longings for the restoration of the predivorced family, and (6) come to feel comfortable and confident in relationships. The successful completion of these tasks, which allows the child to stay on course developmentally, depends on the child's coping resources and the degree of support available to help the child deal with the stressors (Gately & Schwebel, 1991).

FOCUS

Comparisons of African Americans and Whites on Adjustments to Divorce

1. *African Americans, particularly women, are less likely than whites to remarry following marital disruption.* Remarriages are somewhat more stable than first marriages for African Americans, whereas the reverse pattern is evident for whites. Overall, however, remarriage rates for African Americans are lower than for whites because there are fewer African American men than women of comparable socioeconomic status. Also, single-parent status may be more normal among African Americans than it is among whites. Marriage may be less central to the well-being of African Americans than it is to that of whites, and African American women, in contrast to white women, are less con-

strained to marry because of their relative economic independence from men.

2. *Adjustment for African Americans initially, and after four years of separation, is better than for whites.* Divorced African American females have less depression and fewer adjustment difficulties than do divorced white females. African American divorced parents, when compared with white divorced respondents on one study, were more satisfied with being parents and were less likely to indicate that someone in the home had a substance abuse problem.

3. *A third way that African American divorced families differ from their white counterparts is the presence of an extensive kinship sup-*

port network. African Americans in both two-parent and single-parent families are more likely than whites to reside in extended-family households. The presence of extended family members could be helpful to parents because they can perform functions and fulfill roles that might otherwise go unfulfilled. Furthermore, by relieving mothers of household tasks, extended-family members may allow mothers the opportunity to improve their economic situations, primarily through additional employment or education (Fine, McKenry, Donnelly, & Voydanoff, 1992).

Custody—refers to legal custody (who has decision-making rights over the child) and physical custody (where the children live)

Legal custody—right to make decisions regarding the welfare of the child

Physical custody—legal residence of parent that the child lives with

happy." The longing for a reunited family may go on for a long time, until children fully understand the realities of the situation and the reason for the separation.

After children get over the initial upset of divorce, one common reaction is *anger and resentment*, especially against the parent whom they blame for the divorce. Sometimes this is directed against the father—especially if they feel he has deserted the family. The child feels, "I hate you because you have gone off and left me." The resentment or hostility may also be directed at the mother, especially if the children blame her for the divorce. One 5-year-old blamed her mother for her father's absence: "I hate you, because you sent my daddy away." (Actually, the mother hadn't wanted the divorce.) An older girl, age 12, asked her mother, "Why did you leave my father all alone?" It was obvious that the girl did not understand the reason for the divorce. (Author's counseling notes)

Children have other adjustments to make. *They have to adjust to the absence of one parent.* Older children may be required to assume more responsibility for homemaking. Money is tight. *Special adjustments are necessary when*

the parents get emotionally involved with other persons. Now the children must share their parents with another adult. If the parent remarries, as the majority do, the children are confronted with a total readjustment to a stepparent (Baylar, 1988; Rice, 1999).

Child Custody

The term **custody** refers to both **legal custody** (who has decision-making rights) and **physical custody** (where the children will live). In sole legal custody, the noncustodial parent forfeits the right to make decisions about the children's education, health, or religious training; the custodial parent is given control over child-rearing. In joint legal custody, custody is shared between the two parents, with parental obligations and rights left as they were during the marriage. There are advantages and disadvantages to both arrangements.

Traditionally, sole custody has been given to the mother unless she could be declared unfit. In some cases, the father may be more competent than the mother. The children may be closer to the father, and he may be the one who can better afford them and better care for them (Lowrey, 1985). Since both parents usually have to work after divorce, the overriding consideration is what the court considers the best interests of the children. In cases in which two parents are of different races, private prejudices are not permissible considerations if they might inflict injury by removing a child from a competent parent (Myricks & Ferullo, 1986).

In many states, a mediator has to be employed or a child-development expert consulted to investigate the family situation and to recommend custody arrangements to the court. The wishes of older children are often taken into consideration.

In **joint custody,** both parents are responsible. However, the children usually reside with one parent and visit the other often. In joint custody, children have access to both parents, and both are responsible for decisions in relationship to the children. Joint custody fathers are more likely to be actively involved in parenting than are noncustodial fathers (Bowman & Ahrons, 1985). Some research indicates that joint custody increases parental self-esteem, diminishes anxiety, lessens depression, and eases the fathers' feelings of disruption (Coysh et al., 1989). However, joint custody takes great maturity and much cooperation on the part of both parents (Lowrey & Settle, 1985). The parents continue to perpetuate all the squabbles of the unhappy marriage. The effect on the children can be very negative. There is general agreement, however, that joint custody, if desired by both parents and if both are able to get along together, is a good solution to a difficult problem (Melli, 1986). Wives are more likely to prefer joint custody when they are experiencing low levels of conflict with their ex-husbands, having few visitation problems, perceiving the ex-husband to be more competent as a parent, experiencing little psychological distress, and/or receiving social support to maintain the father/child relationship (Wilcox, Wolchik, & Braver, 1998).

Child Support

Under law, child support is an obligation of both the father and the mother whether the parents are married or not. Since nine out of ten custodial parents are women, child-support awards are the most common mechanism by which noncustodial fathers are required to transfer economic resources to their children. However, about one-fifth of divorced mothers are not awarded child-support payments, either because the father was judged unable to pay or because he has run away and cannot be found. Hardly any fathers contribute to their children's support without a court agreement (Peterson & Nord, 1990).

There are various systems for determining the amount of child-support awards: (a) a straight percentage of the noncustodial father's income based on the number of dependent children; (b) calculation of support according to the combined income of both parents, with each paying a percentage that is their share of the combined income; and (c) taking both parents' incomes into consideration, but allowing for exemptions such as work-related expenses, taxes, or new dependents of the noncustodial father. Investigators suggest that many noncustodial fathers can afford to pay substantially more child support than is awarded under any of these three systems (Klitsch, 1989). Under new laws, child-support enforcement amendments require all states to use automatic wage withholdings to collect old/new child support, to withhold state income tax refunds, to use legal processes to enforce the court orders, to impose liens against property, or to require security bonds as guarantees of payment. Such support laws appear to reduce

In joint custody, both parents are legally responsible for the well-being of their children.

Joint custody—both parents share in decisions regarding the welfare of the child

Parenting Issues

Minimizing the Harmful Effects of Divorce

1. File for no-fault divorce and mediate a settlement including financial, property, child custody, and child support arrangements. If the divorce is as amicable as possible, the reduced anger and conflict have a positive effect on both the parents and their children (Kramer & Washo, 1993).

2. Make it clear to the children that you are divorcing your spouse, not the children, that you will always be their parents and continue to take care of them and to see them. One primary goal is to reduce children's anxiety and insecurity.

3. If you are the noncustodial parent, arrange for open access to your children (Depner & Bray, 1990). This means living close to them and seeing them regularly. The primary negative effect of divorce is loss of contact with a parent. Predictable and frequent contact with the noncustodial parent is associated with better adjustment unless the father is poorly adjusted or extremely immature (Seltzer, 1990). Adjustment of the children is enhanced if the custodial mother approves of the father's continued contact and rates the relationship positively.

4. If you are the custodial parent, your psychological adjustment is of great signifi-cance in determining the adjustment of your child (Kitson & Morgan, 1990; Umberson, 1989). If you are disturbed, your child is more likely to be disturbed. Get help if you can't make a happy adjustment yourself (Wallerstein & Kelly, 1980).

5. Keep conflict with your ex-spouse to a minimum (Kline, Johnston, & Tschann, 1991). Reduced conflict after divorce has a major positive effect on children (Demo & Acock, 1988; Tschann, Johnston, Kline, & Wallerstein, 1989). Continued conflict has a negative effect (Amato, 1993; Kelly, 1988).

6. Custody arrangements, whether maternal, paternal, or joint custody, are not as important an issue as the degree of inter-parental conflict. Joint custody is a satisfactory arrangement if ex-spouses get along with one another, but detrimental if it leads to conflict (Donnelly & Finkelhor, 1993; Kolata, 1988; Maccoby, Depner, & Mnookin, 1988; Schwartz, 1987). One study of the effect of custody arrangements on parent-child relationships found no evidence that children in shared custody had less conflictual or better relationships with their parents. Children in sole custody households actually gave their parents more support than those in shared custody, but this tendency may be because they feared losing their remaining parent. The study also found that parents who had high levels of disagreement with each other (regardless of the type of custody) also had more disagreements with their children (Donnelly & Finkelhor, 1992).

7. Parents report high levels of satisfaction with shared (joint) physical custody, and the results run positive for children (Steinman, Zemmelman, & Knoblauch, 1985). This custody arrangement requires that parents reside in the same school district if children are of school age.

8. Don't use children to hurt your spouse or get back at him or her. Children become especially upset if they are used as pawns in angry power plays between divorcing spouses. Don't ask children to take sides or try to turn children against the other parent. Children love both parents; whose side are they supposed to be on?

9. Share in financial child support as much as you are able. It is one way of assuring that your children have the necessities of life and are not affected by the custodial parent's having to live in poverty (Paasch & Teachman, 1991; Teachman, 1991).

delinquency of payments by absent fathers ("Three years after enactment," 1987).

It is important for both parents to make child-support payments. Doing so lets children know that they are loved and cared for by both parents and enables the children to have the necessities of life; to have adequate clothes, food, and education; to live in better neighborhoods and housing; and to prevent the children from being penalized because of the actions of the parents. Children need to know they are loved and nurtured by both parents, regardless of their parents' marital status.

An alarming instance of nonpayment or underpayment of child support obligations ordered by the court has been demonstrated. Only one-half of all noncustodial parents pay the full amount of support that they are ordered to pay, with another one-quarter paying nothing at all. There is also a disturbingly low rate of custodial parent-child contact and a decline in the quality of this relationship over time. The low level of contact is detrimental to children, as contact with noncustodial parents has typically been shown to be conducive to better social, academic, and emotional adjustment, provided that the relationship between the divorced parents is very harmonious (Braver et al., 1993).

Visitation Rights

Visitation rights are given to the parent who was not given custody. These rights may be unlimited, or they may be restrictive, depending on the situation. Although increased visitation is associated with good noncustodial parent-child relationships, the association is mediated by the quality of the postdivorce parental relationship. The frequency and intensity of parental conflict after the divorce have a marked influence on children's psychological adjustment (Schaeffer, 1989). A vindictive spouse can make life miserable by managing to be away when the children are supposed to visit, by poisoning the children's minds against the other parent, by refusing to allow the children to phone or write, or by using visitation rights as a club to wield over the other person's head.

Coparenting

Numerous studies examining the effects of divorce on child development highlight the fundamental importance of conflict between exspouses in explaining variations in child functioning. Children's well-being is inversely correlated with the level of postdivorce conflict that exists and persists between parents. The more that the separated parents are in conflict regarding parenting practices, the poorer adjustment their children are able to make (Belsky, Crnic, & Gable, 1995). A new ideal for cooperative postdivorce parenting has been emerging in recent years. It is **coparenting** by divorced parents. Where there are more than two parenting adults after remarriage, the arrangement is called a **parenting coalition** (Bisher & Bisher, 1989). In coparenting, the two divorced persons cooperate rather than compete in the task of raising their children. In the parenting coalition, the biological parents (now divorced and remarried) plus the stepparents cooperate in raising their own children and the stepchildren. Children have contact with both of their parents and with their stepparents.

There are a number of advantages to these kinds of cooperative parenting. The children's needs as well as those of the parents can be met more adequately than if there is continued antagonism between adults. Children are not caught in the web of hostility; their chances of becoming messengers between two households are greatly reduced; and their fear of losing a parent is minimized. The power struggles between households lessen, the children's self-esteem is enhanced, so that they are easier to live with. Not only that, the parents' responsibilities are lessened, since the task of rearing the children is shared.

Sometimes adults are not aware of the pain they are causing their children by their angry behavior. If they decide to control the anger, the children benefit by the new atmosphere of cooperation.

Emotional Support

Fathers and mothers are important resources for the developing child; both can serve as sources of emotional support, practical assistance, information, guidance, and supervision. Prolonged absence of either parent from the household may be problematic for children. Following divorce, many children experience a decrease in the quantity and quality of contact with the noncustodial parent—usually the father (King, 1994). One research study is based on the *National Survey of Families and Households* (NSFH). Children involved in this study were all boys between the ages of 5 and 18 in divorced families. When the resident parent reported little conflict with the nonresident parent, boys who had a high level of involvement with the nonresident parent were said to have fewer behavioral problems. But when the resident parent reported conflict with the other parent, boys who had a high level of involvement with the nonresident parent were said to have a large number of behavioral problems. The findings clearly showed that frequency of contact with nonresident parents is not as important as the quality of the relationship between the divorced parents, which affects the children in the family (Amato & Rezac, 1994).

The mother is also profoundly affected by what happens. Two factors that result in the greatest impact (including health and mental health) on the mother and child are *payment of child support* and *the frequency and emotional quality of the father's relationship with the child.*

Stepfamilies

Approximately 83% of divorced men and 76% of divorced women remarry. Today, 46% of marriages involve an adult who has been married before (U.S. Bureau of the Census, 1998). Most of these adults have children. This means that 16% of all American children live in stepfamilies (Coleman & Ganong, 1990).

Visitation rights—right to visit the child given by law

Coparenting—cooperation of two parents in rearing their children

Parenting coalition—cooperation of biological and stepparents in the rearing of children

Stepfamily—a family formed when a remarried husband or wife brings children from a former marriage

Many couples enter into stepfamily relations expecting relationships similar to those of primary families. They are soon disappointed, surprised, and bewildered when they find few similarities.

One reason for disappointment is that *stepparents have unrealistically high expectations* of themselves and what to anticipate. After all, they have been married before and have been parents before. They expect they will be able to fit into the stepparent role very nicely. They are shocked when they discover that their stepchildren don't take to them the way that they do to their biological parents. This outcome creates anxiety, anger, guilt, and low self-esteem. The stepparents either blame the children or begin to feel there is something wrong with themselves. They need to realize that it may take several years before satisfactory relationships are worked out. Over a period of time, love and affection may develop (Marsiglio, 1992).

Parents and stepparents enter into their new family with a great deal of guilt and regret over their failed marriage and divorce. They feel sorry for their children, whom they have put through an upsetting experience. This feeling creates several effects. Usually, parents tend to be overindulgent and not as strict as they might otherwise be, and they have more trouble guiding and controlling the children's behavior (Amato, 1987). Often they try to buy the children's affection and cooperation.

A stepparent's role is ill-defined (Hobart, 1988). Stepparents are neither parents nor just friends. Their efforts to try to be parents may be rejected by older children. Stepparents are required to assume many of the responsibilities of parents, yet they have none of the privileges and satisfactions of parenthood (Fine & Fine, 1992). In the beginning, being a stepparent seems all give and no receive. It's frustrating.

The major stress in stepfamilies arises in the stepparent-stepchild relationship.

Fairy tales and folklore have developed the stereotype of the cruel stepmother, a myth that is hard to overcome. Most studies indicate that the stepmother role is more difficult than that of stepfather, primarily because the mother has more responsibilities for direct care of the children (Sauer & Fine, 1988). However, stepfathers are portrayed as being abusive, a stereotype that is also difficult to overcome (Claxton-Oldfield, 1992).

Stepparents confront the necessity of attempting to deal with children who have already been socialized by another set of parents. Stepparents may disagree with the way that their stepchildren are being brought up. But any attempt on their part suddenly to step in and try to change things is deeply resented.

Stepparents expect gratitude and thanks for what they do, but often get rejection and criticism instead. They were expected to support and care for their own biological children, but feel they are being very generous and helpful by offering the same to stepchildren. Yet, stepchildren seem to take help for granted and ask for more, offering little thanks or appreciation for what is done for them.

Stepparents are faced with unresolved emotional issues from the prior marriage and divorce. They need to resolve some of the hostilities that were created through the process of separation and divorce, so that they can make a fresh start.

They must also deal with a network of complex kinship relationships: with their own biological family members, with their former spouse's family members, with their new spouse's family members, plus their own children and stepchildren. This responsibility adds a more difficult dimension to their family involvements.

Stepparents must cope with stepsibling feelings and relationships. Stepchildren are rarely helpful to each other in coping with the strains of the divorce period. Instead, there may be stepsibling rivalry and competition for the attention of parents (Amato, 1987).

Family cohesion tends to be lower in stepfamilies than in intact families (Pill, 1990; Banker & Gaertner, 1998). Life in divorced and reconstituted families tends to be chaotic and stressful during the years following remarriage (Wallerstein & Kelly, 1980). However, as far as the marriages themselves are concerned, in comparison with first-married couples, one study found that if both spouses remarried, stepfather families reported *higher* relationship quality and stronger intrinsic motivations to be in the relationship (Kurdek, 1989; Kurdek & Fine, 1991). One study found that the major strengths for stepfamilies were in the areas of sexual relationships and egalitarian roles. The major stressors were children and parenting (Schultz, Schultz, & Olson, 1991).

Foster Care

The number of children under foster-parent care has skyrocketed from 360,000 in 1990 to an estimated 484,000 in 1998 (U.S. Bureau of the Census, 1998) and could approach 840,000 by the end of the decade (Kools, 1997). The reason for this increase is that child neglect and abuse are prevalent, the number of teenage pregnancies and children born out of wedlock has increased, and the number of parents unable or unfit to care for their children has risen, so that the state has to care for these children by placing them in foster homes. When children are taken from their parents or when parents voluntarily give them up, *foster care becomes the treatment of last resort.* Even the best foster parents may have difficulty coping. The payment they receive from the state is usually inadequate to cover all expenses. They are asked to take children with severe emotional and behavioral problems who are very difficult to manage. Many children have been moved from home to home and therefore have learned not to trust anyone. Although foster care is certainly preferable to staying in an abusive or a neglectful situation, it is still far from ideal. It is supposed to be a temporary arrangement until the child's own parents can care for their own child again, but what is supposed to be short-term care often becomes long-term in a series of foster homes (Wald, Carlsmith, & Leiderman, 1988).

When children are taken from their parents, foster care becomes the treatment of last resort.

Parenting Issues

How to Be a Stepparent

1. Give yourself and your own children ample time before marriage to get acquainted with your prospective stepchildren.

2. Don't try to take the place of your stepchildren's parent. Psychologically, children can accept only one father or mother at a time. Children often reject the stepparent as an intruder if the stepparent tries to compete with the child's natural parent for the child's loyalty.

3. Don't expect instant love (Dainton, 1993). Any affection that develops arises only gradually. In many cases, it takes several years to develop a good relationship. The older the stepchildren, the longer it takes (Hobart, 1987).

4. Winning the friendship of your stepchildren is an important first step. If you can be good friends and learn to like one another, you will have come a long way toward developing a close relationship.

5. Recognize that most stepchildren are jealous of the time and attention that their parent (your spouse) gives you. Encourage your spouse to spend quality time with them.

6. Let the children's natural parent take the lead in guidance and discipline, and then you support the effort. If you as a stepparent try to change the way stepchildren are being taught, they will resent your efforts, especially if they can get their own parent to take their side.

7. Don't try to buy the affection and loyalty of your own children or stepchildren. They will learn to manipulate you to win approval and favors.

8. Since all stepchildren are different, you have to deal with them as individuals.

Current estimates are that 40% of children remain in foster care for more than two years, with an average stay of five years. Multiple placement transitions are not commonplace for the foster-care population. Up to 55% of children in foster care experience three or four placements (Kools, 1997). As the foster-care system has rapidly grown, investigators have begun to gather evidence that severe functional impairment is suffered by children in foster care as a group, including poor academic achievement, behavioral and emotional problems, and health-related problems. A high level of insecurities is experienced by most children who endure conflict between the desire to belong "in the foster family" and the need to maintain loyalty and ties to the biological family. A diminished status and stereotypical views of the foster child contribute to devaluation of the child's self by others, so that foster children have a greater difficulty establishing identity and feelings of self-worth (Kools, 1997).

Peer relationships are important for the development and mental-health functioning of children who have been placed into foster care. Interactions with peers facilitate children's cognitive, moral, affective, and social development, and problematic relationships are linked to a wide variety of adjustment and mental-health problems. Many foster children exhibit social behavioral patterns that undermine their ability to form positive and supportive relationships with their peers. For children to develop normally, they must be exposed to social environments that allow and facilitate the natural unfolding of developmental processes (Price & Brew, 1998). Some authorities feel that some children would be better off in group homes (they used to be called orphanages) where they can live with their siblings and peers. Other authorities maintain that these new orphanages are no better than those of yesteryear, which were warehouses for children (Creighton, 1990). There were some 1,000 group homes in the United States in 1990, each caring for 8 to 125 children.

Adoptive Families

Over half of all women who have adopted have also given birth to a child, so adoption is not always done because of infertility. It is more likely, in fact, for an adoption to follow the birth of a child within a family rather than the reverse (Bachrach, London, & Maza, 1991).

The number of adoptions in the United States increased steadily over the decades and reached a peak of 175,000 in 1970. Since then, however, the number has been declining steadily and is now about 100,000 per year (U.S. Bureau of the Census, 1998). The actual number seeking to adopt a child is about 500,000. Currently, about 974,000 children under 18 years of age are living with adoptive parents. There are fewer infants available for adoption today because of more effective contraceptives and legalized abortion and because more unmarried mothers are keeping their babies (Donnelly & Voydanoff, 1991). The percentage of black mothers relinquishing their children for adoption is low. Relinquishment among Hispanic mothers is virtually nonexistent (Bachrach, Stolley, & London, 1992).

About half of those who petition for adoption are related to the child they wish to adopt. Among women who never married, nonrelated adoption is more common among whites than among blacks or Hispanics, among those with at least a high school edu-

cation, and among those in the high-income brackets. However, related adoption is more common among those who are black, poor, or poorly educated (Bachrach, London, & Maza, 1991).

In 1991 about 8% of adoptions were of orphan children from foreign countries, with Romanian children constituting over 28% of the number. Smaller numbers came from Korea, Peru, Colombia, India, the Philippines, and other countries. Orphan children from Russia were first brought to the United States for adoption in 1992 (personal conversation with a client). Interracial adoptions of minority children in the United States have declined because of the influence of social workers and minority group advocates who are concerned about identity problems in the children and their loss to their ethnic communities.

Among petitioners not related to the child, about 40% of placements are through public agencies, 30% are through private agencies, and another 30% are through independent sources (U.S. Bureau of Census, 1998). About three times the number of people seek unrelated adoptions as are able to get them (Bachrach, London, & Maza, 1991). As a result, there are long waiting periods to get a child through established

Many adoptive parents seek to adopt foreign-born children.

agencies. Some adopting parents turn to private sources, going either to the mother herself or to an agent who is usually a lawyer specializing in open adoption. In **open adoption**, the natural mother is permitted to meet and play an active role in selecting the new adoptive parents. She usually may continue to have some form of contact with her child and with the adoptive parents after her child has been placed. The outcome depends on the agreement. Open adoption is usually expensive, including lawyer fees and birth expenses if state laws allow the charges. Some states—such as California and Texas—support private adoptions, but there are six states that forbid them. Many authorities claim that open adoption eases the pain for the birth mother and is in the best interest of the child (Kallen et al., 1990). Other experts say that it is not in the child's best interest to tell him or her of the adoption unless asked, much less to let the child know who the biological mother and father are. Some states have laws allowing adoptees to get copies of their original birth certificates.

One important consideration is how adoptive parents feel about having adoptive children and how adoptees themselves turn out. *The crucial factor here is not whether a child is adopted or not, but what is the quality of the family environment in which the child is raised* (Stein & Hoopes, 1986). School and behavior problems are more prevalent in adopted children during the elementary years, but by adolescence most adoptive children do not show any such problems (Brodzinsky, Shechter, Braft, & Singer, 1984). In one study of adoptive parents and their adolescent children, the parents were able to identify disadvantages of adoption yet felt their lives and those of their children were no different than those of biological families (Kaye & Warren, 1988). The adolescents themselves acknowledged disadvantages of being adopted even less than their parents.

Adoption reunions have become more common. One study of 67 adult adoptees who had reunions with birth relatives investigated the outcomes of those reunions. In general, the outcomes could be divided into seven categories: those who said that they were *close, were close but not too close, were distant, were tense, were ambivalent, were searching,* and *had no contact.* Those who had close relationships with relatives reported that they had frequent contact with the relatives and that they felt very close to them. Several adoptees had relationships with their relatives that appeared to be close but not too close; these wanted moderate contact. Adoptees who had distant relationships with their birth relatives reported get-

ting together perhaps a couple of times a year. They usually did not have frequent contact over the telephone or through the mail. They were generally satisfied with the amount of contact they had with their birth relatives. Relationships between adoptees and their relatives were sometimes tense. They had limited contact, usually wanted somewhat less or a good deal less contact, and felt not at all close to their relatives. They reported noticeable tension in their relationships. A number of adoptees appeared to have ambivalent relationships with their birth relatives. Contact by telephone and through writing remained limited. Some expressed a desire for more contact and greater closeness, but they were hesitant in terms of how close to become. Some adoptees appeared to be searching for stronger relationships with their birth relatives. Their contact was neither close nor distant, yet they wanted somewhat more or a great deal more contact. They appeared to be highly motivated to search for ways to build a closer relationship. In conclusion, it is obvious that adoptees and birth relatives do not always want to have long-standing relationships or close relationships with one another. The important point is to have opportunities for adoptees and birth relatives to resolve conflicts, negotiate relationships, and reach out to one another for support, if this is what they desire to do (Gladstone & Westhaus, 1998).

There is some evidence, however, that adoptees feel that others perceive their adoption as a social stigma. In one study, when adoptees were asked, "Do you think adoptive families are different than biological families?" almost half of the adoptees said no. Even though they personally saw no difference between adoptive and biological families, they felt that others did. Thus, the adoptees based their belief on others' reaction to their adoptive status. One adoptee stated that

It has little to do with my family. Other people outside the family think this way. I can see it in their reactions when they find out that I am adopted. To them, I am different. To my family, I am family. But, I am still not blood. It shouldn't be important, but it is. Not just to me but to everybody. (March, 1995, page 656)

One woman noted the following:

When someone is told that you are adopted, they usually start to ask you questions about your birth mother. These

Open adoption

questions generally have an underlying implication that she was a loose person. Like, sitting in the back seat of a cab with some guy or something. You carry that image. Because you don't have the information to deny it, it makes you wonder where you come from. (March, 1995, page 656)

Partly because of these attitudes, adoptees desire more complete genealogies; they express curiosity over the events surrounding their conception, birth, and relinquishment; they want information that can be passed on to their children and yearn for more detailed knowledge of their biological family background. Secrecy about biological kinship ties strengthen their sense of stigma by preventing them from being able to respond to other questions or negative assumptions. The adoptees' search for the birth mother can be seen as an attempt to neutralize the stigma by acquiring information about biological kinship ties and thus gaining the sense that they are normal (March, 1995). Research some-

times is conflicting in its analysis of the adjustments of adoptive versus nonadoptive children. Adopted children sometimes show higher levels of adjustment than other children, and at other times, poorer adjustment (Sharma, McGue, & Benson, 1998).

As information grows, there seems to be no significant differences between the behavior of adoptive parents and those of a match group of parents with biological children. Parents see their adoptive children as being equally capable in their social interactions, showing as desirable responsive behavior, and having as high levels of problem behavior and of well-being as those of children from biological parents. In one study, biological parents and adoptive parents were quite similar in terms of their discipline behavior, reported fairly frequent positive behavior such as praise and hugging their children, and said they infrequently used negative behavior such as yelling at or spanking their children. Parents in both groups reported somewhat traditional attitudes about parents' being at home with small children, expressed similar beliefs that parents of young children should try to avoid divorcing, and were somewhat disapproving of unwed mothers. Both groups gave similar instances of desirable behaviors and attitudes that they tried to foster in their children (e.g., to follow rules, to do well in school and athletics, and to be involved in creative activity). Finally, parents in both groups expected their children to complete some college (Borders, Black, & Pasley, 1998).

Parenting Issues

Women Who Place Their Babies for Adoption

One of the questions that arise is how do women feel after they have placed their babies for adoption. Some women say, "I could never give up my baby." Yet, a good number of women do. How do they feel about their decision afterwards? One study was of young, unmarried pregnant women under 21 years of age who were interviewed during the final trimester of pregnancy and again at six months postbirth to determine how they felt about relinquishing their babies (Kalmuss, Namerow, & Bauer, 1992). The results of this study indicated that in respect to short-term consequences, young women who placed their babies for adoption (placers) tended to fare as well as or better than those who kept and parented their babies. The one exception to this pattern was that at six months after birth, those who placed their babies for adoption were relatively less comfortable with their pregnancy resolution decision than were parenters. Despite this, the absolute level of comfort among placers was quite high. Any discomfort that the women experienced regarding their decision to place the baby did not appear to affect their overall psychological well-being. Placers were indistinguishable from parenters on measures of satisfaction with their social relationships, life satisfaction, and a positive future outlook regarding employment and schooling, finances, and marriage. Finally, placers fared somewhat better than parenters on a set of sociodemographic outcomes assessed at six months postbirth.

Adolescent Mothers

There is continuing evidence that adolescent mothers are at greater risk of family instability and negative educational and economic outcomes and that their children are more likely to experience problem behavior. One study investigated predictors of behavior problems in preschool children of inner-city African American and Puerto Rican mothers. One-hundred-twenty adolescent mothers and their children were followed between 1 and 36 months postpartum. The mothers were 13 to 19 years old at the time of delivery of their children. The African American mothers reported the highest levels of problem behaviors in their male children. Puerto Rican mothers reported fewer problem behaviors in male children, perhaps reflecting *machismo* attitudes that afford more tolerance for aggressive behaviors in Hispanic boys. Maternal psychological distress, assessed as depressive symptoms in the first year postpartum, consistently predicted problem behaviors in children 26 to 36 months old. Living with grandmothers or having emotional support from friends might minimize this association (Leadbeater & Bishop, 1994).

THE DEVELOPMENT OF PEER RELATIONSHIPS

Psychosocial Development

The development of friendships with peers is one of the most important aspects of social development of children. In the process of psychosocial development, all normal children pass through four stages.

1. **Autosociality**—infancy and toddler stage of development, in which children's interests, pleasures, and satisfactions are themselves. Toddlers want to be in the company of others, but they play *alongside* of others, not *with* them. A child who is a loner has not yet progressed beyond this stage of psychosocial development.
2. **Childhood heterosociality**—ages 2 to 7, during which children seek the companionship of others regardless of sex.
3. **Homosociality**—ages 8 to 12, or primary school period of development, during which children prefer to play with others of the same sex (not for sexual purposes, but for friendship and companionship). There is some antagonism between the sexes.
4. **Adolescent and adult heterosociality**—age 13 and over, or the adolescent and adult stage of psychosocial development, in which the individual's pleasure, friendships, and companionship are found with those of both sexes. Adolescent boys and girls begin to pair off; most begin dating.

Infants and Toddlers

Babies' first social experiences are usually with parents and siblings (Fiese, 1990; Vandell & Wilson, 1987). Observations of babies and toddlers indicate that they interact with one another from about 5 months onward. Their first social response is simply to notice one another and to smile at one another. When they are able to move around, they crawl all over one another. When they can stand up, they occasionally knock one another down. Six-month-olds reveal little conflict or fussing when infants touch one another's toys, touch one another, or even find

Normal children advance past the first stage of psychosocial development and begin to seek companionship.

themselves trapped beneath a partner (Hay, Nash, & Pedersen, 1983). By 9 months of age, they offer a toy to others and oppose toys' being taken away. They also comfort others in distress and pick up the ones who get pushed over. Personal aggression increases with age, but cooperation also increases as children become more experienced in relating to one another. Observation of children in infant centers indicates that helpfulness is more apparent than are efforts to dominate. By the time children are toddlers, they have learned much about fending for themselves in a group and about how to find satisfaction there. They have made a strong beginning in establishing group relations that are a main source of emotional security and orientation.

Early Childhood

Two-Year-Olds

Children of this age enjoy playing alongside one another, rather than with one another, since cooperative play is not very evident, at least in the beginning. However, 2-year-olds begin to show some preferences in playmates. Individuals interact more with familiar play partners (Brownell, 1990). Twins interact more with one another than with unfamiliar peers (Vandell, Owen, Wilson, & Henderson, 1988). Social interchange becomes more frequent; friendly behavior gradually replaces negative behavior (Brownell & Carriger, 1990; Ross & Lollis, 1989). Sex preferences are not yet evident.

Toddlers are not as forbearing as infants when their toys are touched or taken (Shantz, 1987). Two-year-olds do a lot of grabbing, hitting, and pushing, not usually with an intent to hurt, but for the purpose of protecting their own toy or getting a toy that someone else has

Autosociality—stage of psychosocial development during the first year or so of life, during which infants' interests, pleasures, and satisfactions are themselves

Childhood heterosociality—stage when children seek the companionship of others regardless of sex

Homosociality—stage during which children prefer to play with others of the same sex

Adolescent and adult heterosociality—stage of psychosocial development during which those ages 13 and over find pleasure, friendship, and companionship with those of both sexes

(Caplan, Vespo, Pedersen, & Hay, 1991). Since they are egocentric, they are not aware of the effect that their own actions have on others, nor of the moods and feelings of others. They think in terms of "my ball" or "my book," and they protest when denied what they want. As a result, they inevitably run into conflict from their social interactions. They need supervision and experience in considering the needs and interests of others.

Three-Year-Olds

As children grow older, they engage in fewer solitary activities, do less passive watching of other children, and become less inclined toward isolated play (Bailey, McWilliam, Ware, & Burchinal, 1993). Friendly contacts occur with increasing frequency, and cooperative behavior also increases (Ladd, Price, & Hart, 1988). Children may select one friend, sometimes two, with whom they identify for short periods of time. Aggressive behavior gradually declines (Cummings, Iannotti, & Zahn-Waxler, 1989).

We see the beginning of group play and activity. The development of language makes communication possible, so that when two children play together, they talk about what they are making in the sand, about dressing up their dolls, or about pretending to be a mother or a baby. Group membership, however, is constantly changing, with children moving in and out of a group. (See "Focus" box on facing page.)

Three-year-olds are likely to be victims of aggression by other children in nursery school, so that teachers have to provide supervision and to be careful to reinforce socially acceptable acts.

Four- and Five-Year-Olds

Children at age 4 and 5 gradually develop more socially competent interactions with their peers (Guralnick & Groom, 1987; Park, Lay, & Ramsay, 1993). They begin to depend less on parents and more and more on peers for companionship and social interaction. They now share affection and tangible objects (Farber & Bransetter, 1994). They offer approval of and make demands on one another. Best friends in a group will pair off. Groups of three children are quite common. Occasionally, up to five or six children will form a group and spend most of their playtime with one another. Generally speaking, there is some evidence that boys enjoy group interaction more than girls do. Girls enjoy dyadic (one-on-one) relationships more than boys do (Benenson, 1993).

The behavior of children varies. One moment they are aggressive, the next moment cooperative. Conflict occurs more often between friends than with nonfriends, but the conflict with friends is less intense and resolved more quickly, insuring that the children's relationships will continue once the disagreement ends (Hartup, Laursen, Stewart, & Eastenson, 1988). Children's behavior is affected a lot by the attitude of others at home or in school (Cassidy, Parke, Butkovsky, & Broaungart, 1992). If cooperation is stressed, children become less competitive. If competition is encouraged, rivalry becomes a strong motivator of behavior, and jealousy is quite common. For this reason, most experts try to discourage competitive activities for this age group.

Children vary greatly in their social competence and acceptance by peers (Denham, McKinley, Couehoud, & Holt, 1990). Social status and peer interaction depend partly on children's communication skills (Hazen & Black, 1989). Social acceptance among boys depends partially on their physical abilities (Musun-Miller, 1993). Children develop definite preferences in playmates. Some children in a group become leaders and are quite popular with nearly everyone. Other children are content to be followers. However, those children who are friendly, cooperative, less aggressive, and less difficult to get along with are those who are most well liked (Denham & Holt, 1993; Mendelson, Aboud, & Lanthier, 1994).

There is much intermingling between the sexes and races. There is actually some evidence that children tend to show same-sex preferences more than same race preferences in playmates. One study of preschoolers evaluated their selection of playmate choices. The results show that white boys first preferred playmates who were white boys; they preferred black boys second, white girls

Children prefer same-sex playmates regardless of race.

third, and black girls fourth. White girls first preferred playmates who were white girls, black girls second, black boys third, and white boys fourth. Black boys first preferred white boys, black boys second, black girls third, and white girls last. Black girls first preferred black girls, black boys second, white girls third, and white boys last (Fishbein & Imai, 1993). It is interesting that white boys preferred to play with other boys first and preferred to play with black girls least. Black boys also preferred to play with other boys first and with white girls least. Both white and black girls preferred to play with white boys least. The reason that girls least preferred playing with white boys is that white boys had the highest status, on average, in a classroom and that they would tend to

dominate girls more than would the other groups of boys. Hence, girls would relatively avoid them the most.

As children get acquainted with one another, they become more selective in their playmate contacts. In early childhood classrooms, during the early weeks of the school year, the preschoolers' number of new playmate combinations decline. The similar trend towards selectivity emerges in some yearlong sociometric studies. In the spring, children interact with fewer individuals, in small groups, especially cross-sex peers, than they did in the fall. Sociometric ratings become more negative over the course of the year, suggesting that children reject certain classmates as they learn to distinguish them from their preferred classmates. This

FOCUS

Preschoolers' Play

Preschoolers' play has been classified in a number of ways. In a classic study, Mildred Parten (1932) observed the play of children in a nursery school setting and established categories of play according to the degree of the children's social involvement. This study is as pertinent today as it was 60 years ago. Parten identified six categories of play involvement.

1. *Unoccupied play*—children are not really playing, but instead they are looking around and engaging in random activities.

2. *Solitary play*—children play with toys by themselves, making no effort to relate to other children.

3. *Onlooker play*—children watch others play and are talking to them, but they do not join the play.

4. *Parallel play*—children play alongside of others, not *with* them, but they mimic others' behavior.

5. *Associative play*—children interact with others, borrowing or lending toys, following or leading one another in similar activities.

6. *Cooperative play*—organized groups of children engage in play, such as a game.

Play may also be classified according to the type of activity.

1. *Sensory play*—play that involves sensory experiences such as splashing water, digging in the sand, banging pots and pans, plucking flower petals, or blowing bubbles. Children learn about the world through these sensory experiences.

2. *Motor play*—play that involves physical motion such as running, jumping, skipping, or swinging. This type of play helps to develop muscles and motor coordination, and to release pent-up energy.

3. *Rough-and-tumble play*—motor play that involves mock-fighting and the controlled release of aggression. Children learn to control their impulses and feelings, and to express them in socially acceptable ways. The development of this type of play is often influenced by the way fathers play with their children at home (Levine, 1988). Sometimes this type of play gets out of hand and becomes too rough, and children are hurt.

4. *Cognitive play*—play that involves language, repetition of sounds and words because they sound funny, word games, or

riddles. This play gives children a chance to master word sounds and grammar, to think, and to develop cognitive skills.

5. *Dramatic play or pretend play*—play that involves modeling activities and role-playing, such as playing house, firefighters, nurse or doctor, baby, astronaut, soldier, or truck driver (Doyle et al., 1992; Howes & Matheson, 1992; Lillard, 1993a, 1993b). This play gives children a chance to re-create experiences and to try out roles. It is also called *symbolic play* (Slade, 1987; Wooley & Wellman, 1990). Children of this age also create imaginary companions that become a regular part of their daily routines. Children talk to them, play with them, and treat them as though they were real (Taylor, Cartwright, & Carlson, 1993).

6. *Games and competitive sports*—play that may involve board games such as checkers, games of skill such as darts, or outdoor games and sports such as tag, hide and seek, or baseball. Children learn to follow rules, to take turns, to be able to accept losing or winning, and to cooperate with other children in the group.

increased selectivity has both advantages and disadvantages for children. Stable peer relationships are the optimal context for the development of social skills, but they may pose hardships for children who are trying to enter the social mainstream (Ramsey, 1995).

As preschool children interact with other children of the same age, they gradually discover that they come from a variety of family situations. Some have siblings, others none. Some have young parents, others old parents, and some have only one parent at home. These initial engagements with peers are broadening experiences that stimulate children to ask numerous questions. "How come I don't have any brothers or sisters?" "Why can't I have a big bike like Mary has?" "Why doesn't Johnny have any daddy?"

Research has revealed that experiences in the family have a definite effect on the development of social competence (Youngblade & Belsky, 1992). One study of economically disadvantaged 4- and 5-year-olds in a Midwestern community revealed that the following factors were detrimental to the development of social skills:

- Exposure to aggressive models in the home and parents' endorsement of aggression as a means of solving conflicts
- Restrictive discipline, in which parents used a high degree of constriction
- Parents' hostile reactions to provocation by the child
- Insecure attachment to parents (Turner, 1991)

In contrast to these negative factors, the study found that parents who used preventive teaching and gave their children opportunity for direct peer experience contributed positively to the development of social skills of their children (Ladd & Hart, 1992; Pettit, Dodge, & Brown, 1988). Research also shows that children's friendships make a significant and unique contribution to their adaptation to becoming a sibling. Those who have the most positive relationships with friends are also able to develop the most positive relationships with siblings at home (Kramer & Gottman, 1992).

Middle Childhood

Friendships

The older that children become, the more important that companionship with friends becomes (Buhrmester & Furman, 1987). By the time children start first grade, they are no longer interested in being alone so much of the time. They want to be with friends (Ladd, 1990). They still seek out a special companion, but their circle of friends is widening. During the preschool period, most of their friends were confined to the immediate neighborhood, but now children meet many friends from other areas served by the school. Some of these persons are different from the ones the children are used to playing with. This difference makes it harder for children to get acquainted and to learn to get along, but it is a broadening experience and helps them to mature.

Parents become concerned about the kinds of friends their children want to bring home or want to visit. They worry, and with justification, about the influence of these friends on their children. Parents want to know, "What kind of persons are these children?" Parents are wise to be concerned, because peer-group influence over children becomes more and more important. Certainly, parents need to spell out some ground rules about how far away and where children are allowed to play, about what time to come in, and about the types of activities that are permitted. Because grade-school children need some supervision, it is helpful if there are concerned parents nearby.

However, *some parents are overprotective* and won't allow their children to do what others do or allow them to play with other children in the usual way. This situation is especially likely to happen if children are frail or sickly. The parents try to protect their children from germs, noise, and rough-and-tumble play, but as a result, they keep their children from making friends or from learning how to do what others do.

Others expect too much of their children, try to push them too fast, and are very critical when their children don't measure up. Such attitudes undermine their children's self-confidence. The children become afraid of failure, rejection, ridicule, and criticism, and they react by trying to avoid social groups where they are embarrassed. Thus, in socialization as in other areas, parents need to balance supervision and guidance with freedom and encouragement. Generally speaking, parents who are sociable and agreeable, and who have positive feelings toward their children have children who are sociable and agreeable and who have positive attitudes toward others (Putallaz, 1987).

Discerning parents need to be aware of when their children are not getting along socially or when their children do not seem to have many friends. Parental action such as arranging play opportunities and supervising peer interaction can facilitate peer friendships and help their children develop social skills (Mize, Pettit, & Brown, 1995).

Popularity

Generally speaking, research points to the fact that children generally prefer friends who are like themselves. They are similar in play styles and social participation, and they may be similar in terms of politeness, sense of humor, and sociability (Haselager, Hartup, van Lieshout, & Riksen-Walraven, 1998; Rubin et al., 1994).

Peer acceptance during the elementary years is very important to the children themselves and is predictive of later adjustment during adolescence (Morison & Masten, 1991). Children differ in the degree to which they strive for or achieve popularity. If a group of children are asked individually to name other children whom they most like or with whom they would most like to be associated, it is possible to discover which children are most and least popular (Boulton & Smith, 1990). Usually, such surveys show that even those children who are rated most popular have a few acquaintances who are indifferent to them or dislike them, and those who are least popular are rarely unpopular with everyone.

Nevertheless, since children place such emphasis on being popular, it is helpful to sort out those qualities of personality and character that make for popularity or unpopularity (Gelb & Jacobson, 1988). What types of children are most popular? Generally speaking, popular children (Chance, 1989; Dekovic & Gerris, 1994)

- Are socially aggressive and outgoing (Dodge, Cole, Pettit, & Price, 1990).
- Have a high energy level that they use in activities approved by the group.
- Have positive self-perceptions (Boivin & Begin, 1989).
- Actively participate in social events enthusiastically.
- Are friendly and sociable in relation to others (Dozier, 1991).
- Accept others, and are sympathetic, protective, and comforting toward them.
- Are cheerful, and good-natured, and have a good sense of humor.
- Are above average in intelligence and school performance, but not too high above others.

- Are popular with teachers (White & Kistner, 1992).
- Have superior social-cognitive and communication skills (Burleson, Della, & Applegate, 1992).

There are some social and sex differences in the qualities considered important to popularity. Boys need to show physical prowess, athletic ability, and skill in competitive games. In some antisocial groups, the most popular boys show superior fighting ability. In the upper elementary grades, girls are rated most popular who are considered physically attractive and socially sophisticated and mature. Middle-class children put greater emphasis on scholastic achievement than do lower-class children. A lower-class boy who excels in schoolwork risks alienation from his peers. A lower-class girl can be a good student without alienating her friends. In Chinese culture, shyness is associated with leadership and peer acceptance, whereas in Western culture, it is associated with rejection (Chen, Rubin, & Sun, 1992).

Peer Rejection

Peer relationships within the school setting have a great influence on children's concurrent and later academic, behavioral, and emotional adjustment. Rejected children have been found to be at heightened risk for a number of negative outcomes, including delinquency and criminality, dropping out of school, or needing mental health services. Rejected children have few, if any, neighborhood friends. They maintain distinct negative reputations within their peer group; they are seen as nasty, unpleasant children or actively avoided. Even when rejected children enter new social situations where they are unknown, they rapidly reestablish rejected status. Once a child becomes rejected, there are numerous forces working to maintain the negative status. Reputational biases develop within the peer group so that the peers act toward and think about rejected children more negatively than about nonrejected children. When rejected children attempt to behave more positively, peers fail to reward their efforts. These group dynamics, in turn, are associated with lower self-esteem and loneliness. There are fewer opportunities for rejected children to practice and develop appropriate social skills.

Poor peer relationships are a stressful experience for children because of both the experience itself and the accompanying lack of social support, making children more vulnerable to other life stresses. In fact, children identify peer rejection as a major stressor itself, and any changes in peer acceptance are just as stressful as other life events, such as the failure of a year of school, the death of a close friend, the hospitalization of a parent, or a serious illness (DeRosier, Kupersmidt, & Patterson, 1994).

Least Popular

What types of children are considered least popular (French, 1990)? Generally speaking, the least popular children (Cillessen, van Ijzendoorn, van Lieshout, & Hartup, 1992; Hynel, Bowker, & Woody, 1993; Rogosch & Newcomb, 1989)

- Are self-centered and withdrawn.
- Are anxious, fearful, moody, and inhibited (Asendorpf, 1991).
- Are more likely to be emotionally disturbed (Altmann & Gotlib, 1988; Asarnow, 1988).
- Are impulsive, with poor emotional control (French, 1988).
- Show a lack of sensitivity to others and to social situations.
- Behave in inappropriate ways (Gelb & Jacobson, 1988).
- Are hostile and overaggressive (Coie, Dodge, Terry, & Wright, 1991; Parkhurst & Asher, 1992; Rabiner & Gordon, 1992).
- Behave considerably younger or older than their age groups.
- Are different looking or unconventional in behavior.
- Are more likely to be of low intelligence.
- Are more likely to have a poor self-concept (Rabiner, Keane, & Mackinnon-Lewis, 1993).
- Are members of groups that are not popular (Yee & Brown, 1992).

Conflicts

Conflicts occur more frequently among friends then among nonfriends, and they last longer. They occur more frequently between individuals who are socially interdependent and who interact over substantial periods of time. Disagreements between friends become increasingly salient during middle childhood (Bryant, 1992). Children themselves recognize conflicts as major causes of friendship disruption. Effective conflict management is necessary to both friendship formation and maintenance, and disagreements are commonly seen in interaction between friends (Hartup et al., 1993).

Social Maladjustment

There is a difference between children who are unliked and those who are disliked. *Unliked children* are socially invisible and withdrawn. They are loners (Coie & Dodge, 1988). *Disliked children* are quite visible and aggressive, and they behave in obnoxious, socially unacceptable ways. Younger and Daniels (1992) classified these types of children in two categories: Those that are characterized by *passive withdrawal* and those characterized by *active isolation*. Passive withdrawal and active isolation comprise very different forms of maladjustment. *A child who is socially withdrawn may be isolated from peers because of social anxiety or perceptions of social inefficacy* (Crick & Ladd, 1993). Other children described the socially withdrawn in the following manner:

1. "He wants to play by himself."
2. "Sometimes in class no one can hear her and when they ask her to speak up, her feelings get hurt."
3. "She's always afraid when she meets someone for the first time."
4. "She won't play with other kids because she's shy."
5. "He keeps to himself. He's shy and doesn't want to bother people."
6. "Sometimes she cries because she's so nervous."

Behaviors characteristic of passive withdrawal, such as shyness and oversensitivity, are relatively common in young children. Consequently, young children who display such behavior are not viewed negatively by their peers. With increase in age, however, such behaviors become more conspicuous to the peer group. At higher grades (i.e., fifth to seventh grades), behaviors characteristic of passive withdrawal tend to be associated with peer rejection (Younger & Daniels, 1992).

Children who fit into the actively isolated category experience social isolation that is brought about by behavior that is obnoxious to others. This is associated with long-term maladjustment, including academic difficulty, delinquency, and possibly psychopathology. Socially aggressive children are disliked at all ages (Younger & Piccinin, 1989). These children are described by others in the following manner:

1. "No one wants to play with him."
2. "No one likes her, and when they won't play with her, her feelings get hurt."
3. "The others don't like him and they won't listen to him."
4. "He has trouble making friends because he's really mean."
5. "The other kids don't want to play with her and that makes her sad."

Cruelty and Aggression

Some children of this age can be very cruel (Perry, Williard, & Perry, 1990). They callously exclude one another from their groups, or they say things that shame or belittle others. Bullies who pick on those who are younger or weaker are a problem (Roberts, 1988c). Their primary motive seems to be to gain control of others as a means of feeling important themselves (Boldizar, Perry, & Perry, 1989). Because of their own angry feelings, they often attribute hostile intentions to the actions of others when none exist (Dodge & Somberg, 1987). Under these circumstances, other children need to learn to stand up for themselves and to protect themselves (Ferguson & Rule, 1988).

There is substantial evidence that a small minority of children are consistently targeted for victimization by their peers. One study investigated victimization among six- to eight-year-old boys. There appears to be a strong association between nonassertive behavior and abuse by peers. Victims in the play groups were examined and were found to display a behavioral pattern that was pervasively nonassertive. The submissiveness identified the victims as vulnerable targets for the aggressive and coercive overtures of their peers. Once selected for aggression, victims tended to reward their attackers with submission. Victims were selected for aggression at an increasingly high rate over time. Overall, victims were not well liked by their play-group peers. The behavior of the group towards the victims became more negative as differences in victimization became extreme. Victims were the object of assertive refusals, aggression, and negative responses from peers at an increasingly high rate over time (Schwartz, Dodge, & Coie, 1993).

Loneliness

Those children who are rejected and actively disliked by their peers in school report significantly more loneliness than average-accepted and popular children (Cassidy & Asher, 1992). Lonely children experience feelings of sadness,

School Shooting Suspects

Dylan Klebold   **Eric Harris**

Control over others is often the motivation for violence. On April 20, 1999 the world was in shock with the news of the Columbine High School massacre.

malaise, boredom, and alienation (Parker & Asher, 1993). They often feel excluded, a situation that can be damaging to their self-esteem. There are a number of factors that contribute to loneliness. *The quality of children's attachment to their parents* has been studied extensively (Bullock, 1993). For example, children's early positive attachment to parents is positively correlated with more frequent, sociable, and positive interactions with parents and peers. Conversely, children with insecure attachments are more likely to cling to their parents, show negative interactions with their mothers and peers, show signs of anxiety around them, and are less likely to interact with peers. Children form secure attachments to their parents through positive, reciprocal interaction over time. When attachments with parents are severed by a separation such as divorce, children feel threatened, which can be detrimental to their self-esteem and interpersonal relationships. Children whose parents are going through divorce often report high degrees of sadness and loneliness. Children who are preschool age when their parents split up, report some of the highest feelings of loneliness as adults.

Also, daughters who report a lack of positive parental involvement (reflected by nurturant, positive parental behaviors and affection) have higher loneliness scores than those who report more positive involvement. Those who report low levels of loneliness describe their parents as being close, warm, and supportive (Bullock, 1993). Thus, parent-child interactions influence loneliness later in life.

Several other significant losses throughout childhood also contribute to feelings of

Social cognition—the capacity to understand social relationships

Social role taking—the ability to understand the self and others as subjects and to react to others as like the self

Egocentric undifferentiated stage—the stage of awareness when another person is seen egocentrically, undifferentiated from the self's own point of view

Differentiated or subjective perspective-taking stage—the stage of awareness when the other is seen as different from the self, but the other person's perception of the self is still undifferentiated

loneliness. These may include *moving to a new neighborhood or school; losing an object, possession, or pet; losing a friend; conflict within the home or at school; or experiencing the death of a pet or significant person.*

Interestingly enough, a study by Quay (1992) on personal and family effects on loneliness found *that children in one-parent families were not lonelier than children in two-parent families.* However, *children living in both two-parent and single-parent families were less lonely than children in other arrangements, such as with mother and someone else in the home, with a relative, or in a foster home.* Also, *maternal employment did not affect loneliness.* Children who went home to mother after school and children who went to after-school day-care programs did not differ in loneliness, but these two groups were less lonely than latch-key children (Quay, 1992).

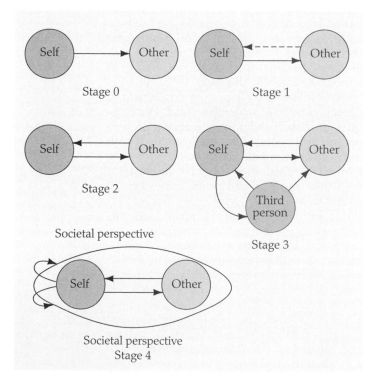

FIGURE 9.6   **Selman's five stages of social role taking.** *Stage 0.* The other person is seen egocentrically, or undifferentiated from the self's own point of view. *Stage 1.* The other is seen as different from the self, but the other person's perception of the self is still undifferentiated. *Stage 2.* The self can take the perspective of another person and becomes aware that the other person can also take the perspective of the self. *Stage 3.* The self can view the self-other interaction from the perspective of a neutral third person. *Stage 4.* The self can take a generalized societal perspective of the self-other interaction.

From *Theories of Adolescence,* 5th ed. (pp. 249, 251, 254, 256, 258), by R. E. Muuss, 1988. New York: McGraw Hill Publishing Company. Copyright © The McGraw-Hill Companies. Used by permission.

Social Cognition

Social cognition is the capacity to understand social relationships. In children, it is the ability to understand others: their thoughts, their intentions, their emotions, their social behavior, and their general point of view (Dunn, Brown, Slomkowski, Desla, & Youngblade, 1991; Zahn-Waxler, Radke-Yarrow, Wagner, & Chapman, 1992). Social cognition is basic to all human interactions. To know what other people think and feel is necessary to understand them and to get along with them (Feldman & Ruble, 1988; Gnepp & Chilamkurti, 1988).

Yet, this ability develops very slowly. Robert Selman (1977, 1980) has advanced a theory of social cognition outlining predictable stages in **social role taking.** To Selman, social role taking is the ability to understand the self and others as subjects, to react to others as like the self, and to react to the self's behavior from the other's point of view.

Selman's five stages of development follow.

Stage 0

Egocentric undifferentiated stage (age 0 to 6). Until about age 6, children cannot make a clear distinction between their own interpretation of a social situation and another's point of view, nor can they understand that their own perception may not be correct (Yaniv & Shatz, 1990). When they are asked how someone else feels in a particular situation, their responses reflect how *they* feel, not how *others* feel (Lewis & Osborne, 1990).

Stage 1

Differentiated or subjective perspective-taking stage (age 6 to 8). Children develop an awareness that others may have a different social perspective, but they have little understanding of the reasons for others' viewpoints (LeMare & Rubin, 1987). Children believe that others would feel the same way if they had the same information. Perspective taking is a one-way street; children cannot accurately judge their own behavior from the perspective of the other person. They do begin to distinguish between intentionality and unintentionality of behavior and to consider causes of actions (Miller & Aloise, 1989). They are capable of inferring other peoples' intentions, feelings, and thoughts (Arsenio & Kramer, 1992) but base their conclusions on physical observations that may not be correct, not realizing that other people may hide their true feelings.

Stage 2

Self-reflective thinking or reciprocal perspective-taking stage (age 8 to 10). A child develops reciprocal awareness, realizing that others have a different point of view and that others are aware that he or she has a particular point of view. The principal change from stage 1 to stage 2 is children's ability to take the perspective of others; to reflect about their own behavior and their own motivation as seen from the perspective of another person. This ability includes an awareness of relativity, that no individual's social perspective is necessarily correct or valid in an absolute sense. Another person's point of view may be as correct as one's own. This awareness also means that individuals may take other persons' points of view into account (Dizon & Moore, 1990).

Stage 3

Third-person or mutual perspective-taking stage (age 10 to 12). Children can see their own perspective, the perspective of their partner, plus assume the perspective of a neutral third person. As third-person observers, they can see themselves as both actor and object. Thus, they can understand a more generalized perspective that might be taken by an "average" member of the group.

Stage 4

In-depth and societal perspective-taking stage (adolescence to adulthood). Young people recognize that there is a group perspective, a point of view reflected in a social system. Law and morality depend on some consensual group perspective that the individual must take into account.

Obviously, the more advanced the stage of social cognition, the more capable children become in understanding and getting along with others.

Family Influences

The question arises as to how social competence develops. As in many other instances, the family plays the primary role. When parents enter into constructive discussions about peer relationships and their children's ability to get along with others and when they coach their children in constructive ways, parents contribute to their children's specific prosocial behavior and problem-solving skills (Mize & Pettit, 1997). Figure 9.7 is a conceptual model that links family characteristics and children's social cognitive knowledge,

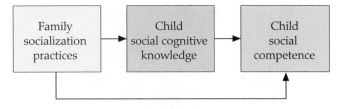

FIGURE 9.7   Conceptual model of the linkages between socialization practices, social cognitive knowledge, and social competence.

From "Social Competence among Low-Income Preschoolers: Emotion Socialization Practices and Social Cognitive Correlates," by P. W. Garner, D. C. Jones, & J. L. Miner, 1994, *Child Development, 685*, pp. 622–637.

with social competence. Family socialization practices are related to children's knowledge about emotions and social behavior. In turn, children's knowledge is expected to relate directly to their social competence. Family socialization practices include the emotional climate in the family that is so important to the development of children's peer relationships. Emotion socialization may be negative, including a high level of conflict, maternal anger, and parental discouragement of children's negative emotional expression. Or emotion socialization may be positive, including warm expressions of affection, moderate levels of conflict that are manageable, and generally positive feelings existing between parents and children. When the parental expressions of emotion are generally positive and when there are good feelings existing between children and their parents, children show more positive relationship with other children and have positive insight as to what friendly relationships should be (Garner, Jones, & Miner, 1994).

TELEVISION AS A SOCIALIZING INFLUENCE

Of all of those factors that have a socializing influence on children, one of the most important is television. Let us take a look at some of the viewing habits of American children and discuss possible influences of television on them.

Viewing Habits

Today, 98% of the households in the United States own at least one television set (U.S. Bureau of the Census, 1998). Seventy-four percent of households in the United States own more than one television set (Nielsen Media Research, 1998). According to a 1987

Self-reflective thinking or reciprocal perspective-taking stage—the stage of awareness when the self can take the perspective of another person and know that the other person can also take the perspective of the self

Third-person or mutual perspective-taking stage—the stage of awareness when children see their own perspective, their partner's, plus a third person's perspective

In-depth and societal perspective-taking stage—the stage of awareness when the self can take a generalized societal perspective of the self-other interaction

Adults have become concerned with the effects that watching television for long hours has on children.

Nielson report, children between the ages of 2 and 11 spend an average of 22 hours and 11 minutes per week watching television (*National Audience Demographics Report*, 1985). Preteen and teenage children 12 to 17 years of age spend an average of 20 hours, 20 minutes per week. By age 18, children will have watched television approximately 20,000 hours, compared with 11,000 hours in the classroom. Singer and Singer (1983) pointed out that children spend more time watching television than they spend in conversation with adults or siblings. They spend more time watching television than engaging in any other activity (including playing and eating) except sleeping (Institute for Social Research, 1985). These figures are startling, so the real question is, *What effect does watching so much television have on children and on their development and relationships?*

Violence and Aggression

A most important concern has been the influence of television as a stimulus of aggressive behavior in children. There is certainly no doubt of the extent of violence on TV. By the time children are in the eighth grade, they will have watched 18,000 human beings killed on television, and violent acts committed against thousands more. The classic research by Bandura on the relationship between television violence and aggressive behavior in children found that children were less likely to imitate the violent behavior of cartoon models than they were the violence of real-people models (Bandura, Ross, & Ross, 1963a). This finding is in keeping with other findings that human portrayal exerts

more influence than cartoon portrayal (Hayes & Casey, 1992). Nevertheless, violent cartoons had a negative effect. One study found that television shows with rapid changes of scene and high action, such as cartoons, increase children's aggression, regardless of content, because the sensory excitement stimulates the children to act without reflection (Greer, Potts, Wright, & Huston, 1982).

The violent acts to which children are exposed on television include war, assassination, murder, shooting, knifing, beating, punching, torture, kicking, choking, burning, rape, cruelty to animals, robbery, violent accidents, and property destruction. Although precise cause and effect relationships are hard to establish, extensive research indicates that *television violence is associated with increased aggressive behavior in children who watch it.* After reviewing the research on the subject, the National Institute on Mental Health (NIMH) (1982) concluded that children who see violence on the screen behave more aggressively, regardless of their geographical location or socioeconomic level. This finding is true of both boys and girls, and of normal children as well as those with emotional problems. The NIMH report concludes that television encourages aggressive behavior in two ways: *Children model and imitate what they see, and they come to accept aggression as appropriate behavior. The effect is interdependent. Aggressive children select more violent television programs and view more of them, and those who watch more violent programs tend to be more aggressive.* Other research substantiates that the effect of violence is interactive and cumulative. Children who watch violence on television are more aggressive than children who do not, and children who are aggressive are likely to watch a lot of TV violence (Friedrich-Cofer & Huston, 1986). The effects may be long lasting. One study concluded that the amount of television violence watched by children when they were in elementary school was associated with how aggressive they were at age 19 and at age 30 (Eron, 1987). Of course, this still does not prove cause and effect.

Factual Versus Fictional

During the years from about 3 to 12, children gradually acquire an understanding of the distinctions between real and fictional television content. It is often assumed that content perceived as real will have a greater effect and greater impact on children than content known to be unreal. But, other than a few studies suggesting that real aggression is more likely to be imitated than fictional aggression, there are few data.

Regardless of whether the experiences depicted are real or fictional, very young children do not have a full understanding of the difference between real and vicarious experience or between appearance and reality, but television can arouse emotions in either case. Children are frightened by threatening stimuli (e.g., a swarm of bees approaching) and by physical transformations (e.g., the change from man to monster in *The Incredible Hulk*). Most emotional reactions to television are probably vicarious responses to the situations of the people portrayed.

Perceived reality of content may mediate emotional responses. When a television program is perceived as factual rather than fictional, children may be more likely to imagine themselves in the role of the people involved or in similar situations. Children 9 to 12 years old, who were interviewed shortly after the explosion of the space shuttle *Challenger*, reported higher levels of emotional distress than they felt when they saw comparable fiction events. Emotional effects of fictional content can be reduced by reminding children that it is not real, but such reassurance is of little help to children younger than 7 years old.

Sometimes dramatic presentations, because of their deliberate attempt to create excitement, identification with characters, and emotional involvement of the viewer, may elicit more affect than the typically dryer, calmer, factual presentations found in news and documentary programs. The small amount of research investigating the effects of perceived reality on emotion is concentrated primarily on frightening television programs and fearful reactions. Even if a program is fictional, it can elicit emotions and empathy with the people shown, particularly if the viewer judges it to be socially realistic. Thus, it is social realism rather than factuality that appears to be important in emotional arousal (Huston, Wright, Albarez, Truglio, Fitch, & Piemyat, 1995).

Family Interaction

Critics argue that television watching has other negative effects on children. One of the effects is felt by the whole family (Fabes, Wilson, & Christopher, 1989). *Extensive viewing has been associated with a decrease in family interaction, social communication, and interpersonal conversation.* Of course, families interact differently depending on the program being watched. Some families talk less but touch more while watching television. Interaction is certainly decreased in those families with more than one television set. The parents watch one program, the children another, in separate locations of the house. Experiments with families that decided to give up television viewing for a period of time revealed that the children played together more, family activities increased, mealtimes were longer, the children read more, and bedtimes were earlier (Chira, 1984).

Increased television viewing has also been associated with dysfunctional families, and increased parent-child conflict (Price & Feshbach, 1982). However, it is likely that increased television viewing is the result of trouble in the family, not the cause. *Children use television as an escape from the stress of the home environment.* One study found that lack of parental empathy, sensitivity, and adaptive role expectations was related to heavy viewing of violent, fantasy-oriented television content (Tangney, 1988). Another study found that parental viewing preferences, habits, and attitudes towards television influence children's viewing habits. The majority of child programs were viewed without parents, whereas the majority of adult programs were watched with parents. Coviewing patterns of adult programs were predicted from parents' individual viewing habits. In other words, the adult programs that children watched depended on what the parents were watching (St. Peters et al., 1991).

Cognitive Development

Heavy television viewing has also been associated with lower school achievement including lower reading comprehension, poorer language usage, and neglect of homework. Certainly, if their parents will let them, many children will stay up until all hours to watch television rather than do their homework. Interestingly, however, *heavy TV viewing by children of low socioeconomic status has been associated with higher scholastic achievement and reading comprehension and at the same time with lower abilities among children of high socioeconomic status.* Apparently, television has a leveling effect. The fact remains that any time spent watching television decreases the amount of time that children spend on other activities, whether it be playing, engaging in hobbies, reading, or talking with friends or family members. Some authorities feel that television makes children less creative, less verbal, less social, and less independent.

Commercials

The question also arises regarding the effects of television commercials on children. *There is no question that television advertising is influential.* Part of the effects are positive. Television warns against smoking and the use of drugs, encourages children to brush their teeth to avoid cavities, and encourages them to eat their cereal. However, one study found that a significant portion of commercials advertised food products high in sugar and that the consumption of these products increased because of television advertising. Television is used to sell every conceivable type of new toy also (Dorr, 1986). Children see a toy advertised, want it, and request it from their parents. If parents refuse, parent-child arguments follow. In one study, when children were presented with a hypothetical scenario of a father refusing to purchase a toy his son had requested, less than 40% of the children who had been exposed to an advertisement of the toy felt the boy would still want to play with his father, whereas over 60% of the children who had not viewed the commercial thought the boy would still want to play with his father (Goldberg & Gorn, 1977). Television is not simply an innocuous form of family entertainment. It is a powerful force.

Positive Effects

Not all effects of television are negative. One of the most watched educational programs is *Sesame Street.* Viewing is highest by children between ages 3 and 5, with a peak between 3½ and 4 and a decline between ages 5 and 7 (Pinon, Huston, & Wright, 1989). A series of studies found the following positive benefits: Viewers showed increased abilities to recognize and name letters, to sort different objects, to name body parts, and to recognize and label geometric forms. However, *Sesame Street* has not reduced the difference between the advantaged and disadvantaged in terms of cognitive functioning. In fact, already advantaged children tend to benefit more. Another children's program, *Mr. Rogers' Neighborhood,* was found to increase prosocial behavior in children (Tower, Singer, Singer, & Biggs, 1979). Television can be used to promote good health and nutrition habits among children (Calvert & Cocking, 1992).

There are many other potential benefits of carefully designed children's programs. Children can be taught cooperation, sharing, affection, friendship, control of aggression, coping with frustration, and the necessity of completing tasks. They can be presented with models of harmonious family relationships and of cooperative, sympathetic, and nurturant behavior. As they get older, they can be exposed to greatness; to various ethnic and cultural groups; to world geography and history; to the world of nature; to a wide variety of interpersonal experiences; to literature and the classics; and to science, art, music, and drama. The potentials are unlimited. Unfortunately, television programs have fallen far short of their potential (*Television and Your Children,* 1985).

COMPUTERS

Some of the same concerns about the effect of TV viewing have been raised regarding the effects of computers. As computers have become smaller, faster, and less expensive, their use has skyrocketed. In a recent year, 28% of students were using computers at home, and over 60% were using computers at school. Amazing as it may seem, 27% of prekindergarten students were using computers at school.

The Internet

One of the most important reasons for using the computer has been the introduction of the *Internet.* Some 25,000 interconnected networks made up of several hundred thousand host computers in their servers span the globe, ready to exchange information and allow you to connect with people all over the world. The result is a decentralized network of data shown on thousands of computers that make up the network. Conservative estimates put more than 100 million users of the Internet by the year 2000 (Carlson, 1996). The Internet is open 24 hours a day, 365 days a year. It is a way to meet people; find adventure; share ideas and experiences; look for a job, a date, or a mate; and ask questions or give advice. The information resources of thousands of university students, government agencies, and researchers are at your fingertips. The Internet is like a shopping mall that never closes, where you can shop for everything.

In addition to its communication role, each of the hundreds of thousands of Internet servers resembles a minilibrary. Each server maintains its own information, catalogues information, and decides what to store and what to discard. Although the Internet is analogous to a library, there is no card catalogue for this library. Each server stores information without indexing or cross-referencing the entire database. To find a particular topic, there are numerous programs called search engines that allow you to search vast depths of database simply by typing in the topic word or words and then hitting the enter key.

The World Wide Web

The *World Wide Web*, which was developed in 1992, has primarily been responsible for the explosion of Internet users in the past several years. If you log onto the Internet using the software product called the browser, you can point and click your way to various web sites, whether they be museums, bookstores, personal home pages, shopping malls, or various businesses. This process makes the whole world available to students literally at their fingertips.

Inappropriate Materials

Unfortunately, some of the materials are inappropriate for children. These may include sexually explicit materials containing examples of beastiality and pedophilia. Sexual encounters may include incest, group sex, or bondage. Catalogues for sexual devices and clothing, as well as advertisements for pay-for-service organizations ranging from phone sex to escort services, are also offered. Recipes for bombs, booby traps, and other destructive devices can be found. The Internet may also contain information on drugs and drug user's devices. Racial activist groups also provide material on the Internet. Parents and lawmakers have sought to install devices in computers that limit the access of children to such materials. Legislation is also proposed to help protect children from these kinds of exposures.

Effects

Just what effects the computer revolution has on children and adolescents is not completely clear. There are untold benefits. Children now may be the best informed generation the United States has ever produced. However, there are negative effects. Many users spend hours a day playing games and browsing through the Internet, searching for various kinds of materials. Many parents now complain that their children are using their computers more time each day than they used to spend watching television. Computer use can become addictive, so that some computer addicts live an isolated existence. The Internet begins to serve a new community, the electronic village, but primary relationships on a face-to-face basis have been superseded by computer relationships. The extent to which this phenomenon has already happened depends on the individual. For some, person-to-person relationships will always be more important than establishing contact over the electronic media. It is up to parents to guide their children in various forms of behavior in relationships so that they get the maximum out of their relationships and contribute the most to the groups of which they are part.

THE DEVELOPMENT OF GENDER ROLES

Meaning

One of the negative effects of television is that it sometimes portrays stereotypical gender roles. **Gender** refers to our biological sex, whether male or female. **Gender roles** are outward expressions of masculinity or femininity in social settings. They are how we act and think as males or females. They are our sex roles.

Sex roles are molded by three important influences: *biological, cognitive,* and *environmental influences.*

Influences on Gender Roles

Biological

The biological bases for gender have already been discussed in Chapter 3. If an ovum is fertilized by a sperm carrying an X chromosome, a female is conceived. If the ovum is fertilized by a sperm carrying a Y chromosome, a male is conceived. *The chromosomal combination is the initial controlling factor in the development of gender.*

Gender development is also influenced by sex hormones. **Testosterone** is the masculinizing hormone secreted by the testes; **estrogen** is the feminizing hormone secreted by the ovaries. If human females are exposed to excessive *androgenic* (masculinizing) influences prenatally, after birth they become more physically vigorous and more assertive than other females. They prefer boys rather than girls as playmates and choose strenuous activities over relatively docile play. Similarly, boys born to mothers who receive estrogen and progesterone during pregnancy tend to exhibit less assertiveness and physical activity and may be rated lower in general masculine-typed behavior. The studies suggest that *changes in prenatal hormonal levels in humans may have marked*

Gender—our biological sex

Gender roles—our outward expressions of masculinity or femininity in social settings

Testosterone—the masculinizing hormone

Estrogen—the feminizing hormone

Gender roles that are outward expressions of masculinity or femininity in social settings are in a state of flux and transition.

effects on gender-role behavior. After birth, hormonal secretions stimulate the development of masculine or feminine physical characteristics, but they have minimal effect on gender-role behavior, usually only accentuating behavior already manifested.

Cognitive

Cognitive theory suggests that *sex-role identity has its beginning in the gender cognitively assigned to the child at birth and subsequently accepted by him or her while growing up.* At the time of birth, gender assignment is made largely on the basis of genital examination. The assignment of gender influences everything that happens thereafter. Kohlberg (1966a), the chief exponent of this view, emphasized that the child's self-categorization (as a boy or girl) is the basic organizer of the sex-role attitudes that develop. A child who recognizes that he is a male begins to value maleness, and a child who recognizes that she is a female begins to value femaleness and to act consistently with gender expectations (Martin & Little, 1990). The child begins to structure experience according to the accepted gender and to act out appropriate sex roles. Sex differentiation takes place gradually as children learn to be male or female according to culturally established sex-role ex-

pectations and their interpretations of them. It is important to emphasize that according to this theory, *girls do not become girls because they identify with or model themselves after their mothers; they model themselves after their mothers because they have realized that they are girls.* They preferentially value their own sex and are motivated to appropriate sex-role behavior.

Environmental Influences

Behaviorists and social learning theorists reason differently. In their view, *a child learns sex-typed behavior the same way he or she learns any other type of behavior: through a combination of rewards and punishment, indoctrination, observation of others, and modeling.* From the beginning, boys and girls are socialized differently (Fagot & Hagan, 1991). Boys are expected to be more active and aggressive. When they act according to these expectations, they are praised; when they refuse to fight, they are criticized for being "sissies." Fathers are more likely to criticize their sons, especially for engaging in nonstereotypical play. Girls are condemned or punished for being too boisterous or aggressive and are rewarded when they are polite and submissive (Williams, 1988). As a consequence, boys and girls grow up manifesting different behaviors.

Traditional sex roles and concepts are taught in many ways as the child grows up (Roopnarine, 1986). *Giving children gender-specific toys may have considerable influence on vocational choices.* Such toys influence boys to be scientists, astronauts, or football players, and girls to be nurses, teachers, or cabin attendants. Without realizing it, *many teachers still develop traditional masculine-feminine stereotypical behavior in school.* Studies of teachers' relationships with boys and girls reveal that teachers encourage boys to be more assertive in the classroom (Sadker & Sadker, 1985). When the teacher asks questions, the boys call out comments without raising their hands, literally grabbing the teacher's attention. Most girls sit patiently with their hands raised, but if a girl calls out, the teacher reprimands her: "In this class, we don't shout our answers; we raise our hands." The message is subtle but powerful: Boys should be assertive academically; girls should be quiet.

Children also find appropriate sex roles through a process of identification, especially with parents of the same sex. Parental identification is the process by which the child adopts and internalizes parental values, attitudes, behavioral traits, and personality characteristics (Weisner

& Wilson-Mitchell, 1990). When applied to sex-role development, parental identification theory suggests that children develop sex-role concepts, attitudes, values, characteristics, and behavior by identifying with their parents, especially with the parent of the opposite sex. Identification begins immediately after birth because of the child's early dependency on parents. This dependency in turn normally leads to a close emotional attachment. Sex-role learning takes place almost unconsciously and indirectly in this close parent-child relationship. Through example and through daily contacts and associations (McHale, Bartko, Crouter, & Perry-Jenkins, 1990), children learn what a mother, a wife, a father, a husband, a woman, or a man is.

The gender-role attitudes that children develop differ, depending on the families in which they are raised. Children from father-headed, single-parent families have the most traditional gender attitudes, and children from mother-headed single-parent families have the most egalitarian. However, family structure is not the only important consideration. Males who have a working mother have a substantially more egalitarian attitude. Even those males from father-headed, single-parent families have more traditional gender attitudes than those from mother-headed, single-parent families. However, the presence of a working mother produces significantly more egalitarian attitudes for females, regardless of the family structure (Wright & Young, 1998).

Peer groups also exert tremendous influence on children in sex-role development. Boys are condemned as "sissies" if they manifest feminine characteristics. Girls are labeled "tomboys" if they are unladylike. Day after day, children are taught to be boys or girls according to the definitions prevalent in their culture (Sroufe, Bennett, Englund, & Urban, 1993).

person must be a man. If someone washes dishes, cooks, or irons clothes, that person must be a woman. By *3 years of age*, children choose gender-typed toys—dolls or cars—and perform sex-typed roles—nurses versus doctors. Yet, at this age, they are unaware that most of the toys they choose are considered appropriate for their gender. There is considerable switching of stereotypical gender-related toys and roles. Three-year-old boys will pretend to be babies, fathers, mothers, or monsters. They will wear mother's high heels or father's cowboy boots. They will play dolls as comfortably as girls do.

By *age 5*, this situation has usually changed. A boy who wants to dress a doll, or a girl who wants to be a space warrior, is criticized by the family (Roopnarine, 1984). Boys will pretend to be monsters or supermen; girls pretend to be princesses or sisters (Paley, 1984).

Sex differences become evident in play. Boys play outdoors more; use more physical space; engage in more rough-and-tumble, noisy play; and more often wrestle, run, push, and tease. Girls more often engage in helping and nurturant play, and more often play house, care for babies, cook, clean, and dress up in hats and other clothes. There is still considerable intermingling of the sexes during play, with some preferences for same-sex companionship becoming evident. By *age 7*, children have developed a sense of **gender constancy:** the understanding of which gender they are and the knowledge that their own sex remains constant. Once a girl, always a girl (Frey & Ruble, 1992). However, research with 4- and 8-year-olds and college-age students revealed that gender-role flexibility increases over these age spans. Children become more flexible regarding certain social transitions (e.g., who can play with trucks) (Levy, Taylor, & Gelman, 1995).

Age and Gender-Role Development

By *2 years of age*, most children are aware that there are boys and girls, mommies and daddies, and that daddies have a penis and mommies have breasts. They use the pronouns *he* and *she* to refer to brothers and sisters and begin to be aware of what constitutes masculine and feminine dress and behavior. Men wear shirts, trousers, suits, and they shave; women wear slacks, dresses, skirts, and blouses, and they put on makeup. Both wear jeans. Children begin to be aware of sex-typed roles (Fagot, Leinbach, & O'Boyle, 1992). If a person drives a truck and is a firefighter, that

Stereotypes

Children's sex-type beliefs develop early and increase rapidly throughout early childhood. They have been found to affect children's play, memory, attributions, and preferences (Bigler, 1995).

Gender stereotypes are common concepts and assumed characteristics of what boys and girls, or men and women, are supposed to be like within the context of the culture in which they live. In our society, when we talk about a "real boy" or a "masculine man," we are expressing value judgments based on an assessment of those personal and

Gender constancy—the understanding of the gender that one is, and the knowledge that gender is going to remain the same: usually achieved by 7 years of age

Gender stereotypes—widespread, assumed gender characteristics of what boys and girls are like

behavioral characteristics of "maleness" according to the defined standards of our culture (Levant, 1992). Similarly, when we are talking about a "feminine woman," we are labeling her according to culturally defined criteria for "femaleness."

Although the standards of maleness and femaleness are undergoing change, *there is still much evidence of traditional stereotypes.* Table 9.1 lists the traditional stereotypes of boys and girls in our culture. These concepts are commonly held by boys and girls themselves (Martin, Wood, & Little, 1990).

There are numerous problems with stereotypes. *First,* they are inaccurate descriptions of those boys and girls who don't fit the stereotypes. To say that all boys are bigger and stronger than girls or that girls are littler and weaker than boys is simply not true. *Second,* stereotypes define what it means to be a boy or girl within narrowly defined limits, and those who don't match the descriptions are criticized or even persecuted because they are different. *Third,* stereotypes tend to perpetuate traditional characteristics, many of which may be undesirable. To say

that real boys are rough and aggressive and like to fight, that girls are passive, gentle, and don't hit, creates numerous problems. Boys may become too physical and girls too passive. A world full of hostile, aggressive males leads to fighting and wars. A world full of passive females leads to exploitation. Similarly, one of the problems between the sexes is that those very traits of sensitivity and emotionality that women are supposed to exhibit and that men are supposed to repress exposes women to the hurts and upsets of intimate living and isolates men from being able to understand why their partners are so upset in the first place. It is difficult for men and women to become real friends and companions.

Fourth, stereotypes limit the roles that men and women play both at home and at work. If women are expected to be breadwinners, as the majority are, then men need to be expected to be homemakers and baby-tenders (Hilton & Haldeman, 1991). Stereotypes also limit the occupations and professions open to men and women. Men can make good nurses and elementary school-

TABLE 9.1	STEREOTYPES OF BOYS AND GIRLS	
	Boys	*Girls*
Physical characteristics	Bigger, stronger, muscular, hard	Weaker, softer, smaller, delicate
	Wear trousers, shirts, suits	Wear dresses, skirts, blouses, makeup, jewelry
	Short hair	Long hair, curls, ribbons
Play	Play war, army, fireman, policeman, cowboy, astronaut, build things	Domestic play: play house, wash dishes, cook, iron, sweep, tend babies
	Play with blocks, cars, trucks, airplanes, boats, soldiers, bulldozers, cranes, tools, space-age toys, video games	Play with dollhouses, dolls, doll carriages, stoves, cooking utensils, pots and pans, board games
	More physical play, sports: football, soccer, hockey, baseball	More interest in art, drawing, music
Domestic work	Mow lawn, build and fix things	Domestic chores, housekeeping, care for children, laundry
Behavior	Rough, aggressive, forceful, tough, daring, brave, competitive, like to fight	Passive, nurturant, helping, caring, compassionate, sympathetic, gentle, kind, scared, like to kiss, don't hit or fight
	Loud, noisy, naughty	Talk a lot
	Not a sissy, unemotional, do not cry, self-confident, independent	Emotional, high-strung, cry, frivolous, impractical, dependent
Cognitive	Better in math, science, visual-spatial skills, mechanical aptitude	Better in verbal skills, grammar, reading, spelling, languages, history

teachers (and men elementary schoolteachers are very much needed), and women can make good scientists and engineers (Jacobs & Eccles, 1992). The important thing is for children to be brought up free to choose their profession.

Androgyny

Gender-role concepts are changing slowly. What seems to be developing is a gradual mixing of male and female traits and roles to produce **androgyny** (male and female in one) (Vannoy, 1991). See Figure 9.8. Male traits emphasize *self-assertion:* leadership, dominance, independence, competitiveness, and individualism. Female traits emphasize *integration:* sympathy, affection, and understanding. Children who possess neither masculine nor feminine characteristics are labeled undifferentiated. Androgynous children have a high degree of both self-assertion and integration: of male and female traits (Ford, 1986). Thus, we have four classifications of gender-role types: *masculine, feminine, undifferentiated,* and *androgynous.* Figure 9.8 shows the possible combinations. A person who is high in both self-assertion and integration is androgynous. Similarly, a person who is high in self-assertion and low in integration is masculine; low in self-assertion and high in integration, feminine; and low in both self-assertion and integration, undifferentiated. *Androgynous persons are not sex-typed with respect to roles (although they are distinctly male or female in gender).* They match their behavior to the situation rather than being limited by what is culturally defined as male or female. An androgynous male feels comfortable cuddling and caring for a young baby; an androgynous female feels comfortable pumping gas and changing the oil in her car. Androgyny expands the range of human behavior, allowing individuals to cope effectively in a variety of situations.

MORAL DEVELOPMENT

Social development includes the development of values and ethical principles as guides of behavior. Social development includes being able to make moral judgments of right or wrong and having a strong sense and desire to do what is considered right and helpful. It also means developing strong moral inhibitions against doing what is wrong and showing higher moral motives and strengths in doing what is right. One aspect of moral development is cultivating

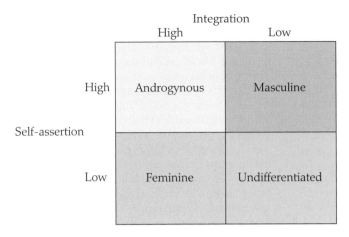

FIGURE 9.8 Classifications of gender-typed roles.

moral judgment, which will be discussed in the next section.

Moral Judgment

The process by which children develop moral judgment is extremely interesting (Walker & Taylor, 1991). The most important early research on the development of moral judgment in children is that of Piaget (1948),

Androgyny—a mixing of male and female traits in one person

Parenting Issues

Parental Roles in Androgynous Development

There are many things that parents can do to encourage development of androgyny in their children (Katz & Walsh, 1991).

- Become androgynous role models for children to imitate. If parents can manifest both self-assertive and integrative traits, and exemplify both masculine and feminine roles in the family, children are likely to adopt both traits and roles themselves.

- Eliminate separating "men's work" and "women's work" in the family, with the whole family performing "our work."

- Encourage children to play games and use toys without regard for traditional sex-typed associations.

- Encourage boys to be integrative and girls to be self-assertive. Let boys know it's all right to have tender feelings and to express emotion, and let girls know they can assert their individualism and independence.

- Teach children that both men and women can engage in traditionally male or traditionally female professions.

(Piaget & Inhelder, 1969). Piaget emphasized the development of moral judgment as a gradual cognitive process, stimulated by increasing social relationships of children as they get older.

Piaget's (1948) work is reported in four sections. The *first section* discusses the attitudes of children to the rules of the game when playing marbles. The *second and third sections* report the results of telling children stories that require them to make moral judgments on the basis of the information given. The *last section* reviews his findings in relation to social psychology, particularly to the work of Durkheim (1960), who argues that the sanctions of society are the only source of morality.

In studying children's attitudes to the rules of the game, Piaget concluded that there is, first of all, a **morality of constraint.** In the early stages of moral development, children are constrained by the rules of the game. These rules are coercive because children regard them as inviolable and because they reflect parental authority. Rules constitute a given order of existence and, like parents, must be obeyed without question. (In actual practice, children's attitudes and behavior don't always coincide, however.) Later, according to Piaget, children learn from social interaction a **morality of cooperation,** that rules are not absolute but can be altered by social consensus (Gabennesch, 1990; Helwig, Tisak, & Turiel, 1990). Rules are no longer external laws to be considered sacred because they are laid down by adults rather are but social creations arrived at through a process of free decision and thus deserving of mutual respect and consent. Children move from *heteronomy* to *autonomy* in making moral judgments (Piaget, 1948).

Piaget also discusses the motives or reasons for judgments. He says there are, first, judgments based solely on the consequences of wrongdoing **(objective judgments)** and, second, judgments that take into account intention or motive **(subjective judgments).** Piaget (1948) claims there is a growing pattern of operational thinking, with children moving from objective to subjective responsibility as they grow older. Piaget would insist that although the two processes overlap, the second gradually supersedes the first. The first stage is superseded when children deem motive or intention more important than consequences.

The child finds in his brothers and sisters or in his playmates a form of society which develops his desire for cooperation. Then a new type of morality will be cre-

ated in him, a *morality of reciprocity* and not of *obedience*. This is true morality of intention. (p. 133)

Piaget (1948) is careful to note that obedience and cooperation are not always successive stages but nevertheless are formative processes that broadly follow one another: "The first of these processes is the moral constraint of the adult, a constraint which leads to heteronomy and consequently to *moral realism*. The second is cooperation which leads to autonomy" (p. 193). (By moral realism Piaget means submitting meekly to the demands of law.)

Before moral judgment moves from the *heteronomous* to the *autonomous* stage, the self-accepted rules must be internalized. This process happens when, in a reciprocal relationship and out of mutual respect, people begin to feel from within the desire to treat others as they themselves would wish to be treated. They pass from *preoperational* to *operational thinking*, from premoral to moral judgment as they internalize the rules that they want to follow.

In the third section of his report, Piaget discusses the child's concept of justice as the child moves from moral restraint to moral cooperation. Two concepts of punishment emerge. The first results from the transgression of an externally imposed regulation; this Piaget calls **expiatory punishment,** which goes hand in hand with constraint and the rules of authority. The second is self-imposed punishment, which comes into operation when the individual, in violation of his or her own conscience, is denied normal social relations and is isolated from the group by his or her own actions. Piaget (1948) calls this the **punishment of reciprocity,** which accompanies cooperation. An ethic of mutual respect, of good as opposed to duty, leads to improved social relationships that are basic to any concept of real equality and reciprocity.

In the last section of his work, Piaget (1948), following Durkheim, asserts that "society is the only source of morality" (p. 326). Morality, to Piaget, consists of a system of rules, but such rules require a sociological context for their development. Thus, "whether the child's moral judgments are heteronomous or autonomous, accepted under pressure or worked out in freedom, this morality is social, and on this point, Durkheim was unquestionably right" (p. 344).

One of the important implications of Piaget's views is that the changes in the moral judgments of children are related to their

Morality of constraint—conduct coerced by rules or by authority

Morality of cooperation—conduct regulated by mutual respect and consent

Objective judgments—judgments based solely on the consequences of wrongdoing

Subjective judgments—judgments that take into account intention or motives

Expiatory punishment—punishment that results from an externally imposed regulation; associated with morality of constraint

Punishment of reciprocity—self-imposed punishment; associated with morality of cooperation

cognitive growth and to the changes in their social relationships. At first children judge the severity of transgressions by their visible damage or harm. They also develop the concept of **imminent justice:** the child's belief that immoral behavior inevitably brings pain or punishment as a natural consequence of the transgression (Jose, 1990). "If you do wrong, you will certainly be punished." Furthermore, children judge the appropriateness of this punishment by its severity rather than by its relevance to the transgression. Only as children get older are they likely to recommend that the transgressor make restitution or that punishment be tailored to fit the wrong done.

As an example, if 6-year-olds are told the story of a little boy who has accidentally dropped a sweet roll into the lake, they are likely to respond: "That's too bad. But it's his own fault for being so clumsy. He shouldn't get another." For them, the punishment implies a crime, and losing a roll in the lake is clearly a punishment in their eyes. They are incapable of taking extenuating circumstances into account. Adolescents, however, make moral judgments on the basis of what Piaget calls **equity,** assigning punishments in accordance with the transgressors' abilities to take responsibility for their crimes.

Another important implication of Piaget's view is that changes in judgments of children must be related to the changes in their social relationships. As peer-group activity and cooperation increase and as adult constraint decreases, the child becomes more truly an autonomous, cooperative, moral person (Kalish, 1998).

Moral Behavior

So far, we have discussed the development of moral judgment. *Moral judgment is the knowledge of right or wrong.* It is quite evident from experience that knowing the right thing to do

Imminent justice—the child's belief that immoral behavior inevitably brings pain or punishment as a natural consequence of the transgression

Equity—assignment of punishments in accordance with transgressors' ability to take responsibility for a crime

---

Parenting Issues

Taking Small Children to Adult Worship Services

Some parents say this: "I'm going to take my children to worship from the time they are young. Then they will get in the habit of going." Other adults say this: "I was forced to go when I was growing up, and I hated it. I'm never going to do that to my children." Assuming that parents want to give their children a firm foundation of religious teaching, what's the wisest approach?

There are some negative aspects to taking small children to adult worship services. The most important consideration is that children are bored; they don't understand what is going on; they are learning to be inattentive, so they either do something else or fall asleep. They are conditioned not to like going to adult worship services and not to get anything out of them.

Letting children stay home until they are old enough to understand adult services is not the answer, either. This teaches them that church, synagogue, mosque, or temple is not important, and they miss out on religious instruction during many of their formative years.

One positive approach is to enroll children in religious classes that meet during the adult service. These should be classes that are divided according to age groups with programs appropriate for each age level. If children like to go and they are learning from the experience, not only are they growing in understanding, but they are also developing positive attitudes and feelings toward going that carry over into adulthood. One mother commented: "Every time we go by the church, my two-year-old says, 'Horsey, horsey.'" The child had made an association between the church and riding on the horsey in the nursery, where she was learning one of the most important religious lessons of all: how to get along with other children. She was getting a helpful beginning.

Worship in church has become part of the tradition of this family.

and doing it are two different things. The discussion of moral development profits from a clear separation of moral judgment and moral motivation. *Moral motivation is the strength of desire to do right*, the intensity of feelings in relationship to doing right. Another facet, *moral inhibition, as it is manifested in a strong conscience, is the strength of desire or feelings not to do wrong*. Moral behavior depends on both positive moral motivation and the strength of inhibitions against doing wrong. *One study showed that the higher that moral motive strength and temperamental inhibitions were, the greater the possibility of moral behavior* (Asendorpf & Nunner-Winkler, 1992). The study showed through group analysis of children low or high in moral motivation and inhibition that cheating or noncheating could be predicted with a rate of about 90% accuracy. *Moral behavior in this study was defined as behavior that did not transgress rules that children clearly knew to be valid.* In this study, when the effects of inhibition and moral motive strength were combined, the prediction of immoral behavior became particularly powerful.

Another study investigated children's concepts, standards, and evaluative reactivity to lying or telling the truth about misdeeds (Bussey, 1992). Children in this study were preschool and second- and fifth-graders. The study produced clear evidence of the development of moral standards associated with lying and storytelling in all children. Children were more disapproving of lies than of truthfulness about misdeeds. All children evaluated lies about misdeeds significantly more negatively than the misdeeds themselves. Truthful statements were, however, not evaluated by preschoolers more favorably than misdeeds. Although young children appreciated the naughtiness of lying, it was more difficult for them to appreciate the value of truthfulness about misdeeds. Older children were able to appreciate the value of truthfulness.

Punishment affected the moral judgment of the preschoolers but not of the older children. Preschoolers placed more value on statements that led to punishment for the misdeed than they did on statements that did not lead to punishment. This finding agrees with social cognitive theory in which *observable physical consequences are predicted to be major determinants of preschoolers' judgments of lies and truthful statements*.

The study demonstrated two important developmental changes. *First, children react initially with censure for lying but, over time, learn to react with feelings of pride for truthfulness.* As a result, eventually children's reactions to lies are negative; with truthful statements, reactions are positive. *Second, there's a change from children's reliance on punishment as a basis for their moral judgments to a greater reliance on internal evaluative reactions.* This greater reliance on internal rather than external factors, with increasing cognitive maturity and social experience, is consistent with the development of self-regulation. Self-evaluative reactions are expected to promote congruence between moral standards and moral conduct. Ideally, if socialization is successful, there is a transfer from external forms of control to more internal controls, so that there is less reliance on external factors such as punishment (Kochanska, Tjebkes, & Forman, 1998).

There are important implications in these ideas. *Young children whose conduct is not regulated to the same extent as older children by internal evaluative reactions, particularly positive evaluative reactions, are helped by adults' actively encouraging and rewarding truthfulness.* If children anticipate punishment for admitting to a misdeed, there's little incentive for them to tell the truth. Parents and other caregivers need to encourage children to accept responsibility for misdeeds and simultaneously feel proud of their truthfulness. Furthermore, adults can promote the development of self-evaluative feelings that unite children's thought and action through the use of reasoning techniques. Punishment may teach fear of doing something wrong, but reasoning can help children to want to do right by feeling good about themselves (Bussey, 1992).

Conscience Development

Much of the child's development of moral judgment and moral behavior depends on the development of conscience. Conscience development has been described as the process of internalization of values. Experts underscore the importance of age 3 as a developmental landmark in the emergence of the "moral self" (Kochanska et al., 1994). The data also indicate that for some signs of early conscience, the important developmental transitions may occur even earlier. Confession and reparation have been described in children as young as 2; for these behaviors, the significant shifts may take place in the second year, paralleling the emergence of self and sensitivity to standards.

Before internalization can take place, the child must perceive the parents' message, and this perception must be accurate. Secondly, the child must also accept the perceived message. The accuracy of perception will depend on getting the child's attention and on the clarity or redundancy of the parents' message. Acceptance is seen to depend especially on the warmth of the relationship between parent and child. Warmth affects the occurrence of acceptance, but not necessarily the accuracy of perception. Clarification is necessary if the child's failure to internalize is the result of not having fully heard or understood the parental message. In Figure 9.9, the variables are grouped according to their impact on (a) the extent to which the child perceives parental behavior to be appropriate, (b) the child's motivation, and (c) the degree to which the child sees the value or standard as self-generated. The first group relates to a child's evaluation of the acceptability of the

parents' intervention. Acceptance is especially likely to be influenced by the child's judgment that the parents' actions are appropriate to the nature of the misdeed; the parents' intervention has truth and value; and due process has been observed, expected procedures followed, seen as well-intentioned, and fitted to the child's temperament, mood, and developmental status.

The second group deals with the extent to which the child is motivated to accept the parental message. High degrees of empathetic arousal, threats to feelings of security, and the extent to which the value is perceived as important to the parent are important contributors to acceptance here. If the child's desire to identify with a parent is promoted, the desire for reciprocal compliance is promoted, and threats to autonomy minimized,

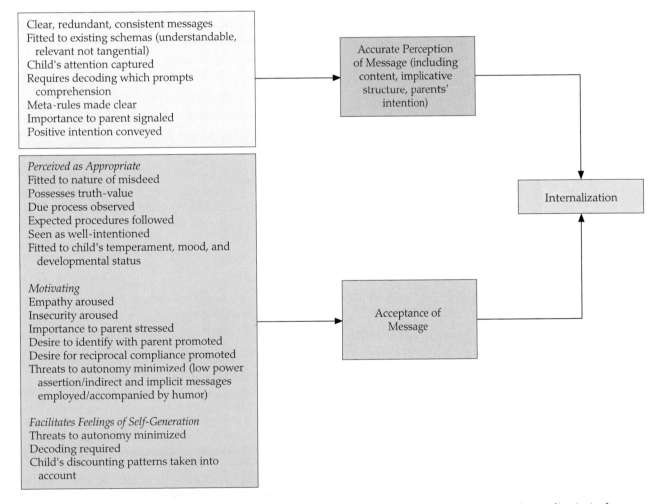

FIGURE 9.9   Features of parental disciplinary actions promoting accurate perception and acceptance (internalization) of a parent's message.

From "Impact of Parental Discipline Methods on the Child's Internalization of Values: A Reconceptualization of Current Points of View," by J. E. Grusec and J. J. Goodnow, 1994, *Developmental Psychology, 30*, pp. 4–19. Copyright 1994 by the American Psychological Association. Adapted with permission.

the child is more likely to be willing to accept the message.

The last group of events involves variables that may lead to feelings on the child's part that their value is self-generated with the feeling promoting acceptance. Overall, internalization takes place to the extent that the child not only has an accurate perception of the message but also has accepted that message (Grusec & Goodnow, 1994; Dunn, Brown, & Maguire, 1995).

Summary

1. Children do not develop in a vacuum. They are influenced by their social relationships in their family, neighborhood, community, country, and the world.

2. Bronfenbrenner developed an ecological model for understanding social influences in the microsystem, mesosystem, exosystem, and macrosystem.

3. There are differences in the way that children are socialized according to socioeconomic status.

4. Socialization is the process by which persons learn the way of society and social groups so that they can function within them.

5. The family is the chief socializing influence on children, but there are many family types, each of which may have a somewhat different influence on children. The influence of the family is also variable because of differences in individual children.

6. The parents' psychological adjustment, parenting style, and the quality of their marriage all have an effect on the child's emotional maturity, social competence, and cognitive development.

7. There are three major styles of parenting in our culture: authoritarian, permissive, and authoritative. Authoritative control seems to work best in our culture.

8. Parental relationships with children can also be divided into four categories according to the degree of control and of affection. These four categories are love-autonomy, love-control, hostility-autonomy, and hostility-control.

9. The one parenting variable that is most related to adjustment is love.

10. The primary purpose of discipline is to teach, not to punish. The ultimate goal is to sensitize the conscience and to develop self-control.

11. Parental control techniques may be divided into seven categories: power-assertive discipline, command, self-oriented induction, other-oriented induction, love withdrawal, advice, and relationship maintenance.

12. Successful parenting seems to depend on the maximum amount of love and the right balance between autonomy and control.

13. Reasoning is the preferred method of discipline with children and must be followed by appropriate punishment if children fail to do what they are supposed to do.

14. Children of mothers who are more responsive during their children's infancy and through early adolescence have higher arithmetic scores, more positive self-esteem, and fewer behavioral and emotional problems than those of less responsive mothers.

15. With more married women working outside the home, fairness would seem to demand that husbands take more responsibility for housework and child care, but equality of roles has not been fully achieved.

16. Fathers tend to be closer to their sons than to their daughters and are less likely to leave the family if they have sons.

17. Social scientists have been trying to evaluate the effect of substitute child care on children's well-being. When social economic status of the parents is taken into consideration, the effect of maternal employment on children is variable. When income of households is high, children are not likely to obtain an environment that is significantly better than that which they have at home. However, children from low-income households may be significantly helped by the developmental opportunities available to them.

18. Siblings exert considerable influence on the socialization of other children in the family. Birth order, the number of children in the family, the gender, and the relationships with brothers and sisters all influence development.

19. Grandparents can help children feel loved and secure; can help children to know, trust, and understand other people; can fill the gap between the past and present; can provide children with experiences and supervision that their own parents cannot give; and can teach children a fine sense of values and wholesome attitudes toward old age.

20. Some problems with grandparents are puzzlement about their roles, having different ideas about raising children, giving unsolicited advice, jealousy, becoming too possessive, and disagreements that need to be discussed.

21. The number of one-parent families is on the increase. The majority are female-headed families. The primary problems of the female family are limited income and pressures to perform all functions well. Like females, single males heading families are concerned about income, not spending enough time with their children, child care, and changes in their social life.

22. Father absence affects boys emotionally, affects their development of masculinity, and affects the level of education they are able to attain. The effect depends partially on the availability of male surrogate models.

23. Father absence affects girls also, especially during adolescence, when girls may develop difficulty with their heterosexual adjustments and with forming a positive and feminine self-concept.

24. Father-absent homes are not always worse for children than father-present homes.

25. One study found no difference in benefits to either males or females in living with a same-sex parent rather than an opposite-sex parent.

26. Many lesbian couples and gay couples seek to raise children in a family.

27. Divorce is often a major, negative event that stimulates painful emotions, confusion, and uncertainty in children. Many children are able to regain psychological equilibrium in a year or so.

28. Wallerstein and Blakeslee found a number of long-term negative consequences for children whose parents divorced, but the consequences depend on a number of important variables.

29. African Americans who are divorced are less likely to marry and make easier adjustments than whites, partly because of extensive kinship support networks.

30. The term *custody* refers to both legal custody and physical custody. In joint custody, both parents are responsible for care and decisions relating to the child.

31. Child support is the obligation of both the mother and the father. Only one-half of all noncustodial parents pay the full amount of support that they are ordered to pay. Also, the low rate of noncustodial parent-child contact is detrimental to children.

32. Ordinarily, visitation rights are given to the parent who does not have physical custody.

33. Children's well-being depends not just on the frequency of visitation but also on the degree of harmony between the husband and wife after divorce.

34. Coparenting involves the cooperation of both parents in rearing the child.

35. Two factors that affect the mental health of mother and child are payment of child support and the frequency and quality of the father's relationship with the child.

36. Parents can do much to minimize the harmful effects of divorce. Postdivorce stressors may have a more important impact on children's mental health than does the occurrence of the divorce per se.

37. The problems of children become more complicated when parents remarry and a stepfamily is formed.

38. Stepfamilies have their own unique set of problems, different from those of primary families. There are many things parents can do to learn to be good stepparents.

39. Foster care is a treatment of last resort for children whose parents can't care for them.

40. The number of adoptions has increased steadily; there is a shortage of children to be adopted; about one-half of those who adopt are related to the child whom they wish to adopt; some adoptions are of children from foreign countries. In open adoption, the natural mother is permitted to play an active role in selecting the new adoptive parents; a crucial factor in relation to the adjustment of adopted children is the quality of the family environ-

ment in which the child is raised. Adoption reunions are becoming more common but prove a disappointment to some when their relative was not as expected.

41. A study of mothers who placed their babies for adoption found that they were indistinguishable from those who did not as to social relationships, life satisfaction, and in having a positive future outlook regarding employment and schooling, finances, and marriage.

42. Adolescent mothers are at a greater risk of family instability and of negative educational and emotional outcome, and they are more likely to experience problem behavior than are older mothers of children.

43. The psychosocial development of children and youth can be divided into four stages: autosociality, childhood heterosociality, homosociality, and adolescent and adult heterosocialty.

44. Children move through progressive stages of social development as they get older. Two-year-olds play alongside one another. Three-year-olds begin group play; four- and five-year-olds gradually develop more socially competent interactions with peers.

45. There is much intermingling of sexes and races, although both boys and girls prefer to play with others of the same sex.

46. The play of preschoolers has been divided into six categories of play involvement: unoccupied play, solitary play, onlooker play, parallel play, associative play, and cooperative play.

47. Play may also be divided into categories according to the type of activity: sensory play, motor play, rough-and-tumble play, cognitive play, dramatic or pretend play, and games and competitive sports.

48. The older that children become, the more important companionship with friends becomes. Popularity, gangs and clubs, competition, and cruelty and aggression all become important considerations during middle childhood.

49. Research points to the fact that children generally prefer friends who are like themselves and who are similar in play styles, social participation, etiquette, and a sense of humor and sociability.

50. Peer relationships within the school setting have a great influence on children's concurrent and later adjustment.

51. Some children are rejected and lonely, and thus they suffer a great deal of stress. Unliked children are socially invisible; disliked children behave in socially unaccepted ways.

52. Once a child is rejected, there are numerous social forces working to maintain the negative status of the child. A small minority of children are consistently targeted for victimization by their peers. Victims who become more submissive become vulnerable targets for continued, aggressive overtures of their peers.

53. Social cognition is the capacity to understand social relationships, an ability that is very important in getting along with others. Robert Selman outlined five stages of development of social cognition: the egocentric undifferentiated stage; differentiated or subjective perspective-taking stage; self-reflective thinking or reciprocal perspective-taking stage; third-person or mutual perspective-taking stage; and the in-depth and societal perspective-taking stage.

54. When parental expressions of emotion are positive and when there are good feelings existing between children and their parents, children show more positive relationships with other children and have insight as to what friendly relationships should be.

55. Television is an important socializing influence. Experts are particularly concerned about its effect on childhood aggression, family interaction, and cognitive development; and about the effects of commercials and video games.

56. During the years from about 3 to 12, children acquire an understanding of the distinctions between real and fictional television content. Both real and fictional television images can directly arouse emotions. Children are frightened by threatening stimuli.

57. Social realism rather than factuality appears to be important in emotional arousal.

58. Television, especially well-designed children's programs, can have a positive effect on children. Some video games that are attached to computer sets are extremely violent and encourage children to participate in killing others as part of the contest.

59. Gender refers to our biological sex; gender roles are outward expressions of masculinity or femininity.

60. There are three important influences on gender-role development: biological, cognitive, and environmental.

61. Gender-role development begins at birth and continues for many years. Children reach gender-role constancy by age 7.

62. Gender stereotypes are inaccurate descriptions of all boys and girls; boys and girls who don't match the descriptions are criticized; stereotypes tend to perpetuate undesirable characteristics; and they limit the roles that men and women play at home and at work.

63. Androgyny is a gradual mixing of male and female traits. Male characteristics emphasize self-assertion; female characteristics emphasize integration. Androgynous persons manifest both sets of traits.

64. According to Piaget, children develop moral judgment in a series of steps. They move from a morality of constraint to a morality of cooperation; from heteronomy to autonomy; from making objective judgments to making subjective judgments; from a morality of obedience to a morality of reciprocity; and from a concept of expiatory punishment to one of punishment of reciprocity. They also move from a concept of imminent justice to a concept of equity.

65. Moral behavior depends on moral motivation—the strength of desire to do right—and on moral inhibition—the strength of desire not to do wrong. As children get older, they rely more on internal evaluative reactions and less on the threat of punishment. Adults can encourage the internalization of values by rewarding and encouraging moral behavior.

66. Conscience development has been described as the process of internalization of values.

67. Before the child can internalize parental values, the message must be fully heard and understood, the child must perceive the parental behavior to be appropriate, and the child must accept the fact that the parents' intervention has truth and value and is well-intentioned.

Key Terms

Discussion Questions

1. In what ways are marriages and families of today better for couples and their children, and in what ways are they worse?

2. What are the most important qualities and characteristics of parents in order for them to do the best job of bringing up children?

3. From your own experience, compare authoritarian, permissive, and authoritative patterns of parenting.

4. Did you have to do family chores when you were growing up? What did you think of doing chores? Did it help you? In what ways did it help, and in what ways did it do harm?

5. What methods of discipline do you believe work the best, and why? Take children's ages into account.

6. If both husband and wife work full-time, how should they divide responsibilities for housework, cooking, and child care?

7. In what ways were your siblings a help to you when growing up, and in what ways were they a hindrance?

8. Do you have grandparents with whom you are close? Describe the relationship and the ways grandparents have helped you, and any problems you have encountered with them.

9. Were you brought up in a one-parent family, or do you know someone who was? What were the effects on you or other children?

10. Were your parents divorced while you were growing up? What were the effects on you while growing up? What effects have you noticed on friends whose parents were divorced or who are now divorced themselves?

11. Have any of you been divorced? How were you and/or your children affected?

12. What are the major advantages and disadvantages of stepfamilies?

13. Do you know anyone who has been brought up in a foster home? How was that person affected?

14. Are any of you adopted? How has being adopted affected your life? Do you have any desire to know your biological parents? What do you think of open adoption? Would you ever want to adopt a child yourself?

15. What are the principal problems of social development of preschoolers and of elementary-school-age children?

16. What are your views on the effects of television on children?

17. What stereotypes of masculine men or feminine women do you think are helpful? Which ones do you object to, and why?

18. What do you think of androgynous personalities? Would you want your child to be androgynous in personality development?

19. What can parents do to raise their children as moral persons? How do you feel about enrolling your children in religious school activities from the time they are little? How do you feel about taking young children to adult worship services?

Suggested Readings

ACOCK, A. C., & DEMO, D. H. (1994). *Family diversity and well-being.* Thousand Oaks, CA: Sage.

ASHER, S. R., & COIE, J. D. (EDS.). (1991). *Peer rejection in childhood.* New York: Cambridge University Press. The nature of peer rejection and ways to help.

ASKEW, W., & ROSS, C. (1988). *Boys don't cry: Boys and sexism in education.* Philadelphia: Open University Press. Sexism and how it can be overcome.

BASSOFF, E. S. (1995). *Between mothers and sons.* New York: Plume. The making of vital and loving men.

BLANKENHORN, D. (1996). *Fatherless America: Confronting our most urgent social problem.* New York: Basic Books. The negative consequences of the United States becoming a fatherless society.

DAMON, W. (1990). *The moral child.* New York: Free Press. The evolution of moral understanding and behavior.

DOYLE, J. A., & PALUDI, M. A. (1991). *Male and female* (2nd ed.). Dubuque, IA: Wm. C. Brown Publishers. Gender and the female role.

EVERETT, S. N., & EVERETT, C. A. (1998). *Healthy divorce.* San Francisco: Jossey-Bass. Making a constructive transition from marriage to divorce with both parents and children able to return to normal, happy functioning.

GILLIGAN, C. (1993). *In a different voice.* Cambridge, MA: Harvard University Press. Pioneering work on women and their moral development.

GOTTFRIED, A. E., & GOTTFRIED, A. W. (EDS.). (1994). *Redefining families: Implications for children's development.* New York: Plenum. The relationship between nontraditional family structures and children's development.

HUESMANN, L. R., & ERON, L. D. (1998). *The development of aggression from infancy to adulthood.* Boulder CO: Westview Press.

KEEN, S. (1991). *Fire in the belly.* New York: Bantam Books. On being a man.

KELLEY, P. (1996). *Developing healthy stepfamilies: Twenty families tell their story.* New York: Hayward. A study of twenty stepfamilies.

KILBRIDE, P. L. (1994). *Plural marriage for our times: A reinvented option?* Westport, CT: Bergin & Garvey. Plural marriage that includes polygyny, polyandry, and group marriage.

KOPECKY, G., & LEVANT, R. F. (1996). *Masculinity reconstructed.* New York: Plume. Changing the rules of manhood at work, in relationships and in family life.

LAMB, M. E. (1987). *The father's role: Cross-cultural perspectives.* Hillsdale, NJ: Erlbaum. Fathers' roles in different cultures.

LIEBERT, R. M., & SPRAKIN, J. N. (1992). *The early window: Effects of television on children and youth* (3rd ed.). Elmsford, NY: Pergamon. Updated research on subject.

McLANAN, S., & SANDFUR, G. (1996). *Growing up with a single parent: What hurts, what helps.* Cambridge, MA: Harvard University Press. The consequences for children growing up in households where only one biological parent is present.

PARCEL, T. L., & MENAGHAN, E. G. (1994). *Parents' jobs and children's lives.* New York: Aldine de Gruyter. How both mothers' and fathers' employment experiences affect children's cognitive and social development.

PASLEY, K., & IHINGER-TALLMAN (Eds.). (1994). *Stepparenting: Issues in theory, research, and practice.* Westport, CT: Auburn House.

REINISCH, J. M., ROSENBLUM, L. A., & SANDERS, S. A. (Eds.). (1987). *Masculinity/feminity.* New York: Oxford University Press. A collection of articles.

SINGER, D. G., & SINGER, J. L. (1992). *The house of make-believe: Children's play and the developing imagination.* Cambridge, MA: Harvard University Press. Children's fantasy play.

WINN, M. (1985). *The plug-in drug* (rev. ed.). New York: Viking. Harmful effects of TV.

WOOD, D., & BECK, R. J. (1994). *Home rules.* Baltimore: The Johns Hopkins University Press. A formidable collection.

http://www.casel.org CASEL The Collaborative to Advance Social and Emotional Learning. Collaborative of educators, scientists, human service providers and policy makers.

Web Resources

Perspectives on Adolescent Development

Chapter
10

INTRODUCTION

In this chapter we are concerned with describing adolescence and a number of terms related to it: maturity, puberty, pubescence, juvenile, and youth. The chapter begins with a discussion of these concepts.

Another way to understand adolescence is to approach it from various points of view: from the studies of the psychobiologist, psychiatrist, psychologist, social psychologist, and anthropologist. This chapter presents the views of theorists from each of these disciplines: psychobiological view— G. Stanley Hall; psychoanalytical view—Anna Freud; sociopsychoanalytical view—Erik Erikson; psychosociological view—Robert Havighurst; and anthropological view—Margaret Mead. By understanding different theories of adolescence, the student can gain a more comprehensive view.

THE MEANING OF ADOLESCENCE

Adolescence

The word *adolescence* comes from the Latin verb *adolescere*, which means "to grow up" or "to grow to maturity." Adolescence is a period of growth beginning with puberty and ending at the beginning of adulthood; it is a transitional stage between childhood and adulthood. The period has been likened to a bridge between childhood and adulthood over which individuals must pass before they can take their places as grown adults. Adolescence ends when youth relinquish their typical student roles and enter into one or more adult roles (marriage, parenthood, full-time employment) (Fasick, 1994). In general, the total period of adolescence has been prolonged in industrial societies as the time span of dependency has increased. The transition from childhood to adulthood is complicated (Hammer & Vaglum, 1990), and the amount of time one takes to pass through this stage is variable, but most adolescents eventually complete the passage.

Puberty and Pubescence

Puberty is the period or age at which a person reaches sexual maturity and becomes capable of having children.

Pubescence is used to denote the whole period during which physical changes relative to sexual maturation are taking place. Literally, it means becoming downy or hairy, describing the growth of body hair that accompanies sexual maturation. Puberty is accompanied not only by biological changes, but by psychological and social changes as well (Adams, Day, Dyk, & Frede, 1992; Lerner, 1992). For example, an adolescent who is an early maturer changes not only in physical appearance but also in friendships and social interests.

Maturity

Maturity is that age, state, or time of life at which a person is considered fully developed socially, intellectually, emotionally, physically, and spiritually. Maturity is not reached in all of these characteristics at the same time. Youths who become physically mature at age 12 are usually not mature in other ways. A person may be mature socially but still be immature emotionally.

Juvenile

The word **juvenile** is a legal term describing an individual who is not accorded adult status in the eyes of the law. In most states, this is a person under 18 years of age. The legal rights of 18-year-olds vary from state to state, however. The 26th Amendment gave them the right to vote. They may obtain credit in their own names at some stores or banks, whereas other banks require cosigners. This status depends on the degree to which they have established a good credit rating in their own names. Many landlords will not rent to minors. Youths have to be 21 years of age to purchase alcoholic beverages. In some states, 18-year-olds can marry without parental consent; in other states, they have to wait until they are older. In Colorado, adolescents can leave home at age 16 but do not attain full legal rights until age 21. The net result is confusion over their status. When do they fully become adults? Some authorities feel that adolescents have to wait too many years to "get into the club."

Keniston (1970) suggested that the law recognize an intermediate legal status between age 15 and 18 when adolescents are accorded more rights than children but fewer than those of adults. Keniston conceptualized a new stage of life, that of *youth*, which he defined as a developmental period that would follow adolescence. In general, his suggestion was never adopted. In modern terminology, however, youth refers to the younger generation, usually adolescence (Sebald, 1984). In this book, it is used in this latter sense.

Transition to Adulthood

The transition to adulthood has been a topic of interest to social scientists for years. Consider what is implied by the use of the phrase "the transition to adulthood." In fact, it implies the existence of a social idea of what it means to be an adult. Also, it implies a commonly held view of the criteria that constitute adult status. Thus, adult status is not merely biological but is socially constructed, and was formed by the members of a culture according to what they deemed to be most important in signifying adult status. As such, the transition to adulthood—the movement into adult status—is also socially constructed. Because adult status is a social concept, the criteria considered important in the transition to adulthood may vary from one culture to another. In our culture, the transition to adulthood has been related to the timing of transition events, which focus on finishing one's education, entering the labor force, establishing an independent household, becoming married, and becoming parents.

The timing of events associated with the transitions to adulthood have been important. Adolescents expectations for the timing of finishing education, marriage, and parenthood have been shown to be related to their families' socioeconomic resources, their parents' expectations, and their own educational aspirations.

Normative events sequences comprise the transition to adulthood. When people are asked what it means to be an adult, they often conceptualize their transition to adulthood differently than just going through a series of timed phases. When a group of college students were asked about their concept of adulthood, they emphasized that the most important characteristics were intangible, gradual, psychological, and individualistic. From this point of view, the transition to adulthood was generally not marked mainly by discrete events but rather by internal and psychological events and attitudes. Thus, the participants in the study said that the transition to adulthood meant accepting responsibility for the consequences of one's own actions: "Decide on personal beliefs and values, independently of parents or other influences," and "establish a relationship with parents as an equal adult." Individualism was perhaps the most dominant characteristics of their conception of the transition to adulthood. The top three criteria emphasized individualistic qualities such as independence and equality. Other criteria endorsed by a majority emphasized individualism, including being "financially independent from parents"

Adolescence is a period of growth beginning with puberty and ending at the beginning of adulthood.

Puberty—the period or age at which a person reaches sexual maturity and becomes capable of reproduction

Pubescence—the whole period during which the physical changes related to sexual maturation take place

Maturity—the time in life when one becomes an adult physically, emotionally, socially, intellectually, and spiritually

Juvenile—one who is not yet considered an adult in the eyes of the law

and "no longer living in your parents' household." Other students have named responsible behavior, autonomous decision making, and financial independence as distinguishing adult characteristics. The transition to adulthood evidently takes place not in the form of discrete transition events but according to the individual's judgment of when various subtle psychological processes have reached fruition (Arnett, 1997).

ADOLESCENCE AND PSYCHIC DISEQUILIBRIUM

One of the ways of understanding adolescence is to describe the period from the viewpoint of different professional disciplines. Let us begin with the discussion of the psychobiologist G. Stanley Hall.

Storm and Stress

G. Stanley Hall (1904), the founder of the child-study movement in North America and the first Ph.D. in psychology in the United States, first described adolescence as a period of great "storm and stress," corresponding to the time when the human race was in a turbulent, transitional stage on the way to becoming civilized. Hall said that the causes of this storm and stress in adolescents are biological, resulting from changes at puberty. To Hall, puberty represents a time of emotional upset and instability in which the adolescents' moods oscillate between energy and lethargy, joy and depression, or egotism and self-depreciation. The end of adolescence marks a birth of adult traits, corresponding to the beginning of modern civilization. Although Hall was a psychologist, his explanation of the changes at adolescence was biological.

Researchers no longer believe that storm and stress are inevitable consequences of adolescence. Many studies have contributed to debunking this idea. The stereotype of adolescence as a tumultuous period of life still appears in the popular media; but, as a result of recent research, adolescence is now considered much more differentiated. For some teenagers, adolescence is a period of development characterized by stress and turmoil, whereas for others, it is a period of relative tranquility. Recent attempts to explain these diversive pathways have been strengthened by considering biological as well as psychological influences on development. One biological influence is indexed by the level of cortisol, which in turn is linked to emotional

FOCUS

Rites of Passage

In some cultures, when a child reaches puberty, ceremonies are conducted to celebrate the passage from childhood to maturity. Once the child successfully passes the prescribed tests, he or she is accepted as a member of adult society.

The ceremonies are often stressful and painful. The most common rite for boys is *circumcision,* usually performed with a sharp stone knife. A tribe in the South Pacific requires that boys leap headfirst from a 100-foot-high platform built in a tree, with nothing but 90-foot-long vines tied to their feet. The vine catches them up short just before their head hits the ground. Sometimes miscalculations result in permanent injury or death. If the boy is brave enough to go through this experience, he is considered worthy to be an adult. The Mandan Indian tribe, living on the plains of the United States, tested the endurance of their pubertal sons by piercing their pectoral muscles under their breasts with sharp sticks and then suspending the boys from the lodge poles by ropes attached to the sticks. Boys who could endure the longest were considered the bravest.

Initiation rites for girls center around the attainment of reproductive capabilities as marked by the onset of menstruation. The girls are prepared ahead of time by instruction on domestic and parental duties, sexual matters, and modes of dress. Some ceremonies are designed to ensure their fertility. In some Arab cultures, a girl's clitoris is removed. In other societies, a girl is scarred while cutting beauty features into the skin.

development in people. Individuals differ in cortisol levels (cortisol reactivity), in different longitudinal changes in cortisol and distress behavior, and by differences in patterns of cortisol reactivity and behavioral and psychological problems. Cortisol is a hormone secreted by the adrenal gland under conditions of stress. It provides the body with the necessary stimulus to deal with the stress. In turn, cortisol provides negative feedback to several glands to decrease the secretion so that the body goes back to normal. Individuals with depression or other affective disorders may have a deficit in the ability to counterregulate or adapt to the negative feedback of increases in cortisol. Adolescents with tendencies toward affective and behavioral problems show deficits in their capability to counterregulate the effects of stressors by decreasing cortisol secretion during novel and challenging situations. Thus, there is a definite relationship between physiological functioning under stress and emotional behavior. This relationship varies with different individuals and depends on the functioning of their bodies (Susman, Dorn, Nottelmann, Inoff-German, & Chrousos, 1997).

The belief that psychological turmoil is normal in adolescence has an unfortunate consequence in that it is often assumed that young people with psychological problems will grow out of them. The evidence is now clear that psychological difficulties in adolescence usually persist and should be treated. They seldom disappear by themselves (Petersen, 1993). One study of fifth- to ninth-graders reported higher rates of negative emotions among adolescents than among preadolescents, but these higher rates of daily distress were partly attributable to the greater number of negative life events encountered by some youths as they got older (Larson & Ham, 1993).

Psychic Conflict

Another contributor to an understanding of adolescence was Anna Freud (1895–1982), daughter of Sigmund Freud (1856–1939). Like her father, she characterized adolescence from a psychoanalytical point of view as a period of psychic disequilibrium, emotional conflict, and erratic behavior. On the one hand, adolescents are egotistic and self-centered, and they believe that everyone's attention is focused on them. On the other hand, they are capable of forgetting themselves while they focus on the needs of others and engage in charitable projects. They can become involved in intense infatuations but can fall out of love just as suddenly. They sometimes want to be with others in their social group, but the next day they seek solitude. They oscillate between rebellion and conformity. Adolescents are not only selfish and materialistic but also morally idealistic. They are ascetic, yet hedonistic; inconsiderate and rude, yet loving and tender. They fluctuate between overflowing confidence and fearful self-doubt, between indefatigable enthusiasm and tired indifference (Freud, 1946).

According to Anna Freud, the reason for this conflicting behavior is sexual maturation at puberty, which causes psychic disequilibrium. At puberty, there is a marked increase in the instinctual drives (the *id*), including a greater interest in genitality and sexual impulses. There is also a rise in other instinctual drives at puberty: exhibitionism and rebelliousness increase; physical hunger intensifies; oral and anal interests reappear; and habits of cleanliness give way to dirt and disorder. Instinctual forces that have remained latent since early childhood reappear at puberty (Freud, 1946, p. 159).

The increasing demands of the id during adolescence create conflict with the *superego* that the *ego* tries to resolve. The task of the ego is to allow the instinctual drives of the id to be satisfied, within the limits of societal expectations as represented by the superego. The ego is a person's power of reasoning. The superego is the conscience that results from internalizing the social values of one's parents and society, according to Anna Freud. The increase in instinctual drives during adolescence directly challenges the reasoning abilities and the powers of conscience of the individual. Open conflict breaks out between the id and superego, and the ego has trouble keeping the peace. If the ego takes the side of the id, "no trace will be left of the previous character of the individual and the entrance into adult life will be marked by a riot of uninhibited gratification of instinct" (Freud, 1946, p. 163). If the ego sides only with the superego, the id impulses are confined within the narrow limits prescribed for a child. Keeping instinctual forces suppressed requires constant expenditure of psychic energy, because defense mechanisms and other measures are used to hold the id in check. *If this id-ego-superego conflict is not resolved during adolescence, emotional disturbance results.*

Anna Freud described the methods of defense (the *defense mechanisms*) that the ego employs to remain in control. The ego denies, rationalizes, or projects the instincts on to others to allow the id to have its way. If conflict over behavior remains, anxiety may result, causing phobias and hysterical symptoms. The appearance of asceticism and intellectualism during adolescence is symptomatic of the mistrust of all instinctual impulses. The rise of neurotic symptoms and excessive inhibitions during adolescence may be a sign of the success of the ego and superego at the expense of the individual.

Anna Freud suggests, however, that *harmony among the id, ego, and superego is possible and does occur finally in most normal adolescents.* The superego needs to be developed during the latency period—but not to the extent that it inhibits the instincts too much, causing extreme guilt and anxiety. The ego needs to be sufficiently strong and wise to mediate the conflict (Freud, 1946).

ADOLESCENCE AND IDENTITY ACHIEVEMENT

One most important modification of Freud's theory of psychosexual development was outlined by Erik Erikson (1902–1994) as a result of findings of modern sociopsychology and anthropology. According to Erikson (1950, 1959), the chief psychosocial task of adolescence is the achievement of identity (Archer, 1990a,b; Bilsker & Marcia, 1991; Lavoie, 1994; Raskin, 1990; Rotheram-Borus, 1990a; Waterman, 1990).

Components of Identity

Identity has many components (Rogow, Marcia, & Slugoski, 1983)—*sexual, social, physical, psychological, moral, ideological,* and *vocational characteristics*—that make up the total self. Thus, individuals may be identified by their physical characteristics, looks, and build; by their biological gender, and enactment of gender roles; by their skills in social interaction and membership in groups; by their career choice and achievement; by their political alignment, religious affiliations, morals, values, and philosophies; and by their ethnic identity (Phinney & Alipuria, 1990), personality characteristics, psychological adjustment, and mental health. Identity is personal and individual: It is not only the "I," but also, socially and collectively, the "we" within groups and society (Hoare, 1991). Adolescents who are able to accept themselves and who have developed a positive identity are more likely to be mentally healthy than those who have a negative identity or do not like themselves.

Some components of identity are established before others (Dellas & Jernigan, 1990). Physical and sexual components of the self seem to be formulated earliest. Early adolescents are concerned with their body image and sexual identity. Later they become concerned about choosing a vocation and about moral values and ideologies. Similarly, they must deal with their social identities fairly early in their development.

Vocational, ideological, and moral identities are formulated gradually. After adolescents reach the formal operational stage of cognitive growth and development, they are able to explore alternative ideas and vocations in systematic ways. The exploration of occupational alternatives is the most immediate and concrete task as adolescents select their high school program and decide whether to continue their education after high school (Kroger, 1993). Political and religious ideologies are usually examined during late adolescence, especially during the college years, but they may be formulated over a period of many years of adulthood (Blustein & Palladino, 1991).

Gender differences are sometimes evident in the identity development process. They align

Achieving sexual identity is one of the psychosocial tasks of adolescence.

along the traditional division between interpersonal and ideological development. Some aspects of interpersonal identity development, such as dating and sexual roles, occur later from a larger proportion of men; and some aspects of ideological identity development, such as politics, occur later for a larger proportion of women (Pastorino et al., 1997). Identity development is viewed both as an

Living Issues

Identity and Sexual Orientation

One seldom-discussed component of identity is one's sexual orientation, which involves the primary source of sexual attraction and arousal, whether male or female. The following comments were made by a professor who has conducted a recent study of the experiences of gays, lesbians, and bisexuals during adolescence.

I just finished an ethnographic study of the experiences of gays, lesbians, bisexuals (gifted) during adolescence and found that almost all wondered about sexual orientation before they left elementary school, were convinced by grade 10, and came out only after age 18 (as they left home or during college.) Almost all experienced depression and suicidal ideation during adolescence. Most had felt in danger at some point, and a percentage of them at school. This study clearly showed that adolescents who were gay/lesbian/bisexual individuals were faced with risk—the most dangerous times seemed to be between grade 10 and age 18. For most, sexual orientation was never discussed by another adult in any meaningful way. As a former high school teacher, I was certainly aware of the preoccupation among most students with sexual orientation, creating much stress and anguish with all the teasing going on even from age 8 and on. Awareness of the phenomenon is there at very early ages these days, there is much talk about it in the schools, and there is much persecution of homosexuals because of prejudices and extreme negative feelings of some others towards them. (Anonymous)

individual process and as a reflection of the larger cultural milieu (Pastorino et al., 1997). Adolescents who have internalized values that they have accepted for themselves and on which they have developed a positive identity are more likely to be mentally healthy than those who have a negative identity or an identity that is not truly theirs, or who do not like themselves.

Initially, behavior is externally controlled; the person reacts to, or complies with, relative immediate situational demands and inducements from others. When introjection occurs, individuals internalize and represent the standards, goals, and values of significant others, including parents. Introjected values, however, may not be fully accepted as the person's own; behavior and actions are motivated internally by concerns about guilt, anxiety, and approval. Integration, in contrast, results when individuals assimilate and organize values and standards within their core sense of self and when the standards become personally valued and the person's actions are volitional and self-determined. Development of identity is related to self-determination, to the extent to which socially endorsed standards and regulatory processes have been internalized (Berzonsky, 1997).

Psychosocial Moratorium

Erikson invented the term **psychosocial moratorium** to describe a period of adolescence during which the individual may stand back, analyze, and experiment with various roles without assuming any one role. According to Erikson (1968), the length of adolescence and the degree of emotional conflict experienced by adolescents will vary among different societies. However, failure to establish identity during this time causes self-doubt and role confusion that may trigger previously latent psychological disturbances. Some individuals may withdraw or turn to drugs or alcohol to relieve anxiety. Lack of a clear identity and lack of personality integration can also be observed in the chronic delinquent (Muuss, 1988b).

Identity Statuses

In the mid-1960s, an extensive body of research had emerged and validated Erikson's psychological construct. Among the many studies of Erikson's concepts, those by James Marcia have been particularly influential (Marcia, 1966, 1976, 1989). Marcia built his model on three assumptions derived from

Adolescents may try out many roles before occupational identity is achieved.

Erikson's theory. *First*, formation of ego identity involves the establishment of firm commitments in such basic identity areas as a vocation or selection of a mate. *Second*, the task of forming identity demands a period of exploration, questioning, and decision making, a period called an identity crisis. *Third*, Western society fosters a period, a psychosocial moratorium, during which the adolescent may experiment with roles and beliefs so as to establish a coherent personal identity (Bilsker, 1992).

From these assumptions, Marcia formulated four identity statuses that are models of dealing with the identity issue characteristic of late adolescence (Marcia, 1980). The statuses are determined by whether there are established commitments and whether there has been a period of exploration and decision making.

The four identity statuses are as follows. **Identity achievement** is the most developmentally advanced status. The individual has gone through a period of exploration of alternatives and has made well-defined commit-

Psychosocial moratorium—socially sanctioned period between childhood and adulthood during which the individual is free to experiment to find a socially acceptable identity and role

Identity achievement—that state resulting from having gone through a crisis in the search for identity and having made a commitment

ments. A **moratorium** precedes identity achievement. Here the person is in the exploration period with commitments only vaguely formed. The word *moratorium* means a period of delay granted to someone who is not yet ready to make a decision or assume an obligation. Adolescence is a period of exploration of alternatives before commitments are made. **Foreclosure** refers to the individual who has undergone no, or very little, exploration and remains firmly committed to childhood-based values. Foreclosure subjects have not experienced a crisis, but they have made commitments to occupations and ideologies that are not a result of their own searching but that are ready-made and handed down to them, frequently by parents. Finally, **identity diffusion,** the least developmentally advanced of the statuses, comprises persons who, whether or not they have explored alternatives, are uncommitted to any definite directions in their lives (Marcia, 1987). Identity-diffused subjects have not experienced a crisis, nor have they made any commitment to a religion, political philosophy, sex role, occupation, or personal standards of behavior (Archer & Waterman, 1990). They have not experienced an identity crisis in relation to any of these issues, nor have gone through the period of searching, reevaluating, and considering alternatives. Diffusion is developmentally the most unsophisticated identity status, and it is usually a normal characteristic of early adolescence.

The identity statuses do not always develop in exact sequence. It was initially believed that a developmental progression would be the norm: Most adolescents would enter the identity crisis from the foreclosure status, moving into a moratorium phase, out of which the achievement status would be attained. Diffusion status during adolescence was seen as an aberration in this natural progression—hopefully, a transient one.

Three important variations from this developmental sequence have been observed. *First,* some individuals seem never to make the transition to the moratorium and identity achievement statuses, remaining firmly entrenched within the foreclosure status. *Secondly, a significant number of individuals enter adolescence in the diffusion status; some of these remain diffused. Third,* certain individuals who attain an achievement status appeared to have regressed to a lower status on follow-up years later (Marcia, 1989). The nature of such a regression to a developmentally prior status is puzzling. Such a regression suggests that *individuals may go through the developmental identity sequence more than once during a life-*

FOCUS

Identity and Personality

The latest research points to the fact that personality type is related to identity status (Clancy & Dollinger, 1993). Research with 190 young adults revealed the following:

1. *Identity-achieved* subjects scored higher than the typical student on extraversion and lower on neroticism, and thus appeared to be "emotionally adjusted" extroverts. Achievement subjects appeared to experience little negative affectivity.

2. *Moratorium and diffused* individuals appeared to be neurotic introverts who lacked conscientiousness. They were more prone to negative emotions and disagreeableness than were typical students.

3. *Foreclosed* subjects were strikingly low on openness. This study raises an interesting question: Does identity resolution influence one's personality, or does preexisting personality influence identity resolution? Actually, there seems to be truth in both possibilities. Such findings would suggest that although not all people may be "created" with equal opportunities to reach achievement status, their identity pathways will have major implications in terms of the kinds of persons they become. Even foreclosure individuals may change their status over a period of time (Kroger, 1995).

time. A person may have found identity achievement at a certain period of life, then later in life go through another moratorium stage, or a stage of identity diffusion, before identity achievement is again accomplished (Stephen, Fraser, & Marcia, 1992).

Ethnic Identity

Members of ethnic minority groups within a society are exposed to two cultures, their ethnic culture and the culture of the larger society. However, the ways in which they actually identify with and participate in these two cultures is far from consistent. Cultural adaptation is the process by which an individual from one culture, the culture of origin, develops competence in another culture, often the dominant majority culture. Early writings on acculturation of European immigrants generally assume that conflict was inevitable between one's ethnic culture and the largest society. It was assumed that these immigrants either had to reject the mainstream and remain embedded within their culture or to assimilate into the mainstream society and reject the ethnic culture. This view was based on a linear, or bipolar, model in which the two cultures were seen as occupying positions at opposite ends of a single continuum.

Moratorium—a period of standing back as one continues to search for an identity

Foreclosure—establishing an identity without going through a crisis or without searching; adopting an identity as prescribed by someone else

Identity diffusion—the situation of the individual who has not experienced an identity crisis nor explored meaningful alternatives in trying to find an identity

Living Issues

Women and Identity

As we have seen, Marcia postulated four potential outcomes of the identity development stage: foreclosure, achievement, moratorium, and diffusion. Some researchers have suggested that identity development is essentially the same regardless of gender (Streitmatter, 1993). Some researchers, such as Gilligan et al., (1988), suggest that the path of identity development for females may be different than that for males. Gilligan et al. argue that Erikson's theory (Erikson, 1959) embodied in the "Eight Stages of Man," is based on a developmental model that is biased to the point of excluding the developmental process of females. The essence of Gilligan's work is the idea that females tend to define themselves through their relationships with others, whereas males follow "traditional masculine" lines of self-definition according to their own occupational selves (Streitmatter, 1993). Identity development for females is quite different from that of males. Intimacy is a primary issue for females. Also, parental attachment plays a considerably more important role in the identity formation process for women than it does for men (Schultheiss & Blustein, 1994).

Still other researchers, especially Josselson (1987), used Marcia's identity research methods to examine how women proceed through Erikson's identity stage and to propose a theoretical model of women's identity development. In so doing, Josselson has sought to integrate opposing viewpoints. She conducted initial interviews with college seniors in the early 1970s and followed their life courses by scheduling second interviews with them in 1980 (Enns, 1991). Approximately one-quarter of Josselson's sample chose a traditional status that was originally identified by Erikson as a universal pattern for women's identity resolution. The pattern was foreclosure in which women often defined their identity in terms of the successful search for a mate. In general, they had high scores on measures of mental health but showed little evidence of a separate self-definition.

Women with an achievement identity status consciously tested their identities, built self-defined paths, and demonstrated flexibility in integrating needs for connection and self-assertion. For them, personal achievement and occupation often became the medium for expressing values that were formed in the context of supportive relationships.

Moratorium women gave up traditional, safe, relational anchors to try out exploratory identities and atypical roles, but they also had greater difficulty resolving identity issues. When they were in their thirties, moratorium women occasionally adopted a self-chosen achievement status, but they often experienced identity diffusion or opted to go back to a foreclosurelike status. Women who displayed characteristics associated with foreclosure or achievement showed higher levels of mental health than women in moratorium or diffusion statuses. Apparently, women were discouraged by social and family pressures to assume extended exploratory identities: If identity was not achieved by the end of the college years, pressure to return to the safety of childhood experiences was strong. For women, the social expectations, choices, self-reflection, conflict, ambivalence, and isolation associated with choosing nontraditional roles was costly.

Josselson's (1987) observation that significant relationships, rather than work, provided the primary anchor for women's identity is disquieting in light of the occupational changes that have emerged in the wake of the feminist movement.

Many women achieve a sense of identity by the end of college.

The more mainstream or acculturated that minority groups were, the less they could retain their ethnic culture, or vice versa. Bicultural individuals are seen as being midway between their ethnic and mainstream cultures (Phinney & Divich-Navarro, 1997; Rotheram-Borus, Lightfoot, Moraes, Dopkins, & LaCour, 1998).

Ethnic identity is the sum total of group members' feelings about those values, symbols, and common histories that identify them as a distinct group. Identity is based on one's perception that he or she shares a common heritage with a particular group (Bagley & Copeland, 1994). Ethnic identity development is an essential human need.

A health identity is related to self-esteem and enhances one's coping strategies for personal problem-solving abilities. It provides a sense of belonging and a sense of historical continuity for an individual (Smith, 1991). In high school and college students, ethnic identity appears to consist of a single factor, including three intercorrelated components: *positive ethnic attitudes, ethnic identity achievement,* and *ethnic behaviors* (Phinney, 1992). **Acculturation** is the adjustment of minority groups to the culture of the dominant group (Sodowsky, Lai, & Plake, 1991).

The problem for adolescents from immigrant or ethnic minority families is that the culture into which they were born is not always valued or appreciated by the culture in which they are raised (Feldman, Mont-Reynaud, & Rosenthal, 1992). In the early stages of forging an identity, ethnic minorities and immigrants often find conflict between their ethnic culture and the values of the larger society in which they live. The central question is the way in which minority ethnic groups relate to the dominant culture and to one another.

There are four possible ways in which ethnic group members can participate in a culturally diverse society. *Assimilation* is the outcome when ethnic group members choose to identify solely with the culture of the dominant society and to relinquish all ties to their ethnic culture. *Integration* is characterized by strong identification and involvement with both the dominant society's culture and the traditional ethnic culture. *Separation* involves exclusive focus on the cultural values and practices of the ethnic group and little or no interaction with the dominant society. *Marginality* is defined by the absence or loss of one's culture of origin and the lack of involvement with the dominant society.

Which type of participation contributes most to the positive development of self-esteem and identity in adolescence? One study of high school and college students from a diverse inner-city school sought to answer this question. The students were Asian, black, Hispanic, of mixed backgrounds, and whites (Phinney, Chavira, & Williamson, 1992). *The results indicate that among the four acculturation options, integration results in better psychological adjustment and higher self-esteem.* The positive relationship between self-esteem and endorsement of integration indicates that a more positive self-concept is associated with identification with both one's own culture and the mainstream culture. In contrast, endorsement of assimilation was found to be related to lower self-esteem, especially among the Asians and the foreign-born subjects. Thus, *giving up*

one's ethnic culture can have a negative impact on self-concept. The concept of separation (that ethnic groups should keep to themselves and not mix with mainstream society) was given little support by the students, with no differences among ethnic groups or by socioeconomic status. *Of all four alternatives, marginality—in which one identifies neither with one's own ethnic group nor with the dominant culture—is the least satisfactory alternative.*

Black Students

Black students tend to encounter more barriers to racial identity development than do white students. Moreover, *gifted black students may experience more psychological and emotional problems than do black students not identified as gifted.* The gifted minority children find themselves "between a rock and a hard place." One gifted black student said, "I had to fight to be gifted and then I had to fight because I am gifted." Another student said, "I am not white and I'm not black. I am a freak" (Ford, Harris, & Schuerger, 1993). Essentially, gifted black children confront conflicting values from which they must choose when forming a racial identity. Gifted black students sometimes consciously decide to underachieve academically so as not to be perceived as "acting white" or as selling out. High-achieving black students must assume a "raceless" persona if they wish to succeed academically. This racelessness occurs when they empty themselves of their culture, believing that the door of opportunity will open if they stand raceless before it. Raceless children adopt characteristics of the dominant culture (such as speaking standard English or straightening their hair). These problems suggest the need for counseling to help gifted black students cope with and appreciate their ability. Group multicultural counseling is especially helpful (Ford, Harris, & Schuerger, 1993).

Native American Students

Research on ethnic identity exploration and commitment among Native American adolescents reveals that school context has a marked effect on ethnic identity commitment. Quite probably, Native American adolescents in schools with a predominantly Native American student body had more Native American peers than did Native American adolescents in the school with a predominantly white student body. Ethnic minority adolescents who can use their ethnicity as a central reference identify more strongly with that ethnic minority group. They tend to have high ethnic pride

Acculturation—the adjustment of minority groups to the dominant group culture

Native Americans, like people from other ethnic groups, are torn by the conflict between cultures.

and are less likely to pursue other ethnic group contacts. Ethnic minority adolescents with lower ethnic identification are found to possess less ethnic pride and view themselves as having a more mainstream identity. The physical location of the Native American high school may have an important influence on ethnic identity exploration and commitment made by Native American adolescents. A school located centrally within reservation boundaries is often used by the Native American community at large for a variety of activities, usually cultural in some aspects. Furthermore, the surrounding community acts as a resource in classrooms in which Native American ethnic identity and culture is explored. Adolescents in a predominantly Native American school complex may have had a greater chance to make contacts with and benefit from traditional Native American activities (Lysne & Levy, 1997).

ADOLESCENCE AND DEVELOPMENTAL TASKS

Another contributor to the meaning of adolescence is Robert Havighurst (1972). The developmental task theory is an eclectic one, combining previously developed concepts. It has been widely accepted and considered useful in discussing adolescent development and education.

Meaning

Havighurst (1972) sought to develop a psychosocial theory of adolescence by combining consideration of societal demands with individuals' needs (Klaczynski, 1990). What society demands and what individuals need constitute **developmental tasks.** These tasks are the knowledge, attitudes, functions, and skills that individuals must acquire at certain points in their lives through physical maturation, personal effort, and social expectations. Mastery of the tasks at each stage of development results in adjustment, preparation for the harder tasks ahead, and greater maturity. Failure to master the developmental tasks results in social disapproval, anxiety, and inability to function as a mature person (Gavazzi, Anderson, & Sabatelli, 1993).

Eight Major Tasks

Havighurst (1972) outlined eight major psychosocial tasks to be accomplished during adolescence, as follows:

1. *Accepting one's physique and using the body effectively.* Adolescents become extremely self-conscious about the changes occurring in their bodies at puberty. Adolescents are concerned about body build, image, and appearance (Newell, Hammig, Jurich, & Johnson, 1990). They need to understand the patterns of growth of their own bodies, to accept their own physiques, to care for their health, and to use their bodies effectively in athletics, recreation, work, and everyday tasks (Havighurst, 1972).

2. *Achieving emotional independence from parents and other adults.* Some adolescents are too emotionally dependent on their parents; others are estranged from their parents. (Cherlin, Scabini, & Rossi, 1997) Part of the task of growing up is to achieve autonomy from parents and establish adult relationships with them at the same time (Brown & Mann, 1990; Daniels, 1990). Adolescents who are rebellious and in conflict with their parents need help in understanding the situation and learning how to improve it.

3. *Achieving a masculine or feminine social-sex role.* What is a woman? What is a man? What are women and men supposed to look like? How are they supposed to act? What roles are they required to play (Kissman, 1990)? Part of the maturing process for adolescents is to reexamine the changing sex roles of their culture and to decide what roles they can adopt (Havighurst, 1972; Nelson & Keith, 1990).

4. *Achieving new and more mature relations with age-mates of both sexes.* One of the

Developmental tasks—the skills, knowledge, functions, and attitudes that individuals have to acquire at certain points in their lives in order to function effectively as mature persons

One of the psychosocial tasks of adolescence is to achieve mature relations with age-mates of both sexes.

tasks of adolescents is to establish heterosocial friendships, as opposed to the same-sex friendships that are more prevalent in middle childhood (Verduyn, Lord, & Forrest, 1990). Maturing also means developing the social skills necessary to get along with others and to participate in social groups.

5. *Desiring and achieving socially responsible behavior.* This goal refers to sorting out social values and goals in our pluralistic society, which also includes assuming more responsibility for community and national affairs. Some adolescents are disturbed by the injustices, social inequities, and problems that they see around them. Some become radical activists; others work in quieter ways to make a difference; others simply refuse to act. Many adolescents struggle to find their niche in society in a way that gives meaning to their lives (Havighurst, 1972).

6. *Acquiring a set of values and an ethical system as a guide to behavior.* This goal includes the development, adoption, and application of meaningful values, morals, and ideals in one's personal life (Harding & Snyder, 1991; Zern, 1991).

7. *Preparing for an economic career.* Determining life goals, choosing a vocation, and preparing for that career are long-term tasks that begin at adolescence (Berzonsky, Rice, & Neimeyer, 1990; Green, 1990; Harding & Snyder, 1991; Steel, 1991).

8. *Preparing for marriage and family life.* The majority of youths consider a happy marriage and parenthood to be important goals in life. However, they need to develop the social skills, positive attitudes, emotional maturity, objective knowledge,

and empathetic understanding to make marriage work. This preparation and development begins in adolescence.

Havighurst feels that many modern youths have not found direction in their lives and therefore suffer from aimlessness and uncertainty. He says that during the first half of the twentieth century, the primary method of identity achievement (especially for boys) was through an occupation. Work was the focus of life. Today, however, many adolescents would say that expressive values have become more important. Identity is established through close, meaningful, and loving relationships with other persons.

ANTHROPOLOGISTS' VIEWS OF ADOLESCENCE

An anthropologist examines the kinds of influences that mold the child as she or he grows up. Anthropologists emphasize the importance of the social environment in determining the personality of the child. Because social institutions, economic patterns, habits, mores, rituals, and religious beliefs vary from society to society, culture is relative.

Developmental Continuity Versus Discontinuity

Anthropologists look at adolescence somewhat differently. *They generally reject age and stage theories of development, which say that children go through various stages of development at different ages.* Instead, anthropologists emphasize continuity of development. Margaret Mead said, for example, that Samoan children follow a relatively continuous pattern of growth with relatively little change from one age to the other. Children are not expected to behave one way and adults another. Samoans never have to abruptly change their ways of acting or thinking as they move from childhood to adulthood, so that adolescence as a transition from one pattern of behavior to another is practically nonexistent. This principle of continuity of development may be illustrated with three examples by Mead (1950).

First, the submissive role of children in Western culture is contrasted to the dominant role of children in primitive society. Children in Western culture are taught to be submissive, but as adults they are expected to be dominant. Mead (1950) showed that the Samoan child is not expected to become dominant on reaching adulthood after being taught submission as a child. On the contrary, the Samoan girl dominates her younger siblings and in turn is dominated by the older ones. The older she gets, the more dominating she becomes and the fewer girls who dominate her (the parents never try to dominate her). When she becomes an adult, she does not experience the conflict of dominance and submission that is found among adolescents in Western society.

Second, the nonresponsible roles of children in Western culture are contrasted to the responsible roles of children in primitive societies. Children in Western culture must assume drastically different roles as they grow up; they shift from nonresponsible play to responsible work and must do it rather suddenly. In contrast, children in primitive societies learn responsibility quite early. Work and play often involve the same activity. By "playing" with a bow and arrow, a boy learns to hunt. His youthful hunting "play" is a prelude to his adult hunting "work."

Third, dissimilarity of sex roles of children and adults in Western culture is contrasted to similarity of sex roles of children and adults in primitive cultures. In Western culture, infant sexuality is denied, and adolescent sexuality is repressed. When adolescents mature sexually, they must unlearn earlier attitudes and taboos and become sexually responsive adults. Mead indicates that the Samoan girl experiences no real discontinuity of sex roles as she passes from childhood to adulthood. She has the opportunity to experiment and become familiar with sex with almost no taboos (except against incest). Therefore, by the time maturity is reached, she is able to assume a sexual role in marriage very easily.

Cultural Influences

Anthropologists say that storm and stress during adolescence is not inevitable. For example, whether or not menstruation is a disturbing experience depends on its interpretation. One tribe may teach that the menstruating girl may dry up the well or scare the game; another tribe may consider her condition a blessing (a priest could obtain a blessing by touching her, or she could increase the food supply). A girl who is taught that menstruation is a curse will react and act differently from a girl who is taught that it is a positive thing. Therefore, the strains and stresses of pubescent physical changes may be caused by negative teachings of the culture and not by any inherited biological tendencies.

Generation Gap

Although anthropologists deny the inevitability of a generation gap (Mead, 1974), they describe the many conditions in Western culture that create such a gap. Those conditions include pluralistic value systems, rapid social change (Dunham & Bengtson, 1992), and modern technology that make the world appear too complex and too unstable to adolescents to provide them with a stable frame of reference. Furthermore, early physiological puberty and the prolongation of adolescence allow many years for the development of a peer-group culture in which adolescent values, customs, and mores may be in conflict with those of the adult world. Mead (1950) felt that parent-adolescent conflict and tension can be minimized by giving adolescents more freedom to make their own choices and to live their own lives, by requiring less conformity and less dependency, and by tolerating individual differences within the family. Also, Mead felt that youth can be accepted into adult society at younger ages. They should be allowed to have sex and to marry, but parenthood should be postponed. Adolescents should be given greater responsibility for community life. These measures would allow for a smoother, easier transition to adulthood by eliminating discontinuities in development.

CRITIQUE

What about the various perspectives on adolescence? Which views are most plausible? Each view adds something to a more complete understanding. Anna Freud made a significant contribution in her emphasis on sexual and psychic drives. Her explanation of the psychic disequilibrium of adolescents helps us understand possible causes of erratic behavior. It is important to remember, however, that not all adolescents go through a period of psychic disequilibrium. Some do, but the majority are not in turmoil, deeply disturbed, at the mercy of their impulses, or rebellious. A survey of 6,000 adolescents from 10 nations found few adolescents who were alienated from their parents. Only 7% said they thought their parents were ashamed of them or would be disappointed in them in the future (Atkinson, 1988).

Erikson's explanation of the adolescent's need for identity and the process by which identity is formed has had a marked influence on adolescent theory and research for years. Although Erikson discusses identity achievement as the principal psychosocial task of adolescence, he emphasizes that the process neither begins nor ends with adolescence. Rather it is a lifelong process.

Havighurst's outline of the developmental tasks of adolescence can help youth to discover some of the things they need to accomplish to reach adulthood. The outline can also help adults who seek to guide adolescents on their road to maturity.

Anthropologists have emphasized that there are few universal patterns of development of behavior, so that general conclusions about adolescents should be formulated to take into account the cultural differences. By making cultural comparisons, anthropologists enable us to see some of the positive and negative elements in each culture that help or hinder the adolescent. In our culture, it is evident from an anthropological point of view that adolescence is a creation, an increasingly prolonged period of transition from childhood to adulthood, during which the individual is edu-

cated and socialized to take his or her adult place in society. In urban, industrialized societies, the process of achieving adulthood is more complicated and takes longer than in primitive cultures. There is fear in the minds of some parents that their adolescents are "never going to grow up." As one father said, "My son is 25 years old and I'm still supporting him." This process does take a long time, especially when years of higher education are involved. Nevertheless, parents can play an important role in the preparatory process as long as they remember that the ultimate goal is mature adulthood.

One perspective of adolescence gives only a partial picture; after all, adolescents are biological creations who are psychologically and sociologically conditioned by the family, community, and society of which they are members. One must stand in many places and look from many points of view to develop the fullest understanding of adolescents (Mead, 1974).

Summary

1. Adolescence means to grow to maturity. Maturity is that age, state, or condition of life in which a person is fully developed physically, emotionally, socially, intellectually, and spiritually. Puberty is the age or period during which a person reaches sexual maturity. Pubescence is the whole period during which sexual maturation takes place. A juvenile is not yet considered an adult in the eyes of the law.

2. The transition to adulthood for some means to complete a series of events, such as getting married or finding a job. To others, it means developing certain psychological characteristics, such as independence.

3. Some tribes have specific initiation ceremonies, or rites of passage, to celebrate the transition from childhood to maturity.

4. G. Stanley Hall said that puberty is a time of upset, emotional maladjustment, and instability that corresponds to the transition of mankind from savagery to civilization.

5. Researchers today conclude that storm and stress are not inevitable consequences of adolescence. Psychological

turmoil may not be normal and ought to be treated.

6. Anna Freud characterized adolescence as a period of internal conflict, psychic disequilibrium, and erratic behavior. The disequilibrium is caused by the increase of instinctual urges (the id) at the time that sexual maturation takes place. The increase in the id presents a direct challenge to the ego and superego, which seek to curtail the id's expression. Only when the id-ego-superego conflict is resolved is psychic equilibrium restored. The ego employs defense mechanisms to protect itself, but excessive use of them is detrimental to the individual.

7. According to Erikson, the chief psychosocial task of adolescence is the achievement of identity. Identity has many components: sexual, social, vocational, moral, ideological, and psychological. Some aspects of identity are more easily formed than others.

8. According to Erikson, adolescence is a period of psychosocial moratorium during which the individual can try out various roles. The adolescent who fails in the search for identity will experience

self-doubt, role diffusion, and role confusion.

9. Marcia elaborated on Erikson's views of identity by outlining four identity statuses: identity achievement, moratorium, foreclosure, and identity diffusion.

10. Gilligan has suggested that the path of identity development for females may be different from that for males. Josselson found that some women at a foreclosure status defined their identity in terms of establishing significant relationships or in the successful search for a mate.

11. Ethnic identity is the subtotal of group members' feelings about those values, symbols, and common histories that identity them as a single group. Ethnic identity includes three components: positive ethnic attitudes, ethnic identity achievement, and ethnic behaviors.

12. There are four possible ways in which ethnic group members can participate in a culturally diverse society: through assimilation, integration, separation, and marginality.

13. Gifted black students have a special problem finding identity and belonging, both because they are black and because they are gifted. Native Americans are torn between conflicting cultures.

14. Havighurst outlined eight major psychosocial tasks that need to be accomplished during adolescence: accepting one's physique and using the body effectively, achieving new and more mature relations with age-mates of both sexes, achieving a masculine or feminine social-sex role, achieving emotional independence from parents and other adults, preparing for an economic career, preparing for marriage and family life, desiring and achieving socially responsible behavior, and acquiring a set of values and an ethical system as a guide to behavior.

15. Anthropologists challenge the basic truths of all age and stage theories of child and adolescent development. They say that in some cultures, children follow a relatively continuous growth pattern, with adult roles evolving as a continuation of the roles they learned as children. In our culture, particular roles are learned as children, and other roles as adults. This discontinuous development results in the creation of a period of adolescence during which roles have to be relearned.

16. Anthropologists also challenge the inevitability of the storm and stress of adolescence and of the generation gap.

17. No one view incorporates the total truth about adolescence. To understand adolescence, one must stand in many places and look from many points of view.

Key Terms

Acculturation   p. 291
Developmental tasks   p. 292
Foreclosure   p. 289
Identity achievement   p. 288
Identity diffusion   p. 289
Juvenile   p. 284

Maturity   p. 284
Moratorium   p. 289
Psychosocial moratorium   p. 288
Puberty   p. 284
Pubescence   p. 284

Discussion Questions

1. Think back to your adolescence. Was this a period of storm and stress and psychic conflict for you? Why, or why not?

2. Name as many rites of passage as you can that mark a transition from childhood into adulthood in our culture. Which one of these was most important to your growing up? Why?

3. Who was the most important person to you in your identity development? In what ways was that person most helpful?

4. Why do some people develop a negative identity? What can they do to form a more positive view of themselves? Which components of identity are most difficult to establish, and why?

5. In what identity stage are you now, according to Marcia's classifications? What problems are you experiencing in achieving an identity?

6. Do you feel that some women can find an acceptable identity primarily through marriage and motherhood? Explain.

7. Are you a member of an ethnic minority group? What are your chief problems in finding an identity?

8. Which one of Havighurst's developmental tasks was hardest for you when you were an adolescent? Explain.

9. What do you think of Mead's concepts of continuity and discontinuity of development? Is it possible to eliminate the discontinuity of development experi-enced by children in our culture? Explain.

10. When you were an adolescent, was there a generation gap between you and your parents? In what respects? Is there a generation gap between you and your parents now? Explain.

DANESI, M. (1994).   *Cool: The signs and meaning of adolescents*. Toronto: University of Toronto Press. Biological, social, psychological, linguistic, and cultural elements of the adolescent experience.

ERIKSON, E. H. (1968).   *Identity: Youth and crisis.* New York: Norton. A classic.

FELDMAN, S. S., & ELLIOTT, G. R. (Eds.). (1993). *At the threshold: The developing adolescent.* Cambridge, MA: Harvard University Press. Results of the Carnegie Foundation study of adolescent development in society.

FRANKEL, R. (1998).   *The adolescent psychic: Jungian & Winnicottian Perspectives.* London: Routledge. Summary of these perspectives.

HAUSER, S. J., POWERS, S. I., & NOAM, G. G. (1991).   *Adolescents and their families: Paths of ego development.* New York: Free Press. The developmental tasks of adolescents and their parents.

LEVY-WARREN, M. (1996).   *The adolescent journey, development, The process of development of identity.* Jason & Aronsom. Answers to questions from 6,000 teenagers in ten countries. Plenum Publishing Company

RICE, F. P. (1999).   *The adolescent: Development, relationships, and culture* (9th ed.). Boston: Allyn and Bacon. The author's comprehensive textbook.

STEINBERG, L. (1994).   *Crossing Paths.* New York: Simon & Schuster. How your child's adolescence triggers your own crisis.

Suggested Readings

http://www.piaget.org The Jean Piaget Society Weblinks, conferences, newsletter, publications and more on issues related to human knowledge and its' development.

Web Resources

Physical Development

Chapter 11

THE ENDOCRINE GLANDS AND HYPOTHALAMUS

An **endocrine gland,** as shown in Figure 11.1, is a gland that secretes **hormones** internally. Because the hormones are secreting into the bloodstream, they reach every cell of the body. However, each hormone has target organs that it influences, telling those organs what to do and when to act.

Only three glands of the endocrine system are discussed here: the *pituitary gland,* the *adrenal glands,* and the *gonads.* The *hypothalamus,* which is a part of the brain, is discussed here as well because it regulates the pituitary secretions.

Pituitary Gland

The **pituitary gland** is only about ½ inch long, weighs less than ½ gram (1/56 oz.), and is located in the base of the brain. Its primary identification is as a master gland producing hormones that regulate growth. The best known hormones secreted by the pituitary gland are discussed here along with their functions.

Gonadotropic hormones (GnRH) are secreted by the anterior pituitary gland and influence gonad (or sex gland) functioning. There are two gonadotropic hormones. **Follicle-stimulating hormone (FSH)** and **luteinizing hormone (LH)** stimulate the growth of egg cells in the ovaries and sperm in the testes. In the female, FSH and LH control the production and release of the feminizing hormone estrogen and of the hormone progesterone. Both are produced in the ovaries. In the male, LH controls the production and release of the masculinizing hormone testosterone by the testes (Rice, 1989b).

The growth hormone, referred to as **human growth hormone (HGH)** or somatotrophic hormone (SH), affects the overall growth and shaping of the skeleton. A deficiency causes dwarfism; an excess causes giantism.

The pituitary gland also secretes a lactogenic hormone, luteotropic hormone (LTH), that contains the hormone **prolactin,** which influences the secretion of milk by the mammary glands of the breast.

Gonads

The **gonads,** or sex glands, include the ovaries in the female and testes in the male. The ovaries in the female secrete a whole group of hormones known as **estrogens** that stimulate the development of the sexual organs themselves and of female secondary sexual characteristics, such as the growth of pubic hair and breasts, and the distribution of fat on the body.

The ovaries also secrete the female hormone **progesterone.** This hormone is produced following the rupture of the **ovum** from the ovarian follicle. When an egg cell is discharged from a follicle in ovulation, the remaining follicular cells multiply rapidly and fill the cavity. This new cell growth becomes the **corpus luteum** ("yellow body"), and it secretes progesterone during the later part of the menstrual cycle. If the ovum has not been fertilized, the corpus luteum disintegrates, and progesterone secretion ceases until the next cycle. Progesterone is of primary importance in preparing the uterus for pregnancy and for maintaining the pregnancy itself.

Under the stimulation of LH from the pituitary, the testes in the male begin the production of the androgenic hormone testosterone. This male hormone is responsible for the development of the male sex organs: the

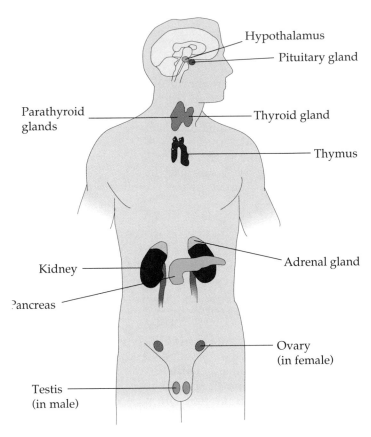

Hypothalamus

Pituitary gland

Parathyroid glands

Thyroid gland

Thymus

Kidney

Adrenal gland

Pancreas

Ovary (in female)

Testis (in male)

FIGURE 11.1   The endocrine glands.

From *Human Anatomy and Physiology*, 5th ed., by John W. Hole, Jr. Copyright © 1990 Wm. C. Brown Publishers, Dubuque, IA. All rights reserved. Reprinted by permission.

penis, scrotum, epididymis, prostate gland, and seminal vesicles. Both FSH and LH secretions from the pituitary gland stimulate the production and growth of sperm cells. Testosterone is also responsible for the development and preservation of masculine secondary sexual characteristics, including muscular and skeletal development, voice changes, and facial and body hair.

As the ovaries mature, ovarian estrogenic hormone levels increase dramatically and begin to show the cyclic variation in level during various stages of the menstrual cycle. The level of androgens in girls' bloodstreams increases only slightly. As the testes mature in the male, testosterone production increases dramatically, whereas the level of the estrogens increases only slightly. Figure 11.2 shows the increase in hormones at puberty. The ratio of the levels of the male to the female hormones is partly responsible for the development of male or female characteristics. When ratios are not normal in a growing child, deviations occur in the development of expected masculine or feminine physical traits. A male with an androgen deficiency and an excess of estrogens may evidence decreased potency and sex drive and an enlargement of the breasts. A female with an excess of androgens may grow body and facial hair, develop masculine musculature and strength, or develop an enlarged clitoris or other masculine characteristics.

Endocrine gland—ductless gland that secretes hormones

Hormones—biochemical substances secreted into the bloodstream by the endocrine glands

Pituitary gland—master gland at the base of the brain that produces growth hormones

Gonadotropic hormones (GnRH)—sex hormones secreted by the gonads

Human growth hormone (HGH)—pituitary hormone that regulates overall body growth

Prolactin—pituitary hormone that stimulates the secretion of milk by the mammary glands

Variations in physical growth.

Living Issues

Use of Steroids by Athletes

Attention has been focused in recent years on the use of **anabolic steroids** by athletes of all ages. A steroid is the male hormone testosterone. Fuller and LaFountain (1987) interviewed 50 athletes, ages 15 to 45 years, who admitted to steroid use. The athletes included both high school and college weight lifters, track stars, body builders, wrestlers, and football players. These athletes said that they used the drugs to be competitive.

> We should be allowed to take them because all those other countries take them . . . the women too. You have no choice if you want to compete in the big time (Fuller & LaFountain, 1987, p. 971).

Steroids increase performance, strength, and muscle mass, and reduce fat deposits and fluid retention by the body. They also increase verbal and physical aggression and hostility (Halpern & Udry, 1992). This increase may result in sexual aggression, fights and arguments with others, and beating up girlfriends or boyfriends.

The use of anabolic steroids causes serious physical harm. This medicine may affect blood sugar levels, especially in diabetics. Males have an increased risk of enlarged prostate or cancer of the prostate. Anabolic steroids may make these conditions worse by causing more enlargement of the prostate or more growth of a tumor already there. The drug may increase the level of cholesterol in the blood, thus causing heart or blood vessel disease. The drug may also cause kidney disease or liver disease; or in patients who already have too much calcium in the blood (in females), anabolic steroids may worsen this condition by raising the total amount of the calcium even more. If used during pregnancy, the drugs may cause the development of male features in the female fetus and premature growth and development of male features in the male fetus. Other side effects in females may include acne or oily skin, an enlarged clitoris, hoarseness, or deepening of the voice, irregular menstrual periods, unnatural hair growth, or unusual hair loss. Some males may experience enlargement of the breasts or breast soreness, frequent or continuing erections, frequent urge to urinate, acne, or unnatural hair growth. It is important to understand that long-term use may cause permanent body damage or become life-threatening (United States Pharmacopeia, 1996.)

Adrenals and Hypothalamus

The **adrenal glands** are located just above the kidneys. In the female, they produce low levels of both androgens (masculinizing sex hormones) and estrogen (feminizing sex hormone), and they partially replace the loss of ovarian estrogen after menopause. Although the adrenals secrete both androgens and estrogens in the male, androgens are produced in greater amounts.

The **hypothalamus** is a small area of the forebrain about the size of a marble. As the motivational and emotional control center of the brain, it regulates such functions as lactation (milk production), pregnancy, menstrual cycles, hormonal production, drinking, eating, and sexual response and behavior. Since it is the pleasure and pain center of the brain, electrical stimulation of the hypothalamus can produce sexual feelings and thoughts.

The hypothalamus plays an important role in hormonal production and regulation. A chemical called **gonadotropin-releasing hormone (GnRH)** is produced to control the secretion of FSH and LH from the pituitary.

MATURATION AND FUNCTIONS OF SEX ORGANS

Male

The primary male sex organs are the **penis, scrotum, testes, prostate gland, seminal vesicles, epididymis, Cowper's glands, urethra,** and **vas deferens.** They are depicted in Figure 11.3. Important changes occur in these organs during adolescence. The testes and scrotum begin to grow faster at about age 11½, with the growth becoming fairly rapid after age 13½, and slowing thereafter. These ages are averages. The testes increase 1½ times in length and about 8½ times in weight during this period. The penis doubles in length and girth during adolescence, with the most rapid growth taking

Gonads—the sex glands: testes and ovaries

Estrogens—female hormones produced by the ovaries and to some extent by the adrenal glands in both males and females

Progesterone—female sex hormone produced by the corpus luteum of the ovary

Ovum—egg cell

Corpus luteum—a new cell formed from an empty follicular cell and which secretes progesterone.

Adrenal glands—ductless glands that secrete androgens and estrogens, as well as adrenalin, in both men and women

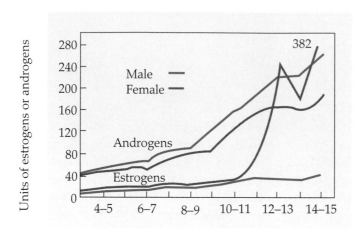

FIGURE 11.2   Hormone secretion with age.

place between ages 14 and 16. Both the prostate gland and the seminal vesicles mature and begin secreting semen. The Cowper's glands mature at this time and begin to secrete the alkaline fluid that neutralizes the acidity of the urethra and lubricates it for safe and easy passage of the sperm. This fluid appears at the opening of the urethra during sexual excitement and before ejaculation. Because this fluid contains sperm in about 25% of the cases examined, conception is possible whenever intercourse occurs, even if the male withdraws prior to ejaculation (McCary & McCary, 1982).

The most important change within the testes is the development of mature sperm cells, which occurs when FSH and LH from the pituitary stimulate their production. The total process of spermatogenesis, from the time the primitive spermatogonium is formed until it grows into a mature sperm, is about 10 days. After production, the sperm ripen and mature and are stored in the epididymis for as long as 6 weeks until ejaculated through the vas deferens and urethra or until absorbed into the body.

Adolescent boys may become concerned about **nocturnal emissions,** or so-called wet dreams. Kinsey, Pomeroy, and Martin (1948) reported that almost all men have erotic dreams, and most of them have dreams that culminate in orgasm. These dreams occur most frequently among males in their teens and twenties, but about half of all adult men continue to have them. Adolescents should be reassured that such experiences are normal, that no harm comes from them, and that they can be accepted as part of their sexuality.

Anxiety may be prevented if adolescents are prepared for nocturnal emissions before they occur (Paddac, 1987).

Female

The primary internal female sex organs are **vagina, fallopian tubes, uterus,** and **ovaries.** They are depicted in Figure 11.4. The external female sex organs are known collectively as the **vulva.** They include the clitoris, the labia majora (major or large outer lips), the labia minora (small inner lips), the mons veneris (mons pubis), and the vestibule (the cleft region enclosed by the labia minora). The **hymen** is a fold of connective tissue that partly closes the vagina in the virginal female. The **Bartholin's glands,** situated on either side of the vaginal orifice, secrete a drop or so of fluid during sexual excitement.

At puberty, the vagina increases in length, and its mucous lining becomes thicker and more elastic, and turns a deeper color. The inner walls of the vagina change their secretion from the alkaline reaction of childhood to an acid reaction in adolescence. The Bartholin's glands begin to secrete their fluids.

The **labia majora,** practically nonexistent in childhood, enlarge greatly, as do the **labia minora** and the **clitoris.** The **mons veneris** becomes more prominent through the development of a fatty pad. The uterus doubles in length showing a straight-line increase during the period from 10 to 18 years of age. The ovaries increase greatly in size and weight. They show a fairly steady growth from birth to age 8, some acceleration of growth from age 8 to the time of ovulation (age 12 or 13), and a very rapid increase after sexual maturity is reached. This is a result, no doubt, of the maturation of the follicles (the structures that produce the eggs) within the ovaries themselves. Every infant girl is born with about 400,000 follicles in each ovary. By the time she reaches puberty, this number has declined to about 80,000 in each ovary. Ordinarily, one follicle produces a mature ovum about every 28 days for a period of about 38 years, which means that fewer than 500 ripen during the woman's reproductive years (McCary & McCary, 1982).

Menstruation

The adolescent girl begins menstruating at an average age of 12 to 13 years, although she may mature considerably earlier or later (from age 9 to age 18 years is an extreme range). **Menarche** (the onset of menstruation) usually

Hypothalamus—small area of the brain controlling motivation, emotion, pleasure, and pain in the body

Gonadotropin-releasing hormone (GnRH)—controls the production and release of FSH and LH from the pituitary

Nocturnal emissions

Menarche—first menstruation

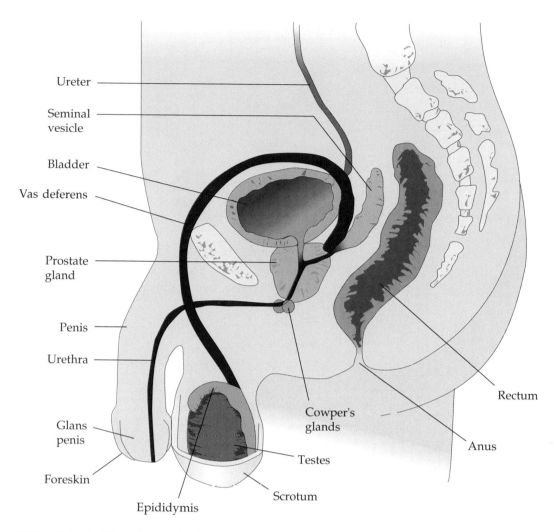

Ureter

Seminal
vesicle

Bladder

Vas deferens

Prostate
gland

Penis

Urethra

Glans
penis

Foreskin

Epididymis

Cowper's
glands

Testes

Scrotum

Rectum

Anus

FIGURE 11.3 The male reproductive system.

does not occur until maximum growth rates in height and weight have been achieved. Because of superior health care and nutrition, girls start menstruating earlier today than in former generations. The average age has decreased from age 14 in 1905 to about age 12½ today (Gilger, Geary, & Eisele, 1991). An increase in body fat may stimulate menarche, whereas vigorous exercise tends to delay it (Stager, 1988). The menstrual cycle may vary in length from 20 to 40 days, with an average of about 28 days. However, there is considerable difference in the length of the cycle when different women are compared, and any one woman may show widespread variations. A regular cycle is quite rare.

The exact time ovulation occurs is an important consideration. *The time of ovulation is ordinarily about 14 days before the onset of the next menstrual period*, which would be on the 12th day of a 26-day cycle and on the 16th day of a 30-day cycle. There is some evidence

that women have become pregnant on any one day of the cycle, including during menstruation itself, and that some women may ovulate more than once during a cycle, possibly because of the stimulus of sexual excitement itself.

Menarche can be a traumatic event for some girls who are not prepared ahead of time (Pillemer, Koff, Rhinehart, & Rierdan, 1987). Other girls are able to accept menstruation because they have been taught the basic facts (McGrory, 1990). The young girl's attitudes and feelings about menstruation are very important (Buchanan, 1991). The more knowledgeable girls are prior to menarche, the more likely they are to report a positive initial experience.

The onset of menstruation may involve a temporary period of disruption and emotional distance in family relationships. One study provides observational evidence that an increase in conflict engagement is associated

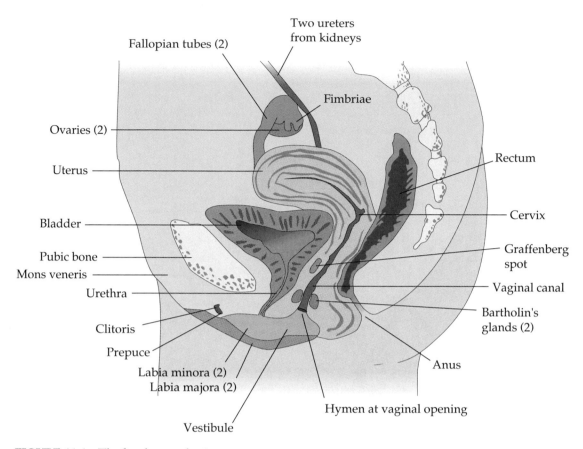

FIGURE 11.4   The female reproductive system.

with menarche, particularly in the mother-daughter dyad (Holmbeck & Hill, 1991a). These findings also imply that pubertal maturation increases emotional distance between youngsters and parents.

A further important question is: Why is there increased conflict and emotional distance shortly after the onset of certain pubertal changes? Direct hormonal and genetic factors may be involved. Just as important, the adolescent girl now sees herself as a more mature person and wants to be treated as such. This desire for more autonomy and freedom brings her into direct conflict with parents, who have trouble accepting her new status.

Factors in Timing

There are many factors that determine the timing of sexual maturation and development (Robertson et al., 1992). Heredity and ethnic factors certainly exert an influence. There is an association between maternal and daughter-aged menarche indicating that heredity has a marked influence (Graber, Brooks-Gunn, & Warren, 1995). Also, nutrition and medical care are important. Those children who receive adequate nutrition and medical care are more likely to mature earlier than those whose care and diet are inadequate. Socioeconomic status seems to have an influence, but the factors are mediated through poor nutrition and medical care received by those of low status. Diet and exercise, because they influence body weight and the percentage of body fat, are influential in the timing of pubertal development. In general, those who tend to be heavier with excess body fat mature earlier (Moffitt, Caspi, Belsky, and Silva, 1992).

The latest research indicates that levels of stress in the adolescent's life also have an influence on the timing of development. One reason is that stress increases the amount of food eaten, thereby increasing body weight, which, in turn, influences the onset of puberty. Therefore, those who are under the most stress tend to mature the earliest (Belsky, Steinberg, & Draper, 1991). For example, girls from divorced families or girls who report higher interparental conflict in the family are more likely to experience earlier menarche compared with girls from intact families (Wierson, Long, & Forehand, 1993).

PHYSICAL GROWTH AND DEVELOPMENT

Development of Secondary Sexual Characteristics

Sexual maturation at puberty also includes development of **secondary sexual characteristics.** These include the development of mature female and male body contours, voice changes, the appearance of body hair, and other minor changes.

The sequence of development for boys and girls is given in Table 11.1. The development of the **primary sexual characteristics** is also included in the table. Primary sexual characteristics are marked with an asterisk. The ages given are averages; actual ages may extend several years before and after these ages. (Akinboye, 1984; Westney, Jenkins, Butts, & Williams, 1984). The average girl matures about 2 years before the average boy, but the time of development is not always consistent. An early-maturing boy may be

Sexual maturation at puberty includes the development of secondary sexual characteristics.

TABLE 11.1	SEQUENCE OF DEVELOPMENT OF PRIMARY AND SECONDARY SEXUAL CHARACTERISTICS		

Boys	Age Span		Girls
Beginning growth of testes, scrotum, pubic hair	11.5–13	10–11	Height spurt begins Slight growth of pubic hair
Some pigmentation, nodulation of breasts (later disappears)			Breasts, nipples elevated to form "bud stage"
Height spurt begins			
Beginning growth of penis*			
Development of straight, pigmented pubic hair	13–16	11–14	Straight, pigmented pubic hair
Early voice changes			Some deepening of voice
Rapid growth of penis, testes, scrotum, prostate, seminal vesicles*			Rapid growth of vagina, ovaries, labia, uterus*
			Kinky pubic hair
First ejaculation of semen*			Age of maximum growth
Kinky pubic hair			Further enlargement, pigmenta-
Age of maximum growth			tion, elevation of nipple, areola
Beginning growth of axillary hair			to form primary breasts
			Menarche*
Rapid growth of axillary hair	16–18	14–16	Growth of axillary hair
Marked voice change			Filling out of breasts to form
Growth of beard			adult conformation, secondary
Indentation of frontal hair line			breast stage

Note: Primary sexual characteristics are marked with an asterisk.

Primary sexual characteristics—changes that involve the sex organs at sexual maturation

Secondary sexual characteristics—changes in the body at sexual maturation that do not involve the sex organs

younger than a late-maturing girl. The mean age for the first ejaculation of semen is 13.7 years. The mean age of menarche is 12.5 years. However, the age of sexual maturity extends over such a wide range (ages 9 to 18 are not unusual) that any age within the range should be considered normal.

Growth in Height and Weight

A growth spurt in height begins in early adolescence, accompanied by an increase in weight and changes in body proportions. The combined data from longitudinal studies of individual adolescents provide a composite picture of growth trends in groups of children.

Boys grow fastest in height and weight at approximately 14 years of age; girls grow fastest at approximately 12 years of age, as shown in Figure 11.5 (Tanner, 1962, 1972). Because girls start to mature earlier, between the ages of 12 and 14 they average slightly taller than boys, and between the ages of 10 and 14 girls are heavier than boys. Whereas girls have reached 98% of adult height at 16¼ years, boys do not reach 98% of their adult height until 17¾ years. These rates vary for different individuals.

One of the most important factors in determining the total mature height of the individual is *heredity* (Gertner, 1986). Short parents tend to have short children; tall parents tend to have tall children. *Nutrition* is the most important environmental factor (Tanner, 1970). Children who receive better diets during the growth years become taller adults than do less well-nourished children. The age when sexual maturation begins also affects the total height finally achieved. Girls and boys who are early maturers tend to be shorter as adults than those who are late maturers. The reason is that a late maturer has a longer time to grow before the sex hormones stop the pituitary from stimulating further growth.

Futhermore, the *growth achieved before puberty is of greater significance to total adult height than is the growth achieved during puberty.* The adolescent growth spurt contributes, in absolute terms, relatively little to the postadolescent skeletal dimensions and only moderately to strength and weight.

The total process of growth is speeding up. Children and adolescents today experience the growth spurt earlier, grow faster, attain a greater total adult height, and attain this height at an earlier age than did children and adolescents 60 or 70 years ago.

Height appears to be an important physical attribute. In the social realm, for example, being short poses some definite handicaps for males in dating relationships. Mate selection seems to rest on the male-taller principle. Among males, height is a factor in occupational opportunities, and there is evidence that this factor extends to later job advancements for both males and females. Moreover, there is a financial advantage in being taller. Taller people are started at higher salaries than shorter people.

The advantages of height begin early. It has been shown that smaller schoolchildren are held back a grade more often than are their taller counterparts. In addition, self-ratings of perceived confidence have been found to be related to height in adolescence. Thus, height appears to be a physical attribute that has many ramifications across a person's lifespan (Hensley, 1998).

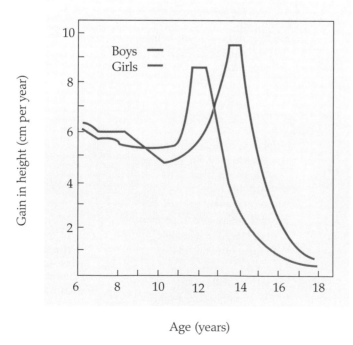

FIGURE 11.5   Increase in height.

From *Growth at Adolescence*, 2nd. ed., by J. M. Tanner (1962). Courtesy of Blackwell Science Ltd., UK.

EARLY AND LATE MATURATION

Figure 11.6 shows the considerable variations in stage of physical development at a given age for each sex. Intensive investigations have been made on the effect of early or

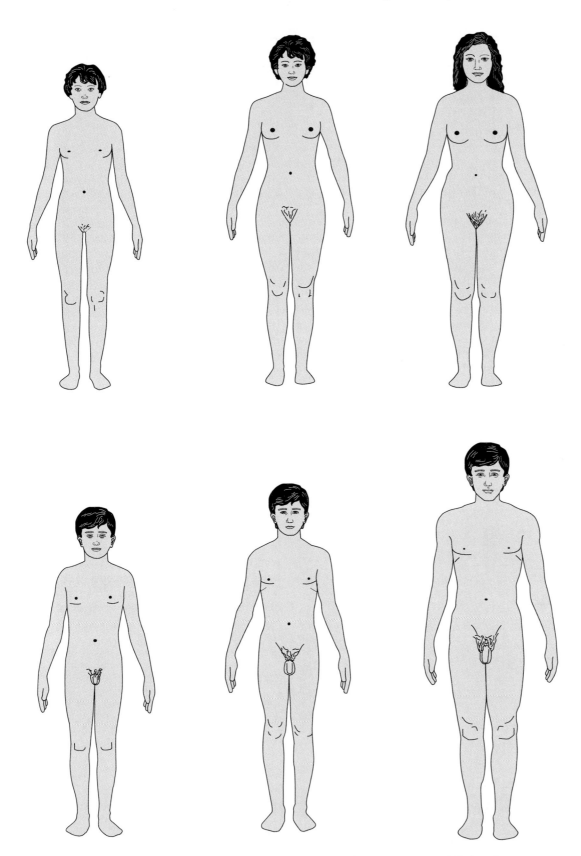

FIGURE 11.6   Variations in pubescent development. All three girls are 12¾ years, and all three boys are 14¾ years of age, but in different stages of puberty.

late physical maturation on psychological and social adjustments. The results of these studies are important for understanding adolescents who differ from the norm in the timing of their development.

Early-Maturing Boys

Because early-maturing boys are large for their age, more muscular, and better coordinated than late-maturing boys, they enjoy both athletic and social advantages. They are better able to excel in competitive sports. Their superior development and athletic skills enhance their social prestige and position. They participate more frequently in extracurricular activities in high school. They are often chosen for leadership roles; their peers tend to give them greater social recognition by appointing them to positions of leadership in school. They tend to show more interest in girls and to be popular with them because of their adult appearance and sophisticated social interests and skills. Early sexual maturation may thrust them into early heterosexual relationships.

Adults, too, tend to favor early-maturing boys by rating them as more physically attractive, better groomed, and more masculine

Acne—pimples on the skin caused by overactive subaceous glands

than late-maturing boys. However, adults tend to expect more of them in terms of adult behavior and responsibilities, thus giving early-maturing boys less time to enjoy the freedom that comes with childhood.

Early-Maturing Girls

Girls who mature early are at a disadvantage during their elementary-school years. Because they are taller and more physically developed, they tend to feel self-conscious and awkward. They enjoy less prestige at this age than do prepubertal girls (Alsaker, 1992b).

However, early-maturing girls come into their own socially by the time they reach junior high and high school age. They tend to look grown up and are envied by other girls because of their looks. They also begin to attract the attention of older boys and to start dating earlier than normal (Phinney, Jensen, Olsen, & Cundick, 1990). However, parents may begin to worry because of their daughters' emerging heterosexual interests and strive to curtail their social activities. The girls may find themselves emotionally unequipped to deal either with sexual enticement or with sophisticated social activities. Early maturation does lead to increased sexual experience at younger ages (Flannery, Rowe, & Gulley, 1993). Parental restriction and outside pressures may create stress, so for some this is a period of upset and anxiety. Nevertheless, usually by the time early-maturing girls have reached 17 years of age, they score higher on tests of total personal and family adjustments, have more positive self-concepts, and enjoy better personal relations than do later maturers. However, the net positive effect of early maturation does not seem to be as pronounced for girls as for boys.

Late-Maturing Boys

Late-maturing boys suffer a number of social disadvantages and may develop feelings of inferiority as a result. At age 15 they may be 8 inches shorter and 30 pounds lighter than early-maturing males, so that they may have less strength and show poorer motor performance, coordination, and reaction time than those who mature earlier. Because physical size and motor coordination play an important role in social acceptance, later maturers may develop negative self-perceptions. They have been characterized as less popular; less well-groomed; less attractive physically; more restless and affected; bossy and rebellious against their parents; and as being dependent,

---

Living Issues

The Problem of Acne

At the onset of puberty, because of an increase in the secretion of androgens in the bloodstream, the glands of the skin increase their activity. Three kinds of skin glands cause problems for the adolescent:

1. *Apocrine sweat glands,* located in the armpits and in the mammary, genital, and anal regions.

2. *Merocrine sweat glands,* distributed over most of the skin surfaces of the body.

3. *Sebaceous glands,* oil-producing glands of the skin.

After puberty, the apocrine and merocrine sweat glands secrete a fatty substance causing body odor. The sebaceous glands develop at a greater speed than the skin ducts through which they discharge their skin oils. As a result, the ducts may become plugged and turn black as the oil oxidizes and dries on exposure to the air, creating a blackhead. This in turn may become infected, causing a pimple or **acne** to form. The acne may be fairly mild with spontaneous remission occurring. Deep acne requires medical management to prevent scarring. A variety of treatment options are available.

with feelings of inadequacy and rejection. They often become self-conscious and withdraw because of their social rejection.

Late-Maturing Girls

Late-maturing girls of junior high or senior high school age are often socially handicapped. Slow-maturing girls, as a group, have less positive views of their physical attractiveness and of their relations with male peers (Rodriguez-Tome, Bariaud, Zardi, Delmas, Jeanvoine, & Szylagyi, 1993). They look and are treated like "little girls." They may not get invited to boy-girl parties and social activities. One study in New York City showed that those who first menstruated at ages 14 to 18 tended to be late-daters. They are often jealous of their friends who are more developed, but they have much in common with normal-maturing boys and look on them as friends. However, their activities reflect the interests of those of younger age groups with whom they spend their time. One advantage for late-maturing girls, compared with those who develop early, is that they may not be criticized by parents and other adults. The chief disadvantage for late-maturers seems to be the temporary loss of social status because of their relative physical immaturity.

BODY IMAGE AND PSYCHOLOGICAL IMPACT

Physical Attractiveness

Physical attractiveness is important in several ways. It affects the adolescent's positive self-esteem and social acceptance (Koff, Rierdan, & Stubbs, 1990; Thornton & Ryckman, 1991). Also, it affects personality, interpersonal attraction, and social relationships. Attractive adolescents are thought of in positive terms: intelligent, desirable, successful, friendly, and warm (Lerner et al., 1990). Partly as a result of differential treatment, attractive adolescents appear to possess a wider variety of interpersonal skills, to be better adjusted socially, and to have higher self-perceptions and healthy personality attributes (Cash & Janda, 1984).

As a result, many adolescents develop concern over physical appearance (appearance anxiety), especially if they have had negative social experiences in childhood and early adolescence (Keelan, Dion, & Dion, 1992). One study of sixth-grade male and female adolescents from Pennsylvania revealed that

those who differed in physical attractiveness were also expected to differ in peer and parent relations, classroom behaviors, and self-perceptions. Adolescents who were higher in physical attractiveness tended to have more favorable ratings by parents, peers, and teachers than adolescents who were lower in physical attractiveness. This is one of the reasons why adolescents give so much attention to how they look (Lerner et al., 1991).

There is a definite link between body esteem and self-esteem. Adolescents who feel positive about their appearance tend to have high global self-worth. Conversely, those with high global self-worth tend to have positive feelings about their appearance and their weight. There is a close interdependence of global self-worth and various dimensions of body esteem (Mendelson, White, & Mendelson, 1996).

Concepts of the Ideal

Research with both adults and adolescents has established that dissatisfaction with one's physical appearance, often termed body image dissatisfaction, is widespread in our society (Wood, Becker, & Thompson, 1996). Adolescents' self-appraisals of their physical attractiveness are determined partly by comparing themselves with other persons around them. One study showed that self-appraisals were more favorable after viewing an unattractive same-sex target than after viewing an attractive same-sex target (Brown, Novick, Lord, & Richards, 1992). Adolescents are influenced by the concepts of the ideal build that are accepted by our culture (Cok, 1990). Most adolescents would prefer to be of medium build (Ogundari, 1985). Adolescents who are tall and skinny are unhappy with their builds, as are those who are short and fat. Because Western culture overemphasizes the importance of being slim, the obese adolescent female is especially miserable (Bozzi, 1985; Lundholm & Littrell, 1986). It is partly because of this obsession with slimness that **anorexia nervosa** and **bulimia** develop among adolescents (Grant & Fodor, 1986). If a girl does not have a slim figure, she is less likely to have dates. Social rejection is hard to live with. Therefore, self-satisfaction and self-esteem are closely related to acceptance of the physical self (Littrell & Littrell, 1990). In general, high school females evidence higher levels of body dissatisfaction than middle school females, indicating that body dissatisfaction increases with age (Phelps, Johnston, Jimenez, Wilczenski, Andrea, & Healy, 1993).

Anorexia nervosa—eating disorder characterized by an obsession with food and being thin

Bulimia—eating disorder characterized by bingeing and purging

Studies of males provide further proof of the social importance of possessing an average physique and of physical attractiveness. Men with muscular body builds are more socially accepted than those with other types of builds (Tucker, 1982). Tall men with good builds are considered more attractive than short men (Feingold, 1982). College-age men with muscular builds are more likely to feel comfortable and confident in interacting with others than those who are skinny or obese (Tucker, 1983). Hensley (1994) found that tall males were at a distinct advantage in attracting dates; however, if males were taller than 6 feet, the height advantage seems to diminish. In another study, adolescents who rated themselves as unattractive were also likely to describe themselves as lonely (Moore & Schultz, 1983).

Sex Education of Adolescents

Goals

The onset of puberty and the changes that take place in the body, along with developing sexual attitudes and interests, awaken adolescents to the need to begin to understand the subject of human sexuality. There are a number of goals in the sexual education of adolescents. *The first goal is to develop knowledge and understanding about the bodily changes that are taking place.* Adolescents need to understand that each person matures at his or her own rate and that the development of girls is different from that of boys. Adolescents need to prepare for these changes because—without adequate preparation—the onset of menstruation, or of ejaculation by males, can be upsetting experiences (Adegoke, 1992). By developing adequate knowledge of the changes that take place, adolescents can not only prepare for these changes but also welcome them and learn how to adjust to them.

Sex education of adolescents also ought to include basic facts about human reproduction and the process of reproduction itself. Actually, the time to give the basic facts about human sexuality is prior to puberty. Adolescents need to know basic facts about conception, pregnancy, and childbirth. They need to know *the process of human sexual response and expression and the role of human sexual expression in their lives.* They need to know the *basic facts about contraception and birth control and how to prevent conception,* along with basic *information about sexually transmitted diseases, especially AIDS.*

But sex education involves more than developing objective knowledge and understanding, important as that may be. *A second goal is to develop adolescent sexual health.* This includes not only physical health but emotional and psychological health as well. Adolescent sexual health is based on esteem and respect for oneself and for other people of both sexes, embracing the view that both males and females are essentially equal, though not necessarily the same. Sexually healthy adolescents take pleasure and pride in their own developing bodies. As they mature, they have an increasing ability to communicate honestly and openly to persons of both sexes with whom they have a close relationship. They grow to feel and understand that their sexuality is not a thing apart but an integral part of their total lives. They accept their own sexual desires as natural but to be acted on with a constraint that takes into account their own values and goals as well as those of significant others. This view of adolescent sexuality includes being sexually responsive and sexually responsible. It does not include the concept that healthy adolescent sexuality involves complete freedom to behave as one wishes so long as contraceptives, including condoms, are used and so long as this behavior is in private with consenting partners. Imposing some constraints on sexual freedom does not necessarily mean unhealthy adolescent sexuality. As a matter of fact, healthy adolescent sexuality is impossible without some constraints (Chilman, 1990).

Another important goal of sex education of adolescents is the prevention of unwanted pregnancy. The incidence of teenage sexual involvement is at an all-time high, producing almost 1 million pregnancies to United States' teenagers each year, most of them unplanned and unwanted. This fact poses a major problem in the lives of adolescents themselves, as well as for society. Sex education ought to include adolescent pregnancy prevention, both through the teaching of responsible sex behavior and by teaching basic facts about contraception and birth control (Christopher & Roosa, 1990).

The rapid increase in AIDS created a monumental health crisis. Although the number of AIDS cases among adolescents has remained relatively low compared with those of older adults. 13- to-24-year-olds who contract HIV through heterosexual contact represent the most rapidly increasing subpopulation of AIDS cases. In 1990, the incidence of AIDS among adolescent women increased by over 67%. AIDS now ranks among the leading causes of death among young people between the ages of 15 and 24. Given the long incubation period prior to the onset of AIDS, many more individuals may be actually becoming infected with HIV during the teens and early twenties and developing AIDS at later ages. The high incidence rates of AIDS are seen in the late twenties and the thirties age groups (Hutchinson & Cooney, 1998). *In response to this crisis, sex education programs for adolescents should provide information about AIDS and about changing AIDS-related behavior.* Such education means teaching the basic facts about AIDS and other sexually transmitted diseases, and trying to get adolescents to adopt behavioral changes that will minimize their risk. Sex education is designed to increase the number of adolescents willing to abstain from sexual intercourse until they are ready to settle down with a permanent partner. It also means that they need to learn to spend a longer time getting to know new partners before engaging in sexual activity. It also means decreasing their number of sex partners so that the possibility of AIDS transmission is minimized. And, lastly, it means that those who are sexually active need to increase their use of condoms as a means of preventing the transmission of AIDS itself (Baldwin, Whiteley, & Baldwin, 1990; Croft & Asmussen, 1992).

Only a minority of parents do a good job of educating their adolescents about sex.

The Parents' Role

The majority of research studies indicate that adolescents are receiving their information about sexuality primarily from peers (Brock & Jennings, 1993; Moran & Corley, 1991). Although increasing numbers of adolescents are receiving information from sex education programs in the schools, the research does not indicate that increasing numbers of parents are providing information themselves. If sex education belongs in the home, then certainly many parents are not assuming their responsibility. There are a number of reasons for this avoidance. *Some parents are too embarrassed to discuss the subject, or they deal with it in negative ways.* They have been brought up to feel uncomfortable whenever the subject of sex comes up. As a result, they are not able to give their children positive attitudes and feelings, or the messages they teach are negative ones that interfere with sexual satisfaction. In general, those parents who were able to have personal talks with their teens about many subjects are the ones who report more frequent communication about a particular sexual topic (Raffaelli, Bogenschneider, & Flood (1998).

Parents also have difficulty overcoming the incest barrier between themselves and their children. The taboo on parent-child sex behavior may be so strong that it is especially difficult for parents to communicate with adolescents about sex. One study showed that parent-daughter communication was more wide-ranging than parent-son communication for each type of sexual discussion. Gender differences were most pronounced for factual and moral discussions—that is, communication that was most likely to transmit sexual information and values directly. Sons were disadvantaged compared with daughters in that they had less communication within the family, less opportunity to discuss sexuality with the same-sex parent, and less discussion of topics likely to teach family values and norms about sexual behavior. Also, sons reported greater discomfort with sexual discussions within the family than did daughters (Nolin & Petersen, 1992).

Another study examined parent-adolescent communication about ten sex-related topics in a sample of 907 Hispanic and black 14- to 16-year-olds. The openness of communication, parent-adolescent agreement about communication of topics, and differences by gender and ethnicity were also examined. Adolescents of both sexes were more likely to report discussions with mothers than with fathers, and parents were more likely to discuss any of the ten topics with an adolescent of the same gender than of the opposite gender. Consistent research among white samples and with mothers of black and Hispanic samples revealed that mothers were the primary parental communicators about sexual topics (Miller, Kotchick, Dorsey, Forehand, & Ham (1998).

Some parents are uninformed and do not know how to explain to their children. Many parents have not received objective sex information themselves. If they don't understand the basic facts about the human body and about reproduction, how can they transmit these facts to their children?

Many parents are afraid that knowledge will lead to experimentation, so that they do not tell their children because they want to keep the children innocent. However, there is no evidence to show that sexual knowledge, per se, leads to sexual experimentation. There is a lot of evidence to show that it is ignorance—not knowledge—that leads to trouble.

Other parents tell too little too late. The time to begin sex education in the home is during the preschool years. I believe that children ought to have all of the basic facts about human reproduction and human sexuality before they reach puberty. Then, during puberty, parents can concentrate on helping to develop positive attitudes and feelings and in dealing with relationships.

Some parents set a negative example at home. It's not just the words parents use that are important; it is also the lives they lead, the example they set. What parents do speaks louder than what they say. One of the most helpful things that parents can do is to back responsible programs of sex education in their schools. Certainly, if parents aren't able to do the task themselves, they need to encourage professionals to help them with it.

The School's Role

Nationwide surveys indicate that about 85% of parents favor sex education in the schools (Kenney, Guardado, & Brown, 1989). Because so many parents do an inadequate job and adolescents need scientific, reliable sources of information, public schools have a real responsibility. There are several reasons why the public schools need to become involved:

1. *Family life and sex education are natural parts of numerous courses already offered to adolescents.* Certainly, sex education ought to be a part of biology classes or health education classes. Home economics classes can deal with parenting relationships, preparation for

The school has an important role to play in the sex education of youth.

marriage, and child care. Social studies courses certainly need to focus on the family as the basic social unit and on such problems as sexually transmitted diseases, early marriage, or divorce. Discussions of sex and sexual behavior are hard to avoid in courses in literature. Even the Bible as literature contains a sexual aspect. Therefore, if existing courses are taught properly and honestly, sex education will have a place in many of them.

2. *Preparing youth for happy marriage and responsible parenthood is an important goal.* School does not prepare youth for this goal as well as for a vocation. Is school preparing students for living as well as for making a living?

3. *The school, as the professional educational institution, can be equipped to do a fine job.* Teachers can be trained, curricula can be developed, and the school can provide necessary resources once the needs are established.

4. *The school is the only social institution that reaches all youth;* therefore, it has a unique opportunity to reach the youth who need sex education the most. Parents who are uneducated themselves can't teach their children, but these children, by and large, attend the public schools where they can be exposed to proper programs of sex education. Some community agencies—such as churches and youth organizations—reach only a fraction of youth. All youth attend public school up to a certain age. It's the school alone that can reach these youth.

5. *Increasing numbers of schools are trying to assume a major responsibility in sex education.* In 1986, Surgeon General C. Everett Koop called for sex education in schools beginning as early as the third grade. He felt that the lives

Education for Abstinence

Recognizing the seriousness and complexity of the teenage pregnancy problem and the problem of increased AIDS transmission, a number of programs have been developed to try to prevent adolescent pregnancy by teaching abstinence. Girls' Clubs of America developed a comprehensive model consisting of two components. The program was designed for 12- to 14-year-old girls. The program's two components were Will Power/Won't Power and a program entitled Growing Together. The Will Power/Won't Power program addresses the social and peer pressures that lead women into early sexual behavior and focuses on building skills that help young teens deal with these issues. This component was offered in cycles of six sessions.

Growing Together is designed to enable parents and daughters to communicate comfortably with each other about human sexuality. This component included five sessions, the first of which was for parents only.

What were the results of the programs? *In the case of Growing Together, nonparticipants were two-and-one-half times as likely as the participants to initiate sexual intercourse during the year being studied.* Factors such as age, religion, race, and having relatives or friends were taken into consideration. The weight of evidence indicated that participation in Growing Together delayed the initiation of sexual intercourse among these young teens.

In the case of Will Power/Won't Power, *those who participated in the program for the longest period of time were less likely to initiate sexual intercourse than those who participated in the program for a lesser period of time.* Those who participated for shorter periods were more than three times as likely to initiate sexual intercourse as those who par-

ticipated for a longer time (Postrado & Nicholson, 1992).

In another study, the effects of three abstinence-emphasis sex education programs on student attitudes toward sexual activity were evaluated. The programs were administered to seventh- and tenth-grade students in three school districts in the state of Utah. There were three types of programs. The Sex Respect program was presented to students in an urban school district. Teen Aid was taught to suburban students. Values and Choices was presented to students in a rural school district. Socioeconomic statistics showed all districts to be relatively representative of the Utah population. *Findings indicate that all three programs increased abstinence values,* with the Sex Respect producing the most attitude change. The findings indicate that junior high students were more positive than were senior high students in rating the three abstinence programs. This information is important to educators in determining the age at which to initiate sex education curriculum. Apparently, younger students are influenced more favorably than older students. Also, the females were more positive in rating the programs than males. All the teachers who presented the programs were given favorable ratings.

One finding focused on individual differences and stated that previous sexual behavior (virginity status) and knowledge (informed or naive) would influence student responses to the abstinence program. The findings indicated that virgin-naive students rated the programs most favorably. The researchers concluded that sex education programs that promote abstinence can be effective in producing a positive attitude change towards abstinence, but females have a more positive attitude towards abstinence than

do males. Also, although the age of the students must be considered, both high school and junior high students will respond. *The results are interpreted as providing support for the feasibility of introducing abstinence-emphasis sex educational programs into the public school curriculum* (Olsen et al., 1992; Olsen et al., 1991).

Another approach to education for abstinence is offered by the *Postponing Sexual Involvement Program (PSI)*, which strongly urges teens to postpone having sex. However, the class also includes information about reproduction, sexually transmitted diseases, and contraceptives, so that teens who do become sexually active can protect themselves from disease and pregnancy. The program is effective in helping teens delay initial sexual intercourse. Eighth-grade participants who had not had sexual intercourse prior to the program were significantly more likely to postpone having coitus at the end of the ninth grade than those who did not participate in the program at all (St. Pierre, Mark, Kaltreider, & Aikin, 1995). Whether the increase in abstinence values resulted in actual abstaining from sexual intercourse depended on the strength of the values and the individual person.

Other programs report both knowledge and attitude changes that are supportive of sexual abstinence, but with no changes in sexual activity. The programs that are most effective in reducing adolescent pregnancy are those that not only emphasize abstinence but also offer the alternative of effective contraception for those who are sexually active. Such programs include classroom presentations, discussion groups, individual counseling, and an after-class school clinic that provides free education and intervention, medical examinations, and contraceptives (Christopher & Roosa, 1990).

of our young people depend on schools' fulfilling their responsibility. The states responded quickly. By the late 1980s, many states required schools to provide instruction about AIDS and other STDs. Some of these states also required instruction in sex education. Since 1998, the Centers for Disease Control and Prevention (CDCP) have provided financial and technical assistance to state and local education agencies, national organizations, and other institutions to improve HIV education in schools. As of December 1997, 19 states and the District of Columbia had established policies that required schools to provide sex education, and 34 states and the District of Columbia had mandated instruction about HIV, AIDS, and other STDs. Some states appear to encourage only limited instruction, however. Twenty-three states specify that all sex education must include instruction about abstinence, and only 13 states require courses to cover contraceptive methods. A large majority of states have developed curricula or guidelines to provide program guidance to local school districts in implementing sex education programs.

As a result of these laws and policies, virtually all teenagers now receive some sex education while they are in high school. In a 1995 national survey, more than nine in ten women ages 18 to 19 said that they received instruction, as did about seven in ten women ages 18 to 24. Most students, however, do not receive any instruction until ninth or tenth grade, by which time they have already become sexually active. Even then, the information they receive may be insufficient. Many programs are short, are not comprehensive, fail to cover important topics, and are less effective than they could be (what is offered depends partially on the teacher's ability, training, and comfort with the subject matter) (Donovan, 1998).

The major problem teachers face in providing sex education is negative pressure from parents, the community, or the school administration (Reis & Seidly, 1989). Teachers of sex education need to be provided with training, support, and agreed-on guidelines on methodology and procedures (Mellanby, Phelps, & Tripp, 1992).

NUTRITION AND WEIGHT

Caloric Requirements

During the period of rapid growth, adolescents need greater quantities of food to take care of bodily requirements. As a consequence, they develop voracious appetites. The stomach increases in capacity to be able to digest the increased amounts of food. The caloric requirement for girls may increase on the average by 25% from ages 10 to 15. The caloric requirement for boys may increase on the average by 90% from ages 10 to 19 (Figure 11.7 shows the increase). As a result, the adolescent boy finds it almost impossible to get enough to eat.

Importance of Nutrition

Health maintenance depends partly on proper eating habits (Carruth & Goldberg, 1990). Attainment of maximum height, strength, and physical well-being depends on proper nutrition. Nerve, bone, muscle, and other tissue growth requires body-building foods. Nutritional deficiencies are related to emotional instability, premenstrual tension (in females), lower resistance to infection, reduced stamina, and physical and mental retardation. Good nutrition also is extremely important during pregnancy.

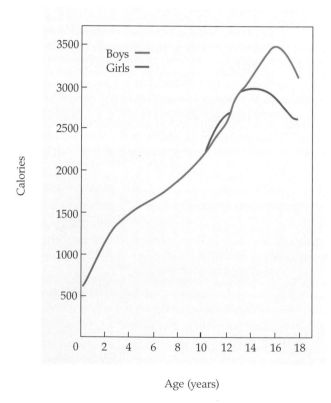

FIGURE 11.7   Daily caloric requirements for both sexes from birth to eighteen years.

Redrawn from "Energy Requirements," by E. L. Holt, Jr., 1972, in H. L. Barnett and A. H. Einhorn (Eds.), *Pediatrics*, 15th ed., p. 131. By permission of Appleton & Lange.

Deficiencies

Many adolescents have inadequate diets (U.S. Departments of Agriculture and of Health and Human Services, 1985). The principal deficiencies are as follows:

1. Insufficient thiamine and riboflavin.
2. Insufficient vitamins—especially A and C—caused primarily by lack of fresh vegetables and fruit in the diet.
3. Insufficient calcium—caused primarily by an inadequate intake of milk.
4. Insufficient iron—especially true in females.
5. Insufficient protein—usually true only in females.

A medical and dietetic assessment of the adolescent's nutritional intake will reveal any deficiencies. This ought to be accompanied by education and counseling about diet and nutrition (Sobal & Marquart, 1994). This action is especially important in cases of adolescent pregnancy. A large proportion of both black and white females have intakes below the recommended allowances. These deficiencies may have an important effect on fetal development (Sargent, Schulken, Kemper, & Hussey, 1994).

Overweight and Underweight

Adolescents often worry about being overweight (Cook, Reiley, Stallsmith, & Garretson, 1991). From 10% to 15% of all adolescents are obese (at least 20% overweight or more), girls more than boys. Being overweight affects the adolescent's emotional adjustment, ego identity development, self-esteem, and social relationships. Being overweight significantly influences adolescents to have negative feelings about their bodies. This is especially true of women's evaluations of themselves (Andersen & LeGrand, 1991). As stated previously, being overweight is also associated with early maturation and affects global, negative self-evaluations of adolescent girls (Alsaker, 1992a). It also is a future health hazard because obesity is related to gynecological disorders, joint disease, hypertension, and cardiovascular disease (Shestowsky, 1983; Stein, 1987).

Underweight adolescents have the opposite condition: They are burning up more calories than they are consuming. Males especially worry about being too skinny or "not having a good build." In one study of 568 adolescent males, over half were dissatisfied with their body, and 71% reported eating to gain weight (Fleischer & Read, 1982). Underweight adolescents need to increase the consumption of fattening foods and to overcome a poor appetite. They also can conserve energy by spending more hours in bed and by omitting strenuous exercise.

Anorexia Nervosa

Anorexia nervosa is a life-threatening emotional disorder characterized by an obsession with being slender. Adolescence represents a particularly vulnerable period with the development of eating disorders (Taub & Blinde, 1994). About 5% to 10% of cases are males, and the remainder are females, usually between ages 12 and 18 (Svec, 1987). However, eating disorders have become quite common on college campuses (Kashubeck, Walsh, & Crowl, 1994). The major symptoms are a constant preoccupation with dieting; body image disturbance (Mallick, Whipple, & Huerta, 1987); excess weight loss (at least 15% below optimal body weight); hyperactivity (excessive exercise) (Warah, 1993); extreme moodiness, loneliness, depression, helplessness, and inadequacy; strong feelings of insecurity; social isolation; and amenorrhea (American Psychiatric Association, 1994). Anorexia is associated with numerous medical conditions: abdominal distress, constipation, metabolic changes, electrolyte abnormalities, hypothermia, dehydration, low blood pressure, sexual dysfunction (Simpson & Ramberg, 1992; Zerbe, 1992), slow heartbeat, and cardiac arrest (which is a frequent cause of death). The anorexic feels cold, even though the body grows fine, silky hair to conserve body heat. Kidney malfunction may occur because of a potassium deficiency (Muuss, 1985).

Once the illness has developed, anorexics become thin and emaciated in appearance. Treichel (1982) found that malnutrition causes brain abnormalities, impaired mental performance, and lengthened reaction time and perceptual speed. Medical problems associated with malnutrition cause death in 5% to 10% of anorexics. Obsession with dieting combined with a compulsion to exercise leads to social isolation and withdrawal from friends and family. Hunger and fatigue are usually denied, and any attempt to interfere with the regime is angrily resisted. Anorexics are very hard to treat (Grant & Fodor, 1984).

Bulimia

Bulimia is a binge-purge syndrome. It is characterized by a compulsive and rapid consumption of large quantities of high-calorie

FOCUS

Five Theories About Causes of Anorexia

1. *Biological theory.* A disturbance in the hypothalamus causes anorexic behavior.

2. *Psychobiologic regression hypothesis.* Once body weight drops below a critical level because of inadequate diet, neuroendocrine functions are impaired, which reverses the developmental changes of puberty. The anorexic regresses to a prepubertal stage of development (Muuss, 1985, pp. 526, 527).

3. *Psychosexual theory.* The fact that anorexia appears at puberty after the development of sexual characteristics suggests that sexual conflict is a central issue in the illness (Romeo, 1984). The anorexic is unwilling to accept her role as a woman and her feminine sexuality. She fears sexual intimacy, so she uses the disorder to delay or regress her psychosexual development.

4. *Social theory.* Anorexics are brainwashed by a culture that emphasizes being slim, so they become obsessed with food and diet (Hertzler & Grun, 1990).

5. *Family systems theory.* Anorexics often have disturbed relationships with their parents (Bailey, 1991; Eisele, Hertsgaard, & Light, 1986). The families are often rigid and overprotective, with a hypochondriacal concern for the child's health (Brone & Fisher, 1988). Often a power struggle develops between the adolescent girl and her parents, particularly with her mother (Goldstein, 1981; Levin, Adelson, Buchalter, & Bilcher, 1983). This desire to guide and control becomes more evident as parental concern grows. The more the parents try to change the pattern, the more intense the power struggle becomes (Russell, Halasz, & Beumont, 1990)

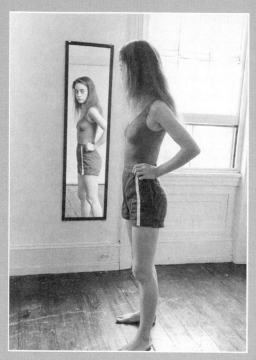

The majority of anorexic victims are female. How would you explain this fact?

food followed by efforts to eliminate the food (Stein & Reichert, 1990). According to one study, bulimic clients in an outpatient setting revealed an average of 13.7 hours spent in binge eating each week, with a range of 15 minutes to 8 hours for each episode (Mitchell, Pyle, & Eckert, 1981). Bingeing and purging could occur many times daily. Caloric consumption ranged from 1,200 to 11,500 calories per episode, with carbohydrates as the primary food. Many clients could not perceive a sense of fullness. Episodes took place secretly, usually in the afternoon, evening, or at night. Induced vomiting was the most common purging method. At other times, bulimics used amphetamines, enemas, diuretics, laxatives, compulsive exercising, or fasting to offset the huge food intake (LeClair & Berkowitz, 1983).

Bulimics feel a compulsion to eat, but because of concern about their weight, they purge afterward. Binges usually follow periods of stress and are accompanied by anxiety, depressed mood, and self-deprecating thoughts during and after the episode (Ledoux, Choquet, & Manfredi, 1993). The illness is most common in college-age females or those in their early twenties (Lachenmeyer & Muni-Brander, 1988), although frequently of occurrence is increasing among high school females (Johnson, Lewis, Love, Lewis, & Stuckey, 1984). Some female athletes use pathogenic weight-control techniques, such as the use of laxatives, vomiting, fasting, and diet aids to control their weight (Taub & Blinde, 1992).

Bulimics have low self-esteem, are anxious and depressed, and have strong moral beliefs (Baird & Sights, 1986; Brouwers, 1988). They wish to be perfect, yet they have negative self-worth and a poor self-image, are shy, and lack assertiveness (Holleran, Pascale, & Fraley, 1988). They are often preoccupied with fear of rejection in sexual relationships and with not being attractive enough to please a man (Van Thorre & Vogel, 1985). Because of the drive for perfection, anxiety builds up, which is relieved through lapses of control during bingeing and purging episodes. This process is followed by feelings of guilt and shame, which contribute to the sense of low self-esteem and depression. Psychological evaluation of adolescent bulimics indicate that they are more depressed, self-punitive, and negativistic than their peers and that they have more disorganized thoughts, inaccurate perceptions, and impaired judgment (Smith, Hillard, & Roll, 1991). There is an especially high correlation between eating disorders and depression (Nagel & Jones, 1992a). Bulimics are often difficult to treat because they resist seeking help or they sabotage treatment. Both bulimics and anorexics need short-term intervention to restore body weight and to save their life, followed by long-term therapy to ameliorate personality and family problems.

For parents and professionals in the educational, physical, and mental health-care fields, the need is to be aware of the influence of social pressures on teenagers' perceptions of body image and appearance. Professionals and parents can help adolescents resist societal pressure to conform to unrealistic standards of appearance, and can provide guidance on nutrition, realistic body ideals, and achievement of self-esteem and self-efficacy (Nagel & Jones, 1992b). There is a need to focus on the prevention of eating disorders before these concerns develop into serious eating problems (Moreno & Thelen, 1995).

Parenting Issues

The Families of Bulimics

The families of bulimics may be characterized by one or more of the following (Felker & Stivers, 1994):

1. Women with bulimia report more negative early mealtime and food-related experiences than women who are not bulimic.

2. There were high levels of stress and conflict during meals, the use of food as a tool for punishment or manipulation, and an emphasis on dieting and weight.

3. Conversations held during family meals were often conflictual. Parents tended to dominate and control the conversations, whereas children were stifled in their attempts to express opinions.

4. The children felt pressured to eat rapidly, to clean their plates, and to finish dinner at the same time as the other family members.

5. Food was used as an instrument of reward or punishment. Daughters would feel stressed or guilty if they refused food offered by other family members.

6. Bulimic women report that their families attach great importance to weight, physical appearance, and attractiveness.

7. Bulimic women report that they thought and worried about their weight when they were young (Miller, McClusky-Fawcett, & Irving, 1993).

Prevention, early intervention, and treatment programs for adolescents who are at risk can sometimes prevent eating disorders from becoming chronic (Scarano & Kalodner-Martin, 1994).

Summary

1. The endocrine glands are ductless glands that secrete hormones directly into the bloodstream. The hormones tell different cells what to do and when to act.

2. The three most important glands related to sexuality are the pituitary gland, the adrenal glands, and the gonads.

3. The pituitary secretes HGH, which regulates growth; gonadotropic hormones (FSH and LH) that stimulate the gonads (ovaries and testes) to function; and LTH, which stimulates milk production.

4. The ovaries secrete estrogen, which is responsible for sexual maturation, and progesterone, which is active in the menstrual cycle.

5. The testes secrete testosterone, which is responsible for sexual maturation in males.

6. Both feminizing and masculinizing hormones (estrogens and androgens) are present in both boys and girls. The ratio of male to female hormones is partly responsible for the development of male or female characteristics.

7. The adrenal glands also secrete both androgens and estrogens in both males and females.

8. The hypothalamus secretes GnRH, which acts on the pituitary to trigger the secretion of the gonadotropic hormones that act on the gonads (the testes and ovaries).

9. The primary sex organs of the male are the testes, scrotum, epididymis, seminal vesicles, prostate gland, Cowper's glands, penis, vas deferens, and urethra, all of which mature at puberty. The most important change within the testes is the production of mature sperm cells. Boys begin ejaculating semen and sperm cells at the mean age of 13.7. Boys need to be prepared for the onset of nocturnal emissions.

10. The primary internal female sex organs that develop during puberty are the ovaries, fallopian tubes, uterus, and vagina. The external female organs, which are known collectively as the vulva, include the mons veneris (mons pubis), labia majora, labia minora, clitoris, vestibule, and hymen.

11. On the average, females begin menstruating at 12 to 13 years of age. Girls need to be prepared in a positive way for menarche (first menstruation).

12. There are a number of factors that influence the timing of sexual maturation: heredity and genetics, nutrition, medical care, socioeconomic status as it influences diet, stress as it influences eating habits and body weight, and percentage of body fat.

13. One of the earliest signs of the physical changes of adolescents is the growth spurt that begins early in adolescence. A number of factors are important in determining the total mature height achieved: heredity, nutrition, age of sexual maturation, and total height achieved before puberty.

14. Some girls and boys are early or late maturers. Early-maturing boys have a physical and social advantage, although parents tend to expect more of them at this age. Although some early-maturing girls are at a disadvantage in elementary school, they come into their own in junior high school, enjoying many social advantages.

15. Late-maturing boys tend to suffer social inferiority because of their delayed growth and development. Late-maturing girls also tend to be at a distinct social disadvantage.

16. Adolescents are very concerned about their body image and physical attractiveness. They have been influenced by images of the ideal build as taught in our culture, which emphasizes medium builds.

17. Acne is a problem for some adolescents.

18. The goals of sex education of adolescents are to develop knowledge and understanding of human sexuality, improve sexual health, to prevent unwanted pregnancy, and to prevent AIDS and other sexually transmitted diseases.

19. Both the parents and the schools have important roles to play in sex education, but studies indicate that adolescents are still receiving their information primarily from peers.

20. A number of programs have been developed that encourage sexual abstinence before marriage. The research data indicate that some programs increase the likelihood that participants will delay the initiation of sexual intercourse and also increase abstinence values.

21. Being either overweight or underweight is a problem.

22. The two most serious eating disorders are anorexia nervosa and bulimia, both of which can be life-threatening diseases and both of which are hard to treat.

Key Terms

Acne   *p. 308*
Adrenal glands   *p. 301*
Anabolic steroids   *p. 301*
Anorexia nervosa   *p. 309*
Bartholin's glands   *p. 302*
Bulimia   *p. 309*
Clitoris   *p. 302*
Corpus luteum   *p. 301*
Cowper's glands   *p. 301*
Endocrine gland   *p. 300*
Epididymis   *p. 301*
Estrogen   *p. 301*

Fallopian tubes   *p. 302*
Follicle-stimulating hormone (FSH)   *p. 299*
Gonadotropic hormones (GnRH)   *p. 300*
Gonadotropin-releasing hormone (GnRH)   *p. 302*
Gonads   *p. 301*
Hormones   *p. 300*
Human growth hormone (HGH)   *p. 300*
Hymen   *p. 302*
Hypothalamus   *p. 302*
Labia majora   *p. 302*
Labia minora   *p. 302*

Luteinizing hormone (LH)   *p. 299*
Menarche   *p. 302*
Mons veneris (mons pubis)   *p. 302*
Nocturnal emissions   *p. 302*
Ovaries   *p. 302*
Ovum   *p. 301*
Penis   *p. 301*
Pituitary gland   *p. 300*
Primary sexual characteristics   *p. 305*
Progesterone   *p. 301*

Prolactin   *p. 300*
Prostate gland   *p. 301*
Scrotum   *p. 301*
Secondary sexual characteristics   *p. 305*
Seminal vesicles   *p. 301*
Testes   *p. 301*
Uterus   *p. 302*
Vagina   *p. 302*
Vas deferens   *p. 301*
Vulva   *p. 302*

Discussion Questions

1. Should athletes be allowed to take steroids to improve their ability? Have you ever known anyone who did? What were the results?

2. To men: When you had your first nocturnal emission, did you understand what was happening? Were you prepared for it? How did you feel?

3. To women: When you first started to menstruate, did you understand what was happening? Were you prepared for it? How did you feel?

4. Comment on the attitudes in American culture toward female breasts and male penis size. What effect do these attitudes have on adolescents?

5. Do you know anyone who matured early? Late? What were the effects?

6. What can be done if a person has acne?

7. What factors prevent some adolescents from getting a balanced diet?

8. What were your principal sources of sex information as you were growing up? Did your parents try to provide sex information for you at home? Describe. What might they have done differently?

9. What is your attitude toward sex education in the schools? What sort of sex education program did you receive in your school? Describe. What did you think of it? How could it have been improved?

10. Do you think a school program in education for abstinence will help prevent early sexual intercourse and pregnancy? Will it change the sex behavior of teenagers?

11. What can be done if a person is overweight? What helps the most? What can be done if a person is underweight? What helps the most?

12. Do you know anyone who has suffered from anorexia nervosa? Describe. What were the results? Do you know anyone who was bulimic? Describe. What were the results?

Suggested Readings

COLMAN, W. (1988).   *Understanding and preventing AIDS.* Chicago: Children's Press. For teenagers and their parents.

LERNER, R. M., & FOCH, T. T. (Eds.). (1987). *Biological-psychological interactions in early adolescence.* Hillsdale, NJ: Erlbaum. Series of articles.

MILLER, B. C., JOSEFINA, J. C., PAIKOFF, R. L., & PETERSON, J. L. (Eds.) (1992).   *Preventing adolescent pregnancy: Model programs and evaluations.* Newbury Park, CA: Sage. Detailed discussions of programs.

RICE, F. P. (1989).   *Human sexuality.* Dubuque, IA: Wm. C. Brown. The author's comprehensive college text on human sexuality. Includes all age groups.

RICE, F. P. (1999).   *The adolescent: Development, relationships, and culture* (7th ed.). Boston: Allyn and Bacon. The author's comprehensive textbook on adolescence.

Web Resources

http://ificinfo.health.org International Food Information Council Nutrition Information, publications and additional resources.

Cognitive Development

Chapter 12

FORMAL OPERATIONAL THOUGHT

As we have seen in Chapter 7, Piaget outlined four stages of cognitive development: the *sensorimotor stage* (birth to 2 years), the *preoperational stage* (2 to 7 years), the *concrete operational stage* (7 to 11 years), and the *formal operational stage* (11 years and up). The formal operational stage is discussed in this section on the cognitive development of adolescents.

Characteristics

During the formal operational stage of development, the thinking of adolescents begins to differ radically from that of children (Piaget, 1972). Children perform concrete operations and arrange things into classes, relations, or numbers, making logical "groupings" and classifications. However, they never integrate their thought into a single, total, logical system. Adolescents, however, are able to use propositional logic. In formal operations, they are able to reason, systematize their ideas, and construct theories. Furthermore, they can test these theories scientifically and logically, considering several variables, and are able to discover truth scientifically (Inhelder & Piaget, 1958). Adolescents are able to assume the role of scientists because they have the capacity to construct and test theories. Elkind (1967) called the formal operational stage *the conquest of thought*.

Piaget conducted an interesting experiment to discover the strategies adolescents use in solving problems. This experiment involved a pendulum suspended by a string (see Figure 12.1). The problem was to find out what would affect the oscillatory speed of the pendulum. The subjects were to investigate four possible effects: starting the pendulum with various degrees of force, releasing the pendulum from various heights, changing its weight, or changing the length of the pendulum. The subjects were free to solve the problem in any way they chose.

The adolescents showed three basic characteristics in their problem-solving behavior. *First*, they planned their investigations systematically. They began to test all possible causes for variation in the pendulum swings: various degrees of force or push, high or low height, light or heavy weight, and long or short string. *Second*, they recorded the results accurately and objectively. *Third*, they formed logical conclusions.

For example, they first observed that both the force and the height of the drop of the pendulum had no effect on oscillatory speed. They next tried different combinations of weight and found out that the oscillation speed remained the same regardless of the weight. They did discover that changing the string length (the pendulum length) alone determined the speed of oscillation. Other researchers have replicated this experiment many times.

By trial and error, children may come up with the right answer, but they fail to use systematic procedures to find the answer and to give logical explanations of the solutions. They often form conclusions that are premature and false because they have not considered all of the important facts and are not able to reason logically about them. Children tend to hold tenaciously to their initial opinions even when presented with contrary evidence. They even try to make the circumstances fit their preconceived notions:

In summary, three interrelated characteristics of adolescent thought have emerged. These are the ability to derive a proposition from two or more variables or a complex relationship; the ability to suggest mentally the possible effect of one or more variables; and the capacity to combine and separate variables in a hypothetical-deductive framework ("if this is so, this will happen") so that a reasonable possibility is recognized

During the formal operational stage of development, the thinking of adolescents begins to differ radically from that of children.

before the test is made in reality. The fundamental property of adolescent thought is this reversible maneuvering between reality and possibility.

To do formal operational thinking, adolescents are able to be *flexible.* They can be quite versatile in their thoughts, and can devise many interpretations of an observed outcome, without relying on preconceived ideas. In contrast, younger children are confused by unexpected results that are inconsistent with their simple preconceptions.

Preoperational children begin to use symbols, but *the formal operational adolescents now begin to use a second symbol system: a set of symbols of symbols.* For example, algebraic signs and metaphorical speech are symbols for numbers and/or words. The capacity to identify symbols makes the adolescent's thought much more flexible than the child's. Words can now carry double or triple meanings. Cartoons can represent a complete story that would otherwise have to be explained in words. Junior high school youth have no difficulty understanding religious symbols or political cartoons that younger children cannot comprehend. Algebra may be understood by adolescents but not by elementary school children.

Adolescents are also able to orient themselves toward what is abstract and not immediately present. This facility enables them to distinguish possibility from present reality, to project themselves into the future, and to think about what might be (Bart, 1983). Adolescents have not only the capacity to accept and understand what is given but also the ability to conceive of what might occur. Because they can construct ideas, they have the ability to elaborate on these ideas and generate new thoughts. They become inventive, imaginative, and original in their thinking, and "possibility dominates reality." "The adolescent is

Educational experiences can be geared toward teaching scientific methods of problem solving.

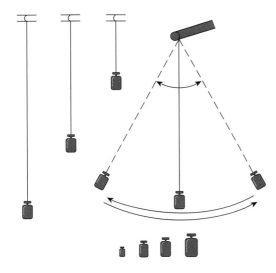

FIGURE 12.1   The pendulum problem. The pendulum problem utilizes a simple apparatus consisting of a string, which can be shortened or lengthened, and a set of varying weights. The other variables that at first might be considered relevant are the height of the release point and the force of the push given by the subject.

From *The Growth of Logical Thinking: From Childhood to Adolescence,* by Jean Piaget and Barbel Inhelder. Copyright © 1958 by Basic Books, Inc. Reprinted by permission of Basic Books, a division of HarperCollins Publishers, Inc., New York.

the person who commits himself to possibilities . . . who begins to build 'systems' or 'theories' in the largest sense of the term" (Inhelder & Piaget, 1958).

In summary, formal thinking, according to Piaget, involves four major aspects: *introspection* (thinking about thought); *abstract thinking* (going beyond the real to what is possible; *logical thinking* (being able to consider all important facts and ideas and to form correct conclusions, such as the ability to determine cause and effect); and *hypothetical reasoning* (formulating hypotheses and examining the evidence for them, considering numerous variables).

Effects on Personality and Behavior

Idealism

Adolescents' power of reflective thinking enables them to evaluate what they have learned as children (Schmidt & Davison, 1983) and to become more capable of moral reasoning. Their ability to distinguish the possible from the real enables them to imagine what the adult world might be like under ideal circumstances. They compare the possible with the actual, recognize that the actual is less than ideal, and so become idealistic rebels.

For a while, some adolescents develop the equivalent of a messianic complex, seeing themselves in a major effort to reform the world. Usually the efforts of young adolescents are confined to verbal discussion, but some older adolescents get caught up in group movements that seek the utopian reconstruction of society. By late adolescence, attention shifts from egocentrism to a newfound **sociocentrism.** Adolescents begin to focus on values that have long-term implications rather than those that emphasize immediate gratification and goal satisfaction. They begin to emphasize values that are more noble and altruistic in nature and achievement in the future rather than just in the present. Their attention begins to be focused on others rather than the inner self.

Adolescents also become champions of the underdog. Adolescents' own inner conflicts account for their empathetic capacities for the suffering of others. They can easily identify with the oppressed, the victims of selfish society, the poor, and the weak. They perceive that social injustices mirror their own internal, individual struggles. One study focused on the fact that those who score high in formal reasoning tend to give a high ranking to value dimensions associated with self-reliance, competence, and independence (Darmody, 1991).

Discrepancy

Adolescents are sometimes accused of hypocrisy because of the discrepancy between what they say and what they actually do. Elkind (1978) illustrated this tendency with two examples. *First,* his son lamented about his brother's going into his room and taking his things. He berated his father for not punishing the culprit; yet the same boy felt no guilt about going into his father's study, using his calculator and typewriter, and playing his own music on his father's stereo without permission. *Second,* a group of young people were involved in a "Walk for Water" drive, in which sponsors were paid for each mile walked. The money was intended for pollution control. The next day, however, a drive along the route that the youths had walked revealed a roadside littered with fast-food wrappers and beverage cans. City workers had to be hired to clean up the mess. The question was, Did the cost of cleaning up amount to more money than was collected? And weren't these adolescents hypocritical? They objected to pollution, yet they were among the chief offenders in defacing their environment (Elkind, 1978).

Sociocentrism—focus of attention on social problems and the concerns of society

The behavior of these adolescents reveals the discrepancy between idealism and behavior. Early adolescents have the capacity to formulate general principles such as "Thou shalt not pollute" but lack the experience to see the application of these general rules to specific practice. Youths believe that if they can conceive and express high moral principles, they have attained them, and that nothing concrete need be done. This attitude upsets and confuses adults, who insist that ideals cannot be attained instantly and that one must work for them (Elkind, 1978).

Adolescents can manifest hypocrisy in another way. They pretend to be what they are not. They are expected to conform to parental viewpoints and beliefs even when they do not agree with them. They are expected to be open and honest but are chastised when they are. They are expected to like school but rarely do. They are expected not to be hurt or angry when they really are. They are expected not to engage in behavior that will hurt or disappoint parents, so they do not talk to them about important things. They are expected to pretend to be what they are not. They are pressured not to be, not to feel, and not to desire. They are expected to deny the self, and so they behave hypocritically.

Self-Consciousness and Egocentrism

Formal operational thinking also results in the development of a new form of egocentrism (deRosenroll, 1987; Hudson & Gray, 1986). The capacity to think about their own thoughts makes adolescents become acutely aware of themselves. As a result, they become egocentric, self-conscious, and introspective. They become so concerned about themselves that they may conclude that others are equally obsessed with their appearance and behavior (Peterson & Roscoe, 1991). "It is this belief that others are preoccupied with his appearance and behavior that constitutes the egocentrism of the adolescent" (Elkind, 1967, p. 1029). Adolescents feel they are "on stage" much of the time, so that much of their energy is spent "reacting to an imaginary audience." As a result, they become extremely self-conscious. Whether in the lunchroom or on the bus going home, youths feel they are the center of attention (Goosens, Seiffge-Krenke, & Marcoen, 1992).

Elkind (1967) also discusses what he terms **personal fable**—adolescents' belief in the uniqueness of their own experiences. Because of their belief that they are important to so many people, they come to regard themselves as special and unique. This perception may be why so many adolescents believe that misfortunes such as unwanted pregnancies or accidents happen only to others, never to them.

Self-consciousness and egocentrism have other manifestations. Adolescents believe that everyone is looking at them, but they feel totally alone, unique in a vast, uncaring universe. To be always on stage, scrutinized but rarely understood, imposes a terrific emotional strain. As a result, they employ numerous psychological mechanisms to protect their frail egos. They become critical and sarcastic, partly as a defense against their own feelings of inferiority and as a way of making themselves look good (Elkind, 1975). Those with low self-esteem tend to present a false front to others and to mask their true feelings by fabricating an image (Hauck & Loughhead, 1985). The intellectualization and newfound asceticism of college students have been explained as just such a defense mechanism.

Whereas adolescents are often self-centered, they are frequently self-admiring, too. Their boorishness, loudness, and faddish dress reflect what they feel others admire. The boy who stands in front of the mirror for two hours combing his hair is probably imagining the swooning reactions he will produce from his girlfriend.

Conformity

One would expect that adolescents who are capable of logical reasoning processes would also be creative. But investigations of the relationship of adolescent thinking processes to creative behavior suggest a negative relation-

Personal fable—belief in the uniqueness of one's own experience

Achievement of formal operational thinking is accompanied by increasing egocentrism and self-consciousness.

ship: Adolescents become less creative, not more so (Wolf, 1981). The reason is not that they are less capable of being creative. They have a greater potential than before. But in actuality they are less creative because of the pressures on them to conform—from both their peers and society in general. The price they pay for acceptance is conformity. As a result, they squelch their individuality and begin to dress, think, and act like others in groups to which they want to belong. One study found that adolescents' self-monitoring behavior increased from early to late adolescence. That is, individuals became more conscious of how others wanted them to behave, and so they adjusted their behavior accordingly (Pledger, 1992). Another study emphasized that adolescents who rate highest in self-trust (who believe in themselves) are more willing to risk doing things that are imaginative and creative (Earl, 1987).

Decentering and a Life Plan

In the process of becoming adults, adolescents gradually begin to develop more cognitive objectivity and perspective. They begin to cure themselves of their idealistic crises and to return to the reality that is the beginning of adulthood. Piaget and Inhelder (1969) go on to emphasize that "the focal point of the decentering process is the entrance into the occupational world or the beginning of serious professional training. The adolescent becomes an adult when he or she undertakes a real job. It is then that the adolescent is transformed from the idealistic reformer into an achiever" (p. 346).

Piaget refers to the importance of adolescent work in the community as a facilitator of human growth. He states that work helps the adolescent meet the storm and stress of that period. Work experience can also stimulate the development of social understanding and socially competent behavior. True integration into society comes when the adolescent begins to affirm a life plan and adopt a social role.

Achieving Formal Operational Thought

Ages and Percentages

Since Piaget formulated his concept of a formal operational stage of cognitive development, researchers have been examining various components of the formulation. The age at which the formal operational stage replaces the concrete operational stage is one question that has to be raised. Piaget (1972)

himself advanced the possibility that in some circumstances, the appearance of formal operations may be delayed to 15 to 20 years of age and "that perhaps in extremely disadvantageous conditions, such a type of thought will never really take shape" (p. 1012). Piaget (1971) acknowledged that social environment can accelerate or delay the onset of formal operations. Fewer economically deprived adolescents achieve formal thought than do their more privileged counterparts, and there is a complete absence of formal operations among the mentally retarded.

Parents, teachers, and other adults need to realize that not all same-age adolescents are at the same stage of development. Some have not yet achieved formal operations. To ask these youths to make decisions from among numerous alternatives or variables that cannot be grasped simultaneously is to ask the impossible. Very few youths may make the transition to formal operations by age 10 or 11, but only about 40% have progressed beyond concrete operations by high school graduation (Bauman, 1978).

Test Level

The measured percentages of people reaching formal operational thinking depend partially on the criteria for formal thinking that are established and the tests employed to evaluate those criteria. Piaget distinguished between an easy level of tests (III-A) and a more advanced level (III-B). Approximately 50% of the adult population actually attain the full stage of formal thinking (III-B). Piaget (1980) readily admitted that the subjects of his study were "from the better schools in Geneva" and that his conclusions were based on a "privileged population." However, he still maintained that "all normal individuals are capable of reaching the level of formal operation" (Piaget, 1980, p. 75) as long as the environment provides the necessary cognitive stimulation. Actually, not all adolescents or adults reach the formal level, but there is still a significant increase in the use of formal operational thinking among adolescents between ages 11 and 15.

Maturation and Intelligence

Maturation of the nervous system plays an important role in cognitive development, because the nervous system must be sufficiently developed for any real thought to take place. This is one reason why a greater percentage of older adolescents exhibit formal thought than do younger adolescents. Webb (1974) tested very bright 6- to 11-year-old children (IQs of 160 and above) to determine their levels of thinking. All subjects performed the concrete operational tasks easily, showing that they were cognitively at their developmental age; but only 4 males, age 10 and older, solved the formal thought problems, indicating that regardless of high intelligence, a degree of maturation was necessary for movement into the next stage of cognitive development. Other research helps explain further the relationship among development, intelligence, and cognition. Other things being equal, individuals with high IQs are more likely to develop formal thought sooner than those with low IQs, but *it is the interaction of age and intelligence that contributes to cognitive ability.*

Cross-Cultural Studies

Formal thought is, however, more dependent on social experience than is sensorimotor or concrete operational thought. Adolescents from various cultural backgrounds show considerable variability in abstract reasoning abilities. Some cultures offer more opportunities to adolescents to develop abstract thinking than others do, by providing a rich verbal environment and experiences that facilitate growth by exposure to problem-solving situations.

Social institutions such as the family and school accelerate or retard the development of formal operations. Parents who encourage academic excellence, ideational explorations, exchanges of thoughts, and the attainment of ambitious educational and occupational goals are fostering cognitive growth. Schools that encourage students to develop problem-

Sociocultural and environmental factors influence the development of formal operational thought.

solving skills and to acquire abstract reasoning enhance cognitive development.

Adolescent Education and Formal Operational Thought

Because many students are used to traditional methods of instruction that involve lectures, memorization, and so forth, they have difficulty adjusting to methods designed to encourage free thinking (Maroufi, 1989). However, development of abstract thinking and formal operations problem solving can be encouraged in a number of ways. Discussion groups, debates, question periods, problem-solving sessions, and science experiments are approaches that encourage the development of formal thinking and problem-solving abilities. Teachers need to be prepared to handle group discussion and stimulate interchange and feedback. Experimental or problematic situations can be presented that allow students opportunities to observe, analyze possibilities, and draw inferences about perceived relationships. Teachers who use authoritarian approaches rather than social interchange stifle real thinking. Some students develop higher cognitive abilities at a relatively slow pace, so that teachers must be willing to give explicit help and encouragement and allow the necessary time for reasoning capacities to develop.

Piaget (1972) sets forth two goals of education that incorporate this philosophy:

> *The principal goal of education is to create men who are capable of doing new things*, not simply of repeating what other generations have done—men who are creative, inventive, and discoverers. *The second goal of education is to form minds which can be critical, can verify and not accept everything they are offered.* . . . We need pupils who are active, who learn early to find out by themselves, partly by their own spontaneous activity and partly through material we set up for them, who learn early to tell what is verifiable and what is simply the first idea to come to them. (p. 5)

Problem-Finding Stage

Progressive changes in thought structure may extend beyond the level of formal operations. The suggestion is that cognitive growth is continuous; there is no end point limiting the possibility for new thought structures to appear. Researchers continue to seek these new structures.

There is some evidence that a fifth stage of development can be differentiated. It has been labeled a **problem-finding stage.** This new stage represents an ability to discover problems not yet delineated, to describe these problems, or to raise general questions from ill-defined problems.

Only some people in the problem-solving stage reach the problem-finding stage. All subjects who score high in problem finding have reached formal operational thinking, but not all subjects who have reached formal thinking score high in problem finding. However, sequencing of development is evident: Formal operations has to be accomplished before persons can move on to the next stage.

Millions of students are given the SAT as a basis of evaluation of aptitude to do college work.

SCHOLASTIC APTITUDE

Scholastic Aptitude Test (SAT)

The *Scholastic Aptitude Test* (**SAT**) was one of the most widely used tests in the United States. The SAT was the predominant college entrance exam in twenty-two states, and 80% of all colleges used it. Over one million high school seniors took the test each year. The combined scores often determined eligibility not only for admission but also for financial aid and scholarships. The *Educational Testing Service* (ETS), which produced the test, claimed that when combined with high school records, the SAT was the better predictor of students' first-year performance in college than any other measurement.

The test was supposed to measure basic abilities acquired over a student's lifetime and was thus supposed to be immune to last-minute cramming and coaching. But a study by the *Federal Trade Commission's Bureau of Consumer Protection* showed that special coaching could improve SAT scores for each part by an average pf 25 points out of the possible 800. In one nationwide chain, more than eighty coaching schools tutored 30,000 students in one year and improved scores on the average of 25 points. In individual cases, these schools claimed that they could improve scores up to 100 points.

The basic question is, If coaching could raise a student's score, should the test be relied on as a basic measure of scholastic aptitude and as a standard for college admission? In all fairness, the College Entrance Examination Board warned against making admission decisions on the basis of the SAT scores alone. The ETS itself had said that an individual's score could vary plus or minus 30 to 35 points, which is a spread of 60 to 70 points. For these reasons, some of the best schools relied more on class rank, high school grades, interviews, student essays, and other admission procedures (Chance, 1988). Even high marks from high school might be questioned, for standards vary from school to school. Also, because grading standards had become more lenient, the number of students with A averages increased so rapidly that there were now as many A students as there were those with C averages. The total SAT scores of college-bound seniors declined until 1980, then showed some increase.

Revisions of the SAT

The College Entrance Examination Board approved changes in the SAT in 1995. The test became known as the *Scholastic Assessment Test*, which the mandatory section labled SAT I. Some educators wanted to require a written essay, but others said that such a section would discriminate against minorities, so the essay was made optional in a separate part known as the SAT II. Also, scoring millions of essays would require enormous amounts of time and money.

The new SAT I has both a verbal and a math part. The verbal section includes longer, critical reading passages about which students must answer questions. The anonym section has been deleted, but the greatest changes are in the math section. Students may use calculators for solving problems, rather than selecting answers from multiple-choice slots. There is a new emphasis in the entire test on critical reasoning and "real-life" problem solving. Although the new test is still coachable, proponents claim that it is less coachable than the old test. Maximum scores are still 1600 or 800 for each of the two parts.

Figure 12.2 shows test score averages from 1967 to 1997. Scores for 1995 and prior years

Problem-finding stage—fifth stage of cognitive development characterized by the ability to create, to discover, and to formulate problems

Scholastic Aptitude Test (SAT)—the most widely used test for youths to determine their aptitude for college work

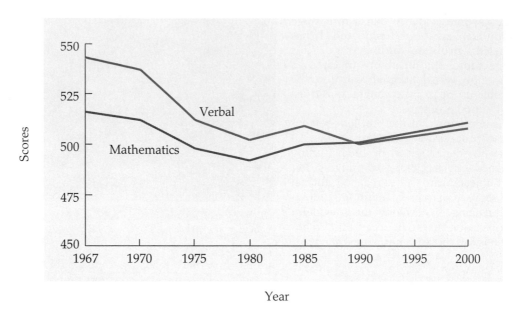

FIGURE 12.2   Scholastic Assessment Test (SAT) Scores and Characteristics of College-Bound Seniors: 1967 to 1997

From College Entrance Examination Board, New York, NY, *National College-Bound Senior*, annual (copyright). (1967–1997)

have been recentered and revised to be comparable to scores on SAT I. Data for 1995 to 1997 are for the SAT I: Reasoning Test. Scores between the two tests have been equated to the same 200 to 800 scale and are thus comparable. The SAT I Reasoning Test replaced the SAT in March 1994.

Total SAT scores of college-bound seniors declined until 1980, then showed some increase at that time. Whenever the scores drop, the schools are criticized for relaxing teaching standards and for not teaching the basics. College Board President Donald M. Stewart commented as follows:

> Students must pay less attention to video games and music videos and begin to read more. The requirement to read through homework has been reduced. Students don't read as much because they don't have to. . . . Reading is in danger of becoming a lost art among too many American students—and that would be a national tragedy. (Mitgang, 1990, pp. 1A, 4A)

Part of the blame for the drop until 1980 was attributed to changes and problems in the family, increased television viewing, and such problems as turbulence in national affairs (Zuckerman, 1985).

ACT

Some authorities suggest that achievement tests would be a better way of predicting college success than SATs. Such tests have several advantages. They evaluate a student's mastery of a particular subject area. They encourage high schools to offer more rigorous courses. Also, they encourage students to work harder in these courses because they would have to pass tests on the subjects to get into college (Chance, 1988).

The **ACT Assessment Program (American College Testing Program,** 1982) is the second most widely used college admissions test, administered to more than a million students each year. The ACT Assessment Program consists of a registration form that includes (a) the Student Profile Section (SPS), (b) the ACT Interest Inventory, and (c) the high school course-grades history. The academic tests include tests in math, English, reading, and science reasoning.

The ACT Interest Inventory is a survey of students' vocational preferences based on Holland's typology (Kifer, 1985). The Student Profile Section (SPS) is a 190-item inventory of demographics, high school activities and accomplishments, and academic and extracurricular plans for college.

The ACT Academic Tests yield standard scores of 1 to 36, which are averaged to

ACT Assessment Program (American College Testing Program)—the second most widely used college admissions test

TABLE 12.1	AMERICAN COLLEGE TESTING (ACT) COMPOSITE ACHIEVEMENT SCORES FOR THE ACADEMIC YEAR ENDING 1999	

Subject	Score
Composite	20.4
M	21.1
F	20.6
English	19.7
M	20.0
F	20.8
Math	20.2
M	21.4
F	20.2
Reading	20.9
M	21.1
F	21.6
Science Reasoning	20.5
M	21.5
F	20.6

Adapted from *High School Profile Report*, Annual Normative Data, 1997. Iowa City, IA: The American College Testing Program.

FOCUS

Gender Differences in Spatial Abilities and Achievement

For a number of years, a variety of tests have shown gender differences in some specific abilities and achievements. Boys generally score higher in spatial and math tests, and girls score higher in reading and verbal tests. This result has been attributed primarily to differences in sex-role socialization (Byrnes & Takahara, 1993). One study predicted that at age 11, those girls who scored high on masculinity would also score high on spatial ability at age 16 (Newcombe & Dubas, 1992). Boys are encouraged to excel in math and spatial skills, but not in reading and verbal skills. Although girls are expected to perform well academically in all subjects, they have not been encouraged to excel either in math or in experiences thought to enhance spatial abilities (e.g., sports). Butcher (1986) reported that girls in grades 6 through 10 ranked "getting good grades" as their primary aspiration at school, well above the choice of "being good at sports." Gender differences may indeed reflect two different sex-role socialization processes (Pearson & Ferguson, 1989).

create the ACT Composite. The mean composite score in 1999 was 20.4. The mean score for males was 21.1, and for females it was 20.9. Table 12.1 shows the scores.

SCHOOL

Trends in American Education

Progressives Versus Traditionalists

The emphasis in American education has shifted from one extreme to the other. **Progressives** have argued that the goal of education is to prepare students for all phases of life: effective personality growth, the effective use of leisure time, physical health, a vocation, home and family living, and citizenship. **Traditionalists** have argued that the goal of education is to teach the basics—foreign languages, history, math, science, and English—to increase student knowledge and intellectual powers.

There are some authorities who insist that education plays an important role in reforming society and addressing social issues. Schools design new programs to deal with social problems as they arise. Driver education was introduced when traffic fatalities rose. Family life and sex education followed a rise in premarital pregnancies, sexually transmitted diseases, and divorce rates. African American studies and school busing were introduced in response to demands for racial integration. Women's studies were introduced in part as a response to women's demands for equality. New social problems courses were offered when crime rates rose. Because social needs change from time to time, the educational pendulum has been pushed first in one direction and then in another.

Goals of Progressive Education

Traditionalism was the dominant emphasis in American schools until the 1930s. When the Depression came, there were no jobs for adolescents, so that many stayed in school instead of seeking employment. Because many of these youths were not bound for college or interested in traditional academic subjects, they needed special programs. Progressive educa-

Progressives—educators emphasizing that education is to prepare pupils for life

Traditionalists—educators who argue that the purpose of education is to teach the basics

Most schools include instruction in the use of computers.

tors like John Dewey said that the schoolroom should be a laboratory of living, preparing students for all of life. As a consequence, many schools introduced vocational and personal service courses, restricting most academic courses to the college preparatory program. These courses included life adjustment education centered around personal concerns, health, leisure activities, vocations, and community problems. Principals boasted that their programs helped students adjust to the demands of real life, freeing them from dry academic studies. Developing an effective personality became as important as improving reading (Wood, Wood, & McDonald, 1988).

After Sputnik

When in the 1950s the Soviet Union launched Sputnik, the first space satellite, our nation became obsessed with the failure of our schools to keep pace with the technological advances of the Soviet Union. Critics accused the schools of offering a watered-down curriculum that left American youth unprepared to challenge a communist country. Congress passed the *National Defense Education Act* and appropriated nearly $1 billion in federal aid to education, which supported the teaching of science, math, and foreign languages. Schools modernized their laboratories, and courses in math and physical sciences were rewritten by leading scholars to reflect advances in knowledge.

1960s and 1970s

The Cold War had abated by the mid-1960s, but the United States was disturbed by increasing racial tension, social unrest, and antiwar protests. The schools were called on to rescue a society that was in turmoil. Major school aid legislation was passed as part of the Johnson administration's "War on Poverty." Once more there was a clamor for

educational relevance. Educators demanded that adolescents spend time not only in the classroom but also in community and work settings. Career and experimental education replaced academic programs so that adolescents could receive "hands-on" experience. Elementary schools knocked down classroom walls, adopted open education, and gave students more choices of what to study. High schools lowered graduation requirements. Enrollments in traditional subjects such as math, science, and foreign language fell and gave way to student-designed courses, independent study, and a flock of electives. By the late 1970s, over 40% of all high school students were taking a general rather than a college preparatory or a vocational course of study, and 25% of their educational credits came from remedial coursework and courses aimed at personal growth and development (National Commission on Excellence in Education, 1983).

1980s and 1990s

By 1980, many people became alarmed at the steady, slow decline in academic indicators. SAT scores had shown a steady decline from 1963. Verbal scores fell over 50 points and average math scores fell 35 points. Parental and public outcry grew, resulting in the appointment of the National Commission on Excellence in Education (1983). The commission's findings were as follows:

- The number and proportion of students demonstrating superior achievement on the SATs (those with math or verbal scores of 650 or higher) had declined.
- Scores on achievement tests in such subjects as physics and English had declined.
- There was a steady decline in science achievement scores of 17-year-olds, by national assessments in 1969, 1973, and 1979.
- Average achievement of high school students on most standardized tests was lower than when Sputnik was launched.
- Nearly 40% of 17-year-olds could not draw inferences from written material; only one-fifth could write a persuasive essay; and only one-third could solve a mathematics problem requiring several steps.
- About 13% of all 17-year-olds were functionally illiterate.

Economic competition from Western Europe and Japan made officials fear that the nation was losing its competitive edge in world markets. Educational reformers demanded more required courses, particularly in math and science; longer school days; more academic rigor in the schools; and tougher standards for graduation. The pendulum began to swing back to a more traditionalist position (Rice, 1990).

Middle Schools and Junior High Schools

One of the problems of modern schools stems partly from their size. Schools with large enrollments tend to be less personal, with less attention devoted to the needs of individual students. Ideally, the best schools seek to combine academic excellence with personalized attention and services to achieve both intellectual rigor and intimacy. Most schools do not function at such a high level of performance (Lipsitz, 1991).

One of the answers has been the formation of schools in which older students are taken out of the upper elementary grades and put in middle schools, and eighth- and ninth-grade students are taken out of high schools and put in junior high schools. One such arrangement is as follows: Grades K through 4, 5 through 7, 8 through 9, and 10 through 12. In this arrangement, the elementary grades are together up through grade 4, middle school students are in grades 5 through 7, junior high school students are in grades 8 through 9, and senior high school students are in grades 10 through 12. All sorts of arrangements may be made, depending on local facilities and policies.

Several comments need to be made. There are tremendous developmental and physical differences between older elementary aged pupils and those in lower grades. Separating older pupils from younger ones provides some advantages on school buses and in school activities and playgrounds. The transition from elementary school to junior high school is particularly traumatic to some pupils. If the transition is made from elementary school to middle school to junior high school, the trauma is reduced. Cotterell (1992) found that school size has an effect on adjustments. As students move from a smaller to a much larger school, adjustments are more difficult. Ninth-graders in junior high school participate significantly more in extracurricular activity and achieve significantly higher academically than do ninth-graders in a senior high school setting (Gifford & Dean, 1990). Most authorities, therefore, recommend taking them out of senior high school and placing them in junior high school. Some authorities feel that even some middle schools are too large and that breaking them up into smaller units will ensure more personalized instruction (Lord, Eccles, & McCarthy, 1994; Scales, 1990).

Enrollment in High School

Prior to 1870, free secondary education was not available to all American youths. There were only 800 public high schools in the whole country. Most youths who were preparing for college attended private secondary schools, then called *preparatory schools*. The now-accepted principle that public education need not be restricted to the elementary schools was established by the famous Kalamazoo decision in 1874. Secondary education began to grow. In 1950, only 33% of those 25 and over had completed 4 or more years of high school. By 1997, the number was 82.1%. Figure 12.3 shows the rise since 1960.

Types of High Schools

In spite of the rise of public education, there are still a wide variety of high schools in the United States. One study compared four types of secondary schools: *public schools, Catholic schools, elite private boarding schools,* and *elite high performance private schools,* in terms of characteristics of the families whose children attend, and the educational and pedagogical characteristics of the schools themselves and their pupils (Persell, Catsambis, & Cookson, 1992). A national sample of 1980

As a group, elite private schools have higher academic standards than public schools.

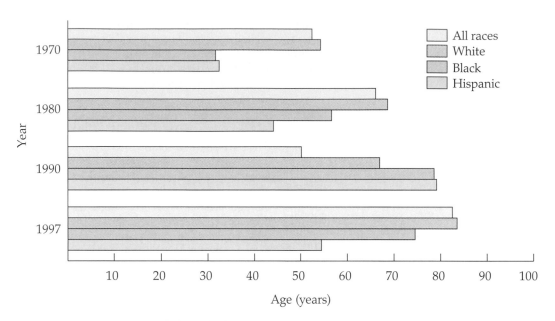

FIGURE 12.3   Percentage of adults who have completed four years of high school or more: 1950–1997.

From *Statistical Abstract of the United States, 1998* (p. 167), by U.S. Department of Commerce, Bureau of the Census, 1998, Washington DC: U.S. Government Printing Office.

high school seniors provided a basic database. There were some 11,500 seniors represented in this study.

Let's look first at family background differences. Actually, 60% of the fathers and 31% of the mothers of adolescents attending elite boarding schools had graduate or professional degrees. The most ethnically diverse student bodies were in the elite high performance private schools.

A look at the educational characteristics by high school type indicates some great differences. The average school size of the private schools was smaller; the private schools had more volumes in their library and a greater percentage of teachers with master's degrees or higher. Fully 100% of students in both the elite private schools and the elite boarding schools were in academic programs, in contrast to only 34% of those in public schools. Private schools also offered superior course programs in terms of academic difficulty. One hundred percent of the private and boarding schools offered calculus. One hundred percent offered French; most of them offered a variety of languages.

It is obvious that the students in the private schools had to work harder than those in the public schools or in the Catholic schools. The students at both the elite private schools and the elite boarding schools were not able to watch TV very much.

A look at Catholic schools indicated that a greater percentage of Catholic parents had graduate or professional degrees than did parents of adolescents attending public schools. Some 71% of the students in the Catholic schools surveyed were in the academic program as compared with only 34% of students in the public schools. A greater percentage of Catholic schools offered advanced courses in math, the social sciences, art, drama, and languages. There were fewer percentages of blacks than in other schools, especially the public schools.

What do these facts mean in terms of practical implications? It is obvious that *those families that can afford private education are more likely to get superior education there for their adolescents than if they sent the students to the average public school.*

Cultural Differences in Achievement

We have seen that the type of school that adolescents attend and the quality of education they receive has a marked influence on their academic achievement. There are also cross-national differences in academic achievement. Students in East Asian countries consistently outperform their American peers, especially in mathematics and science. The question arises as to why this is so: What factors in the educational experiences of East Asian students are important in their superior achievements?

One study of 578 eleventh-grade students, aged 16 to 17 years, from three large metropolitan areas analyzed the waking time that high school students spent going to school and attending after school classes and studies. There were 204 students from Minneapolis, 222 from Taipei (Taiwan), and 152 from Sendai (Japan). Minneapolis was selected because of its high percentage of native-born English-speaking residents. Sendai was selected as the Japanese city most comparable to Minneapolis in terms of socioeconomic and cultural status within the countries. Taipei was the only large Chinese-speaking city in which the study could be done. It is the capital and leading intellectual center of Taiwan. Data were obtained from interviews and tests given to the students as part of a larger study concerning the correlates of academic achievement in three societies. A 46-item mathematics test was constructed to determine math achievement.

Time at School

Researchers sought information about a typical school day by asking students when they arrived and left school on the previous day. The Japanese and Chinese students were at school each school day an hour or two longer than the American students. Some Chinese and Japanese students remained at school for extremely long hours. When only the top percentages are considered, the Japanese eleventh-graders spent over ten hours a day at school, and the Chinese students over eleven-and-a-half hours. In addition to the longer school days in Japan and Taiwan, a half-day of classes on Saturday resulted in substantially more time being spent at school each week by Chinese and Japanese high school students than by American high school students in their five-day week. The longer time that Japanese and Chinese students spent at school was reflected in the greater number of classes they took each semester, which ranged from five to six in the Minneapolis high school and from seven to eight in the Taipei and Sendai high schools. When students were asked specifically about mathematics, Chinese students were spending more time studying math than either the Japanese or the Americans.

Work and Major Activities

Many American eleventh-graders spent much of their time working. While 80% of the American teenagers held part-time jobs, only 26% of the Chinese students and 27%

of the Japanese students worked at jobs outside of school. American students also spent a great deal of time after school socializing with their friends. In fact, they spent about 80% more time with their friends than they did studying. Relative emphasis was reversed for Chinese students, who spent nearly twice as much time studying as they did socializing with their friends. In addition to academic classes, about a third of the students in Taipei and about 15% in Sendai were enrolled in after-school academic classes. The most popular after-school class was mathematics, followed by foreign languages.

Extracurricular Activities

Extracurricular activities were a major part of the lives of many school students in all three cultures. Attending school and studying did not prohibit the majority of Chinese and Japanese students from participating in organized sports, but it did reduce the amount of time spent on sports. The most striking aspect of American students' lives was the amount of time that they spent working and dating, activities that they agreed interfered with schoolwork. Adolescents in Minneapolis reported substantially more time socializing with friends and far greater involvement in dating than did their peers in Sendai and Taipei.

Academic achievement declined in all three cultures as the amount of time students worked, watched television, and socialized with friends increased. Schooling and academic activities appeared to be more important in the lives of East Asian adolescents, especially Chinese adolescents, reflecting the great value placed on education in these societies. Peers and the workplace, in turn, tended to be relatively more common in the lives of most American teenagers (Fuligni & Stevenson, 1995).

Extracurricular activities are emphasized in American schools.

Cross-Cultural Achievement and Psychological Adjustment

It has become increasingly clear that the general level of academic achievement of American elementary and secondary high school students falls below that of their peers in other developed countries or areas such as those in Japan, Taiwan, Hong Kong, and mainland China. Chinese and Japanese students have consistently been among the top performers. When suggestions involve raising academic standards, many American parents and teachers react with grave concern. They often suggest that the East Asian students obtain their impressive levels of academic achievement at an undesirable psychological cost, and that they do not want American students to pay this price. American parents and teachers point to reports that portray East Asian students as nervous, depressed, and generally overburdened by the pressures of trying to maintain high levels of academic excellence.

Psychological maladjustment and its relation to academic achievement, parental expectations, and parental satisfaction were studied in a cross-national sample of 1,386 American, 1,633 Chinese, and 1,247 Japanese eleventh-grade students. Five indices of maladjustment included measures of stress, depressed mood, academic anxiety, aggression, and somatic complaints. In this study, Asian students reported higher levels of parental expectations and lower levels of parental satisfaction concerning academic achievement than their American peers. Nevertheless, Japanese students reported less stress, depressed mood, aggression, academic anxiety, and fewer somatic complaints than did American students. Chinese students reported less stress, academic anxiety, and aggressive feelings than did their American counterparts. High academic achievement as assessed by a test of mathematics was generally not associated with psychological maladjustment. The one exception was in the United States, where high achievers indicated more frequent feelings of stress than did low achievers.

What is the explanation of the higher frequency of stress as reported by American students? One answer is found in the differences in adolescent culture in the different countries. Adolescent culture in the United States is characterized by an abundance of competing interests. American students spend more time dating, working, and socializing than do the students in Taiwan and Japan. Such findings convey the impression that adolescents in the United States feel obliged not only to do well in school but also to have many friends, be good at sports, date, and be employed in some part-time job. In contrast, doing well in school appears to be the major developmental task in Chinese and Japanese teenagers. Despite the demands made on them to maintain high levels of academic achievement, East Asian students seem less conflicted and therefore experience less stress than American students. The major message conveyed by the findings is clear: High academic achievement, such as that exhibited by students in Taiwan and Japan, can be obtained without necessarily increasing students' reports of psychological distress (Crystal, Chen, Fuligni, Stevenson, Hsu, Ko, Kitamura, & Kimura, 1994).

Dropouts

Figure 12.4 shows the percentage of dropouts from school by age and race during 1996. Through age 17, attendance figures are very high, with little difference between whites and blacks. Most dropouts occur during the high school years, especially after age 17, with a greater percentage of Hispanics than blacks or whites leaving school. The total number of dropouts is considerable, though the rate has been decreasing over the years. During 1996, 3.7 million youths were dropouts from school. The overall dropout rate in 1993 was 9.4% (U.S. Bureau of the Census, 1998).

Who Drops Out and Why

There are numerous reasons for youths' dropping out of school or underachieving (Browne & Rife, 1991; Horowitz, 1992). Lack of interest in school, low marks, school failure, misconduct, reading disability, intellectual difficulties or retardation, health problems, financial problems, social maladjustments (Buhrmester, 1990), personality problems, parental influence and relationships, family background (Sarigiani, Wilson, Petersen, & Viocay, 1990), racial and ethnic prejudice and discrimination, and socioeconomic factors were listed (Berndt & Mekos, 1995; Brooks-Gunn, Guo, & Furstenberg, 1993; Connell, Halpern-Felsher, Clifford, Crichlow, & Usinger, 1995; Gregory, 1995; Kupersmidt & Coie, 1990). Usually problems accumulate over the years until withdrawal occurs, after the legal requirements of the number of years of schooling and age have been met. The actual circumstance or event that results in withdrawal may be

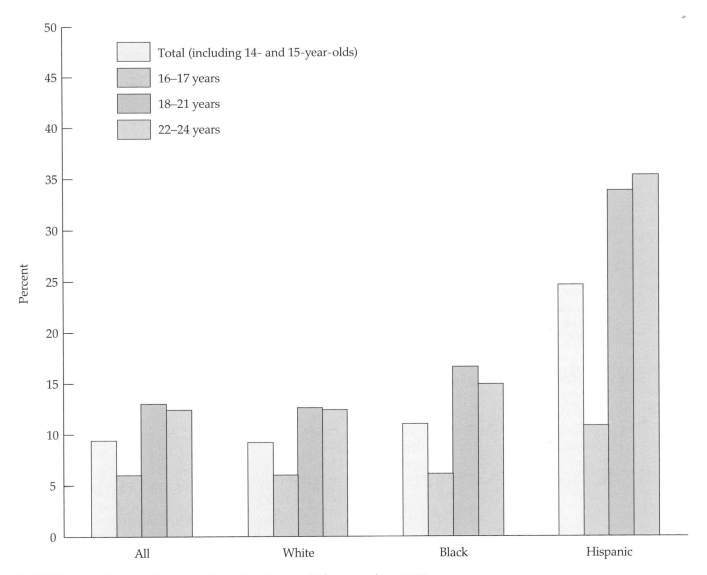

FIGURE 12.4   High school dropouts from 14 to 24 years old, by race and age, 1996.

Statistics from *Statistical Abstract of the United States, 1998* (p. 189) by U.S. Department of Commerce, Bureau of the Census, 1998, Washington DC: U.S. Government Printing Office.

minor: a misunderstanding with a teacher, a disciplinary action, misunderstanding at home, or difficulty with peers. One boy was refused admittance to a class until a late excuse was obtained from his gym teacher in the prior period. The gym teacher would not give an excuse; the boy got angry, walked out of school, and never returned. Another boy withdrew in the last semester of his senior year because his foster parents would not buy him a suit for graduation. In many cases, a whole series of prior events leads to final withdrawal: social maladjustment or isolation, strained family relationships, conduct problems at school, grade retardation, or poor marks. There are a number of factors that correlate with early school withdrawal (Tidwell, 1988).

Family Relationships

The quality of family relationships has a significant impact on school success (DuBois, Eitel, & Felner, 1994; Hurrelmann, Engel, Holler, & Nordlohne, 1988; Snodgrass, 1991). Successful students receive a great deal of social support and encouragement from parents (Cotterell, 1992b; Paulson, 1994). The parents are very involved in school affairs and give their students a lot of encouragement and incentives to do well (Useem, 1991). Bright, high-achieving high

Living Issues

Tracking

Tracking *is an organizational technique that permits schools to create homogeneous groupings of students within a heterogeneous student population in order to facilitate instruction of all students.* Tracking policies can create unequal opportunities for students to learn in a number of ways. One obvious way is by restricting access to higher tracks, which many believe to be characterized by a more interesting curriculum and higher quality instruction. Much theoretical research is critical of tracking, viewing the practice as a means of perpetuating social class and societal values by providing greater learning opportunities for privileged students and fewer opportunities for less privileged ones. From this viewpoint, tracking hinders the attainment of the egalitarian goals associated with American public education.

The problem of how to maximize learning benefits to students when decisions regarding tracking are made is a difficult one. An administrator must make certain tradeoffs in an effort to benefit all students. One administrator may believe that high-ability students benefit more from assignment to a small, homogeneous group, whereas low-ability students might be stimulated by the academic diversity of their peers in a more heterogeneous group. Another administrator may feel that low-ability students have a greater need for homogeneous grouping because of their more limited skills and that high achievers learn regardless of their environment, making homogeneous grouping less critical for them. Because the tracking structures and assignment policies that are established in these two schools will reflect these beliefs, they will differ markedly, with different consequences for student placement and subsequent achievement (Hallinan, 1991).

school students are more likely to describe their parents as less restrictive or severe in discipline, yet authoritative, encouraging (but not pressuring) with respect to achievement, affectionate, trusting, approving, understanding, and typically sharing recreation and ideas (Rosenthal & Feldman, 1991; Steinberg et al., 1992). The extent to which parents offer a warm, accepting environment and provide an emotional support to adolescents plays a critical role in providing a buffer against stressful and anxiety-producing experiences at school. Furthermore, parenting practices appear to influence the degree to which children behave responsibly outside the home. Parents who provide firm guidance by setting clear standards and limits for their young adolescents are especially likely to be successful in having children behave responsibly.

The child's tendency to behave with restraint and in a socially responsible manner is linked to parent-child interactions as well as to academic achievement. Inconsistent par-

enting has been related to childhood aggression and noncompliant behavior, whereas child-centered and responsive parenting has been related to high levels of prosocial and responsible behavior (Wentzel, 1994). Youth from conflict-oriented family environments are more likely to be underachievers and school dropouts than those who come from cohesive, nonconflicting families (Wood, Chapin, & Hannah, 1988).

Pregnancy and Marriage

Pregnancy and marriage are among the most common reasons for girls' dropping out of school (Debolt, Pasley, & Kreutzer, 1990), although pregnancy and marriage are seldom a reason for boys to drop out (Upchurch & McCarthy, 1989).

Money and Employment

Even high school is expensive. This factor, plus financial pressures at home, forces some adolescents to leave school to go to work. For other students, there is the lure of being financially independent. The desire to have money for social activities, a car, or clothes lures many youths to leave school to accept early employment.

Social Adjustment and Peer Associations

Most adolescents want to do what their friends are doing. A student may be persuaded to leave school if friends are dropping out to get jobs earning "big money" or to get married. Students may also withdraw from school if they don't feel that they fit in with their peers. Those students who suffer social maladjustment are those who most likely do not want to continue their school education (Tierno, 1991). Social competence in childhood is often a powerful predictor of academic achievement. Children who are accepted

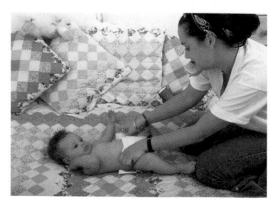

The responsibilities of motherhood may put education on hold.

by their peers, or display postsocial and responsible forms of behavior at school, tend to be high achievers, whereas socially rejected and aggressive children appear to be especially at risk for academic failure. These behavioral and interpersonal forms of competence are often more powerful predictors of achievement than intellectual ability (Wentzel, 1991).

School Apathy, Dissatisfaction, and Failure

A number of scholastic factors are correlated with dropping out of school (O'Sullivan, 1990). Among these are low IQ or mental retardation, low or failing marks, misplacement, grade retardation and repetition, poor reading ability, inability to get along with teachers, and misconduct. Many of these students have lost all confidence in their ability to succeed in school (Nunn & Parish, 1992).

Transition to a new school often precipitates a whole series of events that lead to school failure and dropout. There may be an increase in disengagement from school, accompanied by a decline in class preparations and in grade-point averages. Daily contention with teachers and school personnel seems to increase, while social support and extracurricular involvement decrease over the transition. Conflicts with peers increase as students seek to make adjustments to new friends. The more that youths experience conflicts with the transition to a new school, the lower their expectations of academic prowess become, the less they are prepared for class, and the poorer are their grades (Seidman, Allen, Aber, Mitchell, & Feinman, 1994).

Some students actually anticipate failure even before it begins. Dropouts' perceptions of their situation is the outcome of cumulative experience in the educational system; that is, their feelings of alienation and failure are already internalized when they enter a new school (Horowitz, 1992).

Some students are not necessarily emotionally or socially maladjusted but are not motivated (Elmen, 1991). They simply lack interest in schoolwork, feel it is a waste of time, and would rather get married or go to work. Sometimes such students have been placed in the wrong type of program. A switch to a vocational course that students find appealing is helpful to the adolescent wrongly placed in the college prep program. Students who have to repeat grades, causing them to miss friends and feel like social misfits, may develop an intense dislike for school and lose all interest in learning. Similarly, students who have a history of low marks and failure find school to be an unrewarding experience and cannot wait to get out.

Many students do not drop out; they are either thrown out or given a temporary suspension and never come back. Teachers and administrators often breathe a sigh of relief when the student does not come back. In the case of expulsion, the student has no choice and is not allowed to return.

Truancy

Those who drop out may have a higher rate of truancy from school. Truants, in turn, are less likely to live with both parents and more likely to have more siblings and to score lower in academic ability and achievement than those who attend school regularly (Sommer & Nagel, 1991). School officials are concerned about truancy because of the relationship between truancy and delinquency. School truants are often characterized by unstable employment and higher levels of antisocial behavior than nontruants. There seems to be a connection therefore, between delinquency, lack of school achievement or school success, and truancy. Delinquents are often students of low ability who give little in school and are truant as well. Another study showed that students who were at risk for dropping out had significantly less positive attitudes toward their school experience, lower self-concepts, more external control orientations, and that they viewed their parents as less demanding and more casual in their expectations (Browne & Rife, 1991).

Personality

Dropouts are more likely to be emotionally immature and less well adjusted than high school graduates. They manifest symptoms of defective ego functioning: emotional instability; excessive fear and anxiety; feelings of inferiority; low self-esteem; deep-seated feelings of hostility and resentment; and rebellion, negativism, and alienation (Cairns, Cairns, & Neckerman, 1989). What is so often described as lack of willpower or laziness may actually be resentment toward punitive parents, unfair treatment at school, or social rejection, all of which can cause such feelings of rebellion that the adolescent refuses to do anything demanded by authority. Some of these students develop a real phobia about school (Paccione-Dyszlewski & Contessa-Kislus, 1987). Five traits have been identified as common among underachievers: (a) overprotectiveness, (b) boredom, (c) anxiety, (d) inferiority, and (e) negativism (Stevens & Pihl, 1987).

FOCUS

Student Alienation

One of the reasons that students drop out of school is that they begin to feel alienated from the total school environment. Mau (1992) outlined four dimensions of alienation that seemed applicable to a school context: *powerlessness, meaninglessness, normlessness,* and *social estrangement.*

People feel powerless when they are controlled and manipulated by authority figures and the rules of social institutions. In school, some students experience powerlessness when they can neither control nor change school policies, tracking, or their marginal academic positions. Such students choose not to compete for rewards such as praise and academic grades, and instead rebel against rules, play truant from classes, or merely attend but do not participate in the classes themselves. Other students, occupying better positions in the academic and tracking hierarchies, experience less powerlessness.

Meaninglessness is a second dimension of student alienation. *Some students may be unclear on the connection between subjects taught in school and their future roles in society.* Students who are in this category of meaninglessness simply do not find school relevant to their own lives.

A third dimension of alienation, *normlessness, occurs when individuals have little sense of the cohesive norms and goals of the social institution.* School norms reward students who achieve academically and who intend to pursue higher education. Official school norms seem less fair to students from low socioeconomic status and minority groups. Alienated students may readily reject official school norms in favor of peer and/or counterschool norms.

Finally, *the fourth dimension of alienation, social estrangement, refers to a lack of involvement and minimal association with others in the school context.* When schoolwork is monotonous, when peers are unfriendly, when school officials are uninspiring, then students become dissatisfied with school. Some manifest their feelings by withdrawing or rebelling (Mau, 1992).

Many students feel alienated from their school environment often because they have lost all confidence in their ability to succeed in school.

Stress

Research has indicated that stress has an effect on students' adjustment at school. Stress causes anxiety, depression, and a sense of loss of control. These factors, in turn, have an influence on students' academic success. Decreased confidence, as demonstrated in the classroom by less appropriate attention to tasks or social skills and failing to follow rules, is sometimes the first clue to teachers that children are having a negative reaction to stress. Boys have been found to be more likely than girls to respond with aggression to stress, whereas girls are more likely to withdraw. Furthermore, aggression is more likely to be rated by teachers as maladjustment than the withdrawn behaviors that are more typical of girls under stress (Goodman, Brumley, Schwartz, & Purcell, 1993).

Socioeconomic Factors

Low socioeconomic status correlates positively with early withdrawal from school. There are a number of reasons why this connection is so. The role models presented by parents may not be conducive to finishing school. Many low socioeconomic parents want their children to have more education than they did, but if parents finished only the seventh grade, they may consider graduating from junior high school sufficient. Also, daughters still tend to receive less encouragement to finish school than do sons.

Teachers are sometimes prejudiced against youth from low socioeconomic families and show preferential treatment to students from high-status families. Students from a low socioeconomic background tend to receive less encouragement to do well and to stay in school than do students from higher-status families. They often do not possess the verbal skills of their middle-class peers. This lack in itself presents a handicap in learning to read and in almost all other academic work. Peer influences on low socioeconomic youth are often antischool and delinquency prone. Some low socioeconomic youths reject adult institutions and values, and become involved with groups composed of jobless dropouts.

Ethnic Identity

Students from minority groups, especially those from inner-city schools, have a much higher dropout rate than do white students (U.S. Bureau of the Census, 1989). The value orientation and the familial, social, and economic conditions under which they live tend not to be conducive to continuing education.

Youths from poor neighborhoods are frequently truant and tend to drop out as soon as they reach age 16. However, race, per se, is not the important factor in the high dropout rate of minority students. Low economic status is what makes the difference (Nettles, 1989). For example, the dropout rate among black adolescents in poverty is 33%, compared with 13% for middle-class black adolescents (Children's Defense Fund, 1988).

Intervention

Intervention programs can reduce the dropout rate considerably. That is, the conditions that cause the student to drop out need to be corrected. One study of juvenile delinquents and school dropouts revealed four factors that predicted school dropout: poor relationships with parents, negative influence of peers, disliking school, and misbehavior in school (Dunham & Alpert, 1987). Specific interventions are needed to correct these conditions if the likelihood of dropping out is to be reduced (Bloch, 1989; Kammer, Fouad, & Williams, 1988). One approach is to get youths who have dropped out of school to return by offering them some special programs such as those represented by the Job Corps (Johnson & Troppe, 1992).

Academic Success

One research project was designed to identify those factors that contributed to the ability of at-risk high school students to make the transition from academic failure to academic success. On the basis of open-ended interviews with 66 students, the following factors were important in enabling students to turn around and achieve school success.

1. Schools need to be kept small and their adult populations accessible. Students need both guidance and caring adults in their lives. This study shows that in many cases, students simply need someone to recognize and single them out. Thus, a large number of youth need a lot more attention than they are presently getting in school, especially when they are making transitions from one school to another.
2. Schools need to create an atmosphere that promotes positive peer relationships and helps students to develop social skills. This study totally demonstrates the power of the group among adolescents. It also shows that the group can have both positive and negative influences. Schools and other youth-serving agencies can promote

positive peer relationships by focusing time and energy on the social aspects of development.
3. Schools need to provide youth with an authentic experience of personal success. Once students have had an experience that they trust and an experience that helps them to become successful, they are able to rethink their self-destructive behavior and begin their efforts to turn around (Gregory, 1995).

Full-Service Schools

The plight of young people growing up in inner cities or in poor rural areas has been well documented. The effects of sex, drugs, violence, depression, and stress account for a vast number of youth who will never make it without immediate intervention. These disadvantaged young people, who live in run-down, resource-poor communities, cannot overcome the odds without substantial assistance. Some lack family nurturing and require individual attention from other caring adults. Many go to schools in which they are expected to fail. Both the health system and the educational system are called on to respond to these social deficiencies. Thus, the rationale for creating new kinds of institutional arrangements crosses several domains: health, education, and social services integration.

One emerging program to meet these needs is called a full-service school. A full-

Parenting Issues

Middle-Class Parenting and Underachievement

Metcalf and Gaier (1987) studied patterns of parenting among middle-class parents of underachieving eleventh- and twelfth-graders and found four patterns that contributed to academic underachievement.

- *Conflicted parents*—parents disagree on child-rearing.
- *Indifferent parents*—parents set no consistent limits or standards, and show little interest.
- *Overprotective parents*—parents are perfectionist, domineering, overdirecting, overrestrictive, and constantly expecting their children to do better.
- *Upward-striving parents*—parents criticize, nag, and pressure adolescents to get good marks.

Parenting Issues

Changes in Parents' Work Status and Adolescents' Adjustment to School

Research has indicated that the transition from elementary to junior high school is a time of stress because the adolescent must adjust to a new school environment and new peer networks. We also know that a decline in work status of family members, which affects family income, has disruptive effects on marital and parent-child relationships, increasing parents' depression, discipline, and conflict with children, and decreasing feelings of nurturance and integration in the family. The loss of a family's income or a parent's job security is associated with children's adjustment problems, such as loneliness, depression, antisocial tendencies, and decreases in academic aspirations and self-esteem.

One study examined the patterns of change or stability in parental work status during a two-year period to determine the effect on adolescents who were at the same time going from sixth to seventh grade in school. The families of 432 girls and 451 boys were examined and were divided into four different groups.

The first, the *deprived group,* reported permanent layoffs during the two years of the study. The second, the *declining group,* experienced a layoff or demotion between the time of the first and the second study. The third, the *stable group,* were families who reported no layoffs or demotions at either time of measure. The fourth, the *recovery group,* were families that reported a layoff or demotion at the first study and reemployment at comparable jobs at the second study. Studies one and two were the times that the data were obtained; these times were about two years apart.

The results show that work status and family income were strongly related to each other both times. The stable group had significantly higher, and the deprived group significantly lower, incomes than any other group. The adolescents in stable families reported significantly less worry than the other three groups. By the time of the second study, the financial boost that the recovery families had obtained was obvious in the decline of financial concern to the point where there was no longer a significant difference between the stable and the recovery groups. According to the teachers, adolescents in the deprived, and especially in the declining, families, exhibited significantly lower social competence than their peers in the stable or recovery families. Moreover, a decline in parental work status that occurred during the same period that the adolescent made the transition to junior high school was associated with an increase in school adjustment problems between the sixth and seventh grades; this was especially true of the students in the deprived or declining families. After the transition to junior high school took place, the adolescents in the declining families had the lowest level of social competence of any group. Although the absolute level of income for this group was not as low as that for the deprived groups, they now were worse off in terms of both income and security relative to their accustomed standards (Flanagan & Eccles, 1993).

Parental unemployment has a profound effect on adolescent-parent relationships and adolescent adjustment.

service school integrates education, medical, social, and/or human services that are beneficial to children and youth and their families on school grounds or at other locations that are easily accessible. Full-service schools provide the types of prevention, treatment, and support services that children and families need to succeed: services that are high-quality and comprehensive and are built on interagency partnerships, among state, local, public, and private entities. Their emphasis includes education, health care, transportation, job training, child care, housing, employment, and various other types of social services. School doors are open before and after school, on weekends, and over the summer. A full-time coordinator or program director runs the support service in conjunction with school and community agencies (Dryfoos, 1995).

Summary

1. According to Piaget, the fourth stage of cognitive development is the formal operational stage, achieved by some during adolescence and adulthood.

2. During the formal operational stage, adolescents are capable of introspection (thinking critically about their thoughts); logical thinking (considering all important variables and forming correct conclusions); abstract thinking (going beyond the real to the possible); and hypothetical reasoning (formulating hypotheses, examining the evidence for them, and determining whether they are correct). They are able to use symbols of symbols, so that words can carry double or triple meanings, and their thinking is flexible.

3. As a result of formal operational thinking, adolescents' thoughts and behavior are characterized by idealism and sociocentrism, hypocrisy, egocentrism and self-consciousness, and conformity. Gradually adolescents become decentered as they enter into the adult world and begin an occupation.

4. There are several considerations in relation to Piaget's views: The ages and percentages are not precise and not all adolescents or adults achieve formal operations. The test criteria for operational thinking depend partly on the level of the tests employed; environmental influences, as well as maturation, play a role in cognitive development. There is considerable variability in abstract reasoning abilities, depending on cultural background. Social institutions such as the family and school accelerate or retard the development of formal operations.

5. There is some evidence of a fifth stage of development known as a problem-finding stage. This stage represents an ability to discover and formulate new problems.

6. One of the most widely used tests in the United States has been the SAT— a two-part test consisting of a verbal part and a math part, each scored from 200 to 800. The Educational Testing Service has insisted that in combination with high school records, the SAT is a better predictor of a student's first-year performance in college than any other measurement. Objections to the test have centered around the fact that students can be taught through coaching to do better on the test, and that it is not fair, therefore, to use it as the sole basis for college admission.

7. Some authorities feel that achievement test scores are a more valid measure of scholastic aptitude. The most widely used test of this type is the ACT Assessment Program.

8. The College Entrance Examination Board approved changes in the SAT. The test is now known as the *Scholastic Assessment Test*, with a mandatory section labeled SAT I. The new SAT I has both a verbal part and a math part. Significant changes have been made in the verbal section in terms of the questions that students have to answer. The greatest changes are in the math section. Students may use calculators. There is a new emphasis in the test on critical reasoning and "real-life" problem solving. Although the new test is still coachable, proponents claim it is less coachable than the old tests.

9. During the past 50 years, the emphasis in American education has shifted from one extreme to another: from traditionalism to progressivism and back again. Until the 1930s, traditionalism was the dominant emphasis in American schools. Then came the Depression and the shift to progressive education. After Sputnik, the call was to return to basics: especially math, science, and foreign languages. In the 1960s and 1970s, the call was to do something about social problems and to achieve relevancy. During the 1980s and 1990s, the cry was to return to basics again.

10. Some schools put older students in middle schools and/or junior high school with grades 10 through 12 in senior high schools. Such divisions have many advantages.

11. A comparison of public schools with Catholic schools, elite private high schools, and elite boarding schools reveals superior education in all the types of private schools.

12. There are considerable cultural differences in achievement of students from various parts of the world. Students from Asian countries consistently surpass students from the United States in math and science. Asian students spend more time studying and in school than do U.S. students, who are more involved with extracurricular activities, social life, and working.

13. In spite of longer hours spent studying, Asian students report less stress than U.S. students, who are stressed out from so many different activities.

14. Tracking is an organizational technique for creating homogeneous groupings of students within a heterogeneous student population in order to facilitate instruction of all students.

15. Over 4 million youths are dropouts from school with the greatest percentage among Hispanics, a lesser percentage among blacks, and the lowest percentage among whites.

16. Some students drop out because of alienation, which may be described in four dimensions: powerlessness, meaninglessness, normlessness, and social estrangement.

17. There are a number of factors that correlate with early school withdrawal: misconduct, health problems, ethnic prejudices, truancy, stress, low socioeconomic status, quality of family relationships, personality, social adjustments and peer associations, financial considerations, school failure, apathy and dissatisfaction, and pregnancy and marriage.

18. Schools that establish intervention programs can reduce the dropout rate considerably.

19. Academic success is increased if schools are kept small, if students get personal attention, if schools promote an atmosphere of positive peer relationships, and if youth are given an authentic experience of school success.

20. Full-service schools integrate education, medical, social, and human services that are beneficial to students and their families.

Key Terms

ACT Assessment Program (American College Testing Program)   *p. 328*
Personal fable   *p. 324*
Problem-finding stage   *p. 327*
Progressives   *p. 329*

Scholastic Aptitude Test (SAT)   *p. 327*
Sociocentrism   *p. 323*
Tracking   *p. 336*
Traditionalists   *p. 329*

Discussion Questions

1. Give some examples of adolescents you know who are self-conscious and egocentric.

2. Do adolescents think logically? Why, or why not? Give some examples.

3. How does the idealism of adolescents compare with that of adults?

4. What evidence is there that adolescents are hypocritical?

5. Comment on this statement: "Adolescents are able to escape the concrete present and think about the abstract and the possible."

6. Why do adolescents tend to be conformists?

7. When you were in high school, did your teachers encourage original thinking? Give examples of ways they did and ways they did not.

8. What do you think of the SAT I? Should it be used as a basis for admission to college? What criteria would you use for selection?

9. What do you think of requiring certain performance on achievement tests as a basis for college admission?

10. Did any of you attend a private school when you were an adolescent? What did you think of the experience? Would you want your child to attend a private school? Why, or why not?

11. Should bright pupils be put in a track along with others like themselves, or should they be kept in classes with average students? What about slow learners? Should they be taught in their own sections or placed with others?

12. In your opinion, what are the principal reasons for pupils dropping out of school?

13. What can schools do to reduce the number of dropouts?

14. Should pupils be required by law to stay in school through the twelfth grade? Why, or why not?

15. What can and should parents do if their adolescent is not doing well in school?

CSIKSZENTMIHALYI, M., RATHUNDE, K., & WHALEN, S. (1996). *Talented Teenagers: The Roots Of Success and Failure.* New York: Cambridge University Press.

DRYFOOS, J. G. (1998). *Full-service Schools: A Revolution in Health and Social Services for Children, Youth, and Families.* San Francisco: Jossey-Bass Publishers.

FARRELL, E. (1994).   *Self and School Success: Voices and Lore of Inner-City Students.* Albany: University of New York Press.

GREENBERG, D. (1993).   *Education in America: A View from Sudbury Valley.* Framingham, MA: Sudbury Valley School Press.

NATRIELLO, G., MCDILL, E. L., & PALLAS, A. M. (1990).   *Schooling Disadvantaged Children: Racing against Catastrophe.* New York: Teachers College Press.

NEWMAN, B. M., & NEWMAN, P. R. (1992). *When Kids Go to College: Parents' Guide to Changing Relationships.* Columbus: Ohio State University Press.

RYAN, B. A., & ADAMS, G. R. (Eds.) (1997).   *The Family-School Connection: Theory, Research, and Practice.* Newbury Park, CA: Sage.

Suggested Readings

http://www.davidsonfilms.com Davidson Films Teaching guides, films and research materials about cognitive development and developmental psychology for students and instructors.

Web Resources

Emotional Development

ADOLESCENTS' EMOTIONS

The Components of Emotions

Emotions are subjective feelings an individual experiences in response to stimuli. The word *emotion* literally means "the act of being moved out, or stirred up." An **emotion** is a state of consciousness that is felt as an integrated reaction of the total organism. As discussed in Chapter 8, emotions are accompanied by physiological arousal and result in behavioral responses. Emotional growth and development refer to the development of subjective feelings and to the conditioning of physiological and behavioral responses to these feelings.

The kinds of feelings that develop, the intensity with which they are felt, and the period of time that they persist are important for several reasons. *One's emotional state affects physical well-being and health.* The entire body participates in and reacts to an emotional experience. The autonomic nervous system, the system that is not under voluntary control, carries stimuli to the adrenal glands, which, in turn, secrete adrenalin that acts on the internal organs—the heart, lungs, stomach, intestines, colon, kidneys, liver, pancreas—and glands such as the tear glands, salivary glands, the gonads, and the genitals. Through this network of connections, emotional stimuli can inhibit or increase the rate of respiration or heartbeat. They can contract the blood vessels, dilate the pupils of the eyes, release blood sugar from the liver, secrete perspiration from the glands of the skin, tense the muscles, cause the skin to blush, result in loss of bladder control, or produce a wide variety of other physical reactions. The more intense the emotional stimulus and the longer it persists, the greater and longer the physical reactions will be. Furthermore, emotional states that persist over long periods of time either enhance or destroy physical well-being and health. For example, intense emotional stimuli that cause the stomach to secrete large amounts of acidic fluids over a long period of time may eventually result in those acids' eating away the inner lining of the stomach.

Emotions are also important because they affect behavior in relationships with others (Wintre, Polivy, & Murray, 1990). How adolescents feel partially controls how they act. Those who feel loving, consciously or unconsciously, act more kindly toward others. Those who feel angry may strike out at others or hurt them. Adolescents who feel fearful may try to run away or escape.

The behavior of adolescents can be partly understood by studying and understanding their emotions and feelings. Behavior is caused, in part, by feeling and emotion. In this sense, emotions are a source of motivation; that is, they drive the individual to action. Fear of failure can result in the adolescent's striving for achievement; excessive fear may result in paralysis and prevent action. Emotions, therefore, may have either a positive or a negative effect on behavior, depending on the type of emotion and its intensity.

Emotions are important because they can be sources of pleasure, enjoyment, and satisfaction. They can add color and spice to living. A feeling of joy or happy excitement makes an otherwise routine day bearable. The warmth of love and affection, given or received, gives inner satisfaction and genuine pleasure. The individual who can feel may also fully appreciate the beauty and joy that life can offer.

Emotions During Adolescence

Adolescence is considered by some to be a time of increased emotional lability and intensity. Although this possibility may be true of a minority of adolescents, it is certainly not true of all. For most adolescents, affect with friends becomes more positive, whereas affect experience with family members (especially parents) at home becomes more negative. Research on

Emotions, such as the joy exhibited by this adolescent boy, are subjective feelings and individual experiences in response to stimuli.

As seen in Chapter 8, emotions are classified into different types of categories. One helpful classification is to divide them into three categories according to their effect and result:

1. *Joyous states*—positive emotions of affection, love, happiness, and pleasure
2. *Inhibitory states*—fear or dread, worry or anxiety, sadness or sorrow, embarrassment, regret or guilt, and disgust
3. *Hostile states*—anger, hatred, contempt, and jealousy

Each person experiences these three states at some time, but the ones that predominate are going to be the ones that have the most influence over the person's behavior and life. Moreover, the choice of which ones predominate depends, in turn, on the people and events a person is exposed to during the lifetime.

Joyous States

Children are born with an unlimited capacity to love, but the actual development of warm, affectionate, caring, optimistic, and happy feelings comes from a secure environment, pleasurable events, and close interpersonal relationships. According to Maslow (1970), children first need to satisfy physiological needs and the need for physical protection from harm. As these needs are supplied, children experience positive feelings of comfort, satisfaction, and well-being. However, the basic needs of children are not only physical but also emotional and social. They need love and affection, companionship, approval, acceptance, and respect. If these emotional supports are supplied, their capacity to show positive feelings toward others grows, and they become loving, affectionate, friendly, sociable, approving, accepting, and respecting people. Whether or not adolescents are joyous, happy, and loving will depend on the events taking place around them and on the influence of the people with whom they relate. Certainly, happiness is contagious (Olson, 1992). The continued repetition of pleasant experiences and relationships builds positive emotions, whereas the continued repetition of unpleasant experiences and relationships builds negative emotions.

The important point is that *by the time children reach adolescence, they already exhibit well-developed patterns of emotional responses to events and people.* They may already be described as warm, affectionate, and friendly, or as cold,

emotional expression has demonstrated consistently that as adolescents physically mature, they express more negative affect toward their parents. This trend is paralleled by parent expression of negative affect toward adolescents. Observational studies also report findings of declines in positive emotional expression from early to late puberty. In spite of the increase of negative emotions expressed among family members during adolescence, the majority of adolescents still maintain affectively positive relations with their parents and continue to be warmly engaged with their families.

Changes in the action style are typically viewed as transitory perturbations, whereas adolescents perceive less closeness and acceptance in their relationships with parents. Observational studies point to an increase in expression of negative affect and a parallel decrease in expression of positive emotions across puberty (Flannery, Torquati, & Lindemeier, 1994).

Parental emotions are highly associated with the quality of parenting, with parental warmth predicting favorable developmental outcomes, and with parental hostility predicting unfavorable outcomes. Because strong emotion is a daily concomitant of parenting, even average parents report high levels of conflict and anger with their adolescents. Sometimes these family conflicts increase during adolescence, thus bringing skill in resolving these issues to the forefront during this developmental phase. Families that fail to stay problem-focused and instead resort to the exchange of negatively charged emotions during family problem-solving discussions tend to have more distressed adolescents (Capaldi, Forgatch, & Crosby, 1994).

Emotion—state of consciousness, or a feeling, felt as an integrated reaction of the total organism, accompanied by physiological arousal, and resulting in behavioral responses

unresponsive, and distant. The pattern of emotional response shown during adolescence is only a continuation of the pattern that has been emerging slowly during childhood.

Adolescents who become warm, affectionate, and friendly people have some distinct advantages (Paul & White, 1990). Not only do they derive far greater potential satisfaction from human relationships, but also they engage in social relationships that are more harmonious. Love encourages a positive response from others; it minimizes the individual's aggressive behavior; it acts as a therapeutic force in healing hurts; and it is a creative power in individual accomplishment and in social movements. Love stimulates human vitality and longevity; it is the driving force in positive biological and social relationships in marriage. For adolescents, it is necessary as a binding power in their friendships or in relationships with their parents.

One way of coping with emotional difficulties during adolescence is to develop a sense of humor. A sense of humor is an effective coping style for a variety of emotions. It has been shown to be associated with decreased feelings of anxiety, stress, and negative mood states in response to stressful situations. Humor may be related to negative stressors by cognitively and effectively distancing individuals from the stressor, providing them with a more objective view of the situation. This process also may be helpful in copying with a depressed mood. When depressed individuals are able to find the irony or humor in stressful situations, the level of depression may decrease. Humor may also be associated with individuals' positive view of themselves in the future (Freiheit, Overholser, & Lehnert, 1998).

Inhibitory States

Fear

Fear is one of the most powerful negative human emotions. The psychologists Watson and Raynor (1920) observed that the infant, by nature, shows fear responses to only two types of situations: when threatened with loss of support or falling, and when startled with a loud noise. They found that children do not naturally fear the dark, fire, snakes, or strangers without either having had frightening exposure to them or having been otherwise conditioned to fear them.

Many of the fears that children develop carry over into adolescence. Sometimes, however, the nature and content of fears change as one gets older.

Fears may be divided into four categories:

Living Issues

Is It Love or Infatuation?

An adolescent can develop very intense feelings for another person. However, there is a difference between infatuation, which is an emotional crush on another person, and a deep love. Some of the differences are the following:

- Infatuation is associated with immaturity and is more frequent among young adolescents than mature adults.

- Infatuation may develop toward someone the adolescent doesn't even know. The romance may be entirely fantasized. Mature love is based on knowledge of the other individual.

- Infatuation may be felt toward an unsuitable person; love more likely develops in relation to an appropriate partner.

- Infatuation may cause frustration, insecurity, upset, and anguish; love is more likely to result in fulfillment and happiness (Hatfield and Sprecher, 1986).

- Infatuation is more likely to arise very quickly; love grows slowly. Infatuation can fade as quickly as it arises. Love is more lasting.

- Infatuation centers on intense emotion and strong sexual feelings; love involves the whole personality and includes friendship, admiration, care, and concern as well as sexual attraction.

1. *Fear of material things and natural phenomena*—bugs, snakes, dogs, storms, strange noises, fire, water, closed spaces, heights, trains, airplanes, and the like.
2. *Fear relating to the self*—failure in school, inadequacy in vocational situations, illness, being hurt, death, personal inadequacy, immoral drives or wrongdoings, or temptations.
3. *Fear involving social relationships*—parents, meeting people, loneliness, personal appearance, crowds, the opposite sex, adult groups or situations, dates, parties, certain types of people, speaking before a group, or other situations arising when in social groups.
4. *Fear of the unknown*—supernatural phenomena, world events, unpredictable future, or tragedies.

Generally, as adolescents grow, they lose some of their fears of material things and natural phenomena (although usually not all of them), but they develop other fears, such as the fear that parents are angry, fear of failure, or fear of particular social situations, persons, or groups. Adolescents become more concerned with the effect they have on others, with what others think of them, and of being disliked or rejected by others. Being ignored by a group or being put on the spot in front of a class is a terrifying experience for some adolescents.

Phobias

A **phobia** is an irrational fear that exceeds normal proportions and has no basis in reality. The *Diagnostic and Statistical Manual of Mental Disorders* (4th edition) (American Psychiatric Association, 1994) divides phobias into three categories: (a) simple phobias, (b) social phobias, and (c) agoraphobia. *Simple phobias* include *acrophobia*, fear of high places, and *hematophobia*, fear of blood. Other simple phobias are *hydrophobia*, fear of water, and *zoophobia*, fear of animals (usually a specific kind).

Social phobias are characterized by fears of social situations, such as meeting strangers, going to a party, or applying for a job. Since this kind of phobia limits social relationships, it can interfere with normal living.

Agoraphobia means literally "fear of open spaces" and involves fear of going outside one's own home. It can include fear of going shopping, to church, to work, or to any kind of public place because of a fear of crowds. For this reason, it is a very handicapping phobia. Table 13.1 lists some common phobias.

Worry and Anxiety

Worry and anxiety are closely allied to fear, but they may arise from imagined unpleasant situations as well as from real causes (Moore, Jensen, & Hauck, 1990). The mind imagines what might happen. Many times the worst never happens, so the worry has been unnecessary.

Some worry is directed to a specific person, thing, or situation. Adolescents may worry about what their parents will do because the car battery ran down; they may worry about an examination or about having to give a speech in front of the class. Other causes of adolescent anxiety include not being asked to dance, having friends criticizing their dress, or having friends making fun of the braces on their teeth. These worries arise out of specific things, but the imagined "happening" has not yet occurred or maybe never takes place.

There are wide variations in the extent to which adolescents worry. Some adolescents are more resistant to worry than others. Some are fairly worry free, not only because of constitutional and hereditary factors, but also be-

Phobia—anxiety disorder characterized by excessive, uncontrolled fear of objects, situations, or living creatures of some type

TABLE 13.1   TYPES OF PHOBIAS

Name	Object or Situation Feared
Acrophobia	Heights
Agoraphobia	Open places
Algophobia	Pain
Anthophobia	Flowers
Astraphobia	Storms, thunder, lightning
Cardiophobia	Heart attack
Claustrophobia	Enclosed spaces or confinement
Cyberphobia	Computers
Decidophobia	Making decisions
Ergophobia	Work
Gephydrophobia	Crossing bridges
Hematophobia	Blood
Hydrophobia	Water
Iatrophobia	Doctors
Lalophobia	Public speaking
Monophobia	Being alone
Mysophobia	Contamination or germs
Nyctophobia	Darkness
Ochlophobia	Crowds
Ombrophobia	Rain
Pathophobia	Disease
Peccatophobia	Sinning
Phobophobia	Fear
Photophobia	Light
Pyrophobia	Fire
Syphilophobia	Syphilis
Taphophobia	Being buried alive
Thanatophobia	Death
Toxophobia	Being poisoned
Trichophobia	Hair
Xenophobia	Strangers
Zoophobia	Animals (usually a specific kind)

cause of an environment in which they have had little to worry about as they were growing up. All of their physical needs were supplied; they were loved, accepted, respected, and admired by their parents. They had normal opportunities for companionship, social contacts, and new experiences. They received the necessary guidance and discipline to help them become socialized people. They found success in school experiences, learned

A worried facial expression is often an indication of anxiety.

acceptable standards of conduct, and adjusted well to society. They did not have to be anxious.

Some adolescents are reared in conditions that are just the opposite. They learned early that they could not depend on their parents to supply their basic needs for food, protection from harm, or physical contact. They were never really loved, accepted, praised, or encouraged. Instead, they were rejected, criticized, belittled, or ignored. These experiences stimulated repeated doubts about their self-worth and their own capabilities and talents. They were denied opportunities for ego building and for fulfilling social experiences and relationships. School was a disaster, and friendships were lacking. Tension, turmoil, and conflict in the family were almost continual and extremely upsetting (Stern & Zevon, 1990). Uncontrollable life events stimulate worry and anxiety and thus make these adolescents more prone to depression (Ge, Lorenz, Conger, Elder, & Simons, 1994; Masten, Neemann, & Andenas, 1994).

Under these circumstances, adolescents grow up in an almost constant state of tension and anxiety (Daniels & Moos, 1990). Worry has become a way of life, so much so that they overreact to everyday frustrations or happenings and are anxious about every-

thing that is going to happen. They doubt themselves, other people, and the outcomes of most situations. Whether people or circumstances justify it or not, these adolescents bring anxiety with them to their relationships and to the events that they encounter (Frydenberg & Lewis, 1991). Adolescents who have low levels of family and peer support are more prone to worry and anxiety (Licitra-Kleckler & Waas, 1993).

Hostile States

Anger

Hostile states, which are characterized primarily by feelings of ill will, may be manifested as anger, hatred, contempt, or jealousy (Buss

Generalized anxiety disorder—Exaggerated worry and fear that something terrible is going to happen even though there is nothing to worry about

FOCUS

Generalized Anxiety Disorder

Anxiety is not a mental illness. However, when anxiety becomes so intense and persistent that it interferes with everyday functioning, it is an illness called **generalized anxiety disorder.** Symptoms of generalized anxiety disorder include extreme worry about the smallest mishap, dread that something terrible is going to happen, and anxiety when there is no reason for it to exist. Adolescents suffering from this disorder do not think rationally, so one cannot calm their feelings by presenting all the facts and reasons why they have nothing to worry about. Such intense anxiety may be accompanied by somatic symptoms such as digestive or respiratory disturbances, tearfulness, sweating, shaking and trembling, nervousness, sleep disturbances, feelings of inferiority, or an increase in activity to try to cover up or to escape the fear. It may also result in behavior disturbances.

& Perry, 1992). They have been classified as hostile states because there is a natural tendency to express these emotions through various forms of hostility: fighting, swearing, arguing, or temper tantrums. Adolescents may seek to express their hostility in physical activity, such as work or sports. Sometimes they hold in their feelings, but sulk, become withdrawn, or get moody. Many times they express their anger through verbal aggression (Kubany, Richard, Bauer, & Muraoka, 1992). At other times, their anger results in aggressive acts of violence in which damage is inflicted on inanimate objects, the self, or others. In fits of rage, adolescents will vent their anger by attacking family furniture, school property, a teacher, or a helpless victim. Figure 13.1 illustrates some typical responses to anger-producing stimuli during the adolescent years.

Some time ago, newspapers carried headlines of a father and his 12-year-old son who had been shot by a 16-year-old boy. Their bodies were covered over with leaves in the woods. The father had been shot 32 times. What prompted such rage and violence? Later investigation revealed that the boy who committed the murders was deeply disturbed emotionally and in desperate need of psychiatric help.

Hartocollis (1972) described the quieter, but still destructive, expression of anger of a group of four young patients from the mental ward of a hospital:

> One night after bedtime and when nearly everybody had retired . . . four young patients, three boys and a girl, gathered in front of the nurses' central station. They sat down in a circle and, pouring some coke on the carpet, proceeded to deposit the ashes of their cigarettes on the round wet spot as if it were an ashtray. They did this casually, without saying much, as if performing a ritual, smiling in a mocking way at the nurses who were inside the station. (p. 483)

Whenever excessive or uncontrollable anger builds up and is not expressed in socially constructive ways, it takes impulsive, irrational, and destructive forms, and the adolescent becomes a menace (Hart, 1990). This is one explanation for the wanton violence and vandalism found in many communities. Anger that turns into destructive violence usually builds up through a person's repeated and long-standing negative involvement with other people. A father may reject, belittle, and treat his son cruelly for years before the son's anger finally explodes in an act of violence.

Anger in adolescents has many causes. They may get angry when restricted in physical movement or social activity. They become especially resentful when denied opportunities for social life; for example, when they are not allowed to go out on a date or when they are denied the use of the car. They become angry at any attack on their ego, status, or position. Criticism (especially if they feel it is unjust or unfair), shaming, belittling, or rejection arouses their anger, partly because any such negative stimulus is a real threat to an already overly sensitive ego and a precarious social position. Anger stimuli in adolescents are mostly social. People—their personalities and behavior—stimulate anger responses more often than do things. Hypocritical, inconsiderate, intolerant, dishonest, unfair, nosy, selfish, irresponsible people who ridicule, criticize, hurt, snub, boss, gossip about, or take advantage of other people are the major cause of anger.

To a lesser extent, situations as well as things may cause anger. Situations may include such things as injustices in the world, war, and on-the-job frustrations. Petty situations cause anger: A car or lawnmower won't start, a flashlight won't work, the weather turns unfavorable and interrupts a planned picnic, a guitar string breaks, a baked cake falls, or a low door

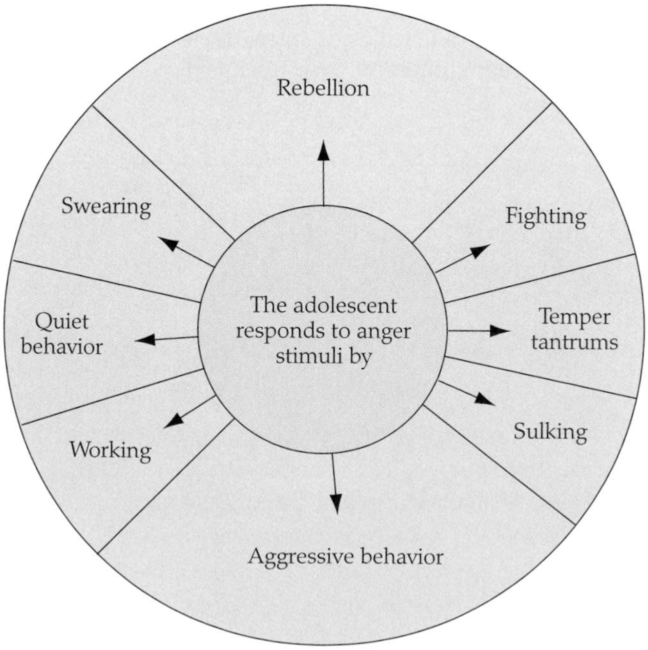

FIGURE 13.1   Responses to anger-producing stimuli during the adolescent years.

Adapted from *Adolescent Development and Adjustment*, 2nd ed. (p. 146), by L. D. Crow and A. Crow, 1965. New York: McGraw-Hill Book Company. Used by permission.

causes a blow to the head. Males are usually more angered by things that don't work than are females. Most females tend to be angered by people and social situations.

Adolescents' anger is sometimes aroused because of their own inability to perform a task or do something that they are trying to do. They become angry at their own mistakes, frustrated when they can't paint a picture that they imagine or achieve a school grade that they desire. They're angry because they receive a low score on a test or because they are unable to hit a tennis ball the way that they feel they should.

There is a wide range of individual differences in the tendency to become angry. Some people are very laid back, seldom getting angry at anything, unless they are given extreme provocation. Other people have almost daily anger reactions and greater tendencies to express verbal and physical aggression when provoked. These high-trait angry people usually describe their family environments as having been less cohesive, having been less tolerant of self-expression, having more conflict, and being more disorganized when they were growing up than the typical family (Lopez & Thurman, 1993).

Hatred

Hatred can be a more serious emotion than anger (at least temporary anger), because it can persist over a longer period of time and can be a result of repeated exposure to a particular person or persons. Adolescents who grow up with parents who do things they detest may develop hatred toward their parents that is not easy to overcome. Hatred is difficult to hide and almost impossible to suppress over a period of time. The feelings are there, and they may be expressed either in subtle ways through words or actions, or in violent ways through explosive, aggressive behavior.

SELF-CONCEPT AND SELF-ESTEEM

As we have seen, how adolescents feel about themselves, about situations, and about other people is very important, because their behavior is often an expression of how they feel. A person's attitudes about himself or herself can be called a self-concept and the way that the person feels about himself or herself can be labeled self-esteem. In this section, we are concerned about both self-concept and self-esteem as they relate to the total life of the adolescent.

Living Issues

Anger and Gender

Both men and women have a problem with anger. But men and women express anger differently. Women are supposed to be emotionally expressive, with the exception of anger. That is, women are socialized to show their emotions more openly than are men, but women's open expressions of anger are viewed as unfeminine. Many women find the idea of anger unthinkable, no matter how much justification there might seem to be. Taught to hide or suppress anger or, at most, to release it indirectly, most women find their anger terrifying.

Because girls are encouraged in relationship skills, they may have heightened awareness of both the personal and interpersonal consequences of anger experiences and thus be more sensitive to the impact of potential responses. Females tend to be more verbal, more facilitative and cooperative, and more focused on interpersonal relationships and the consequences of conflict for such relationships. This finding suggests that girls are more likely to talk to the offender or to talk to someone else about the events, as well as to think about the problem and the way that it may be solved (Whitesell, Robinson, & Harter, 1993).

In contrast to women, men are generally viewed as emotionally inexpressive, with the exception of anger. That is, men tend to exhibit a limited array of emotions except anger, which is considered to be the primary male emotion. Men are, quite simply, taught to be emotionally inexpressive except for the emotions of anger and rage. Men tend to transform all negative or painful emotions into anger again and again (Sharkin, 1993).

Boys are likely to use physical means of expressing anger, such as hitting or yelling. Because their anger is less socially constrained, they think that they have less need to control it. Boys sometimes get mixed messages concerning the control of anger. On the one hand, there is pressure to limit anger responses; on the other hand, there is also pressure to stand up for one's self and fight back. In the social world of school, male dominance is an important aspect of the male subculture. Boys' aggressive strategies may be related to goals for conflict resolution that focus on dominance and self-assertion.

In our culture, males are encouraged to express their anger, females to repress theirs.

Definitions

Self-Concept

The **self** has been defined as a person's perception of his or her nature, character, and individuality. **Self-concept** is the view or impression people have of themselves; it is their "self-hypothesized identity," which develops over a period of many years. Self-concept is the cognitive perceptions and attitudes people have about themselves. It is the sum total of their self-descriptions or self-appraisals.

Self-concept is multidimensional, with each dimension describing different roles. A person may rate himself or herself as a husband or wife, professional person, community leader, relative, friend, and so forth. These different aspects of the self describe the total person (Niedenthal, Setterlund, & Wherry, 1992).

Individuals may have different self-concepts that change from time to time and that may or may not be accurate portrayals of their real selves. Self-concepts are constantly being formulated depending on the circumstances and relationships confronting the individual (Palazzi, deVito, Luzzati, Guerrini, & Torre, 1990). Research findings reveal that the self becomes increasingly differentiated with age. Contradictions and conflict within the self are lowest in early adolescence, peak in middle adolescence, and then begin to decline in later adolescence. During midadolescence, youth develops the ability to compare—but not to resolve—contradictory self-attributes. In later adolescence, the capacity to coordinate, resolve, and normalize contradictory attributes emerges, reducing the experience of conflict over what type of self the person really wants to be (Harter & Monsour, 1992).

A number of years ago, in *Becoming: Basic Considerations for a Psychology of Personality*, Gordon W. Allport (1950) said that personality has some stability, but it never remains exactly the same; it is always in transition, undergoing revisions. Allport used the word **proprium,** which is defined as "all aspects of personality that make for inward unity." This is one's personal identity, one's self that is developing over a period of time.

Ruth Strang (1957) said that there are four basic dimensions of the self. *First,* there is a general self-concept, which is an adolescent's overall "perceptions of his abilities and his status and roles in the outer world" (p. 68).

Second, there are temporary or changing self-concepts, which are influenced by current experiences. A critical remark from a teacher may produce a temporary feeling of deflated self-worth.

The self is a person's perception of his or her nature, character, and individuality.

Third, there are adolescents' social selves: their selves in relationships with others, and their selves that others react to (Lackovic-Grgin & Dekovic, 1990). As one adolescent said, "I like the way others respond to me; it makes me feel good about myself." Some adolescents think of themselves only in negative ways because they feel others don't like them. One important influence on self-concept is the way adolescents feel in social groups.

Fourth, adolescents would like to be their conceptualized ideal self. These projected images may or may not be realistic. Imagining themselves to be selves they never can be sometimes leads to frustration and disappointment. At other times, adolescents project an idealized self and then strive to be that person. Those who are in the healthiest emotional state are those whose real selves approximate their projected ideal selves and who are able to accept the selves who they are.

Self-Esteem

Self-esteem is a vital human need (Greenberg et al., 1992). Self-esteem is the value individuals place on the selves whom they perceive. If their self-appraisal leads to self-acceptance and approval, to a feeling of self-worth, they have high self-esteem. If they view themselves negatively, their self-esteem is low. At various times, adolescents make a thorough assessment of themselves, comparing not

Self—overall perception of one's personality, nature, and individuality

Self-concept—individual's conscious, cognitive perception and evaluation of self; one's thoughts and opinions about oneself

Proprium—the self's core of identity that is developing in time

only their body parts, but also their motor skills, intellectual abilities, talents, and social skills with those of their peers and their ideals or heroes. If their self-appraisal is negative, it may result in self-conscious, embarrassed behavior. They become unhappy because they can't measure up to their ideal selves. Hopefully, they will learn to accept themselves as they are, to formulate a positive view of themselves, and to integrate their goals into their ideal selves (Mandelson, White, & Mendelson, 1996).

Correlations

Relationships with Others

Those who can accept themselves are more likely to be able to accept others and to be accepted by them. There is a positive correlation between self-acceptance, social adjustment, and social support (Blain, Thompson, & Whiffen, 1993). Research indicates that adolescents who are slightly older than their classmates at a particular grade level have more self-esteem than those who tend to be younger than their classmates. Other students tend to look up to the older adolescent (Fenzel, 1992). Adolescents who are more flexible and adaptable in their relationships with others are better liked by others, and these qualities are associated with higher self-esteem (Klein, 1992).

Low self-concept and self-esteem affect social relationships in a number of ways. Adolescents with low self-esteem more often develop feelings of isolation and are more often afflicted with pangs of loneliness. Because they often feel awkward and tense in social situations, it is more difficult for them to communicate with others. And because they want to please others, they are more easily led and influenced by them.

Emotional Well-Being

Adversity or stressful environmental conditions within the home are related to developmental problems for children in adolescence. Adversive or stressful environments might include marital conflict, divorce, family economic stress, or parental psychopathology. The risk of child psychopathology is even greater among children who are exposed to two or more stressful conditions. Discordance within the home, which may precede separation or divorce, may be a more significant factor than the breakup of the marriage in the development of child behavioral or emotional problems (Harold & Conger, 1997).

FOCUS

Self-Esteem in Adolescent Girls

In one research study, the *Mooney Problem Check List* and *Rosenberg's Self-Esteem Scale* were administered to 201 adolescents, ages 14 to 16 years (Harper & Marshall, 1991). Both sex differences in the number and nature of problems reported, and the relationship to self-esteem were examined. There were no significant differences between girls and boys in the areas of *educational* and *vocational future*. Relative to other areas, *adjustment to school-work* was identified as being of considerable concern for both sexes. However, there was a significant relationship between self-esteem and the number of reported problems. And different problem areas were related to self-esteem for girls and boys.

The two problem areas that influenced the self-esteem of girls were *health and physical development* and *home and family*. In both cases, high levels of problems were associated with lower self-esteem. The association between low self-esteem and problematic health and physical development partly reflects the potency of the media in determining the ideal body-image of women and the extreme difficulty that adolescent girls have in trying to obtain this image. The association between low self-esteem of girls and having problems with home and family replicates a common finding reflecting the effects on girls of the restrictions imposed on them, as compared with boys, by parents.

Negative self-esteem is related to parental punitiveness and control (Lackovic-Grgin, Dekovic, & Opacic, 1994). In contrast to the multiple interaction of the influences of problems on the self-esteem of girls, only one problem area, *social and psychological relations*, predicted the self-esteem of boys (Harper & Marshall, 1991).

This research study duplicates what other studies have found: that the self-esteem of men and women arise from different sources (Josephs, Markus, & Tafarodi, 1992).

Self-esteem grows out of human interaction in which the self is considered important to someone. The ego grows through small accomplishments, praise, and success. As a result, high self-esteem is associated with positive psychological adjustment in adolescence (Schweitzer, Seth-Smith, & Callan, 1992). Individuals with low self-esteem often manifest a number of symptoms of emotional ill-health (Ehrenberg, Cox, & Koopman, 1991; Koenig, 1988). They may evidence psychosomatic symptoms of anxiety and stress (Youngs, Rathge, Mullis, & Mullis, 1990). Low self-esteem has also been found to be a factor in drug abuse and in pregnancy among unwed mothers (Black & de-Blassie, 1985; Blinn, 1987; Horn & Rudolph, 1987). In fact, pregnancy among unwed mothers may be an effort on the part of young women to enhance their self-esteem (Streetman, 1987).

Sometimes adolescents with low self-esteem try to compensate and overcome the feeling of worthlessness by putting on a false front to convince others that they are worthy. "I try to cover up so that others won't know I'm afraid." But putting on an act is a strain. To act confident, friendly, and cheerful when one feels the opposite is a constant struggle. The anxiety that one might make a false step and let his or her guard slip creates considerable tension.

Adolescents with low self-esteem are vulnerable to criticism, rejection, or any other evidence in their daily lives that testifies to their inadequacy, incompetence, or worthlessness. They may be deeply disturbed when laughed at, scolded, and blamed, or when others have a poor opinion of them. The more vulnerable they feel themselves to be, the higher are their anxiety levels. Such adolescents report, "Criticism hurts me terribly" or "I can't stand to have anyone laugh at me or blame me when something goes wrong." As a result, they feel awkward and uneasy in social situations and avoid embarrassment whenever they can.

Achievement

There is a correlation between self-concept and achievement in school (Garzarelli, Everhart, & Lester, 1993). Students' level of achievement is related to the perceptions that they have of themselves as learners (Hamachek, 1995). A high self-concept contributes to school success, and scholastic achievement builds a positive self-concept (Liu, Kaplan, & Risser, 1992; Mooney, Sherman, & Lopresto, 1991). The relationship is reciprocal (Roberts, Sarigiani, Petersen, & Newman, 1990).

This relationship between school achievement and self-concept begins in the early grades. Because those who already have negative self-images before they enter school feel that they may not be able to do well, consequently they do not. Older siblings, close friends, fathers, mothers, grandparents, teachers, and school counselors can have an important influence on students' academic self-concepts. If these people manifest positive attitudes in relation to the academic ability of students, the students are more likely to have confidence in their abilities and do well in school.

Goals

There is a positive correlation between the degree of self-esteem and the level of vocational aspirations (Chiu, 1990). Adolescents

with either low or high self-esteem consider it important to get ahead, but those with low self-esteem are less likely to expect that they will succeed. They are more likely to say, "I never get any breaks, which is why I don't get ahead, but I really don't care anyhow." Underneath, they are afraid that they don't possess those qualities essential to success.

Acting-Out Behavior

Juvenile delinquency and low self-esteem seem to be related. In fact, delinquency is sometimes an attempt to compensate for lower self-esteem. The theory is that those who have low self-esteem sometimes adopt deviant patterns of behavior to reduce self-rejecting feelings (Burr & Christensen, 1992). By making their behavior match their low self-concept, they confirm their own rejection of themselves. In these instances, adolescents ally themselves with deviant groups that give them the recognition that society does not give. Those who see themselves as "nondelinquents" or "good people" don't have to prove their own inner worth by becoming delinquent (Krueger & Hansen, 1987).

Parental Roles in Development

Parent-Adolescent Relationships

A number of family variables are related to the development of self-concept and self-esteem (Demo, Small, & Savin-Williams, 1987; Hoelter & Harper, 1987). Adolescents who identify closely with parents strive to model their personality and behavior after them. Consequently, adolescents whose parents have high self-esteem are more likely to have self-esteem themselves (Brown & Mann, 1991). Erikson (1968) said, however, that too close an identification with parents stifles the ego and retards identity development. However, children with minimal parental identification will also have poor ego development. Overall, the degree of maternal identification is related to self-concept. Thus, ego identity of girls is weak if they have poor maternal identification and weak again if there is over-identification.

Fathers also influence identity development. Girls who have a warm relationship with their fathers are more comfortable with their own femininity and with their relationships with other men. They are able to make more mature heterosocial adjustments. Similarly, if the adolescent boy identifies closely with his father and also has very positive, warm feelings toward his mother, his relationships with other women are more likely to be positive.

Self-concept and self-esteem are influenced partly by identification with parents.

Adolescents whose parents provide emotional support and who use democratic reasoning methods of control are more likely to have positive self-esteem than those whose parents offer little support or only negative means of control (Barber, Chadwick, & Oerter, 1992). Parents who reject their children contribute to the development of a negative self-concept (Whitbeck et al., 1992).

Parental Control and Adolescent Self-Esteem

The warmth, concern, and interest parents show adolescents is important in helping youth build a positive ego identity. Parents who show interest and care are more likely to have adolescents who have high self-esteem. Furthermore, parents who are democratic but not permissive are also more likely to have adolescents with high self-esteem. The best parents are strict consistently, demanding high standards, but they are also flexible enough to allow necessary deviations from rules as needed. There seems to be a combination of firmness and emotional warmth. The parent-adolescent relationship is characterized by ties of affection, strong identification, and good communication. Parents who are often inconsistent in expectations and discipline are more likely to have adolescents with low self-esteem.

Some parents are too restrictive or critical of their children. For example, adolescents who are under excessive pressure from their parents to achieve in school are likely to have low self-esteem and feel they are incapable of reaching the goals set for them by their families (Eskilson, Wiley, Muehlbauer, & Dodder, 1986). Certainly adolescents who are physically abused by their parents develop low self-esteem (Allen, Hauser, Bell, & O'Connor, 1994).

Family Happiness

The family represents a basic human support system within which various needs are met. Thus, the degree of family happiness has been found to be related to individuals' levels of esteem. It is reported that college students' self-concepts are significantly related to how their fathers act toward their mothers and how their mothers act toward their fathers (Parish & Necessary, 1994). When all family members get along well and meet one another's needs, the result is higher self-esteem of adolescents within the family (Nielsen & Metha, 1994).

Divided Families

There are a number of factors that mediate the influence of divorce on a growing child (Sessa & Steinberg, 1991). If the mother has custody of the children, the mother's age at the time of

Living Issues

Perfectionism

The wish to excel is an admirable attribute. However, there is a difference between normal and neurotic perfectionism. Normal perfectionists derive a real sense of pleasure from painstaking effort, but feel free to be less precise if needed. Neurotic perfectionists pursue excellence to an unhealthy extreme. Their standards are far beyond reach or reason; they strain unremittingly toward impossible goals and measure their own worth in terms of productivity and accomplishment. They are plagued by self-criticism. When faced with "imperfect" actions, their self-worth is lowered. Recurrent and persistent dissatisfaction with themselves leaves perfectionists feeling unrelenting stress. They fear and anticipate rejection when they are judged imperfect; they are overly defensive when criticized. When contradicted, they become angry. Their behavior alienates others who show the very disapproval that the perfectionist fears. Thus, the irrational belief is reinforced that they must be perfect to be accepted.

Perfectionism evolves from interactions with perfectionistic parents. In a desperate pursuit of parental love and acceptance, the children strive to be flawless. When they are less than perfect, they feel terrible, so they are caught up in compulsively striving to avoid failure (Halgin & Leahy, 1989).

divorce is important. If the mother is young at the time of divorce, the effect on the children will be more negative than if the mother is older because younger mothers are less able to cope with the upset of divorce. The child's age at the time of the marital rupture is also a factor. Young children are more negatively influenced than are older children. Remarriage also influences self-esteem. In one study, children whose parents remarried ("reconstituted families") evaluated themselves more positively than children whose parents had divorced but not remarried (Parish & Dostal, 1980). However, children who did not get along with their stepparents tended to evaluate themselves more negatively than children whose mothers did not remarry. Children from intact families tend to have the most positive self-esteem of all (Parish, 1991).

In one study, no significant differences in self-concept scores were found in third-, sixth-, and eighth-grade children from intact, single-parent, and reconstituted families (Raschke & Raschke, 1979). However, children who reported higher levels of family conflict also had significantly lower self-concept scores regardless of family type. Thus, the quality of interpersonal relationships is more important than the type of family structure. Parish and Parish (1983) also found that whether a child came from an intact, reconstituted, or single-parent family was not as important as whether the existing family was happy or unhappy. Conflicts between parents or between children and parents often result in lower self-esteem in the children. Amato (1986) also found lower self-esteem among adolescents from conflicting families and from those where the parent-adolescent relationship was poor.

One significant finding is that loss of self-esteem when parents divorce may or may not be temporary (Parish & Parish, 1991). Amato (1988a) found little correlation between adult

self-esteem and the experience of parental divorce or death during childhood. However, in a longitudinal study of 60 divorced families, Wallerstein (1989) found that more than half of the adolescents entered adulthood as underachieving, self-deprecating, and sometimes angry young men and women. They showed high levels of delinquency, promiscuity, and alcohol abuse both 10 and 15 years after the divorce. Not surprisingly, they had trouble with intimacy in relationships.

Unfortunately, Wallerstein did not study a control group from intact families for a comparison of her findings. The findings were predicated on the assumption that these problems would not occur as often in intact families. Also, because her findings were from an affluent sample living in Marin County, California, they might not apply to those of other groups. However, Wallerstein's provocative study has shattered the complacent feeling that divorce never has long-term consequences for children.

Socioeconomic Variables

Socioeconomic status (SES) has an inconsistent effect on self-esteem (Orr & Dinur, 1995). One comparison between college and noncollege youths indicated that college youths had higher self-esteem than noncollege youths (Greene & Reed, 1992). Generally, students with higher SES have higher self-esteem than those with lower SES. However, in their study of 11th-grade students from three North Carolina high schools, Richman, Clark, and Brown (1985) found that females with higher SES had lower self-esteem than those with middle or low SES. In this instance, females with higher SES felt pressured to excel in social activities, physical attractiveness, academics, and so on. Perceived failure in any one of these areas led to feelings of inadequacy and loss of self-esteem. Females with lower SES were more used to failure, so it was not as traumatic for them as for those with higher SES.

Economic hardship has been found to have a negative effect on adolescent self-esteem. The adverse effect of economic hardship on adolescent self-esteem is mediated through the parent-adolescent relationship. Economically stressed parents are more likely to display inconsistent discipline, more rejection behavior, less nurturance, less support, and to be more autocratic (Ho, Lempers, & Clark-Lempers, 1995).

Socioeconomic status of the parents alone does not produce the same level of

Coming from an intact family is not as important to childhood self-esteem as the level of conflict in the family.

self-esteem (Martinez & Dukes, 1991) in every case. Families with low SES can raise high self-esteem children if the parents have high self-esteem. Similarly, parents from minority groups can raise high self-esteem children if the parents have high self-esteem. One example is that of Jewish adolescents, who, though they come from a minority religious group in American society, tend to have high self-esteem, probably because of the high self-esteem of the Jewish parents and the generally adequate parent-child relationship, measured by the concern and care that Jewish parents show for their children.

Racial Considerations

Self-esteem among blacks has risen, partly as civil rights and black consciousness movements have encouraged racial pride. A study of public high school black and white adolescents from Tennessee showed that the black students had significantly higher levels of self-esteem than did the white students (Rust & Mc-Craw, 1984). Richman, Clark, and Brown (1985) found this same situation in North Carolina. However, when blacks are exposed to white prejudices, their self-esteem declines. If black adolescents are surrounded by those with similar social class standing, family background, and school performance, they rate themselves much higher in self-esteem than when surrounded by prejudiced white people.

Understandably, some black adolescents have high self-esteem, and others have low self-esteem. Black adolescents who have established close friendships and achieved some degree of intimacy have high self-concepts and feel good about themselves. This finding emphasizes an important factor in self-esteem. Social adjustments are important to adolescents' developing high self-concepts. Those who have difficulty maintaining close friendships and gaining group acceptance also show signs of low self-concepts.

Short-Term and Longitudinal Changes

The self-esteem of adolescents is affected by important changes and events in their lives. Adolescents who get involved with the wrong crowd and begin to adopt deviant behavior may show less self-respect and an increase in their own self-derogation. High school juniors had a lower self-concept after they had moved with their families a long distance to another town. One study showed that self-esteem was lowest at around 12 years of age (Protinsky & Farrier, 1980). By applying careful statistical controls, researchers showed that the onset of puberty itself was not the determining factor. Twelve-year-olds in junior high school had lower self-esteem, higher self-consciousness, and greater instability of self-image than did 12-year-olds in elementary school. When differences in race, socioeconomic class, or marks in school were considered, none of these variables was found to be conclusive. The one factor that was significant was whether the students had entered junior high school. The move from a protected elementary school, where a child had one set of classmates and few teachers, to a more impersonal and larger junior high school, where classrooms, classmates, and teachers were constantly shifting, was disturbing to the self-image. Males, particularly, were much more likely to be harassed or beaten up after they entered junior high school. This study clearly illustrates that self-image can be affected, at least temporarily, by disturbing events (Wigfield & Eccles, 1994).

Different schools have a different effect on self-concepts. If pupils aren't doing well in one school, transferring them to another school sometimes changes their behavior, attitudes, and self-concepts. Transferring pupils to different schools is, however, more effective with junior high school pupils than with those in senior high schools.

Self-image and self-esteem can also be improved by helpful events. Positive summer camp experiences can improve the self-concepts of young adolescents. Stake, DeVille, and Pennell (1983) and Waksman (1984a,b) offered assertion training to secondary school and college-level students who were timid and withdrawn. Good results were reported by Stake and colleagues (1983) at 3-month

Self-esteem among blacks has risen, partly because of increased opportunities and partly because of black consciousness movements that encourage racial pride.

follow-up, and by Waksman at 7-week follow-up, in helping students to maintain eye contact, talk to others, greet them, ask questions, refuse some requests, and express their feelings when they dealt with other students, teachers, or relatives. Wehr and Kaufman (1987) report improved assertiveness of ninth-grade boys and girls after only four hours of training.

Overall, self-concept gradually stabilizes (Chiam, 1987). A 10-year longitudinal study of adolescents, beginning in grade 5 and 6 and continuing until they were out of high school, showed only a slight increase in positive self-concept. For the majority of youths, those who had a negative self-concept in early adolescence entered adulthood with the same negative feelings (Barnes & Farrier, 1985). This finding is in keeping with another study that indicates no age differences in self-esteem (Mullis, Mullis, & Normandin, 1992).

Longitudinal studies addressing change and self-esteem over time reveal that adolescent males tend to show higher levels of self-esteem than do females. Explanations of males' relatively higher levels of self-esteem often center on body image, which tends to be more positive for adolescent males than for females. There is some evidence for declining self-confidence in other areas for adolescent girls, including confidence in mathematical abilities (Thorne & Michaelieu, 1996). Stability of self-esteem is necessary in making mature, emotional adjustments (Tevendale, DuBois, Lopez, & Prindiville, 1997).

EMOTIONS AND BEHAVIORAL PROBLEMS

Sometimes negative emotions result in behavioral problems. Three such problems discussed here are drug abuse, delinquency, and running away.

Drug Abuse

Commonly Abused Drugs

The drugs most commonly abused may be grouped into a number of categories: alcohol, nicotine, narcotics, stimulants, depressants, hallucinogens, marijuana, and inhalants. Out of these groups, the most frequently used drugs in the United States are alcohol, tobacco, and marijuana, in that order. Table 13.2 shows the percentage of 12- to 17-year-olds who have ever used and who are current users (past month) of various types of drugs in 1985, 1990, 1995, and 1996.

Black adolescent males are significantly less likely than white adolescent males to drink alcohol, get drunk, smoke cigarettes, or use smokeless tobacco, hallucinogens, and sedatives. Black adolescent females are significantly less likely than white adolescent females to drink alcohol, get drunk, smoke cigarettes, and use marijuana (Allen & Page, 1994).

Addiction and Dependency

A distinction must be made between **physical addiction,** or physical dependency, and **psychological dependency.** An addictive drug is one that causes the body to build up a chemical dependency to it, so that withdrawal results in unpleasant physical symptoms (Ralph & Morgan, 1991). Psychological dependency is the development of a powerful psychological need for a drug, resulting in a compulsion to take it. Drugs become a means of finding relief, comfort, or security. The use of alcohol, for example, becomes self-reinforcing when individuals come to believe that it enhances social and physical pleasure or sexual performance, leads to arousal, or to increased social assertiveness, or reduces tension (Webb et al., 1992).

Some individuals become psychologically dependent on drugs that are also physically addicting, such as crack cocaine, barbiturates, alcohol, heroin, and nicotine. Dependence is strongly reinforced by the desire to avoid the pain and distress of physical withdrawal. Sometimes physical dependency is broken, but individuals go back to the drug because of psychological dependency on it. It is a mistake, therefore, to assume that the only dangerous drugs are those that are physically addictive.

Trends in Drug Abuse

Youths are trying drugs at young ages. It is not unusual for children 8 to 10 years old to use drugs. An elementary school official in Washington, D.C., complained that he had not been able to keep one third-grader from smoking marijuana every day at recess. Threats of expulsion did not help because the child insisted he could not break the habit. He did refuse to share his cigarettes with classmates because, he said, "the habit is dangerous" ("Drug Pushers," 1979). One longitudinal study in the San Francisco area showed that socially precocious females were more likely to become involved with drugs earlier than were males, although for both boys and girls, the transition to junior high school played an important role in initiating drug use (Keyes & Block, 1984).

Physical addiction—the body's chemical dependency on a drug built up through its use

Psychological dependency—an overpowering emotional need for a drug

| TABLE 13.2 | PERCENTAGE OF YOUTH, AGES 12–17, USING DRUGS | | | | | | | |

Drug	Ever Used				Used in Past Month			
	1985	1990	1995	1996	1985	1990	1995	1996
Marijuana*	20.1	12.7	16.2	16.8	10.2	4.4	8.2	7.1
Inhalants†	7.9	5.7	10.3	5.6	0.6	0.4	0.4	0.4
Hallucinogens†	6.9	7.9	9.5	9.7	1.2	0.4	0.7	0.6
Cocaine†	11.2	11.2	10.3	10.3	3.0	0.9	0.7	0.8
Heroin†	0.9	0.8	1.2	1.1	0.1	0.6	0.4	0.1
Stimulants†	7.3	5.5	4.9	4.7	1.8	0.6	0.4	0.4
Sedatives†	4.8	2.8	2.7	2.3	0.5	0.2	0.2	0.1
Tranquilizers†	7.6	4.0	3.9	3.6	2.2	0.6	0.4	0.4
Analgesics†	7.6	6.3	6.1	5.5	1.4	0.9	0.6	0.8
Alcohol*	56.1	48.8	40.6	38.8	41.2	32.5	21.1	18.8
Cigarettes*	50.7	45.1	38.1	36.3	29.4	22.4	20.2	18.3

*Youth ages 12 to 17.
†Youth 12 years old and older.
Statistics from U.S. Bureau of the Census (1998). U.S. Government Printing Office, p. 151.

Patterns of Drug Use

Five patterns of drug use may be identified (Pedersen, 1990):

1. *Social-recreational use* occurs among acquaintances or friends as a part of socializing. Usually this use does not include addictive drugs and does not escalate in either frequency or intensity to become uncontrolled use.

2. *Experimental use* is motivated primarily by curiosity or by a desire to experience new feelings on a short-term basis. Users rarely use any drug on a daily basis and tend not to use drugs to escape the pressures of personal problems. However, if users experiment with physically addictive drugs, they may become addicted before they realize it.

3. *Circumstantial-situational use* is indulgence to achieve a known and desired effect. A person may take stimulants to stay awake while driving or may take sedatives to relieve tension and go to sleep. Some persons use drugs to try to escape problems. The danger is that such use will escalate to intensified use.

4. *Intensified drug use* generally involves using drugs at least once daily over a long period of time to achieve relief from a stressful situation or a persistent problem. Drugs become a customary part of the daily routine. Use may or may not affect functioning depending on the frequency, intensity, and amount of use.

5. *Compulsive drug use* involves both extensive and frequent use for relatively long periods, producing psychological dependence and physiological addiction with discontinuance resulting in psychological stress or physiological discomfort. The threat of psychological and physical discomfort from withdrawal becomes the motivation for continued use. Users in this category include not only the skid-row alcoholic and street "junkie" but also the crack-dependent adolescent, the alcohol-dependent businessman, the barbiturate-dependent

Drug abuse education tries to prevent children and youths from starting to use drugs.

housewife, the opiate-dependent physician, and the habitual smoker (Rice, 1990a).

Family Origins

The following family factors correlate closely with excessive drug use by adolescents while growing up (Beman, 1995; Bettes, Dusenbury, Kerner, James-Ortiz, & Botvin, 1990; Denton & Kampfe, 1994; Foshee & Bauman, 1994). In comparison with nonabusers,

- Drug abusers are less likely to have open communication with parents (Kafka & London, 1991).

- Abusers are usually not as close to their parents, are more likely to have negative adolescent-parent relationships, and have a low degree of parental support (Anderson & Henry, 1994; Unger, Kipke, Simon, Johnson, Montgomery, & Iverson, 1998; Weigel, Devereux, Leigh, & Ballard-Reisch, 1998).

- Abusers are more likely to have parents who drink excessively and/or use other psychotropic drugs (Andrews, Hops, Ary, Tildesley, & Harris, 1993; Doherty & Allen, 1994; Wodarski, 1990).

- Adolescents are more likely to smoke if their parents smoke (Kandel & Wu, 1995).

FOCUS

The Role of Smoking in the Lives of Low-Income Pregnant Adolescents

Over the past decade, increased cigarette smoking among female adolescents has emerged as a major social issue. This is a particular problem because smoking during pregnancy is detrimental to the health of the fetus, the newborn, and the infant. Smoking has been associated with low infant birth rate and with perinatal and neonatal mortality. Smoking contributes to intrauterine growth retardation, delayed reading ability, and short attention span.

Smoking during pregnancy is detrimental to the health of the baby.

One study describes the beliefs and attitudes of smoking among low-income pregnant teenagers (Lawson, 1994). The sample consisted of 20 first-pregnant adolescents who received prenatal care at a public health center. They were between the ages of 16 and 18 (mean 16 years) with two years of high school education (mean 10 years). Of the group, 70% were white, and 30% were African American; 65% were single, 30% were married, and 5% were separated or divorced.

A structured interview of 40 open-ended questions was administered. The questionnaire was designed for the teenagers' beliefs about and perceptions of tobacco use. Examples from the questionnaire were, "Tell me what you think about smoking during pregnancy. What are the benefits you derive from smoking? Would you start smoking again? What do you like most about smoking?" Additionally, at the beginning of the first interview, subjects were asked the amount they currently smoked, the length of time they had smoked, and the type of cigarettes they used. Data were collected during two years of field research. The interviews, which were held weekly until six-weeks postpartum, lasted for more than two hours and were audiotaped in the respondents' homes. Participant observations were conducted over one year in prenatal classes, at high school dances, and at community locations such as pool halls, playgrounds, and bowling alleys, in order to explore the use of tobacco in a social environment. Sixty-five percent of the sample reported smoking a pack of cigarettes daily. Seventy percent began smoking between the ages of 10 and 11.

The beliefs about why the teenagers smoked were very interesting. The study population believed that cigarette smoking controlled body weight and that cessation consistently produced marked weight gain. As a

continued ▶

- Parent use of a substance is the most powerful influence on an adolescent's initiation of use of the same substance (Andrews, Hops, & Duncan, 1997).
- Abusers are more likely to come from broken homes or not to live with both parents (Doherty & Needle, 1991).
- Abusers are more likely to be dissatisfied with parents and experience parental deprivation (Hundleby & Mercer, 1987).
- Abusers' parents less often praise, encourage, and counsel and set limits to adolescents' behavior (Coombs & Landsverk, 1988; Hauser, Bornan, Jacobson, Powers, & Noam, 1991).
- Parental conflict in child-rearing practices, inconsistent discipline, restrictive discipline, and maternal rejection are all associated with marijuana and alcohol use in older adolescents (Vicary & Lerner, 1986).
- Harsh and inconsistent parental child-rearing strategies are related to tobacco use by adolescents (Melby, Conger, Conger, & Lorenz, 1993).
- Abusers are likely to experience parental physical and sexual abuse, which leads to self-derogation (Dembo et al., 1987).
- The family relationships of adolescents who abuse drugs are similar to those of

result, they endorsed smoking to pacify their craving for "junk foods" and to control their appetite. One subject, for example, explained in this way: "When I smoke, I don't eat cakes and candy bars. Just think how much weight I would gain if I did not smoke." Another remark was, "I don't snack as much when I smoke, so I keep my weight under control." Furthermore, these young women believed that cigarette smoking helped them avoid dieting postpartum. For example, subjects who smoked one pack daily before pregnancy and started to smoke additional cigarettes in their second trimester commented: "I smoked one pack a day before I got pregnant. I smoke more now since I am pregnant. If I put on too much weight, it would be hard to lose after delivery."

One reason that these young women were concerned about weight gain was peer harassment about body size. One respondent claimed she was called names because she was fat, and another said she was not invited to parties because of her weight gain. Thus, she smoked to maintain her weight and to win approval.

Another recurrent theme in the respondents' perception of smoking was the belief that weight gain inhibited future relationships. One girl explained, "I won't get another boyfriend if I gain too much weight. I smoke so I'll be slim and boys will ask me out."

These young women reported fear of anticipated labor pain and the time that it would last. They saw cigarette smoking as a way to control the pain. Without exception, all believed that cigarette smoking would ensure having a smaller baby, which would result in shorter labor and less painful delivery. One said, "I want a small baby so my labor will not be hard." These women also reported about other women who smoked during pregnancy. One recalled, "Five of my friends smoke a pack everyday. Their babies are healthy."

These girls also described the extent of their dependency on cigarettes and the role that they played in their lives. One girl who had lived in eleven foster homes since birth described her "bond" to cigarettes: "I just gotta have cigarettes by my side because they are the only stable thing in my life." One said, "Cigarettes are my best friends." Their commitment to cigarettes was analogous to a child's clinging to a favorite blanket or doll.

Some teenagers smoked because they were having difficulty achieving an identity. One reason for the difficulty was the lack of positive role models. They believed that tobacco use distinguished them from peers who smoked marijuana and used drugs. One girl noted this: "I have friends who use drugs and smoke pot but I just smoke cigarettes. It's better to smoke

cigarettes than to be using drugs." Another one remarked, "I'm better than other girls in the projects who were running around with different boys, selling their bodies for drugs, and writing cold checks, because I just smoke." In addition, these young women contrasted smoking to conduct that involved their peers in a criminal justice system: "I won't go to jail for smoking. Two of my friends are in juvenile detention for stealing, I'm glad to be just a smoker." Some of the girls compared their smoking with their parents' alcohol and drug abuse. As one noted: "I'm proud to be just a smoker cause my parents are alcoholics."

In summary, this study showed that teenagers smoked in order to cope with increased weight gain; to deliver smaller infants, which, in turn, would decrease the duration of labor and reduce the pain of delivery. They smoked because they formed an attachment to cigarettes that partially fulfilled their need for security in their lives. Tobacco use was also related to identity formation. The respondents believed that cigarette smoking distinguished them from peers and family members who abuse drugs (Lawson, 1994).

adolescents who are emotionally disturbed. In one study, all substance abusing/mood disordered families rated themselves as dysfunctional in major areas of family life (Yeh & Hedgespeth, 1995).

- In one study, adolescent mothers who abuse drugs during pregnancy reported more mental and physical problems, more problematic family and peer relationships, poorer social skills, more negative behavior, less constructive use of leisure time, and a lower educational and vocational status than did non-drug-abusing adolescent mothers (Scafidi, Fieod, Prodromidis, & Rahdert, 1997).

- Siblings are significant contributors to the early development of adolescent problem behavior, including substance use. A sibling's level of concurrent use is significantly related to the level of use of the younger adolescent. These findings suggest that siblings can be a significant continuing source of influence on adolescent substance use as the adolescent's use increases with age (Duncan, Duncan, & Hops, 1996).

- Drug abuse among Native American adolescents is higher than among white adolescents and continues to increase (Gfellner, 1994).

These types of family situations create personality problems that cause individuals to be more likely to turn to drugs. Numerous other studies associate drug addiction and dependency with disturbed family relationships and personality problems (Page, 1990).

Other Social and Psychological Correlates

A number of studies concerning illicit substance abuse among adolescent and preadolescent populations have been conducted and identify specific risk factors associated with the initiation and use of substances by these adolescents. Of particular interest are those studies that focus on individual attributes, characteristics, situations, and environmental conditions that may increase the probability of substance use and abuse by school-age youth (Zapata, Katims, & Yin, 1998).

1. Those who abuse drugs are more likely to have peers who use and approve of drug use (Alberts, Hecht, Miller-Rassulo, & Krizek, 1992; Dinges & Oetting, 1993; Stanton & Silva, 1992; van Roosmalen & McDaniel, 1992; Webb et al., 1991).

Abusers spend a lot of time with drug-abusing friends (Shilts, 1991).

2. Abusers are more likely to be involved with deviant peers (Simons & Whitbeck, 1991).
3. Abusers are more likely to suffer psychological distress and feelings of depression (Eisen, Youngman, Grob, & Dill, 1992; Simons & Whitbeck, 1991).
4. Abusers are more likely to show interpersonal distress, lack of self-confidence, self-rejection, and devaluation.
5. Abusers are more likely to have disturbed relationships with others and to be disruptive in the school classroom (Dobkin, Tremblay, Masse, & Vitaro, 1995).
6. Abusers are more likely to be in rebellion against social sanctions (Kaplan & Fukurai, 1992).
7. Abusers are more likely to be lonely (Page & Cole, 1991).
8. Abusers are more likely to be truant from school (Pritchard, Cotton, & Cox, 1992).
9. Abusers are more likely to have frequent sex, have a greater number of coital partners, and show a greater percentage of unprotected sex (Jemmott & Jemmott, 1993).
10. Drug abusers are considered more likely to be at risk for AIDS infection than those who do not use drugs (Li, Stanton, Feigelman, Black, & Romer, 1994).
11. Religion is a protective factor against alcohol abuse by black adolescents. White adolescents are more susceptible to beer drinking influences than are black adolescents (Barnes, Farrell, & Banerjee, 1994).

Delinquency

Incidence

Of all persons arrested in 1998, 19% were juveniles—under age 18. Figure 13.2 shows the percentages. As seen in Figure 13.3, the incidence of delinquency among males under 18 is nearly 4 times that among females of the same age (U.S. Bureau of the Census, 1998). When just serious crimes are considered, 31% of these were committed by persons under age 18. This includes 15% of all murders, 16% of all rapes, 32% of all robberies, 42% of all automobile thefts, and 53% of all arrests for arson. When they are arrested, females are more likely to be arrested for minor crimes and status offenses such as running away from home, incorrigibility, truancy, and other noncriminal offenses (Rhodes & Fischer, 1993).

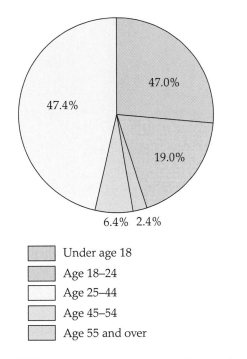

47.0%

47.4%

19.0%

6.4% 2.4%

- Under age 18
- Age 18–24
- Age 25–44
- Age 45–54
- Age 55 and over

FIGURE 13.2   Age distribution of all people arrested, 1996.

From *Statistical Abstract of the United States, 1998* (p. 220), by U.S. Bureau of the Census, Department of Commerce, 1998, Washington, DC: U.S. Government Printing Office.

Psychological Causes

In general, the causes of delinquency may be grouped into three major categories (Farrington, 1990): psychological factors that include emotional and personality factors and difficulties in interpersonal relationships; sociological factors that include societal and cultural influences; and biological factors that include the effects of organic and physical elements (Caspi et al., 1993).

There have been efforts to determine whether certain personality factors predispose the adolescent to delinquency (Holcomb & Kashani, 1991; Weaver & Wooten, 1992). Generally speaking, no one personality type is related to delinquency, but those who become delinquent are more likely to be impulsive, destructive, suspicious, hostile, resentful, ambivalent to authority, defiant, socially assertive, and lacking in self-control (Ashford & LeCroy, 1990; Thompson and Dodder, 1986). Aggressive conduct is associated with delinquent behavior (Pakiz, Reinherz, & Frost, 1992).

Delinquency is sometimes a manifestation of hostilities, anxieties, fears, or of deeper neuroses. One important cause is love deprivation while growing up (Walsh & Beyer, 1987). In other instances, delinquency occurs in basically healthy adolescents who have been misled by others. In some cases, delinquency is the result of poor socialization that results in adolescents' not developing proper impulse controls. The psychodynamics of delinquents' behavior are different, although the results of that behavior are similar (Hoffman, 1984).

Sociological Causes

Family factors, such as strained family relationships and lack of family cohesion, are important sources of delinquency (Kroupa, 1988; Mas, Alexander & Turner, 1991; Nory et al., 1992; Tolan, 1988; Tygart, 1991). The families of violent delinquent adolescents report poorer discipline, less cohesion, and less involvment that nonviolent families of adolescents (Gorman-Smith, Tolan, Zelli, & Huesmann, 1996).

Broken homes have been associated with delinquency, but are no worse than, and sometimes not as detrimental as, intact but unhappy or disturbed family relationships. Studies of delinquency often compare the rates for adolescents from broken homes with those from intact happy homes. However, if comparisons are made between adolescents from broken homes with adolescents from intact but unhappy homes, the effects on adolescents are similar, indicating that family environment is more important in delinquency than is family structure (LeFlore, 1988).

One study demonstrates that *parental controls are significant inhibitors of delinquency*. But this is true more often for males than for females. For males, these controls are more effective in midadolescence, (ages 13 through 16 years); for females, they are better deterrents in later adolescence (ages 15 through 18 years). Attachment varies with age, and parental control decreases as adolescents become older. This pattern means that parental power, in its influence on delinquency or in its influence in preventing delinquency, becomes less as male adolescents get older (Seydlitz, 1991). However, later study suggests that rebellion against parental control is highest when the adolescent is less attached to the parent. The pattern suggests that adolescents who feel more distant from their parents are less accepting of parental rules and resent parents' controlling actions (Seydlitz, 1993). When parents use consistent, child-centered, and nonaversive parenting when their sons are in the sixth grade, their boys' relative level of self-restraint is higher, and the level of delinquency is lower (Feldman & Weinberger, 1994).

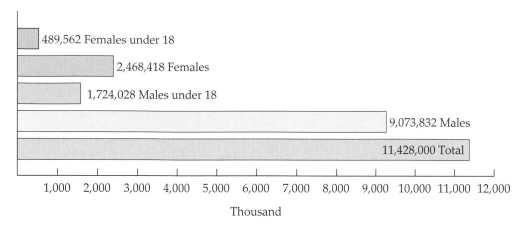

FIGURE 13.3   People arrested, by sex and age, 1996.

Statistics from *Statistical Abstract of the United States, 1998*, by U.S. Bureau of the Census, Department of Commerce, 1998; Washington, DC: U.S. Government Printing Office.

Juvenile delinquency is distributed through all socioeconomic status levels (Lempers & Clark-Lempers, 1990). In fact, as great an incidence of some forms of delinquency among adolescents of middle classes exists as among those of lower classes. Tygart (1988) found, for example, that youths of high socioeconomic status (SES) were more likely to be involved in school vandalism than youths of low SES. One big difference is that middle-class adolescents who commit delinquent offenses are less often arrested and incarcerated than are low-class youths. However, family poverty inhibits informal social control and in turn, increases the likelihood of juvenile delinquency. Also, erratic, threatening, and harsh discipline, low supervision, and weak parent-child attachment mediate the effects of poverty on delinquency (Sampson & Laub, 1994). Not only is juvenile delinquency found in poverty-stricken families, but also it is distributed through all socioeconomic status levels.

Community and neighborhood influences are also important. Most larger communities have areas in which delinquency rates are higher than in other neighborhoods. A larger than average percentage of adolescents growing up in these areas become delinquent because of the negative influence of the neighborhood. Adolescents who grow up in these neighborhoods are also more likely to be victims of crimes themselves.

Some adolescents become delinquent because of antisocial influences of peers (Pryor & McGarrell, 1993). A high degree of peer orientation is sometimes associated with a high level of delinquency. In fact, association with delinquent peers is the strongest single predictor of delinquency (Pabon, Rodriguez, & Gurin, 1992).

The absence of either a parent or a teacher as an adequate role model is an important predictor of gang membership (Wang, 1994). Many youths become involved with juvenile gangs and commit a number of illegal acts that they wouldn't dare to do without the pressure of gang membership (Winfree, Backstrom, & Mays, 1994). Contemporary researchers studying gang activities emphasize that such activity is increasing at a meteoric rate (McConnell, 1994). The youth gang is becoming a complex, variable, and highly significant institution in society that needs to be understood better so that we can prevent or at least control its development and impact. Adolescent female participation in violent crime and illegal gang activities has become more common (Sommers & Baskin, 1994).

Modern youths are also influenced by affluent and hedonistic values and lifestyles in our culture. Youths may be encouraged to keep late hours, get into mischief, and become involved in vandalism or delinquent acts just for kicks.

Violent youths may have been influenced by the violence they see in our culture and in the media (Snyder, 1991). May (1986) found that youths who behave in a violent manner give more selective attention to violent cues. They tend to choose to attend movies that are more violent, and then to imitate what they have seen and heard. Today's adolescents are also living in a period of unrest, disorganization, and rapid cultural change, all of which tend to increase delinquency rates.

Drinking is strongly associated with serious delinquency among both white and black youths, especially when other factors such as drug use, association with drug users, and previous arrests are present (Watts & Wright, 1990).

The level of school performance is also correlated with delinquency (Grande, 1988). Inability to get along with teachers and administrators, difficulty adjusting to the school program, classroom misconduct, poor grades, and a lack of school success are associated with delinquency.

Biological Causes

Biological causes may play a role in delinquency. Mednick and Christiansen (1977) showed that the autonomic nervous system (ANS) in criminals recovers more slowly from environmental stimulation as compared with that of noncriminals. Slow recovery time reduces the ability to alter their behavior through punishment; thus, it becomes more difficult to unlearn delinquent behavior.

There is a possibility that a maturational lag in the development of the frontal lobe of the brain results in neurophysiological dysfunction and delinquent behavior. Juveniles are not able to act on the basis of the knowledge they have.

We know also that certain personality characteristics, such as temperament, are

Seventeen percent of all persons arrested in a recent year were under age 18.

FOCUS

Profile of Youthful Offenders

A summary of the characteristics of adolescent felons in a prison treatment program in California revealed the following characteristics (Eisenman, 1993):

1. The youth had all developed antisocial orientation. They saw crime as the right thing to do and considered people as objects to be manipulated for their own purposes.

2. They attempted to be hostile toward all authorities.

3. Most of them had no idea how to be anything other than full-time, hard-core criminals. They lacked any sense of how they could change themselves to be something else.

4. Almost all of them had been subjected to physical, psychological, or sexual abuse while growing up, and typically, from one or both parents, usually the father. Original authority figures had failed miserably in the socialization process.

5. Often the parents were either criminals themselves or were less than totally law-abiding.

6. Over half of the black and Hispanic prisoners were members of street gangs. These gangs resembled the Mafia in that once someone was in, there was no leaving. Less than half of the white inmates were gang members, but of those who were, they tended to be either skinheads or stoners. Skinheads are members of racist, neo-Nazi, proviolent groups that are extremely anti-black and anti-Jewish. Stoners are prodrugs, their name derived from the expression "getting stoned." Most were mainly involved in burglary to support their drug habits.

7. The felons were typically of low intelligence, at least as measured by the standardized tests.

partly inherited, so that a child may have a predisposition to behave poorly. If the parents do not know how to cope, the problem is compounded because the child develops a psychological disturbance.

According to Sheppard (1974), at least 25% of delinquency can be blamed on organic causes. He cited the case of a 15-year-old girl whose blood sugar level was too low because of an excess of insulin. The girl was fidgety, jumpy, restless, and unable to think or act rationally. Proper diet and medication corrected the difficulty. Sheppard cited other examples of delinquency caused by abnormal brain wave patterns, hyperactivity from hyperthyroidism, and hearing impairment. Other research indicates a definite relationship between delinquency and health problems such as neurological, speech, and hearing and vision abnormalities. Prenatal and perinatal complications may also be the cause of later behavior problems.

Living Issues

Teens Who Kill

As indicated earlier, *15% of all murders committed in 1996 were committed by teenagers under 18 years of age* (U.S. Bureau of the Census, 1998). Recently, a 13-year-old Maine boy was indicted for bludgeoning to death a 3-year-old boy in his neighborhood. This crime is but one of a growing number of senseless murders. In Madison, Indiana, four teenage girls doused 12-year-old Sandra Shrer with gasoline and burned her alive in January 1992 because she was trying to "steal" the friendship of another girl. Henry James, 19, opened fire on a passing car on a Washington-area interstate because he felt like "busting somebody." The somebody turned out to be a 32-year-old woman driving home from work. It seems that in some communities, every teenager has a gun. When everyone has a gun, every argument carries the potential for deadly violence. The FBI reports that, in 1990, nearly three out of four juvenile murderers used guns to commit their crimes. The gun in the hands of a 14-year-old is a very dangerous weapon. A 14-year-old has little investment in life and doesn't really know the meaning of death.

In the inner cities, where weapons are as common as household appliances, the lessons in cruelty usually start at home. Psychologist Charles Patrick Ewing, author of *Kids Who Kill,* has found that many young people committing seemingly motiveless killings were themselves sexually or physically abused. To brutalize another human being, a youngster has to have been brutalized himself or herself. Ewing finds that teenage murderers often don't recall or won't admit that they were once victims. A street tough often would rather go to the gas chamber than admit to having been beaten or sodomized by a male relative (Traver, 1992).

Drug-Related Causes

A high percentage of juvenile crime is drug-related. Drugs influence crime in several ways. *First,* youths who cannot otherwise afford drugs commit crimes in order to feed their drug habits. *Second,* youths are more likely to commit crimes when they are under the influence of drugs (McMurran, 1991). Steroids, for example, increase verbal and physical aggression and hostility, resulting in fights with others or beating up a girlfriend.

Prevention

Those who work with delinquents are very concerned about prevention. One of the ways to prevent delinquency is to identify children (such as hyperactive ones) who may be predisposed to getting into trouble, and then to plan intervention programs to help them. Another preventative measure is to focus on dysfunctional family relationships and assist parents in learning more effective parenting skills. Antisocial youths may be placed in groups of prosocial peers, such as at day camps, where their behavior is influenced positively. Young children may be placed in preschool settings before problems arise. Older children need help with learning disabilities before they develop behavior problems. Social skills training may be helpful with some offenders (Cunliffe, 1992). Programs such as *Big Brothers/Big Sisters* have also been found to be beneficial. Many children need intensive programs with one-on-one therapy or group therapy (Garrett, 1995).

Evidence is mounting that the effective prevention and treatment of juvenile violence is possible. Programs that intervene in multiple social systems that involve the offending youth have begun to show positive effects, even with violent offenders. There is also evidence that systematic changes in juvenile justice policies that emphasize treatment and rehabilitation regardless of the seriousness of offense can result in a system that is more humane, more cost-effective, and more effective in reducing rates of juvenile crime and recidivism (Kuperminc, & Reppucci, 1996).

Hurley (1985) wrote: "A partial list of the links to crime includes television, poor nutrition, eyesight problems, teenage unemployment or employment, too little punishment, too much punishment, high or low IQ, allergies and fluorescent light" (p. 680). Great commitment is required to sort out the various links to crime and to correct these causes. Certainly incarceration, although it may be necessary, does not really solve the problem of juvenile delinquency (Armistead, Wierson, Forehand, & Frame, 1992).

Unfortunately, there has been a decline in efforts at rehabilitation through juvenile justice throughout much of the United States in the past 20 years. Contrary to expectations, emphasis on justice has promoted an unprecedented rise in the number of incarcerated youth and a deterioration in institutional conditions. This situation has occurred in spite of the fact that rehabilitation is superior in effectiveness in altering patterns of delinquency (MacAllair, 1993).

Effective prevention rests on making a comprehensive assessment of the causes of delinquency in the first place. Psychological, familial, sociological, and community factors may interact in various ways to produce delinquent behavior. The kinds of intervention must be tailored to the problem profiles of the youth, the families, and the community. Treating all delinquents with the same set of intervention techniques and resources is doomed to partial success at best (Sullivan & Wilson, 1995).

Gun Violence

A higher incidence of weapon-carrying, of guns in particular, among youth has been identified as a key factor in recent increases of violence. According to the 1990 *Youth Risk Behavior Survey*, one in twenty high school students carries firearms, usually a handgun, and one in five carried a weapon of some type during the thirty days preceding the survey (Page & Hammermeister, 1997).

Running Away

Incidence

Over 700,000 youths, ages 10 to 17, run away from home for at least one night without adult consent (Crespi & Sabatelli, 1993). Almost 60% of these youths are females, many of whom are assisted by boyfriends. An analysis of the youths served under the *National Runaway Youth Program* across the United States revealed the following profile (U.S. Department of Health and Human Services, 1980).

- *Race/ethnic origin:* White (74%)
- *Age:* 16 years (25%)
- *Sex:* Female (59%)
- *Living situation past 3 years:* Home with parents or legal guardians (82.4%)
- *Length of stay:* Less than 14 days (84.1%)
- *Juvenile justice system involvement:* No involvement (59.4%)
- *Reasons for seeking services:* Poor communication with parent figures (51.8%)
- *Parent participation:* One or both parents (51.9%)
- *Disposition:* Home with parents or legal guardian (30.4%)

Runaways come from the full range of American families: white black, Latino, Native American, and Asian-American families; single-parent and two-parent households; and privileged, middle-class, working-class, low-income, and even homeless families. Furthermore, they do not always run away from home; "youth run from foster care, shelters, group homes, and traditional treatment facilities" (Schaffner, 1998). The fact that these youths come from a variety of social classes and home backgrounds indicates that the reasons for running away are not a result of any one cause.

Living Issues

Parricide

One form of intrafamilial violence that is attracting more attention is child-to-parent violence. **Parricide,** the killing of one's mother or father, is becoming increasingly publicized, although it remains relatively infrequent. It now accounts for less than 2% of all homicides in the United States. **Patricide,** the killing of one's father, accounts for less than 1% of all homicides; **matricide,** the killing of one's mother, accounts for a slightly lower percentage (Young, 1993). Most of the research emphasizes a common theme: Parricide is often a response to a long-standing child-abuse problem. Typically, children who kill their parent are from 16 to 18 years old, from a white, middle-class family. Most have above-average intelligence, although their schoolwork may be below average. They generally are well-adjusted in school and the community, though they tend to be isolated without many friends. They commonly have had no prior run-in with the law.

Their target is most often the father—usually a biological or stepparent rather than adoptive or foster parent—and the typical weapon is a gun kept in the home. In most cases of parricide, a bizarre, neurotic relationship exists between the victim and the assassin in which the parent-victim mistreats the child excessively and pushes the child to the point of explosive violence. Offenders know they are doing wrong, but they're desperate and helpless, and they don't see alternatives. In fact, dispatching their tormenter can be seen as an act of sanity, a last-resort effort at self-preservation (Toufexis, 1992).

Shannon and Melissa Garrison, and Allen Goul (background) are escorted away from the courthouse in Gulfport, Mississippi, after their preliminary charges of killing the girls' mother.

Classification

Roberts (1982) made a helpful classification of different types of runaways according to the degree of conflict with parents. Figure 13.4

Some adolescents who run away from home become street kids.

illustrates the categories. The 0 to 1 categories include youths who wanted to travel and received permission from parents. Runaway explorers wanted adventure and to assert their independence. They left their parents word about where they had gone and then left without permission. They generally returned home on their own if they were not picked up by the police. Social pleasure-seekers usually had conflict with parents over such issues as dating a certain person, attending an important event, being grounded, or having an early curfew. They sneaked out to engage in the forbidden activity and then either sneaked back or stopped by a friend's house overnight. They usually telephoned the parents the next morning to ask to come home.

Runaway manipulators tried to maneuver their parents by running away to force them to permit return on the runaways' own terms. They had serious conflict with parents over choice of friends, home chores, and other issues.

Runaway retreatists came from families where there was conflict, hitting or throwing objects, frequent yelling, and other manifestations of tension. Some of the homes were broken. In addition, the majority of adoles-

cents had one or more school problems, or problems with alcohol or other types of drugs. They and their families needed counseling help to correct the situations that resulted in running away in the first place.

Endangered runaways left to escape abusive parents or stepparents (Kurtz, Kurtz, & Jarvis, 1991). These youths often used drugs and had drinking problems. A beating or the threat of a beating may have precipitated running away (Roberts, 1982). Physical or sexual abuse of both males and females is often a reason for running away (Janus, Burgess, & McCormack, 1987). Girls often become involved in prostitution, and males in drug dealing. Once on the street, runaways tend to become involved in a social network composed of other runaways and street people who engage in deviant, often illegal, acts of various sorts to support themselves (Simons & Whitbeck, 1991).

The simplest classification of runaways is to divide them into two groups: the running from and the running to (Miller, Eggertson-Tacon, & Quigg, 1990; Roberts, 1982). The running-from adolescents could not tolerate one or both parents, or their home situation. The running-to adolescents were pleasure-seekers, impulsive, running to places or people providing exciting and different activities. Some enjoyed running away and liked the friends they met on the way. They usually stay away longer and do not return until picked up by the police (Sharlin & Mor-Barak, 1992).

Not all runaways are the same or leave home for similar reasons (Hier, Korboot, & Schweitzer, 1990). However, clusters of personal or situational variables appear repeatedly in their case histories. One study in Hawaii found that children from single-parent families had less chance of becoming chronic runaways than those from intact families (Matthews & Ilon, 1980). This is the case because there was more quarreling in

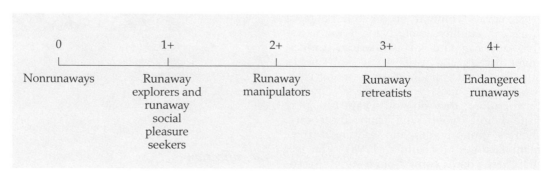

FIGURE 13.4   Formulation of the degree of parent-youth conflict continuum.

From "Adolescent Runaways in Suburbia: A New Typology," by A. R. Roberts, Summer 1982, *Adolescence, 17,* pp. 379–396.

the two-parent families, which the child felt powerless to prevent and from which escape seemed the only solution.

Assistance

The *National Runaway Youth Program*, with the U.S. Youth Development Bureau, has promoted nationwide assistance to youths who are vulnerable to exploitation and to dangerous encounters. The program offers a national toll-free communication system to enable youths to telephone their families and/or centers where they can get help. Most of the individual programs throughout the United States have developed different services to meet various needs. Social service agencies and juvenile justice/law enforcement systems also use their services to assist runaways and their families.

Summary

1. Emotions are subjective feelings and individual experiences in response to stimuli, which are accompanied by physiological arousal and which result in behavioral responses.

2. Emotions affect physical well-being and behavior, and are important sources of pleasure and satisfaction.

3. Adolescence may be a time of increased mood swings and emotional lability for some adolescents, but certainly not for all. Positive affect with friends may increase at the same time that it is decreasing with parents. Still, the majority of adolescents maintain positive relationships with their parents.

4. Adolescents' emotions are associated with the quality of parenting.

5. Emotions may be classified into three categories: joyous states including affection, love, happiness, and pleasure; inhibitory states including fear or dread, worry or anxiety, sadness or sorrow, embarrassment, regret or guilt, and disgust; and hostile states including anger, hatred, contempt, and jealousy.

6. Joyous states also include feelings of warmth and well-being.

7. By the time that children reach adolescence, they already exhibit well-developed patterns of emotional responses to events and people. They may already be described as warm, affectionate, and friendly, or as cold, unresponsive, and distant.

8. One way of coping with emotional difficulties is to develop a sense of humor.

9. Fear may be divided into four categories: fear of material things and natural phenomena, fear relating to the self, fear involving social relationships, and fear of the unknown.

10. A phobia is an excessive, uncontrolled fear. Phobias may be divided into three categories: simple phobias, social phobias, and agoraphobia.

11. Worry and anxiety are closely allied with fear but may arise from imagined unpleasant situations as well as from real causes.

12. Generalized anxiety disorder occurs when anxiety becomes so pervasive and tenacious that it interferes with normal functioning.

13. One of the ways of relieving emotional distress is by talking out feelings.

14. Hostile states may be manifested as anger, hatred, contempt, or jealousy.

15. Anger in adolescents has many causes: restrictions on social life, attacks on their ego or status, criticism, shaming, rejection, or the actions or treatment of other people. Situations, as well as the adolescents' own ineptitude, also cause anger.

16. Both men and women have a problem with anger. However, women are taught to inhibit anger; men, to express it. There is a wide range of differences in the tendency to become angry.

17. Hatred can be more serious than anger because it persists over a long period of time, is difficult to suppress, and may be expressed through words or actions in violent, aggressive, and explosive ways.

18. Self-concept may be defined as a person's perception of his or her nature, character, and individuality.

19. Ruth Strang said that there are four basic dimensions of the self: basic, overall self-concepts; transitory or temporary self-concepts; social selves; and ideal selves.

20. Self-esteem is the value that people place on themselves. There is a positive correlation between self-esteem, social acceptance, and social support.

21. One study revealed that high levels of problems in the areas of health and physical development and home and family were associated with low self-esteem in adolescent girls.

22. A positive self-esteem is important to interpersonal competence and social adjustments, and to emotional well-being, progress in school, and vocational aspirations. Negative self-esteem is related to delinquency.

23. A number of factors are important to the development of a positive self-concept: the quality of parent-adolescent relationships, the type of parental control, the atmosphere of the home—whether happy or unhappy, the self-esteem of the parents, and the quality of social relationships and friendships.

24. Neurotic perfectionists pursue excellence to an unhealthy extreme, are plagued by self-criticism and low self-worth, and by the stress of having to be perfect.

25. Self-concept gradually stabilizes during adolescence, although adolescents are sensitive to important events and changes in their lives.

26. The most frequently abused drugs are alcohol, tobacco, and marijuana, in that order.

27. A physically addictive drug is one that builds up a chemical craving for it, so that denial results in withdrawal symptoms. Psychological dependence is the development of a persistent, psychological need for a drug. Those who use physically addictive drugs may develop a chemical dependency before they realize it. Those who use nonaddictive drugs to solve emotional problems may become psychologically dependent on them.

28. Youths are trying drugs at younger ages.

29. Drug use may be divided into five patterns: social-recreational use, experimental use, circumstantial-situational use, intensified use, and compulsive use.

30. There is a correlation between drug addiction and dependency and disturbed family relationships. Other social and psychological correlates with drug use in adolescents are: peer approval of drug use, involvement with deviant peers, psychological distress and depression, lack of self-confidence, disturbed relationships with others, rebellion against social sanctions, truancy, and frequent, permissive, unprotected sex.

31. Alcoholism is dependence on alcohol: uncontrolled, compulsive, and excessive drinking leading to functional impairment. Alcohol abuse is the use of alcohol to a degree that causes physical damage or impairs functioning.

32. A considerable number of pregnant adolescent mothers continue to smoke during pregnancy, endangering their health and that of their baby.

33. Nineteen percent of all arrests during 1998 were of people under age 15. Delinquency among males under age 18 is 3½ times that among females of the same age.

34. The causes of delinquency may be grouped into three categories: psychological, sociological, and biological.

35. Psychological causes include emotional and personality factors.

36. Sociological causes include family background influences, socioeconomic status levels, neighborhood and community influences, peer group involvement, affluence and hedonistic values and lifestyles, violence in our culture, cultural change and unrest, drinking and drug use, and school performance.

37. Teens who kill were often themselves sexually or physically abused.

38. Biological or organic factors may also be involved in delinquency.

39. Parricide is the killing of one's mother or father. Patricide is the killing of one's father; matricide is the killing of one's mother.

40. Any efforts to curb delinquency need to focus on prevention.

41. Adolescents who run away from home have been classified along a continuum as runaway explorers, social pleasure seekers, runaway manipulators, runaway retreatists, and endangered runaways. The simplest classification is to divide them into two groups: the running from and running to. Thus, not all runaways leave home for the same reasons.

42. The National Runaway Youth Program has been developed to provide multiple-service assistance to runaways.

Key Terms

Discussion Questions

1. What sort of things make you the happiest? most afraid? most worried? most angry?

2. Do you have any phobias? Describe. How did they arise? What do you do about them?

3. Why do some adolescents hate their parents? What can or should they do about these feelings?

4. Do you have a positive or negative self-concept? What factors have been most influential in molding your ideas about yourself?

5. If you could be any type of person you wanted, what would you be like?

6. Is there any possibility you can become your ideal self? Explain why or why not.

7. Do you have a different self-concept from when you were younger? Explain.

8. What role have your parents played in influencing your self-esteem?

9. Do you accept what your friends say about you? Why, or why not?

10. Who have been the most significant others in your life in influencing your self-conception?

11. Does parental divorce or remarriage influence self-esteem? Explain with personal examples.

12. Did you or your friends use drugs when you were in high school? With what effects?

13. What type of drug education programs in high school would help the most?

14. If you were a parent and discovered that your adolescent was using alcohol, tobacco, marijuana, narcotics, or cocaine, what would you do?

15. To those who have stopped smoking: What helped the most in being able to stop?

16. Why do far fewer females than males become delinquent?

17. If you were a parent, would you forbid your adolescent to run around with a friend who was a convicted delinquent? How would you handle the situation?

18. What factors are the most important in causing delinquency?

19. Do you have any firsthand knowledge of gangs in the town where you live, or where you grew up? Describe.

20. Have you or has a member of your family ever run away from home? Why? What happened?

AMMERMAN, R. T., & HERSEN, M. (Eds.). (1991). *Case studies in family violence.* New York: Plenum. Different types of family violence and their treatment.

DAVIES, J., & COGGANS, N. (1991). *The facts about adolescent drug abuse.* London: Cassell. What drug abuse is, and what can be done about it.

GOLDSTEIN, A. P. (1991). *Delinquent gangs: A psychological perspective.* Champaign, IL.: Research Press. The gang phenomenon and how to deal with it.

NEWCOMB, M. D., & BENTLER, P. M. (1988). *Consequences of adolescent drug use: Impact on the lives of young adults.* Newbury Park, CA: Sage. How does adolescent drug use affect later life?

STRAUS, N. D. (1994). *Violence in the lives of adolescents.* New York: Norton. Suicide, running away from home, delinquency, sexual offending, and physical abuse.

Suggested Readings

http://www.aacap.org The American Academy of Child & Adolescent Psychiatry. Up to date information on child and adolescent development and issues, especially behavioral and emotional mental disorders.

Web Resources

Social Development

Chapter 14

ADOLESCENTS IN THEIR FAMILIES

The family is the chief socializing influence on adolescents. Therefore, the family is the principal transmitter of knowledge, values, attitudes, roles, and habits that one generation passes on to the next. Through word and example, the family shapes an adolescent's personality and instills modes of thought and ways of acting that become habitual. But what adolescents learn from parents depends partly on the kinds of people the parents are (McKenry, Kotch, & Browne, 1991).

What Adolescents Expect of Parents

The following is a compilation of research findings that indicate that youths want and need parents who

1. "Treat us as grown-ups, not like children."
2. "Have faith in us to do the right things."
3. "Love us and like us the way we are."
4. "We can talk to."
5. "Listen to us and try to understand us."
6. "Are interested in us."
7. "Guide us."
8. "Are fun and have a sense of humor."
9. "We can be proud of."

These characteristics need closer examination (Williamson & Campbell, 1985).

Reasonable Freedom and Privileges

One goal of every adolescent is to be accepted as an autonomous adult (Fasick, 1994). This acceptance is accomplished through a process called separation-individuation, during which the parent-adolescent bond is transformed but maintained. The adolescent establishes individuality from and connectedness with parents at the same time. The adolescent seeks a differentiated relationship with parents, while communication, affection, and trust continue (Quintana & Lapsley, 1990).

One of the complaints of adolescents is that their parents treat them like kids (Kobak, Cole, Ferenz-Gillies, & Fleming, 1993). Most adolescents push as hard as they can for adult privileges and freedom. They want to feel that they can make their own decisions and run their own lives, without their parents always telling them what to do (Pardeck, 1990). However, adolescents need parents who will grant them autonomy in slowly increasing amounts as they learn to use it responsibly (Dornbusch, Ritter, Mont-Reynaud, & Chen, 1990; Gavazzi, Anderson, & Sabatelli, 1993; Gavazzi & Sabatelli, 1990). In his research with adolescent boys, Steinberg (1981) found that assertiveness increases from early puberty to middle adolescence, after which it tapers off as adolescents begin to exert more influence in family decision making (Ellis, 1991; Papini, Roggman, & Anderson, 1990). Too much freedom granted too early may make them think that the parents aren't interested. Youth want freedom—but do not want it all at once. Those who have freedom suddenly worry about it because they realize they do not know how to use it. Adolescents who have good relationships with their parents still look to them for guidance and advice (Greene & Grimsley, 1990; Papini & Roggman, 1992).

One of the most important ways a parent can assist the adolescent's successful transition into adulthood is to maintain a balance between the adolescent's need for individuality and for remaining emotionally

The family is the chief socializing influence on adolescents.

connected to the family (Gavazzi, Anderson, & Sabatelli, 1993). A lack of parental attachment seems to be associated with increased depression in adolescence (Sabatelli & Anderson, 1991). The ideal seems to be to have a moderate degree of emotional attachment to parents (Papini & Roggman, 1992).

Faith

Adolescents say,

> "My parents don't trust me. They always seem to expect the worst. I even have trouble getting them to believe me when I tell them where I'm going or what I'm going to do. I might as well not do right; they already accuse me anyhow. If they could expect me to do the right thing, I wouldn't disappoint them."

Some parents seem to have more trouble than others in trusting their adolescents. They tend to project their own guilt, anxieties, and fears onto the adolescent. They worry most about problems that they experienced while growing up.

Approval

All adolescents want their parents to like them, approve of them, and accept them in spite of faults. Adolescents don't want to feel that they have to be perfect before they receive their parents' approval. No adolescent can thrive in an atmosphere of constant criticism and disapproval (Vangelisti, 1992). However, parents do not have to accept everything that their adolescents do. Ideally, adolescents need both family acceptance and

family control (Kurdek & Fine, 1994). One research study found that family bonding, family flexibility, and parental support were positively related to adolescent family life satisfaction, whereas parental punitiveness was negatively related to adolescent family life satisfaction (Henry, 1994).

Willingness to Communicate

Many of the problems between parents and adolescents can be solved if both are able to communicate with one another (Masselam, Marcus, & Stunkard, 1990; Papini, Farmer, Clark, Micka, & Barnett, 1990). Parents complain that their adolescents never listen to them. Adolescents say that their parents lecture them or preach to them rather than to discuss issues with them. One adolescent comments as follows:

> "My parents aren't really willing to listen to what I have to say. They don't understand me. I'm not even allowed to express my point of view. They will tell me to be quiet and not to argue. That's the end of the discussion."

When parents show respect for adolescents' opinions, conflict is minimized and the atmosphere of the home is enhanced. Some parents don't give their adolescents a chance to express their feelings or point of view, with the result that resentment and tension build up (Rubenstein & Feldman, 1993). The ability to communicate and solve problems keeps tension at a minimum (Openshaw et al., 1992).

Parental Concern and Support

Adolescents want their parents to be interested in what they are doing and to give moral and emotional support when necessary (Windle & Miller-Tutzauer, 1992; Young, Miller, Norton, & Hill, 1995). One boy, a baseball player, was angry because his parents never attended a game to see him play ball. Adolescents especially resent parents who are so involved with their own activities that they don't have time for their children or are not around when they are needed (Jensen & Borges, 1986). The term "latch-key" children applies to youth who have to let themselves into the house after school because parents are working outside the home. For a full discussion of parental employment and adolescents, see *The Journal of Adolescence* (Volume 10, August 1990).

Guidance

Research on parenting during adolescence is focused primarily on effects of parenting styles on adolescent development. Parenting styles are usually divided into four dimensions: Authoritative parents are both responsive and demanding; authoritarian parents are demanding but not responsive; permissive parents are responsive but not demanding; and more recently, rejecting-neglecting parents are disengaged and neither demanding nor responsive (Smetana, 1995).

All adolescents need guidance and discipline, but some methods work better than others (Holmbeck & Hill, 1991b; Nurmi & Pulliainen, 1991). Research generally indicates that parental explanations and reasoning (induction) are strongly associated with adolescents' internalizing ethical and moral principles. To talk with adolescents is the most frequent disciplinary measure used and the one considered best for the age group. The parents and adolescents who are most successful at conflict resolution are those who show mutual respect and exchange and high regard for the needs of one another, and who exchange ideas and information (McCombs, Forehand, & Smith, 1988). Use of physical punishment, deprivation, and threats (power-assertive discipline) is associated with children's aggression, hostility, and delinquency (Feldman & Wentzel, 1990). Power-assertive discipline is effective in producing short-term compliance but does not have beneficial long-term effects (Smetana & Berent, 1993). It impedes the development of emotional, social, and intellectual maturity.

The authoritative but democratic home, where parents encourage individual responsibility, decision making, initiative, and autonomy but still exercise authority and give guidance, has a positive effect on adolescents (Lamborn et al., 1991). The home atmosphere has the character of respect, appreciation, warmth, and acceptance (Kurdek & Fing, 1993). This type of home, where there is warmth, fairness, and consistency of discipline, is associated with conforming, trouble-free, nondelinquent behavior for both boys and girls (Fischer & Crawford, 1992). One study showed that adolescents whose parents are accepting, firm, and democratic earn higher grades in school, are more self-reliant, report less anxiety and depression, and are less likely to engage in delinquent behavior (Steinberg et al., 1991).

Inconsistent or sporadic parental control also has a negative effect on adolescents (Parish & McCluskey, 1992). Adolescents be-

FOCUS

Parental Bonding Instrument

The Parental Bonding Instrument (PBI) measures mothers' and fathers' care and control as perceived by the adolescent. The instrument requires respondents to report perceptions of their parents when the adolescents were up to 16 years old. Questionnaires consist of 25 statements where the degree of agreement can be indicated by using a Likert scale (scored 0–3). One group of statements is connected with care ("They have been affectionate towards me"), and another with control ("They had allowed me to decide things myself"). A high care-score implied that parents were considered to be empathetic, warm, understanding, and friendly. They were usually present and talked with and understood the child. On the other hand, a low score indicates that parents were very cold, not very helpful, rejecting, and failing to provide sufficient care. At one end of the control scale, the parents were described as overprotective, causing the child to remain dependent and infantile, and were also invading and controlling. At the other end of the scale, parents gave the child autonomy. A high score, which implies too much control, is considered to be the primary risk factor. Some findings indicate, however, that a very low score may represent indifference by the parents (Parker, 1990). The combination of Parker's two dimensions gives us four quadrants, as shown in Figure 14.1. The combination of low control and high care is usually called optimal parenting and is the most favorable combination; that of high control and high care is termed affectionate constraint; that of high control and low care is called affectionless control, and is considered to be the worst combination; and that of low control and low care is often called neglectful (Pedersen, 1994).

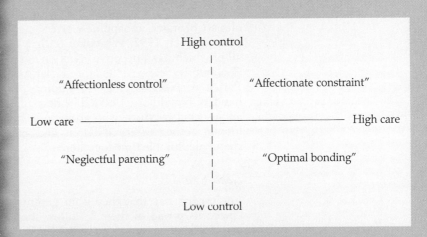

FIGURE 14.1   Four PBI-quadrants.

From "Parental Relations, Mental Health, and Delinquency in Adolescents," by W. Pedersen, 1994. *Adolescence, 29,* pp. 975–990.

come insecure and confused when they lack boundaries and clear guidelines (Ferrari & Olivette, 1993). Such youths may show antisocial, delinquent behavior, and may rebel against conflicting expectations (Steinberg,

Lamborne, Darling, Mounts, & Dornbusch, 1994). A distinction is sometimes made between psychological control and behavioral control (Barber, Olsen, & Shagle, 1994). Adolescents need a mixture of both types of control. They need an adequate degree of psychological autonomy so that they can learn through their social interactions that they are effective, competent individuals with a clear sense of personal identity. They also need sufficient regulation of behavior to enable them to learn that social interaction is governed by rules and structures that must be recognized and adhered to in order for them to be competent members of society.

A Happy Home

The most important contribution that parents can make to their adolescent children is to create a happy home environment in which to bring them up (Fauber, Forehand, Thomas, & Wierson, 1990; Parish, 1990). One adolescent remarked,

> "I love it at home because we always have such a good time together. Mom and Dad are always laughing and joking. We seldom argue, but when we do, we get over it quickly. No one holds a grudge. We are really happy together."

In contrast to this, some families live in a home climate of anger, unhappiness, stress, and hostility (Barber, 1992; Whittaker & Bry, 1991), all of which has a negative effect on everyone (Galambos, Sears, Almeida, & Kolaric, 1995; Parish & Necessary, 1993; Thomas, Forehand, & Neighbors, 1995). The best-adjusted adolescents are those who grow up in happy, loving homes where children and parents spend pleasurable time together.

Good Example

Adolescents say that they want parents who "make us proud of them," "follow the same principles they try to teach us," "set a good example for us to follow," and "who practice what they preach." They want parents they can admire. As one adolescent expressed it, "It's good to feel our parents are trying to teach us right from wrong and set a good example for us to follow" (Clark-Lempers, Lempers, & Ho, 1991). Research indicates that mothers and fathers convey their parenting beliefs to their adolescent children via their parenting practices. For example, if parents use harsh discipline with their adolescents, these discipline beliefs—for both boys

and girls—are likely to be the beliefs that they carry into family living themselves (Simons et al., 1992).

Parent-Adolescent Disagreements

Most parents get along fairly well with their adolescent children. When disagreement occurs, it is often because there are significant discrepancies in adolescents' and parents' judgments of the boundaries of legitimate parental authority (Smetana & Asquith, 1994). Disagreement may occur in one or more of the areas described in the following sections (Galambos & Almeida, 1992; Hall, 1987; Smetana, Braeges, & Yau, 1991).

Moral, Ethical Behavior

Parents are concerned about their adolescents' going to church, synagogue, or temple; obeying the law and staying out of trouble; sexual behavior; honesty; language and speech, drinking, smoking, and use of drugs.

Relationships with Family Members

Disagreements arise over the amount of time adolescents spend with the family (Jurich, Schumm, & Bollman, 1987); relationships with relatives, especially with aged grandparents in the home; quarreling with siblings; the general attitude and level of respect shown to parents (Flint, 1992); and temper tantrums and other manifestations of childish behavior.

Academics

Parents are concerned about adolescents' behavior in school; general attitudes toward school studies and teachers; regularity of attendance, study habits and homework; and grades and level of performance.

Fulfilling Responsibilities

Most parents expect adolescents to show responsibility in the following areas: use of family property or belongings, furnishings, supplies, tools, and equipment; use of the telephone; use of the family automobile; care of personal belongings, clothes, and room; earning and spending money; and performance of family chores (Light, Hertsgaard, & Martin, 1985; Sanik & Stafford, 1985).

Social Activities

Adolescents' social activities probably create more conflict with parents than any other areas of concern. The most common sources

Adolescent social activities probably create more conflict with parents than any other areas of concern.

of friction are the following: choice of clothes and hair styles; going steady and age allowed to date, riding in cars and participating in certain events; curfew hours and places where they are allowed to go; how often they are allowed to go out, going out on a school night, or frequency of dating; and choice of friends or dating partners.

Work Outside the Home

Most parents expect adolescents to do some work outside the home to earn money, and most do, but sometimes the amount of work is excessive so that the adolescent neglects the family and school and is away from home too much.

Correlations with Conflict

A number of factors relate to the focus and extent of conflict with parents. Discussed below are the type of discipline that parents use, the socioeconomic status of the family, the number of children in the family, and the stage of development and gender of the adolescent.

The type of *discipline* that parents use has an effect on conflict (Johnson, Shulman, & Collings, 1991). Authoritarian discipline results in more conflict with parents over home chores, activities outside the home, friends, and spending money than does a democratic approach to guidance.

The *socioeconomic status* of the family influences the focus of conflict. Parents of low socioeconomic status are more often concerned with respect, politeness, and obedience, whereas middle-income families are more concerned with developing initiative and independence. Parents of low socioeconomic status worry about keeping children out of trouble at school, whereas middle-class parents are more concerned about achievement and grades (McKenry, Kotch, & Browne, 1991).

One study of 1,828 white, black, and Hispanic families with adolescents reported the frequency of parent-adolescent conflict on ten issues. Parental adolescent conflict was consistent in each of the ethnic groups, although whites reported more frequent conflict than did either the blacks or the Hispanics. Disagreements about helping around the house were most frequently reported for each group, and conflicts about family relations, school, dress, and money were reported in similar decreasing frequency. Regardless of cultural background, parents disagreed with their adolescents over issues that were central to the day-to-day experience of living together. There was far less conflict over substantive issues such as sex and drugs (Barber, 1994).

The *number of children* in the family is a significant factor, at least in middle-class families. The more children in the middle-class family, the more parent-youth conflict there is and the more parents use physical force to control adolescents.

The *stage of development* of adolescents is another factor. From age 12 on, girls are increasingly in conflict with parents over boyfriends, with the peak years being 14 and 15. The peak age of boys for conflict with parents over girlfriends is around age 16.

The *gender* of the adolescent relates to conflict. The fact that boys report more unresolved conflict with families than do girls is an indication of gender differences in communication skills used in conflict resolution (Smetana, Yau, & Hanson, 1991). The gender of the parent also relates to conflict. Adolescents are usually closer to their mothers than to their fathers (Paulson, Hill, & Holmbeck, 1990). As a result, they usually get along better with their mothers, and the mothers exert more influence over them in such areas as educational goals. Most adolescents report more difficulties getting along with their fathers than with their mothers (Miller & Lane, 1991).

The level of parent-adolescent conflict is, in large part, determined by family atmosphere. An atmosphere of warmth and supportiveness, which promotes successful negotiation of disagreements between parents and adolescent children, helps to keep conflict at low to moderate levels. Under hostile, coercive conditions, however, parents and adolescents will be unlikely to resolve disagreements, and conflict will therefore escalate to dysfunctional levels (Rueter & Conger, 1995).

The variables associated with parent-adolescent conflict are numerous (Flanagan, 1990), but the ones discussed here are representative. Not all parents and adolescents quarrel about the same things or to the same extent.

If conflict between parents and adolescents becomes excessive, parents ought to seek outside help (Raviv, Maddy-Weitzman, & Raviv, 1992). This recommendation is particularly important, since adolescent adjustment is related to the degree and intensity of family conflict (Nelson et al., 1993) and family adjustment (Ohannessian, Lerner, Lerner, & von Eye, 1994).

Relationships with Siblings

The relationships between brothers and sisters have a considerable influence on the social development of the adolescent (Buhrmester & Furman, 1990). This development is affected in a number of ways.

Siblings often provide friendship and companionship and meet one another's needs for meaningful relationships and affection. They act as confidants for one another, share many experiences, and are able to help one another when there are problems. However, this situation is not as true if siblings are 6 or more years apart in age.

On the negative side, if there is less than 6 years' difference in their ages, siblings tend

FOCUS

Parental Functions and Support

Raising adolescent children in contemporary society is a complex process. This process is influenced by numerous factors that reside both within individuals and families and outside them. These parental functions and social supports are illustrated in Figure 14.2. This figure is in the form of an ecological map (not unlike Bronfenbrenner's, 1979).

In this map, the parenting functions are arranged hierarchically at the center. In the *innermost circle,* we see four parenting functions. The first is the function of *meeting basic needs* of the children. This includes a wide array of resources necessary for survival, such as a safe and secure place to live, adequate food and nutrition, clothing, and access to medical services. Basic needs would also include emotional needs.

The second parental function is that of *protection.* Parents are usually responsible for protecting the physical, psychological, spiritual, ethnic, and cultural integrity of their children from threats from the natural environment and other persons, groups, and institutions.

The third function involves *guidance*—guiding and promoting all aspects of the child's development, including cognitive, social, physical, emotional, moral, sexual, spiritual, cultural, and educational aspects.

Finally, a fourth function refers to *advocacy,* which is the parents' role both as advocates and supporters of their children and as coordinators and links to experts, individuals, groups, and institutions that help them raise their children.

In the innermost circle surrounding the parenting functions are the most immediate factors that can affect a parent's ability to carry out these functions: *the parent's personal characteristics, characteristics of the adolescent, and the presence and quality of the marital relationship.*

The *second level* in the map involves factors outside the individual and family, such as the neighborhood, the parent's work situation, and informal networks. All these also impinge on the parent's ability to function.

The *outer ring* of Figure 14.2 represents broader social influences, such as cultural val-

ues, formal social programs, and factors related to social class. While these *"macrosystem"* factors seem far removed from the parenting function, they often help to define the entire context in which parenting takes place; for example, social class is known to be related to family size and the division of labor in marriage, and it is also likely to affect which parental functions are deemed most important, how they are performed, and by whom.

It is important to recognize that there is a hierarchy of parenting functions and that not all families will view them as equally important. For example, some parents, as a result of economic or other personal circumstances, may have their energies focused more on performing basic parental functions such as providing a safe environment or adequate food to eat, than on higher-level functions, such as improving parent-child communications. Families are different, and the functions, that they perform partially reflect these differences (Small & Eastman, 1991).

continued ▶

to be more jealous of one another than if they are farther apart in age. Also, sibling rivalry is greater during early adolescence than later. As adolescents mature, conflicting relationships with siblings tend to subside (Goodwin & Roscoe, 1990).

The focus box accompanying this section points out some myth-shattering research on sibling relationships. The effects of sibling violence have been found to profoundly influence emotional adjustment in certain individuals. Depending on gender and age differences, reports of sibling violence confirm the disclosures of recent studies. Not surprisingly, trends that are evident in today's society appear to be mirrored within the family unit.

Older siblings often serve as confidants, playmates, teachers, caregivers, and surrogate parents (Seginer, 1992). Pleasant relationships can contribute to younger children's sense of acceptance, belonging, and security. Rejecting, hostile relationships may create deep-seated feelings of hostility, resentment, insecurity, or anxiety that may be carried into adulthood. Many adolescents learn adult responsibilities and roles by having to care for younger sisters and brothers while growing up. However, some adolescents are given too much responsibility and provide most of the care that parents ought to be providing. They may grow to resent this responsibility, which prevents them from having any free time of their

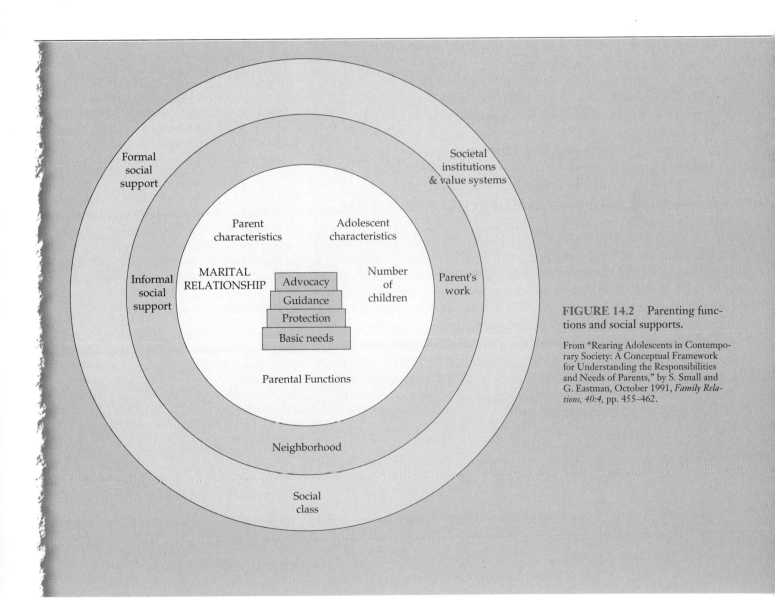

FIGURE 14.2   Parenting functions and social supports.

From "Rearing Adolescents in Contemporary Society: A Conceptual Framework for Understanding the Responsibilities and Needs of Parents," by S. Small and G. Eastman, October 1991, *Family Relations, 40:4*, pp. 455–462.

FOCUS

Sibling Violence

Recent research has disclosed the extent of violence present in American families, thus shattering the myth that the family is a haven of safety and support. But one important finding has nearly been overlooked, namely, that sibling abuse is the most common form of abuse in the family. It occurs more frequently than parental child abuse and more frequently than spousal or female abuse. One study examined the conflict and violence in childhood sibling relationships and its effect on later, emotional adjustment. The subjects of the study included 1,450 students from a graduate psychology school who had one or more siblings, who were not a twin, and who answered all of the prescreening questions. Of the total sample, 54% reported that there was one brother or sister in the family who used to pick on and bother them a lot when they were growing up. Forty-eight percent reported not having such a sibling in the family. When asked whether there was one brother or sister in the family whom they used to pick on or to bother a lot, 48% said yes. Out of the totals, 20% of the subjects reported higher levels of victimization by a sibling in relation to other families they knew, and 17% of the subjects said they picked on a sibling much more than did people in other families. Not surprisingly, older siblings were much more likely to be the perpetrators of conflict with younger siblings than they were to be the victims. Sex differences also existed. The finding of gender differences in both perpetrator and victim roles suggests that the dyad most at risk of serious sibling conflict was one with a male older sibling and a female younger sibling.

This study confirms that higher levels of conflict among siblings is remembered and appears to be a source of long-term dissatisfaction for almost 30% of the students sampled. For women, having been the target of a sibling's emotional aggression, high violence, or severe violence is associated with feelings of anxiety in young adults. Male students are not likely to report negative emotional consequences to these same events.

There is a significant relationship between parental use of severe violence to resolve conflict within the parental dyad and children's use of severe violence to resolve conflict in the sibling dyad. There appears to be a greater incidence of sibling violence when parents use violence, and such violence appears to have a developmental pattern. Also, violence between siblings affects emotional adjustment, because the history of violence with a sibling is consistent with difficulties in emotional adjustments with college-aged women. Interventions early in the life of such families with sibling violence may serve to reduce the long-term emotional damage that can occur (Graham-Bermann, Cutler, Litzenberger, & Schwartz, 1994).

own. Older siblings represent masculine or feminine personalities and behavior to young siblings. Through appearance, character, and overall behavior, they exemplify a type of person the younger child might become. This process can have either a positive or a negative effect, depending on the example set.

SOCIAL RELATIONSHIPS

Friendship during adolescence has a strategic function. Friendship is a factor in the socialization of adolescents. It is important as a means of learning social skills and plays a central role in the adolescent's quest for self-knowledge and self-definition. Furthermore, the absence of friendships or conflictual relations with friends constitutes predictors of later psychological problems (Claes, 1992). Friends are important sources of companionship and recreation, share advice and valued possessions, serve as trusted confidants and critics, act as loyal allies, and provide stability in times of stress or transition (Lempers & Clark-Lempers, 1993). Friendship is important in achieving emancipation from parents, the establishment of heterosexual relationships, and the affirmation of one's identity.

Early adolescence represents a time of significant changes in children's relationships with both their peers and their parents. Children have increased unsupervised contact with peers and begin to place greater importance on their approval, views, and advice. At the same time, they spend less time with their parents and appear to distance themselves emotionally from them. A realignment of a power balance and authority in parent-child relationships takes place during adolescence. For most early adolescents, parent-child relationships need to begin providing greater mutuality and more opportunities for adolescents' participation and decision making.

A study of a sample of 1,771 early adolescents in the sixth and seventh grades examines the relationships with their parents. The subjects were asked to complete self-report questionnaires during the spring of their sixth and seventh grades. Early adolescents agreed that their parents asserted and did not relax their power. Restrictiveness was higher in an extreme form of peer orientation. Also, those adolescents who perceived but little opportunity to be involved in decision-making were higher in both extreme peer orientation and peer advice (Fuligni & Eccles, 1993).

Friendships of Young Adolescents

Adolescents' need for close friends is different from that of children (Pombeni, Kirchler, & Palmonari, 1990). Children need playmates of their own age to share common activities and games. However, they do not depend primarily on one another for love and affection. They look to their parents for filling their emotional needs, and seek praise, affection, and love from them. Only if they have been rejected and unloved by parents will they have turned to parent substitutes and friends for emotional fulfillment.

Needs change with the advent of puberty. The adolescent desires emotional independence and emancipation from parents and emotional fulfillment from friends (Larson & Richards, 1991; Quintana & Lapsley, 1990). Peers now provide part of the emotional support formerly provided by families (Cotterell, 1992b; DuBois & Hirsch, 1990; Howes & Wu, 1990).

One study found that mothers and fathers were seen as the most frequent providers of support in the fourth grade. Same-sex friends were perceived to be as supportive as parents in the seventh grade and were the most frequent providers of support in the tenth grade. Romantic partners moved up in rank with age until college, where they, along with friends and mothers, received the highest ratings for support (Furman & Buhrmester, 1992).

Young adolescents begin to form a small group of friends, often choosing one or several very best friends. Usually these best friends are of the same sex in the beginning (Beneson, 1990). Mutual activities become important in friendships during the early school years (Clark & Ayers, 1993). Adolescents attend school, go to athletic events, and share in recreational activities with these friends (Dubois & Hirsch, 1993; Zarbatany, Hartmann, & Rankin, 1990). Best friends strive to dress alike, look alike, and act alike. They are often similar in personality traits and behavior (Bukowski, Gauze, Hoza, & Newcomb, 1993; Tolson & Urberg, 1993). After spending all day together, they may come home and talk for additional hours on the telephone.

Early adolescent friendships are sometimes upsetting if expectations are not fulfilled. The more intense and narcissistic the emotions that drive adolescents to seek companionship, the more likely it is that sustained friendships will be difficult and tenuous. Once disappointed, the frustrated, immature, and unstable adolescent may react with excessive emotions, thereby possibly disrupting friendships, at least temporarily. Friendships that can be a valuable source of social support sometimes end up as a means of social stress (Moran & Eckenrode, 1991).

Heterosocial Development

Both same-sex and opposite-sex friendships are important by simultaneously providing for many of the social needs of adolescents (Lempers & Clark-Lempers, 1993). Heterosociality means

Adolescents turn to their friends for companionship and emotional fulfillment.

forming friendships with those of both sexes (Goff, 1990). Getting to know and feel comfortable with the opposite sex is a difficult process for some adolescents (Miller, 1990). Here are typical questions from adolescents who are trying to form heterosocial relationships:

1. "Why is it that I'm so shy when I'm around girls?"
2. "How can you get a girl to like you?"
3. "How old do you have to be before you can start dating?"
4. "How can I get boys to think of me as more than a friend?"
5. "If a girl likes a boy, should she tell him?"
6. "How can I become more sexy?"
7. "How can I overcome my fear of asking a girl out?"
8. "How do you go about talking to a girl?"

Puberty brings on a biological and emotional awareness of the opposite sex, the beginning of sexual attraction, and a decline in negative attitudes. The girl who was looked on before as a giggly kid now becomes strangely alluring. On the one hand, the now-maturing male is attracted to and fascinated by this young woman; on the other hand, he is perplexed, awed, and terrified. No wonder he ends up asking, "How do you go about talking to a girl?" Girls, who used to feel that boys were too rough and ill-mannered, now feel a strange urge to be near them: "If a girl likes a boy, should she tell him?"

Some boys show their interest through physical contact and teasing: by pulling the

FOCUS

Do Males Value Intimacy?

Research indicates that *males continue to have difficulty with intimacy* and that this gender difference may emerge as early as middle adolescence. The gender differences in intimacy, both expressed and wanted, confirm that females value closeness in relationships more than males and that males exhibit tendencies toward autonomy within relationships (Bakken & Romig, 1992).

These differences between males and females are highlighted by McGill (1985, pp. 157, 158):

To say that men have no intimate friends seems on the surface too harsh, but the data indicates that it is not far from the truth. Even the most intimate of male friendships (of which there are very few) rarely approached the depth of disclosure a woman commonly has with many other women. One man in ten has a friend with whom he discusses work, money, marriage; only one in more than twenty has friendships in which he discloses feelings about himself, or his sexual feelings. The most common male friendship pattern is for a man to have many friends, each of whom knows something of the man's public self, and therefore little about him, but not one of whom knows more than a small piece of the whole. Most often, they are created in the context of common occupational or recreational interests and pursued very cautiously.

By contrast, women typically have many friends who know everything there is to know about them. Theirs is an open, fully disclosing interaction, not constrained by circumstance or content.

members of a group or clique to which they are attracted. At this stage, adolescents are sensitive to criticism or to others' negative reaction to them. They are concerned about what people think because they want to be accepted and admired by them. Also, their degree of self-worth is partly a reflection of the opinions of others.

The following questions are real-life examples of questions asked by adolescents in the seventh, eighth, and ninth grades. The questions reflect adolescents' concern about group involvement.

1. "What do you have to do to become a member of a group you like?"
2. "Why are some kids not friendly? Is there something wrong with me?"
3. "When other kids ignore you, what do you do?"
4. "Are kids born popular, or do they learn to be that way?"
5. "If you are too fat, will other kids not accept you?"

Social Acceptance

Considerable evidence shows that personal qualities and social skills such as conversational ability, ability to empathize with others, and poise are the most important factors in social acceptance (Meyers & Nelson, 1986). One study of 204 adolescents in the seventh, ninth, and twelfth grades revealed that personal factors such as social conduct, personality, and character traits were more important in social acceptance than either achievement or physical characteristics. This was true of adolescents at all grade levels (Tedesco & Gaier, 1988). It is especially important to peer group acceptance that adolescents' personality and behavioral characteristics provide a good match with peer group norms. To be accepted by the group, adolescents have to manifest characteristics similar to those of other members of the group (East et al., 1992).

Achievement, which included academic success and athletic prowess, also contributed to popularity. And physical characteristics, including appearance and material things such as money or autos, also affected social acceptance. However, the older they became, the more adolescents emphasized personal factors and deemphasized achievement and physical characteristics in friendship. Other research also emphasizes the importance of personal qualities as a criterion of popularity.

girl's hat off, putting snow down her neck, or chasing after her. Girls, too, find ways of attracting attention. Gradually, these initial contacts are replaced by more mature behavior: attempts at conversation, considerate acts to win favor, or other means of expressing interest. The effort is to act more grown-up and mannerly in social situations. The group boy-girl relationships change into paired relationships, and these deepen into affectionate friendships and romance as the two sexes discover one another.

Group Involvement

Need to Belong to a Group

Finding acceptance in social groups also becomes a powerful motivation in the lives of adolescents (Borja-Alvarez, Zarbatany, & Pepper, 1991; Woodward & Kalyan-Masih, 1990). A primary goal of adolescents is to be accepted by

Thus, one of the primary ways in which adolescents find group acceptance is by developing and exhibiting personal qualities that others admire and by learning social skills that ensure acceptance (Miller, 1991; Wise, Bundy, Bundy, & Wise, 1991). In general, popular youths are accepted because of their character, sociability, and personal appearance. They have good reputations and exhibit qualities of moral character that people admire (Gillmore, Hawkins, Day, & Catalano, 1992). They usually possess high self-esteem and positive self-concepts. They are appropriately groomed and dressed according to the standards of their group. They are acceptable-looking youths who are friendly, happy, fun-loving, outgoing, and energetic; who have developed a high degree of social skills; and who like to participate in many activities with others (Gifford & Dean, 1990). They may be sexually experienced but are not promiscuous.

Prestige

In one study, 271 college students who graduated from high school in 1979 to 1982 and 225 college students who graduated from high school in 1988 to 1989 were asked to list five ways in which male and female students could gain prestige in the high schools from which they had graduated. The findings indicated relatively little change in gender norms across the decade. The overall patterns showed that boys and girls continued to acquire prestige through fairly similar means. The findings showed that boys gained prestige primarily through (a) sports, (b) grades and intelligence, (c) access to cars, (d) sociability, (e) popularity with the opposite sex, (f) physical appearance, and (g) participation in school activities (e.g., school government, clubs). In contrast, girls gained prestige primarily through (a) physical attractiveness, (b) sociability, (c) grades and intelligence, (d) popularity with the opposite sex, (e) clothes, (f) participation in school activities, and (g) cheerleading.

The noteworthy differences between the reports in the early and the late 1980s were an increase in girls' acquisition of prestige through participation in sports and sexual activity, a decrease in the role of cheerleading, and a reduction in the importance of car ownership as a means by which boys approved prestige. Most of the change that occurred in the way that girls accrued prestige could be accounted for by changes in boys' rather than girls' perceptions. Contributors

to prestige that boys viewed as important were those that traditionally had been avenues by which men, rather than women, gained prestige: participation in sports and engaging in sexual activity. Thus, much of the change that occurred involved a greater acceptance of girls in traditionally "male" activity rather than the reverse (Suitor & Reavis, 1995).

Deviant Behavior

So far we have been talking about youths who are in the mainstream of group participation. There are other adolescents, however, who find acceptance in deviant groups by conforming to the antisocial standards adopted by their members (Downs & Rose, 1991). Whereas delinquent or antisocial behavior may be unacceptable in society as a whole, it may be required as a condition of membership in a ghetto gang. What might be considered causes of a bad reputation in some adolescent groups (sexual promiscuity, antisocial behavior, being uncooperative, making trouble, or fighting) might be considered causes of a good reputation among a group of delinquents. Standards of group behavior vary with different groups and that popularity depends not so much on a fixed standard as on group conformity.

Sometimes peer groups are formed because of hostility to family authority and a desire to rebel against it. When this situation happens, the peer groups may become antisocial gangs that are hostile to all established authority, yet supportive of the particular deviancy accepted by the group.

Dating

Dating in American culture is not equivalent to courtship, at least during the early and middle years of adolescence. Traditionally, courtship was for purposes of mate sorting and selection. Today, however, dating has other purposes in the eyes of adolescents (Roscoe, Diana, & Brooks, 1987).

Values

One major purpose of dating is to have *fun*. Dating provides amusement; it is a form of recreation and a source of enjoyment; it can be an end in itself. Wanting the *friendship, acceptance, affection, and love* of the opposite sex is a normal part of growing up. Dating is also used to achieve and *maintain status*. However, adolescents of higher socioeconomic status

FOCUS

School-Based Adolescent Peer Network

Adolescents are imbedded in a rich network of peer relations, including best friendships, other close friends, cliques or friendship groups, social crowds, and perhaps romantic relationships. One study examined the structure of school-based peer networks of adolescents in sixth through twelfth grade in three school systems. The study reveals some interesting findings. One finding is that female students were more integrated into social school networks than male students. Girls made and received more choices and had more mutual choices of friendships than boys. Girls were also more likely than boys to have a best friend and to be a clique member, and they were less likely than boys to be unconnected to the school networks. A larger percentage of girls' friendship lists had the same network role and the same social crowd affiliation compared with boys. Girls, then, participated more in school networks and were more similar to their friends in the type of participation that they had, compared with boys.

With increasing grade, adolescents appeared to become more selective in naming friends. They made and received fewer choices and had fewer mutual friends, although mutual friends became a larger proportion of their friendship list. This increased selectivity is probably the result of the social-cognitive changes reported in adolescents, such as definitions of friendship that emphasized reciprocity and intimacy as well as improved social-cognitive skills. This change allowed the adolescent to make more accurate reports about who liked them.

When African Americans were examined, the research tended to show that they were less connected to the school network than were whites. In addition, the school with an African American majority had the lowest level of school network participation and the highest percentage in the unconnected group of any of the three systems. This finding suggests that almost all ethnic groups who were in a numeric minority in a school were less integrated in the school peer networks than were majority groups (Urberg, Degirmencioglu, Tolson, & Halliday-Scher, 1995).

Dating is not equivalent to courtship in its early stages.

tionship sooner than women, with the discrepancy a source of potential conflict.

One of the major purposes of dating is to find *intimacy*. Intimacy is the development of affection, respect, loyalty, mutual trust, sharing, openness, love, and commitment (Roscoe, Kennedy, & Pope, 1987). Some adolescent relationships with friends are superficial. Other relationships are close ones, in which adolescents are sensitive to the innermost thoughts and feelings of their partner and are willing to share personal information, private thoughts, and feelings. Heterosocial relationships vary greatly in intensity of feeling and in depth of communication. Dating can provide the opportunity for intimacy, but whether it develops varies with the individuals and with different pairs. Boys who are socialized to hide feelings may have trouble developing intimate relationships with girls.

As youths get older, dating becomes more a means of *mate sorting and selection*, whether the motive is conscious or not. Those who are similar in personality characteristics are more likely to be compatible than are those who are dissimilar in social characteristics, psychological traits, and physical attractiveness. Thus, dating can result in sorting out compatible pairs and can contribute to wise mate selection.

Dating Concerns

A study of 107 men and 227 women, who comprised a random sample of students at East Carolina University, sought to identify dating problems (Knox & Wilson, 1983). Table 14.1 shows the problems experienced by the men. *The most frequently mentioned problems of the men were communication, where to go and what to do on dates, and shyness. The most frequent problems expressed by the women (see Table 14.2) were unwanted pressure to engage in sexual behavior, where to go and what to*

more often use dating as a symbol of their status than do those of lower socioeconomic status. Membership in certain cliques is associated with the status-seeking aspects of dating. Dating is also a *means of social and personal growth*. It is a way of learning to get along with others and to know and understand many different types of people.

Dating has become more *sex-oriented* as increasing numbers of adolescents have sexual intercourse. Dating is sometimes used to have sex; at other times, sex develops out of dating experiences. Most research indicates that men want sexual involvement in a rela-

TABLE 14.1	DATING PROBLEMS EXPERIENCED BY 107 UNIVERSITY MEN

Problem	Percentage
Communication with date	35
Place to date	23
Shyness	20
Money	17
Honesty, openness	8

Adapted from "Dating Problems of University Students," by D. Knox and K. Wilson, 1983, *College Student Journal*, *17*, pp. 225–228.

do on dates, and communication (Knox & Wilson, 1983). Some of the women complained that the men wanted to move toward a sexual relationship too quickly.

The problem of communication was mentioned frequently by both women and men. Students complained that they didn't know what to talk about and that they ran out of things to say. After they had discussed school, classes, teachers, jobs, or the weather, the conversation lagged and they had trouble filling in long gaps of silence.

Both college women and men look for honesty and openness in a relationship. Part of the problem is caused by the fact that both the man and the woman strive to be on their best behavior. This effort involves a certain amount of pretense or playacting called **imaging,** to present oneself in the best possible manner.

PREMARITAL SEXUAL BEHAVIOR

Sexual Interests

Intensified interest in sex accompanies sexual maturation (Weinstein & Rosen, 1991). At first this interest focuses on the adolescent's bodily changes and observable happenings. Most adolescents spend time looking in the mirror and examining body parts in minute detail. Accompanying this self-centered concern is the desire to develop an acceptable body image.

TABLE 14.2	DATING PROBLEMS EXPERIENCED BY 227 UNIVERSITY WOMEN

Problem	Percentage
Unwanted pressure to engage in sexual behavior	23
Places to go	22
Communication with date	20
Sexual misunderstandings	13
Money	9

Adapted from "Dating Problems of University Students," by D. Knox and K. Wilson, 1983, *College Student Journal*, *17*, pp. 225–228.

Gradually young adolescents become interested not only in their own development and that of others of the same gender, but also in the opposite sex (Frydenberg & Lewis, 1991). Curiosity motivates them to try to learn as much as possible about the sexual characteristics of the opposite sex. Adolescents also become fascinated with basic facts about human reproduction. Both boys and girls gradually become aware of their own developing sexual feelings and drives and of the way in which

Imaging—being on one's best behavior to make a good impression

Living Issues

Sexual Activity, Dating, and Marriage Desirability

Over 750 students from three universities were asked to judge the dating and marriage desirability of a person on the basis of information provided about his or her current sexual activity. Overall, the results indicated that a person portrayed as engaging in low sexual activity in a current relationship was perceived to be more desirable as a marriage partner than a person engaging in moderate or high sexual activity, whereas moderate or high sexual activity was preferred more in a dating partner. Evidence was found for a reverse double standard in rating dating desirability: Males were perceived as more desirable as a date when they engaged in moderate sexual activity, whereas females were perceived as more desirable as a date when they engaged in high sexual activity (Sprecher, McKinney, & Orbuch, 1991).

Masturbation—self-stimulation for purposes of sexual arousal

Coitus—sexual intercourse

these are aroused and expressed. Most adolescents begin some experimentation: touching themselves, playing with their genitals, or exploring various parts of the body. Often by accident they experience orgasm through self-manipulation. From that time on, interest in sex as erotic feeling and expression increases. Adolescents begin to compare their ideas with those of others and spend a lot of time talking about sex, telling jokes, using sex slang, and exchanging sex-oriented literature. Adults are sometimes shocked at the language and jokes. Many parents have been horrified at finding sex-related books hidden under the mattress. But these activities are motivated by a desire to understand human

sexuality; they are a means of understanding, expressing, and gaining control over sexual feelings. Wise parents can play a positive role in the sex education of their children (Mueller & Powers, 1990).

Masturbation

One of the common practices of adolescents is **masturbation,** which is any type of self-stimulation that produces erotic arousal, whether or not arousal results in orgasm. After adolescents discover that they can sexually arouse themselves through self-manipulation, masturbation may become a regular part of their self-expression. The incidences of masturbation vary somewhat among studies. In a recent study of female and male college students, twice as many males as females said they had masturbated, and of the males that masturbated, they did so more frequently then the females (Leitenberg, Detzer, & Sribnik, 1993). This and other studies indicate that a greater percentage of males than females masturbate. Among those who masturbate, males do so more often than females and more frequently fantasize erotic experiences (Jones & Barlow, 1990). According to one survey, teenage boys masturbate about five times a week (LoPresto, Sherman, & Sherman, 1985).

Practically all authorities now say that masturbation is a normal part of growing up and does not have any harmful physical and mental effects. Masturbation provides sexual release and serves a useful function in helping the individual to learn about his or her body, to learn how to respond sexually, and to develop sexual identity. The only ill effect that masturbation may stimulate is guilt, fear, or anxiety stemming from the belief that the practice will do harm or create problems. Negative emotions concerning masturbation can lead to great anxiety if a youth continues to practice it and to feel guilty about it.

Premarital Sexual Intercourse

Studies have indicated a rapid rise in the percentage of youths engaging in heavy petting and premarital sexual intercourse (**coitus**). Data from the *National Survey of Family Growth* in 1995 revealed the percentages of never-married women 15 to 19 years of age who had ever had sexual intercourse after menarche, by age, race, and Hispanic origin. Figure 14.3 shows the data. Accumulated percentage of those having sexual intercourse is as follows: 15 years of age, 21.4%; 16 years of age, 38%; 17 years of age, 49.6%; 18 years of

Parenting Issues

When Parents Object to a Dating Partner

Since our system of courtship emphasizes individual freedom, the question arises as to how much influence parents have in the dating process. In a study by Knox and Wilson (1981) of 334 university students, women were significantly more likely than men to report that their parents tried to influence their choice of dates. About 60% of the women, compared with 40% of the men, said parental influence was involved. Daughters also were more likely than sons to say that parents interfered with dating relationships. However, daughters were also more likely than sons to say it was important to them that they dated the kinds of people their parents approved of. About 30% of men versus 10% of women said they didn't care what their parents thought.

Parental objections are usually based on one or more of the following:

- *The parents don't like the person* because "he's rude; she's impolite; she has a bad reputation; he's not a nice person." These objections are based on dislike of the other's personality.

- *The parents feel the other person has a problem:* "He drinks too much; she has a drug problem; she's too emotional; he has a bad reputation."

- *The other person's family is different from the parents' family.* "His family are rather common people; he's not of our religion; why couldn't he have picked some fine Italian (or Irish, Jewish, or Spanish) girl?"

- *There is a significant age difference.* "He's too old for her."

- *Parents object because they are too possessive of their offspring and are unwilling to let them grow up.* In this case, the parents might object no matter whom their child wanted to go out with.

There are several approaches adolescents can take. They can try to get their parents to like their choice. If objections are based on a lack of knowledge, they can invite the person over to get acquainted. Sometimes parents end up approving. At other times, parents object even more. Parents are not always wrong. The situation needs to be discussed, employing the aid of a counselor if the parents and adolescent are not able to find a solution.

age, 62.7%; and 19 years of age, 72.4%. All together, 52% of Hispanic women 15 to 19 years of age, 47% of non-Hispanic whites 15 to 19 years of age, and 58% of non-Hispanic blacks 15 to 19 years of age had sexual intercourse.

An earlier survey, conducted in 1992, called the *National Health and Social Life Survey* (NHSLS), is based on 3,432 interviews with people across the United States who were willing to sit down and answer a 90-minute questionnaire about their sexual behavior and other aspects of their sex lives (Michael, Gagnon, Laumann, and Kolata, 1994). One of the trends revealed by the results was a steadily declining age at first sexual intercourse. Half of all black men have had intercourse by age 15, half of all Hispanic men by age 16-and-a-half, and half of all white men by age 17. Half of all black women have had intercourse by about age 17, and half of white women and Hispanic women have had intercourse by about age 18. By age 22, about 90% of each group has had intercourse.

When asked why they had intercourse the first time, 51% of the men attributed it to curiosity and readiness for sex, and 25% indi-cated affection for their partner. Among the women, it was the reverse: about half cited affection for their partner, and about 25% curiosity and readiness for sex. A very small percentage of both men and women said they had sex because of a desire for physical plea-sure. Most of the men said they were not in love with their first sexual partner; most of the women, in contrast, said they were.

Today, American teenagers are having sex earlier than their parents did, but they do not necessarily have more partners. About half of today's adolescents begin having intercourse with a partner sometime between the ages of 15 and 18, and at least four out of five have had intercourse by the time they are 21. Since the average age of marriage is now in the mid-twenties, most Americans are not waiting to marry to have sex, but most sexu-ally active young people show no signs of having large numbers of partners. More than half the men and women between ages 18 and 24 in 1992 had had just one sex partner in the previous year, and 11% had had none.

Later data from the 1995 *National Survey of Family Growth* revealed that 30½% of

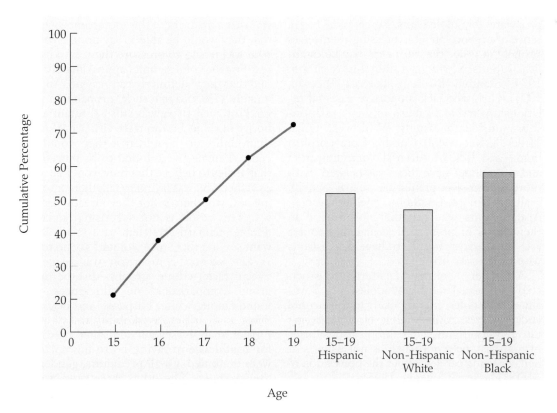

FIGURE 14.3 Percentage of never-married women 15 to 19 years of age who have ever had sexual inter-course after menarche by age at interview and by age and race and Hispanic origin.

From *Fertility, Family Planning, and Women's Health: New Data from the 1995 National Survey of Family Growth.* Hyattsville, Maryland: U.S. Department of Health and Human Services, 1997.

unmarried women 15 to 19 years of age had two or more partners in the last twelve months (1995 *National Survey of Family Growth*, 1995). Seventy-six percent of unmarried women 15 to 19 years of age had one or zero sexual partners during the year. Some reported that they or their partners used no contraceptive method or that they used an ineffective method (withdrawal, douching, or rhythm) at last intercourse (U.S. Bureau of Census, Statistical Abstract of the United States, 1998).

One of the explanations for the increase in early sexual activity is that it is an expression of cultural norms (Slonin-Nevo, 1992). For many youths, particularly boys, sexual activity may be normative and abstinence nonnormative. Social policies and community characteristics may actually condone sexual expression (Billy, Brewster, & Grady, 1994). On the other hand, religiosity and a lower level of sexual permissiveness go together. Sexual socialization of younger adolescents by older youths may be a factor in early initiation into sexual activities, since adolescents tend to form sexual standards close to peer standards.

Some youths, especially girls, appear to regard sex as a mechanism for establishing an intimate relationship. Because establishing an intimate relationship is developmentally appropriate for adolescents, some girls feel a sense of urgency about expressing themselves sexually in order that intimacy may be established (Salts, Seismore, Lindholm, & Smith, 1994; Stanton, Black, Kaljee, & Ricardo, 1993). Girls who lack supportive parental relationships try to establish intimate relationships outside the family (Whitbeck, Hoyt, Miller, & Kao, 1992). Coming from a broken home and lack of parental communication and discipline have been associated with more permissive premarital sexual activity (Salts, Seismore, Lindholm, & Smith, 1994). Also, parents who are the most liberal in their views of premarital sexual intercourse are those most likely to have adolescents whose views are liberal.

A number of behavioral patterns are associated with sexual activity of adolescents. Sexually active adolescents are likely to use alcohol and cigarettes, exhibit high levels of stress, get into physical fights, and exhibit various forms of high-risk behavior, such as not using seat belts or being careless about the prevention of AIDS (Harvey & Spigner, 1995).

One study of 1,330 white, Hispanic, and African American male and female middle-school and high-school students emphasized the importance of unconventionality in sexual behavior. Relative to the behavior of virgins, those who were premaritally sexually active placed a higher value on independence, had lower expectations for success in school, a greater tolerance of deviance, were influenced more by peers than by parents, and showed lower parental disapproval of problem behavior, such as delinquency, problem drinking, and marijuana use (Costa, Jessor, & Donovan, 1995).

Saying No

One study examined adolescents' competence for perceived ability at saying no to unwanted sex with a boyfriend or girlfriend. The focus was on examining how gender, race, and other variables predicted adolescents' ability to say no. The sample consisted of 2,472 tenth-grade students from eight public high schools in Dade County, Florida. The mean age of the final sample was 15-and-a-half years. The sample consisted of about half females and half males and a fairly even distribution by ethnic groups. The sample included 29% white, 38% Hispanic, and 28% non-Hispanic black. About 6% of adolescents were in other categories. The sample was about equally divided between those who had not had sex and those who had. The first major finding of the study was that a majority of the adolescents believed that they would be able to say no to a partner who was trying to pressure them into having sex. For the total sample, approximately 50% said that they "definitely can" say no. Approximately 17% said that they "probably can" say no. However, there was still a substantial minority of subjects who were either not sure of their ability or thought that they would succumb. Females were found to be more likely than males to believe that they would say no to a partner who was trying to talk them into having sex, whether or not they already had had sex. This result is not surprising, since the double standard says that "real men" always want sex and that "nice women" say no to sex.

The second comparison was made between racial-ethnic groups. In the initial group comparisons, no differences were found among white, Hispanic, and black students in their perceived ability to say no. In further analysis, several additional predictors for confidence in saying no to unwanted sex were examined. Of all predictors, gender was the strongest. The other three predictors of confidence in saying no were a positive attitude toward initiation of sexual activity, peer influence, and generalized self-efficacy. Peer influence had a negative effect in saying no. That is, the respondents believed it was important to do what their friends wanted and to be like their friends. High self-efficacy was significant and had a positive effect on one's confidence in saying no, especially for females. In other words, if adolescents set their minds to it, they more likely thought that they would succeed. The racial or ethnic background of subjects was a predictor of confidence in saying no for females but not for males. Hispanic and black females were less confident in their perceived ability to say no to unwanted sex than were white females.

The results of this study have implications for the implementation of educational programs. For example, programs that attempt to instill responsible sexual behavior in adolescents need to focus on the development of a generalized sense of self-efficacy (confidence, particularly in females) and the development of an identity separate from that of peers. Also, programs should continue to focus on attitudes about early sexual activity (Zimmerman, Sprecher, Langer, & Holloway, 1995).

FOCUS

Family Relationships and Sexual Behavior Among Black Male Adolescents

According to one study, black male adolescents who lived with both of their parents reported using condoms more consistently in the past year, and were less likely to report fathering a pregnancy, as compared with adolescents who did not live with both of their parents. Adolescents who perceived that their mothers were more strict than did other adolescents reported less frequent coitus, and with fewer women. Adolescents who perceived that their fathers were more strict than did other adolescents reported using condoms more consistently in the past year (Jemmott & Jemmott, 1992).

Use of Contraceptives

With large numbers of adolescents having premarital sex (DiBlasio & Benda, 1990), the rate of use of contraceptives becomes important. What percentage of these young people are using some form of protection against pregnancy? The NSFG in 1995 revealed that 58% of 15- to 19-year-olds used any methods of contraception (including withdrawal) at first intercourse. Only 30% of 15- to 19-year-old females or their partners reported that they were currently using contraceptives. According to the 1988 *National Survey of Adolescent Males*, of males who were 15 to 19 years old, 23% reported either that they or their partners used no contraceptive method, or that they used an ineffective method (withdrawal, douching, or rhythm) at last intercourse (Sonenstein, Pleck, & Ku, 1991).

These figures indicate that large numbers of adolescents are not protected against unwanted pregnancy. As a result, 1 out of every 10 women age 15 to 19 becomes pregnant each year in the United States (Trussell, 1988), and 4 out of 5 of these young women are unmarried. Among teenage men and women who use contraceptives, the most popular method is the pill, followed by the condom (Beck & Davies, 1987; Segest, Mygind, Jergensen, Bechgaard, & Fallov, 1990). Withdrawal and rhythm, both relatively ineffective methods, are the next most commonly used methods. Only small percentages of adolescents use the diaphragm, sponge, IUD, or foam (U.S. Bureau of the Census, 1998).

One Canadian study examined the sexual behavior and condom use of suburban male adolescents from 12 to 19 years of age. The study showed that male adolescents became sexually active, on average, at 13.9 years. Furthermore, 60% of the adolescent males used a condom at their first intercourse; however, their use decreased to one third when utilization at each intercourse was examined. Overall, condom use was greatest in 14-year-olds and decreased in older adolescents, being replaced by the pill. The study further reveals that 12- to 13-year-olds were less likely to use condoms and were more likely to use ineffective methods than were 14-year-olds (Hayes, 1994).

Potential Problems

Teenage Pregnancy and Parenthood

The net increase in premarital sexual intercourse accompanied by a lack of efficient use of contraceptives has resulted in an increase in the incidence of out-of-wedlock pregnancies, now estimated at 1 million each year among women less than 20 years of age (Jemmott & Jemmott, 1990; Paikoff, 1990). Of this number, 104,000 are miscarriages or stillbirths, 407,000 (41%) are induced abortions, and the remaining 489,000 babies are born alive. About 167,000 expectant mothers marry hastily before their babies are born, leaving 322,000 babies born out of wedlock in 1988 (Trussell, 1988). Recent data indicate that for women under 20 years of age, 83.4% had a

Living Issues

Convincing Teens to Use Condoms

Convincing adolescents to use condoms to lower their risk of contracting the HIV virus and other sexually transmitted diseases has become a major goal for most family planning practitioners (Poppen, 1994; Wilson, Kastrinakis, D'Angelo, & Getson, 1994). Planned Parenthood of Maryland (PPM) has developed a peer-support program that goes beyond teaching teenagers the basic hows and whys of condom use. It gets them thinking about how they make decisions and what the consequences of those decisions can be. It helps them to understand their own values and the importance of understanding others, and provides them with a supportive atmosphere in which they can talk and ask questions. The project is called STARS: *Students Taking Responsibility About Sexuality* (Rind, 1992a).

first birth that was unintended. Of these births, 16.6% were unwanted. The pregnancy was classified as unwanted at conception if the woman had become pregnant while using contraception and had not wanted to have another baby ever in her life. Pregnancy was classified as mistimed if the woman became pregnant either at a younger age than she desired or at an older age. If she had a first child at age 22 but had become pregnant at 17, her pregnancy was classified as mistimed (National Survey of Family Growth, 1995).

Over 90% of unwed mothers decide to keep their babies (Guttmacher, 1983). Some let their parents or other relatives adopt their babies, but the remainder want to raise their children themselves, assisted by whatever family or other help they can get (Culp, Culp, Osofsky, & Osofsky, 1991; Hanson, 1990). They have many motives for keeping their babies. One motive is to have someone to love. One mother said: "I wanted to get pregnant because I always wanted a baby so that I could have someone to care for and to care for me." Other motives are to find identity or a feeling of importance, or to try to be an adult by having a child.

Unmarried motherhood among young teenage girls is a tragedy in most instances (Christmon, 1990; Moore & Stief, 1991). The single mother who decides to keep her baby may become trapped in a self-destructive cycle consisting of dependence on others for support, failure to establish a stable family life, repeated pregnancies, and failure to continue her education (Blinn, 1990; Ohannesian & Crocket, 1993). Marriage is not the answer, because only 20% of those who

marry are still together after five years. Only a minority complete their high school education and are able to get a good job to support themselves and their family, so most are likely to require welfare assistance for years.

AIDS and Other Sexually Transmitted Diseases

Adolescents who are sexually active may be exposed to sexually transmitted diseases (STDs) (Holmbeck, Waters, & Brookmen, 1990; Moore & Rosenthal, 1990). *Chlamydial infections* are the most common. The incidence of *gonorrhea* exceeds that of chicken pox, measles, mumps, and rubella combined. About 1 in 4 cases of gonorrhea involves an adolescent. *Genital herpes* is found in 1 out of every 35 adolescents. *Syphilis* and other STDs are also found among adolescents. Those 20 to 24 years old have the highest incidence of STDs, followed by 15- to 19-year-olds.

Because adolescents are sexually active, the AIDS epidemic is severely affecting this specific age group ("Kids and Contraceptives," 1987). The Secretary of Health and Human Services of the United States has announced that the rate of AIDS among heterosexual young women is growing faster than in any other group. HIV/AIDS is the fifth leading killer of young women, who are most likely to be poor, from minority groups, and from metropolitan areas (Stiffman, Dore, & Cunningham, 1994). Many adolescents are unrealistic (Roscoe & Kruger, 1990; Slonin-Nevo, Ozaga, & Auslander, 1991). They can't imagine that it will happen to them, so they take unnecessary chances (Andre & Bormann, 1991; Peterson & Murphy, 1990). Adolescents who report homosexual experience are placing themselves at high risk exposure to AIDS. Those adolescents who are most heterosexually active, who use alcohol and drugs during sexual activity, who are

Prenatal education classes are vitally important in preparing pregnant teens for motherhood.

intravenous drug users, or who engage in homosexual contacts comprise a high-risk group for contracting AIDS (Jemmott & Jemmott, 1993). They can easily become infected and transmit the disease to others, if they do not take necessary precautions. There is a widespread need for education to prevent the further spread of AIDS (Hobart, 1992; Maticka-Tyndale, 1991).

Because the incubation period for AIDS may be from a few years to up to ten years, adolescents can be exposed to the virus and carry it for years without knowing it if blood tests have not been done. During this period they can transmit the disease to others. Because of the long incubation period, few cases of active AIDS are reported during adolescence itself.

Unwanted Sexual Activity

Fifteen percent of a sample of sixth- to twelfth-graders in Los Angeles reported that they had had an unwanted sexual experience, which may or may not have ended in intercourse. Eighteen percent of this group were females, and 12% were males. High school students were more likely to report an unwanted sexual experience (17%) than were middle school students (11%). Of the ethnic groups, Asians were the least likely to report such an experience (7%), while Hispanics and non-Hispanic whites were equally likely to do so (16%), and blacks were most likely to do so (19%) (Turner, 1991).

One study of 507 university men and 486 university women revealed that 97.5% of the men and 93.5% of the women had experienced unwanted sexual activity (Muehlenhard & Cook, 1988). More women than men were likely to have engaged in unwanted kissing. The ten most important reasons given for engaging in unwanted sexual activity were verbal coercion, physical coercion, threat to terminate the relationship, sex-role concern (afraid of appearing unmasculine or unfeminine), peer pressure, reluctance (felt obligated, under pressure), intoxication, inexperience (desire to build experience), altruism (desire to please partner), and enticement by partners.

Another survey of 275 undergraduate single women at Arizona State University revealed that over 50% of the participants reported being pressured into oral contact with their partners' genitals, genital and breast manipulation, and kissing (Christopher, 1988). Both the use of physical force and the verbal threat of force were uncommon. However, persistent attempts and verbal pressure were frequent.

Is Sex Becoming Depersonalized?

The question arises regarding the meaning attached to sexual relationships experienced by adolescents: Do adolescents have premarital sexual intercourse as an expression of emotional intimacy and loving feelings accompanied by commitment (Shaughnessy & Shakesby, 1992)?

Past studies have shown that the preferred sexual standard for youth has been permissiveness with affection. However, there is a significant number of adolescents today who engage in coitus without affection or commitment (Roche & Ramsbey, 1993; Wilson & Medora, 1990). Figure 14.4 shows the results of a survey among 237 (male and female) undergraduate students enrolled in 1986 at Illinois State University (Sprecher, McKinney, Walsh, & Anderson, 1988). The students ranged in age from 18 to 47, with a mean age of 20. All four undergraduate classes were represented. About 90% of the respondents were white, 8% black, and 2% other. About 49% were Catholic, 22% Protestant, 3% Jewish, and the remainder either another religion or no religion.

As indicated, 45% agreed that heavy petting was acceptable on a first date, 28% agreed that sexual intercourse was acceptable on a first date, and 22% found oral-genital sex to be acceptable on a first date. For those engaged in casual dating, 61% approved of heavy petting, 41% approved of intercourse, and 37% approved of oral-genital sex. The largest increase in acceptability for various types of sexual behavior occurred between the casual and

FOCUS

Sexual Abuse and Adolescent Pregnancy

Two-thirds of a sample of 535 young women from the state of Washington who became pregnant as adolescents had been sexually abused. Fifty-five percent had been molested, 42% had been victims of attempted rape, and 44% had been raped. Sexually victimized teenagers began intercourse a year earlier than the norm, were more likely to abuse drugs and alcohol, and were less likely to practice contraception. Abused adolescents were also more likely to have been hit, slapped, or beaten by a partner, and to have exchanged sex for money, drugs, or a place to stay (Boyer & Fine, 1992).

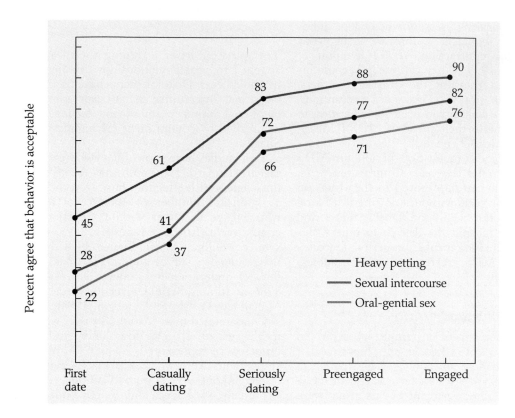

FIGURE 14.4   Acceptance of sexual activity by relationship stage.

From "A Revision of the Reiss Premarital Sexual Permissiveness Scale," by S. Sprecher, K. McKinney, R. Walsh, and C. Anderson, August 1988, *Journal of Marriage and the Family, 50*, pp. 821–828. Copyright 1988 by the National Council on Family Relations, 1910 West County Road B, Suite 147, St. Paul, Minnesota 55113. Reprinted by permission.

serious dating stages. Surprisingly, there were no significant differences according to gender, although there were differences according to age. The 18-year-olds were less sexually permissive than those 21 years of age.

Adolescent Marriage

Frequency

Figure 14.5 gives a detailed picture of U.S. statistics on marriage ages between 1890 and 1993. The median age at first marriage stopped declining for males in 1959 and for females in 1956, and has been increasing slowly since. The median age at first marriage in 1993 was 24.5 for females and 26.5 for males (Witmer, 1993). It appears that the steady drop in median age at marriage that was especially noticeable in the 1940s has been arrested. However, there are still numbers of youth, especially females, who are marrying young. Census figures for 1995 show that 4.5% of females and 2.3% of males age 15 to 19 are (or have been) married (U.S. Bureau of the Census, 1998).

Success Rates

To evaluate whether adolescent marriage is desirable or undesirable, one must ask how successful these marriages are. There is no cause for concern if these marriages are strong, happy, and satisfying; but if they are weak, unhappy, and frustrating, causing much personal suffering and numerous social problems, there is ample cause for concern.

Using divorce statistics as the measure of success, adolescent marriages do not work out well. Numerous studies indicate that the younger people are when married, the greater the chance of unhappy marriage and of divorce (Teti, Lamb, & Elster, 1987). The older the couple is at first marriage, the more likely that the marriage will succeed. But this direct correlation between age at first marriage and marital success diminishes for men at about age 27, when the decline in divorce rates with advancing age slows considerably. For women, the divorce rate declines with each year they wait to marry until a gradual leveling off occurs at about age 25. Therefore, strictly from the standpoint of marital stability, men who wait to marry until at least

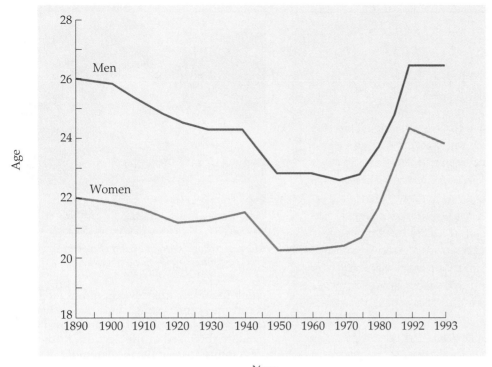

FIGURE 14.5   Median age at first marriage, by sex: 1890–1993.

From *Statistical Abstract of the United States*, 1995, by U.S. Bureau of the Census, 1995, Washington, DC: U.S. Government Printing Office.

age 27 and women who wait until about age 25 are old enough to maximize their chances of success.

Motivations

The most influential motivations for adolescents to marry young are

- Overly romantic, glamorous views of marriage
- Social pressure
- Early dating, acceleration of adult sophistication
- Sexual stimulation and unwed pregnancy
- Escape; attempt to resolve personal or social problems.

The Problem of Immaturity

Many of the adjustments young couples must make become more difficult because of the immaturity of the couple. The less mature are less likely to make a wise choice of mate. The less mature are less likely to evidence the ultimate direction of their personality growth. They change as they get older and so have nothing in common with their partners after a while. The less mature are less likely to be able to deal with the complex adjustments and problems of marriage. They are immature and insecure, oversensitive, unstable, and rebellious against authority—characteristics that make it harder for them to get along with their mate and to solve problems that arise. Booth and Edwards (1985) found that the principal sources of marital dissatisfaction among couples who married young were lack of faithfulness, presence of jealousy, lack of understanding, disagreement, and lack of communication. Attempts by one partner to dominate or a refusal to talk made communication difficult.

Most youths have not become responsible enough for marriage. One of the major problems of early marriage is financial worry. The primary difficulties are inadequate income and the fact that income has not reached the level expected. Little education, inexperience, and youth do not bring high wages (Grindstaff, 1988). Some couples marry without any income. In many cases, education is interrupted or terminated, so that the young person never achieves as much as the person who is able to continue an education.

Another real problem in early marriage is that it often results in *early parenthood*. A

FOCUS

School Birth Control Clinics

Faced with a desperate situation, some high school administrators offer contraceptive education services in birth control clinics right on the school premises. This idea is shocking to many people. Opponents insist that providing such services condones teenage sex, but advocates say that such programs in high schools are responses to emergency situations. A clinic in DeSable High School in Chicago was established after more than one-third of the 1,000 female students in the school became pregnant each year (Plummer, 1985). A 50% dropout rate from school resulted from the high rate of pregnancies. One of the most important services of the clinic was to keep pregnant girls in school to continue their education. Similar programs have been established in other cities across the country. This approach is pragmatic. Its purpose is to protect adolescents against unwanted pregnancy and from sexually transmitted diseases, without necessarily reducing sexual activity.

One study of schoolwide birth rates in St. Paul, Minnesota, both before and after the opening of school-based health clinics, indicated that birth rates were not significantly lower in the years immediately following the opening of the clinic than in the preceding years (Kirby et al., 1993). These results indicate that there is no easy way to change adolescent sexual behavior.

Another study analyzed the results of programs of six school-based clinics from around the country. The clinics were in Gary, Indiana; San Francisco, California; Muskeegan, Michigan; Jackson, Mississippi; Quincy, Florida; and Dallas, Texas (Kirby, Waszak, & Ziegler, 1991). Survey data collected both before the clinics opened and two years later indicated that the clinics neither hastened the onset of sexual activity nor increased its frequency. The clinics had varying effects on contraceptive use. The data suggest that the clinics probably prevented small numbers of pregnancies at some schools, but none of the clinics had a statistically significant effect on schoolwide pregnancy rates. Condom use did rise sharply at one clinic school that had a strong AIDS education program and was located in a community where AIDS was an important issue.

Married teenagers need a variety of support services to help them succeed in their marriages.

children and youths develop moral judgment is extremely interesting. Two major theories, those of Lawrence Kohlberg and Carol Gilligan, are discussed in this section. Both theories emphasize that the development of moral judgment is a gradual cognitive process, stimulated by increasing, changing social relationships of children as they get older (Hayes, 1994). For a newer theory of morality for everyday life, see the discussion by Shelton and McAdams (1990).

Lawrence Kohlberg

Lawrence Kohlberg has made a lasting contribution to the study of the development of moral judgment in children and youth (Kohlberg, 1963, 1966b, 1969, 1970; Kohlberg & Gilligan, 1971; Kohlberg & Kramer, 1969; Kohlberg & Turiel, 1972).

Initially, Kohlberg (1963) studied 72 boys aged 10, 13, and 16. Boys in the different age groups were all similar in IQ with half of them from upper middle classes. Ten moral dilemmas were presented to each subject. Each dilemma presented a choice of whether to obey authority figures even though the action violated legal-social rules, or to do what was best for the welfare of others and meet human needs. The choices were taped, and the subjects were then questioned about the reasons for their choices. Kohlberg's technique and material were Piagetian in form. In this study, Kohlberg was concerned not with behavior, but with moral judgment and the process of thought by which the individual made a judgment. There were no wrong or right answers expected; the individual was scored according to modes of reasoning, regardless of the direction of the given response.

majority of teenage brides are pregnant at the time of marriage. In fact, the earlier the age at marriage, the greater is the percentage of brides who are premaritally pregnant, and the sooner they start having children (Miller & Heaton, 1991). Yet marriage because of pregnancy has a poor prognosis of success (Kahn & London, 1991).

DEVELOPMENT OF MORAL JUDGMENT

An important part of social development is developing the ability to make moral judgments or decisions. The process by which

Kohlberg (1970) identified three major levels of development of moral judgment, each level with two types of motivation. The levels and subtypes are listed in Table 14.3. Kohlberg found that *Level I* of premoral thinking declined sharply from the younger to the older age groups. *Level II* thinking increased until age 13, then stabilized. *Level III* thinking also increased markedly between 10 and 13 years of age, with some additional increase between ages 13 and 16.

Kohlberg cautioned that each type should not be equated with only one age. Individuals of different ages are at different levels of development in their moral thinking: Some are advanced, others are retarded. No person fits neatly into any one of the six types. Kohlberg (1970) indicated that moral thought develops gradually as the individual passes through a sequence of increasingly sophisticated moral stages.

At Level I, the **premoral level,** children respond to the definitions of good and bad provided by parental authority figures. Decisions are made on the basis of self-interest; children interpret acts as good or bad in terms of physical consequences. There are two types under Level I. *Type 1* obeys rules to avoid punishment. *Type 2* conforms to obtain rewards or have favors returned.

Level II, the level of **morality of conventional role conformity,** comprises *type 3* and *type 4* and is less egocentric and more socio-

FOCUS

TV, Sex, and Marriage

Sexual content on television has risen steadily, and is now a stable part of many television programs. Sexual activity is most likely to take place between unmarried partners with numerous adulterous liasions. There is also an obsession with sexual relationships in both the prime-time and daytime serials, with the prime-time serials likely to be steamier and their characters more sexually active. Yet both genres of serial drama are deeply sentimental about marriage. The greatest esteem is awarded to monogamous individuals. Television images thus present an ambivalent picture of marriage and intimate, interpersonal relationships. Numerous programs, especially sitcoms, present happily married husbands and wives in a positive view of marriage. Serial dramas, on the other hand, present a less positive view of marriage and monogamy. They often revolve around characters who may be divorced, who do not express positive notions about marriage, or who may partake in sexual activity outside marriage. For large segments of the population, television may be the single most important influence in forming concepts of marriage and interpersonal relationships (Signorielli, 1991).

centric in orientation, and is based on a desire to justify, support, and maintain the existing social structure (Muuss, 1988b). *Type 3* under this level is the good boy–nice girl orientation in which the child conforms to avoid

---

TABLE 14.3	KOHLBERG'S LEVELS OF DEVELOPMENT OF MORAL THOUGHT

Level I. *Premoral level*

    Type 1. Punishment and obedience orientation
    (Motivation: to avoid punishment by others)

    Type 2. Naive instrumental hedonism
    (Motivation: to gain rewards from others)

Level II. *Morality of conventional role conformity*

    Type 3. Good-person morality of maintaining good relations with and approval of others
    (Motivation: to avoid disapproval of others)

    Type 4. Authority-maintaining morality
    (Motivation: to maintain law and order and to show concern for the community)

Level III. *Morality of democratically accepted laws*

    Type 5. Morality of democratically accepted laws
    (Motivation: to gain the respect of an individual community)

    Type 6. Morality of individual principles of conduct
    (Motivation: to avoid self-condemnation for lapses)

From Kohlberg, L. (1963). The development of children's orientations toward a moral order. I: Sequence in the development of thought. *Vita humana, 6,* pp. 11–33. Used by permission. Reproduced with permission of S. Karger AG, Basel.

disapproval and dislike by others; *type 4* conforms because of a desire to maintain law and order or because of concern for the larger community.

Level III, the level of **morality of self-accepted moral principles,** is made up of individuals who accept democratically recognized principles of universal truths, not because they have to but because they believe in the principles or truths. *Type 5* under this level conforms to maintain mutual respect with another person or group. At this stage, the individual defines moral thinking in terms of general principles such as mutual obligations, contractual agreement, equality, human dignity, and individual rights. Finally, *type 6* conforms to avoid self-condemnation. The motivation is to uphold universal principles of justice that are valid beyond existing laws, peer mores, or social conditions.

Kohlberg's stage concept implies sequence: Each child must go through successive levels of moral judgment. Kohlberg also said that the sequence of development of his stages is universal, even under varying cultural conditions. Developing moral judgment is not merely a matter of learning the rules of a particular culture; it reflects a universal process of development. Kohlberg (1966b) tested and validated his theory with boys aged 10, 13, and 16 in a Taiwanese city, in a Malaysian (Atayal) aboriginal tribal village, and in a Turkish village, as well as in the United States, Canada, and Great Britain.

Kohlberg (1966b) found that the sequence of development was similar in all cultures, but that the last two stages of moral thought did not develop clearly in tribal and preliterate communities. Data from the United States showed that the great majority of American adults never reached Level III either, even by age 24. Research has indicated that adolescents can be trained in the process of moral reasoning and in making moral judgments (Santilli & Hudson, 1992).

Kohlberg (1966b) tested his hypothesis with boys and girls of different classes and religions, and with both popular and socially isolated children. The same general stages of development were found among all groups, with middle-class children of all ages in advance of the working-class children. Middle-class children moved faster and farther in development compared with working-class children. Working-class children had less understanding of the broader social order and had less participation in it; thus, their development of moral judgment was retarded. This explanation is further substantiated by the fact that children with extensive social participation advance

considerably more quickly through the successive stages of development.

In general, researchers have found an increase in the sophistication of moral reasoning through adolescence due in part to an increase in perspective taking, intelligence, and the ability to think abstractly (Carlo, Eisenberg, & Knight, 1992). However, which moral dilemmas adolescents become most concerned about depends partially on their own individual experiences. Research indicates that early adolescents who are the products of divorce, for example, may not advance as soon as other early adolescents from concern about the family to concern about the peer and social culture (Breen & Crosbie-Burnett, 1993).

Moral judgment also correlates highly with IQ, indicating that it is partly cognitive in nature. Children who participate in social groups lose some of their cognitive naïveté and adopt a more sophisticated view of authority and social relationships (Mason & Gibbs, 1993). They acquire a greater capacity for moral thinking, but whether such knowledge leads to better behavior depends on emotional and social influences in their backgrounds and relationships. The point is, the ability to make moral judgments does not always result in more moral behavior.

Carol Gilligan

Kohlberg conducted his research on moral development on male subjects. His scoring method was developed from male responses,

Moral development includes developing sensitivity to the needs of others and a willingness to care for them.

Premoral level—the first level of development of moral judgment, based on rewards and punishments, according to Kohlberg

Morality of conventional role conformity—the second level of development of moral thought, based on a desire to conform to social convention, according to Kohlberg

Morality of self-accepted moral principles—the third level of development of moral thought, based on adherence to universal principles, according to Kohlberg

with the average adolescent female attaining a rating corresponding to type 3 (the good boy–nice girl orientation). The average adolescent male was rated as type 4 (the law-and-order orientation).

Carol Gilligan (1977), an associate of Kohlberg, found that females approach moral issues from a different perspective (Linn, 1991). Women emphasize sensitivity to others' feelings and rights, and show concern and care for others (Skoe & Gooden, 1993). Women emphasize care of human beings rather than obedience to abstract principles. Men emphasize justice—preserving principles, rules, and rights. Thus, women and men speak with two different voices (Gilligan, 1982). In summarizing six studies, including four longitudinal ones, Gilligan (1984) revealed that women rely on an inter-personal network of care orientation, and men rely more heavily on a justice orientation (Muuss, 1988a).

As a result of the difference in the way women and men think, Gilligan proposed a female alternative to Kohlberg's stages of moral reasoning. Table 14.4 compares Kohlberg and Gilligan.

At *Level I*, women are concerned with survival and self-interest. Gradually, they become aware of the differences between what they want (selfishness) and what they ought to do (responsibility). This leads to *Level II*, in which the need to please others takes precedence over self-interest. Women begin sacrificing their own preferences and become responsible for caring for others. They begin to wonder whether they can remain true to themselves while fulfilling the needs of

TABLE 14.4	KOHLBERG'S VERSUS GILLIGAN'S UNDERSTANDING OF MORAL DEVELOPMENT	

Kohlberg's Levels and Stages	Kohlberg's Definition	Gilligan's Levels
Level I. *Preconventional morality*		Level I. *Preconventional morality*
Stage 1. Punishment orientation	Obey rules to avoid punishment	Concern for the self and survival
Stage 2. Naive reward orientation	Obey rules to get rewards, share in order to get returns	
Level II. *Conventional morality*		Level II. *Conventional morality*
Stage 3. Good boy–good girl orientation	Conform to rules that are defined by others' approval/disapproval	Concern for being responsible, caring for others
Stage 4. Authority orientation	Rigid conformity to society's rules, law-and-order mentality, avoid censure for rule-breaking	
Level III. *Postconventional morality*		Level III. *Postconventional morality*
Stage 5. Social-contract orientation	More flexible understanding that we obey rules because they are necessary for social order, but the rules could be changed if there were better alternatives	Concern for self and others as interdependent
Stage 6. Morality of individual principles and conscience	Behavior conforms to internal principles (justice, equality) to avoid self-condemnation, and sometimes may violate society's rules	

From Hyde, Janet S., *Half the Human Experience: The Psychology of Women*, Third Edition. Copyright © 1985 by D. C. Heath and Company. Reprinted with permission of Houghton Mifflin Company.

others. Still, they place others' needs before their own. At *Level III*, which many never attain, women develop a universal perspective, in which they no longer see themselves as powerless and submissive, but as active in decision making. They become concerned about the consequences for all, including themselves, in making decisions.

Obviously, Gilligan's and Kohlberg's stages are parallel. Gilligan does not contend that her theory should replace Kohlberg's. She insists only that her theory is more applicable to the moral reasoning of females and that the highest form of moral reasoning can interpret, use, and combine the female emphasis on responsibility and care with the male emphasis on rights and justice (Muuss, 1988a).

WORK

An important part of socialization is to learn to work and hold responsible positions. Of today's high school seniors, 75% hold a part-time job during the school year (Bachman, Johnston, & O'Malley, 1987; Johnston, O'Malley, & Bachmen, 1987). The proportion of high school students who work has been rising steadily. Generally speaking, teachers, social scientists, and parents have encouraged students to work. The conventional wisdom seems to argue, "Working is good for them" (Otto, 1988).

Among high school seniors, one of four females works at least 20 hours a week, and among males, one of three does the same (Bachman et al., 1987). These students are working half-time while going to school full-time.

Seventy-five percent of today's high school seniors hold a part-time job during the school year.

Some authorities, however, are beginning to say that some adolescents are devoting too much time to jobs and not enough to school (Bills, Helm, & Ozcam, 1995). Greenberger and Steinberg (1981) emphasize that when high school students work more than 15 to 20 hours a week, the disadvantages include diminished involvement with peers, family, and school, and increased use of marijuana, alcohol, cigarettes, and other drugs.

Some adolescents today grow up so used to working after school and on weekends that they never have time for fun with peers, health recreation, or extracurricular activities. They become adult workaholics who have never learned how to play or relax. Such habits can be detrimental to personal health and marital and family relationships.

Summary

1. Adolescents want parents who will treat them as adults, have faith in them, love and like them the way they are; whom they can communicate with; who are interested in them; who will guide them; who are fun and have a sense of humor; who have a happy home; and whom they can be proud of.

2. Research indicates that fathers are more involved with raising sons than daughters and that noncustodial fathers are less close to their children than custodial fathers are.

3. The Parental Bonding Instrument measures mothers' and fathers' care and control as perceived by the adolescent.

4. Adolescent-parent conflict usually revolves around six areas: values and morals, family relationships, school, responsibilities, social activities, and work outside the home.

5. Parental functions are fourfold: meeting basic needs of children, protection, guidance, and advocacy.

6. The parents' ability to carry out their functions depends on the personal

characteristics of the parents, characteristics of the adolescent, and the quality of the marital relationship.

7. Factors outside the family, such as the neighborhood, the parents' work situation, and informal networks, also influence the parents' ability to function. Also, broader social values, social programs, social class, and other cultural influences define the context in which parenting takes place.

8. Relationships with brothers and sisers are vitally important because they have a considerable influence on the development of the adolescent. Older siblings provide companionship; serve as surrogate parents, acting as caretakers, teachers, playmates, and confidants; and can serve as role models.

9. Some families report a high level of sibling violence, with older siblings picking on younger ones. Such violence may be a long-term source of unhappiness while growing up.

10. The need for close friendships becomes crucial during adolescence. Young adolescents choose a best friend, a chum or two, usually of the same sex in the beginning. Early adolescent friendships are emotional, intense, sometimes characterized by conflict.

11. One of the most important social goals of midadolescence is to achieve heterosociality in which the individual's pleasure and friendships are found with those of both sexes.

12. Adolescents become increasingly aware of their need to belong to a group and to find peer acceptance. Personality and social skills have been found to be very important in gaining social acceptance.

13. Boys and girls gain prestige through grades and intelligence, sociability, popularity with the opposite sex, physical appearance including clothes, and participation in school activities. In addition, boys gain prestige through sports and access to cars. Girls gain prestige through cheerleading. During the 1980s, sports and sexual activity became more important as a means whereby girls found prestige. Cheerleading for girls and car ownership for boys became less important.

14. Some youths gain social acceptance by joining deviant groups.

15. Adolescents become imbedded in a rich network of peer relations, cliques and groups, social crowds, and romantic relationships.

16. Dating has many purposes: It provides amusement, enjoyment, friendship, affection; is a means of achieving social status and personal and social growth; provides sexual intimacy and emotional intimacy; and is a means of mate sorting and selection.

17. The most frequent dating problems reported in one study of college women were unwanted pressure to engage in sex, where to go and what to do on dates, communication, sexual misunderstandings, and money. The most common dating problems reported in one study of college men were communication, where to go and what to do on dates, shyness, money, and honesty/openness. Both men and women report problems in communication, due partly to imaging—presenting oneself in the best possible manner.

18. One study showed that persons who ranked low in sexual activity were more desirable as marriage partners than those who ranked moderate or high in sexual activity, but those who ranked moderate or high in sexual activity were preferred as dating partners. Males were perceived as more desirable dating partners when they engaged in moderate sexual activity, whereas females were perceived as more desirable dates when they engaged in high sexual activity.

19. Parents sometimes object to their adolescent's selection of a dating partner because they don't like the person, they feel the person has a problem, the other person's family is different from the parents' family, or there is a significant age difference.

20. The onset of puberty is accompanied by an increasing interest in sex.

21. Masturbation is commonly practiced by both adolescent men and women and is a normal part of growing up.

22. Data from the *National Survey of Family Growth* in 1995 revealed the percentages of never-married women 15 to 19 years of age who had ever had sexual intercourse after menarche, by age, race, and Hispanic origin.

23. Results from the NHSLS indicated the following percentages having heterosexual intercourse by the designated birthday: half of all black men have had intercourse by age 15, half of all Hispanic men by age 16-and-a-half, and half of all white men by age 17. Half of all black women have had intercourse by about age 17, and half of white women and

Hispanic women have had intercourse by about age 18. By age 22, about 90% of each group has had intercourse.

24. More females than males are able to say no to unwanted sex. Those who had more self-confidence and self-efficacy and who were less pressured by friends found it easier to say no.

25. According to the NSFG, only 58% of 15- to 19-year-olds used any method of contraception at first intercourse, and only 30% reported they were currently using contraceptives. According to the NSAM, only 23% of males 15 to 19 years old used no method or an ineffective method of contraception. Convincing sexually active teens to use condoms is important in preventing AIDS.

26. The net result of the increase in premarital sexual intercourse accompanied by a lack of efficient use of contraceptives has been an increase in out-of-wedlock pregnancies, now estimated at over 1 million per year.

27. Authorities are also concerned about the increase in sexually transmitted diseases among adolescents: especially chlamydia, gonorrhea, genital herpes, syphillis, and AIDS.

28. Faced with the rising tide of teenage pregnancies and the threat of AIDS, some schools offer birth control clinics on the school premises. The high rate of pregnancies is partly responsible for high dropout rates. One of the goals of the clinic programs is to keep pregnant girls in school.

29. There is some evidence that sex among many adolescents is becoming depersonalized, without affection or commitment.

30. The median age at first marriage has been increasing, but there are still large numbers of adolescents who marry. The prognosis for success in most adolescent marriages is poor. Many young marrieds express deep dissatisfaction with their marriage. Many of the problems of early marriage are due to the immaturity of the couple.

31. Sexual content on TV has risen steadily and often presents sex between unmarried partners or in adulterous liaisons. Ambivalent views of marriage are presented. For large segments of the population, TV is important in forming concepts related to marriage and interpersonal relationships.

32. Kohlberg has identified three levels of moral development. Level I is the premoral level; Level II is a morality of conventional role conformity; Level III is a morality of self-accepted moral principles.

33. Although Kohlberg's findings show a similar sequence of development in all cultures, not all persons reach the higher levels of development. This is true in preliterate communities, and among youth from various socioeconomic classes, especially among the working classes of adolescents.

34. The development of moral judgment also correlates highly with IQ.

35. Following rules as the guide to morality is referred to as a *justice choice*, whereas taking into account human situations and needs is labeled an *interpersonal choice*.

36. Carol Gilligan emphasized that women approach moral issues from a different perspective than do men. Men rely more heavily on a justice orientation, women on an interpersonal network or care orientation.

37. Gilligan outlined three levels of development: Level I—self-interest, Level II—caring for the needs of others, and Level III—a universal perspective that takes into account consequences for all people.

38. The theory of reasoned action says that moral behavior is determined by two factors that influence behavioral intentions: personal attitudes and social norms.

39. Among high school seniors, one of three males, and one of four females work at least 20 hours a week, leading some authorities to feel that many adolescents are devoting too much time to work and not enough to school.

Key Terms

Coitus   *p. 386*
Imaging   *p. 385*
Masturbation   *p. 386*
Morality of conventional role conformity
    p. 395

Morality of self-accepted moral
    principles   *p. 396*
Premoral level   *p. 396*

1. When you were growing up, how did you get along with your parents? Explain.

2. What did you like about your parents? What did you dislike?

3. When adolescents disobey their parents, what should the parents do?

4. How many brothers and sisters did you have? How did you get along with them?

5. How can an adolescent get over being shy in groups?

6. What qualities are most important in being popular and accepted by others?

7. At what age should adolescents be allowed to start dating?

8. What do you think of going steady in high school?

9. Should seventh-graders be allowed to go to school dances? Explain.

10. Should girls initiate dates? How do boys feel about girls asking them out?

11. Is it all right to date several persons at once?

12. Is it necessary for a girl to be sexually responsive to be popular with boys? Will boys ask a girl out if she is not willing to go all the way?

13. What should a 15-year-old girl do if her parents object to her going out with a boy who is 18?

14. Have sexual attitudes and behavior become more liberal since you were in high school? How, or how not?

15. Why don't more sexually active adolescents use contraceptives?

16. What can be done to reduce the number of unwed pregnancies? To reduce the spread of AIDS?

17. Should adolescents marry because of premarital pregnancy? What are some alternatives? Which would you choose?

18. What sort of sex education did you receive from parents when you were growing up? Describe.

19. Should school teach sex education? Why, or why not? Are there any sex subjects that high schools should not teach? Why?

20. What do you think about having birth control clinics in high schools?

21. Explain Kohlberg's three levels of moral development.

22. Do you agree or disagree with Gilligan's idea that the level of moral judgment of women ought to be evaluated differently from that of men?

23. How do you feel about adolescents' working 20 or more hours per week when in high school?

DEKOVIC, M. (1992). *The role of parents in the development of a child's peer acceptance.* The Netherlands: Van Goreum. Factors that cause or contribute to peer acceptance or rejection. Contributions of parents.

GIBBS, J. C., BASSINGER, K. S., & FULLER, D. (1992). *Moral maturity: Measuring the development of sociomoral reflection.* Hillsdale, NJ: Erlbaum. Discussion of the Sociomoral Reflection Measure–Short Form (SRM-SF).

GULLOTTA, T. P., ADAMS, G., & MONTEMAYOR, R. (Eds.). (1992). *Adolescent sexuality.* Newbury Park, CA: Sage. Overview.

LARSON, R., & RICHARDS, M. Y. (1994). *The divergent realities: The emotional lives of mothers, fathers, and adolescents.* New York: Basic Books. Interpersonal relationships between adolescents and their parents during an average week.

LINDSAY, J. W. (1995a). *Teenage couples: Coping with reality, dealing with money, in-laws, babies,* *and other details of daily life.* Buena Park, CA: Morning Glory Press. A practical guide to managing the realities of living, such as paying bills, developing workable budgets, living with in-laws, deciding how to share homework roles, finding jobs, learning about child care, sexual needs, pregnancy, and childbirth, and making decisions about the future.

LINDSAY, J. W. (1995b). *Teenage couples: Caring, commitment, and change.* How to build a relationship that lasts. Buena Park, CA: Morning Glory Press. Relevant issues for couples rather than professionals.

MONTEMAYOR, R., ADAMS, G. R., & GULLOTA, T. P. (Eds.). (1994). *Personal relationships during adolescence.* Thousand Oaks, CA: Sage. Interpersonal relationships of adolescents with families, peers, at school, and in the community.

http://nces.ed.gov/pubs/yi/ Youth Indicators 1996 Trends in the Wellbeing of American Youth. A statistical compilation of data put together by the Department of Education; involving psychological elements that comprise the world of the adolescent.

Perspectives on Adult Development

DEMOGRAPHICS

Age Periods

For purposes of analysis in this book, the span of adulthood has been divided into three age periods: *early adulthood* (the 20s and 30s), *middle adulthood* (the 40s and 50s), and *late adulthood* (age 60 and over). Because there is no general agreement among researchers as to when adolescence ends and early adulthood begins or when middle age begins and ends, the divisions proposed here are somewhat arbitrary. However, Levinson and colleagues describe middle adulthood as 40 to 59 years of age and late adulthood as age 60 and over (Levinson, Darrow, Klein, Levinson, & McKee, 1978). These age groupings are adopted in this book.

Population Trends

Figure 15.1 shows the population distribution in the United States, by age, in 1994 (U.S. Bureau of the Census, 1998). As can be seen, people 19 and younger are 29% of the population, early adults comprise 30% of the total; middle adults, 25%; and those 60 and over, 17%. *The median age of the U.S. population continues to increase as life expectancy increases.* Though it seems almost unbelievable, in 1850 the median age of people in this country was only 18.9 years. As shown in Figure 15.2, the comparable figure was 34 years in 1994 (U.S. Bureau of the Census, 1998). As seen on the graph, the decline in median age between 1950 and 1970 was due to the huge cohort of babies born during the post–World War II years. By the year 2000, the median age is expected to increase to 35.5 years (Kii, 1982). The aging of the population is the most important demographic event occurring in the United States today (Ahmed & Smith, 1992). It is due partly to declining mortality rates and partly to declining

Middle-age adults, in their 40s and 50s, comprise 25% of the population, and adults over 60 comprise 17%.

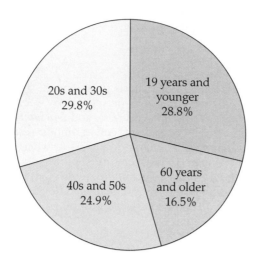

FIGURE 15.1   Distribution of resident population by age, United States, 1997.

Statistic from *Statistical Abstract of the United States, 1997.* (p. 21) by U.S. Bureau of the Census, 1998, Washington, DC: U.S. Government Printing Office.

Baby boomers—the huge cohort of babies born during the postwar period between 1945 and 1960

birthrate during the early 1900s was followed by a sharp decline from the mid-1920s to mid-1930s, during the Great Depression. This was followed by a baby boom after World War II, between the years 1945 and 1960.

Implications

The birthrate cycles have important implications. The small cohort born between 1930 and 1945 (the depression- and war-period babies) were 45 to 60 years old in 1990. As a generation, they enjoyed little job competition and an exceptionally high degree of prosperity and social stability. They succeeded, primarily because of their small numbers and superior opportunities.

But the teeming ranks of **baby boomers** have had a more difficult time. They were the restless generation in the 1960s and early 1970s—the activists, protesters, and hippies rebelling against society—and were unwilling to accept the status quo handed down by their prosperous parents. They attended college in huge numbers but had to compete for jobs. Many remained underemployed, forced to accept lower-level positions than those for which they had been trained. They married later than their parents, often not until their

fertility rates. Fewer babies are being born, with the general result being an increase in age of the population.

Figure 15.3 shows the birthrates in the United States between 1910 and 1993. This graph reveals several major cycles. The high

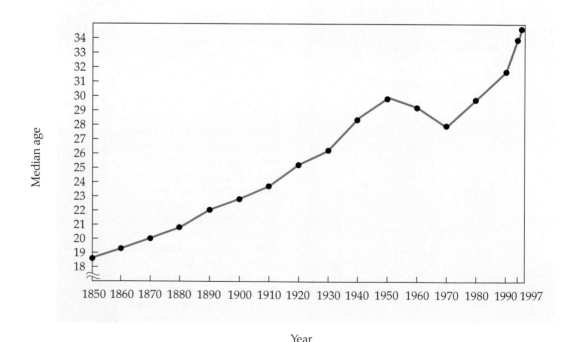

FIGURE 15.2   Median age of the population, United States.

Statistics from *Statistical Abstract of the United States, 1997* (p. 15) by U.S. Bureau of the Census, 1998, Washington, DC: U.S. Government Printing Office.

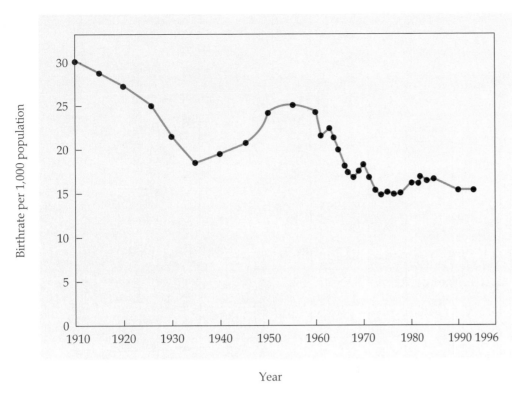

FIGURE 15.3   Birthrates, 1910–1996, United States.

From U.S. Bureau of the Census. (1998) Statistical Abstract of the United States, 1997. Washington, DC: U.S. Government Printing Office.

The large cohort born between 1945 and 1960 are known as the baby boomers.

late 20s or early 30s. Because of their sheer numbers, they have borne a huge number of children. The pressure on elementary school enrollments has been especially intense. The population of 5- to 17-year-olds shown in Figure 15.4 are the children of baby boomers. The baby boomers were 35 to 50 years of age in 1995; as also shown, they are a large portion of the total population.

Once married, this cohort exerted great pressure on the housing market, making rents and housing prices skyrocket. The competition this group has faced has also contributed to their materialistic ambitions and to creating pressures reflected in high divorce rates and continued drug use. In the year 2020, this group will be 60 to 75 years of age. The projection for this cohort in the year 2020 is, as shown in Figure 15.4, to remain large. As the entire group reaches age 60 and over (in the year 2020), the prospects are staggering (Butler, 1983). (See Figure 15.5.)

Because the elderly get a disproportionate share of health care, medical costs will keep soaring unless drastic measures are taken. Already, people 65 and older consume more than half of tax-supported health expenditures, although they are only one-tenth of the population. The pressure on the nation's Social

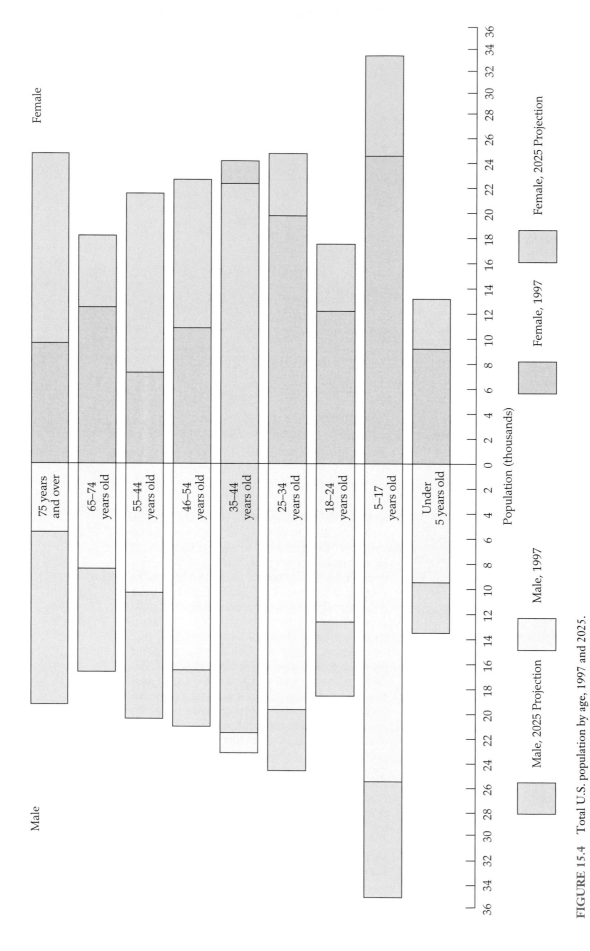

FIGURE 15.4 Total U.S. population by age, 1997 and 2025.

Statistics from *Statistical Abstract of the United States, 1998*, by U.S. Bureau of the Census, 1998, Washington, DC: U.S. Government Printing Office.

Security and pension systems is already surfacing with the retirement of large numbers of people born before the Depression of the 1930s. What will happen to the system when the postwar baby-boom generation retires? In 1990, one beneficiary drew Social Security for every three workers paying into the system. By 2030, that ratio will decrease to one beneficiary for every two workers paying into the system under the present law (*Aging in America*, 1989). If revenue sources remain unchanged, the Social Security tax rate, already high, would become exorbitant.

To reduce slightly the extent of these tax rate increases, Social Security amendments in 1983 increased the retirement age for full benefits to 66 in the year 2008 and to age 67 in the year 2027 (Chen, 1987).

Another way to look at the situation is through examining dependency ratios. The **dependency ratio** is the number of dependents for each person in the labor force. This includes both child and elderly dependents. In 1990, that ratio was 1.02 dependents for each person working. In the year 2025, the ratio will be 1.20 to 1 (Crown, 1985). The only reason it won't increase more is that the large increase in elderly dependents will be partially offset by a decrease in child dependents.

As large numbers of Americans move into older adulthood, the problem will intensify because their political power will increase (Hudson, 1987). If society tries to infringe on their rights or reduce their benefits and services, they will present formidable opposition. Because a greater percentage of the elderly vote than do younger adults, they already exhibit considerable power. The *American Association of Retired Persons* (AARP) currently has 12 million members. Other senior citizens' groups have increased their total political power. This generation has always fought for its rights and will continue to do so. However, as high expectations collide with reality, some degree of frustration is bound to set in.

Some Positive Developments and Challenges

Developments

As a result of the demographic and social and political forces shaping our lives, some positive changes are also taking place. The *divorce rate*, which peaked in 1979, has leveled off and is decreasing slightly as the baby-boom generation moves through the crucial early years of marriage. The aging of the population has caused a shift from a youth-oriented culture to

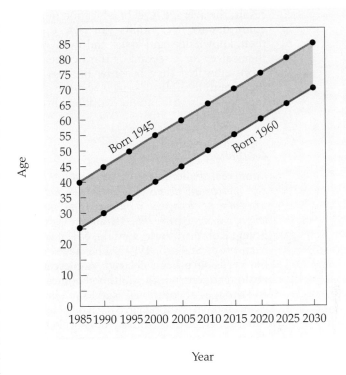

FIGURE 15.5   Aging of the postwar baby-boom generation.

an adult-centered society. *Clothing* styles are increasingly geared to the needs of young and middle-aged adults. Demands for *automobiles* reflect the practical requirements of adults and their families. Even tastes in *music* have changed, with increasing emphasis on the big-band sound and the love ballads of the 1940s and 1950s. The *food* industry, which for years catered to the demands of the young, now courts middle-aged and older adults who want to stay healthy and trim and add years to their lives. *Aerobic classes and fitness centers* enroll adults by the millions. The *recreational industry*, after emphasizing the sports pursuits and leisure-time activities of the young, now appeals to adults to take up tennis, golf, fishing, and skiing; to rent or buy a recreational home; or to engage in aerobics, jogging, or other physical fitness activities. *Travel agencies* cater to adults who prefer tours or more leisurely cruises. Because of increasing *housing* costs, more and more adults are moving into condominiums and other group housing arrangements. This arrangement frees them from some of the responsibilities of home ownership, allows them more time for leisurely pursuits, and offers companionship and camaraderie to those who enjoy social living.

Colleges, which experienced a drop in enrollments because of the declining numbers of teenagers, have expanded their continuing education and other programs for adults. As a

Dependency ratio—the number of dependent persons for each person in the labor force

result, the average level of education of adults continues to rise. Adults can now upgrade their knowledge and skills and even retrain themselves for a second or third career. The more educated they become, the less likely they are to face obsolescence, and the greater their chances to continue working throughout life.

Challenges

Some real challenges remain. *One is to alter our age-appropriate norms of behavior and make the necessary psychological adjustments to living a longer, more active life* (Branch, Guralnik, Foley, Kohout, Wetle, Ostfeld, & Katz, 1991; Manton & Stallard, 1991). The stages of the life cycle have been delayed. Adolescence is prolonged; entry into adulthood comes later; and the ages of vocational establishment, marriage, and parenthood have been delayed. Yet, America still suffers from a "rocking chair syndrome," a notion that disengagement should come early, even though poor health and death come later. A man conditioned toward early retirement, who decides to retire at age 60, still has an average of 18 more years to live; a woman has 23. These are long periods of time to live without working regularly and to be supported by the rest of society. Society will not be able to support the whole generation of baby-boom dependents. For the most part, they will have to continue to struggle to look after themselves.

   Society needs a new orientation to the concept of who is old. A person of 60 should no longer be considered old. Perhaps 80 is old, but in a short span of time, this concept may be outdated, and 80-year-olds may be considered "young-old." We know that sexual enjoyment can continue into this age, that a high proportion of intellectual capacity is retained, that an ability to learn remains, and that many health problems of late adulthood are being cured, allowing the majority of people to be healthy, active, and productive throughout their lives. Therefore, we need to revise our age norms, or our social age clock. We have to rethink the time schedule of our life—the time to go to school, the time to work, the time to marry, and the time to die (Horn & Meer, 1987).

MEANING OF ADULTHOOD

Adulthood means different things to different people. To a child, it means special privileges like staying up late or not having to go to school. To a child's parents, being an adult means acting grown up and assuming responsibility. To an adolescent, adulthood means being on one's own, establishing an apartment, and having freedom from parental control.

Social Dimensions

Whatever else it is, *the primary meaning of adulthood is social.* One cannot declare oneself an adult; one is perceived as such. Inevitably this perception reflects a mature, rational, and responsible person. It is unthinkable to call an undisciplined, irrational, undependable, socially irresponsible person an adult.

Biological Dimensions

Dictionaries define an adult as one who has attained *full size and strength; a fully grown person.* This definition implies biological maturity, reaching the limits of physical development and attaining reproductive capacity. But this biological definition alone is inadequate. Adolescents in our culture may attain their full height and strength and become sexually mature but still behave childishly and dependently, with nebulous identities and undetermined stations in life.

Emotional Dimensions

Being an adult also includes *emotional maturity.* It implies a high degree of emotional stability, including good impulse control, a high frustration tolerance, and freedom from violent

Establishing a separate residence, whether it is a dormitory room or an apartment in the community, is an important step for young adults in achieving autonomy.

mood swings. Another requirement of adulthood is to break childish dependency ties with parents and to function autonomously.

Legal Dimensions

Laws attempt to differentiate between who should and who should not be *accorded adult rights and responsibilities.* They designate chronological ages at which privileges are granted and duties required. Thus, the 26th Amendment to the U.S. Constitution established the legal voting age as 18. Child labor laws partially define whether one is permitted to be gainfully employed and what type of work one is allowed to perform at age 16, 18, or 21. Federal law restricts the age for military service and for obtaining contraceptives. Constitutional law limits election to the U.S. House of Representatives to people 25 and over, to the Senate to people age 30 and over, and to the presidency of the United States to those 35 and over.

The states retain the privilege of deciding at what age to grant some other rights; for example, the age a person may purchase alcoholic beverages, obtain a driver's license, or marry without parental consent. States also decide the legal age for making binding contracts, obtaining credit, disposing of property, or being tried in court as an adult. Whatever age that legislatures select, the decision also affects when adolescents may make decisions without parental consent and when they no longer are legally entitled to financial support from parents.

One problem of deciding adult status by law is that chronological age is not always the best determinant of capability. An 18-year-old may be eligible to vote but be completely unqualified to do so. The only positive value of automatic entitlement at 18 is that all persons are treated equally. Although the law can bestow adult status in one way, the person may not be an adult in other ways.

TRANSITION TO ADULTHOOD

Difficulties

Becoming an adult is a complicated process, especially in the pluralistic and highly industrialized society in which we live. Different segments of society seek to protect their own interests by erecting barriers to admission. Trade unions may require long periods of apprenticeship; businesses may require employees to have years of formal education. Until one fulfills the preparatory requirements of a

This Apache puberty rite serves as a rite of passage into adulthood.

group, one is denied adult membership in that society. As these requirements become more stringent, the age of admission to the adult labor force is delayed, and the period between childhood and adulthood lengthens.

Passages and Rites

In our culture, numerous rites of passage take place before adulthood can be reached. They include religious confirmations, Bar or Bas Mitzvahs, driver's license tests, and school graduation ceremonies. Unlike primitive cultures, however, each rite in our culture is only one small part of the process of reaching adulthood. Even if a person passes various tests, there may still be some question whether the individual is an adult in other ways (Rice, 1990a). This process makes the passage more ambiguous and lengthy than in primitive societies.

Socialization

An important part of becoming an adult is the accompanying socialization. *Socialization involves learning and adopting the norms, values, expectations, and social roles required by a particular group.* It is the process that grooms a person for life in companionship with others.

Part of socialization is anticipatory: preparing for certain tasks. Education for a specific profession is one example. At other times, resocialization is required. An adult must relearn something or learn something new in anticipation of a new task or role. Thus, a college graduate may have to return to school before taking a job requiring additional knowledge. Resocialization may be necessitated by role changes, occupational transfers, changes in family structure, relocation, retirement, or other reasons. Socialization does not happen only to children and adolescents in preparation for adulthood; it occurs throughout adulthood, particularly during periods of transition and preparation for new experiences.

DEVELOPMENTAL TASKS

Becoming an adult also involves the successful completion of a number of developmental tasks. A *developmental task* is a "task which arises at or about a certain period of life of the individual, successful achievement of which leads to his happiness and to success with later tasks, while failure leads to unhappiness in the individual, disapproval by society, and difficulty with later tasks" (Havighurst, 1972, p. 2). Each society defines what tasks must be accomplished and at what ages. Once these tasks are completed, the individual can enter another period or phase of life. Developmental tasks of early, middle, and late adulthood are shown in Table 15.1 and are discussed in detail in the following sections.

The Twenties and Thirties

Detaching oneself from parents is an important step in becoming an adult. During their teens, adolescents turn to their peers for companionship, emotional fulfillment, and guidance. This step helps break the dependent ties with parents. *Establishing a separate residence*, whether in a dormitory room at school or an apartment in the community, also helps in achieving autonomy. *Achieving emotional autonomy* is even more important than physical separation. The task is to break the close, dependent emotional ties that have been formed, realigning those ties on the basis of equality—one adult to another (Thornton, Young-DeMarco, & Goldscheider, 1993).

Breaking the emotional ties does not mean that young adults become emotionally estranged from parents. Research indicates the existence of positive and supportive relationships between most parents and their children. Only a minority of parent-child relationships are not characterized by positive sentiment and affection. The generally positive relationships between children and parents suggest that the role of parents in the lives of young adults may include not only the provision for some financial support but also other kinds of emotional and social assistance. There is a general improvement in parent-child relationships as young people make the transition to adulthood. This improvement tends to be greater for mother-child relationships than for father-child relationships. As young people

TABLE 15.1	DEVELOP-MENTAL TASKS OF ADULTHOOD

Early Adulthood
1. Achieving autonomy
2. Molding an identity
3. Developing emotional stability
4. Establishing and consolidating a career
5. Finding intimacy
6. Becoming part of congenial social groups and of a community
7. Selecting a mate and adjusting to marriage
8. Establishing residence and learning to manage a home
9. Becoming a parent and rearing children

Middle Adulthood
1. Adjusting to the physical changes of middle age
2. Finding satisfaction and success in one's occupational career
3. Assuming adult social and civic responsibility
4. Launching children into responsible, happy adulthood
5. Revitalizing marriage
6. Reorienting oneself to aging parents
7. Realigning sex roles
8. Developing social networks and leisure-time activities
9. Finding new meaning in life

Late Adulthood
1. Staying physically healthy and adjusting to limitations
2. Maintaining an adequate income and means of support
3. Adjusting to revised work roles
4. Establishing acceptable housing and living conditions
5. Maintaining identity and social status
6. Finding companionship and friendship
7. Learning to use leisure time pleasurably
8. Establishing new roles in the family
9. Achieving integrity through acceptance of one's life

begin to experience adult roles and have more independence, there are increases in respect, understanding, affection, confidence, and enjoyment between them and their parents. These parent-child relationships may continue to be important as the children establish their own careers and families and as the parents mature into old age (Thornton, Orbuch, & Axinn, 1995).

In detaching themselves from their families, adolescents gain an opportunity to *form their personal identities.* Separation at least provides the opportunity to become a unique person. However, Erikson (1968) suggests that identity formation neither begins nor ends with adolescence. It is a lifelong process of selection and assimilation of parental, peer, social, and self-perceptions and expectations. Becoming an adult involves integrating various aspects of identity, resolving conflicts among them, and developing a complete personality.

A major task in becoming a mature adult is *developing the capacity to tolerate tensions and frustrations.* Frustrations are recognized as a part of life and are either overcome or accepted without undue hostility and aggression. The ability to control emotions is one measure of the degree of maturity achieved.

Young adults are also involved in *making an occupational commitment*, completing their education, entering the work world, gaining proficiency in their work, and becoming economically independent. Career success provides a sense of fulfillment and worth. Enjoyable work contributes to personal happiness and adds meaning to life.

Erikson (1968) says that the chief psychosocial task of early adulthood is the *achievement of intimacy.* "Intimacy includes the ability to experience an open, supportive, tender relationship with another person, without fear of losing one's own identity in the process of growing close" (Newman & Newman, 1984, p. 384). Intimacy suggests the capacity to give of oneself, to share feelings and thoughts, and to establish mutual empathy. It may involve expressing sexual feelings; it does involve giving up isolation and complete independence and developing some dependent emotional ties. *Participation in congenial social groups*, another psychosocial need of young adults, begins in childhood, continues during adolescence, and is consolidated during young adulthood.

In 1997, the median age for *marriage* was 24 for females and 27 for males. This finding means that half of all persons who marry do so in their early 20s, often finding themselves unprepared for the responsibilities (U.S. Bureau of the Census, 1998). The earliest years of marriage are the most difficult, requiring extensive adjustments and readjustments as couples learn to live together harmoniously (Schumm & Bugaighis, 1986).

About 33 percent of all first marriages dissolve within five years if the woman marries before age 18, compared with only 14 percent of marriages in which the woman marries at age 23 or older (National Survey of Family Growth, 1995).

Young adults must also decide where and in what type of housing to live. More young adults are moving to the West and South than to other sections of the United States. First, they must choose among urban, suburban, and rural areas. About 60% of the total population live in urban areas, but not necessarily in the inner city (U.S. Bureau of the Census, 1998). Second, depending partly on the type of area, they need to select an apartment or other rented unit, a mobile home, condominium, single-family home, or multiple-family dwelling. As the price of single-family homes skyrockets, more couples are forced to rent or buy into multiple-family dwellings. *Learning to manage and maintain their own residence* is a new experience for most young adults. It often requires years of experience before they can do it efficiently.

The numbers of persons remaining voluntarily childless are increasing, but they are only about 4% of married couples (Rice, 1990a). The others turn their attention to *becoming parents and raising a family.* This task requires major economic, social, and emotional adjustments as family responsibilities increase and marital roles are realigned. Because of the increasing pressures, marital satisfaction declines, usually reaching its lowest point when the children reach school age (Anderson, Russell, & Schumm, 1983). The majority of couples are between their late 20s and mid-30s during this period. Once these years pass, family responsibilities decline and pressures ease.

Middle Age

Middle age presents a number of challenges or developmental tasks. If individuals are to fulfill these developmental tasks, they need a great deal of emotional support from members of their family, from friends, and from colleagues at work. Expressions of affection encouragement, and concern from different sources have been shown to be related to psychological well-being. Another source of family support to midlife men and women is aging parents. Older parents often provide emotional support to their adult children in the form of expressions of affection and concern. Even the older parent who has some form of impairment continues to be an important source of support to the adult children who are the older parent's caregivers. Employed people may also benefit from the support provided by individuals in their work setting. Support from one's work supervisor encourages psychological well-being and gives a greater sense of mastery in a given role. Feeling integrated and supported both by one's supervisor and by coworkers has been linked to reduced depressive symptoms and less anxiety for workers (Martire, Stephens, & Townsend, 1998). If these challenges are met and the conflicts resolved, middle age can be a time of continued growth, personal satisfaction, and happiness. If these psychosocial tasks are not accomplished, however, the period can be one of stagnation and increasing disillusionment (Erikson, 1959). Again, Table 15.1 lists the developmental tasks (Klohmen, Vandewater, & Young, 1996).

The day comes when many adults realize that they are out of shape; they cannot run as fast, lift as much, or perform as much physical work without tiring. Some women equate their loss of reproductive capacity at menopause with a loss of sexuality and youthfulness. These *physical changes require psychological adjustments and adjustments in lifestyle and health habits* to keep as fit and healthy as possible.

Ordinarily, middle age is the most fruitful period of *professional and creative work*. Middle-agers become the senior persons at the office, who receive a certain amount of respect and deference because of experience and seniority. But several things can happen. They may find that their superiors take them for granted and pass them over for promotions, or else they

Middle age can be a time of continued growth, personal satisfaction, and happiness by doing volunteer service in the community.

may become bored or disillusioned with their work. Middle age may be a time of unfulfilled expectations. The realization that the dreams of earlier years are not going to come true comes as quite a shock.

A more positive awareness may also develop. Realizing that they no longer find their work interesting and challenging, adults begin to rethink what they want to do for the second half of their lives. They modify their dreams in terms of new directions or locations in their present occupation, or in terms of a completely different career.

Adults 40 to 60 years old have been called "the ruling class" or "the command generation" (Stevenson, 1977). Although they make up only one-fifth of the population, they control our society and social institutions. They are the norm bearers, the decision makers, and the office holders. Their *participation in community life* is essential for society's progress. Ordinarily, community concerns and participation increase during these years.

When men marry at the median age of 27 and women at the median age of 24, the average father is 50 and the average mother 48 when the last child leaves home (Rice, 1999). But before this day occurs, there are long years preparing dependent children for independent adult living. Ordinarily children's dependency on parents gradually lessens and parental control slowly wanes, until the children are capable of managing their own lives. Part of the developmental task at this point is to *let go of the responsibility for, as well as the control of, the children.*

For many midlife adults, these years are a time of reflection about how well their children have turned out. As might be expected, children's adjustment and well-being are positively linked with parents' well-being.

Living Issues

Parental Support and the Transition to Young Adulthood

Developmental life transitions, as times of dramatic life change, provide unique opportunities for the study of the role of the family in adaptive functioning. Transition to young adulthood, which entails the developmental tasks of leaving the parental home and forming new social networks outside the family of origin, presents significant adaptive challenges for many individuals.

Family support is associated with less psychological strain and emotional dysfunction during periods of stressful life change. Although a restructuring of the parent-child relationship occurs during the transition to young adulthood, parental acceptance, empathy, and support remain an essential foundation for healthy adjustment during this period. A study of 175 college students, who were followed for two years beginning at 18 years of age, showed that social support from both mother and father played an important, adaptive role during the transition to young adulthood. Students adjusting to college experience more psychological problems when their families are characterized by less supportive and more conflictual interactions (Holahan, Valentiner, & Moos, 1994).

Parents feel a great personal satisfaction when they see evidence of their children's accomplishments, such as educational achievements and occupational pursuits, and when they understand that their children are happy and well adjusted. How one's children turn out constitutes a powerful statement about one's successes or failings as a parent (Ryff, Lee, Essex, & Schmutte, 1994).

Marital needs depend on what the marriage has experienced over the years. It is common for marital satisfaction to decline during the early and middle years of the life cycle. A couple whose children are independent now have only one another. They face the task of working out problems, eliminating resentments, getting reacquainted, and being close all over again. Goldstine (1977) suggests that there are three cycles in most marriages—falling in love, falling out of love, and falling back in love—and that the last cycle is both the most difficult and the most rewarding. Many people whose marriages failed during early adulthood have since remarried. The challenge is to *revitalize troubled, intact marriages.* Some cannot be revitalized, and the couple may *divorce* in midlife, often *remarrying* and starting over. The small percentage of people who are widowed during middle adulthood have to *adjust to living without a spouse.*

By the time adults reach 40, their parents are anywhere from 58 to 80 years of age, with 65 to 70 being most common. Therefore, during middle adulthood, children watch their parents grow old, retire, perhaps become ill, and die. *Middle-agers become more responsible for providing assistance to aging parents:* economic support, personal care, transportation, food, companionship, medical help, housekeeping or yard care, or a place to live. However, only 10% of married elderly couples and 17% of widows and widowers actually live with married children.

Once children are independent, *crossing of adult sex roles* becomes more apparent. Women are freer after the children are launched; they are not as tied down; some who have not worked before now take jobs outside the home. This increasing personal and economic independence gives them more authority, and the husband is called on to perform more services formerly provided by the wife. Some husbands object to their wives' independence and to their own revised roles.

Middle age brings a shift in the focus of social activities. Parents previously involved in family-centered social activities find an *increasing need for couple-centered activities.* Teenagers go out with friends. Grown children move out of the house, leaving the couple to their own resources. As a result, adult friendships assume greater importance.

Midlife may bring *increased interest in having fun, in pursuing one's own interests and hobbies, or in developing entirely new leisure-time pursuits.* It is not unusual for middle-agers to explore interests that they ignored during their child-rearing years. Some travel to places they always longed to visit.

One goal of the middle years is to find new meaning in life. This can be a period of introspection, in which to examine one's feelings, attitudes, values, and goals. There is a need to redefine one's identity, and to answer the questions: Who am I? Where do I go from here? These years can be a time of rejuvenation of the self and enrichment of one's life.

According to Erikson (1963, 1982) the chief psychosocial task of middle age is the realization of generativity. Generative people have prosocial personality characteristics, express generative attitudes through their work, are invested in the parenting process, and exhibit an expanded radius of care (Peterson & Klohnen, 1995). People become concerned about contributing to future generations. These contributions may involve passing on cultural traditions or ways of doing things, as well as furnishing others with new ideas and products. It is important to pass on ideas to the next generation and to show care and concern for others. Thus, there is a movement from concern for oneself to concern for other individuals and for society.

Late Adulthood

As adults enter late adulthood, they are faced with a number of developmental tasks. The task of *staying physically healthy* becomes more difficult as people age (Speare, Avery, & Lawton, 1991). Older people dread physical problems that impair mobility, their senses, and the capacity to take care of themselves (Longino, Jackson, Zimmerman, & Bradsher, 1991). As a consequence, maintaining good health is one of the most important predictors of life satisfaction in the elderly (Clark & Madox, 1992).

Many adults face the problem of *having adequate income* in their old age. Despite massive Social Security programs aimed at protecting retired people, older women are still the most vulnerable members of society. The failure of Social Security programs to provide sufficient protection to women following the death of their husbands is, in large part, responsible for the relatively poor economic well-being of older women (Burkhauser, Duncan, & Hauser, 1994). Elderly who feel they are better off financially than their relatives report higher life satisfaction than do those who are not so well off. Most older adults want financial independence, but this requires careful long-term planning. Retirement at age 65 is no longer compulsory, but many workers must retire at 70. Forced retirement has been ranked among the top ten crises in terms of the amount of stress that it causes the individual. People who elect retirement, plan for it, and look forward to it, feel that they have directed their own lives and are not being pushed or manipulated. Those most satisfied with retirement are people who have been preparing for it for a number of years. Certainly, retirement should be retirement to, not from. Retirees who are most satisfied seem to be those most involved in meaningful activity following retirement.

For some of the elderly, *being able to keep their own home is of great importance* (Worobey & Angel, 1990). It allows them independence and usually more satisfactory relationships with their children. American elders have been moving less frequently since World War II, and they are expressing ever-stronger preferences to age in the dwellings that they have occupied for a long time (Golant & LaGreca, 1994).

Statistics from 1997 reveal that almost 79% of households maintained by persons 65 years old and over are owned by them. In the remaining households, the elderly are renting. Of course, about 1 out of 10 men and 1 out of 5 women aged 65 and older are not heads of household because they go to live with married children (U.S. Bureau of the Census, 1998).

When the elderly have to depend on community-based care because of illness or physical frailty, it is important that the care institution encourage independence and help the elderly contribute to their own care as much as possible. Baltes, Neumann, & Zank (1994) emphasize that institutions should provide environments that are both stimulating and protective at the same time. This means that staff behavior is tailored to the individual competence level of elderly residents, that is, the staff should provide security and support only when needed and otherwise support autonomy and stimulation, by letting the elderly residents compensate for their deficits with the help of staff and by maintaining and even optimizing remaining competencies. In this sense, institutions do not need to provide total care but should serve as age-friendly environments allowing for positive aging.

The elderly have high status and prestige in primitive societies because they possess the greatest knowledge of traditions and ceremonies considered essential for group survival. The elderly also have high status in agricultural societies because they control the property, have the greatest knowledge of farming skills, are able to perform useful tasks, and are the leaders of the extended family. But as our society becomes more industrialized, technological, and modern, the elderly lose their economic advantages and their leadership roles in industry and the extended family. Consequently, they lose their *status and prestige* (Ishii-Kuntz & Lee, 1987).

Part of the loss of status comes when people retire (Floyd et al., 1992). When they leave their work role, they have the feeling that they have lost their main identity. As Bell (1975) said, "A former mechanic is no longer a mechanic—he is occupationally nothing" (p. 332). Those who are able to develop a meaningful identity through avocations, social life, their marriage, their children, or other activities adjust more easily. Some older adults go back to work part-time, whereas others engage in volunteer activities in their communities (Chambre, 1993). It is helpful if elders are able to set new goals and to maintain a lifestyle that they feel comfortable with (Rapkin & Fisher, 1992b). Their life satisfaction depends partly on the extent to which their current circumstances match their own personal standards or ideals (Rapkin & Fisher, 1992a).

Loneliness is one of the most frequent complaints of some older people, especially of the formerly married (Essex & Nam, 1987). Seventeen percent of men and 42% of women over 65 years of age live alone. Some older adults move to retirement communities so that they can share a variety of activities with others of their own age (Haas & Serow, 1993). Their challenge is to *find meaningful relationships with others*. Developing and maintaining friendships with peers seems to be more important to the emotional well-being of the elderly than interaction with kin. Late adulthood offers most people an opportunity to enjoy themselves. As work roles decline, more leisure time is available for preferred pursuits. Life satisfaction in late adulthood is very much dependent on social activity. People need *worthwhile, pleasurable activities* to help them feel good about themselves and about life in general.

Several events bring about the *adjustment of family roles:* children marrying and moving away, grandparenthood (Miller & Cavanaugh, 1990), retirement, the death of a spouse, or becoming dependent on one's children. All of these circumstances require

Pleasurable activities, such as collecting model trains, can enhance life satisfaction in late adulthood.

major adjustments and a realignment of family roles and responsibilities.

Erikson (1959) says that *the development of ego integrity* is the chief psychosocial task of the final stage of life. This includes life review, being able to accept the facts of one's life without regret and being able to face death without great fear. It entails appreciating one's own individuality, accomplishments, and satisfactions, as well as accepting the hardships, failures, and disappointments that one has experienced. Ultimately, it means contentment with one's life as it is and has been (Reker, Peacock, & Wong, 1987).

THEORIES OF ADULT DEVELOPMENT OVER THE LIFE SPAN

In addition to outlining the various developmental tasks of early, middle, and late adulthood, another approach to the study of adult development is to divide the process into a series of phases or stages of life. Several psychologists have sought to divide life into phases, to outline the transitions from one phase to another, and to define the major adjustments required during these different stages. Three theories have been selected for discussion here: those of *Gould* (1972, 1978), *Levinson et al.* (1976, 1977, 1978), and *Vaillant* (1977a, 1977b).

Gould: Phases of Life

Psychiatrist Roger Gould (1972, 1978) reported on two studies. One was a descriptive report of cross-sectional observations of psychiatric outpatients divided into 7 age-homogeneous groups. At the end of six months, a second set of 7 groups was constituted. Each of the 14 groups was observed continuously over a period of months. The second study was based on questionnaire answers of 524 middle-class adults not in psychotherapy. (See Figure 15.6.)

Gould's seven arbitrary age groupings and descriptions were as follows:

1. *Ages 16 to 18.* Desire for autonomy, to get away from parents, for deep, close relationships with peers.
2. *Ages 18 to 22.* Desire not to be reclaimed by family, to be intimate with peers, to re-create with peers the family they are leaving; real living is just around the corner.
3. *Ages 22 to 29.* Engage in work of being adults, in proving competence as adults; now is the time for living as well as growing and building for future; on guard against extreme emotions.
4. *Ages 29 to 35.* Role confusion; question self, marriage, career; begin to question what they are doing; weary of devoting themselves to the task of doing what they are supposed to do; desire to be what they are, to accept their children for what they are becoming.
5. *Ages 35 to 43.* Increasing awareness of time squeeze; realignment of goals, increasing urgency to attain goals; realization that control over children is waning.
6. *Ages 43 to 50.* Acceptance of finite time as reality, settling-down stage, acceptance of one's fate in life; desire for social activities and friends, need for sympathy and affection from spouse; watchful of young adult children's progress.
7. *Ages 50 to 60.* Mellowing, warming, more accepting of parents, children, friends, past failures; also renewed questioning about meaningfulness of life; hunger for personal relationships.

Gould admitted the danger in reporting cross-sectional data, because changing cultural values, rather than age, could influence results. Gould's reported fluctuations are not necessarily age specific for one individual. That is, changes occurring over certain periods of time do not necessarily occur at the

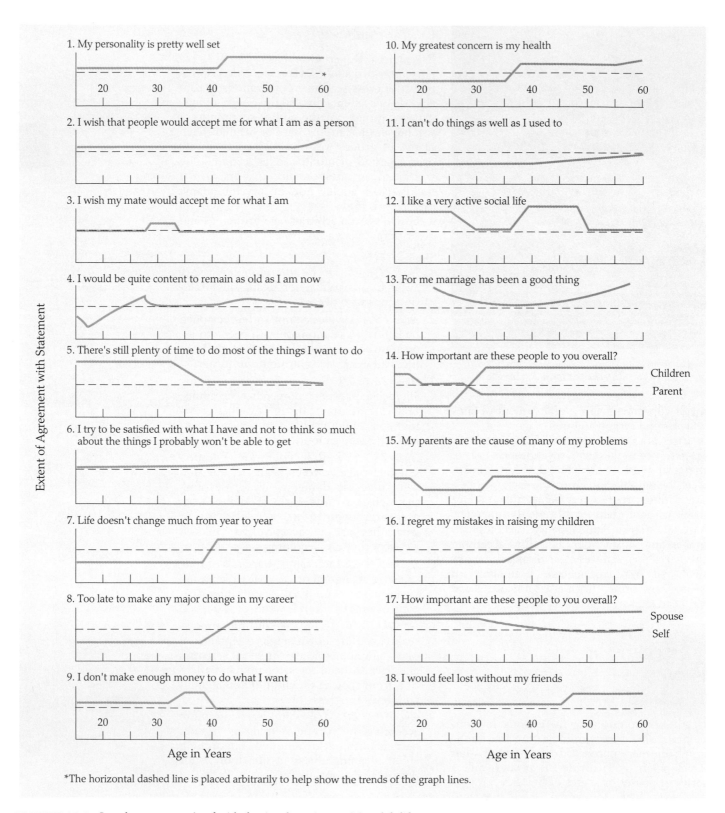

*The horizontal dashed line is placed arbitrarily to help show the trends of the graph lines.

FIGURE 15.6   Sample curves associated with the time boundaries of the adult life span.

Reprinted from "The Phases of Adult Life: A Study in Developmental Psychology," by R. J. Gould, 1972, *The American Journal of Psychiatry, 129* (November), pp. 521–531. Copyright © 1972 by the American Psychiatric Association. Reprinted by permission.

same ages in all individuals. He acknowledged that his studies were designed to cancel out individual differences to highlight sameness existing in an age group. But he defended his findings on the basis that many of them were supported by other studies using different methodologies and populations.

Some findings from Gould's second study are illustrated in Figure 15.6. In this study, the subjects were asked to respond to a series of statements in a questionnaire. Gould concluded his discussion by stating that strong evidence indicated that a series of distinct stages could be demarcated.

Levinson: Seasons of Life

Men

Daniel Levinson (1978), a social psychology professor from Yale, and his associates made a cross-sectional study of 40 men between 35 and 45 years of age over a period of several years. The subjects were divided into four groups: 10 hourly workers, 10 Ph.D. biologists, 10 novelists, and 10 executives from two companies. Of the 40 men, 70% had completed college, all had married at least once, 20% were divorced, 80% had children, and 50% were Protestants. Subjects were interviewed weekly for several months, with a follow-up interview after two years. The interviews were taped and interpretations made from the data. The interviews included much retrospective data from childhood on, as well as information about the present. *Thematic Apperception Test* pictures were used to recall personal experiences. Most of the subjects' wives were interviewed once. Extensive biographical information was also used in interpreting the data.

Levinson proposed a model of adult development that included periods of relative stability (periods of structure building) interspersed with periods of transition (periods of structure changing) (Kanchier & Unruh, 1988). Figure 15.7 shows the developmental periods outlined by Levinson.

The periods can be described as follows:

1. *Ages 17 to 22*. Early adult transition: Leaving the family and adolescent groups, going to college, military service, marrying,
2. *Ages 22 to 28*. Entering the adult world: Time of choices, defining goals, establishing occupation and marriage; conflict between desire to explore and desire to commit.
3. *Ages 28 to 33*. Age 30 transition: Period of reworking, modifying life structure; smooth transition for some, disruptive crisis for others; growing sense of need for change before becoming locked in because of commitments.
4. *Ages 33 to 40*. Settling down: Accepting a few major goals, building the structure around central choices; establishing one's niche, working at advancement.
5. *Ages 40 to 45*. Midlife transition: Midlife crisis, link between early and middle adulthood; review and reappraise early adult period; modify unsatisfying aspects of life structure; adjust psychologically to the final half of life; intense reexamination that causes emotional upset, tumultuous struggles with self, questioning every aspect of life.

Because Levinson's (1978) original groups were younger than 45, his descriptions basically end with the midlife transition. However, he does give some brief and tentative descriptions of subsequent periods based primarily on speculation.

1. *Ages 45 to 50*. Entering middle adulthood: End of reappraisal, time of choices, forming a new life structure in relation to occupation, marriage, locale; wide variations in satisfactions and extent of fulfillment.
2. *Ages 50 to 55*. Age 50 transition: Work further on the tasks of midlife transition and modification of structure formed in the mid-40s; crisis if there was not enough change during midlife transition.
3. *Ages 55 to 60*. Culmination of middle adulthood: Building a second middle adult structure; time of fulfillment for those who can rejuvenate themselves and enrich their lives.
4. *Ages 60 to 65*. Late adult transition: Conclude efforts of middle adulthood, prepare for era to come; major turning point in life cycle.
5. *Ages 65 and over*. Late adulthood: Confrontation with self, life: need to make peace with the world.

Levinson also observed that the entire period after age 65 is often regarded as a single era, primarily because of a lack of research data. However, with many people living to be well past 80, there is a period of late-late adulthood that can be either a period of further psychosocial development or of senescence.

Levinson emphasized that periods are defined in terms of developmental tasks, not in terms of such concrete events as marriage or

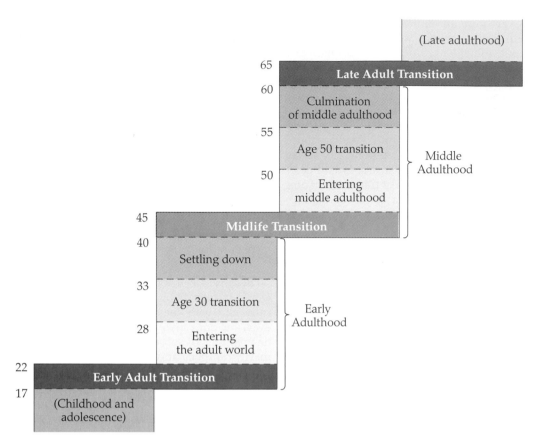

FIGURE 15.7   Developmental periods in early and middle adulthood.

From *The Seasons of a Man's Life*, by Daniel J. Levinson et al. Copyright © 1978 by Daniel J. Levinson. Reprinted by permission of Alfred A. Knopf, Inc.

retirement. Each stable life period has certain developmental tasks and life issues crucial to the evolution of that period. A period ends when its tasks lose their primacy and new tasks emerge, initiating a new period. Transitional periods are the times to question and reappraise, to search for new possibilities in the self and the world. Furthermore, there are ranges of variations when periods begin or end. Thus, the age 30 transition can start between 26 and 29 and end between 30 and 34. The exact ages Levinson cited are averages for his samples. Levinson also acknowledged that some men who suffer defeats (such as in their marriage or occupation) in previous periods lack the inner and outer resources to create even minimally adequate structures. Their lives lack meaning, and they face future periods with feelings of constriction and failure.

Women

In 1979, the year after the publication of *The Season of a Man's Life*, Levinson (1996) began work on the study of women. He and his colleagues undertook lengthy and exhaustive interviews with 45 randomly chosen women—businesswomen, academics, and homemakers. Levinson died on April 12, 1994, after he had completed the manuscript for his epic work, *The Seasons of a Woman's Life*.

Levinson found that he could divide the life cycle of women into similar periods to those for men—childhood and adolescence (ages 0 to 17), early adulthood (17 to 40), middle adulthood (40 to 60), late adulthood (60 to 85), and late-late adulthood (85 to ?). For women as for men, the eras are separate seasons, each with its own distinctive character. Within each era, women and men go through the same sequence of periods in adult life structure development and at the same ages. Between the major life periods, there are periods of transition; thus, there is the period of early adult transition between the ages of 17 and 22, midlife transition between the ages of 40 and 45, and late adulthood transition between the ages of 60 and 65. Although the periods of transition and of the life cycle for men and women are similar, Levinson emphasizes that women's lives are much harder than men's, partly because of the rigid division between female and male roles, between the feminine and masculine in all aspects of our lives. Of particular importance is the split between the domestic sphere and the public occupational sphere, between female homemaker and male provider. Ours is a patriarchal society in which women are generally subordinate to men and in which the splitting of roles is still acknowledged.

Gender splitting continues to predominate, although the general direction of change is clear: The lives and personality of men and women are becoming more alike. For most women, permanent, full-time homemaking is less feasible and less desirable than in previous generations. More women are working outside the home and are playing a less subordinate part in the public occupational sphere. Some 15 homemakers in this study were traditional women who wanted to live within a traditional marriage enterprise. However, the study emphasizes that the traditional pattern of the homemaker's role is difficult to sustain. Many women who tried to maintain the traditional pattern found the process relatively unsatisfactory, because that pattern is not viable in today's world and is not suitable for the self. The few who were more or less content paid a considerable price in the restriction of self-development.

The career women, in contrast, attempted to modify the traditional pattern. A recurrent theme in their lives was the intense conflict between the traditional homemaker figure and the internal antitraditional figure. Career women tried to reduce gender splitting, to enter formerly male occupations, to work on equal terms with men, and to establish a family life in which homemaking and work were more equally divided.

Every one of the women in both groups had her share of both suffering and joy. At the worst, each woman was engaged in a bitter struggle for survival; at the best, in a struggle for greater meaning and self-fulfillment. The study revealed much hardship: anguish, stressful experiences, and difficulty in marriage, motherhood, occupation, and personal relationships. The researchers made great efforts to maximize demographic diversity and not to include a disproportionately large number of women with serious problems. As a consequence, the women represented a cross-section of the American population. As a result, in every person's life, there was a mixture of joy and sorrow, success and failure, self-fulfillment and self-defeat.

The conditions of life for women now, however, are better in some ways and worse in other ways than those for women in former generations. Nevertheless, the great majority of women are still employed in low-pay, unskilled jobs and predominantly female occupations. Although advances are being made, women are still generally paid lower wages then men, and they are still advanced at a lower pace than men in the same occupations. Sexual harassment and discrimination are still widely practiced. There is a growing public awareness that many women are abused, discriminated against, and hindered in their personal development. Also, there is a growing incidence of singlehood and single-parent households in which women play very difficult roles. The past few centuries have seen some remarkable advances made in legal rights, education, suffrage, control of reproduction, occupational choice, and development. Yet, paradoxically, the recurrent advances have brought new forms of restriction and subordination that have been referred to as backlash. It will probably take another century to see how far the gender transformation will go and to discover what various meanings may be ascribed to gender in our culture. Levinson's book emphasizes the struggle for gender equality, which will benefit both women and men. Men must understand women better, and women must do likewise for men, if we are to understand ourselves.

Vaillant: Adaptation to Life

George Vaillant (1977a, 1977b), a psychiatrist teaching at Harvard Medical School, conducted a longitudinal study of 94 males who had been graduated from Harvard College between 1942 and 1944. These white males were among 268 college sophomores who had been carefully selected for the *Grant Study*, begun in 1938. The average age in 1969 was 47. The average income was substantial ($30,000), 95% had married, 15% were divorced, and 25% were doctors and lawyers. Most had served in World War II, 71% viewed themselves as liberals, and most were "extremely satisfied" with their professions.

A variety of research methods were used. Childhood histories were obtained by interviewing parents. Physical, physiological, and psychological examinations were conducted during the college years. After graduation, questionnaires were sent each year until 1955, and every 2 years after that. A social anthropologist conducted in-depth, home interviews with each subject between 1950 and 1952. Vaillant interviewed each man in 1967, usually at home, using identical interview questionnaires with each (Muson, 1977).

This study provides thorough histories of the life cycles of specific men who were among the nation's best and brightest. It is a long view of maturational processes, ego development, and coping strategies and adaptation mechanisms, as these men reacted to life's challenges. Some succeeded, whereas others remained locked in patterns of defeat. Vaillant (1977b) also said the study confirmed the principal developmental tasks in Erikson's life stages, especially those of adolescence (identity), young adulthood (intimacy), and middle adulthood (generativity).

One of the study's most interesting aspects was the comparison of the childhoods, family backgrounds, and earlier years of the men who, in their 50s, were labeled *Best Outcomes* and *Worst Outcomes*. Table 15.2 presents the results (Vaillant, 1977a). The table shows that *about one-half of the men who had experienced unsatisfactory (poor) childhood environments were among the 30 worst outcomes. However, 17% with poor childhood environments were among the 30 best outcomes*, indicating that childhood environment was not the sole determinant of adult success.

Some details were surprising. Fingernail biting, early toilet training, and mental illness failed to predict adult emotional illness. However, the comparison of 23 men whose childhoods were bleak and loveless with 23 men whose childhoods were happy and fortunate yielded four conclusions. Men with unhappy childhoods were (1) unable to play, (2) dependent and lacking in trust, (3) more likely to become mentally ill, and (4) lacking friends.

Similarly, it was difficult to predict successful midlife adaptation from negative traits seen during adolescence. Descriptions such as shyness, ideation, introspection, and lacking purpose and values did not predict the worst outcomes. Rather, these traits were merely characteristic of many adolescents. However, late adolescents labeled "well-integrated" and "practical and organized" were best adapted at 50, whereas those labeled "asocial" were least likely to be best outcomes (Vaillant, 1977b).

The study underlined the importance of achieving intimacy during young adulthood. The majority who married between 23 and 29 were happily married, and 28 of the 30 best outcomes had achieved a stable marriage before age 30 and remained married at 50, whereas 23 of the 30 worst outcomes had either married after 30 or separated from their wives before 50. Those who married before 23 (before developing a capacity for intimacy) and those who delayed marriage until after 30 were both likely to have the worst marriages (Vaillant, 1977b).

Between 25 and 35, the men tended to work hard, consolidate their careers, and devote themselves to the nuclear family. The most frequent psychological complaints of the men in their 20s reflected a retreat from intimacy, whereas the emotional complaints of those in their 30s reflected conflicts about success (occupational overachievement or neurotic defeat). Many found nonparental role models or mentors during this period of career consolidation.

TABLE 15.2	**COMPARISON OF BEST AND WORST OUTCOMES IN THE GRANT STUDY**	
	The 30 Best Outcomes	*The 30 Worst Outcomes*
Poor childhood environment	17%	47%
Pessimism, self-doubt, passivity, and fear of sex at 50	3%	50%
In college, personality integration put in bottom fifth	0%	33%
Career choice reflected identification with father	60%	27%
Dominated by mother in adult life	0%	40%
Failure to marry by 30	3%	37%
Bleak friendship patterns at 50	0%	57%
Current job has little supervisory responsibility	20%	93%
Children admitted to father's college	47%	10%
Children's outcome described as good or excellent	66%	23%
Average yearly charitable contribution	$3,000	$500

At 40 (plus or minus 10 years), men left the compulsive, unreflective busywork of their occupational apprenticeship and once more explored the world within. The pain of this age was preparation for a new life stage. Some men who were bland and colorless during adolescence became vibrant and interesting.

> In his early 40s, one man took up underwater archaeology and deep-sea diving in the Mediterranean. Another built a dramatic, shamelessly exhibitionistic house. A third man whose projective tests at 24 suggested an inner life like "some Brazilian jungle spilling out onto a North Dakota plain" was at 50 finally able to let the Brazilian jungle emerge into his conscious life, yet, he was the last man that the study ever expected to have an exciting love affair. (Vaillant, 1977b, p. 41)

The enrichment of these years also extended into the lives of the most successful businessmen. Their career patterns suddenly broadened in middle life; they assumed tasks for which they were untrained. The men who enjoyed the best marriages and richest friendships became the company presidents.

Vaillant continued to study these men in their 50s. Most of them reported having attained a certain tranquillity, perhaps suffused with a mild undercurrent of regret.

Comparison and Critique of Studies

Table 15.3 compares the results of the Gould, Levinson, and Vaillant studies. It must be emphasized that *Gould* purposely used arbitrary age grouping to organize the outpatients into age-homogeneous groups. Although he divided them into seven groups with particular age ranges, he could have used fewer or more groups, changing the age range of each. The age ranges, therefore, are themselves not important.

Levinson used five time periods (5 to 6 years each) between the ages of 17 and 45. Each major time period, which is a period of settling down and becoming established, was interspersed with an unsettling, restless period of transition and change. The beginning and the end of the age periods were averages for Levinson's samples; he acknowledged that for individuals, the beginning and end of each period may differ. Levinson also projected 5-year age periods to 65 and over, interspersing main periods with transition periods.

Vaillant used much broader life periods in seeking to confirm Erikson's description of the psychosocial task of each life stage. Young adulthood is a period of intimacy achievement and career consolidation. But although Vaillant related restlessness and desire for change with the age of 40, he said that some individuals experience this as much as 10 years earlier or later. Again, the exact age is not as important as the actual step in development.

All three researchers described a period of transition between adolescence and early adulthood, a period according to Levinson in which "The Dream" is formed. The Dream is a concept of what one wishes to accomplish. Some envision riches and fame, others a home and children.

These researchers also described a period of struggle, achievement, and growth as individuals in their 20s enter the adult world, striving to succeed in their occupations and in marriage.

One question that arises when comparing these studies is whether there are dual crisis periods during early and middle adulthood; one during the age 30 transition, followed by a period of settling down, and a midlife crisis as one enters the 40s. For Gould, there was one period from 29 to 43 of role confusion and realignment, and questioning of oneself, one's marriage, and one's career plans. Gould gave the impression that this entire period was devoted to reworking and adjusting one's life. Levinson (1978) made the clearest distinction between an age 30 transition period, about 7 years of settling down, and another transition period in the early 40s. But he also found that only 62% of the men experienced a moderate or severe crisis during the age 30 transition period. The rest did not report a crisis at age 30. Vaillant described no age 30 transition period; for him, the period from 20 to 40 was one of intimacy and career consolidation.

All three described a midlife crisis. For Gould, it occurred between 35 and 43, for Levinson between 40 and 45, and for Vaillant at 40 (give or take a decade). Gould and Levinson reported a marked crisis. According to Vaillant, severe crises were rare. Mild upsets occurred that created some anxiety, which often resulted in new challenges and vigor. One man of 47 commented,

> I am into a whole new life, a personal renaissance, which has got me excited most of the time. If I can make it pay adequate to my family responsibility, I will "really be livin'," man (Vaillant, 1977a, p. 221).

Psychologically healthy adults were able to reorganize their life patterns during their 40s and emerge with a new sense of personal happiness and fulfillment.

TABLE 15.3   STAGES OR PHASES OF THE LIFE CYCLE

Age in Years	Gould	Levinson	Vaillant
60	Mellowing, warming; acceptance of parents, friends, past failures; but renewed questions about life's meaning; hunger for personal relationships		Middle adulthood: mild midlife crisis around 40, inner exploration, reassessment, reawakening of instinctual urges including sex, throwing off some overrestraint of 30s, intergenerational conflict, establishing generativity versus stagnation
50	Settling down stage; acceptance of one's life, finite time; desire for social activity, friends; need for spousal affection; watch children	Midlife transition: crisis, review, reappraisal, modify life, emotion turmoil, upset	
40	Time squeeze, realignment of goals, urgency to attain goals; realization that control over children is waning.	Settling down: acceptance of a few major goals, central choices, establish niche, work at advancement	Young adulthood: achieve intimacy, career consolidation
30	Role confusion, question self, marriage, career; waning of duty, desire to be self; accept children as are	Age 30 transition: reworking, modifying life structure, need for change now	
	Working, proving competence as adults; living, growing for future; control of emotions	Entering adult world: choices, defining goals, occupation, marriage, explore versus commit	
20	Getting away from parents; desire for intimacy with peers	Early adult transition: leaving family, adolescent groups, college, service, marriage	
16	Desire for autonomy		Adolescence: search for identity

Adapted from R. L. Gould, "The Phases of Adult Life: A Study in Developmental Psychology," *American Journal of Psychiatry* 129 (November 1972): 33–43; D. J. Levinson et al., *The Seasons of a Man's Life* (New York: Knopf, 1978); G. E. Vaillant, *Adaptation to Life* (Boston: Little, Brown, 1977).

These findings were derived primarily from studies of middle- and upper-middle-class segments of the population. Gould's subjects included two groups: psychiatric outpatients and middle-class adults. Levinson's male subjects included only 10 hourly workers. The remaining 30 were all professional people. Vaillant's subjects were 94 males, all of whom had graduated from Harvard University.

Whether the findings apply to lower socioeconomic status adults, especially to those of minority groups, and to women of different backgrounds and ages, is uncertain. Nevertheless, there is a great need for longitudinal studies of adults of a variety of socioeconomic, racial, and ethnic groups to shed light on the changes and challenges that they face as they go through various phases of the life cycle (Whitbourne, Zuschlag, Elliot, & Waterman, 1992).

CAUSES OF CHANGE AND TRANSITION

The theories just described help us to understand what happens during various life stages, but they don't deal with the basic question of why these changes and transitions take place. There are basically two theoretical models that explain the causes of change and transition in our lives (Baltes, Reese, & Lipsett, 1980).

Normative-Crisis Model

One model is called the **normative-crisis model.** This model describes human development in terms of a definite sequence of age-related biological, social, and emotional changes. The three theories already discussed come under this category. Thus, Gould, Levinson, and Vaillant all describe a midlife crisis around age 40. Because the majority of persons experienced this crisis, it could be called a normative happening. Some normative crises are biologically based. Thus, puberty and menopause are determined by a **biological time clock,** which includes a specific range of ages for everyone.

Other normative crises occur because of social norms that define what is appropriate for people to do at various ages. Each society establishes a **social clock** that specifies when various life events and activities are supposed

Normative-crisis model—a model based on a definite sequence of age-related changes

Biological time clock—life events regulated by maturation and biological changes

Social clock—each society's specification as to when various life events and activities are supposed to happen

to happen. There is a best age to go to college, to marry, to begin a vocation, to have children (Greene, Wheatley, & Aldava, 1992). However, social clocks are not set the same for everyone in our culture, or in different cultures. Low socioeconomic status people in our society generally leave school, begin work, marry, and become parents at younger ages than those of higher socioeconomic status. Similarly, it may be appropriate for a woman in some other cultures to marry much younger than women in our country. When people do things earlier or later than society prescribes, pressures are put on them to conform to expectations.

The normative-crisis model also takes into account emotional factors that influence behavior and changes. People must be emotionally ready to make changes or to accept various responsibilities, such as going to college, getting married, or becoming parents.

As seen in the "Focus" box on p. 424 there has been a dramatic decline in consensus regarding the "right time" for various things to happen.

Timing-of-Events Model

The **timing-of-events model** says that development is not the result of a set plan or schedule of crises but is a result of the time in people's lives when important events take place. People develop in response to specific events that occur at various times in their lives. Neugarten, the chief exponent of this view, suggests that this development results in much variation in the time when events happen (Neugarten, Moore, & Lowe, 1965; Neugarten & Neugarten, 1987).

Generally speaking, life events that are expected **(normative influences)** create few problems for people. If people have time to prepare for a job or for marriage or parenthood, they are usually able to make the transition more easily. But unexpected events

(nonnormative or idiosyncratic influences) are the ones that create the most stress. Thus, the unexpected divorce, job layoff, automobile accident, heart attack, or death may create a great deal of stress. There is no time to prepare for these nonnormative influences, yet these critical events may define a turning point in one's life.

Some events are *sociohistorical*. These would include wars, economic depression, revolutions, or epidemics. They would also include events in the physical world such as fires, hurricanes, earthquakes, or volcanic eruptions. These events may alter significantly the lives of many people.

Sociohistorical events affect different age cohorts significantly. A small child during the Great Depression of the 1930s may have been largely unaware of unemployment and financial hardships that caused her father and mother to lie awake nights worrying about how they were going to make ends meet. Similarly, a 21-year-old who was subject to the draft in 1968 during the Vietnam War was affected far differently from his 75-year-old grandfather.

PERSONALITY THROUGH ADULTHOOD

So far, we have emphasized developmental changes that take place in people's lives as they grow older. Each stage of life requires its own adjustments and challenges. But what about the basic structure of personality itself? What happens to it? Does it change or remain constant? We have said that personality is the sum total of the physical, mental, emotional, and social characteristics of an individual. Personality is a global concept that includes all those characteristics that make every person an individual, different from every other person. We have said that personality is not static, that it develops over the years and is always in the process of becoming. There is considerable evidence that provides substantial support for continuity of personality in adulthood, although there are indications of change. Converging evidence from several investigations reveals that individuals exhibit change as well as stability in various personality traits through adulthood and that certain individuals are more likely to exhibit changing personal characteristics than are other individuals. On the basis of longitudinal data, there is at least as much evidence for changing continuity through adulthood as there is for stability and continuity (Manen & Whitbourne, 1997).

Counseling often helps people deal with important changes in their lives.

Normative influences—expected life events that occur at customary times

Nonnormative or idiosyncratic influences—life events that occur at unexpected times or that are unusual, both of which have a major impact on development

Timing-of-events model—a model of development based on responses to the occurrences and timing of normative and nonnormative events

FOCUS

The Right Time for Life Events

Two surveys asked Americans 20 years apart (late 1950s and late 1970s) what is the right age for various major events and achievements of adult life. A dramatic decline occurred in the consensus among middle-class, middle-aged people.

TABLE 15.4   CONCEPTS OF "THE RIGHT TIME"

Activity/Event	Appropriate Age Range	Late 1950s Study (% Who Agree)		Late 1970s Study (% Who Agree)	
		Men	Women	Men	Women
Best age for a man to marry	20–25	80%	90%	42%	42%
Best age for a woman to marry	19–24	85	90	44	36
When most people should become grandparents	45–50	84	79	64	57
Best age for most people to finish school and go to work	20–22	86	82	36	38
When most men should be settled on a career	24–26	74	64	24	26
When most men hold their top jobs	45–50	71	58	38	31
When most people should be ready to retire	60–65	83	86	66	41
When a man has the most responsibilities	35–50	79	75	49	50
When a man accomplishes most	40–50	82	71	46	41
The prime of life for a man	35–50	86	80	59	66
When a woman has the most responsibilities	25–40	93	91	59	53
When a woman accomplishes most	30–45	94	92	57	48

Adapted from "Age Norms and Age Constraints Twenty Years Later," by P. Passuth, D. Maines, and B. I. Neugarten, *Psychology Today 21* (May 1987), 72, pp. 29–33. Paper first presented at the Midwest Sociological Society meeting, Chicago, April 1984.

It is apparent that people behave differently in different situations and then make adjustments to the various problems and tasks that arise over the different stages of their lives. However, much longitudinal research over the decades of adulthood has found considerable continuity in basic personality characteristics and traits that people possess. Part of the research has utilized the so-called *Five-Factor Model* of personality dimensions. This Five-Factor Model (FFM) divides the dimensions of personality into the following five categories: extraversion, agreeableness, conscientiousness, neuroticism, and openness/intellect (John, Caspi, Robins, Moffitt, & Stouthamer-Lober, 1994). Various adjectives have been used to describe the big five factors as follows (McCrae & John, 1992):

1. *Extraversion (E):* active, assertive, energetic, enthusiastic, outgoing, and talkative

2. *Agreeableness (A):* affectionate, forgiving, generous, kind, sympathetic, and trusting

3. *Conscientiousness (C):* efficient, organized, planful, reliable, responsible, thorough

4. *Neuroticism (N):* anxious, self-pitying, tense, touchy, unstable, worrying

5. *Openness/Intellect (O):* artistic, curious, imaginative, insightful, original, and having wide interests

These big five factors in personality have been influenced both by heredity and childhood experiences and by experiences during adolescence and early adulthood. During these formative years, traits are more likely to fluctuate than they do later in life. By about age 30, traits usually become quite stable and are likely to remain so throughout the rest of adulthood. By age 30, many people have settled into their vocations, selected a mate, and adopted a certain lifestyle that reflects their particular personality traits. McCrae & Costa (1990) suggest that personality shapes people's lives rather than the other way around. Let us see how personality traits influence behavior and lifestyle. If people are *extraverted*, this quality most likely has some influence on their choice of friends. They are usually outgoing people who behave assertively and are very gregarious; they are usually very talkative, energetic, and enthusiastic. Their characteristics would influence not only the kind of friends that they keep but also the kind of mate that they are likely to marry and their selection of employment. Extraverted people make very good managers and salespeople; also, they make very good workers in professions that require the kind of person who gets along well with others.

Other people may exhibit the trait of *conscientiousness*. Such people are generally dependable, reasonable, and very productive; also, they are very careful about the way that they do things and about getting them done on time. They behave ethically, have a high aspiration level, and are the kind of workers whom people enjoy hiring because they are so particular about the way that they work. When assigned a task, they will see to it that they get it done.

Or, supposing people are described as *agreeable*. Such people are sympathetic, considerate, warm, and compassionate. They behave in a given way and are easy to get along with. They are pleasant persons to have around.

On the other hand, people who are *neurotic* are usually supersensitive to criticism, get upset very easily, and are thin-skinned. Basically they are anxious persons who show fluctuation of moods; you never know when they are going to get upset and when not. In extreme cases, they are very difficult, almost impossible, to get along with because they feel so anxious all the time.

Finally, the *openness* and *intellect* of some people indicate that they are very receptive to new ideas and have a wide range of interests. Being introspective, they don't always agree with everybody else and thus can be very different in the way that they think and in the way that they do things.

The research indicates that these five basic clusters of personality traits remain quite stable throughout adulthood. If a person tends to be neurotic early in life, chances are he or she will be neurotic, anxious, moody, and self-punishing throughout life. Such a person will still worry about the future and be anxious about events that have not yet happened. Life might somewhat modify the extent of these traits, but the basic structure of personality seems to be there over the life span.

Summary

1. The span of adulthood may be divided into three age periods: early adulthood (20s and 30s), middle adulthood (40s and 50s), and late adulthood (60 and over).

2. The median age of the population, which continues to increase, was 34 years in 1997.

3. Graphs of birthrates reveal a large cohort born during the early 1900s, a small cohort of Depression babies born between 1930 and 1945, and a large cohort of baby boomers born after World War II, between 1945 and 1960. Because of their large numbers, the baby boomers have had to struggle for jobs, have had large numbers of children, have exerted great pressure on the housing market, and have reacted to the stress with high divorce rates and drug use. When they age, medical and Social Security costs will be staggering. They will exert considerable political power in demanding their rights.

4. As the dependency ratio increases, the burden of responsibility for supporting dependents is great and is partially shifting from men to women.

5. As a result of these demographics, there are various positive developments that are taking place: a leveling off of divorce rates and society's turning its attention from a youth-oriented to an adult-conscious culture.

6. Adulthood means different things to different people, but it has social, biological, emotional, and legal dimensions; its primary meaning is social.

7. The transition to adulthood is a complicated process in our highly industrialized society, with individuals having to go through various rites of passage as they

become socialized (learning and adopting the norms, values, expectations, and social roles of their group).

8. Becoming an adult means the successful completion of a number of developmental tasks. Development continues and the tasks change during early, middle, and late adulthood.

9. Early adults face the tasks of achieving autonomy, molding an identity, developing emotional stability, establishing a career, finding intimacy, becoming part of social groups, selecting a mate and adjusting to marriage, establishing and managing a residence, becoming parents and rearing children.

10. Middle-aged adults are faced with the tasks of adjusting to physical changes, finding satisfaction in their career, assuming social and civic responsibilities, launching children, revitalizing marriage, reorienting to aging parents, realigning sex roles, developing social networks and leisure-time activities. Their overall goal is to find new meaning in life.

11. According to Erikson, the chief psychosocial task of middle age is the realization of generativity.

12. Late adults are faced with the tasks of staying physically healthy and adjusting to limitations, maintaining an adequate income, adjusting to revised work roles, establishing acceptable housing and living conditions, maintaining identity and social status, finding companionship, learning to use leisure time pleasurably, establishing new roles in the family, and achieving integrity through acceptance of one's life.

13. Three major theories of adult development over the life span are discussed here: those of Roger Gould, Daniel Levinson, and George Vaillant.

14. Gould used seven homogeneous age groups to define the changes and adjustments required as people go through various life phases.

15. Levinson proposed a model of adult development that outlines periods of relative stability interspersed with major periods of transition beginning at ages 17, 40, and 60, and lesser transitions at 30 and 50.

16. Levinson found that he could divide the life cycle of women into similar periods to those for men. Although the periods of transition and of the life cycle for men and women are similar, Levinson emphasizes that women's lives are much harder than men's, partly because of the rigid division between female and male roles. The traditional pattern of the homemaker's role is difficult to sustain. Many women who tried to do so found the process relatively unsatisfactory. The career women, in contrast, attempted to modify the traditional pattern. A recurrent theme in their lives was the intense conflict between the traditional homemaker figure and the internal antitraditional figure. As a result, in every person's life, there was a mixture of joy and sorrow, success and failure, self-fulfillment and self-defeat.

17. Vaillant made a longitudinal study of the histories of the life cycles of men who were among the nation's best and brightest. One important contribution was the comparison of childhood background with adult success. Half the men who had poor childhood environments were among the 30 worst outcomes, and 17 with poor childhood environments were among the 30 best outcomes, indicating that childhood environment alone was not the sole determinant of adult success. However, those with unhappy childhoods were (a) unable to play, (b) dependent and lacking in trust, (c) more likely to become mentally ill, and (d) lacking friends.

18. It was difficult to predict successful adaptation from negative traits during adolescence. The study revealed the importance of achieving intimacy during young adulthood in terms of later marital success.

19. The age divisions in the three studies are purely arbitrary. All three researchers described a period of transition between adolescence and early adulthood, and a midlife crisis around age 40.

20. Two theoretical models describe the causes of change and transition in life: the normative-crisis model and the timing-of-events model.

21. The normative-crisis model describes normative happenings according to a biological time clock and a social clock. These happenings result in changes in our lives. This model also takes into account emotional factors that influence behavior and change.

22. The timing-of-events model says that development is a result of the times in people's lives when important events take place. Some events are normative; others are nonnormative, or idiosyncratic. In this model, the latter type of events are often the most critical to a person's development.

23. According to the Five-Factor Model of personality development, certain clusters of personality traits remain quite stable throughout adulthood.

Key Terms

Discussion Questions

1. When were you born, and how does your age cohort differ from others who are younger or older?

2. Were your parents part of the baby boomers' cohort? What difference might it have made in their lives?

3. What are some things that are likely to happen because of increasing dependency ratios? What is your reaction to the idea that the responsibility for taking care of dependents is shifting from men to women?

4. What are the most important qualities in an adult? Which rite of passage is most important to you in achieving adulthood?

5. To those in your 20s and 30s: Which developmental tasks are most important to you? Which ones are the most difficult?

6. To those in your 40s, 50s, or 60s: Which developmental tasks are most important to you? Which ones are the most difficult?

7. Are any of your parents or grandparents age 60 or over? Which developmental tasks seem to be most important to them? Which are the most difficult?

8. Look at Figure 15.6 based on Gould's findings. Which findings do you find most significant? Explain. Are there any findings that you find surprising? Are

there any findings that seem different from those of your own experiences? Explain.

9. What do you think of Levinson's theory? What aspects do you feel are most important? Which ones agree with your own experience? Which do you disagree with? Explain.

10. Think about your own childhood background. How has it affected you in the process of becoming an adult? In what ways have you been handicapped by your childhood background? In what ways have you been helped by your childhood background?

11. Why do some people overcome the effects of being brought up in a dysfunctional family, but others do not? What factors are important in overcoming the negative effects?

12. Is it possible to have too happy a childhood as far as later adult success is concerned?

13. In what ways has your biological time clock affected your life? In what ways has your social clock affected your life?

14. What events in your life have been most significant in influencing change and transitions? Describe.

Suggested Readings

COWAN, P. A., HETHERINGTON, E. M. (Eds.). (1991). *Family transitions*. Hillsdale, NJ: Erlbaum. Normative and nonnormative transitions.

KEITH, P. M., & SCHAFER, R. B. (1991). *Relationships and well-being over the life stages*. New York: Praeger. Four different stages of family life.

LEVINSON, D. J. (1996). *The seasons of a woman's life*. New York: Alfred Knopf. Adult development of women.

McCRAE, R. P., & COSTA, P. T. (1990). *Personality in adulthood*. New York: Guilford Press. The continuity of personality characteristics.

RICE, F. P. (1986). *Adult development and aging*. Boston: Allyn and Bacon. The author's comprehensive textbook on the subject.

SHERMAN, E. (1987). *Meaning in midlife transitions*. Albany: State University of New York Press. Case studies of individuals making the transitions during middle age.

VAUGHN, M. E., & SKINNER, B. F. (1997). *Enjoy Old Age: A Practical Guide*. W. W. Norton & Co. By B. F. Skinner, the famous psychologist, and his colleague.

Web Resources

http://www.iog.wayne.edu/APADIV20/APADIV20.htm   Web Pages of The American Psychological Association's Division 20 which is dedicated to studying the psychology of adult development and aging. Offers research, employment, pre- and post-doctorial programs, instructional resources, institutes and more.

Physical Development

PHYSICAL ATTRACTIVENESS, ABILITIES, AND FITNESS

Growth and Aging

Sometime during the mid-20s, the human body is usually at the peak of its physical development. Height is at a maximum, bones and teeth are strong, muscles are powerful, the skin is supple, senses are keen, and the mind is sharp. Table 16.1 shows the ages of peak performance of athletes (Horn, 1988). An analysis of the relationship between age and major league baseball performance showed that performance rises relatively quickly from age 19 to a peak age of 27 and then declines (Schulz, Musa, Stascewski, & Siegler, 1994). Ironically, at the same time that peak performance is reached, aging is taking place. Every human being is born with a fantastic reserve of tissue and cells, but this reserve is gradually depleted with age. Some types of cells, such as liver and kidney cells, replace themselves over a long period of time. Other cells, such as muscle cells, have a limited replicative potential. All cells and tissue have limited lives, and the older a person gets, the weaker the regenerative process becomes. Slowly, almost imperceptibly for years, the human body ages.

One characteristic of middle age is a growing awareness of personal mortality accompanying the first physical signs of aging. Most young adults are concerned about their appearance because "they want to look nice," but middle-aged adults are concerned for a different reason. For the first time, they begin to look older, with noticeable alteration in appearance. However, the extent of changes depends partly on the individual. Superior nutrition and health care, with close attention to exercise and physical fitness, help people look much younger than was the case a generation ago. Everyone eventually ages physically, but some people look 20 or 30 years younger than their actual age would suggest.

Robust Aging

Robust aging, which is referred to by various terms such as "successful aging," "productive aging," and "vitality," is attracting increasing attention by gerontological researchers. This research has helped in redirecting attention from the sole distinction between impaired and nonimpaired older persons to include further identification of those who age particularly well, for what has been termed "successful" versus usual aging. No longer is older age viewed necessarily as a phase of waning health or declining resources in which the absence of such detrimental declines is the best that one could hope for. Rather, it is now recognized that people who do not suffer any known illnesses or severe impairments can exhibit quite a range of levels of functioning. For example, older people who compete in athletic events, hold full-time responsible employment, or contribute their expertise to political or social causes are quite different from fully retired, largely passive and sedentary older persons. The emphasis on aging well is consistent with the *World Health Organization's* definition of health as a state of complete physical, mental, and social well-being, rather than simply the absence of disease (Garfein & Herzog, 1995).

Attitudes of Society

The prevalence of age stereotypes shows that age plays an important role as an organizing principle in social perception (Slotterback & Saarnio, 1996). However, age categories have no clearly socially defined boundaries. Although age is a continuous chronological variable, people tend to break down the life span and categorize themselves and others into

TABLE 16.1	AGES OF PEAK PERFORMANCE OF ATHLETES	

	Age	
Sport	*Men*	*Women*
Baseball		
Pitchers	27 years	
Batters	26.5–28	
Swimming	20	18
Short-distance running	23	22
Medium-distance running	24	24
Long-distance running	27	27
Tennis	24	24
Golf	31	30

Adapted from "The Peak Years," by J. C. Horn, 1988, *Psychology Today, 22*, pp. 62–63.

During the mid-20s, the body is at the peak of its physical development.

discrete age segments. Segments of young, middle-aged, and old adulthood are associated with the network of stereotyped expectations about social roles, life events, and stages of personality development. Research shows that stereotypic age-related beliefs affect judgments about individuals at least as much as do gender stereotypes (Krueger, Heckhausen, and Hundertmark, 1995). Aging is partly subjective: how old a person perceives himself or herself to be (Goldsmith & Heiens, 1992). However, *self-consciousness about one's changing physique is accentuated by society's attitudes.* In the United States, attractiveness is equated with youthfulness. To be beautiful is to be young and slender. Female models of cosmetics and clothes are thin and sinewy; male models are slender and muscular. The middle-aged adults conclude from these ads that their bodies are crumbling (Hooker & Kaus, 1994). The roof is in trouble, the mortar is coming out of the joints, the floors are sagging, and the doors creak. As a result, some people will go to extreme lengths, including cosmetic surgery, to look more youthful (Hamburger, 1988). Those who have a poor concept of their body image, even if they are reasonably attractive, become self-conscious and socially inhibited and anxious because they can't accept the way that they look (Cash & Butters, 1988).

Generally speaking, our society accepts a double standard for men and women. The signs of aging tend to be seen as less attractive for women than for men, and women therefore are more likely to try to conceal them. The assumption is that aging is viewed as worse for women than for men, perhaps because of the tendency for women to be judged so greatly on their appearance (Harris, 1994). It helps if a man is slim and youthful, but it is practically obligatory for a woman. Most modern women reject this sexist philosophy, but many are still taught that physical attractiveness is their most valuable asset. As a result, women—in general—are less satisfied with their physical appearance than are men (Cash, Winstead, & Janda, 1986; Thompson, 1986).

Physical Fitness and Health

Chronological Age Versus Functional Age

Each person has a different biological time clock, some aging faster than others. Men age more quickly than women up to the age of 50. Both biological and environmental influences are important in health (Harris et al., 1992; Seeman, Berkman, Charpentier, Blazer, Albert, & Tinetti, 1995).

Psychological and social factors such as relationships with family members also have a profound influence on health (Field et al., 1993). Cross-cultural studies indicate wide variations (Markides & Lee, 1991).

Ageism—profound, widespread prejudice against the elderly resulting in discrimination

Ageism in Our Society

The term **ageism** was coined in 1968 by Robert Butler, a physician and former director of the National Institute of Aging. He used the word to describe profound, widespread prejudice against the elderly. Like sexism and racism, ageism represents discrimination of one group against another, in this case on the basis of age. When applied to the elderly, it reflects negative attitudes toward them, unfair and false stereotyping, differential medical or employment treatment, and emotional rejection (Ferraro, 1992).

Ageism assumes many forms in our society. An examination of prescription drug advertising in two journals (*Medical Economics* and *Geriatrics*) generally showed the elderly as active people, but the written descriptions of them were negative. They were described as aimless, apathetic, debilitated, disruptive, hypochondriacal, insecure, needing insatiable reassurance, low in self-esteem, out of control, sluggish, reclusive, and temperamental (Smith, 1975).

Ageism is evident in various professions. One study of 69 graduate students in the fields of social work, law, and medicine showed that not one student registered a first-choice preference for working with the elderly (Geiger, 1978).

The preceding suggests that the aging of society will have a major impact on the professional careers of today's medical students. Familiarity with the essentials of geriatric medicine is critical for these future physicians. Clearly there is an urgent need to incorporate geriatric training into the medical education process. Literature provides evidence that the attitudes of health care professionals toward the geriatric population affects the quality of care that they receive. It is alarming to note that numerous researchers have found that health care workers, in general, have negative attitudes toward the elderly (Duerson, Thomas, Chang, & Stevens, 1992).

Television used to perpetuate a negative image of the elderly. Commercials portrayed nice 80-year-old grandmothers (today many are 40) in old-fashioned clothes. Most often they were shown buying laxatives or denture cleansers. The elderly were often pictured living in nursing homes, when actually only 6% of people over 65 are institutionalized (U.S. Bureau of the Census, 1989). Today there are a few exceptions to these negative images. Problems of the aged have become a more viable subject for television; they are now being shown as misunderstood by the young and perfectly capable of getting along without their children's help. In fact, the capabilities of the aged, especially as represented by national leaders and entertainment figures, are gaining recognition.

A number of studies have analyzed the humorous portrayal of the elderly in jokes, birthday cards, and cartoons. Birthday cards deal most often with the subject of age itself: the associated physical and mental characteristics, the inevitability of growing older, the concealment of age, aging as a state of mind, the aging of others but not of oneself, and concern about age (Demos & Jache, 1981). The emphasis on decline in physical appearance is illustrated by the following quote from a greeting card:

> Another birthday? You're not old until you go to the beauty parlor on Tuesday, come home on Thursday . . . And still look like you did on Monday. (Demos & Jache, 1981, p. 212)

Demos and Jache conclude their study by suggesting that birthday messages appear to reflect stereotypes about aging and consequently may reinforce ageist ideas.

An analysis of contemporary American poetry showed that a number of poems equate growing old with diminishment, whereas others express a striving for continued change, growth, and self-realization in old age (Clark, 1980). The elderly are sometimes portrayed as having a "vigor beyond their youth"; even though bones may creak, eyes grow bleary, and breasts wither, the aging are endowed with strength arising from their individuality. Age is referred to as "the hour for praise . . . praise that is joy." There is also a keen sense of the passage of years, and the desire in the time left, with the strength given, to do "that which is worthy of heaven." There is a realization, too, that age offers opportunities for love that are not available to the young.

> Ours is the late, last wisdom of the afternoon. We know that love, like light, grows dearer toward the dark. (Clark, 1980, p. 190)

The aged are described negatively as having "no faces," "no voices," with "riches gone." The old are diminished in value "as merchandise marked down." They are "sitters by the wall," and the poet asks: "Is there a song left then for aged voices?" (Clark, 1980). Still, despite the emphasis on loss, the retention of pleasant memories is often mentioned. The older person learns to become patient, placid, tranquil, content, and quiet (Donow, 1992). Some older people will weave "nets of dreams," laugh, and appreciate the beauty of nature; the fortunate even retain the poet's ability to "sing" (Sohngen & Smith, 1978, p. 183).

Differences also exist within a particular culture. Black males age faster than do white males (Morgan, 1968). Much depends on heredity, but diet, climate, exercise, and health habits are also influential. Thus, chronological age alone is a poor measure of physical condition or aging.

Obviously, overall health depends partially on the extent to which people are able to be free of major diseases. One major finding of a longitudinal study found that 30% of 60-year-old men who were free of three major illnesses associated with aging (heart disease, cancer, and stroke) could be expected to survive and be free of these medical problems some twenty years later (Metter et al., 1992).

The important emphasis should be on **functional age,** that is, the ability of the adult to perform regardless of age. Some 40-year-olds act, think, and behave like 60-year-olds, and some at 60 live and perform better than those in their 20s. One study of 1,146 healthy men, ages 25 to 83, revealed a 42% differential between functional age and chronological age when personality factors, abilities, and blood chemistry were considered (Nuttal, Fozard, Rose, & Spencer, 1971).

As part of the ongoing *Minnesota Twin-Study of Adult Development and Aging (MTSDA)*, twin analyses were conducted to determine the relative influence of genetic and environmental factors on functional aging. The investigation revealed twelve variables that could be divided into three categories—*physiological measures, cognitive abilities,* and *processing speed*—that were related to functional age. The physiological variables included pulse rate and both systolic and diastolic blood pressure. Speed variables included reaction time, conductive reasoning and digit symbols; and cognitive variables included verbal IQ, performance IQ, forward digit span, block design, and text recall. The three factors, physiological variables, speed variables, and cognitive variables, accounted for 66% of the variance in chronological age. The relative influence of genetic and environmental factors varied for different components of functional aging. The existence of common genetic and shared environmental influences from the components of functional aging suggests that both genetic and nongenetic theories of aging are appropriate (Finkel, Whitfield, & McGue, 1995).

Other extensive studies attempted to measure different aspects of functional age, such as body chemistry, anthropometric descriptions, perceptual and motor abilities, and other factors (Bell, Rose, & Danon, 1972). These measurements, along with subjective evaluations of age (how old people say they

Functional age—age as measured by the ability to perform physical or mental functions

Cross-cultural studies indicate wide variations in the speed of aging. Functional age emphasizes the ability of the adult to perform regardless of age. Speed of aging depends on heredity, diet, climate, exercise, and health habits.

actually look, feel, think, and act), enable researchers to make more accurate age determinations than are possible with chronological evaluations.

Reaction Time

One measurement of functional ability in the older adult is **reaction time,** the interval between stimulation and response. If a person is driving a car and the traffic light turns red, reaction time is the interval between the time the light changes and the time the person steps on the car brake. Numerous studies have been done to discover how this time interval changes as persons age. *In general, reaction time decreases from childhood to about age 20, remains constant until the mid-20s, and then slowly increases.* This increase has been estimated at approximately 17% between 20 and 40 years of age. Whether this increase has any practical significance depends on the type of activity in which a person engages. Most active sports require quick reactions as well as good coordination. Consequently, most professional athletes in their 30s are considered old. Advance in age is accompanied by reduced ability to execute rapid aimed hand movements (Teeken, Adam, Paas, van Boxtel, Houx & Jolles, 1996). However, those who play various sports for pleasure can continue to enjoy themselves and benefit from the activity.

Adults whose jobs involve physical skill, quick movements, and speed will slow down as they get older. However, they can often do as much work as younger adults because they work steadily and conscientiously. Older adults are also safer drivers than young adults, even though their reactions have slowed. Young adults respond more quickly in emergencies, but they can create problems by driving too fast.

Comparisons of athletes with nonathletes have shown the importance of regular exercise and practice in improving both physical fitness and reaction time (Bunce, Warr, & Cochran, 1993). Although older adults fatigue more easily than do young adults, suitable rest periods minimize fatigue and improve reaction time. Another reason why older adults respond more slowly is that they are more cautious about making errors. They may show superior performance on tasks requiring accuracy without emphasizing speed.

Motor Ability, Coordination, and Dexterity

Other measurements of functional ability include motor ability, coordination, and dexterity (Rogers, Kukulka, & Soderberg, 1992).

Regular exercise is important in improving reaction time.

Motor ability implies the ability to move the fingers, hands, arms, legs, or other parts of the body. This ability requires muscular strength (Phillips et al., 1992), coordination, dexterity, and proper functioning of the central nervous system, which carries the messages from the brain to the muscles. Motor skills vary from the mundane (walking, running, or dressing) to the dramatic (gymnastics or ballet). All of these abilities eventually decline with age, but *the decline is minimal during early adulthood. Most of the decline occurs after the 30s.* It becomes more difficult to compete in such sports as boxing, baseball, tennis, or basketball, which require good motor ability (Horn, 1988). Inflexibility in the joints is a major cause of discomfort and disability in elderly people (Vandervoort, 1992). Typically, older adults show a decline in motor coordination and speed (Morgan, Phillips, Bradshaw, Mattingley, Iansek, & Bradshaw, 1994).

Psychomotor ability affects numerous skills, including writing skill (Slavin, Phillips, & Bradshaw, 1996). Research on writing speed in relation to age reveals some decline with age, but this depends partially on occupation. There is little decline in typing speed among clerical workers, indicating the importance of practice. One study showed that low-skill, older typists exhibited a deficit in motor performance, whereas high-skill older typists did not show a decline in typing speed (Bosman, 1993).

Gait Adjustment

In a typical day, individuals make numerous adjustments in their gaits in order to avoid obstacles, maintain balance, and navigate successfully over uneven or cluttered surfaces.

Reaction time—the interval between stimulation and response

Motor ability—the ability to move fingers, hands, arms, legs, and other parts of the body in a useful, coordinated way

With increased age, individuals have greater difficulty negotiating these situations, placing the older adult at risk for falling. The manner in which older adults adjust their gait to step over obstacles has been found to differ in a number of important ways from those of younger adults. Specifically, older adults typically walk more slowly, most likely because of an overall decrease in step or stride length. These changes may lead to improve balance by increasing time in double support (the interval time when both feet are in contact with the ground). When confronted with obstacles, older adults have been found to exhibit slower crossing speeds as well as shorter step lengths and greater obstacle-to-heel sight distances, compared with younger adults (Rosengren, McAuley, & Mihalko, 1998).

Strength

The potential of increases in strength remains until almost age 30. There is usually very little loss of muscular strength during the 30s. Beyond the age of 50 years, there are progressive declines in exercise performance and muscle strength. Reductions in muscle strength may compromise activities of daily living and bring individuals close to, or beyond, the threshold for dependency. In the frail elderly, there is a strong association between muscle weakness and falls. The resulting fractures are a common source of disability in this group. Interventions to increase muscle strength in the elderly are potentially very useful, and in recent years, systematic techniques of aggressive resistance overload training have been applied to this population (McCartney, Hicks, Martin, & Webber, 1995).

Endurance and Fatigue

The maximum work rate one can achieve without fatigue begins to decline at about 35, as related to such activities as climbing stairs, using a treadmill, or cranking a wheel. The capacity for hard work at high temperatures falls off sharply by age 30. But here again, physical condition is an important factor causing abilities to overlap considerably over a broad age range. Some older adults do more physical work than younger adults half their age.

Exercise

Benefits

Exercise is one of the best ways to prevent ill health and maintain body fitness (Harris, 1988; Rakowski & Mor, 1992; Sharpe & Connell, 1992). Some researchers have suggested that about 50% of aging decline is preventable through improved lifestyle habits such as participation in regular exercise (O'Brien & Vertinsky, 1991). One of the secrets of the abundance of energy and drive of the chief executive officers of America's top corporations is their devotion to exercise as well as to other good health habits such as not smoking, eating a good diet, and getting adequate sleep (Rippe, 1989). Many corporations have developed whole programs to encourage their workers to stay healthy. L. L. Bean in Maine has three fitness rooms, rewards persons who have logged 200 miles jogging, and gives gift certificates to those who attend exercise classes (Roberts & Harris, 1989). Without exercise, bodies literally waste away. Muscles grow weak, bones become more porous, arteries clog up, and the heart is pressed to cope with sudden demands. A study of 16,936 men (ages 35 to 74) showed that those who took part in strenuous sports had fewer heart attacks than those who were sedentary (Boeckman, 1979). Furthermore, exercise is quite beneficial to patients who have already had heart attacks. In one study, older coronary patients who participated in a formal exercise training program showed great increases in peak exercise capacity and exercise efficiency (Ades, Waldmann, & Gillespie, 1995).

In addition to the physiological effects of exercise, considerable literature suggests that a number of psychological conditions are also influenced, including cognitive functioning, anxiety, and perceptions of personal efficacy. Individuals feel better about themselves when they are exercising (McAuley, Lox, & Duncan, 1993). Exercise can improve mental processing speeds and memory functions (Wang, Bashore, & Friedman, 1995). Exercise may be the most effective fountain of youth yet discovered (Doan & Scherman, 1987).

Aerobic exercise is particularly important in improving cardiovascular fitness (Hill, Storandt, & Malley, 1993). It improves respiration and feeds more oxygen to the whole body, increasing circulation and metabolism (Poehlman, Melby, & Badylak, 1991); nourishing the brain (Shay & Roth, 1992); improving digestion and bowel functioning; preserving the bones; toning the muscles; and relieving nervous tension, depression, and anxiety (McAuley, Courneya, & Lettunich, 1991). Moderate exercise can even improve one's sex life (Whitten & Whiteside, 1989). Without exercise, the cardiovascular system's capacity to deliver oxygen to working muscles is reduced relatively early in the aging process, and the weakness and fatigability of the muscles advances rapidly. One of the secrets of

Aerobic exercise helps to maintain cardiovascular and respiratory fitness.

good health is to adopt an exercise program and to stick with it (Blumenthal et al., 1991; Emery, Huck, & Blumenthal, 1992; Williams & Lord, 1995). Unfortunately, it is often those who are younger and most fit who get the most exercise. They need it, too, but the aged need it even more (Koval et al., 1992).

Habits

According to one national survey, about 29% of adults 18 years of age and older do not participate in any physical activity. Only 22% of males and 19% of females participate in regular sustained activity, which would comprise activity for at least five times or more per week. Adults 65 to 74 years of age have the highest participation rate, at 27%, of all the age groups (U.S. Bureau of the Census, 1998). With those who exercise, walking in the most pupular, and it is one of the best forms of exercise. Swimming ranks second in popularity, followed by bicycling, riding, exercising with equipment, and camping. Bowling, fresh-water fishing, playing billiards, playing basketball, hiking, aerobic exercising, golfing, running or jogging, playing softball, and hunting with firearms come next in popularity (U.S. Bureau of Census, 1998, p. 266). Many adults of all ages become couch potatoes, spending long hours in front of the television set ("Couch Potato Physique," 1989).

Pulse Rate

One of the simplest measures of health and physical fitness is pulse rate. **Pulse rate** is the number of times the heart beats per minute. It can be felt in various parts of the body, but the area commonly used is the wrist artery. Count the number of pulse beats for 6 seconds and then add a zero; or count the beats for 15 seconds and multiply by 4. This procedure gives the heartbeats per minute. The pulse rate is the body's

Living Issues

Monitoring Pulse Rate During Exercise

There are some indexes of how much the pulse rate should increase during exercise to make certain an individual is not exerting too much or too little (Blanding, 1982). For instance, take the figure of 220 beats per minute (the theoretical maximum pulse rate), subtract your age, and multiply by a percentage. People in poor physical condition should multiply by 60%, those in moderate condition by 70%, and those in good physical condition by 80%. The result is a target pulse rate.

Suppose a person is 40 years old and in moderate physical condition.

220 (maximum pulse rate)
−40 (age)
180 × .70 (for moderate condition) = 126 beats per minute

The target rate of 126 is the rate the person should strive to achieve while exercising. If the rate is not reached, more strenuous exercise is needed. If the rate is much higher, the exertion may be too great for one's fitness level. Furthermore, the target rate should be sustained for at least 15 to 30 minutes of continuous exercise. Some authorities advise exercise at least 3 or 4 times per week. Some recommend daily exercise to maintain cardiovascular fitness. As fitness improves, the target rate will increase, requiring one to exercise more strenuously to raise the pulse rate. Once a person is in good physical condition (using an 80% multiple), maintenance is achieved by raising the pulse rate to the target figure, or slightly above, during exercise.

most important single indicator of well-being, stress, or illness. In the average adult male, the resting pulse rate averages 72 to 76 beats per minute. In adult females, the resting pulse rate averages 76 to 80 beats per minute. In general, the lower the resting rate, the healthier the person, unless there is a major heart problem. Resting pulse rates higher than 80 beats per minute suggest poor health and fitness; the heart is working hard just to maintain the circulation in the body. For example, the mortality rate for men and women with resting pulse rates of 92 is 4 times greater than for those with pulse rates lower than 67.

The pulse rate goes up during exercise and indicates the intensity of exertion as well as one's fitness. A rate of about 120 per minute borders on intensive exertion. However, the more physically fit you are, the more strenuously you can exercise without increasing your pulse rate excessively. A person whose resting pulse is racing at 100 or 110 cannot tolerate much exertion; the heart is already strained. But a person who exercises strenuously and whose pulse rate rises very little is in excellent physical

Pulse rate—the number of heartbeats per minute

condition, unless significant problems are preventing the heartbeat from increasing. The healthy person's heart is already working strongly, pumping a large volume of blood with each beat, so that the pumping rate does not have to rise much even under considerable exertion. Ordinarily, the more a person exercises over a period of time, the stronger the heart becomes, and the slower the pulse rate is at rest or under exertion.

Diet and Nutrition

Requirements and Deficiencies

Proper nutrition is another important factor in maintaining good health (Hallfrisch, Muller, Drinkwater, Tobin, & Andres, 1990). It results in feelings of well-being, high energy levels to carry on daily activities, and maximum resistance to disease and fatigue. Proper nutrition may mitigate existing health problems, improve the management of many chronic conditions, prevent adverse complications of acute and chronic illnesses, accelerate wound healing and recovery from trauma, improve functional capacity, and extend years of healthy living. Poor nutrition may accelerate the aging process, accentuate physical handicaps, and result in generally poorer health. The saying "You are what you eat" is certainly true.

A broad spectrum of nutritional problems exist among the elderly, ranging from nutrient deficiencies, such as protein malnutrition, to nutritional excesses, including excessive intakes of calories or alcohol. Elderly people who live alone or who are institutionalized are more likely to suffer nutritional deficiencies of various kinds (Posner, Jette, Smigelski, Miller, & Mitchell, 1994).

Although energy requirements decrease with advancing age, middle-aged and older adults need as many nutrients as do younger adults. Thus, the older person's diet must provide foods of great **nutrient density,** relative to calories. Therefore, it is necessary to cut back on fats and sugars, especially on fats (Brownell, 1989; Gurin, 1989; Simon, 1989).

Unfortunately, reduced caloric intake with age is sometimes accompanied by progressive decreases in the intake of necessary minerals, vitamins, and proteins. A number of different studies have indicated that calcium, zinc, magnesium, and potassium are the minerals most likely to be deficient. Vitamins A, B_6, C, E, thiamin (Smidt, Cremin, Grivetti, & Clifford, 1991), and riboflavin are the vitamins most likely to be deficient (Horwath, 1991; Ryan, Craig, & Finn, 1992). Vitamin and

mineral deficiencies are responsible for a wide range of problems. For example, low levels of vitamin B_{12} and folic acid combined interfere with episodic memory performance in very old age (Wahlin, Hill, Winblad, & Backman, 1996).

Metabolism, Eating Behavior, and Obesity

The average adult in the United States is 20 or more pounds overweight (Meyers et al., 1991; Schwartz et al., 1990). Although the average 50-year-old woman weighs 154 pounds and the average 50-year-old man weighs 177 pounds, these are not ideal weights. Ideal weights range from 20 to 40 pounds less, depending on body frame. (See Table 16.2.)

TABLE 16.2	**HEIGHT-WEIGHT REFERENCE CHART FOR ADULTS***	
Height	**Weight (pounds)** Women	Men
4′ 10″	92–121	—
4′ 11″	95–124	—
5′ 0″	98–127	—
5′ 1″	101–130	105–134
5′ 2″	104–134	108–137
5′ 3″	107–138	111–141
5′ 4″	110–142	114–145
5′ 5″	114–146	117–149
5′ 6″	118–150	121–154
5′ 7″	122–154	125–159
5′ 8″	126–159	129–163
5′ 9″	130–164	133–167
5′ 10″	134–169	137–172
5′ 11″	—	141–177
6′ 0″	—	145–182
6′ 1″	—	149–187
6′ 2″	—	153–192
6′ 3″	—	157–197

*Height is without shoes; weight is without clothes.

Adapted from *The Merck Manual of Medical Information,* Home Edition, by R. Berkow (1997). Whitehouse Station, NJ: Merck Research Laboratories.

Nutrient density—percentage of essential nutrients in food in relation to calories

In order to lose weight, either exercise must be increased, or caloric intake reduced, preferably both.

Losing weight is difficult unless caloric intake is reduced. Figure 16.1 shows the daily caloric intake and expenditure in normal males. **Basal calories** are those metabolized by the body to carry on its physiological functions and maintain normal body temperature. **Activity calories** are those expended through physical activities. Because of reduced exercise, the need for activity calories falls somewhat more rapidly than for basal calories, requiring a corresponding reduction in caloric intake to avoid weight gain. *In order to lose weight, either exercise must be increased, or caloric intake reduced, preferably both* (Fisher, 1988). Rapid weight-loss diets are usually followed by rapid weight gain once the diet is discontinued. Permanent reduction in weight requires a basic restructuring of eating habits (Brownell, 1988). Some people eat when they are under stress or upset. In such a case,

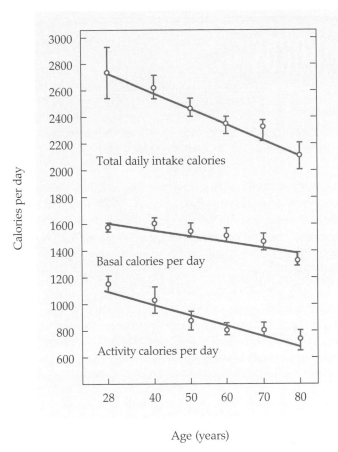

FIGURE 16.1   Daily caloric intake and expenditure in normal males.

Adapted from "Systems Integration," by N. W. Shock, 1977, in *Handbook of the Biology of Aging* (p. 644), C. E. Finch and L. Hayflick, Eds. New York: Van Nostrand Reinhold Co.

weight reduction is possible only when alternative means of handling this stress are found (Heatherton, Herman, & Polivy, 1992).

Special Needs of Adults

Adults may require special diets; for example, diets low in **saturated fats** and **cholesterol** (Lowik et al., 1991), a chemical found in all animal fats (Roberts, 1989). Excesses of these substances in the bloodstream contribute to atherosclerosis by building up fatty deposits in the arteries (Fritzsche, Tracy, Speirs, & Glueck, 1990). The result is a higher incidence of heart disease and heart attack (Wohl, 1988). Diets high in fiber help combat the risk of cancer and heart disease (Hickey & Stilwell, 1991). Some people cannot reduce cholesterol through either dieting or exercise. The level of cholesterol seems to have a hereditary base, so that no matter what some people do, they are not able to reduce the amount to acceptable levels. Fortunately, helpful

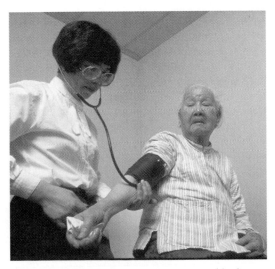

If arteries become constricted, an increase in blood pressure may strain the heart and damage it.

Basal calories—energy metabolized by the body

Activity calories—energy expended through physical activities

Saturated fats—animal fats

Cholesterol—chemical in all animal fats that is a major cause of atherosclerosis

FOCUS

Fat Liberation

In our society, women are showing an increasing concern and dissatisfaction with their body image. Many appear to be preoccupied with conforming to unrealistic standards of slenderness that have been perpetuated by media images that drive women to pursue weight loss and weight control strategies, some of which are suspect and dangerous from a public health perspective (McAuley, Baine, Rudolph, & Lox, 1995). "The Famine Within," a documentary on American women's collective obsession with body weight, suggests that many women fear being fat more than they fear death (Maslin, 1991). In light of the large percentage of women who either are—or perceive themselves to be—overweight, and the negative social consequences of being "fat," the overweight may be the most frequently and severely stigmatized group in this country.

This possibility suggests that the overweight might benefit from the type of social movement that has changed public attitudes about prejudice and discrimination against women. In light of evidence that weight is not merely a matter of will power, a social change that counters prejudice and discrimination against the overweight may ultimately be the most effective strategy for erasing the stigma associated with being overweight (Crocker, Cornwell, & Major, 1993).

medication is now available to help those adults reduce their cholesterol level who are not able to do so by other means.

Adults have other special nutritional needs. One of these needs is a *diet low in sodium.* Sodium from salt, sodium nitrates, sodium nitrites, and other sources encourages fluid retention and edema. This condition, in turn, may cause high blood pressure and other problems. One major treatment for hypertension is the administration of *diuretics,* which help the body eliminate excess fluids. Limiting sodium intake will minimize fluid retention.

Most adults get *too much sugar* in their diets. This is certainly a problem for diabetics, but everyone should be cognizant of sugar intake. Sugar is considered "empty calories" because it contains no proteins, vitamins, or minerals. More than that, it forms acids that deplete the body's source of calcium and destroy important B vitamins. Most people get enough sugar from fresh fruits and other natural foods. In addition, carbohydrates are converted into sugar during the process of digestion, so that the body often gets too much sugar if the diet is rich in starches.

Rest and Sleep

Patterns

Adequate amounts of sleep and rest help to stave off physical fatigue by replenishing energy burned up while awake. Rest also helps maintain maximum intellectual functioning. A positive correlation has been found, for example, between adequate rest and high scores on the *Wechsler Adult Intelligence Scale (WAIS)* (Prinz, 1977). Lack of sleep has also been correlated with an increase in accidents such as that at Three Mile Island (Adessa, 1988). Most adults regularly need 7 or 8 hours of sleep at night to stay healthy. *But sleeping habits change as one ages, and the rest received may not be adequate* (Reynolds, Mon, Hoch, Jennings, Buysee, Houck, Jarrett, & Kupfer, 1991). Bedtime and wake time tend to be earlier, with sleep fragmentation and early morning awakening tending to characterize the night, and a preponderance of naps characterizing the day (Monk et al., 1991). On the average, people over 50 sleep an hour less, and among the elderly, deep sleep generally disappears. Consequently, older adults sleep more fitfully and are more easily disturbed (Bliwise, 1992). Generally, the hours spent in bed are not as restful as they once were. (Riedel, Lichstein, & Dwyer, 1995).

In addition, older adults usually wake earlier than when they were younger. One adult male in his 40s reported, "When I was younger, I used to stay in bed all morning on the weekends. Now, I can't sleep past 8 o'clock." If the adult goes to bed later than usual, he or she may not get adequate sleep because of the tendency to wake up early.

Insomnia

More than 25% of people 60 years of age or older complain of sleep difficulties (Morin, Stone, Trinkle, Mercer, & Remsberg, (1993). The greater prevalence of disturbed sleep with increasing age has been found in laboratory survey studies. Insomnia is often a product of multiple factors that can be difficult to separate. Insomnia can be viewed as a product of predisposing precipitating, and perpetuating factors. *Predisposing factors* antedate the origin of sleep problems and can be viewed as constituting a susceptibility to insomnia. *Precipitating factors* usually coincide with insomnia onsets and can be viewed as triggers or initiators of sleep disturbance. *Perpetuating factors* serve to maintain insomnia long after the occurrence of precipitating factors. Life stress can play a role both in initiating and in perpetuating chronic poor sleep (Friedman. Brooks, Bliwise, Yesavage, & Wicks, 1995). Researchers have documented at least five groups of factors that contribute to insomnia: (a) underlying biological predisposition, (b) psychological factors, (c) use of drugs and alcohol, (d) disturbing environment and bad habits, and (e) negative conditioning (Hopson, 1986).

Some researchers believe that people can be *biologically predisposed to insomnia*. Wakefulness and sleep are controlled by two systems in the hypothalamus: an *arousal system* and a *sleep, or hypnagogic, system*. Insomniacs seem to have an overly active arousal system and an underactive hypnagogic system. They are predisposed to be light sleepers and are more easily aroused. In addition, they may have various medical problems, such as physical pain, that contribute to their insomnia.

Psychological factors include a variety of emotional problems: anxiety, chronic anger, worry, or depression. Insomnia may be triggered by a variety of upsetting circumstances, such as a death in the family or job loss. Emotional arousal causes physiological arousal that keeps people awake (Libman, Creti, Amsel, Brender, & Fichten, 1997).

Alcohol and many other drugs are major causes of insomnia. Various stimulants, sedatives, antidepressants, thyroid drugs, contraceptives, and heart medicines may cause insomnia. Both sleeping pills and alcohol, while seeming to put one to sleep, actually lead to shallow, fragmented, disturbed sleep with shortened, abnormal REM-sleep periods and early morning awakening.

Living Issues

Controlling Cholesterol

The best way to reduce cholesterol and saturated fat is to reduce the intake of animal fats and oils. The American Heart Association recommends a maximum of 300 mg of cholesterol daily. One medium chicken egg has 274 mg of cholesterol and 1.7 g of saturated fat. The following quantities are in a 3 oz serving of each food: Beef liver has 327 mg of cholesterol and 2.5 g of saturated fat. Of all the fish, squid has the highest cholesterol (152 mg) but only .4 g of saturated fat. There is not much difference in the amount of cholesterol in beef, pork, lamb, veal, and chicken, provided the meat is lean. But the total saturated fat content of red meat is considerably higher than that of poultry and much higher than that of fish. Lean fish, clams, oysters, and scallops have the lowest amounts of overall cholesterol and saturated fat. Crabs, lobster, and shrimp have somewhat higher levels of cholesterol but are still very low in saturated fats. Saturated fats have been included in this discussion because they tend to raise the levels of harmful cholesterol.

The harmful cholesterol is **LDL (low-density lipoprotein)**. Another type of cholesterol, known as **HDL (high-density lipoprotein),** plays a salutary role by helping to remove LDL from circulation and reducing the risk of heart disease. The higher the HDL in relation to LDL, the less risk of heart disease. Most physicians feel that a total cholesterol (LDL plus HDL) over 200 mg is too high and that the person should cut back on fat and cholesterol consumption, and that a ratio of LDL to HDL ought to be 4.6 to 1 or lower (Ives, Bonino, Traven, & Kuller, 1993).

Another way to reduce LDL is to increase the amount of fiber in the diet. Dr. Jon Story of Purdue University says, "LDL cholesterol can be reduced 20% in people with high levels just by consuming a cup of oat bran a day" (Wallis, 1984). Regular, sustained aerobic exercise is a healthy way to increase protective HDL.

Some people may be biologically predisposed to insomnia.

Bad sleep habits such as irregular bedtimes or awake times, frequent afternoon naps, going to bed too early, or sleeping too late in the morning, may confuse the sleeping mechanism, so that insomnia results.

Negative conditioning may also cause insomnia. If a person doesn't fall asleep right away and thus begins to worry and try too hard to sleep, the thought of going to bed triggers stress and fear of insomnia, which becomes a self-fulfilling prophecy.

The most effective insomnia treatment programs use a multidimensional approach, including initially a hypnotic drug to relieve the symptoms, counseling to improve sleep habits and environment, training in stress reduction and relaxation techniques, and psychology (Edinger, 1992; Hopson, 1986; Lichstein & Johnson, 1993).

LDL (low-density lipoprotein)—harmful cholesterol which increases the risk of heart disease

HDL (high-density lipoprotein)—beneficial cholesterol which reduces the risk of heart disease

Drug Abuse

Patterns

Few social problems have caused more concern in recent years than drug abuse. Currently, *the greatest abusers of drugs are young adults between the ages 18 and 25.* Table 16.3 compares the use of various drugs by adults from different age groups (U.S. Bureau of the Census, 1997). The figures include the total percentages of those who have ever used the drug and the percentages of those who used the drug within the past month.

As shown in Table 16.3, young adults 18 to 25 years of age have the greatest percentages of current users in every drug category mentioned except inhalants, analgesics, stimulants, and tranquilizers, which have been used by a slightly greater percentage of adolescents age 12 to 17. More than two-thirds of young adults 18 to 25 years of age report experience with an illicit substance.

Drugs and the Elderly

The figures cited describe the abuse of drugs for nonmedical purposes. But sometimes drugs are abused even when legally prescribed by a doctor for medical reasons. In addition, many over-the-counter drugs are taken for other reasons than intended, and in larger amounts or at more frequent intervals than prescribed.

Although national surveys show only small percentages of older persons taking drugs for nonmedical purposes, *these same studies do indicate widespread drug abuse among the elderly who report taking them for medical reasons.* These drugs are most commonly obtained through prescriptions; also, they may be nonprescription drugs that are widely available. Those over 65 years of age use three times as many prescription medications per capita as any other age group (Chrischilles et al., 1992).

The drugs most commonly prescribed for the elderly can be classified into five groups:

1. *Hypertensives and diuretics:* those used to control high blood pressure.
2. *Heart medicines:* those that act either on the heart itself or on the blood vessels.
3. *Psychotropics:* mood-altering drugs, such as tranquilizers, antidepressants, sedatives, hypnotics, or stimulants.
4. *Painkillers:* analgesics with codeine.
5. *Miscellaneous:* a variety of drugs, including antacids and antibiotics (tetracycline is one of the most popular).

TABLE 16.3   **DRUG USE, BY TYPE OF DRUG AND AGE GROUP: 1974 AND 1994**

| Type of Drug | Percentage of Persons 12–17 Years Old | | | | Percentage of Persons 18–25 Years Old | | | | Percentage of Persons 26 Years Old and Older | | | |
| | Ever Used | | Current User | | Ever Used | | Current User | | Ever Used | | Current User | |
	1974	1994	1974	1994	1974	1994	1974	1994	1974	1994	1974	1994
Marijuana	23.0	16.0	12.0	7.3	52.7	43.4	25.2	12.2	9.9	35	2.0	3.0
Inhalants	8.5	6.2	0.7	2.0	9.2	9.6	(NA)	0.4	1.2	9.3	(NA)	0.5
Hallucinogens	6.0	4.0	1.3	1.2	16.6	11.7	2.5	1.5	1.3	8.8	(NA)	0.1
Cocaine	3.6	1.3	1.0	0.4	12.7	9.6	3.1	1.0	0.9	10.8	(NA)	0.6
Heroin	1.0	0.4	(NA)	1.3	4.5	0.2	0.1	0.1	0.5	1.3	(NA)	B
Analgesics	(NA)	4.7	(NA)	1.3	(NA)	7.1	(NA)	0.7	(NA)	4.7	(NA)	0.4
Stimulants	5.0	2.6	1.0	0.4	17.0	5.3	3.7	0.3	3.0	6.0	(NA)	0.1
Sedatives	5.0	3.2	1.0	0.3	15.0	1.9	1.6	0.3	2.0	3.5	(NA)	0.1
Tranquilizers	3.0	2.0	1.0	0.2	10.0	4.5	0.5	0.4	2.0	4.3	(NA)	0.1
Alcohol	54.0	41.2	34.0	6.3	81.6	83.8	69.3	63.8	73.2	74.1	54.5	55.6
Cigarettes	52.0	35.5	25.0	9.8	68.5	68.6	48.8	26.5	65.4	76.8	39.1	24.1

NA = Not available. B = base too small to get a reliable figure. Nonmedical Use. (Current users are those who used drugs at least once within month prior to this study. Based on national samples of respondents residing in households. Subject to sampling variability.)
From *Statistical Abstract of the United States* (p. 144), by U.S. Bureau of the Census, 1997, Washington, DC: U. S. Government Printing Office.

Living Issues

How to Stop Smoking

Recent research indicates that the only way to quit smoking is to stop completely. Cutting down doesn't work. Smokers who decide to have "just one" go right back to their former habit. One study showed that of 348 people who quit smoking on their own, 58% had relapsed by the end of the first month, 83% by year's end. One-quarter who relapsed during the first month smoked a single cigarette and then immediately resumed their previous level of smoking. About 42% reached their previous level gradually but never abstained for more than 24 hours. About 30% experienced at least one period of more than 1 day of abstinence between their first cigarette and full resumption (Simon, 1988). The most likely candidates for quitting are those who are highly motivated to stop. Tell yourself that you can't smoke under any circumstances.

Here are some suggestions:

1. Accept the fact that if you have even so much as a puff, you're right back to smoking all over again.

2. Read all you can about the harmful effects of smoking. Look at a video on quitting smoking.

3. Use oral substitutes such as sugarless gum, mints, toothpicks, or dummy cigarettes (Bozzi, 1986).

4. Immerse yourself in activities such as sports, running, reading, working, or watching TV.

5. Don't keep any cigarettes or ashtrays or other cigarette-associated objects in the house or office. Not having them available helps you to stop. Resolve never to borrow from another smoker.

6. Join a support group or enlist in an antismoking clinic if you can't stop on your own.

7. While you're breaking the chemical dependency on nicotine, use the patch, chew nicotine gum, and gradually cut down on its use until you're off completely.

8. Remember that the first few weeks are the hardest. Resolve to avoid a relapse during these critical weeks. The craving will gradually subside so that not smoking becomes easier.

9. Don't use weight gain as an excuse to resume smoking. Most smokers who quit gain some weight but do not "balloon," contrary to popular belief. Lick the smoking habit first, then deal with the weight (Meer, 1986a).

10. Each week or month that you abstain, reward yourself by buying something you want with the money you saved by not smoking (Hall, 1986).

11. Once you've stopped, remember never to take a puff again, or you'll be right back to the habit.

Smoking is one of the greatest preventable hazards to health.

The widespread use of **psychotropics** among the aged, especially among institutionalized patients, is causing concern (Garrard et al., 1992). Either the aged in institutions have more psychological problems or develop more psychological problems while institutionalized, or the drugs are administered more for the benefit of the institutions. Certainly, too many institutions use drugs as chemical restraints in the absence of adequate help, to keep patients quiet and avoid trouble.

All kinds of drugs are potentially more harmful for older persons than for younger persons. Older adults metabolize drugs more slowly, and because of decreased renal (kidney) and liver functions, the safety margin between therapeutic and toxic doses is considerably narrowed. Drugs taken regularly can easily build up to toxic levels. For example, 24 hours after taking *Valium,* half the drug is still in the system. If another dose is taken at this time, the remaining Valium will escalate the action.

The greater the number of drugs taken, the greater the possibilities of adverse reactions. Some drugs are antagonistic to one another or heighten the action of other drugs.

Psychotropics—mood-altering drugs

Another factor leading to drug abuse is patients' use of the services of different physicians and pharmacists. Prescriptions from several physicians may cause confusion about instructions for individual drugs. Multiple or conflicting explanations may lead to information overload, which could interfere with appropriate drug-taking behavior. Many drugs that the elderly abuse are nonprescription medicines bought over the counter and taken improperly. Such drugs may include *analgesics, bromides, antihistamines,* and *anticholinergics.*

Another common type of inappropriate drug use among the elderly is underuse. Some deliberately omit and others forget to take needed medication (Park et al., 1992). The elderly need clear instructions in taking their medication (Morrow et al., 1991).

SOME BODILY SYSTEMS AND THEIR FUNCTIONING

Nervous System

To understand what happens to various parts of the nervous system as people grow older, let us first examine the *brain.* The largest part of the brain, the *cerebrum,* contains about 14 billion nerve cells (neurons) that are located in its outer layer (*cortex*). The cortex is associated with three major functions. The *motor cortex* coordinates voluntary movements of the body through direct action on the skeletal muscles. The *sensory cortex* is the center of perception, where changes in the environment, which are received through the senses of vision, hearing, smell, taste, touch, and pain, are interpreted. The *associational cortex* includes areas involved in cognitive functions (reasoning, abstract thinking, memory), as well as general consciousness.

As aging progresses, brain weight declines as gray matter declines, but this process is due to a decline in the size of brain cells and not because of cell death (Lin et al., 1992). For some reason, the neurons shrink, resulting in fewer large neurons. This shrinkage may contribute to some loss of mental vigor, but normal elderly people are largely intact intellectually (Chollar, 1988a).

The brain's efficiency depends primarily on the amount of blood and oxygen it receives. If **arteriosclerosis** (hardening of the arteries) occurs or if damage to the heart or vascular system diminishes the blood supply, the brain cannot work properly. If, however, the blood supply is gradually lowered, the brain reacts by growing additional and larger blood vessels. The adjustments result in an increased blood supply to the cerebral cortex during old age.

Almost all bodily functions slow down with age. As a result, people talk, read, write, walk, and jump more slowly as they get older. The most widely accepted explanation for this slowing down is that *nerve impulses are transmitted more slowly as people age.* This slowing is due primarily to an increase in the time required to transmit impulses across nerve connections (synapses) via the neurochemical transmitters. Information is also processed more slowly before appropriate impulses can be sent to areas of the body that must respond. Thus, older people become disproportionately slower than younger ones as tasks become more difficult and choices increase. Research has indicated that practice can improve neuro-psychological performance (Dustman et al., 1992).

Cardiovascular System

The cardiovascular system consists of the *heart* and *blood vessels.* The heart itself is a muscular organ that works constantly throughout life. During a 70-year lifetime, the average human heart pumps about 900 million gallons of blood.

With age, several changes occur in the heart. Fat deposits form around the heart and at the entry points of the blood vessels. The number and size of heart muscles decline as muscle cells age and die. Collagen replaces more flexible tissues in valves and artery walls, causing hardening and thickening. Arterial walls become calcified, causing the arteries to dilate, lengthen, and lose elasticity. The walls of the aorta, the largest artery, become less elastic, producing a typical increase in **systolic blood pressure** (pressure produced by the heart forcing out blood) (Harris et al., 1991). **Diastolic blood pressure** is the lower of the two blood pressure readings. It represents the pressure of the blood returning to the heart.

Changes in the heart and blood vessels cause a decline in the heart's pumping power and stroke volume (the amount of blood pumped out with each beat) (Kitzman & Edwards, 1990). In addition, the heartbeat rate (pulse rate) diminishes gradually. The net result is a decrease in cardiac output. From age 20 to 75, this output typically declines by only 30%. It must be emphasized, however, that cardiac output is not a function of age alone in all individuals. The described changes may not occur in the most physically fit individuals.

Arteriosclerosis—hardening of the arteries by a buildup of calcium in the middle muscle layer of arterial tissue, resulting in decreased elasticity

Systolic blood pressure

Diastolic blood pressure

The heart can lose its ability to respond to stress, such as vigorous exercise (Schwartz, Gibb, & Tran, 1991). People in their 20s exhibit a greater increase in heart rate during vigorous exercise than do older persons. The younger heart can also pump more blood per heartbeat, enabling it to respond better to demands for an increased blood supply.

The health of the heart depends partially on the health of the blood vessels that transport the blood. Several types of conditions can impede the flow of blood (Mukerji, 1988). The arteries consist of three layers: a lining, a middle muscular layer, and an outer layer. In arteriosclerosis, progressive deposits of calcium in the middle muscular layer cause the arteries to become rigid (hardening of the arteries). Because they cannot expand as readily when blood is pumped through them, their cross-sectional volume is reduced.

As the arteries stiffen and peripheral resistance increases, hypertension, or elevated blood pressure, results as the heart works harder to force the blood through smaller openings. This puts additional strain on the heart and, in extreme cases, may cause enlargement of the heart and damage to it. This type of heart trouble is called **hypertensive heart disease.** In the United States, the prevalence of either borderline or definite hypertension increases with each decade between the ages of 20 and 70 years. Consequently, more than 50% of individuals over age 65 have at least mild hypertension. Because cardiovascular related morbidity and mortality progressively increase with an elevation in blood pressure, even small changes in systolic and dystolic pressures of age may have profound health implications (Gardner & Poehlman, 1995). In **atherosclerosis,** fatty deposits collect between the artery lining and the middle muscular layer. If these deposits break through into the artery, rough spots form on which blood may clot, reducing blood flow. When this happens in the coronary arteries, which supply the heart muscle with blood, the oxygen supply to the heart muscle is reduced (Williams & Spark, 1988). The heart struggles to get more oxygen, resulting in chest pains known as **angina pectoris** (Chun, 1988). A complete cutoff of the blood supply to any area of the heart, as with a blood clot, is called a **coronary occlusion with myocardial infarction** (heart attack) (Fiske, Coyne, & Smith, 1991). Since there are three major coronary arteries, an occlusion of one does not ordinarily cause death (12% die following a first heart attack). However, each succeeding attack becomes more risky. These types of **ischemic heart**

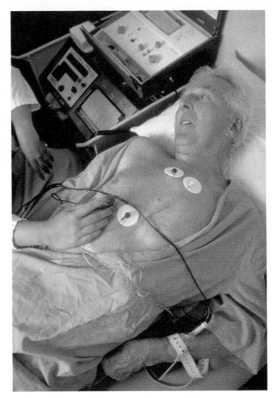

An electrocardiogram (EKG) is a valuable diagnostic tool when heart trouble is suspected.

disease (that impede the flow of blood and oxygen to the heart) are the most common and serious heart diseases of the elderly.

Congestive heart failure is also common among the elderly (Benotti, 1988). Diminished cardiac output accompanied by increased blood pressure results in a buildup of fluid **(edema)** in other organs, particularly the lungs, liver, and legs. Symptoms include shortness of breath, severe discomfort when lying down, and swelling of the ankles.

Cardiac arrhythmias are irregularities in the normal heartbeat sequence. They can be dangerous when they alter the heart's normal contraction cycle. Irregular contractions may result in reduced pumping capacity and inadequate nourishment of the heart muscle, which leads to ischemia (inadequate oxygen supply) conditions (Vlay & Fricchione, 1987).

Heart disease is the number-one killer of the elderly. Furthermore, the incidence of heart disease increases with advancing age. However, rapid advances have been made in the treatment of heart and circulatory disorders, and the incidence of these diseases is declining (Roberts, 1988b). With good medical care and proper health habits, the average older person can minimize the risks of heart

Hypertensive heart disease—caused by high blood pressure

Atherosclerosis—buildup of fatty deposits

Angina pectoris

Coronary occlusion with myocardial infarction

Ischemic heart disease

Congestive heart failure

Edema—condition characterized by buildup of fluid in the body

Cardiac arrhythmias

problems (Harris, 1989; Krone & Hodson, 1988; Williams, 1989).

When the brain is the site of vascular disease **(cerebrovascular disease),** an accident can occur in the form of a **thrombosis** (blockage from any kind of undissolved material in the blood), an **embolism** (blockage from a blood clot), or a **hemorrhage** (a ruptured blood vessel). A **stroke** is a paralysis that occurs when the blood supply to the brain is cut off and affected brain cells die. Loss of speech and paralysis commonly result, depending on the part of the brain affected.

Stroke is the major cause of adult disability in the United States; however, survival from stroke is more prevalent than ever before. Up to 50% of elderly stroke victims experience permanent loss of function. Recovery function after stroke is influenced by many factors, however. Those most clearly identified focus on the severity, location, and type of stroke. In addition to clinical features, psychosocial interventions have led to improved psychosocial adjustment in stroke patients and longer survival in patients with chronic illnesses. These interventions focus on improving or providing support to patients with chronic illness and improving family functioning (Colantonio, Kasl, Ostfeld, & Berkman, 1993). When a blockage of blood vessels to the lung occurs, **pulmonary thrombosis** results. A blockage due to a blood clot is called a **pulmonary embolism.**

Respiratory System

The respiratory system includes the *lungs* and related *air passageways.* Several significant things occur during aging to reduce lung efficiency. The rib cage and muscles become increasingly rigid, reducing the expansion and contraction capacity of the lungs (Teramoto, Fukuchi, Nagase, Matsuse, & Orimo, 1995). Air passageways become calcified and rigid. The result, together with changes in the rib cage, is a 55% to 60% reduction in maximum breathing capacity from 25 to 85 years of age. *The breathing rate remains constant while breathing capacity declines.* This change means that the volume inhaled with each breath **(vital capacity)** declines considerably. For this reason the elderly do not have as great a tolerance for exercise as do younger people (McConnell & Davies, 1992).

Several other changes occur that reduce lung efficiency. The air sacs lose elasticity, hindering their ability to expand on inhalation and contract on exhalation. Furthermore, deterioration in the capillaries and air sacs reduces the effectiveness of gas exchange between the air sacs and their blood supply.

Various studies have shown that oxygen conductance in the elderly can be increased through intensive training efforts. Part of the improvement is due to improved blood circulation, which brings more oxygen to the lungs. However, since genetic factors account for between one-half and two-thirds of variability in pulmonary functions, not all individuals can be brought up to the same rate of pulmonary efficiency (McClearn, Svartengren, Pedersen, Heller, & Plomin, 1994).

The changes just described commonly accompany aging. Various environmental factors can aggravate these changes. Long-term exposure to concentrations of air pollutants destroys the functional capability of the **alveoli** (lung cells) and capillaries. Acute respiratory distress and even death may result from such conditions. Such respiratory diseases as **tuberculosis** (Van der Brande, Vijgen, & Demedts, 1991), **bronchial pneumonia,** and **pulmonary infections** are most frequent in persons over 65. Smoking is one of the greatest hazards. It is a principal cause of **emphysema** and of lung cancer.

Gastrointestinal System

The gastrointestinal system consists of the *mouth, esophagus, stomach, small intestine, large intestine, liver, pancreas,* and *gallbladder.*

The liver is the single most important organ in digestion. It is involved in the intermediate metabolism of all three nutrients: fats, proteins, and carbohydrates (which are reduced to sugars.) It is also important in detoxifying drugs like morphine and steroids and in converting uric acid into urea, which then passes out of the body in urine.

The liver receives blood from the stomach and intestines and removes waste matter and poisons from it. It stores **glycogen** and emits it as sugar when the blood needs it. It stores vitamins A and D and those of the B-complex group, including vitamin B_{12}, which helps produce red blood cells and prevent **pernicious anemia.** The liver stores iron needed to produce **hemoglobin,** the red blood pigment. It also makes many blood proteins that prevent edema, provide resistance to disease, and ensure blood clotting to prevent extensive bleeding. The liver shrinks about 20% by age 75, yet half of the organ can be removed and it will still function effectively. It has remarkable power to grow new cells as needed.

Cerebrovascular disease

Thrombosis

Embolism

Hemorrhage

Stroke

Pulmonary thrombosis

Pulmonary embolism

Vital capacity

Alveoli

Tuberculosis

Bronchial pneumonia

Pulmonary infections

Emphysema

Glycogen—starchlike substance stored by the liver and released when the body needs sugar

Pernicious anemia—severe anemia with a great reduction in red blood cells

Hemoglobin

The liver is subject to damage, disease, and infections. **Jaundice,** in which the skin tissues turn yellow, develops if the liver is not functioning properly. **Cirrhosis** is a condition in which the connective tissue thickens and then shrinks, causing the liver to become hard, lumpy, and shriveled. Alcohol, which irritates the liver, is a major cause of cirrhosis. Certain infections and poisons, an excess of fat, lack of protein in the diet, and lack of B-complex vitamins also can cause cirrhosis, the eighth leading cause of death among diseases of the elderly (U.S. Bureau of the Census, 1998).

Gall bladder trouble is also fairly common in old age. The gallbladder stores about 1½ ounces of **bile** at one time. It receives the bile from the liver and releases it when needed for digestion. Disease can block the bile duct and cause extreme pain. If the bile becomes highly concentrated, **gallstones** form that must be removed.

The pancreas is also important to digestion because it secretes enzymes and salts that help digest proteins, sugars, and fats. It also secretes **insulin** directly into the bloodstream. All body cells need insulin to help them use sugar (glucose), their main fuel. If the pancreas secretes too little insulin, as sometimes happens with advancing age, the cells cannot function properly. Sugar accumulates and is passed out of the body in urine. Sugar in urine is one of the primary symptoms of **diabetes mellitus,** the ninth leading cause of death among diseases of the elderly (Perlmutter, 1991; U.S. Bureau of the Census, 1998). Cancer of the pancreas has only a 3% survival rate among those afflicted.

Older persons often complain of indigestion and gas. This may be a result of chronic inflammation of the stomach lining. This condition **(gastritis)** is also characterized by a reduced secretion of digestive juices. The incidence of stomach cancer increases with age (Atillasoy & Holt, 1993). Although the frequency of gastric (stomach) ulcers increases in middle age, few new cases develop after age 60.

Urinary System

The urinary system includes the *kidneys,* the *bladder* (which stores the urine), the *ureters* (tubes that transport the urine from the kidneys to the bladder), and the *urethra* (excretory tube that passes urine to the outside). The overall functions of the system are to eliminate wastes from the blood, maintain the proper balance of water and salts in the body, and regulate the pH level (the measure of acidity or alkalinity) of body fluids, which should be slightly alkaline.

The kidneys filter the waste products of metabolism from the blood. They slowly lose their filtering ability and function less efficiently with advancing age. Filtration declines as much as 50% from 25 to 80 years of age, with very little change occurring before age 40. However, the capacity is so great that if one kidney is removed, the other takes over completely. Therefore, most changes with age are not debilitating.

Diseases of the kidney can be serious, however, because poisons collect in the body if the kidneys function improperly. Various types of diseases and inflammations reduce kidney functioning, and if too many wastes accumulate in the blood, the result can be fatal.

The bladder's ability to store urine diminishes at advanced ages. Consequently, older people have to urinate more often. Almost one third of adults over 65 become **incontinent,** losing bladder control, which results in bed wetting (Herzog, Diokno, Brown, Normolle, & Brock, 1990). This is most common after strokes and in cases of organic brain syndrome. About 3% of women and 13% of men over 65 lose all control of urination and void involuntarily. This symptom is often associated with prostate gland problems in men. Incontinence can begin gradually, may appear intermittently, and may be seen as socially undesirable because it is thought to herald old age dependency. These factors make it difficult to diagnose by health care professionals. Patients may be either unable or unwilling to report on their condition (Fultz & Herzog, 1993). Biofeedback and pelvic muscle exercises have been shown to improve incontinence in older women (Burns, Pranikoff, Nochajski, Hadley, Levy, & Ory, 1993).

Skeletal-Dental Systems

One of the most noticeable signs of advancing age is a change in stature and posture. Investigations have shown that white males lose approximately ½ inch in height every 20 years after age 30. This loss is accelerated in blacks. It is also greater in females of both races than in males.

There are several reasons for this loss in stature. There is some loss of bone mass itself and a flattening of vertebral discs. Muscles shrink; ligaments and tendons lose elasticity, shrink, and harden. The result is a posture slump or stoop, with the head, neck, and upper torso bent forward. Accordingly,

Jaundice

Cirrhosis

Gall bladder trouble—any kind of trouble that prevents the gall bladder from functioning properly

Bile

Gallstones

Insulin—hormone secreted by the pancreas that regulates the blood sugar level

Diabetes mellitus—disease characterized by excess sugar in the system due to insufficient insulin production

Gastritis—inflammation of the stomach lining

Incontinent—unable to control passage of urine

Osteoporosis

Decalcification and loss of bone is called **osteoporosis.** It occurs in both sexes but is more extensive in females. Females show a 25% bone loss, as compared with a 12% loss in males, over a 30-year period. However, in the United States, black women have a lower rate of adult bone loss than do white women. In extreme cases of osteoporosis, the upper spinal vertebrae collapse, causing what is referred to in women as *dowager's hump.* Although the disease affects both men and women, females are 4 times more likely to be affected with severe osteoporosis than are men. The wisest approach to osteoporosis is to try to prevent it through diet, hormonal supplements, and exercise, and by the practice of other good health habits (Mitchell & Lyles, 1990).

Rheumatoid arthritis— chronic disease marked by painful inflammation and swelling of the small joints of the hands and wrists, and often accompanied by deformities

Osteoarthritis— degenerative joint disease

Periodontal disease— disease of the gums in which they become infected, swell, and shrink away from the teeth

height diminishes with advancing age. This loss in height and compression of the skeleton may interfere with the actions of some of the internal organs of the body, such as the lungs (Smith et al., 1992).

One important disease that affects the skeletal systems of the elderly is **osteoarthritis** (Ehrlich, 1988). Osteoarthritis is a degenerative joint disease (Verbrugge, Kepkowski, & Konkol, 1991). It occurs in different bones, including weight- and non-weight-bearing types, but it seems more common in parts of the body bearing the greatest weight. Males seem to have the disease with greater severity than females, and blacks appear more susceptible than whites. The incidence and severity of osteoarthritis increases to the age of 80, with a striking decrease after 90. Hereditary factors may have some influence on the probability of the disease. Loss of bone mass is a major cause of fractures in elderly people (Roberto, 1992). The risk of a fall and injury increases with age (Nevitt, Cummings, & Hudes, 1991; Ward, Hubert, Shi, & Bloch, 1995). By their ninth decade, 17% of men and 32% of women will have suffered a hip fracture (Wolinsky & Fitzgerald, 1994). Arthritis is a major contributor to disability in elderly persons (Hughes, Dunlop, Edelman, Chang, & Singer, 1994).

Rheumatoid arthritis, a second disease affecting the joints (Ehrlich, 1988), is less common than osteoarthritis. It characteristically affects the small joints of the hands and wrists, is marked by a swelling or disfigurement of the affected area, and is accompanied by a higher level of pain than most other

types of arthritis. There is considerable evidence that the causes are partly psychosomatic, related to reactions to stress. At the present time, arthritis cannot be cured, but it can be managed, allowing people to function. Unfortunately, many older people seek out all kinds of quack cures that do not help.

Years ago, women believed that they would lose at least one tooth for each child born. This loss often happened because nutritional demands of pregnancy and nursing depleted the mother's nutrients. Because these nutrients were not replaced through vitamin and mineral supplements, the mother's body suffered. Many older people resigned themselves to losing all their teeth by 65 and having to wear dentures. Even today, as many as 50% of people over 65 have lost all their teeth.

Periodontal disease (formerly called pyorrhea) is a major reason for tooth loss (Douglass et al., 1993). It is a disease in which the gums become infected, swell, and shrink away from the teeth. Tooth decay is also a significant factor in tooth loss in the elderly. Yet these diseases are not inevitable results of aging. They are primarily caused by neglect of the teeth and lack of proper dental care. Almost 70% of the elderly receive no dental care.

Dental health is important not only in preserving the teeth but also in maintaining the body's health. Improperly chewed food affects digestion. People with sore gums

Without proper care, older people face greater problems.

become less interested in eating, thus receiving inadequate amounts of nutrients needed to maintain bodily health.

Reproductive System

Menopause

Menopause is derived from two Greek words meaning "month" and "cessation," and it refers to the cessation of the monthly menstrual period. Common use of the term has given it a wider meaning that includes the entire period during which periodic menstrual flow stops.

The cessation of menstruation takes place over a period of years. The ovaries gradually atrophy, become less able to fulfill their double function of hormonal secretion and housing of egg cells. The pituitary gland continues to secrete FSH on a cyclic basis, but the ovaries are not able to respond to FSH, so ovulation ceases. The production of estrogen and progesterone gradually declines, the endometrium does not build or slough off, and the regular rhythmic cycle of menstrual bleeding gradually ceases (Cutler, Garcia, & McCoy, 1987).

Symptoms sometimes associated with menopause are hot flashes, profuse perspiration, numbness or tingling of fingers and toes, headaches, dizziness, insomnia, fatigue, palpitations, weakness, gastrointestinal upset, joint pain, backaches, bladder difficulties, thickening and drying of the skin and relaxation of tissues under it, itching, and dryness of vaginal tissue causing pain during intercourse. There can also be nervous tensions, irritability, and depression (Schmitt et al., 1991). These symptoms can also develop and exist independently of the hormonal imbalance characteristic of menopausal changes, so that they may not be due to menopause per se but become manifest at the age when menopause commonly occurs and are precipitated by other life events (King, 1989).

About 75% of menopausal women do not exhibit these symptoms at all. Therefore, the symptoms are not inevitable results of the change. Neither are abnormal physiological conditions associated with the menopausal state per se. Menopause is neither a disorder nor a disease, but is simply a normal change. Almost one-half of all women having a natural menopause do so by 49.76 years of age. One hundred percent have gone through menopause by age 58. If symptoms become too severe, they are often treated with estrogen and progesterone therapy (Bellantoni et al., 1991).

Male Climacteric

The **climacteric**, derived from a Greek word meaning "rung of a ladder," implies the passage from one stage of life to another, and so can apply to any period of life. When applied to a man's middle years, it refers to the many changes he experiences during this period. The decline in reproductive function in the male is generally a gradual process. Sperm cells constantly replenish themselves from puberty to old age. Consequently, *reproduction is often possible into extreme old age.* Men as old as 94 have fathered children. About half of all men between 80 and 90 have viable sperm in their semen.

Testosterone secretion decreases in some elderly men. The level remains constant until about age 60, after which it declines. This change may cause some decline in sexual drive and erectile ability; however, wide individual variations exist. Testosterone levels in some 80- and 90-year-olds are in the high-normal range. Levels fluctuate over a period of time, ranging from 3 to 30 days. Generally speaking, in younger men, testosterone levels are at the highest during the early morning, but daily fluctuations tend to decrease as males age (Tenover & Bremner, 1991). The male climacteric is sometimes associated with depression, anxiety, headache, insomnia, irritability, tremors, palpitations, and digestive and urinary disturbances. Many of the reactions that men have toward aging are psychological.

HUMAN SEXUALITY

Sexual Relationships

Sexual expression is an important component of the total relationship. Certainly, the positive expression of sexuality contributes to a couple's satisfaction with each other and to their satisfaction in life (Maddock, 1989; McCann & Biaggio, 1989). Healthy sexuality is meant to be a blessing, not a problem (Dyk, 1990).

A question often asked is, how frequently do couples have intercourse and how long does it continue as people get older? One study of women in the early years of marriage showed that the frequency of intercourse declined from an average of over 15 times per month during the first years of marriage to about 6 times per month during the sixth year (Greenblat, 1993). However, there was a wide range of frequency: from 4 times to 45 times per month for couples married under one year. Typically, most couples start out

Menopause—the permanent cessation of menstruation at midlife

Climacteric—often, a man's middle years' changes; also, menopause or changes marking the transition from one stage of life to another

For most couples, sexual interest continues well into old age.

of the women were having intercourse once a month or more often (Bergstrom-Walan & Nielsen, 1990). Twenty-nine percent of the men and 16% of the women were having intercourse once a week or more often. Ordinarily, healthy men and women continue sexual activity well into old age.

Another study of sexual interest and behavior of white men and women 80 to 102 years old revealed that the most common activity was caressing and touching without intercourse (Bretschneider & McCoy, 1988). Masturbation was the second most common activity. Sexual intercourse was the third most common activity, with 62% of the men and 30% of the women saying that they had sexual intercourse at least sometimes. Only a minority of men and women in their 80s reported having no interest in sex.

The question arises regarding the incidence and frequency of marital sex. The 1988 *National Survey of Families and Households* presented data on marital sex. The sample was representative of adults in the United States and included some 7,463 subjects. Consistent with previous research, the study showed a decline in marital sex incidence and frequency. As revealed in Figure 16.2, the average number of times a married couple had sex was 11.7 times a month at ages 19 to 24, 8.5 times a month at ages 30 to 34, 5.5 times a month at ages 50 to 54, 2.4 times a month at ages 65 to 69, and .8 times a month at age 75 or older. Among respondents over 75 who

engaging very frequently in intercourse, but then the incidence begins to decline, and they settle into their own individual patterns.

This decline does not mean that couples lose interest in sex. An investigation of 4,000 respondents revealed that 75% of the men and 61% of the women were sexually active and enjoying sex even at age 70 and over (Brecher, 1984). When asked for reasons for stopping sexual intercourse, many women reported that they lacked a capable and interested male partner. A study of Swedish men and women 60 to 79 years of age with partners revealed that 53% of the men and 38%

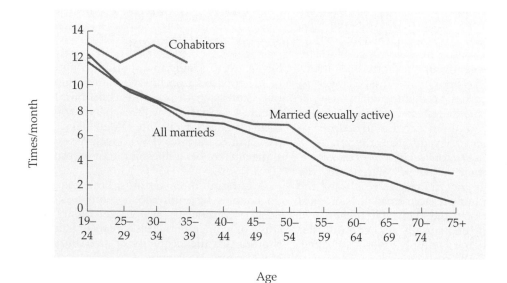

FIGURE 16.2   Frequency of Sex Last Month by Age and Marital Status

From "The Incidence and Frequency of Marital Sex in a National Sample," by V. Call, S. Sprecher, and P. Schwartz, 1995, *Journal of Marriage and the Family, 57*, pp. 639–652. Reprinted by permission of the National Council of Churches.

were sexually active, the frequency was about 3 times a month (Call, Sprecher, & Schwartz, 1995). Several factors contributed to sexual decline, including biological aging, diminished health, and habituation to sex. Age was the single factor most highly associated with marital sexual frequency. Marital happiness was the second most important predictor. Some factors found to be related to sexual frequency were associated with life changes that reduced or increased the opportunity to have sex, including pregnancy, the presence of small children, and sterilization.

Homosexuality

Homosexuality refers to the sexual orientation of a person who is sexually attracted to a person of the same sex. The word "homosexual" comes from the Greek word "homo," meaning "same." Thus, literally homosexuality means "same sex." Homosexuals can be either male or female, with the further designation of males as gay and females as lesbian. Homosexuality does not describe physical appearance, sex roles, or personality traits any more than does heterosexuality. One cannot tell by appearance or behavioral characteristics if a person is homosexual or heterosexual. Fulfilling the stereotypical or traditional roles of one's gender, that is, men as masculine and women as feminine, is not dependent on sexual orientation. Thus, many gay men, like many heterosexual men, are quite masculine in appearance, and many lesbians, like many heterosexual women, are quite feminine in appearance.

A homosexual is a person who is sexually attracted to a person of the same sex.

Years ago, Alfred Kinsey emphasized that there are degrees of heterosexuality and homosexuality (Patterson, 1995). He developed a scale ranging from 0 to 6 on which individuals were categorized on a continuum between exclusively heterosexual at one extreme and exclusively homosexual at the other extreme. He also suggested that some people fall in the middle of the scale and can therefore be considered bisexual because they are equally attracted to men and women.

Until recently, most of the research on human development has focused primarily on heterosexual patterns of development, ignoring nonheterosexual pathways (Baumrind, 1995). This neglect was mainly due to ignorance about sexual orientation and to homophobic attitudes—both of which still exist in our society. Today, however, many developmental psychologists are challenging these attitudes and are approaching the question of sexuality with a more scientific approach that stresses inclusiveness in relation to sexuality and that seeks to understand and investigate the many aspects of homosexual development (Gonsiorek and Weinrich, 1991).

Causes of Homosexuality

There is no conclusive evidence or accepted theory for the development of homosexuality. In all probability there is no single cause of homosexuality; rather, many experts believe that sexual orientation develops as the result of a complicated interplay of genetic, physiological, and environmental factors (Gladue, 1994). Still, there are many theories that attempt to account for the existence of homosexuality. The two major theories that seek to explain the origins of homosexuality can be divided into two broad categories: biological factors and psychosocial causes.

Biological factors point both to differences in neural structures as well as to the different influences of sex hormone levels on the body between homosexuals and heterosexuals. One genetic theory was proposed by LeVay of the Salk Institute in San Diego (Begley and Gilman, 1991). He found that one bundle of neurons in the hypothalamus was three times larger in heterosexual men and women than in homosexual men and women. The lack of neural structures correlated with the altered sexual interests in homosexuals. Experiments on male primates found that lesions in the hypothalamus caused the males to lose interest in females even though their sexual drive was vigorous. Of course, the question arises regarding cause and effect. Did the small bundle of neurons cause homosexuality, or did homosexuality cause that portion of the brain to shrink? Or was there an unknown factor that influenced both (LeVay, 1993)?

The unknown factor might relate to the levels of testosterone prenatally. Studies of women with congenital adrenal hyperplasia (CAH) who have been exposed to high levels of androgens prenatally and postnatally tend to be somewhat masculine with increased bisexuality and homosexuality (Bailey and Zucker, 1995). Meyer-Bahlburg (1995) and his colleagues conclude that their data are compatible with the hypothesis that prenatal estrogen may play a role in the development of human sexual orientation. One study implies that our bodies respond differently to changes in hormonal levels. These levels, in turn, may have differential effects on development and behavior. Part of sexual differentiation takes place in the hypothalamus of the brain (Money, 1987).

Psychosocial theories of homosexuality include both psychoanalytic and social learning theories. Traditionally, in the Freudian psychoanalytic model, homosexuality was thought to be caused by the relationship between parent and child; however, there is not sufficient evidence to assert that parent-child relationships are the primary cause of homosexuality (Pillard, 1990).

The second type of psychosocial explanation stresses the role of parental socialization. Although parental socialization may account for some of the sex differences in childhood sex-typed behavior, the effect appears to diminish by the preschool years (Fagot and Hagan, 1991). Social learning theories emphasize that homosexuality is simply the result of learning. Psychosocial theory emphasizes that conditioning through the reinforcement of early sexual thoughts, feelings, and behavior is what influences sexual attraction. Thus, a person may lean toward homosexuality if he or she has unpleasant heterosexual experiences and rewarding same-sex experiences.

Once again, however, there probably is no single cause of homosexuality. For some people, the sexual orientation seems to be there from childhood. In most cases, the children of homosexuals do not grow up to be homosexual, indicating that modeling and imitation alone cannot account for a person's becoming homosexual or heterosexual. In fact, many people are forced to deny their sexual identity for years because they are afraid of public and personal discrimination, outrage, rejection, or violence (Meyer-Bahlburg et al., 1995).

Sexual Dysfunction

Under most circumstances, the body functions quite smoothly, reacting in predictable ways to certain sexual stimulus. Sometimes, however, the sex organs do not respond; a particular stimulus does not produce the expected response. Any malfunction of the human sexual response system is termed **sexual dysfunction,** because a person is not reacting as would normally be expected. Both male and female sexual dysfunctions are addressed in the following sections.

Male Sexual Dysfunction

Male sexual dysfunctions include inhibited sexual desire, ejaculatory inhibition, erectile dysfunction, and premature ejaculation.

There is little reference in the literature to the fact that men can experience **inhibited sexual desire** (also called hypoactive sexual desire) or almost nonexistent sexual drive. Sexual drive in women is discussed at length, but men are assumed to have ample drive, healthy sexual appetites, and a persistent desire for intercourse. A few men do not fit this stereotype, however, because they seldom have any interest in sexual expression. The man who has inhibited sexual desire may create a great deal of misery for a partner who desires regular sexual expression.

A minority of males suffer from **ejaculatory inhibition.** They are able to become sexually aroused and have a firm erection and normal intercourse but are unable to reach a climax. As a result, intercourse becomes frustrating. Even though a man desires an orgasm and is stimulated enough to trigger a climax, he cannot do so.

If a male is unable to produce an erection so that coital connection can take place or maintain one long enough to complete the sexual act, he has **erectile dysfunction.** Actually, this situation occurs in most men at some time or another but is temporary in nature. However, if the problem persists, it can become a real difficulty.

Premature ejaculation has been defined as a condition in which a man is unable to exert voluntary control over his ejaculatory reflex, with the result that once he is sexually aroused, he reaches orgasm very quickly (Kaplan, 1974). A man's ability to control ejaculation helps a couple attain satisfaction. A couple need to be able to engage in sexual play and in intercourse until both partners are sufficiently aroused for orgasm to take place. If the man climaxes and his penis becomes flaccid before the woman is aroused

Sexual dysfunction

Inhibited sexual desire

Ejaculatory inhibition

Erectile dysfunction

Premature ejaculation

sufficiently, the couple may have to rely on other means of stimulation to bring her to orgasm. At best, prematurity restricts the couple's sexuality.

Female Sexual Dysfunction

Female sexual dysfunctions include general sexual dysfunction, orgasm dysfunction, vaginismus, and painful intercourse (dyspareunia).

Women who experience **general sexual dysfunction** lack desire for or lack pleasure in sexual relations. Some may have little or minimal interest in sexual activity. If they participate, they derive no erotic pleasure from the experience. The dysfunction may be situational; that is, a woman may be unresponsive in a particular situation or with a certain partner but not on other occasions or with another partner. The degrees of sexual interest and responsiveness vary. Complete and permanent lack of sexual interest is rare.

Some women are able to become sexually aroused but are unable to reach a climax. This condition, referred to as **orgasm dysfunction,** is one of the most common sexual dysfunctions in women.

Vaginismus, which is rather rare, refers to an involuntary contraction and spasm of the vaginal muscles. If vaginismus exists even in a mild form, sexual intercourse may be very unpleasant.

Another common female difficulty is **dyspareunia,** or painful intercourse (Semmens & Tsai, 1984). The pain may be severe or slight, the degree depending on its origin and the woman's condition.

Causes of Sexual Dysfunction

In general, physical or emotional causes can result in sexual dysfunctions in men and women (Lopiccolo, 1985). For purposes of clarity, the causes of sexual dysfunction may be grouped into six categories:

1. *Ignorance and lack of knowledge and understanding* regarding sexual anatomy, sexual response, and lovemaking techniques may be reasons why couples have problems.
2. *Situational and environmental circumstances* can prevent couples from achieving satisfactory sexual function.
3. *Inadequate stimulation,* which is usually due to improper techniques, inappropriate ways, or insufficient time given to lovemaking, can cause sexual dysfunctions.
4. *Psychological blocks* that include negative attitudes toward sex or the human body are fre-

quent causes. Fear and anxiety are also psychological blocks. Fear of pregnancy, hurt, rejection, or failure are common causes of difficulties, as are feelings of guilt, embarrassment, or disgust. Emotional illness can also cause sexual dysfunction.

5. *Negative feelings toward one's partner or disturbance in the relationship* can result in sexual dysfunction. The quality and emotional tone of a couple's relationship influence sexual function.
6. *Physical abnormality, illness, surgery, or drugs* can also cause sexual difficulties.

Getting Help

At some time in their lives, most people experience temporary sexual dysfunction. If the dysfunction persists and is left untreated, the problem can wreck a relationship. However, most difficulties can be cleared up by obtaining the proper help. Basically there are four types of help: (a) *psychotherapy* for emotional problems and hang-ups, (b) *marriage counseling* to deal with the total marriage relationship, (c) *medical treatment* for physical problems, and (d) *sex therapy,* which emphasizes sensate-focus or symptom-focus approaches to immediate sexual problems. Sex therapy assigns couples sexual tasks that enable them to learn how to caress or "pleasure" each

General sexual dysfunction

Orgasm dysfunction

Vaginismus

Dyspareunia

Hypoactive Sexual Desire

An investigation of 69 men and women was undertaken to explore those factors associated with hypoactive sexual desire. The picture that emerged of the "typical" woman who experienced hypoactive sexual desire was someone who is in her early to middle 30s, of higher than average socioeconomic status, and who has a long-lasting primary arousal problem. She experiences a significant level of life stress, feels satisfaction with her marriage relationship, and has a significantly elevated level of psychological distress. The typical man with hypoactive sexual desire is older, in his late forties to early fifties, of higher socioeconomic status, who usually experiences this and other sexual dysfunctions (most often erectile dysfunction). His level of psychological distress is only slightly higher than the "normal" male norm. He also experiences only slightly more distress in the relationship than males with acceptable marital satisfaction. For both the majority of men and women, problems with hypoactive sexual desire coexisted with arousal disorders (Donahey & Carroll, 1993).

other in a nondemanding way until they are able to respond to each other. Usually, help involves a combination or one or more of these approaches. Most therapists use conjoint therapy involving both the wife and the husband, because sexual functioning necessarily affects them both. For this reason, couples that are having problems need to decide to get help together (Rice, 1989b).

THE SENSES AND PERCEPTION

Sensory Acuity

Maintaining a high level of sensory acuity enables us to participate actively in the life about us. Sustaining the ability to see, hear, taste and smell, keep a sense of balance, touch and feel pain, and regulate the body temperature during exposure to heat or cold are important factors in enabling people to maintain contact with the outside world and to adjust to the information that they receive (Marsiske, Klumb, & Baltes, 1997).

Visual Acuity

Visual acuity, the ability to perceive small details, reaches a maximum around age 20 and remains relatively constant to 40 (Sekuler & Blake, 1987). It then begins to decline. Although most older people need corrective lenses, about 70% have fair to adequate visual acuity to age 80 and beyond.

There are various kinds of visual impairments. One of the most common is **presbyopia** (farsightedness). As the lens becomes less elastic, it begins to lose some power of **accommodation** (the power to focus so that distinct vision is assured at both near and far distances). Accommodation declines from age 6 to 60, after which it levels off until extreme old age. Farsighted adults must wear corrective lenses for reading, writing, knitting, or other close work.

One of the changes that takes place in the visual system is a linear decline in motion perception with age. Elderly adults have expressed more difficulty with tasks involving dynamic vision, such as reading moving signs or television credits (Gilmore, Wenk, Naylor, & Stuve, 1992). Many elderly have trouble visually tracking moving objects (Moschner & Baloh, 1994).

Another common problem is a decrease in pupil size, allowing less light to reach the retina. The pupil also declines in ability to open and close with changes in light intensity

Although most older people need eyeglasses, about 70% have fair to adequate visual acuity.

(loss of **adaptation**). This ability decreases linearly from age 20 to age 60. As a result, older people have difficulty seeing at night or in dimly lit places. At the same time, glare in intense light is a problem because the eye cannot close enough to block out the excess. **Peripheral vision,** or ability to see toward the sides when looking straight ahead, also begins to show meaningful decrements when people reach their 50s and 60s. Color vision is also affected by age (Cooper, Ward, Gowland, & McIntosh, 1991). The lens gradually yellows and filters out the violet, blue, and green colors toward the dark end of the spectrum. For this reason, older people see yellow, orange, and red colors more easily than darker colors.

A number of diseases affect vision in old age. Among these are **cataracts** (clouding of the lenses); **glaucoma** (loss of vision from excess pressure inside the eyes); and **macular diseases** (of the retina) and damage to the cornea.

Hearing Acuity

An impairment of hearing ability can profoundly affect individual well-being. Hearing impairment can produce hearing difficulties and the perception of speech and environmental sounds that, in turn, can adversely affect functions such as social interactions, maintenance of personal relationships, and communicative efficiency (Slawinski, Hartel, & Kline, 1993). Hearing ability reaches its maximum around age 20. Hearing impairment associated with advancing age is called **presbycusis**. Usually, hearing loss occurs gradually from childhood on, with severe loss occurring first in the ability to hear high-pitched sounds. A

Visual acuity

Presbyopia

Accommodation

Adaptation—ability of the eye to adjust to different intensities of light

Peripheral vision—ability to see objects to either side of the line of sight in front of one's face

Cataracts

Glaucoma

Macular diseases

Presbycusis—impaired hearing due to old age

In-the-ear hearing aids are designed to correct moderate to profound hearing loss.

10-year-old, for example, can hear high-pitched sounds and upper frequencies of almost 20,000 cycles per second (Hz). But at 65, persons hear sound only up to about 8,000 Hz. They have more difficulty hearing high-pitched voices and perceiving certain high-frequency consonants, such as *z*, *s*, *g*, *f*, and *t*. The elderly person may hear *ave* instead of *save*, *ame* instead of *game*, *alk* instead of *talk*, or *pa* instead of *pat*. Such words as *gaze*, *first*, *stop*, or *grass*, with two or more high-frequency consonants, may not be understood at all.

A noticeable decline begins in the 50s, and by 70 there is a loss in hearing at all frequencies, even those below 1,000 Hz. After 55, men show a greater incidence of hearing loss than do women. However, when speech is clear, undistorted, and presented without competing noise, most older subjects suffer very little loss in ability to understand. Distorted and noise-masked speech is difficult for many older people to decipher. Shouting at them usually does not help, because this involves raising the voice to higher pitches. Fortunately, some hearing problems are treatable or correctable. Approximately 10% of all hearing losses can be helped medically or surgically. Most of the remaining 90% can be helped with amplification: through the use of hearing aids. Most important, many hearing problems are preventable by avoiding overexposure to loud noises.

Taste and Smell

Eating is such an important part of our physical and social lives that any change in the ability to taste various foods is significant. Evidence indicates that the ability to perceive

Living Issues

Vision, Aging, and Driving

Laboratory and field studies have been only moderately successful in demonstrating a relationship between age-related visual decline and the increased automobile accident rate of older drivers. Although older drivers as a group do not contribute excessively to the overall number of automobile accidents or of traffic violations, their rate of traffic accidents and citations per mile is higher than that of all but their youngest colleagues. They also differ in the types of accidents that they are likely to experience. Compared with their younger colleagues, older drivers are infrequently involved in accidents attributable to speed, equipment problems, or major violations (such as driving under the influence). They are considerably more likely, however, to participate in accidents and violations involving failure to heed signs, to give right of way, or to turn appropriately. Elderly drivers appear to be involved in fewer single-vehicle accidents and more two-vehicle accidents than are young or middle-aged drivers. Once involved in an accident, they are also more likely than younger groups to be injured or killed (Kline et al., 1992). (See Figure 16.3.)

The decision to stop driving involves a severe contraction of independence. Among elderly persons, driving cessation is likely to signify lost independence. An examination of medical conditions associated with the decision to stop driving included six conditions that explained about 50% of the decisions to stop driving: Macular degeneration, retinal hemorrhage, any deficit in activities of daily living, Parkinson's Disease, stroke-related residual paralysis or weakness, and syncope. Syncope involves the loss of consciousness (Campbell, Bush, & Hale, 1993; Marottoli, Ostfeld, Merrill, Perlman, Foley, & Kooney, 1993). Figure 16.3 shows the proportion of at-fault collisions and single accidents by sex and age group (Hakamies-Blomquist, 1994).

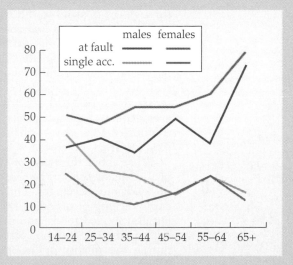

FIGURE 16.3 Proportion of at-fault collisions and single accidents by sex and age group.

From "Aging and Fatal Accidents in Male and Female Drivers," by L. Hakamies-Blomqvist, 1994, *Journal of Gerontology, 49*, S286–S290. Copyright © The Gerontological Society of America.

FOCUS

Environmental Hazards and the Sense of Smell

Optimal performance in and appreciation of one's environment require adequate functioning sensory systems. The interaction of sensory systems with the environment entails certain hazards. Noxious stimuli, in the form either of repetitive, low-intensity exposures or of a single major exposure, can impair the functioning of a sensory system. One study reported data from 712,000 respondents aged 20 to 79 as part of the *National Geographic Smell Survey* that suggest that exposure to the factory workplace adversely affects the sense of smell and that these effects depend on age. Men and women with histories of factory work reported poorer senses of smell relative to other workers. They also demonstrated objective evidence of greater impairment in odor detection. Effects were greater for men. Factory workers of all ages more frequently reported olfactory loss than did workers in other environments (Corwin, Loury, & Gilbert, 1995).

Tactile acuity—sensitivity of touch

Thermoregulation—maintenance of correct body temperature during exposure to heat or cold

all four taste qualities—sweet, salt, bitter, and sour—declines in later life, although the decrement is small. Actually, taste buds continually replace themselves, but taste sensitivity shows some decline (Weiffenbach, Tylenda, & Baum, 1990); the number of taste buds is not as crucial as are their responsiveness and ability to transmit taste sensations through the neurons to the brain.

The taste for sweet and salty flavors declines faster than that for bitter and sour. As a result, older people complain that their food tastes bitter and sour. Or, they require more highly seasoned food to experience the same taste satisfactions they had when younger. On the average, elderly people prefer higher concentrations of food flavors than do young subjects (deGraaf, Polet, & van Staveren, 1994).

What about the sense of smell? Olfaction plays a major role in the sensory experiences of food and beverages, and it provides an early warning of fire, dangerous fumes, leaking gas, spoiled foods, and polluted environments. Smell dysfunction can significantly diminish the quality of life and can even be life-threatening. Age-related declines in various aspects of olfactory functioning have been documented. Since food flavor arises largely from olfactory stimulation, the poorer flavor discrimination and the decreased ability to identify foods in the mouth by older persons likely reflect age-related declines in olfactory function (Ship & Weiffenbach, 1993). Another study showed some age-

related changes in odor perception (Russel et al., 1993). Young adults consistently outperform older adults in odor recognition and odor naming (Larsson & Backman, 1993).

Tactile Sensitivity: Touch, Temperature, and Pain

Research reveals some decrease in **tactile acuity** with increasing age; the loss is small, though, and a number of individuals over 60 retain high sensitivity. Temperature and pain sensitivity are impaired in only a small percentage of the elderly.

Thermoregulation

Thermoregulation is the maintenance of body temperature during exposure to heat or cold. Body temperature is usually regulated within narrow limits. Experiments have shown that young adults can regulate body heat under adverse temperature conditions, whereas older adults show significant changes in body temperature. Such changes explain why older adults suffer more in extremes of hot or cold. Elderly people may require a more intense thermal stimulus to elicit the appropriate behavior responses in the home. Such stimuli may result in greater heat flow and elevated risk of dysthermia in the aged (Taylor, Allsopp, & Parkes, 1995). The elderly are at high risk of mortality from excessive heat and excessive cold. Psychological as well as behavioral changes contribute to the increased vulnerability of the elderly to temperature-related mortality. Diminished perception, impairment of thermal regulatory capacity, and a reduced ability to depict temperature change, along with an associated lack of decision in adjusting the thermal environment, have been reported. Even when older people are aware of their inability adequately to judge internal environment, few employ remedial care measures. Some even consciously threatened their own health by trying to save money on heating and electric bills. In particular, low-income urban elderly have been found to engage in energy curtailment behaviors. The elderly also generally occupy older dwelling units that are prone to have less insulation, with greater loss of heat or air-conditioning through cracks and leaks (Macey & Schneider, 1993).

Sense of Balance

Hairlike projections in the inner ear, which are activated by the flow of fluids as the body changes positions, act as sensory perceptors that pick up and pass on information to the brain about body positions and orientations that constitute our sense of balance. A maximum sense of balance is achieved between 40 and 50, followed by decline, and an increase in postural sway (Teasdale, Stelnach, & Breunig, 1991). One consequence is that older people tend to fall more often (Judge, King, Whipple, Clive, & Wolsson, 1995). We are not certain exactly why balance declines. Inner ear tissues may deteriorate with age, but not always. Possibly a diminishing blood supply causes dizziness. Declines in nervous reflexes, psychomotor coordination, and muscular strength are undoubtedly factors (Chen, Ashton-Miller, Alexander, & Schultz, 1991). Or, failing eyesight and improper illumination may cause older adults to have more accidents (Simoneau et al., 1992). Most injurious falls occur during the performance of routine daily activities such as walking, transferring, stooping, bending, or reaching, rather than doing high-risk activities such as climbing ladders or standing on step stools (King, Judge, & Wolsson, 1994). The fact that women lose their balance more than men explains their greater frequency of falling as they get older (Wolsson, Whipple, Derby, Amerman, Nashner, 1994).

BIOLOGICAL AGING

Senescence

Senescence is the term that biologists, gerontologists, and others use to describe biological aging. It should not be confused with *senility*, which is a disease. Disease is not inevitable as people age. Senescence describes the processes that lead to a decline in the viability of the human organism and increase its vulnerability. There is no known animal species whose individual members do not age. However, rates of senescence for most species vary from individual to individual. These individual variations increase with chronological age. Some persons exhibit traits similar to those chronologically older or younger than themselves. Furthermore, senescence is not one process but many, with decline occurring in different parts of the body at different rates.

Theories of Biological Aging

Exactly why physical aging occurs has been the subject of much investigation and discussion. Do people have to age? Under ideal condi-

tions, could they stay young forever? Or, does a built-in time clock control longevity, so that living much beyond an allotted time is impossible? There are no answers, but a number of different theories have attempted to explain the causes of physical aging.

Theories of aging are typically divided into two major categories: *genetic* and *nongenetic*. Genetic theories of aging emphasize that aging occurs as a result of a genetic program that produces both physical and mental deterioration in late adulthood. Nongenetic theories emphasize that aging is due to disease and lifestyle factors and insist that accumulation of environmental damage over the life span is the source of physical and mental deterioration.

Heredity Theory

The most obvious explanation is that the theoretical length of life is hereditary (Vaillant, 1991). The life span of a species is set by genetic characteristics that have evolved over countless years. Thus, each species has its own life expectancy. Elephants may live 60 years, hippopotamuses 50, and primates reach or exceed 30 years. Heredity also plays an important role in human longevity, so that children whose parents and grandparents are long lived may also live longer. Apparently, they inherit certain traits (e.g., increased resistance to disease) that contribute to a longer life (McGue, Baupel, Holm, & Harvald, 1993).

Cellular Aging Theory

Some cells in the body, such as those in the brain and nervous system, never reproduce. Other cells reproduce, but only a finite number of times. Hayflick (1970) studied the aging of living cells maintained in cultures. He found that lung tissues, for example, multiply rapidly, at first doubling every 24 hours. But as the process progresses, the length of time between doublings increases; after about 50 doublings (about 6 months), the cells fail to double and start to die. Other cells of the body double fewer times. This fact suggests that aging is programmed by the limited capacity of cells to replace themselves (Lockshin & Zakeri, 1990).

Wear-and-Tear Theory

The wear-and-tear theory emphasizes that the organism simply wears out, like a machine that has run for too many years. Metabolic rate seems to be a factor. Modestly underfed

Senescence—biological aging

warm-blooded animals (including humans), as well as cold-blooded animals living at lower than normal temperatures, tend to live longer because metabolism slows down.

Metabolic Waste, or Clinker, Theory

The metabolic waste, or clinker, theory suggests that aging is caused by the accumulation of deleterious substances (by-products of cellular metabolism) within various cells of the body. The accumulation of these substances interferes with the normal tissue functioning. One such substance is collagen, a fibrous protein associated with connective tissue. It builds up slowly in most organs, tendons, skin, and blood vessels, and it is eliminated gradually, if at all. It also stiffens with age. Therefore, tissues containing collagen lose elasticity, causing deterioration in organ functions.

Autoimmunity Theory

The autoimmunity theory of aging describes the process by which the body's immune system rejects its own tissues through the production of autoimmune antibodies. When foreign substances enter the body, the immune system produces antibodies to neutralize their effects. The response to invasion is called an immune reaction. When antibodies respond to mutations within the body, their response is an autoimmune reaction. The net result is self-destruction. This promising theory may lead to the discovery of methods that will retard this action and modify the aging process.

Homeostatic Imbalance Theory

The homeostatic imbalance theory emphasizes the gradual inability of the body to maintain vital physiologic balances. For example, the body gradually loses its ability to maintain the proper temperature during exposure to heat or cold; similarly, it loses its ability to maintain the proper blood sugar level. Older people have difficulty adapting to emotional stress; thus, many older persons die soon after their spouses. This loss of efficiency of the physiologic response to stress is perhaps the most general theory of aging and provides the closest link between the physiological, social, and psychological aspects of aging.

Mutation Theory

The mutation theory describes what happens when more and more body cells develop mutations. Rates of genetic mutation increase with age. One cause is radiation, which damages the genetic material and shortens the organ's life span in direct proportion to the amount of genetic damage incurred. Cell functioning is controlled by the genetic material DNA (deoxyribonucleic acid), which is found in each cell. When mutations occur in DNA, subsequent cell divisions replicate them, and an appreciable percentage of an organ's cells become mutated. Since most mutations are harmful, mutated cells function less efficiently, and the organs made up of these cells become inefficient and senescent (Whitehead & Grigliatti, 1993).

Error Theory

The error theory is a variation of the mutation theory. The error theory includes the cumulative effects of a variety of mistakes that may occur; mistakes in RNA (ribonucleic acid) production, which affect enzymic synthesis, which affects protein synthesis, and so on. Research indicates a loss of DNA from the cells of aging animals, which impairs the production of RNA and DNA. This process, in turn, impairs cell functioning and eventually leads to cellular death (Johnson & Strehler, 1972).

Which Theory?

No single theory proposed to date adequately explains the complex events that occur in aging. Aging involves a number of processes that produce time-dependent changes in an organism. In addition to hereditary factors and intrinsic changes (those occurring from within), environmental stresses, bacteria, viruses, and other influences affect the organism from without, sometimes reducing the abilities of various organs to continue functioning.

PROLONGEVITY

Possibilities

Longevity refers to the duration of life, usually implying a long or extended life. The term *prolongevity* was introduced in 1966 by Gerald J. Gruman, a physician and historian, to describe deliberate efforts to extend the length of life by human action (Gruman, 1966). Some prolongevitists have been optimistic in their predictions. They assert that the problems of death and aging can be overcome, virtually removing limits on the length of human life. More conservative prolongevitists have proposed a more limited increase in the length of life: usually to age 100 or over. They look forward to breaking the 110-year limit, which is a formidable barrier. Dr. Roy

Implications

At 122, Jeanne Calment was thought to be the world's oldest person at the time of her death on August 4, 1997.

Walford, professor of pathology at UCLA's medical school, asserts that in the foreseeable future we may be able to retard the rate of aging so that people will live to be 100 years of age or more ("How People Will Live to Be 100 or More," 1983).

The goal of prolongevitists is not simply to increase the maximum life span, but to retard both disease and the aging process. The goal is to improve the overall health of older people (Hickey & Stilwell, 1991). If people were physically young and healthy, even though advanced in years, heart disease, cancer, and diabetes would practically be eliminated. Instead of being sick, disabled, and dependent, people would have their health and vigor for years and live active, useful lives (Rothenberg, Lentzener, & Parker, 1991).

Equally important, the wisdom and experience amassed by the young-old could be used to solve societal problems and create a better life for all. There is no telling what a person might become or achieve given a significant number of extra years. Those who live a long time not only can learn more but also can synthesize their learning in new ways to create new systems of thought and ideas. If the lives of some of the world's geniuses were prolonged, what might they achieve?

Summary

1. During the mid-20s, the human body is at the peak of its physical development, but at the same time, aging is already taking place.

2. Robust aging, or successful aging, means getting older but maintaining physical, mental, and social well-being.

3. Self-consciousness about one's changing physique is accentuated by society's attitudes that equate attractiveness with youthfulness.

4. Ageism is prejudice and discrimination against the elderly, which is so widely reflected in advertising, professional attitudes, television, humorous greeting cards, and poetry.

5. Since some people age more rapidly than others, the important emphasis should be on functional age, not on chronological age.

6. Functional age is reflected in reaction time, motor ability, coordination, dexterity, strength, and endurance and fatigue.

7. Aging is influenced by both genetic and environmental influences.

8. Exercise is one of the best ways to prevent ill health and maintain body fitness, but only about half of 20- to 39-year-old adults, and less than half of adults 45 to 64, engage in any form of exercise at least weekly.

9. Pulse rate is one of the simplest measures of health and physical fitness. It should be monitored during exercise so that the target rate is reached and maintained for periods of 15 to 30 minutes.

10. The prevalent view is that overweight people could lose weight if they exerted voluntary control over their eating, but since they are thought not to control their eating, they are stigmatized. The overweight could benefit from a social movement that removed the stigma from obesity and that countered the prejudice and discrimination against them.

11. Proper nutrition is another important factor in maintaining good health. Older adults need diets with greater nutrient density in proportion to the number of calories consumed. Weight gain occurs

because fewer basal and activity calories are burned up in relation to those eaten.

12. Adults require diets low in saturated fats and cholesterol, sodium, and sugar.

13. Exercise training can cause a total reduction in body fat content with a preferential loss of fat from the central regions of the body.

14. Adequate amounts of sleep and rest maximize healthful functioning, but sleep patterns change with age, so that some older adults do not get adequate rest.

15. There are 5 groups of factors that contribute to insomnia: biological, psychological, drugs and alcohol, disturbing environment and bad habits, and negative conditioning. The most effective insomnia treatments utilize a multidimensional approach.

16. Couples whose sleep/wake patterns are out of sync are more likely to have troubled marriages than couples whose patterns are similar.

17. Drug abuse is highest in young adults ages 18 to 25.

18. Many elderly abuse drugs that are prescribed for them for medical purposes. The elderly are especially susceptible to drugs because their bodies do not metabolize them readily and the drugs remain in their system. Also, the greater the number of drugs taken, the greater the possibility of adverse reactions as the drugs interact with one another.

19. Research has revealed that the only effective way to quit smoking is to give it up entirely, rather than trying to cut down.

20. As aging progresses, brain weight declines, arteriosclerosis may cut down on the blood supply, and nerve impulses are transmitted more slowly.

21. Significant changes may occur in the heart and blood vessels with age. The following cardiovascular and heart diseases are common: atherosclerosis, coronary occlusion with myocardial infarction, congestive heart failure, and cardiac arrhythmias. Heart disease is the number-one killer of the elderly.

22. Other vascular diseases include thrombosis, embolism, hemorrhage, and stroke. When the brain is the site of the vascular disease, it is called cerebrovascular. When the lung is the site, it is called a pulmonary thrombosis or pulmonary embolism.

23. Changes in the respiratory system with age include a decline in vital capacity of the lungs, and lower efficiency in air exchange and oxygen conductance. Important respiratory diseases include tuberculosis, bronchial pneumonia, emphysema, pulmonary infections, and lung cancer.

24. The liver is the most important organ in digestion, since it removes waste matter from the blood; stores glycogen and makes sugar available as needed; stores vitamins and iron; and makes many blood proteins that prevent edema, resist disease, and ensure blood clotting.

25. Jaundice, in which the skin tissues turn yellow, occurs when the liver is not functioning properly. Cirrhosis of the liver is the eighth leading cause of death among the elderly.

26. The gall bladder stores bile and releases it as needed for digestion. Gallstones form when the bile duct becomes blocked.

27. Diabetes mellitus occurs when the pancreas does not secrete enough insulin to regulate the sugar level in the blood. Diabetes is the ninth leading cause of death among diseases of the elderly.

28. Gastritis is a chronic inflammation of the stomach lining causing indigestion and gas.

29. The urinary system includes the kidneys, bladder, ureters, and urethra. The kidneys filter the waste products of metabolism. Since the body can live with one kidney, most changes in age are not debilitating, although various diseases reduce kidney functioning.

30. The bladder's ability to store and hold urine diminishes at advanced ages. Incontinence or loss of bladder control is common in adults over 65 years of age.

31. Common diseases of the skeletal system include osteoarthritis, rheumatoid arthritis, and osteoporosis.

32. Periodontal disease of the gums and tooth decay, along with neglect of the teeth, cause many elderly to lose some or all of their teeth.

33. Menopause is cessation of menstruation as the ovaries gradually atrophy and become less able to secrete hormones and develop egg cells. The median age of natural menopause is 49.76 years. About 75% of women do not exhibit the common symptoms of menopause.

34. The male climacteric is primarily psychological, although the secretion of

testosterone declines very slowly in some men as they age.

35. Sexual relations and interest in sex often continue well into old age.

36. Homosexuality refers to sexual orientation in which a person is sexually attracted to a person of the same sex. The causes of homosexuality may be either biological or psychosocial.

37 Sexual dysfunction is any malfunction of the human sexual response system. Male sexual dysfunctions include inhibited sexual desire, erectile dysfunction, premature ejaculation, and ejaculatory inhibition. Female sexual dysfunctions include general sexual dysfunction, orgasm dysfunction, vaginismus, and dyspareunia.

38. Causes of sexual dysfunction may be grouped into six categories: ignorance and lack of knowledge; circumstances; inadequate stimulation, psychological blocks; negative feelings toward one's partner; and physical abnormality, illness, surgery, and drugs.

39. Treatment for sexual dysfunction includes four types: psychotherapy, marriage counseling, medical treatment, and sex therapy.

40. With age, changes occur in visual acuity, loss of accommodation, adaptation, and peripheral vision. Common diseases of the eye that affect vision are cataracts, glaucoma, macular diseases, and damage to the cornea.

41. There is only a moderate relationship between vision in the elderly and automobile accident rates. Elderly drivers are more likely to be involved in fewer single-vehicle accidents and more two-vehicle accidents than are young or middle-aged drivers; however, once involved in an accident, they are more likely than younger groups to be injured or killed.

42. Hearing acuity declines with age, especially in relation to high-pitched sounds. Ninety percent of losses can be corrected by amplification, that is wearing a hearing aid.

43. Ability to taste declines somewhat with age, though the taste for sweet and salty flavors declines faster than that for bitter and sour.

44. People who are exposed to smells over a period of time gradually become desensitized to those odors. The ability to detect various odors declines with age.

45. Tactile acuity and temperature and pain sensitivity are impaired in only a small percentage of the elderly. Thermoregulation declines, as does the sense of balance.

46. Senescence refers to biological aging. Rates vary from individual to individual, with decline occurring in different parts of the body at various rates.

47. The principal theories of biological aging include the following: heredity, cellular aging, wear-and-tear, metabolic waste or clinker, autoimmunity, homeostatic imbalance, mutation, and error. No single theory adequately explains the complex events that occur in aging.

48. Longevity refers to the duration of life; prolongevity refers to efforts to extend the length of life. The goal is not simply to maximize the life span, but to retard the aging process itself.

Key Terms

Accommodation *p. 452*
Activity calories *p. 437*
Adaptation *p. 452*
Ageism *p. 431*
Alveoli *p. 444*
Angina pectoris *p. 443*
Arteriosclerosis *p. 442*
Atherosclerosis *p. 443*
Basal calories *p. 437*
Bile *p. 445*
Bronchial pneumonia *p. 444*
Cardiac arrhythmias *p. 443*
Cataracts *p. 452*
Cerebrovascular disease *p. 444*
Cholesterol *p. 437*
Cirrhosis *p. 445*
Climacteric *p. 447*

Congestive heart failure *p. 443*
Coronary occlusion with myocardial infarction *p. 443*
Diabetes mellitus *p. 445*
Diastolic blood pressure *p. 442*
Dyspareunia *p. 451*
Edema *p. 443*
Ejaculatory inhibition *p. 450*
Embolism *p. 444*
Emphysema *p. 444*
Erectile dysfunction *p. 450*
Functional age *p. 432*
Gall bladder trouble *p. 445*
Gallstones *p. 445*
Gastritis *p. 445*
General sexual dysfunction *p. 451*
Glaucoma *p. 452*

Discussion Questions

1. How do you feel about the aged? About getting old? Why does society equate worth with youthfulness? What evidence of ageism do you see in our society?

2. What images of the elderly are portrayed in the TV programs that you watch?

3. What can be done to change negative feelings toward the elderly? What can the elderly do to help?

4. What factors do you feel are most important in maintaining physical fitness and health? What do you do to stay healthy? What habits do you have that are detrimental to your health?

5. What sort of exercise do you engage in? For what reasons? With what results?

6. What do you think of a movement to eliminate the stigma of being obese? Why are fat people discriminated against? What should be done about it?

7. What factors are important to you in maintaining proper nutrition? What factors prevent you from getting an adequate diet? Have you tried the liquid diets? What do you think of them? What factors have been most helpful to you in losing weight?

8. Do you know anyone who has insomnia? Describe. What can be done to eliminate the problem?

9. What drugs are abused most frequently among adults whom you know? Have you ever had serious problems with drug abuse? What happened, and what did you do?

10. What factors help you the most in stopping smoking? What factors prevent you from stopping smoking?

11. Have any members of your family had cardiovascular diseases, heart attacks, or brain disorders? Describe.

12. Do you know anyone who now has or has had tuberculosis? Lung cancer? Bronchial pneumonia? Emphysema? Describe.

13. Does any member of your family have liver disease? Cirrhosis of the liver? Gall bladder trouble? Diabetes? Stomach cancer? Describe.

14. Does any member of your family have kidney, bladder, or bowel problems? Describe. What can be done to help elderly people who are incontinent?

15. Does any member of your family have arthritis? Osteoporosis? What can be done?

16. Is your mother or any female member of your family going through menopause? Describe. Is your father or any male member of your family going through a male climacteric?

17. How do you react to the fact that most adults have sexual interests and engage in sex well into old age? Why do young adults have trouble accepting the fact that their parents are sexual beings?

18. Does any member of your family have problems with one or more of the following senses: vision, hearing, taste, smell, tactile sensitivity, thermoregulation, or sense of balance? Describe the condition, its consequences, and what is being done or can be done about it.

19. Of the various theories of aging, which ones have the greatest validity? Explain.

20. What do you think of trying to prolong the length and quality of life and of trying to delay the aging process? What are some of the implications of people living to be over 100 years old?

Suggested Readings

CARLSON, K. J., EINSENTENSTAT, S. A., & ZIPORYN, T. (1996). *The Harvard guide to women's health*. Cambridge, MA: Harvard University Press. Answers questions that physicians hear every day from their women patients.

CLAYMAN, C. B., ed. (1994). *American Medical Association Family Medical Guide* (3rd. ed.). New York: Random House. A comprehensive reference.

COOPER, K. H. (1989). *Controlling cholesterol*. New York: Bantam Books. An important book on this subject.

COOPER, R. K., FERGUSON, T. (1990). *Health and physical fitness excellence*. Boston: Houghton Mifflin. Stress, exercise, nutrition, fat control, wellness.

GERSHOFF, S. (1996). *The Tufts University guide to total nutrition*. New York: Harper & Collins. An authoritative guide on all aspects of nutrition.

LOGUE, A. W. (1991). *The psychology of eating and drinking*. New York: W. H. Freeman. Eating behavior, obesity, and weight loss.

Our Bodies, Ourselves for the New Century: A Book by and for Women (1998). New York: Touchstone Books, Women's health.

RICE, F. P. (1986). *Adult development and aging*. Boston: Allyn and Bacon. Basic college textbook by the author.

RICE, F. P. (1989). *Human sexuality*. Dubuque, IA: Wm. C. Brown. The author's comprehensive textbook on the subject.

SPENCE, A. P. (1995). *Biology of human aging*. Englewood Cliffs, NJ: Prentice-Hall. Theories plus changes in the bodily systems.

WHITBOURNE, S. K. (1985). *The aging body: Physiological changes and psychological consequences*. New York: Springer-Verlag. Review of physical aging and how to cope.

Web Resources

http://physicaldevelopmenta.health-personal md.com/history/PERSONALMD.COM One stop health destination featuring comprehensive medical records, customized health and medical news on physical development.

Cognitive Development

Chapter 17

COGNITIVE DEVELOPMENT

Cognitive development includes the changes that take place in the way people think. It includes a consideration of the *qualities of those thought processes* themselves, as individuals seek to comprehend information, solve problems, and engage in the thought that is necessary to survive and to live. Some individuals are able to comprehend better than others, showing much wisdom in the way they control their lives and in the way they go about solving their problems and thinking of any alternatives that are presented to them.

Cognitive development also includes *the development of intelligence.* What does it mean to be an intelligent person, and what are the implications of this trait in everyday living? How are those abilities that constitute intelligence developed? To what extent do heredity and environment have an influence on the development of these qualities? How is intelligence measured? And how does it change as people get older?

In addition, cognitive development includes *the ability to process information,* to learn, to remember, and to utilize this information as needed. What is involved in the ability to remember, and how might this ability be developed? What factors influence learning, and how might this knowledge be used in enhancing the learning process in adults? And, finally, how might cognitive development contribute to productivity and creativity in our lives? What is the role of education, especially adult education, in the learning process, and how might the concept of lifelong education be utilized to help individuals be more productive in their lives? All these aspects of cognitive development are discussed in this chapter.

Formal Operational Thinking

As discussed in Chapter 12, the achievement of formal operational thinking means the individual has developed the ability to engage in four distinct thought processes: (a) introspection (to think about thought); (b) abstract thinking (to go beyond the real to what is possible); (c) logical thinking (to gather facts and ideas to form correct conclusions); and (d) hypothetical reasoning (to formulate hypotheses and examine the truth of them, considering numerous variables). According to Piaget (1972), the ability develops during adolescence from approximately age 11 to 15, although Piaget admits that the appearance of formal operations may be delayed until 15 to 20 years of age, and in disadvantaged conditions, may never take shape. According to other research using advanced criteria (Kuhn, 1979), *approximately half of the adult population may never attain the full stage of formal thinking.*

Some adults are able to use formal operational thinking in their particular field of specialization, but not in other fields. DeLisi and Staudt (1980) found that although physics students could solve the pendulum problem easily, they had trouble in political-socialization tasks or in literary-styles tasks. English majors were successful in applying formal operations only in the literary-styles tasks. The years of formal education, intelligence level, and numerous cultural factors also influence the development of formal operational thinking. Brodzinsky (1985) suggested that cognitive style affects the ability to do well on Piagetian-type tasks. *Reflective people,* who are cautious and systematic in problem solving, and **field-independent people,** who can sort out relevant from irrelevant information, do well in such tasks, whereas those who are *impulsive* or who are **field-dependent** (who have trouble isolating the relevant information in solving a problem) do relatively poorly on Piagetian-type tasks.

There is some evidence that older adults approach problems at a lower level of abstraction than do adolescents or younger adults (Johnson, 1990). Hartley (1981) tested four age groups of adults on their abilities to solve a problem requiring deductive reasoning or drawing specific conclusions from a premise. The younger adults (mean age 20) were enrolled in college. The middle-aged adults (mean age 41.4) were college graduates. The younger group of older adults (mean age 65.4) were also college graduates. The older, community-dwelling adults (mean age 71.5) had an average of 14.33 years of education. Figure 17.1 shows that a significantly smaller percentage of those in the older two adult groups were able to solve the problem. The older nonsolvers were less able to separate relevant from irrelevant information; they based solutions on hunches rather than on available evidence, processed information on only one dimension at a time, and generally showed a reduced ability to do formal operational thinking.

Field-independent people— people who sort out relevant from irrelevant information in solving problems

Field-dependent people— people who have trouble isolating relevant information in solving problems

Other researchers generally find that *older adults do poorly on measures of formal reasoning ability, but this is because they approach problems differently.* Older adults tend to be more pragmatic, more attuned to social and economic realities (Labouvie-Vief, 1986), so that abstract questions don't seem meaningful or important. Older people tend to ignore some things as unimportant. They also tend to personalize learning tasks (Datan, Rodeheaver, & Hughes, 1987). Instead of applying logico-deductive methods, they rely more on subjective, intuitive thinking. Labouvie-Vief (1986) insisted that this characteristic is not inferior to formal logic; it is just different. She found that when older people are asked to summarize fables they have read, they excel at recalling the metaphorical meaning, whereas college students try to remember the precise text.

Practical Problem-Solving Abilities

When adults over 65 were asked how they thought their abilities to reason, think, and solve problems had changed throughout their adult lives, 76% thought their abilities had increased with age, 20% reported no change, and only 4% reported that their abilities had declined with age (Williams, Denney, & Schadler, 1980). But these people were talking about practical problems of everyday

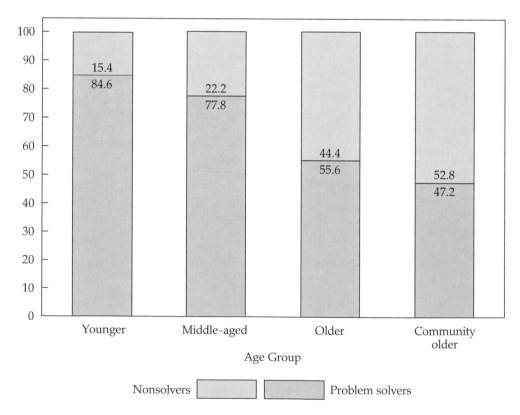

FIGURE 17.1   Percentage of problem solvers as a function of age group. Copyright © The Gerontological Society of America.

Adapted from "Adult Age Differences in Deductive Reasoning Processes," by A. A. Hartley, 1981, *Journal of Gerontology, 36*, pp. 700–706. Reprinted by permission.

With formal operational thinking comes the ability to employ scientific methods and logical reasoning in solving problems.

living, not about abstract reasoning problems traditionally used in laboratory experiments.

Denney and Palmer (1981) found a diminution with age in capacity to do abstract problems but an improvement in ability to solve practical problems that might actually be encountered. They presented two types of problem-solving tasks to adults between 20 and 79 years of age. The first task was a 20 questions type of test typically used in problem-solving research. The test results showed that such ability peaked in the late 20s. The second task was designed to measure the ability to solve problems presented in real-life situations. The test results showed that the ability to solve practical problems increased during early adulthood and did not peak until the late 40s. The researchers cautioned that since this was a cross-sectional study, one must be careful about drawing strong conclusions with reference to age. Because cross-sectional studies usually overemphasize decline with age, the fact that the ability to solve practical problems actually increased is even more significant. Age differences in problem-solving abilities are highly dependent on the degree to which situations are emotionally salient. Older adults do best on problems that have meaning and emotional interest for them (Blanchard-Fields, Jahnke, & Camp, 1995).

Other problem-solving research shows similar results. *Young adults do not appear to be solving the practical problems of everyday living as efficiently as older adults.* Research indicates that this trait may occur because there's a tendency on the part of young adults to give less than their optimal performance unless explicitly instructed and motivated to do so (Denney, Tozier, & Schlotthauer, 1992). Problem-solving abilities may also be improved with training.

Comprehension

Word Familiarity

A number of studies have been conducted to determine age-related abilities of adults to comprehend linguistic meanings of individual words, sentences, or paragraphs (Emery & Breslau, 1989; Laver & Burke, 1993). *Tests of word familiarity have shown that adults generally show improvement to ages 50 through 59 (mean age 55), after which scores decline.* However, the scores of people with high education (above high school) were never as low as the scores of those with low education (high school or less), regardless of age. Thus, educational level was found to be more important than age itself.

Sentence Comprehension

Sentence comprehension research has revealed that the *ability to comprehend relativized sentences (complex sentences with a number of relative clauses) remains stable until the 60s, after which ability declines with age.* However, comprehension of sentences presented auditorily depends on the complexity of the sentences (Norman et al., 1991) and partially on the rate of presentation. Material presented either too rapidly or too slowly is not comprehended as readily as material presented at a normal rate. Similarly, adults don't do well ,on reading tests when they are ordered to finish the test in an allotted time. However, when no time constraints are imposed, adults read more slowly, but their comprehension improves (Norman, Kemper, & Kynette, 1992).

Prose Comprehension

Belmore (1981) tested the ability of adults to process and comprehend linguistic meanings of short prose passages that they were asked to read. *Older adults (mean age 66.5) were able to comprehend the meanings almost as well as younger adults (mean age 18.3).* The older subjects were correct on 83% of the trials, the younger subjects on 91% of the trials. However, when testing for levels of comprehension was delayed, older adults showed impairment in retaining the information over a period of time. They comprehended almost as well initially, but they could not remember the material as long as the younger subjects could. In another study, both young (18 to 33 years of age) and old (65 to 80) adults were able to recall narrative passages better than expository passages, but older subjects recalled less than young subjects (Tun, 1989). This finding is in keeping with other research that indicates that working memory capacity declines with age (Hamm & Hasher, 1992).

Wisdom

One of the advantages of getting older is that people develop pragmatic knowledge that we call wisdom (Luszki & Luszki, 1985). Wisdom goes beyond book learning and factual knowledge. It involves the accumulation of a lifetime of expertise in dealing with life tasks, managing situations, and solving problems (Staudinger, Smith, & Baltes, 1992). Wisdom involves using sound judgment in the conduct of life; it is the developing of understanding through experience and the capacity to apply that understanding to the issues of life (Baltes, Smith, Staudinger, & Sowarka, 1988). Wisdom may be defined as the expert-level of knowledge in the fundamental pragmatics of life.

One comparative study of wisdom-related knowledge focused on a group of distinguished individuals nominated as being wise. The groups included both older clinical psychologists and highly educated old and young control groups. Wisdom-related knowledge was assessed by two tasks and evaluated with a set of five wisdom criteria. Older clinical psychologists (average age of 66 years) and wisdom nominees (average age of 64 years) significantly outperformed young and older adult comparison groups on both tasks. The fact that clinical psychologists outperformed control groups demonstrated the expected wisdom-enhancement effect associated with being a member of a profession oriented towards matters of the human condition—the planning, conduct, and the interpretation of life. The finding is novel, however, in regard to the wisdom nominees. Although none of the wisdom nominees were psychologists, the fact that they performed as well as the professional group trained for the kind of problems under studies is noteworthy (Baltes, Staudinger, Maercker, & Smith, 1995).

Problem Finding

In some ways, adulthood requires a different kind of thinking. Schoolchildren learn to solve teacher-determined problems. Adults need to learn to identify problems that exist and to delineate those that need solving. This involves going beyond formal operational thinking to a fifth stage of development that has been labeled a *problem-finding stage*. This fifth stage represents an ability to discover problems not yet delineated, to formulate these problems, and to raise general questions from ill-defined problems. *This fifth stage is a postformal operational thinking stage.*

Investigations of the Piagetian stage of formal operations suggest that progressive changes in thought structures may extend beyond the level of formal operations. *The suggestion is that formal structures may not be the final equilibrium; they may be building blocks for new structures that might be identified.* The implication is that cognitive growth in adulthood is continuous; there is no end point beyond which new structures may not appear. Researchers continue to seek these new structures.

Dialectical Thinking

A number of theorists have described an advanced form of adult thought that they call **dialectical thinking** (Leadbeater, 1986). According to this view, every idea, truth, or **thesis** implies an opposing idea or **antithesis.** *Dialectical thinking involves being able to consider both sides of an issue simultaneously* and to be able to accept the existence of contradictions. Dialectical thinking sometimes leads to integrating one's beliefs and experiences with the

Dialectical thinking—the view that every idea implies its opposite; the ability to consider opposing viewpoints simultaneously

Thesis—the principal point or idea

Antithesis—the idea or point directly opposing a stated idea, or thesis

One advantage of getting older is that people develop pragmatic knowledge that we call wisdom.

inconsistencies and contradictions that are discovered, so that a continuously new view evolves. The new view recognizes that answers need to be constantly updated to take into account new information. At each stage, however, the dialectical theorist commits himself or herself to the best that is known, realizing that knowledge and values will change tomorrow. In other words, the unifying premise of dialectical thinking is that change itself is the universal truth.

Not only are adult dialectical thinkers more sensitive to contradictions—and more appreciative of opposing points of view—but also they have learned to live with them. In marriage, dialectical thinkers can appreciate their spouses' viewpoints that are opposite to their own. They have an ability, not common in all people, to evaluate personal, social, and political viewpoints. *Although they can accept contradictions as a basic property of thought, they are sometimes able to synthesize new formulations of ideas that are superior to both opposites.* The result is a continuously evolving view of truths about the world.

Schaie's Stages of Adult Cognitive Development

One of the most interesting models of cognitive development was described by Schaie (1977–1978), who identified five stages people go through in acquiring knowledge and then in making increased use of it.

1. *Acquisitive stage* (childhood and adolescence)—learning information and skills without regard for their usefulness in one's life.
2. *Achieving stage* (late teens to early 20s or 30s)—recognition of the need to apply knowledge to achieve long-term goals.
3. *Responsibility stage* (late 30s to early 60s)—use of cognitive abilities in caring for family, for others on the job, and in the community.
4. *Executive stage* (another stage during the 30s or 40s through middle age)—development of the ability to apply complex knowledge at a number of different levels; becoming responsible for businesses, academic institutions, churches, government, and other organizations.
5. *Reintegrative stage* (late adulthood)—increasingly selective acquisition and application of knowledge to specific tasks: to interests and purposes one thinks have

value; becoming less likely to expend effort to solve problems that have no meaning for them and that they do not personally face.

As can be seen, Schaie emphasized that *people typically switch from acquiring knowledge to applying knowledge in their own lives.*

INTELLIGENCE

Berg & Sterberg (1992) asked 140 adults of various ages to describe their concept of an intelligent person. The dimensions that adults perceived to characterize intelligence during adulthood consisted of an ability to deal with novelty everyday competence and verbal competence. When Alfred Binet addressed the problem of intelligence, he defined it as a general capacity for comprehension, reasoning, judgment, and memory, and he described this capacity as mental age (Binet & Simon, 1916). In England, Charles Spear originated the two-factor theory of intelligence. He concluded that there is a *general intellectual factor*, which he labeled g, and *a number of specific abilities*, which he called s factors, that are useful for different tasks, for example, arithmetic or spatial relations. Gardner (1983) divides intelligence into seven dimensions: linguistic, logical mathematical, spatial, musical, body-kinesthetic, and interpersonal. Gardner objected to measuring people according to some unitary dimension that is called intelligence. Instead, he preferred to think in terms of different intellectual strengths (1983).

Like Gardner, Thurstone (1938) preferred to think of many kinds of intelligence. Thurstone identified distinct *primary mental abilities*, which were tested separately in five subtests. The mental abilities were word fluency, number, reasoning, space, and verbal meaning. Each score represented a different mental ability. Knowledge of primary mental abilities is a useful tool for teachers in planning educational programs, for employers in making a wise selection of workers for particular jobs, and for parents in having a realistic expectation of the capabilities of their children. Scores on intelligence tests, especially when a test is designated as *IQ*, have sometimes been used to label people unfairly, thus working to their disadvantage. However, when used along with results from other types of tests, intellectual measurements can be a useful tool.

Any attempt to measure intelligence with advancing age depends on the types of tests used, their research design, and what they purport to measure. Some intellectual functions increase with age; some peak early and are maintained well into old age; others show decline beginning in early adulthood. Clearly, conclusions regarding changes in intellectual ability will differ, depending on which functions are evaluated. Furthermore, there are increasing differences among individuals as they get older (Albert, Jones, Savage, Berkman, Seeman, Blazer, & Rowe, 1995). Older people are more variable than younger people when it comes to intelligence, thus making it increasingly difficult to categorize older people regarding the level of their intelligence (Morse, 1993).

Scores on the WAIS-III as a Function of Age

The *Wechsler Adult Intelligence Scale (WAIS-III)* is the most widely used measure of adult intelligence (Wechsler, 1981). It includes 11 subtests. Of these, 6 of the tests, *Information, Comprehension, Arithmetic, Similarities, Digit Span,* and *Vocabulary,* comprise the verbal scores. The other 5 tests, *Digit Symbol, Picture Completion, Block Design, Picture Arrangement,* and *Object Assembly,* comprise the performance scores. In general, *verbal scores tend to hold up with increasing age, whereas performance scores tend to decline after the mid-20s.* The decline of performance scores is partially due to a loss of speed and psychomotor coordination (Salthouse, 1992a). Generally speaking, all studies of age-related cognitive slowing indicate that for any given cognitive task at any level of complexity, the response times of older adults are slower than those of young adults (Sliwinski, 1997).

Cross-Sectional Versus Longitudinal Measurements

As discussed in Chapter 1, longitudinal measurements tend to minimize intellectual decline with age, whereas cross-sectional measurements tend to maximize it. However, *longitudinal and cross-sectional measurements both show that verbal scores remain the most stable and that performance scores decline the most* (Wechsler, 1981). Scores on information, vocabulary, and comprehension from the verbal section remain the most stable. Scores on block design, object assembly, and digit symbol from the performance section decline the most with age.

Some longitudinal studies emphasize that intellectual decline of a number of abilities is not inevitable, even by age 50 and over. Extreme care must be taken when interpreting the results of any testing, or faulty conclusions will be drawn (Hayslip & Brookshire, 1985). For example, the health status of elderly samples and the method by which they are recruited may have significant effects on results of research on cognition (Christensen et al., 1992). As the longitudinal research continued, selective subject dropout obscured decline patterns that otherwise might have been present earlier. In general, the elderly subjects who are the healthiest score the highest. These healthiest individuals survive the longest; their scores are higher than those of the subjects who have dropped out along the way. Decline is not apparent until much later in life. As the longitudinal research continues, selective subject dropouts obscure the decline patterns that otherwise might have been present earlier.

Scores on the PMA as a Function of Age

Thurstone's (1949) *Primary Mental Abilities Test (PMA)* is constructed so that scores are derived from 5 subtests: *Word Fluency, Number, Reasoning, Space,* and *Verbal Meaning.* Each score represents a different mental ability relatively unrelated to the others. Schaie & Colleagues in their *Seattle Longitudinal Study* used the PMA to test subjects and make comparisons between cross-sectional and longitudinal results (Schaie et al., 1998). The principal database for this study consisted of more than 5,000 subjects, on whom cognitive and other collateral data were acquired during six major testing cycles (1956, 1963, 1970, 1977, 1984, and 1991). The data from the 1991 testing period present results of cross-sectional comparisons as given in Figure 17.2 (Schaie, 1994; Schaie et al., 1998). The cross-sectional data showed two different patterns: (1) Three of the abilities peak in young adulthood and show linearly accelerated age differences that are steepest for *Spatial Orientation* and *Inductive Reasoning,* but are less pronounced for *Word Fluency.* (2) *Verbal Meaning* and *Number* peak in midlife. However, *Verbal Meaning,* at somewhat speeded tests, begins to show negative age differences by early old age, whereas *Number* has an almost level age-differences profile through adulthood.

The longitudinal gradients in Figure 17.3 show at least modest gain for all abilities from young adulthood to early middle age. However, there remain differences among abilities with respect to the attainment of peak age as well as the degree to which age-changes accelerate with advance in age. The longitudinal data collected over thirty-five years indicate that average age decrements in psychometric ability cannot be reliably confirmed prior to age 60, except for *Word Fluency*, which shows a significant decline by age 53. However, reliable average decrement is indeed found for all abilities by age 67. This decrement is modest until the 80s are reached, and for most individuals, it is not a linear phenomenon that occurs in a stair-step fashion. Even at age 81, fewer than one-half of all observed individuals showed reliable decrements over the preceding seven years (Schaie, 1994; Schaie et al., 1998).

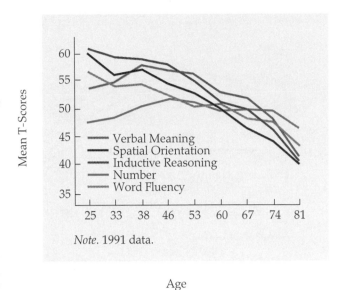

Note. 1991 data.

FIGURE 17.2   Cross-sectional mean T-scores for single markers of the primary mental abilities.

From "The Course of Adult Intellectual Development," by K. W. Schaie, 1994, *American Psychologist, 49,* 1–9.

Fluid and Crystallized Intelligence

Horn and Cattell (1967) felt that the reason that studies of the kinds made by Schaie and Labouvie-Vief (1974) show a plateau in intelligence test scores during the early adult years is that the studies do not separate the data for *fluid* and *crystallized intelligence. Horn and Cattell found that fluid intelligence declined after age 14 and that the sharpest decline came in early adulthood.* The decline in fluid intelligence was evidenced by poorer performance on tests requiring abstract thinking, inductive reasoning, relational thinking, and short-term memory, and on tests requiring figural classification, analogy, and the completion of logical series. Horn and Cattell also reported that *at least 20 studies, both cross-sectional and longitudinal, showed increases in crystallized intelligence through adulthood.* They reasoned that learning through experience and acculturation continues for many years. Therefore, intelligence, defined as knowledge, increases until at least age 60. However, when the scores on the tests for both fluid and crystallized intelligence were combined, the composite intelligence score remained substantially the same or increased very slightly from age 14 to 60.

The same is not true for the elderly over age 70. The cognitive test performance of 897 community-dwelling elderly subjects, aged 70 years and older, was examined for age trends and interindividual variations in intelligence. Over the age span sampled, crystallized intelligence, fluid intelligence, and memory all decreased, with the decrease being the greatest for fluid intelligence and the least for crystallized intelligence. These findings give support to the view that even crystallized intelligence begins to decline in the very old and that there is a greater degree of variability in test performance with advancing age (Christensen, MacKinnon, Jorn, Henderson, Scott, & Korten, 1994).

Schaie (1978) did not accept Horn and Cattell's arguments as valid, because the data were based on cross-sectional studies. He felt that *the apparent decline in fluid intelligence was due to generational differences:* Older subjects were more poorly educated and had less exposure to intellectual stimulation and fewer opportunities to grow during their lifetime than did the younger subjects (Cockburn & Smith, 1991). The increase in crystallized intelligence could be expected because a greater number and variety of life experiences would increase their knowledge over many years.

Taken together, these findings show that the measurement of intelligence is a complex undertaking and that it is difficult to sort out age-related differences from other causes. Whether intellectual capabilities change depends a lot on what is measured and how (Cornelius, 1984). Some intellectual functions decline; others improve. But the two-

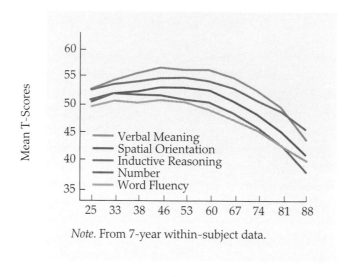

Note. From 7-year within-subject data.

Age

FIGURE 17.3 Longitudinal estimates of mean T-scores for single markers of the primary mental abilities.

From "The Course of Adult Intellectual Development," by K. W. Schaie, 1994, *American Psychologist, 49,* 1–9.

factor model of Cattell and Horn, helpful as it is, may oversimplify the complexity of intellectual change over the life span.

Criticisms

The WAIS and other tests have been criticized primarily on the basis that they are not relevant for the purposes for which the tests are used. Scores on the WAIS can be converted into IQ, using a table in the test manual. But *IQ is only one important factor necessary to carry out responsible tasks.* To succeed, a successful businessperson needs drive and motivation, social adeptness, courage, patience, self-confidence, practical wisdom, organizational and administrative ability, and a variety of skills, in addition to intelligence. People should not be selected for a job on the basis of intelligence alone. It would be a mistake to assume that people of any age could be successfully evaluated for responsibility only by test scores.

Another criticism of adult intelligence tests is that the test items are *more familiar to children or very young adults* than to older adults. When tests are constructed comprising practical information items related more to the needs of adults, scores rise through the middle and older adult years. Furthermore, intelligence tests show a *cultural and economic bias.* They are more suited to middle-class adults than to minorities and low socioeco-

nomic groups, who tend to score poorly because they are unfamiliar with the vocabulary and examples used.

The original WAIS (1955) is outdated and no longer used. It was tested originally on only a very small adult sample. The new, revised WAIS (1981) was tested on a much larger adult sample and is an improvement over the original.

IQ can be quite misleading. It does not measure innate capacity; it measures the score on a test at a particular time with reference to one's own age group. Thus, an IQ of 100 at age 50 indicates an average level of performance relative to other adults the same age. But the 50-year-old person actually has performed less well than a 20-year-old person, because an age correction is added to the score. The older person is given a handicap in expectation that his or her score will decline.

Factors Affecting Scores

How, by whom, to whom, and under what circumstances tests are administered can affect scores. Adults score better if test items are *relevant* to their daily lives. For example, the Block Design subtest of the WAIS-III requires the rearranging of assorted red and white blocks according to a design on a printed card, while the examiner checks a stopwatch. If adults find this activity irrelevant, their scores will be lower than on tests that they consider more meaningful. Motivation may affect an older adult's performance, particularly if the tasks are meaningless and unfamiliar (Dickerson & Fisher, 1997). Generally speaking, the more complex the task, the greater the adult age differences in scores (Salthouse, 1992b).

Other factors, such as the *degree of motivation,* affect performance. Such *personality traits* as cautiousness, rigidity, or dogmatism negatively affect test scores. Self-confidence can improve scores, as can experience and practice in taking tests. *Physical factors* such as physical fitness, lower limb strength, activity level, cardiovascular health, brain functioning, overall health (Hultsch, Hammer, & Small, 1993; Perlmutter & Nyquist, 1990), sleep, eyesight, hearing, motor ability, and reaction time are especially important on subtests measuring performance (Manton, Siegler, & Woodbury, 1986). Sensory functioning, especially visual and auditory acuity, is a strong late-life predictor of individual differences in intellectual functioning (Lindenberger & Baltes, 1994). Research has generally found that high blood pressure may

Heart Disease and Intelligence

The *Duke Longitudinal Study of Aging* sought to demonstrate a relationship between heart disease and brain impairment of aged persons (Wang & Busse, 1974). Figure 17.4 shows the relationship between heart disease and WAIS verbal and performance scores (Wang & Busse,

1974). Verbal and performance scores were significantly higher for persons with no heart disease than for those with compensated heart disease (those who have received remedial treatment) or decompensated heart disease. This difference in scores was due partly to the

fact that subjects with heart disease were slightly older than those without. When age, race, and education differences were considered, however, WAIS scores of the diseased group were still slightly lower, particularly on performance tests.

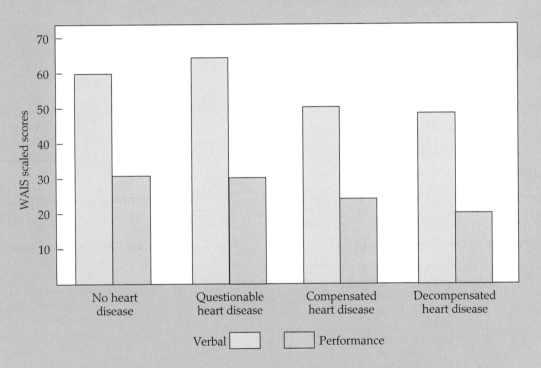

FIGURE 17.4 Mean WAIS verbal and performance scaled scores.

From "Heart Disease and Brain Impairment Among Aged Persons," by H. S. Wang and E. W. Busse, 1974, in *Normal Aging II: Reports from the Duke Longitudinal Studies*, 1970–73. E. Palmore, Ed. Durham, NC: Duke University Press. Copyright © 1974 by Duke University Press. Reprinted with permission.

have a negative effect on intellectual functioning (Sands & Meredith, 1992), as does expiratory volume (Salthouse, Hambrick, & McGuthry, 1998).

Furthermore, *emotional factors* such as low morale, depression, learning apprehension, and tension may result in lower scores. One study showed that *hypertension* (Elias, Robbins, Schultz, & Pierce, 1990) had a more negative effect on the WAIS-III scores of young adults than on the scores of older subjects (Schultz, Elias, Robbins, Streeten, &

Blakeman, 1986). One explanation for the decline of cognitive functioning of the aged, particularly verbal comprehension, is a decline in *hearing acuity*. Even a slight hearing loss imposes handicaps in receiving and understanding verbal messages. Many older people show poor intelligibility of fast speech and low-volume speech. Research has shown a fairly clear-cut relationship between auditory acuity and a decline in level of cognitive functioning (Sands & Meredith, 1989).

The relationship between the test administrator and the test takers also affects performance. In general, the administrator who develops good rapport, puts subjects at ease, and offers supportive comments can maximize test performance. *General intellectual level and years of school completed* are also related to test performance. People with superior intelligence and education either show little decline or show improvement, at least to age 60. Those of average intelligence and low educational level show increasingly poorer performance between 40 and 60.

Personality, Behavior, and Mental Abilities

To what extent is the decline in intellectual functioning with age related to personality factors? Unfortunately, only limited objective information is available to answer this question. Part of the problem is the difficulty of classifying and measuring personality types and trying to describe personality changes with age.

Emotional Health

In general, there is a positive relationship between mental health and cognitive ability. The emotionally healthy seem to show less cognitive decline with age than the emotionally ill. The extreme example is the seriously depressed person whose severe withdrawal precludes any type of testing. Kleban and associates (1976) found that in comparison with subjects exhibiting declines in functioning levels, stable subjects comprehended their situations better (more awareness, coherence, verbalization, better memory), were more socially reactive, manifested fewer neurotic conditions, and had greater control over impulses and aggression.

Personality Types

Personality indirectly affects intellectual functioning by influencing life cycle changes. People who are more open and imaginative, outgoing and highly interactive socially, more open to new ideas, curious, and highly motivated to learn are likely to accumulate a great variety of cognitive experiences over a lifetime. Therefore, they score higher on measures dependent on accumulated knowledge and abilities, such as crystallized intelligence measures. If the elderly show negative personality changes with old age, becoming short-tempered, stubborn, or suspicious, these qualities cause maladaptations that are often accompanied by distinct intellectual decline. Sometimes organic brain pathologies underlie such personality changes.

Cautiousness and Rigidity

Individuals become more cautious with advancing age. They take longer to answer questions on cognitive tests because they want to avoid mistakes. As their response time increases, they do progressively worse on timed tests. But, conversely, cautiousness in later life may be a function of intellectual decline, making either interpretation tenable.

Rigidity, or resistance to change, may have a negative effect on changes in one's ideas, attitudes, habits, and tasks. The rigid person refuses to relinquish attitudes, opinions, or tasks, despite plentiful evidence that this persistence is wrong or unrewarding.

There is no such thing as global rigidity, that is, inflexibility in all aspects of one's personality or life. The notion that one's whole being or lifestyle can be characterized as rigid or inflexible is not supported by research results. There are a variety of rigidities. An engineer who is very rigid in his ideas of marital roles can be very open-minded about the results of his scientific research. And a person with inflexible habits may show tolerance to new ideas.

The statement that rigidity increases with age is simplistic. Rigid behavior in older people tends to be marginal. Many studies that indicate increasing rigidity with age fail to differentiate among other deficits in cognitive performance. For example, older people have difficulty shifting from one task to another, but this is partially because of slowness and the increased time that they need to switch tasks. This slowness results in higher rigidity scores. When the elderly are given step-by-step instructions regarding which function to perform next, their slowness in shift performance is minimized, and they score higher.

Some studies also fail to consider cultural change factors. Cross-sectional studies comparing older and younger subjects show the former to be more rigid. But longitudinal studies fail to show consistent results or extensive rigidity (Schaie & Labouvie-Vief, 1974). Thus, rigidity may or may not be intrinsic to maturational age changes. Rigidity is influenced greatly by intelligence and educational level. *The person with more intelligence and education will exhibit less rigidity.*

Expectations

The maintenance of intellectual abilities with advancing age depends partly on what people expect will happen. Those who believe they are becoming senile, whether they are or not, who believe they can't remember or learn, and who make little effort to find intellectual stimulation, may find their expectations have become self-fulfilling prophecy. They become less competent because of disuse, not because of any changes inherent in the aging process itself. Elderly people can often greatly improve their intellectual abilities if they can become convinced that cognitive loss is not inevitable (Perlmutter, 1987).

Socioenvironmental Effects

Stimulating Environment

Older adults who are exposed to intellectually stimulating environments maintain a higher level of cognitive ability with increasing age than those who are not. Social contacts with family, friends, social groups, or at work; interesting activities that provide a variety of experiences in different settings; and opportunities to look at books, magazines, art, or television all help maintain cognitive powers. A person who is isolated from other people, with little opportunity for meaningful interpersonal contacts, becomes generally divorced from social interaction. In all probability, that person's mental abilities will evidence decline.

Educational Level and Socioeconomic Status

People with high education levels and superior socioeconomic status show less decline in cognitive abilities with age, especially verbal abilities, than do those with less education and lower socioeconomic status. Superior education and socioeconomic status are both causes and effects. The most educated people have superior intellectual abilities to start with, as measured by intelligence tests. This characteristic is true regardless of age. In fact, educational level is as important to intellectual functioning as is age. Those with high status and education are more likely to maintain an active interest in learning and to remain involved in various rewarding activities. They also have more opportunities and resources to participate. As a result, they manifest fewer signs of mental deterioration in old age (Inouye, Albert, Mohs, Sun, & Berkman, 1993). In fact, they may show improvement, at least to age 60. Although they decline in perceptual-integrative abilities and in performance functions, the extent of the decline is not enough to reduce them to the level of their less intellectually capable age peers.

Older adults with a high level of education are likely to maintain an active interest in learning.

Life Crises and Stress

Mental deterioration is also related to the frequency and intensity of people's life crises. The greater and more frequent the stress, the greater the probability of mental deterioration. Amster and Krauss (1974) found that elderly females from 65 to 95 who showed mental deterioration had been exposed to almost twice as many crises as the women in a control group who showed no deterioration.

Training

Efforts have been made to improve the cognitive abilities of older adults through training (Dittmann-Kohli, Lachman, Kliegl, & Baltes, 1991). Such efforts reflect the philosophy that reduced intellectual performance is an experiential or performance deficit that can be reduced by training in certain component skills. However, current opinion emphasizes that the extent to which different intellectual abilities are trainable differs markedly, depending on the degree to which abilities represent the effects of acculturation or of the individual's biological-maturational well-being. Those abilities most dependent on acculturation, such as the components of crystallized intelligence, are considered the most trainable.

To show, however, that other abilities may also be trainable, Labouvie-Vief and Gonda (1976) attempted to improve the scores of 60 females, ages 63 to 95, in solving complex problems requiring inductive reasoning. The results showed that training could produce significant increments in intellectual performance of the elderly, even with skills linked primarily with biological-maturational factors (i.e., fluid intelligence). Plemons and associates (1978) tried to determine to what extent fluid intelligence could be modified in subjects aged 59 to 85. A training program was devised to enhance the figural relations component to fluid intelligence. Posttraining assessments after one week, one month, and six months showed improved performance as a result of training. This improvement carried over to other tasks related to fluid intelligence. These significant findings suggest that *intellectual performance on fluid intelligence tests is more modifiable through short-term intervention than traditionally assumed* (Blackburn, Papalia-Finlay, Foye, & Serlin, 1988).

Several studies have also shown that *scores on performance-type tests requiring speed and motor coordination can also be improved with practice* (Grant, Storandt, & Botwinick, 1978). The Digit Symbol Substitution subtest of the WAIS was administered to older women (mean age 69) and to younger women (mean age 23) on each of 5 training days. The older women improved substantially, but equally large gains were made by the younger women. Therefore, age differences were not reduced by training when both groups were trained. However, as a result of training, scores of the older women on this subtest increased from the 19th to the 25th percentile, relative to norms for young adults in general. These scores were maintained during a follow-up test 10 days later.

The notion that adults cannot or will not learn, or that little can be done about the decline of cognitive abilities, is fallacious. The fact that a variety of performance deficits typically observed in the elderly are amenable to intervention suggests that *adult cognitive functioning can be more proficient if adequate environmental support is provided.* Moreover, the degree of plasticity revealed in intervention studies (Baltes & Schaie, 1976) has contributed to a deeper, more positive understanding of adult cognitive potential.

Berlin Aging Study

The *Berlin Aging Study* documents age trends and interrelations, and also correlates intellectual ability in the old and the very old (ages 70 to 103 years). Fourteen tests were used to assess five abilities. Three of them, reasoning, memory, and perpetual speed, were from the mechanic (broad fluid) domain; and the other two, knowledge and fluency, were from the pragmatic (broad crystallized) domain. Intellectual abilities had negative linear age relations, with more pronounced age reductions in mechanics than in pragmatic abilities. Interrelations among intellectual abilities were highly positive and did not follow the mechanic-pragmatic distinction. Sociobiographical indicators were less closely linked to intellectual functioning and sensorimotor variables, which predicted 59% of the total reliable variance in general intelligence. Results suggested that age-induced biological factors are a prominent source of individual differences in intelligence in old and very old age. Thus, both sociobiographical factors and mental biological factors are significantly related to intelligence in general and to knowledge in particular (Lindenberger & Baltes, 1997).

INFORMATION PROCESSING

Another important aspect of cognitive development is broadening the ability to process information. This involves exposure to information, learning, remembering, and utilization of these in helpful ways.

Memory

What Memory Involves

The ability to remember is basic to all learning and to intellectual and social functioning. It is also basic to making sound judgments (Moser, 1992). Stated very simply, this fact means that people make sounder judgments when they are able to remember both the pros and the cons of a discussion (MacLeod & Campbell, 1992).

One group of researchers divided memory into *prospective memory* and *retrospective memory*. Retrospective memory is memory for past events, for example, remembering the contents of a newspaper article or someone's name. Many memory studies measure retrospective memory. Prospective memory is memory for activities to be performed in the future, for example, remembering to give someone a message or to keep an appointment (Einstein, Smith, McDaniel, & Shaw (1997). Obviously, prospective memory is extremely important in everyday functioning (Einstein, Holland, McDaniel, & Guynn, 1992).

Studies of memory during adulthood are extremely important because they enable us to determine what happens to this basic process throughout the adult life cycle. All studies of memory recognize three basic processes: **acquisition, storage,** and **retrieval** (Holland & Rabbitt, 1992).

The process of acquisition begins with exposure to stimuli so that information can be learned. The process involves making an impression on memory receptors and registering and recording information. Acquisition is the learning or input phase of memory. Unless something is acquired, it cannot be remembered.

In the process of storage, information is cycled, processed, organized, rehearsed, and stored until needed.

In the process of retrieval, stored information is obtained by searching, finding, and remembering, either through recall or recognition.

Memory efficiency depends on all three of these processes. Loss of memory represents a decline with advancing age. This is true whether learning is measured in terms of speed (Hertzog, Raskind, & Cannon, 1986) or by the amount revealed or recognized. When younger adults (20 to 39 years) were compared with older adults (60 to 83 years), the older adults were not as efficient in reading and were not able to answer comprehension questions as successfully as younger adults; moreover, they were not able to retrieve as much information when asked explicitly for recall from a text (Hartley, Stojack, Mushaney, Annon, & Lee, 1994). The older that people become, the more likely they are to show age-dependent deficits. Age-related differences in memory for facts, their source, and contextual details decline over time to a greater extent in the elderly than in the young.

However, there are many exceptions to this generalization (Rebok, Montaglione, & Bendlin, 1988). *Age-related differences may not be great.* If ample time is given for registering, assimilating, coding, categorizing, rehearsing, and reinforcing short-term holdings, many older persons do as well as or better than younger ones (Bowles, 1994). A decline in basic processing efficiency that affects memory is slow (Bieman-Copland & Charness, 1994). Much depends on the neuropsychological health of the subjects being tested (Moehle & Long, 1989; Parkin & Walter, 1992). In one national health survey, only 15% of adults age 55 and over reported having trouble remembering things during the past year. About 36% indicated having no trouble at all (Cutler & Grams, 1988). Most elderly adults feel that they are not at all handicapped by forgetfulness (Erber & Rothberg, 1991; Sunderland, Watts, Baddeley, & Harris, 1986).

One study investigated the speed of information processing as a mediator between age and free-recall performance in young adults (age 21) and older adults (age 73). Participants were required to encode three lists of words for immediate recall by rehearsing the words aloud one, twice, and three times. Participants' speed of information processing was assessed. Working memory was also recorded. As predicted, younger adults recalled more words after rehearsing words three times rather than once, whereas older adults' recall did not increase with increasing numbers of rehearsals. The age differences in recall performance appear to be mediated by speed of processing. Even when older adults engage in the same number of rehearsals as do younger adults, the recall performance does not match that of younger adults. Furthermore, younger adults' recall performance increased with increasing numbers of rehearsals, whereas the older adults did not. This finding is consistent with the hypothesis that faster processing leads to better memory performance than does that of slower processing. Also, this finding can explain why increased study time often fails to compensate for age differences in memory performance (Bryan & Luszcz, 1996).

There may be considerable difference between laboratory tests of memory and the actual ability to exercise memory functions in everyday life. Laboratory tests of speed of search in short-term memory, memory span, missed recall, paired-associate recall, and prose recall showed that age difference may be quite large, depending on the task. However, the laboratory memory tasks mentioned here may be only loosely predictive of everyday memory functioning. Salient everyday memory tasks, such as retrieving the name of some vague acquaintance, buying all items needed on a shopping trip, making sure not to forget to post that letter, keeping appointments, or remembering who is who in a Tolstoy novel may be only loosely related to the aspects of memory discussed here (Berhaeghen, Marcoen, & Goossens, 1993).

Part of memory ability is inherited. Data from the *Minnesota Twin Study of Adult Development and Aging* (Finkel & McGue, 1993) and from the *Swedish Adoption Twin Study of Aging* (Pedersen, Plomin, Nesselroade, & McClearn, 1992) revealed that there was no significant differences in the inheritability of memory performance across cohorts. This finding means that there was no suggestion that environmental influences on memory increased to a significant extent across age cohorts. The influence of heredity measured

Acquisition—the process by which information is recorded, encoded, and stored

Storage—the process by which acquired information is put away for later use

Retrieval—the process of recalling or of being able to remember or recognize information that has been stored

the same in comparing younger, middle-aged, and older twins within each study (Finkel, Pedersen, & McGue, 1995).

Sensory Memory

Sensory memory abilities of older adults depend partially on the extent to which their sensory receptors are functioning at normal levels. Those who show some decrement in visual or auditory functioning cannot be expected to remember what they have not acquired. Less information is passed from sensory to short-term stores.

Information received by the senses is held very briefly in one of several specific sensory stores. For example, auditory information is held in an *auditory sensory store*, and visual information is held in a *visual sensory store*. The auditory sensory store is referred to as **echoic memory,** and the visual sensory store as **iconic memory.** Other sensory stores include those for tactual information and for smell.

Most investigations of visual or iconic memory have shown a rapid decay in less than a second. But other studies have confirmed that the durability of a memory trace depends on how intensively the stimulus was presented and how deeply it was processed (Gilmore, Allan, & Royer, 1986). Studies of auditory, or echoic, memory as contrasted to visual, or iconic, memory and **tactual memory** show variable results (Zacks, Hasher,

Echoic memory—the auditory sensory store

Iconic memory—the visual sensory store

Tactual memory—memory of touch

Doren, Hamm, & Attig, 1987). *All three sensory memory stores show some decline with age, but tactual memory seems to decline the fastest.* Figure 17.5 shows the average performances of groups of volunteers divided on the basis of age decades. *Visual sensory memory did not decline much before age 50 but did so fairly rapidly after that.* It also declined after 60, whereas auditory memory did not. This situation is particularly true in older subjects if any interference or disruption occurs while the stimuli are being presented. Visual memory tasks require close attention while the images are being presented; auditory inputs can be heard and held briefly whether they are attended to or not.

However, *the durability of an audio memory trace depends on the attention given it when heard, and therefore the depth at which the stimulus is processed* (Wingfield, Lahar, & Stine, 1989). When attention is diverted during a stimulus, older subjects in particular remember less because the information is processed less deeply (Allen, Madden, Webber, & Crozier, 1992). Thus, if they are asked to listen to two things at once, or to hold some information while reporting other information, or to receive some input while recalling and reporting information previously given, older subjects tend to concentrate on only one task. Performance on the other task deteriorates badly. Older subjects are penalized more when they must divide their attention.

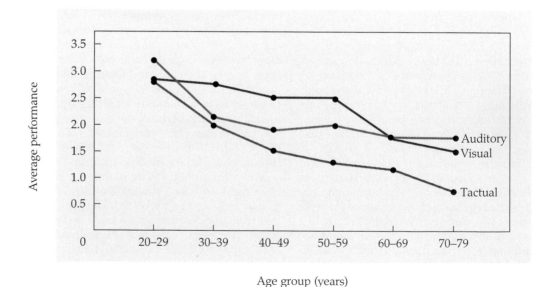

FIGURE 17.5   Average performances on nonverbal recognition tests, by age group.

Adapted from "Age Differences in Nonverbal Memory Tasks," by W. H. Riege and V. Inman, January 1991, *Journal of Gerontology, 36,* pp. 51–58. Copyright 1981 by The Gerontological Society. Adapted by permission of the publisher.

Short-Term, or Primary, Memory

There is some confusion in various studies about the difference between short-term and long-term memory. One helpful distinction was given by Waugh and Norman (1965). They used the terms **primary memory (PM)** and **secondary memory (SM).** Primary memory, considered synonymous with short-term memory, involves information still being rehearsed and focused on in one's conscious mind. Secondary memory, or long-term memory, is characterized by how deeply the information has been processed, not by how long the information has been held. Deep processing, in which perceived information has been passed into layers of memory below the conscious level, constitutes secondary memory (Allen, 1993). For example, when a subject memorizes a word list, the words under immediate consideration are at the primary, or short-term, memory stage. Words already looked at, memorized, and tucked away are at the secondary, or long-term, memory level, even though they were learned only a short time before. Specific words recalled several days or months later are recalled from secondary memory. Secondary memory can last for 30 seconds or for years. The terms *primary* and *secondary* memory are used synonymously in this discussion with short-term and long-term memory, even though some secondary memory stores may be recalled after relatively short time intervals.

In measuring primary memory, the subject is presented a short string of digits, letters, or words and then tested for the total that can be recalled immediately. When measured in this way, *primary memory span does not change with age, or it decreases only slightly,* unless ability has been seriously impaired by physical deterioration (Kausler, Wiley, & Lieberwitz, 1992).

Long-Term, or Secondary, Memory

Many studies show that *older subjects perform less well than younger subjects when secondary memory is involved* (Allen & Coyne, 1989; Guttentag & Hunt, 1988). For example, if subjects are asked to recall a list of 12 to 30 words in any order, no age differences appear in the recall of the last four items (retrieved from primary memory). However, older subjects recall fewer words from the beginning and middle of the list, where secondary memory is involved.

It should not be assumed, however, that aging always brings memory deficits (Erber, 1989). Many factors can eliminate age differences. Overall *verbal ability* is a better predictor of prose recall than is age (Rice & Meyer,

1986). *Material organized, categorized, or associated* with what is already familiar is remembered more readily, because acquisition is enhanced (Hess, Flanagan, & Tate, 1993; Wingfield, Aberdeen, & Stine, 1991). Also, if a list of words is presented in one category (for example, animals), age differences in recall are slight, suggesting that grouping words under one concept offers cues that enhance retrieval (Allen & Crozier, 1992). Retrieval is also enhanced if the *same cues* are given at retrieval as given when the material was learned (Gerard, Zacks, Hasher, & Radvansky, 1991; Puglisi, Park, Smith, & Dudley, 1988; Taylor, 1992). Furthermore, other *studies have shown greater age losses in free recall than in recognition performance* (Backman & Larsson, 1992), suggesting that retrieval from storage without any cues constitutes a special problem for older subjects (Fisher & McDowd, 1993; McEvoy, Nelson, Holley, & Stelnicki, 1992). Recognition does not require retrieval, because cues are given, so that smaller age decrements are found in recognition than in recall. Figure 17.6 shows age-related differences in recall and recognition.

Older subjects are at their greatest disadvantage when materials to be learned are meaningless or unfamiliar, or cannot be associated with what is already known (Hess & Flannagan, 1992). For example, it is more difficult to remember nonsense syllables than meaningful words. Similarly, if random materials can be sorted out or arranged in some logical order, such as alphabetically, they are easier to remember. However, *general recall ability decreases with age.*

Facial recognition memory also declines across the adult life span, with significant decline sometimes seen as early as 50 years of age (Crook & Larrabee, 1992; Maylor & Valentine, 1992). One study of subjects over 50 years of age found that the ability to recognize and name tunes on television programs declined with increased age (Maylor, 1991).

The spatial memory of older adults, measured by being asked to remember object location, depends partly on how meaningful are the objects that they are expected to remember (Cherry & Park, 1989; Sharps & Gollin, 1988) and on the total context in which the objects are placed (Denney, Miller, Dew, & Levav, 1991). In general, however, memory for spatial information declines over age in adulthood (Bowling & Browne, 1991). One study showed an age-related decline in spatial memory performance and placed the onset of this decline in the sixth decade of life (Uttl & Graf, 1993).

Primary memory—short-term memory

Secondary memory—long-term memory

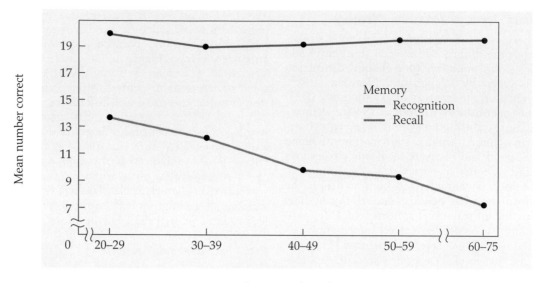

FIGURE 17.6   Mean recall and recognition scores as a function of age.

Adapted from "Memory Changes with Age," by D. Schonfield, 1965, *Nature 28*, p. 918. Reprinted by permission from *Nature*, Vol. 28, p. 918. Copyright © 1965 Macmillan Magazines Limited.

Three Kinds of Long-Term Memory

There appear to be three kinds of long-term memory storage, each with distinctly different properties, and each probably based on different brain mechanisms.

1. **Procedural memory** is memory for skills and other procedures. Our memories show us how to ride a bike, to cook, or to kiss. These are procedural memories.
2. **Semantic memory** is memory for meaning. We remember what a father is, what ice cream is, and what the phrase "peace of mind" means.
3. **Episodic memory** is the kind of long-term memory that stores information about specific experiences that took place at specific times and in specific places (Luszez, Bryan, & Kent (1997).

Most adults are able to store procedural and semantic memories quite effectively, but long-term memory handles episodic information less well. It has been documented that age-related changes in memory are found primarily in episodic tasks, with little or no differences found in either semantic or procedural memory (Brown & Mitchell, 1991).

False Recall

Recently there has been increasing interest in whether or not memories of childhood experience can suddenly be recalled after being buried for a number of years. This question

is especially important in a situation in which an adult has been accused of something, such as abuse of children. Are the children able to bury this memory, only to have it suddenly arise at a particular time later in their lives? Usually something happens that brings this early memory to light. Some researchers have found that reviewing photographs of events seen earlier in a videotaping increases the likelihood of both younger and older adults' remembering specific details from the reviewed event (Schacter, Koutstaal, Johnson, Gross, & Angell, 1997).

In general, memory can achieve extremely high levels of accuracy, but people are sometimes susceptible to a variety of memory distortions and illusions. Several studies suggested that elderly adults may be especially prone to false memories. For example, older adults are sometimes more likely than younger adults to claim mistakenly that a recently seen nonfamous name or face is famous. The aged are more prone to the distorting influences of postevent suggestion than are younger adults. For example, in a courtroom, a lawyer may suggest to an older adult that he or she has seen a particular event happen, and then the older adult begins to have doubts about his or her testimony and may suggest that he or she actually thinks that the event did happen. Older adults often have trouble remembering the source of recently acquired information, thus likely making them more susceptible to false recognition than younger adults. Most older adults do not deliberately

Procedural memory

Semantic memory

Episodic memory

construct totally false memories of events that never happened; rather, they sometimes confuse the origin of distinct events that did happen, thereby leading to an incorrect or false claim of recognition.

Memory Training

Can training improve the memory of older adults (Menich & Baron, 1990)? Evidence indicates that it can (Hill, Storandt, & Simeone, 1990; LeBreck & Baron, 1987; Verhaegen, Marcoen, & Goossens, 1992). Fortunately, memory function does appear to retain plasticity, and numerous studies have demonstrated the efficacy of memory strategies (mnemonics) training in improving memory functions in older adults (Floyd & Scogin, 1997). Using this approach, the typical training program involves teaching in mnemonic strategy, such as the method of loci, and administering both objective and subjective measures of memory performance. Improvement is determined by the analysis of the difference between the pretraining and post-training scores of the participants or the difference between treatment and control groups. Objective measures of memory ability include tasks such as paired-associates and word-list recall. Subjective measures involve the use of self-report questionnaires to elicit the participants' evaluation of their memory functioning. Recall ability, in particular, can be improved if adults are trained in such recall strategies as repetition, association, and categorical material arrangement. In one experiment, training classes were held weekly for 4 weeks, during which institutionalized adults, 60 to 89 years of age, were exposed to 90-minute training sessions (Zarit, Cole, & Guider, 1981). At the end of the training, retesting revealed considerable improvement in their ability to recall related items, names, and faces, and unrelated items. No improvement was found in the recall of paragraph material or in recognition performance. Training did cause some decline in subject complaints about their memory ability, regardless of whether performance improved. This finding indicates that elderly complaints about memory may not be related objectively to actual memory decrements (Taylor, Miller, & Tinklenberg, 1992). Overall, adults with good memory self-perceptions anticipate better memory performance, and this anticipation increases competency (Ryan, 1992).

Learning to remember depends partially on the ability to give one's undivided attention to the task at hand. When attention is divided at encoding, memory performance

suffers relative to full attention conditions. Divided attention disrupts strategic encoding processes that take place in learning and memory, and these encoding processes require close attention (Anderson, Craik, & Naveh-Benjamin, 1998).

Learning

Most people maintain the ability to learn through adulthood. Such capacity is vitally necessary because each new event in an adult's life requires new knowledge and abilities. Getting married, becoming parents, assuming a new job, moving to another house or community, retiring, and adjusting to a rapidly changing world all require learning.

Learning and Memory

Learning and memory are inextricably intertwined. Unless individuals learn well, they have little to recall. Conversely, if their

FOCUS

Spatial Cognition and Neighborhood Use

With the rise in the number of people over the age of 65 living in the United States, it becomes increasingly important for the older people in the population to remain independent and community-dwelling as long as possible. One of the factors that contribute to an older person's ability to live independently is his or her continued use of neighborhood resources (shops, services, recreational facilities, and so forth).

However, the ability to use neighborhood resources has been found to depend on a number of factors. Overall, the results of one study indicate that spatial cognitive ability makes a practical difference in older adults' use of their neighborhoods. This study found four direct predictors and one indirect predictor of neighborhood use. The number of years that a person had lived in the neighborhood and the person's mobility predicted neighborhood use. An important finding of this study was that no-context placement, a laboratory test of special cognition, directly predicted the subjects' use of their neighborhood. Furthermore, the no-context placement test was a better predictor of the subjects' use of their neighborhoods than either the number of years that they had lived there or their mobility. The indirect predictor of neighborhood was the ETS Building Memory Task. This test taps the ability to remember the spatial location and orientation of objects. The ETS Building Memory Task predicted neighborhood knowledge that, in turn, was predictive of the participants' neighborhood use. These results suggest that training designed to increase the ability of older adults to learn and to remember spatial relationships could increase their ability to make use of their neighborhoods (Simon, Walsh, Regnier, & Krauss, 1992).

Living Issues

Do Men Show More Age-Associated Memory Decline Than Women?

Recent magnetic resonance imaging data suggest that men show more rapid age-associated atrophy of the left hemisphere of the brain than do women. But research suggests that although gender-based differences in the rate of left-hemisphere structural decline may occur with normal aging, this decline apparently does not translate into differential functional decline in simulated everyday verbal memory (Larrabee & Crook, 1993).

Learning is a lifelong process.

Paired-associate learning— learning to make associations between pairs of items

Serial learning tasks— learning items in a list in the exact order of presentation

Intrinsic motivation— motivation coming directly from physical and psychological needs

Extrinsic motivation— motivation influenced by external rewards

memory is poor, they cannot learn much. Learning is the acquisition of knowledge; memory is the storage, processing, and retrieval of knowledge. Each ability depends on the other.

A distinction must be made between learning as an internal process and performance as an external act. If performance declines, we assume, often incorrectly, that learning has decreased. Performance, not learning ability, may decline because of many environmental factors, lack of motivation, or psychological disturbances. Before making definitive statements about changes in learning ability as one ages, it is necessary to sort out factors that affect performance. Much of what was previously regarded as learning ability deficiency in later life is now seen as a problem in the ability to express learned information—as a difficulty older people have in adapting to a task and demonstrating what they know. There is little disagreement regarding performance declines in later life, but controversy exists about the extent to which learning ability declines with age.

Verbal Learning Research

Verbal learning research uses two different types of tasks: **paired-associate learning** and **serial learning tasks.** In paired-associate learning tasks, subjects must learn associations between pairs of verbal items (for example, *book-car*), and then be able to supply the correct word to complete the pair when a particular stimulus word is given. Paired-associate verbal learning ability is measured by the number of trials required for perfect recitation, or for reaching a designated level of proficiency, or by the number of errors made per trial (Rogers & Gilbert, 1997).

In serial learning tasks, subjects must learn a list of simple words, usually in the exact order presented. Learning ability is measured by the number of errors per trial or by the number of trials required for one or more perfect recitations of the list (Howard & Howard, 1992).

Learning is also sometimes measured by divided-attention situations. These are situations in which two or more stimuli are presented to the subject at once, and he or she is subsequently asked to remember what had been heard or seen (Tun, Wingfield, Stine, & Mecsas, 1992). Obviously, being able to remember something means having been able to focus on that which one wants to remember (Madden, Pierce, & Allen, 1992).

Motivation, Relevance, Meaning

Every teacher knows that the desire to learn (the degree of motivation) is an important key to success. **Intrinsic motivation** comes from within, from physical and psychological drives. Thus, a person who has an emotional need to excel is driven to learn; so is a person who learns to achieve status. These people are driven by personal needs for ego satisfaction, and they strive harder than those who have lesser needs and desires.

Motivation is also enhanced through outside incentives (**extrinsic motivation**). The promise of promotion or increased financial rewards, or even verbal praise, may stimulate greater efforts. However, no amount of incentive works unless the subjects feel that the rewards are attainable. Prizes seen as virtually unattainable result in lower performance scores because the subjects do not try. Even among students of high ability, there is no significantly different effect between virtually unattainable prizes and no prizes at all. Motivation is also enhanced if assigned tasks are more meaningful and personally relevant. For example, it is easier to learn and remember words that are concrete rather than words that are abstract (Dirkx & Craik, 1992).

Associative Strength

The degree of association, or so-called **associative strength,** also affects learning. Some words go together naturally. For example, *table* goes with *chair* more than with *hat.* Thus, *table-chair* has greater associative strength. The higher the associative strength, and the more meaningful and familiar the word lists, the less likely older adults are to show a decline in learning ability.

Autonomic Arousal

Autonomic arousal is stimulation of the autonomic nervous system. The degree of autonomic arousal has been measured in a number of ways: by the level of free fatty acids (FFA) in the blood (the higher the level, the greater the degree of arousal) and by heart rate, blood pressure, and skin conductance. It was assumed in the past that older persons showed less autonomic arousal during learning tasks because they did not get as involved as younger persons. Consequently, they did not learn as much as younger subjects. Actually, just the opposite may occur. Powell and associates (1980) showed that the blood pressure of older subjects (between 55 and 70) increased during serial learning tasks and that this increase was positively related to serial learning ability and better performance on the easier tasks. If, however, learning tasks became too complex, the positive relationship to an increase in autonomic arousal was obscured. Subjects did less well because of anxiety. Older adults can become so emotionally aroused and anxious that their energies are dissipated in undifferentiated, haphazard ways, and learning performance declines. When given a drug that suppresses the action of the autonomic nervous system (anxiety and upset), learning performance improves.

Pacing, Speed

Pacing refers to the time intervals between stimuli. In paired-associate tasks, subjects must learn a series of paired words or letters, such as *ball-bat* or *boy-girl.* These paired associates may be presented at 2-second, 4-second, or longer intervals. It has been found that *older adults take more time to learn than do younger adults.* When older adults are allowed to study paired associates on a slower or self-paced schedule, their learning ability improves. The total time needed to learn continues to increase with advancing age.

FOCUS

Extremely Long-Term Memory

The ability to remember over a long period of time depends partially on how often the material is recalled and used in the intervening years. For example, if words are periodically recalled, held in working memory, and then tucked away again, they can be remembered more easily than if they were never used after initial learning took place (Howard, Lasaga, & McAndrews, 1980). Retrieval from very long-term memory is also enhanced if the information is familiar (Wahlin et al., 1993). In one experiment, 20-year-olds remembered the names of unique contemporary pictures faster than did the older subjects, but the 65-year-old group retrieved the names of unique but dated pictures faster. The speed of 50-year-old subjects fell between that of the two other groups (Poon & Fozard, 1978). Each age group best recalled pictures with which they were familiar.

It is commonly assumed that older people are not good at recalling recent events but that their memory for remote events is unimpaired. One flaw in this assumption is that childhood events usually have been recalled many times since they occurred; the older person is remembering from the time of the last rehearsal, not from 40 years before (Rabinowitz & Craik, 1986). Even so, objective studies show that *older subjects are poorer than younger controls at recalling and recognizing events from the past* (Holding, Noonan, Pfau, & Holding, 1986). Performance declines with the remoteness of events and with increasing age.

It must be emphasized, however, that decline is very slow. Warrington and Siberstein (1970) found that adults under 40 were able to recall 32% of the news items one-and-a-half years after they had happened. Adults over 55 were able to recall 26% of the items. No differences were found in recognition performance between the two different age groups.

The ability to recall may depend partially on the subjects' age when the events occurred. *Subjects of all ages (20 to 79) can best remember sociohistoric events that occurred when the subjects were 15 to 25 years old* (Hyland and Ackerman, 1988). These ages may be the most impressionable years, so that persons of 60 remember events that occurred 35 to 45 years earlier better than they recall events that happened before or after.

Once the pairs are learned, older adults also take longer to respond to the stimulus word. Thus, if the word *ball* is presented, older adults take longer to respond with the correct word *bat.* Older adults need more time to show what they have learned; otherwise, it appears that they have not learned as well as younger adults.

Learning and Age

The most extensive body of longitudinal data on adult learning appears in the *Baltimore Longitudinal Study of Men* (Arenberg & Robertson-Tshabo, 1977). For the most part, these were well-educated men of high socioeconomic status. The data consisted

Associative strength— degree of association, as between two words

Autonomic arousal—stimulation of the autonomic, or involuntary, nervous system—found to be positively associated with serial learning at all ages, particularly for learning simpler tasks

Pacing—time intervals between stimuli

FOCUS

Enhancing Learning

One purpose of research is to provide practical knowledge that can be used. The research on adult learning can be beneficial to adult education. People who teach adults and adults who seek to learn can benefit from understanding and practicing the following important principles:

1. Task performance and learning improve as adult anxiety regarding proficiency decreases. Establishing rapport and offering assurance, moral support, and assistance help to reduce anxiety.

2. Adults need opportunities to express what they do know and to exhibit their talents. They often know and are capable of more than they show. A natural cautiousness about doing something wrong makes them wary of exhibiting their skills.

3. Careful instruction and directions help overcome adult cautiousness and stimulate performance.

4. Adults do much better with material and tasks that are relevant and meaningful to them. They can hardly be expected to show their intelligence on tests of tasks they consider stupid.

5. Adults are able to perform better with materials and tasks that are organized into logical categories or sequences. They benefit from organizational aids and suggestions that help them categorize and group materials into meaningful associations.

6. Motivation is increased if adults comprehend the reasons for learning or for performance. Offering explanations about the relevance of the material or task and providing rewards and incentives, within the realm of possibility, stimulate effort (Hartley & Walsh, 1980).

7. Because adults value accuracy more than speed, tasks must be paced to allow maximum learning and performance. Self-paced assignments are often accomplished more proficiently than those with severe time limitations.

8. Maximum and repeated exposure to material or tasks to be learned encourages deeper processing and enhances learning and performance.

9. Reducing all forms of interference and distracting stimuli enhances learning. If present materials and tasks are completely learned before new ones are introduced, interference effects are minimized and learning is enhanced.

10. The use of both visual and auditory presentations in the teaching process enhances learning more than the use of only one method. When studying, repeating information out loud enhances learning (Rissenberg & Glanzer, 1986).

11. Adult performance declines as fatigue increases. Offering appropriate breaks and rest periods may actually improve learning and performance.

of paired-associate and serial-performance learning data measured at two different speed intervals for each task. Cross-sectional analysis showed small age differences before age 60 and large age differences thereafter, particularly at the faster pacing speeds. Analysis of the longitudinal data for both the paired-associate and serial-performance learning tasks showed similar results: *The great increases in learning er-* *rors occurred after age 60, using both the slow- and fast-paced intervals.* The youngest group of men (initially between 30 and 38) showed either a slight improvement in scores or the smallest mean decline (depending on the speed of pacing) over a 7-year period. The two groups of men between 39 and 54 years of age showed moderate mean declines; the two oldest groups, initially 61 to 74, showed the largest mean declines. Even among men who learned at the slower pace, the earliest-born cohorts showed the most decline, and the latest-born cohorts the least. Mean errors were consistently greater for older subsamples within each cohort, indicating that they performed less effectively than younger subsamples from the same cohort. *This evidence indicates a verbal learning deficit in the later years of life* (Allen & Crozier, 1992).

PRODUCTIVITY AND CREATIVITY

Ultimately, cognitive development should result in increased productivity and creativity in our daily lives. Productivity is among the oldest and most cherished values in American culture. In our stories and language, we extol the virtues of productive activity and scorn the failings of those who do not carry their own weight. We now speak of an aging process that can be successful, productive, and dynamic. The emerging picture of the productive activity of elderly persons shows considerable variation, with a substantial proportion of older persons remaining productive well into their later years. Productive activity declines on average with increasing age, but controls for health status and education sharply reduce the magnitude of these age-related declines. In part, declines of productivity in older age is a result of the cessation of paid work.

There is some evidence that certain domains of productivity remain quite stable over time. Most of the decline that we see in older ages is the result of increases in the numbers of older persons who, for reasons of disability and impairment, stop engaging in any activity at all. Those who remain active tend to diminish relatively little in the intensity of that activity. Cross-sectional comparisons and patterns of longitudinal change of productive activities among 1,192 adults aged 70 to 79 sought to discover changes in productive activity during later adulthood (Glass, Seeman, Herzog, Kahn, & Berkman, 1995). Overall, 15% of the group became less productive, while another 12.7% became more productive. Risk factors for decline in productivity included hospital admission and stroke. Age, functional ability, marriage, and increased mastery were protective against declines. One finding was that fully one-quarter of the successful agers engaged in some child care. Additionally, among more successful agers, men engaged in child-care activities as often as did women, suggesting that child care may be an especially important and significant social role for elderly persons of both genders. One important emphasis in this study was that older people do not see themselves as "old" and are not treated as "old" by their family and friends as long as they remain active and productive in some meaningful sense. Continued productive activity may be a key to following the path of successful aging.

Creativity in Late Adulthood

Much has been written about developing creativity in children but little about creativity in adulthood. Do educators and psychologists equate creativity with youthfulness? If so, the notion is fallacious. Outstanding contributions have been made by many people during late adulthood, as the following examples show:

Many older adults are highly creative.

- Will and Ariel Durant completed their 11-volume work *The Story of Civilization* when he was 90 and she was 77.
- Sophocles wrote *Oedipus Rex* at 75.
- Sigmund Freud wrote his last book at 83.
- Von Benden discovered the reduction of chromosomes at 74.
- Mahatma Gandhi launched his movement to gain India's independence at 72.
- Cecil B. DeMille directed *The Ten Commandments* at 75.
- Claude Monet began his *Water Lily* series at 73.

Creativity as Quality of Production

The lack of attention to creativity in adulthood has resulted in a paucity of research. The work by Lehman (1962, 1966) is usually cited as the most important on the subject, even though it is now more than 3 decades old. Lehman is still cited because little subsequent research is available to supplement his work. Lehman measured creativity by the quality of work achieved by adults in the various fields of science, medicine, philosophy, psychology, art, invention, and other areas. His method was to tabulate by age groups the frequency with which high-quality production was listed in historical accounts covering a period of

more than 400 years. He found that in most fields, people produced the greatest proportion of superior work during their 30s. After that there was a decline in high-quality production. About 80% of superior work was completed by age 50. The rate of lower-quality work peaked somewhat later. He also found that some fields of endeavor peaked earlier than others. However, in all fields, individual variations were so great that Lehman emphasized that usefulness was not limited to age and that age was not always a causative factor in the decline of creative quality. *People made valuable contributions at all ages.*

Creativity as Quantity of Work

Lehman has had his critics. Dennis (1966) maintained that it is almost impossible to make objective judgments of the quality of a person's work. A person's early, pioneering work is more likely to be mentioned than later work. Older work is usually designated masterwork more often than recent work. Thus, investigations tend to show that earlier work at younger ages is superior. Besides, competition increases as the years pass, making it difficult for a person's later work to be labeled superior. Dennis (1966) maintained that Lehman's analysis of quality through bibliographies and citations favored early work and distorted the findings. He insisted that quantity of output, not quality, is a far better measure of creativity.

Dennis's research revealed that peak performance years occurred much later than Lehman maintained, that the performance often continued over many years of the life cycle, and that *the quantity of output at each age varied depending on the field of endeavor.* Output in creative arts and science peaked in the 40s and declined thereafter, with artistic output declining the most and scientific output falling only a little. Output of adults in the humanities continued to rise from the 30s to the 60s, with little decline even through the 70s. Figure 17.7 shows the data presented by Dennis and represented graphically by Botwinick (1967).

Another study analyzed the productivity of scientists in the math, physics, and economics departments at the University of California at Berkeley, and in the math, physics, and chemistry departments at the University of Illinois at Urbana. Productivity was measured by the number of citations made in a year to all of the scientists' earlier work, as listed in the *Science Citation Index.* The mean peak age for the greatest number of citations was 59, but the ages ranged from 39 for the Berkeley physics professors to 89 for the Urbana math professors. The mean peak age of salaries of all of the professors was in the mid-60s (Diamond, 1986).

Individual Variations

Why individuals in the humanities remain creative into late adulthood, whereas the output of artists and scientists declines with age,

remains a question. Certainly, individual variations exist in every field. Some people remain intellectually alive, active, and inventive, continuing to question, search, and participate fully in life. Others become stagnant at an early age. What happens depends partly on individual attitudes about oneself and the aging process. Life can be a fascinating challenge throughout the adult life span.

EDUCATION

Learning is a lifelong endeavor. There is no specific age at which people can or should cease learning.

> Learning is not something outside life. It is something within life waiting to be understood. Learning is a kind of big umbrella over everything else that happens to you. And it can help you whether you are buying a house, reading about heart trouble, studying your social security rates, or even trying to understand what's happening in Congress (Schuckman, 1975, p. 85).

Increasingly, serious consideration is being given to adult education. Many opportunities exist to learn through adult courses in high schools, vocational schools, community colleges, universities, and self-taught or self-directed home study programs. In addition, thousands of older adults attend regular university classes with younger students. Some universities provide gold card registrations that offer free tuition to people over 65.

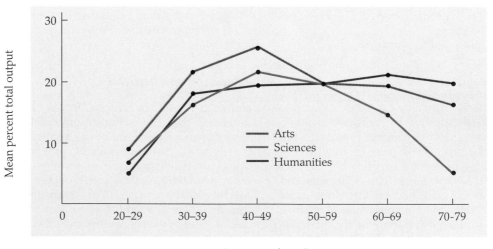

FIGURE 17.7   Creative output of people in the humanities, sciences, and arts over the life cycle.

Adapted from *Cognitive Processes in Maturity and Old Age,* by J. Botwinick, 1967. Springer Publishing Co., Inc. New York: 10012. Used with permission.

A variety of nonacademic organizations also offer courses for older people, notably *The Institute for Lifetime Learning*, sponsored by the *American Association for Retired Persons (AARP)* and the *National Retired Teachers' Association (NRTA)*.

In spite of the progress, the total number of older persons with a secondary or college education is limited. Figure 17.8 shows the percentages of people 25 and older who have completed various levels of education (U.S. Bureau of the Census, 1998). The number of older people taking some type of formal education is also limited. The major reasons older people give for not participating in educational courses are lack of interest, being too old, poor health, and lack of time. Other barriers are vision and hearing problems, and lack of transportation. For handicapped adults, courses must be carefully planned, considering numerous learning, personality, and environmental factors.

The concept of lifelong education is taken seriously today by educators and administrators. Exposure to schooling throughout life enables adults to maintain their cognitive skills, morale, self-image, and abilities to deal with the complex problems of the future. The rate of change of our knowledge base in most fields is so rapid that workers need refresher and retraining courses several times during a career.

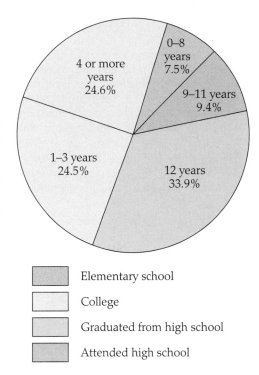

Elementary school

College

Graduated from high school

Attended high school

FIGURE 17.8 Years of school completed by adults, 25 years of age or older, 1997.

Statistics from *Statistical Abstract of the United States, 1998* (p. 51), by U.S. Bureau of the Census, 1998, Washington, DC: U.S. Government Printing Office.

Summary

1. About half the adult population attains the full stage of formal operational thinking. Some adults are able to use formal thinking in their field of specialization but not in others.

2. Older adults approach problems at a lower level of abstraction than do young adults or adolescents.

3. Older adults approach problems differently; they tend to be more pragmatic and subjective, and to personalize learning tasks.

4. Older adults appear to solve practical problems of living more efficiently than do younger adults.

5. Tests of word familiarity and of sentence and prose comprehension reveal that older adults are able to comprehend almost as well as younger adults, with comprehension declining some after age 60.

6. Older people develop pragmatic knowledge that we call wisdom.

7. Some adults seem to go beyond formal operational thinking to reach a problem-finding stage.

8. Dialectical thinkers are able to consider opposing viewpoints simultaneously without need to resolve the inconsistencies, and they are sometimes able to formulate new ideas that are superior to both opposites.

9. Schaie has outlined five stages of adult cognitive development in which people move from acquiring knowledge to applying it in their own lives.

10. Any attempt to measure intelligence depends on the types of tests used, their research design, and what they purport to measure.

11. Verbal scores on the WAIS-III tend to hold up with increasing age, whereas

performance scores tend to decline after the mid-20s.

12. Longitudinal measurements tend to minimize intellectual decline with age, whereas cross-sectional measurements tend to maximize it. Some longitudinal studies emphasize that intellectual decline is not inevitable even by age 50 and over.

13. Scores on the PMA also show that intellectual decline does not always occur, and when it does, it usually takes place after age 50.

14. Psychometric intelligence declines with age, but the extent of decline depends on the particular type of ability measured. Verbal and numerical abilities hold up better than some others.

15. Fluid intelligence seems to decline from early adulthood on, but this decline is probably due to generational differences and not to aging itself. Scores on crystallized intelligence increase through adulthood.

16. A chief criticism of intelligence tests is that IQ is only one of the important factors necessary to carry out responsible tasks. Other criticisms include the familiarity of test items to children and young adults, and the cultural and economic bias.

17. A large number of factors affect test scores: the circumstances of test administration, motivation, personality traits of the subjects, physical factors, emotional factors, sensory abilities, the relationship with the test administrator, and general intellectual level and years of school completed.

18. Socioenvironmental factors that influence intellectual abilities include educational level, socioeconomic status, stress, and training.

19. Memory is sometimes divided into prospective and retrospective memory.

20. Memory involves acquisition, storage, and retrieval of information.

21. There are three memory stores: sensory stores, short-term storage, and long-term storage. Information passes from one compartment to another.

22. Sensory memory stores show some decline with age, with tactual memory declining the fastest, visual memory declining the next fastest, and audio memory showing the least decline.

23. Primary memory, or short-term memory, does not change much with age, but secondary, or long-term, memory may decline some. There are greater losses in recall ability than in recognition ability.

24. There is some age-related decline in spatial memory, particularly after the sixth decade of life. Spatial ability makes a practical difference in older adults' use of their neighborhoods.

25. There appear to be three kinds of long-term memory: procedural, semantic, and episodic.

26. Men show more rapid age-associated atrophy of the left hemisphere than women do, but this decline apparently does not translate into differential functional decline in everyday verbal memory.

27. Memory training can enhance the memory of elderly adults.

28. Flashbulb memory denotes unusually vivid and detailed memories that persist unchanged over long periods of time.

29. Young adults have greater long-term memory ability than do older adults, but subjects of all ages best remember sociohistoric events that occurred when the subjects were 15 to 25 years old.

30. Learning and memory are intertwined, but the performance of adults is not always indicative of what they have learned.

31. Learning research has revealed the importance of motivation, relevance, meaning, associative strength, autonomic arousal, and pacing and speed in learning ability.

32. Research reveals some decline in learning ability after age 60, particularly at faster pacing speeds.

33. Some elderly remain productive throughout their lives, but others less so, depending on whether they have disabilities and impairments. Fully one-quarter of older adults engage in some type of child care.

34. Creative ability measured as quality of production shows that about 80% of superior work is completed by age 50, with the peak occurring during the 30s.

35. Creativity as quantity of production shows a peak in the 40s in the sciences and arts, and in the 60s in the humanities. In another study, the mean peak age for the greatest number of science citations was 59, with age ranges from 39 to 89; however, there are wide individual variations.

36. Because learning is a lifelong endeavor, increasing attention is being given to education of adults throughout life.

Key Terms

Discussion Questions

1. Do you know any adults over 55 or 60? How does their thinking differ from your own? Do they have greater practical problem-solving abilities than younger adults?

2. How does your word comprehension now compare with your ability when you were younger?

3. Do you think people become wiser as they get older? Why, or why not?

4. One of the tasks of marriage counselors is to try to get couples to identify their problems. What evidence do you have that some adults are better at problem finding than others?

5. What are some advantages and disadvantages of being able to think dialectically?

6. Schaie says that as people age, they move from acquiring knowledge to using knowledge in their everyday lives. Do you think that all adults use their knowledge to the fullest? Explain. Give examples.

7. What do you think of evaluating the intellectual ability of people in terms of IQ? What are some pros and cons?

8. Why do cross-sectional measurements of intelligence maximize decline with age, whereas longitudinal measurements minimize it?

9. Give some examples of fluid versus crystallized intelligence.

10. What personality factors do you feel are most important in affecting intelligence?

11. What socioenvironmental factors are most important in maintaining intellectual abilities as one ages?

12. Talk about the memory ability of some adult whom you know. Has this ability changed as the person has aged? How?

13. Do you agree that people best remember events that happen when they are 15 to 25 years of age? What events do you best remember that happened during this age period of your life?

14. To older students: Do you feel you can learn as well now as when you were younger? Discuss.

15. To younger students: Of the principles for adult learning outlined in the Focus: Enhancing Learning, which items are most important for people of all ages? for children? for older people? Discuss.

16. What helps you the most when you are trying to learn something?

17. Give examples of people whose greatest period of creativity was after they were 50 years or more old.

COMMONS, M. L., RICHARDS, F. A., & ARNON, C. (Eds.) (1984). *Beyond formal operations: Late adolescent and adult cognitive development.* New York: Praeger. A fifth stage.

POON, L. W., RUBIN, D. C., & WILSON, B. C. (Eds.) (1992). *Everyday cognition in adulthood and later life.* New York: Cambridge University Press. Cognitive processes in aging.

SCHOOLER, C., & SCHAIE, K. W. (Eds.) (1987). *Cognitive functioning and social structure over the life course.* Norwood, NJ: Ablex. Articles about cognitive development, change.

Suggested Readings

http://www.cis.udel.edu/cogsci/worldwide
.html   Cognitive Science World Wide Links to journals, conferences, newsgroups and more.

Web Resources

Emotional Development

*A*s we have seen in Chapters 8 and 13, emotions are concerned with the development of feelings and the expression of them in relation to other people. We are concerned with what feelings develop, how they develop, and what the consequences of these feelings are to the individual. The kinds of feelings that develop, the way that they are expressed, and the extent to which they are controlled are important considerations in a person's life, and especially so in relationships with other people. There is an expression in psychology that "behavior is caused," and one of the causes of behavior is how people feel. People who feel angry express their anger; those who feel sad are likely to express this sadness; and those who feel warm and loving are likely to act in a warm and loving way. Thus, to understand the behavior of an individual requires us to understand the inner emotional life that motivates the individual to act as he or she does.

In this chapter, we are particularly concerned with the development of emotional maturity. What is emotional maturity? How is it developed? And why is it important? Certainly, to become a mature adult requires that adults be mature not only physically, cognitively, and socially, but also emotionally. In general, we might classify emotional maturity in these three categories: being *emotionally secure*, being *emotionally stable*, and having *the capacity to feel for others* and to form relationships. These three concepts will be discussed in the first part of this chapter.

EMOTIONAL MATURITY

Emotional Security

Being an emotionally secure person means having freedom from excessive, negative emotions and from crippling anxieties, doubts, and fears. All individuals experience some anxiety, doubts, and fear, but the extent to which these emotions are expressed determines the relative degree of **emotional maturity** that the individual reaches. An individual who feels a lot of anxiety about many things to the degree that the anxiety is all-pervasive is going to be affected negatively by his or her emotional insecurity. Some people seem to worry about everything: about themselves, their health, their relationships with other people, their jobs, their financial situation, their social relationships, and problems in the world. This behavior becomes undesirable because it affects their overall relationships with others, as well as their general contentment and happiness. When carried to extreme, this behavior is called **general anxiety disorder.** Individuals with general anxiety disorder worry about the smallest happenings, are concerned

Crying is a way of expressing emotion.

that something terrible is going to happen, and are anxious when there is no reason for the anxiety to exist. They cannot be reasoned into thinking that everything is going to be all right and that there is nothing to worry about. Their anxiety affects their physical well-being, so that they may complain about stomach upset, shortness of breath, sweating, shaking and trembling, nervousness, sleep disturbances, headaches, tiredness, or a variety of other physical difficulties that have a psychological origin.

An example of such emotional insecurity is that of Joanne, who complains about a number of difficulties. In general, she doesn't feel very good about herself, is afraid that she is not capable of doing a good job at her office, and is always anxious that she is going to get fired although she is actually a very good worker. Joanne has very little faith in her own abilities and sense of accomplishment. She feels that what she does is never good enough and that others criticize her and look down on her for her poor performance. Also, she has anxieties about her physical appearance even though she is a very attractive woman. She is always complaining that she is too fat, that her hair is too long, or that her general appearance is unacceptable. At work she feels that there is always somebody who doesn't like her. No matter where she goes, Joanne points out somebody who she feels is criticizing her. She is constantly concerned with what others are saying about her and is convinced that they are talking about her behind her back. Feeling as she does about herself, she is miserable in most situations because she can never feel that she is adequate and secure, or that she is accepted as she is. She is very sensitive to criticism and is threatened by feelings of rejection. If when walking into a room, somebody doesn't say hello to her, she is deeply hurt and believes she is being rejected, when actually that person might not have even seen her go into the room. Her emotional insecurity is obviously interfering with her functioning in life.

Emotionally insecure people may become very possessive in their relationships with others. They hang onto and depend on other people to give them some feeling of security and adequacy. Hesitating to strike out on their own, they are afraid they will fail at what they do; therefore, they try to overcompensate by clinging to and depending on others. Children who are very emotionally insecure will not let their parents out of their sight or will be very upset when the parents do have to leave temporarily.

Jealousy is a common symptom of emotional insecurity in relationships. In one case,

a husband had great difficulty with his wife. The couple ran a ma-and-pa store, and every time a woman came into the store, the wife was convinced that her husband was flirting with the woman, even though he did not know the woman. The wife claimed that her husband and the woman were sending signals to one another through their eyes. She made her husband's life miserable by accusing him of a number of extramarital relationships that in fact did not exist. No amount of reasoning could convince her that she did not have any reason to be jealous.

Emotionally secure people may have some negative emotions and feelings about themselves, about others, and about relationships, but these negative feelings are overpowered by more positive feelings. Such people have adequate self-concept, are convinced that others like them, and get along pretty well with others. They think that they perform adequately at work, and they generally do not have unreasoned feelings or fears about the future. Because they have self-confidence, feel adequate, and do not have unreasonable fears about what might happen, they are able to be productive and to prove themselves to other people. One study of relationship problems during different stages of marriage showed that jealousy was the number two problem before marriage, the number seven problem during the first year of marriage, and the number eight problem after the birth of the first child. Gradually, as the marriage continued, the problem of jealousy declined (Storaasli & Markman, 1990).

Emotional Stability

Emotional maturity also means that a person has **emotional stability,** which is a relative degree of freedom from drastic ups and downs of

Excessive jealousy can be a major problem in relationships.

Emotional maturity—Being emotionally secure, stable, and with a capacity to feel emotion

General anxiety disorder—Mental illness characterized by pervasive anxiety that is way out of proportion to the stimulus and that lasts well beyond reasonable expectations

Emotional stability—Being free of excessive and crippling ups and downs of mood emotions. Mature people do not usually show positive emotions one day and negative emotions the next. The feelings of emotionally unstable people often go up and down like a yoyo, so that others do not know what to expect of them. They are so unstable that they may explode at any time. Emotionally unstable people cause many problems in relationships because their behavior causes hard feelings and conflicts. In extreme cases, emotional instability is called *bi-polar disorder*, in which individuals go from manic phases to depressive phases, with drastic changes of mood, emotion, and feeling. Emotionally stable people are generally free from violent temperamental or emotional outbursts that have little cause. Stable people usually have a high frustration tolerance and can stand a certain degree of denial and frustration without becoming excessively upset.

Emotionally unstable people, however, get very upset when crossed, thus making it harder for others to get along with them. There are a number of situations that might describe emotional instability in relationships. While driving a car, emotionally unstable people are likely to honk the horn or to curse the driver ahead when that person doesn't go immediately after the light has

Emotionally unstable people have a low tolerance for frustration.

turned green. Emotionally unstable people get upset when a date is late or when things have not gone exactly as desired. Such people usually have very little patience with children and become angry when children are annoying or do things that are upsetting.

What happens to emotional stability as individuals age? In general, studies indicate that *the intensity of emotion declines subjectively as people get older*. Emotion becomes increasingly salient but better controlled with age. Compared with younger adults, older adults typically describe themselves as less emotionally labile and more moderate in their affective responses. In one study, participants were asked to rate statements such as the following on a scale ranging from always true to never true: "Others tend to get more excited about things than I do" and "I try hard to stay in a neutral state and to avoid emotional situations" (Lawton, Kleban, Rajagopal, & Dean, 1992); Levine & Bluck, 1997). These findings, as well as popular stereotypes, suggest that people become less emotional as they age. Exuberance from abundant emotional energy in early adulthood is replaced by the moderation of calm rationality in middle adulthood and older age. Another study that confirmed these findings examined three domains of potential change in emotion as people get older: *emotional experience, emotional expression*, and *emotional control* (Gross, Carstensen, Tsai, Pasupathi, Skorpen, & Hsu, 1997).

An examination of emotional experience in age generally suggests that there are decreases in the frequency and intensity of self-reported emotional experience. On the whole, older participants report feeling emotions that are less intense and less frequent.

Researchers have examined whether emotion-expressive behavior decreases over the life span. Behavioral evidence from examining older couples suggests that older couples express less interest, humor, anger, disgust, belligerence, and whining about a conflict in their relationship than do middle-age couples. However, older couples show greater affection than do middle-age couples, suggesting that some positive emotions may be exempted from the general age-related decline in emotional expressivity.

Age-related decline in emotional experience and expression suggests increased emotional control with age. Older participants are more likely to agree with the following statements: "I try hard to stay in a neutral state and to avoid emotional situations" and "I try to avoid reacting emotionally whether the emotion is positive or negative." Thus, the elderly seem to have increased emotional control (Gross, Carstensen, Pasupathi, Tsai, Skorpen, & Hsu, 1997).

Capacity to Feel

The emotionally mature person has the capacity to feel, whether to feel love or to feel hate. Without the capacity to feel, emotions are dead. People grow up by forming attachments, giving and receiving affection, relating in warm and understanding ways to one another, and developing empathy and the ability to ascertain one another's feelings. Feeling genuine emotions in their relationships with other people, they are able to express these emotions in positive, mature ways. They are able to form emotional relationships based on love, affection, and companionship. Some people who have experienced much abuse, rejection, and negative relationships with other people sometimes learn to shut off their emotions, so that they reach a nonfeeling state in which they will not be hurt. Because of this absence of positive feelings, they miss out on some of the great pleasures of life. Some people have so successfully learned to suppress their feelings that you never know what they are thinking or how they are feeling (Gross & Levenson, 1997).

In extreme instances, the person who is emotionally cold and loses all capacity to express feelings is classified as a **psychopath.** One such person that the author counseled was a returning Vietnam veteran. He was extremely cruel to his wife, whom he said was a nothing. He said, "I treat her like a thing, like an it and that she's a nobody." Because she was a little overweight, he would call her on the phone and go "oink oink oink oink, you fat pig" and hang up. When asked why he did this, he said that he just enjoyed getting his wife upset. When I asked about his experiences in Vietnam, he said that he had enrolled for a second hitch. I asked him why he had done so, and he said, "Well, I love it over there. I can rape, I can pillage, I can burn, and it's really quite exciting." The wife's problem was what to do about his abuse. Like a lot of other abused wives, she thought that the abuse was partly her fault and that if she only acted differently, he might not hurt her. She asked, "Why does he do it?" I could reply only that he was a sick person and that unless he got extreme help, there was nothing that anybody could do about it. I suggested that he come in for counseling, and at that point, I suggested he go see a psychiatrist, but he refused to do so. Unfortunately,

Many serial killers are psychopaths.

then, I had to tell the wife that I didn't think there was any hope for his getting better, since he wasn't willing to get any medical help. Therefore, the best thing that she could do was to leave him. Although she was extremely frightened of her husband, she fortunately left him and, with her two children, moved to another state, where she rejoined her family.

It is regrettable when people lose all capacity to feel positive emotions: They are indeed emotionally dead.

SUBJECTIVE WELL-BEING

Another important consideration in emotional development is how people feel about themselves. In this section, we are concerned especially with identifying what psychologists call **subjective well-being** and with an understanding of the many factors that influence it (Stacey & Gatz, 1991).

A number of definitions of subjective well-being have been proposed. Horley (1984) defines it as "a self-perceived positive feeling or state" (p. 127). Liang (1985) describes subjective well-being as "an individual's cognitive as well as affective assessments about life as a whole" (p. 552). Most psychologists agree that subjective well-being is an abstract, multidimensional concept that can best be

Psychopath—Mentally ill person incapable of the development of conscience or feelings for others

Subjective well-being—self-perceived positive feeling or state; a cognitive and affective assessment about life as a whole

Subjective well-being describes how adults feel about themselves, others, and life in general.

measured by specific indicators such as *life satisfaction, morale, happiness, congruence,* and *affect* (Liang, 1984). Let's look at some of these indicators.

Life Satisfaction

Neugarten, Havighurst, and Tobin (1961) conducted the most influential initial research on life satisfaction (Krause, 1991b) and developed the *Life Satisfaction Index A* (LSIA) to measure it in older adults. The researchers viewed life satisfaction as having five dimensions:

1. *Zest versus apathy*—the degree of involvement in activity, either with other persons or with ideas.
2. *Resolution and fortitude*—the extent to which persons take responsibility for their own lives.
3. *Congruence*—the extent to which goals are achieved. Studies of all ages of adults show that what happens in the present remains more important than what happens in the past or future as far as its contribution to life satisfaction. However, as people age, past accomplishments become more important in allowing the elderly to reconcile

themselves to hardships in the present and diminishing resources in the future (Shmotkin, 1991).
4. *Self-concept*—the extent to which a person has a positive concept of self, physically, psychologically, and socially.
5. *Mood tone*—whether the person holds optimistic attitudes and happy feelings.

Thus, an individual possesses positive psychological well-being

to the extent that he (a) takes pleasure from whatever round of activities that constitutes his everyday life; (b) regards his life as meaningful and accepts resolutely that which life has been; (c) feels he has succeeded in achieving his major goals; (d) holds a positive image of self; and (e) maintains happy and optimistic attitudes and mood (Neugarten, Havighurst, & Tobin, 1961, p. 137).

Research has only partially supported the LSIA as originally constructed as a valid measure of life satisfaction among older adults (Hoyt & Creech, 1983). Other researchers emphasize that rating scales ought to contain questions regarding the future in evaluating important factors in adult life satisfaction (Shmotkin, 1992). In other words, life satisfaction now depends not only on one's present feelings and living conditions but also on the way that one views the future.

Sociodemographic Factors

The LSIA completely leaves out sociodemographic factors in measuring life satisfaction. The question arises as to the effect of such factors as race, religion, residence, and socioeconomic status on life satisfaction. Let's look at these three variables.

Race

Several studies measure the effect of race on life satisfaction (Liang, Lawrence, & Bollen, 1987). One study showed that most factors influencing life satisfaction affected both whites and blacks, but that the negative effects of various physical impairments are considerably stronger among blacks than among whites (Usui, Keil, & Phillips, 1983).

Krause (1993) examined racial differences in life satisfaction among aged men and women. Findings from his nationwide survey revealed that older blacks had lower levels of life satisfaction than older whites. Lower feelings of life satisfaction of blacks emerged

FOCUS

Life Satisfaction Among African Americans

Marguerite Coke (1992) conducted a study of 166 male and female African Americans ranging from 65 to 88 years of age. The mean income was $7,100 a year. The mean number of years of education was 9 years. The majority of respondents were retired and had been engaged in blue-collar occupations throughout their lives. The majority of respondents (61%) indicated that they attended church. More were living with family members than with nonfamily members, although the greatest percentage (64%) were living alone or with a spouse. The respondents were recruited at senior citizen centers that they attended. The purpose of this study was to find out what factors correlated with life satisfaction among these African Americans.

The results of the study indicate striking differences between male and female respondents. The women in this study were generally involved in family roles, engaged in church activities, and satisfied with life. The variability in life satisfaction that did occur among women was due to an intangible quality, the importance of religion. In contrast, among men, there were considerable differences in life satisfaction, and these differences were related not only to attitudinal factors such as the importance of religion but also to more objective, observable factors such as family roles and socioeconomic achievement.

It would appear that the continued fulfillment of meaningful social roles is an important determinant of life satisfaction among the African American elderly. The findings also support the conclusions of others regarding the importance of the church and religion among African American seniors (Coke, 1992).

from comparing past aspirations to subsequent achievements. Blacks were more often frustrated in their achievements that did not measure up to their goals.

Religion

Religion has gained prominence as a topic for gerontological research in recent years, with work reflecting the writing of preeminent scholars who regard religion as central to physical, mental, and emotional well-being. Increasing evidence indicates that religious involvement is especially central to the lives of black Americans. Religion has promoted individual well-being for blacks and has been instrumental in the development of black communities. Black churches have provided social and psychological support and facilitated linkages to community health resources. Religion plays a supportive role in enhancing the mental health and well-being of black adults. Religious attendance and strength of affiliation are associated with life

satisfaction among black adults. High scores on indices reflecting subjective religiosity (feelings and attitudes towards religion) are associated with fewer psychological symptoms among black men and women. Using data from the *National Survey of Black Americans* (a nationally representative sample of blacks at least 18 years old), reveals statistically significant effects of organizational religiosity on life satisfaction. The findings suggest that the association between religion and well-being is consistent over the life course (Levin, Chatters, & Taylor, 1995).

Socioeconomic Status

Cross-sectional studies consistently reveal a positive relationship between income and overall satisfaction with life. But longitudinal and cross-national studies reveal a more complex relationship. Life satisfaction in the United States does not automatically rise as income and consumption levels increase. Furthermore, persons in richer nations are not happier than those in poorer nations (Usui, Keil, & Durig, 1985).

The key seems to be the standard by which one judges satisfaction. People compare their own financial status with that of others. Their satisfaction then reflects the extent to which reality matches what is considered necessary or desirable. Fernandez and Kulik (1981) suggested that people compare their situation with the standard of others in their neighborhood, assuming that the neighborhood provides a relative basis for comparison. One study of persons 60 years and older living in Kentucky in 1980 showed that the adults compared themselves with the nearest or closest relatives (Usui, Keil, & Durig, 1985). If they felt they were better off than their relatives, their sense of well-being was heightened. Interestingly, comparison with close friends and neighbors did not seem to affect subjective well-being, but this was probably the situation because neighbors and friends were usually similar to each other in status. Certainly, if people feel they are considerably poorer than others in their neighborhood, most would feel some dissatisfaction. Other research on marital satisfaction has shown that *it is not the level of income that is important, but whether people are satisfied with the level they have reached* (Berry & Williams, 1987).

Urban Versus Rural Living

Another study sought to sort out the effects of urban versus rural living on life satisfaction (Liang & Warfel, 1983). Even though no

Whether people live in urban or rural areas is not the key determinant of life satisfaction.

direct effect of urbanism on life satisfaction was found, *urbanism influenced life satisfaction indirectly and interactively because it influenced health, financial satisfaction, and social integration.* In general, the better the health, the greater the financial satisfaction; and the higher the social integration, the greater was life satisfaction. But the influence of the size of the city on these is variable. One study found that the health and welfare of elderly persons living in urban areas has deteriorated during the past decades (Ford et al., 1992).

Some urban areas have better health care than do rural areas, but many rural residents see their services as more accessible. Income is lower in rural than in urban areas, but many rural residents don't see themselves as financially deprived. The level of social integration in urban areas is lower than in rural areas. Social relationships in rural communities tend to be more personal, so that social integration in large cities may contribute less to life satisfaction. Overall, *the effects of urban living on life satisfaction are inconsistent.*

Acculturation Stress

Minority groups that move to the United States have special problems because of language barriers. Not knowing the language of the majority culture, they feel a sense of social isolation from the rest of society. Low income and financial strain place a lot of stress on minorities. Lack of education is also a factor in preventing them from getting good jobs. Krause and Goldenhar (1992) found considerable psychological distress in adults who had immigrated from Mexico, Cuba, and Puerto Rico. Hispanic immigrants experienced considerable prejudice and discrimination while they resided in the United States. Levels of psychological distress tend to vary across

Hispanic groups, and these differences may be attributed, in part, to the complex interplay between educational attainment, language acculturation, financial strain, and social isolation (Krause & Goldenhar, 1992).

Family Relationships

The quality of a marriage has a strong effect on happiness and satisfaction with life (White, 1992; Zollar & Williams, 1987). Similarly, marital dissatisfaction in distressed families is highly related to the occurrence of marital tensions (Margolin, Christensen, & John, 1996). Data from six national studies conducted in the United States revealed that marital happiness contributes more to personal overall happiness than does any other kind of satisfaction, including satisfaction from work. At the same time, an unhappy marriage can also have a negative effect on life satisfaction and subjective well-being. Marital relationships are seldom static. Most couples have some ups and downs in their relationships. What is important, however, is the general quality of the relationship over periods of time and the extent to which partners report satisfaction with it (Mills, Grasmick, Morgan, & Wenk, 1992).

Family relationships earlier in life also have an important influence on subjective well-being as adults. Andersson and Stevens (1993) explored the impact of early experiences with parents on health and well-being in old age. An interview survey was conducted with a representative sample of 267 elderly community residents in the age group of 65 to 74. The foremost conclusion of the study was that early experiences with parents had an impact on the well-being of elderly persons. The effect is stronger among those

Family relationships have an important influence on subjective well-being.

older persons who do not currently have an attachment to an affectionate partner; also, it is stronger for unattached older men than for unattached older women (Carstensen, Gottman, & Levenson, 1995).

Differences in well-being in old age can be at least partially explained by differences in early experiences in interaction with primary caregivers or parents. Some adults are better able to develop and maintain supportive relationships through the life cycle, which serve them well when faced with adversity. When parental care is recalled as neither warm nor attentive, the unattached elderly experience lowered well-being as measured in terms of self-esteem and loneliness. Unattached older men also experience worse subjective health and greater anxiety and depression when their recollections of parental care are negative. For unattached women, the association between recalled quality of parenting and their current well-being is weaker and less extensive. The interpretation is that the impact of recalled parenting is somewhat diluted by the influence of other close relationships for many of these women; these other relationships contributed to a revision of feelings since childhood and had a stronger impact on current well-being than did the memories of parental behavior (Andersson & Stevens, 1993).

The effect of present parent status also has an influence on subjective well-being of older adults. Data from a quota sample of adults, age 55 and older, were used to examine the effect of parent status on subjective well-being. Unlike other studies, this study employed four categories of parent status: those who had close parents, those who had distant parents, those who chose not to have children, and those who were childless by circumstances (Connidis & McMullin, 1993). The study found that those who were emotionally close to their children and those who were childless by choice reported greater happiness, fewer depressive symptoms, and greater life satisfaction than those who were distant from their children or those who were childless by circumstances over which they had little control. The well-being of older adults who had close relationships with their children was higher because such ties are likely to be supportive and may act to protect older adults from harmful stress. Conversely, older adults who had relatively distant ties with their children did not enjoy the potential support of closer ties and experienced stress and unhappiness because of their poor relationships. Those who were childless by choice had higher scores and measures of subjective well-being than the childless by circumstance. Older persons who

were childless by circumstance reported levels of subjective well-being that were lower than those of older adults with close ties to their children and higher than those of older adults with distant ties to children. In summary, this study found significant differences in subject well-being between close parents and distant parents and between close parents and the childless by circumstance, but not the childless by choice.

Morale

Subjective well-being has also been described in terms of **morale,** which is defined as one's emotional or mental condition with respect to cheerfulness, confidence, zeal, and the like. Older adults who are high in extraversion and low in tension have higher morale than others (Adkins, Martin, & Poon, 1996). The *Philadelphia Geriatric Center (PGC) Morale Scale* is the most commonly used instrument to measure morale among the elderly (Lawton, 1975). The PGC Morale Scale evaluates three components of morale:

1. *Agitation*—as revealed by such phrases as "Little things bother me more this year," "I worry so much that I can't sleep," "I am afraid of a lot of things," "I get mad more than I used to," "I take things hard," and "I get upset easily."
2. *Dissatisfaction*—as revealed by such phrases as "Life isn't worth living," "Life is hard for me," "How satisfied am I with life today?" and "I have a lot to be sad about."
3. *Attitudes toward aging*—as revealed by such phrases as "Things get worse as one ages," "I have as much pep as last year," "As one ages, he gets less useful," "Things are better/worse than I thought," and "I am as happy as when I was younger."

The *PGC Morale Scale* has been found to be a helpful measure of subjective well-being (Liang & Bollen, 1983). In slightly modified form, it has been found useful in comparing the morale of American and Japanese elderly (Liang, Asano, Bollen, Kahana, & Maeda, 1987). The level of morale varies greatly, depending on the group studied.

Happiness

Happiness has been listed as another dimension of subjective well-being. It has been described as a quality or state characterized by

Morale—one's moral or mental condition with respect to cheerfulness, confidence, zeal, and the like

Happiness—quality or state characterized by pleasure, delight, joy, gladness, and contentment

pleasure, delight, joy, gladness, and contentment. In more technical terms, it has been referred to as "a long-term positive affect or a cognitive measurement of positive affect" (Liang, 1985, p. 552). It is a sense of subjective well-being.

Much has been written about happiness: what it is and how to achieve it. Researchers have examined the role that genetics plays in happiness and unhappiness. Interestingly, twin studies have indicated a genetic predisposition for unhappiness that runs in families (Goleman, 1986; Thomas & Chess, 1984). Some people seem to be born to be sad. However, happiness itself is not inherited; it is a capacity that must be developed.

What are the happiest years? One survey of 216 men and women, ages 16 to 67, showed that approximately 40% of the respondents regarded the 20s as the best age of life. About 18% chose the 30s. The middle years of life (the 40s and 50s) were considered best by 19%. Only 2% chose the 60s (Chiriboga, 1978). This finding agrees with other studies showing the young adult years to be the happiest.

When broken down into age groups, however, this same study indicated that *each group reported the present to be a satisfying time of life.* Most young adults felt that their age was the best age; but among those of preretirement age, 44% of the men and 61% of the women felt that the 40s and after were the best periods of life (Chiriboga, 1978). Because life expectancy at 40 is still more than 38 years, these individuals had nearly half a lifetime ahead. It is encouraging that most looked forward to those years with expectation and optimism.

One study sought to investigate the sources of overall life happiness and marital happiness in dual-career black couples. Investigation examined the contribution of 10 aspects of life, ranging from marriage to leisure activities. For both husbands and wives, marital happiness was the strongest determinant of overall life happiness. Further analysis indicated that family cohesion was the strongest determinant of marital happiness for the husbands, whereas quality communication was the strongest determinant of marital happiness for the wives (Thomas, 1990). These findings suggest that among these black couples, overall marital happiness was an important contributor to psychological well-being. Happiness with their work and career also took on added significance as a determinant of overall life happiness.

Happiness is a quality or state characterized by pleasure, delight, joy, gladness, and contentment.

Living Issues

Who Is Happiest?

The following is a compilation of research findings on happiness (Swanbrow, 1989).

1. People who plan to be happier tend to be, by making happiness a priority in their lives.
2. People are happy who have control over their own lives (Aldwin, 1991; Eizenman, Nesselroade, Featherman, & Rowe, 1997; Heckhausen & Baltes, 1991; Nurmi, Palliainen, & Salmela-Aro, 1992).
3. Poverty makes people miserable; having enough money makes them happier; but having more than enough doesn't guarantee happiness.
4. Love and intimacy—sharing loving relationships—are important ingredients to happiness.
5. Maintaining a positive attitude of optimism toward life contributes to happiness.
6. Novelty, doing new things, contributes to happiness.
7. The frequency and duration of emotional highs contributes more to happiness than does the intensity of positive feelings.
8. Keeping busy at work that is enjoyable, and accomplishing it, contributes to happiness.
9. Altruism, doing good, enhances self-esteem, makes people feel good about themselves, and contributes to happiness.
10. Maintaining physical fitness through exercise and good health habits is an important road to happiness.
11. Having meaning and purpose in life is one component of a happy life.

Congruence

Congruence means that, when assessed cognitively, there is an agreement between a person's desired goals and the goals that have been, or are being, attained in life (Rapkin & Fisher, 1992a). Congruence begins with

Congruence—cognitive agreement between a person's desired goals and the goals that have been, or are being, attained in life

Living Issues

Personal Goals of Older Adults

As the older population becomes larger and more diverse, it is imperative that psychologists understand the variety of goals and lifestyles that different elders want to pursue. An explicit description of personal goals is fundamental to an appreciation of elders as active participants in adaptation to the circumstances and transitions of later life. Rapkin & Fischer (1992a) divide the personal goals of older adults into four categories, as follows.

Achievement Goals

Young adults' concerns are heavily dominated by achievement pertaining to open-ended careers. For older adults as well, focusing on a goal that one is actively trying to attain makes much sense. At all ages, adults need goals that they are trying to achieve.

Maintenance Goals

Despite their relevance, exclusive emphasis on achievement-oriented strivings may not provide a complete portrait of elders' personal goals. Aspirations change as a function of the individual's accumulated achievements and changing circumstances. The goals of elders, in contrast to those of younger adults, necessarily entail maintaining what has already been achieved. This may involve keeping up well-established activities or social roles that provide satisfaction. Maintenance goals do not imply passivity or lower aspirations relative to achievement goals. Indeed, maintenance may require considerable effort and serve as an important source of self-esteem.

Disengagement Goals

Elders in Western culture may sometimes be motivated to participate in their own disengagement from social roles. Social pressures often lead elders to choose to abandon needs and concerns that they had as younger adults. However, they do not withdraw from all activities and roles simultaneously, and there are considerable individual differences in the patterns and circumstances of disengagement. Withdrawal of elders from society is at least partly shaped by personal priorities and preferences.

Compensation Goals

When maintenance of roles or resources is not possible, elders may shift their goals to compensate for losses that they have experienced. Relative to younger people, elders report a low level of concern with many goals and pursuits except for adaptation and avoidance of hardships. They want to cope with actual and potential losses in various aspects of their lives (Rapkin & Fischer, 1992a).

Affect—one's feelings, whether positive or negative

Social networks—social ties with children, family, and friends

finding meaning in life, making sense, order, or coherence out of one's existence, having a purpose and then striving toward a goal or goals (Reker, Peacock, & Wong, 1987). The search for meaning remains a significant and universal human motive. Meaninglessness in life, if left unresolved, can lead to symptoms of anxiety, depression, hopelessness, or physical decline.

Affect

Affect has been included as a dimension of subjective well-being in most research on the subject (Lawton, Kleban, Rajagopal, & Dean, 1992). Affect may be positive, which is a transitory feeling or emotional state of active pleasure. *Negative affect*, which is also transitory, includes anxiety, depression, agitation, worry, pessimism, and other distressing psychological symptoms (Liang, 1985). The primary content of affect is emotion, feeling. *On the Affect Balance Scale (ABS), positive affect* is described by such feelings as "excited," "pleased," "on top of the world," or "going my way." Negative affect is described by such feelings as "restless," "very lonely," "bored," or "depressed." Affect has been found to be an important dimension of subjective well-being. It has also been found to have both a hereditary and an environmental base (Baker et al., 1992).

Social Networks

Social supports are an important resource for older adults, not only for protecting them against stress and its symptoms but also for enhancing their lives (Murrell, Norris, & Chipley, 1992). Subjective well-being has been found to relate to the quality of **social networks,** that is, to the quality of social ties with children, family, and friends (Ward, Sherman, & LaGory, 1984). Past research has investigated the quality (number, frequency, and proximity) of relationships and has found that the number of ties and frequency of social interaction were relatively unimportant to life satisfaction (Bowling & Browne, 1991). Family availability and interaction particularly seemed to have little relation to the subjective well-being of older adults. The quantity of friendship interaction was only a little more consistently related to well-being.

More research by Ward and associates (1984) revealed that *whether older persons had enough social ties in the objective sense was less important than whether they perceived that they had enough.* Thus a subjective quality of social relationships is more important to well-being than objective quantity (Krause, 1990). Children play an important role in social networks of older adults, but whether children are nearby and seen regularly is less

Subjective well-being is related to the quality of social relationships.

important than whether they are seen enough and whether interaction with children has the quality desired by the older individual. The same is true in relation to friends and family. If adults expressed satisfaction with present levels and quality of social interaction and support, these social networks bore a strong association with subjective well-being.

Some research indicates that having a variety of social networks and supports, both kin and non-kin, contributes to psychological well-being (Felton & Berry, 1992). Here again, it is the quality of social networks that is important. Sometimes negative social networks may increase psychological depression and stress (Finch & Zautra, 1992).

Health

Numerous research studies point to health as one of the most important factors related to subjective well-being (Hooker, 1992). Certainly a decrease in life satisfaction and an increase in depression have been associated with a decline in perceived health (Rodin & McAvay, 1992). Also, people who are sick or physically disabled are much less likely to express contentment about their lives (Revicki & Mitchell, 1990). Willits and Crider (1988) evaluated the relationship between health rating and other satisfaction measures of adults 50 to 55 years of age and found that

health rating was significantly related to four satisfaction measures: life satisfaction, community satisfaction, job satisfaction, and marital satisfaction. Furthermore, these relationships held true regardless of gender, education, marital status, income, number of relatives in the area, number of friends nearby, or frequency of leisure involvement.

Stability of Subjective Well-Being

One question that arises is to what extent subjective well-being changes with age (McCulloch, 1991). How are different times of life perceived and evaluated? Is old age as bleak a period as younger people commonly assume? What changes take place in the affective (emotional) life of the adult? Is there a blunting of both positive and negative feelings, leading to tranquillity or even emotional blandness?

One of the most important efforts to answer these questions was a research study known as the *National Health and Nutrition Examination Survey (NHANES) I Epidemiologic Follow-up Study* (Costa et al., 1987). This survey consisted of a 9-year longitudinal study of 4,942 men and women initially aged 25 to 74. This survey was supplemented by cross- and time-sequential analysis of an independent sample of 4,986 participants (ages 32 to 87) who were first administered the *General Well-Being Schedule (GWB)* at the

Living Issues

Helping Others and Subjective Well-Being

There is now voluminous literature on supportive relationships in later life and their importance in contributing to subjective well-being. Krause, Herzog, & Baker (1992) conducted a nationwide survey on how helping others benefited one's own subjective well-being. The findings suggested that helping others bolstered feelings of personal control in later life, and this in turn resulted in lower levels of depression and increased well-being among those surveyed.

There are at least three reasons why help-giving may promote these effects. First, the realization that one has helped an individual in need is a fulfilling and self-validating experience and can bolster feelings of psychological well-being. Second, giving aid to others fosters intimacy and trust, thereby strengthening existing social bonds. Finally, giving support to significant others increases the probability that one's own need for assistance will be met in the future. Research indicates that this sense of anticipated support may be an important correlate of psychological well-being in later life.

Helping others contributes to personal well-being.

Stress—physical, mental, or emotional strain

Type A personality—personality characterized by intense competitiveness, hostility, overwork, and a sense of time urgency; one who has extreme bodily reactions to stress

time of follow-up. Although older participants tended to be lower in both positive and negative affect when measured cross-sectionally, longitudinal changes in these two measures were not found. Total well-being showed no significant age, birth cohort, or time effects in any of the analyses. Given the size and representativeness of the sample, *this is strong evidence of the stability of mean levels of*

psychological well-being in adulthood, and points to the importance of enduring personality dispositions. The finding also suggests that many adults are able to adapt to varying circumstances of life so that levels of well-being stay fairly constant (Markides & Lee, 1990).

There is a growing consensus among personality psychologists that personality stabilizes in adulthood (McGue, Bacon, & Lykken, 1993). There is a stable core of personality strongly associated with genetic factors that ensures some stability of emotionality throughout adult life. When personality change occurs, it may largely reflect environmental influences that may or may not be temporary.

STRESS

Most people function adequately and positively during their lives. They may experience difficulty, however, when exposed to excessive stress.

Meaning

Stress is physical, mental, or emotional strain or tension caused by environmental, situational, or personal pressure and demands. A woman late for work becomes tense and anxious when caught in a traffic jam. She is needed for an important meeting and paces nervously until her arrival. Her children were upset that morning because she pushed them to dress in a hurry. Her husband became angry when he could not find a clean shirt. These stresses were minor and temporary and soon forgotten by those involved.

Other stresses involve more pressure, tension, strain, and upheaval for longer periods of time: A family member becomes critically ill or a soldier is exposed to violent combat over several months. The amount of stress depends partially on the severity of the circumstances and the duration of the exposure. Generally, more stress occurs when events happen suddenly than when the individual has advance warning and can make preparations. Unpredictable and uncontrollable events cause more stress than those over which individuals exercise more control.

Also, people react differently to stress. Some have a very high frustration tolerance, others a low one. Tolerance depends partially on one's hereditary makeup and past experiences. A so-called **type A personality,** or one characterized by extreme competitiveness, overwork, hostility, and urgency, also seems to have extreme bodily reactions to stress, including increased heart rate, blood pressure, and blood flow to the muscles (Fischman, 1988). People raised in tense family environments over a period of years usually react more strongly to stressful situations. *The amount of stress experienced depends not only on the severity and duration of exposure, but also on one's previous conditioning.*

Causes

Job Related

Stress arises from various causes. Some stress is job related (Wilson, Larson, & Stone, 1993). Long hours, heavy responsibilities, and continued pressure can make a job stressful. However, these factors do not always cause stress. People who like their occupation, whose work offers opportunities to use their talents and skills and provides status, recognition, and pleasant associations, are less likely to experience job-related stress than those who are dissatisfied with their jobs. Equally important is the fact that stress in the family can have serious effects on children (Taylor, Roberts, & Jacobson, 1997).

Work that requires constant vigilance and exposes the worker to uncertainty or danger can result in stress. The work of air traffic controllers is one example. They never know when an accident is imminent. On the job, they must be alert at all times.

When the results of one's work are uncertain, stress is increased. Farm families never know whether the weather will be favorable to their crops. Drought or floods can ruin a whole year's work (Davis-Brown & Salamon,

The work of air traffic controllers involves a high degree of stress.

1987). Actors never know whether the critics will give them good reviews or whether the plays they are in will be a success. Writers never know whether their works will sell and how much their royalty checks will be. Workers who never know whether they will have a job tomorrow experience a great deal of stress.

Retirement is also considered a major source of stress, depending on whether or not a person is really ready and wants to retire. Even those who want to retire mention feelings of uselessness and of missing work after retirement. Others refer to feelings of boredom, missing contacts with work colleagues, and not knowing what to do with their time (Szinovacz & Washo, 1992). A full discussion of retirement is found in Chapter 19.

Role Strain

Stress can result from role strain. The busy homemaker and mother with four children, who is constantly under pressure from family members to run errands, provide personal services, supervise children's activities, stay up all night with a sick child, maintain a home, and give moral support to other family members, may find these demands exhausting and stressful over a long period of time (Franks & Stephens, 1992).

> Mrs. L. prided herself on her ability to run her home, take care of her three children and her husband, and work at the same time. But then things began to pile up. Her aging mother became ill and required daily care and attention. Her boss expected overtime work until his accounts were caught up. Her youngest child became seriously ill and had to be hospitalized. After several weeks, Mrs. L. was physically and emotionally exhausted. She became nervous and distraught. She cried for no special reason. She became so distressed that she had to take a leave of absence from her job to remove part of the pressure on her. (Author's counseling notes)

Job stressors may have their strongest impact on the behavior of mothers who generally experience higher levels of emotional distress, depression, and anxious mood, and, in particular, of mothers who report more type A behaviors (Repetti & Wood, 1997).

As long as people can manage their situations and feel in control, stress can be kept to a minimum (Krause, 1994). When the demands placed on one become too much to handle, stress develops (Emmons, 1992).

Interpersonal Relationships

Stress is likely to arise out of interpersonal relationships that are unpleasant and conflicting over a period of time.

> Mr. and Mrs. S. were married young. She was only 16, he was 21 when she became pregnant. She dropped out of school to have her baby, and he worked at two jobs to try to make ends meet. After the baby was born, she had no car, little money, and no close friends where they lived. She would become particularly upset if her husband spent his time off going out with his friends, leaving her alone in their apartment to take care of the baby. If she tried to talk to him, he would accuse her of being a nag and storm out the door. They began to argue about everything. No matter what they discussed, it ended up in a fight.
>
> Mrs. S. began to show physical symptoms of the tension she was under. She was exhausted most of the time, frequently sick, and despondent and depressed. Many mornings she didn't feel like getting out of bed. One morning she was shocked when she found herself slapping the baby because he cried. (Author's counseling notes).

Transition or Change

Any kind of transition or change is also stressful for some people. They get along fine if life moves routinely on the same schedule, involving the same responsibilities, the same people, and familiar surroundings. But if something changes that routine, they became upset and confused.

Major transitions in the life cycle, such as going to school, getting a job, getting married, moving to a new community, becoming a parent, switching jobs, facing retirement, or similar transitions, may require considerable adjustment. Desired changes have a much different effect than do unwanted events; however, even happy events can cause stress. People have suffered heart attacks from good news as well as bad. An older man died of a heart attack after winning $10 million in the lottery. Having a baby can be a delightful experience, but it still causes stress, especially for the couple who did not plan on children.

Life Crises

Numerous life crises cause stress (Hurwicz et al., 1992). A **crisis** may be defined as a drastic change in the course of events; it is a turning point that affects the trend of future events. It is a time of instability, necessitating decisions and adjustments. Sometimes the crisis develops because of *external events:* a hurricane, earthquake, flood (Phifer & Norris, 1989), war, national economic depression, or the closing of a plant where a person works (Thompson, Norris, & Hanacek, 1993). At other times, a crisis occurs within the family system: the loss of a family member, conflict that erupts in family violence, divorce, or alcoholism (Weigel, Weigel, & Blundall, 1987). *Internal crises* tend to demoralize a family, increasing resentment, alienation, and conflict. Sometimes a crisis develops out of a whole series of smaller external and internal events that build up to the point where people cannot cope (Lavee, McCubbin, & Olson, 1987). Broderick (1984) explained as follows:

> Even small events, not enough by themselves to cause any real stress, can take a toll when they come one after another. First an unplanned pregnancy, then a move, then the big row with the new neighbors over keeping the dog tied up, and finally little Jimmy breaking his arm in a bicycle accident, all in three months, finally becomes too much. (p. 310)

Broderick calls this situation **crisis overload.**

Sarason and colleagues (1981) developed a *Life Experience Survey* measuring the impact of various life events. People are asked to check events that occurred during the past year and to evaluate the effect of each on their lives, the extent to which they expected the event to happen, and the extent to which they had control over the event's occurrence (Friedland, Keinan, & Regev, 1992; Helgeson, 1992). Some of the events, such as death of a spouse, were more stressful than others. People who experienced multiple events, whose troubles "came in bunches," became more depressed, anxious, hostile, and fatigued, performed more poorly, and experienced more of an increase in physical symptoms. If they are able to get therapeutic help, and talk out their feelings, their mental health is improved and stress is reduced (Greenberg & Stone, 1992).

Chronic Illness

Chronic illness can be viewed as a stressor that affects the entire family. Statistics indicate that approximately 35% of deaths among adults between 25 and 44 years of age result from chronic medical conditions, such as cancer, heart disease, chronic liver

Crisis—drastic change in the course of events; a turning point that affects the trend of future events

Crisis overload—series of crises happening one after the other so that the person has difficulty in coping

diseases, pulmonary diseases, cerebral vascular diseases, and diabetes. In addition, many adults in this age range experience other chronic illnesses that are debilitating but may not be life-threatening, such as migraine headaches or chronic fatigue. It is clear that chronic illness can be identified as a major stressor for all family members. Indeed, illness demands and severity have been found to relate to higher levels of psychological distress in chronically ill adults and their partners and, at least to some extent, in their children (Kotchick, Forehand, Armistead, Klein, & Wierson, 1996).

Self-Induced Stress

One of the major sources of stress lies within an individual. A great deal of stress is self-induced: people take on more of a load than they can carry, they react very pessimistically to events that happen, or they get involved in situations that they know almost from the beginning are doomed to fail. Some people have a talent for getting themselves involved in situations that cause them trouble and that they are not able to handle, yet they do it time and time again because they believe that next time will be different. They do not seem to have the capacity to evaluate situations before they undertake them, to determine their chances of success (Epstein & Katz, 1992).

Effects of Stress

Stress produces physiological reactions within the body (Spiro, Aldwing, Levenson, & Bosse, 1990). The body goes through three stages in adapting to stress. The first stage is an *alarm reaction*, in which the body prepares to cope. Large quantities of the hormones *adrenaline* (*epinephrine*) and *noradrenaline* (*norepinephrine*) are secreted into the bloodstream to prepare the body for action. This secretion is accompanied by an increase in activity in the sympathetic nervous system, along with an increase in blood sugar, heart rate, blood pressure, and blood flow to the muscles (Blascovitch et al., 1992; Uchino, Kiecolt-Glaser, & Cacioppo, 1992).

If stress continues, the body enters a *resistance stage* during which it begins to recover from the initial stress and to cope with the situation. Secretion of adrenaline decreases, and other body functions decrease. During the final stage, a state of *exhaustion* is reached as bodily resources are depleted and the body begins to break down.

Repeated stress can result in physical damage, decline in health, and an increase in ill-

Living Issues

Financial Stress

Economic distress has a significant effect on individuals involved. Employment uncertainty or unemployment is associated with depression, psychological distress, anxiety, and state hospital admissions (Dooley, Catalano, & Rook, 1988; Ensminger & Celentano, 1988). There is considerable evidence that men's unemployment is associated with psychological distress among their wives (Liem & Liem, 1988). In fact, wives show more anxiety and depression when their husbands are unemployed than when they themselves are out of work (Voydanoff & Donnelly, 1989a). Some studies show that unemployment lowers self-esteem, a condition that, in turn, is related to a lower level of self-mastery and to an increase in depression (Perrucci, 1988). Research findings reveal that financial problems are associated with diminished feelings of control, and that these in turn are related to increased stress, regardless of how highly economic success is valued (Krause & Baker, 1992).

ness (Bigbee, 1992; Willis, Thomas, Gary, & Goodwin, 1987). High blood pressure (hypertension); some types of heart disease (Brodsky & Allen, 1988; Rubin, 1988); migraine headaches, respiratory problems such as asthma; gastrointestinal disorders such as peptic ulcers; rheumatoid arthritis; and skin disorders such as eczema and dermatitis are stress related. Stress can play a role in muscle cramps, backaches, and menstrual problems. Also, it can cause a decrease in testosterone levels as men get older (Ottenweller, Tapp, Creighton, & Natelson, 1988). If this decrease happens, it may play a role in decreased sexual functioning. Stress can adversely affect any part of the body. Stress can make people more subject to disease because it weakens the immune system (Stone, 1987). Even the incidence of cancer is higher in people who are exposed to stress that they can't handle (Smith, 1988). Some people seem to have the type of personality that is cancer prone. These individuals exhibit two major features. *One* is an inability to express emotions such as anger, fear, and anxiety. The *other* is an inability to cope with stress and a tendency to develop feelings of hopelessness, helplessness, and finally depression (Eyseneck, 1988).

Stress can interfere with psychological functioning. Depression (Krause, 1986c), panic disorder (Roberts, 1988a), anxiety, paranoia, aggression, painful guilt feelings, and insomnia are often post-traumatic stress reactions.

FOCUS

Post-Traumatic Stress Disorder

The combat experiences and reaction of soldiers during war have been the subject of much research. Soldiers must deal with the fear of death or injury. They witness other people being blown up or maimed. There is the strain of combat vigilance against unexpected attack or capture. These situations, plus separation from family; loss of sleep; physical exhaustion; and exposure to hunger, heat, or cold, produce high levels of stress, some-

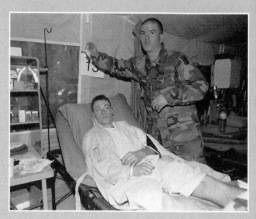

Long-term effects of combat may remain in the form of post-traumatic stress disorder.

times over long periods. Long-term effects in the form of post-traumatic stress disorder may remain. Combat veterans report terrifying nightmares and other psychological disturbances years after the war ended for them (Fontana & Rosenheck, 1994).

The relationship of post-traumatic stress disorder (PTSD) symptoms to combat exposure was examined in 1,210 veterans of World War II and the Korean War. Over 55% of World War II and 19% of Korean War veterans reported combat experience. The relationship between combat exposure and PTSD symptoms was stronger in the World War II cohorts. The World War II veterans who had been exposed to moderate to heavy combat had 13.3 times greater risk of PTSD symptoms measured 45 years later, compared with noncombat veterans (Spiro, Schnurr, & Aldwin, 1994).

Coping with Stress

Coping Strategies

Coping has been broadly defined as the constellation of responses that serve to control or reduce emotional distress in the face of some externally imposed life strain such as chronic illness. Coping strategies have been conceptualized as being either active or avoidant in nature. *Active coping* consists of those strategies that are intended to affect directly the stressor, either behaviorally (such as doing something to eliminate the source of the problem) or cognitively (such as thinking about the stressor in a more positive light). *Avoidant coping* strategies are behaviors and cognitions intended to draw attention away from the stressful event; such avoidant strate-

gies include doing something to keep from thinking about the problem or denying the presence or impact of the stressor.

The use of active coping strategies, such as information seeking or cognitive restructuring, have been associated with better psychological adjustment in chronically ill adults. Avoidant coping has traditionally been associated with poor individual adjustment in both children and adults. Avoidant coping strategies, such as self-blame and wishful thinking, are related to higher levels of distress among women suffering from rheumatoid arthritis, for example. Similarly, fantasizing, emotional discharge, and self-blame were associated with poor adjustments, with patients with hypertension, diabetes, or rheumatoid arthritis. A person's use of avoidant coping strategies has been associated with elevated levels of depression and anxiety (Kotchick, Forehand, Armistead, Klein, & Wierson, 1996).

Task-Oriented Approach

Adults deal with stress in various ways. In a task-oriented approach, they make a direct effort to alleviate the source of the stress. A person having financial problems gets an additional part-time job to earn extra money. The parent who is worried about a child consults a specialist for a solution. Couples with marital problems seek marriage counseling. In this way, stress can provide an opportunity for growth. The stressed person who believes that his or her own behavior makes a difference in the outcome of a stressful situation and then "takes charge" is pursuing an effective way of coping with stress (Preston & Mansfield, 1984). Individuals who perceive themselves as being "in control" become less demoralized in stress situations and are less likely to develop illness symptoms. There is one exception, however: When people who are in control fail and then blame themselves, stress is increased (Krause, 1986b).

The task-oriented approach requires reality testing, that is, being aware of what is going on, undistorted by anxiety, hostility, or other negative feelings. The first step in alleviating stress is to discover its roots. Then, constructive problem solving and objective evaluation must be used to discover methods that will relieve stress.

Cognitive Effort

Another approach to stress is a deliberate, cognitive effort to change one's internal response (Lohr, Essex, & Klein, 1988). Events alone do not determine the amount of stress.

What people strive to do, what they tell themselves, and how they evaluate situations all influence the amount of anxiety that they experience. Mind-set and expectations also have a great deal to do with the success that people have in accomplishing goals or in overcoming a health problem (Langer, 1989).

Meichenbaum (1972) instituted a **cognitive modification program** to help students suffering from high test-taking anxiety. Worries about the test, fear of failure, and feeling of inadequacy kept these students from doing well on exams. Some would freeze and forget facts that they actually knew. Meichenbaum explained to the students what their anxiety was doing to them. He helped them identify their negative thoughts and feelings: "I'm certain I'm going to flunk"; "I don't believe I know this stuff"; "If I don't do well, my parents will kill me." He instructed the students to restructure their thoughts, to think positively, and to direct their attention to the task at hand: "I can handle this"; "I've studied hard"; "All I have to do is quit worrying and pay attention to the questions"; "Relax, don't be afraid." During group instruction, the students had to imagine test situations and practice eliminating negative self-statements, focusing their attention on the task at hand. As a result, the students reported large decreases in anxiety and improved test performance.

Yoga is one form of relaxation training.

Living Issues

Stress and the Common Cold

It is commonly believed that life's stresses increase susceptibility to infectious disease by weakening the immune system. When demands imposed by events exceed one's ability to cope, a psychological stress response is elicited. This response is composed of negative, cognitive, and emotional states. These states stimulate autonomic nerves that connect the nervous system to immune tissue.

In one study, 394 healthy subjects completed questionnaires assessing stressful life events, perceived stress, and negative affect. They were then intentionally exposed to the common cold virus, quarantined, and monitored for the development of biologically verified clinical illness. Consistent with the hypothesis that psychological stress increases susceptibility to infectious agents, higher scores on each of the three stress scales was associated with greater risk of developing a cold (Cohen, Tyrrell, & Smith, 1993).

Relaxation Training

Relaxation training is used widely to cope with stress (Scogin et al., 1992). A one-year follow-up of relaxation training for elders with subjective anxiety showed that the older adults demonstrated relaxation within each of four training sessions; they reported greater post-training relaxation, less anxiety, and fewer psychological symptoms than those in a control group (Rickard, Scogin, & Keith, 1994). One approach is to lie down on a comfortable couch or bed, putting a small pillow under each knee and a large one under each arm. Arms should be slightly flexed alongside the body. Starting with the toes of each foot, make a deliberate effort to relax the muscles. Flex the muscles and relax them, telling each muscle to let go, to relax. Do the same thing with each foot, leg, thigh, and so on up the whole body, ending with the muscles of the neck, face, head, and scalp. By focusing attention on separate parts of the body, it is possible to relax each part and ultimately the whole body. Deep breathing during the process also helps one to relax. Deep relaxation has been used successfully in reducing headaches; in treating insomnia, high blood pressure, and body pains; and in natural childbirth. Some people use techniques like **transcendental meditation,** designed to direct one's consciousness away from thoughts and toward a state of relaxation, to accomplish the same purpose. Business executives are encouraged to take catnaps, lie down on the floor, or take a seventh-inning stretch between meetings.

Cognitive modification program—therapeutic program designed to teach restructuring of thought patterns, positive thinking, and focusing on immediate tasks; one such program, designed by Meichenbaum, helps students with high test-taking anxiety

Relaxation training—techniques to relax the body in order to combat stress

Transcendental meditation—technique to direct one's consciousness away from thoughts and toward a state of relaxation

Physical Activity and Exercise

Physical activity and exercise are wonderful ways to relieve stress. Dr. G., a dentist, finds his profession tiring and stressful. When he gets very tense, he takes time off to jog, often running 6 to 7 miles before beginning to relax. Other people walk or play tennis, racquetball, or other sports. Some climb mountains; others go fishing or hunting. Physical labor of any kind can be very relaxing after a tense day.

Sublimation

Another way to deal with stress is to sublimate it through indirect means, such as psychotherapy, work, sex, hobbies, or recreation. Some people bury themselves in their work, paint the house, or work in the garden. Others escape through hobbies or through sexual release. One husband who was under great emotional strain at work joined a local theater group and relieved his pent-up emotions on stage. Another would hammer on an old metal water tank in his basement whenever he became upset.

Medication

A common way of dealing with stress is to medicate it. Judging from the millions of tranquilizers and sedatives sold each year, this seems to be a popular source of relief. Reasonable medication on a temporary basis may provide appropriate and welcome relief. The danger is developing dependency or addiction that relieves symptoms but never gets to the root of the problem and ends up creating problems of its own.

Social Interest

Another way to minimize stress is to increase one's social interest—one's interest in and concern for others. Zarski, Bubenzer, and West (1986) found that there is a positive relationship between high social interest and life adjustment, and between high social interest and overall health, high energy level, and fewer somatic symptoms. Those adults who scored high on social interest were also lower on measures of day-to-day hassles and frustrations.

Self-Efficacy and Social Support

Perceived self-efficacy is the beliefs that people have about their capabilities to execute behavior needed to achieve desired ends. Perceived self-efficacy is viewed as an important determinant of how much effort people will exert and how long they will persevere in the face of significant challenges. One study examined perceived self-efficacy in men 6 months after a *myocardial infarction (heart attack)* (Coyne & Smith, 1994). Efficacy was positively correlated with the men's degree of dependence on their wives. Men who actively engaged the support of their wives, provided that the wife did not do too much protective buffering, had higher self-efficacy than did men who tried to do it on their own. Patient efficacy was related to the wives' social support without being overprotective. Higher self-ratings of dependence was associated with higher self-efficacy and a better quality of marriage before the myocardial infarction. Both the quality of marriage before the myocardial infarction and the patient's use of active engagement and protective buffering as strategies for dealing with their wives were important.

Social Support

Seeking social support helps in managing stress (Arling, 1987; Krause, 1986a, 1988). Family members, friends, or counselors who listen empathetically provide moral support and emotional assistance (Krause, 1991a). Because some people need support groups when they have problems, groups like *Al-Anon*, *Parents Without Partners*, and *Divorce Perspectives* are very successful. People band together to learn how to cope and to overcome their difficulties.

Of course, there is always the possibility when one turns to friends or family for social support that stress may be increased. There are both negative and positive aspects of social relationships. Some friends and family members add to the conflict and increase stress rather than alleviate it (Lepore, 1992). Mothers who are stressed because of the impact of economic strain and the demands placed on them by their children are able to handle their stress and be far better parents if they have their husbands' support (Simons, et al., 1993). Unfortunately, there are people who will not let others help them when they really need support. They avoid physical contact, reject supportive comments, and refuse all efforts to seek and give emotional support. This behavior makes it very difficult for friends and family members to know how to help them (Simpson, Rholes, & Nelligan, 1992).

Hostile Reactions

Hostile reactions to stress may or may not be helpful in relieving the stress (McCrae, 1982). If anger motivates people to do something positive about their situation, it can be very helpful, but if anger leads to distrustful, hurtful behavior, it may make the situation worse and aggravate the stress.

Other Coping Mechanisms

Generally speaking, middle-aged and older adults use more positive coping mechanisms in dealing with stress than do adolescents or young adults. Positive mechanisms might include *direct confrontation, planful problem solving, positive reappraisal, seeking social support,* and sometimes *distancing, self-controlling,* and *showing care and concern.* Negative coping mechanisms might include *escape-avoidance, some hostile reactions,* or *self-blame* (Irion & Blanchard-Fields, 1987).

PATTERNS OF FAMILY ADJUSTMENT TO CRISES*

A family crisis may be an important source of stress. There are definable stages to such crises (Boss, 1987; Lavee, McCubbin, & Patterson, 1985). The stages of adjustment to a family crisis are shown in Figure 18.1 and are discussed separately in this section.

First Stage: Definition and Acceptance

The *first stage* is the onset of the crisis and the increasing realization that a crisis has occurred. An initial reaction may include disbelief. Family members may define a situation differently; what is a major crisis to one person may not be to another. In the case of a married couple having difficulties, for example, one spouse may be on the verge of a divorce; the other refuses to accept the fact that there is a problem, believing that the other is "making too big a deal out of it." The first step, therefore, involves defining the problem and gradually accepting that a crisis exists: for example, the gradual realization and acceptance of a child's disability. Therefore, the impact of the crisis will depend on the nature of the precipitating event and the interpretation and cognitive perception of it, the degree of hardship and stress that the crisis produces, and the existing resources available to handle the problem.

*The material in this section is excerpted from the author's book *Intimate Relationships, Marriages, and Families,* Mountain View, CA: Mayfield Publishing Co., 1999. Used by permission of the publisher.

Second Stage: Disorganization

The *second stage* of a crisis is a period of disorganization. Shock and disbelief may make it impossible to function at all or to think clearly in the beginning. "I don't know what I'm going to do" is a common reaction. The period of disorganization may last for only a few hours, or it may stretch into days or weeks. During this period, the family's normal functioning is disrupted. Tempers are short, loyalties are strained, tensions fill the air, friction increases, and family morale declines. When it occurs, child and spousal abuse is more likely to develop during the time of maximum disorganization than at any other time. When Mount St. Helens erupted on May 18, 1980, thousands of people felt the stress. Associated Press reports from Washington state after the eruption indicated that criminal assaults rose 25%, suicide threats and attempts doubled, and the number of cases of battered wives increased 45% (Blumenthal, 1980). The situation was particularly stressful because of the violence of the explosion (500 times the force of the atom bomb at Hiroshima) and the uncertainty of subsequent explosions. People did not know what would happen next or how long the catastrophe would last. The effects of stress were delayed, however. The greatest increase in cases of spouse abuse did not occur until about 30 days after the major eruption.

Other studies have shown that the use of alcohol and other drugs sharply increases during times of stress and may lead to a deeper level of disorganization or serve to handicap the family's capacity to bounce back from the crisis (Miller, Turner, & Kimball, 1981).

Third Stage: Reorganization

The *third stage* is one of gradual reorganization, during which family members try to take remedial action. If the crisis is a financial one (Larson, 1984), family members may borrow money, sell the family car, or cash in some savings. Other family members get temporary employment to help out, or a primary provider who is out of work starts drawing unemployment. If the financial crisis persists, the stock of resources begins to run out. The family has to think about a second mortgage, selling the house, or moving to another neighborhood.

Once the crisis "hits bottom," things begin to improve. The family providers get new jobs, and bills are gradually paid off; the family begins to recoup its emotional and physical resources. Eventually, after a period

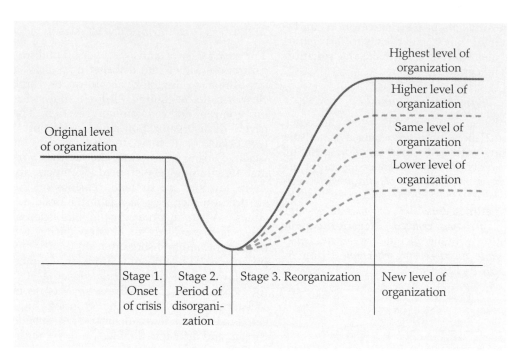

FIGURE 18.1   Family adjustment to a crisis.

that may range from days to months, the family is reorganized at a new level. Sometimes the new level is never as satisfactory as the old one; at other times, the level of organization is superior to the old. (In the case of a financial crisis, family money management improves and/or total income is higher.) At any rate, the level is high enough and stable enough to mark the end of the period of crisis. (See Figure 18.1.)

Summary

1. The kind of feelings that develop and the way that they are expressed and controlled are important considerations in a person's life and behavior.

2. To be emotionally mature means being emotionally secure, being emotionally stable, and having the capacity to feel.

3. Emotional security involves freedom from crippling negative emotions such as anxiety, doubt, and fear, which are present in excess and keep a person from functioning as a healthy individual.

4. Emotional stability means a relative degree of freedom from drastic ups and downs of emotions that interfere with a person's functioning with other people in appropriate ways. Emotionally unstable people get upset easily, so that they are hard to get along with.

5. Research generally supports the conclusion that emotional experience and expression decline with age and that emotional control increases.

6. Being an emotionally mature person also means having the capacity to feel, whether to love or to hate.

7. In extreme cases, a person who has lost all capacity to express feelings and who has no conscience is considered a psychopath.

8. Subjective well-being is a multidimensional concept that can best be measured by specific indicators such as life satisfaction, morale, happiness, congruence, and effect.

9. The Life Satisfaction Index A measures five dimensions of the concept: zest versus

apathy, resolution and fortitude, congruence, self-concept, and mood tone.

10. Continued fulfillment of meaningful social roles is an important determinant of life satisfaction among African American elderly. The church and religion also play an important role in their lives.

11. Most factors influencing life satisfaction affect both blacks and whites, but the negative effects of impairments are considerably stronger among blacks than among whites.

12. Life satisfaction does not automatically increase as income rises. The key seems to be whether people are satisfied with the level of income that they have reached.

13. Urbanism influences life satisfaction indirectly and interactively because it influences health, financial satisfaction, and social integration; however, the effects of urban living on life satisfaction are inconsistent.

14. Hispanic immigrants find considerable psychological stress because of social isolation, language barriers, acculturation problems, and prejudice and discrimination against them.

15. The quality of a marriage has a strong effect on happiness and life satisfaction. Family relationships early in life also have an important influence on subjective well-being as adults.

16. Subjective well-being has also been described in terms of morale, which is one's mental or emotional condition with respect to cheerfulness, confidence, zeal, and the like.

17. Happiness is listed as another dimension of subjective well-being. Genetics may play a role in unhappiness, but happiness itself is a capacity that must be developed. One study reported that each age group said that the present was a satisfying time of life.

18. Congruence is another element of subjective well-being. It means that there is an agreement between a person's desired goals and the goals that have been or are being attained. Congruence begins by trying to find meaning in life, establishing a purpose, and striving toward goals.

19. Results of testing a group of adults, age 16 to 75, with the Life Attitude Profile (LAP) showed that both life purpose and death acceptance increased with age; goal seeking and future meaning decreased with age; and existential vacuum showed a curvilinear relationship with age. Women scored higher on life control and will to meaning than men.

20. Older adults as well as younger ones need personal goals to strive for. These goals have been divided into four categories: achievement, maintenance, disengagement, and compensation.

21. Affect is another dimension of subjective well-being. Positive affect (emotions) indicates well-being; negative affect indicates lack of well-being.

22. Social networks also relate to subjective well-being. The important consideration is not the quantity of such networks, but the quality, and whether adults perceive that they have enough social ties with friends and family.

23. Numerous research studies point to health as one of the most important factors related to subjective well-being.

24. Subjective well-being is fairly stable throughout adulthood.

25. Stress is physical, mental, or emotional strain or tension caused by environmental, situational, or personal pressure and demands. The amount of stress experienced depends on the severity and duration of exposure, one's cognitive perception of it, one's previous conditioning, and one's hereditary makeup.

26. Stress may be job-related or may result from role strain; the degree of stress experienced depends on the degree of control that people feel they have over their situations. Stress may arise from interpersonal relationships, be created by transition or change, or be precipitated by life crises. Crises may develop because of external events, or arise internally within the family.

27. There are three stages in adapting to stress: alarm, resistance, and exhaustion.

28. Repeated stress can have a negative effect on health or even weaken the immune system so that one is more susceptible to the common cold.

29. There are a variety of approaches in dealing with stress: a task-oriented approach, cognitive effort and modification, relaxation training, transcendental meditation, physical activity and exercise, sublimation, medication, increasing social interest, and seeking social support.

30. A number of other positive mechanisms to cope with stress include confrontation, planful problem solving, positive reappraisal, seeking social support,

distancing, self-controlling, and showing care and concern.

31. Negative coping mechanisms include escape-avoidance, some hostile reactions, or self-blame.

32. There are three stages of family adjustment to a crisis: definition and acceptance of the crisis, disorganization, and reorganization.

Key Terms

Affect   *p. 498*
Cognitive modification program   *p. 505*
Congruence   *p. 497*
Crisis   *p. 502*
Crisis overload   *p. 502*
Emotional maturity   *p. 490*
Emotional stability   *p. 490*
General anxiety disorder   *p. 490*
Happiness   *p. 496*

Morale   *p. 496*
Psychopath   *p. 492*
Relaxation training   *p. 505*
Social networks   *p. 498*
Stress   *p. 500*
Subjective well-being   *p. 492*
Transcendental meditation   *p. 505*
Type A personality   *p. 500*

Discussion Questions

1. In what ways are you emotionally mature? Immature? In what ways are you secure or insecure? Stable or unstable? Do you have the capacity to feel emotion?

2. Have you ever known another person who suffered from general anxiety disorder? What was the person like? Were you able to relate to that person? Were there any particular problems you encountered?

3. Have you ever known a psychopath? Describe.

4. To what extent do you feel positive, subjective well-being? What makes you most satisfied and happy? What makes you most dissatisfied and unhappy?

5. Identify a person whom you know who seems to be very happy and satisfied with life. Why is that person that way?

6. Identify a person whom you know who is never happy or satisfied. Why?

7. Can you be happier in the city or in rural areas? Explain.

8. How much of an income do you feel you need in order to be satisfied? Would you be happier if you won a million dollars in the lottery? Explain.

9. Describe your morale. Is it high, low, or medium? Why?

10. What factors do you feel are most important to happiness?

11. Why is it important to find meaning, purpose, and goals in life to be satisfied? What are your most important goals in life?

12. Do you know anyone who is always cheerful and pleased and who shows positive affect? Describe that person. Do you know anyone who seems always to show negative affect? Describe that person.

13. How do social networks relate to life satisfaction? Can you be happy without friends? Without seeing members of your family? Explain.

14. Do you know anyone who has poor health who is still happy? Describe.

15. What factors in your life have you found most stressful? What have you done or are you doing to relieve this stress? Does it help? Explain.

16. What factors cause you the most stress: school, job, interpersonal relationships with friends or with family, changes in your life, or life crises? Explain.

17. Describe a very stressful experience that you have gone through, and compare your reactions with the three stages in adapting to stress.

18. In your opinion, what are the most effective means of dealing with stress?

19. Describe a major crisis that occurred in your family and the adjustments that were made to it.

Suggested Readings

BLECHMAN, E. A. (Ed.). (1990). *Emotions and the family: For better or for worse.* Hillsdale, NJ: Lawrence Erlbaum. The nature of emotions in the context of the family and their relationship to behavior.

COOPER, C. L. (Ed.). (1985). *Psychosocial stress and cancer.* New York: Wiley. The relationship between stress and cancer.

EDELSTEIN, B. A., & DOMBRANDT, I. (Eds.). (1996). *The Practical Handbook of clinical geron-*

tology. California: Sage. Alzheimer's disease and depression; treatment. Mental health problems.

KEITH, P. M., & SCHAEFER, R. B. (1991). *Relationships and well-being over the life stages*. New York: Praeger. Comparisons of couples over four different life stages.

POTTER-EFRON, R., & POTTER-EFRON, P. (1995). *Letting go of anger*. Oakland, CA: New Harbinger Publications.

TAYLOR, S. E. (1998). *Health psychology*. New York: McGraw-Hill. Overview of the field.

http://www.mentalhealth.org   Center for Mental Health Services Knowledge exchange network and information and resources on prevention, treatment, and rehabilitation services for mental illness.

Web Resources

Social Development

Chapter 19

SINGLEHOOD

Marital Status and Delay

Figure 19.1 illustrates the marital status of the U.S. population, 18 years of age and older, in 1997. Overall, 60% were married, 23.5% were single (never married), 7% were widowed, and 9.9% were divorced. Obviously, the great majority of adults were married, and an additional number had been married at one time. Nevertheless, a bit more than 1 in 5 adults had never been married, but these were primarily in the youngest age groups.

The unmarried status of most in the singles group is only temporary because by age 45 to 54 only 8.6% of males and 7.1% of females have never been married. (See Figure 19.2.) However, the trend is for adults to get married at older ages than they used to.

Typology of Singles

There are various categories of single persons. Stein (1981) has developed a typology of single persons based on whether their status is voluntary or involuntary. Table 19.1 shows four major categories of singles according to Stein.

Voluntary Temporary Singles

This is a category that includes young persons who have never been married and are not currently looking and those who are postponing marriage even though they are not opposed to the idea of marriage. It includes cohabitors who will eventually marry each other or someone else. It includes recently divorced or widowed persons who need time to be single, though they may eventually want to marry again. It also includes older never-marrieds who are not actively looking but who would marry if the right person came along.

Voluntary Stable (Permanent) Singles

This is a category that includes never-marrieds and former-marrieds of all ages who have no intention of marrying or of remarrying.

Involuntary Temporary Singles

Included in this category are young adults who have never been married but are actively seeking a mate, and divorced or widowed persons who want to remarry soon.

Involuntary Stable (Permanent) Singles

This category includes never-married persons or widowed or divorced persons who wanted to marry or remarry and who have not found a mate (South & Lloyd, 1992); they have become reconciled to their single state. It also includes physically or mentally impaired persons.

Advantages and Disadvantages of Being Single

People find both advantages and disadvantages in being single.

Advantages

Reputed advantages include the following:

1. Greater opportunities for *self-development and personal growth and fulfillment.* If singles want to take a course or travel, they are freer to do so than are married people.

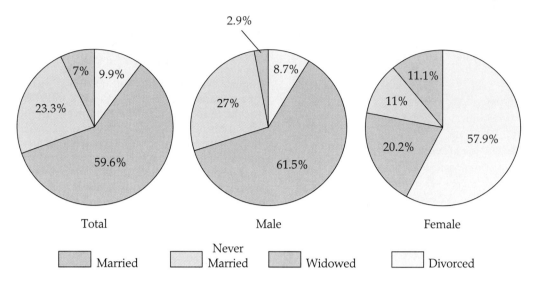

FIGURE 19.1   Marital status of the population, 18 years old and over, 1997.

Adapted from *Statistical Abstract of the United States, 1998* (p. 58) by U.S. Bureau of the Census, 1998, Washington, DC: U.S. Government Printing Office.

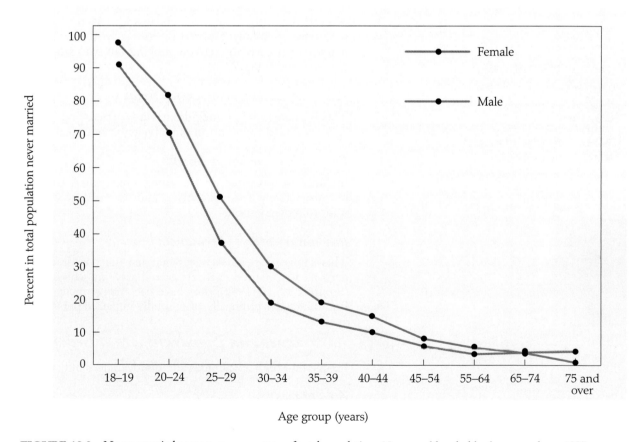

FIGURE 19.2   Never-married persons as percentage of total population, 18 years old and older by age and sex, 1997.

Adapted from *Statistical Abstract of the United States, 1998* (p. 58) by U.S. Bureau of the Census, 1995, Washington, DC: U.S. Government Printing Office.

TABLE 19.1   TYPOLOGY OF SINGLES

	Voluntary	*Involuntary*
Temporary	Never-marrieds and previously married who are not opposed to the idea of marriage but are not currently seeking mates	Those who have actively been seeking mates but have not found them
Stable (permanent)	All those (never-marrieds and former-marrieds) who choose to be single	Never-marrieds and former-marrieds who wanted to marry, who have not found a mate, and who have more or less accepted being single

Adapted from *Single Life: Unmarried Adults in Social Context*, by P. Stein, 1981, New York: St. Martin's Press. Used by permission of Haworth Press.

2. Opportunities to *meet different people and develop and enjoy different friendships*. Singles are free to pursue friendships with either men or women, according to their own preferences.

3. *Economic independence and self-sufficiency*. One woman said: "I don't have to depend on a husband for money. I earn it myself and I can spend it as I want."

4. *More sexual experience*. Singles are free to seek experiences with more than one partner.

5. *Freedom to control one's own life*, to do what one wants without answering to a spouse; more psychological and social autonomy.

6. *More opportunities for career change, development, and expansion*. Singles are not locked in by family responsibilities and so can be more mobile and flexible in the climb up the career ladder.

Not all of these advantages can be applied to all singles. For example, not all singles have opportunities to meet different people. Not all are economically well off, nor are all free of family responsibilities. Nevertheless, some singles would list some of these or even all of these items as advantages for them.

Disadvantages

Those who are not in favor of remaining single describe a number of disadvantages:

1. *Loneliness and lack of companionship*. This is one of the most pressing problems of singles.

2. *Economic hardship*, especially for single women. Single women earn less than single or married men and, without access to a husband's income, have a lower standard of living than do married men or women. Also, employers tend to feel that unmarried persons are less stable than are those who are married, so top positions are more often given to married persons, especially to men.

3. *Feeling out of place in many social gatherings* because social life is organized around married couples. In addition, singles may not be invited to some social events.

4. *Sexual frustration* for some persons.

5. *Not having children*, or lacking a family in which to bring up children.

6. *Prejudices* against single persons in our society and social disapproval of their lifestyles. This creates problems for singles if society considers them a threat to the established social order or to other people's marriages. Much pressure is put on them to get married.

People find both advantages and disadvantages in being single.

Lifestyles

Research on lifestyles of singles reveals a variety of patterns. An in-depth study of never-married college-educated men and women over age 36 describes six lifestyle patterns (Schwartz, 1976).

Professional

These persons organized their lives around work and identified with their occupational roles. Most of their time and energy was spent on their careers.

Social

These persons had extensive social lives and many personal relationships. Friends and social activities were given priority over work. They were deeply involved in hobbies, organizations, and family activities.

Individualistic

These persons focused their attention on self-growth. They enjoyed freedom, privacy, living alone, and not having to answer to anyone. They enjoyed hobbies, reading, and other solitary pursuits, along with classes on self-improvement.

Activist

The lives of these persons were centered on community and political causes. Work was important, but much time was devoted to trying to create a better world.

Passive

These were loners who spent much free time alone, in solitary pursuits such as shopping or attending movies. They had negative outlooks on life and showed little initiative in using their lives creatively.

Supportive

These persons spent their time in service to others. The few persons in this category were mostly women who were very satisfied with their lives.

It is obvious that not all single adults fit into the same lifestyle. There is as great a variation among members of this group as among other segments of the population, and so it is misleading to try to describe singles as a homogeneous group.

Living Arrangements

Singles Communities

In the stereotyped fantasy, groups of singles occupy apartments or condominiums that cater especially to their needs. A case in point is Carl Sandburg Village in Chicago, transformed from a skid-row neighborhood with run-down apartments, greasy-spoon taverns, and transient hotels, into nine high-rise buildings surrounded by townhouses and renovated apartments. Nearly three-quarters of the residents 18 and older are unmarried. Occupants enjoy an indoor swimming pool, gymnasiums, restaurants, and other built-in amenities. Rents have skyrocketed, but people who cannot afford the leases often get roommates, increasing the number of unwed couples living together.

Shared Living Spaces

Although a large number of unmarrieds live in singles areas or apartments, more live with the general population. The majority occupy individual apartments, usually with roommates. The usual pattern is to share apartments and living expenses with one or more persons who provide emotional support and companionship.

Leaving Home

One of the most fascinating transition points in the relationship between parents and their children occurs when children are on the brink of leaving home. Prior to that time, the two generations are part of a single family. The process of leaving home is an important part of the transition to adult life. Whereas in the past leaving home was usually associated with marriage, now the move out of the parental home is increasingly concerned with a preference for independence. Both the destination and the timing of young people's home-leaving are likely to be crucial in determining later life opportunities. For example, children who make the final break with their parental home at a very early age may incur detrimental economic and social consequences much the same way as has been observed with teen-aged motherhood. In addition, moves to independent living are likely to delay marriage and may result in young people's adopting less traditional family values and more egalitarian gender role attitudes than those who remain in the parental home (Buck & Scott, 1993).

We are increasingly coming to recognize that young adults remain dependent in some ways even after they leave home (e.g., they are likely to return home when things get particularly rough), suggesting that parental power and support remain highly important during the transition to adulthood (Gold-scheider & Goldscheider, 1993).

Living Alone

Table 19.2 shows the percentage distribution, by age group, of singles living alone (U.S. Bureau of the Census, 1998). However, this table includes divorced, separated, or widowed people, as well as the never-married. As illustrated, greater percentages of males than females in the 15 to 44 age group live alone. With each succeeding age group (55 to 64 and 65 and over), the relative numbers and percentage of females living alone increase rapidly, because of the greater numbers of older females in the population.

Friendships and Social Life

Companionship

One of the greatest needs of single people is to develop interpersonal relationships, networks of friendships that provide emotional fulfillment, companionship, and intimacy. Single people value freedom and varied activities, but they also place a high value on enduring, close friendships. Social interaction occupies a position of considerable impor-

One of the greatest advantages of being married is to be able to share companionship.

tance in the lives of young adults. Much waking time is spent participating in and thinking about social activities with friends, family, and romantic partners. Satisfying social bonds are a primary source of psychological well-being and happiness. Moreover, the absence of desired levels of social contact and closeness with friends and relatives typically produces distress (Reis, Lin, Bennett, & Nezlek, 1993).

When Cargan and Melko (1982) asked both marrieds and singles to describe the greatest advantage of being married, most replied in terms of shared feelings: "companionship and someone to share decisions with," "companionship," "love and companionship," "the opportunity to converse with someone every day," "being able to share your life with someone you love," "togetherness is very important to me," "love is caring and having children and sharing things, and doing things together." The concept that turned up most frequently was companionship.

Loneliness

Loneliness is a problem for a significant minority of never-marrieds (Cargan, 1981). Some evidence suggests that among single young adults, male-male friendships are less intimate and spontaneous than are female-female friendships. Single males are more isolated and have fewer intimate relationships than do single females. Although men sometimes exceed women in the number of voluntary associations in which they hold memberships, they spend less time in group activities, and their participation is less stable. The norms of competition and fear of homosexuality have hindered the development of male friendships. Yet, *males as well as females need*

Age	Both Sexes	Male	Female
15–24 yrs old	1	1	1
25–34	9	11	7
35–44	8	10	7
45–54	10	10	10
55–64	14	10	18
65 years and older	30	16	40
All ages	12	10	14

TABLE 19.2 **PERCENTAGE OF PERSONS LIVING ALONE BY AGE AND SEX, 1997**

Adapted from *Statistical Abstract of the United States, 1998* (p. 70) by U.S. Bureau of the Census, 1998, Washington, DC: U.S. Government Printing Office.

Living Issues

Unmarried Cohabitation

The government now defines **unmarried cohabitation** as two unrelated adults of the opposite sex sharing the same living quarters in which there is no other adult present (Spanier, 1983). According to this definition, referred to as Persons of the Opposite Sex Sharing Living Quarters, or POSSLQ (S. Davidson, 1983), there were 4,130,000 unmarried cohabiting couples in the United States in 1997 (U.S. Bureau of the Census, 1998), a 160% increase since 1980. About 36% of these couples had some children in the household under 15 years of age. About 19% of all the householders were under 25 years of age; 59% were 25 to 44 years old; 18% were age 45 to 64; and 5% were 65 years or over.

One of the important questions is, To what extent has cohabitation resulted in greater satisfaction in subsequent marriage? Researchers (Thompson & Colella, 1992) have consistently found that physical aggression is more common among cohabiting couples compared with married couples. Part of the reason may be that cohabitors are more likely to be socially isolated than married persons. The isolation may lift restraints on being aggressive, either because of lack of social support or lack of social control. Cohabitors, especially men, report significantly more alcohol problems than both

married and single adults (Horwitz & White, 1998). Certainly then, these characteristics of cohabitors do not make them more eligible to become marriageable people (Stets, 1991).

Actually, there is no evidence that premarital cohabitation weeds out incompatible couples and prepares people for successful marriage. According to the 1987–1988 National Survey of Families and Households (Thomson and Colella, 1992), couples who had cohabited before marriage reported lower quality marriages, lower commitment to the institution of marriage, more individualistic views of marriage (wives only), and a greater likelihood of divorce than couples who had not cohabited. These consequences were generally more likely for those who had cohabited for longer periods before marriage. (Shelton & John, 1993). According to the *1995 National Survey of Family Growth,* by ten years after first marriage, only 15% of couples who had never cohabited at all before their first marriage had their marriage dissolved by separation, divorce, or annulment. This finding is in contrast to 30% of marriages dissolved when the woman cohabited with her first husband and 83% of marriages dissolved when a woman had cohabited after she first married (1995 National Survey of Family Growth, 1997).

The results seem to be affected partially by how long people have been married at the time of the evaluation. Most research indicates that a period of disillusionment in relation to marriage occurs after the initial glow and excitement have worn off and couples have settled down to daily living. Presumably, the longer couples have lived together before marriage, the earlier in the marriage relationship the period of disillusionment sets in (DeMaris & Rao, 1992).

Comparisons of married couples who had and who had not cohabited showed that those who had lived together before marriage scored significantly lower in marital communication, consensus, and satisfaction.

The finding that cohabitation is associated with a decrease in marital quality, especially for serial cohabitors, may be explained by less commitment to marital permanence (Teachman and Polonko, 1990). For others, the association of cohabitation with greater odds of marital dissolution is the result of the increased exposure to the problems of living together. DeMaris and Rao (1992) found that cohabiting prior to marriage, regardless of the nature of that cohabitation, is associated with an enhanced risk of later marital dissolution.

---

close, caring friendships that develop into a sense of mutuality and constitute a major source of social support.

Social Activities

Is it true that singles have more leisure time and more fun than marrieds? It is easy for married persons to envy their apartment-dwelling single friends. But singles who work all week still have to clean their living quarters, make beds, cook, and do laundry. They go bicycling or to an art gallery, but if they want company, they may have to call friends

and encounter some rejections before plans are completed, just as marrieds do.

In spite of this, *singles do have more time for optional activities.* They can make more choices and devote more time to leisure activities if they choose. Marrieds are more likely to have houses and children requiring time and attention (Cargan & Melko, 1982).

According to Cargan & Melko (1982), visiting friends was the preferred social activity of never-marrieds, followed (in declining order of preference) by going to movies, restaurants, nightclubs, theaters, or social clubs, or visiting relatives. Couples married once preferred going to restaurants or visiting relatives. The entertainment preference of never-marrieds was more a preference of youth. Both never-marrieds and marrieds spent a lot of time watching television. Never-marrieds spent more time on hobbies.

Despite the fact that singles spent more time on social activities, *a greater percentage of marrieds than never-marrieds said they got a lot of fun out of life and that they were happy* (Cargan & Melko, 1982). Marrieds may derive happiness and fun in different ways. Gardening or taking the children on a picnic can be fun. When asked what was most important to their happiness, marrieds mentioned health first, then marriage, children, love, religion, and friends, in that order. Only the category of friends was more important to singles than to marrieds. Surprisingly, success and money were not listed as important to happiness in either group (Cargan & Melko, 1982).

Dating and Courtship

Attraction

The most important element in attraction—at least in initial encounters—is physical attractiveness. We are attracted positively to those who are pleasing to look at, have good builds and well-proportioned bodies, and other physical characteristics that appeal to our aesthetic sensibilities. Study after study finds physical appearance to be one of the chief ingredients in early attraction (Shea & Adams, 1984).

Factors other than physical appearance also attract people to one another. A study of 30 men and 30 women who were married (not to each other) for 2 to 8 years measured factors that the subjects found most attractive in their spouse (Whitehouse, 1981). The subjects were asked what attracted them to their spouse on first meeting, what attracted them after a few months, and what attracted them at the time of the interview. The factors were divided into five categories: *extroversion, agreeableness, conscientiousness, emotional stability*, and *culture*. Various traits under each category are shown in Table 19.3. Upon initial meeting, the most important factor was extroversion: being talkative, frank, open, adventurous, and social. However, the importance of these traits declined with the years, whereas characteristics listed under agreeableness became much more important. The traits under conscientiousness also became slightly more important.

Other studies have confirmed that *personality traits and the way people act are significant factors in whether others find them attractive or not.*

TABLE 19.3	FACTORS THAT MARRIED PERSONS FOUND ATTRACTIVE IN THEIR SPOUSES

Category	Traits
Extroversion	Talkative
	Frank, open
	Adventurous
	Sociable
Agreeableness	Good-natured
	Not jealous
	Mild, gentle
	Cooperative
Conscientiousness	Fussy, tidy
	Responsible
	Scrupulous
	Persistent
Emotional stability	Poised
	Not nervous
	Calm
	Composed
	Not hypochondriacal
Culture	Artistic
	Sensitive
	Intellectual
	Polished, refined
	Imaginative

From "Toward an Adequate Taxonomy of Personal Attributes: Replicated Factor Structure in Peer Nomination Personality Ratings," by W. T. Norton, 1963, *Journal of Abnormal and Social Psychology, 66*, p. 577.

People who are generally warm, kind, generous, intelligent, interesting, poised, confident, or humorous, or who exhibit generally admired qualities, are more attractive than those who are rude, insecure, clumsy, insensitive, unstable, or irresponsible, or who manifest other negative traits. Orlofsky (1982) found that conformity to the cultural standards of approved femininity or masculinity was a powerful component of attractiveness.

Parents and friends exert a considerable influence on the quality and stability of romantic relationships. Support from parents and friends affects the quality of these relationships and the likelihood that they will break up or continue over a period of time (Sprecher & Felmlee, 1992).

Finding and Meeting Dates

One of the major problems of those who want to date is where and how to meet prospective partners (Ahuvia & Adelman, 1992). Knox and Wilson (1981) surveyed a random sample of 334 students at East Carolina University to find out how they met, where they went, and what they did on dates. About a third of the students met their current dating partner "through a friend." The next most frequently mentioned way of meeting was "at a party." A lesser number met "at work" or "in class." Those not meeting in these ways checked "other," which included "I grew up with him/her" and "We met on the school newspaper" (p. 256).

Gender Roles in Dating

Male-female roles in the dating process are changing rapidly. Traditionally, males controlled initiation, planning, and paying for the date. This arrangement encouraged an unspoken agreement in which females were expected to reciprocate for benefits received

Present trends emphasize egalitarian relationships in dating while maintaining some desirable customs.

by allowing expressions of affection and sexual intimacies (Sprecher, 1985).

With the development of the feminist movement, women became increasingly aware of the inequalities between the sexes and suspicious of the power distribution in heterosexual relationships. They have sought to equalize control within the dating situation by initiating and paying for dates, thereby altering any alleged male sexual expectations and female sexual obligations on dates. In a study of 400 college women, Korman and Leslie (1982) found that approximately 55% of their sample reported that they helped pay the expenses of dates at least some of the time. Korman (1983) compared the initiation and expense-sharing behavior on dates of feminists and nonfeminists. The subjects were 258 unmarried, undergraduate women attending classes at a large Southeastern university. Feminists and nonfeminists were grouped according to overall scale scores on the *FEM Scale*. In comparison with nonfeminists, feminists were more likely to initiate dates and to share the financial obligations of women-initiated dates. However, their motives were to achieve more egalitarian relationships and not necessarily to reduce sexual obligations. Although both feminists and nonfeminists believed that men who paid for dates were more likely to expect sexual favors, both groups said that they were unlikely to engage in unwanted sexual activity.

Dating Anxiety

Dating is usually an important part of the social life of young people. Yet many haven't learned the social skills and developed the self-confidence to succeed. A survey of 3,800 undergraduates at the University of Arizona found that a third (37% of men and 25% of women) were "somewhat" or "very anxious"

Living Issues

Opening Lines

Psychologist Chris Kleinke asked several hundred students at colleges in California and Massachusetts to suggest opening lines that they might use to meet those of the opposite sex in general situations, at beaches, supermarkets, and bars. Kleinke divided approaches into three groups: "direct," "innocuous," or "cute/flippant." Men and women both claimed to prefer direct and innocuous approaches to cute/flippant ones. The top-rated openers were:

- *In general situations:* "I feel a little embarrassed, but I'd like to meet you." (direct)
- *At the beach:* "The water is beautiful today, isn't it?" (innocuous)
- *At a supermarket:* "Can you help me decide here? I'm a terrible shopper." (direct)
- *At a bar:* "What do you think of the band?" (innocuous)

The least-favored of the cute/flippant openers were:

- *In general situations:* "Is that really your hair?" "Your place or mine?" "You remind me of a woman I used to date."
- *At the beach:* "Let me see your strap marks."
- *At a supermarket:* "Do you really eat that junk?"
- *At a bar:* "Bet I can outdrink you."

(Rice, 1981)

Living Issues

Date Rape

Date rape refers to rape that occurs between two people who go on a voluntary, prearranged date or who meet at a social occasion and voluntarily leave together. This type of sexual aggression is very common. Estimates of the incidence of rape by acquaintances range from 15% to 27% (Killian & Busby, 1995). Data from various findings lend support to the fact that only a few date rapes are officially reported and that most survivors do not acknowledge the date rape as a rape experience. In light of the phenomenon of underreporting, the actual prevalence of date rape is much higher than one-fourth of all women. One student writes the following:

> Charlie and I went parking after the movie. He asked me to get in the back seat with him, which I did, because I trusted him and felt safe with him. We necked and petted awhile, and then he became violent. He ripped off my panties, pinned me down on the seat, and forced himself on me. I couldn't do anything about it, yet he had the

nerve to ask me afterward if I enjoyed it. (From a student paper)

Women are told frequently: "Don't go out with a man you don't know. If you do, you're taking a big chance." This is probably sound advice, but one of the purposes of dating is to get to know other people. Unfortunately, no matter how well you know an individual, problems can arise.

Date rapes can occur in relationships where two people have gone together for a long period of time. As familiarity grows, the sexually aggressive male may become more insistent and try verbally and/or physically to coerce his partner into sexual activity that she finds objectionable. This behavior may reflect lack of communication and lack of understanding in the man-woman relationship. Some men are brought up to believe that when a woman says "no" she really means "yes," and it's up to the man to do what he feels she really wants to do anyhow. This attitude reflects the same myth that exists in relation to other types of rape—the myth that women want to be forced. It also

reflects the social learning in our culture; that men are supposed to be the sexual aggressors and overcome the reluctance and hesitancy of women. Men rape their dates out of anger, hostility, and contempt, as an expression of negative feelings, certainly not as an act of caring. Many such men engage repeatedly in acts of sexual aggression with a series of partners (Heilbrun & Loftus, 1986).

Devastating effects of sexual assault can include symptoms of anxiety, depression, and increased instance of sexual dysfunction. Most rape psychological symptoms experienced by the victim of stranger and acquaintance rape really don't differ; both groups manifest scores of high depression and anxiety. With a basic belief destroyed (that the world is a safe place and people are trustworthy), a victim's capacity for openness and trust in her intimate relationships may be severely curtailed during the recovery process. When the rapist is a friend or date, not only has her whole body been violated, but also her trust in another human being is betrayed. Her faith in her own judgment has been shaken (Killian & Busby, 1995).

about dating. Half the students in a University of Indiana survey rated dating situations "difficult." Nearly a third of Iowa students said they feared meeting new people (Timnick, 1982).

Sexual Behavior

If we are to believe the media, all young, healthy Americans are having a great deal of sex. The truth is far more complex. According to the *National Health and Social Life Survey* (NHSLS), 94% to 98% of men and women have had sexual intercourse by the time they have reached 25 (Michael, Gagnon, Laumann, & Kolata, 1994). These statistics include everybody who has ever had sex. When the researchers inquired about the fre-

quency of sex in the past 12 months, they got a completely different picture. According to the NHSLS Survey, 25% of never-married, noncohabiting men and women had no sex partners during the past 12 months. Thirty-eight percent had only one partner, 28% had two to four. Only a small percentage of the population (9%) had as many as five sex partners during the past year; most of this group were young men who have never been married and were not living with anybody. These findings give no support to media images of a promiscuous society. The findings present evidence that most people do, in fact, form a partnership and ultimately get married.

One serious consideration is whether or not those who are having sex are protecting themselves against sexually transmitted diseases, especially against AIDS. In a national survey of

Date rape—forced, unwanted sexual intercourse while on a date.

Living Issues

AIDS

AIDS is of special concern today not only because it is incurable but also because it is always fatal once a person contracts it. A blood test measures the presence of AIDS virus antibodies in the bloodstream. A person who tests positive for the AIDS virus antibodies has been exposed to the virus, is infected, can get it, and can transmit it to others (Wallis, 1987). Persons may spread the virus without knowing they are infected. The incubation period may be from several years to as long as 10 years.

The AIDS virus is found in semen, blood, urine, vaginal secretions, saliva, tears, and breast milk, and is transmitted from male to female, female to male, male to male, and female to female during the exchange of body fluids (Communicable Disease Summary, 1985). Transmission is through direct sexual contact, by getting HIV positive blood in an open wound or in the eyes, and by use of infected needles or syringes. The AIDS virus can also pass from mother to fetus during pregnancy and through breast milk to a nursing infant (Koop, 1986). Although the AIDS virus has been found in tears and saliva, only one instance of transmission from saliva has been reported, and none from tears. However, physicians and dentists have transmitted the disease to patients, and patients to them, through blood exchanges. AIDS is not transmitted through casual, nonsexual social contact such as occurs at home, in offices, restaurants, or schools (Friedland et al., 1986). It is not transmitted through touching, holding, shaking hands, or playing together; nor by sneezing, breathing, or coughing; nor through food or biting insects; nor through towels, toilet seats, eating utensils, or water fountains ("Health Services," 1985). AIDS is a disease of heterosexuals as well as homosexuals and bisexuals. It also occurs frequently among intravenous drug users (Smilgis, 1987). The more sex partners that one has, male or female, the greater the risk of becoming infected.

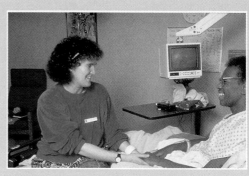

AIDS attacks the immune system and makes the person susceptible to opportunistic diseases.

10,630 people, aged 18 to 75, among respondents with multiple partners, only 18% of men and 22% of women always used condoms with their primary partner. Twenty-eight percent of men and 32% of women always used them with their secondary partners. In general, almost half of men and women with multiple partners never used condoms (Dolcini, Catania, Cotes, Stall, Hudes, Gagnon, & Pollack, 1993). This finding places the sexually active people at high risk for AIDS.

LOVE AND INTIMACY

Each person defines love differently according to his or her background and experience. One person may describe love in terms of strong feelings and emotions. Another may describe it as sexual attraction. Another may emphasize that love is a way of behaving and a way of treating other people. Someone else may emphasize love as friendship and liking of another person. Another may say it is primarily care or concern for someone else. Still another person may say that there's no such thing as love, that it is just a delusion and a myth (Rice, 1996).

Type of Love

In fact, there are many different definitions of love. The point of view reflected here is that love is not a single concept but has different dimensions. This author has found it convenient to divide love into five different elements as follows: *romantic love, erotic love, dependent love, friendship love,* and *altruistic love.* **Romantic love** has been described as a profoundly tender or passionate affection for another person. Its chief characteristic is strong emotions, marked by intensity of feelings. If love is mutual and fulfilling, there is a great sense of joy, ecstasy, exhilaration, and well-being, and there is a desire to be together so that the couple can continue to enjoy the pleasure of love. However, if romantic love is taken as the only criterion for marriage, love can become very dysfunctional. Feelings alone are not an accurate indication of suitability or marriageability.

Romantic love

Love is not just a feeling; it is how people treat one another.

People can fall in love with imprisoned rapists, drug addicts, wife abusers, or emotionally immature, unstable, hostile individuals. If they marry persons who have these faults, they certainly are minimizing their chances of being happily married. Yet, at the time they married, they said they were wildly in love. However, the idealism of romantic love is not dysfunctional if it approaches reality. What is dysfunctional is the inability of some people to separate the idealized from realistic and real-life relationships.

The second element of love is **erotic love.** Erotic love is sensual love. This type of love can be defined as sexual attraction to another person. It is the biological component of love relationships. Erotic love is an important part of love. Certainly, sexual attraction is an important beginning, and sexual satisfaction strengthens the bond between two people. Ordinarily, sex and love are interdependent. A loving relationship becomes a firm foundation for a happy sexual life, and a fulfilling sexual relationship reinforces the love of a couple for each other.

The third type of love is **dependent love.** It is valuable as a basis for a strong relationship, but it involves mutual dependency. This type of love is functional in a relationship to the extent that each person meets the needs of the other. Unless people need each other and fulfill each other's needs, why have a relationship? The difficulty arises when the needs of one person are so excessive that neurotic, possessive dependency becomes the basis for the relationship. Most people need to receive as well as to give if they are to remain emotionally healthy.

The fourth type of love is **friendship love,** which is based on companionship and common interests. It's an enduring bond between two people who like each other and enjoy each other's company. It can endure for many years. For most people, friendship alone is not enough for marriage, but it is an important ingredient in loving relationships.

The fifth type of love is **altruistic love,** which adds genuine concern and care to the total relationship. The criterion as to whether the person is in love or not in this sense is the extent to which that person shows he or she cares and is concerned about the other person. As in dependent love, receiving and giving must be mutual. Altruistic love allows the person expressing it to gain satisfaction through caring for another. It allows the receiving person to be loved and cared about for his or her own sake (Rice, 1996).

The five elements of love just described are all important in the most complete love. The more one's love contains all five of these elements, the stronger and deeper it is and the more functional it becomes as a sound basis for a permanent marriage relationship.

Other researchers categorize the elements of love a little differently. Sternberg (1986) asked subjects to describe their relationships with friends, siblings, parents, and lovers. Analysis of the results revealed three components of close relationships: intimacy, passion, and decision/commitment to maintain the relationships. *Intimacy* with another person involves emotional bonding: having loving, close, warm feelings for another, receiving and giving understanding and support, and being able to communicate with each other. It involves feeling happy with a partner, valuing that person's presence in one's life, and holding that person in high regard. It involves trust, being able to count on a partner in time of need. It also involves altruism: the desire to promote the person's welfare and to share oneself and one's possessions with a partner (Sternberg & Grajek, 1984).

The *passion* component refers to sexuality, romance, and attraction in a relationship.

The *decision/commitment* component involves both short-term and long-term factors. The short-term factor includes a decision made consciously to love another person. The long-term factor is commitment to maintain the love. Sometimes people fall in love but do nothing afterwards to maintain it. Sternberg emphasizes that the most complete love, which he calls **consummate love,** results from a combination of all three components. The love relationship is balanced when all three elements are present in relatively equal degrees.

Sternberg and Barnes (1988) describe eight different combinations of these three components of love:

Erotic love

Dependent love

Friendship love

Altruistic love

Consummate love

1. *Absence of intimacy, passion, and commitment*—no love.
2. *Intimacy only*—liking (but no passion or commitment)
3. *Passion only*—infatuation (but little intimacy or commitment)
4. *Decision/commitment only*—empty love (with no passion or intimacy)
5. *Intimacy and passion*—romantic love (no commitment)
6. *Intimacy and commitment*—companionate love (without passion)
7. *Passion and commitment*—fatuous love (foolish love, without real intimacy)
8. *Balanced match of intimacy, passion, and commitment*—Sternberg and Barnes found that people are more likely to be satisfied with their relationships if their love triangles match, that is, if they have fairly equal amounts of the same components of love (Sternberg & Barnes, 1988).

There have been efforts made to measure differences in love styles and love attitudes across family life stages. Research by Montgomery and Sorrel (1997) reveals the following love styles. Manic and ludus styles are held more strongly by young singles and adolescents than by any of the married adult groups, and at the same time, unmarried youths were the lowest in agape love attitudes. Ludic attitudes and obsessive, uncertain, manic attitudes that are characteristic of courtship are more common in the younger age groups. Marriage encourages agapic, altruistic, or self-giving love attitudes. Couples who have children in the home hold less pragmic love attitudes than couples who are in all other stages of family life. This is the case probably because the demands of children in the home stimulate a very practical, pragmatic approach to family relationships. Older couples also have very pragmatic attitudes that reflect pressures to form partnerships with social and economic viability. Those couples who reported being in love endorsed eros to a greater degree than those who did not report being in love. Storgic love was evident in couples of any age, who reported long-lasting friendships. Agape or an altruistic selfless love was reported only by those couples who gave priority to partners' needs as a principal love style. Endorsement of both passionate (eros) and friendship/companionship love attitudes (storge) was high for all groups and did not differ by family life stages. All stages of the life-course adults endorsed passion, friendship, and self-giving love attitudes as highly salient for them. Pas-

sion and friendships/companionship were not consecutive in a romantic relationship, after all—they appeared to exist concurrently in both dating and married life-stage groups (Montgomery & Sorell, 1997).

Mate Selection

According to developmental process theory, mate selection is a process of filtering and weeding out ineligibles and incompatible people until one person is selected. This theory describes various factors that are used in the selection process.

Propinquity

One of the factors in mate sorting is propinquity. That is, geographical nearness is a major factor influencing mate selection (South, 1991). Obviously, we're more likely to marry someone who lives nearby, with whom we come into contact. Mate availability is also an important factor in mate selection. Is there an adequate supply of eligible men and women in the local areas in which one resides (Fossett & Kiecolt, 1993)?

Attraction

People are drawn to those whom they find attractive. This category includes both physical attraction and attraction because of specific personal characteristics or traits.

Homogamy and Heterogamy

People tend to choose mates who share social and personal characteristics such as religion, social economic class, education, ethnicity, race, and age. This tendency to choose a mate similar to one's self is called **homogamy.** Choosing a mate different from one's self is called **heterogamy.** In general, homogamous marriages tend to be more stable than heterogamous marriages, although there are exceptions. The major reasons that marriages are generally homogamous is that we tend to prefer people who are like us, and we feel uncomfortable around those who are different.

Compatibility

Compatibility means the capability of living together in harmony. Compatibility may be evaluated according to habit systems, role conceptions and enactment, needs, attitudes and values, and temperament. In the process of mate selection, couples strive to sort out those with whom they are compatible in these various ways.

Homogamy

Heterogamy

The Filtering Process

Figure 19.3 shows a schematic representation of the filtering process. The figure is based on numerous research studies and theories.

Beginning at the top of the figure, we begin the process of filtering with a very wide field of eligibles. This total group goes through a series of filters, each of which eliminates ineligibles, so that the numbers are reduced before passing to the next filter. Before making a final decision, two people may go through a final trial period either through a formal engagement or through cohabitation or both. If they survive this filtering process, the final filter is the decision to marry.

Note that the order is approximate. Obviously, partners are selected according to propinquity first, but physical attraction plays a significant role very early in the relationship, followed by attraction because of other personality traits. Gradually, couples begin to sort out homogamous mates according to religion, socioeconomic class, education, race, and age. As the relationship develops, they find out whether they're compatible according to habit systems, role concepts, needs, attitudes and values, and temperament. Some couples place more emphasis on some factors than on others. Some may explore compatibility without regard for homogamy. Others are more interested in selecting someone with the same socioeconomic background. Generally speaking, however, both compatibility factors and homogamous factors are important. A testing of the relationship provides further evidence of whether the choice is a wise one or not.

Mate selection, therefore, can be a complex process by which people sort out various personal, psychological, social, and emotional factors until the final choice is made.

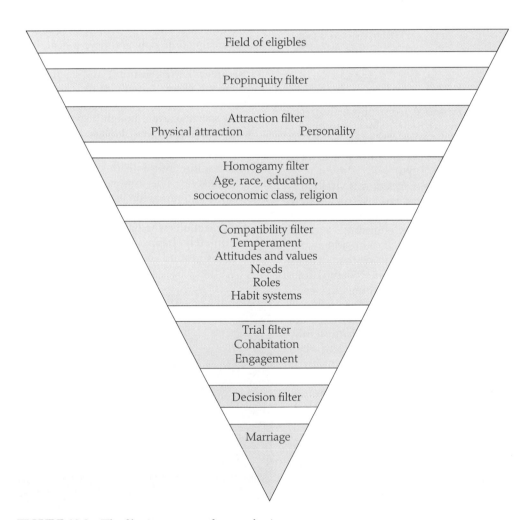

FIGURE 19.3   The filtering process of mate selection.

Living Issues

Marriage Rates Among Blacks

Overall, both black men and black women are significantly less likely to marry than are their white counterparts. The situation is not caused by any deficiency in ideology in relation to the family. African Americans believe strongly in the institution of the family. When black men and women are unable to fulfill their family roles, it is often because of situations beyond their control. There is an acute shortage of African American males who are of marriageable age or who are economically ready for marriage. There are one-half million fewer black men than women over age 18 (U.S. Bureau of the Census, 1998). Many of the young, unmarried men are not good marriage prospects. The problem is especially acute for college-educated African American women. More black women than black men are obtaining undergraduate and master's degrees, and the gap is widening. Not wanting to marry someone with less education than they have, almost one-third of college-educated black women remain unmarried past the age of 30. Compared with white women, African American women place greater importance of having economic support in place prior to marriage and are more resistant to marrying someone who has few resources (Bulcroft & Bulcroft, 1993).

Unfortunately, some people are not this thorough. They move from physical attraction to marriage without going through the intervening filters; or outside factors, such as pregnancy, pressure them into a marriage that is unwise (Rice, 1996).

When couples get married, it is vitally important that they be ready to take such a step. Background factors and sociodemographic characteristics of income, education, and age are strongly related to perceived readiness for marriage. Being ready is more than having found a person with whom one is compatible. It also is a matter of having things in order: Thus, when a person is older, is financially and educationally in a position to get married, and feels that he or she has support from family and friends for the choice of partner, and when the quality of that couple's relationship is good, then he or she feels ready to marry. Interaction factors such as the quality of communication and the level of agreement are significantly and positively related to perceived readiness for marriage. Approval by significant others (parent and peers) increases the quality of couple communication, results in a greater level of agreement, and thus culminates in a greater perceived readiness for marriage. It is interesting that approval by significant others is one of the most powerfully related variables to perceived readiness for marriage (Holman & Li, 1997).

The Older, Never-Married Adult

The major difference between younger and older adults who have never married is that most younger singles consider their status temporary, whereas older singles are often well adjusted to their situation. Older singles may or may not be interested in dating, but they usually have some social life and a variety of things to do with a few friends. A study of older singles between 60 and 94 found that they saw nothing special about being married; it was "just another way of life" (Gubrium, 1976). They valued being independent, were relatively isolated (but not lonely), and were generally satisfied with their activities. They did not have to face widowhood or divorce and tended to accept and take for granted their lifestyle. They were unique persons, not misfits, who had adjusted to life differently from most others.

The following comments from a 71-year-old male are typical:

> I have been single all my life (71 years). I am living alone now and have a beautiful, well-furnished, two-and-a-half room apartment. I work at home and keep the apartment clean. I don't think I would like to live together presently. I'd rather not be married, even though I have plenty of opportunities (Hite, 1982, p. 266).

It's hard to find fault with this man's point of view or lifestyle. The important thing is that he is happy and satisfied.

In contrast to the situation of this man, other single adults who have never married are not completely happy with their situation. Keith (1986) found that a sizable minority of

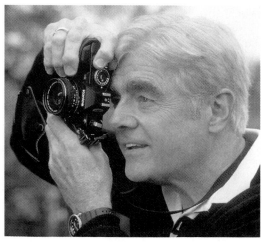

When older singles are satisfied with their activities, they tend to be happy.

unmarried aged people felt isolated from neighbors, friends, and relatives. Men were more likely to be isolated from family than were women. Divorced and never-married men and women were more isolated from family than were those who were widowed. Both never-married men and women, however, compensated for their isolation from relatives by maintaining more ties with friends.

Overall, however, *the happiness of these older adults was very dependent on satisfaction with their level of living and with their level of activity rather than just on the extent of social contacts.* Adequate financial resources permitted mobility and reciprocation in the development and maintenance of friendships. Also, if persons were satisfied with their level of activity even though they might be isolated from family or friends, they tended to express greater happiness.

Marriage and Family Living

Marriage and Personal Happiness

There are significant mental health benefits to being married. People who maintain close social relationships in marriage are happier, live longer, have fewer mental and physical illnesses, and have lower levels of substance abuse than those who are socially isolated. Compared with people who remain unmarried, the married have less distress, mental illness, alcoholism, and drug abuse, as well as less morbidity and mortality. In addition, a number of factors, including greater social integration, social support, social control over health-threatening behaviors, and economic well-being, appear to account for the mental health benefits of marriage (Horwitz & White, 1998). Few married people would disagree with the thesis that the quality of marriage has a strong effect on their happiness and satisfaction with life (Lee, Seccombe, & Shehan, 1991; Mastekaasa, 1992; Ross, 1995; Zollar & Williams, 1987). Data from six national studies conducted in the United States revealed that *marital happiness contributed more to personal global (overall) happiness than did any other kinds of satisfaction, including satisfaction from work* (Glenn & Weaver, 1981). At the same time, an unhappy marriage can also have a negative effect on life satisfaction and subjective well-being (Haring-Hidore, Stock, Okun, & Witler, 1985). People who are having severe marital problems may not be able to eat properly; they often can't sleep; and they may

become debilitated and run-down during the period of upset.

The Family Life Cycle

Stages

One of the most helpful ways of examining marital relationships over periods of time is to look at them over various phases of the **family life cycle.** The family life cycle divides the family experience into phases or stages over the life span and seeks to describe changes in family structure and composition during each stage. The cycle can also be used to show the challenges, tasks, and problems that people face during each stage, as well as the satisfactions derived.

Figure 19.4 shows the family life cycle of a husband and wife in an intact marriage. The ages of the husband and wife are median ages for the U.S. population. Thus, the husband is married at 26, the wife at 24. They wait 2 years and then have 2 children. The husband is 50 and the wife 48 when the youngest child is 20 and leaves home. The empty-nest years until retirement are from age 50 to 65 for the husband and age 48 to 65 for the wife. The wife lives to be age 79, the last seven years as a widow (U.S. Bureau of the Census, 1998). The husband dies at 72.

Marital Satisfaction Over the Family Life Cycle

How does marital satisfaction change over various phases of the family life cycle? One study found that marital quality as measured

Family life cycle—the family experience divided into phases or stages over the life span; a description of the changes in family structure and composition, and of the challenges, tasks, problems, and satisfactions involved during each stage

Living Issues

Marriage and Personal Control

Research indicates that people are much happier if they have control over their own lives. The question arises: How does marriage affect people's sense of control over their lives? On the one hand, marriage increases social and economic resources that may increase perceived control. People have more finances to do the things they would like to do. On the other hand, marriage limits autonomy, freedom, and independence. Furthermore, the relative effects may differ for men and women. Both spouses' sense of control (or lack thereof) may be due ultimately to the fact that many men still earn more than women, thus making some women dependent on men for their economic well-being (Ross, 1991).

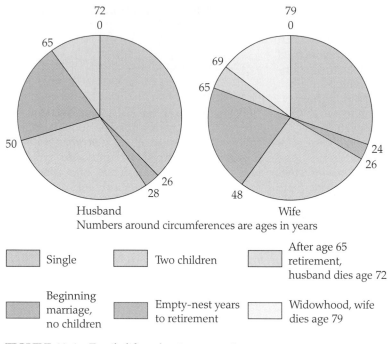

Numbers around circumferences are ages in years

Single

Two children

After age 65 retirement, husband dies age 72

Beginning marriage, no children

Empty-nest years to retirement

Widowhood, wife dies age 79

FIGURE 19.4 Family life cycle—intact marriage.

Statistics from *Statistical Abstract of the United States, 1998*, by U.S. Bureau of the Census, 1998, Washington, DC: U.S. Government Printing Office.

Marital adjustment tasks— areas of concern in marriage in which adjustments need to be made

by divorce proneness, marital problems, marital happiness, marital interaction, and marital disagreements remained fairly stable over an 8-year period (Johnson, Amoloza, & Booth, 1992). Those who had poor marriages at the beginning of the period were more likely to have poor marriages at the end of the period. However, other research shows that marital satisfaction does change over longer periods of time that encompass various phases of the family life cycle. The studies are quite consistent in showing a decline in marital satisfaction during the early years of marriage, particularly following the birth of the first child and continuing to the end of the preschool or school-age period (Schumm & Bugaighis, 1986). These findings are consistent with other research that parental hassles increase during the childbearing years. It seems that as children develop and acquire more abilities, they present a greater range of behaviors and situations that parents find stressful (Crnic & Booth, 1991). A few studies show the decline extending to the end of the teenage period. Other studies show a decline in marital satisfaction throughout the years of marriage (Vaillant & Vaillant, 1993).

Practically all studies show an overall increase in marital satisfaction after children have reached school age or finished their teenage years. Some also show another slight decline in satisfaction prior to retirement (An-

derson, Russell, & Schumm, 1983). *The general trend is for marital satisfaction to decline or to be somewhat curvilinear—to be high at the time of marriage, lowest during the child-rearing years, and higher again after the youngest child has passed beyond the teens.* Apparently, bearing and rearing children interfere with marital satisfaction (Anderson, Russell, & Schumm, 1983).

When the question is raised as to why marital satisfaction is at an ebb when the children are of school age, the most plausible explanation seems to be that the demands placed on the couple during these years are at their greatest. One study showed that discordant family relationships and disharmonious marital and parent-child relationships increase as children get older (Stattin & Klackenberg, 1992).

Adjustments Early in Marriage

All couples discover that their marriage never lives up to all of their expectations. As a result, couples go through a series of adjustments in which they try to modify their behavior and relationship to achieve the greatest degree of satisfaction with a minimum degree of frustration. The various areas of adjustment are called **marital adjustment tasks** and may be divided into 12 areas as shown in Table 19.4. The extent to which couples need to make adjustments after marriage depends partially on the extent to which some of these tasks are confronted during courtship.

Adjustments to Parenthood

"First Pregnancy," says psychiatrist Eldred, "is a 9-month crisis. Thank God it takes 9 months, because a child's coming requires enormous changes in a couple's ways of adjusting to each other" (Maynard, 1974, p. 139). In recent years, there has been less of a tendency to refer to the addition of a first child as a crisis and more of an inclination to refer to it as a period of stress and transition. The amount of stress will vary from couple to couple. *The more stressful a couple's marriage before parenthood, the more likely it is that they will have difficulty in adjusting to the first child.* Moreover, if parental expectations do not match realities, stress arises because parents are disappointed (Kalmuss, Davidson, & Cushman, 1992).

Sometimes stress arises if the pregnancy was not planned. Part of the stress comes from the fact that most couples are inadequately prepared for parenthood. As one mother states, "We knew where babies came from, but we didn't know what they were like." When their first child is born, many parents have absolutely no

---

TABLE 19.4   MARITAL ADJUSTMENT TASKS

Emotional fulfillment and support
Learning to give and receive affection and love
Development of sensitivity, empathy, closeness
Giving emotional support, building morale, fulfilling ego needs

Sexual adjustments
Learning to satisfy, fulfill one another sexually
Working out mode, manner, timing of sexual expression
Finding, using acceptable means of birth control

Personal habits
Adjusting to one another's personal habits, speech, cleanliness, grooming, manners, eating, sleeping, promptness
Reconciling differences in smoking, drinking, drug habits
Elimination or modification of personal habits that annoy one another
Adjusting to differences in body rhythms, schedules
Learning to share space, time, belongings, work

Sex roles
Establishing husband's and wife's roles in and outside the home
Balancing employment and parenthood by both the husband and wife (Berry & Rao, 1997; Robinson & Milkie, 1998)
Working out sex roles in relation to income production, housekeeping, household maintenance, homemaking, caring for children (Brayfield, 1992)
Agreement on division of labor

Material concerns, finances (Clark-Nicolas & Gray-Little, 1991)
Finding, selecting a residence: geographical area, community, neighborhood, type of housing
Equipping, maintaining a household
Earning adequate income
Managing money

Work, employment, achievement
Finding, selecting, maintaining employment
Adjustment to type, place, hours, conditions of employment

Working out schedules when one or both are working
Arranging for child care when one or both are working

Social life, friends, recreation
Learning to plan, execute joint social activities
Learning to visit, entertain as a couple
Deciding on type, frequency of social activities as individuals and as a couple
Selecting, relating to friends
Finding the time to be together (Zuo, 1992)

Family, relatives
Establishing relationships with parents, in-laws, relatives
Learning how to deal with families

Communication
Learning to disclose and communicate ideas, worries, concerns, needs
Learning to listen to one another and to talk to one another in constructive ways

Power, decision-making (Zietlow & Van Lear, 1991)
Achieving desired balance of status, power
Learning to make, execute decisions
Learning cooperation, accommodation, compromise
Learning to accept responsibility for actions

Handling conflict, solving problems
Learning to identify conflict causes, circumstances
Learning to cope with conflict constructively
Learning to solve problems
Learning where, when, how to obtain help if needed

Morals, values, ideology
Understanding and adjusting to individual morals, values, ethics, beliefs, philosophies, and goals in life
Accepting one another's religious beliefs and practices
Decisions in relation to religious affiliation, participation

Living Issues

Tremendous Trifles

In the beginning, couples notice every minute detail about the way the other person walks, talks, dresses, eats, sleeps, bathes, and so on. Everything one does comes under the close scrutiny and observation of the other. The newness of the experience makes the two people very observant and sometimes critical. One husband complained because his wife never wanted to sleep with a window open, whereas he liked a lot of fresh air. One meticulous wife discovered that her husband never liked to take a bath or to use deodorant. Another discovered that her husband always threw his dirty socks and underwear in a corner of the room. Gradually, couples begin to get used to one another, to overlook some of these things, and to learn how not to annoy one another. Early in the marriage, however, these "tremendous trifles" can be quite aggravating.

experience in caring for infants. One study showed that men who are prepared for fatherhood, who have been prepared for parenthood by attending classes, reading books, and so forth, found far greater satisfaction in being a parent than did those who had not been so prepared (Cooney, 1993).

There are three factors that contribute toward first-time fathers' readiness for parenthood: (a) a sense of stability in the couple's relationship, (b) relative financial security, and (c) a sense of closure to the childless part of the couple's relationship (Garrison, Blalock, Zarski, & Merrit, 1997).

Part of the stress arises, also, because of the abrupt transition to parenthood. Rossi (1968) wrote the following:

> The birth of a child is not followed by any gradual taking on of responsibility, as in the case of a professional work role. It is as if the woman shifted from a graduate student to a full professor with little intervening apprenticeship experience of slowly increasing responsibility. The new mother starts out immediately on 24-hour duty, with responsibility for a fragile and mysterious infant totally dependent on her care (p. 35).

For this reason, it is vital that the husband share the care with the mother. Direct assistance from relatives in the early days after birth can also reduce stress.

Wives often prefer to have husbands participate in child care to a greater degree than husbands actually participate. How does a woman respond if she finds that her husband stubbornly resists sharing the work of caring for the new baby? If a husband consistently fails to be moved by his wife's preferences, she usually makes unfavorable attributions about his character and love. High prenatal expectations about postnatal sharing of housework eventually lead first-time mothers to feel less close to their husbands. In many instances, when the husband and the wife do not agree about child care, the woman changes her expectations and her feelings are moderated by the level of love she has for her husband. Over a period of time, many wives are able to change their husbands' willingness to help with child care, especially when the husbands discover that there are many positive benefits both to themselves and to their children because of their participation. Considerate husbands who love their wives will try to please them, just as the wives try to please their husbands. Increased correlation between the husbands' and the wives' attitude about child care may enable them to work out an understanding about child-care responsibilities that is satisfactory to each of them. Whether the wives pursue a strategy of demanding more from their husbands or of lowering their expectations, it is the husbands' strategies that are critically important to wives, because they provide evidence of either their husbands' love or their self-interest. The wives' sense of fairness is a predictor of their satisfaction with the relationship (Johnson & Huston, 1998). Even the egalitarian couples have to make a conscious confrontation of both gender and equality issues before they can fulfill the prerequisites for the possibility of marital equality (Knudson-Martin & Mahoney, 1998).

Stress will vary from child to child depending on each child's temperament and how easy each child is to care for. Some children give a minimum of trouble. Others, such as hyperactive or sick children, require an abnormal amount of care. However, all babies require considerable care, and significant stress necessarily occurs with every new baby.

In the past two decades, there has been a growing trend for couples to delay parenthood. Many reasons account for this trend, but three primary factors are *educational attainment*, *economic stability*, and *careers*, particularly for women.

Voluntary Childlessness

The vast majority of couples want to have children, but voluntary childlessness is increasing, and society is more accepting of this lifestyle (Thornton, 1989). In general, women who have a post–high school education are less likely to have children than are those who have less education. Race is not a significant determinant of childlessness, but childhood residence is. Rural women are less likely to remain childless than those growing up in urban centers or in nonrural areas. Other research indicates little difference in the happiness in the family of origin between those who want to remain childless and those who do not. However, the childless are less traditional and less sexist in their views of women. Other surveys reveal similar results: Women who want to remain childless are less likely to want to be housewives only; they have higher social mobility goals; they are more likely to prefer urban residence; and they expect to marry at later ages than women who want children (Kenkel, 1985). Couples who are voluntarily childless have some convincing arguments against having children. They say that having children contributes to the population problem; children make it difficult for a woman to work outside the home; they require a drastic change in lifestyle; they cost too much; they cause too much disorder in the household and have a negative effect on one's health and stamina; they cause too much worry and tension; and child care takes too much time (Neal, Groat, & Wicks, 1989).

The amount of stress in child rearing varies, depending on how easy each child is to care for.

One of the principal arguments against having children is the restriction on freedom that rearing children entails. Having children means readjusting one's lifestyle to take into account their needs and activities. There is no question that the woman who finds self-fulfillment through her own career might find life much easier if she does not have children. As a result, women brought up to find personal fulfillment primarily through career pursuits do not often feel dissatisfied or distressed that they do not also have children. In fact, research does support the contention of the voluntarily child-free couple that they do have a higher level of cohesion and a significantly higher level of dyadic satisfaction (Somers, 1993).

Adjustments During Middle Adulthood

The Time Squeeze

The most noticeable changes of midlife are physical ones, which have already been described in Chapter 16. Body monitoring increases as individuals concern themselves with the dimensions of their middle-aged bodies. Health concerns are increasingly related to life satisfaction (Willits & Crider, 1988). Perhaps for the first time, adults are confronted with their own mortality (Kercher, Kosloski, & Normoyle, 1988). Up to this point in their lives, adults have counted how old they are. Now, they begin to count the years that they have remaining. The midlife crisis is precipitated by the awareness that the years are numbered. Paradoxically, people are entering the stage of fulfillment, the prime of life. But the fulfillment and the prime are limited in time.

This personalization of mortality leads to an awareness that life is a race against time, that there is a sense of urgency to accomplish all that one wants to achieve, that time is finite. Many middle-agers intensify efforts to live life while they can before it is too late. This crucial shift of time orientation in the life cycle may lead to self-appraisal, self-analysis, and introspection. Middle-agers engage in an existential questioning of values, self, and life itself. They ask, "Is there anything else for me? What am I here for? What is the purpose of life? Where is my life going? What have I done with my life?" They ask, "Who am I?" They try to find a new identity they feel comfortable with. Concern with these identity issues is an important cause of personal dissatisfaction during the middle years (Steinberg & Silverberg, 1987).

This assessment of self extends to an examination of marriage, career, and responsibilities. As one middle-ager expressed it: "I'm tired of doing what I'm supposed to do. Now I'd like to start doing what I want to do." Financial responsibilities tend to be heavy in middle age. Some men at midlife become obsessed with financial security for themselves and their wives in retirement. Many middle-agers are under considerable stress. This is the time of heaviest responsibilities in the community and at work. The main stressors for men are economics and work. Job burnout may occur during this time (Arthur, 1990). Middle-aged women typically feel stress about lack of companionship with their husbands, the possibilities of their young adult children's making bad marriages, and concern about their work. As far as work is concerned, employment for middle-aged women may serve as a buffer against other stresses in their lives.

Thus, midlife is a time when existential, practical, and personal issues are all in focus. It can become a time for reexamination, a time to chart new courses for life ahead (Rice, 1996).

Marital Adjustments

As we have discussed, marital satisfaction tends to be at its lowest ebb when the children are of school age or in their teenage years. On the average, the wife is 41 and the husband is 43 when the youngest child is age 13. If the husband and wife have been busy

Middle-aged couples begin to feel a time squeeze, a sense of urgency to do all of the things they want to do.

Postparental years—the years after the last child leaves home and until the husband's and wife's retirement

working and raising children, as well as being active in community affairs, they may have drifted apart, spending less time communicating, playing, and being together. It is easy to get so absorbed with other activities that the marriage suffers from lack of attention. Parents who stayed together until their children were grown now feel freer to dissolve their relationship. Some do get divorced (Wu & Penning, 1997).

For others, however, *middle age can become a time for revitalizing a tired marriage, for rethinking their relationship, and for deciding that they want to share many things in life together.* If the couple can learn to communicate and express tender feelings, especially feelings of love and affection that they have neglected, they can develop greater intimacy than they have experienced in a long time. This improved communication can also uncover troublesome issues that have been denied. Once faced and resolved, they need no longer prevent improved companionship and togetherness.

The Postparental Years

The term **postparental years** usually refers to the ages after the last child leaves home and until the husband's and wife's retirement. If the woman gets married at the median age of 24 and has two children, she is 48 when the last child leaves home. The husband who married at age 26 and has two children will be 50 when the last child leaves. Some writers prefer the term the *empty-nest years;* for them, after children are born, one is always a parent.

The biggest adjustment for the wife if her whole life has been wrapped up in her children is in filling the gap after the children leave. However, *ever greater numbers of women breathe a sigh of relief after the last child leaves* (Cooper & Gutmann, 1987). At last, these women are now free to live their own lives. Many husbands don't feel too great a loss when the children leave, especially if they have reasons to be proud of them and their accomplishments.

There is considerable evidence to show that adults in the postparental period are happier than are those earlier or later in life. The period has been described as "a time of freedom." One husband showed his relief at not having such a great financial burden: "It took a load off me when the boys left. I didn't have to support 'em anymore" (Deutscher, 1964, p. 55). It would appear, therefore, that while there are adjustments to be made during the empty-nest years, there are increased opportunities to enjoy life as a couple.

One postscript needs to be added. The empty nest may not stay that way. High divorce rates and financial need have resulted in increasing numbers of adult children returning home to live with their parents. The fledglings are returning to the nest. This situation has important ramifications for parents, adult children, and grandchildren. Most parents do not welcome the return of their children and view their stay as a short-term arrangement (Clemens & Axelson, 1985). Sometimes the adult child reverts to the role of the dependent child, and the parents return to superordinate roles of earlier times. In these cases, increasing evidence points to a lessening of life satisfaction for all parties involved (Clemens & Axelson, 1985). Even if adult children do not live with their parents, many of them depend on parents for financial and/or social support. Many young adults are not able to make it on their own without fi-

nancial help from parents, or some young adults who get divorced find it difficult to get along and therefore return to their parents for help (Marks, 1995). Middle-aged parents have been called the "sandwich generation," because they are caught between care-giving responsibilities for their children and their elderly parents (Loomis & Booth, 1995).

Adjustments During Late Adulthood

Marital Status

As health and longevity of the elderly increase, an increasing proportion of adults over age 65 are still married and living with their spouse. In 1997, 79% of men 65 to 74

Misogynists—persons who have a hatred of women

Living Issues

Domestic Violence

Spouse abusers may seem to be ordinary citizens in various aspects of their lives, but they typically have poor self-images that they express by being outwardly violent (Goldstein & Rosenbaum, 1985). They also rank higher in general aggression than do mates that do not engage in such action. Excessive jealousy and alcohol abuse are also common. Because they are insecure individuals, abusers typically choose partners who are passive and compliant, whom they can bully and whom they can blame for all their own personal problems. Their abused partners become their scapegoats because the abusers cannot accept responsibility for their own actions.

Some male abusers—called **misogynists**—have an underlying hatred of women. Misogynists are hostile, cruel in their relationships with women, and contemptuous and aggressive. They show their hatred through (1) their abuse of women and (2) their efforts to control them. The misogynist seeks total control of a woman's life: how she thinks and feels, how she behaves, and what she does. His con-

trol is established through fear, humiliation, and psychological and physical abuse. Physical abuse includes violence and bodily harm; it also includes constant criticism, name calling, verbal attacks, threatening harm, and yelling. If the misogynist is confronted with what he does, he blames the woman. He may exercise sexual control by criticizing his partner's lovemaking or by sexually brutalizing her. He seeks financial control by withholding money or even controlling what she earns as well. He seeks to control her social life by limiting her contacts with her family and friends, and limiting her social activities. He may be jealous of his own children and may abuse them as well as attack their mother. In families characterized by more extreme battering, it has been found that boys were more often victims of aggression than girls (Jouriles & Norwood, 1995).

What about the abused woman herself? She usually is confused about herself and her partner. Sometimes her partner says he loves her and needs her and is nice to her; at other times, he is abusive. He tries to make her feel

that the reason he gets angry is that she makes him angry, that she's done something wrong. She comes to feel that it's her fault, that he's only trying to make her a better person (Andrews & Brewin, 1990). She doesn't want to be hurt, so she searches for the right way to behave so that her partner will be consistently loving. She doesn't confront him or question his behavior. Because her security depends on his approval, she renounces her own wishes and is compliant. She gives up her freedom if he demands that she quit her job or give up her friends, interests, and activities. Every part of her life is affected by his control. Because she blames herself, her self-confidence and self-esteem continue to drop because he makes her feel that she is a bad person. She doesn't leave him because she hopes things will change, or because she is fearful of what he might do to her, or because she feels that if she just tries harder, everything will be all right. She's afraid that she will lose his love and that no one else will have her (Forward, 1986; Rice, 1996).

years old and 67% of men 75 and older were married. Figures for women of comparable ages were 54% and 29% respectively. Obviously, there are far greater numbers of unmarried women than men.

Marital Satisfaction

For many older adults, marriage continues to be a major source of life satisfaction. *Marital happiness and satisfaction usually increase during a second honeymoon stage after the children are launched and after retirement.* The spouses usually have more leisure time to spend together and with adult children and grandchildren. The adults may still be in good health. They depend more on one another for companionship. As one wife remarked: "I feel closer to Bill than I have for years. We had forgotten what it meant to have real companionship." (Author's counseling notes)

Sometimes during the last stages of old age, marital satisfaction again declines (Gilford, 1984). Some wives complain that their husbands are always underfoot and expect to be waited on. Some wives are busier than ever completing and reorganizing household tasks, so they have little time to respond to their husband's needs as well. Some retired husbands take on a few additional household tasks, but others don't share more than when they were working. Much of a retired husband's time at home is spent in his own pursuits. Therefore, although the retired couple is together more, retirement does not ensure that the husband will spend much additional time in household chores.

Declining physical health and financial resources begin to take their toll. The couple find it harder to cope with their life situation. Declining status and involuntary disengagement from society result in increasing discontent. Spouses now have fewer physical, social, and emotional resources to reward one another in mutual marital exchange. Figure 19.5 shows the trend. When studies show a higher mean level of marital quality in late-term marriages than in shorter-term marriages, the results are usually influenced by cohort differences in marital success. The more unhappily married couples have dropped out, leaving surviving couples with greater satisfaction. Thus, the longer couples stay married, the greater is the bias towards greater satisfaction (Glenn, 1998).

Gender Roles in the Family

There is some evidence that there is a reversal of sex roles in relation to authority in the family as people get older. The man who retires loses some status and authority in family governance. The woman often assumes a more dominant role as an authority figure. This reversal is especially true in relation to planning activities for herself and her husband and in assuming a nurturing role that has not been possible since the children were launched.

Parent–Adult Child Relationships

The image of parents growing older without the contact and concern of their adult children does not coincide with the facts (Connidis & Davies, 1990). A 1984 survey of the elderly (Kovar, 1986) revealed that half of the aged with children had seen one of them on the day of the interview or the day before. If the time period covered the previous week, the proportion of elderly parents in contact with children increased to three-fourths. Thus, "the finding that most older persons are not isolated from their children is well supported in the existing literature" (Bengston & Roberts, 1991). In fact, some elderly parents complain that their children are too close. They ask, "Will I ever escape my child's problems?" Frequent exposure to adult children's problems can have a depressive effect on elderly parents (Pillemer & Suitor, 1991).

Other studies have reported important factors in parent–adult child relationships (Hamon & Blieszner, 1990):

- The frequency of contact is not the key factor in satisfactory relationships; quality of contact is.
- Emotional support is important and can be more significant than whether adult children provide financial support (Houser & Berkman, 1984).
- The morale of elderly individuals is higher if they feel that they can reciprocate some of the help their children or friends give them (McCulloch, 1990; Roberto & Scott, 1986).
- Providing extensive care for severely functionally impaired parents causes extreme stress and hardship for the caregivers. Community personal care services, day care, home nursing, and homemakers' services are needed.
- Studies of attitudes regarding obligations to assist an older parent or stepparent following later life remarriage indicates that relationship closeness was an important consideration when making judgments about obligations to stepparents but not to parents. Men and women were equally obligated to their elders, and obligations

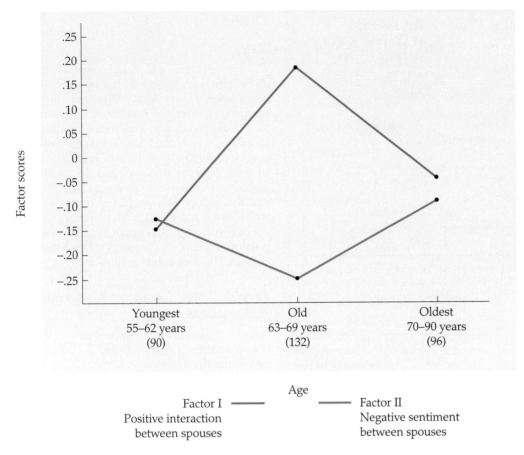

Factor I ——— Positive interaction between spouses

Factor II ——— Negative sentiment between spouses

Age

FIGURE 19.5   Mean levels of marital satisfaction by age group (N = 318). Group sample sizes are shown in parentheses.

From "Contrasts in Marital Satisfaction Throughout Old Age: An Exchange Theory Analysis," by R. Gilford, 1984, *Journal of Gerontology, 39,* p. 331. Copyright © The Gerontological Society of America.

to help stepmothers were slightly less than obligations to help stepfathers and biological parents (Ganong, Coleman, McDaniel, & Killian, 1998).

- Adults with one living parent generally report feeling more obligations to provide assistance than adults with two living parents (Stein, Wemmerus, Ward, Gaines, Freeberg, & Jewell, 1998).

Widowhood

The greater longevity of women means that the number of widows exceeds widowers at all levels. Table 19.5 shows the ratios at different ages (U.S. Bureau of the Census, 1998). Partly as a result of these ratios, the remarriage rates for widows is lower than for widowers. The younger a person is when a mate dies, the greater the chances of remarriage. The death of a spouse is recognized as one of life's most traumatic events. The survivor often confronts emotional, economic, and/or physical

problems precipitated by the spouse's death (Bound, Duncan, Laren, & Oleinick, 1991). One of the keys to successful widowhood is to be able to maintain intimate relationships with friends over a period of time. Apparently, widowed women are able to do this better than men (Hatch & Bulcroft, 1992).

One report analyzes friendship patterns of individuals 85 and older, 77% of whom were women. In spite of high levels of disability and the loss of age peers, the majority were in frequent contact with friends. Over 31 months, however, the predictors of friendship involvement changed. Increased disability was the most important barrier to continued friendships (Johnson & Troll, 1994).

Two of the questions that arise are how are women able to get along financially, and where will they live? Shared living arrangements are an important source of social and economic support for older people. During the last three decades, there has been a substantial increase in the prevalence of living alone. The change appears mainly to reflect

TABLE 19.5	RATIO OF WIDOWS TO WIDOWERS AT DIFFERENT AGES
Age	*Ratio of Widows to Widowers*
45–54	4.2 to 1
55–64	4.5 to 1
65–74	4.3 to 1
75 years and over	3.9 to 1

Adapted from *Statistical Abstract of the United States, 1998* (p. 58), by U.S. Bureau of the Census, 1998, Washington, DC: U.S. Government Printing Office.

reduced likelihood of living with grown children. However, the "old-old" (those over age 75) have higher rates of functional impairment and are most likely to need personal care assistance. One survey estimated the impact of coresidence on the economic well-being of elderly widows and the impact of coresidence on family members. Coresidence improved well-being for both the widow and other participants in 51% of the cases; improved it for the widow and diminished it in others in 28% of the cases; and improved it for the others while diminishing it for the widows in 21% of the cases. Although coresidence is often thought of as a response to an elderly widow's needs, her presence typically contributes rather than diminishes the economic well-being of the household (Waehrer & Crystal, 1995).

One key to successful widowhood is to be able to maintain friendships over a period of time.

Divorce

Rates

Divorce rates increased steadily from 1958 until 1979. After 1979, they leveled off and even declined. (See Figure 19.6.) Whether rates will continue to decline remains to be seen. As they now stand, the high rates mean that a large number of marriages end in divorce. A survey in 1985 showed that nearly one-third of ever-married women aged 35 to 39 had ended a first marriage in divorce by the survey date and that a projected figure of 56% would eventually end a first marriage in divorce (Norton & Moorman, 1987). The proportion for this age group is greater than for women 10 years younger or older.

Problems Most Damaging to Marital Relationships

A survey among 116 members of the *American Association of Marriage and Family Therapists* rates the frequency, severity, and treatment difficulty of 29 problems commonly experienced by distressed couples. The therapists were asked to choose and give the rank order of only the top 5 areas most damaging to the marital relationship and the 5 most difficult to treat successfully (Geiss & O'Leary, 1981). A value of 5 was assigned to an item for each first-place ranking that it received, a value of 4 was given for each second-place ranking, and so on. These values were summed for each item. The 10 areas rated by respondents as having the most damaging effect on marital relationships were as follows (Geiss & O'Leary, 1981, p. 516):

1. Communication (361)
2. Unrealistic expectation of marriage or spouse (197)
3. Power struggles (135)
4. Serious individual problems (126)
5. Role conflict (95)
6. Lack of loving feelings (92)
7. Demonstration of affection (90)
8. Alcoholism (81)
9. Extramarital affairs (80)
10. Sex (10)

On the basis of these responses from marital therapists, lack of communication was ranked as having the most damaging effect. In a further analysis of data from the study, *communication problems were also rated as the most frequently occurring problems in distressed*

Living Issues

Stable, Unhappy Marriages

Divorce has become a fact of life in an ever-increasing number of households. Yet many comparatively unhappy and unrewarding marriages have not ended in divorce. Age, lack of prior marital experience, commitment to marriage as an institution, low social activity, lack of control over one's life, and belief that divorce would detract from happiness are all predictive of stability in unhappy marriages. As might be expected, both older age and longer marriage duration are associated with stability. The investment of many years in a relationship does contribute somewhat to its stability even if not to its satisfaction. Midlife divorce can be particularly costly for the woman who has contributed to her husband's success and career over much of her adult life and who may see few alternatives to the current marriage. In such cases, divorce can become a very high-cost proposition.

Attitudinal and belief patterns also seem to be quite important. The belief that marriage is a lifetime commitment contributes to stability, as does the expectation that one's life would be even less happy if one divorced. Both men and women are willing to leave an unhappy marriage if they feel that they have some sense of control over their lives. The person who is willing to act often does so because of the belief that he or she has more control over the possible outcomes (Heaton & Albrecht, 1991).

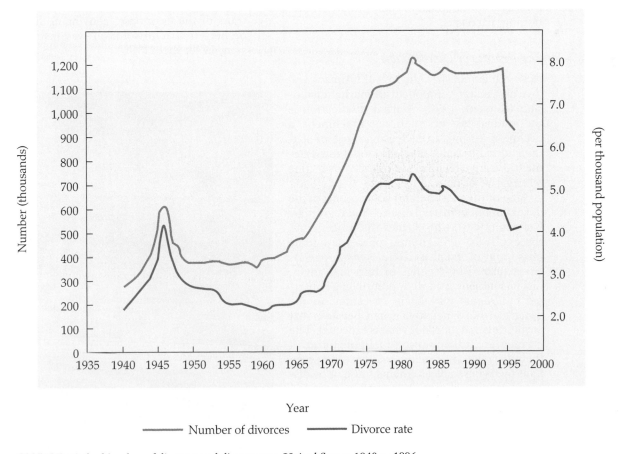

FIGURE 19.6   Number of divorces and divorce rate: United States, 1940 to 1996.

From *Statistical Abstract of the United States, 1998*, by U.S. Bureau of the Census, 1998, Washington, DC: U.S. Government Printing Office, p. 76.

Living Issues

The Role of Commitment

One of the things the author of this book has discovered as a marriage counselor is that he can never predict ahead of time who is going to get divorced and who is not. Some couples have tremendous problems that seem to be impossible to overcome; yet, with a high degree of commitment and a lot of hard work, they are able to straighten out their relationship over a period of time. Other couples, whose problems seem more superficial, could work out the relationship very easily, but because of a lack of commitment or motivation, decide to split up very soon, and the marriage fails. This observation does not mean that all failures are due to a lack of commitment—some couples are extremely committed but are not able to work out their relationships because of insurmountable problems and almost complete incompatibility—but it does illustrate the importance of commitment in terms of whether a couple will try to make their marriage work or not (Stanley & Markman, 1992).

marriages. These responses suggest the vital role that communication plays in well-functioning marriages.

The Process of Disaffection

Research emphasizes the loss of intimacy and love as a major component of marital disillusion (Kersten, 1990). Marital disaffection is the gradual loss of emotional attachment, a decline in caring, an increasing sense of apathy and indifference, and emotional estrangement. Positive feelings are replaced over time by negative or neutral feelings.

One of the most helpful descriptions of the development of marital disaffection is given by Kersten (1990), who divides the process into three phases: a beginning phase, a middle phase, and an end phase. The *beginning phase* is characterized by feelings of hurt and anger, disillusionment, and disappointment. A partner's thoughts may begin to center on the other partner's negative traits because that partner's behavior is not what is expected. The partners are still optimistic about the future of their marriage and attempt to solve their problems by trying to please their spouse or by discussing their feelings.

The *middle phase* is characterized by increased anger and hurt. Spouses begin to expect their partner to behave in certain negative ways; an increase in apathy begins to be reported. Some partners begin to weigh whether to stay or leave the marriage, and

they sort out factors relating to religion, finances, or children. Attempts to please the partner are less frequently made, but problem-solving attempts such as entering a drug-abuse treatment program increase.

In the *end phase*, anger is again the most frequently reported feeling. Feelings of helplessness and apathy increase, and feelings of trust and hope decline. The most frequent thoughts during this stage concern wanting to end the marriage and determining exactly how it can be dissolved. However, feelings are still ambivalent. Often counseling is pursued as couples seek marital therapy in a last attempt to save the marriage or to get assistance in leaving it.

Basic to the dissolution of the relationship is the perception that the costs of staying together outweigh the rewards. Each partner focuses on the negative traits of his or her spouse, and it's difficult to change one's feelings. To do so requires the partner to make drastic changes. Sometimes the partner is willing to make these changes, and feelings become positive again; but such a change takes a lot of maturity, insight, and hard work. If the marriage is dissolved, the disaffected spouse continues to focus on the negative traits of the ex-spouse, convincing himself or herself that dissolution was justified (Kersten, 1990; Rice, 1996).

The process of disaffection is characterized by increased feelings of hurt, anger, and disappointment.

Alternatives to Divorce

Before couples decide to divorce, there are several other possibilities they might consider. These options are marriage counseling, marriage enrichment programs, separation, and reconciliation.

Marriage Counseling

One alternative to divorce is marriage counseling (Bringles & Byers, 1997). Couples cannot be expected to live together unhappily, but breaking up the marriage may not always be the best or only answer to a problem. Divorce often substitutes one set of problems for another. An alternative answer is to see whether the unhappy marriage can become a satisfying one by seeking professional help. Couples are often skeptical about the outcome of counseling—especially if they have had an unhappy experience with therapists of if they have never been to a counselor before. Not all therapists are equally competent. However, one summary of the benefits of marital and family therapy found that therapy involves beneficial outcomes in about two-thirds of the cases; that there's a greater chance of positive outcome when spouses are treated conjointly rather than individually; and that positive results typically occur in treatments of fairly short duration, from about 1 to 20 sessions (Piercy & Sprenkle, 1990).

Usually, the earlier that couples with a troubled marriage seek counseling, the more likely it is that it will succeed. Many couples never seek help until the relationship has deteriorated to the point where it is very difficult to straighten things out. Actually, couples need help the most during the first year of their marriage. One suggestion is that professional practitioners schedule monthly sessions with newlyweds (either as couples or groups of couples) during the first year of marriage.

Marriage Enrichment Programs

Marriage enrichment programs combine education with group discussion to assist couples in improving problem solving, relationships, and marital communication. Programs are conducted in groups shortly before or after the wedding or any number of years after it. The central purpose of such programs is preventative: to address issues before they get out of hand and become unmanageable (Guerney & Maxson, 1990; Mace, 1987).

Separation

A trial separation is another option before divorce. It can be an effective treatment in some instances, but usually only if the separation is carefully structured and if marital therapy continues during the separation itself (Granvold, 1983). **Structured separation** may be defined as a time-limited approach in which the couple terminates cohabitation, agrees to regular interpersonal contact, commits to regularly scheduled therapy with a therapist, and has a moratorium on a final decision either to reunite or to divorce (Granvold & Tarrant, 1983). The objective of separation is change. It is designed to interrupt old interactional patterns with the creation of an environment conducive to change. The anticipated result is that spouses will move closer together or further apart (Morgan, Lye, & Condran, 1988). One cannot tell at the beginning of separation what the outcome will be. The important thing, though, is for couples to give the separation their very best try.

Separation is not to be taken lightly. It is a time of extreme stress and emotional upheaval. It is also a time of upset and stress for the children and has both potential benefits and risks. It is, however, one alternative that may be considered.

Reconciliation

Another alternative to divorce is to try to attempt reconciliation. Some couples decide to give their marriage another chance. In other cases, couples may give it numerous chances before they go through with divorce.

One survey of families examined the prevalence of successful reconciliations among 506 white women in the United States (Wineberg, 1994). Approximately one-third of the women attempted reconciliation and were still married more than one year after the reconciliation began. The probability of having successful reconciliation varied among subgroups of women. Religion was the strongest predictor of the success of reconciliation. In particular, women having the same religion as their spouse had a significantly increased probability of having a successful reconciliation. In the case of mixed marriage, when one spouse changed religious affiliation, there was increased probability of successful reconciliation in the marriage. Additionally, religious conversion suggested a strong commitment to the marriage. Couples who are highly committed to marriage may exhaust all possible options in order to save their marriage, and they will tolerate substantial marital discord before deciding to end the marriage.

If attempts at reconciliation are to succeed, most couples need some kind of therapeutic help to work out the differences. They may get

Marriage enrichment programs

Structured separation

back into the same relationship that they had before, find that nothing has changed, and see that the problems that split them up are still there, with very little success of saving the marriage. But if through therapy they are able to discover what went wrong in the marriage and what needs to be changed, and when they are highly motivated to make those changes, then reconciliation is more possible.

Adult Adjustments After Divorce

The problems of adjustment after divorce may be grouped into a number of categories.

- *Getting over the emotional trauma of divorce.* Under the best of circumstances, divorce is an emotionally disturbing experience (Plummer & Koch-Hattem, 1986). Under the worst conditions, it may result in a high degree of shock and disorientation. The trauma is greater when one spouse wants the divorce and the other doesn't, when the idea comes unexpectedly, when one continues to be emotionally attached to the other after the divorce, or when friends and family disapprove of the whole idea. For most couples, the decision to divorce is viewed as an "end of the rope" decision, which is reached, on the average, over a period of about 2 years.

- *Dealing with the attitudes of society.* Part of the trauma of divorce is experienced because of the attitudes of society toward divorce and divorced persons. In the eyes of some, in spite of increasing liberal attitudes, divorce represents moral failure or evidence of personal inadequacy. The immediate feeling stemming from the divorce is a sense of loss and failure. Some men experience social ostracism following divorce. Crucial social support networks may be lost. One man reported that he lost his friends, family, and church membership. Since much of his social identity during his marriage was based on his ties to his church and since the church regarded divorce as absolutely wrong, the man was forced to give up his church ties as a result (Umberson & Williams, 1993).

- *Loneliness and the problem of social readjustment.* Even if two married people did not get along, they kept one another company. Part of the time, at least, they knew that someone else was in the home. After divorce, they begin to realize what it is like to live alone. Numerous authorities suggest that the friendship and companionship of other people is one of the most essential

ingredients for a successful readjustment after divorce, so getting involved with others is important (Leslie & Grady, 1985).

- *Finances.* In spite of some advances, working women still receive only 62% of the income of males, assuming that both have the same occupation, education, working experience, and hours. Furthermore, the mother still ends up with custody of the children in 9 out of 10 cases. Some mothers get only a little or irregular support from their ex-husbands. As a result of these factors, most divorced mothers have to work, but do so at inadequate wages (Uhlenberg, Cooney, & Boyd, 1990). It is estimated that women who get divorced and do not remarry experience a 50% decline in family income. The irony is that whereas divorce lowers the living standards of both mothers and children, it typically raises that of fathers (Pett & Vaughan-Cole, 1986).

- *Realignment of responsibilities and work roles.* The divorced person with children is faced with the prospect of an overload of work. Now that person must perform all family functions, which were formerly shared by two persons.

- *Sexual readjustments.* Research reveals that most divorced persons are sexually active. This does not mean, however, that all of these sexual contacts are emotionally satisfying. Some divorced persons speak of meaningless sex, that is, using sex to find companionship, to prove sexual attractiveness, or to escape from problems.

- *Contacts with the ex-spouse* (Masheter, 1997). The more upsetting the divorce has been and the more vindictive the spouse, the less the other person wants to have any postdivorce contact. This is particularly true in cases of remarriage.

- *Kinship interaction.* Divorce is a multigenerational process that affects grandparents and other kin as well as the divorcing couple and their children (Ferreiro, Warren, & Konanc, 1986).

- *Relationships with children.* Sixty percent of divorces involve minor children; in a vast majority of cases, mothers are granted residential custody of their children, and fathers are granted visitation rights. It is estimated that more than one-half of fathers eventually become noncustodial fathers. Once this event occurs, many noncustodial divorced fathers will not regularly visit their children, or they may visit them regularly for a while after the divorce, and then the visitations gradually taper off.

About half of all divorced men fail to meet court-ordered child support obligations to their children (Pirog-Good & Amerson, 1997). When they fail to pay child support, they are thus less likely to visit their children. Some fathers are forbidden to see their children on a regular basis, or the visitation allowed comes at infrequent intervals, so that the chief source of strain on the father is the emotional strain from not seeing his own offspring. Others hesitate to visit their children because it involves contacts with the ex-spouse and may therefore involve conflict. Some men are upset about noncustodial fathering because it entails a loss of control over their children. When the ex-wife establishes a new intimate relationship, it is often threatening to the ex-husband's identity as a father, sometimes because the ex-wife's remarriage limits the father's access to his children (Umberson & Williams, 1993).

If parents divorce when the children are older, research suggests that sons are somewhat less close to both parents, whereas daughters are considerably less close to fathers, and only slightly less close to mothers. This finding suggests that the father-daughter relationship is especially vulnerable, whereas the mother-daughter tie is especially resilient. Once reaching adulthood, children who leave the custodial parents' home have freedom to initiate and sustain contact with parents that they did not have while growing up. This circumstance may be especially likely in cases in which fathers avoid conflict with ex-wives (Booth & Amato, 1994; Cooney, 1994).

Remarriage

Adults who remarry after divorce have some real advantages over those married for the first time. Remarrieds are older, more mature and experienced, and often highly motivated to make their marriages work. They ought to be able to make a better go of marriage the second time around. But divorce rates are about the same as for those in first marriages. However, Furstenberg and Spanier (1984) concluded that successful remarrieds stated that their new marriage was better than their first marriage. These people felt they had married the right person, "someone who allows you to be yourself" (p. 83). They felt they had learned to communicate and that they handled problems maturely. Better communication also led to better decision making. Both partners tended to feel that they were more equal in

FOCUS

Extramarital Affairs

The majority of Americans still enter marriage expecting and committed to sexual fidelity. Americans place a high value on sexual exclusiveness as important to a healthy marriage relationship (Stayton, 1983). In spite of these attitudes, the meager data available indicate an increase in extramarital sexual relationships since the 1960s (Saunders & Edwards, 1984).

Extramarital affairs have varying effects on married people and their marriages. Some marriages are never the same afterward. Guilt, anger, jealousy, loss of respect, and the destruction of love and intimacy are common. One wife remarked: "I don't know if I can ever trust him again. Every time he's out of town I wonder what he is doing and who he's with."

Sometimes, however, the crisis of an affair stimulates the couple finally to accept the fact that their marriage is in deep trouble and that they need help. One wife explained in this way:

> I've been trying to tell my husband for years that I was unhappy in our marriage, but he didn't listen. Now, I've met someone else, and for the first time my husband is listening and is willing to go to a marriage counselor. (Author's counseling notes)

In this case, the affair resulted in something positive.

There are some couples whose marriages are not affected very much by an affair. One of the spouses is having an affair, but the other doesn't care. These are often marriages in which the emotional bonds between the couples are already broken, so that the extramarital relationship is just evidence of the fractured marriage. These couples have either lost or have never had a meaningful relationship with each other (Voth, Perry, McCranie, & Rogers, 1982).

In some situations, a wife discovers that her husband is unfaithful but chooses not to confront him with his actions because they have children and she does not feel equipped to support herself and the children (Saul, 1983). Or, a husband discovers his wife is having an affair, but he chooses not to confront her because he's afraid he'll lose her.

The affairs that are most threatening to the marriage are ongoing affairs that include emotional involvement as well as sexual relations (Thompson, 1984). Persons who believe that they have fallen deeply in love don't want to give up the affairs, which seem so meaningful and exciting. Some people report: "I haven't felt like this for years. I can't give up something that makes me feel alive again" (Author's counseling notes). Of course, what people don't realize in the beginning is that the intense emotional excitement tends to pass; and if the relationship is to endure, the couple needs to have many other things going in the relationship.

remarriage and that the division of labor was more equitable.

All of these last comments came from those who had successful remarriages. *For others, remarriage introduces some complications that were not present in first marriage* (Montgomery,

Living Issues

Problems of Stepfathers

Although the situation is slowly changing, about 90% of children of divorced parents live with their mothers after divorce. If the mother remarries, the children inherit a stepfather. A summary of studies indicates that the most frequently cited problems of stepfathers include the following (Robinson, 1984).

1. Uncertainty about the degree of authority that they have in the role of stepfather.

2. The amount of affection to give stepchildren and ways to show it. Stepfathers report feeling uncomfortable kissing their stepchildren.

3. The discipline of stepchildren and enforcement of rules.

4. Money conflicts.

5. Guilt over leaving children from a previous family.

6. Loyalty conflicts—how much time children spend with natural parents versus with stepparents.

7. Sexual conflict—the incest taboo is present but is not as strong in stepfather families as it is in biological families.

8. Conflict over surnames—different names of stepfathers and stepchildren may lead to problems, but some stepchildren and stepfathers don't want the same names (Robinson, 1984, p. 382).

Anderson, Hetherington, & Clingempeel, 1992). The biggest complication is children. Having children of school age from prior marriages increases the likelihood of divorce among remarried couples (Fine, 1986; Wineberg, 1992). When remarrieds divorce, it is often because of problems with the stepchildren, not the spouse (Meer, 1986b). In a majority of cases, at least one partner already has children when the remarriage begins (Cherlin & McCarthy, 1985). Being a stepparent is far more difficult than being a natural parent, because children have difficulty accepting a substitute parental figure (Kurdek & Fine, 1991). However, if the remarried couple have a child between them after marriage, the chances of marital dissolution become less.

Not all couples experience conflict because of children. Using national representative data on 2,655 black and white married couples with children, the impact of remarriage and stepchildren on the frequency of marital conflict was examined. Contrary to expectations, the findings suggested that remarriage and children were not necessarily associated with more frequent marital conflict and in some cases were associated with less frequent conflict (MacDonald & DeMaris, 1995).

WORK AND CAREERS

Another major component of social adjustment is to successfully pursue a career. This section traces career development through early, middle, and late adulthood.

Career Establishment

Vocational Identity

Two major psychosocial tasks of early adulthood are to mold an identity and to choose and consolidate a career. These two goals are intertwined because vocational choice is one way to establish identity. Adults are associated with their work: "She is a branch manager of the bank." "He is superintendent of schools." Vocational achievement is important in a society that emphasizes individualism, personal fulfillment, and material success. Success and job satisfaction reaffirm one's identity and provide social recognition. One important task of this period, therefore, is to become established in an occupation (Levinson et al., 1978).

Vocation and Life Satisfaction

Discontentment with jobs or money also affects other aspects of life. Discontent with one's work is strongly associated with unhappiness at home. People who are most troubled about money or who derive little pleasure from their work are most unhappy with their love and sexual relationships.

Aspirations

One goal of early adulthood is to succeed according to individual criteria with which one feels comfortable within the context of one's community. Everyone has to be somebody—somehow, somewhere, sometime. It is important to strive toward personalized goals and to experience some success.

Vocational Development

During the years of early adulthood, primarily the 20s, adults can be grouped into five different categories according to the status of their vocational development.

One group consists of *vocational achievers.* They are highly involved in a vocation of their choice and are actively pursuing established career goals. They have completed their formal education and training and are applying their knowledge and skill in their work. They are fairly contented with their work and look forward to continued development.

Vocational achievement reaffirms identity and provides social recognition.

A second group are the *vocationally frustrated*. They have in mind particular vocational goals that they have not been able to attain, at least at present. This group includes a large number who want to go on to higher education or some type of postsecondary training, but they are hampered by economic, family, or personal circumstances. Also included are those who dropped out of school to get married and those locked into jobs they dislike because they cannot afford to leave them to pursue other goals.

A third group consists of the *noncommitted*: people who are still uncertain what they want to do. They are confused and anxious, unable to decide which direction to pursue. Some are still in school. They change majors frequently, trying a lot of different courses, but they cannot select a preference. Some of these persons are interested in so many things that they are unable to narrow down their interests to one program. Some are not particularly interested in any one thing. They take job after job but never find one type of work they prefer. They are concerned and confused. Some are so emotionally insecure that they have trouble making decisions about anything.

People in the fourth group are *vocational opportunists*. They do not have a clear-cut vocational plan or specific goals. They have not selected any particular occupation or profession, but instead accept jobs as opportunities arise. If they can get a job as a salesperson, they take it. If they find a better job doing factory work, they try that. Their employment record is usually erratic, with no real planning involved.

Members of the fifth group are *social dropouts*. Some of them do not care whether they work. They have no occupational goals

and little personal ambition. Most of the time they are unemployed, or they work long enough to be eligible for unemployment and then get fired to collect. Some beg, some steal, some live off of others, and some have drug problems. Others live at home, expecting their parents to support them. Certain people have a nonmaterialistic philosophy of life, rejecting the work ethic, or preferring to work as little as possible to maintain themselves. Some young adults move in with others who have adopted a "hang-loose" ethic. For many, this is a phase to be worked through before they become established members of society.

Women's Careers

Employment and Income

The number and percentage of wives and mothers in the labor force are increasing (Menaghan & Parcell, 1990). In 1997, 62% of all married women over age 16, 78% of married women with the youngest child of 6

Living Issues

Problems of Mothers in Remarriages

The mother in a remarriage has a whole set of problems that are unique to her situation.

1. She is often placed in the role of mediator between her own children and her husband. Her children want her to take their side; her husband wants her to take his side. The mother is drawn into the conflict and is in the middle, trying to please both.

2. Her children are often jealous of the time and attention given to the husband, resenting his intrusion into the family, and the fact that he takes their mother away from them. The mother is placed in a difficult situation. No matter whom she pleases, she displeases the other part of the family.

3. She has to adjust to the fact that her husband may have other children and will be spending money for their support, money that she and her family may need; and that he will be seeing his children.

4. She may have to adjust to the fact that her husband was married to another woman before, and that he will be contacting her, especially when visiting the children or having them come to visit.

5. She has a difficult adjustment to make with her husband's children because she spends little time with them, and they may resent her taking their place in relation to their father.

6. She may have to mediate relationships between the stepsiblings, being careful not to show partiality.

(Author's counseling experience)

to 17 years of age, and 64% of married women with the youngest child under 6 years of age were in the labor force (U.S. Bureau of the Census, 1998). In the same year, 60% of women with babies under 1 year old were also in the labor force.

What about the impact of this employment on women's lives? Are employed wives happier, more satisfied with life, and more fulfilled than housewives? Research on life satisfaction of married women who work versus those who do not work shows slightly greater satisfaction among those working, but the results depend on a number of variables (Tiedje et al., 1990). *One of the important considerations in the life satisfaction of working wives is whether they have been able to integrate their home life and their work life, and whether or not there is conflict between their family and job roles* (Walters & McKenry, 1985). The maternal role holds the most potential conflict with employment outside the home. If children's needs are not met satisfactorily, then role dissatisfaction and conflict can easily result. One individual source of role strain is the woman's own conflict over the fact that she is working at all (Greenberger & O'Neil, 1990). If the woman prefers being at home but has to work for various reasons, her ambivalent feelings become an inner source of tension and conflict (MacEwen & Barling, 1991).

A family-related source of strain is the presence of young children in the family (Eggebeen & Hawkins, 1990). The more young children in the family, the more stress is introduced. Some women feel guilty about leaving their children, especially when their children are small. However, mothers feel less stress if they are satisfied with the quality of substitute child care. Stress is also reduced if mothers with young children have social support. Most mothers need transportation assistance and certainly assistance with child care, especially if children are sick or out of school. Social support can come from friends, neighbors, coworkers, and especially from parents, brothers and sisters, adult children, or other relatives in the family. Unfortunately, many of the mothers who need support the most are the ones who are least likely to receive it. One research study examined the social support of employed African American and Anglo mothers and found that mothers whose income was below the poverty line were no more likely to receive support than were more affluent mothers. Employed African Americans were less likely to receive general baby-sitting assistance and help with transportation than were Anglo mothers of young children. However, African American

Fifty-nine percent of married women over age 16 are in the labor force.

mothers were more likely than Anglo mothers to receive help in caring for sick and out-of-school children. The findings indicated that both African American and Anglo employed mothers reported moderate levels of transportation and help from friends and even lower levels from family members. For both groups, living closer to respondent's mother increased the odds of receiving support from the family with transportation. Being above the poverty level also increased the chances of both groups in receiving help from family. It is not surprising that the more affluent mothers received more support: They were both more likely to have relatives who had reliable sources of transportation and were in a better position to reciprocate assistance. However, mothers living closer to or in poverty were the least likely to receive assistance (Benin & Keith, 1995).

Another source of conflict is the strain of having to fulfill too many roles at once (Voydanoff & Donnelly, 1989b). Most working wives understand that they do not have as much time for leisure-time activities and housework as they would if they were not working (Firestone & Shelton, 1988). This is the reason why the husband's support and help are necessary to alleviate part of the stress. One large-scale study of married women and men in Canada revealed that the women spent more total time in work and family activities than did the men. They experienced higher levels of overload, spent more time in family activities, and experienced higher levels of family interference with work. They also experienced significantly more interference from work with family than did the men (Duxbury, Higgins, & Lee, 1994).

The job itself may be a source of stress and strain (Sears & Galambos, 1992). Inflexible job demands, long hours, inconvenient schedules, and job pressures all create strain (Wethington & Kessler, 1989). The fact that women get paid only 62% of the wages that men receive for the same experience, education, and tenure certainly does not help to make them satisfied with their work.

For many women, however, working outside the home enhances their lives, especially if they love their job and have children and a husband who helps or if they are able to hire some assistance. Some of these women are more relaxed at work than at home. In fact, some go to work to get away from their families.

Dual Careers

The problems of role strain and conflict are highlighted in dual-career families. In the dual-career family, there are two career-committed individuals, both of whom are trying to fulfill professional and family roles. A career ordinarily requires full-time employment, especially if one is working for someone else. The greater the responsibility and the higher the position achieved, the greater is the commitment of the individual—leaving less time to devote to child and mate. The dual-career marriage is difficult to achieve from a strictly managerial point of view. It is difficult to balance father-mother and husband-wife role relationships and responsibilities, to find adequate child care, or to maintain the expected husband-wife companionship and intimacy so that the marriage itself remains a viable relationship. In spite of these difficulties, some couples are able to succeed in pursuing careers and in being good mates and parents.

There are some real satisfactions and gains in a dual-career marriage (Hanson & Ooms, 1991). The *financial rewards* in a dual-career marriage are considerable. Furthermore, many women who want a career in addition to a family have a great need for *creativity, achievement, recognition, and self-expression*. The woman who is trained for a profession wants the satisfaction of using that training. The most successful dual-career marriages are those in which the husband and wife treat each other as *equal partners*. As a result, they share not only in earning income but also in caring for children and performing household tasks.

There are some important issues for dual-career couples. *The first issue is that of moving.* If one spouse is offered a promotion that means moving to another town, what will be the effect on the other spouse's career? The pres-

sure to move about frequently while one's career is becoming established presents a difficulty for the dual-career family. It is not always easy for both partners to find suitable employment in one area, especially in less populated areas where there are fewer opportunities.

The second issue is that of travel. Professionals often attend out-of-town meetings or conferences or consult with others in different locales. The question is, what is the effect on marriage companionship, and what arrangements for child care can be made? Some couples commute long distances when their home and the base for their careers are in different locations. They may work all week in separate places and get together on weekends. Most commuting couples report that they feel lonely and have more difficulty being emotionally intimate and close.

The third issue is that of child care. The crucial consideration, of course, is the kind of substitute care provided when the parents are gone. The quality and consistency of the substitute care provided is paramount. One solution being considered by increasing numbers of career couples is to remain childless (Cooney & Uhlenberg, 1989).

A fourth issue is that of household responsibilities and roles. The strains of a dual-career

The primary problem of dual-career marriages is finding and providing quality child care.

marriage are considerable (Galambos & Silbereisen, 1989). One source of strain is overwork. The demands of the career, children, marriage, and home are great and also leave couples exhausted and tense. Most couples try to hire some sort of domestic worker on a regular basis.

The fifth issue is that of scheduling. Most couples admit that they have to budget their time very carefully and that they don't have as much time for social activities and for pursuing their own interests as they did before they were working.

A sixth issue is that of identity and competitiveness. Career husbands and wives each sacrifice a great deal to make it possible for the other to pursue a career. For this reason, they have to learn to accept the high value that the other places on career pursuits. If two people compete, each trying to outperform the other, or resent the other's working overtime, the relationship may become tense. However, if two people are certain of their own identities and are secure within themselves, they're able to work out compromises so that each is not threatened by the successes and demands of the other.

Midlife Careers and Employment

A Time of Fruition

For most people, middle adulthood is the fruition of a long period of professional work, when years of training and experience culminate in positions of maximum authority and responsibility. People appointed to leadership positions usually achieve these positions by their early 50s. The important point is that the middle years of the 40s and 50s are years of high productivity. They can be quite satisfying years to those who gain widespread recognition of their accomplishments.

Second Careers

Sometimes middle-aged people do not keep abreast in our increasingly technological society, where change is so rapid that their skills become completely outdated unless they attend refresher courses every several years. Companies are forced to hire new employees who are familiar with the latest technology.

When a person is shut out of a career or is at a dead end, one answer is to begin a second career. Thousands of middle-agers make midlife career changes, sometimes voluntarily after months or years of reevaluation and thought, or other times because of losing a job.

Opera star Beverly Sills gave up her active singing career at 50 to take on a second career as general director of the New York City Opera: "I may be considered old as an opera singer," she remarked, "but I'm thought of as a young manager. That's one of the corporate perks of this job" (Heymont, 1980, p. 64).

Work and Emotional Stress

Whereas the middle years can be productive and rewarding for many, they can also be years of upset and anxiety for others. Job-related emotional problems are common among middle-agers. One source of stress, which was discussed earlier, is *being laid off or fired.* Although the economic impact of job loss may be severe, the emotional impact may be even more serious. Such psychosomatic symptoms as diarrhea, headaches, sleep disturbances, or depression are common. Middle-aged persons whose main gratifications in life came from work may panic when they find their primary source of emotional support terminated. The frustration of *unfulfilled expectations* is a source of stress for other people.

The Older Worker

Job Satisfaction

Most research has pointed to a high and positive correlation between job satisfaction and age; that is, *job satisfaction tends to increase with the worker's age.* There are several explanations for this satisfaction. The most likely one is that older workers have better jobs with higher incomes, more occupational prestige, and greater skills. Also, older workers more likely have remained in jobs that they liked and for which they were best suited. They left unsatisfactory jobs earlier in their careers.

Increased Numbers

Because of increased longevity, better health care, and legislation extending the mandatory retirement age, the possible span of an adult's working life in the United States is increasing. The mandatory retirement age of 70 will allow millions of workers to remain on the job after age 65. Workers in certain types of jobs can remain even longer if they desire. It is still true that a lot of workers are taking early retirement (Gohmann, 1990), but many take other kinds of jobs (Myers, 1991). The gradual increase in age of retirement to draw maximum Social Security will have an influence in encouraging a longer work life. Accordingly, *the numbers of older workers in the workforce may increase in the years ahead.*

Using data from the *National Longitudinal Surveys of Older Men* (NLS), one study examined the extent and character of the work experience of men who chose to continue labor force participation well beyond conventional retirement age. The results show that good health, a strong psychological commitment to work, and the corresponding distaste for retirement were among the most important characteristics related to continued employment in old age. The probability of employment was also found to be positively related to educational attainment and being married to a working wife. Of the men in the sample who were not working, very few gave evidence of the desire to work (Parnes & Sommers, 1994).

Another study examined women's labor force participation in later life. The findings generally support an attachment hypothesis, showing that women who were the most work-oriented throughout their life course were more likely than women who experienced spells of non–labor market activity to participate in the labor force, either full-time or part-time, later in life (Pienta, Burr, & Mutchler, 1994).

Retirement

Forced retirement has been ranked among the top 10 crises in terms of the amount of stress it causes the individual (Bosse, Aldwin, Levenson, & Workman-Daniels, 1991). People who elect early retirement, plan for it, and look forward to it feel that they have directed their own lives and are not being pushed or manipulated (Ferraro, 1990). They have some adjustment problems, but far fewer than do those who retire unwillingly (Gibson, 1991). For people who want to continue working, forced retirement is a bitter pill to swallow. The resulting stress can precipitate various physical and emotional problems (Reitzes, Mutran, & Pope, 1991). Morale drops, the mortality rate rises as disillusionment sets in, and individuals who identified very closely with their work sometimes suffer prolonged depression and other ailments. Without the stabilizing influence of work, old emotional conflicts can reemerge, and the person often acquires feelings of inadequacy and worthlessness that generate behavior sometimes regarded as "senile."

The real issue of retirement is whether people have a choice. They should be able to decide for themselves. Actually, the earlier fears of industry that large numbers of less efficient workers would remain on the payrolls have not materialized. Workers with good health

Living Issues

Burnout

Burnout is a term that describes the condition of a person emotionally and physically exhausted from too much job pressure. Burnout can occur at any stage of adult life, but middle-aged people seem particularly prone. They have devoted their efforts to their careers and families, often not finding the replenishment they hoped for. Burned-out men and women describe their overwhelming depletion, saying: "I don't care any more," "I have nothing left to give," "I'm drained," or "I'm exhausted."

Job pressures often combine with personal and family circumstances to create an overload. Added together, family tensions and conflicts, financial pressures, illness, and problems with children or other family members can create stress. Poor health habits over a period of time can cause havoc. Unless people take time off for rest and relaxation and diversionary social activities, they forget how to relax, and stress builds up. When burnout becomes advanced and prolonged and turns into severe depression or chronic anxiety, then psychotherapy or counseling is in order.

and superior performance are the ones most likely to stay on the job.

SOCIAL-PSYCHOLOGICAL THEORIES OF AGING

One task of social scientists is to develop theories explaining social phenomena. Theories of aging attempt to explain the process of aging in its many dimensions. The biological theories of aging were described in Chapter 16. This chapter discusses five social-psychological theories of aging.

Disengagement Theory

The **disengagement theory** of aging was originally formulated by Cummings and Henry (1961). The theory states that as people approach and enter old age, they have a natural tendency to withdraw socially and psychologically from the environment. According to the theory, older people tend to detach themselves voluntarily from outside social activities and to become less involved with other people (Carstensen, 1992). At the same time, they withdraw emotionally, turning inward to their own thoughts and feelings. This disengagement frees older people from the stress that arises from numerous

Burnout—physical, mental, and emotional exhaustion that is attributable to work related stress

Disengagement theory—theory of aging saying that aging people have a natural tendency to withdraw socially and psychologically from the environment, social activities, and other people

role obligations and family and community responsibilities. It also allows them more time and opportunity to pursue those activities, values, and ideas that they consider important. Thus, disengagement enhances their life satisfaction as they grow older.

Since its conception, disengagement theory has been criticized severely (Achenbaum & Bengtson, 1994). *Critics argue that disengagement is not universal, inevitable, or inherent in the aging process.* Some older people never disengage; they remain active and productive all their lives. Benjamin Franklin was 70 when he helped draft the *Declaration of Independence.* Giuseppe Verdi, the distinguished Italian opera composer, was 73 when he composed *Othello,* and 80 when *Falstaff* was first performed in Milan. Karl Menninger, the outstanding psychiatrist who received countless awards, wrote *The Crime of Punishment* at 75. In his 80s, Arthur Fiedler was directing the Boston Pops Orchestra.

Critics also insist that the theory does not consider those individual differences in health and personality that influence activity. Further, it is continued activity, not disengagement, that produces the most life satisfaction for older people.

Activity Theory

Activity theory suggests that continuance of an active lifestyle will have a positive effect on the sense of well-being and satisfaction of older people. This personal satisfaction depends on a positive self-image, which is validated through continued participation in middle-aged roles. When these roles end, they must be replaced to avoid feelings of decline and uselessness.

Psychologists and social gerontologists give only partial support to this oversimplified theory (Lee & Markides, 1990). Simply engaging in activities does not automatically maintain one's feeling of self-worth, especially if those activities are less meaningful than the roles that one has given up. Will a retired corporation president have as adequate a self-concept playing bingo as he did when working? It is unlikely. Busywork alone is not the answer.

Another difficulty is that *activity theory neglects persons who cannot maintain middle-aged standards physically, mentally, or emotionally.* Some people are forced to shift roles for health or other reasons, yet still find great satisfaction. Not everyone must maintain a high level of activity to be happy. Overall, there is an association among morale, personality adjustment, and activity

levels; but *different persons may prefer different types of activities and different degrees of participation to be satisfied.*

Personality and Lifestyle Theory

Because of individual differences in activity and disengagement, many gerontologists seek a **personality and lifestyle theory** to describe what constitutes successful aging. Neugarten (1968), who investigated older people between the ages of 70 and 79, identified four major personality types and categorized the role activities of those comprising the major types. Table 19.6 shows the four major personality types: *integrated, armored-defended, passive-dependent,* and *unintegrated.* The *integrated* include three subtypes. The *reorganizers* are those who substitute new activities for lost ones and engage in a wide variety of activities. The *focused* have integrated personalities with high life satisfaction. They are selective in their activities and derive major satisfaction from one or two role areas. The *disengaged* are integrated personalities with high life satisfaction but with low activity. They have voluntarily moved away from role commitments because of preference.

The *armored-defended* include two types: the *holding on* and the *constricted.* Because aging is a threat to the holding-on group, they maintain middle-age patterns as long as possible. They are successful in their attempts and maintain high life satisfaction at medium or high activity levels. Moreover, they say, "I'll work until I drop" or "So long as you keep busy, you will get along all right" (Neugarten, 1968, p. 176). Those people in the *constricted* group deal with losses by constricting their social interactions and energies and by closing themselves off from experiences. This tactic works fairly well, giving them high or medium life satisfaction.

Those in the *passive-dependent* group are either *succorance-seeking* or *apathetic.* The succorance-seeking have high dependency needs and are fairly satisfied, as long as they have others to lean on who can meet their emotional needs. The apathetic are the "rocking chair types" who have disengaged; they have low role activity and only medium or low life satisfaction.

The *unintegrated,* or *disorganized,* exhibit gross defects in psychological functions, loss of emotional control, and deterioration of thought processes.

Neugarten and associates concluded from their research that the activity and disengaged theories did not adequately explain

Activity theory—theory of aging suggesting that continuance of an active lifestyle has a positive effect on the sense of well-being and satisfaction of older people

Personality and lifestyle theory—theory of aging that shows the relationship between personality type and patterns of aging

Continuing an active lifestyle contributes to a sense of well-being and satisfaction among some older people.

what happened as people grow older. People are not at the mercy of their social environment or intrinsic processes. They continue to make choices, selecting in accordance with their long-established needs. Personality is "the pivotal dimension in describing patterns of aging and in predicting relationships between level of social role activity and life satisfaction" (Neugarten, 1968, p. 177). Other personality theorists group individuals into different categories.

Exchange Theory

Exchange theory rests on these four basic assumptions:

1. Individuals and groups act to maximize rewards and minimize costs.

2. The individual uses past experience to predict the outcome of similar exchanges in the present.

3. An individual will maintain an interaction if it continues to be more rewarding than costly.

4. When one individual is dependent on another, the latter accrues power.

According to this theory, social exchanges involve not only financial transactions but also psychological satisfaction and need gratification. *The person having the greater needs loses power; the other person gains power.* Power is thus derived from unequal needs or imbalances in social exchange.

Exchange theory was not formulated originally as a theory of aging. The first person to apply the theory to the aged was Martin (1971). He used the theory to describe visiting patterns among family members. The aged who have financial resources that younger persons need or who can offer valuable services such as baby-sitting hold positions of power and put their children in dependent positions. Those who have little to offer—who, for example, have to beg others to visit—are forced to pay a high price. Their relatives visit reluctantly and begrudgingly, demonstrating to the elderly that visiting is a chore or burden.

Social Reconstruction Theory

Kuypers and Bengtson (1973) have used the social breakdown model as developed by Zusman (1966) to show how our society

TABLE 19.6 PERSONALITY AND THEORIES OF AGING

Personality Type	Role Activity	Life Satisfaction	Number
1. Integrated			
—Reorganizers	High	High	9
—Focused	Medium	High	5
—Disengaged	Low	High	3
2. Armored-defended			
—Holding on	High or medium	High	11
—Constricted	Low or medium	High or medium	4
3. Passive-dependent			
—Succorance-seeking	High or medium	High or medium	6
—Apathetic	Low	Medium or low	5
4. Unintegrated			
—Disorganized	Low	Medium or low	7

Based on statistical material by B. L. Neugarten, R. J. Havighurst, and S. S. Tobin, in "Personality and Patterns of aging," *Middle Age and Aging* (pp. 173–177), B. L. Neugarten, Ed., 1968, Chicago: University of Chicago Press.

Exchange theory—theory that, as applied to the aged and their families, maintains that persons with the greatest needs lose the most power and those supplying needs gain power

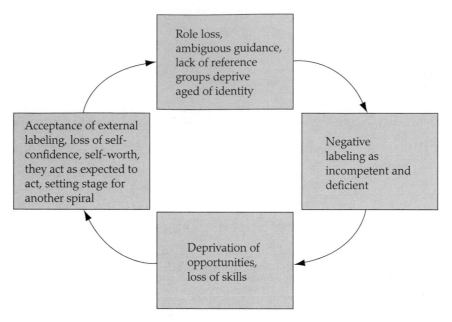

FIGURE 19.7   Social breakdown and the aged.

Adapted from "Social Breakdown and Competence: A Model of Normal Aging," by J. A. Kuypers and V. L. Bengtson, 1973, *Human Development, 16*, pp. 181–201. Reproduced with permission of S. Karger AG, Basel.

causes negative changes in the self-concept of the aged. Four steps are involved (see Figure 19.7):

1. *Our society brings about role loss*, offers only sparse normative information and guidance, and deprives the elderly of reference groups, so that they lose the sense of who they are and what their roles are.
2. *Society then labels them negatively* as incompetent and deficient.
3. *Society deprives them of opportunities* to use their skills, which atrophy in the process.
4. *The aged accept the external labeling*, identify themselves as inadequate, and begin to act as they are expected to act, setting the stage for another spiral (Kuypers & Bengtson, 1973).

According to the **social reconstruction theory** of Kuypers and Bengtson, people can change the system and break the cycle through three types of action. *First*, we must eliminate the idea that work is the primary source of worth. The Protestant work ethic is inappropriate to old age. People need to be

Social reconstruction theory—theory of aging describing how society reduces the self-concept of the aged, and proposing ways to reverse this negative cycle

judged by their character, personality, and humanitarianism. *Second*, the social services, housing, health care, and financial status of the aged need to be improved. *Finally*, we must give the elderly greater powers of self-rule; they need to be the ones who determine the political and social policies and programs that affect them. In this way, they can develop greater self-confidence and feelings of self-worth and can help maintain their personal competency and social power.

Which Theory?

Each of these theories contributes something to the total understanding of the aging process. No one theory can explain the process in every individual. People are different; they live in different environments; their personalities and needs are different; and they act and react in different ways to social pressures. The more thoroughly we analyze these different determinants, the more clearly we will understand the process of aging in our culture. Finally, the better we understand our own needs and concerns as we age, the more likely we are to achieve satisfaction in our later years.

Summary

1. A bit fewer than 1 in 5 adults over 18 years of age have never been married, but these are primarily in the youngest age groups. However, the unmarried status of most adult singles is only temporary, because by age 45 to 54, only 8.6% of males and 7.1% of females have never been married.

2. Singles have been divided into four categories: voluntary temporary singles, voluntary permanent singles, involuntary temporary singles, and involuntary permanent singles.

3. There are both advantages and disadvantages in being single.

4. One study describes six lifestyle patterns of singles: professional, social, individualistic, activist, passive, and supportive.

5. Some singles live in singles communities; others live in housing among the general population; others live with parents; and others live alone.

6. Young people leave home because they prefer independence, but increasing numbers are returning to the nest when things get rough on the outside.

7. One of the greatest needs of single people is for friendship and companionship. Loneliness is a problem for a significant majority.

8. Singles seem to have more time for optional activities than married couples, but married people report that they have more fun than singles.

9. The number of singles cohabiting with members of the opposite sex continues to increase, but there is no evidence that premarital cohabitation weeds out incompatible couples or prepares people for successful marriage.

10. Couples who have cohabited before marriage score significantly lower in marital satisfaction after marriage than couples who have not cohabited; in addition, they often have less commitment to marital permanence.

11. The most important element in initial attraction is physical attractiveness, but personality factors become increasingly important as relationships develop.

12. One of the major problems for singles is finding and meeting dates. One survey reported that the most frequent way of meeting dates was through friends, at parties, at work or in class, and other ways (in decreasing order of frequency).

13. Gender roles in dating have been changing, with more females initiating dating and sharing part of the expenses. Among other things, this method helps alter male-female sexual expectations.

14. Date rape is a very common type of sexual aggression; it can occur in various kinds of relationships, and it reflects the myth that women want to be forced and that it is up to the male to overcome female resistance. Of course, many men engage in such acts as an expression of anger, hostility, and contempt.

15. AIDS is of special concern today because it is incurable and fatal.

16. According to the NHSLS survey, 94% to 98% of men and women have had sexual intercourse by age 25. However, 25% of never-married, noncohabiting men and women had no sex partners in the past 12 months; 38% had only one partner; 28% had two to four. In another national survey of people aged 18 to 75 with multiple sex partners, only 18% of men and 22% of women always used condoms with their primary partner. Twenty-eight percent of men and 32% of women always used condoms with their secondary partner. In general, almost half of men and women with multiple partners never used condoms. This practice places sexually active people at high risk of getting AIDS.

17. Love may be divided into five different elements: romantic love, erotic love, dependent love, friendship love, and altruistic love. Love is most complete when it contains all of these elements. Sternberg and Barnes divide love into three components: intimacy, passion, and decision/commitment.

18. There are various factors that are considered in the mate selection process: propinquity, attraction, homogamy or heterogamy, and compatibility.

19. Marriage rates among both black men and black women are significantly lower than are those for their white counterparts.

20. According to the filter process theory of mate selection, the search for a mate starts with a broad field of eligibles and goes through a series of filters, each of which eliminates ineligibles before going on to the next filter, ending up with a final trial period before marriage.

21. The primary difference between older never-marrieds and younger ones is that

the former are often well adjusted to their situation.

22. A minority of unmarried aged feel socially isolated. Their happiness depends a lot on their satisfaction with their level of living and their level of social activity.

23. Marital happiness contributes more to overall personal happiness than does any other kind of satisfaction, including satisfaction from work.

24. The family life cycle divides the family experience into phases or stages over the life span. In general, marital satisfaction declines; it is high at the time of marriage, lowest during the child-rearing years, and higher again after the youngest child has passed beyond the teens.

25. All couples are faced with marital adjustment tasks early in marriage.

26. Adjustments to parenthood are less stressful if the marriage is not stressful, if parenthood was planned, if couples are prepared ahead of time, and if a child is easy to care for.

27. In the beginning of marriage, couples watch every detail about one another. Gradually, they learn to adjust to these trifles.

28. The vast majority of couples want to have children, but voluntary childlessness is increasing. Couples who are childless by choice offer some convincing arguments why they don't want children.

29. Middle-agers start to face a time squeeze in which they begin to count the years remaining and to see life as a race against time in which to accomplish all they want. This leads to an assessment of self, relationships, and life goals in which existential, practical, and personal issues come into focus.

30. The task during middle adulthood may be to revitalize a tired marriage.

31. Some couples have trouble adjusting to the empty-nest years, but even greater numbers breathe a sigh of relief after the last child leaves. There is considerable evidence to show that adults in the post-parental period are happier than are those earlier or later in life.

32. Spouse abusers are insecure individuals who can't take responsibilities for their own actions and who blame all their problems on their spouse. They are misogynists who express their hatred of women through abuse and through efforts to control. Abused women have poor self-images, come to feel that all is their own fault, that they deserve to be abused, and that if they will just try harder, everything will be all right. Such a woman doesn't leave because she hopes for change if she tries harder or because she is afraid of what her partner will do.

33. Marital satisfaction usually increases during a second honeymoon period after the children are launched and after retirement. However, during the last stages of old age, marital satisfaction may again decline.

34. Other adjustments during late adulthood are readjusting sex roles in the family, working out older parent-adult child relationships, contacts, and aid.

35. The greater longevity of women means that the number of widows exceeds widowers at all levels. Survivors often confront a variety of emotional, economic, and physical problems.

36. Some couples live in stable but unhappy marriages for a wide variety of reasons.

37. Divorce rates increased steadily from 1958 until 1979, but have since leveled off and declined. However, projections show that among women age 35 to 39, 56% may eventually divorce.

38. Surveys among marriage and family therapists show the following ten areas as being most damaging to marital relationships (in decreasing frequency): communication, unrealistic expectations, power struggles, serious individual problems, role conflict, lack of love, lack of demonstration of affection, alcoholism, extramarital affairs, and sex.

39. The process of disaffection may be divided into three stages: the beginning phase, middle phase, and end phase.

40. Commitment and hard work enable some very troubled couples to work out their situations. Lack of commitment prevents some couples from working out minor problems that can really be solved.

41. There are several possible alternatives to divorce: marriage counseling, attending marriage enrichment programs, reconciliation, or structured separation. It is important for couples to explore alternatives to see whether they can work out problems before they make a decision to divorce.

42. The most important adult adjustments after divorce are getting over the emotional trauma, dealing with the attitudes of society, loneliness, finances, realignment of work responsibilities and sex

roles, sexual readjustments, contacts with ex-spouse, and kinship and children interaction.

43. Extramarital affairs have varying effects on marriage; some marriages are never the same afterward. Affairs sometimes stimulate the couple to seek help in solving unresolved problems. Sometimes affairs have no effect; at other times they hurt the wronged person, who chooses not to make an issue. Other times, affairs result in divorce. The most damaging affairs are ongoing ones that include emotional involvement as well as sexual relations.

44. Adults who remarry have some real advantages over those married for the first time.

45. Remarriage introduces some complications not present in first marriage, the most important of which is stepchildren.

46. One of the major psychosocial tasks of young adulthood is to seek and find vocational identity, which is necessary to life satisfaction. It is important to aspire toward goals and to experience some success.

47. Adults have been grouped into five categories according to the status of their vocational development: vocational achievers, vocationally frustrated, noncommitted, vocational opportunists, and social dropouts.

48. The numbers and percentages of wives and mothers in the labor force are increasing. This increase includes mothers of preschool and school-age children.

49. There are several sources of stress for working wives and mothers: conflict between home life and work life, the presence of young children in the family, the strain of role fulfillment, or the job itself.

50. There are some real satisfactions and gains in dual-career marriages: financial rewards, satisfaction of the urge for creativity, achievement, recognition and self-expression, and the establishment of equality in the relationship.

51. There are some important issues in dual-career marriages: moving, travel, child care, household responsibilities and roles, scheduling, and the issue of identity and competitiveness.

52. The overall conclusion one can draw from research is that no consistent negative effects accrue to the children of employed mothers, unless the effect on the mother is negative.

53. Midlife should be a time of vocational fruition. Some middle-agers lose their jobs because they do not keep abreast of their fields. Those who feel at a dead end in their career might start a second career.

54. Midlife careers can also be a source of stress. One source is being fired. Too much job pressure and stress can result in burnout.

55. Job satisfaction tends to increase with a worker's age.

56. Because of increased longevity, raising of the mandatory retirement age and the age when workers can draw maximum social security, the numbers of older workers in the workforce may increase in the years ahead.

57. Forced retirement has been ranked among the top ten crises in terms of the amount of stress caused. Workers ought to have a choice in deciding when to retire.

58. Social-psychological theories of aging include disengagement theory, activity theory, personality and lifestyle theory, exchange theory, and social reconstruction theory.

59. Each of the social-psychological theories of aging has merit. The truth is not found in one theory alone.

Key Terms

Activity theory p. 548
Altruistic love p. 523
Burnout p. 547
Cohabitation p. 518
Consummate love p. 523
Date rape p. 521
Dependent love p. 523
Disengagement theory p. 547
Erotic love p. 523
Exchange theory p. 548
Family life cycle p. 527
Friendship love p. 523
Heterogamy p. 524
Homogamy p. 524
Marital adjustment tasks p. 528
Marriage enrichment program p. 539
Misogynist p. 533
Personality and lifestyle theory p. 548
Postparental years p. 532
Romantic love p. 522
Social reconstruction theory p. 550
Structured separation p. 539

Discussion Questions

1. What, in your view, are the greatest advantages and disadvantages to being single?

2. To singles: What are your greatest problems of adjustment? Describe.

3. What do you think of single young adults living with parents? living alone?

4. Describe the pros and cons of nonmarital cohabitation. Are you cohabiting with someone now? How is it working out? What are the biggest problems you have? Do you think that premarital cohabitation helps to sort out compatible mates? helps to prepare for a happy marriage? Explain.

5. To be happy, do you need close friends? a lot of social life? Do marrieds or singles have more fun? What are the greatest advantages to you of being married? What are the greatest disadvantages?

6. What are the biggest problems in dating?

7. To women: Have you ever been exposed to unwanted male sexual aggression? How has the experience affected you since then? What are the real issues in date rape? If you were date raped, would you go to the police? Explain.

8. To men: Are men today taught to believe that when women say no, they really mean yes, and that it is up to the man to overcome the woman's resistance? What can you do to ensure that you do not become guilty of date rape?

9. What particular problems are most associated with the high rate of premarital sexual intercourse? Would you marry a virgin? Explain your views.

10. How can you tell whether you're in love?

11. What to you are the most important qualities in a mate?

12. Do you know any older, never-married adults? Describe. What are their reasons for not marrying? Are they happy? Are you aware of any particular problems they face? Have you thought of never getting married? Explain your views.

13. In your opinion, what are the greatest adjustment problems early in marriage?

14. Are you a parent? What are your greatest problems in relation to parenthood? What are your greatest satisfactions?

15. Will you elect never to become a parent? Explain.

16. Have you ever known anyone who was an abused spouse? Tell about the situation.

17. What are the greatest problems your parents face as married adults? Are any of your parents widowed? divorced? What are the most important problems they face?

18. Have you ever been to a marriage counselor? To a marriage enrichment program? Describe. What were the results?

19. If your spouse got involved in an extramarital affair, what would you do?

20. Was either of your parents remarried after divorce or widowhood? How did the remarriage work out? If you are a stepchild, what have been the most important adjustments you have had to make?

21. What are the primary problems and challenges you face in becoming established in your career?

22. How do you feel about mothers of infants being employed outside the home?

23. Are you an employed mother, or is your spouse one? How is it working out?

24. Has either of your parents established a second career in midlife? Describe. How has it worked out?

25. Have you ever known anyone who suffered from job burnout? Tell about it.

26. How do you feel about retirement at age 65? Is either of your parents retired? How has the retirement worked out?

27. Which theory of aging best explains to you what happens as people get older?

28. What socioeconomic and political trends and conditions in the United States make growing old more difficult than it needs to be?

Suggested Readings

ANDERSON, J. (1990). *The single mother's book.* Atlanta: Peachtree Publishers. A guide for the single mother.

ARENDELL, T. T. (1995). *Fathers and divorce.* Thousand Oaks, CA: Sage. In-depth interviews with a volunteer sample of 75 divorced fathers in New York.

BOOTH, A., & DUNN, J. (Eds.). (1994). *Stepfamilies: Who benefits? Who does not?* Hillsdale, NJ: Lawrence Erlbaum Associates. A collection of invited papers that were presented at the National Symposium on Stepfamilies in 1993 at Pennsylvania State University.

BREHM, S. S. (1991).   *Intimate relationships.* New York: McGraw-Hill. Intimate relationships from beginning to dissolution and how to improve them.

DORESS-WORTERS, P. B. (1996).   *The New Ourselves Growing Older.* New York: Peter Smith. Women aging with knowledge and power.

GANONG, L. H., & COLEMAN, M. (1994).   *Remarried family relationships.* Thousand Oaks, CA: Sage. Advances our understanding of remarried families.

GOTTMAN, J. (1994).   *What predicts divorce?* Hillsdale, NJ: Erlbaum. A detailed, in-depth account of the most significant studies of marriage to date.

GOTTMAN, J. (1995).   *Why marriages succeed or fail.* New York: Fireside. Marital stability and satisfaction results on teachable conflict-management skills.

HENDRICK, S. S., & HENDRICK, C. (1992).   *Romantic love.* Newbury Park, CA: Sage. A social-psychological approach to romantic love.

HUNTER, S., & SUNDEL, M. (Eds.). (1989).   *Midlife myths.* Newbury Park, CA: Sage. Issues of middle adulthood.

KAYSER, K. (1999).   *When love dies: The process of marital disaffection.* New York: Guilford. The process by which individuals fall out of love with their partners.

KISSMAN, K., & ALLEN, J. A. (1993).   *Single-parent families.* Newbury Park, CA: Sage. A therapist's experience with single-parent families.

KITSON, G. C. (with W. M. HOLMES). (1992).   *Portrait of divorce: Adjustment to marital breakdown.* New York: The Guilford Press. The consequences of divorce.

LEWIS, S., IZRAELI, D. N., & HOOTSMANS, H. (Eds.). (1991).   *Dual-earner families:* International perspectives. London: Sage. Thirteen articles on dual-earner families.

MOEN, P. (1992).   *Women's two roles: A contemporary dilemma.* New York: Auburn House. The difficulties of two roles and some solutions.

RANK, M. R. (1994).   *Living on the edge: The realities of welfare in America.* New York: Columbia University Press. The book focuses on the struggle to live with public assistance among those who are not urban underclass.

RICE, F. P. (1998).   *Intimate relationships, marriages, and families* (4th ed.). Mountain View, CA: Mayfield Publishing Co. Comprehensive look at all aspects.

RILEY, G. (1992).   *Divorce: An American tradition.* University of Nebraska Press. Historical evolution of divorce.

SCARF, M. (1996).   *Intimate partners: Patterns in love and marriage.* New York: Random House. Love, relationships, and marriage, and the way earlier lives affect these.

SCHIFF, H. S. (1996).   *How did I become my parents' parent?* New York: Penguin USA. For caregivers of parents.

SHAPIRO, J. L. (1995).   *The measure of a man.* New York: Perigee. Becoming the father you wish your father had been.

STACEY, W. A., HAZLEWOOD, L. R., & SHUPE, A. (1994).   *The violent couple.* Westport, CT: Greenwood. The dynamics of domestic violence.

STERNBERG, R. J. (1988).   *The triangle of love.* New York: Basic Books. His theory of love.

SZINOVACZ, M. E., EKERDT, D. J., & VINICK, B. H. (Eds.). (1992).   *Families and retirement.* Newbury Park, CA: Sage. Effects of retirement on individuals.

TANNEN, D. (1991).   *You just don't understand.* New York: Ballantine Books. Women and men in conversation.

http://www.ijpa.org/International journal of psychoanalysis. Peer reviewed journal published six times a year, dealing with many issues including research and life cycle development.

Web Resources

Death, Dying, and Bereavement

LEADING CAUSES OF DEATH

Figure 20.1 shows the leading causes of death in the United States in 1995. *Heart disease was the number-one killer.* If all of the major cardiovascular diseases were added together (including heart diseases, hypertension, cerebrovascular disease, and atherosclerosis), these would account for 39% of all deaths. However, rapid progress in the treatment of these diseases has caused the associated death rate to decrease steadily (U.S. Bureau of the Census, 1998).

Cancer was the number-two killer, and in spite of advances in treatment, the death rate continues to be fairly steady.

Death rates from accidents continue to decline. Death rates from homicides have stayed fairly constant.

There is a marked difference in death rates among different groups of people:

1. Males die at a higher rate than females at all ages.
2. The nonwhite population has a higher death rate than the white population.
3. The death rate among nonwhite infants under 1 year of age is 2 times greater than among white infants.
4. Accidents are the leading cause of death among youths 15 to 24 years old.
5. Deaths from suicide reach a peak among adults in the 75- to 84-year-old age group.

The causes of death have changed radically in the past 100 years. At one time, infectious diseases such as *influenza, pneumonia,* and *tuberculosis* were the leading causes of death (Hendricks & Hendricks, 1986). Childhood infections such as *diphtheria, whooping cough, measles, scarlet fever,* and *acute infectious gastroenteritis* claimed the lives of many children. Acute infectious gastroenteritis with vomiting and diarrhea is still the leading cause of death in children less than 4 years old in developing countries (Berkow, 1997).

ATTITUDES TOWARD DEATH AND DYING

Cultural Antecedents

The dominant feature of death in the twentieth century has been its invisibility. We try to solve the problems of death by hiding it or denying it. We lie to dying people about their condition because death is unmentionable. They, in turn, try to convince us that they are getting better. Or, we use machines to keep organs functioning, even when people are clinically dead. When people die, they are made to look healthy and alive, as though they were sleeping. We sometimes discourage mourning and the natural expression of grief at a time of great loss. The denial of death has become the orthodoxy of our culture.

In earlier times, death was more a part of everyday life. People who were critically ill were usually cared for at home, with family members providing the service. Death often occurred at home. Relatives prepared the body for burial, built the coffin, and buried it. Services were by the graveside. The burial itself may have taken place in a family graveyard next to other relatives who had died. Death was stressful to all, but it was an accepted part of life.

Today, the critically ill usually die in the hospital with medical staff members attending them. The body is transported to the funeral home, where professionals prepare it for viewing. The undertaker feels proud if

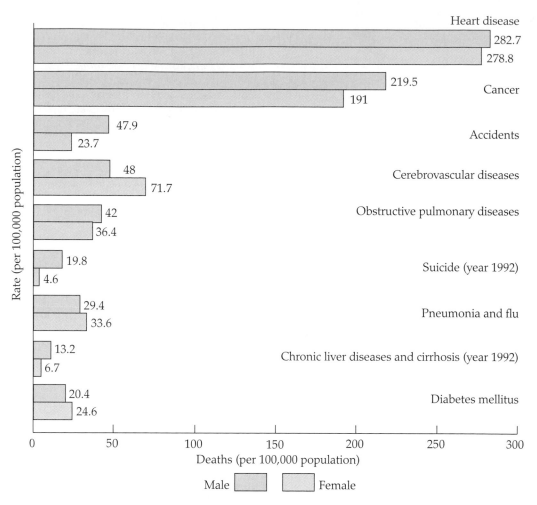

FIGURE 20.1   Death rates by cause and sex, United States, 1995.

Statistics from *Statistical Abstract of the United States, 1995* (p. 104), by U.S. Bureau of the Census, 1998, Washington, DC: U.S. Government Printing Office.

the deceased looks natural and seems to be sleeping. The graveside is prepared with plastic green carpet and flowers to hide the soil. Usually, the casket is not lowered into the grave until family members have left. Everything is done to hide the fact and reality of death.

Denial can be an important coping mechanism. The way that some people deal with loss is to believe it doesn't exist, but *it is this very denial, when carried to extremes, that prevents acceptance and positive adjustments.* There are so many positive things that the dying want to do and say before they die. There are so many positive things that family members want to do and say, but when the living and dying both deny that death is taking place, the words are never spoken.

After death, one of the most important ways of dealing with grief is to be able to express it and talk about the loved one. When people try, they are hushed up, or the subject is changed. Death is considered too unpleasant a subject for polite conversation. Even children have to struggle to understand because their curiosity and questions are reprimanded or avoided. They are forced to try to cope as best they can (Kalish, 1985a).

Criticisms

Modern trends involving the denial of death have led to increasing examination of our philosophies of death and dying, to a deluge of courses on the subject, and to a flood of literature, much of it protesting modern practices. Tentler (1977) provided a comparative critique of writings about death in American culture, drawn from the fields of psychology, sociology, anthropology, religion, and literature. He observed a common

There is a need for an expression of grief at a time of great loss.

ASPECTS OF DEATH

What Is Death?

theme in these essays: a "moralist, reformist approach" characterized by criticism of the denial of death. Dishonesty with dying people, lack of care for the aged, and American funeral practices are common subjects of scorn. *Currently, there is a swing away from the denial of death toward the notion of death with dignity.*

Although they did not fear death, few of the elderly subjects indicated a resignation to or desire for death. Only 5% said they frequently wished for death. About 82% thought about things related to living and looked forward to the future. About 69% reported that they perceived death as rescuing them from pain and difficulty. However, only 33% looked forward to death for that reason. The one fear of the respondents was that death would be painful (45%), but only 6% believed this would be the case.

In relation to an afterlife, 62% believed it existed, but 94% said it did not worry them. About 75% reported they would not change their way of life even if they were certain there were no life after death (Myska & Pasewark, 1978). These results indicated an affirmation of life and a realistic acceptance of death, with little anxiety or preoccupation.

Determining when a person is dead is not simple. A distinction is made between **physiological death** and **clinical death.** With physiological death, all the vital organs cease to function and the organism can no longer live, in any sense of the word. Deprived of oxygen and nutrients, the cells of the body gradually die. Clinical death is the cessation of all brain activity as indicated by an absence of brain waves. There is no consciousness, no awareness. The organism ceases to function as a self-sustaining, mind-body human, even though the heart and lungs can function with artificial support.

There are other aspects of death. **Sociological death** involves withdrawal and separation from the patient by others. This may occur weeks before terminus if patients are left alone to die. It happens when families desert the aged in nursing homes, where older people may live for years as if dead. As a resident of one nursing home expressed it,

What have I to live for? I have two children who don't care about me. They are so busy with their own lives that they haven't been in to see me in two years. My health is not good. I have arthritis, no appetite, and a weak heart. There is nothing to do here. It's the same old thing day after day. I might as well be dead.

Physiological death—the ceasing to function of all the vital organs

Clinical death—the cessation of all brain activity

Sociological death—the withdrawal and separation by other people as though one were dead, often long before physiological death

FOCUS

Children's and Adolescents' Conceptions of Death

Maria Nagy (1948) conducted the first investigation of children's attitudes toward death. The following is a summary of her findings:

- *Ages 3 to 5.* Children are curious about death, but they see it as temporary and reversible. The dead person will return.

- *Ages 5 to 9.* Children only gradually realize that death is final, irreversible, and permanent (Lazur & Torney-Purta, 1991). They begin to realize that they could die, but they don't necessarily have to. Older people die because they can't run fast enough or hide from death in the way that younger, smaller people can.

- *Ages 9 to 10.* Death is final, inevitable, and universal. They become concerned about how death affects them and their family. They can show a lot of anger, guilt, and

grief over someone's dying (Schaefer & Lyons, 1986).

- *Adolescents.* A few adolescents who have experienced the death of a close member of the family or of a close friend try to fathom its meaning and nature. For most, death is so remote that it doesn't have much relevance. Little thought is given to it because it is always something that happens to someone else.

The adolescent's sense of immortality makes it difficult for him or her to deal with death (Hetzel, Winn, & Tolstoshev, 1991).

Parents can help children to understand death by answering their questions.

Psychic death occurs when the patient accepts death and regresses into the self. Often this occurs long before physiological death. The psychic acceptance of death can actually cause a person to die. Death comes through the power of suggestion because the will to live is gone.

Attitudes Among Different Age Groups of Adults

Detailed studies of groups of adults reveal variations in attitudes toward death among different age groups. One study examined the attitudes toward death of black, white, and Mexican-American adults of low, medium, and high socioeconomic status, from three different age groups (45 to 54; 55 to 64; and 65 to 74). It revealed little variation in attitudes toward death with respect to race, socioeconomic status, or sex, but it did show substantial differences according to age (Bengtson, Cuellar, & Ragan, 1977). *Middle-aged respondents age 45 to 54 expressed the greatest fear of death; the elderly, 65 to 74, reflected the least.* The re-

searchers suggested that middle-aged adults are more frightened of death because they experience a middle-aged crisis and become aware of the finitude of their lives.

The researchers also indicated that in old age, adults do resolve their death fear. This attitude is exemplified by a 67-year-old widower, who said: "I know I'm going to die, it's something that we all have to go through. When it happens, it happens, and there's nothing I can do. I'll cross that bridge when I come to it" (Bengtson et al., 1977).

Attitudes toward death depend partly on attitudes toward life. Keith (1979) surveyed 214 men and 254 women, median age 79, from small towns in a midwestern state, and found that those who experienced continuity in marital status, good health, church involvement, and informal contacts with family and friends viewed life and death more positively.

Attitudes Among the Elderly

The elderly are often more philosophical, more realistic, and less anxious about death than are others in our culture. Many studies underscore these

Psychic death—the acceptance of death and regression into self, often long before physiological death

attitudes. Questionnaires were administered to 40 voluntarily institutionalized ambulatory residents of the *Wyoming Pioneer Home* for senior citizens, and to 40 others who were non-institutionalized ambulatory persons, members of the *Senior Citizen's Center* in Laramie, Wyoming, a center providing meals, nursing services, recreations, and social activities (Myska & Pasewark, 1978). Subjects ranged in age from 61 to 97. There were few differences between the institutionalized and noninstitutionalized in their views of death. Generally, fear of death was not suggested by the respondents (see Table 20.1).

Patterns of Death

Figure 20.2 illustrates five different patterns of death (Pattison, 1977). In *pattern one*, the terminal phase begins when the person starts to give up. There is still some element of desirable hope for life, but gradually other people withdraw (sociological death), the patient acquiesces (psychic death), the brain ceases to function (clinical death), and the body dies (physiological death).

In *pattern two*, other people reject the patient and withdraw (sociological death) long before death occurs. This circumstance leads to psychic death, which ultimately results in clinical and physiological death.

In *pattern three*, both the patient and others refuse to accept impending death. When death comes, it may precipitate a shocked reaction. The same thing occurs when deterioration is sudden and death occurs contrary to expectations.

In *pattern four*, the patient rejects life and becomes psychically dead. This condition is met with social disapproval and efforts by family and friends to motivate the person to live.

Finally, in *pattern five*, there is social denial of the fact that both psychic and clinical death have occurred, and the patient is kept physiologically alive by artificial means. The morality and ethics of such artificial procedures are currently the subject of much controversy.

VARYING CIRCUMSTANCES OF DEATH

Death, especially that of a spouse or other close relative, is among life's most stressful events. It creates considerable physical, mental, and emotional stress and tension, which may take a long period of time to subside.

There are various circumstances of death. These include the following:

1. *Uncertain death*
2. Certain death, at either a known or an unknown time
3. *Untimely death*, which may be *premature*, *unexpected*, and/or *calamitous*

Each of these circumstances is discussed in this section.

Uncertain Death

Everyone will die, but the exact time is uncertain for most people. The circumstances of uncertain death can be very stressful if people have been badly injured and are in critical condition, or if they have had radical surgery with the result uncertain. During such times, the patient and family members must live through a continuing period of acute crisis.

> Harvey is lying in a hospital bed in the intensive care unit. He has just suffered a major heart attack. He is hooked up to a machine that beeps and registers a blip on a television screen every time his heart beats. His wife is beside him, holding his hand. He is receiving oxygen. He is scared. His wife is scared. They both know the days ahead are crucial. (Rice, 1999b, p. 505)

The most difficult part about such uncertainty is the waiting: dreading something

TABLE 20.1	FEAR OF DEATH AMONG ELDERLY RURAL RESIDENTS

Attitude	Percentage Affirming Attitude
Strong fear of death	1%
Absolutely unafraid of death	51%
Indifferent toward death	40%
Did not respond	8%

Reprinted with permission of authors and publisher from "Death Attitudes of Residential and Non-residential Rural Aged Persons," by M. J. Myska and R. A. Pasewark, December 1978, *Psychological Reports*, *43*, pp. 1235–1238.

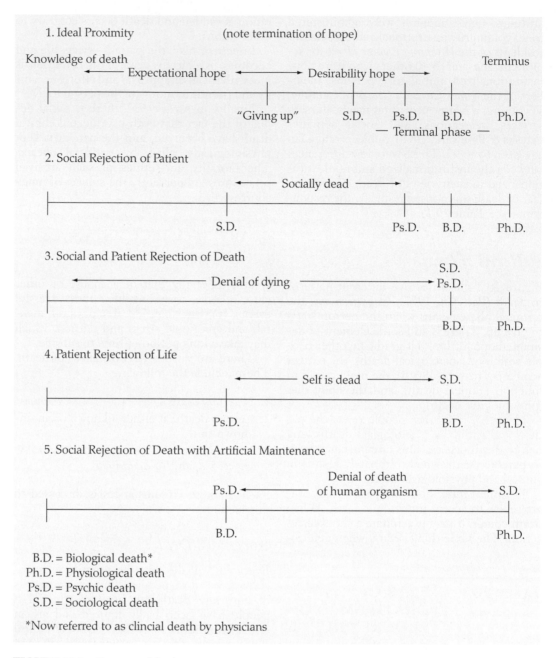

1. Ideal Proximity   (note termination of hope)

Knowledge of death   Terminus

2. Social Rejection of Patient

3. Social and Patient Rejection of Death

4. Patient Rejection of Life

5. Social Rejection of Death with Artificial Maintenance

B.D. = Biological death*
Ph.D. = Physiological death
Ps.D. = Psychic death
S.D. = Sociological death

*Now referred to as clincial death by physicians

FIGURE 20.2   Patterns of death.

adverse; hoping for improvement; waiting anxiously for other family members to arrive. The patient needs to avoid panic, to relax, and to let healing take place. The wife and family need relief from the continued anxiety and worry; they need sleep and reassurance that their loved one will be all right.

The question of whether the patient will live or die is resolved eventually: "The next 48 hours will tell us whether she is going to make it or not." At other times, there are long-term uncertainties, as is the case with treatments of cancer that may or may not have arrested the disease. Ambiguity may remain for years: "If there is no return in 5 years, the outlook is very positive." Long years of waiting can be difficult. However, some people learn to go about being as happy and optimistic as possible and not to worry about what might happen.

FOCUS

Hospice Care for the Terminally Ill

The hospice has emerged as a viable alternative to hospital deaths that are depersonalizing, lonely, and painful experiences for dying persons and their families. The term **hospice** means literally a "way station" to care for travelers on their journey. In this case, the travelers are on the way to dying.

Hospice care originated in London at St. Christopher's and spread to the United States in the early 1970s. *New Haven Hospice* in New Haven, Connecticut, was the first in the United States. Since then, thousands of hospices have sprung up around the country. Hospice care can take place at home or in the center. It includes physician-directed services, an interdisciplinary team, the use of volunteers, 24-hour-a-day treatment for the patient and family,

pain-symptom control, and bereavement follow-up of the family after death (Dubois, 1980; Mor & Masterson-Allen, 1987). Patients have the same rights to quality care as those receiving hospital care. Medicare, Medicaid, and some other insurance plans may pay part of the bill.

There are several other important features of hospice care. Bringing pain under control helps the dying person face death comfortably. Family members are welcome, and keeping the dying patient and family together comforts the patient and minimizes the guilt and anxiety of the family. The hospice permits patients and family to make decisions and to experience control over their lives

in a warm, caring atmosphere. They decide family matters, funeral planning, wills, and *where,* with *whom,* under *what* conditions, and *how* death will happen (Hayslip & Leon, 1988).

Hospice care is available in thousands of places around the country.

Certain Death

Certain death requires a different adjustment. The approximate time of death may be known or unknown or can only be surmised. Such might be the case in a deadly disease such as cancer of the pancreas. Whether the approximate time of death is known or not, the adjustments to terminal illness are difficult.

Kübler-Ross: Five Stages of Dying

One of the best descriptions of the process of dying was given by Kübler-Ross, (1969, 1974), a psychiatrist at the University of Chicago, who spent considerable time talking with 200 dying patients to try to understand and describe their reactions to terminal illness. She found considerable resistance among medical personnel to the idea of talking with patients about dying, but she also found that the patients were relieved to share their concerns.

Kübler-Ross identified five stages of dying that did not necessarily occur in a regular sequence. She said, "Most of my patients have exhibited two or three stages simultaneously and these do not always occur in the same order" (1974).

The five stages she identified are *denial, anger, bargaining, depression,* and *acceptance.*

The *denial* response of patients is this: "No, not me. It can't be true." Some accuse their doctor of incompetence, and some think a mistake was made in the lab or in diagnosis. Others seek the advice of other physicians or of faith healers, or look for miracle cures. Some simply deny the reality of impending death and proceed as if nothing were wrong. Only a few patients maintain denial to the very end; most accept reality gradually.

As they acknowledge reality, their next reaction is one of *anger:* "Why me? It's not fair it should be happening to me." Patients in this stage become very hostile, resentful, and highly irritable, often quarreling with doctors, nurses, and loved ones.

As terminally ill patients begin to realize that death may be coming, they try *bargaining* to win a reprieve. The patient propositions God, the staff, and family, sometimes just to live a while longer to attend a wedding or complete a task. The patient says to God, "If you give me 6 more months, I'll leave most of my money to the church." If the person lives beyond the requested period, however, the agreement is usually broken.

Hospice—an organization caring for the needs of the dying

Once patients lose hope that life is possible and accept death as inevitable, *depression* may set in. Depression may be caused by regret at leaving behind everything and everybody that one loves. It may be caused by guilt over one's life. It may result from shame over bodily disfigurement or because of the inability to die with dignity. Some patients need to express their sorrow to overcome it. Others need cheering up and support to improve their morale and to regain their self-esteem.

The final stage of the dying process is *acceptance*. The patient has worked through denial, anger, bargaining, depression, and fear of death; he or she is now exhausted and weak. This is the time for friends or family members to sit quietly holding the patient's hands, to show that death is not such a frightening experience (Rice, 1986).

Pattison: The Living-Dying Trajectory

Pattison (1977) presented the dying process in a somewhat different way. He said that all of us project a trajectory of our life involving a certain anticipated life span within which we arrange our activities and our lives (see Figure 20.3). And then we are abruptly confronted with a crisis—the crisis of the knowledge of death. Our potential trajectory is suddenly changed. We shall die in days, weeks, months, or several years. Our life has been foreshortened. Our activities must be rearranged. We cannot plan for the potential; we must deal with the actual. The period between the "crisis and knowledge of death" and the "point of death" is the **living-dying interval.** This interval is divided into three phases: (a) *the acute crisis phase*, (b) *the chronic living-dying phase*, and (c) *the terminal phase*. Family members can help the person respond to the acute crisis so that it does not result in a chaotic disintegration of the person's life during the chronic living-dying phase. The following is an example of **disintegrated dying** during the living-dying phase.

> Martha was told she had an incurable cancer. She shut herself up in her house, refused to talk to her family and friends or to see them. She never went out. Her husband couldn't stand to see her upset, so he went out most of the time. She spent most of her days depressed and crying. Finally, one afternoon her husband came home early and found that she had slashed her wrists in an effort to kill herself. Emergency treatment saved her life.

The following is an example of **integrated dying,** following psychiatric treatment that Martha received.

> Martha alternated between feeling terrible (when she was given chemotherapy) and feeling fairly well at other times. Her husband began to stay home more and to provide moral support and companionship. Martha and her husband started to go out to dinner occasionally. She began to call family members and friends and let them come visit. She finally decided that she was going to make the best of her life during the time she had.

The last task of family members is to give the person comfort and support as the person moves inevitably into the terminal phase (Pattison, 1977).

Needs of the Dying

Dying people have a number of needs (Kalish, 1985b). They have the same need for food, clothing, shelter, rest, and warmth that

Living-dying interval— period of time between the knowledge of the crisis of death and death itself

Disintegrated dying—going to pieces emotionally and not being able to function after learning of impending death

Integrated dying—being able to put one's life together, to make satisfactory adjustments to the dying process

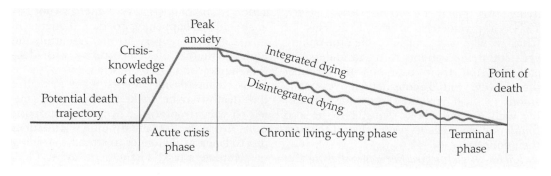

FIGURE 20.3   The living-dying trajectory.

Reprinted with the permission of Simon & Schuster. Adapted from *The Experience of Dying*, by E. Mansell Pattison. Copyright © 1977 by Prentice-Hall, Inc.

we all have. In addition, they often have the need for freedom from pain. They also need reassurance that their close friends and family will not let them die alone.

The dying person usually has a number of tasks to complete. These include getting insurance and financial affairs in order, dealing with medical care needs, especially when alternate forms of treatment are proposed, arranging for distribution of possessions after death, making a will, and making funeral suggestions; some people even make their own funeral arrangements (Kalish & Reynolds, 1981).

Telling Patients They Are Dying

Should patients be told that they are dying? A survey among physicians, nurses, chaplains, and college students concerning their attitudes toward informing patients of their terminal condition revealed that all groups felt the patients had a right to be told (Carey & Posavac, 1978–1979). Yet, there is a lack of socialization for dying in many hospitals. People are not oriented toward the process of dying and are left to cope with their problems in ambiguity and isolation. Moreover, not all patients should be approached and told in the same manner. There are no prescribed norms for dealing with dying patients. The basic intent should be to help, not harm, the patient. There is no need for a long discussion about the severity of the illness with an acutely ill patient who is barely conscious. That person often knows death is imminent. Care and comfort are the primary concerns. But the patient who is experiencing physical deterioration and who is told there is nothing to worry about may say nothing but wonder much (Pat-

This cancer patient, who is dying, receives reassurance from the doctor about the dying process.

tison, 1977). Some people absolutely do not want to know, and some would literally die of shock if they did know. *The goal is to ease the dying process, not to apply a dogma of always telling the truth.* Patients must be aware of the significance of their illness and helped to adjust. Respect for their feelings and the use of tact are extremely important.

Untimely Death: Premature Death

Grief may be considerable following a miscarriage, stillbirth, ectopic pregnancy, or neonatal death (DeFrain, 1991). Women are likely to show their grief, and men to hide it (Stimson et al., 1992). The psychological reactions to death are more extreme when death occurs in childhood or at a comparatively young age (Wass & Corr, 1984). People have trouble accepting a child's death or understanding it. People feel that the death of a small child is a greater injustice than the death of an older adult, and they experience correspondingly greater sorrow, anger, regret, or bitterness when a very young person dies (Jecker & Schneiderman, 1994). Such a death seems so unfair. The child has not had a chance at life. It is difficult to reconcile *what is* with *what might have been.* Parental reactions are variable. Many parents feel guilty: "If only I had not let him play in the front yard." "I should have watched her more care-

Sick and dying patients need the support and love of family members.

fully." "It's my fault for not taking him to the doctor sooner." "God is punishing me." Parents become angry and resentful and lash out at whomever they can blame for the loss: "I told him not to put the baby in the front seat." "If she had not been talking on the telephone, this would never have happened." Guilt and blame can destroy a family at the time that they need one another's help. Sometimes blame is put on hospitals, doctors, and nurses. Medical personnel themselves get caught up in the struggle to save a child's life, and—when this fails—they are filled with sorrow and feelings of helplessness, or with self-recrimination for failure.

While the family is focusing on saving the dying child, other siblings may be overlooked. Siblings often are frightened, bewildered, and jealous, and they may feel rejected. Parents need to keep them informed about what's going on and pay attention to them also (Wallinga, Paguio, & Skeen, 1987). Adult family members need to support one another (Smart, 1992).

Sudden Infant Death Syndrome (SIDS)

Sudden infant death syndrome, or when infants die mysteriously while asleep, is the most common cause of death in infants between 2 weeks and 1 year of age, accounting for 30% of all deaths in the age group. SIDS is one type of unexpected death that shocks

and disorganizes the family system. Survivors experience grief somatophysically and as intense, subjective mental pain. Parents experience despondency, concentration difficulties, time confusion, loss of appetite, or inability to sleep. They may dread being alone and fear the responsibilities of caring for other children. They feel helpless, angry, and guilty. Parents often blame themselves.

Research is being conducted on the best way to help families cope with the death of a child (Joyce, 1984). John Spinetta, professor of psychology at San Diego State University, has followed the course of bereavement in 120 families in which children have died of cancer, trying to distinguish the families that bounce back quickly from those that languish in grief. He asks whether the family can talk about or see reminders of the child without shedding tears, whether they have returned to normal activities like jobs, clubs, and hobbies. Are they still filled with questions about why it happened? It is hoped that some guidelines for the best ways to help grieving parents will be provided (Joyce, 1984).

Untimely Death: Unexpected Death

Unexpected death refers to the sudden death of a healthy person. The emotional impact on survivors is gauged by how vital, alive, and distinctive the person is at the time of death.

Sudden infant death syndrome—the sudden and mysterious death of infants in their sleep, usually between 2 weeks and 1 year of age

South Africans attend the funeral of a young child.

The more vital and alive the person, the harder it is to imagine that person as dead. When a young adult dies, relatives react with frustration, disappointment, and anger. Career, marriage, children, and home were probably yet to come. Unexpected death of a middle-aged person can also be tragic, but for different reasons. The middle-aged person has assumed responsibilities for family, job, and home, as well as in the community. Financial obligations are at a peak. There is extensive involvement with spouse, children, relatives, business associates, and friends. Death leaves the survivors with continuing obligations and no one to assume the responsibilities. Coping with dying involves coping with obligations already assumed.

Untimely Death: Calamitous Death

Calamitous death is not only unpredictable but also can be violent, destructive, demeaning, and even degrading. It includes *accidents, involuntary manslaughter, homicide,* and *suicide.* Accidents are the leading cause of death in the United States among people 15 to 34 years of age (U.S. Bureau of the Census, 1998). Most accidents have identifiable causes and are preventable, so that family members are left with the knowledge that the accident need not have happened. The revelation of death comes as a shock, causing an extended period of disorganization before relatives can reorganize their lives to living without their loved one.

Calamitous Death: Homicide

Most of the stereotypes about murders and murderers have no foundation in fact. The following facts help to clear up the myths (Kastenbaum & Aisenberg, 1976).

- Most murderers are not mysterious strangers. In at least two-thirds of the cases of willful homicide and violent assault, the perpetrator and the victim were at least acquainted. A sizable minority of homicides are committed by relatives of the victim.
- Family members or acquaintances behave more violently toward their victims than do total strangers.
- Senseless assaults by complete strangers are rare.
- Police officers are more likely to be killed while investigating domestic disturbances than in any other type of duty.

Accidents are the leading cause of death among people 15 to 34 years of age.

- The incidence of violent crime decreases with increases in neighborhood income.
- In most cases of violence, the perpetrator and the victim are of the same race.

These facts suggest that homicide is most often an outgrowth of quarrels and violence among family members or friends. The quarrels get out of hand, resulting in people's slaying one another in the privacy of their own homes. Police officers who are summoned to quell domestic disturbances are sometimes killed themselves.

Calamitous Death: Suicide

Suicide is acting out behavior that is often an indication of severe emotional upset. The rate increases with advancing age, reaching a peak in males over 85 years of age and in females 45 to 54 (U.S. Bureau of the Census, 1998). Figure 20.4 shows the trends. Suicide is rare in children under age 15. Children are still dependent on love objects for gratification. They have not yet completed the process of identification within themselves; thus, the thought of turning hostility toward themselves is too painful and frightening. Only as children find more self-identity can they be independent enough to commit suicide.

As can be seen in the figure, the rate among males is far greater than among females. *Females attempt suicide much more frequently than do males, but many more males than females are successful in completing the suicide.* Males more frequently use violent

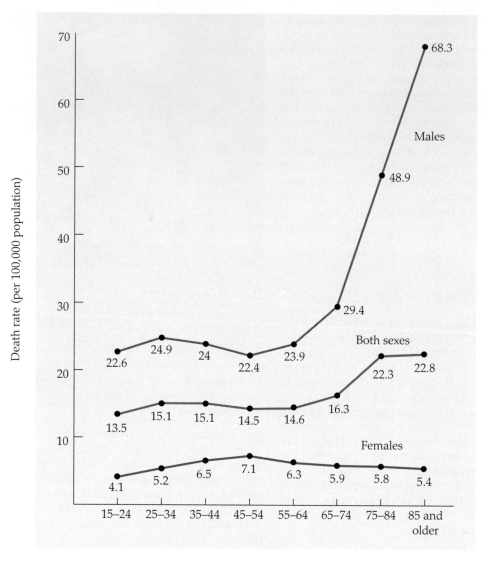

FIGURE 20.4   U.S. suicide rates, 1993, by age and sex.

Statistics from *Statistical Abstract of the United States, 1996–1997* (p. 97) by U.S. Bureau of the Census, 1996–1997, Washington, DC: U.S. Government Printing Office.

means—hanging, jumping from heights, shooting, or stabbing themselves—whereas females more often use passive and less dangerous methods, such as taking pills. Females more often make multiple threats but less often want to kill themselves or actually do it (Suicide Prevention Center, 1984).

There are a variety of motivations and reasons for suicide among the elderly. Many senile persons kill themselves in such a way that intention cannot be proven. They forget to light the gas stove after turning it on, or they overdose with medicine, having forgotten how much they have already taken. Sometimes the elderly make a deliberate and rational decision to end their lives, rather than to die a slow death or live alone and penniless. Married couples may make a pact to commit suicide together or to commit mercy killing and suicide.

More single males commit suicide than married ones. Often they have been forced into unwanted retirement. Poor planning for retirement and poor adjustment to it are major factors in the suicides of older men. Very low income seems to have a significant impact on elderly white males who commit suicide.

Older people who attempt suicide fail much less often than younger people, and any threats or symptoms must be taken seriously. Relatives and friends should be especially alert to signs of depression or suicidal preoccupation. Few human beings can sustain a meaningless life, and suicide is evidence of that fact. Some people do not attempt to take their lives with one act; rather, they neglect themselves, refuse to eat, or show other self-destructive behavior as an alternative to suicide.

Suicide is one of the most upsetting of family crises because it leaves family members feeling so remorseful, so guilty, so confused and hurt. Survivors inevitably ask:

- Why did he or she do it?
- Why didn't I sense that something was wrong?
- Why didn't I do something to prevent it?

Survivors who are left with dependent children, large financial responsibilities, and other obligations are also justifiably resentful.

- How could he or she do such a thing?
- I hate him or her for doing this and leaving me all the responsibility of caring for the children.

If family members blame themselves for letting suicide happen, or for not preventing it from happening, or for causing it to happen, it may take considerable therapy to get over the self-incrimination. Group therapy is often helpful for those bereaved by suicide (Freeman, 1991).

Socially Accelerated Dying

In the broadest sense, **socially accelerated dying** is allowing any condition or action of society that shortens life and hastens death. This includes industrial pollution, unhealthy mine conditions that lead to black lung disease, asbestos or radiation exposure that causes cancer, and subsidizing tobacco farmers. In a narrow sense, it includes withholding health care from the elderly or abandoning them in nursing homes or other institutions. Hospitals that are unconcerned with geriatric medicine or curing illnesses in elderly people are socially accelerating the dying process.

In the *Northwestern Arnhem Land of Australia*, a doomed member of the *Murngin tribe* is socially rejected by other members. All relatives withdraw their sustaining support. Other tribe members change their attitudes, placing the sick member in a sacred, taboo category. No longer a member of the group, and alone and isolated, the person can

---

Living Issues

Theories of Suicide

In an effort to understand the reasons for suicide, five general theories have been postulated. *Biological theories* of suicide focus on biochemical and genetic causes. For instance, clinical depression has been identified in as many as 60% of individuals who commit suicide. Similarly, difficulties in specific parts of the brain, such as the hypothalamus, and decreases in neurotransmitter production may predispose people to impulsive acts of self-aggression. *Characterological theories* stress the importance of personality traits. For instance, individuals prone to suicide may have low self-esteem; intense feelings of worthlessness, self-reproach, and futility may create dangerous feelings that can propel a person to commit suicide to escape the unbearable responsibilities of the self.

Cognitive theories concentrate on content of thought, that is, how suicidal people view themselves in the world. Events, relationships, and outcomes are either good or bad. Life is either pleasant or intolerable. Suicidal individuals' thinking is rigid, and their ability to see alternatives is crippled.

Psychodynamic theories invoke the subconscious processes formulated by Freud that emphasized the contest between pleasure-driven instinct for life, *Eros,* and the death instinct, *Thanatos.* More recent psychodynamic views regard suicide as aggression towards others that was redirected toward the self.

Sociological theories highlight the social forces that can prompt suicide. These effects might include the breakup of family or the widening gap between the wealthy and the poor. One element that these experiences have in common is an underlying disapproval of suicide itself (Carpenter, 1993).

---

escape only by death. The fact that the community has drawn away from the person suggests in countless ways that the condition is irreversible. It takes little imagination to see that some institutionalized elderly suffer a similar fate. They too may feel cast aside with little support and condemned to die. No wonder that people relocated to a nursing home sometimes die quickly. About half the deaths take place in the first 3 months after admission (Watson & Maxwell, 1977).

*E*UTHANASIA

Meaning

Some people want to die because they are crippled or in pain and have nothing left to live for, or because they are terminally ill or are being kept alive only by artificial life support. In such cases, questions arise as to the moral obligations of society, family, and medical personnel to keep them alive.

Socially accelerated dying—allowing any condition or action of society that shortens life and hastens death

FOCUS

Factors Contributing to Adolescent Suicide

The following situations or factors contribute to suicide among adolescents (Greuling & De-Blassie, 1980; Rice, 1990).

- Suicidal adolescents tend to come from *disturbed family backgrounds* (Wright, 1985). There may have been much conflict between the parents or between the parents and children, and considerable family violence, or the parents may have manifested negative, rejecting attitudes toward the children (Wade, 1987).

- Other studies relate adolescent suicide with *frequent parental absence* because of employment (Stack, 1985). As a consequence, there is often an absence of any warm, parental figure with whom to identify and a sense of emotional and social isolation (Stivers, 1988).

- The background of *social isolation* makes these adolescents particularly vulnerable to a loss of love object, which may trigger the suicide attempt (Neiger & Hopkins, 1988).

- One frequent component of suicidal tendencies is *depression*.

- The risk of suicide among adolescents is increased with *alcohol and drug abuse* (Rogers, 1992; Sommer, 1984). Or adolescents sometimes overdose and kill themselves without intending to do so (Gispert, Wheeler, Marsh, & Davis, 1985).

- Some suicidal adolescents have been categorized as *immature personalities* with poor impulse control.

- Other suicidal adolescents have been shown to be highly *suggestible* in following the directions or examples of others.

- Suicide may be a direct result of *mental illness*. Some adolescents experience hallucinations that tell them to kill themselves.

- *Guilt* and/or *anger* and *hostility* are important emotional components of suicide. The adolescents may be in the terminal stages of a romance. Girls may believe they are pregnant. Guilt and shame over an out-of-wedlock pregnancy can be powerful motivating factors in suicides.

- Suicide may be an attempt to escape the pain and shame caused by exposure of unacceptable behavior (Shreve & Kunkel, 1991).

- Suicide is a cry for help to get *attention* or *sympathy* or is an attempt to manipulate other people.

Contrary to common opinion, suicide attempts in a great majority of cases are considered in advance and weighed rationally against other alternatives. Having tried these alternatives and failed, the person turns to suicide attempts. Most adolescents who attempt suicide talk about it first (Pfeffer, 1987; Shafi, 1988). If others are alerted in time, and if they pay attention to these developments and take them seriously enough to try to remedy the situation, a death may be prevented (Fujimura, Weis, & Cochran, 1985; Gispert, 1987; Hazell, 1991).

Suicide is rare among children under age 16.

Euthanasia—allowing a terminally ill patient to die naturally without life support; putting to death a person who suffers from an incurable disease (mercy killing); or killing a person who is no longer considered socially useful (death selection)

The word **euthanasia** conjures up many images, from so-called mercy killing to pulling the plug when there is no hope of recovery. Euthanasia is sometimes described as a positive/active process (forcing a person to die) or a negative/passive process (doing nothing, allowing death to come naturally). But as medical science advances, these distinctions are no longer clear. There is a difference between doing everything possible to cure a person's illness, but allowing death to come if the efforts fail, and using artificial means to prolong life even after ultimate death is certain. Although technology allows the prolongation of life in patients with terminal illness, many patients and professionals expressed relief that treatment decisions should take into account a patient's quality of life and should not necessarily aim to prolong life in all cases. Patients are now legally able to refuse unwanted medical treatment. Home-care facilities are required to inform patients of their right to make decisions about their own medical treatment. However, the process of deciding to forgo life-support treatment continues to pose difficult ethical, legal, clinical, and emotional challenges.

Respect for individual autonomy or self-determination is the principle currently guiding most ethical and legal decisions in decision making. However, many patients for whom such decisions must be made are no longer capable of expressing their treatment preferences because of severe cognitive impairments or loss of consciousness. In such cases, the principle of substituted judgment has been promoted, in which an attempt is made to determine what treatment choices the patient would have made under the circumstances. The emphasis on respecting patient preferences has led to the use of living wills, in which individuals can state treatment preferences while they are competent to do so. Another legal instrument is the durable power of attorney for health care, whereby an individual appoints a person to be his or her surrogate decision-maker in cases of future mental incapacity (Karel & Gatz, 1996).

In one study, 388 black and white older adults ages 60 to 100 responded to seventeen decision-making situations depicting terminal and nonterminal conditions with a very low quality of life. Despite the low quality of life, maintaining life (striving to live and seeking treatment) was the most acceptable option, but a significant minority of the participants wished to end life (suicide, assisted suicide, or euthanasia), and a moderate number wished to defer the decision to others (Cicirelli, 1997).

Death with Dignity

Euthanasia includes three different concepts: death with dignity, mercy killing, and death selection. **Death with dignity** allows a terminally ill patient to die naturally without mechanized prolongation that could turn death into an ordeal. The concept rejects extraordinary means when a person has irrevocably entered the dying process. This is referred to as "pulling the plug." Some families refuse to do this, and physicians have sometimes been forbidden by courts to do it. When asked whether they believed in the right of a patient and/or family to terminate medical care in the case of irreversible illness, three-fourths of 418 persons surveyed (ages 17 to 91) agreed with this right (Haug, 1978). There was a strong belief in the right of self-determination. This is why patients need to make their wishes known before they are no longer capable of making a reasoned decision.

Most medical and some church groups have no trouble accepting the concept of death with dignity (Ward, 1980). In March 1986, after two years of study, the *Council on Ethical and Judicial Affairs of the American Medical Association* issued the opinion that it is ethically permissible for doctors to withhold all life-prolonging treatment, including artificial nutrition and hydration, from patients in irreversible comas and from dying patients.

A Living Will

Thirty-eight states plus the District of Columbia now have statutes that approve the use of a **living will;** often a suggested form is included in the statute. And in every state, constitutional law and common law support the right of any competent adult to refuse medical treatment in any situation (Annas & Densberger, 1984). Without a living will, however, it is sometimes hard to know what treatment a patient wants (Zweibel & Cassel, 1989).

Physicians are required to comply with living-will legislation or to transfer the patient to a doctor who will comply. If a state has no living-will legislation, a person may still draw up such a document because court decisions give weight to individual choice (Sullivan, 1987).

Living wills usually apply only when the person's condition is incurable. They direct in such cases that life-extending procedures be withdrawn or withheld. Living wills are not honored in situations in which a person has a slow, degenerative disease or in which a very old person has "multiple systems failure."

Mercy Killing

Mercy killing is positive, direct euthanasia, either voluntary or involuntary. Whereas death with dignity permits a natural death, mercy killing actively causes death or at least speeds up death, for example, by lethal injection (Sinnett, Goodyear, & Hannemann, 1989). The nurse who deliberately gives an overdose of medication because the nurse does not want to see the patient suffer is performing mercy killing.

Mercy killing also includes abandonment or withdrawal of ordinary medical care—that is, the withdrawal of any medical or surgical procedures commonly used to relieve suffering and problems caused by injuries or illness, based on the condition of the individual patient, the circumstances, and the available medical technology. As medical science advances, the interpretation of this principle becomes more confused. Artificial heart machines and respirators, artificial kidneys, intravenous feeding, and other advanced technologies can keep patients alive for weeks,

Death with dignity—allowing a terminally ill patient to die naturally without artificial life support that could turn death into an ordeal

Living will—written request by a patient that life-sustaining procedures be withdrawn if there is no reasonable expectation of recovery or regaining a meaningful quality of life

Mercy killing—putting to death a person who suffers from an incurable disease

months, or years. Not too long ago, these patients would have died much sooner. What constitutes ordinary care? Most persons insist that keeping a clinically dead person physiologically alive does not constitute ordinary care. Others feel that sustaining life indefinitely by artificial means should not be permitted.

Death Selection

Opponents of euthanasia are especially concerned about **death selection**—that is, the involuntary or even mandatory killing of persons who are "no longer considered socially useful" or who are judged to be a burden on society. This type of euthanasia poses a real threat to many groups in our society, especially the aged, the severely handicapped, and the retarded. It is strongly opposed by all religious groups.

BEREAVEMENT

The loss of a loved one is among life's most stressful events. Loss is followed by a period of mourning for the deceased and grief over the departed. The grieving process may occur over a short period of time, or it may never be finished. One 54-year-old woman comments as follows:

> My husband died 18 years ago, and even though today I have a happy, full life, I still miss him. I am often reminded of what he is missing, especially at happy moments, such as the children's high school and college graduations, which are tinged with the wish that he were alive to share the joy (Howell, Allen, & Doress, 1987).

Grief Reactions

Grief reactions are dealt with on four levels:

1. Physical
2. Emotional
3. Intellectual
4. Sociological

Physical Reactions

A wide range of physical reactions accompany grief. These can include insomnia, loss of appetite or overeating, stomach upset, constipation or diarrhea, fatigue, headaches, shortness of breath, excessive perspiration,

and dizziness. Stress from grief tends to lower immunologic effectiveness and to leave the bereaved less resistant to infection and disease (Norris & Murrell, 1987). This condition explains why some studies show an increase in the number of sick days of survivors (Lundin, 1984) and a worsening of physical health following the death of a spouse (Thompson, Breckenridge, Gallagher, & Peterson, 1984).

Adults who have been taking care of an elderly person during a long illness usually experience a profound sense of grief, although the actual death may come as a relief from having to take care of that person. The death of a parent, even if expected, is a profound loss to the relative who is taking care of that person. However, daughters report that their feelings of distress such as emotional shock, helplessness, anger, and guilt, lessen over time from 2 to 6 months following the mother's death (Pratt, Walker, & Wood, 1992). Health of the caregiver may have deteriorated during care and then may improve after the actual death (George & Gwyther, 1984).

Emotional Reactions

Emotional reactions to grief include depression, despondency, crying, shock and disbelief, anger, guilt, anxiety, irritability, preoccupation with thoughts of the deceased, feelings of helplessness, difficulty concentrating, forgetfulness, apathy, indecisiveness, and withdrawal or feelings of aloneness. A study of grief among 162 health-care workers found these to be the two most common psychological grief reactions: About 92% reported thinking or talking about the patient, and 84% reported feelings of helplessness (Lerea & LiMauro, 1982).

Intellectual Reactions

Intellectual reactions to grief include efforts to explain and accept the causes of death of the deceased and sometimes to rationalize, or try to understand, the reasons for the death. People want to know what happened and why. Sometimes, reasons concluded are never satisfactory, but people nevertheless try to find causes and meaning in the death.

One common intellectual reaction to bereavement is **idealization:** the attempt to purify the memory of the deceased by mentally diminishing that person's negative characteristics. One woman who disliked her husband remarked, "My husband was an unusually good man." If this idealization continues, it

Death selection—the involuntary or mandatory killing of a person who is no longer socially useful

Idealization—the attempt to purify the memory of the deceased

FOCUS

Bereavement in Children

The reaction of children to loss depends partially on their age and understanding of what has taken place and how close they have been to the deceased. As mentioned in an earlier section, children under 5 believe that death is reversible and that the loved one will return. Because they do not see death as final, they are not too disturbed, but they become rather anxious about when the loved one will return.

I used to direct a nursery school and kindergarten and teach a class of 5-year-olds. When the grandfather of one of the girls died, the mother asked me to break the news to the granddaughter. I explained to her that her grandfather had been sick, and that when our bodies become old and sick, they die. After my careful explanation, the girl turned to her mother and asked, "OK, can I go outside and play now?" The mother was devastated at her daughter's callous reaction. It was obvious that the girl did not completely understand or accept the finality of death because for months afterward, she would ask her mother when her grandfather was going to return home.

Unless they have been exposed to frightening experiences, young children are not afraid of bodies or funerals. I remember one girl whose brother had been killed by lightning while playing golf. She saw her brother's body in the casket, stroked his cheek very soothingly, but did remark that he seemed cold.

Young children are not completely grief-stricken at death, partly because they don't understand the finality of it. However, when children begin to realize the permanence of death, they become more upset. Often 9- or 10-year-olds can show a lot of grief, anxiety, anger, and guilt, especially if in any way they believe that the death is their fault. They may become very upset, as evidenced by nightmares, sleeping, eating, and academic problems. They may have temper tantrums, get in fights easily, and show other symptoms of emotional disturbance and physical upset. They sometimes show a great deal of anxiety about death itself, and, if one parent has died, about the other parent's leaving. Also, the reactions of children depend partly on how upset other family members are with whom they are living. If children are not upset by funerals per se, they are upset by the crying and distress of the people there. Children can cope with death if they have the support of other loved ones (Furman, 1984; Horn, 1986).

The reaction of children to death depends partially on their age and level of understanding.

can prevent the formation of new intimate friendships. Extended bereavement can result in a sentimentalized, nostalgic, and morose style of life.

Sociological Reactions

Sociological reactions to grief include the efforts of family and friends to band together to share the experience, and to offer support and aid to one another. Sociological reaction also includes all efforts to reorganize one's life after the loss: financial readjustments, reorientation of family and community roles, the return to work, resumption of social and community activities. Death may necessitate making a number of important decisions: taking a job or changing jobs, moving, or selling a house. Sometimes such decisions are made hastily while one is still in a state of shock. Hurried decisions made during the grieving period are often wrong decisions.

The Stages of Grief

There are usually three stages of grief (Hiltz, 1978). *The first is a short period of shock* during which the surviving family members are stunned and immobilized with grief and disbelief. The survivors frequently weep and become easily agitated. This stage occurs soon after death and usually lasts several days. *The second stage is a period of intense suffering* during which individuals show physical and emotional symptoms of great disturbance. There is a painful longing for the dead, including memories and visual images of the deceased, sadness, insomnia, irritability, and restlessness. Beginning not long after the death of the family member, this stage often peaks in the second to fourth weeks following the death and may subside after several months, but it can persist for one to two years. Being able to talk about the decreased person enables the individual to overcome grief more quickly (Rosenblatt & Elde, 1990).

During the third stage there is a gradual reawakening of interest in life. Stage three usually appears within a year after the death. This stage is marked by a resumption of ordinary activities, a greater likelihood that the deceased will be recalled with pleasant memories, and the establishment of new relationships with others.

Gender Differences

Most researchers say that men and women share equal feelings of pain and grief. However, there are important cultural differences in the way grief is expressed. *Men have been conditioned not to show their emotions.* They fear uncontrolled expression of emotion and appearing to be "unmanly" in front of other people. Men may put on a big show at the office and then go home and stare at the walls. As a consequence, a widowed man often may become terribly isolated because his sole confidante had been his wife, who is now lost. Widowers are more likely to feel lonely and depressed than are widows, and they are less willing to talk about their feelings associated with their loss.

Not only do women have more friends than men, but also women more often use these friends as supports in time of loss. The pain of loss is eased by talking to others about the loss, and women seem to be better able to do this than men (Cole, 1988).

This funeral for a Buddhist monk in South Korea included a cremation ceremony.

Cultural Differences

Cultural differences play a part in the way that people are able to cope with death. One study at the *Philadelphia Geriatric Center* examined the differences between 12 elderly Jewish and 17 non-Jewish women in dealing with the death of an adult child. The data collection included in-depth life histories and quantitative evaluations of well-being, affect, generativity, and personality variables associated with mothering. Qualitatively, Jewish women were depressed and fixed in grief, with the loss remaining central to their lives. From the point of view of these Jewish women, the children continued to occupy a central part of their lives in death as they had in life. Non-Jewish women articulated veracities of acceptance, putting the death in a perspective that enabled them to move beyond their children's lives. Perhaps the philosophical attitudes toward life and death as revealed in differences in religion may explain the difference in the way the two groups adjusted to death. For the Christian women, the belief that children were in God's hands, that life is preparation for death, and that the resurrection leads to eternal life, might have been instrumental in easing the burden of loss for these women (Goodman et al., 1991).

1. In 1989, heart disease was the number-one cause of death; cancer was the number-two.

2. The causes of death have changed radically in the past one hundred years. Infectious diseases used to be the primary killers.

3. The dominant feature of death in the twentieth century is its invisibility; we try to solve the problem of death by denying it. In earlier times, death was more accepted as a part of everyday life. Currently, there is a swing away from the denial of death toward a notion of death with dignity.

4. Middle-agers express the greatest fear of death among the different age groups of adults; the elderly are less anxious about death than others.

5. Children under age 5 see death as temporary and reversible; between ages 5 and 9 they gradually realize that death is final and permanent; those 9 and over see it as final, inevitable, and universal. Adolescents usually give little thought to it, unless they have personal experience with someone's dying.

6. There are four aspects of death: physiological death, clinical death, sociological death, and psychic death.

7. Pattison outlined five different patterns of death.

8. Varying circumstances of death include uncertain death, certain death, and untimely death, which may be premature, unexpected, and/or calamitous.

9. Uncertain death occurs when a person has become seriously ill or injured and it is not known for certain whether that person will live or die.

10. Hospice care for the terminally ill is a viable alternative to hospital care.

11. In certain death, the person is terminally ill, and the approximate time of death may be known or unknown or can only be surmised. Kübler-Ross identified five stages of dying in terms of personal reactions: denial, anger, bargaining, depression, and acceptance.

12. Pattison outlined the living-dying trajectory that included three phases: acute crisis, chronic living-dying phase, and terminal phases.

13. Disintegrated dying occurs when a person learns of pending death and goes all to pieces, unable to function. Integrated dying involves being able to put one's life together to make satisfactory adjustments to the dying process.

14. Dying people have the same need for food, clothing, shelter, rest, and warmth that we all have, plus the need for reassurance that family members will not let them die alone. The dying person also usually has a number of tasks to complete in making arrangements for death.

15. Many people want to be told that they are dying; others do not. The goal is to ease the dying process and the adjustments that must be made, rather than to apply a dogma of always telling the truth.

16. Anticipatory grief is a process of emotional detachment from a dying person while emotional involvement is still maintained.

17. The psychological reactions of adults to death are more extreme when a child or a comparatively young person dies.

18. Sudden infant death syndrome, or when infants die mysteriously while asleep, is the most common cause of death in infants between 2 weeks and 1 year of age. The syndrome often causes intense mental pain and disruption among the survivors.

19. Unexpected death is the sudden death of a normal and healthy person. Calamitous death includes death from accidents, involuntary manslaughter, homicide, and suicide. Involuntary manslaughter is the unintentional killing of another human being.

20. Most stereotypes about murders and murderers have no foundation in fact. A sizable minority of homicides are committed by relatives or acquaintances of the victim. Homicide is most often an outgrowth of quarrels and violence among family members or friends.

21. The rate of suicide increases with advancing age, reaching a peak in males over 85 years of age and in females 45 to 54. Females attempt suicide more frequently than males, but males more often succeed. Suicide is one of the most upsetting of family crises because it leaves family members feeling remorseful, guilty, confused, and hurt.

22. Five theories of suicide have been postulated: biological, characterological, cognitive, psychodynamic, and sociological theories.

23. Socially accelerated dying is allowing any condition or action of society that shortens life and hastens death.

24. Euthanasia includes three different concepts: death with dignity, mercy killing, and death selection.

25. Death with dignity allows terminally ill patients to die naturally without mechanized prolongation.

26. Mercy killing is actively causing death or speeding it up rather than letting a patient suffer.

27. Death selection is involuntary or mandatory killing of persons who are no longer socially useful. It is considered a real threat to many groups in society, and it is opposed by all religious groups.

28. Grief reactions take place on four levels: physical, emotional, intellectual, and sociological.

29. The reaction of a child to grief depends on the age, understanding of death, reactions of family members, and the child's relationship with the deceased.

30. There are usually three stages of grief: shock, intense suffering, and a gradual reawakening of interest in life.

31. Though feelings of pain and grief are equal among men and women, there are gender differences in the extent and ways of expressing grief practiced by men and women.

32. Cultural differences play a part in the way that people are able to cope with death.

Key Terms

Clinical death   *p. 559*
Death selection   *p. 572*
Death with dignity   *p. 571*
Disintegrated dying   *p. 564*
Euthanasia   *p. 570*
Hospice   *p. 563*
Idealization   *p. 572*
Integrated dying   *p. 564*

Living-dying interval   *p. 564*
Living will   *p. 571*
Mercy killing   *p. 571*
Physiological death   *p. 559*
Psychic death   *p. 560*
Socially accelerated dying   *p. 569*
Sociological death   *p. 559*
Sudden infant death syndrome   *p. 566*

Discussion Questions

1. What do you think of the whole idea of making death as invisible as possible? Explain your views.

2. How do you feel about children attending funerals?

3. What are the differences between physiological death, clinical death, psychic death, and sociological death?

4. Have you or has any member of your family faced the prospect of uncertain death? What were the reactions, feelings, and biggest problems?

5. Should terminally ill patients be told that they are dying? Why? Why not?

6. Have there been any premature deaths, unexpected deaths, or calamitous deaths in your family? With what results?

7. How do you feel about the use of artificial life-support systems to prolong the life of a terminally ill patient? Under what circumstances would you pull the plug, and under what circumstances would you not?

8. How do you feel about mercy killing, or giving a terminally ill patient who is suffering an injection to speed death?

9. When people are grieving for the loss of a loved one, what helps the most? What are the types of things that other people do or say that make things worse?

10. How do present funeral practices help or hinder people getting over their grief? Explain.

11. How do you feel about men's weeping at a funeral?

12. How do you feel personally about death? About the fact that one day you will die? If you knew you were dying within one year, what would you do? How would you react?

Suggested Readings

KÜBLER-ROSS, E. (1997). *On death and dying.* New York: Simon and Schuster. Classic on the subject.

LEVINE, S. (1989). *Meetings at the edge: Dialogues with the grieving and the dying, the healing and the healed.* New York: Anchor.

MAHEADY, J., & REIMER, R. (1985).   Comparative analysis of state statutes recognizing a patient's right to die a natural death. Washington, DC: Congressional Research Service.

MUNLEY, A. (1983).   The hospice alternative: A new context for death and dying. New York: Basic Books. The hospice movement and its benefits to patients and their families.

SAUNDERS, C. M., BAINES, S. M., & DUNLOP, R. C. (1983).   Living with dying. New York: Oxford University Press. Home health care for the dying.

WEIZMAN, S. G., & KAMM, P. (1986).   About mourning: Support and guidance for the bereaved. New York: Human Sciences Press. For mental health workers.

http://www.death-dying.com Death And Dying a website that offers support and education about issues surrounding death.

Web Resources

Glossary

Accommodation according to Piaget, adjusting to new information by creating new structures when the old ones will not do (pp. 34, 452)

Accommodation the power of the eye's lens to focus (p. 34)

Acculturation the adjustment of minority groups to the dominant group culture (p. 291)

Acne pimples on the skin caused by overactive sebaceous glands (p. 308)

Acquisition the process by which information is recorded, encoded, and stored (p. 475)

ACT Assessment Program (American College Testing Program) the second most widely used college admissions test (p. 328)

Activity calories energy expended through physical activities (p. 437)

Activity theory theory of aging suggesting that continuance of an active lifestyle has a positive effect on the sense of well-being and satisfaction of older people (p. 548)

Adaptation according to Piaget, the process by which individuals adjust their thinking to new conditions or situations (p. 34)

Adaptation ability of the eye to adjust to different intensities of light (p. 452)

Adolescence the period of transition from childhood to young adulthood, from about 12 to 19 years of age (p. 5)

Adolescent and adult heterosociality period of psychosocial development during which those ages 13 and over find pleasure, friendships, and companionship with those of both sexes (p. 255)

Adrenal glands ductless glands that secrete androgens and estrogens, as well as adrenalin, in both men and women (p. 301)

Affect one's feelings, whether positive or negative (p. 498)

Ageism prejudice and discrimination against the elderly (p. 431)

Alleles genes that govern alternate expressions of a particular characteristic (p. 55)

Altruistic love unselfish care and concern for another person (p. 523)

Alveoli air cells of the lungs (p. 444)

Amniocentesis removal of cells from the amniotic fluid to test for abnormalities (p. 60)

Amniotic sac (bag of waters) sac containing the liquid in which the fetus is suspended during pregnancy (p. 78)

Anabolic steroids the masculinizing hormone testosterone taken by athletes to build muscle mass (p. 301)

Anal stage Freud's second psychosexual stage of development (2 to 3 years), in which the child's chief source of pleasure is from anal activity (p. 25)

Androgyny mixing of male and female traits in one person (p. 271)

Angina pectoris pain caused by constriction of blood vessels leading to the heart, causing an insufficient blood supply (p. 443)

Animism ascribing lifelike qualities to inanimate objects (p. 163)

Anorexia nervosa eating disorder characterized by an obsession with food and being thin (p. 309)

Anoxia oxygen deprivation to the brain, causing neurological damage or death (p. 82)

Antithesis the idea or point directly opposing a stated idea, or thesis (p. 466)

Apgar score method of evaluating the physical condition of the neonate, developed by Dr. Virginia Apgar (p. 82)

Arteriosclerosis hardening of the arteries by a buildup of calcium in the middle muscle layer of arterial tissue, resulting in decreased elasticity (p. 442)

Artificial insemination injection of sperm cells into the vagina or uterus for the purpose of inducing pregnancy (p. 52)

Assimilation according to Piaget, the process of acquiring new information by using already existing structures in response to new stimuli (p. 34)

Associative strength degree of association, as between two words (p. 481)

Associativity the understanding that operations can reach a goal in various ways (p. 167)

Atherosclerosis buildup of fatty deposits between the middle muscular layer and lining layer of arterial tissue (p. 443)

Attachment the feeling that binds a child to a parent or caregiver (p. 194)

Attachment theory the description of the process by which infants develop close emotional dependence on one or more adult caregivers (p. 37)

Attention-deficit hyperactive disorder (ADHD) child's hyperactivity, characterized by excessive activity, inattentiveness, and impulsivity (p. 216)

Autistic phase age during which children are aware of their mother only as an agent to meet their basic needs (p. 201)

Autonomic arousal stimulation of the autonomic, or involuntary, nervous system—found to be positively associated with serial learning at all ages, particularly for learning simpler tasks (p. 481)

Autonomy versus shame and doubt Erikson's second stage of psychosocial development (1 to 2 years), in which toddlers learn that they are capable of some independent actions, or they develop the fear that they are not capable (p. 36)

Autosociality stage of psychosocial development during the first year or so of life, during which infants' interests, pleasures, and satisfactions are themselves, when they play alongside of others, not with them (p. 255)

Autosomes twenty-two pairs of chromosomes that are responsible for most aspects of the individual's development (p. 54)

Babbling one-syllable utterances containing vowels and consonants in combination (p. 150)

Baby boomers the huge cohort of babies born during the postwar period between 1945 and 1960 (p. 404)

Bartholin's glands glands on either side of the vaginal opening that secrete fluid during sexual arousal (p. 302)

Basal calories energy metabolized by the body to carry on physiological functions and to maintain normal body temperature (p. 437)

Behaviorism the school of psychology that emphasizes that behavior is modified through conditioning (p. 28)

Bile liquid secreted by the liver that aids in the digestion and absorption of fats (p. 445)

Binuclear family original family divided into two by divorce (p. 227)

Biological time clock life events regulated by maturation and biological changes (p. 422)

Blastocyst inner layer of the blastula that develops into the embryo (p. 46)

Blastula zygote after the cells have divided into 100 to 150 cells (p. 46)

Blended or reconstituted family family formed by any widowed or divorced person remarrying another person who may or may not have children (p. 226)

Bonding the formation of a close relationship between a person and a child through early and frequent association (p. 37)

Brazelton Neonatal Behavior Assessment Scale method of evaluating the neurological condition and behavior of the neonate, developed by Dr. T. Berry Brazelton (p. 82)

Bronchial pneumonia infectious disease of the bronchial tubes (p. 444)

Bulimia eating disorder characterized by bingeing and purging (p. 309)

Burnout the situation of being emotionally and physically exhausted from too much job pressure (p. 547)

Canalization tendency for inherited characteristics to persist along a certain path regardless of environmental conditions (p. 57)

Cardiac arrhythmia irregular heartbeat (p. 443)

Case studies research method involving in-depth, longitudinal investigations and records of individuals (p. 14)

Cataracts abnormality of the eye in which the lens becomes cloudy and opaque (p. 452)

Centration focusing attention on one aspect of a situation or one detail, and being unable to take into account other details (p. 164)

Cephalocaudal principle downward distribution of physical growth, starting in the head and proceeding, by stages, down the body to the feet (p. 112)

Cerebral cortex two large hemispheres of the forebrain, which control intellectual, motor, and sensory functions (p. 114)

Cerebrovascular disease vascular disease in the brain (p. 444)

Cesarean section removal of the fetus through a surgical incision of the abdominal and uterine walls (p. 80)

Child development all aspects of human growth from birth to adolescence; the study of this growth (p. 98)

Childhood heterosociality stage when children seek the companionship of others regardless of sex (p. 255)

Cholesterol chemical in all animal fats that is a major cause of atherosclerosis (p. 437)

Chorionic villi sampling (CVS) removal of a sample of chorionic villi from the membrane enclosing the fetus, to be analyzed for possible birth defects (p. 62)

Chromosomes rodlike structures in each cell, occurring in pairs, that carry the hereditary material (p. 53)

Chronological age (CA) age in years (p. 173)

Chunking dividing material into meaningful parts to remember it (p. 172)

Cirrhosis disease of the liver in which the connective tissue becomes hard, lumpy, and shriveled (p. 445)

Classical conditioning form of learning through association, in which a previously neutral stimulus is paired with an unconditioned stimulus to stimulate a conditioned response that is similar to the unconditioned response (p. 28)

Classification arranging objects into categories or classes (p. 165)

Class inclusion relationships the inclusion of objects in different levels of hierarchy at the same time (p. 166)

Client-centered therapy Rogers's approach to humanistic therapy, in which the discussion focuses on the client's thoughts and feelings and the therapist creates an atmosphere of acceptance so that the client can gain insight and grow toward his or her full potential (p. 32)

Climacteric often, a man's middle years' changes; also, menopause or other changes marking the transition from one stage of life to another (p. 447)

Clinical death the cessation of all brain activity (p. 559)

Clitoris the small shaft containing erectile tissue located above the vaginal and urethral openings and that is highly responsive to sexual stimulation (p. 302)

Cognition the act of knowing (p. 34)

Cognitive development all the changes in the intellectual processes of thinking, learning, remembering, judging, problem solving, and communicating (p. 6)

Cognitive modification program therapeutic program designed to teach restructuring of thought patterns, positive thinking, and focusing on immediate tasks; one such program, designed by Michenbaum, helps students with high test-taking anxiety (p. 505)

Cohabitation two unrelated adults of the opposite sex sharing the same living quarters in which there is no other adult present—according to the U.S. government; other adults may actually live with the couple (p. 518)

Cohabiting family family formed by two people of the opposite sex who live together, with or without children; who are committed to the relationship, without formal legal marriage, within the general definition in this book (p. 227)

Cohort group of subjects born during the same time period (p. 16)

Coitus sexual intercourse (p. 386)

Colostrum high-protein liquid secreted by the mother's breasts prior to her milk coming in; contains antibodies to protect the nursing infant from diseases (p. 89)

Combinativity ability to combine two or more classes into one larger class (p. 166)

Communal family group of people who live together and who qualify as a family according to the general definition in this book (p. 227)

Concrete operational stage Piaget's third stage of cognitive development (7 to 11 years), during which the child gains some mastery over classes, relations, and quantities (p. 35)

Conditional positive regard giving love, praise, and acceptance only if the individual conforms to parental or social standards (p. 32)

Conditioning simple process of learning (p. 28)

Congenital deformity defect present at birth, which may be the result of hereditary factors, conditions during pregnancy, or damage occurring at the time of birth (p. 58)

Congestive heart failure reduced cardiac output accompanied by increased blood pressure, which results in a buildup of fluids on the body (p. 443)

Congruence cognitive agreement between a person's desired goals and the goals that have been, or are being, attained in life (p. 497)

Conservation the idea that properties of objects such as weight and mass stay the same regardless of how the shape or arrangement changes (p. 164)

Consummate love according to Sternberg, it is complete love derived by combining three types of love: intimacy, passion, and decision/commitment (p. 523)

Cooing the initial vowel-like utterances by young infants (p. 150)

Coparenting cooperation of two parents in rearing their children (p. 249)

Coronary occlusion with myocardial infarction heart attack, a cutoff of blood from a coronary artery, causing death of a localized area (an infarct) of heart muscle (p. 443)

Corpus luteum yellow body that grows from the ruptured ovarian follicle and becomes a mass of progesterone-secreting endocrine tissue (p. 301)

Correlation the extent to which two factors are associated or related to one another (p. 16)

Cowper's glands small twin glands in the male that secrete a fluid to neutralize the acid environment of the urethra (p. 301)

Crisis drastic change in the course of events; a turning point that affects the trend of future events (p. 502)

Crisis overload series of crises happening one after the other so that the person has difficulty in coping (p. 502)

Cross-modal perception the ability to perceive objects with more than one sense (p. 128)

Cross-sectional study comparing one age group with others at one time of testing (p. 17)

Crystallized intelligence Cattell's concept that knowledge and skills arise out of acculteration and education (p. 175)

Custody refers to legal custody (who has decision-making rights over the child) and physical custody (where the children live) (p. 246)

Date rape forced sexual compliance on a person while on a date, whether or not intercourse occurs (p. 521)

Death selection the involuntary or mandatory killing of a person who is no longer considered socially useful (p. 572)

Death with dignity allowing a terminally ill patient to die naturally without artificial life support that could turn death into an ordeal (p. 571)

Deductive reasoning beginning with a hypothesis or premise and breaking it down to see whether it is true (p. 163)

Defense mechanisms according to Freud, unconscious strategies used by the ego to protect itself from disturbance and to discharge tension (p. 24)

Deferred imitation imitating someone or something no longer present (p. 162)

Denial Freudian defense mechanism in which the individual refuses to admit that something exists (p. 25)

Dependency ratio the number of dependent persons for each person in the labor force (p. 407)

Dependent love involves mutual dependency and need for one another (p. 523)

Dependent variable in an experiment, a factor that is influenced by the independent or manipulated variable (p. 15)

Developmental pediatrics new field of study that integrates medical knowledge, psychological understanding, health care, and parental guidance in relation to children (p. 106)

Developmental quotient (DQ) score developed by Gesell to evaluate an infant's behavioral level in four categories: motor, language, adaptive, and personal-social (p. 178)

Developmental tasks the skills, knowledge, functions, and attitudes that individuals have to acquire at certain points in their lives in order to function effectively as mature persons (p. 292)

Diabetes mellitus disease characterized by excess sugar in the system due to insufficient insulin production in the pancreas (p. 445)

Dialectical thinking the view that every idea implies its opposite; the ability to consider opposing viewpoints simultaneously (p. 466)

Diastolic blood pressure the pressure produced when the chambers of the heart dilate and fill with blood (p. 442)

Differentiated or subjective perspective-taking stage the stage of awareness when the other is seen as different from the self, but the other person's perception of the self is still undifferentiated—stage 1 in Selman's theory (p. 262)

Discipline process of learning by which socialization takes place; its purpose is instruction in proper conduct (p. 232)

Disengagement theory theory of aging saying that aging people have a natural tendency to withdraw socially and psychologically from the environment, social activities, and other people (p. 547)

Disintegrated dying going to pieces emotionally and not being able to function after learning of impending death (p. 564)

Displacement Freudian defense mechanism in which an individual diverts aggressive, sexual, or disturbed feelings away from a primary object to something useful (p. 24)

Dizygotic (fraternal) twins two-egg, or fraternal, twins (p. 54)

DNA complex molecules in genes that form the basis for the genetic structure, deoxyribonucleic acid (p. 53)

Dominant gene gene that exerts its full characteristic regardless of its gene pair (p. 55)

Duos two-word utterances (p. 152)

Dyslexia developmental language disorder in which the person reads from right to left, reverses letters and words, omits words, or loses his or her place (p. 184)

Dyspareunia painful intercourse (p. 451)

Dysphoria generalized unhappiness (p. 230)

Early adulthood the young adult years, including the 20s and 30s (p. 5)

Early childhood the preschool period of development from ages 3 to 5 years (p. 4)

Echoic memory the auditory sensory store (p. 476)

Ectopic pregnancy attachment and growth of the embryo in any location other than inside the uterus (p. 49)

Edema retention of excess fluids in body tissues and cavities (p. 443)

Ego according to Freud, the rational part of the mind, which uses the reality principle to satisfy the id (p. 24)

Egocentricism the inability to take the perspective of another, to imagine the other person's point of view (p. 163)

Egocentric undifferentiated stage the stage of awareness when another person is seen egocentrically, undifferentiated from the self's own point of view—stage 0 in Selman's theory of development of social cognition (p. 262)

Ejaculatory inhibition inability of the man to reach a sexual climax (p. 450)

Electra complex according to Freud, the unconscious love and sexual desire of female children for their father, after they blame the mother for the fact that they have no penis (p. 25)

Embolism blockage from a blood clot (p. 444)

Embryo growing baby from the end of the second week to the end of the eighth week after conception (p. 46)

Embryonic period period from 2 weeks to 8 weeks after conception (p. 46)

Embryo transplant insemination of a volunteer female with the sperm of an infertile woman's partner; the resulting zygote is transferred, about 5 days later, into the uterus of the mother-to-be, who carries the child during pregnancy (p. 53)

Emotion state of consciousness, or a feeling, felt as an integrated reaction of the total organism, accompanied by physiological arousal, and resulting in behavioral responses (p. 346)

Emotional development the development of attachment, trust, love, feelings, temperament, concept of self, autonomy, and emotional disturbances (p. 6)

Emotional maturity being emotionally secure and stable, with a capacity to feel emotion (p. 490)

Emotional stability   being free of excessive of crippling ups and downs of mood (p. 490)

Emphysema   degenerative disorder of the walls separating the air sacs in the lungs so that they become distended, inelastic, and incapable of expelling stale air (p. 444)

Endocrine gland   ductless gland that secretes hormones (p. 300)

Epididymis   system of ducts, running from the testes to the vas deferens, in which sperm ripen, mature, and are stored (p. 301)

Epinephrine   hormone secreted by the adrenal glands that produces physiological arousal (p. 206)

Episiotomy   surgical incision of the perineum to allow room for passage of the baby from the birth canal without tearing the mother's tissue (p. 80)

Episodic memory   long-term memory that stores information about specific experiences that took place at specific times and in specific places (p. 478)

Equilibrium   Piagetian concept meaning a balance between schemas and accommodation, a state in which children feel comfortable because what they find in their environment is compatible with what they have been taught to believe (p. 34)

Equity   assignment of punishments in accordance with transgressors' ability to take responsibility for a crime (p. 273)

Erectile dysfunction   inability of the male to maintain an erection so that coitus can take place (p. 450)

Erotic love   sensual, sexual love (p. 523)

Estrogen   female hormone produced by the ovaries and to some extent by the adrenal glands in both males and females (pp. 267, 301)

Ethology   the view that behavior is a product of evolution and biology (p. 36)

Euthanasia   allowing a terminally ill patient to die naturally without life support; putting to death a person who suffers from an incurable disease (mercy killing); or killing a person who is no longer considered socially useful (death selection) (p. 570)

Exchange theory   theory that, as applied to the aged and their families, maintains that persons with the greatest needs lose the most power and those supplying needs gain power (p. 548)

Exosystem   social settings in which the child usually is not an active participant, but that influence the child indirectly through their effects on the microsystem (p. 226)

Experimental methods   methods of gathering scientific data, in which procedures are closely controlled and the experimenter manipulates variables to determine how one affects the other (p. 15)

Expiatory punishment   punishment that results from an externally imposed regulation; associated with morality of constraint (p. 272)

Extended family   family consisting of one person, a possible mate, their children, and other relatives who live with them in the household; more broadly, can include relatives living in close proximity or who are in regular or frequent contact with a household's members (p. 226)

Extrinsic motivation   motivation influenced by external rewards (p. 480)

Fallopian tubes   tubes that transport the ova from the ovaries to the uterus (p. 302)

Family   any group of persons united by the ties of marriage, blood, or adoption, or any sexually expressive relationship, in which (1) the people are committed to one another in an intimate, interpersonal relationship, (2) the members see their identity as importantly attached to the group, and (3) the group has an identity of its own (p. 226)

Family life cycle   the family experience divided into phases or stages over the life span; a description of the changes in family structure and composition, and of the challenges, tasks, problems, and satisfactions involved during each stage (p. 527)

Fertilization or conception   union of sperm and ovum (p. 44)

Fetal period   period of prenatal development from the beginning of the third month through the remainder of the pregnancy (p. 46)

Fetoscope   scope passed through a narrow tube inserted into the uterus to observe the fetus and placenta directly (p. 62)

Fetus   growing baby from the beginning of the third month of development to birth (p. 46)

Field-dependent people   people who have trouble isolating relevant information in solving problems (p. 464)

Field-independent people   people who sort out relevant from irrelevant information in solving problems (p. 464)

Fixated   according to Freud, remaining at a particular psychosexual stage because of too much or too little gratification (p. 25)

Fluid intelligence   Cattell's concept of inherited ability to think and reason abstractly (p. 175)

Follicle-stimulating hormone (FSH)   pituitary hormone that stimulates the maturation of the follicles and ova in the ovaries and of sperm in the testes (p. 299)

Foreclosure   establishing an identity without going through a crisis or without searching; adopting an identity as prescribed by someone else (p. 289)

Formal operational stage   Piaget's highest stage of cognitive development (11 years and up), during which individuals are able to use logic and abstract concepts (p. 35)

Free association   method of treatment of Freud in which the patient is encouraged to say anything that comes to mind, allowing unconscious thoughts to slip out (p. 24)

Friendship love   loved based on companionship and common interests and liking of one another (p. 523)

Full-term infant   infant who is born with a gestational age between 37 and 42 weeks (p. 85)

Functional age   age as measured by the ability to perform physical or mental functions (p. 432)

Gall bladder trouble   any kind of trouble that prevents the gall bladder from functioning properly; gallstones, for example (p. 445)

Gallstones   stones formed in the gall bladder or bile passages when the bile becomes overconcentrated (p. 445)

Gamete intrafallopian transfer (GIFT)   inserting sperm cells and an egg cell directly into the fallopian tube, where fertilization is expected to occur (p. 53)

Gametes   sex cells (p. 44)

Gap threshold   the minimum detectable gap between sounds (p. 129)

Gastritis   inflammation of the stomach lining (p. 445)

Gay or lesbian family   family formed by adults of the same sex who live together, with their children, and who share sexual expression and commitment according to the general definition in this book (p. 227)

Gender   our biological sex (p. 267)

Gender constancy   the understanding of the gender that one is, and the knowledge that gender is going to remain the same; usually achieved by 7 years of age (p. 269)

Gender roles   our outward expressions of masculinity or femininity in social settings (p. 267)

Gender stereotypes   widespread, assumed gender characteristics of what boys and girls are like (p. 269)

General anesthesia   drug acting on the central nervous system and used to suppress pain during childbirth; affects the fetus also (p. 79)

Generalized anxiety disorder   mental illness characterized by pervasive anxiety that is way out of proportion to the stimulus and that lasts well beyond reasonable expectations (pp. 349, 490)

General sexual dysfunction woman's lack of desire for or pleasure in sexual relations (p. 451)

Generational transmission transmitting of knowledge, values, attitudes, roles, and habits from one generation to the next (p. 227)

Generativity versus stagnation Erikson's seventh psychosocial stage of development (middle adulthood), during which adults assume responsible, adult roles in their community and in caring for the younger generation, or they lead impoverished, self-centered lives (p. 26)

Genes the hereditary material of the chromosomes (p. 53)

Genital stage Freud's fifth psychosexual stage of development (puberty through adulthood), in which sexual urges are directed toward one's peers in a desire to relieve sexual tension (p. 25)

Genotype underlying genetic pattern of an individual (p. 56)

Germinal period the period from conception to 14 days later (p. 46)

Glaucoma disease of the eye in which the fluid pressure within the eyeball increases, causing progressive vision loss (p. 452)

Glycogen starchlike substance stored by the liver and released when the body needs sugar (p. 444)

Gonadotropic hormones sex hormones secreted by the gonads (p. 300)

Gonadotropin-releasing hormone (GnRH) controls the production and release of FSH and LH from the pituitary (p. 302)

Gonads the sex glands: testes and ovaries (p. 301)

Grammar the formal description of structure and rules that a language uses to communicate meaning (p. 153)

Habituation the tendency to get used to a repeated stimulus and to lose interest in it (p. 168)

Handedness preference for using one hand rather than another (p. 121)

Happiness quality or state characterized by pleasure, delight, joy, gladness, and contentment (p. 496)

HDL (high-density lipoprotein) beneficial cholesterol that helps lower the level of LDL in the blood (p. 439)

Hemoglobin the red pigment of the blood (p. 444)

Hemorrhage copious blood flow, rapid loss of blood (p. 444)

Heterogamy choice of a mate different from oneself (p. 524)

Heterologous insemination (AID) artificial insemination using the sperm from a donor (p. 52)

Heterozygous having paired alleles that are different (p. 56)

Hierarchical classification arranging objects into categories according to level (p. 166)

Holistic view emphasizes the functioning of the total individual to try to grow, improve, and reach his or her full potential (p. 31)

Holophrases single words that infants use to convey different meanings, depending on the context in which they are used (p. 151)

Homogamy choice of a mate similar to oneself (p. 524)

Homologous insemination (AIH) artificial insemination with the husband's sperm (p. 52)

Homosociality stage during which children prefer to play with others of the same sex (p. 255)

Homozygous having paired alleles that are alike (p. 55)

Hormones biochemical substances secreted into the bloodstream by the endocrine glands that act as an internal communication system telling the different cells what to do (p. 302)

Hospice institution committed to making the end of life free from pain and as comfortable and supportive as possible in a homelike environment with family members present (p. 563)

Human growth hormone (HGH) pituitary hormone that regulates overall body growth (p. 300)

Humanistic theory psychological theory that emphasizes the ability of individuals to make the right choices and to reach their full potential (p. 31)

Hymen tissue partly covering the vaginal opening (p. 302)

Hypertensive heart disease caused by high blood pressure (p. 443)

Hypothalamus small area of the brain controlling motivation, emotion, pleasure, and pain in the body; that is, controls eating, drinking, hormonal production, menstruation, pregnancy, lactation, and sexual response and behavior (p. 302)

Iconic memory the visual sensory store (p. 476)

Id according to Freud, the inborn instinctual urges that a person seeks to satisfy (p. 24)

Idealization the attempt to purify the memory of the deceased (p. 572)

Identity achievement that state resulting from having gone through a crisis in the search for identity and having made a commitment (p. 288)

Identity diffusion the situation of the individual who has not experienced an identity crisis, nor explored meaningful alternatives in trying to find an identity (p. 289)

Identity or nullifiability the understanding that an operation that is combined with its opposite becomes nullified, and the element remains unchanged (p. 167)

Identity versus role confusion Erikson's fifth psychosocial stage of development (12 to 19 years), during which the adolescent develops a strong sense of self or becomes confused about identity and roles in life (p. 26)

Imaging being on one's best behavior to make a good impression (p. 385)

Imitation copying the behavior of another (p. 162)

Imminent justice the child's belief that immoral behavior inevitably brings pain or punishment as a natural consequence of the transgression (p. 273)

Implantation attachment of the blastocyst to the uterine wall (p. 46)

Imprinting biological ability to establish an attachment on first exposure to an object or a person (p. 37)

Inanition starvation (p. 133)

Incomplete dominance when one paired allele is not completely dominant over the other (p. 56)

Incontinent unable to control passage of urine (p. 445)

Independent variable in an experiment, a factor that is manipulated or controlled by the experimenter to determine its effect on the subjects' behavior (p. 15)

In-depth and societal perspective-taking stage the stage of awareness when the self can take a generalized societal perspective of the self-other interaction (p. 263)

Inductive reasoning gathering individual items of information and putting them together to form a hypothesis or conclusions (p. 163)

Industry versus inferiority Erikson's fourth psychosocial stage of development (6 to 11 years), during which children develop feelings of adequacy and self-worth for accomplishments or begin to feel inadequate (p. 26)

Infancy the first two years of life (p. 4)

Infantile amnesia the lack of memory of events experienced before age 3 (p. 170)

Infertile unable to conceive or to effect pregnancy (p. 50)

Information-processing approach approach to cognition that emphasizes the steps, actions, and operations by which persons receive, perceive, remember, think about, and utilize information (pp. 35, 160)

Inhibited sexual desire　low sexual libido or drive (p. 450)

Initiative versus guilt　Erikson's third psychosocial stage of development (3 to 5 years), during which children are encouraged to assume responsibility for planning and carrying out actions, or are criticized and made to feel guilty for such actions (p. 26)

Insecurely attached children　children who are overly dependent on parents or caregivers because of insufficient attachment (p. 195)

Insulin　hormone secreted by the pancreas that regulates the blood sugar level (p. 445)

Integrated dying　being able to put one's life together, to make satisfactory adjustments to the dying process (p. 564)

Integrity versus despair　Erikson's eighth psychosocial stage of development (late adulthood), in which adults evaluate their lives and either accept them for what they are, or despair because they have not found meaning in life (p. 26)

Intelligence quotient (IQ)　MA divided by CA $\times$ 100 (p. 173)

Interviews　research method conducted face-to-face between an interviewer and subject where information is obtained through recorded responses to questions (p. 14)

Intimacy versus isolation　Erikson's sixth psychosocial stage of development (young adulthood), during which the young adult develops close relationships with others, or is unable to, resulting in feelings of isolation (p. 26)

Intrinsic motivation　motivation coming directly from physical and psychological needs (p. 480)

In vitro fertilization　removal of the ovum from the mother and fertilizing it in the laboratory, then implanting the zygote within the uterine wall (p. 52)

Irreversibility　failure to recognize that an operation can go both ways (p. 166)

Ischemic heart disease　diseases that impede blood flow to the heart, resulting in inadequate oxygen supply (p. 443)

Jaundice　abnormal liver condition causing increase in bile pigments in the blood and thus a yellowing of the skin and whites of the eyes (p. 445)

Joint custody　both parents share in decisions regarding the welfare of the child (p. 247)

Juvenile　one who is not yet considered an adult in the eyes of the law (p. 284)

Kwashiorkor　protein deficiency (p. 134)

Labia majora　the major or large lips of tissue on either side of the vaginal opening (p. 302)

Labia minora　the smaller lips of tissue on either side of the vagina (p. 302)

Labor　rhythmic muscular contractions of the uterus that expel the baby through the birth canal (p. 78)

Lamaze method　natural childbirth method emphasizing education, physical conditioning, controlled breathing, and emotional support, developed by the French obstetrician Fernand Lamaze (p. 78)

Language acquisition device　the inherited characteristics that enable children to listen to and imitate speech sounds and patterns (p. 148)

Late adulthood　age 60 and over (p. 5)

Latency stage　Freud's fourth psychosexual stage of development (6 years to puberty), during which sexual interests are sublimated and concentrated on social and education activities (p. 25)

Lateralization　the preference for using one side of the body more than the other in performing special tasks, depending on which hemisphere is dominant for the task (p. 115)

Law of dominant inheritance　Mendel's law that says that when an organism inherits competing traits, only one trait will be expressed (p. 55)

LDL (low-density lipoprotein)　harmful cholesterol that contributes to the buildup of fatty deposits in the arteries (p. 439)

Learning disabilities　problems with reading, arithmetic, spelling, and written expression even in a person with normal intelligence (p. 184)

Legal custody　right to make decisions regarding the welfare of the child (p. 246)

Living-dying interval　period of time between the knowledge of the crisis of death and death itself (p. 564)

Living will　written request by a patient that life-sustaining procedures be withdrawn if there is no reasonable expectation of recovery or regaining a meaningful quality of life (p. 571)

Local or regional anesthesia　drug injected into localized areas or regions to block pain during childbirth; some types may have little effect on the fetus (p. 79)

Longitudinal research　the repeated measurement of a group of subjects over a period of years (p. 17)

Long-term storage　the process by which information is perceived and processed deeply so that it passes into the layers of memory below the conscious level—the third stage in a three-stage memory model (p. 170)

Low socioeconomic status　low social class, including cultural deprivation and low income (p. 228)

Luteinizing hormone (LH)　pituitary hormone that stimulates the development of the ovum and estrogen and progesterone in females and of sperm and testosterone in males (p. 299)

Macrosystem　influences of a particular culture (p. 226)

Macular diseases　diseases of the macula, the part of the retina that possesses maximum visual acuity (p. 452)

Marasmus　starvation in young children (p. 133)

Marital adjustment tasks　areas of concern in marriage in which adjustments need to be made (p. 528)

Marriage enrichment program　group discussion program designed to help couples improve their marriage (p. 539)

Masturbation　self-stimulation for purposes of sexual arousal (p. 386)

Matricide　the killing of one's mother (p. 367)

Maturation　the unfolding of the genetically determined patterns of growth and development (p. 101)

Maturity　the time in life when one becomes an adult physically, emotionally, socially, intellectually, and spiritually (p. 284)

Mechanistic or deterministic　as applied to behaviorism, a criticism that behavior is a result of mindless reactions to stimuli (p. 28)

Meiosis　process of cell division by which gametes reproduce (p. 44)

Menarche　first menstruation (p. 302)

Menopause　the permanent cessation of menstruation at midlife (p. 447)

Mental age (MA)　measure that expresses the intellectual level of a person (p. 173)

Mental retardation　below normal intelligence (p. 179)

Mercy killing　putting to death a person who suffers from an incurable disease (p. 571)

Mesosystem　social influences involving reciprocal relationships among the child's microsystem settings; for example, reciprocal influences of the home and school (p. 226)

Metamemory　knowledge of memory strategies people employ to learn and remember information (p. 172)

Method of loci　remembering by visualizing the position of something (p. 172)

Microsystem   the child's immediate contacts (p. 226)

Middle adulthood   middle age, including the 40s and 50s (p. 5)

Middle childhood   the elementary school years, from 6 to 11 years (p. 4)

Misogynist   person who hates women (p. 533)

Mnemonic   memory-aiding (p. 172)

Modeling   learning through observing and imitating the behavior of others (p. 30)

Monozygotic (identical) twins   one-egg, or identical, twins (p. 54)

Mons veneris (mons pubis)   the mound of flesh (mound of Venus) located above the vagina in the female, over which pubic hair grows (p. 302)

Morale   one's moral or mental condition with respect to cheerfulness, confidence, zeal, and the like (p. 496)

Morality of constraint   conduct coerced by rules or by authority (p. 272)

Morality of conventional role conformity   the second level of development of moral thought, based on a desire to conform to social convention, according to Kohlberg (p. 395)

Morality of cooperation   conduct regulated by mutual respect and consent (p. 272)

Morality of self-accepted moral principles   the third level of development of moral thought, based on adherence to universal principles, according to Kohlberg (p. 396)

Moratorium   period of standing back as one continues to search for an identity (p. 289)

Morpheme   the smallest unit of meaning in a language (p. 148)

Morula   zygote after a number of cell divisions have taken place, resembling a mulberry (p. 46)

Motor ability   the ability to move fingers, hands, arms, legs, and other parts of the body in a useful, coordinated way (p. 433)

Myelinization   the process by which neurons become coated with an insultating, fatty substance called myelin (p. 133)

Nativist view   says that children have a predisposition to learn language at a certain age (p. 148)

Naturalistic observation   research conducted in a natural setting by watching and recording behavior (p. 14)

Natural selection   Charles Darwin's concept that certain species have been selected to survive because of characteristics that help them adapt to their environment; part of the process implying that the human species has evolved from lower forms of life (p. 101)

Nature   biological and genetic factors that influence development (p. 7)

Neurons   nerve cells (p. 91)

Nightmares   frightening dreams during REM (rapid eye movement) sleep (p. 136)

Night terrors   upsetting nocturnal experiences during sleep that often cause children to wake up terrified and screaming (p. 136)

Noble savages   beings endowed with a sense of right and wrong; a term used by Jean-Jacques Rousseau to describe his view of children (p. 101)

Nocturnal emissions   male ejaculations during sleep (p. 302)

Nonattached children   children who have not developed a close emotional relationship with parents or caregivers (p. 195)

Nonnormative or idiosyncratic influences   life events that occur at unexpected times or that are unusual, both of which have a major impact on development (p. 423)

Normative-crisis model   model based on a definite sequence of age-related changes—typified by Gould, Levinson, and Vaillant (p. 422)

Normative influences   expected life events that occur at customary times (p. 423)

Nuclear family   family consisting of a mother, father, and their children (p. 226)

Nurture   the influence of environment and experience on development (p. 7)

Nutrient density   percentage of essential nutrients in food in relation to calories (p. 436)

Objective judgments   judgments based solely on the consequences of wrongdoing (p. 272)

Object permanence   the concept that an object continues to exist independently of our perceiving it (p. 161)

Oedipal complex   according to Freud, the unconscious love and sexual desire of male children for their mother, and jealousy, hostility, and fear of the father (p. 25)

Oogenesis   process by which ova mature (p. 44)

Open adoption   adoption system in which the natural mother is permitted to meet and play an active role in selecting the new adoptive parents (p. 253)

Operant conditioning   learning from the consequences of behavior so that the consequences change the probability of the behavior's recurrence (p. 29)

Oral stage   Freud's first psychosexual stage of development (0 to 1 year), in which the child's chief source of pleasure is from oral activity (p. 25)

Orgasm dysfunction   inability of the woman to reach a climax (p. 451)

Original sin   the Christian doctrine that, because of Adam's sin, a sinful nature has been passed on to succeeding generations (p. 100)

Osteoarthritis   degenerative joint disease (p. 446)

Osteoporosis   decalcification and loss of bone mass (p. 446)

Otitis media   middle-ear disease in children often causing partial hearing loss (p. 124)

Ova   female egg cells (p. 44)

Ovaries   female gonads, or sex glands, which secrete estrogen and progesterone and produce mature egg cells (p. 302)

Ovulation   process by which the mature ovum separates from the ovarian wall and is released from the ovary (p. 44)

Ovum   egg cell (p. 301)

Pacing   time intervals between stimuli (p. 481)

Paired-associate learning   learning to make associations between pairs of items (p. 480)

Parentese   baby talk that adults use in speaking to infants (p. 152)

Parenting coalition   cooperation of biological and stepparents in the rearing of children (p. 249)

Parricide   the killing of one's mother or father (p. 367)

Patricide   the killing of one's father (p. 367)

Penis   the male sexual organ for coitus and urination (p. 301)

Perineum   area of skin between the vagina and anus (p. 80)

Periodontal disease   disease of the gums in which they become infected, swell, and shrink away from the teeth (p. 446)

Peripheral vision   ability to see objects to either side of the line of sight in front of one's face (p. 452)

Pernicious anemia   severe anemia with a great reduction in red blood cells, an increase in their size, and the presence of large, primitive cells containing no hemoglobin (p. 444)

Personal fable   beliefs in the uniqueness of one's own experience (p. 324)

Personality   the sum total of the physical, mental, social, and emotional characteristics of an individual (p. 213)

Personality and lifestyle theory   theory of aging that shows the relationship between personality type and patterns of aging (p. 548)

Phallic stage Freud's third psychosexual stage of development (4 to 5 years), in which the child's chief source of pleasure is through exploration and self-manipulation of the genitals (p. 25)

Phenotype observed characteristics of an individual (p. 56)

Phobia anxiety disorder characterized by excessive, uncontrolled fear of objects, situations, or living creatures of some type (p. 348)

Phoneme the smallest unit of sound in a language (p. 148)

Phonics approach method of teaching reading by teaching the child to sound out the various phonemes of the word (p. 157)

Physical addiction the body's chemical dependency on a drug built up through its use (p. 358)

Physical custody legal residence of parent whom the child lives with (p. 246)

Physical development the genetic foundations of development, the physical growth of all of the components of the body, their functioning and care (p. 6)

Physiological death the ceasing to function of all the vital organs, such as the lungs and heart (p. 559)

Piagetian approach the approach to the study of cognitive development emphasizing the qualitative changes in the ways children think, created by Jean Piaget (p. 160)

Pituitary gland master gland at the base of the brain that produces growth hormones (p. 300)

Pleasure principle the motivation of the id to seek pleasure and avoid pain, regardless of the consequences (p. 24)

Polygenic system of inheritance number of interacting genes that produce a phenotype (p. 56)

Postmature infant infant who is born with a gestational age over 42 weeks (p. 85)

Postparental years the years after the last child leaves home and until the husband's and wife's retirement (p. 532)

Postpartal depression feelings of sadness, crying, depression, insomnia, irritability, and fatigue commonly experienced by the mother several days after her baby is born (p. 83)

Posttraumatic stress disorder psychological disorder characterized by extreme emotional upset after a traumatic experience is over (p. 504)

Pragmatics the practical use of language to communicate with others in a variety of social contexts (p. 148)

Premature ejaculation inability to exert voluntary control over the ejaculatory reflex, causing climax to be reached very quickly (p. 450)

Premature infant infant who is born with a gestational age less than 37 weeks (p. 85)

Premoral level the first level of development of moral judgment, based on rewards and punishments, according to Kohlberg (p. 396)

Prenatal period the period from conception to birth (p. 4)

Preoperational stage Piaget's second stage of cognitive development (2 to 7 years), during which the child gains some conquest over symbols (p. 35)

Prepared childbirth the physical, social, intellectual, and emotional preparation for the birth of a baby (p. 78)

Presbycusis hearing impairment associated with advancing age (p. 452)

Presbyopia farsightedness characterized by lack of clear focus at close distances (p. 452)

Primary memory short-term memory (p. 477)

Primary mental abilities seven basic abilities described by Thurstone (p. 174)

Primary sexual characteristics changes that involve the sex organs at sexual maturation (p. 305)

Problem-finding stage fifth stage of cognitive development characterized by the ability to create, to discover, and to formulate problems (p. 327)

Procedural memory memory for skill and other procedures (p. 478)

Progesterone female sex hormone produced by the corpus luteum of the ovary (p. 301)

Progressives educators emphasizing that education is to prepare pupils for life (p. 329)

Prolactin pituitary hormone that stimulates the secretion of milk by the mammary glands (p. 300)

Prolapsed umbilical cord squeezing of the umbilical cord between the baby's body and the wall of the birth canal during childbirth, causing oxygen deprivation to the fetus (p. 82)

Proprium the self's core of identity that is developing in time (p. 352)

Prostate gland gland that secretes a portion of the seminal fluid (p. 301)

Proximodistal principle outward distribution of physical growth, starting in the center of the body and proceeding out to the extremities (p. 112)

Psychic death the acceptance of death and regression into self, often long before physiological death (p. 560)

Psychoanalytical theory Freud's theory that the structure of personality is composed of the id, ego, and superego, and that mental health depends on keeping the balance among them (p. 24)

Psychological dependency overpowering emotional need for a drug (p. 358)

Psychometric approach the approach to the study of cognitive development that measures the quantitative changes in children's intelligence (p. 160)

Psychopath mentally ill person incapable of the development of conscience or feelings for others (p. 492)

Psychosexual theory theory developed by Freud in which development occurs in stages as the center of sensual sensitivity shifts from one body zone to another as children mature (p. 25)

Psychosocial moratorium socially sanctioned period between childhood and adulthood during which the individual is free to experiment to find a socially acceptable identity and role (p. 288)

Psychosocial theory the term used to describe Erikson's stage theory of development in which there are psychosocial tasks to master at each level of development (p. 26)

Psychotropics mood-altering drugs (p. 441)

Puberty the period or age at which a person reaches sexual maturity and becomes capable of reproduction (p. 284)

Pubescence the whole period during which the physical changes related to sexual maturation take place (p. 284)

Pulmonary embolism blockage of blood vessels to the lungs by a blood clot (p. 444)

Pulmonary infections lung infections (p. 444)

Pulmonary thrombosis blockage of blood vessels to the lungs (p. 444)

Pulse rate the number of heartbeats per minute (p. 435)

Punishment of reciprocity self-imposed punishment; associated with morality of cooperation (p. 272)

Questionnaires research method whereby the subject writes out answers to written questions (p. 14)

Random sample research subjects selected at random (p. 15)

Rationalization Freudian defense mechanism in which excuses are given for one's behavior (p. 25)

Reaction formation Freudian defense mechanism in which an individual deals with an unacceptable impulse by overemphasizing the exact opposite in thought and behavior (p. 24)

Reaction range   range of possible phenotypes given a particular genotype and environmental influences (p. 57)

Reaction time   the interval between stimulation and response (p. 433)

Recall   remembering without cues (p. 170)

Recessive gene   gene whose characteristic is masked by a dominant gene, and is expressed only when paired with a matching recessive gene (p. 55)

Recognition   remembering after cues have been given (p. 170)

Reflexes   unlearned behavioral responses to particular stimuli in the environment (p. 90)

Regression   Freudian defense mechanism in which there is a reverting to an earlier, childish form of behavior in response to anxiety (p. 24)

Relaxation training   techniques to relax the body in order to combat stress (p. 505)

Reliability   the extent to which a test reveals the same scores with repeated administration and when given by two or more examiners (p. 14)

Representative sample   population sample that includes the same percentage of people with specific personal or background characteristics as contained in the population studied (p. 15)

Repression   Freudian defense mechanism in which unpleasant thoughts are pushed down into the unconscious (p. 24)

Retrieval   the process of recalling or of being able to remember or recognize information that has been stored (p. 475)

Reversibility   the concept that every operation has an opposite operation that reverses it (p. 167)

Rheumatoid arthritis   chronic disease marked by painful inflammation and swelling of the small joints of the hands and wrists, and often accompanied by deformities (p. 446)

Romantic love   profoundly tender or passionate affection for another person whose chief characteristic is emotion (p. 522)

Sample   the group of subjects chosen for research (p. 15)

Saturated fats   animal fats; fats saturated with hydrogen, such as oleomargarine (p. 437)

Schema   according to Piaget, the original patterns of thinking that people use for dealing with specific situations in their environment (p. 34)

Scholastic Aptitude Test (SAT)   the most widely used test for youths to determine their aptitude for college work (p. 327)

Scientific method   series of steps used to obtain accurate data; these include formulating the problem, developing a hypothesis, testing the hypothesis, and drawing conclusions that are stated in the form of a theory (p. 13)

Scrotum   the pouch of skin containing the testes (p. 301)

Secondary memory   long-term memory (p. 477)

Secondary sexual characteristics   changes in the body at the time of sexual maturation that do not involve the sex organs (p. 305)

Self   overall perception of one's personality, nature, and individuality (p. 352)

Self-actualization   according to Buhler, the drive of individuals to try to grow, improve, and reach their full potential (p. 31)

Self-concept   individual's conscious, cognitive perception and evaluation of self; one's thoughts and opinions about oneself (p. 352)

Self-efficacy   our perceptions of our actual skill and personal effectiveness (p. 219)

Self-esteem   our perception of our worth, abilities, and accomplishments; our view of ourselves: negative or positive (p. 219)

Self-reference   estimates of our abilities and of how effectively we deal with others and the world (p. 219)

Self-reflective thinking or reciprocal perspective-taking stage   the stage of awareness when the self can take the perspective of another person and know that the other person can also take the perspective of the self (p. 263)

Semantic memory   memory for meaning (p. 478)

Semantics   the meaning of words and sentences (p. 148)

Seminal vesicles   twin glands that secrete fluid into the vas deferens to enhance sperm viability (p. 301)

Senescence   biological aging (p. 455)

Sensitive period   period during which a given effect can be produced more readily than at other times (p. 38)

Sensorimotor stage   Piaget's first stage of cognitive development (birth to 2 years), during which the child coordinates motor actions with sensory experiences (p. 35)

Sensory storage   the process by which information is received and transduced by the senses, usually in a fraction of a second—the first stage in a three-stage model of memory (p. 170)

Separation anxiety   anxiety experienced by children when they are separated from caregivers to whom they are emotionally attached (p. 135)

Separation-individuation   period during which the infant gradually develops a self apart from the mother, a concept of Mahler (p. 217)

Sequential study   combination of cross-sectional and longitudinal research designs that attempts to sort out age, cohort, and time effects; age changes are not measured (p. 18)

Serialization   arranging objects into a hierarchy of classes (p. 166)

Serial-learning tasks   learning items in a list in the exact order of presentation (p. 480)

Sex chromosomes   twenty-third pair of chromosomes that determines the gender of the offspring (p. 54)

Sex-linked disorders   disorders carried only by the mother, through defective, recessive genes on the X chromosome (p. 57)

Sexual dysfunction   malfunctioning of the human sexual response system (p. 450)

Short-term storage   the process by which information is still in the conscious mind and being rehearsed and focused on—the second stage in a three-stage memory model (p. 170)

Show   blood-tinged mucus expelled from the cervix, usually when labor and contractions begin (p. 78)

Siamese twins   monozygotic twins where complete separation did not occur during development (p. 54)

Sibling rivalry   the competition of brothers and sisters for the attention, approval, and affection of the parents (p. 238)

Single-parent family   family consisting of one parent and one or more children (p. 226)

Skills approach   method of teaching reading that involves either a phonics approach or a word recognition approach (p. 157)

Sleepwalking   walking and carrying on various activities during deep sleep (p. 136)

Social clock   each society's specification as to when various life events and activities are supposed to happen (p. 426)

Social cognition   the capacity to understand social relationships (p. 262)

Social cognitive and learning theory   how people think and reason about their social world as they watch and interact with others; their understanding the ability to get along with other people (p. 30)

Social development   the socialization process, moral development, and relationships with peers, family, and at work (p. 6)

Socialization   the process by which persons learn the ways of society or social groups so that they can function within them (p. 227)

Socially accelerated dying   allowing any condition or action of society that shortens life and hastens death (p. 569)

Social networks   social ties with children, family, and friends (p. 498)

Social reconstruction theory   theory of aging describing how society reduces the self-concept of the aged, and proposing ways to reverse this negative cycle (p. 550)

Social role taking   the ability to understand the self and others as subjects and to react to others like the self (p. 262)

Sociocentrism   focus of attention on social problems and the concerns of society (p. 323)

Sociological death   the withdrawal and separation by other people as though one were dead, often long before psysiological death (p. 559)

Sonogram   visual image of fetus, produced from sound waves, used to detect fetal abnormalities (p. 62)

Spermatogenesis   process by which sperm are produced (p. 44)

Stepfamily   family formed when a husband remarries or wife remarries bringing children from a former marriage (p. 249)

Storage   the process by which acquired information is put away for later use (p. 475)

Stress   physical, mental, or emotional strain (p. 500)

Stroke   paralysis that occurs when the blood supply to part of the brain is cut off and affected brain cells die (p. 444)

Structured separation   time-limited approach in which the couple terminate cohabitation, agree to regular personal contact and scheduled therapy, with a moratorium on a final decision either to reunite or to divorce (p. 539)

Subjective judgments   judgments that take into account intention or motives (p. 272)

Subjective well-being   self-perceived positive feeling or state; a cognitive and affective assessment about life as a whole (p. 492)

Sublimation   Freudian defense mechanism in which a socially acceptable goal or action is substituted for an unacceptable, socially harmful one (p. 24)

Sudden infant death syndrome   the sudden and mysterious death of infants in their crib, usually between 2 weeks and 1 year of age (p. 566)

Superego   according to Freud, the socially induced moral restrictions that strive to keep the id in check and help the individual attain perfection (p. 24)

Surrogate mother   woman whose services are obtained by a couple, who is to be inseminated with the man's sperm, to carry the resulting baby until birth, and then to give the baby and all rights to it to the couple (p. 52)

Survival of the fittest   Darwin's concept that only the fittest live to pass on their superior traits to future generations, thereby evolving into higher and higher forms of life (p. 101)

Symbiosis   period in which children establish a close dependency on their mothers, to the extent that there is almost a fusing of personalities (p. 201)

Symbolic play   using one object to represent another in play (p. 162)

Syncretism   trying to link ideas together that are not always related (p. 163)

Syntax   the grammatical rules of a language (p. 148)

Systolic blood pressure   the pressure produced by the heart pumping blood out to the body (p. 442)

Tabula rasa   literally, a blank slate; refers to John Locke's view that children are born morally neutral (p. 100)

Tactile acuity   sensitivity of touch (p. 454)

Tactual memory   memory of touch (p. 476)

Telegraphic speech   several-word utterances that convey meaning (p. 152)

Temperament   the relatively consistent, basic dispositions inherent in people that underlie and modulate much of their behavior (p. 213)

Teratogen   harmful substance that crosses the placenta barrier and harms the embryo or fetus and causes birth defects (p. 62)

Testes   the male gonads that produce sperm and male sex hormones (p. 301)

Testosterone   the masculinizing hormone (p. 267)

Theory   tentative explanation of facts and data that have been observed (p. 24)

Thermoregulation   maintenance of correct body temperature during exposure to heat or cold (p. 454)

Thesis   the principal point or idea of a statement (p. 466)

Third person or mutual perspective-taking stage   the stage of awareness when children see their own perspective, their partner's, plus a third person's perspective (p. 263)

Thrombosis   blockage from any kind of undissolved material in the blood (p. 444)

Timing-of-events model   model of development based on responses to the occurrences and timing of normative and nonnormative events—typified by Neugarten (p. 423)

Tracking   organizational technique that permits schools to create homogeneous groupings of students within a heterogeneous student population in order to facilitate instruction of all students (p. 336)

Traditionalists   educators who argue that the purpose of education is to teach the basics (p. 329)

Transcendental meditation   technique to direct one's consciousness away from thoughts and toward a state of relaxation (p. 505)

Transductive reasoning   proceeding from particular to particular in thought, without making generalizations (p. 163)

Triarchic theory of intelligence   three components of intelligence described by Sternberg (p. 174)

Trimester   one-third of the gestation period, or about 12.7 weeks (p. 48)

Trust versus distrust   Erikson's first stage of psychosocial development (0 to 1 year) in which the infant learns that needs will be met or becomes anxious that needs will be frustrated (p. 26)

Tuberculosis   infectious disease of the lungs (p. 444)

Two-factor theory of intelligence   concept developed by Spearman that intelligence consists of a general factor "g" and a number of specific abilities—"s" factors (p. 174)

Type A personality   personality characterized by intense competitiveness, hostility, overwork, and a sense of time urgency; one who has extreme bodily reactions to stress (p. 500)

Unconditional positive regard   giving acceptance and appreciation of the individual regardless of socially unacceptable behavior (p. 33)

Urethra   the tube that carries urine from the bladder to the outside; in males it also carries the semen to the outside (pp. 302, 445)

Uterus   womb, in which the baby grows and develops (p. 302)

Vagina   canal from the cervix to the vulva that receives the penis during intercourse and acts as the birth canal through which the baby passes to the outside (p. 302)

Vaginismus   involuntary contraction and spasm of the muscles of the vagina (p. 451)

Validity   the extent to which a test measures what it claims to measure (p. 14)

Vas deferens   the tubes running from the epididymis to the urethra that carry semen and sperm to the ejaculatory duct (p. 301)

Vernix caseosa   waxy substance covering the skin of the neonate (p. 89)

Viable   capable of living on its own (p. 51)

Vicarious reinforcement   observing that the positive consequences of another's behavior increase the probability of the behavior in the observer (p. 30)

Visitation rights   right to visit the child given by law (p. 249)

Visual acuity   the ability to see small details (p. 452)

Vital capacity   volume of air inhaled by the lungs with each breath (p. 444)

Vulva   a collective term for the external genitalia of the female (p. 302)

Whole-language approach   method of teaching reading that presents reading materials as a whole so the child learns the meaning of the passage before learning individual words (p. 157)

Word recognition approach   method of teaching reading by teaching the child to recognize the whold word (p. 157)

Zone of proximal development   the distance between a child's actual development level reached through individual problem solving and a higher level of potential development (p. 167)

Zygote   fertilized ovum (p. 44)

References

ABBEY, A., ANDREWS, F. M., & HALMAN, L. J. (1992). Infertility and subjective well-being: The mediating roles of self-esteem, internal control, and interpersonal conflict. *Journal of Marriage and the Family, 54,* 408–417.

ABRAHAM, K. G., & CHRISTOPHERSON, V. A. (1984). Perceived competence among rural middle school children: Parental antecedents and relations to locus of control. *Journal of Early Adolescence, 4,* 343–351.

ABRAMOVITCH, R., FREEDMAN, J. L., THODEN, K., & NIKOLICH, C. (1991). Children's capacity to consent to participation in psychological research: Empirical findings. *Child Development 62,* 1100–1109.

ACHENBACH, T. M., PHARES, V., & HOWELL, C. T. (1990). Seven-year outcome of the Vermont intervention program for low-birthweight infants. *Child Development, 61,* 1672–1681.

ACHENBAUM, W. A., & BENGTSON, B. L. (1994). The reengaging the disengagement theory of aging: On the history and assessment of theory development in gerontology. *The Gerontologist, 34,* 756–761.

ADAMS, G. R., DAY, T., DYK, P. H., & FREDE, E. (1992). On the dialectics of pubescence and psychosocial development. *Journal of Early Adolescence, 12,* 348–365.

ADEGOKE, A. (1992). Relationship between parental socioeconomic status, sex, and initial pubertal problems among school-going adolescents in Nigeria. *Journal of Adolescence, 15,* 323–326.

ADES, P. A., WALDMANN, M. L., & GILLESPIE, C. (1995). A controlled trial of exercise training in older coronary patients. *Journal of Gerontology, 50A,* M7–M11.

ADESSA, M. (1988). Sleep in and smell the coffee. *Psychology Today, 22,* 18.

ADKINS, G., MARTIN, P., & POON, L. W. (1996). Personality traits and states as predictors of subjective well-being in centenarians, octogenarians, and sexagenarians. *Psychology and Aging, 11,* 408–416.

ADLER, S. A., GERHARDSTEIN, P., & ROVEE-COLLIER, C. (1998). Levels-of-processing effects in infant memory? *Child Development, 69,* 280–294.

ADOLPH, K. E., VEREIJKEN, B., & DENNY, M. A. (1998). Learning to crawl. *Child Development, 69,* 1299–1312.

AFFLECK, G., TENNEN, H., ROWE, J., ROSCHER, B., & WALKER, L. (1989). Effects of formal support on mother's adaptation to the hospital-to-home transition of high-risk infants: The benefits and costs of helping. *Child Development, 60,* 488–501.

AGING IN AMERICA. (1989). Washington, DC: Congressional Quarterly.

AHMED, B., & SMITH, S. K. (1992). How changes in components of growth affect the population aging of states. *Journal of Gerontology, 47,* S27–S37.

AHRONS, C., & RODGERS, R. (1987). *Divorced families: A multidisciplinary view.* New York: W. W. Norton.

AHUVIA, A. C., & ADELMAN, M. B. (1992). Formal intermediaries in the marriage market: A typology and review. *Journal of Marriage and the Family, 54,* 452–463.

AINSWORTH, M. D. S. (1988, August). *Attachment beyond infancy.* Paper presented at the meeting of the American Psychological Association.

AINSWORTH, M. D. S., & BOWLBY, J. (1991). An ethological approach to personality development. *American Psychologist, 46,* 331–341.

AKINBOYE, J. O. (1984, Summer). Secondary sexual characteristics and normal puberty in Nigerian and Zimbabwian adolescents. *Adolescence, 19,* 483–492.

ALAN GUTTMACHER INSTITUTE. (1983). *Teenage pregnancy.* New York: Alan Guttmacher Institute.

ALBERT, M. S., JONES, K., SAVAGE, C. R., BERKMAN, L., SEEMAN, T, BLAZER, D., & ROWE, J. W. (1995). Predictors of cognitive change in older persons: MacArthur Studies of Successful Aging. *Psychology and Aging, 10,* 578–589.

ALBERTS, J. K., HECHT, M. L., MILLER-RASSULO, M., & KRIZEK, R. L. (1992). The communicative process of drug resistance among high school students. *Adolescence, 27,* 203–226.

ALBRIGHT, A. (1992). Postpartum depression: An overview. *Journal of Counseling and Development, 71,* 316–320.

ALDWIN, C. M. (1991). Does age affect the stress and coping process? Implications of age differences in perceived control. *Journal of Gerontology, 46,* P174–P180.

ALLEN, J. P., HAUSER, S. T., BELL, K. L., & O'CONNOR, T. G. (1994). Longitudinal assessment of autonomy and relatedness in adolescent-family interactions as predictors of adolescent ego development and self-esteem. *Child Development, 65,* 179–194.

ALLEN, K. E., HART, R. M., BUELL, J. S., HARRIS, F. R., & WOLF, M. M. (1964). Effects of social reinforcement on isolate behavior of a nursery school child. *Child Development, 35,* 511–518.

ALLEN, K. R., & DEMO, D. A. (1995). The families of lesbians and gay men: A new frontier in family research. *Journal of Marriage and the Family, 57,* 111–127.

ALLEN, O., & PAGE, R. M. (1994). Variance in substance use between rural Black and White Mississippi high school students. *Adolescence, 29,* 401–404.

ALLEN, P. A. (1993). On age differences in processing variability and scanning speed. *The Journals of Gerontology, 46,* P191–P201.

ALLEN, P. A., & COYNE, A. C. (1989). Are there age differences in chunking? *Journal of Gerontology, 44,* 181–183.

ALLEN, P. A., & CROZIER, L. C. (1992). Age and ideal chunk size. *The Journals of Gerontology, 47,* P47–P51.

ALLEN, P. A., MADDEN, D. J., WEBER, P., & CROZIER, L. C. (1992). Age differences in short-term memory: Organization or internal noise? *The Journals of Gerontology, 47,* P281–P288.

ALLERS, C. T., & BENJACK, K. J. (1991). Connections between childhood abuse and HIV infection. *Journal of Counseling and Development, 70,* 309–313.

ALLPORT, G. W. (1950). *Becoming: Basic considerations for a psychology of personality.* New Haven, CT: Yale University Press.

ALSAKER, F. D. (1992). Pubertal timing, overweight, and psychological adjustments. *Journal of Early Adolescence, 12,* 396–419.

ALSAKER, F. D. (1992a). Being overweight and psychological adjustment. *Journal of Early Adolescence, 12,* 396–419.

ALSAKER, F. D. (1992b). Pubertal timing, overweight, and psychological adjustment. *Journal of Early Adolescence, 12,* 396–419.

ALTHAUS, F. (March/April, 1991a). Expansion of Medicaid alone may not result in healthier newborns. *Family Planning Perspectives, 23,* 91–92.

ALTHAUS, F. (November/December, 1991b). A woman's risk of ectopic pregnancy varies according to the contraceptive she chooses. *Family Planning Perspectives, 23,* 291–292.

ALTMANN, E. O., & GOTTLIEB, I. H. (1988). The social behavior of depressed children: An observational study. *Journal of Abnormal Child Psychology, 16,* 29–44.

AMABILE, T. A., & ROVEE-COLLIER, C. (1991). Contextual variation and memory retrieval at six months. *Child Development, 62,* 1155–1166.

AMATO, P. R. (1986). Marital conflict, the parent-child relationship, and self-esteem. *Family Relations, 35,* 403–410.

AMATO, P. R. (1987). Family process in one-parent, stepparent, and intact families: The child's point of view. *Journal of Marriage and the Family, 49,* 327–337.

AMATO, P. R. (1988a). Long-term implications of parental divorce for adult self-concept. *Journal of Family Issues, 9,* 201–213.

AMATO, P. R. (1988b). Parental divorce and attitudes toward marriage and family life. *Journal of Marriage and the Family, 50,* 453–461.

AMATO, P. R. (1990). Dimensions of the family environment as perceived by children: A multidimensional scaling analysis. *Journal of Marriage and the Family, 52,* 613–620.

AMATO, P. R. (1991a). The "child of divorce" as a person prototype: Bias in the recall of information about children in divorced families. *Journal of Marriage and the Family, 53,* 59–69.

AMATO, P. R. (1991b). Psychological distress and the recall of childhood family characteristics. *Journal of Marriage and the Family, 53,* 1011–1019.

AMATO, P. R. (1993). Children's adjustment to divorce: Theories, hypothesis, and empirical support. *Journal of Marriage and the Family, 55,* 23–38.

AMATO, P. R., & BOOTH, A. (1991). The consequences of divorce for attitudes towards divorce and gender roles. *Journal of Family Issues, 12,* 306–322.

AMATO, P. R., & REZAC, S. J. (1994). Contact with nonresident parents, interparental conflict, and children's behavior. *Journal of Family Issues, 15,* 191–207.

AMERICAN ACADEMY OF PEDIATRICS. (1982, March). Guidelines for health supervision. *News and Comment.*

AMERICAN ACADEMY OF PEDIATRICS. (1986). *Positive approaches to daycare dilemmas: How to make it work.* Elk Grove Village, IL: American Academy of Pediatrics.

AMERICAN ACADEMY OF PEDIATRICS (August 1995). Recommendations for preventive health care. *Pediatrics,* 96, No. 2.

AMERICAN ACADEMY OF PEDIATRICS, COMMITTEE ON NUTRITION. (1986). Prudent life-style for children: Dietary fat and cholesterol. *Pediatrics, 78,* 521–525.

AMERICAN ACADEMY OF PEDIATRICS, COMMITTEE ON PEDIATRIC ASPECTS OF PHYSICAL FITNESS, RECREATION, AND SPORTS. (1981). Competitive athletics for children of elementary school age. *Pediatrics, 67.*

AMERICAN PSYCHIATRIC ASSOCIATION. (1994). *Diagnostic and statistical manual of mental disorders* (4th ed., rev.). Washington, DC: American Psychiatric Association.

AMERICAN PSYCHOLOGICAL ASSOCIATION (APA). (1982). *Ethical principles in the conduct of research with human participants.* Washington, DC: American Psychological Association.

AMES, L. B., GILLESPIE, C., HAINES, J., & ILG, F. L. (1978). *The Gesell Institute's child from one to six.* New York: Harper & Row.

AMSTER, L. E., & KRAUSS, H. H. (1974). Life crises and mental deterioration. *International Journal of Aging and Human Development, 5,* 51–55.

ANDERSEN, B. L., & LeGRAND, J. (1991). Body image for women: Conceptualization, assessment, and a test of its importance to sexual dysfunction and to mental illness. *The Journal of Sex Research, 28,* 457–477.

ANDERSON, A. R., & HENRY, C. S. (1994). Family system characteristics and parental behaviors as predictors of adolescent substance use. *Adolescence, 29,* 405–420.

ANDERSON, D. R., CHOI, H. P., & LORCH, E. P. (1987). Attentional inertia reduces distractibility during young children's TV viewing. *Child Development, 58,* 798–806.

ANDERSON, N. D., CRAIK, S. I. M., & NAVEH-BENJAMIN, M. (1998). The attentional demands of encoding and retrieval in younger and older adults. 1. Evidence from divided attention costs. *Psychology and Aging, 13,* 405–423.

ANDERSON, S. A., RUSSELL, C. S., & SCHUMM, W. R. (1983). Perceived marital quality and family-life cycle categories: A further analysis. *Journal of Marriage and the Family, 45,* 227–239.

ANDERSSON, B. E. (1992). Effects of day-care on cognitive and socioemotional competence of thirteen-year-old Swedish schoolchildren. *Child Development, 63,* 20–36.

ANDERSSON, L., & STEVENS, N. (1993). Associations between early experiences with parents and well-being in old age. *Journal of Gerontology, 48,* P109–P116.

ANDRE, T., & BORMANN, L. (1991). Knowledge of acquired immune deficiency syndrome and sexual responsibility among high school students. *Youth and Society, 22,* 339–361.

ANDREWS, B., & BREWIN, C. R. (1990). Attributions of blame for marital violence: A study of antecedents and consequences. *Journal of Marriage and the Family, 52,* 757–776.

ANDREWS, J. A., HOPS, H., & DUNCAN, S. C., (1997). Adolescent modeling of parent substance: The moderating effect of the relationship with the parent. *Journal of Family Psychology, 11,* 259–270.

ANDREWS, J. A., HOPS, H., ARY, D., TILDESLEY, E., & HARRIS, J. (1993). Parental influence on early adolescent substance use: Specific and nonspecific effects. *Journal of Early Adolescence, 13,* 285–310.

ANDREWS, S. R., BLUMENTHAL, J. B., JOHNSON, D. L, KAHN, A. J., FERGUSON, C. J., LASATER, T. M., MALONE, P. E., & WALLACE, D. B. (1982). The skills of mothering—a study of parent-child develop-

ment centers. *Monographs of the Society for Research in Child Development, 47* (6, Serial No. 198).

ANISFELD, E., CASPER, V., NOZYCE, M., & CUNNINGHAM, N. (1990). Does infant carrying promote attachment? An experimental study of the effects of increased physical contact on the development of attachment. *Child Development, 61,* 1617–1627.

ANNAS, G., & DENSBERGER, J. (1984). Competence to refuse medical treatment: Autonomy v. paternalism. *University of Toledo Law Review, 15,* 561–596.

ANSBACHER, R., & ADLER, J. P. (1988). Infertility workup and sexual stress. *Medical Aspects of Human Sexuality, 22,* 55–63.

APGAR, V. A. (1953). A proposal for a new method of evaluation of a newborn infant. *Anesthesia and Analgesia, 32,* 260–267.

APTITUDE TEST SCORES. Grumbling gets louder. (1979, May 14). *U.S. News and World Report,* pp. 76ff.

ARCHER, S. L. (1990a). Adolescent identity: An appraisal of health and intervention. *Journal of Adolescence, 13,* 341–344.

ARCHER, S. L. (1990b). The status of identity: Reflections on the need for intervention. *Journal of Adolescence, 13,* 345–360.

ARCHER, S. L., & WATERMAN, A. S. (1990). Varieties of identity diffusions and foreclosures: An exploration of subcategories of the identity statuses. *Journal of Adolescent Research, 5,* 96–111.

ARENBERG, D., & ROBERTSON-TSHABO, E. A. (1977). Learning and aging. In J. A. Bireen & K. W. Schaie (Eds.), *Handbook on the psychology of aging* (pp. 421–449). New York: Van Nostrand-Reinhold.

ARIES, P. (1981). *The hour of death.* New York: Alfred A. Knopf.

ARKIN, E. B. (1989, July). *Infant care.* U.S. Department of HHS, Public Health Service, Health Resources and Services Administration, Bureau of Maternal and Child Health and Resources Development. Washington, DC: U.S. Government Printing Office.

ARLING, G. (1987). Strain, social support, and distress in old age. *Journal of Gerontology, 42,* 107–113.

ARMISTEAD, L., WIERSON, M., FOREHAND, R., & FRAME, C. (1992). Psychopathology in incarcerated juvenile delinquents: Does it extend beyond externalizing problems? *Adolescence, 27,* 309–314.

ARNETT, J. J. (1997). Young people's conceptions of the transition to adulthood. *Youth and Society, 29,* 3–23.

ARSENIO, W. F., & KRAMER, R. (1992). Victimizers and their victims: Children's conceptions of the mixed emotional consequences of moral transgressions. *Child Development, 63,* 915–927.

ARTHUR, N. M. (1990). The assessment of burnout: A review of three inventories useful for research in counseling. *Journal of Counseling and Development, 69,* 186–189.

ASARNOW, J. R. (1988). Peers status and social competence in child psychiatric inpatients: A comparison of children with depressive, externalizing, and concurrent depressive and externalizing disorders. *Journal of Abnormal Child Psychology, 16,* 151–162.

ASENDORPF, J. B. (1991). Development of inhibited children's coping with unfamiliarity. *Child Development, 62,* 1460–1474.

ASENDORPF, J. B., & NUNNER-WINKLER, G. (1992). Children's moral motive strength and temperamental inhibition reduce their immoral behavior in real moral conflicts. *Child Development, 63,* 1223–1235.

ASHFORD, J., & LeCROY, C. W. (1990). Juvenile recidivism: A comparison of three prediction instruments. *Adolescence, 25,* 441–450.

ASHMEAD, D. H., & DAVIS, D. L. (1996). Measuring habituation in infants: An approach using regression analysis. *Child Development, 67,* 2677–2690.

ASHMEAD, D. H., DAVIS, D. L., WHALEN, T., & ODOM, R. D. (1991). Sound localization and sensitivity to interaural time differences in human infants. *Child Development, 62,* 1211–1226.

ASLIN, R. N., & SMITH, L. B. (1988). Perceptual development. *Annual Review of Psychology, 39,* 435–473.

ATILLASOY, E., & HOLT, P. (1993). Gastrointestinal proliferation and aging. *The Journals of Gerontology, 48,* B43–B49.

ATKINSON, M. B., & BLACKWELDER, S. B. (1993). Fathering in the 20th century. *Journal of Marriage and the Family, 55,* 975–986.

ATKINSON, R. (1988). *Teenage world: Adolescent self-image in ten countries.* New York: Plenum.

AUERBACH, J. G., LERNER, Y., BARASCH, M., TEPPER, D., & PALTI, H. (1995). The identification in infancy of children at cognitive and behavioral risk: The Jerusalem kindergarten project. *The Journal of Applied Developmental Psychology, 16,* 319–338.

BACHARACH, B. R., & BAUMEISTER, A. A. (1998). Direct and indirect effects of maternal intelligence, maternal age, income, and home environment on intelligence of preterm, low-birth-weight children. *Journal of Applied Developmental Psychology, 19,* 361–375.

BACHMAN, J. G., JOHNSTON, L. D., & O'MALLEY, P. M. (1987). *Monitoring the future: Questionnaire responses from the nation's high school seniors, 1986.* Ann Arbor, MI: Institute for Social Research.

BACHRACH, C. A., LONDON, R. A., & MAZA, P. L. (1991). On the path to adoption: Adoption seeking in the United States, 1988. *Journal of Marriage and the Family, 53,* 705–718.

BACHRACH, C. A., STOLLEY, K. S., & LONDON, K. A. (1992, January/February). Relinquishment of premarital births: Evidence from national survey data. *Family Planning Perspectives, 24,* 27–32.

BACKMAN, L., & LARSSON, M. (1992). Recall of organizable words and objects in adulthood: Influences of instructions, retention interval, and retrieval cues. *The Journals of Gerontology, 47,* P273–P278.

BACKSCHEIDER, A. D., SHATZ, M., & GELMAN, S. A. (1993). Preschoolers' ability to distinguish living kinds as a function of regrowth. *Child Development, 64,* 1242–1257.

BAGLEY, C. A., & COPELAND, E. J. (1994). African and African-American graduate students' racial identity and personal problem-solving strategies. *Journal of Counseling and Development, 1994, 73,* 167–171.

BAHR, S. J., HAWKS, R. D., & WANG, G. (1993). Family and religious influences on adolescent substance abuse. *Youth and Society, 24,* 443–465.

BAHRICK, L. E., NETTO, D., & HERNANDEZ-REIF, M. (1998). Intermodal perception of child faces and voices by infants. *Child Development, 69,* 1263–1275.

BAI, D. O., & BERTENTHAL, B. I. (1992). Locomotor status and the development of spatial search skills. *Child Development, 63,* 215–226.

BAILEY, C. A. (1991). Family structure and eating disorders: The family environment scale and bulimic-like symptoms. *Youth and Society, 23,* 251–272.

BAILEY, D. B., JR., MCWILLIAM, R. A., WARE, W. B., & BURCHINAL, M. A. (1993). Social interactions with toddlers and preschoolers in same-age and mixed-age play groups. *Journal of Applied Developmental Psychology, 14,* 261–276.

BAILEY, J. M., AND ZUCKER, K. J. (1995). Childhood sex-typed behavior and sexual orientation: A conceptual analysis and quantitative review. *Developmental Psychology, 31,* 43–55.

BAILLARGEON, R. (1987). Object permanence in 3½–4½-month-old infants. *Developmental Psychology, 23,* 655–664.

BAILLARGEON, R., & DEVOS, J. (1991). Object permanence in young infants: Further evidence. *Child Development, 62,* 1227–1246.

BAIRD, P., & SIGHTS, J. R. (1986). Low self-esteem as a treatment issue in the psychotherapy of anorexia and bulimia. *Journal of Counseling and Development, 64,* 449–451.

BAKER, L. A., et al. (1992). Genetic and environmental influences on positive and negative affect: Support for a 2-factor theory. *Psychology and Aging, 7,* 158–163.

BAKKEN, L., & ROMIG, C. (1992). Interpersonal needs in middle adolescents: Companionship, leadership, and intimacy. *Journal of Adolescence, 15,* 301–316.

BALDWIN, D. A. (1991). Infants' contribution to the achievement of joint references. *Child Development, 62,* 875–890.

BALDWIN, D. A. (1993). Early referential understanding: Infants' ability to recognize referential acts for what they are. *Developmental Psychology, 29,* 832–843.

BALDWIN, J. I., WHITELEY, S., & BALDWIN, J. D. (1990). Changing AIDS- and fertility-related behavior: The effectiveness of sexual education. *The Journal of Sex Research, 27,* 245–262.

BALLARD, M. E., CUMMINGS, E. M., & LARKIN, K. (1993). Emotional and cardiovascular responses to adults' angry behavior and to challenging tasks in children of hypertensive and normotensive parents. *Child Development, 64,* 500–515.

BALTES, M. M., NEUMANN, E., & ZANK, S. (1994). Maintenance and rehabilitation of independence in old age: An intervention program for staff. *Psychology and Aging, 9,* 179–188.

BALTES, P. B. (1987). Theoretical propositions of life-span developmental psychology: On the dynamics between growth and decline. *Developmental Psychology, 23,* 611–626.

BALTES, P. B., & SCHAIE, K. W. (1976). On the plasticity of intelligence in adulthood and old age: Where Horn and Donaldson fail. *American Psychologist, 31,* 720–725.

BALTES, P. B., REESE, H. W., & LIPSITT, L. (1980). Life span developmental psychology, In M. Rosenzweig & L. Portor (Eds.), *Annual review of psychology* (Vol. 31). Palo Alto, CA: Annual Reviews.

BALTES, P. B., SMITH, J., STAUDINGER, V. M., & SOWARKA, D. (1988). Wisdom: One facet of successful aging? In M. Perlmutter (Ed.), *Late-life potential.* Washington, DC: Gerontological Society of America.

BALTES, P. B., STAUDINGER, U. N., MAERCKER, A., & SMITH, J. (1995). People nominated as wise: A comparative study of wisdom-related knowledge. *Psychology and Aging, 10,* 155–166.

BANDURA, A. (1977). *Social learning theory.* Englewood Cliffs, NJ: Prentice-Hall.

BANDURA, A. (1986). *Social foundations of thought and action: A social cognitive theory.* Englewood Cliffs, NJ: Prentice-Hall.

BANDURA, A. (1989). Human agency in social cognitive theory. *American Psychologist, 44,* 1175–1184.

BANDURA, A., ROSS, D., & ROSS, S. A (1963). Imitation of film-mediated aggressive models. *Journal of Abnormal and Social Psychology, 66,* 3–11.

BANKER, D. S., & GAERTNER, S. L. (1998). Achieving step-family harmony: An intergroup-relation's approach. *Journal of Family Psychology, 12,* 310–325.

BANKS, M. S., & SALAPATEK, P. (1983). Infant visual perception. In P. H. Mussen (Ed.), *Handbook of child psychology* (4th ed., Vol. 2). New York: Wiley.

BARBER, B. K. (1992). Family, personality, and adolescent problem behaviors. *Journal of Marriage and the Family, 54,* 69–79.

BARBER, B. K. (1994). Cultural, family, and personal contexts of parent-adolescent conflicts. *Journal of Marriage and the Family, 56,* 375–386.

BARBER, B. K., CHADWICK, B. A., & OERTER, R. (1992). Parental behaviors and adolescent self-esteem in the United States and Germany. *Journal of Marriage and the Family, 54,* 128–141.

BARBER, B. K., OLSEN, J. E., & SHAGLE, S. C. (1994). Associations between parental psychological and behavioral controls and youth internalized and externalized behavior. *Child Development, 65,* 1120–1136.

BARNES, G. M., FARRELL, M. P., & BANERJEE, S. (1994). Family influences on alcohol abuse and other problem behaviors among Black and White adolescents in a general population sample. *Journal of Research on Adolescence, 4,* 183–201.

BARNES, M. E., & FARRIER, S. C. (1985, Spring). A longitudinal study of the self-concept of low-income youth. *Adolescence, 20,* 199–205.

BARRANTI, C. C. R. (1985). The grandparent-grandchild relationship: Family resource in an era of voluntary bonds. *Family Relations, 34,* 343–352.

BARRETT, K. C., & CAMPOS, J. J. (1987). A functionalist approach to emotions. In J. D. Osofsky (Ed.), *Handbook of infant development.* New York: Wiley.

BARRETT, M. D. (1986). Early semantic representations and early word-usage. In S. A. Kuczaj & M. C. Barrett (Eds.), *The development of word meaning: Progress in cognitive developmental research.* New York: Springer-Verlag.

BART, W. M. (1983, Winter). Adolescent thinking and the quality of life. *Adolescence, 18,* 875–888.

BARTON, M. C., & TOMASELLO, M. (1991). Joint attention and conversation in mother-infant-sibling triads. *Child Development, 62,* 517–529.

BATES, J. E., DODGE, K. A., PETTIT, G. S., & RIDGE, B. (1998). Interaction of temperamental resistance to control and restrictive parenting in the development of externalized behavior. *Developmental Psychology, 34,* 982–995.

BAUER, P. J., & HERTSGAARD, L. A. (1993). Increasing steps in recall of events: Factors facilitating immediate and long-term memory in 13.5- and 16.5-month-old children. *Child Development, 64,* 1204–1223.

BAUER, P. J., & MANDLER, J. M. (1992). Putting the horse before the cart: The use of temporal order in recall of events by one-year-old children. *Developmental Psychology, 28,* 441–452.

BAUMAN, R. P. (1978, Spring). Teaching for cognitive development. *Andover Review, 5,* 83–98.

BAUMRIND, D. (1978). Parental disciplinary patterns and social competence in children. *Youth and Society, 9,* 239–276.

BAUMRIND, D. (1980). New directions in socialization research. *American Psychologist, 35,* 639–652.

BAUMRIND, D. (1995). Commentary on sexual orientation: Research and social policy implications. *Developmental Psychology, 31,* 130–136.

BAYDAR, N., BROOKS-GUNN, J., & FURSTENBERG, F. F. (1993). Early warning signs of functional illiteracy: Predictors in childhood and adolescence. *Child Development, 64,* 815–829.

BAYLAR, N. (1988). Effects of parental separation and re-entry into union on the emotional well-being of children. *Journal of Marriage and the Family, 50,* 967–981.

BAYLES, K. A., & TROSSET, M. W. (1992). Confrontation naming in Alzheimer's patients: Relation to disease severity. *Psychology and Aging, 7,* 197–203.

BAYLEY, N. (1969). *Manual for the Bayley Scales of infant development.* New York: The Psychological Corporation.

BEAUCHAMP, G., & COWART, B. (1985). Congenital and experiential factors in the development of human flavor preferences. *Appetite, 6,* 357–372.

BECK, J. G., & DAVIES, D. K. (1987). Teen contraception: A review of perspectives on compliance. *Archives of Sexual Behavior, 16,* 337–368.

BECKWITH, L., RODNING, C., & COHEN, S. (1992). Preterm children at early adolescence and continuity and discontinuity in maternal responsiveness from infancy. *Child Development, 63,* 1198–1208.

BEGLEY, S., AND GILMAN, D. (Sept. 9, 1991). What causes people to be homosexual? *Newsweek, 118,* 52.

BEHRMAN, R. E., & VAUGHN, B. E. (Eds.). (1983). *Nelson textbook of pediatrics* (12th ed.). Philadelphia, PA: Saunders.

BEILIN, H. (1992). Piaget's enduring contribution to developmental psychology. *Developmental Psychology, 28,* 191–204.

BELL, B., ROSE, C. L., & DANON, A. (1972). The normative aging study: An interdisciplinary and longitudinal study of health and aging. *Aging and Human Development, 3,* 5–18.

BELL, M. A., & FOX, N. A. (1992). The relations between frontal brain electrical activity and cognitive development during infancy. *Child Development, 63,* 1142–1163.

BELL, R. R. (1975). *Marriage and family interaction* (4th ed.). Homewood, IL: Dorsey.

BELLANTONI, M. F., et al. (1991). Transdermal estradiol with oral progestin: Biological and clinical effects in younger and older postmenopausal women. *The Journals of Gerontology, 46,* M216–M222.

BELLINGER, D., LEVITON, A. A., WATERMAUX, C., NEEDLEMAN, H., & RABINOWITZ, M. (1987). Longitudinal analyses of prenatal and postnatal lead exposure and early cognitive development. *New England Journal of Medicine, 316,* 1037–1043.

BELMORE, S. M. (1981). Age-related changes in processing explicit and implicit language. *Journal of Gerontology, 36,* 316–322.

BELSKY, J. (1987, August). *Mother care, other care, and infant-parent attachment security.* Paper presented at the annual meeting of the American Psychological Association, New York.

BELSKY, J. (1990). Parental and nonparental child care and children's socioemotional development: A decade in review. *Journal of Marriage and the Family, 52,* 885–903.

BELSKY, J., & BRAUNGART, J. M. (1991). Are insecure-avoidant infants with extensive day-care experience less stressed by and more independent in the strange situation? *Child Development, 62,* 567–571.

BELSKY, J., & ROVINE, M. J. (1988). Nonmaternal care in the first year of life and the security of infant-parent attachment. *Child Development, 59,* 157–167.

BELSKY, J., CRNIC, K., & GABLE, S. (1995). The determinants of coparenting in families with toddler boys: Spousal differences and daily hassles. *Child Development, 66,* 629–642.

BELSKY, J., STEINBERG, L., & DRAPER, P. (1991). Further reflections on an evolutionary theory of socialization. *Child Development, 62,* 682–685.

BEMAN, D. S., (1995). Risk factors leading to adolescent substance abuse. *Adolescence, 30,* 201–208.

BENAZON, N., WRIGHT, J., AND SABOURIN, S. (1992). Stress, sexual satisfaction, and marital adjustment in infertile couples. *Journal of Sex and Marital Therapy, 18,* 273–284.

BENENSON, J. F. (1990). Gender differences in social networks. *Journal of Early Adolescence, 10,* 472–495.

BENENSON, J. F. (1993). Greater preference among females and males for dyadic interaction in early childhood. *Child Development, 64,* 544–555.

BENGSTON, V. L., & ROBERTS, R. E. L. (1991). Intergenerational solidarity in aging families: An example of formal theory construction. *Journal of Marriage and the Family, 53,* 856–870.

BENGSTON, V. L., CUELLAR, J. B., & RAGAN, P. K. (1977, January). Stratum contrasts and similarities in attitudes toward death. *Journal of Gerontology, 32,* 76–88.

BENIN, M., & KEITH, V. M., (1995). The social support of employed African American and Anglo mothers. *Journal of Family Issues, 16,* 275–297.

BENOTTI, J. R. (1988). Living with congestive heart disease. *Medical Aspects of Human Sexuality, 22,* 47–48.

BERCH, D. B., & BENDER, B. G. (1987). Margins of sexuality. *Psychology Today, 21,* 54–57.

BERENBAUM, S. A., AND SNYDER, E. (1995). Early hormonal influences on childhood sex-typed activity and playmate preferences: Implications for the development of sexual orientation. *Developmental Psychology, 31,* 31–42.

BERG, C. A., & STERNBERG, R. J. (1992). Adults; conceptions of intelligence across the adult life span. *Psychology and Aging, 7,* 221–231.

BERGSTROM-WALEN, M., & NIELSEN, H. H. (1990). Sexual expression among 60- to 80-year-old men and women: A sample from Stockman, Sweden. *The Journal of Sex Research, 27,* 289–295.

BERHAEGHEN, P., MARCOEN, A., & GOOSSENS, L. (1993). Facts and fiction about memory aging: A quantitative integration of research findings. *Journal of Gerontology, 48,* P157–P171.

BERKOW, R. (Ed.). (1987). Postpartum care. *The Merck Manual* (15th ed. Revis.). Rahway, NJ: Merck, Sharp and Dohme Research Laboratories.

BERKOW, R. (Ed.) (1997). *The Merck manual of medical information* (Home ed.). Whitehouse Station, NJ: Merck Research Laboratories.

BERMAN, P. W., O'NAN, B. A., & FLOYD, W. (1981). The double standard of aging and the social situation: Judgments of attractiveness of the middle-aged woman. *Sex Roles, 7,* 87–96.

BERNDT, T. J., & MEKOS, D. (1995). Adolescents' perceptions of the stressful and desirable aspects of the transition to junior high school. *Journal of Research on Adolescence, 5,* 123–142.

BERRY, J. O., & RAO, J. M. (1997). Balancing employment and fatherhood. *Journal of Family Issues, 18,* 386–402.

BERRY, R. E., & WILLIAMS, F. L. (1987). Assessing the relationship between the quality of life and marital income satisfaction. *Journal of Marriage and the Family, 49,* 107–116.

BERSCHUEREN, K., MARCOEN, A., & SCHOEFS, Y. (1996). The internal working model of the self, attachment, and competence in five-year-olds. *Child Development, 67,* 2493–2511.

BERTENTHAL, B. I., & BRADBURY, A. (1992). Infants' detection of shearing motion in random-dot displays. *Developmental Psychology, 28,* 1056–1066.

BERZONSKY, M. D., (1997). Identity development, control theory, and self-regulation: An individual's differences perspective. *Journal of Adolescent Research, 12,* 347–353.

BERZONSKY, M. D., RICE, K. G., & NEIMEYER, G. J. (1990). Identity status and self-construct systems: Process × structure interactions. *Journal of Adolescence, 13,* 251–264.

BEST, D. L. (1993). Inducing children to generate mnemonic organizational strategies: An examination of long-term retention and materials. *Developmental Psychology, 29,* 324–336.

BETTES, B. A., DUSENBURY, L., KERNER, J., JAMES-ORTIZ, S., & BOTVIN, G. J. (1990). Ethnicity and psychosocial factors in alcohol and tobacco use in adolescence. *Child Development, 61,* 557–565.

BIALYSTOK, E. (1992). Attentional control in children's metalinguistic performance and measures of field independence. *Developmental Psychology, 28,* 654–664.

BIBACE, R., SAGARIN, J. D., & DYL, J. (1998). The heuristic value of Werner's co-existence concept of development. *Journal of Applied Developmental Psychology, 19,* 153–163.

BIEMAN-COPLAND, S., & CHARNESS, N. (1994). Memory knowledge and memory monitoring in adulthood. *Psychology and Aging, 9,* 287–302.

BIGBEE, J. L. (1992). Family stress, hardiness, and illness: A pilot study. *Family Relations, 41,* 212–217.

BIGLER, R. S. (1995). The role of classification skill in moderating environmental influences on children's gender stereotyping: A study of the functional use of gender in the classroom. *Child Development, 66,* 1072–1087.

BILLS, D. B., HELMS, L. B., & OZCAN, M. (1995). The impact of student employment on teachers' attitudes and behaviors toward working students. *Youth and Society, 27*, 169–193.

BILLY, J. O. G., BREWSTER, K. L., & GRADY, W. R. (1994). Contextual effects on the sexual behavior of adolescent women. *Journal of Marriage and the Family, 56*, 387–404.

BILSKER, D. (1992). An existentialist account of identity formation. *Journal of Adolescence, 15*, 177–192.

BILSKER, D., & MARCIA, J. E. (1991). Adaptive regression and ego identity. *Journal of Adolescence, 14*, 75–84.

BINET, A., & SIMON, T. (1916). *The development of intelligence in children.* Baltimore, MD: William & Wilkins.

BIRINGEN, Z., EMDE, R. N., CAMPOS, J. J., & APPLEBAUM, M. I. (1995). Affective reorganization in the infant, the mother, and the dyad: The role of upright locomotion and its timing. *Child Development, 66*, 499–514.

BIRNHOLZ, J. C., & BENACERRAF, B. R. (1983). The development of human fetal hearing. *Science, 222*, 516–518.

BISHER, E. B., & BISHER, J. S. (1989). Parenting coalition after remarriage: Dynamics and therapeutic guidelines. *Family Relations, 38*, 65–70.

BISPING, R., STEINGRUEBER, H. J., OLTMANN, M., & WENK, C. (1990). Adults' tolerance of cries: An experimental investigation of acoustic features. *Child Development, 61*, 1218–1229.

BJORKLUND, D. F., SCHNEIDER, W., CASSEL, W. S., & ASHLEY, E. (1994). Training an extension of a memory strategy: Evidence for utilization deficiencies in the acquisition of an organizational strategy in high- and low-IQ children. *Child Development, 65*, 951–965.

BLACK, C., & deBLASSIE, R. R. (1985). Adolescent pregnancy: Contributing factors, consequences, treatment, and plausible solutions. *Adolescence, 20*, 281–290.

BLAIN, M. D., THOMPSON, J. M., & WHIFFEN, V. E. (1993). Attachment and perceived social support in late adolescence: The interaction between working models of self and others. *Journal of Adolescent Research, 8*, 226–241.

BLAKE, J. (1989). *Family size and achievement.* Berkeley: University of California Press.

BLAKE, J. (1991). Number of siblings and personality. *Family Planning Perspectives, 23*, 273–274.

BLANCHARD-FIELDS, F., JAHNKE, II. C., & CAMP, C. (1995). Age differences in problem-solving style: The role of emotional salience. *Psychology and Aging, 10*, 173–180.

BLANDING, F. H. (1982). *Pulse point plan.* New York: Random House.

BLASCOVICH, J., et al. (1992). Affect intensity and cardiac arousal. *Journal of Personality and Social Psychology, 63*, 164–174.

BLASS, E. M., & SMITH, B. A. (1992). Differential effects of sucrose, fructose, glucose, and lactose on crying in 1- to 3-day-old human infants: Qualitative and quantitative considerations. *Developmental Psychology, 28*, 804–810.

BLECKE, J. (1990). Exploration of children's health and self-care behavior within a family context through qualitative research. *Family Relations, 39*, 284–291.

BLEWITT, P. (1994). Understanding categorical hierarchies: The earliest levels of skill. *Child Development, 65*, 1259–1298.

BLINN, L. M. (1987). Phototherapeutic intervention to improve self-concept and prevent repeat pregnancies among adolescents. *Family Relations, 36*, 252–257.

BLINN, L. M. (1990). Adolescent mothers' preceptions of their work lives in the future: Are they stable? *Journal of Adolescent Research, 5*, 206–221.

BLIWISE, N. (1992). Factors related to sleep quality in healthy elderly women. *Psychology and Aging, 7*, 83–88.

BLOCH, D. P. (1989). Using career information with drop-outs and at-risk youth. *Career Development Quarterly, 38*, 160–171.

BLOCK, J., BLOCK, J. H., & KEYES, S. (1988). Longitudinally foretelling drug usage in adolescence: Early childhood personality and environmental precursors. *Child Development, 59*, 336–355.

BLUMENTHAL, J. A., et al. (1991). Long-term effects of exercise on psychological functioning in older men and women. *The Journals of Gerontology, 46*, P352–P361.

BLUMENTHAL, L. (1980, July 25). Upsurge in violence, stress, blamed on eruptions. *Seattle Times*, A1.

BLUSTEIN, D. L., & PALLADINO, D. E. (1991). Self and identity in late adolescence: A theoretical and empirical integration. *Journal of Adolescent Research, 6*, 437–453.

BOECKMAN, C. (1979). Your health as you get older. *Dynamic Years, 14*, 24–27.

BOIVIN, M., & BEGIN, G. (1989). Peer status and self-perceptions among early elementary school children: The case of the rejected children. *Child Development, 60*, 571–579.

BOLDIZAR, J. P., PERRY, D. G., & PERRY, L. C. (1989). Outcomes, values and aggression. *Child Development, 60*, 591–596.

BOOTH, A., & AMATO, P. R. (1994). Parental marital quality, parental divorce, and relations with parents. *Journal of Marriage and the Family, 56*, 21–34.

BOOTH, A., & EDWARDS, J. N. (1985). Age at marriage and marital instability. *Journal of Marriage and the Family, 47*, 67–75.

BOOTH, C. L., RUBIN, K. H., & ROSE-KRASNOR, L. (1998). Perceptions of emotional support from mother and friends in middle childhood: Links with social-emotional adaptation and preschool attachment security. *Child Development, 69*, 427–442.

BORDERS, L. D., BLACK, L. K., & PASLEY, B. K. (1998). Are adopted children and their parents at greater risks for negative outcomes? *Family Relations, 47*, 237–241.

BORJA-ALVAREZ, T., ZARBATANY, L., & PEPPER, S. (1991). Contributions of male and female guests and hosts to peer group entry. *Child Development, 62*, 1079–1090.

BORNSTEIN, M. H. (1985a). How infant and mother jointly contribute to developing cognitive competence in the child. *Proceedings of the National Academy of Sciences of the U.S.A., 82*, 7470–7473.

BORNSTEIN, M. H. (1985b). Human infant color vision and color perception. *Infant Behavior and Development, 8*, 109–113.

BORNSTEIN, M. H. (1987). *Sensitive periods of development.* Hillsdale, NJ: Erlbaum.

BORNSTEIN, M. H., & HAYNES, O. M. (1998). Vocabulary competence in early childhood: Measurement, latent construct, & predictive validity. *Child Development, 69*, 654–671.

BORNSTEIN, M. H., & SIGMAN, M. D. (1986). Continuity in mental development from infancy. *Child Development, 57*, 251–274.

BORNSTEIN, M. H., TAL, J., RAHN, GALPERIN, C. Z., PECHEUX, M., LAMOUR, M., TODA, S., AZUMA, H., OGINO, M., & TAMIS-LEMONDA, C. S. (1992). Functional analysis of the contents of maternal speech to infants of 5 and 13 months in four cultures: Argentina, France, Japan, & the United States. *Developmental Psychology, 28*, 593–603.

BOROVSKY, D., & ROVEE-COLLIER, C. (1990). Contextual constraints on memory retrieval at six months. *Child Development, 61*, 1569–1583.

BORSTELMANN, L. J. (1983). Children before psychology: Ideas about children from antiquity to the late 1800s. In P. H. Mussen (Ed.), *Handbook of child psychology* (4th ed., Vol. 1). New York: Wiley.

BOSMAN, E. A. (1993). Age-related differences in the motoric aspects of transcription typing skill. *Psychology and Aging, 8*, 87–102.

BOSS, P. B. (1987). Family stress. In M. B. Sussman & S. K. Steinmetz (Eds.), *Handbook of marriage and the family* (pp. 695–723). New York: Plenum.

BOSSE, R., ALDWIN, C. M., LEVENSON, M. R., & WORKMAN-DANIELS, K. (1991). How stressful is retirement? Findings from the normative aging study. *Journal of Gerontology, 46*, P9–P14.

BOSTON WOMEN'S HEALTH BOOK COLLECTIVE. (1984). *The new our bodies, ourselves.* New York: Simon & Schuster.

BOTWINICK, J. (1967). *Cognitive processes in maturity and old age* (1st ed.). New York: Springer-Verlag.

BOTWINICK, J., & STORANDT, M. (1980). Recall and recognition of old information in relation to age and sex. *Journal of Gerontology, 35*, 70–76.

BOUCHARD, T. J., JR. (1984). Twins reared together and apart: What they tell us about human diversity. In S. W. Fox (Ed.), *Individuality and determinism: Chemical and biological bases* (pp. 147–184). New York: Plenum.

BOUCHARD, T. J., JR., & McGUE, M. (1981). Familial studies of intelligence: A review. *Science, 212*, 1055–1059.

BOULTON, M. J., & SMITH, P. K. (1990). Affective bias in children's perceptions of dominance relationships. *Child Development, 61*, 221–229.

BOUND, J., DUNCAN, G. J., LAREN, D. S., & OLEINICK, L. (1991). Poverty dynamics in widowhood. *Journal of Gerontology, 46*, S115–S124.

BOWLBY, J. (1969). *Attachment and loss: Vol. 1. Attachment.* London: Hogarth.

BOWLBY, J. (1971). *Child care and the growth of love.* Baltimore, MD: Pelican Books.

BOWLBY, J. (1973). *Attachment and loss: Vol. 2. Separation.* London: Hogarth.

BOWLBY, J. (1980). *Attachment and loss: Vol. 3. Loss, sadness, and depression.* London: Hogarth.

BOWLBY, J. (1982). *Attachment and loss: Vol. 1. Attachment* (2nd ed.). London: Hogarth.

BOWLES, N. L. (1994). Age and rate of accusation in semantic memory. *Psychology and Aging, 9,* 414–429.

BOWLING, A., & BROWNE, P. D. (1991). Social networks and emotional well-being among the oldest old in London. *Journal of Gerontology, 46,* S20–S32.

BOYER, D., & FINE, D. (1992). Sexual abuse as a factor in adolescent pregnancy and child maltreatment. *Family Planning Perspectives, 24,* 4–11.

BOZZI, V. (1985). Body talk. *Psychology Today, 19,* 20.

BOZZI, V. (1986). The stress alibi won't fly. *Psychology Today, 20,* 14.

BRAINE, L. G., SCHAUBLE, L., KUGELMASS, S., & WINTER, A. (1993). Representation of depth by children: Spatial strategies and lateral biases. *Developmental Psychology, 29,* 466–479.

BRAINERD, C. J., & REYNA, V. F., (1995). Learning rate, learning opportunities, and the development of forgetting. *Developmental Psychology, 31,* 251–262.

BRANCH, L. G., GURALNIK, J. M., FOLEY, D. J., KOHOUT, F. H., WETLE, T. T., OSTFELD, A., & KATZ, S. (1991). Active life expectancy for 10,000 Caucasian men and women in three communities. *Journal of Gerontology, 26,* M145–M150.

BRAUNGART, J. M., PLOMIN, R., DeFRIES, J. C., & FULKER, D. W. (1992). Genetic influence on tester-rated infant temperament as assessed by Bayley's infant behavior record: Nonadoptive and adoptive siblings and twins. *Developmental Psychology, 28,* 40–47.

BRAUNGART-RIEKER, J. M., & STIFTER, C. A. (1996). Infants' responses to frustrating situations: Continuity and change in reactivity and regulation. *Child Development, 67,* 1767–1779.

BRAVER, S. L., WOLCHIK, S. A., SANDLER, I. M., SHEETS, V. L., FOGAS, B., & BAY, R. C. (1993). A longitudinal study of noncustodial parents: Parents without children. *Journal of Family Psychology, 7,* 9–23.

BRAYFIELD, A. A. (1992). Employment resources and housework in Canada. *Journal of Marriage and the Family, 54,* 19–30.

BRAZELTON, T. B. (1974). *Toddlers and parents.* New York: Delacorte Press.

BRAZELTON, T. B. (1983). *Infants and mothers.* New York: Delacorte Press.

BRAZELTON, T. B. (1984). *Neonatal behavior assessment scale.* Philadelphia: Lippincott.

BRAZELTON, T. B. (1990). Saving the bathwater. *Child Development, 61,* 1661–1671.

BREADY, J. W. (1926). *Lord Shaftesbury and social industrial progress.* London: Allen & Unwin.

BRECHER, E. M. (1984). *Love, sex, and aging.* Boston: Little, Brown.

BREDEKAMP, S. (Ed.). (1987). *Developmentally appropriate practice* (pp. 50, 51). Washington, DC: National Association for the Education of Young Children.

BREEN, D. T., & CROSBIE-BURNETT, M. (1993). Moral dilemmas of early adolescents of divorced and intact families: A qualitative and quantitative analysis. *Journal of Early Adolescence, 13,* 168–182.

BRESLER, E. (1998). Women with too closely spaced pregnancies risk early delivery, especially if the first ends in a term birth. *Family Planning Perspectives, 30,* 252.

BRETHERTON, I. (1992). The origins of attachment theory: John Bowlby and Mary Ainsworth. *Developmental Psychology, 28,* 759–775.

BRETSCHNEIDER, J. G., & McCOY, N. L. (1988). Sexual interest and behavior in healthy 80- to 102-year-olds. *Archives of Sexual Behavior, 17,* 109–129.

BRIDGES, L. H., CONNELL, J. P., & BELSKY, J. (1988). Similarities and differences in infant-mother and infant-father interaction in the strange situation: A composite process analysis. *Developmental Psychology, 24,* 92–100.

BRINGLE, R. D., & BYERS, D. (1997). Intentions to seek marriage counseling. *Family Relations, 46,* 299–304.

BROBERG, A., LAMB, M. E., & HWANG, P. (1990). Inhibition: Its stability and correlates in sixteen- to forty-month-old children. *Child Development, 61,* 1153–1163.

BROCK, L. J., & JENNINGS, G. H. (1993). Sexuality education: What daughters in their thirties wish their mothers had told them. *Family Relations, 42,* 61–65.

BRODERICK, C. B. (1984). *Marriage and the Family* (2nd ed.). Englewood Cliffs, NJ: Prentice-Hall.

BRODSKY, M. A., & ALLEN, B. J. (1988). Stress-related sudden cardiac death. *Medical Aspects of Human Sexuality, 22,* 82–94.

BRODY, G. H., & FLOR, D. L. (1998). Maternal resources, parenting practices, and child competence in rural, single-parent African American families. *Child Development, 69,* 803–816.

BRODY, L., ZELAGO, P. R., & CHAIKE, M. (1984). Habituation-dishabituation to speech in the neonate. *Developmental Psychology, 20,* 114–119.

BRODZINSKY, D. M. (1985). On the relationship between cognitive styles and cognitive structures. In E. Neimark & R. DeLisi (Eds.), *Moderators of competence.* Hillsdale, NJ: Erlbaum.

BRODZINSKY, D., SCHECHTER, D., BRAFF, A., & SINGER, L. (1984). Psychological and academic adjustment in adopted children. *Journal of Consulting and Clinical Psychology, 52,* 582–590.

BRONE, R. J., & FISHER, C. B. (1988). Determinants of adolescent obesity: A comparison with anorexia nervosa. *Adolescence, 23,* 155–169.

BRONFENBRENNER, U. (1979). *The ecology of human development.* Cambridge, MA: Harvard University Press.

BRONFENBRENNER, U. (1987, August). *Recent advances in theory and design.* Paper presented at the meeting of the American Psychological Association, New York.

BRONSON, G. W. (1991). Infant differences in rate of visual encoding. *Child Development, 62,* 44–54.

BROOKS-GUNN, J., GUO, G., & FURSTENBERG, F. F., JR. (1993). Who drops out of and who continues beyond high school? A twenty-year follow-up of black, urban youth. *Journal of Research on Adolescence, 3,* 271–294.

BROUWERS, M. (1988). Depressive thought content among female college students with bulimia. *Journal of Counseling and Development, 66,* 425–428.

BROWN, A. L., BRANSFORD, J. D., FERRARA, R. A., & CHAMPIONE, J. C. (1983). Learning, remembering, and understanding. In P. H. Mussen (Ed.), *Handbook of child psychology* (4th ed., Vol. 3). New York: Wiley.

BROWN, A. S., & MITCHELL, D. B. (1991). Age differences in retrieval consistency and response dominance. *The Journals of Gerontology, 46,* P332–P339.

BROWN, J. D., NOVICK, N. J., LORD, K. A., & RICHARDS, J. M. (1992). When Gulliver travels: Social context, psychological closeness, and self appraisals. *Journal of Personality and Social Psychology, 62,* 717–727.

BROWN, J. E., & MANN, L. (1990). The relationship between family structure and process variables and adolescent decision making. *Journal of Adolescence, 13,* 25–38.

BROWN, J. E., & MANN, L. (1991). Decision-making competence and self-esteem: A comparison of parents and adolescents. *Journal of Adolescence, 14,* 363–371.

BROWN, J. R., & DUNN, J. (1992). Talking with your mother or your sibling? Developmental changes in early family conversations about feelings. *Child Development, 63,* 336–349.

BROWNE, C. S., & RIFE, J. C. (1991). Social, personality, and gender differences in at-risk and not-at-risk sixth-grade students. *Journal of Early Adolescence, 11,* 482–495.

BROWNELL, C. A. (1990). Peer social skills in toddlers: Competencies and constraints illustrated by same-age and mixed-age interaction. *Child Development, 61,* 838–848.

BROWNELL, C. A., & CARRIGER, M. S. (1990). Changes in cooperation and self-other differentiation during the second year. *Child Development, 61,* 1164–1174.

BROWNELL, K. D. (1988). Yo-yo dieting. *Psychology Today, 22,* 20–23.

BROWNELL, K. D. (1989). When and how to diet. *Psychology Today, 23,* 40–46.

BRYAN, J., & LUSZCZ, M. A. (1996). Speed of information processing as a mediator between age and free-recall performance. *Psychology and Aging, 11,* 3–9.

BRYANT, B. K. (1992). Conflict resolution strategies in relation to children's peer relations. *Journal of Applied Developmental Psychology, 13,* 35–50.

BUCHANAN, C. M. (1991). Pubertal status in early-adolescent girls: Relations to moods, energy, and restlessness. *Journal of Early Adolescence, 11,* 185–200.

BUCK, N., & SCOTT, J. (1993). She's leaving home: But why? An analysis of young people leaving the parental home. *Journal of Marriage and the Family, 55,* N63–N64.

BUGENTAL, D. B., BLUE, J., CORTEZ, V., FLECK, K., & RODRIGUES, A. (1992). Influences of witnessed affect on information processing in children. *Child Development, 63,* 774–786.

BUHLER, C. (1935). The curve of life as studied in biographies. *Journal of Applied Psychology, 19,* 405–409.

BUHLER, C., & MASSARIK, F. (1968). *The course of human life: A study of goals in the humanistic perspective.* New York: Springer.

BUHRMESTER, D. (1990). Intimacy of friendships, interpersonal competence, and adjustment during preadolescence and adolescence. *Child Development, 61,* 1101–1111.

BUHRMESTER, D., & FURMAN, W. (1987). The development of companionship and intimacy. *Child Development, 58,* 1101–1113.

BUHRMESTER, D., & FURMAN, W. (1990). Perceptions of sibling relationships during middle childhood and adolescence. *Child Development, 61,* 1387–1398.

BUKOWSKI, W. M., GAUZE, C., HOZA, B., & NEWCOMB, A. F. (1993). Differences and consistency between same-sex and other-sex peer relationships during early adolescence. *Developmental Psychology, 29,* 255–263.

BULCROFT, R. A., & BULCROFT, K. A. (1993). Race differences in attitudinal and motivational factors in their decision to marry. *Journal of Marriage and the Family, 55,* 338–355.

BULLOCK, J. R. (1993). Children's loneliness and their relationships with family and peers. *Family Relations, 42,* 46–49.

BULLOCK, M. (1985). Animism in childhood thinking: A new look at an old question. *Developmental Psychology, 21,* 217–225.

BUNCE, D. J., WARR, T. B., & COCHRAN, T. (1993). Blocks in choice responding as a function of age and physical fitness. *Psychology and Aging, 8,* 26–33.

BURKHAUSER, R. B., DUNCAN, G. J., & HAUSER, R. (1994). Sharing prosperity across the age distribution: A comparison of the United States and Germany in the 1980's. *The Gerontologist, 34,* 150–160.

BURLESON, B. R., DELLA, J. G., & APPLEGATE, J. L. (1992). Effects of maternal communication and children's social-cognitive and communication skills on children's acceptance by the peer group. *Family Relations, 41,* 264–272.

BURNS, P. A., PRANIKOFF, K., NOCHAJSKI, T. H., HADLEY, E. C., LEVY, K. J., & ORY, M. G. (1993). A comparison of the effectiveness of biofeedback and pelvic muscle exercise treatment of stress incontinence in older community-dwelling women. *Journal of Gerontology, 48,* M167–M174.

BURR, W. R., & CHRISTENSEN, C. (1992). Undesirable side effects of enhancing self-esteem. *Family Relations, 41,* 460–464.

BURT, C. (1993). Concentration and academic ability following a transition to university: An investigation of the effects of homesickness. *Journal of Environmental Psychology, 13,* 333–342.

BUS, A. B., & IJZENDOORN, M. H. (1988). Mother-child interaction, attachment, and emergent literacy: A cross-sectional study, *Child Development, 59,* 1262–1272.

BUSHNELL, E. W., MCKENZIE, B. E., LAWRENCE, D. A., & CONNELL, S. (1995). The special coding strategies of 1-year-old infants in a locomotor search task. *Child Development, 66,* 937–958.

BUSHNELL, H. (1988). *Christian nurture.* New Haven, CT: Yale University Press.

BUSS, A. H., & PERRY, M. (1992). The aggression questionnaire. *Journal of Personality and Social Psychology, 63,* 452–459.

BUSS, A. H., & PLOMIN, R. (1984). *Temperament: Early developing personality traits.* Hillsdale, NJ: Erlbaum.

BUSS, K. A., & GOLDSMITH, H. H. (1998). Fear and anger regulation in infancy: Effects on the temporal dynamics of an affective expression. *Child Development, 69,* 359–374.

BUSSEY, K. (1992). Lying and truthfulness: Children's definitions, standards, and evaluative reactions. *Child Development, 63,* 129–137.

BUTCHER, J. (1986). Longitudinal analysis of adolescent girls' aspirations at school and perceptions of popularity. *Adolescence, 21,* 133–143.

BUTLER, R. N. (1983, July/August). A generation at risk: When the baby boomers reach golden pond. *Across the Boards,* 37–45.

BUTLER, R. N. (1990). The effects of mastery and competitive conditions on self-assessment at different ages. *Child Development, 61,* 201–210.

BYRNES, J. P., TAKAHARA, S. (1993). Explaining gender differences on SAT-Math items. *Developmental Psychology, 29,* 805–810.

CADKIN, A., GINSBERG, N., PERGAMENT, E., & VERLINSKI, Y. (1984). Chorionic villi sampling: A new technique for detection of genetic abnormalities in the first trimester. *Radiology, 151,* 159–162.

CAGGIULA, A. R., & HOEBEL, B. G. (1966). Copulation-record site in the posterior hypothalamus. *Science, 153,* 1284–1285.

CAHAN, E. D. (1992). John Dewey and Human Development. *Developmental Psychology, 28,* 205–214.

CAIRNS, R. B., CAIRNS, B. D., & NECKERMAN, H. J. (1989). Early school dropout: Configuration and determinants. *Child Development, 60,* 1436–1452.

CAIRNS, R. B., CAIRNS, O. D., XIE, H., LEUNG, M-C., & HEARNE, S. (1998). Paths across generations: Academic competence and aggressive behaviors in young mothers and their children. *Developmental Psychology, 34,* 1162–1174.

CALDERONE, M. S. (1983). Fetal erection and its message to us. *SIECUS Report, II*(5/6), 9–16.

CALKINS, S. D., & FOX, N. A. (1992). The relations among infant temperament, security of attachment, and behavioral inhibition at twenty-four months. *Child Development, 63,* 1456–1472.

CALL, B., SPRECHER, S., & SCHWARTZ, P. (1995). The incidence and frequency of marital sex in a national sample. *Journal of Marriage and the Family, 67,* 639–652.

CALVERT, S. L., & COCKING, R. R. (1992). Health promotion through mass media. *Journal of Applied Developmental Psychology, 13,* 143–149.

CAMASSO, M. J., & ROCHE, S. E. (1991). The willingness to change to formalized child care arrangements: Parental considerations of cost and quality. *Journal of Marriage and the Family, 53,* 1071–1082.

CAMPBELL, F. A., & RAMEY, C. P. (1994). Effects of early intervention on intellectual and academic achievement: A follow-up study of children from low-income families. *Child Development, 65,* 684–698.

CAMPBELL, F. A., BREITMAYER, B., & RAMEY, C. T. (1986). Disadvantaged single teenage mothers and their children: Consequences of free educational day care. *Family Relations, 35,* 63–68.

CAMPBELL, M. L., & MOEN, P. (1992). Job-family role strain among employed, single mothers of preschoolers. *Family Relations, 41,* 205–211.

CAMPBELL, M. P., BUSH, T. L., & HALE, W. E. (1993). Medical conditions associated with driving cessation in the community-dwelling, ambulatory elders. *Journal of Gerontology, 48,* S230–S234.

CAMPOS, J., BARRETT, K. C., LAMB, M. E., GOLDSMITH, H., & STENBERG, C. (1983). Socioemotional development. In P. H. Mussen, M. M. Haith, & J. J. Campos (Eds.), *Handbook of child psychology: Vol. 2. Infancy and developmental psychobiology.* New York: Wiley.

CANAVAN, M. M., MEYER, W. J., III, & HIGGS, D. C. (1992). The family experience of sibling incest. *Journal of Marital and Family Therapy, 18,* 129–142.

CAPALDI, D. M., & CLARK, S. (1998). Prospective family predictors of aggression towards female partners or at-risk young men. *Developmental Psychology, 34,* 1175–1188.

CAPALDI, D. M., FORGATCH, M. S., & CROSBY, L. (1994). Affective expression in family problem-solving discussions with adolescent boys. *Journal of Adolescent Research, 9,* 28–49.

CAPELLI, C. A., NAKAGAWA, N., & MADDEN, C. M. (1990). How children understand sarcasm: The role of context and intonation. *Child Development, 61,* 1824–1841.

CAPLAN, F. (1973). *The first twelve months of life.* New York: Grosset & Dunlap.

CAPLAN, M., VESPO, J., PEDERSEN, J., & HAY, D. F. (1991). Conflict and its resolution in small groups of one- and two-year-olds. *Child Development, 62,* 1513–1524.

CARDON, L. R., FULKER, D. W., DEFRIES, J. C., & PLOMIN, R. (1992). Continuity and change in general cognitive ability from 1 to 7 years of age. *Developmental Psychology, 28,* 64–73.

CAREY, R. G., & POSAVAC, E. J. (1978–1979). Attitudes of physicians on disclosing information to and maintaining life for terminal patients. *Omega: Journal of Death and Dying, 9,* 67–77.

CARGAN, L. (1981). Singles: An examination of two stereotypes. *Family Relations, 30,* 377–385.

CARGAN, L., & MELKO, M. (1982). *Singles: Myths and realities.* Beverly Hills, CA: Sage.

CARLISTE, E. R. (1984, Fall). The effect of a twelve-week dropout intervention program. *Adolescence, 19,* 649–657.

CARLO, G., EISENBERG, N., & KNIGHT, G. P. (1992). An objective measure of adolescents' prosocial moral reasoning. *Journal of Research on Adolescence, 2,* 331–349.

CARLSON, M. (1996). *Childproof Internet: A Parent's Guide to Safe and Secure Online Access.* New York: Mis Press.

CARMINES, E. G., & BAXTER, D. J. (1986). Race, intelligence, and political efficacy among school children. *Adolescence, 22,* 437–442.

CARPENTER, B. D. (1993). A review and new look at ethical suicide in advanced age. *The Gerontologist, 33,* 359–365.

CARRUTH, B. R., & GOLDBERG, D. L. (1990). Nutritional issues of adolescents: Athletics and the body image mania. *Journal of Early Adolescence, 10,* 122–140.

CARSTENSEN, L. L. (1992). Social and emotional patterns in adulthood: Support for socioemotional selectivity theory. *Psychology and Aging, 7,* 331–338.

CARSTENSEN, L. L., GOTTMAN, J. M., & LEVENSON, R. W. (1995). Emotional behavior in long-term marriage. *Psychology and Aging, 10,* 140–149.

CARUSO, G.-A. L. (1992). Patterns of maternal employment and child care for a sample of two-year-olds. *Journal of Family Issues, 13,* 297–311.

CASAS, J. M., & PONTEROTTO, J. G. (1984, February). Profiling an invisible minority in higher education: The Chicano. *Personnel and Guidance Journal, 62,* 349–353.

CASEY, R. (1993). Children's emotional experience: Relations among expression, self-report, and understanding. *Developmental Psychology, 29,* 119–129.

CASH, T. F., & BUTTERS, J. W. (1988). Poor body image: Helping the patient to change. *Medical Aspects of Human Sexuality, 22,* 67–70.

CASH, T. F., & JANDA, L. H. (1984, December). The eye of the beholder. *Psychology Today, 18,* 46–52.

CASH, T. F., WINSTEAD, B. A., & JANDA, L. H. (1986). The great American shape-up. *Psychology Today, 20,* 30–37.

CASPI, A., HENRY, B., MCGEE, R. O., MOFFITT, T. E., & SILVA, P. A. (1995). Temperamental origins of child and adolescent behavior problems: From age three to age fifteen. *Child Development, 66,* 55–68.

CASPI, A., LYNAM, D., MOFFITT, T. E., & SILVA, P. A. (1993). Unraveling girls' delinquency: Biological, dispositional, and contextual contributions to adolescent misbehavior. *Developmental Psychology, 29,* 19–30.

CASSIDY, J., & ASHER, S. R. (1992). Loneliness and peer relations in young children. *Child Development, 63,* 350–365.

CASSIDY, J., PARKE, R. D., BUTKOVSKY, L., & BROAUNGART, J. M. (1992). Family-peer connections: The roles of emotional expressiveness within the family and children's understanding of emotions. *Child Development, 63,* 603–618.

CATES, W., JR., & STONE, K. M. (March/April 1992a). Family planning, sexually transmitted diseases and contraceptive choice: A literature update—Part I. *Family Planning Perspectives, 24,* 75–84.

CATES, W., JR., & STONE, K. M. (May/June 1992b). Family planning, sexually transmitted diseases and contraceptive choice: A literature update—Part II. *Family Planning Perspectives, 24,* 122–128.

CATHERWOOD, D. (1993). The robustness of infant haptic memory: Testing its capacity to withstand delay and haptic interference. *Child Development, 64,* 702–710.

CATTELL, R. B. (1963). Theory of fluid and crystallized intelligence: A critical experiment. *Journal of Educational Psychology, 54,* 1–22.

CENTER FOR SCIENCE IN THE PUBLIC INTEREST. Copyright 1998 CSPI. Reprinted/Adapted from *Nutrition Action Healthletter* (1875 Connecticut Ave., N.W., Suite 300, Washington, DC 20009-5728. $24.00 for 10 issues.).

CERNOCH, J. M., & PORTER, R. H. (1985). Recognition of maternal axillary odors by infants. *Child Development, 56,* 1593–1598.

CHAMBRE, S. M. (1993). Volunteerism by elders: Past trends and future prospects. *The Gerontologist, 33,* 221–228.

CHAN, R. W., RABOY, B., & PATTERSON, C. J. (1998). Psychosocial adjustments among children conceived via donor insemination by lesbians and heterosexual mothers. *Child Development, 69,* 443–457.

CHANCE, P. (1988). Testing education. *Psychology Today, 22,* 20–21.

CHANCE, P. (1989). Kids without friends. *Psychology Today, 23,* 29–31.

CHANDRA, A., & STEPHEN, E. H. (1998). Impaired fecundity in the United States: 1982–1995. *Family Planning Perspectives, 30,* 34–42.

CHARLESWORTH, W. R. (1992). Darwin and developmental psychology: Past and present. *Developmental Psychology, 28,* 5–16.

CHASE-LANSDALE, P. L., & OWEN, M. T. (1987). Maternal employment in a family context: Effects on infant-mother and infant-father attachments. *Child Development, 58,* 1505–1512.

CHASNOFF, I. J., BURNS, W. J., SCHNOLL, S. H., & BURNS, K. A. (1985). Cocaine use in pregnancy. *New England Journal of Medicine, 313,* 666–669.

CHEAL, D. (1993). Unity and difference in postmodern families. *Journal of Family Issues, 14,* 5–19.

CHEN, H., ASHTON-MILLER, J. A., ALEXANDER, N. B., & SCHULTZ, A. B. (1991). Stepping over obstacles: Gait patterns of healthy young and old adults. *The Journals of Gerontology, 46,* M196–M203.

CHEN, X., RUBIN, K. H., & SUN, Y. (1992). Social reputation and peer relationships in Chinese and Canadian children: A cross cultural study. *Child Development, 63,* 1336–1343.

CHEN, Y. (1987). Making assets out of tomorrow's elderly. *The Gerontologist, 27,* 410–417.

CHERLIN, A. J., SCABINI, E., & ROSSI, G. (1997). Still in the nest. *Journal of Family Issues, 18,* 572–575.

CHERLIN, A., & FURSTENBERG, F. F., JR. (1986). *The new American grandparent.* New York: Basic Books.

CHERLIN, A., & MCCARTHY, J. (1985). Remarried couple households: Data from the June 1980 current population survey. *Journal of Marriage and the Family, 47,* 23–30.

CHERRY, K. E., & PARK, D. C. (1989). Age-related differences in three-dimensional spatial memory. *Journal of Gerontology, 44,* 16–22.

CHESS, S., & THOMAS, A. (1986). *Temperament in clinical practice.* New York: Guilford.

CHIAM, H. (1987). Changes in self-concept during adolescence. *Adolescence, 16,* 613–620.

CHILDERS, J. S., DURHAM, R. W., BOLEN, L. M., & TAYLOR, L. H. (1985). A predictive validity study of the Kaufman Assessment Battery for children taking the California Achievement Test. *Psychology in the Schools, 22,* 29–33.

CHILDREN'S DEFENSE FUND (1988). *A children's defense budget.* Washington, DC: Children's Defense Fund.

CHILMAN, C. S. (1990). Promoting healthy adolescent sexuality. *Family Relations, 39,* 123–131.

CHILMAN, C. S. (1991). Working poor families: Trends, causes, effects, & suggested policies. *Family Relations, 40,* 191–198.

CHIPUER, H. M., PLOMIN, R., PERSENSEN, N. L., MCCLEARN, G. E., & NESSELROADE, J. R. (1993). Genetic influence on family environment: The role of personality. *Developmental Psychology, 29,* 110–118.

CHIRA, S. (1984, February 11). Town experiment cuts TV. *New York Times.*

CHIRIBOGA, D. A. (1978). Evaluated time: A life course perspective. *Journal of Gerontology, 33,* 388–393.

CHIU, L. H. (1990). The relationship of career goal and self-esteem among adolescents. *Adolescence, 25,* 593–598.

CHOLLAR, S. (1988a, April). Older brains don't fade away. *Psychology Today, 22,* 22.

CHOLLAR, S. (1988b, April). Food for thought. *Psychology Today, 22,* 30–34.

CHOLLAR, S. (1988c, December). Stuttering: The parental influence. *Psychology Today, 22,* 12–16.

CHOMSKY, N. (1968). *Language and mind.* New York: Harcourt, Brace, World.

CHOMSKY, N. (1980). *Rules and representations.* New York: Columbia University Press.

CHRISCHILLES, E. A., et al. (1992). Use of medications by persons sixty-five and older: Data from the established populations for epidemiologic studies of the elderly. *The Journals of Gerontology, 47,* M137–M144.

CHRISTENSEN, H., MACKINNON, A., JORN, A. F., HENDERSON, A. S., SCOTT, L. R., & KORTEN, A. E. (1994). The differences and interindividual variation in cognition in community-dwelling elderly. *Psychology and Aging, 9,* 381–390.

CHRISTENSEN, K. J., MOYE, J., ARMSON, R. R., & KERN, T. M. (1992). Health screening and random recruitment for cognitive aging research. *Psychology and Aging*, 7, 204–208.

CHRISTMON, K. (1990). Parental responsibility of African-American unwed adolescent fathers. *Adolescence*, 25, 645–654.

CHRISTOPHER, F. S. (1988). An initial investigation into a continuum of premartial sexual pressure. *Journal of Sex Research*, 25, 255–266.

CHRISTOPHER, F. S., & ROOSA, M. W. (1990). An evaluation of an adolescent pregnancy prevention program: Is "Just say no" enough? *Family Relations*, 39, 73–80.

CHRISTOPHER, F. S., FABES, R. A., & WILSON, P. M. (1989). Family television viewing and implications for family life education. *Family Relations*, 38, 210–214.

CHUGANI, H. T., & PHELPS, M. E. (1986). Maturational changes in cerebral function in infants determined by FFG positron emission tomography. *Science*, 231, 840–843.

CHUN, P. K. L. (1988). Angina pectoris. *Medical Aspects of Human Sexuality*, 22, 65–66.

CICIRELLI, V. G. (1997). Relationship to psychosocial and background variables to older adults' end-of-life decisions. *Psychology and Aging*, 12, 72–83.

CILLESSEN, A. H. N., VAN IJZENDOORN, H. W., VAN LIESHOUT, C. F. M., & HARTUP, W. W. (1992). Heterogeneity among peer-rejected boys: Subtypes and stabilities. *Child Development*, 63, 893–905.

CLAES, M. E. (1992). Friendship and personal adjustment during adolescence. *Journal of Adolescence*, 15, 39–55.

CLANCY, S. M., & DOLLINGER, S. J. (1993). Identity, self, and personality: Identity status and the five-factor model of personality. *Journal of Research on Adolescence*, 3, 227–245.

CLARK, A. J. (1991). The identification and modification of defense mechanisms in counseling. *Journal of Counseling and Development*, 69, 231–235.

CLARK, D. O., & MADDOX, G. L. (1992). Racial and social correlates of age-related changes in functioning. *Journal of Gerontology*, 47, S222–S232.

CLARK, E. V., GELMAN, S. A., & LANE, N. M. (1985). Compound nouns and category structure in young children. *Child Development*, 56, 84–94.

CLARK, M. (1980). The poetry of aging: Views of old age in contemporary American poetry. *Gerontologist*, 20, 188–191.

CLARK, M. L., & AYERS, M. (1993). Friendship expectations and friendship evaluations. Reciprocity and gender effects. *Youth and Society*, 24, 299–313.

CLARK, M. L., CHEYNE, J. A., CUNNINGHAM, C. E., & SIEGEL, L. S. (1988). *Journal of Abnormal Child Psychology*, 16, 1–15.

CLARK, R., HYDE, J. S., ESSEX, M. J., & KLEIN, M. H. (1997). Length of maternity leave and quality of mother-infant interactions. *Child Development*, 68, 364–383.

CLARK-LEMPERS, D. S., LEMPERS, J. D., & HO, C. (1991). Early, middle, and late adolescents' perceptions of their relationships with significant others. *Journal of Adolescent Research*, 6, 296–315.

CLARK-NICOLAS, P., & GRAY-LITTLE, B. (1991). Effect of economic resources on marital quality and black married couples. *Journal of Marriage and the Family*, 53, 645–655.

CLAXTON-OLDFIELD, S. (1992). Perceptions of stepfathers. *Journal of Family Issues*, 13, 378–389.

CLEMENS, A. W., & AXELSON, L. J. (1985). The not-so-empty nest: The return of the fledgling adult. *Family Relations*, 34, 259–264.

CLINGENPEEL, W. G., COLYAR, J. Y., BRAND, E., & HETHERINGTON, E. M. (1992). Children's relationships with maternal grandparents: A longitudinal study of family structure and pubertal status effects. *Child Development*, 63, 1404–1422.

COATES, D. L., & LEWIS, M. (1984). Early mother-infant interaction and infant cognitive status as predictors of school performance and cognitive behavior in six-year-olds. *Child Development*, 55, 1219–1230.

COCKBURN, J., & SMITH, P. T. (1991). The relative influence of intelligence and age on everyday memory. *Journal of Gerontology*, 46, P31–P36.

COFFMAN, S., LEVITT, M. J., DEETS, C., & QUIGLEY, K. L. (1991). Close relationships in mothers of distressed and normal newborns: Support, expectancy, confirmation, and maternal well-being. *Journal of Family Psychology*, 5, 93–107.

COHEN, D., EISDORFER, C., GORELICK, P., PAVEZA, G, LUCHINS, B. J., FREELS, S., ASHFORD, J. W., SEMLA, T., LEVY, P., & HIRSCHMAN, R. (1993). Psychopathology associated with Alzeimer's Disease and related disorders. *Journal of Gerontology*, 48, M255–M260.

COHEN, S. TYRELL, D. A. J., & SMITH, A. P. (1993). Negative life events, perceived stress, negative affect, and susceptibility of the common cold. *Journal of Personality and Social Psychology*, 64, 131–140.

COIE, J. D., & DODGE, K. A. (1988). Multiple sources of data on social behavior and social status in the school: A cross-age comparison. *Child Development*, 59, 815–829.

COIE, J. D., DODGE, K. A., TERRY, R., & WRIGHT, B. (1991). The role of aggression in peer relations: An analysis of aggression episodes in boys' playgroups. *Child Development*, 62, 812–826.

COK, F. (1990). Body image satisfaction in Turkish adolescents. *Adolescence*, 25, 409–414.

COKE, M. M. (1992). Correlates of life satisfaction among elderly African Americans. *The Journals of Gerontology*, 47, P316–P320.

COLANTONIO, A., KASL, S. B., OSTFELD, A. M., & BERKMAN, L. F. (1993). Psychosocial predictors of stroke outcomes in an elderly population. *Journal of Gerontology*, 48, S261–S268.

COLE, D. (1988). Grief lessons: His and hers. *Psychology Today*, 22, 60–61.

COLE, J. W. (1990). *Human Anatomy and Physiology*, 5th ed. Dubuque, IA: Wm. C. Brown Co.

COLE, P. M., BARRETT, K. C., & ZAHN-WAXLER, C. (1992). Emotion displays in two-year-olds during mishaps. *Child Development*, 63, 314–324.

COLE, P. M., ZAHN-WAXLER, C., & SMITH, K. D., (1994). Expressive control during a disappointment: Variations related to preschoolers' behavior problems. *Developmental Psychology*, 30, 835–846.

COLEMAN, M., & GANONG, L. H. (1990). Remarriage and step-family research in the 1980s: Increased interest in an old family form. *Journal of Marriage and the Family*, 52, 925–940.

COLEMAN, M., GANONG, L. H., CLARK, J. M., & MADSEN, R. (1989). Parenting perceptions in rural and urban families. *Journal of Marriage and the Family*, 51, 329–335.

COLL, C. T. G. (1990). Developmental outcome of minority infants: A process-oriented look into our beginnings. *Child Development*, 61, 270–289.

COLLEGE ENTRANCE EXAMINATION BOARD (Annual, 1967–1997). *National College-Bound Senior.*

COLOMBO, J. MITCHELL, D. W., COLDREN, J. T., & FREESEMAN, L. J. (1991). Individual differences in infant visual attention: Are short lookers faster processors or feature processors? *Child Development*, 62, 1247–1257.

COMMUNICABLE DISEASE SUMMARY (1985, November). *AIDS update* (Vol. 34, pp. 1–3). Oregon Health Division.

CONNELL, J. P., HALPERN-FELSHER, B. L., CLIFFORD, E., CRICHLOW, W., & USINGER, P. (1995). Hanging in there: Behavioral, psychological, and contextual factors affecting whether African American adolescents stay in high school. *Journal of Adolescent Research*, 10, 41–63.

CONNIDIS, I. A., & DAVIES, L. (1990). Confidants and companions in later life: The place of family and friends. *Journal of Gerontology*, 45, S141–S149.

CONNIDIS, I. A., & MCMULLIN, J. A. (1993). To have or have not: Parent status and the subjective well-being of older men and women. *The Gerontologist*, 33, 630–636.

COOK, K. V., REILEY, K. L., STALLSMITH, R., & GARRETSON, H. B. (1991). Eating concerns on two Christian and two nonsectarian college campuses: A measure of sex and campus differences in attitudes toward eating. *Adolescence*, 26, 273–286.

COOKE, R. A. (1982). The ethics and regulation of research involving children. In B. B. Wolman (Ed.), *Handbook of developmental psychology*. Englewood Cliffs, NJ: Prentice-Hall.

COOMBS, R. H., & LANDSVERK, J. (1988). Parenting styles and substance use during childhood and adolescence. *Journal of Marriage and the Family*, 50, 473–482.

COONEY, T. M. (1993). Timing of fatherhood: Is "on-time" optimal? *Journal of Marriage and the Family*, 55, 205–215.

COONEY, T. M. (1994). Young adult's relations with parents: The influence of recent parental divorce. *Journal of Marriage and the Family*, 56, 45–56.

COONEY, T. M., & Uhlenberg, P. (1989). Family-building patterns of professional women: A comparison of lawyers, physicians, and postsecondary teachers. *Journal of Marriage and the Family*, 51, 749–758.

COOPER, D. A., WARD, M., GOWLAND, C. A., & McINTOSH, J. M. (1991). The use of the Lanthony new color test in determining the effects of aging on color vision. *The Journals of Gerontology, 46,* P320–P324.

COOPER, K. L., & GUTMANN, D. L. (1987). Gender identity and ego mastery style in middle-aged pre- and post-empty nest women. *Gerontologist, 27,* 347–352.

COOPER, R. P., & ASLIN, R. N. (1990). Preference for infant-directed speech in the first month after birth. *Child Development, 61,* 1584–1595.

COOPER, R. P., & ASLIN, R. N. (1994). Developmental differences in infant attention to the spectral properties of infant-directed speech. *Child Development, 65,* 1663–1677.

COOPERSMITH, S., & GILBERTS, R. (1982). *BASE: Behavioral Academic Self-Esteem.* Palo Alto, CA: Consulting Psychologists Press.

COREN, S., & HALPERN, D. F. (1991). Left-handedness: A marker for decreased survival fitness. *Psychological Bulletin, 109,* 90–106.

CORNELIUS, S. W. (1984). Classic pattern of intellectual aging: Test familiarity, difficulty, and performance. *Journal of Gerontology, 39,* 201–206.

CORTER, C. M. (1976, September). The nature of the mother's absence and the infant's response to brief separations. *Developmental Psychology, 12,* 428–434.

CORWIN, J., LOURY, N., & GILBERT, A. M. (1995). Work place, age, and sex as mediators of olfactory function: Data from the National Geographic Smell Survey. *Journal of Gerontology, 50B,* P179–P186.

COSTA, F. M., JESSOR, R., & DONOVAN, J. E. (1995). Early initiation of sexual intercourse: The influence of psychosocial unconventiality. *Journal of Research on Adolescence, 5,* 93–121.

COSTA, P. P., ZONDERMAN, A. B., McCRAE, R. R., CORNONI-HUNTLEY, J., LOCKE, B. Z., & BARBANO, H. E. (1987). Longitudinal analysis of psychological well-being in a national sample: Stability of mean levels. *Journal of Gerontology, 42,* 50–55.

COTRELL, V., & SCHULZ, R. (1993). The perspective of the patient with Alzheimer's Disease: A neglected dimension of dementia research. *The Gerontologist, 33,* 405–211.

COTTERELL, J. L. (1992a). The relation of attachments and supports to adolescent well-being and school adjustment. *Journal of Adolescent Research, 7,* 28–42.

COTTERELL, J. L. (1992b). School size as a factor in adolescents' adjustment to the transition to secondary school. *Journal of Early Adolescence, 12,* 28–45.

COUCH POTATO PHYSIQUE. (1989). *Psychology Today, 23,* 8.

THE COURT EDGES AWAY FROM ROE V. WADE. (1989). *Family Planning Perspectives, 21,* 184–187.

COVERMAN, S., & SHELEY, J. F. (1986). Change in men's housework and child-care time, 1965–1975. *Journal of Marriage and the Family, 48,* 413–422.

COX, M. J., OWEN, M. T., HENDERSON, V. K., & MARGAND, N. A. (1992). Prediction of infant-father and infant-mother attachment. *Developmental Psychology, 28,* 474–483.

COYNE, J. C., & SMITH, D. A. F. (1994). Couples coping with myocardial infarction: Contextual perspective on patient self-efficacy. *Journal of Family Psychology, 8,* 43–54.

COYSH, W. S., JOHNSTON, J. R., TSCHANN, J. M., WALLERSTEIN, J. S., & KLINE, M. (1989). Parental postdivorce adjustment in joint and sole physical custody families. *Journal of Family Issues, 10,* 52–71.

CRAIN-THORESON, C., & DALE, P. S. (1992). Do early talkers become early readers? Linguistic precocity, preschool language, and emergent literacy. *Developmental Psychology, 28,* 421–439.

CRAMER, P., & STEINWERT, T. (1998). Thin is good, fat is bad: How early does it begin? *Journal of Applied Developmental Psychology, 19,* 429–451.

CREASEY, G., & REESE, M. (1996). Mothers' and fathers' perceptions of parenting hassles: Association with psychological symptoms, nonparenting hassles, and child behavior problems. *Journal of Applied Developmental Psychology, 17,* 393–406.

CREIGHTON, L. L. (1990, October 8). The new orphanages. *U.S. News and World Report,* 37–41.

CRESPI, T. D., & SABATELLI, R. M. (1993). Adolescent runaways and family strife: A conflict-induced differentiation framework. *Adolescence, 28,* 867–878.

CRICK, N. R., & GROTPETER, J. K. (1995). Relational aggression, gender, and social-psychological adjustment. *Child Development, 66,* 710–722.

CRICK, N. R., & LADD, G. W. (1993). Children's perceptions of their peer experiences: Attributions, loneliness, social anxiety, and social avoidance. *Developmental Psychology, 29,* 244–254.

CRNIC, K. A., & BOOTH, C. L. (1991). Mothers' and fathers' perceptions of daily hassles of parenting across early childhood. *Journal of Marriage and the Family, 53,* 1042–1050.

CRNIC, K. A., & GREENBERG, M. T. (1990). Minor parenting stresses with young children. *Child Development, 61,* 1628–1637.

CROCKER, J., CORNWELL, B., & MAJOR, B. (1993). The stigma of overweight: Affective consequences of attributional ambiguity. *Journal of Personality and Social Psychology, 64,* 60–70.

CROFT, C. A., & ASMUSSEN, L. (1992). Perception of mothers, youth, and educators: A path towards detente regarding sexuality education. *Family Relations, 41,* 452–459.

CROOK, T. H., III, & LARRABEE, G. J. (1992). Changes in facial recognition memory across the adult life span. *The Journals of Gerontology, 47,* P138–P141.

CROW, L. D., & CROW, H. (1965). *Adolescent development and adjustment* (2nd ed.). New York: McGraw-Hill.

CROWN, W. H. (1985). Some thoughts on reformulating the dependency ratio. *Gerontologist, 25,* 166–171.

CRUM, C., & ELLNER, P. (1985). Chlamydial infections: Making the diagnosis. *Contemporary Obstetrics and Gynecology, 25,* 153–159, 163, 165, 168.

CRYSTAL, D. S., CHEN, C., FULIGNI, A. J., STEVENSON, H. W., HSU, C., KO, H. J., KITAMURA, S., & KIMURA, S. (1994). Psychological maladjustment and academic achievement: A cross-cultural study of Japanese, Chinese, and American high school students. *Child Development, 65,* 738–753.

CSPI, *Fast Food Eating Guide* (1991). Washington, DC: Center for Science in the Public Interest.

CUETO, S., JACOBY, E., & POLLITT, E. (1998). Breakfast prevents delays of attention and memory functions among nutritionally at-risk boys. *Journal of Applied Developmental Psychology, 19,* 219–233.

CULP, R. E., CULP, A. M., OSOFSKY, J. D., & OSOFSKY, H. J. (1991). Adolescent and older mothers' interaction patterns with their six-month-old infants. *Journal of Adolescence, 14,* 195–200.

CUMMINGS, E. M. (1987). Coping with background anger in early childhood. *Child Development, 58,* 976–984.

CUMMINGS, E. M., IANNOTTI, R. J., & ZAHN-WAXLER, C. (1989). Aggression between peers in early childhood: Individual continuity and developmental change. *Child Development, 60,* 887–895.

CUMMINGS, E., & HENRY, W. (1961). *Growing old: The process of disengagement.* New York: Basic Books.

CUMMINS, J. (1986). Empowering minority students: A framework for intervention. *Harvard Education Review, 56,* 18–36.

CUMMINS, J., & SWAIN, M. (1986). *Bilingualism in education: Aspects of theory, research, and practice.* London: Taylor & Fry.

CUNLIFFE, T. (1992). Arresting youth crime: A review of social skills training with young offenders. *Adolescence, 27,* 891–900.

CURTIS, S. (1977). *Genie: A psychological study of a modern-day "wild child."* New York: Academic Press.

CUTLER, S. J., & GRAMS, A. E. (1988). Correlates of self-reported everyday memory problems. *Journal of Gerontology, 43,* S82–S90.

CUTLER, W. B., GARCIA, C. R., & McCOY, N. (1987). Perimenopausal sexuality. *Archives of Sexual Behavior, 16,* 225–234.

D'ODORICO, L., & FRANCO, F. (1985). The determinants of baby talk: Relationships and context. *Journal of Child Language, 12,* 567–586.

DAINTON, M. (1993). The myth and misconceptions of the stepmother identity. Descriptions and prescriptions for identity management. *Family Relations, 42,* 93–98.

DAMON, W. (1983). *Social and personality development.* New York: W. W. Norton.

DANIELS, D., & MOOS, R. H. (1990). Assessing life stressors and social resources among adolescents: Applications to depressed youth. *Journal of Adolescent Research, 5,* 268–289.

DANIELS, J. A. (1990). Adolescent separation-individuation and family transitions. *Adolescence, 25,* 105–116.

DANILUK, J. C. (1991). Strategies for counseling infertile couples. *Journal of Counseling and Development, 69,* 317–320.

DARLING-FISHER, C. S., & TIEDJE, L. B. (1990). The impact of maternal employment characteristics on fathers' participation in child care. *Family Relations, 39,* 20–26.

DARMODY, J. P. (1991). The adolescent personality, formal reasoning, and values. *Adolescence, 26,* 731–742.

DARWIN, C. A. (1877). A biographical sketch of an infant. *Mind, 2,* 285–294.

DARWIN, C. A. (1936). *On the origin of species.* New York: Modern Library. (Original work published in 1859.)

DATAN, N., RODEHEAVER, D., & HUGHES, F. (1987). Adult development and aging. *Annual Review of Psychology, 38,* 153–180.

DAVIDSON, S. (1983). Proliferating POSSLQ. *Psychology Today, 17,* 84.

DAVIES, C. T., & CUMMNINGS, E. M. (1998). Exploring children's emotional security as a mediator of the link between marital relations and child adjustment. *Child Development, 69,* 124–139.

DAVIS, M., & EMORY, E. (1995). Sex differences in neonatal stress reactivity. *Child Development, 66,* 14–27.

DAVIS-BROWN, K. & SALAMON, S. (1987). Farm families in crisis: An application of stress theory to farm family research. *Family Relations, 36,* 368–373.

DAWSON, D. A. (1991). Family structure and children's health and well-being: Data from the 1988 National Health Interview Survey on child health. *Journal of Marriage and the Family, 53,* 573–584.

DAWSON, G., MELTZOFF, A. N., OSTERLING, J., & RINALDI, J. (1998). Neuropsychological correlates of early symptoms of autism. *Child Development, 69,* 1276–1285.

DAY, R. D, PETERSON, G. W., & MCCRACKEN, C. (1998). Predicting spanking of younger and older children by mothers and fathers. *Journal of Marriage and the Family, 60,* 79–94.

DEAL, J. E., HALVERSON, C. F., & WAMPLER, K. S. (1989). Parental agreement on child-rearing orientations: Relations to parental, marital, family, and child characteristics. *Child Development, 60,* 1025–1034.

DEBOLT, M. E., PASLEY, B. K., & KREUTZER, J. (1990). Factors affecting the probability of school dropout: A study of pregnant and parenting adolescent females. *Journal of Adolescent Research, 5,* 190–205.

DECASPER, A., & FIFER, W. (1980). Newborns prefer their mothers' voices. *Science, 208,* 1174–1176.

DECASPER, A. J., & SPENCE, M. J. (1986). Prenatal maternal speech influences newborns' reception of speech sounds. *Infant Behavior and Development, 9,* 133–150.

DEFRAIN, J. (1991). Learning about grief from normal families: SIDS, stillbirth, and miscarriage. *Journal of Marriage and Family Therapy, 17,* 215–232.

DEGRAAF, C., POLET, P., & VAN STAVEREN, W. A. (1994). Censured perception and pleasantness of food flavors in elderly subjects. *Journal of Gerontology, 49,* P93–P99.

DEHAAN, N., & NELSON, C. A. (1997). Recognition of the mother's face by six-month-old infants: A neurobehavioral study. *Child Development, 68,* 187, 210.

DEKOVIC, M., & GERRIS, J. R. M. (1992). Parental reasoning complexity, social class, and child-rearing behaviors. *Journal of Marriage and the Family, 54,* 675–685.

DEKOVIC, M., & GERRIS, J. R. M. (1994). Developmental analysis of social cognitive and behavioral differences between popular and rejected children. *Journal of Applied Developmental Psychology, 15,* 367–386.

DEKOVIC, M., & JANSSENS, J. M. A. M. (1992). Parents' child-rearing style and child's sociometric status. *Developmental Psychology, 28,* 925–932.

DELISI, R., & STAUDT, J. (1980). Individual differences in college students' performance on formal operational tasks. *Journal of Applied Developmental Psychology, 1,* 201–208.

DELLAS, M., & JERNIGAN, L. P. (1990). Affective personality characteristics associated with undergraduate ego identity formation. *Journal of Adolescent Research, 5,* 306–324.

DELOACHE, J. S. (1991). Symbolic functioning in very young children: Understanding of pictures and models. *Child Development, 62,* 736–752.

DEMARIE-DREBLOW, D. (1991). Relation between knowledge and memory: A reminder that correlation does not imply causality. *Child Development, 62,* 484–498.

DEMARIE-DREBLOW, D., & MILLER, P. H. (1988). The development of children's strategies for selective attention: Evidence for a transitional period. *Child Development, 59,* 1504–1513.

DEMARIS, A., & RAO, K. V. (1992). Premarital cohabitation and subsequent marital stability in the United States: A reassessment. *Journal of Marriage and the Family, 54,* 178–190.

DEMBO, R., DERTKE, M., LAVOIE, L., BORDERS, S., WASHBURN, M., & SCHMEIDLER, J. (1987). Physical abuse, sexual victimization and illicit drug use: A structural analysis among high risk adolescents. *Journal of Adolescence, 10,* 13–33.

DEMO, D. H. (1992). Parent-child relations: Assessing recent changes. *Journal of Marriage and the Family, 54,* 104–117.

DEMO, D. H., & ACOCK, A. C. (1988). The impact of divorce on children. *Journal of Marriage and the Family, 50,* 619–648.

DEMO, D. H., SMALL, S. A., & SAVIN-WILLIAMS, R. C. (1987). Family relations and the self-esteem of adolescents and their parents. *Journal of Marriage and the Family, 49,* 705–715.

DEMOS, V., & JACHE, A. (1981). When you care enough: An analysis of attitudes toward aging in humorous birthday cards. *Gerontologist, 21,* 209–215.

DEMPSTER, F. N. (1981). Memory span: Sources of individual and developmental differences. *Psychological Bulletin, 80,* 63–100.

DENHAM, S. A., & HOLT, R. W. (1993). Preschoolers likeability as cause or consequence of their social behavior. *Developmental Psychology, 29,* 271–275.

DENHAM, S. A., MCKINLEY, M., COUEHOUD, E. Z., & HOLT, R. (1990). Emotional and behavioral predictors of preschool peer ratings. *Child Development, 61,* 1145–1152.

DENHAM, S. A., RENWICK, S. M., & HOLT, R. W. (1991). Working and playing together: Prediction of preschool social-emotional competence from mother-child interaction. *Child Development, 62,* 242–249.

DENHAM, T. E., & SMITH, C. W. (1989). The influence of grandparents and grandchildren: A review of the literature and resources. *Family Relations, 38,* 345–350.

DENNEY, N. W., & PALMER, A. M. (1981). Adult age differences on traditional and practical problem-solving measures. *Journal of Gerontology, 36,* 323–328.

DENNEY, N. W., MILLER, B. V., DEW, J. R., & LEVAV, A. L. (1991). An adult developmental study of contextual memory. *Journal of Gerontology, 46,* P44–P50.

DENNEY, N. W., TOZIER, T. L., & SCHLOTTHAUER, C. A. (1992). The effect of instructions on age differences in practical problem solving. *The Journals of Gerontology, 47,* P142–P145.

DENNIS, W. (1966). Creative productivity between the ages of 20 and 80 years. *Journal of Gerontology, 21.*

DENTON, R. E., & KAMPFE, C. N. (1994). The relationship between family variables and adolescent substance abuse: A literature review. *Adolescence, 29,* 475–495.

DEPNER, C. E., & BRAY, J. H., (1990). Modes of participation for non-custodial parents: The challenge for research, policy, practice and education. *Family Relations, 39,* 379–381.

DEROSENROLL, D. A. (1987). Creativity and self-trust: A field of study. *Adolescence, 22,* 419–432.

DEROSIER, M. E., CILLESSEN, A. H. M., COIE, J. D., & DODGE, K. A. (1994). Group social context in children's aggressive behavior. *Child Development, 65,* 1068–1079.

DEROSIER, M. E., KUPERSMIDT, J. B., & PATTERSON, C. J. (1994). Children's academics and behavioral adjustment as a function of the chronicity and proximity of peer rejection. *Child Development, 65,* 1799–1813.

DEUTSCHER, I. (1964). The qualities of postparental life: Definitions of the situation. *Journal of Marriage and the Family, 26,* 52–59.

DIAMOND, A. M. (1986). The life-cycle research productivity of mathematicians and scientists. *Journal of Gerontology, 41,* 520–525.

DIBLASIO, F. A., & BENDA, B. B. (1990). Adolescent sexual behavior: Multivariate analysis of a social learning model. *Journal of Adolescent Research, 5,* 449–466.

DICKERSON, A. E., & FISHER, A. G. (1997). Effects of familiarity of tasks and choice on the functional performance of younger and older adults. *Psychology and Aging, 12,* 247–254.

DICKSTEIN, S., & PARKE, R. D. (1988). Social referencing in infancy: A glance at fathers and marriage. *Child Development, 59,* 506–511.

DIETZ, W. H., & GORTMACHER, S. L. (1985). Do we fatten our children at the television set? Obesity and television watching in children and adolescents. *Pediatrics, 75,* 807–812.

DILL, D., FELD, E., MARTIN, J., BEUKEMA, S., & BELLE, D. (1980). The impact of the environment on the coping effects of low-income mothers. *Family Relations, 29,* 503–509.

DINGES, M. M., & OETTING, E. R. (1993). Similarity in drug use patterns between adolescents and their friends. *Adolescence, 253–266.*

DIPIETRO, J. A., & ALLEN, M. C. (1991). Estimation of gestational age: Implications for developmental research. *Child Development, 62,* 1200–1208.

DiPietro, J. A., Porges, S. W., & Uhly, B. (1992). Reactivity and developmental competence in preterm and full-term infants. *Developmental Psychology, 28,* 831–841.

Dirkx, E., & Craik, F. I. M. (1992). Age-related differences in memory as a function of imagery processing. *Psychology and Aging, 7,* 352–358.

Dishion, T. J. (1990). The family ecology of boys' peer relations in middle childhood. *Child Development, 61,* 874–892.

Dittman-Kohli, F., Lachman, M. E., Kliefl, R., & Baltes, P. B. (1991). Effects of cognitive training and testing on intellectual efficacy beliefs in elderly adults. *Journal of Gerontology, 46,* P162–P165.

Dizon, J. A., & Moore, C. F. (1990). The development of perspective taking: Understanding differences in information and weighting. *Child Development, 61,* 1502–1513.

Doan, R. E., & Scherman, A. (1987). The therapeutic effect of physical fitness on measures of personality: A literature review. *Journal of Counseling and Development, 66,* 28–36.

Dobkin, P. L., Tremblay, R. E., Masse, L. C., & Vitaro, F. (1995). Individual and peer characteristics in predicting boys' early onset of substance abuse: A seven-year longitudinal study. *Child Development, 66,* 1198–1214.

Dodge, K. A., & Somberg, D. R. (1987). Hostile attributional biases among aggressive boys are exacerbated under conditions of threats to self. *Child Development, 58,* 215–224.

Dodge, K. A., Cole, J. D., Pettit, G. S., & Price, J. M. (1990). Peer status and aggression in boys' groups: Developmental and contextual analyses. *Child Development, 61,* 1289–1309.

Dodge, K. A., Pettit, G. S., & Bates, J. E. (1994). Socialization mediators or the relation between socioeconomic status and child conduct problems. *Child Development, 65,* 649–665.

Dodwell, P., Humphrey, G. K., & Muir, D. (1987). Shape and pattern perception. In P. Salapatek & L. Cohen (Eds.), *Handbook of Infant Perception.* New York: Academic Press.

Doherty, W. J., & Allen, W. (1994). Family functioning and parental smoking as predictors of adolescent cigarette use: A six-year prospective study. *Journal of Family Psychology, 8,* 347–353.

Doherty, W. J., & Needle, R. H. (1991). Psychological adjustment and substance use among adolescents before and after a parental divorce. *Child Development, 62,* 328–337.

Dolan, L. J., et al. (1993). The short-term impact of two classroom-based preventive interventions on aggressive and shy behavior and poor achievement. *Journal of Applied Developmental Psychology, 14,* 317–345.

Dolcini, M. M., Catania, J. A., Cotes, T. J., Stall, R., Hudes, E. S., Gagnon, J. H., & Pollack, L. M. (1993). Demographic characteristics of heterosexuals of multiple partners: The National Age Behavioral Survey. *Family Planning Perspectives, 25,* 208–214.

Donahey, K. M., & Carroll, R. A., (1993). Gender differences in factors associated with hypoactive sexual desire. *Journal of Sex and Marital Therapy, 19,* 25–40.

Donnelly, D., & Finkelhor, D. (1992). Does equality and custody arrangements improve the parent-child relationship? *Journal of Marriage and the Family, 54,* 837–845.

Donnelly, D., & Finkelhor, D. (1993). Who has joint custody? Class differences in the determination of custody arrangements. *Family Relations, 42,* 57–60.

Donnely, B. W., & Voydanoff, P. (1991). Factors associated with releasing for adoption among adolescent mothers. *Family Relations, 39,* 311–316.

Donovan, P. (1994). Experimental prenatal care program reduced preterm deliveries by 20%, saves $1,800 per high-risk woman. *Family Planning Perspectives, 26,* 280–281.

Donovan, P. (1998). School-based sexuality education: The issues and challenges. *Family Planning Perspectives, 30,* 189–193.

Donovan, W. L., & Leavitt, L. A. (1989). Maternal self-efficacy and infant attachment: Integrating physiology, perceptions, and behavior. *Child Development, 60,* 460–472.

Donovan, W. L., Leavitt, L. A., & Walsh, R. O. (1990). Maternal self-efficacy: Illusory control and its effect on susceptibility to learned helplessness. *Child Development, 61,* 1638–1647.

Donovan, W. L., Levitt, L. A., & Walsh, R. O. (1997). Cognitive set and coping strategy affect mothers' sensitivity to infants' cry: A single detection approach. *Child Development, 68,* 760–772.

Donow, H. S. (1992). "To everything there is a season": Some Shakespearean models of normal and anomalous aging. *The Gerontologist, 32,* 728–733.

Dooley, D., Catalano, R., & Rook, K. S. (1988). Personal and aggregate unemployment and psychological symptoms. *Journal of Social Issues, 47,* 107–123.

Dornbusch, S. M., Ritter, P. L., Mont-Reynaud, R., & Chen, Z. (1990). Family decision making and academic performance in a diverse high school population. *Journal of Adolescent Research, 5,* 143–160.

Dorr, A. (1986). *Television and children.* Beverly Hills, CA: Sage.

Dorval, B., & Eckerman, C. O. (1984). Developmental trends in the quality of conversation achieved by small groups of acquainted peers. *Monographs of the Society for Research in Child Development, 49* (2, Serial No. 206).

Douglass, C. W., et al. (1993). Oral health status of the elderly in New England. *The Journals of Gerontology, 48,* M39–M46.

Doussard-Roosevelt, J. A., Porges, S. W., Scanlon, J. W., Alemi, B., & Scanlon, K. B. (1997). Vagal regulation of heart rate in the prediction of developmental outcomes for very low birth weight premature infants. *Child Development, 68,* 173–186.

Downey, D. B. (1994). The school performance of children from single-mother and single-father families. *Journal of Family Issues, 15,* 129–147.

Downey, D. B., & Powell, B. (1993). Do children in single-parent households fare better living with the same-sex parents? *Journal of Marriage and the Family, 55,* 55–71.

Downey, G., Lebolt, A., Rincon, C., & Freitas, A. L. (1998). Rejection sensitivity and children's interpersonal difficulties. *Child Development, 69,* 1074–1091.

Downs, W. W., & Rose, S. R. (1991). The relationship of adolescent peer groups to the incidence of psychosocial problems. *Adolescence, 26,* 473–492.

Doyle, A. B., Doehring, P., Tessier, O., deLorimier, S., & Shapiro, S. (1992). Transitions in children's play: A sequential analysis of states preceding and following social pretense. *Developmental Psychology, 28,* 137–144.

Dozier, M. (1991). Functional measurement assessment of young children's ability to predict future behavior. *Child Development, 62,* 1091–1099.

Drug pushers go for even younger prey. (1979, August 13). *U.S. News and World Report,* p. 31.

Dryfoos, J. G. (1995). Full-Service Schools: Revolution or fad? *Journal of Research on Adolescence, 5,* 147–172.

Dubey, D. R., O'Leary, S. G., & Kaufman, K. F. (1983). Training parents of hyperactive children in child management: A comparative outcome study. *Journal of Abnormal Child Psychology, 11,* 229–246.

DuBois, D. L., Eitel, S. K., & Felner, R. D. (1994). Effects of family environment and parent-child relationships on school adjustment during the transition to early adolescence. *Journal of Marriage and the Family, 56,* 405–414.

DuBois, D. L., & Hirsch, B. J. (1990). School and neighborhood friendship patterns of blacks and whites in early adolescence. *Child Development, 61,* 524–536.

DuBois, D. L., & Hirsch, B. J. (1993). School/nonschool friendship patterns in early adolescence. *Journal of Adolescence, 13,* 102–122.

DuBois, P. M. (1980). *Hospice way of death.* New York: Human Sciences Press.

Duerson, M. C., Thomas, J. W., Chang, J., & Stevens, C. B. (1992). Medical students' knowledge and misconceptions about aging: Responses to Palmore's facts on aging quizzes. *The Gerontologist, 32,* 171–174.

Duffy, F. H., Als, H., & McAnulty, G. B. (1990). Behavioral and electrophysiological evidence for gestational age effects in healthy preterm and full-term infants; studies two weeks after expected due date. *Child Development, 61,* 1271–1286.

Duncan, T. E., Duncan, N. C., & Hops, H. (1996). The role of parents and old siblings in predicting adolescent substance use: Modeling development via structural equation latent growth mythology. *Journal of Family Psychology, 10,* 158–172.

Dunham, C. C., & Bengston, V. L. (1992). The long-term effects of political activism on intergenerational relations. *Youth and Society, 24,* 31–51.

DUNHAM, P., DUNHAM, F., HURSHMAN, A., & ALEXANDER, T. (1989). Social contingency effects on subsequent perceptual-cognitive tasks in young infants. *Child Development, 60*, 1486–1696.

DUNHAM, R. G., & ALPERT, G. P. (1987). Keeping juvenile delinquents in school: A prediction model. *Adolescence, 23*, 45–57.

DUNN, J. (1977). *Distress and comfort.* Cambridge, MA: Harvard University Press.

DUNN, J., BROWN, J. R., & MAGUIRE, M. (1995). The development of children's moral sensibility: Individual differences and emotion understanding. *Developmental Psychology, 4*, 649–659.

DUNN, J., BROWN, J., SLOMKOWSKI, C., DESLA, C., & YOUNGBLADE, L. (1991). Young children's understanding of other people's feelings and beliefs: Individual differences and their antecedents. *Child Development, 62*, 1352–1366.

DUNN, P. C., RYAN, I. J., & O'BRIEN, K. (1988). College students' acceptance of adoption and five alternative fertilization techniques. *Journal of Sex Research, 24*, 282–287.

DURKHEIM, E. (1960). *Moral education.* New York: Free Press.

DUSTMAN, R. E., EMMERSON, R. Y., STEINHAUS, L. A., SHEARER, D. E., & DUSTMAN, T. J. (1992). The effects of videogame playing on neuropsychological performance of elderly individuals. *The Journals of Gerontology, 47*, P168–P171.

DUXBURY, L., HIGGINS, C., & LEE, C. (1994). Work-family conflicts. A comparison by gender, family type, and perceived control. *Journal of Family Issues, 15*, 449–466.

DYK, P. A. H. (1990). Healthy family sexuality: Challenge and assessment. *Family Relations, 39*, 216–220.

EAKINS, P. S. (Ed.). (1986). *The American way of birth.* Philadelphia, PA: Temple University Press.

EARL, W. L. (1987). Creativity and self-thrust: A field of study. *Adolescence, 22*, 419–432.

EASLEY, M. J., & EPSTEIN, N. (1991). Coping with stress in a family with an alcoholic parent. *Family Relations, 40*, 218–224.

EAST, P. L., LERNER, R. M., LERNER, J. B., SONI, R. T., OHANNESSIAN, C. M., & JACOBSON, L. P. (1992). Early adolescent–peer group fit, peer relations, and psychosocial competence: A short-term longitudinal study. *Journal of Early Adolescence, 12*, 132–152.

EASTERBROOKS, M. A. (1989). Quality of attachment to mother and to father: Effects of perinatal risk status. *Child Development, 60*, 825–830.

EATON, W. O., & YU, A. P. (1989). Are sex differences in child motor activity level a function of sex differences in maturational status? *Child Development, 60*, 1005–1011.

EBELING, K. S., & GELMAN, S. A. (1994). Children's use of context in interpreting "big" and "little." *Child Development, 65*, 1178–1192.

EBERHARDT, C. A., & SCHILL, T. (1984). Differences in sexual attitudes and likeliness of sexual behavior of black lower-socioeconomic father-present versus father-absent female adolescents. *Adolescence, 19*, 99–105.

ECKENRODE, J., LAIRD, M., & DORIS, J. (1993). School performance and disciplinary problems among abused and neglected children. *Developmental Psychology, 29*, 53–62.

EDER, R. A. (1989). The emergent personologist: The structure and content of 3½, 5½, and 7½-year-olds' concepts of themselves and other persons. *Child Development, 60*, 1218–1228.

EDER, R. A. (1990). Uncovering young children's psychological selves: Individual and developmental differences. *Child Development, 61*, 849–863.

EDINGER, J. D. (1992). Cognitive-behavioral therapy for sleep-maintenance insomnia in older adults. *Psychology and Aging, 7*, 282–289.

EDWARDS, S. (1992). Use of coffee, alcohol, cigarettes raises risk of poor birth outcomes. *Family Planning Perspectives, 24*, 188–189.

EGELAND, B., & FARBER, E. A. (1984). Infant-mother attachment: Factors related to its development and changes over time. *Child Development, 55*, 753–771.

EGELAND, B., JACOBVITZ, D., & SROUFE, L. A. (1988). Breaking the cycle of abuse. *Child Development, 55*, 1080–1088.

EGELAND, B., & VAUGHN, B. (1981). Failure of "bond formation" as a cause of abuse, neglect, and maltreatment. *American Journal of Orthopsychiatry, 51*, 78–84.

EGGEBEEN, D. J., & HAWKINS, A. J. (1990). Economic need and wives' employment. *Journal of Family Issues, 11*, 48–66.

EHRENBERG, M. F., COX, D. N., & KOOPMAN, R. F. (1991). The relationships between self-efficacy and depression in adolescents. *Adolescence, 26*, 361–374.

EHRLICH, G. E. (1988). Sexual concerns of patients with arthritis. *Medical Aspects of Human Sexuality, 22*, 104–107.

EICHORN, D. M., HUNT, J. V., & HONZIK, M. P. (1981). Experience, personality, and IQ: Adolescence to middle age. In D. Eichorn, J. Clausen, N. Haan, M. Honzik, & P. H. Mussen (Eds.), *Present and past in middle life.* New York: Academic Press.

EINSTEIN, G. O., HOLLAND, L. J., McDANIEL, M. A., & GUYNN, M. J. (1992). Age-related deficits in prospective memory: The influence of task complexity. *Psychology and Aging, 7*, 471–478.

EINSTEIN, G. O., SMITH, R. E., McDANIEL, M. A., & SHAW, P. (1997). Aging and prospective memory: The influence of increased task demands and encoding and retrieval. *Psychology and Aging, 12*, 479–488.

EISELE, J., HERTSGAARD, D., & LIGHT, H. K. (1986). Factors related to eating disorders in young adolescent girls. *Adolescence, 82*, 283–290.

EISEN, S. B., YOUNGMAN, D. J., GROB, M. C., & DILL, D. L. (1992). Alcohol, drugs, and psychiatric disorders: A current view of hospitalized adolescents. *Journal of Adolescent Research, 7*, 250–265.

EISENBERG, N., FABES, R. A., CARLO, G., TROYER, D., SPEER, A. L., KARBON, M., & SWITZER, G. (1992). The relations of maternal practices and characteristics to children's vicarious emotional responsiveness. *Child Development, 63*, 583–602.

EISENBERG, N., FABES, R. A., & MURPHY, B. C. (1996). Parents' reactions to children's negative emotions: Relations to children's social confidence and comforting behavior. *Child Development, 67*, 2227–2247.

EISENBERG, N., FABES, R. A., SCHALLER, M., CARLO, G., & MILLER, P. A. (1991). The relations of parental characteristics and practices to children's vicarious emotional responding. *Child Development, 62*, 1393–1408.

EISENBERG, N., FABES, R. A., SHEPPARD, S. A., MURPHY, B. C., JUTHRIE, I. K., JONES, S., FRIEDMAN, J. O., POULIN, R., & MASZK, P. (1997). Contemporaneous and longitudinal predictions of children's social functioning from regulation and emotionality. *Child Development, 68*, 642–664.

EISENMAN, R. (1993). Characteristics of adolescent felons in a prison treatment program. *Adolescence, 28*, 695–699.

EIZENMAN, D. R., NESSELROADE, J. R., FEATHERMAN, D. L., & ROWE, J. W. (1997). Intraindividual variability in perceived control in an older sample: MacArthur successful aging studies. *Psychology and Aging, 12*, 4489–4502.

EKMAN, P. (1972). Universals in cultural differences in facial expressions of emotions. In J. K. Cole (Ed.), *Nebraska symposium on motivation* (Vol. 19). Lincoln: University of Nebraska Press.

ELIAS, M. F., ROBBINS, M. A., SCHULTZ, N. R., & PIERCE, T. W. (1990). Is blood pressure an important variable in research on aging and neuropsychological test performance? *Journal of Gerontology, 45*, P128–P135.

ELKIND, D. (1967). Egocentrism in adolescence. *Child Development, 38*, 1025–1034.

ELKIND, D. (1970). *Children and adolescents: Interpretive essays on Jean Piaget.* New York: Oxford University Press.

ELKIND, D. (1975). Recent research on cognitive development in adolescence. In S. E. Dragastin & G. H. Elder, Jr. (Eds.), *Adolescence in the life cycle.* New York: Wiley.

ELKIND, D. (1978, Spring). Understanding the young adolescent. *Adolescence, 13*, 127–134.

ELLIS, N. B. (1991). An extension of the Steinberg accelerating hypothesis. *Journal of Early Adolescence, 11*, 221–235.

ELMEN, J. (1991). Achievement orientation in early adolescence: Developmental patterns and social correlates. *Journal of Early Adolescence, 11*, 125–151.

EMDE, R. N. (1992). Individual meaning and increasing complexity: Contributions of Sigmund Freud and Rene Spitz to developmental psychology. *Developmental Psychology, 28*, 347–359.

EMDE, R. N., PLOMIN, R., ROBINSON, J., CORLEY, R. DEFRIES, J., FULKER, D. W., REZNICK, J. S., CAMPOS, J., KAGAN, J., & ZAHN-WAXLER, C. (1992). Temperament, emotion, and cognition at fourteen months: The MacArthur Longitudinal Twin Study. *Child Development, 63*, 1437–1455.

EMERY, C. F., HUCK, E. R., & BLUMENTAHL, J. A. (1992). Exercise adherence or maintenance among older adults: 1-year follow-up study. *Psychology and Aging, 7*, 466–470.

EMERY, O. B., & BRESLAU, L. D. (1989). Language deficits in depression: Comparisons with SDAT and normal aging. *Journal of Gerontology, 44*, M85–M92.

EMMONS, R. A. (1992). Abstract versus concrete goals: Personal striving level, physical illness, and psychological well-being. *Journal of Personality and Social Psychology, 62*, 292–300.

ENGLISH, O. S., & PEARSON, G. H. J. (1945). *Emotional problems of living.* New York: W. W. Norton.

ENNS, C. Z. (1991). The "new" relationship models of women's identity: A review and critique for counselors. *Journal of Counseling and Development, 69*, 209–217.

ENSMINGER, M. E., & CELENTANO, D. D. (1988). Unemployment and psychiatric distress. *Social Science Medicine, 27*, 239–247.

ENTWISLE, D. R., ALEXANDER, K. L., PALLAS, A. M., & CADIGAN, W. (1987). The emergent academic self-image of first graders: Its response to social structure. *Child Development, 58*, 1190–1206.

ENTWISLE, G. R., & ALEXANDER, K. L. (1996). Family type and children's growth in reading and math over the primary grades. *Journal of Marriage and the Family, 58*, 341–355.

EPSTEIN, S., & KATZ, L. (1992). Coping ability, stress, productive load, and symptoms. *Journal of Personality and Social Psychology, 62*, 813–825.

ERBER, J. T., & ROTHBERG, S. T. (1991). Here's looking at you: The relative effect of age and attractiveness on judgments about memory failure. *Journal of Gerontology, 46*, P116–P123.

ERIKSON, E. (1950). *Childhood and society.* New York: W. W. Norton.

ERIKSON, E. (1959). *Identity and the life cycle.* New York: International Universities Press.

ERIKSON, E. (1963). *Childhood and society* (2nd ed.). New York: W. W. Norton.

ERIKSON, E. (1968). *Identity: Youth and crisis.* New York: W. W. Norton.

ERIKSON, E. (1982). *The life cycle completed.* New York: W. W. Norton.

ERON, L. D. (1987). The development of aggression from the perspective of a developing behaviorism. *American Psychologist, 42*, 435–442.

ESKILSON, A., WILEY, M. G., MUEHLBAUER, G., & DODDER, L. (1986). Parental pressure, self-esteem, and adolescent reported deviance: Bending the twig too far. *Adolescence, 21*, 501–515.

ESSEX, M. J., & NAM, S. (1987). Marital status and loneliness among older women: The differential importance of close family and friends. *Journal of Marriage and the Family, 49*, 93–106.

EYSENCK, H. J. (1988, December). Health's character. *Psychology Today, 22*, 28–35.

FABES, R. A., WILSON, P., & CHRISTOPHER, F. S. (1989). A time to reexamine the role of television in family life. *Family Relations, 38*, 337–341.

FABRICIUS, W. V., & WELLMAN, H. M. (1993). Two roads diverged: Young children's ability to judge distance. *Child Development, 64*, 399–414.

FAGAN, J. F., III. (1977, March). Infant recognition memory: Studies in forgetting. *Child Development, 48*, 68–78.

FAGOT, B. I., & HAGAN, R. (1991). Observations of parent reactions to sex-stereotype behaviors: Age and sex effects. *Child Development, 62*, 617–628.

FAGOT, B. I., & KAVANAGH, K. (1990). The prediction of antisocial behavior from avoidant attachment classifications. *Child Development, 61*, 864–873.

FAGOT, B. I., & KAVANAGH, K. (1993). Parenting during the second year. Effects of children's age, sex, and attachment classification. *Child Development, 64*, 258–271.

FAGOT, B. I., LEINBACH, M. D., & O'BOYLE, C. (1992). Gender labeling, gender stereotyping, and parenting behaviors. *Developmental Psychology, 28*, 255–260.

FARBER, J. A. M., & BRANSETTER, W. H. (1994). Preschoolers' prosocial responses to their peers' distress. *Developmental Psychology, 30*, 331–334.

FARMER, A. E., McGUFFIN, P., & GOTTESMAN, I. I. (1987). Twin concordance for DSM-III schizophrenia. Scrutinizing the validity of the definition. *Archives of General Psychiatry, 44*, 634–641.

FARO, S. (1985). Chlamydia trachomatic infection in women. *Journal of Reproductive Medicine, 30* (Suppl.), 273–278.

FARRAR, M. J. (1992). Negative evidence and grammatical morpheme acquisition. *Developmental Psychology, 28*, 90–98.

FARRAR, M. J., & GOODMAN, G. S. (1992). Developmental changes in event memory. *Child Development, 63*, 173–187.

FARRAR, W. J., RANEY, G. E., & BOYER, M. E. (1992). Knowledge, concepts, and inferences in childhood. *Child Development, 63*, 673–691.

FARRINGTON, D. P. (1990). Implications of criminal career research for the prevention of offending. *Journal of Adolescence, 13*, 93–114.

FASICK, F. A. (1994). On the "Invention" of adolescence. *Journal of Early Adolescence, 14*, 6–23.

FAUBER, R., FOREHAND, R., THOMAS, A. M., & WIERSON, M. (1990). A mediational model of the impact of marital conflict on adolescent adjustment in intact and divorced families: The role of disrupted parenting. *Child Development, 61*, 1112–1123.

FEAGANS, L. B., KIPP, E., & BLOOD, I. (1994). The effects of otitis media on the attention skills of day-care-attending toddlers. *Developmental Psychology, 30*, 701–708.

FEINGOLD, A. (1982). Do taller men have prettier girlfriends? *Psychological Reports, 50*, 810.

FELDMAN, H. (1981). A comparison of intentional parents and intentionally childless couples. *Journal of Marriage and the Family, 43*, 593–600.

FELDMAN, N. A., & RUBLE, D. N. (1988). The effect of personal relevance on psychological inference: A developmental analysis. *Child Development, 59*, 1339–1352.

FELDMAN, S. S., MONT-REYNAUD, R., & ROSENTHAL, D. A. (1992). When East moves West: The acculturation of values of Chinese adolescence in the United States and Australia. *Journal of Research on Adolescence, 2*, 147–173.

FELDMAN, S. S., & WEINBERGER, D. A. (1994). Self-restraint as a mediator of family influences on boys' delinquent behavior: A longitudinal study. *Child Development, 65*, 195–211.

FELDMAN, S. S., & WENTZEL, K. R. (1990). The relationship between parenting styles, sons' self-restraint, and peer relations in early adolescence. *Journal of Early Adolescence, 10*, 439–454.

FELKER, K. R., & STIVERS, C. (1994). The relationship of gender and family environment, eating disorder risk in adolescents. *Adolescence, 29*, 821–834.

FELSON, M., & GOTTFREDSON, M. (1984). Social indicators of adolescent activities near peers and parents. *Journal of Marriage and the Family, 46*, 709–714.

FELSON, R. B., & ZIELINSKI, M. A. (1989). Children's self-esteem and parental support. *Journal of Marriage and the Family, 51*, 727–735.

FELTON, B. J., & BERRY, C. A. (1992). Do the sources of the urban elderly's social support determine its psychological consequences? *Psychology and Aging, 7*, 89–97.

FENZEL, L. M. (1992). The effect of relative age on self-esteem, role strain, GPA, and anxiety. *Journal of Early Adolescence, 12*, 253–266.

FERGUSON, T. J., & RULE, B. G. (1988). Children's evaluations of retaliatory aggression. *Child Development, 59*, 961–968.

FERNANDEZ, R. M., & KULIK, J. C. (1981). A multilevel model of life satisfaction: Effects of individual characteristics and neighborhood composition. *American Sociological Review, 46*, 840–850.

FERRARI, J. R., & OLIVETTE, M. J. (1993). Perceptions of parental control and the development of indecision among late adolescent females. *Adolescence, 28*, 963–970.

FERRARO, K. F. (1990). Cohort analysis of retirement preparation, 1974–1981. *Journal of Gerontology, 45*, S21–S31.

FERRARO, K. F. (1992). Cohort change in images of older adults, 1974–1981. *The Gerontologist, 32*, 296–304.

FERREIRA, F., & MORRISON, F. J. (1994). Children's meta-linguistic knowledge of syntactic constituents: Effects of age and schooling. *Developmental Psychology, 30*, 663–678.

FERREIRO, B. W., WARREN, N. J., & KONANC, J. T. (1986). ADAP: A divorce assessment proposal. *Family Relations, 35*, 439–449.

FERRISS, L. (1989, October 30). *Women's life crisis deepens says author.* Portland, ME: Portland Press Herald.

FIELD, D., MINKLER, M., FALK, R. F., & LEINO, E. V. (1993). The influence of health on family contact and family feelings in advanced old age: A longitudinal study. *The Journals of Gerontology, 48*, P18–P28.

FIELD, T., HEALY, B., GOLDSTEIN, S., PERRY, S., & BENDELL, D. (1988). Infants of depressed mothers show "depressed" behavior even with nondepressed adults. *Child Development, 59*, 1569–1579.

FIELD, T. M. (1991a). Quality infant day-care and grade school behavior and performance. *Child Development, 62*, 863–870.

FIELD, T. M. (1991b). Young children's adaptations to repeated separations from their mothers. *Child Development, 62*, 539–547.

FIESE, B. H. (1990). Playful relationships: A contextual analysis of mother-toddler interaction and symbolic play. *Child Development, 61*, 1648–1656.

FINCH, J. F., & ZAUTRA, A. J. (1992). Testing latent longitudinal models of social ties and depression among the elderly: A comparison of distribution-free and maximum likelihood estimates with nonnormal data. *Psychology and Aging, 7,* 107–118.

FINCHER, J. (1982). Before their time. *Science, 82.*

FINE, M. A. (1986). Perceptions of stepparents: Variation in stereotypes as a function of current family structure. *Journal of Marriage and the Family, 48,* 537–543.

FINE, M. A., & FINE, D. R. (1992). Recent changes in laws affecting stepfamilies: Suggestions for legal reform. *Family Relations, 41,* 334–340.

FINE, M. A., MCKENRY, P. C., DONNELLY, B. W., & VOYDANOFF, P. (1992). Received adjustment of parents and children: Variations by family structure, race, and gender. *Journal of Marriage and the Family, 54,* 118–127.

FINKEL, D., & MCGUE, M. (1993). The origins of individual differences in memory among the elderly: A behavior genetic analysis. *Psychology and Aging, 8,* 527–537.

FINKEL, D., PEDERSEN, N., & MCGUE, M. (1995). Genetic influences on memory performance in adulthood: Comparison of Minnesota and Swedish twin data. *Psychology and Aging, 10,* 437–446.

FINKEL, D., WHITFIELD, K., & MCGUE, M. (1995). Genetic and environmental influences on functional age: A twin study. *Journal of Gerontology, 50B,* P104–P113.

FINKELHOR, D. (1994). Current information on the scope and nature of child sexual abuse. *The Future of Children, 4,* 31, 53.

FIRESTONE, J., & SHELTON, B. A. (1988). An estimation of the effect of women's work on available leisure time. *Journal of Family Issues, 9,* 478–495.

FISCHER, J. L., & CRAWFORD, D. W. (1992). Codependency and parenting styles. *Journal of Adolescent Research 7,* 352–363.

FISCHMAN, J. (1988, September). Type A situations. *Psychology Today, 22,* 22.

FISH, M., STIFLER, C. A., & BELSKY, J. (1991). Conditions of continuity and discontinuity in infant negative emotionality: Newborn to five months. *Child Development, 62,* 1525–1537.

FISHBEIN, H. D., & IMAI, S. (1993). Preschoolers select playmates on the basis of gender and race. *Journal of Applied Developmental Psychology, 14,* 303–316.

FISHER, J. (1988). The "fitness factor" in individual and family health: One doctor's prescription. *Medical Aspects of Human Sexuality, 22,* 45–48.

FISHER, L. M., & MCDOWD, J. M. (1993). Item and relational processing in young and older adults. *The Journals of Gerontology, 48,* P62–P68.

FISHER, T. D., & HALL, R. G. (1988). A scale for the comparison of the sexual attitudes of adolescents and their parents. *Journal of Sex Research, 24,* 90–100.

FISKE, V., COYNE, J. C., & SMITH, D. A. (1991). Coping with mild myocardial infarction: An impirical reconsideration of the role of overprotectiveness. *Journal of Family Psychology, 5,* 4–20.

FITNESS FINDERS. (1984). *Feelin' good.* Spring Arbor, MI: Fitness Finders.

FITZGERALD, H. E., SULLIVAN, L. A., HAM, H. P., ZUCKER, R. A., BRUCKEL, S., & SCHNEIDER, A. M. (1993). Predictors of behavior problems in three-year-old sons of alcoholics: Early evidence for the onset of risk. *Child Development, 64,* 110–123.

FIVUSH, R., KUEBLI, J., & CLUBB, P. A. (1992). The structure of events and event representations: A developmental analysis. *Child Development, 63,* 188–201.

FLANAGAN, C. A. (1990). Change in family work status: Effects on parent-adolescent decision making. *Child Development, 61,* 163–177.

FLANAGAN, C. A., & ECCLES, J. S. (1993). Change in parents' work status in adolescents' adjustment at school. *Child Development, 64,* 246–257.

FLANNERY, D. J., ROWE, D. C., & GULLEY, B. L. (1993). Impact of pubertal status, timing, and age on adolescent sexual experience and delinquency. *Journal of Adolescent Research, 8,* 21–40.

FLANNERY, D. J., TORQUATI, J. C., LINDEMEIER, L. (1994). The method and meaning of emotional expression and experience during adolescence. *Journal of Adolescent Research, 9,* 8–27.

FLAVELL, J. H., GREEN, F. L., FLAVELL, E. R., & GROSSMAN, J. B. (1997). The development of children's knowledge about inner speech. *Child Development, 68,* 39–47.

FLAVELL, J. H., MUMME, D. L., GREEN, F. L., & FLAVELL, E. R. (1992). Young children's understanding of different types of beliefs. *Child Development, 63,* 960–977.

FLEISCHER, B., & READ, M. (1982, Winter). Food supplement usage by adolescent males. *Adolescence, 17,* 831–845.

FLINT, L. (1992). Adolescent parental affinity-seeking: Age- and gender-mediated strategy use. *Adolescence, 27,* 417–444.

FLORSHEIM, P., TOLAN, P., & GORMAN-SMITH, D. (1998). Family relationships, parenting practices, the availability of male family members, and the behavior of inner-city boys in single-mother and two-parent families. *Child Development, 69,* 1437–1447.

FLOYD, F. J., GILLIOM, L. A., & COSTIGAN, C. L. (1998). Marriage and the parenting alliance: Longitudinal prediction of change in parenting perceptions and behaviors. *Child Development, 69,* 1461–1479.

FLOYD, F. J., & ZMICH, D. E. (1991). Marriage and the parenting partnership: Perceptions and interactions of parents with mentally retarded and typically developing children. *Child Development, 62,* 1434–1448.

FLOYD, M., & SCOGIN, S. (1997). Effects of memory training on the subjective memory functioning and mental health of older adults: A meta-analysis. *Psychology and Aging, 12,* 150–161.

FONAGY, P., STEELE, H., & STEELE, M. (1991). Maternal representations of attachment during pregnancy predict the organization of infant-mother attachment at one year of age. *Child Development, 62,* 891–905.

FONTANA, A., & ROSENHECK, R. (1994). Traumatic war stressors and psychiatric symptoms among World War II, Korean, & Vietnam war veterans. *Psychology and Aging, 9,* 27–33.

FORD, D. Y., HARRIS, J., & SCHUERGER, J. N. (1993). Racial identity development among gifted black students: Counseling issues and concerns. *Journal of Counseling and Development, 71,* 409–416.

FORD, H. B., et al. (1992). New cohorts of urban elders: Are they in trouble? *The Journals of Gerontology, 47,* S297–S303.

FORD, M. E. (1986). *Androgyny as self-assertion and integration: Implications for psychological and social competence.* Unpublished manuscript, Stanford University School of Education, Stanford, CA.

FORWARD, S. (1986). *Men who hate women: The women who love them.* New York: Bantam.

FOSHEE, D., & BAUMAN, K. E. (1994). Parental attachment and adolescent cigarette smoking initiation. *Journal of Adolescent Research, 9,* 88–104.

FOSSETT, M. A., & KIECOLT, K. J. (1993). Mate availability and family structure among African Americans in U. S. metropolitan areas. *Journal of Marriage and the Family, 55,* 288–302.

FOX, N. A., KIMMERLY, N. L., & SCHAFER, W. D. (1991). Attachment of mother/attachment to father: A meta-analysis. *Child Development, 62,* 210–225.

FRANÇOIS, G. R. (1990). *The lifespan* (3rd ed.). Belmont, CA: Wadsworth.

FRANKEL, K. A., & BATES, J. E. (1990). Mother–toddler problem solving: Antecedents in attachment, home behavior, and temperament. *Child Development, 61,* 810–819.

FRANKENBURG, W. K., FRANDAL, A., SCIARILLO, W., & BURGESS, D. (1981). The newly abbreviated and revised Denver Developmental Screening Test. *Journal of Pediatrics, 99,* 995–999.

FRANKS, M. M., & STEPHENS, M. A. P. (1992). Multiple roles of middle-generation care givers: Contextual effects and psychological mechanisms. *The Journals of Gerontology, 47,* S123–S129.

FREEMAN, S. J. (1991). Group facilitation of the grieving process with those bereaved by suicide. *Journal of Counseling and Development, 69,* 328–331.

FREIDLAND, N., KEINAN, G., & REGEV, Y. (1992). Controlling the uncontrollable: Effects of stress on illusory perceptions of controllability. *Journal of Personality and Social Psychology, 63,* 923–931.

FREIHEIT, S. R., OVERHOLSER, J. C., & LEHNERT, K. L. (1998). The association between humor and depression in adolescent psychiatric inpatient in high school students. *Journal of Adolescent Research, 13,* 32–48.

FRENCH, D. C. (1988). Heterogeneity of peer-rejected boys: Aggressive and nonaggressive subtypes. *Child Development, 59,* 976–985.

FRENCH, D. C. (1990). Heterogeneity of peer-rejected girls. *Child Development, 61,* 2028–2031.

FREUD, A. (1946). *The ego and the mechanism of defense.* New York: International Universities Press.

FREUD, S. (1917). *A general introduction to psychoanalysis.* New York: Washington Square Press.

FREY, K. S., & RUBLE, D. N. (1992). Gender constancy and the "cost" of sex-typed behavior: a test of the conflict hypothesis. *Developmental Psychology, 28*, 714–721.

FRIEDLAND, G. SALTZMAN, G., ROGERS, M., KAHL, P., LESSER, M., MAYERS, M., & KLEIN, R. (1986). Lack of transmission of HLTLV-III/LAV infection to household contacts of patients with AIDS or AIDS-related complex with oral candidiases. *New England Journal of Medicine, 314*, 344–349.

FRIEDMAN, L., BROOKS, J. O., III, BLIWISE, B. L., YESAVAGE, J. A., & WICKS, D. S. (1995). Perceptions of life stress and chronic insomnia in older adults. *Psychology and Aging, 10*, 352–357.

FRIEDRICH-COFER, L., & HUSTON, A. C. (1986) Television violence and aggression: The debate continues. *Psychological Bulletin, 100*, 364–371.

FRITZSCHE, V., TRACY, T., SPEIRS, J., & GLUECK, C. J. (1990). Cholesterol screening in 5,719 self-referred elderly subjects. *Journal of Gerontology, 45*, M198–M202.

FRODI, A., & SENCHAK, M. (1990). Verbal and behavioral responsiveness to the cries of atypical infants. *Child Development, 61*, 76–84.

FRYDENBERG, E., & LEWIS, R. (1991). Adolescent coping: The different ways in which boys and girls cope. *Journal of Adolescence, 14*, 119–134.

FUJIMARA, L. E., WEIS, D. M., & COCHRAN, J. R. (1985, June). Suicide: Dynamics and implications for counseling. *Journal of Counseling and Development, 63*, 612–615.

FULIGNI, A. J., & ECCLES, J. S. (1993). Perceived parent-child relationships in early adolescents' orientation toward peers. *Developmental Psychology, 29*, 622–632.

FULIGNI, A. J., & STEVENSON, H. W. (1995). Time use and mathematics achievement among American, Chinese, and Japanese high school students. *Child Development, 66*, 830–842.

FULLER, D., HOLLOWAY, S. D., & LIANG, X. (1996). Family selection of child-care centers: The influence of hosuehold support, ethnicity, and parental practices. *Child Development, 67*, 3320–3337.

FULLER, J. R., & LAFOUNTAIN, M. J. (1987). Performance-enhancing drugs in sport: A different form of drug abuse. *Adolescence, 22*, 969–976.

FULTZ, N. H., & HERZOG, A. R. (1993). Measuring urinary incontinence in surveys. *The Gerontologist, 33*, 708–713.

FURMAN, E. (1984). Children's patterns in mourning the death of a loved one. In H. Wass & C. Corr (Eds.), *Childhood and death* (pp. 185–203). Washington, DC: Hemisphere/McGraw-Hill.

FURMAN, W., & BUHRMESTER, D. (1992). Age and sex differences in perceptions of networks of personal relationships. *Child Development, 63*, 103–115.

FURSTENBERG, F. F., & SPANIER, G. (1984). *Recycling the family: Remarriage after divorce.* Beverly Hills, CA: Sage.

GABENNESCH, H. (1990). The perception of social conventionality by children and adults. *Child Development, 61*, 2047–2059.

GABLE, S., BELSKY, J., & CRNIC, K. (1992). Marriage, parenting, and child development: Progress and prospects. *Journal of Family Psychology, 5*, 276–294.

GAENSBAUER, T., & HIATT, S. (1984). *The psychobiology of affective development.* Hillsdale, NJ: Erlbaum.

GALAMBOS, N. L., & ALMEIDA, D. N. (1992). Does parent-adolescent conflict increase in early adolescence? *Journal of Marriage and the Family, 54*, 737–747.

GALAMBOS, N. L., SEARS, H. A., ALMEIDA, D. M., & KOLARIC, G. C. (1995). Parents' work overload and problems of behavior in young adolescents. *Journal of Research on Adolescents, 5*, 201–223.

GALAMBOS, N. L., & SILBEREISEN, R. K. (1989). Role strain in West German dual-earner households. *Journal of Marriage and the Family, 51*, 385–389.

GANONG, L., COLEMAN, M., MCDANIEL, A. K., & KILLIAN, T. (1998). Attitudes regarding obligations to assist an older parent or stepparent following later-life remarriage. *Journal of Marriage and the Family, 60*, 595–610.

GARDNER, A. W., & POEHLMAN, E. P. (1995). Predictors of the age-related increase in blood pressure in men and women. *Journal of Gerontology, 50A*, M1–M6.

GARDNER, H. (1983). *Frames of mind.* New York: Basic Books.

GARDNER, J. M., ZARMEL, B. Z., & MAGNANO, C. L. (1992). Arousal/visual preference interactions in high-risk neonates. *Developmental Psychology, 28*, 821–830.

GARDNER, L. I. (1972). Deprivation dwarfism. *Scientific American, 227*, 76–82.

GARFEIN, A. J., & HERZOG, A. R. (1995). Robust aging among the young-old, old-old, and oldest-old. *Journal of Gerontology, 50B*, S77–S87.

GARNER, P. W., & POWER, T. G. (1996). Preschoolers' emotional control and the disappointment paradigm in its relation to temperament, emotional knowledge, and family expressiveness. *Child Development, 67*, 1406–1419.

GARNER, P. W., JONES, D. C., & MINER, J. L. (1994). Social competence among low-income preschoolers: Emotion socialization practices and social cognitive correlates. *Child Development, 65*, 622–637.

GARRARD, J., et al. (1992). Longitudinal study of psychotropic drug use by elderly nursing home residents. *The Journals of Gerontology, 47*, M183–M188.

GARRETT, D. (1995). Violent behaviors among African-American adolescents. *Adolescence, 30*, 209–216.

GARRISON, B. M. E., BLALOCK, L. D., ZARSKI, J. J., & MERRITT, P. B. (1997). Delayed parenthood: An exploratory study of family functioning. *Family Relations, 46*, 281–290.

GARZARELLI, P., EVERHART, B., & LESTER, D. (1993). Self-concept and academic performance in gifted and academically weak students. *Adolescence, 28*, 233–237.

GATELY, D. W., & SCHWEBEL, A. I. (1991). The challenge model of children's adjustment to parental divorce: Explaining favorable post-divorce outcomes in children. *Journal of Family Psychology, 5*, 60–81.

GATHERCOLE, S. E., WILLIS, C. S., EMSLIE, H., & BADDELEP, A. D. (1992). Phonological memory and vocabulary development during the early school years: A longitudinal study. *Development Psychology, 28*, 887–898.

GAVAZZI, S. M., ANDERSON, S. A., & SABATELLI, R. M. (1993). Family differentiation, peer differentiation, and adolescence adjustment in a clinical sample. *Journal of Adolescent Research, 8*, 205–225.

GAVAZZI, S. M., & SABATELLI, R. M. (1990). Family system dynamics, the individuation process, and psychosocial development. *Journal of Adolescent Research, 5*, 500–519.

GE, X., LORENZ, F. O., CONGER, R. D., ELDER, G. H., JR., & SIMONS, R. L. (1994). Trajectories of stressful life events and depressive symptoms during adolescence. *Developmental Psychology, 4*, 467–483.

GEASLER, M. J., DANNISON, L. L., & EDLUND, C. J. (1995). Sexuality education of young children. Parental concerns. *Family Relations, 44*, 184–188.

GEIGER, D. L. (1978). Note: How future professionals view the elderly: A comparative analysis of social work, law, and medical students' perceptions. *Gerontologist, 18*, 591–594.

GEISS, S. K., & O'LEARY, K. D. (1981). Therapists ratings of frequency and severity of marital problems: Implications for research. *Journal of Marital and Family Therapy, 7*, 515–520.

GELB, R., & JACOBSON, J. L. (1988). Popular and unpopular children's interaction during cooperative and competitive peer group activities. *Journal of Abnormal Child Psychology, 16*, 247–261.

GELLES, R. J., & CONTE, J. R. (1990). Domestic violence and sexual abuse of children: A review of research in the eighties. *Journal of Marriage and the Family, 52*, 1045–1058.

GELLES, R. J., & HARROP, J. W. (1991). The risk of abusive violence among children with nongenetic caretakers. *Family Relations, 40*, 78–83.

GELLMAN, E., et al. (1983). Vaginal delivery after Cesarean section. *JAMA, Journal of American Medical Association, 249*, 2935–2937.

GENESEE, F. (1985). Second language learning through immersion: A review of U.S. programs. *Review of Educational Research, 55*, 541–546.

GEORGE, L., & GWYTHER, L. (1984). The dynamics of caregiving burden: Changes in caregiver well-being over time. *Gerontologist, 23*, 249.

GERARD, L., ZACKS, R. T., HASHER, L., & RADVANSKY, G. A. (1991). Age deficits in retrieval: The fan effect. *Journal of Gerontology, 46*, P131–P136.

GERKEN, L., & MCINTOSH, B. J. (1993). Interplay of function morphemes and prosody in early language. *Developmental Psychology, 29*, 448–457.

GERTNER, M. (1986). Short stature in children. *Medical Aspects of Human Sexuality, 20*, 36–42.

GESELL, A. (1934). *An atlas of infant behavior.* New Haven, CT: Yale University Press.

GESELL, A., & AMES, L. B. (1956). *Youth: The years from ten to sixteen.* New York: Harper & Row.

GESELL, A., & ILG, F. L. (1943). *Infant and child in the culture of today.* New York: Harper.

GESELL, A., & ILG, F. L. (1946). *The child from five to ten.* New York: Harper.

GFELLNER, B. M. (1994). A matched-group comparison of drug use and problem behavior among Canadian Indians and White adolescents. *Journal of Early Adolescence, 14,* 24–48.

GIBSON, R. C. (1991). The subjective retirement of black Americans. *Journal of Gerontology, 46,* S204–S210.

GIFFORD, V. D., & DEAN, M. M. (1990). Differences in extracurricular activity participation, achievement, and attitudes toward school between ninth-grade students attending junior high school and those attending senior high school. *Adolescence, 25,* 799–802.

GILFORD, R. (1984). Contrasts in marital satisfaction throughout old age: An exchange theory analysis. *Journal of Gerontology, 39,* 325–333.

GILGER, J. W., GEARY, D. C., & EISELE, L. M. (1991). Reliability and validity of retrospective self-reports of the age of pubertal onset using twin, sibling, and college student data. *Adolescence, 26,* 41–54.

GILLIGAN, C. (1977). In a different voice: Women's conceptions of self and of morality. *Harvard Educational Review, 47,* 481–517.

GILLIGAN, C. (1982). *In a different voice: Psychological theory and women's development.* Cambridge, MA: Harvard University Press.

GILLIGAN, C. (1984). *Remapping the moral domain in personality research and assessment.* Invited address presented to the American Psychological Association Convention, Toronto.

GILLIGAN, C., WARD, J. V., TAYLOR, J. M., & BARDIGE, B. (1988). *Mapping the moral domain.* Cambridge, MA: Harvard University Press.

GILLMORE, M. R., HAWKINS, J. D., DAY, L. E., & CATALANO, R. F. (1992). Friendship and deviance: New evidence on an old controversy. *Journal of Early Adolescence, 12,* 80–95.

GILMORE, G. C., ALLAN, T. M., & ROYER, F. L. (1986). Iconic memory and aging. *Journal of Gerontology, 41,* 183–190.

GILMORE, G. C., WENK, H. E., NAYLOR, L. A., & STUVE, T. A. (1992). Motion perception and aging. *Psychology and Aging, 7,* 654–660.

GINSBURG, G. S., & BRONSTEIN, P. (1993). Family factors related to children's intrinsic/extrinsic motivational orientation and academic performance. *Child Development, 64,* 1461–1474.

GISPERT, M. (1987). Preventing teenage suicide. *Medical Aspects of Human Sexuality, 21,* 16.

GISPERT, M., WHEELER, K., MARSH, L., & DAVIS, M. S. (1985). Suicidal adolescents: Factors in evaluation. *Adolescence, 20,* 753–762.

GIUDUBALDI, J., & PERRY, J. D. (1985). Divorce and mental health sequelae for children. A two-year follow-up of a nationwide sample. *Journal of the American Academy of Child Psychiatry, 24,* 531–537.

GLADSTONE, J. W. (1988). Perceived changes in grandmother-grandchild relations following a child's separation or divorce. *The Gerontologist, 28,* 66–72.

GLADSTONE, J., & WESTHUES, A. (1998). Adoption reunions: A new side to intergenerational family relationships. *Family Relations, 47,* 177–184.

GLADUE, B. A. (1994). The biopsychology of sexual orientation. *Current Directions in Psychological Science, 3,* 150–154.

GLASS, T. A., SEEMAN, T. E., HERZOG, A. R., KAHN, R., & BERKMAN, L. F. (1995). Change in productive activity in late adulthood: MacArthur studies of successful aging. *Journal of Gerontology, 50B,* S65–S76.

GLENN, N. D. (1998). The course of marital success and failure in five American ten-year marriage cohorts. *Journal of Marriage and the Family, 60,* 569–576.

GLENN, N. D., & KRAMER, K. B. (1987). The marriages and divorces of children of divorce. *Journal of Marriage and the Family, 49,* 811–825.

GLENN, N. D., & WEAVER, C. N. (1981). The contribution of marital happiness to global happiness. *Journal of Marriage and the Family, 43,* 161–168.

GLOVINSKY-FAHSHOLTZ, D. (1992). The effect of free or reduced-price lunches on the self-esteem of middle school students. *Adolescence, 27,* 633–638.

GNEPP, J., & CHILAMKURTI, C. (1988). Children's use of personality attributions to predict other people's emotional and behavioral reactions. *Child Development, 59,* 743–754.

GNEPP, J., & KLAYMAN, J. K. (1992). Recognition of uncertainty in emotional inferences: Reasoning about emotionally equivocal situations. *Developmental Psychology, 28,* 145–158.

GOELMAN, H., SHAPIRO, E., & PENCE, A. R. (1990). Family environment and family day care. *Family Relations, 39,* 14–19.

GOFF, J. L. (1990). Sexual confusion among certain college males. *Adolescence, 25,* 599–614.

GOHMANN, S. F. (1990). Retirement differences among the respondents to the retirement history survey. *Journal of Gerontology, 45,* S120–S127.

GOLANT, S. M., & LAGRECA, A. J. (1994). Housing quality of U.S. elderly households: Does aging in place matter? *The Gerontologist, 34,* 803–814.

GOLBECK, S. L. (1992). Young children's memory for spatial locations in organized and unorganized rooms. *Journal of Applied Developmental Psychology, 13,* 75–96.

GOLDBERG, M. E., & GORN, G. J. (1977, March). *Material vs. social preferences, parent-child relations, and the child's emotional responses.* Paper presented at the Telecommunications Policy Research Conference, Raleigh House, VA.

GOLDBERG, W. A., GREENBERGER, E., HAMILL, S., O'NEIL, R. (1992). Role demands in the lives of employed single mothers with preschoolers. *Journal of Family Issues, 13,* 312–333.

GOLDMAN, J. A., LERMAN, R. H., CONTOIS, J. H., & UDALL, J. N. (1986). Behavioral effects of sucrose on preschool children. *Journal of Abnormal Child Psychology, 14,* 565–577.

GOLDMAN, J. A., ROSENZWEIG, C. M., & LUTTER, A. D. (1980, April). Effect of similarity of ego identity status on interpersonal attraction. *Journal of Youth and Adolescence, 9,* 153–162.

GOLDSCHEIDER, F., & GOLDSCHEIDER, C. (1993). Whose nest? A two-generational view of leaving home during the 1980's. *Journal of Marriage and the Family, 55,* 851–862.

GOLDSMITH, H. H. (1983). Genetic influences on personality from infancy to adulthood. *Child Development, 54,* 331–355.

GOLDSMITH, H. H., BUSS, A. H., PLOMIN, R., ROTHBURT, M. K., THOMAS, A., CHESS, S., HINDE, R. A., & MCCALL, R. B. (1987). Roundtable: What is temperament? Four approaches. *Child Development, 58,* 505–529.

GOLDSMITH, H. H., & CAMPOS, J. J. (1990). The structure of temperamental fear and pleasure in infants: A psychometric perspective. *Child Development, 61,* 1944–1964.

GOLDSMITH, H. H., & GOTTESMAN, I. I. (1981). Origins of variation in behavioral style: A longitudinal study of temperament in young twins. *Child Development, 52,* 91–103.

GOLDSMITH, R. E., & HEIENS, R. A. (1992). Subjective age: A test of five hypotheses. *The Gerontologist, 32,* 312–317.

GOLDSTEIN, C., & ROSENBAUM, A. (1985). An evaluation of the self-esteem of maritally violent men. *Family Relations, 34,* 425–428.

GOLDSTEIN, M. J. (1981, October). Family factors associated with schizophrenia and anorexia nervosa. *Journal of Youth and Adolescence, 10,* 385–405.

GOLDSTINE, D. (1977). *The dance-away lover.* New York: Morrow.

GOLEMAN, D. (1980, February). 1,528 little geniuses and how they grew. *Psychology Today, 13,* 28–143.

GOLEMAN, D. (1985). Spacing of siblings strongly link to success in life. *New York Times* (May 28th), 17, 18.

GOLEMAN, D. (1986, December 2). Major personality study finds that traits are mostly inherited. *New York Times,* pp. 17–18.

GOLEMAN, D. (1989, October 22). Pushing preschoolers may not be a good idea. *Maine Sunday Telegram,* p. 20.

GOLINKOFF, R. M., HIRSH-PASEK, K., BAILEY, L. M., & WENGER, N. R. (1992). Young children and adults use lexical principles to learn new nouns. *Developmental Psychology, 28,* 99–108.

GOLOMB, C. & GALASSO, L. (1995). Make believe and reality: Explorations of the imaginary realm. *Developmental Psychology, 31,* 800–810.

GOMEL, J. N., TINSLEY, B. J., PARKE, R. D., & CLARK, K. M. (1998). The effects of economic hardship on family relationships among African American, Latino, and Euro-American families. *Journal of Family Issues, 19,* 436–467.

GONSIOREK, J. C., & WEINRICH, J. D. (1991). *Homosexuality: Research implications for public policy.* Beverly Hills, CA: Sage.

GOODMAN, G. A., & HAITH, M. M. (1987). Memory development and neurophysiology: Accomplishments and limitations. *Child Development, 58,* 713–717.

GOODMAN, M., et al. (1991). Cultural differences among elderly women in coping with the death of an adult child. *The Journals of Gerontology, 46,* S321–S329.

GOODMAN, S. H., BROGAN, D., LYNCH, M. E., & FIELDING, B. (1993). Social and emotional competence in children of depressed mothers. *Child Development, 64,* 516–531.

GOODMAN, S. H., BRUMLEY, H. E., SCHWARTZ, K. R., & PURCELL, D. W. (1993). Gender and age in the relation between stress and children's school adjustment. *Journal of Early Adolescence, 13,* 329–345.

GOODWIN, M. P., & ROSCOE, B. (1990). Sibling violence and agonistic interactions among middle adolescents. *Adolescence, 25,* 451–468.

GOODWYN, S. W., & ACREDOLO, L. P. (1993). Symbolic gesture versus word: Is there a modality advantage for onset of symbol use? *Child Development, 64,* 688–701.

GOOSSENS, F. A., & VAN IJZENDOORN, M. H. (1990). Quality of infant's attachments to professional caregivers: Relation to infant-parent attachment and day-care characteristics. *Child Development, 61,* 832–837.

GOOSSENS, L., SEIFFGE-KRENKE, I., & MARCOEN, A. (1992). The many faces of adolescent egocentrisim: Two European replications. *Journal of Adolescent Research, 7,* 43–58.

GOPNIK, A., & MELTZOFF, A. N. (1992). Categorization and naming: Basic-level sorting in eighteen-month-olds and its relation to language. *Child Development, 63,* 1091–1102.

GORMAN-SMITH, D., TOLAN, P. H., ZELLI, A., & HUESMANN, L. R. (1996). The relation of family functioning to violence among inner-city minority youth. *Journal of Family Psychology, 10,* 115–129.

GOSWAMI, U. (1991). Learning about spelling sequences: The role of onsets and rimes in analogies to reading. *Child Development, 62,* 1119–1123.

GOTTMAN, J. M., KATZ, L. F., & HOOVEN, C. (1996). Parental meta-emotion philosophy and the emotional life of families: Theoretical models and preliminary data. *Journal of Family Psychology, 10,* 243–268.

GOULD, R. L. (1972). The phases of adult life: A study in developmental psychology. *American Journal of Psychiatry, 129,* 521–531.

GOULD, R. L. (1978). *Transformations: Growth and change in adult life.* New York: Simon & Schuster.

GRABER, J. A., BROOKS-GUNN, J., & WARREN, M. P. (1995). The antecedents of menarcheal age: Heredity, family environment, and stressful life events. *Child Development, 66,* 346–359.

GRAHAM, S. (1986, August). *Can attribution theory tell us something about motivation in blacks?* Paper presented at the meeting of the American Psychological Association, Washington, DC.

GRAHAM, S., & HOEHN, S. (1995). Children's understanding of aggression and withdrawal as social stigmas: An attributional analysis. *Child Development, 66,* 1143–1161.

GRAHAM-BERMANN, S. A., CUTLER, S. E., LITZENBERGER, B. W., SCHWARTZ, W. E. (1994). Perceived conflict and violence in childhood sibling relationships and later emotional adjustment. *Journal of Family Psychology, 8,* 85–97.

GRALINSKI, J. H., & KOPP, C. B. (1993). Everyday rules for behavior: Mothers' requests to young children. *Developmental Psychology, 29,* 573–584.

GRANDE, C. G. (1988). Delinquency: The learning disabled students' reaction to academic school failure. *Adolescence, 23,* 209–219.

GRANT, C. L., & FODOR, J. G. (1984, April). *Body image and eating disorders: A new role for school psychologist in screening and prevention.* Mimeographed paper, New York University, School of Education, Health, Nursing, and Arts Profession.

GRANT, C. L., & FODOR, J. G. (1986). Adolescent attitudes toward body image and anorexic behavior. *Adolescence, 21,* 269–281.

GRANT, E. A., STORANDT, M., & BOTWINICK, J. (1978). Incentive and practice in the psychomotor performance of the elderly. *Journal of Gerontology, 33,* 413–415.

GRANVOLD, D. K. (1983). Structured separation for marital treatment and decision-making. *Journal of Marital and Family Therapy, 9,* 403–412.

GRANVOLD, D. K., & TARRANT, R. (1983). Structured marital separation as a marital treatment method. *Journal of Marital and Family Therapy, 2,* 189–198.

GRATTAN, M. P., DEVOS, E., LEVY, J., & MCCLINTOCK, M. K. (1992). Asymmetric action in the human newborn: Sex differences in patterns of organization. *Child Development, 63,* 273–289.

GREEN, D. L. (1990). High school student employment in social context: Adolescents' perceptions of the role of part-time work. *Adolescence, 25,* 425–434.

GREEN, J. A. (1992). Testing whether correlation matrices are different from each other. *Developmental Psychology, 28,* 215–224.

GREENBERG, J., PYSZCZYNSKI, T., BURLING, J., SIMON, L., SOLOMON, S., ROSENBLATT, A., LYON, D., & PINEL, E. (1992). Why do people need self-esteem? Converging evidence that self-esteem serves an anxiety-buffering function. *Journal of Personality and Social Psychology, 63,* 913–922.

GREENBERG, J. S., BRUESS, C. E., & SANDS, D. W. (1986). *Sexuality: Insights and issues.* Dubuque, IA: Wm. C. Brown.

GREENBERG, M. A., & STONE, A. A. (1992). Emotional disclosure about traumas and its relation to help: Effects of previous disclosure and trauma and severity. *Journal of Personality and Social Psychology, 63,* 75–84.

GREENBERGER, E., & O'NEIL, R. (1990). Parents' concerns about their child's development: Implications for fathers' and mothers' well-being and attitudes towards work. *Journal of Marriage and the Family, 52,* 621–635.

GREENBERGER, E., & STEINBERG, L. (1981). The work-place as a context for the socialization of youth. *Journal of Youth and Adolescence, 10,* 185–210.

GREENBLAT, C. S. (1993). The salience of sexuality in the early years of marriage. *Journal of Marriage and the Family, 45,* 289–299.

GREENE, A. L., & GRIMSLEY, M. D. (1990). Age and gender differences in adolescents' preferences for parental advice: Mum's the word. *Journal of Adolescent Research, 5,* 396–413.

GREENE, A. L., & REED, E. (1992). Social context differences in the relation between self-esteem and self-concept during late adolescence. *Journal of Adolescent Research, 7,* 266–282.

GREENE, A. L., WHEATLEY, S. M., & ALDAVA, J. F., IV. (1992). Stages on life's way. Adolescents' implicit theories of the life course. *Journal of Adolescent Research, 7,* 364–381.

GREENOUGH, W. T., BLACK, J. R., & WALLACE, C. S. (1987). Experience and brain development. *Child Development, 58,* 539–559.

GREENSTEIN, T. N. (1993). Maternal employment and child behavioral outcomes. *Journal of Family Issues, 3,* 323–354.

GREER, D., POTTS, R., WRIGHT, J. C., & HUSTON, A. (1982). The effects of television commercial form and commercial placement on children's social behavior and attention. *Child Development, 53,* 611–619.

GREER, T., & LOCKMAN, J. J. (1998). Using writing instruments: Invariances in young children and adults. *Child Development, 69,* 888–902.

GREGORY, L. W. (1995). The "Turn Around" process: Factors influencing the school success of urban youth. *Journal of Adolescent Research, 10,* 136–154,

GREIF, G. L. (1988). Single fathers: Helping them cope with day-to-day problems. *Medical Aspects of Human Sexuality, 22,* 18–25.

GREULING, J. W., & DEBLASSIE, R. R. (1980, Fall). Adolescent suicide. *Adolescence, 59,* 589–591.

GRINDSTAFF, C. F. (1988). Adolescent marriage and childbearing: The long-term economic outcome: Canada in the 1980s. *Adolescence, 23,* 45–58.

GRINGLAS, M., & WEINRAUB, M. (1995). The more times change . . . single parenting revisited. *Journal of Family Issues, 16,* 29–52.

GROBSTEIN, C. (1989). When does life begin? *Psychology Today, 23,* 42–46.

GROSS, J. J., CARSTENSEN, L., TSAI, J., PASUPATHI, M., SKORPEN, C. G., & HSU, A. Y. C. (1997). Emotion and aging: Experience, expression, and control. *Psychology and Aging, 12,* 590–599.

GROSS, J. J., & LEVENSON, R. W. (1997). Hiding feelings: The acute effects of inhibiting negative and positive emotions. *Journal of Abnormal Psychology, 106,* 95–103.

GROSSMAN, J. H. (1986). Congenital syphilis. In J. L. Sever & R. L. Brent (Eds.), *Teratogen update: Environmentally induced birth defect risks.* New York: Liss.

GRUMAN, G. J. (1966). A history of ideas about the prolongation of life. The evolution of prolongevity hypothesis to 1800. *Transactions of the American Philosophical Society, 56,* Pt. 9.

GRUSEC, J. E. (1992). Social learning theory and developmental psychology: The legacies of Robert Sears and Albert Bandura. *Developmental Psychology, 28,* 776–786.

GRUSEC, J. E., & GOODNOW, J. J. (1994). Impact of parental discipline methods on the child's internalization of values: A reconceptualization of current points of view. *Developmental Psychology, 30,* 4–19.

GRYCH, J. H., & FINEHAM, F. D. (1993). Children's appraisal of marital conflict: Initial investigations of the cognitive-contextual framework. *Child Development, 64,* 215–230.

GRYCH, J. H., SEID, M., AND FINEHAM, F. D. (1992). Assessing marital conflict from the child's perspective: The children's perception of interparental conflict scale. *Child Development, 63*, 558–572.

GUBRIUM, J. F. (1976). Being single in old age. In J. F. Gubrium (Ed.), *Times, roles and self in old age.* New York: Human Sciences Press.

GUERNEY, B., & MAXSON, P. (1990). Marital and family enrichment research: A decade review and look ahead. *Journal of Marriage and the Family, 52*, 1127–1135.

GUILFORD, J. P. (1967). *The nature of human intelligence.* New York: McGraw-Hill.

GUNNAR, M. R., & NELSON, C. A. (1994). Event-related potentials in year-old infants: Relations with emotionality and cortisol. *Child Development, 65*, 80–94.

GURALNICK, M. J., & GROOM, J. M. (1987). The peer relations of mildly delayed and non-handicapped preschool children in mainstream playgroups. *Child Development, 58*, 1556–1572.

GURIN, J. (1989). Leaner not lighter. *Psychology Today, 23*, 32–36.

GUTIERREZ, J., & SAMEROFF, A. (1990). Determinants of complexity in Mexican-American and Anglo-American mothers' conceptions of child development. *Child Development, 61*, 384–394.

GUTIERREZ, J., SAMEROFF, A. J., & CARRER, B. M. (1988). Acculturation and SES effects on Mexican American parents' concepts of development. *Child Development, 59*, 250–255.

GUTTENTAG, R. E., & HUNT, R. R. (1988). Adult age differences in memory for imagined and performed actions. *Journal of Gerontology, 43*, P107–P108.

GUTTMACHER, A. F. (1983). *Pregnancy, birth and family planning* (rev. ed.). New York: New American Library.

HAAS, W. H., III, & SEROW, W. J. (1993). Amenity retirement migration process: A model and preliminary evidence. *The Gerontologist, 33*, 212–220.

HACK, M. B., BRESLAU, M., ARAM, D, WEISSMAN, B., KLEIN, N., & BORAWSKI-CLARK, E. (1992). The effect of very low birth weight and social risks on neurocognitive abilities at school age. *Journal of Developmental and Behavioral Pediatrics, 13*, 412–420.

HACK, M., TAYLOR, G., KLEIN, N., EIBEN, R., SCHATSCHNEIDER, C., & MERCURI-MINICH, N. (1994). School-age outcomes in children with birth weight under 750 grams. *The New England Journal of Medicine, 331*, 753–759.

HAGAN, P. (1983, May). Does 180 mean supergenius? *Psychology Today, 17*, 18.

HAITH, M. M. (1986). Sensory and perceptual processes in early infancy. *Journal of Pediatrics, 109*, 158–171.

HAKAMIES-BLONQVIST, L. (1994). Aging and fatal accidents in male and female drivers. *Journal of Gerontology, 49*, S286–S290.

HAKUTA, K., & GARCIA, E. E. (1989). Bilingualism and education. *American Psychologist, 44*, 374–379.

HALGIN, R. P., & LEAHY, P. M. (1989). Understanding and treating perfectionistic college students. *Journal of Counseling and Development, 68*, 222–225.

HALL, D. G. (1991). Acquiring proper nouns for familiar and unfamiliar animate objects: Two-year-olds' word-learning biases. *Child Development, 62*, 1142–1154.

HALL, D. G. (1994). Semantic constraints on word learning: Proper names and adjectives. *Child Development, 65*, 1299–1317.

HALL, D. G., & WAXMAN, S. R. (1993). Assumptions about word meaning: Individuation and basic-level kinds. *Child Development, 64*, 1550–1570.

HALL, E. G., & LEE, A. M. (1984). Sex differences in motor performances of young children: Fact or fiction? *Sex Roles, 10*, 217–230.

HALL, G. S. (1891). The contents of children's minds on entering school. *Pedagogical Seminary, 1*, 139–173.

HALL, G. S. (1904). *Adolescence: Its psychology and its relation to physiology, anthropology, sociology, sex, crime, religion, and education* (2 vols.). New York: Appleton.

HALL, H. (1986). A pat on the back helps smokers quit. *Psychology Today, 20*, 20.

HALL, J. A. (1987). Parent-adolescent conflict: An empirical review. *Adolescence, 22*, 767–789.

HALLFRISCH, J., MULLER, D., DRINKWATER, D., TOBIN, J., & ANDRES, R. (1990). Continuing diet trends in men: The Baltimore longitudinal study of aging (1961–1987). *Journal of Gerontology, 45*, M186–M191.

HALLINAN, M. T. (1991). School differences in tracking structures and track assignments. *Journal of Research on Adolescence, 1*, 251–275.

HALPERN, C. T., & UDRY, J. R. (1992). Variation in adolescent hormone measures and implications for behavioral research. *Journal of Research on Adolescence, 2*, 103–122.

HAMACHEK, D. (1995). Self-concept and school achievement: Interaction dynamics and a tool for assessing the self-concept component. *Journal of Counseling and Development, 73*, 419–425.

HAMACHEK, D. E. (1988). Evaluating self-concept and ego development with Erikson's psychosocial framework: A formulation. *Journal of Counseling and Development, 66*, 354–360.

HAMBURGER, A. C. (1988). Beauty quest. *Psychology Today, 22*, 28–32.

HAMM, V. P., & HASHER, L. (1992). Age and the availability of inferences. *Psychology and Aging, 7*, 56–64.

HAMMER, T., & VAGLUM, P. (1990). Use of alcohol and drugs in the transitional phase from adolescence to young adulthood. *Journal of Adolescence, 13*, 129–142.

HAMMIL, S. B. (1994). Parent-adolescent communication in sandwich generation families. *Journal of Adolescent Research, 9*, 458–482.

HAMON, R. R., & BLIESZNER, R. (1990). Filial responsiblity expectations among adult child–older parent pairs. *Journal of Gerontology, 45*, P110–P112.

HANSEN, J., & BOWEY, J. A. (1994). Phonological analysis skills, verbal working memory, and reading ability in second-grade children. *Child Development, 65*, 938–950.

HANSON, R. A. (1990). Initial parent attitudes of pregnant adolescents and a comparison with the decision about adoption. *Adolescence, 25*, 629–645.

HANSON, S. L., & OOMS, T. (1991). The economic costs and rewards of two-earner, two-parent families. *Journal of Marriage and the Family, 53*, 622–634.

HARDING, G., & SNYDER, K. (1991). Tom, Huck, and Oliver Stone as advocates in Kohlberg's just community: Theory-based strategies for moral education. *Adolescence, 26*, 319–330.

HARE, J., & RICHARDS, L. (1993). Children raised by lesbian couples: Does context of birth affect father and partner involvement? *Family Relations, 42*, 249–255.

HARING-HIDORE, M., STOCK, W. A., OKUN, M. A., & WITLER, R. A. (1985). Marital status and subjective well-being: A research synthesis. *Journal of Marriage and the Family, 47*, 947–953.

HARKNESS, S. (1992). Cross-cultural research in child development: A sample of the state of the art. *Developmental Psychology, 28*, 622–625.

HAROLD, G. T., & CONGER, R. D. (1997). Marital conflict and adolescent distress: The role of adolescent awareness. *Child Development, 68*, 333–350.

HARPER, J. F., & MARSHALL, E. (1991). Adolescents' problems and their relationship to self-esteem. *Adolescence, 26*, 799–808.

HARRIS, A., JACKSON, C. M., PATERSON, D. G. and SCAMMON, R. E. (1930). *The measurement of man.* Minneapolis: University of Minnesota Press, p. 193.

HARRIS, J. R., PEDERSEN, M. L., McCLEARN, G. E., PLOMIN, R., & NESSELROADE, J. R. (1992). Age differences in genetic and environmental influences for health from the Swedish adoption/twin study of aging. *The Journals of Gerontology, 47*, P213–P220.

HARRIS, K. M. (1991). Teenage mothers and welfare dependency: working off welfare. *Journal of Family Issues, 12*, 492–519.

HARRIS, M. B. (1994). Growing old gracefully: Age concealment and gender. *Journal of Gerontology, 49*, P149–P158.

HARRIS, P. L., BROWN, E., MARRIOT, C., WHITTAL, S., & HARMER, S. (1991). Monsters, ghosts, and witches: Testing the limits of the fantasy-reality distinction in young children. *British Journal of Developmental Psychology, 9*, 105–123.

HARRIS, P. L., KADANAUGH, R. D., & MEREDITH, M. C. (1994). Young children's comprehension of pretend episodes: The integration of successive actions. *Child Development, 65*, 16–30.

HARRIS, R. (1988). Exercise and sex in the aging patient. *Medical Aspects of Human Sexuality, 22*, 148–159.

HARRIS, T., et al. (1991). Postural change in blood pressure associated with age and systolic blood pressure. *The Journals of Gerontology, 46*, M159–M163.

HARRIS, T. G. (1989). Heart disease in retreat. *Psychology in Retreat, 23*, 46–48.

HARRISON, A. O., WILSON, M. N., PINE, C. J., CHAN, S. Q., & BURIEL, R. (1990). Family ecologies of ethnic minority children. *Child Development, 61,* 347–362.

HART, B., & RISLEY, T. R. (1992). American parenting of language-learning children: Persisting differences in family-child interactions observed in natural home environments. *Developmental Psychology, 28,* 1096–1105.

HART, C. H., DEWOLF, M., WOZNIAK, P., & BURTS, D. C. (1992). Maternal and paternal disciplinary styles: Relations with preschoolers, playground behavioral orientations and peer status. *Child Development, 63,* 790–892.

HART, C. H., LADD, G. W., & BURLESON, B. R. (1990). Children's expectations of the outcomes of social strategies: Relations with sociometric status and maternal disciplinary styles. *Child Development, 61,* 127–137.

HART, K. E. (1990). Coping with anger-provoking situations: Adolescent coping in relation to anger reactivity. *Journal of Adolescent Research, 6,* 357–370.

HARTER, S., & MONSOUR, A. (1992). Developmental analysis of conflict caused by opposing attributes in the adolescent self-portrait. *Developmental Psychology, 28,* 251–260.

HARTER, S., & PIKE, R. (1984). The pictorial scale of perceived competence and social acceptance for young children. *Child Development, 55,* 1969–1982.

HARTLEY, A. A. (1981). Adult age differences in deductive reasoning processes. *Journal of Gerontology, 36,* 700–706.

HARTLEY, J. T., STOJACK, C. C., MUSHANEY, T. J., ANNON, T. A. K., & LEE, D. W. (1994). Reading speed in prose memory in older and younger adults. *Psychology and Aging, 9,* 216–223.

HARTLEY, J. T., & WALSH, D. A. (1980). The effect of monetary incentive on amount and rate of free recall in older and younger adults. *Journal of Gerontology, 35,* 899–905.

HARTMAN, E., RUSS, D., OLDFIELD, M., SIVIAN, I., & COOPER, S. (1987). Who has nightmares? The personality of the lifelong nightmare sufferer. *Archives of General Psychiatry, 44,* 49–56.

HARTOCOLLIS, P. (1972). Aggressive behavior and the fear of violence. *Adolescence, 7,* 479–490.

HARTSOUGH, C. S., LAMBERT, N. M. (1985). Medical factors in hyperactive and normal children: Prenatal developmental and health history findings. *American Journal of Orthopsychiatry, 55,* 190–201.

HARTUP, W. W., FRENCH, D. C., LAURSEN, B., JOHNSTON, M. K., & OGAWA, J. R. (1993). Conflict and friendship relations in middle childhood: Behavior in a closed-field situation. *Child Development, 64,* 445–454.

HARTUP, W. W., LAURSEN, B., STEWART, M. I., & EASTENSON, A. (1988). Conflict and the friendship relations of young children. *Child Development, 59,* 1590–1600.

HARVEY, M. A. S., MCRORIE, M. M., & SMITH, D. W. (1981). Suggested limits to the use of the hot tubs and sauna by pregnant women. *Canadian Medical Association Journal, 125,* 50–53.

HARVEY, S. M., & FABER, K. S. (Jan./Feb. 1993). Obstacles to prenatal care following implementation of a community-based program to reduce financial barriers. *Family Planning Perspectives, 25,* 32–36.

HARVEY, S. M., & SPIGNER, C. (1995). Factors associated with sexual behavior among adolescents: A multivariate analysis. *Adolescence, 30,* 253–264.

HARWOOD, R. L. (1992). The influence of culturally derived values on Anglo and Puerto Rican mothers' perceptions of attachment behavior. *Child Development, 63,* 822–839.

HARWOOD, R. L., SCHOELMERICH, A., VENTURA-COOK, E., SCHULZE, P. A., & WILSON, S. T. (1996). Culture and class influences on Anglo and Puerto Rican mothers' beliefs regarding long-term socialization goals and child behavior. *Child Development, 67,* 2446–2461.

HASELAGER, G. J. T., HARTUP, W. W., VAN LIESHOUT, C. F. M., & RISKEN-WALRAVEN, J. M. A. (1998). Similarities between friends and nonfriends in middle childhood. *Child Development, 69,* 1198–1208.

HASKETT, M. E., & KISTNER, J. A. (1991). Social interactions and peer perceptions of young physically abused children. *Child Development, 62,* 979–990.

HATCH, L. R., & BULCROFT, K. (1992). Contact with friends in later life: Disentangling the effects of gender and marital status. *Journal of Marriage and the Family, 54,* 222–232.

HATCHER, P. J., HULME, C., & ELLIS, A. W. (1994). Ameliorating early reading failure by integrating the teaching of reading and phonological skills: The phonological linkage hypothesis. *Child Development, 65,* 41–57.

HATFIELD, E., & SPRECHER, S. (1986). Measuring passionate love in intimate relationships. *Journal of Adolescence, 9,* 383–410.

HATTON, D. D., BAILEY, D. B., JR., BURCHINAL, M. R., & FERRELL, K. A. (1997). Developmental growth curves of preschool children with vision impairments. *Child Development, 68,* 788–806.

HAUCK, W. E., & LOUGHEAD, M. (1985). Adolescent self-monitoring. *Adolescence, 20,* 567–574.

HAUG, M. (1978, July). Aging and the right to terminate medical treatment. *Journal of Gerontology, 33,* 586–591.

HAUSER, S. T., BORNAN, E. H., JACOBSON, A. M., POWERS, S. I., & NOAM, G. G. (1991). Understanding family contexts of adolescent coping: A study of parental ego development and adolescent coping strategies. *Journal of Early Adolescence, 11,* 96–124.

HAVERKAMP, B., & DANILUK, J. C. (1993). Child sexual abuse: Ethical issues for the family therapist. *Family Relations, 42,* 134–139.

HAVIGHURST, R. J. (1972). *Developmental tasks and education* (3rd ed.). New York: David McKay.

HAWKINS, A. J., EGGEBEEN, D. J. (1991). Are fathers fungible? Patterns of co-resident adult men in maritally disruptive families and young children's well-being. *Journal of Marriage and the Family, 53,* 958–972.

HAY, D. F., NASH, A., & PEDERSEN, J. (1983). Interaction between six-month-old peers. *Child Development, 54,* 557–562.

HAYES, D. S., & CASEY, D. M. (1992). Young children and television: The retention of emotional reactions. *Child Development, 63,* 1423–1436.

HAYES, R. L. (1994). The legacy of Lawrence Kohlberg: Implications for counseling in human development. *Journal of Counseling and Development, 72,* 261–267.

HAYFLICK, L. (1970). Aging under glass. *Experimental Gerontology, 5,* 291–303.

HAYNE, H., & ROBEE-COLLIER, C. (1995). The organization of reactivated memory in infancy. *Child Development, 66,* 893–906.

HAYNE, H., ROBEE-COLLIER, C., & PERRIS, E. E. (1987). Categorization and memory retrieval by three-month-olds. *Child Development, 58,* 750–767.

HAYS, S. (1998). The relationship assumptions and unrealistic prescriptions of attachment theory: A comment on parent's socioemotional investment in children. *Journal of Marriage and the Family, 60,* 782–795.

HAYSLIP, B., & BROOKSHIRE, R. G. (1985). Relationships among abilities in elderly adults: A time lag analysis. *Journal of Gerontology, 40,* 748–750.

HAYSLIP, B., & LEON, J. (1988). *Geriatric care practice in hospice settings.* Beverly Hills, CA: Sage.

HAZELL, P. (1991). Postvention after teenage suicide: An Australian experience. *Journal of Adolescence, 14,* 335–342.

HAZEN, N. L., & BLACK, B. (1989). Preschool peer communication skills: The role of social status and interaction context. *Child Development, 60,* 867–876.

HEALTH SERVICES ISSUES AIDS GUIDELINES (1985, November 15). Portland, ME: *Portland Press Herald.*

HEATH, A. C., KESSLER, R. C., NEALE, M. C., EAVES, L. J., & KENDLER, K. S. (1992). Evidence for genetic influences on personality from self-reports and informant ratings. *Journal of Personality and Social Psychology, 63,* 85–96.

HEATHERINGTON, L., FRIEDLANDER, M. L., & JOHNSON, W. F. (1989). Informed consent in family therapy research: Ethical dilemmas and practical problems. *Journal of Family Psychology, 2,* 373–385.

HEATHERTON, T. F., HERMAN, C. P., & POLIVY, J. (1992). The effects of distress on eating: The importance of ego-involvement. *Journal of Personality and Social Psychology, 62,* 801–803.

HEATON, T. B., & ALBRECHT, S. L. (1991). Stable, unhappy marriages. *Journal of Marriage and the Family, 53,* 747–758.

HECKHAUSEN, J. (1997). Developmental regulation across adulthood: Primary and secondary control of age-related challenges. *Developmental Psychology, 13,* 176–187.

HECKHAUSEN, J., & BALTES, P. B. (1991). Perceived controllability of expected psychological change across adulthood and old age. *Journal of Gerontology, 46,* P165–P173.

HECKHAUSEN, J., & KRUEGER, J. (1993). Developmental expectations for the self and most other people: Age grading in three functions of social comparison. *Developmental Psychology, 29,* 539–548.

HEILBRUN, A. B. (1984). Identification with the father and peer intimacy of the daughter. *Family Relations, 33,* 597–605.

HEILBRUN, A. B., & LOFTUS, M. P. (1986). The role of sadism and peer pressure in the sexual aggression of male college students. *Journal of Sex Research, 22,* 320–332.

HEIM, S. C., & SNYDER, D. K. (1991). Predicting depression from marital distress and attributional processes. *Journal of Marriage and Family Therapy, 17,* 67–72.

HELGESON, V. S. (1992). Moderators of the relation between perceived control and adjustment to chronic illness. *Journal of Personality and Social Psychology, 63,* 656–666.

HELWIG, C. C., TISAK, M. S., & TURIEL, E. (1990). Children's social reasoning in context: Reply to Gabennesch. *Child Development, 61,* 2068–2078.

HENDRICKS, J., & HENDRICKS, C. D. (1986). *Aging in mass society: Myths and realities* (3rd ed.). Boston: Little, Brown.

HENRY, C. S. (1994). Family system characteristics, parental behaviors, and adolescent family life satisfaction. *Family Relations, 43,* 447–455.

HENSHAW, S. K. (1998). Unintended pregnancy in the United States. *Family Planning Perspectives, 30,* 24.

HENSLEY, W. E. (1994). Height as a basis for interpersonal attraction. *Adolescence, 29,* 469–474.

HENSLEY, W. E. (1998). The measurement of height. *Adolescence, 33,* 629–635.

HEPWORTH, J., RYDER, R. G., & DREYER, A. S. (1984). The effects of parental loss on the formation of intimate relationships. *Journal of Marital and Family Therapy, 10,* 73–82.

HERMAN, M. A., & MCHALE, S. M. (1993). Coping with parental negativity: Links with parental warmth and child adjustment. *Journal of Applied Developmental Psychology, 14,* 121–136.

HERTZLER, A. A., & GRUN, I. (1990). Potential nutrition message in magazines read by college students. *Adolescence, 25,* 717–724.

HERTZOG, C., RASKIND, C. L., & CANNON, C. J. (1986). Age-related slowing in semantic information processing speed: An individual difference analysis. *Journal of Gerontology, 41,* 500–502.

HERZOG, A. R., DIOKNO, A. C., BROWN, M. B., NORMOLLE, D. P., & BROCK, B. M. (1990). Two-year incidence, remission, and change patterns of urinary incontinence in noninstitutionalized older adults. *Journal of Gerontology, 45,* M67–M74.

HESS, T. M., & FLANNAGAN, D. A. (1992). Schema-based retrieval processes in young and older adults. *The Journals of Gerontology, 47,* P52–P58.

HESS, T. M., FLANNAGAN, D. A., & TATE, C. S. (1993). Aging and memory for schematically vs. taxonomically organized verbal materials. *The Journals of Gerontology, 48,* P37–P44.

HESTON, L. L., & MASTRI, A. R. (1982). Age at onset of Pick's and Alzheimer's dementia: Implication for diagnosis and research. *Journal of Gerontology, 37,* 422–424.

HETHERINGTON, E. M. (1989). Coping with family transitions: Winners, losers, and survivors. *Child Development, 60,* 1–14.

HETZEL, S., WINN, D., & TOLSTOSHEV, H. (1991). Loss and change: New directions in death education for adolescents. *Journal of Adolescence, 14,* 323–334.

HEYMONT, G. (1980, July–August). A star is reborn. *Dynamic Years, 15,* 61–64.

HICKEY, T., & STILWELL, D. L. (1991). Health promotion for older people: All is not well. *The Gerontologist, 31,* 822–829.

HICKLING, A. K., & GELMAN, S. A. (1995). How does your garden grow? Early conceptualization of seeds and their place in the plant growth cycle. *Child Development, 66,* 856–876.

HIER, S. J., KORBOOT, P. J., & SCHWEITZER, R. D. (1990). Social adjustment and symptomatology in two types of homeless adolescents: Runaways and throwaways. *Adolescence, 25,* 761–772.

HIGGINS, B. S. (1990). Couple infertility: From the perspective of the close-relationship model. *Family Relations, 39,* 81–86.

HIGH SCHOOL PROFILE REPORT. *Annual Normative Data.* (1997). Iowa City, IA: The American College Testing Program.

HILL, L. M., BRECKLE, R., & GEHRKING, W. C. (1983). The prenatal detection of congenital malformations by ultrasonography. *Mayo Clinic Proceedings, 58,* 805–826.

HILL, R. D., STORANDT, M., & MALLEY, M. (1993). The impact of long-term exercise training on psychological functions in older adults. *The Journals of Gerontology, 48,* P12–P17.

HILL, R. D., STORANDT, M., & SIMEONE, C. (1990). The effects of memory skills training and incentives on free recall in older learners. *Journal of Gerontology, 45,* P227–P232.

HILTON, J. N., & HALDEMAN, V. A. (1991). Gender differences in the performance of household tasks by adults and children in single-parent and two-parent, two-earner families. *Journal of Family Issues, 12,* 114–130.

HILTZ, S. R. (1978, November/December). Widowhood: A roleless role. *Marriage and the Family Review, 1,* 1–10.

HIMELSTEIN, S., GRAHAM, S., & WEINTER, B. (1991). An attributional analysis of maternal beliefs about the importance of child-rearing practices. *Child Development, 62,* 301–310.

HINDE, R. (1983). Ethology and child development. In P. H. Mussen (Ed.), *Handbook of child psychology* (4th ed., Vol. 2). New York: Wiley.

HINDE, R. A. (1991). When is an evolutionary approach useful? *Child Development, 62,* 671–675.

HINDE, R. A. (1992). Developmental psychology in the context of other behavioral sciences. *Developmental Psychology, 28,* 1018–1029.

HINDS, M. D. (1982, May 2). Countries acting on baby formula. *New York Times,* p. 10.

HINES, M., & KAUFMAN, F. R. (1994). Androgen and the development of human sex-typical behavior: Rough-and-tumble play and sex of preferred playmates in children with congenital adrenal hyperplasia (CAH). *Child Development, 65,* 1042–1053.

HITE, S. L. (1981). *The Hite report: A nation-wide study of female sexuality.* New York: Dell.

HITE, S. L. (1982). *The Hite report on male sexuality.* New York: Ballantine.

HO, C. S., LEMPERS, J. D., & CLARK-LEMPERS, D. S. (1995). Effects of economic hardship on adolescent self-esteem: A family mediation model. *Adolescence, 30,* 118–131.

HOARE, C. H. (1991). Psychosocial identity development and cultural others. *Journal of Counseling and Development, 70,* 45–53.

HOBART, C. (1987). Parent-child relations in remarried families. *Journal of Family Issues, 8,* 259–277.

HOBART, C. (1988). The family system in remarriages: An exploratory study. *Journal of Marriage and the Family, 50,* 649–661.

HOBART, C. (1992). How they handle it: Young Canadians, sex, and AIDS. *Youth and Society, 23,* 411–433.

HOCK, E., & SCHIRTZINGER, M. B. (1992). Maternal separation anxiety: Its developmental course and relation to maternal mental health. *Child Development, 63,* 93–102.

HOELTER, J., & HARPER, L. (1987). Structural and interpersonal family influences on adolescent self-conception. *Journal of Marriage and the Family, 49,* 129–139.

HOFF-GINSBERG, E. (1991). Mother-child conversation in different social classes and communicative settings. *Child Development, 62,* 782–796.

HOFFMAN, L. W., & YOUNGBLADE, L. M. (1998). Maternal employment, morale, and parenting style: Social class comparisons. *Journal of Applied Developmental Psychology, 19,* 389–413.

HOLAHAN, C. J., VALENTINER, D. P., & MOOS, R. H. (1994). Parental support and psychological adjustment during the transition to young adulthood in a college sample. *Journal of Family Psychology, 8,* 215–223.

HOLCOMB, W. R., & KASHANI, J. H. (1991). Personality characteristics of a community sample of adolescents with conduct disorders. *Adolescence, 26,* 579–586.

HOLDEN, G. W., & RITCHIE, K. L. (1991). Linking extreme marital discord, child rearing, and child behavior problems: Evidence from battered women. *Child Development, 62,* 311–327.

HOLDEN, G. W., & WEST, M. J. (1989). Proximate regulation by mothers: A demonstration of how differing styles affect young children's behavior. *Child Development, 60,* 64–69.

HOLDING, D. H., NOONAN, R. K., PFAU, H. D., & HOLDING, C. S. (1986). Date, attribution, age, and the distribution of lifetime memories. *Journal of Gerontology, 41,* 481–485.

HOLE, J. W. (1987). *Human anatomy and physiology* (4th ed.). Dubuque, IA: Wm. C. Brown.

HOLLAND, C. A., & RABBITT, P. M. A. (1992). Effects of age-related reductions in processing resources on text recall. *The Journals of Gerontology, 47,* P129–P137.

HOLLERAN, P. R., PASCALE, J., & FRALEY, J. (1988). Personality correlates of college-age bulimics. *Journal of Counseling and Development, 66,* 378–381.

HOLMAN, T. B., & LI, B. D. (1997). Premarital factors influencing perceived readiness for marriage. *Journal of Family Issues, 18,* 124–144.

HOLMBECK, G. N., & HILL, J. P. (1991a). Conflictive engagement, positive affect, and menarche in families with seventh-grade girls. *Child Development, 62,* 1030–1048.

HOLMBECK, G. N., & HILL, J. P. (1991b). Rules, rule behaviors, and biological maturation in families with seventh-grade boys and girls. *Journal of Early Adolescence, 11,* 236–257.

HOLMBECK, G. N., WATERS, K. A., & BROOKMEN, R. R. (1990). Psychosocial correlates of sexually transmitted diseases and sexual activity in black adolescent females. *Journal of Adolescent Research, 5,* 431–448.

HOLT, E. L. (1972). Energy requirements. In H. L. Barnett & A. H. Einhorn (Eds.), *Pediatrics* (15th ed.). New York: Appleton-Century-Crofts.

HOOKER, K. (1992). Possible selves and perceived health in older adults and college students. *The Journals of Gerontology, 47,* P85–P95.

HOOKER, K., & KAUS, C. R. (1994). Health-related possible selves in young and middle adulthood. *Psychology and Aging, 9,* 126–133.

HOPSON, J. L. (1986). The unraveling of insomnia. *Psychology Today, 22,* 62–63.

HORLEY, J. (1984). Life satisfaction, happiness, and morale: The problems with the use of subjective well-being indicators. *Gerontologist, 24,* 124–127.

HORN, J. C. (1986). When a parent dies. *Psychology Today, 20,* 15.

HORN, J. C. (1988). The peak years. *Psychology Today, 22,* 62–63.

HORN, J. C., & MEER, J. (1987). The vintage years. *Psychology Today, 21,* 76, 77, 80–84, 88–90.

HORN, J. L., & CATTEL, R. B. (1967). Age differences in fluid and crystallized intelligence. *Acta Psychologica, 26,* 107–129.

HORN, J. M. (1983). The Texas Adoption Project. *Child Development, 54,* 268–275.

HORN, M. E., & RUDOLPH, L. B. (1987). An investigation of verbal interaction knowledge of sexual behavior and self-concept in adolescent mothers. *Adolescence, 87,* 591–598.

HOROWITZ, F. D. (1992). John B. Watson's legacy: Learning and environment. *Developmental Psychology, 28,* 360–367.

HOROWITZ, T. R. (1992). Dropout—Mertonian or reproduction scheme? *Adolescence, 27,* 451–459.

HORWATH, C. C. (1991). Nutrition goals for older adults: A review. *The Gerontologist, 31,* 811–821.

HORWITZ, A. B., & WHITE, H. R. (1998). The relationship of cohabitation and mental health: A study of a young adult cohort. *Journal of Marriage and the Family, 60,* 505–514.

HOUSER, B. B., & BERKMAN, S. L. (1984). Aging parent/mature child relationships. *Journal of Marriage and the Family, 46,* 245–299.

HOWARD, D. V., & HOWARD, J. H., JR. (1992). Adult age differences in the rate of learning serial patterns: Evidence from direct and indirect tests. *Psychology and Aging, 7,* 232–241.

HOWARD, D. V., LASAGA, M. I., & MCANDREWS, M. P. (1980). Semantic activation during memory encoding across the life span. *Journal of Gerontology, 35,* 884–890.

HOWE, N. (1991). Sibling-directed internal state language, perspective taking, and affective behavior. *Child Development, 62,* 1503–1512.

HOWELL, M. C., ALLEN, M. C., & DORESS, P. B. (1987). Dying and death. In P. B. Doress & D. L. Siegal and the Midlife and Older Women Book Project (Eds.), *Ourselves, growing older* (pp. 392–403). New York: Simon & Schuster.

HOWES, C., & HAMILTON, C. E. (1992). Children's relationships with child care teachers: Stability and concordance with parental attachments. *Child Development, 63,* 867–878.

HOWES, C., HAMILTON, C. E., & MATHESON, C. C. (1994). Children's relationships with peers: Differential associations with aspects of the teacher-child relationship. *Child Development, 65,* 253–263.

HOWES, C., & MATHESON, C. C. (1992). Sequences in the development of competent play with peers: Social and social pretend play. *Developmental Psychology, 28,* 961–974.

HOWES, C., & RUBENSTEIN, J. (1985). Determinants of toddler experiences in day care: Age of entry and quality of setting. *Child Care Quarterly, 14,* 140–151.

HOWES, C., UNGER, O., & SEIDNER, L. B. (1989). Social pretend play in toddlers: Parallels with social play and solitary pretend. *Child Development, 66,* 77–84.

HOWES, C., & WU, F. (1990). Peer interactions and friendships in an ethnically diverse school setting. *Child Development, 61,* 531–541.

HOW PEOPLE WILL LIVE TO BE 100 OR MORE. (1983, July 4). *U.S. News and World Report, 73,* 74.

HOYT, D. R., & CREECH, J. C. (1983). The life satisfaction index: A methodological and theoretical critique. *Journal of Gerontology, 38,* 111–116.

HUDLEY, C., & GRAHAM, S. (1993). An attributional intervention to reduce peer-directed aggression among African-American boys. *Child Development, 64,* 124–138.

HUDSON, J. A., & SHEFFIELD, E. G. (1998). Déjà vu all over again: Effects of re-enactment on toddlers' event memory. *Child Development, 69,* 51–67.

HUDSON, L. M., & GRAY, W. M. (1986). Formal operations, the imaginary audience and the personal fable. *Adolescence, 84,* 751–765.

HUDSON, R. B. (1987). Tomorrow's able elders: Implications for the state. *Gerontologist, 27,* 405–409.

HUGHES, S. L., DUNLOP, D., EDELMAN, P., CHANG, R. W., & SINGER, R. H. (1994). Impact of joint impairment on longitudinal disability in elderly persons. *Journal of Gerontology, 49,* S291–S300.

HULTSCH, D. F., Hammer, M. & Small, B. J. (1993). Age differences in cognitive performance in later life: Relationships to self-reported health and activity lifestyle. *The Journals of Gerontology, 48,* P1–P11.

HUNDLEBY, J. D., & MERCER, G. W. (1987). Family and friends as social environments and their relationship to youth adolescents' use of alcohol and marijuana. *Journal of Marriage and the Family, 49,* 151–164.

HUNT, M. (1974a). *Sexual behavior in the 1970s.* New York: Dell.

HUNT, M. (1974b). Sexual behavior in the 1970s. *Playboy,* p. 204.

HURLEY, D. (1985, March). Arresting delinquency. *Psychology Today, 19,* 62–68.

HURRELMANN, K., ENGEL, U., HOLLER, B., & NORDLOHNE, E. (1988). Failure in school, family conflicts, and psychosomatic disorders in adolescence. *Journal of Adolescence, 11,* 237–249.

HURWICZ, M., et al. (1992). Salient life events in three-generation families. *The Journals of Gerontology, 47,* P13.

HUSTON, A. C., WRIGHT, J. C., ALBAREZ, M., TRUGLIO, R., FITCH, M., & PIEMYAT, S. (1995). Perceived television reality in children's emotional and cognitive responses to its social content. *Journal of Applied Developmental Psychology, 16,* 231–251.

HUTCHINS, E. (1991). The social organization of distributed cognition. In J. M. Levine and S. D. Teasley (Eds.), *Perspectives on Socially Shared Cognition.* Washington, DC: American Psychological Association.

HUTCHINSON, M. K., & COONEY, T. M. (1998). Patterns of parent-teen sexual risk communication: Implications for intervention. *Family Relations, 47,* 185–194.

HUTTENLOCHER, J., LEVINE, S., & VEVEA, J. (1998). Environmental input and cognitive growth: A study using time-period comparisons. *Child Development, 69,* 1012–1029.

HYDE, J. S. (1985). *Half the human experience.* Lexington, MA: D.C. Heath.

HYLAND, D. T., & ACKERMAN, A. M. (1988). Reminiscence and autobiographical memory in the study of personal past. *Journal of Gerontology, 43,* P35–P39.

HYNEL, S., BOWKER, A., & WOODY, C. (1993). Aggressive versus withdrawn, unpopular children. Variations in peer and self-perceptions in multiple domains. *Child Development, 64,* 879–896.

HYSON, M. C., & IZARD, C. E. (1985). Continuities and changes in emotional expressions during brief separations at 13 and 18 months. *Developmental Psychology, 21,* 1065–1170.

INAGAKI, K., & HATANO, G. (1993). Young children's understanding of the mind-body distinction. *Child Development, 64,* 1534–1549.

INHELDER, B., & PIAGET, J. (1958). *The growth of logical thinking from childhood to adolescence.* New York: Basic Books.

INOUYE, S. K., ALBERT, M. S., MOHS, R., SUN, K., & BERKMAN, L. F. (1993). Cognitive performance in high-functioning community-dwelling elderly population. *Journal of Gerontology, 48,* M146–M151.

INSTITUTE FOR SOCIAL RESEARCH. (1985). How children use time. In *Time, goals, and well-being*. Ann Arbor: University of Michigan.

IOSUB, S., BAMJI, H., STONE, R. K., GROMISCH, D. S., & WASERMAN, E. (1987). More on human immune deficiency virus embryopathy. *Pediatrics, 80,* 512–516.

IRION, J. C., & BLANCHARD-FIELDS, F. (1987). A cross-sectional comparison of adaptive coping in adulthood. *Journal of Gerontology, 42,* 502–504.

ISABELLA, R. A., & BELSKY, J. (1991). Interactional synchrony and the origins of infant-mother attachment: A replication study. *Child Development, 62,* 373–384.

ISHII-KUNTZ, M. (1994). Parental involvement and perception toward fathers' roles: A comparison between Japan and the United States. *Journal of Family Issues, 15,* 30–48.

ISHII-KUNTZ, M., & LEE, G. R. (1987). Status of the elderly: An extension of the theory. *Journal of Marriage and the Family, 49,* 413–420.

ISTVAN, J. (1986). Stress, anxiety, and birth outcomes: A critical review of the evidence. *Psychological Bulletin, 100,* 331–348.

IVES, D. G., BONINO, P., TRAVEN, N. D., & KULLER, L. H. (1993). Morbidity and mortality in rural community-dwelling elderly with low total serum cholesterol. *The Journals of Gerontology, 48,* M103–M107.

IZARD, C. E. (1977). *Human emotions.* New York: Plenum.

IZARD, C. E. (1980). The young infant's ability to produce discreet emotion expression. *Developmental Psychology, 16,* 132–140.

IZARD, C. E., HAYNES, O. M., CHISHOLM, G., & BAAK, K. (1991). Emotional determinants of infant-mother attachment. *Child Development, 62,* 906–917.

IZARD, C. E., HEMBREE, E. A., & HUEBNER, R. R. (1987). Infants' emotion expressions to acute pain: Developmental change and stability of individual differences. *Developmental Psychology, 23,* 105–113.

JACOB, T. (1992). Family studies of alcoholism. *Journal of Family Psychology, 5,* 319–338.

JACOBS, J. E., & ECCLES, J. S. (1992). The impact of mothers' gender-role stereotypic beliefs on mothers' and children's ability perceptions. *Journal of Personality and Social Psychology, 63,* 932–944.

JACOBS, J. E., & POTENZA, M. (1991). The use of judgment heuristics to make social and object decisions: A developmental perspective. *Child Development, 62,* 166–178.

JACOBSEN, T., & HOFMANN, V. (1997). Children's attachment representation: Longitudinal relations to school behavior and academic competency in middle childhood and adolescence. *Developmental Psychology, 33,* 703–710.

JACOBSON, J. E., & WILLIE, D. E. (1986). The influence of attachment pattern on developmental changes in peer interaction from the toddler to the preschool period. *Child Development, 57,* 338–347.

JACOBSON, J. L., JACOBSON, S. W., FEIN, G. G., SCHWARTZ, P. M., & DOWLER, J. K. (1984). Prenatal exposure to an environmental toxin: A test of multiple effects. *Developmental Psychology, 20,* 523–532.

JACOBSON, S. W., & FRYE, K. F. (1991). Effects of maternal support on attachment: Experimental evidence. *Child Development, 62,* 572–582.

JACOBVITZ, D., & SROUFE, L. A. (1987). The early caregiver-child relationship and attention-deficit disorder with hyperactivity in kindergarten: A prospective study. *Child Development, 58,* 1496–1504.

JAKAB, I. (1987). Growing up in the 80s: Prescriptions for raising a happy and successful child. *Medical Aspects of Human Sexuality, 21,* 53–63.

JAMIESON, D. J., & BUESCHER, P. A. (Sept./Oct., 1992). The effect of family planning participation on prenatal care use and low birth weight. *Family Planning Perspectives, 24,* 214–218.

JANUS, M., BURGESS, A. W., & McCORMACK, A. (1987). Histories of sexual abuse in adolescent male runaways. *Adolescence, 22,* 405–417.

JEAN-GILLIS, M., & CRITTENDEN, P. M. (1990). Maltreating families: A look at siblings. *Family Relations, 39,* 323–329.

JECKER, N. S., & SCHNEIDERMAN, L. J. (1994). Is dying young worse than dying old? *The Gerontologist, 34,* 66–72.

JEMMOTT, J. B., III., & JEMMOTT, L. S. (1993). Alcohol and drug use during sexual activity. Predicting the HIV-risk-related behaviors of inner-city black male adolescents. *Journal of Adolescent Research, 8,* 41–57.

JEMMOTT, L. S., & JEMMOTT, J. B., III (1990). Sexual knowledge, attitudes, and risky sexual behavior among inner-city black male adolescents. *Journal of Adolescent Research, 5,* 346–369.

JEMMOTT, L. S., & JEMMOTT, J. B., III (1992). Family structure, parental strictness, and sexual behavior among inner-city black male adolescents. *Journal of Adolescent Research, 7,* 192–207.

JENNINGS, K. D., STAGG, V., & CONNORS, R. E. (1991). Social networks and mothers' interactions with their preschool children. *Child Development, 62,* 966–978.

JENNINGS, K. D., STAGG, V., CONNORS, R. E., & ROSS, S. (1995). Social networks of mothers of physically handicapped preschoolers: Group differences and relations to mother-child interaction. *Journal of Applied Developmental Psychology, 16,* 193–209.

JENSEN, G. F. (1986). Explaining differences in academic behavior between public-school and Catholic-school students. A quantitative case study. *Sociology of Education, 59,* 32–41.

JENSEN, L., & BORGES, M. (1986). The effect of maternal employment on adolescent daughters. *Adolescence, 21,* 659–666.

JOESCH, J. M. (1994). Children and the timing of women's paid work after childbirth: A further specification of the relationship. *Journal of Marriage and the Family, 56,* 429–440.

JOESCH, J. M. (1997). Paid leave and the timing of women's employment before and after birth. *Journal of Marriage and the Family, 59,* 1008–1021.

JOHN, O. P., CASPI, A., ROBINS, R. W., MOFFITT, T. E., & STOUTHAMER-LOEBER, M. (1994). "The Little Five": Exploring the nomological network of the five-factor model of personality in adolescent boys. *Child Development, 65,* 160–178.

JOHNSON, B. M., SHULMAN, S., & COLLINGS, W. A. (1991). Systemic patterns of parenting as reported by adolescents: Developmental differences and implications for psychosocial outcomes. *Journal of Adolescent Research, 6,* 235–252.

JOHNSON, C., LEWIS, C., LOVE, S., LEWIS, L., & STUCKEY, M. (1984, February). Incidence and correlates of bulimic behavior in a female high school population. *Journal of Youth and Adolescence, 13,* 15–26.

JOHNSON, C. L., & TROLL, L. E. (1994). Constraints and facilitators to friendships in late late life. *The Gerontologist, 34,* 79–87.

JOHNSON, D. R., AMOLOZA, T. O., & BOOTH, A. (1992). Stability a developmental change in marital quality: A three-wave panel analysis. *Journal of Marriage and the Family, 54,* 582–594.

JOHNSON, E. M., & HUSTON, T. L. (1998). The perils of love, or why wives adapt to husbands during the transition to parenthood. *Journal of Marriage and the Family, 60,* 195–204.

JOHNSON, M. M. S. (1990). Age differences in decision making: A process methodology for examining strategic information processing. *Journal of Gerontology, 45,* P75–P78.

JOHNSON, R., & STREHLER, B. L. (1972). Loss of genes coding for ribosomal RNA in aging bring cells. *Nature (London), 240,* 412–414.

JOHNSON, S. C., & SOLOMON, G. E. A. (1997). Why dogs have puppies and cats have kittens: The role of birth in young children's understanding of biological origins. *Child Development, 68,* 404–419.

JOHNSON, T. R., & TROPPE, N. (1992). Improving literacy and employability among disadvantaged youths. The Job Corps model. *Youth and Society, 23,* 335–355.

JOHNSTON, L. D., O'MALLEY, P. M., & BACHMAN, J. G. (1987). *National trends in drug use and related factors among American high school students and young adults, 1975–1986.* Washington, DC: U.S. Government Printing Office.

JONES, J. C., & BARLOW, D. H. (1990). Self-report frequency of sexual urges, fantasies, and masturbatory fantasies in heterosexual males and females. *Archives of Sexual Behavior, 19,* 269–279.

JONES, S. S. (1996). Imitation or exploration? Young infants matching of adults' oral gestures. *Child Development, 67,* 1952–1969.

JONES, S. S., & RAAG, T. (1989). Smile production in older infants. The importance of a social recipient for the facial signal. *Child Development, 60,* 811–818.

JONES, S. S., SMITH, L. B., & LANDAU, B. (1991). Object properties and knowledge in early lexical learning. *Child Development, 62,* 499–516.

JOSE, P. E. (1990). Just-world reasoning in children's immanent justice judgments. *Child Development, 61,* 1024–1033.

JOSEPHS, R A., MARKUS, H. R., & TAFARODI, R. W. (1992). Gender and self-esteem. *Journal of Personality and Social Psychology, 63,* 391–402.

JOSSELSON, R. (1987). *Finding herself: Pathways to identity development in women.* San Francisco: Jossey-Bass.

JOURILES, E. N., & NORWOOD, W. O. (1995). Physical aggression towards boys and girls in families characterized by the battering of women. *Journal of Family Psychology, 9,* 69–78.

JOURILES, E. N., MURPHY, C. M., FARRIS, A. M., SMITH, D. A., RICHTERS, J. E., & WATERS, E. (1991). Marital adjustment, parental disagreements about child rearing, and behavior problems in boys: Increasing the specificity of the marital assessment. *Child Development, 62,* 1424–1433.

JOYCE, E. (1984). A time of grieving. *Psychology Today, 18,* 42–46.

JUDGE, J. O., KING, M. B., WHIPPLE, R., CLIVE, J., & WOLSSON, L. I. (1995). Dynamic balance in older persons: Effects of reduced visual and proprioceptive input. *Journal of Gerontology, 50A,* M263–M270.

JUDGE, S. L. (1998). Parental coping strategies and strengths in families of young children with disabilities. *Family Relations, 47,* 263–268.

JULIAN, T. W., MCKENRY, P. C., & MCKELVEY, M. W. (1994). Cultural variations in parenting: Perceptions of Caucasian, African-American, Hispanic, and Asian-American parents. *Family Relations, 43,* 30–37.

JURICH, A. P., POLSON, C. J., JURICH, J. A., & BATES, R. A. (1985). Family factors in the lives of drug users and abusers. *Adolescence, 20,* 143–159.

JURICH, A. P., SCHUMM, W. R., & BOLLMAN, S. R. (1987). The degree of family orientation perceived by mothers, fathers, and adolescents. *Adolescence, 22,* 119–238.

JUSEZYK, P. W., CUTLER, A., & REDANZ, N. J. (1993). Infants' preference for the predominant stress patterns of English words. *Child Development, 64,* 675–687.

KAFKA, R. R., & LONDON, B. (1991). Communication and relationships in adolescent substance use: The influence of parents and friends. *Adolescence, 26,* 587–598.

KAGAN, J., ARCUS, D., SNIDMAN, N., YUFENG, W., HENDLER, J., & GREENE, S. (1994). Reactivity in infants: A cross-national comparison. *Developmental Psychology, 30,* 342–345.

KAGAN, J., REZNICK, J. S., CLARKE, C., SNIDMAN, N., & GARCIA-COLE, C. (1984). Behavioral inhibitors to the unfamiliar. *Child Development, 55,* 2212–2225.

KAGAN, J., REZNICK, J. S., & SNIDMAN, N. (1987). The physiology and psychology of behavioral inhibition in children. *Child Development, 58,* 1459–1473.

KAGAN, J., REZNICK, J. S., SNIDMAN, N., GIBBONS, J., & JOHNSON, M. (1988). Childhood derivatives of inhibition and lack of inhibition to the familiar. *Child Development, 59,* 1580–1589.

KAHN, J. R., & LONDON, K. A. (1991). Premarital sex and the risk of divorce. *Journal of Marriage and the Family, 53,* 845–855.

KAIL, R. (1992). Processing speed, speech rate, and memory. *Developmental Psychology, 28,* 899–904.

KAITZ, M., LAPIDOT, P., BRONNER, R., & EIDELMAN, A. I. (1992). Parturient women can recognize their infants by touch. *Developmental Psychology, 28,* 35–39.

KAITZ, M., MESCHAULACH-SARFATY, O., AUERBACH, J., & EIDELMAN, A. (1988). A reexamination of newborn ability to imitate facial expressions. *Developmental Psychology, 24,* 3–7.

KALISH, C. (1998). Reasons and causes: Children's understanding of conformity to social rules and physical laws. *Child Development, 69,* 706–720.

KALISH, C. W., & GELMAN, S. A. (1992). On wooden pillows: Multiple classifications and children's category-based inductions. *Child Development, 63,* 1536–1557.

KALISH, R. A. (1985a). The social context of death and dying. In R. H. Binstock & E. Shanas (Eds.), *Handbook of aging and the social sciences.* New York: Van Nostrand-Reinhold.

KALISH, R. A. (1985b). *Death, grief, and caring relationships* (2nd ed.). Monterey, CA: Brooks/Cole.

KALISH, R. A., & REYNOLDS, D. K. (1981). *Death and ethnicity: A psychocultural study.* Farmington, NY: Baywood.

KALLEN, D. J., GRIFFORE, R. J., POPOVICH, S., & POWELL, V. (1990). Adolescent mothers and their mothers view adoption. *Family Relations, 39,* 311–316.

KALMUSS, D., DAVIDSON, A., & CUSHMAN, L. (1992). Parenting expectations, experiences, and adjustment to parenthood: A test of the violated expectations framework. *Journal of Marriage and the Family, 54,* 516–526.

KALMUSS, D., NAMEROW, P. B., & BAUER, U. (1992). Short-term consequences of parenting versus adoption among young, unmarried women. *Journal of Marriage and the Family, 54,* 80–90.

KALMUSS, D., & SELTZER, J. A. (1989). A framework for studying family socialization over the life cycle. *Journal of Family Issues, 10,* 339–358.

KALTER, N. (1983). How children perceive divorce. *Medical Aspects of Human Sexuality, 17,* 18–45.

KAMMER, P. P., FOUAD, N., & WILLIAMS, R. (1988). Follow-up of a precollege program for minority and disadvantaged students. *Career Development Quarterly, 37,* 40–45.

KANCHIER, C., & UNRUH, W. R. (1988). The career cycle meets the life cycle. *Career Development Quarterly, 37,* 127–137.

KANDEL, D. B. (1990). Parenting styles, drug use, and children's adjustment in families of young adults. *Journal of Marriage and the Family, 52,* 183–196.

KANDEL, D. B., & WU, P. (1995). The contributions of mothers and fathers to the intergenerational transmission of cigarette smoking in adolescents. *Journal of Research on Adolescence, 5,* 225–252.

KAPLAN, E. A. (1990). Sex, work, and motherhood: The impossible triangle. *The Journal of Sex Research, 27,* 409–425.

KAPLAN, H. B., & FUKURAI, H. (1992). Negative social sanctions, self-rejection, and drug use. *Youth and Society, 23,* 275–298.

KAPLAN, H. S. (1974). *The new sex therapy.* New York: Brunner/Mazel.

KAREL, M. J., & GATZ, M. (1996). Factors influencing life-sustaining treatment decisions in a community sample of families. *Psychology and Aging, 11,* 226–234.

KASARI, C., SIGMAN, M., MUNDY, P., & YIRMIYA, N. (1988). Caregiver interactions with autistic children. *Journal of Abnormal Child Psychology, 16,* 45–56.

KASHUBECK, S., WALSH, B., & CROWL, A. (1994). College atmosphere and eating disorders. *Journal of Counseling and Development, 72,* 640–645.

KASTENBAUM, R., & AISENBERG, R. (1976). *The psychology of death.* New York: Springer.

KATAINEN, S., RAIKKONEN, K., & KELTIKANJAS-JARBINEN, L. (1998). Development of temperament, childhood temperament, and the mother's childrearing attitudes as predictors of adolescent temperament in a nine-year follow-up study. *Journal of Research on Adolescents, 8,* 485–509.

KATZ, P. H., & WALSH, P. V. (1991). Modification of children's gender-stereotypes behavior. *Child Development, 62,* 338–351.

KAUSLER, D. H., WILEY, J. G., & LIEBERWITZ, K. J. (1992). Adult age differences in short-term memory and subsequent long-term memory for actions. *Psychology and Aging, 7,* 309–316.

KAYE, K., & WARREN, S. (1988). Discord about adoption in adoptive families. *Journal of Family Psychology, 1,* 406–433.

KEE, D. W., GOTTFRIED, A. W., BATHURST, K., & BROWN, K. (1987). Left-hemisphere language specialization and consistency in hand preference and sex differences. *Child Development, 58,* 718–724.

KEELAN, J. P. R., DION, K. K., & DION, K. L. (1992). Correlates of appearance anxiety in late adolescents and early adulthood among young women. *Journal of Adolescence, 15,* 193–205.

KEITH, P. M. (1979, November). Life changes and perceptions of life and death among older men and women. *Journal of Gerontology, 34,* 870–878.

KEITH, P. M. (1986). Isolation of the unmarried in later life. *Family Relations, 35,* 389–395.

KELLEY, M. L., POWER, T. G., & WIMBUSH, D. D. (1992). Determinants of disciplinary practices in low income black mothers. *Child Development, 63,* 573–582.

KELLY, J. B. (1988). Longer-term adjustment in children of divorce: Converging findings and implications for practice. *Journal of Family Planning, 2,* 119–140.

KENISTON, K. (1970). Youth: A new stage of life. *American Scholar, 39,* 4.

KENKEL, W. F. (1985). The desire for voluntary childlessness among low-income youth. *Journal of Marriage and the Family, 47,* 509–512.

KENNEY, A. M., GUARDADO, S., & BROWN, L. (1989). Sex education and AIDS education in the schools: What states and large school districts are doing. *Family Planning Perspectives, 21,* 56–64.

KENNY, T. J., CLEMMENS, R. L. (1997). Mental retardation. In R. A. Houkelman (Ed.), *Primary pediatric care.* St. Louis: C. V. Mosby Company, p. 410.

KERCHER, K., KOSLOSKI, K. D., & NORMOYLE, J. B. (1988). Reconsideration of fear of personal aging and subjective well-being in later life. *The Journals of Gerontology, 43,* P170–P172.

KERSHNER, J. G., & COHEN, N. J. (1992). Maternal depressive symptoms and child functioning. *Journal of Applied Developmental Psychology, 13,* 51–63.

KERSTEN, K. K. (1990). The process of marital disaffection: Intervention at various stages. *Family Relations, 39,* 257–265.

KESTENBAUM, R. (1992). Feeling happy versus feeling good: The processing of discrete and global categories of emotional expressions by children and adults. *Developmental Psychology, 28,* 1132–1142.

KETTERLINUS, R. D., HENDERSON, S., & LAMB, M. E. (1991). The effects of maternal age-at-birth on children's cognitive development. *Journal of Research on Adolescence, 1,* 173–188.

KEYES, S., & BLOCK, J. (1984, February). Prevalence and patterns of substance use among early adolescents. *Journal of Youth and Adolescence, 13,* 1–13.

KIDS AND CONTRACEPTIVES. (1987, February 16). *Newsweek,* pp. 54–65.

KIFER, E. (1985). Review of the ACT Assessment Program. In J. V. Mitchell (Ed.), *Ninth mental measurement yearbook* (pp. 31–45). Lincoln: University of Nebraska Press, Buros Mental Measurement Institute.

KII, T. (1982). A new index for measuring demographic aging. *Gerontologist, 22,* 438–442.

KILLIAN, K. D., & BUSBY, D. N. (1995). Premarital sexual coercion: Treatment issues for family therapists. *Journal of Marital and Family Therapy, 21,* 167–181.

KING, B. (1994). Nonresident father involvement and child well-being: Can dads make a difference? *Journal of Family Issues, 15,* 78–96.

KING, M. B., JUDGE, J. O., & WOLSSON, L. (1994). Functional base of support decreases with age. *Journal of Gerontology, 49,* M258–M263.

KING, P. (1989). The (meno)pause that refreshes. *Psychology Today, 22,* 11.

KINNEY, D. K., & MATTHYSSE, S. (1978). Genetic transmission of schizophrenia. *Annual Review of Medicine, 29,* 459–473.

KINSEY, A. C., POMEROY, W., & MARTIN, C. (1948). *Sexual behavior in the human male.* Philadelphia, PA: Saunders.

KIRBY, D., RESNICK, M. D., DOWNES, B., KOCHER, T., GUNDERSON, P., POTTHOFF, S., ZELTERMAN, D., BLUM, R. W. (1993). The effects of school-based health clinics in St. Paul on school-wide birth rates. *Family Planning Perspectives 25,* 12–16.

KIRBY, D., WASZAK, C., & ZIEGLER, J. (1991). Six school-based clinics: The reproductive health services and impact on sexual behavior. *Family Planning Perspectives, 23,* 6–16.

KISILEVSKY, B. S., MUIR, D. W., & LOW, J. A. (1992). Maturation of human fetal responses to vibroacoustic stimulation. *Child Development, 63,* 1497–1508.

KISSMAN, K. (1990). Social support and gender role attitude among teenage mothers. *Adolescence, 25,* 709–716.

KIT-FONG AU, T., SIDLE, A. L., & ROLLINS, K. B. (1993). Developing an intuitive understanding of conservation and contamination: Invisible particles as a plausible mechanism. *Developmental Psychology, 29,* 286–299.

KITSON, G. C., & MORGAN, L. A. (1990). The multiple consequences of divorce: A decade review. *Journal of Marriage and the Family, 52,* 913–924.

KITZMAN, D. W., & EDWARDS, W. D. (1990). Minireview: Age related changes in the anatomy of the normal human heart. *Journal of Gerontology, 45,* M33–M39.

KLACZYNSKI, P. A. (1990). Cultural-developmental tasks and adolescent development: Theoretical and methodological considerations. *Adolescence, 25,* 811–824.

KLAUS, M., & KENNEL, J. (1982). *Parent-infant bonding* (2nd ed.). St. Louis, MO: Mosby.

KLEBAN, H. H., LAWTON, M. P., BRODY, E. M., & MOSS, M. (1976). Behavioral observations of mentally impaired aged: Those who decline and those who do not. *Journal of Gerontology, 31,* 333–339.

KLEIN, H. A. (1992). Treatment and self-esteem in late adolescence. *Adolescence, 27,* 689–694.

KLINE, D. W., et al. (1992). Vision, aging, and driving: The problems of older drivers. *The Journals of Gerontology, 47,* P27–P34.

KLINE, M., JOHNSTON, J. R., & TSCHANN, J. M. (1991). The long shadow of marital conflict: A model of children's postdivorce adjustment. *Journal of Marriage and the Family, 53,* 297–309.

KLITSCH, M. (1989). Noncustodial fathers can probably afford to pay far more for child support than they now provide. *Family Planning Perspectives, 21,* 278–279.

KLITSCH, M. (1991). Hispanic ethnic groups face variety of serious health, social problems. *Family Planning Perspectives, 23,* 186–188.

KLITSCH, M. (March/April 1992). Maternal cocaine use raises delivery costs, need for neonatal care. *Family Planning Perspectives, 24,* 93–95.

KLITSCH, M. (1993). Close to half of women aged 13–44 are at risk of unintended pregnancy. *Family Planning Perspectives, 25,* 44–45.

KLITSCH, M. (1994). Prenatal exposure to tobacco, alcohol, and other drugs found in more than one in ten California newborns. *Family Planning Perspectives, 26,* 95–96.

KLOHMEN, E. C., VANDEWATER, E. A., & YOUNG, A. (1996). *Psychology and Aging, 11,* 441–442.

KNOX, D., & WILSON, K. (1981). Dating behavior of university students. *Family Relations, 30,* 255–258.

KNOX, D., & WILSON, K. (1983). Dating problems of university students. *College Student Journal, 17,* 225–228.

KNUDSON-MARTIN, C., & MAHONEY, A. R. (1998). Language and processes in the construction of equality in new marriages. *Family Relations, 47,* 81–91.

KOBAK, R. R., COLE, H. E., FERENZ-GILLIES, R., & FLEMING, W. S. (1993). Attachment and emotional regulation during mother-teen problem solving: A controlled theory analysis. *Child Development, 64,* 231–245.

KOCHANSKA, G. (1990). Maternal beliefs as long-term predictors of mother-child interaction and rapport. *Child Development, 61,* 1934–1943.

KOCHANSKA, G. (1991). Patterns of inhibition to the unfamiliar in children of normal and affectively ill mothers. *Child Development, 62,* 250–263.

KOCHANSKA, G. (1992). Children's interpersonal influence with mothers and peers. *Developmental Psychology, 28,* 491–499.

KOCHANSKA, G., COY, K. C., TJEBKES, T. L., & HUSAREK, S. J. (1998). Individual differences in emotionality in infancy. *Child Development, 64,* 375–390.

KOCHANSKA, G., DeVET, K., GOLDMAN, M., MURRAY, K., & PUTNAM, S. P. (1994). Maternal reports of conscience development and temperament in young children. *Child Development, 65,* 852–868.

KOCHANSKA, G., & KUCZYNSKI, L. (1991). Maternal autonomy granting: Predictors of normal and depressed mothers' compliance and noncompliance with the requests of five-year-olds. *Child Development, 62,* 1449–1459.

KOCHANSKA, G., KUCZYNSKI, L., & RADKE-YARROW, M. (1989). Correspondence between mothers' self-reported and observed child-rearing practices. *Child Development, 60,* 56–63.

KOCHANSKA, G., MURRAY, K., JACQUES, U. Y., KOENIG, A. L., & VANDEGEEST, K. A. (1996). Inhibitory control in young children and its role in emerging internalization. *Child Development, 67,* 490–507.

KOCHANSKA, G., TJEBKES, T. L., & FORMAN, D. R. (1998). Children's emerging regulation of conduct: Restraint, compliance, and internalization from infancy to the second year. *Child Development, 69,* 1378–1389.

KOENIG, L. J. (1988). Self-image of emotionally disturbed adolescents. *Journal of Abnormal Child Psychology, 16,* 111–126.

KOFF, E., RIERDAN, J., & STUBBS, M. L. (1990). Gender, body image, and self-concept in early adolescence. *Journal of Early Adolescence, 10,* 56–68.

KOHLBERG, L. (1963). The development of children's orientation toward a moral order. *Vita Humana, 6,* 11–33.

KOHLBERG, L. (1966a). A cognitive-developmental analysis of children's sex role concepts and attitudes. In E. Maccoby (Ed.), *The development of sex differences.* Palo Alto, CA: Stanford University Press.

KOHLBERG, L. (1966b). Moral education in the schools: A developmental view. *School Review, 74,* 1–30.

KOHLBERG, L. (1969). *Stages in the development of moral thought and action.* New York: Holt, Rinehart, & Winston.

KOHLBERG, L. (1970). Moral development and the education of adolescents. In R. F. Purnell (Ed.), *Adolescents and the American high school.* New York: Holt, Rinehart, & Winston.

KOHLBERG, L., & GILLIGAN, C. (1971, Fall). The adolescent as a philosopher: The discovery of the self in a postconventional world. *Daedalus,* 1051–1086.

KOHLBERG, L., & KRAMER, M. S. (1969). Continuities and discontinuities in childhood and adult development. *Human Development, 12,* 93–120.

KOHLBERG, L., & TURIEL, E. (Eds.). (1972). *Recent research in moral development.* New York: Holt, Rinehart, & Winston.

KOHN, A. (1988). Make love, not war. *Psychology Today, 22,* 34–38.

KOLATA, G. (1986). Obese children: A growing problem. *Science, 232,* 20–21.

KOLATA, G. (1988).   Child splitting. *Psychology Today, 22,* 34–36.

KOLODNY, R. C. (1980, November).   *Adolescent sexuality.* Paper presented at the annual convention of the Michigan Personnel and Guidance Association, Detroit.

KONTOS, S., HSU, H., & DUNN, L. (1994).   Children's cognitive and social competence in child-care centers and family day-care homes. *Journal of Applied Developmental Psychology, 15,* 387–411.

KOOLS, S. M. (1997).   Adolescent identity development in foster care. *Family Relations, 46,* 263–271.

KOOP, C. E. (1986).   *Surgeon general's reports on acquired immune deficiency syndrome.* Washington, DC: U.S. Department of Health and Human Services.

KOPP, C. B., & KALER, S. R. (1989).   Risk in infancy: Origins and implications. *American Psychologist, 44,* 224–230.

KORMAN, S. (1983).   Nontraditional dating behavior: Date initiation and date expense-sharing among feminists and non-feminists. *Family Relations, 32,* 575–581.

KORMAN, S., & LESLIE, G. (1982).   The relationship between feminists ideology and date expense-sharing to perceptions of sexual aggression in dating. *Journal of Sex Research, 18,* 114–129.

KORNER, A. F. (1996).   Reliable individual differences in preterm infants' excitation management. *Child Development, 67,* 1793–1805.

KORNER, A. F., CONSTANTINOU, J., DIMICELI, S., & BROWN, B. W., JR. (1991).   Establishing the reliability and developmental validity of a neurobehavioral assessment for preterm infants: A methodological process. *Child Development, 62,* 1200–1208.

KOST, K., LANDRY, D. J., & DARROCH, J. E. (1998).   The effects of pregnancy planning status on birth outcomes and infant care. Family Planning Perspectives, 30, 223–230.

KOTCHICK, V. A., FOREHAND, R., ARMISTEAD, L., KLEIN, K., & WIERSON, M. (1996).   Coping with illness: Interrelationships across family members and predictors of psychological adjustment. *Journal of Family Psychology, 10,* 358–370.

KOVAL, J. J., ECCLESTON, N. A., PATERSON, D. H., BROWN, B., CUNNINGHAM, D. A., & RECHNITZER, P. A. (1992).   Response rates in a survey of physical capacity among older persons. *The Journals of Gerontology, 47,* S140–S147.

KOVAR, M. G. (1986).   *Aging in the eighties: Age 65 years and over and living alone, contacts with family, friends, and neighbors,* advance data from vital and health statistics, No. 116 (DHHS Publication No. [PHS] 86–1250). Washington, DC: National Center for Health Statistics.

KRAMER, L., & GOTTMAN, J. M. (1992).   Becoming a sibling: "With a little help from my friends." *Developmental Psychology, 28,* 685–699.

KRAMER, L., & WASHO, C. A. (1993).   Evaluation of a court-mandated prevention program for divorcing parents. The children first program. *Family Relations, 42,* 179–186.

KRAUSE, C. M., & SAARNIO, D. A. (1993).   Deciding what is safe to eat: Young children's understanding of a parent's reality, and edibleness. *Journal of Applied Developmental Psychology, 14,* 231–244.

KRAUSE, M. (1993).   Race differences and life satisfaction among aged men and women. *Journal of Gerontology, 48,* S234–S235.

KRAUSE, M. (1994).   Stressors in salient social roles and well-being in later life. *Journal of Gerontology, 49,* P137–P148.

KRAUSE, N. (1986a).   Social support, stress, and well-being among older adults. *Journal of Gerontology, 41,* 512–519.

KRAUSE, N. (1986b).   Stress and coping: Reconceptualizing the role of locus of control beliefs. *Journal of Gerontology, 41,* 617–622.

KRAUSE, N. (1986c).   Stress and sex differences in depressive symptoms among older adults. *Journal of Gerontology, 41,* 727–731.

KRAUSE, N. (1988).   Stressful life events and physician utilization. *Journal of Gerontology, 43,* S53–S61.

KRAUSE, N. (1990).   Perceived health problems, formal/informal support, and life satisfaction among older adults. *Journal of Gerontology, 45,* S193–S205.

KRAUSE, N. (1991a).   Stress and isolation from close ties in later life. *Journal of Gerontology, 46,* S183–S194.

KRAUSE, N. (1991b).   Stressful events and life satisfaction among elderly men and women. *Journal of Gerontology, 46,* S84–S92.

KRAUSE, N., & BAKER, E. (1992).   Financial strain, economic values and somatic symptoms in later life. *Psychology and Aging, 7,* 4–14.

KRAUSE, N., & GOLDENHAR, L. N. (1992).   Acculturation and psychological distress in three groups of elderly Hispanics. *The Journals of Gerontology, 47,* S279–S288.

KRAUSE, N., HERZOG, A. R., & BAKER, E. (1992).   Providing support to others and well-being in later life. *The Journals of Gerontology, 47,* P300–P311.

KREIN, S. F., & BELLER, A. H. (1988).   Educational attainment of children from single-parent families: Differences by exposure, gender, and race. *Demography, 25,* 221–224.

KRIESHOK, S. I., & KARPOWITZ, D. H. (1988).   A review of selected literature on obesity and guidelines for treatment. *Journal of Consulting and Development, 66,* 326–330.

KROGER, J. (1993).   The role of historical context in the identity formation process of late adolescence. *Youth and Society, 24,* 363–376.

KROGER, J. (1995).   The differentiation of "firm" and "developmental" foreclosure identity statuses: A longitudinal study. *Journal of Adolescent Research, 10,* 317–337.

KRONE, R. J., & HODSON, R. (1988).   Exercising and the heart. *Medical Aspects of Human Sexuality, 22,* 21–22.

KROUPA, S. E. (1988).   Perceived parental acceptance and female juvenile delinquency. *Adolescence, 23,* 171–185.

KRUEGER, J., HECKHAUSEN, J., & HUNDERTMARK, J. (1995).   Perceiving middle-aged adults: Effects of stereotype-congruent and incongruent information. *Journal of Gerontology, 50B,* P82–P93.

KRUEGER, R., & HANSEN, J. C. (1987).   Self-concept changes during youth-home placement of adolescents. *Adolescence, 86,* 385–392.

KUBANY, E. S., RICHARD, D. C., BAUER, G. B., & MURAOKA, M. Y. (1992).   Verbalized anger and accusatory "you" messages as cues for anger and antagonism among adolescents. *Adolescence, 27,* 505–516.

KÜBLER-ROSS, E. (1969).   *On death and dying.* New York: Macmillan.

KÜBLER-ROSS, E. (1974).   *Questions and answers on death and dying.* New York: Macmillan.

KUCZAJ, S. A. (1986).   Thoughts on the intentional basis of early object word extension. Evidence from comprehension and production. In S. A. Kuczaj & M. D. Barrett (Eds.), *The development of word meaning. Progress in cognitive developmental research.* New York: Springer-Verlag.

KUGLER, D. E., & HANSSON, R. O. (1988).   Relational competence and social support among parents at risk of child abuse. *Family Relations, 37,* 328–332.

KUHN, D. (1979).   The significance of Piaget's formal operations stage in education. *Journal of Education, 161,* 34–50.

KUPERMINC, G. P., & REPPUCCI, M. D. (1996).   Contributions of new research on juvenile delinquency to the prevention and treatment of antisocial behavior: Comment on Gorman-Smith et al. *Journal of Family Psychology, 10,* 130–136.

KUPERSMIDT, J. B., & COIE, J. D. (1990).   Preadolescent peer status, aggression, and school adjustment as predictors of externalizing problems in adolescence. *Child Development, 61,* 1350–1362.

KUPERSMIDT, J. B., GRIESLER, P. C., DEROSIER, M. E., PATTERSON, C. J., & DAVIS, P W. (1995).   Childhood aggression and peer relations in the context of family and neighborhood factors. *Child Development, 66,* 360–375.

KURDEK, L. A. (1989).   Relationship quality for newly married husbands and wives: Marital history, stepchildren, and individual-difference predictors. *Journal of Marriage and the Family, 51,* 1053–1064.

KURDEK, L. A., & FINE, M. A. (1991).   Cognitive correlates of satisfaction for mothers and stepfathers in stepfather families. *Journal of Marriage and the Family, 53,* 565–572.

KURDEK, L. A., & FINE, M. A. (1993).   The relation between family structure and the young adolescent's appraisals of family climate and parenting behavior. *Journal of Family Issues, 14,* 279–290.

KURDEK, L. A., & FINE, M. A. (1994).   Family acceptance and family control as predictors of adjustment in young adolescents: Linear, curvilinear, or interactive effects? *Child Development, 65,* 1137–1146.

KURTZ, P. D., KURTZ, G. L., & JARVIS, S. B. (1991).   Problems of maltreated runaway youths. *Adolescence, 26,* 543–555.

KUYPERS, J. A., & BENGSTON, V. L. (1973).   Social breakdown and competence: A model of normal aging. *Human Development, 16,* 181–201.

LABOUVIE-VIEF, G. (1986).   Modes of knowledge and organization of development. In M. L. Commens, L. Kohlberg, F. A. Richards, & J. Sinnott (Eds.), *Beyond formal operations: Models and methods in the study of adult and adolescent thought* (Vol. 3). New York: Praeger.

LABOUVIE-VIEF, G., & GONDA, J. N. (1976).   Cognitive strategy training and intellectual performance in the elderly. *Journal of Gerontology, 31,* 327–332.

LACHENMEYER, J. R., & MUNI-BRANDER, P. (1988). Eating disorders in a nonclinical adolescent population: Implications for treatment. *Adolescence, 23*, 303–312.

LACKOVIC-GRGIN, K., & DEKOVIC, M. (1990). The contribution of significant others to adolescents' self-esteem. *Adolescence, 25*, 839–846.

LACKOVIC-GRGIN, K., DEKOVIC, M., & OPACIC, G. (1994). Pubertal status, interaction with significant others, and self-esteem of adolescent girls. *Adolescence, 29*, 691–700.

LADD, G. W. (1990). Having friends, keeping friends, making friends, and being liked by peers in the classroom: Predictors of children's early school adjustment? *Child Development, 61*, 1081–1100.

LADD, G. W., & HART, C. H. (1992). Creating informal play opportunities: Are parents' and preschoolers' initiations related to children's confidence with peers? *Developmental Psychology, 28*, 1179–1187.

LADD, G. W., PRICE, J. M., & HART, C. H. (1988). Predicting preschoolers' peer status from their playground behaviors. *Child Development, 9*, 986–992.

LAGERCRANTZ, H., & SLOTKIN, T. A. (1986). The "stress" of being born. *Scientific American, 254*, 100–107.

LAING, J., VALIGA, M., & EBERLY, C. (1986). Predicting college freshman major choices from ACT Assessment Program data. *College and University, 61*, 198–205.

LAMAZE, F. (1970). *Painless childbirth.* Chicago, IL: Regency.

LAMBORN, S. D., MOUNTS, N. S., STEINBERG, L., & DORNBUSCH, S. N. (1991). Patterns of competence and adjustment among adolescents from authoritative, authoritarian, indulgent, and neglectful families. *Child Development, 62*, 1049–1065.

LANDAU, S., & MILICH, R. (1988). Social communication patterns of attention-deficit-disordered boys. *Journal of Abnormal Child Psychology, 16*, 69–81.

LANDERS, A. (1985, June 11). Is affection more important than sex? *Family Circle.*

LANDRY, R. (1987). Additive bilingualism, schooling, and special education: A minority group perspective. *Canadian Journal for Exceptional Children, 3*, 109–114.

LANGE, G., & PIERCE, S. H. (1992). Memory-strategy learning and maintenance in preschool children. *Developmental Psychology, 28*, 453–462.

LANGER, E. J. (1989, April). The mindset of health. *Psychology Today, 23*, 48–51.

LAROSSA, R. (1988). Fatherhood and social change. *Family Relations, 37*, 451–457.

LAROSSA, R., GORDON, B. A., WILSON, R. J., BAIRAN, A., & JARET, C. (1991). The fluctuating image of the 20th-century American father. *Journal of Marriage and the Family, 53*, 987–997.

LARRABEE, G. J., & CROOK, T. H., III. (1993). Do men show more rapid age-associated decline in simulated, everyday verbal memory than do women? *Psychology and Aging, 8*, 68–71.

LARSEN, J. W. (1986). Congenital toxoplasmas. In J. L. Sever & R. L. Brent (Eds.), *Teratogen update: Environmentally induced birth defect risks.* New York: Liss.

LARSON, J. H. (1984). The effect of husband's unemployment on marital and family relations in blue-collar families. *Family Relations, 33*, 503–511.

LARSON, R., & HAM, M. (1993). Stress and "storm and stress" in early adolescence: Relationship of negative events with dysphoric effect. *Developmental Psychology, 29*, 130–140.

LARSON, R., & RICHARDS, M. H. (1991). Daily companionship in later childhood and early adolescence: Changing developmental contexts. *Child Development, 62*, 284–300.

LARSSON, M., & BACKMAN, L. (1993). Semantic activation episodic odor recognition in young and older adults. *Psychology and Aging, 8*, 582–588.

LARZELERE, R. E., AMBERSON, T. G., & MARTIN, J. A. (1992). Age differences in perceived and discipline problems from nine to 48 months. *Family Relations, 41*, 192–199.

LARZELERE, R. E., SATHER, P. R., SCHNEIDER, W. N., LARSON, D. B., & PIKE, P. L. (1998). Punishment enhances reasoning's effectiveness as a disciplinary response to toddlers. *Journal of Marriage and the Family, 60*, 388–403.

LAVEE, Y., MCCUBBIN, H. I., & OLSON, D. H. (1987). The effect of stressful life events and transitions on family functioning and well-being. *Journal of Marriage and the Family, 49*, 857–873.

LAVEE, Y., MCCUBBIN, H. I., & PATTERSON, J. M. (1985). The double ABCX model of family stress and adaptation: An empirical test by analysis of structural equations with latent variables. *Journal of Marriage and the Family, 47*, 811–825.

LAVER, G. D., & BURKE, D. M. (1993). Why do semantic priming effects increase in old age? A meta-analysis. *Psychology and Aging, 8*, 34–43.

LAVIN, J., STEPHENS, R., MIODOVNIK, M., & BARDON, T. (1982). Vaginal delivery in patients with a prior cesarean section. *Obstetrics and Gynecology, 59*, 135–148.

LAVOIE, J. C. (1994). Identity in adolescence: Issues of theory, structure, and transition. *Journal of Adolescence, 17*, 17–28.

LAWSON, E. J. (1994). The role of smoking in the lives of low-income pregnant adolescents: A field study. *Adolescence, 29*, 60–79.

LAWTON, M. P. (1975). The Phildadelphia center morale scale: A revision. *Journal of Gerontology, 30*, 85–89.

LAWTON, M. P., et al. (1992). Dimensions of affective experience in three age groups. *Psychology and Aging, 7*, 171–184.

LAWTON, M. P., KLEBAN, M. H., RAJAGOPAL, P., & DEAN, J. (1992). Dimensions of affective experience in three age groups. *Psychology and Aging, 7*, 171–184.

LAZAR, A., & TORNEY-PURTA, J. (1991). The development of the subconcepts of death in young children: A short-term longitudinal study. *Child Development, 62*, 1321–1333.

LEADBEATER, B. (1986). The resolution of relativism in adult thinking: Subjective, objective, and conceptual. *Human Development, 29*, 291–300.

LEADBEATER, B. J., & BISHOP, S. J., (1994). Predictors of behavior problems in preschool children of inner-city Afro-American and Puerto Rican adolescent mothers. *Child Development, 65*, 638–648.

LEAPER, C. (1991). Influence and involvement in children's discourse: Age, gender, and partner effects. *Child Development, 62*, 797–811.

LEBRECK, D. B., & BARON, A. (1987). Age and practice effects in continuous recognition memory. *Journal of Gerontology, 42*, 89–91.

LECLAIR, N., & BERKOWITZ, B. (1983, February). Counseling concerns for the individual with bulimia. *Personnel and Guidance Journal, 61*, 352–355.

LEDOUX, S., CHOQUET, M., & MANFREDI, R. (1993). Associated factors for self-reported binge eating among male and female adolescents. *Journal of Adolescence, 16*, 75–91.

LEE, D. J., & MARKIDES, K. S. (1990). Activity and mortality among aged persons over an eight-year period. *Journal of Gerontology, 45*, S39–S42.

LEE, G. R., SECCOMBE, K., & SHEHAN, C. L. (1991). Marital status and personal happiness: An analysis of trend data. *Journal of Marriage and the Family, 53*, 839–844.

LEE, J. A. (1973). *The colors of love: An exploration of the ways of loving.* Don Mills, Ontario: New Press.

LEE, V. E., BROOKS-GUNN, J., SCHNUR, E., & LIAW, F. (1990). Are Head Start effects sustained: A longitudinal follow-up comparison of disadvantaged children attending Head Start, no preschool, and other preschool programs. *Child Development, 61*, 495–507.

LEFLORE, L. (1988). Delinquent youths and family. *Adolescence, 23*, 629–642.

LEHMAN, H. C. (1962). The creative production rates of present versus past generations of scientists. *Journal of Gerontology, 17*, 409–417.

LEHMAN, H. C. (1966). The psychologist's most creative years. *American Psychologist, 21*, 363–369.

LEITENBERG, H., DETZER, & SCRIBNIK. (1993). *Archives of Sexual Behavior, 22*, 87–98.

LEMPERS, J. D., & CLARK-LEMPERS, D. (1990). Family economic stress, maternal and paternal support and adolescent distress. *Journal of Adolescence, 13*, 217–230.

LEMPERS, J. D., & CLARK-LEMPERS, D. S. (1993). A functional comparison of same-sex and opposite-sex friendships during adolescence. *Journal of Adolescent Research, 8*, 89–108.

LENNEBERG, E. H. (1973). *Biological Foundations of Language.* New York: Wiley.

LEO, J. (1987, January 12). Exploring the traits of twins. *Time*, p. 63.

LEPORE, S. J. (1992). Social conflict, social support, and psychological distress: Evidence of cross-domain buffering effects. *Journal of Personality and Social Psychology, 63*, 857–867.

LEREA, L. E., & LIMAURO, B. F. (1982). Grief among healthcare workers: A comparative study. *Journal of Gerontology, 37*, 604–608.

LERNER, J. V., HERTZOG, C., HOOKER, K., HASSIBI, M., & THOMAS, A. (1988). Longitudinal study of negative emotional states and adjustment from early childhood through adolescence. *Child Development, 59*, 356–366.

LERNER, R. M. (1992). Dialectics, developmental contextualism, and the further enhancement of theory about puberty and psychosocial development. *Journal of Early Adolescence, 12*, 366–388.

LERNER, R. M., DELANEY, M., HESS, L. E., JOVANOVIC, J., & VON EYE, A. (1990). Early adolescent physical attractiveness and academic competence. *Journal of Early Adolescence, 10*, 4–20.

LERNER, R. M., LERNER, J. V., HESS, L. E., SCHWAB, J., JOVANOVIC, J., TALWAR, R., & KUCHER, J. S. (1991). Physical attractiveness and psychosocial functioning among early adolescents. *Journal of Early Adolescence, 11*, 300–320.

LESLIE, L. A., & GRADY, K. (1985). Changes in mothers' social networks and social support following divorce. *Journal of Marriage and the Family, 47*, 663–673.

LESTER, B. M. (1987). Prediction of developmental outcome from acoustical cry analysis in term and preterm infants. *Pediatrics, 80*, 529–534.

LESTER, B. M., CORWIN, M. J., SEPKOSKI, C., SEIFER, R., PEUCKER, M., McLAUGHLIN, S., & GOLUB, H. L. (1991). Neurobehavioral syndromes in cocaine-exposed newborn infants. *Child Development, 62*, 694–705.

LESTER, B. M., & DREHER, M. (1989). Effects of marijuana use during pregnancy on newborn cry. *Child Development, 60*, 765–771.

LEUPNITZ, D. A. (1982). *Child custody: A study of families after divorce.* Lexington, MA: Lexington Books.

LEVANT, R. F. (1992). Toward the reconstruction of masculinity. *Journal of Family Psychology, 5*, 379–402.

LEVANT, R. F., SLATTERY, S. C., & LOISELLE, J. E. (1987). Fathers' involvement in housework and child care with school-age daughters. *Family Relations, 36*, 152–157.

LE VAY, S. (1993). *The Sexual Brain.* Cambridge, MA: MIT Press.

LEVE, L. D., WINEBARGER, A. A., FAGOT, B. I., REID, J. B., & GOLDSMITH, H. H. (1998). Environmental and genetic variance in children's observed and reported maladaptive behavior. *Child Development, 69*, 1286–1298.

LEVIN, E., ADELSON, S., BUCHALTER, G., & BILCHER, L. (1983, February). Karen Carpenter, *People.*

LEVIN, J. S., CHATTERS, L. M., & TAYLOR, R. J. (1995). Religious effects on health status and life satisfaction among Black Americans. *Journal of Gerontology, 50B*, S154–S163.

LEVINE, J. B. (1988). Play in the context of the family. *Journal of Family Psychology, 2*, 164–187.

LEVINE, L. J., & BLUCK, S. (1997). Experience and remembered emotional intensity in older adults. *Psychology and Aging, 12*, 514–523.

LEVINSON, D. J. (1977). The midlife transition: A period in adult psychosocial development. *Psychiatry, 40*, 99–112.

LEVINSON, D. J., DARROW, C. N., KLEIN, E. B., LEVINSON, M. H., & McKEE, B. (1976). Periods in the adult development of men: Ages 18 to 45. *Counseling Psychologist, 6*, 21–25.

LEVINSON, D. J., DARROW, C. N., KLEIN, E. B., LEVINSON, M. H., & McKEE, B. (1978). *The seasons of a man's life.* New York: Alfred A. Knopf.

LEVINSON, T. J., IN COLLABORATION WITH LEVINSON, J. D. (1996). *The Seasons of a Woman's Life.* New York: Alfred A. Knopf.

LEVY, J. (1985, May). Right brain, left brain. Fact and fiction. *Psychology Today, 19*, 28–44.

LEVY, T. B., & TAYLOR, M. G., & GELMAN, S. A. (1995). Traditional and evaluative aspects of flexibility in gender roles, social conventions, moral rules, and physical laws. *Child Development, 66*, 515–531.

LEVY-SHIFF, R., SHARIR, H., & MOGILNER, M. B. (1989). Mother- and father-preterm infant relationships in the hospital preterm nursery. *Child Development, 60*, 93–102.

LEW, A. R., & BUTTERWOTH, G. (1995). The effects of hunger on hand-mouth coordination in newborn infants. *Developmental Psychology, 31*, 456–463.

LEWIS, C., & OSBORNE, A. (1990). Three-year-olds' problems with false belief: Conceptual deficit or linguistic artifact? *Child Development, 61*, 1514–1519.

LEWIS, M., ALESSANDRI, S. M., & SULLIVAN, M. W. (1992). Differences in shame and pride as a function of children's gender and task difficulty. *Child Development, 63*, 630–638.

LEWIS, M., & FEIRING, C. (1989). Infant, mother, and mother-infant interaction behavior and subsequent attachment. *Child Development, 60*, 831–837.

LI, X., STANTON, B., FEIGELMAN, S., BLACK, M. M., & ROMER, D. (1994). Drug trafficking and drug use among urban African-American early adolescents. *Journal of Early Adolescence, 14*, 491–508.

LIANG, J. (1984). Dimensions of the Life Satisfaction Index A: A structural formation. *Journal of Gerontology, 39*, 613–622.

LIANG, J. (1985). A structural integration of the affect balance scale and the Life Satisfaction Index A. *Journal of Gerontology, 5*, 552–561.

LIANG, J., ASANO, H., BOLLEN, K. A., KAHANA, E. F., & MAEDA, D. (1987). Cross-cultural comparability of the Philadelphia Geriatric Center Moral Scale: An American-Japanese comparison. *Journal of Gerontology, 42*, 37–43.

LIANG, J., & BOLLEN, K. A. (1983). The structure of the Philadelphia Geriatric Center Moral Scale: A reinterpretation. *Journal of Gerontology, 38*, 181–189.

LIANG, J., LAWRENCE, R. H., & BOLLEN, K. A. (1987). Race differences in factorial structures of two measures of subjective well-being. *Journal of Gerontology, 42*, 426–428.

LIANG, J., & WARFEL, B. L. (1983). Urbanism and life satisfaction among the aged. *Journal of Gerontology, 38*, 977–1006.

LIBMAN, E, CRETI, L., AMSEL, R., BRENDER, W., & FICHTEN, C. S. (1997). What do older good and poor sleepers do during periods of normal wakefulness? The sleep behavior scale: 60+. *Psychology and Aging, 12*, 170–182.

LICHSTEIN, K. L., & JOHNSON, R. S. (1993). Relaxation for insomnia and hypnotic medication use in older women. *Psychology and Aging, 8*, 103–111.

LICITRA-KLECKLER, D. M., & WAAS, G. A. (1993). Perceived social support among high-stress adolescents. The role of peers and family. *Journal of Adolescent Research, 8*, 381–402.

LIEBERMAN, A. F., WESTON, D. R., & PAWL, J. H. (1991). Preventive intervention and outcome with anxiously attached dyads. *Child Development, 62*, 199–209.

LIEM, R., & LIEM, J. H. (1988). Psychological effects of unemployment on workers and their families. *Journal of Social Issues, 44*, 87–105.

LIGHT, H. K., HERTSGAARD, D., & MARTIN, R. E. (1985). Farm children's work in the family. *Adolescence, 20*, 425–432.

LILLARD, A. S. (1993a). Pretend play skills and the child's theory of mind. *Child Development, 64*, 348–371.

LILLARD, A. S. (1993b). Young children's conceptualization of pretense: action or mental representational state? *Child Development, 64*, 372–386.

LILLARD, A. S., & FLAVELL, J. H. (1992). Young children's understanding of different mental states. *Developmental Psychology, 28*, 626–634.

LIN, K. O., et al. (1992). Decreased gray matter in normal aging: In vivo magnetic resonance study. *The Journals of Gerontology, 47*, B26–B30.

LINDE, E. V., MORRONGIELLO, B. A., & ROVEE-COLLIER, C. (1985). Determinants of retention in 8–week-old infants. *Developmental Psychology, 21*, 601–613.

LINDENBERGER, U., & BALTES, P. B. (1994). Sensory functioning and intelligence in old age: A strong connection. *Psychology and Aging, 9*, 339–355.

LINDENBERGER, U., & BALTES, P. D. (1997). Intellectual functioning in old and very old age: Cross-sexual results from the Berlin Aging Study. *Psychology and Aging, 12*, 410–432.

LINN, R. (1991). Sexual and moral development of Israeli female adolescents for city and kibbutz: Perspectives of Kohlberg and Gilligan. *Adolescence, 26*, 59–72.

LIPS, H. M. (1991). *Women, men, and power.* Mountain View, CA: Mayfield.

LIPSITT, L. (1986). Learning in infancy: Cognitive development in babies. *Journal of Pediatrics, 109*, 172–182.

LIPSITZ, J. (1991). Public policy and young adolescents. A 1990's context for researchers. *Journal of Early Adolescence, 11*, 20–37.

LITTRELL, M. L. D., & LITTRELL, J. M. (1990). Clothing interests, body satisfaction, and eating behavior of adolescent females: Related or independent dimensions? *Adolescence, 25*, 77–96.

LIU, X., KAPLAN, H. B., & RISSER, W. W. (1992). Decomposing the reciprocal relationships between academic achievement and general self-esteem. *Youth and Society, 24*, 123–148.

LOCKE, J. (1982). Some thoughts concerning education. In P. H. Quick (Ed.), *Locke on education* (pp. 1–236). Cambridge, England: Cambridge University Press.

LOCKSHIN, R. A., & ZAKERI, Z. F. (1990). Minireview: Programmed cell death: New thoughts and relevance to aging. *Journal of Gerontology, 45,* B135–B140.

LOEHLIN, J. C. (1985). Fitting heredity-environment models jointly to twin and adoption data from the California Psychological inventory. *Behavior Genetics, 15,* 199–221.

LOHR, M. J., ESSEX, M. J., & KLEIN, M. H. (1988). The relationship of coping resources to physical health status and life satisfaction among older women. *Journal of Gerontology, 43,* P54–P60.

LOLLIS, S. P. (1990). Effects of maternal behavior on toddler behavior during separation. *Child Development, 61,* 99–103.

LONGINO, C. F., JR., JACKSON, D. J., ZIMMERMAN, R. C., & BRADSHER, J. E. (1991). The second move: Health and geographical mobility. *Journal of Gerontology, 46,* S218–S225.

LOOMIS, L. S., & BOOTH, A., (1995). Multi-generational care-giving and well-being: The myth of the beleaguered sandwich generation. *Journal of Family Issues, 16,* 131–148.

LOPEZ, A., GELMAN, S. A., GUTHEIL, G., & SMITH, E. E. (1992). The development of category-based induction. *Child Development, 63,* 1070–1090.

LOPEZ, F. G., & THURMAN, C. W. (1993). High-trait and low-trait angry college students: A comparison of family environments. *Journal of Counseling and Development, 71,* 524–527.

LOPICCOLO, J. (1985, September 22). Advances in diagnosis and treatment of sexual dysfunction. Paper presented at the 28th annual meeting of the Society for the Scientific Study of Sex, San Diego.

LOPRESTO, C., SHERMAN, M., & SHERMAN, N. (1985). The effects of masturbation seminar on high school males' attitudes, false beliefs, guilt, and behavior. *Journal Sex Research, 21,* 142–156.

LORCH, E. P., BELLACK, D. R., & AUGSBACH, L. H. (1987). Young children's memory for televised stories: Effects of importance. *Child Development, 58,* 453–463.

LORD, S. E., ECCLES, J. S., & MCCARTHY, K. A. (1994). Surviving the junior high school transition. Family processes and self-perceptions as protective and risk factors. *Journal of Early Adolescence, 14,* 162–199.

LORENZ, K. Z. (1965). *Evolution and the modification of behavior.* Chicago, IL: University of Chicago Press.

LOVELL, J. (1984, October 21). Why sexual abusers often get away with it. *Maine Sunday Telegram,* Portland, ME.

LOWERY, C. R. (1985). Child custody in divorce: Parents' decisions and perceptions. *Family Relations, 34,* 241–249.

LOWERY, C. R., & SETTLE, S. A. (1985). Effects of divorce on children: Differential impact on custody and visitation patterns. *Family Relations, 34,* 455–463.

LOWIK, M. R. H., WEDEL, M., KOK, F. J., ODINK, J., WESTENBRINK, S., & MEULMEESTER, J. F. (1991). Nutrition and serum cholesterol levels among elderly men and women (Dutch Nutrition Surveillance System). *Journal of Gerontology, 46,* M23– M28.

LUDEMANN, P. M. (1991). Generalized discrimination of positive facial expression by seven- and ten-month-old infants. *Child Development, 62,* 55–67.

LUNDHOLM, J. K., & LITTRELL, J. M. (1986). Desire for thinness among high school cheerleaders. Relationship to disordered eating and weight control behavior. *Adolescence, 21,* 573–579.

LUNDIN, T. (1984). Morbidity following sudden and unexpected bereavement. *British Journal of Psychiatry, 144,* 84–88.

LUSTER, T., RHOADES, K., & HAAS, B. (1989). The relation between parental values and parenting behavior: A test of the Kohn hypothesis. *Journal of Marriage and the Family, 51,* 139–147.

LUSTER, T., & SMALL, S. A. (1997). Sexual abuse history and problems in adolescence: Exploring the effects of moderating variables. *Journal of Marriage and the Family, 59,* 131–142.

LUSZEZ, M. A., BRYAN, J., & KENT, P. (1997). Predicting episodic memory performance of very old men and women: Contributions from age, depression, activity, cognitive ability, and speed. *Psychology and Aging, 12,* 340–351.

LUSZKI, M., & LUSZKI, W. (1985). Advantages of growing older. *Journal of the American Geriatric Society, 33,* 216–217.

LYONS-RUTH, K., CONNELL, D. B., & GRUNEBAUM, H. U. (1990). Infants at special risk: Maternal depression and family support services as mediators of infant development and security of attachment. *Child Development, 61,* 85–98.

LYSNE, M., & LEVY, G. D. (1997). Differences in ethnic identity in Native American adolescents as a function of school context. *Journal of Adolescent Research, 13,* 372–388.

MACALLAIR, D. (1993). Reaffirming rehabilitation in juvenile justice. *Youth and Society, 25,* 104–125.

MACCOBY, E. E. (1992). The role of parents in the socialization of children: An historical overview. *Developmental Psychology, 28,* 1006–1017.

MACCOBY, E. E., DEPNER, C., & MNOOKIN, R. (1988). *Family functioning in three forms of residence: Maternal, paternal, and joint.* Paper presented at the annual meeting of the American Orthopsychiatry Association, San Francisco, CA.

MACDONALD, K. (1992). Warmth as a developmental construct: An evoluntary analysis. *Child Development, 63,* 753–773.

MACDONALD, W. L., & DEMARIS, A. (1995). Remarriage, stepchildren, and marital conflict: Challenges to the incomplete institutionalization hypothesis. *Journal of Marriage and the Family, 56,* 387–398.

MACE, D. (1987). Three ways of helping married couples. *Journal of Marital and Family Therapy, 13,* 179–185.

MACEWEN, K. E. & BARLING, J. (1991). Effects of maternal employment experiences on children's behavior via mood, cognitive difficulties, and parenting behavior. *Journal of Marriage and the Family, 53,* 635–644.

MACEY, S. M., & SCHNEIDER, D. F. (1993). Deaths from excessive heat and excessive cold among the elderly. *The Gerontologist, 33,* 497–500.

MACHIDA, S., & HOLLOWAY, S. D. (1991). The relationship between divorced mothers' perceived control over child rearing and children's post-divorce development. *Family Relations, 40,* 272–278.

MACKENZIE, B. (1984). Explaining race differences in IQ: The logic, the methodology, and the evidence. *American Psychologist, 39,* 1214–1233.

MACKINNON-LEWIS, C., VOLLING, B. L., LAMB, M. E., DECHMAN, K., RABINER, D., & CURTNER, M. E. (1994). A cross-contextual analysis of boys' social competence: From family to school. *Developmental Psychology, 30,* 325–333.

MACKLIN, E. D. (1983). Nonmarital heterosexual cohabitation: An overview. In E. D. Macklin & R. H. Rubin (Eds.), *Contemporary families and alternate lifestyles: Handbook on research and theory* (pp. 49–73). Beverly Hills, CA: Sage.

MACLEOD, C,. & CAMPBELL, L. L. (1992). Memory accessibility and probability judgments: An experimental evaluation of the availability heuristic. *Journal of Personality and Social Psychology, 63,* 890–902.

MADDEN, D. J., PIERCE, T. W., & ALLEN, P. A. (1992). *Psychology and Aging, 7,* 594–601.

MADDOCK, J. W. (1989). Healthy family sexuality: Positive principles for educators and clinicians. *Family Relations, 38,* 130–136.

MADISON, L. S., MADISON, J. K., & ADUBATO, S. A. (1986). Infant behavior and development in relation to fetal movement and habituation. *Child Development, 57,* 1475–1482.

MAHLER, M. S., PINE, F., & BERGMAN, A. (1975). *The psychological birth of the human infant: Symbiosis and individuation.* New York: Basic Books.

MAIN, M., & CASSIDY, J. (1988). Categories of response in reunion with the parent at age 6: Predictable from infant attachment classifications and stable over a 1-month period. *Developmental Psychology, 24,* 415–426.

MAKIN, J. W., & PORTER, R. H. (1989). Attractiveness of lactating females' breast odors to neonates. *Child Development, 60,* 803–810.

MALATESTA, C. Z., GRIGORYEV, P., LAMB, C., ALBIN, M., & CULVER, C. (1986). Emotion socialization and expressive development in preterm and full-term infants. *Child Development, 57,* 316–330.

MALLICK, M. J., WHIPPLE, T. W., & HUERTA, E. (1987). Behavioral and psychological traits of weight-conscious teenagers: A comparison of eating-disordered patients and high- and low-risk groups. *Adolescence, 85,* 157–168.

MANEN, K. Z., & WHITBOURNE, S. K. (1997). Psychosocial development and life experiences in adulthood: A 22-year sequential study. *Psychology and Aging, 12,* 239–246.

MANGELSDORF, S., GUNNAR, M., KESTENBAUM, R., LANG, S., & ANDREAS, D. (1990). Infant proneness-to-distress temperament, maternal personality, and mother-infant attachment: Associations and goodness of fit. *Child Development, 61,* 820–831.

MANTON, K. B., & STALLARD, E. (1991). Cross-sectional estimates of active life expectancy for the U.S. elderly and oldest-old populations. *Journal of Gerontology, 46,* S170–S182.

MANTON, K. G., SIEGLER, I. C., & WOODBURY, M. A. (1986). Patterns of intellectual development in later life. *Journal of Gerontology, 4,* 486–499.

MARCH, T. (1995). Perception of adoption as social stigma: Motivation for search and reunion. *Journal of Marriage and the Family, 57,* 653–660.

MARCIA, J. E. (1966). Development and validation of ego identity status. *Journal of Personality and Social Psychology, 3,* 551–558.

MARCIA, J. E. (1976). Identity six years after: A follow-up study. *Journal of Youth and Adolescence, 5,* 145–160.

MARCIA, J. E. (1980). Identity in adolescence. In J. Adelson (Ed.). *Handbook of Adolescence.* New York: John Wiley & Sons.

MARCIA, J. E. (1987). The identity status approach to the study of ego development. In T. Honess & K. Yardley (Eds.), *Self and identity: Perspectives across the life span.* London & New York: Routledge & Kegan Paul.

MARCIA, J. E. (1989). Identity and intervention. *Journal of Adolescence, 12,* 401–410.

MAREAN, G. C., WERNER, L. A., & KUHL, P. K. (1992). Vowel categorization by very young infants. *Developmental Psychology, 28,* 396–405.

MARGOLIN, G., CHRISTENSEN, A., & JOHN, R. S. (1996). The continuance and spill over of everyday tensions in distressed and nondistressed families. *Journal of Family Psychology, 10,* 304–321.

MARGOLIN, L. (1991). Abuse and neglect in nonparental child care: A risk assessment. *Journal of Marriage and the Family, 53,* 694–704.

MARGOLIN, L. (1992). Beyond maternal blame. *Journal of Family Issues, 13,* 419–423.

MARION, R. W., WIZNIA, A. A., HUTCHEON, G., & RUBINSTEIN, A. (1986). Human T-cell lymphotropic virus type III (HTLV-III) embryopathy. *American Journal of Diseases of Children, 140,* 638–640.

MARKIDES, K. S., & LEE, D. J. (1990). Predictors of well-being and functioning in older Mexican Americans and Anglos: An eight-year follow-up. *Journal of Gerontology, 45,* S69–S73.

MARKIDES, K. S., & LEE, D. J. (1991). Predictors of health status in middle-aged and older Mexican Americans. *The Journals of Gerontology, 46,* S243–S249.

MARKMAN, H. J., LEBER, B. D., CORDOVA, A. B., & ST. PETERS, N. (1995). Behavioral observations in family psychology—strange bedfellows for a healthy marriage? Comments on Alexander et al. (1995). *Journal of Family Psychology, 9,* 371–379.

MARKS, N. F. (1995). Mid-life marital status differences in social support relationships with adult children and psychological well-being. *Journal of Family Issues, 16,* 5–28.

MARKUS, H. J., & NURIUS, P. S. (1984). Self-understanding and self-regulation in middle childhood. In W. A. Collins (Ed.), *Development during middle childhood: The years from six to twelve* (pp. 147–183). Washington, DC: National Academy Press.

MARKUS, H. R., & KITAYAMA, S. (1991). Culture and the self: Implications for cognition, emotion, and motivation. *Psychological Review, 98,* 224–253.

MARLIER, L., SCHAAL, B., & SOUSSIGNAN, R. (1998). Responsiveness to the odor of amniotic and lacteal fluids: A test of paranatal chemosensory continuity. *Child Development, 69,* 611–623.

MAROTTOLI, R. A., OSTFELD, A. M., MERRILL, S. S., PERLMAN, G. D., FOLEY, D. J., & COONEY, L. M., JR. (1993). Driving cessation and changes in mileage driven among elderly individuals. *Journal of Gerontology, 48,* S255–S260.

MAROUFI, C. (1989). A study of student attitude toward traditional and generative models of instruction. *Adolescence, 24,* 65–72.

MARSH, H. W., CRAVEN, R., & DEBUS, R. (1998). Structure, stability, and development of young children's self-concepts: A multicohort-multioccasion study. *Child Development, 69,* 1030–1053.

MARSIGLIO, W. (1991a). Male procreative consciousness and responsibility: A conceptual analysis and research agenda. *Journal of Family Issues, 12,* 268–290.

MARSIGLIO, W. (1991b). Paternal engagement activities with minor children. *Journal of Marriage and the Family, 53,* 973–986.

MARSIGLIO, W., (1992). Stepfathers with minor children living at home. *Journal of Family Issues, 13,* 195–214.

MARSISKE, M., KLUMB, P., & BALTES, M. M. (1997). Everyday activity patterns and sensory functioning in old age. *Psychology and Aging, 12,* 444–457.

MARTIN, C. L., & LITTLE, J. K. (1990). The relation of gender understanding to children's sex-typed preferences and gender stereotypes. *Child Development, 61,* 1427–1439.

MARTIN, C. L., WOOD, C. H., & LITTLE, J. K. (1990). The development of gender stereotype components. *Child Development, 61,* 1861–1904.

MARTIN, J. D. (1971). Power, dependence, and the complaints of the elderly: A social exchange perspective. *Aging and Human Development, 2,* 108–112.

MARTIN, P., HAGESTAD, G. O., & DIEDRICH, P. (1988). Family stories: Events (temporarily) remembered. *Journal of Marriage and the Family, 40,* 533–541.

MARTINEZ, R., & DUKES, R. L. (1991). Ethnic and gender differences in self-esteem. *Youth and Society, 22,* 318–338.

MARTIRE, L. N., STEPHENS, A. P., & TOWNSEND, A. L. (1998). Emotional support and well-being of midlife women: Role-specific mastery as a mediational mechanism. *Psychology and Aging, 13,* 396–404.

MARTLEW, M. (1992). Pen grips: Their relationship to letter/word formation and literacy knowledge in children starting school. *Journal of Human Movement Studies, 4,* 165–185.

MAS, C. H., ALEXANDER, J. F., & TURNER, C. W. (1991). Dispositional attributions and defensive behavior in high- and low-conflict families. *Journal of Family Psychology, 5,* 176–191.

MASATAKA, N. (1992). Early ontogeny of vocal behavior of Japanese infants in response to maternal speech. *Child Development, 63,* 1177–1185.

MASHETER, C. (1997). Healthy and unhealthy friendships and hostility between ex-spouses. *Journal of Marriage and the Family, 59,* 463–475.

MASLIN, J. (1991, July 17). A false goddess: Thinness for women: Review of "The famine within." *New York Times,* p. C13.

MASLOW, A. H. (1968). *Toward a psychology of being* (2nd ed.). Princeton, NJ: Van Nostrand.

MASLOW, A. H. (1970). *Motivation and personality* (2nd ed.). New York: Harper.

MASLOW, A. H. (1971). *The farther reaches of human nature.* New York: Viking.

MASON, G., & GIBBS, J. C. (1993). Social perspective taking and moral judgment among college students. *Journal of Adolescent Research, 8,* 109–123.

MASSELAM, V. S., MARCUS, R. F., & STUNKARD, C. L. (1990). Parent-adolescent communication, family functioning, and school performance. *Adolescence, 25,* 725–738.

MASTEKAASA, A. (1992). Marriage and psychological well-being: Some evidence on selection into marriage. *Journal of Marriage and the Family, 54,* 901–911.

MASTEN, A. S., NEEMANN, J., & ANDENAS, S. (1994). Life events and adjustment in adolescents: The significance of event independence, desirability, and chronicity. *Journal of Research on Adolescence, 4,* 71–97.

MATHEW, A., & COOK, M. (1990). The control of reaching movements by young infants. *Child Development, 61,* 1238–1257.

MATIAS, R., & COHN, J. F. (1993). Are Max-specified infant facial expressions during face-to-face interaction consistent with differential emotions theory? *Developmental Psychology, 29,* 524–531.

MATICKA-TYNDALE, E. (1991). Modification of sexual activities in the era of AIDS: A trained analysis of adolescent sexual activities. *Youth and Society, 23,* 31–49.

MATTHEWS, L. J., & ILON, L. (1980, July). Becoming a chronic runaway: The effects of race and family in Hawaii. *Family Relations, 29,* 404–409.

MAU, R. Y. (1992). The validity and devolution of a concept: Student alienation. *Adolescence, 27,* 731–741.

MAY, J. M. (1986). Cognitive processes and violent behavior in young people. *Journal of Adolescence, 9,* 17–27.

MAYLOR, E. A. (1991). Recognizing and naming tunes: Memory impairment in the elderly. *The Journals of Gerontology, 46,* P207–P217.

MAYLOR, E. A., & VALENTINE, T. (1992). Linear and nonlinear effects of aging on categorizing and naming faces. *Psychology and Aging, 7,* 317–323.

MAYNARD, F. (1974). Understanding the crisis in men's lives. In C. E. Williams & J. F. Crosby (Eds.), *Choice and challenge* (pp. 135–144). Dubuque, IA: Wm. C. Brown.

McADAMS, D. P. & DE ST. AUBIN, E. (1992). A theory of generativity and its assessment through self-report, behavioral acts, and narrative themes in autobiography. *Journal of Personality and Social Psychology, 62,* 1003–1015.

McAULEY, E., BAINE, S. M., RUDOLPH, D. L., & LOX, C. L. (1995). Physique anxiety and exercise in middle-aged adults. *Journal of Gerontology, 50B,* P229–P235.

MCAULEY, E., COURNEYA, K. S., & LETTUNICH, J. (1991). Effects of acute and long-term exercise on self-efficacy responses in sedentary, middle-aged males and females. *The Gerontologist, 31*, 534–542.

MCAULEY, E., LOX, C., & DUNCAN, T. E. (1993). Long-term maintenance of exercise, self-efficacy and physiological change in older adults. *Journal of Gerontology, 48*, P218–P224.

MCBRIDE, B. A., & RANE, T. R. (1998). Parenting alliance as a predictor of family involvement: An exploratory study. *Family Relations, 47*, 229–236.

MCCALL, R. B., & CARRIGER, M. S. (1993). A meta-analysis of infant habituation and recognition memory performance as predictors of later IQ. *Child Development, 64*, 57–79.

MCCALL, R. B., GROARK, C. J., STRAUSS, M. S., & JOHNSON, C. N. (1995). An experiment promoting interdisciplinary applied human development: The University of Pittsburgh Model. *Journal of Applied Developmental Psychology, 16*, 593–612.

MCCANN, J. T., & BIAGGIO, M. K. (1989). Sexual satisfaction in marriage as a function of life meaning. *Archives of Sexual Behavior, 18*, 59–72.

MCCARTNEY, N., HICKS, A. L., MARTIN, J., & WEBBER, C. E. (1995). Long-term resistance training in the elderly: Effects on dynamic strength, exercise capacity, muscle, and bones. *Journal of Gerontology, 50A*, B59–B66.

MCCARY, J. L., & MCCARY, S. P. (1982). *McCary's human sexuality* (4th ed.). Belmont, CA: Wadsworth Publishing Co.

MCCAULEY, E., KAY, T., ITO, J., & TREDER, R. (1987). The Turner syndrome: Cognitive deficits, affective discrimination, and behavior problems. *Child Development, 58*, 464–473.

MCCLEARN, B. E., SVARTENGREN, M., PEDERSEN, N. L., HELLER, D. A., & PLOMIN, R. (1994). Genetic and environmental influences on pulmonary functions of aging Swedish twins. *Journal of Gerontology, 49*, M264–M268.

MCCOMBS, A., FOREHAND, A., & SMITH, K. (1988). The relationship between maternal problem-solving style and adolescent social adjustment. *Journal of Family Psychology, 2*, 57–66.

MCCONNELL, A., & DAVIES, C. T. M. (1992). A comparison of the ventilatory responses to exercise of elderly and younger humans. *The Journals of Gerontology, 47*, B137–B141.

MCCONNELL, E. H. (1994). High school students. An assessment of their knowledge of gangs. *Youth and Society, 26*, 256–276.

MCCORMICK, C. M., & MAURER, D. M. (1988). Unimanual hand preferences in 6–month-olds: Consistency and relation to familial handedness. *Infant Behavior and Development, 11*, 21–29.

MCCRAE, R. R. (1982). Age differences in the use of coping mechanisms. *Journal of Gerontology, 37*, 454–460.

MCCRAE, R. R., & COSTA, P. T. (1990). *Personality in adulthood.* New York: Guilford.

MCCRAE, R. R., & JOHN, O. T. (1992). An introduction to the five-factor model and its applications. *Journal of Personality, 60*, 175–215.

MCCULLERS, J. C., & LOVE, J. M. (1976). The scientific study of the child. In B. J. Taylor & T. J. White (Eds.), *Issues and ideas in America.* Norman: Oklahoma University Press.

MCCULLOUGH, B. J. (1990). The relationships of intergenerational reciprocity of aid to the morale of older parents: Equity and exchange theory comparisons. *Journal of Gerontology, 45*, S150–S155.

MCCULLOUGH, B. J. (1991). A longitudinal investigation of the factor structure of subjective well-being: The case of the Philadelphia geriatric center morale scale. *The Journals of Gerontology, 46*, P251–P258.

MCDERMOTT, D. (1984, Spring). The relationship of parental drug use and parents' attitude concerning adolescent drug use to adolescent drug use. *Adolescence, 19*, 89–97.

MCEVOY, C. L., NELSON, D. L., HOLLEY, P. E., & STELNICKI, G. S. (1992). Implicit processing in the cued recall of young and old adults. *Psychology and Aging, 7*, 401–408.

MCGILL, M. (1985). *The McGill report on male intimacy.* New York: Harper and Row.

MCGRAW, M. B. (1940). Neural maturation as exemplified in achievement of bladder control. *Journal of Pediatrics, 16*, 580–590.

MCGRORY, A. (1990). Menarche: Response of early adolescent females. *Adolescence, 25*, 265–270.

MCGUE, M., BACON, S., & LYKKEN, D. T. (1993). Personality stability and change in early adulthood: A behavioral genetic analysis. *Developmental Psychology, 29*, 96–109.

MCGUE, M., BAUPEL, J. W., HOLM, N., & HARVALD, B. (1993). Longevity is moderately heritable in a sample of Danish twins born 1870–1880. *Journal of Gerontology, 48*, B237–B244.

MCHALE, S. M., BARTKO, W. T., CROUTER, A. C., & PERRY-JENKINS, M. (1990). Children's housework and psychosocial functioning: The mediating effects of parents' sex-role behaviors and attitudes. *Child Development, 61*, 1413–1426.

MCHALE, S. M., & PAWLETKO, T. M. (1992). Differential treatment of siblings in two family contexts. *Child Development, 63*, 68–91.

MCKENRY, P. C., KOTCH, J. B., & BROWNE, D. H. (1991). Correlates of dysfunctional parenting attitudes among low-income adolescent mothers. *Journal of Adolescent Research, 6*, 212–234.

MCKENZIE, B. E., SKOUTERIS, H., DAY, R. H., HARTMAN, B., & YONAS, A. (1993). Effective action by infants to contact objects by reaching and learning. *Child Development, 64*, 415–429.

MCKITRICK, L. A., CAMP, C. J., & BLACK, F. W. (1992). Prospective memory intervention in Alzheimer's disease. *The Journals of Gerontology, 47*, P337–P343.

MCKUSICK, V. A. (1986). *Mendelian inheritance in man* (7th ed.). Baltimore, MD: Johns Hopkins University Press.

MCLANAHAN, S., & BOOTH, K. (1989). Mothers-only families: Problems, prospects, and politics. *Journal of Marriage and the Family, 51*, 557–580.

MCLAUGHLIN, B. (1985). *Second language acquisition in childhood: Vol. 2. School-age children* (2nd ed.). Hillsdale, NJ: Erlbaum.

MCLOYD, V. C. (1990). The impact of economic hardship on black families and children: Psychological distress, parenting, and socioemotional development. *Child Development, 61*, 311–346.

MCMURRAN, M. (1991). Young offenders and alcohol-related crime: What interventions will address the issues? *Journal of Adolescence, 14*, 245–253.

MCNALLY, S., EISENBERG, N., & HARRIS, J. E. (1991). Consistency and change in maternal child-rearing practices and values: A longitudinal study. *Child Development, 62*, 190–198.

MCNEILL, D. (1970). Language development in children. In P. H. Mussen (Ed.), *Handbook of child psychology* (3rd ed.). New York: Wiley.

MCWHIRTER, E. H. (1991). Empowerment in counseling. *Journal of Counseling and Development, 69*, 222–227.

MEAD, M. (1950). *Coming of age in Samoa.* New York: New American Library.

MEAD, M. (1974). Adolescence. In H. V. Kraemer (Ed.), *Youth and culture: A human development approach.* Monterey, CA: Brooks/Cole.

MEDNICK, S. S., & CHRISTIANSEN, K. O. (1977). *Biosocial bases of criminal behavior.* New York: Gardner Press.

MEER, J. (1986a). The smoking diet plan. *Psychology Today, 20*, 12.

MEER, J. (1986b). Yours, mine, and divorce. *Psychology Today, 20*, 13.

MEICHENBAUM, D. (1972). Cognitive modification of test anxious college students. *Journal of Consulting and Clinical Psychology, 39*, 370–380.

MEIER, B. (1987, February 5). Companies wrestle with threats to workers' reproductive health. *Wall Street Journal*, p. 21.

MELBY, J. N., CONGER, R. D., CONGER, K. J., & LORENZ, F. O. (1993). Effects of parental behavior on tobacco use by young male adolescents. *Journal of Marriage and the Family, 55*, 439–454.

MELLANBY, A., PHELPS, F., & TRIPP, J. (1992). Sex education: More is not enough. *Journal of Adolescence, 15*, 449–466.

MELLI, M. S. (1986). The changing legal status of the single parent. *Family Relations, 35*, 31–35.

MELTZOFF, A. N. (1988). Infant imitation after a 1-week delay: Long-term memory for novel acts and multiple stimuli. *Developmental Psychology, 24*, 470–476.

MENAGHAN, E. G., & PARCEL, T. L. (1990). Parental employment and family life: Research in the 1980s. *Journal of Marriage and the Family 52*, 1079–1098.

MENDELSON, B. J., WHITE, D. R., & MENDELSON, M. J. (1996). Self-esteem and body esteem: Effects of gender, age, and weight. *Journal of Applied Developmental Psychology, 17*, 321–346.

MENDELSON, B. K., WHITE, D. R., & MENDELSON, M. J. (1996). Self-esteem and body esteem: Effects of gender, age and weight. *Journal of Applied Developmental Psychology, 17*, 321–346.

MENDELSON, M. J., ABOUD, F. E., & LANTHIER, R. P. (1994). Personality predictors of friendship and popularity in kindergarten. *Journal of Applied Developmental Psychology, 15*, 413–435.

MENICH, S. R., & BARON, A. (1990). Age-related effects of reinforced practice on recognition memory: Consistent versus varied stimulus-response relations. *Journal of Gerontology, 45*, P88–P93.

MEREDITH, D. (1986).   Day care: The nine-to-five dilemma. *Psychology Today, 20*, 36–44.

MESSER, A. A. (1989).   Boys' father hunger: The missing father syndrome. *Medical Aspects of Human Sexuality, 23*, 44–50.

METCALF, K., & GAIER, E. L. (1987).   Patterns of middle-class parent and adolescent underachievement. *Adolescence, 23*, 919–928.

METTER, E. J., WALEGA, D., METTER, E. L., PEARSON, J., BRANT, L. J., HISCOCK, B. S., & FOZARD, J. L. (1992).   How comparable are healthy sixty- and eighty-year-old men? *The Journals of Gerontology, 47*, M73–M78.

MEYER-BAHLBURG, H. F. L., EHRHARDT, A. A., ROSEN, L. R., GRUEN, R. S., VERIDIANO, N. P., VANN, F. H., & NEUWALDER, H. (1995).   Prenatal estrogens and the development of homosexual orientation. *Developmental Psychology, 31*, 12–21.

MEYERS, D. A., GOLDBERG, A. P., BLEECKER, M. L., COON, P. J., DRINKWATER, D. T., & BLEECKER, E. R. (1991).   Relationship of obesity and physical fitness to cardiopulmonary and metabolic function in healthy older men. *Journal of Gerontology, 46*, M57–M65.

MEYERS, J. E., & NELSON, W. M., III (1986).   Cognitive strategies and expectations as components of social competence in young adolescents. *Adolescence, 21*, 291–303.

MICHAEL, R. T., GAGNON, J. H., LAUMANN, E. O., & KOLATA, G. (1994).   *Sex in America.* Boston: Little, Brown.

MICHEL, G. F., HARKINS, D. A., & OVRUT, M. R. (1986, April).   Assessing infant (6–13 months old) handedness status. Paper presented at the 5th International Conference on Infant Studies. Los Angeles, CA.

MIDDLETON, D. (1987).   Collective memory and remembering: Some issues and approaches. *Quarterly Newsletter of the Laboratory of Comparative Human Cognition, 9*, 2–5.

MILLER, A. T., EGGERTSON-TACON, C., & QUIGG, B. (1990).   Patterns of runaway behavior within a larger systems context: The road to empowerment. *Adolescence, 25*, 271–290.

MILLER, B. C., & HEATON, T. B. (1991).   Age at first sexual intercourse and the timing of marriage and childbirth. *Journal of Marriage and the Family, 53*, 719–732.

MILLER, D. A. F., McCLUSKEY-FAWCETT, K., & IRVING, L. M. (1993).   Correlates of bulimia nervosa: Early family mealtime experiences. *Adolescence, 28*, 621–635.

MILLER, J. A., TURNER, J. G., & KIMBALL, E. (1981).   Big Thompson flood victims: One year later. *Family Relations, 30*, 111–116.

MILLER, J. B., & LANE, M. (1991).   Relations between young adults and their parents. *Journal of Adolescence, 14*, 179–194.

MILLER, J. E. (1991).   Birth intervals and perinatal health: An investigation of three hypotheses. *Family Planning Perspectives, 23*, 63–70.

MILLER, K. E. (1990).   Adolescents' same-sex and opposite-sex peer relations: Sex differences in popularity, perceived social competence, and social cognitive skills. *Journal of Adolescent Research, 5*, 222–241.

MILLER, K. S., KOTCHICK, B. A., DORSEY, S., FOREHAND, R., & HAM, A. Y. (1998).   Family communication about sex: What are parents saying and are there adolescents listening? *Family Planning Perspectives, 30*, 218–222.

MILLER, L. (1988).   The emotional brain. *Psychology Today, 22*, 34–42.

MILLER, M. W. (1985, January 17).   Study says birth defects more frequent in areas polluted by technology firms. *Wall Street Journal*, p. 6.

MILLER, N. B., COWAN, P. A., COWAN, C. P., HETHERINGTON, E. M., & CLINGEMPEEL, W. G. (1993).   Externalizing in preschoolers and early adolescents. A cross-study replication of a family model. *Developmental Psychology, 29*, 3–18.

MILLER, P. H., & ALOISE, P. A. (1989).   Young children's understanding of the psychological causes of behavior: A review. *Child Development, 60*, 257–285.

MILLER, S. A., & DAVIS, T. L. (1992).   Beliefs about children: A comparative study of mothers, teachers, peers, and self. *Child Development, 63*, 1251–1265.

MILLER, S. S., & CAVANAUGH, J. C. (1990).   The meaning of grandparenthood and its relationship to demographic, relationship, and social participation variables. *Journal of Gerontology, 45*, P244–P247.

MILLS, R. J., et al. (1992).   The effects of gender, family satisfaction, and economic strain on psychological well-being. *Family Relations, 41*, 440–445.

MILLS, R. S. L., & RUBIN, K. H. (1990).   Parents' beliefs about problematic social behaviors in early childhood. *Child Development, 61*, 138–151.

MISTRY, J. J., & LANGE, G. W. (1985).   Children's organization and recall of information in scripted narratives. *Child Development, 56*, 953–961.

MITCHELL, D. R., & LYLES, K. W. (1990).   Minireview: Glucocorticoid-induced osteoporosis: Mechanisms for bone loss; evaluation of strategies for prevention. *Journal of Gerontology, 45*, M153–M158.

MITCHELL, J. E., PYLE, R. L., & ECKERT, E. D. (1981).   Frequency and duration of binge-eating episodes in patients with bulimia. *American Journal of Psychiatry, 138*, 835, 836.

MITGANG, L. (1990, April 28).   *Student SAT scores decline for third year.* Portland, ME: Portland Press Herald.

MIZE, J., & PETTIT, G. S. (1997).   Mothers' social coaching, mother-child relationship style, and children's peer competence: Is the medium the message? *Child Development, 68*, 312–332.

MIZE, J., PETTIT, G. S., & BROWN, E. G. (1995).   Mothers' supervision of their children's peer play: Relations with beliefs, perceptions, and knowledge. *Developmental Psychology, 31*, 311–321.

MOEHLE, K. A., & LONG, C. (1989).   Models of aging and neuropsychological test performance decline with aging. *Journal of Gerontology, 44*, P176–177.

MOELY, B. E., HART, S. S., LEAL, L., SANTULLI, K. A., RAO, N., JOHNSON, T., & HAMILTON, L. B. (1992).   The teacher's role in facilitating memory and study strategy development in the elementary school classroom. *Child Development, 63*, 653–672.

MOFFITT, T. E. (1990).   Juvenile delinquency and attention deficit disorder: Boys' developmental trajectories from age 3 to 15. *Child Development, 61*, 893–910.

MONAHAN, S. C., BUCHANAN, C. N., MACCOBY, E. E., & DORNBUSCH, S. M. (1993).   Sibling differences in divorced families. *Child Development, 64*, 152–168.

MONEY, J. (1980).   *Love and love sickness.* Baltimore, MD: Johns Hopkins University Press.

MONEY, J. (1987).   Sin, sickness or status? Homosexual gender identity and psychoneuroendocrinology. *American Psychologist, 42*, 384–399.

MONK, T. H., et al. (1991).   Circadian characteristics of healthy eighty-year-olds and their relationship to objectively recorded sleep. *The Journals of Gerontology, 46*, M171–M175.

MONTGOMERY, D. E. (1993).   Young children's understanding of interpretive diversity between different-age listeners. *Developmental Psychology, 29*, 337–345.

MONTGOMERY, M. J., et al. (1992).   Patterns of courtship for remarriage: Implications for child adjustment and parent-child relationships. *Journal of Marriage and the Family, 54*, 686–698.

MONTGOMERY, M. J., & SORELL, G. T. (1997).   Differences in love attitudes across family life stages. *Family Relations, 46*, 55–61.

MOONEY, S. P., SHERMAN, M. F., & LOPRESTO, C. T. (1991).   Academic locus of control, self-esteem, and perceived distance from home as predictors of college adjustment. *Journal of Counseling and Development, 69*, 445–448.

MOORE, D., & SCHULTZ, N. R. (1983).   Loneliness at adolescence: Correlates, attributions, and coping. *Journal of Youth and Adolescence, 12*, 95–100.

MOORE, J. W., JENSEN, B., & HAUCK, W. E. (1990).   Decision-making processes of youth. *Adolescence, 25*, 583–592.

MOORE, K. A., & STIEF, T. M. (1991).   Changes in marriage and fertility behavior: Behavior versus attitudes of young adults. *Youth and Society, 22*, 362–386.

MOORE, S., & ROSENTHAL, D. (1990).   Adolescent invulnerability and perceptions of AIDS risk. *Journal of Adolescent Research, 6*, 164–180.

MOR, V., & MASTERSON-ALLEN, S. (1987).   *Hospice care systems: Structure, process, costs, and outcome.* New York: Springer.

MORAN, G. F., & VINOVSKIS, M. A. (1986).   The great care of godly parents: Early childhood in Puritan New England. *Monographs of the Society for Research in Child Development, 50*, (4–5, Serial No. 211).

MORAN, J. R., & CORLEY, M. D. (1991).   Sources of sexual information and sexual attitudes and behaviors of Anglo and Hispanic adolescent males. *Adolescence, 26*, 857–864.

MORAN, P. B., & ECKENRODE, J. (1991).   Gender differences in the costs and benefits of peer relations during adolescence. *Journal of Adolescent Research, 6*, 396–409.

MORELL, P., & NORTON, W. T. (1980).   Myelin. *Scientific American, 24*, 88–118.

MORENO, A. B., & THELEN, M. H. (1995).   Eating behavior in junior high shcool females. *Adolescence, 30*, 171–174.

MORGAN, M., PHILLIPS, J. G., BRADSHAW, J. L., MATTINGLEY, J. G., IANSEK, R., & BRADSHAW, J. A. (1994). Age-related motor slowness: Simple strategic? *Journal of Gerontology, 49,* M133–M139.

MORGAN, R. E. (1968). The adult growth examination: Preliminary comparison of physical aging in adults by sex and race. *Perceptual and Motor Skills, 27,* 595–599.

MORGAN, S. P., LYE, D. & CONDRAN, G. (1988). Sons, daughters, and the risk of marital disruption. *American Journal of Sociology, 90,* 1053–1077.

MORIN, C. M., STONE, J., TRINKLE, D., MERCER, J., & REMSBERG, S. (1993). Dysfunctional beliefs and attitudes about sleep among older adults with and without insomnia complaints. *Psychology in Aging, 8,* 463–467.

MORISON, P., & MASTEN, A. S. (1991). Peer reputation in middle childhood as a predictor of adaptation in adolescence: A seven-year follow up. *Child Development, 62,* 991–1007.

MORROW, D., LEIRER, V., ALTIEVI, P., & TANKE, E. (1991). Elder's schema for taking medication: Implications for instruction design. *The Journals of Gerontology, 46,* P378–P385.

MORSE, C. K. (1993). Does variability increase with age? An archival study of cognitive measures. *Psychology and Aging, 8,* 156–164.

MOSCHNER, C., & BALOH, R. W. (1994). Age-related changes in visual tracking. *Journal of Gerontology, 49,* M235–M238.

MOSER, D. V. (1992). Does memory affect judgment? Self-generated versus recall memory measures. *Journal of Personality and Social Psychology, 62,* 555–563.

MOTT, F. L. (1994). Sons, daughters, and fathers' absence: Differentials in father-leaving probabilities and in home environments. *Journal of Family Issues, 15,* 97–128.

MUEHLENHARD, C. L., & COOK, S. W. (1988). Men's self-reports of unwanted sexual activity. *The Joy of Sex Research, 24,* 58–72.

MUELLER, D. P., & COOPER, P. W. (1986). Children of single parent families: How they fare as young adults. *Family Relations, 35,* 169–172.

MUELLER, K. E., & POWERS, W. G. (1990). Parent-child sexual discussion: Perceived communicator style and subsequent behavior. *Adolescence, 25,* 469–482.

MUKERJI, V. (1988). Peripheral vascular disease. *Medical Aspects of Human Sexuality, 22,* 83–84.

MULLIS, A. K., MULLIS, R. L., & NORMANDIN, D. (1992). Cross-sectional and longitudinal comparisons of adolescent self-esteem. *Adolescence, 27,* 51–61.

MURRELL, S. A., NORRIS, F. H., & CHIPLEY, Q. T. (1992). Functional versus structural social support, desirable events, and positive affect in older adults. *Psychology and Aging, 7,* 562–570.

MUSON, H. (1977). The lessons of the Grant study. *Psychology Today, 11,* 42, 48, 49.

MUSUN-MILLER, L. (1993). Social acceptance and social problem-solving in preschool children. *Journal of Applied Developmental Psychology, 14,* 59–70.

MUUSS, R. E. (1985). Adolescent eating disorder: Anorexia nervosa. *Adolescence, 20,* 525–536.

MUUSS, R. E. (1988a). Carol Gilligan's theory of sex differences in the development of moral reasoning during adolescence. *Adolescence, 23,* 229–243.

MUUSS, R. E. (1988b). *Theories of adolescence* (5th ed.). New York: McGraw-Hill.

MYERS, D. A. (1991). Work after cessation of career job. *Journal of Gerontology, 46,* S93–S102.

MYRICKS, N., & FERULLO, D. L. (1986). Race and child custody disputes. *Family Relations, 35,* 325–328.

MYSKA, M. J., & PASEWARK, R. A. (1978, December). Death attitudes of residential and non-residential rural aged persons. *Psychological Reports, 43,* 1235–1238.

NACHMIAS, M., GUNNAR, M., MAGELSDORF, S., PARRITZ, R. H., & BUSS, K. (1966). Behavioral inhibition and stress reactivity: The moderating role of attachment security. *Child Development, 67,* 508–522.

NAGATA, Y., & DANNEMILLER, J. L. (1996). The selectivity of motion-driven visual attention in infants. *Child Development, 67,* 2608–2620.

NAGEL, K. L., & JONES, K. H. (1992a). Predisposition factors in anorexia nervosa. *Adolescence, 27,* 381–386.

NAGEL, K. L., & JONES, K. H. (1992b). Sociological factors in the development of eating disorders. *Adolescence, 27,* 107–113.

NAGY, M. H. (1948). The child's theories concerning death. *Journal of Genetic Psychology, 73,* 3–27.

NAMAY, L. L., & WAXMAN, S. R. (1998). Words and gestures: Infants' interpretations at different forms of symbolic reference. *Child Development, 69,* 295–308.

NATIONAL AUDIENCE DEMOGRAPHICS. REPORT 1985. (1985). Northrock, IL: A. C. Nielsen Co.

NATIONAL CHILDREN AND YOUTH FITNESS STUDY. (1984). Washington, DC: U.S. Public Health Service, Office for Disease Prevention and Health Promotion.

NATIONAL COMMISSION FOR THE PROTECTION OF HUMAN SUBJECTS OF BIOMEDICAL AND BEHAVIORAL RESEARCH. (1978). Institutional review boards: Report and recommendations. *Federal Register, 43,* 56174–56198.

NATIONAL COMMISSION ON EXCELLENCE IN EDUCATION. (1983). *A nation at risk: The imperative for educational reform.* Washington, DC: Department of Education.

NATIONAL FOUNDATION FOR THE MARCH OF DIMES. (1997). *Birth defects: Tragedy and hope.*

NATIONAL INSTITUTE ON ALCOHOL ABUSE AND ALCOHOLISM (NIAA). (1986). *Media alert: FAS awareness campaign: My baby . . . strong and healthy.* Rockville, MD: National Clearinghouse for Alcohol Information.

NATIONAL INSTITUTE ON MENTAL HEALTH (NIMH). (1982). *Television and behavior: Ten years of scientific progress and implications for the eighties:* Vol. 1. *Summary Report* (DHHS Publication No. ADM 82–1195). Washington, DC: U.S. Government Printing Office.

NATIONAL SURVEY OF FAMILY GROWTH, SERIES 23, No. 19. (1997). *Fertility, family planning and women's health: New data from the 1995 National Survey of Family Growth.* U.S. Department of Health and Human Services: National Center for Health Statistics.

NEAL, A. G., GROAT, H. T., & WICKS, J. W. (1989). Attitudes about having children: A study of 600 couples in the early years of marriage. *Journal of Marriage and the Family, 51,* 313–328.

NEIGER, B. L., & HOPKINS, R. W. (1988). Adolescent suicide: Character traits of high-risk teenagers. *Adolescence, 23,* 469–475.

NEILSEN, D. M., & METHA, A. (1994). Parental behavior and adolescent self-esteem in clinical and nonclinical samples. *Adolescence, 29,* 525–542.

NELSON, C., & KEITH, J. (1990). Comparison of female and male early adolescent sex role attitude and behavior development. *Adolescence, 25,* 183–204.

NELSON, C. A., & DOLGIN, K. G. (1985). The generalized discrimination of facial expressions by seven-month-old infants. *Child Development, 56,* 58–61.

NELSON, W. L., HUGHES, H. M., HANDAL, P., KATZ, B., & SEARIGHT, H. R. (1993). The relationship of family structure and family conflict to adjustment in young adult college students. *Adolescence, 28,* 29–40.

NEMETH, P. (1990, April). Kids on ritalin: Are they better off? *On campus.* Washington, DC: American Federation of Teachers.

NETTLES, S. M. (1989). The role of community involvement in fostering investment behavior in low-income black adolescents: A theoretical perspective. *Journal of Adolescent Research, 4,* 190–201.

NEUGARTEN, B. L. (Ed.). (1968). *Middle age and aging: A reader in social psychology.* Chicago, IL: University of Chicago Press.

NEUGARTEN, B. L., HAVIGHURST, R. J., & TOBIN, S. (1961). The measurement of life satisfaction. *Journal of Gerontology, 16,* 134–143.

NEUGARTEN, B. L., HAVIGHURST, R. D., & TOBIN, S. S. (1968). Personality and patterns of aging. In B. L. Neugarten (Ed.), *Middle age and aging* (pp. 173–177). Chicago, IL: University of Chicago Press.

NEUGARTEN, B. L., MOORE, J. W., & LOWE, J. C. (1965). Age norms, age constraints, and adult socialization. *American Journal of Sociology, 40,* 710–717.

NEUGARTEN, B. L., & NEUGARTEN, D. A. (1987). The changing meanings of age. *Psychology Today, 21,* 29–33.

NEVITT, M., CUMMINGS, S. R., & HUDES, E. S. (1991). Risk factors for injurious falls: A prospective study. *The Journals of Gerontology, 46,* M164–M170.

NEWCOMBE, N., & DUBAS, J. S. (1992). A longitudinal study of predictors of spatial ability in adolescent females. *Child Development, 63,* 37–46.

NEWCOMBE, N., & FOX, N. A. (1994). Infantile amnesia: Through a glass darkly. *Child Development, 65,* 31–40.

NEWCOMBE, N., & HUTTENLOCHER, J. (1992). Children's early ability to solve perspective-taking problems. *Developmental Psychology, 28*, 635–641.

NEWELL, G. K., HAMMIG, C. L., JURICH, A. P., & JOHNSON, D. E. (1990). Self-concept as a factor in the quality of diets of adolescent girls. *Adolescence, 25*, 117–130.

NEWMAN, B. M., & NEWMAN, P. R. (1984). *Development through life: A psychosocial approach* (2nd ed.). Homewood, IL: Dorsey Press.

NEWMAN, D. L., CASPI, A., & MOFFITT, T. E. (1997). Antecedents of adult interpersonal functioning: The effects of individual differences in age three temperament. *Developmental Psychology, 33*, 206–217.

NIEDENTHAL, P. M., SETTERLUND, M. B., & WHERRY, M. B. (1992). Possible self-complexity and affective reactions to goal-relevant evaluation. *Journal of Personality and Social Psychology, 63*, 5–16.

NIELSEN MEDIA RESEARCH (1998). Report on television. *National Audience Demographic Report*, February 1997.

NOCK, S. L. (1988). The family and hierarchy. *Journal of Marriage and the Family, 50*, 957–966.

NOLIN, M. J., & PETERSEN, K. K. (1992). Gender differences in parent-child communication about sexuality. *Journal of Adolescent Research, 7*, 59–71.

NOLL, R. B., ZUCKER, R. A., FITZGERALD, H. E., & CURTIS, W. J. (1992). Cognitive and motor functioning of sons of alcoholic fathers and controls: The early childhood years. *Developmental Psychology, 28*, 665–675.

NORMAN, S., KEMPER, S., & KYNETTE, D. (1992). Adults' reading comprehension: Effects of syntactic complexity and working memory. *The Journals of Gerontology, 47*, P258–P265.

NORMAN, S., KEMPER, S., KYNETTE, D., CHEUNG, H., & ANAGNOPOULOS, C. (1991). Syntactic complexity in adults' running memory span. *The Journals of Gerontology, 46*, P346–P351.

NORRIS, F. H., & MURRELL, S. A. (1987). Older adult family stress and adaptation before and after bereavement. *Journal of Gerontology, 43*, 606–612.

NORTON, A. J., & GLICK, P. B. (1986). One-parent families: A social and economic profile. *Family Relations, 35*, 9–13.

NORTON, A. J., & MOORMAN, J. E. (1987). Current trends in marriage and divorce among American women. *Journal of Marriage and the Family, 49*, 3–14.

NORTON, W. T. (1963). Toward an adequate taxonomy of personal attributes: Replicated factor structure in peer nomination personality ratings. *Journal of Abnormal and Social Psychology, 66*, 577.

NORY, D. M., GAA, J. P., FRANKIEWICZ, R. G., LIBERMAN, D., & AMERIKANER, M. (1992). The association between patterns of family functioning and ego development of the juvenile offender. *Adolescence, 27*, 25–35.

NUCCI, L., & SMETANA, J. B. (1996). Mothers' concepts of young children's areas of personal freedom. *Child Development, 67*, 1870–1886.

NUNN, G. D., & PARISH, T. S. (1992). The psychosocial characteristics of at-risk high school students. *Adolescence, 27*, 435–440.

NURMI, J., et al. (1992). Age differences in adults' control beliefs related to life goals and concerns. *Psychology and Aging, 7*, 194–196.

NURMI, J. A., & PULLIAINEN, H. (1991). The changing parent-child relationships, self-esteem, and intelligence as determinants of orientation to the future during early adolescence. *Journal of Adolescence, 14*, 17–34.

NUTTAL, R. L., FOZARD, J. L., ORSE, C. L., & SPENCER, B. (1971). *The ages of man: Ability age, personality age, and blood chemistry age.* Proceedings of the 79th annual convention of the American Psychological Association (Vol. 6, pp. 605–606).

O'BRIEN, S. J., & VERTINSKY, P. A. (1991). Unit survivors: Exercise as a resource for aging women. *The Gerontologist, 31*, 347–357.

O'CONNOR, T. G., HAWKINS, N., DUNN, J., THORPE, K., GOLDING, J., & THE ALSPAC STUDY TEAM (1998). Family type and depression in pregnancy: Factors mediating risk in a community sample. *Journal of Marriage and the Family, 60*, 757–770.

O'CONNOR, T. G., HETHERINGTON, E. M., REISS, D., & POLOMIN, R. (1995). A twin-sibling study of observed parent adolescent interactions. *Child Development, 66*, 812–829.

OGUNDARI, J. T. (1985, Spring). Somatic deviations in adolescence: Reactions and adjustments. *Adolescence, 20*, 179–183.

OHANNESSIAN, C. M., & CROCKETT, L. J. (1993). A longitudinal investigation of the relationship between educational investment and adolescent sexual activity. *Journal of Adolescent Research, 8*, 167–182.

OHANNESSIAN, C. M., LERNER, R. M., LERNER, J. D., & VON EYE, A. (1994). A longitudinal study of perceived family adjustment and emotional adjustment in early adolescence. *Journal of Early Adolescence, 14*, 371–390.

OLSEN, J., WEED, S., NIELSEN, A., & JENSEN, L. (1992). Student evaluation of sex education programs advocating abstinence. *Adolescence, 27*, 369–380.

OLSEN, J. A., JENSEN, L. C., & GREAVES, P. M. (1991). Adolescent sexuality and public policy. *Adolescence, 26*, 419–430.

OLSEN, J. A., WEED, S. E., RITZ, G. M., & JENSEN, L. C. (1991). The effects of three abstinence sex education programs on student attitudes towards sexual activity. *Adolescence, 26*, 631–641.

OLSON, J. M. (1992). Self-perception of humor: Evidence for discounting and augmentation effects. *Journal of Personality and Social Psychology, 62*, 369–377.

OLSON, S. L., & BANYARD, V. (1993). Sources of daily stress in the lives of low-income single mothers of young children. *Family Relations, 42*, 50–56.

OLTHOF, T., FERGUSON, T. J., & LUITEN, A. (1989). Personal responsibility antecedents of anger and blame reactions on children. *Child Development, 60*, 1328–1336.

OLVERA-EZZELL, N., POWER, T. G., & COUSINS, J. H. (1990). Maternal socialization of children's eating habits: Strategies used by obese Mexican-American mothers. *Child Development, 61*, 395–400.

OPENSHAW, D. K., MILLS, P. A., ADAMS, G. R., & DURSO, D. D. (1992). Conflict resolution in parent-adolescent dyads: The influence of social skills training. *Journal of Adolescent Research, 7*, 457–468.

ORLOFSKY, J. L. (1982). Psychological androgyny, sex typing, and sex role ideology as predictors of male-female interpersonal attraction. *Sex Roles, 8*, 1057.

ORR, E., & DINUR, B. (1995). Actual and perceived parental status: Effects on adolescent self-concept. *Adolescence, 30*, 603–616.

OSTER, H., HEGLEY, D., & NAGEL, L. (1992). Adult judgments and fine-grained analysis of infant facial expressions: Testing the validity of a priori coding formulas. *Developmental Psychology, 28*, 1115–1131.

O'SULLIVAN, R. G. (1990). Validating a method to identify at-risk middle school students for participation in a dropout prevention program. *Journal of Early Adolescence, 10*, 209–220.

OTTENWELLER, J. E., TAPP, W. W, CREIGHTON, D., & NATELSON, B. H. (1988). Aging, stress, and chronic disease interact to suppress plasma testosterone in Syrian hamsters. *Journal of Gerontology, 43*, M175–M180.

OTTO, L. B. (1988). America's youth: A changing profile. *Family Relations, 37*, 385–391.

OVERPECK, M. D., et al. (1989). A comparison of the childhood health status of normal birth weight and low birth weight infants. *Public Health Reports, 104*, 58.

OYSERMAN, D., RADIN, N., & BENN, R. (1993). Dynamics in a three-generational family: Teens, grandparents and babies. *Developmental Psychology, 29*, 564–572.

P. C. GAMES. (1997, January). 4, 1.

PAASSCH, K. M., & TEACHMAN, J. D. (1991). Gender of children and receipt of assistance from absent fathers. *Journal of Family Issues, 12*, 450–466.

PABON, E., RODRIGUEZ, O., & GURIN, G. (1992). Clarifying peer relations and delinquency. *Youth and Society, 24*, 149–165.

PACCIONE-DYSZLEWSKI, M. R., & CONTESSA-KISLUS, M. A. (1987). School phobia: Identification of subtypes as a prerequisite to treatment intervention. *Adolescence, 22*, 277–384.

PADDAC, C. (1987). Preparing a boy for nocturnal emissions. *Medical Aspects of Human Sexuality, 21*, 15, 16.

PAGE, R. M. (1990). Shyness and sociability: A dangerous combination for illicit substance use in adolescent males? *Adolescence, 25*, 803–806.

PAGE, R. M., & COLE, G. E. (1991). Loneliness and alcoholism risk in late adolescence: A comparison study of adults and adolescents. *Adolescence, 26*, 924–930.

PAGE, R. M., & HAMMERMEISTER, J. (1997). Weapon-carrying and youth violence. *Adolescence, 32*, 505–513.

PAIKOFF, R. B. (1990). Attitudes toward consequences of pregnancy in young women attending a family planning clinic. *Journal of Adolescent Research, 5*, 467–484.

PAKIZ, B., REINHERZ, H. Z., & FROST, A. K. (1992). Antisocial behavior in adolescence: A community study. *Journal of Early Adolescence, 12*, 300–313.

PALAZZI, S., DEVITO, E., LUZZATI, G., GUERRINI, A., & TORRE, I. (1990). A study of the relationships between life events and disturbed self-image in adolescents. *Journal of Adolescence, 13,* 53–64.

PALEY, V. G. (1984). *Boys and girls: Superheroes in the doll corner.* Chicago, IL: University of Chicago Press.

PAPINI, D. R., FARMER, F. F., CLARK, S. M., MICKA, J. C., & BARNETT, J. W. (1990). *Adolescence, 25,* 958–976.

PAPINI, D. R., & ROGGMAN, L. A. (1992). Adolescent perceived attachments to parents in relation to competence, depression, and anxiety: A longitudinal study. *Journal of Early Adolescence, 12,* 420–440.

PAPINI, D. R., ROGGMAN, L. A., & ANDERSON, J. (1990). Early-adolescent perceptions of attachment to mother and father: A test of the emotional-distancing and buffering hypotheses. *Journal of Early Adolescence, 11,* 258–275.

PAPPAS, B. A., et al. (1992). Alzheimer's disease and feeling-of-knowing or knowledge and episodic memory. *The Journals of Gerontology, 47,* P159–P164.

PARACHINI, A. (1987, August, 19). Condoms fail government tests. *Portland Press Herald,* Portland, ME.

PARDECK, J. T. (1990). Family factors related to adolescent autonomy. *Adolescence, 25,* 311–320.

PARISH, J. G., & PARISH, T. S. (1983, Fall). Children's self-concepts as related to family structure and family concept. *Adolescence, 18,* 649–658.

PARISH, T. S. (1990). Evaluations of family by youth: Do they vary as a function of family structure, gender, and birth order? *Adolescence, 25,* 353–356.

PARISH, T. S. (1991). Ratings of self and parents by youth: Are they affected by family status, gender, and birth order? *Adolescence, 26,* 105–112.

PARISH, T. S., & DOSTAL, J. W. (1980, August). Evaluations of self and parent figures by children from intact, divorced and reconstituted families. *Journal of Youth and Adolescence, 9,* 347–351.

PARISH, T. S., & MCCLUSKEY, J. J. (1992). The relationship between parenting styles and young adults' self-concepts and evaluations of parents. *Adolescence, 27,* 915–918.

PARISH, T. S., & NECESSARY, J. R. (1993). Received actions of parents and attitudes of youth. *Adolescence, 28,* 185–198.

PARISH, T. S., & NECESSARY, J. R. (1994). Parents' actions: Are they related to children's self-concepts, evaluations of parents, and to each other? *Adolescence, 29,* 943–947.

PARISH, T. S., & PARISH, J. G. (1991). The effects of family configuration and support system failures during childhood and adolescence on college students' self-concepts and social skills. *Adolescence, 26,* 441–448.

PARK, D. C., MORRELL, R. W., FRIESKE, D., & KINCAID, D. (1992). Medication adherence behaviors in older adults: Effects of external cognitive supports. *Psychology and Aging, 7,* 252–256.

PARK, K. A., LAY, K., & RAMSAY, L. (1993). Individual differences and developmental changes in preschoolers' friendships. *Developmental Psychology, 29,* 264–270.

PARK, K. A., & WATERS, E. (1989). Security of attachment and preschool friendships. *Child Development, 60,* 1076–1081.

PARKER, G. (1990). The Parental Bonding Instrument. A decade of research. *Social Psychiatry and Psychiatric Epidemiology, 25,* 281–282.

PARKER, J. G., & ASHER, S. R. (1993). Friendship and friendship quality in middle childhood: Links with peer group acceptance and feelings of loneliness and social dissatisfaction. *Developmental Psychology, 29,* 611–621.

PARKER, R. D. (1995). The role of family emotional expressiveness in the development of children's social competence. *Journal of Marriage and the Family, 57,* 593–608.

PARKHURST, J. T., & ASHER, S. R. (1992). Peer rejection in middle school: Subgroup differences in behavior, loneliness, and interpersonal concerns. *Developmental Psychology, 28,* 231–241.

PARKIN, A. J., & WALTER, B. M. (1992). Recollective experience, normal aging and frontal dysfunction. *Psychology and Aging, 7,* 290–298.

PARNES, H. S., & SOMMERS, D. G. (1994). Shunning retirement: Work experience of men in their seventies and early eighties. *Journal of Gerontology, 49,* S117–S124.

PARTEN, M. B. (1932). Social participation among preschool children. *Journal of Abnormal and Social Psychology, 27,* 243–269.

PASSUTH, P., MAINES, D., & NEUGARTEN, B. L. (1984, April). *Age norms and age constraints twenty years later.* Paper presented at the Midwest Sociological Society meeting, Chicago, IL.

PASTORINO, E., DUNHAM, R. M., KIDWELL, J., BACHO, R., & LAMBORN, S. D. (1997). Domain-specific comparisons in identity development among college youth: Ideology and relationships. *Adolescence, 32,* 559–577.

PATTERSON, C. J. (1995). Sexual orientation and human development: An overview. *Developmental psychology, 31,* 3–11.

PATTERSON, C. J., KUPERSMIDT, J. B., & VADEN, N. A. (1990). Income level, gender, ethnicity, and household composition as predictors of children's school-based competence. *Child Development, 61,* 485–494.

PATTISON, E. M. (1977). The experience of dying. Englewood Cliffs, NJ: Prentice-Hall.

PAUL, E. L., & WHITE, K. M. (1990). The development of intimate relationships in late adolescence. *Adolescence, 25,* 375–400.

PAULSON, S. E. (1994). Relations of parenting style and parental involvement with ninth-grade students' achievement. *Journal of Early Adolescence, 14,* 250–267.

PAULSON, S. E., HILL, J. P., & HOLMBECK, G. N. (1990). Distinguishing between perceived closeness and parental warmth in families with seventh-grade boys and girls. *Journal of Early Adolescence, 11,* 276–293.

PEARSON, J. L., & FERGUSON, L. R. (1989). Gender differences in patterns of spatial ability, environmental cognition, and math and English achievement in late adolescence. *Adolescence, 24,* 421–431.

PEARSON, J. L., HUNTER, A. G., ENSMINGER, M. E., & KELLAM, S. G. (1990). Black grandmothers in multigenerational households: Diversity in family structure and parenting involvement in the Woodlawn community. *Child Development, 61,* 434–442.

PEDERSEN, N. L., PLOMIN, R., NESSELROADE, J. R., & MCCLERN, G. E. (1992). Quantitative genetic analysis of cognitive abilities during the second half of their lifespan. *Psychological Science, 3,* 346–353.

PEDERSEN, W. (1990). Adolescents initiating cannabis use: Cultural opposition or poor mental health? *Journal of Adolescence, 13,* 327–340.

PEDERSEN, W. (1994). Parental relations, mental health, and delinquency in adolescents. *Adolescence, 29,* 975–990.

PEDERSON, B. R., GLEASON, K. E., MORAN, G., & BENTO, S. (1998). Maternal attachment representations, maternal sensitivity, and the infant-mother attachment relationship. *Developmental Psychology, 34,* 925–933.

PEDERSON, D. R., MORAN, G., SITKO, C., CAMPBELL, K., GHESQUIRE, K., & ACTON, H. (1990). Maternal sensitivity and the security of infant–mother attachment: A Q-sort study. *Child Development, 61,* 1974–1983.

PELAEZ-NOGUERAS, M., FIELD, T., HOSSAIN, D., & PICKENS, J. (1996). Depressed mothers' touching increases infants' positive affect and attention in still-faced interactions. *Child Development, 67,* 1780–1792.

PELAEZ-NOGUERAS, M., GEWIRTZ, J. L., FIELD, T., CIGALES, M., MALTHURS, J., CLASKY, S., & SANCHEZ, A. (1996). Infants' preference for touch stimulation in face-to-face interactions. *Journal of Applied Developmental Psychology, 17,* 199–213.

PELLEGRINI, A. D., PERLMUTTER, J. C., GALDA, L., & BRODY, G. H. (1990). Joint reading between black Head Start children and their mothers. *Child Development, 61,* 443–453.

PEPE, M. V., & BYRNE, T. J. (1991). Women's perceptions of immediate and long-term effects of failed infertility treatment on marital and sexual satisfaction. *Family Relations, 40,* 303–309.

PEPLER, D. J., & CRAIG, W. M. (1995). A peek behind the fence: Naturalistic observations of aggressive children with remote audio visual recording. *Developmental Psychology, 31,* 548–553.

PERKINS, H. W., & BERKOWITZ, A. D. (1991). Collegiate COAs and alcohol abuse: Problem drinking in relation to assessments of parent and grandparent alcoholism. *Journal of Counseling and Development, 69,* 237–240.

PERLMUTER, L. C. (1991). Choice enhances performance in non-insulin dependent diabetics and controls. *The Journals of Gerontology, 46,* P218–P223.

PERLMUTTER, M. (1987). Aging and memory. In K. W. Schaie & K. Eisdorfer (Eds.), *Annual review of gerontology and geriatrics* (Vol. 7). New York: Springer Publishing Co.

PERLMUTTER, M., & NYQUIST, L. (1990). Relationships between self-reported physical and mental health and intelligence performance across adulthood. *Journal of Gerontology, 45,* P145– P155

PERRIS, E. E., MYERS, N. A., & CLIFTON, R. K. (1990). Long-term memory for a single infancy experience. *Child Development, 61,* 1796–1807.

PERRUCCI, C. C. (1988). *Plant closing*. New York: Aldine de Gruyter.

PERRY, D. G., WILLIARD, J. C., & PERRY, L. C. (1990). Peers' perceptions of the consequences that victimized children provide aggressors. *Child Development, 61,* 1310–1325.

PERSELL, C. H., CATSAMBIS, S., & COOKSON, P. W., JR. (1992). Family background, school type, and college attendance: A conjoint system of cultural capital transmission. *Journal of Research on Adolescence, 2,* 1–23.

PETERSEN, A. C. (1993). Presidential address: Creating adolescence: The role of context and process in developmental trajectories. *Journal of Research on Adolescence, 3,* 1–18.

PETERSON, B. E., & KLOHNEN, E. C. (1995). Realization of generativity in two samples of women at midlife. *Psychology and Aging, 10,* 20–29.

PETERSON, C., & MCCABE, A. (1994). A social interactionist's account of developing decontextualized narrative skill. *Developmental Psychology, 30,* 937–948.

PETERSON, C. C., & MURPHY, L. (1990). Adolescents' thoughts and feelings about AIDS in relation to cognitive maturity. *Journal of Adolescence, 13,* 185–188.

PETERSON, G. W., & ROLLINS, B. C. (1987). Parent-child socialization. In M. B. Sussman & S. K. Steinmetz (Eds.), *Handbook of marriage and the family* (pp. 471–507). New York: Plenum.

PETERSON, J. L., & NORD, C. W. (1990). The regular receipt of child support: A multistep process. *Journal of Marriage and the Family, 52,* 539–551.

PETERSON, K. L., & ROSCOE, B. (1991). Imaginary audience behavior in older adolescent females. *Adolescence, 26,* 195–200.

PETRILL, S. A., SAUDINO, K., CHERNY, S. S., EMDE, R. N., FULKER, D. W., HEWITT, J. K., & PLOMIN, R. (1998). Exploring the genetic and environmental etiology of high general cognitive ability in fourteen-to-thirty-six-month-old twins. *Child Development, 69,* 68–74.

PETT, M. B., & VAUGHAN-COLE, B. (1986). The impact of income issues and social status in post-divorce adjustment of custodial parents. *Family Relations, 35,* 103–111.

PETTIT, G. S., DODGE, K. H., & BROWN, M. M. (1988). Early family experience, social problem solving patterns, and children's social competence. *Child Development, 59,* 107–120.

PEZDEK, K. (1987). Memory of pictures: A life-span study of the role of visual detail. *Child Development, 58,* 807–815.

PFEFFER, C. (1987). Suicidal children announce their self-destructive intentions. *Medical Aspects of Human Sexuality, 21,* 14.

PHELPS, L., JOHNSTON, L. S., JIMENEZ, D. P., WILCZENSKI, F. L., ANDREA, R. K., & HEALY, R. W. (1993). Figure preference, body dissatisfaction, and body distortion in adolescence. *Journal of Adolescent Research, 8,* 297–310.

PHIFER, J. G., & NORRIS, F. H. (1989). Psychological symptoms in older adults following natural disaster: Nature, timing, duration, and course. *Journal of Gerontology, 44,* S207–S217.

PHILLIPS, D. A. (1987). Socialization of perceived academic competence among highly competitive children. *Child Development, 58,* 1308–1320.

PHILLIPS, S. K., BRUCE, S. A., NEWTON, D., & WOLEDGE, R. C. (1992). The weakness of old age is not due to failure of muscle activation. *The Journals of Gerontology, 47,* M45–M49.

PHINNEY, J. S. (1992). The multigroup ethnic identity measure. A new scale for youths with diverse groups. *Journal of Adolescent Research, 7,* 156–176.

PHINNEY, J. S., & ALIPURIA, L. L. (1990). Ethnic identity in college students from four ethnic groups. *Journal of Adolescence, 13,* 171–184.

PHINNEY, J. S., CHAVIRA, V., & WILLIAMSON, L. (1992). The acculturation attitudes and self-esteem among high-school and college students. *Youth and Society, 23,* 299–312.

PHINNEY, J. S., & DEVICH-NAVARRO, M. (1997). Variations in bicultural identification among African American and Mexican American adolescents. *Journal of Research on Adolescence, 7,* 3–32.

PHINNEY, V. G., JENSEN, L. C., OLSEN, J. A., & CUNDICK, B. (1990). The relationship between early development and psychosexual behaviors in adolescent females. *Adolescence, 25,* 321–332.

PIAGET, J. (1926). *The language of the child* (M. Warden, Trans.). New York: Harcourt.

PIAGET, J. (1948). *The moral judgment of the child* (1932 reprint). Glencoe, IL: Free Press.

PIAGET, J. (1950). *The psychology of intelligence*. London: Routledge and Kegan Paul.

PIAGET, J. (1954). *The construction of reality in the child*. New York: Basic Books.

PIAGET, J. (1962). *Play, dream, and imitation in childhood*. New York: W. W. Norton.

PIAGET, J. (1963). *The origins of intelligence in children*. New York: W. W. Norton.

PIAGET, J. (1967a). *The child's construction of the world*. Totowa, NJ: Littlefield, Adams.

PIAGET, J. (1971). The theory of stages in cognitive development. In D. R. Green (Ed.), *Measurement and Piaget*. New York: McGraw-Hill.

PIAGET, J. (1972). Intellectual evolution from adolescence to adulthood. *Human Development, 15,* 1012.

PIAGET, J. (1980). Intellectual evolution from adolescence to adulthood. In R. E. Muuss (Ed.), *Adolescent behavior and society: A body of readings* (3rd ed.). New York: Random House.

PIAGET, J., & INHELDER, B. (1958). *The Growth of Logical Thinking: From Childhood to Adolescence*. New York: Basic Books.

PIAGET, J., & INHELDER, B. (1969). *The psychology of the child*. (H. Weaver, Trans.). New York: Basic Books.

PIANTA, R. C., & BALL, R. M. (1993). Maternal support as a predictor of child adjustment in kindergarten. *Journal of Applied Developmental Psychology, 14,* 107–120.

PICCININO, L. J., & MOSHER, W. D. (1998). Trends in contraceptive use in the United States: 1982–1995. *Family Planning Perspectives, 30,* 4–10, 46.

PIENTA, A. M., BURR, J. A., & MUTCHLER, J. E. (1994). Women's labor force participation in later life: The effects of early work and family experiences. *Journal of Gerontology, 49,* S231–S239.

PIERCE, J. W., & WARDLE, J. (1993). Self-esteem, parental appraisal and body size in children. *Journal of Child Psychology and Psychiatry, 34,* 725–1136.

PIERCY, F. P., & SPRENKLE, D. H. (1990). Marriage and family therapy: A decade review. *Journal of Marriage and the Family, 52,* 1116–1126.

PIERS, M. W. (1978). *Infanticide: Past and present*. New York: W. W. Norton.

PILL, C. J. (1990). Stepfamilies: Redefining the family. *Family Relations, 39,* 186–193.

PILLARD, R. C. (1990). The Kinsey scale: Is it familial? In D. P. McWhirter, S. A. Saunders, & J. M. Reinisch (Eds.), *Homosexuality/heterosexuality: Concepts of sexual orientation* (pp. 88–100). New York: Oxford University Press.

PILLEMER, D. B., KOFF, E., RHINEHART, E. D., & RIERDAN, J. (1987). Flashbulb memories of menarche and adult menstrual distress. *Journal of Adolescence, 10,* 187–199.

PILLEMER, K., & SUITOR, J. J. (1991). "Will I ever escape my child's problems?" Effects of adult children's problems on elderly parents. *Journal of Marriage and the Family, 53,* 585–594.

PILLOW, B. H. (1988). Young children's understanding of attentional limits. *Child Development, 58,* 38–46.

PILLOW, B. H., & HENRICHON, A. J. (1996). There's more to the picture than meets the eye: Young children's difficulty understanding biased interpretation. *Child Development, 67,* 803–819.

PINES, M. (1981, September). The civilizing of Genie. *Psychology Today, 14,* 28–34.

PINES, M. (1984). In the shadow of Huntington's. *Science, 84, 5,* 32–39.

PINNEAU, S. R. (1961). *Changes in intelligent quotient*. Boston, MA: Houghton Mifflin.

PINON, M. F., HUSTON, A. C., & WRIGHT, J. C. (1989). Family ecology and child characteristics that predict young children's educational television viewing. *Child Development, 60,* 846–856.

PIPP, S., EASTERBROOKS, M. A., & HARMON, R. J. (1992). The relation between attachment and knowledge of self and mother in one- to three-year-old infants. *Child Development, 63,* 738–750.

PIPP, S., & HARMON, R. J. (1987). Attachment as regulation: A commentary. *Child Development, 58,* 648–652.

PIROG-GOOD, M. A., & AMERSON, L. (1997). The long arm of justice: The potential for seizing the assets of child support obligors. *Family Relations, 46,* 47–54.

PLEDGER, L. M. (1992). Development of self-monitoring behavior from early to late adolescence. *Adolescence, 27,* 329–338.

PLEMONS, J. K., WILLIS, S. L., & BALTES, P. (1978). Modifiability of fluid intelligence in aging: A short-term longitudinal training approach. *Journal of Gerontology, 33,* 224–231.

PLUMERT, J. N., EWERT, J., & SPEAR, S. J. (1995). The early development of children's communication about nested spatial relations. *Child Development, 66,* 959–969.

PLUMERT, J. N., PICK, H. L., JR., MARKS, R. A., KINTSCH, A. S., WEGESIN, D. (1994). Locating objects and communicating about locations: Organizational differences in children's searching and direction-giving. *Developmental Psychology, 30,* 443–453.

PLUMMER, L. D., & KOCH-HATTEM, A. (1986). Family stress and adjustment to divorce. *Family Relations, 35,* 523–529.

PLUMMER, W. (1985, October 28). A school's Rx for sex. *People,* pp. 39–41.

POEHLMAN, E. T., MELBY, C. L., & BADYLAK, S. F. (1991). Relation of age and physical exercise status on metabolic rate in younger and older healthy men. *Journal of Gerontology, 46,* B54–B58.

POLLITT, E. (1995). Does breakfast make a difference in school? *Journal of the American Dietetic Association, 95,* 734–1139.

POMBENI, J. L., KIRCHLER, E., & PALMONARI, A. (1990). Identification with peers as a strategy to muddle through the troubles of the adolescent years. *Journal of Adolescence, 13,* 351–370.

POON, L. W., & FOZARD, J. L. (1978). Speed of retrieval from long-term memory in relation to age, familiarity, and datedness of information. *Journal of Gerontology, 33,* 711–717.

POPPEN, P. J. (1994). Adolescent contraceptive use and communication: Changes over a decade. *Adolescence, 29,* 503–514.

PORJESZ, B., & BEGLEITNER, H. (1985). Human brain electrophysiology and alcoholism. In R. Tarter & D. Thiel (Eds.), *Alcohol and the brain.* New York: Plenum.

PORRECO, R., & MEIER, P. (1983). Trials of labor in patients with multiple previous cesarean sections. *Journal of Reproductive Medicine, 28,* 770–772.

PORTER, N. L., & CHRISTOPHER, F. S. (1984). Infertility: Toward an awareness of a need among family life practitioners. *Family Relations, 33,* 309–315.

POSNER, B. M., JETTE, A., SMIGELSKI, C., MILLER, D., & MITCHELL, P. (1994). Nutritional risk in New England elders. *Journal of Gerontology, 49,* M123–M132.

POSTRADO, L. T., & NICHOLSON, H. J. (1992). Effectiveness in delaying the initiation of sexual intercourse in girls aged 12–14. *Youth in Society, 23,* 356–379.

POWELL, D. A., MILLIGAN, W. L., & FURCHTGOTT, E. (1980). Peripheral autonomic changes accompanying learning and reaction time performance in older people. *Journal of Gerontology, 35,* 57–65.

POWELL, M. B., & THOMSON, D. M. (1996). Children's memory of an occurrence of a repeated event: Effects of age, repetition, and retention intervals across three question types. *Child Development, 67,* 1988–2004.

POWERS, P. S. (1980). *Obesity: The regulation of weight.* Baltimore, MD: Williams & Wilkins.

PRATT, C. C., WALKER, A. J., & WOOD, D. L. (1992). Bereavement among former caregivers to elderly mothers. *Family Relations, 31,* 278–283.

PRESSER, H. D. (1989). Some economic complexities of child care provided by grandmothers. *Journal of Marriage and the Family, 51,* 581–591.

PRESTON, D. B., & MANSFIELD, P. K. (1984). An exploration of stressful life events, illness, and coping among the rural elderly. *Gerontologist, 24,* 490–495.

PRICE, D. W. W., & GOODMAN, G. S. (1990). Visiting the wizard: Children's memory for a recurring event. *Child Development, 61,* 664–680.

PRICE, J., & FESHBACH, S. (1982, August). *Emotional adjustment correlates of televising viewing in children.* Paper presented at the meeting of the American Psychological Association, Washington, DC.

PRICE, J. M., & BREW, V. (1998). Peer relationships of foster children: Developmental and mental health service implications. *Journal of Applied Developmental Psychology, 19,* 199–218.

PRINZ, P. A. (1977). Sleep patterns in the healthy aged: Relationship with intellectual function. *Journal of Gerontology, 32,* 179–186.

PRITCHARD, C., COTTON, A., & COX, M. (1992). Truancy and illegal drug use, and knowledge of HIV infection in 932 14- to 16-year-old adolescents. *Journal of Adolescence, 15,* 1–17.

PRITCHARD, J., MACDONALD, D., & GRANT, N. (1985). *Williams obstetrics* (17th ed.). New York: Appleton-Century-Crofts.

PROTINSKY, H., & FARRIER, S. (1980, Winter). Self-image changes in pre-adolescence and adolescents. *Adolescence, 15,* 887–893.

PRYOR, D. W., & MCGARRELL, E. F. (1993). Public perceptions of youth gang crime: An exploratory analysis. *Youth and Society, 24,* 399–418.

PUGLISI, J. T., PARK, D. C., SMITH, A. D., & DUDLEY, W. N. (1988). Age differences in encoding specificity. *Journal of Gerontology, 43,* P145–P150.

PUTALLAZ, M. (1987). Maternal behavior and children's sociometric status. *Child Development, 58,* 324–340.

QUAY, L. C. (1992). Personal and family effects on loneliness. *Journal of Applied Developmental Psychology, 13,* 97–110.

QUAYHAGEN, M. P., & QUAYHAGEN, M. (1989). Differential effects of family based strategies on Alzheimer's disease. *Gerontologist, 29,* 150–155.

QUINN, P., & ALLEN, K. R. (1989). Facing challenges and making compromises: How single mothers endure. *Family Relations, 38,* 390–395.

QUINTANA, S. M., & LAPSLEY, D. K. (1990). Rapprochement in late adolescent separation-individuation: A structural equations approach. *Journal of Adolescence, 13,* 371–386.

QUITTNER, A. L., & OPIPARI, L. C. (1994). Differential treatment of siblings: Interview and diary analyses comparing two family contexts. *Child Development, 65,* 800–814.

RABINER, D. L., & GORDON, L. B. (1992). The coordination of conflicting social goals: Differences between rejected and nonrejected boys. *Child Development, 63,* 1344–1350.

RABINER, D. L., KEANE, S. P., & MACKINNON-LEWIS, C. (1993). Children's beliefs about familiar and unfamiliar peers in relation to their sociometric status. *Developmental Psychology, 29,* 236–243.

RABINOWITZ, J. C., & CRAIK, F. I. M. (1986). Prior retrieval effects in young and old adults. *Journal of Gerontology, 41,* 368–375.

RADOMSKI, M. (1981). Stereotypes, stepmothers, and splitting. *American Journal of Psychoanalysis, 41,* 121–127.

RAFFAELLI, M, BOGENSCHNEIDER, K., & FLOOD, M. F. (1998). Parent-teen communication about sexual topics. *Journal of Family Issues, 19,* 315–333.

RAINE, A., HULME, C., CHADDERTON, H., & BAILEY, P. (1991). Verbal short-term memory span in speech disordered children: Implications for articulatory coding in short-term memory. *Child Development, 62,* 415–423.

RAKOWSKI, W., & MOR, V. (1992). The association of physical activity with mortality among adults in the longitudinal study of aging (1984–1988). *The Journals of Gerontology, 47,* M122–M129.

RALOFF, J. (1986). Even low levels in mom affect baby. *Science News, 130,* 164.

RALPH, N., & MORGAN, K. A. (1991). Assessing differences in chemically dependent adolescent males using the child behavior checklist. *Adolescence, 26,* 183–194.

RAMSEY, B. G. (1995). Changing social dynamics in early childhood classrooms. *Child Development, 66,* 764–773.

RAMSEY, D. S. (1985). Fluctuations in unimanual hand preference in infants following the onset of duplicated syllable babbling. *Developmental Psychology, 21,* 318–324.

RAMSEY, D. S., & WEBER, S. L. (1986). Infants' hand preference in a task involving complementary roles for the two hands. *Child Development, 57,* 300–307.

RAPKIN, B. D., & FISCHER, K. (1992b). Framing the construct of life satisfaction in terms of older adults' personal goals. *Psychology and Aging, 7,* 138–149.

RAPKIN, B. D., & FISHER, K. (1992a). Framing the construct of life satisfaction in terms of older adults' personal goals. *Psychology and Aging, 7,* 138–149.

RAPKIN, B. D., & FISHER, K. (1992b). Personal goals of older adults: Issues in assessment and prediction. *Psychology and Aging, 7,* 127–137.

RAPP, G. S., & LLOYD, S. A. (1989). The role of "home as haven" ideology in child care use. *Family Relations, 38,* 426–430.

RASCHKE, H. J., & RASCHKE, V. J. (1979, May). Family conflict and children's self-concepts: A comparison of intact and single-parent families. *Journal of Marriage and the Family, 41,* 367–374.

RASKIN, P. M. (1990). Identity status research: Implications for career counseling. *Journal of Adolescence, 13,* 375–388.

RAUH, V. A., ACHENBACH, T. M., NURCOMBE, B., HOWELL, C. T., & TETI, D. M. (1988). Minimizing adverse effects of low birth-weight:

Four-year results of an early intervention program. *Child Development, 59,* 544–553.

RAVIV, A., MADDY-WEITZMAN, E., & RAVIV, A. (1992). Parents of adolescents: Help-seeking intentions as a function of health sources and parenting issues. *Journal of Adolescence, 15,* 115–135.

REAVES, J., & ROBERTS, A. (1983). The effects of the type of information on children's attraction to peers. *Child Development, 54,* 1024–1031.

REBOK, G. W., MONTAGLIONE, C. J., & BENDLIN, G. (1988). Effects of age and training on memory for pragmatic implications in advertising. *Journal of Gerontology, 43,* P75–P78.

RECCHIA, S. L. (1997). Social communication and response to ambiguous stimuli in toddlers with visual impairments. *Journal of Applied Developmental Psychology, 18,* 297–316.

REED, E. S. (1988). *James J. Gibson and the psychology of perception.* New Haven, CT: Yale University Press.

REICH, P. A. (1986). *Language development.* Englewood Cliffs, NJ: Prentice-Hall.

REICHMAN, N. E., & PAGNINI, D. L. (1997). Maternal age and birth outcomes: Data from New Jersey. *Family Planning Perspectives, 29,* 268–272.

REIS, H. T., LIN, Y., BENNETT, M. E., & NEZLEK, J. B. (1993). Change in consistency in social participation during early adulthood. *Developmental Psychology, 29,* 633–645.

REIS, J., & SEIDLY, A. (1989). School administrators, parents, and sex education: A resolvable paradox? *Adolescence, 24,* 639–645.

REISSLAND, N. (1988). Neonatal imitation in the first hour of life: Observations in rural Nepal. *Developmental Psychology, 24,* 464–469.

REITZES, D. C., MUTRAN, E., & POPE, H. (1991). Location and well-being among retired men. *Journal of Gerontology, 46,* S195–S203.

REKER, G. T., PEACOCK, E. J., & WONG, P. T. P. (1987). Meaning and purpose in life and well-being: A life-span perspective. *Journal of Gerontology, 42,* 44–49.

REMEZ, L. (1991, July/August). Decision on Cesarean can often be influenced by nonclinical factors. *Family Planning Perspectives, 23,* 191–193.

REMEZ, L. (1992, January/February). Children who don't live with both parents face more behavior problems. *Family Planning Perspectives, 24,* 41–43.

REMEZ, L. (1992, May/June). Infant mortality on Oregon Indian reservation is almost three times higher than the overall U.S. rate. *Family Planning Perspectives, 24,* 138–139.

REMLEY, A. (1988). From obedience to independence. *Psychology Today, 22,* 56–59.

RENSHAW, P. D., & BROWN, P. J. (1993). Loneliness in middle childhood: Concurrent longitudinal predictors. *Child Development, 64,* 1271–1284.

REPETTI, R. L., & WOOD, J. (1997). Effects of daily stress at work on mothers' interaction with pre-schoolers. *Journal of Family Psychology, 11,* 90–108.

RESMAN, B. (1986). Can men "mother"? Life as a single father. *Family Relations, 35,* 95–102.

RESNICK, L. A., LEVINE, R., & BEHREND, A. (1991). *Perspectives on socially shared cognition.* Washington, DC: American Psychological Association.

REVICKI, D. A., & MITCHELL, J. P. (1990). Strain, social support, and mental health in rural elderly individuals. *Journal of Gerontology, 45,* S267–S274.

REYNOLDS, C. F., III, MON, T. H., HOCH, C. C., JENNINGS, J. R., BUYSEE, D. J., HOUCK, P. R., JARRETT, D. B., & KUPFER, D. J. (1991). Electroencephalographic sleep in the healthy "old old": A comparison with the "young old" in visually scored and automated measures. *Journal of Gerontology, 46,* M39–M46.

REZNICK, J. S., & GOLDFIELD, B. A. (1992). Rapid change in lexical development in comprehension and production. *Developmental Psychology, 28,* 406–413.

REZNICK, J. S., KAGAN, J., SNIDMAN, N., GERSTEN, M., BAAK, K., & ROSENBERG, A. (1986). Inhibited and uninhibited children: A follow-up study. *Child Development, 57,* 660–680.

RHODES, J. E., & FISCHER, K. (1993). Spanning the gender gap: Gender differences in delinquency among inner-city adolescents. *Adolescence, 112,* 879–889.

RICE, B. (1981). How not to pick up a woman. *Psychology Today, 23,* 15–17.

RICE, F. P. (1986). *Adult development and aging.* Boston, MA: Allyn & Bacon.

RICE, F. P. (1989b). *Human sexuality.* Dubuque, IA: Wm. C. Brown.

RICE, F. P. (1990). *The adolescent: Development, relationships, and culture* (6th ed.). Boston, MA: Allyn & Bacon.

RICE, F. P. (1996a). *The adolescent: Development, relationships, and culture* (8th ed.). Boston, MA: Allyn & Bacon.

RICE, F. P. (1996b). *Intimate relationships, marriages, and families* (3rd ed.). Mountain View, CA: Mayfield Publishing Co.

RICE, F. P. (1999). *Intimate relationships, marriages, and families* (4th ed.). Mountain View, CA: Mayfield Publishing Co.

RICE, G. E., & MEYER, B. J. F. (1986). Prose recall: Effects of aging, verbal ability, and reading behavior. *Journal of Gerontology, 41,* 469–480.

RICHMAN, A. L., MILLER, P. M., & LEVINE, R. A. (1992). Cultural and educational variations in maternal responsiveness. *Developmental Psychology, 28,* 614–621.

RICHMAN, C. L., CLARK, M. L., & BROWN, K. P. (1985). General and specific self-esteem in late adolescent students: Race and gender × SES effects. *Adolescence, 20,* 555–566.

RICKARD, H. C., SCOGIN, F., & KEITH, S. (1994). A one-year follow-up of relaxation training for elders with subjective anxiety. *The Gerontologist, 34,* 121–122.

RICKARDS, A. L., KITCHEN, W. H., DOYLE, L. W., FORD, G. W., KELLY, E. A., & CALLANAN, C. (1993). Cognition, school performance, and behavior in very low birth weight and normal weight children at eight years of age: A longitudinal study. *Developmental and Behavioral Pediatrics, 14,* 363–368.

RIEDEL, B. W., LICHSTEIN, K. L., & DWYER, W. O. (1995). Sleep compression and sleep education for older insomniacs: Self-help versus therapist guidance. *Psychology and Aging, 10,* 54–63.

RIEGE, W. H., & INHAM, V. (1991). *Age differences in nonverbal learning tasks.* Washington, DC: The Gerontological Society of America.

RIESE, M. L. (1990). Neonatal temperament in monozygotic and dizygotic twin pairs. *Child Development, 61,* 1230–1237.

RIND, P. (1992a). Peer support to keep teenagers alive and well. *Family Planning Perspectives, 24,* 36–37.

RIND, P. (1992b). Smoking in pregnancy nearly triples women's risk of placenta praevia. *Family Planning Perspectives, 24,* 47–48.

RIND, P. (January/February 1992c). Program Spotlight: Teens and toddlers' aims to reduce child abuse among adolescent parents. *Family Planning Perspectives, 24,* 37, 40.

RIPPE, J. M. (1989). CEO fitness: The performance plus. *Psychology Today, 23,* 50–53.

RISSENBERG, M., & GLANZER, M. (1986). Picture superiority in free recall: The effects of normal aging and primary degenerative dementia. *Journal of Gerontology, 41,* 64–71.

RITTER, J. M., CASEY, R. J., & LONGLOIS, J. H. (1991). Adults' responses to infants varying in appearance of age and attractiveness. *Child Development, 62,* 68–82.

RITVO, E. R., FREEMAN, B. J., MASON-BROTHERS, A., MO, A., & RITVO, A. M. (1985). Concordance for the syndrome of autism in 40 pairs of afflicted twins. *American Journal of Psychiatry, 142,* 74–77.

RIZZO, T. A., METZGER, B. E., DOOLEY, S. L., & CHO, N. H. (1997). Early malnutrition and child neurobehavioral development: Insights from the study of children of diabetic mothers. *Child Development, 68,* 26–38.

ROBERTO, K. A. (1992). Coping strategies of older women with hip fractures: Resources and outcomes. *The Journals of Gerontology, 47,* P21–P26.

ROBERTO, K. A., & SCOTT, J. P. (1986). Equity considerations in the friendships of older adults. *Journal of Gerontology, 41,* 241–247.

ROBERTS, A. R. (Summer, 1982). Adolescent runaways in suburbia: A new typology. *Adolescence, 17,* 379–396.

ROBERTS, L. R., SARIGIANI, P. A., PETERSEN, A. C., & NEWMAN, J. L. (1990). Gender differences in the relationship between achievement and self-image during early adolescence. *Journal of Early Adolescence, 10,* 159–175.

ROBERTS, M. (1988a, May). Heartfelt panic. *Psychology Today, 22,* 13.

ROBERTS, M. (1988b). Comeback from bypass. *Psychology Today, 22,* 18–20.

ROBERTS, M. (1988c). School yard menace. *Psychology Today, 22,* 52–56.

ROBERTS, M. (1989). Minding your health. Mind over cholesterol. *Psychology Today, 23,* 21–33.

ROBERTS, M., & HARRIS, T. G. (1989). Wellness at work. *Psychology Today, 23,* 54–58.

ROBERTSON, E. B., SKINNER, M. L., LOVE, M. M., ELDER, G. H., CONGER, R. D., DUBAS, J. S., & PETERSEN, A. C. (1992). The pubertal development scale: A rural and suburban comparison. *Journal of Early Adolescence, 12,* 174–186.

ROBINSON, B. E. (1984). The contemporary American stepfather. *Family Relatioins, 33,* 381–388.

ROBINSON, J. L., REZNICK, J. S., KAGAN, J., & CORLEY, R. (1992). The heritability of inhibited and uninhibited behavior: A twin study. *Developmental Psychology, 28,* 1030–1037.

ROBINSON, J. P., & MILKIE, M. A. (1998). Back to the basics: Trends in and role determinants of women's attitudes towards housework. *Journal of Marriage and the Family, 60,* 205–215.

ROBINSON, S. I. (1983, January). Nader versus ETS: Who should we believe? *Personnel and Guidance Journal, 61,* 260–262.

ROCHE, J. P., & RAMSBEY, T. W. (1993). Premarital sexuality: A five-year follow-up study of attitudes and behavior by dating stage. *Adolescence, 28,* 67–80.

RODGERS, J. (1988). Pains of complaint. *Psychology Today, 22,* 26, 27.

RODIN, J., & MCAVAY, G. (1992). Determinants of change in perceived health in a longitudinal study of older adults. *The Journals of Gerontology, 47,* P373–P384.

RODRIGUEZ-TOME, H., BARIAUD, F., ZARDI, M. F. C., DELMAS, C., JEAN-VOINE, B., & SZYLAGYI, P. (1993). The effects of pubertal changes on body image in relations with peers of the opposite sex in adolescence. *Journal of Adolescence, 16,* 421–438.

ROE V. WADE, 410 U.S. 113 (1973).

ROGERS, C. R. (1951). *Client-centered therapy: Its current practice, implications, and theory.* Boston, MA: Houghton Mifflin.

ROGERS, C. R. (1961). *On becoming a person.* Boston, MA: Houghton Mifflin.

ROGERS, C. R. (1980). *A way of being.* Boston, MA: Houghton Mifflin.

ROGERS, J. R. (1992). Suicide and alcohol: Conceptualizing the relationship from a cognitive-social paradigm. *Journal of Counseling and Development, 70,* 540–543.

ROGERS, M. F. (1985). AIDS in children: A review of the clinical, epidemiological and public health aspects. *Pediatric Infectious Disease, 4,* 230–236.

ROGERS, M. W., KUKULKA, C. G., & SODERBERG, G. L. (1992). Age-related changes in postural responses preceding rapid self-paced and reaction-time arm movements. *The Journals of Gerontology, 47,* M159–M165.

ROGERS, S. J., & WHITE, L. K. (1998). Satisfaction with parenting: The role of marital happiness, family structure, and parents' gender. *Journal of Marriage and the Family, 60,* 293–308.

ROGERS, W. A., & GILBERT, D. K. (1997). Do performance strategists mediate age-related differences in associative learning? *Psychology and Aging, 12,* 620–633.

ROGOSCH, F. A., & NEWCOMB, A. F. (1989). Children's perceptions of peer reputation and their social reputations among peers. *Child Development, 60,* 597–610.

ROGOW, A. M., MARCIA, J. E., & SLUGOSKI, B. R. (1983, October). The relative importance of identity status interview components. *Journal of Youth and Adolescence, 12,* 387–400.

ROHNER, R. P., KEAN, K. J., & CORNOYER, D. E. (1991). Effects of corporal punishment, perceived caretaker warmth, and cultural beliefs on the psychological adjustment of children in St. Kitts, West Indies. *Journal of Marriage and the Family, 53,* 681–693.

ROMAINE, S. (1984). *The language of children and adolescents. The acquisition of communication competence.* Oxford: Blackwell.

ROMEO, F. F. (1984, Fall). Adolescence, sexual conflict, and anorexia nervosa. *Adolescence, 19,* 551–555.

ROOPNARINE, J. L. (1984). Sex-typed socialization in mixed age preschool classrooms. *Child Development, 55,* 1078–1084.

ROOPNARINE, J. L. (1986, January). Mothers' and fathers' behavior toward the toy play of their infant sons and daughters. *Sex Roles: A Journal of Research, 14,* 59.

ROOSA, M. W., TEIN, J., CROPPENBACHER, N., MICHAELS, M., & DUMEA, L. (1993). Mothers' parenting behavior and child mental health in families with a problem drinking parent. *Journal of Marriage and the Family, 55,* 107–118.

ROSCOE, B., DIANA, M. S., & BROOKS, R. H., II. (1987). Early, middle, and later adolescents' views on dating and factors influencing partner selection. *Adolescence, 87,* 511–516.

ROSCOE, B., KENNEDY, D., & POPE, H. (1987). Distinguishing intimacy from nonintimate relationships. *Adolescence, 87,* 511–516.

ROSCOE, B., & KRUGER, T. L. (1990). AIDS: Late adolescents' knowledge and its influence on sexual behavior. *Adolescence, 25,* 39–48.

ROSE, S. A. (1994). Relation between physical growth and information processing in infants born in India. *Child Development, 65,* 889–902.

ROSE, S. A., & FELDMAN, J. F. (1996). Memory and processing speed in preterm children at 11 years: A comparison with full-terms. *Child Development, 67,* 2005–2021.

ROSE, S. A., & FELDMAN, J. S. (1995). Prediction of IQ and specific cognitive abilities at 11 years of infancy measures. *Developmental Psychology, 31,* 685–696.

ROSE, S. A., FELDMAN, J. F., & WALLACE, I. F. (1992). Infant information processing in relation to six-year cognitive outcomes. *Child Development, 63,* 1126–1141.

ROSE, S. A., & ORLIAN, E. K. (1991). Asymmetries in infant cross-modal transfer. *Child Development, 62,* 706–718.

ROSEN, A. B., & ROZIN, P. (1993). Now you see it, now you don't: The preschool child's conception of invisible particles in the context of dissolving. *Child Development, 29,* 300–311.

ROSEN, K. S., & ROTHBAUM, F. (1993). Quality of parental caregiving and security of attachment. *Developmental Psychology, 29,* 358–367.

ROSENBLATT, P., & ELDE, C. (1990). Shared reminiscence about a deceased parent: Implications for grief education and grief counseling. *Family Relations, 39,* 206–210.

ROSENFELD, A., & STARK, E. (1987). The prime of our lives. *Psychology Today, 21,* 62–70.

ROSENGREN, K. S., GELMAN, S. A., KALISH, C. W., & MCCORMICK, M. (1991). As time goes by: Children's early understanding of growth in animals. *Child Development, 62,* 1302–1320.

ROSENGREN, K. S., & HICKLING, A. K. (1994). Seeing is believing: Children's explanations of commonplace, magical, and extraordinary transformations. *Child Development, 65,* 1605–1626.

ROSENGREN, K. S., MCAULEY, E., & MIHALKO, S. L. (1998). Gait adjustments in older adults: Activity and efficacy influences. *Psychology and Aging, 13,* 375–386.

ROSENSTEIN, D., & OSTER, H. (1988). Differential facial responses to four basic tastes in newborns. *Child Development, 59,* 1555–1568.

ROSENTHAL, D., & HANSEN, J. (1980, October). Comparison of adolescents: Perception and behavior in single- and two-parent families. *Journal of Youth and Adolescence, 9,* 407–414.

ROSENTHAL, D. A., & FELDMAN, S. S. (1991). The influence of perceived family and personal factors on self-reported school performance of Chinese and Western high school students. *Journal of Research on Adolescence, 1,* 135–154.

ROSOFF, J. I. (1989, July/August). The Webster decision: A giant step backwards. *Family Planning Perspectives, 21,* 148–149.

ROSS, C. E. (1991). Marriage and the sense of control. *Journal of Marriage and the Family, 53,* 831–838.

ROSS, C. E. (1995). Reconceptualizing marital status as a continuum of social attachment. *Journal of Marriage and the Family, 57,* 129–140.

ROSS, G., LIPPER, E. G., & AULD, P. A. M. (1991). Educational status and school-related abilities of very low birth weight premature children. *Pediatrics, 88,* 339–346.

ROSS, G., TESMAN, J., AULD, P. A. M., & NASS, R. (1992). Effects of subependymal and mild intraventricular lesions on visual attention and memory in premature infants. *Developmental Psychology, 28,* 1067–1074.

ROSS, H. S., & LOLLIS, S. P. (1989). A social relations analysis of toddler peer relationships. *Child Development, 60,* 1082–1091.

ROSSIE, A. S. (1968). Transition to parenthood. *Journal of Marriage and the Family, 30,* 26–39.

ROTHBART, M. K. (1988). Temperament and the development of inhibited approach. *Child Development, 59,* 1249–1250.

ROTHENBERG, R., LENTZENER, H. R., & PARKER, R. A. (1991). Population aging patterns: The expansion of mortality. *Journal of Gerontology, 46,* S66–S70.

ROTHERAM, M. J., & ARMSTRONG, M. (1980, Summer). Assertiveness training with high school students. *Adolescence, 15,* 267–276.

ROTHERAM-BORUS, M. J. (1990a). Ethnic differences in adolescents' identity status and associated behavior problems. *Journal of Adolescence, 13,* 361–374.

ROTHERAM-BORUS, M. J. (1990b). Patterns of social expectations among black and Mexican-American children. *Child Development, 61,* 542–556.

ROTHERAM-BORUS, M. J., LIGHTFOOT, M., MORAES, A., DOPKINS, S., & LACOUR, J. (1998). Developmental ethnic and gender differences in ethnic identity among adolescents. *Journal of Adolescent Research, 13,* 487–507.

ROUSSEAU, J. J. (1955). *Emile.* New York: Dutton. (Original work published 1762.)

ROVEE-COLLIER, C. K. (1987a). Learning and memory in infancy. In J. D. Osofsky (Ed.), *Handbook of infant development* (2nd ed.). New York: Wiley.

ROVEE-COLLIER, C. K. (1987b). Learning and memory in children. In J. D. Osofsky (Ed.), *Handbook of infant development* (2nd ed.). New York: Wiley.

ROVEE-COLLIER, C., SCHECTER, A., SHYI, G. C. W., & SHIELDS, P. (1992). Perceptual identification of contextual attributes and infant memory retrieval. *Developmental Psychology, 28,* 307–318.

RUBENSTEIN, J. L., & FELDMAN, S. S. (1993). Conflict-resolution behavior in adolescent boys: Antecedent and adaptational correlates. *Journal of Research on Adolescence, 3,* 41–66.

RUBIN, D. H., CRASKILNIKOFF, P. A., LEVENTHAL, J. M., WEILE, B., & BERGET, A. (1986, August 23). Effect of passive smoking on birth weight. *Lancet,* pp. 415–417.

RUBIN, J. (1988, October). Stress: From heart to heart. *Psychology Today, 22,* 14.

RUBIN, K. E., LYNCH, D., COPLAN, R., ROSE-KRASNOR, L., & BOOTH, C. L. (1994). "Birds of a feather . . .": Behavioral concordances and preferential personal attraction in children. *Child Development, 65,* 1778–1785.

RUBLE, D. N., & FLETT, G. L. (1988). Conflicting goals in self-evaluative information seeking: Developmental and ability level analysis. *Child Development, 59,* 97–106.

RUETER, M. A., & CONGER, R. D. (1995). Antecedents of parent-adolescent disagreements. *Journal of Marriage and the Family, 57,* 435–448.

RUFF, H. A., LAWSON, K. R., PARRINELLO, R., & WEISSBERG, R. (1990). Long-term stability of individual differences in sustained attention in the early years. *Child Development, 61,* 60–75.

RUFF, H. A., SALTARELLI, L. M., CAPOZZOLI, M., & DUBINER, K. (1992). The differentiation of activity in infants' exploration of objects. *Developmental Psychology, 28,* 851–861.

RUSSELL, B., & RUSSELL, A. (1987). Mother-child and father-child relationships in middle childhood. *Child Development, 58,* 1573–1585.

RUSSELL, J., HALASZ, G., & BEAUMONT, P. J. V. (1990). Death related themes in anorexia nervosa: A practical exploration. *Journal of Adolescence, 13,* 311–326.

RUSSELL, J. A. (1990). The preschooler's understanding of the causes and consequences of emotion. *Child Development, 61,* 1872–1881.

RUSSELL, M. J., et al. (1993). Life-span changes in the verbal categorization of olders. *The Journals of Gerontology, 48,* P49–P53.

RUST, J. O., & MCCRAW, A. (1984, Summer). Influence of masculinity-femininity on adolescent self-esteem and peer acceptance. *Adolescence, 19,* 357–366.

RUTTER, M. (1983). School effects on pupil progress: Research findings and policy implications. *Child Development, 54,* 1–29.

RUTTER, M., & SCHOPHER, E. (1987). Autism and persuasive developmental disorders: Concepts and diagnostic issues. *Journal of Autism and Developmental Disorders, 17,* 159–186.

RYAN, A. S., CRAIG, L. D., & FINN, S. C. (1992). Nutrient intakes and dietary patterns of Americans: A national study. *The Journals of Gerontology, 47,* M145–M150.

RYAN, E. D. (1992). Beliefs about memory changes across the adult life span. *The Journals of Gerontology, 47,* P41–P46.

RYFF, C. D., LEE, Y. H., ESSEX, M. J., & SCHMUTTE, P. S. (1994). My children and me: Midlife evaluations of grown children and of self. *Psychology and Aging, 9,* 195–205.

SABATELLI, R. M., & ANDERSON, S. A. (1991). Family system dynamics, peer relationships, and adolescents' psychological adjustment. *Family Relations, 40,* 363–369.

SADKER, M., & SADKER, M. (1985, March). Sexism in the schoolroom of the 80s. *Psychology Today, 19,* 54–57.

SALK, L. (1974). *Preparing for parenthood.* New York: David McKay Co.

SALTHOUSE, K. A., HAMBRICK, B. D., & MCGUTHRY, K. E. (1998). Shared age-related influences on cognitive and noncognitive variables (1998). *Psychology and Aging, 13,* 486–500.

SALTHOUSE, T. A. (1992a). What do adult age differences in the digit symbol substitution test reflect? *The Journals of Gerontology, 47,* P121–P128.

SALTHOUSE, T. A. (1992b). Why do adult age differences increase with task complexity? *Developmental Psychology, 28,* 905–918.

SALTS, C. J., SEISMORE, M. D., LINDHOLM, B. W., & SMITH, T. A. (1994). Attitudes toward marriage and premarital sexual activity of college freshmen. *Adolescence, 29,* 775–779.

SALZINGER, S., FELDMAN, R. S., & HAMMER, M. (1993). The effects of physical abuse on children's social relationships. *Child Development, 64,* 169–187.

SAMEROFF, A. J., SEIFER, R., BALDWIN, A., & BALDWIN, C. (1993). Stability of intelligence from preschool to adolescence: The influence of social and family risk factors. *Child Development, 64,* 80–97.

SAMPSON, R. J., & LAUB, J. H. (1994). Urban poverty and the family context of delinquency: A new look at structure and process in a classic study. *Child Development, 55,* 523–540.

SANDLER, D. P., EVERSON, R. B., WILCOX, A. J., & BROWDER, J. P. (1985). Cancer risk in adulthood from early life exposure to parents' smoking. *American Journal of Public Health, 75,* 487–492.

SANDLER, I. N., TEIN, J., & WEST, S. G. (1994). Coping, stress, and the psychological symptoms of children of divorce: A cross-sectional and longitudinal study. *Child Development, 65,* 1744–1763.

SANDS, L. P., & MERIDITH, W. (1989). Effects of sensory and motor functioning on adult intellectual performance. *Journal of Gerontology, 44,* P56–P58.

SANDS, L. P., & MEREDITH, W. (1992). Blood pressure in intellectual functioning in late mid-life. *The Journals of Gerontology, 47,* P81–P84.

SANIK, M. M., & MAULDIN, T. (1986). Single- versus two-parent families: A comparison of mothers' time. *Family Relations, 35,* 53–56.

SANIK, M. M., & STAFFORD, D. (1985). Adolescents' contributions to household production: Male and female differences. *Adolescence, 20,* 207–215.

SANTEE, B., & HENSHAW, S. K. (July/August 1992). The abortion debate: Measuring gestational age. *Family Planning Perspectives, 24,* 172–173.

SANTILLI, M. R., & HUDSON, L. N. (1992). Enhancing moral growth: Is communication the key? *Adolescence, 27,* 145–160.

SANTROCK, J. W. (1970a). Paternal absence, sex-typing, and identification. *Developmental Psychology, 6,* 264–272.

SANTROCK, J. W. (1970b). Influence of onset and type of paternal absence on the first four Eriksonian developmental crises. *Developmental Psychology, 6,* 273–274.

SARASON, I. G. (1981). *The revised life experiences survey.* Unpublished manuscript, University of Washington, Seattle.

SARGENT, R. G., SCHULKEN, E. D., KEMPER, K. A., & HUSSEY, J. A. (1994). Black and white adolescent females' pre-pregnancy nutrition status. *Adolescence, 29,* 845–858.

SARIGIANI, P. A., WILSON, J. L., PETERSEN, A. C., & VIOCAY, J. R. (1990). Self-image and educational plans of adolescents from two contrasting communities. *Journal of Early Adolescence, 10,* 37–55.

SAUDINO, K. J., & EATON, W. O. (1991). Infant temperament and genetics: An objective twin study of motor activity level. *Child Development, 62,* 1167–1174.

SAUER, L. E., & FINE, M. A. (1988). Parent-child relationships in stepparent families. *Journal of Family Psychology, 1,* 434–451.

SAUL, L. J. (1983). How to cope with adultery. *Medical Aspects of Human Sexuality, 17,* 90–106.

SAUNDERS, J. M., & EDWARDS, J. N. (1984). Extramarital sexuality, a predictive model of permissive attitudes. *Journal of Marriage and the Family, 46,* 825–835.

SCAFIDI, F. A. (1986). Effects of tactile/kinesthetic stimulation on the clinical course and sleep/wake behavior of preterm neonates. *Infant Behavior and Development, 9,* 91–105.

SCAFIDI, F. A., FIEOD, T., PRODROMIDIS, M., & RAHDERT, E. (1997). Psychosocial stressors of drug-abusing disadvantaged adolescent mothers. *Adolescence, 32,* 93–100.

SCALES, P. (1990). Developing capable young people: An alternative strategy for prevention programs. *Journal of Early Adolescence, 10,* 420–438.

SCARANO, G. M., & KALODNER-MARTIN, C. R. (1994). A description of the continuum of eating disorders: Implications for intervention and research. *Journal of Counseling and Development, 72,* 357–361.

SCARR, S. (1984, May). What's a parent to do? *Psychology Today, 18,* 58–63.

SCARR, S. (1992). Developmental theories for the 1990's: Development and individual differences. *Child Development, 63,* 1–19.

SCARR, S., & WEINBERG, R. A. (1983). The Minnesota adoptions studies: Genetic differences and malleability. *Child Development, 54,* 260–267.

SCHACTER, D. L., KOUTSTAAL, W., JOHNSON, M. K., GROSS, M. S., & ANGELL, K. A. (1997). False recollection induced by photogaphs: A comparison of older and younger adults. *Psychology and Aging, 12,* 203–215.

SCHAEFER, D., & LYONS, C. (1986). *How do we tell the children?* New York: Newmarket Press.

SCHAEFER, E. S. (1959). A circumplex model for maternal behavior. *Journal of Abnormal and Social Psychology, 59,* 226–235.

SCHAEFFER, N. C. (1989). The frequency and intensity of parental conflict: Choosing response dimensions. *Journal of Marriage and the Family, 51,* 759–766.

SCHAFER, G., & PLUNKETT, K. (1998). Rapid word learning by 15-month-olds under tightly controlled conditions. *Child Development, 69,* 309–320.

SCHAFFER, H. R. (1984). *The child's entry into the social world.* Orlando, FL: Academic Press.

SCHAFFNER, L. (1998). Searching for connection: A new look at teenaged runaways. *Adolescence, 33,* 619–627.

SCHAIE, K. W. (1977–1978). Toward a stage theory of adult cognitive development. *Journal of Aging and Human Development, 8,* 129–138.

SCHAIE, K. W. (1978). External validity in the assessment of intellectual development in adulthood. *Journal of Gerontology, 33,* 695–701.

SCHAIE, K. W. (1994). The course of adult intellectual development. *American Psychologist, 49,* 1–9.

SCHAIE, K. W., & LABOUVIE-VIEF, G. (1974). Generational versus ontogenetic components of change in adult cognitive behavior: A fourteen-year cross-sectional study. *Developmental Psychology, 10,* 305–320.

SCHAIE, K. W., MAITLAND, S. B., WILLIS, S. L., & INTRIERI, R. C. (1998). Longitudinal invariance of adult psychometric ability factors structures across seven years. *Psychology and Aging, 13,* 8–20.

SCHALLENBERGER, M. E. (1894). A study of children's rights as seen by themselves. *Pedagogical Seminary, 3,* 87–96.

SCHMETZ, S., SAUDINO, K. J., PLOMIN, R., FULKER, D. W., & DeFRIES, J. C. (1996). Genetic and environmental influences on temperament in middle childhood. Analyses of teacher and tester ratings. *Child Development, 67,* 409–422.

SCHMIDT, J. A., & DAVISON, M. L. (1983, May). Helping students think. *Personnel and Guidance Journal, 61,* 563–569.

SCHMITT, N., GOGATE, J., ROTHERT, M., ROVENER, D., HOLMES, M., TALARCYZK, G., GIVEN, B., & KROLL, J. (1991). Capturing and clustering women's judgment policies: The case of hormonal therapy for menopause. *Journal of Gerontology, 46,* P92–P101.

SCHNEIDER, W., & BJORKLUND, D. F. (1992). Expertise, aptitude, and strategic remembering. *Child Development, 63,* 461–473.

SCHNEIDER-ROSEN, K., & WENZ-GROSS, M. (1990). Patterns of compliance from eighteen to thirty months of age. *Child Development, 61,* 104–112.

SCHONFIELD, D. (1965). Memory changes with age. *Nature* (London), *28,* 918.

SCHRECK, L. (1998). After early amniocentesis, chances of fetal loss and foot deformity rise. *Family Planning Perspectives, 30,* 249–250.

SCHUCKIT, M. A. (1985). Genetics and the risk for alcoholism. *JAMA, Journal of the American Medical Association, 254,* 2614–2617.

SCHUCKIT, M. A. (1987). Biological vulnerability to alcoholism. *Journal of Consulting and Clinical Psychology, 55,* 301–309.

SCHUCKMAN, T. (1975). *Aging is not for sissies.* Philadelphia, PA: Westminster Press.

SCHULMAN, S. (1986). Facing the invisible handicap. *Psychology Today, 20,* 58–64.

SCHULTHEISS, D. P., & BLUSTEIN, D. L. (1994). Contributions of family relationship factors to the identity formation process. *Journal of Counseling and Development, 73,* 159–166.

SCHULTZ, N. C., SCHULTZ, C. L., & OLSON, D. H. (1991). Couple strengths and stressors in complex and simple stepfamilies in Australia. *Journal of Marriage and the Family, 53,* 555–564.

SCHULTZ, N. R., ELIAS, M. F., ROBBINS, M. A., STREETEN, D. H. P., & BLAKEMAN, N. (1986). A longitudinal comparison of hypertensives and normotensives on the Wechsler Adult Intelligence Scale: Initial findings. *Journal of Gerontology, 41,* 169–175.

SCHULZ, R., MUSA, B., STASCEWSKI, J., & SIEGLER, R. S. (1994). The relationship between age and major league baseball performance: Implications for development. *Psychology and Aging, 9,* 274–286.

SCHUMM, W. R., & BUGAIGHIS, M. A. (1986). Marital quality over the marital career: Alternative explanations. *Journal of Marriage and the Family, 48,* 165–168.

SCHUNK, D. H. (1984). Self-efficacy perspective on achievement behavior. *Educational Psychologist, 19,* 48–58.

SCHWARTZ, D., DODGE, K. A., & COIE, J. D. (1993). The emergence of chronic peer victimization in boys' play groups. *Child Development, 64,* 1755–1772.

SCHWARTZ, J. B., GIBB, W. J., & TRAN, T. (1991). Aging effects on heart rate variation. *Journal of Gerontology, 46,* M99–M106.

SCHWARTZ, J. C. (1979). Childhood origins of psychopathology. *American Psychologist, 34,* 879–885.

SCHWARTZ, J. I. (1981). Children's experiments with language. *Young Children, 36,* 16–26.

SCHWARTZ, L. L. (1987). Joint custody: Is it all right for all children? *Journal of Family Psychology, 1,* 120–134.

SCHWARTZ, M. A. (1976). *Career strategies of the never-married.* Paper presented at the 71st annual meeting of the American Sociological Association, New York.

SCHWARTZ, R. S., SHUMAN, W. P., BRADBURY, V. L., CAIN, K. C., FELLINGHAM, G. W., BEARD, J. C., KAHN, S. E., STRATTON, J. R., CERQUEIRA, M. D., & ABRASS, I. B. (1990). Body fat distribution in healthy young and older men. *Journal of Gerontology, 45,* M181–M185.

SCHWEINHART, L. J., & WEIKART, D. P. (1985). Evidence that good early childhood programs work. *Phi Delta Kappan, 66,* 545–551.

SCHWEITZER, R. D., SETH-SMITH, M., & CALLAN, V. (1992). The relationship between self-esteem and psychological adjustment in young adolescents. *Journal of Adolescence, 15,* 83–97.

SCOGIN, F., et al. (1992). Progressive and imaginal relaxation training for elderly persons with subjective anxiety. *Psychology and Aging, 7,* 419–424.

SEARLEMAN, A., PORAC, C., & CORAN, S. (1989). Relationship between birth order, birth stress, and lateral preferences: A critical review. *Psychological Bulletin, 105,* 397–408.

SEARS, H. A., & GALAMBOS, N. L. (1992). Women's work conditions and marital adjustment in two-earner couples: A structural model. *Journal of Marriage and the Family, 54,* 789–997.

SEBALD, H. (1984). *Adolescence: A social psychological analysis* (3rd ed.). Englewood Cliffs, NJ: Prentice-Hall.

SEEMAN, T. E., BERKMAN, L. F., CHARPENTIER, P. A., BLAZER, D. G., ALBERT, M. S., & TINETTI, M. E. (1995). Behavioral and psychosocial predictors of physical performance: MacArthur studies of successful aging. *Journal of Gerontology, 50A,* M177–M183.

SEGEST, E., MYGIND, O., JERGENSEN, W., BECHGAARD, M., & FALLOV, J. (1990). Free condoms in youth clubs in Copenhagen. *Journal of Adolescence, 13,* 17–24.

SEGINER, R. (1992). Sibling relationships in early adolescence: A study of Israeli-Arab sisters. *Journal of Early Adolescence, 12,* 96–110.

SEIDMAN, E., ALLEN, L., ABER, J. L., MITCHELL, C., & FEINMAN, J. (1994). The impact of school transitions in early adolescence on the self-system and perceived as social context of poor, urban youth. *Child Development, 65,* 507–522.

SEITZ, V., & APFEL, N. H. (1994). Parent-focused intervention: Diffusion effects on siblings. *Child Development, 65,* 677–683.

SEKULER, R., & BLAKE, R. (1987). Sensory underload. *Psychology Today, 21,* 48–51.

SELMAN, R. L. (1977). A structural-developmental model of social cognition: Implications for intervention research. *Counseling Psychologists, 6,* 3–6.

SELMAN, R. L. (1980). *The growth of interpersonal understanding: Development and clinical analysis.* New York: Academic Press.

SELTZER, J. A. (1990). Relationships between fathers and children who live apart: The father's role after separation. *Journal of Marriage and the Family, 53,* 79–101.

SEMMENS, J. P., & TSAI, C. C. (1984). Some gynecological causes of sexual problems. *Medical Aspects of Human Sexuality, 18,* 174–181.

SESSA, F. M., & STEINBERG, L. (1991). Family structure and the development of autonomy during adolescence. *Journal of Early Adolescence, 11,* 38–55.

SEYDLITZ, R. (1991). The effects of age and gender on parental control and delinquency. *Youth and Society, 23,* 175–201.

SEYDLITZ, R. (1993). Complexity in the relationships among direct and indirect parental controls and delinquency, *Youth and Society, 24,* 243–275.

SHAFI, M. (1988). Suicidal children. *Medical Aspects of Human Sexuality, 22,* 63.

SHANAN, J. (1991). Who and how: Some unanswered questions in adult development. *Journal of Gerontology, 46,* P309–P316.

SHANTZ, C. U. (1987). Conflicts between children. *Child Development, 58,* 283–305.

SHAPIRA, J., & CUMMINGS, J. L. (1989). Alzheimer's disease: Changes in sexual behavior. *Medical Aspects of Human Sexuality, 23,* 32–36.

SHARKIN, B. S. (1993). Age and gender: Theory, research, and implications. *Journal of Counseling and Development, 71,* 386–389.

SHARLIN, S. A., & MOR-BARAK, M. (1992). Runaway girls in distress: Motivation, background, and personality. *Adolescence, 27,* 387–405.

SHARMA, A. R., McGUE, M. K., & BENSON, P. L. (1998). The psychological adjustment of United States adopted adolescents and their nonadopted siblings. *Child Development, 69,* 791–802.

SHARPE, P. A., & CONNELL, C. M. (1992). Exercise beliefs and behaviors among older employees: A health promotion trial. *The Gerontologist, 32,* 444–449.

SHARPS, M. J., & GOLLIN, E. S. (1988). Aging and free recall for objects located in space. *Journal of Gerontology, 43,* P8–P11.

SHAUGHNESSY, M. F., & SHAKESBY, P. (1992). Adolescent sexual and emotional intimacy. *Adolescence, 27,* 475–480.

SHAY, K. A., & ROTH, D. L. (1992). Association between aerobic fitness and visuospatial performance in healthy older adults. *Psychology and Aging, 7,* 15–24.

SHEA, J. A., & ADAMS, G. R. (1984). Correlates of romantic attachment: A path analysis study. *Journal of Youth and Adolescence, 13,* 27–44.

SHEINGOLD, D. K., & TENNEY, Y. J. (1982). Memory for a salient childhood event. In U. Neisser (Ed.), *Memory observed.* San Francisco, CA: Freeman.

SHEK, D. T. L. (1998). Linkage between marital quality and parent-child relationship. *Journal of Family Issues, 19,* 687–704.

SHELL, R. M., & EISENBERG, M. (1996). Children's reactions to the receipt of direct and indirect help. *Child Development, 67,* 1391–1405.

SHELTON, B. A. (1990). The distribution of household tasks. *Journal of Family Issues, 11,* 115–135.

SHELTON, B. A., & JOHN, D. (1993). Does marital status make a difference? Housework among married and cohabiting men and women. *Journal of Family Issues, 14,* 401–420.

SHELTON, C. M., & McADAMS, D. P. (1990). In search of everyday morality: The development of a measure. *Adolescence, 25,* 923–944.

SHEPPARD, B. J. (1974). Making the case for behavior as an expression of physiological condition. In B. L. Kratonile (Ed.), *Youth in trouble.* San Rafael, CA: Academic Therapy Publications.

SHESTOWSKY, B. J. (1983, Fall). Ego identity development and obesity in adolescent girls. *Adolescence, 18,* 551–559.

SHIELDS, P. J., & ROVEE-COLLIER, C. (1992). Long-term memory for context-specific category information at six months. *Child Development, 63,* 245–259.

SHILTS, L. (1991). The relationship of early adolescent substance use to extracurricular activities, peer influence, and personal attitudes. *Adolescence, 26,* 613–617.

SHINN, M. W. (1900). *The biography of a baby.* Boston, MA: Houghton Mifflin.

SHIP, J. A., & WEIFFENBACH, J. M. (1993). Age, gender, medical treatment, and medication effects on smell identification. *The Journals of Gerontology, 48,* M26–M32.

SHMOTKIN, D. (1991). The role of time orientation in life satisfaction across the life span. *The Journals of Gerontology, 46,* P243–P250.

SHMOTKIN, D. (1992). The apprehensive respondent: Failing to rate future life satisfaction in older adults. *Psychology and Aging, 7,* 484–486.

SHOCK, N. W. (1977). Systems integration. In C. E. Finch and L. Hayflick (Eds.) *Handbook of the biology of aging,* p. 644. New York: Van Nostrand Reinhold Co.

SHREVE, B. W., & KUNKEL, M. A. (1991). Self-psychology, shame, and adolescent suicide: Theoretical and practical considerations. *Journal of Couseling and Development, 69,* 305–311.

SIEGEL, A., & WHITE, S. H. (1982). The child study movement: Early growth and development of the symbolized child. In H. W. Reese (Ed.), *Advances in child development and behavior* (Vol. 17). New York: Academic Press.

SIEGLER, R. S. (1989). Mechanisms of cognitive development. *Annual Review of Psychology, 40,* 353–379.

SIEGLER, R. S. (1992). The other Alfred Binet. *Developmental Psychology, 28,* 179–190.

SIGNORIELLI, N. (1991). Adolescents and ambivalence towards marriage: A cultivation analysis. *Youth and Society, 23,* 121–149.

SILVERMAN, W. K., LaGRECA, A. M., & WASSERSTEIN, S. (1995). What do children worry about? Worries and their relation to anxiety. *Child Development, 66,* 671–686.

SIM, H., & BUCHINICH, S. (1996). The declining effects of family stressors and antisocial behavior from childhood to adolescence and early adulthood. *Journal of Family Issues, 17,* 408–427.

SIMCOCK, B. (1985). Sons and daughters—a sex preselection study. *Medical Journal of Australia, 142,* 541–542.

SIMON, C. (1988). One is too much. *Psychology Today, 22,* 10.

SIMON, C. (1989). The triumphant dieter. *Psychology Today, 23,* 48–52.

SIMON, L. (1988). Freud, in his time and ours. *Psychology Today, 22,* 68, 69.

SIMON, S. L., WALSH, D. A., REGNIER, D. A., & KRAUSS, I. K. (1992). Spatial cognition and neighborhood use: The relationship in older adults. *Psychology and Aging, 7,* 389–394.

SIMONEAU et al. (1992). The effects of visual factors and head orientation on postural steadiness on women 55 to 70 years of age. *The Journals of Gerontology, 47,* M151–M158.

SIMONEAU, G. G., CAVANAGH, P. R., ULBRECHT, J. S., LEIBOWITZ, H. W., & TYRELL, R. A. (1991). Influence of visual factors on fall-related kinematic variables during stair descent by older women. *The Journals of Gerontology, 46,* M188–M195.

SIMONS, R. L., BEAMAN, J., CONGER, R. D., & CHAO, W. (1992). Gender differences in the intergenerational transmission of parenting beliefs. *Journal of Marriage and the Family, 54,* 823–836.

SIMONS, R. L., BEAMAN, J., CONGER, R. D., & CHAO, W. (1993). Childhood experience, conceptions of parenting, and attitudes of spouse as determinants of parental behavior. *Journal of Marriage and the Family, 55,* 91–106.

SIMONS, R. L., et al. (1993). Social network and marital support as mediators and moderators of the impact of stress and depression on parental behavior. *Developmental Psychology, 29,* 368–381.

SIMONS, R. L., & WHITBECK, L. B. (1991). Sexual abuse as a precursor to prostitution and victimization among adolescent and adult homeless women. *Journal of Family Issues, 12,* 361–379.

SIMPSON, J. A., RHOLES, W. S., & NELLIGAN, J. S. (1992). Support seeking and support giving within couples in an anxiety-provoking situation: The role of attachment styles. *Journal of Personality and Social Psychology, 62,* 434–446.

SIMPSON, W. S., & RAMBERG, J. A. (1992). Sexual dysfunction in married female patients with anorexia and bulimia nervosa. *Journal of Sex and Marital Therapy, 18,* 44–54.

SINGER, J. L., & SINGER, D. G. (1983). Implications of childhood television viewing for cognition, imagination, and emotion. In J. Bryant & Dr. R. Anderson (Eds.), *Children's understanding of television: Research on attention and comprehension* (pp. 265–297). New York: Academic Press.

SINGER, J. M., & FAGAN, J. W. (1992). Negative affect, emotional expression, and forgetting in young infants. *Developmental Psychology, 28,* 48–57.

SINGER, L. T., DAVILLIER, M., BRUENING, P., HAWKINS, S., & YAMASHITA, T. S. (1996). Social support, psychological distress, and parenting strains in mothers of very low birth weight infants. *Family Relations, 45,* 343–350.

SINNETT, E. R., GOODYEAR, R. K., & HANNEMAN, V. (1989). Voluntary euthanasia and the right to die: A dialogue with Derek Humphry. *Journal of Counseling and Development, 67,* 568–572.

SISTLER, A. K., & GOTTFRIED, N. W. (1990). Shared child development knowledge between grandmother and mother. *Family Relations, 39,* 92–96.

SKANDHAN, K. P., PANDYA, A. K., SKANDHAN, S., & MEHTA, Y. B. (1988). Menarche: Prior knowledge and experience. *Adolescence, 89,* 149–154.

SKINNER, B. F. (1953). *Science and human behavior.* New York: Macmillan.

SKINNER, B. F. (1957). *Verbal behavior.* New York: Appleton-Century-Crofts.

SKINNER, B. F. (1983). *A matter of consequences. Part 3 of an autobiography.* New York: Alfred A. Knopf.

SKOE, E. E., & GOODEN, A. (1993). Ethic of care and real-life moral dilemma content in male and female early adolescents. *Journal of Early Adolescence, 13,* 154–167.

SLADE, A. (1987). A longitudinal study of maternal involvement and symbolic play during the toddler period. *Child Development, 58,* 367–375.

SLAUGHTER-DEFOE, D. T., NAKAGAWA, K., TAKANISHI, R., & JOHNSON, D. J. (1990). Toward cultural/ecological perspectives on schooling and achievement in African- and Asian-American children. *Child Development, 61,* 363–383.

SLAVIN, M. J., PHILLIPS, J. G., & BRADSHAW, J. L. (1996). Visual queues and handwriting of older adults: A kinematic analysis. *Psychology and Aging, 11,* 521–526.

SLAWINSKI, E. B., HARTEL, D. M., & KLINE, D. W. (1993). Self-reported hearing problems in daily life throughout adulthood. *Psychology and Aging, 8,* 552–561.

SLIWINSKI, M. (1997). Aging and counting speed: Evidence for process-specific slowing. *Psychology and Aging, 12,* 38–49.

SLOMKOWSKI, C. L., NELSON, K., DUNN, J., & PLOMIN, R. (1992). Temperament and language: Relations from toddlerhood to middle childhood. *Developmental Psychology, 28,* 1090–1095.

SLONIN-NEVO, B. (1992). First premarital intercourse among Mexican-American and Anglo-American adolescent women. Interpreting ethnic differences. *Journal of Adolescent Research, 7,* 332–351.

SLONIN-NEVO, V., OZAGA, M. N., & AUSLANDER, W. F. (1991). Knowledge, attitudes and behaviors related to AIDS among youths in residential centers: Results from an exploratory study. *Journal of Adolescence, 14,* 1–16.

SLOTTERBACK, C. S., & SAARNIO, D. A. (1996). Attitudes towards older adults reported by young adults: Variation based on attitudinal tasks and attribute categories. *Psychology and Aging, 11,* 563–571.

SMALL, S. A., & EASTMAN, G. (1991). Rearing adolescents in contemporary society: A conceptual framework for understanding the responsibilities and needs of parents. *Family Relations, 40,* 455–462.

SMART, L. S. (1992). Marital helping relationship following pregnancy loss and infant death. *Journal of Family Issues, 13,* 81–98.

SMETANA, J. G. (1995). Parenting styles and conceptions of parental authority during adolescence. *Child Development, 66,* 299–316.

SMETANA, J. G., & ASQUITH, P. (1994). Adolescents' and parents' conceptions of parental authority and personal autonomy. *Child Development, 65,* 1147–1162.

SMETANA, J. G., & BERENT, R. (1993). Adolescents' and mothers' evaluations of justifications for disputes. *Journal of Adolescent Research, 8,* 252–273.

SMETANA, J. G., BRAEGES, J. L., & YAU, J. (1991). Doing what you say and saying what you do: Reasoning about adolescent-parent conflict in interviews and interactions. *Journal of Adolescent Research, 6,* 276–295.

SMETANA, J. G., YAU, J., & HANSON, S. (1991). Conflict resolution in families with adolescents. *Journal of Research on Adolescence, 1,* 189–206.

SMIDT, L. J., CREMIN, F. M., GRIVETTI, L. E., & CLIFFORD, A. J. (1991). Influence of thiamin supplementation on the health and general well-being of an elderly Irish population with marginal thiamin deficiency. *Journal of Gerontology, 46,* M16–M22.

SMILEY, T. A., & DWECK, C. S. (1994). Individual differences in achievement goals among young children. *Child Development, 65,* 1723–1743.

SMILGIS, M. (1987, February 16). The big chill: Fear of AIDS. *Time,* pp. 58–59.

SMITH, B. A., STEVENS, K., TORGERSON, W. S., & KIM, J. H. (1992). Diminished reactivity of postmature human infants to sucrose compared with term infants. *Developmental Psychology, 28,* 811–820.

SMITH, E. (1988, May). Fighting cancerous feelings. *Psychology Today, 22,* 22–23.

SMITH, E. J. (1991). Ethnic identity development: Toward the development of a theory within the context of majority/minority status. *Journal of Counseling and Development, 770,* 181–188.

SMITH, H. L., & MORGAN, S. P. (1994). Children's closeness to father as reported by mothers, sons, and daughters: Evaluated subjected assessments with the Rasch model. *Journal of Family Issues, 15,* 3–29.

SMITH, J. E., HILLARD, M. C., & ROLL, S. (1991). Rorschach evaluation of adolescent bulimics. *Adolescence, 26,* 687–696.

SMITH, L. B., JONES, S., & LANDAU, B. (1992). Count nouns, adjectives, and perceptual properties in children's novel word interpretations. *Developmental Psychology, 28,* 273–286.

SMITH, M. C. (1975). Portrayal of the elderly in prescription drug advertising. *Gerontologist, 16,* 329–334.

SMITH, P. B., & PEDERSON, D. R. (1988). Maternal sensitivity and patterns of infant-mother attachment. *Child Development, 59,* 1097–1101.

SMITH, T. E. (1988). Parental control techniques. *Journal of Family Issues, 9,* 155–176.

SMITH, W. D. F., et al. (1992). Forced expiratory volume, height, and demispan in Canadian men and women aged 55–86. *The Journals of Gerontology, 47,* M40–M44.

SNODGRASS, D. M. (1991). The parent connection. *Adolescence, 26,* 83–88.

SNYDER, S. (1991). Movies and juvenile delinquency. *Adolescence, 26,* 121–132.

SOBAL, J., & MARQUART, L. F. (1994). Vitamin/mineral supplement use among high school athletes. *Adolescence, 29,* 835–843.

SOBEL, D. (1981, June 29). Surrogate mothers: Why women volunteer. *New York Times,* p. B-5.

SODIAN, B., TAYLOR, C., HARRIS, P. L., & PERNER, J. (1991). Early deception and the child's theory of mind: False trails and genuine markers. *Child Development, 62,* 468–483.

SODIAN, B., ZAITCHIK, D., & CAREY, S. (1991). Young children's differentiation of hypothetical beliefs from evidence. *Child Development, 62,* 753–766.

SODOWSKY, G. R., LAI, E. W. M., & PLAKE, B. S. (1991). Moderating effects of sociocultural variables on acculturation attitudes of Hispanics and Asian Americans. *Journal of Counseling and Development, 70,* 195–204.

SOHNGEN, M., & SMITH, R. J. (1978). Images of old age in poetry. *Gerontologist, 18,* 181–186.

SOKEN, N. H., & PICK, A. D. (1992). Intermodal perception of happy and angry expressive behaviors by seven-month-old infants. *Child Development, 63,* 787–795.

SOLOMON, G. E. A., JOHNSON, S. C., ZAITCHIK, D., & CAREY, S. (1996). Like father, like son: Young children's understanding of how and why offspring resemble parents. *Child Development, 67,* 151–171.

SOMERS, M. D. (1993). A comparison of voluntarily child-free adults and parents. *Journal of Marriage and the Family, 55,* 643–650.

SOMMER, B. (1984). The troubled teen: Suicide, drug use, and running away. *Women's Health, 9,* 117–141.

SOMMER, B., & NAGEL, S. (1991). Ecological and typological characteristics in early adolescent truancy. *Journal of Early Adolescence, 11,* 379–392.

SOMMERS, I., & BASKIN, D. R. (1994). Factors related to female adolescent initiation into violent street crime. *Youth and Society, 25,* 468–489.

SONENSTEIN, F. L., PLECK, J. H., & KU, L. C. (1989). Sexual activity, condom use and AIDS awareness among adolescent males. *Family Planning Perspectives, 21,* 152–158.

SONENSTEIN, F. L., PLECK, J. H., & KU, L. C. (1991). Levels of sexual activity among adolescent males in the United States. *Family Planning Perspectives, 23,* 162–167.

SOSTEK, A. M., SMITH, Y. F., KATZ, K. S., & GRANT, E. G. (1987). Developmental outcome of preterm infants with intraventricular hemorrhage at one and two years of age. *Child Development, 58,* 779–786.

SOUTH, S. J. (1991). Sociodemographic differentials in mate selection preferences. *Journal of Marriage and the Family, 53,* 928–940.

SOUTH, S. J., & LLOYD, K. M. (1992). Marriage opportunities and family formation: Further implications of imbalanced sex ratios. *Journal of Marriage and the Family, 54,* 440–451.

SOUTHARD, B. (1985). Interlimb movement control and coordination in children. In J. E. Clark & J. H. Humphrey (Eds.), *Motor development: Current selected research.* Princeton, NJ: Princeton Book Co.

SPANIER, G. B. (1983). Married and unmarried cohabitation in the United States: 1980. *Journal of Marriage and the Family, 45,* 277–288.

SPEARE, A., JR., AVERY, R., & LAWTON, L. (1991). Disability, residential mobility, and changes in living arrangements. *Journal of Gerontology, 46,* S133–S142.

SPEARMAN, C. (1927). *The abilities of man: Their nature and measurement.* New York: Macmillan.

SPENCER, M. B., & MARKSTROM-ADAMS, C. (1990). Identity processes among racial and ethnic minority children in America. *Child Development, 61*, 290–310.

SPETNER, N. B. & OLSHO, L. W. (1990). Auditory frequency resolution in human infancy. *Child Development, 61*, 632–652.

SPIKER, D., KRAEMER, H. C., CONSTANTINE, N. A., & BRYANT, D. (1992). Reliability and validity of behavior problem checklists as measures of stable traits in low birth weight, premature preschoolers. *Child Development, 63*, 1481–1496.

SPINILLO, A. G., & BRYANT, P. (1991). Children's proportional judgments: The importance of "half." *Child Development, 62*, 427–440.

SPIRO, A., III, ALDWING, C. M., LEVENSON, M. R., & BOSSE, R. (1990). Longitudinal findings from the normative aging study: II. Do emotionality and extraversion predict symptom change? *Journal of Gerontology, 45*, P136–P144.

SPIRO, A., III, SCHNURR, P. P., & ALDWIN, C. M. (1994). Combat-related post-traumatic stress disorder symptoms in older men. *Psychology and Aging, 9*, 17–26.

SPOCK, B. (1946). Commonsense book of baby and child care. New York: Duell, Sloan & Pearce.

SPOCK, B., & ROTHENBERG, M. B. (1992). *Dr. Spock's baby and child care.* New York: Pocket Books.

SPORNS, O., & EDELMAN, G. M. (1993). Solving Bernstein's problem: A proposal for the development of coordinated movement by selection. *Child Development, 64*, 960–981.

SPRECHER, S. (1985). Sex differences in bases of power in dating relationships. *Sex Roles, 12*, 449–462.

SPRECHER, S., & FELMLEE, D. (1992). The influence of parents and friends on the quality and stability of romantic relationships: A three-wave longitudinal investigation. *Journal of Marriage and the Family, 54*, 888–900.

SPRECHER, S., MCKINNEY, K., & ORBUCH, T. L. (1991). The effect of current sexual behavior on friendship, dating, and marriage desirability. *The Journal of Sex Research, 28*, 387–408.

SPRECHER, S., MCKINNEY, K., WALSH, R., & ANDERSON, C. (1988). A revision of the Reiss premarital sexual permissiveness scale. *Journal of Marriage and the Family, 50*, 821–828.

SPRINGER, K. (1992). Children's awareness of the biological implications of kinship. *Child Development, 63*, 950–959.

SROUFE, L. A. (1985). Attachment classification from the perspective of infant-caregiver relationships and infant temperament. *Child Development, 56*, 1–14.

SROUFE, L. A., BENNETT, C., ENGLUND, M., & URBAN, J. (1993). The significance of gender boundaries in preadolescents: The contemporary correlates and antecedents of boundary violations and maintenance. *Child Development, 64*, 455–466.

SROUFE, L. A., EGELAND, B., & KREUTZER, T. (1990). The fate of early experience following developmental change: Longitudinal approaches to individual adaptation in childhood. *Child Development, 61*, 1363–1373.

STACEY, C. A., & GATZ, M. (1991). Cross-sectional age differences and longitudinal change on the Bradburn affect balance scale. *Journal of Gerontology, 46*, P76–P78.

STACK, S. (1985, May). The effect of domestic/religious individualism in suicide, 1954–1978. *Journal of Marriage and the Family, 47*, 431–447.

STAGER, J. M. (1988). Menarche and exercise. *Medical Aspects of Human Sexuality, 22*, 118, 133.

STAKE, J. E., DEVILLE, C. J., & PENNELL, C. L. (1983, October). The effects of assertive training on the performance self-esteem of adolescent girls. *Journal of Youth and Adolescence, 12*, 435–442.

STANLEY, B. K., WEIKEL, W. J., & WILSON, J. (1986). The effects of father absence on interpersonal problem-solving skills of nursery school children. *Journal of Counseling and Development, 64*, 383–385.

STANLEY, S. M., & MARKMAN, H. J. (1992). Assessing commitment in personal relationships. *Journal of Marriage and the Family, 54*, 595–608.

STANTON, B. F., BLACK, M., KALJEE, L., & RICARDO, I. (1993). Perceptions of sexual behavior among urban early adolescents: Translating theory through focus groups. *Journal of Early Adolescence, 13*, 44–66.

STANTON, W. R., & SILVA, P. A. (1992). A longitudinal study of the influence of parents and friends on children's initiation of smoking. *Journal of Applied Developmental Psychology, 13*, 423–434.

STARRELS, M. E. (1994). Gender differences in parent-child relations. *Journal of Family Issues, 15*, 148–165.

STATTIN, H., & KLACKENBERG, G. (1992). Discordant family relations in intact families: Developmental tendencies over 18 years. *Journal of Marriage and the Family, 54*, 940–956.

STAUDINGER, U. M., SMITH, J., & BALTES, P. B. (1992). Wisdom-related knowledge in a life review task: Age differences and the role of professional specialization. *Psychology and Aging, 7*, 271–281.

STAYTON, W. R. (1983). Preventing infidelity. *Medical Aspects of Human Sexuality, 17*, 36C–36D.

STEEL, L. (1991). Early work experience among white and nonwhite youths: Implications for subsequent enrollment and employment. *Youth and Society, 22*, 419–447.

STEIN, C. H., WEMMERUS, V. A., WARD, M., GAINES, M. E., FREEBERG, A. L., & JEWELL, T. C. (1998). "Because they're my parents": An intergenerational study of felt obligation and parental care giving. *Journal of Marriage and the Family, 60*, 611–622.

STEIN, D. M., & REICHERT, P. (1990). Extreme dieting behaviors in early adolescence. *Journal of Early Adolescence, 10*, 108–121.

STEIN, J. A., NEWCOMB, M. D., & BENTLER, P. M. (1993). Differential effects of parent and grandparent drug use on behavior problems of male and female children. *Developmental Psychology, 29*, 31–43.

STEIN, L., & HOOPES, J. (1986). *Identity formation in the adopted child.* New York: Child Welfare League of America.

STEIN, P. J. (Ed.). (1981). *Single life: Unmarried adults in social context.* New York: St. Martin's Press.

STEIN, R. F. (1987). Comparison of self-concept of non-obese and obese university junior female nursing students. *Adolescence, 22*, 77–90.

STEINBERG, L., LAMBORN, S. D., DARLING, N., MOUNTS, N. S., & DORNBUSCH, S. M. (1994). Over-time changes in adjustment and competence among adolescents from authoritative, authoritarian, indulgent, and neglectful families. *Child Development, 65*, 754–770.

STEINBERG, L., LAMBORN, S. D., DORNBUSCH, S. M., & DARLING, M. (1992). Impact of parenting practices on adolescent achievement: Authoritative parenting, school involvement, and encouragement to succeed. *Child Development, 63*, 1266–1281.

STEINBERG, L., MOUNTS, N. S., LAMBORN, S. D., & DORNBUSCH, S. M. (1991). Authoritative parenting and adolescent adjustment across varied ecological niches. *Journal of Research on Adolescence, 1*, 19–36.

STEINBERG, L., & SILVERBERG, S. B. (1987). Influences on marital satisfaction during the middle stages of the family life cycle. *Journal of Marriage and the Family, 49*, 751–760.

STEINBERG, L. D. (1981). Transformations in family relations at puberty. *Developmental Psychology, 17*, 833–840.

STEINMAN, S., ZEMMELMAN, S., & KNOBLAUCH, T. (1985). A study of parents who sought joint custody and who returns to court. *Journal of the American Academy of Child Psychiatry, 24*, 554–562.

STEPHEN, J., FRASER, E., & MARCIA, J. E. (1992). Moratorium achievement (Mama) cycles in lifespan identity development: Value orientations and reasoning systems correlates. *Journal of Adolescence, 15*, 283–300.

STERN, J. A., OSTER, P. J., & NEWPORT, K. (1980). Reaction time measure, hemisphere specialization, and age. In L. W. Poon (Ed.), *Aging in the 80's: Psychological issues.* Washington, DC: American Psychological Association.

STERN, M., & ZEVON, M. A. (1990). Stress, coping, and family environment: The adolescent's response to naturally occurring stressors. *Journal of Adolescent Research, 5*, 290–305.

STERNBERG, K. J., LAMB, M. E., GREENBAUM, C., CICCHETTI, D., DAWUD, S., CORTES, R. M., KRISPIN, O., & LOREY, F. (1993). Effects of domestic violence on children's behavior problems and depression. *Developmental Psychology, 29*, 44–52.

STERNBERG, R. (1986). A triangular theory of love. *Psychological Review, 93*, 119–135.

STERNBERG, R., & BARNES, M. (Eds.). (1988). *The psychology of love.* New Haven, CT: Yale University Press.

STERNBERG, R., & GRAJEK, S. (1984). The nature of love. *Journal of Personality and Social Psychology, 47*, 312–329.

STERNBERG, R. J. (1985). *Beyond IQ.* Cambridge, England: Cambridge University Press.

STERNBERG, R. J., & WAGNER, R. K. (Eds.). (1986). *Practical intelligence: Nature and origins of competence in the everyday world.* Cambridge, England: Cambridge University Press.

STETS, J. E. (1991). Cohabiting and marital aggression: The role of social isolation. *Journal of Marriage and the Family, 53*, 669–680.

STEVENS, J. H., JR. (1988). Social support, locus of control, and parenting in three low-income groups of mothers: Black teenagers, black adults, and white adults. *Child Development, 59*, 635–642.

STEVENS, R., & PIHL, R. O. (1987). Seventh-grade students at risk for school failure. *Adolescence, 22*, 333–345.

STEVENSON, H. W., CHEN, C., & UTTAL, D. H. (1990). Beliefs and achievement: A study of black, white, and Hispanic children. *Child Development, 61*, 508–523.

STEVENSON, J. S. (1977). *Issues and crises during middlescence.* New York: Appleton-Century-Crofts.

STEVENSON, M. R., & BLACK, K. N. (1988). Paternal absence and sex-role developments: A meta-analysis. *Child Development, 59*, 793–814.

STEVENSON-HINDE, J. (1998). Parenting in different cultures: Time to focus. *Developmental Psychology, 34*, 698–700.

STEWART, S. D. (1998). Economic and personal factors affecting women's use of nurse-midwives in Michigan. *Family Planning Perspectives, 30*, 231–235.

STIFFMAN, A. R., DORE, P., & CUNNINGHAM, R. M. (1994). Inner-city youths and condom use: Health benefits, clinic care, welfare, and the HIV epidemic. *Adolescence, 29*, 805–820.

STILES, W. B., SHUSTER, P. L., & HARRIGAN, J. A. (1992). Disclosure and anxiety: A test of the fever model. *Journal of Personality and Social Psychology, 63*, 980–988.

STIMSON, K. M., et al. (1992). Parents' grief following pregnancy loss: A comparison of mothers and fathers. *Family Regulations, 41*, 218–223.

STIPEK, D., FEILER, R., DANIELS, D., & MILBURN, S. (1995). Effects of different instructional approaches on young children's achievement and motivation. *Child Development, 66*, 209–223.

STIPEK, D. J., & HOFFMAN, J. (1980). Development of children's performance-related judgments. *Child Development, 51*, 912–914.

STIPEK, D., & MacIVER, D. (1989). Developmental change in children's assessment of intellectual competence. *Child Development, 60*, 521–538.

STIVERS, C. (1988). Parent-adolescent communication and its relationship to adolescent depression and suicide proneness. *Adolescence, 23*, 291–295.

ST. JAMES-ROBERTS, I., & Plewis, I. (1996). Individual differences, daily fluctuations, and developmental changes in amounts of infants waking, fussing, crying, feeding, and sleeping. *Child Development, 67*, 2527–2540.

STJERNFELDT, M., BERGLUND, K., LINDSTEN, J., & LUDVIGSSON, J. (1986). Maternal smoking during pregnancy and risk of childhood cancer. *Lancet*, pp. 1350–1352.

STOCKMAN, I. J., & COOKE-VAUGHN, F. (1992). Lexical elaboration in children's locative action expressions. *Child Development, 63*, 1104–1125.

STOKOLS, D. (1992). Environmental quality, human development, and health: An ecological view. *Journal of Applied Developmental Psychology, 13*, 121–124.

STONE, A. A. (1987, November). Moody immunity. *Psychology Today, 21*, 14.

STORAASLI, R. D., & MARKMAN, H. J. (1990). Relationship problems in the early stages of marriage. *Journal of Family Psychology, 4*, 80–98.

ST. PETERS, M., FITCH, M., HUSTON, A. C., WRIGHT, J. C., & EAKINS, D. J. (1991). Television and families: What do young children watch with their parents? *Child Development, 62*, 1409–1423.

ST. PIERRE, T. L., MARK, M. M., KALTREIDER, D. L., & AIKIN, K. J. (1995). A 27–month evaluation of a sexual activity prevention program in boys and girls clubs across the nation. *Family Relations, 44*, 69–77.

STRANG, R. (1957). *The adolescent views himself.* New York: McGraw-Hill.

STRAYER, J. (1993). Children's concordant emotions and cognitions in response to observed emotions. *Child Development, 64*, 188–201.

STREETMAN, L. G. (1987). Contrasts in self-esteem of unwed teenage mothers. *Adolescence, 23*, 459–464.

STREISSGUTH, A. P., MARTIN, D. C., BARR, H. M., SANDMAN, B. M., KIRSHNER, G. L., & DARBY, B. L. (1984). Intrauterine alcohol and nicotine exposure: Attention and reaction time in 4–year-old children. *Developmental Psychology, 20*, 533–541.

STREITMATTER, J. (1993). Gender differences in identity development: An examination of longitudinal data. *Adolescence, 28*, 55–66.

STRONGMAN, K. T. (1987). *The psychology of emotion* (3rd ed.). New York: Wiley.

STUNKARD, A. J., FOCH, T. T., & HRUBEC, Z. (1986). A twin study of human obesity. *JAMA, Journal of the American Medical Association, 256*, 51–54.

SUBAK-SHARPE, G. J. (Ed.). (1984). Genital herpes. *The physicians manual for patients* (pp. 370–372). New York: Times Books.

SUICIDE PREVENTION CENTER. (1984). *Suicide statistics.* Los Angeles, CA.

SUITOR, J. J., & REAVIS, R. (1995). Football, fast cars, and cheerleading: Adolescent gender norms, 1978–1989. *Adolescence, 30*, 265–272.

SULLIVAN, J. F. (1987, June 25). Wishes of patient in refusing care backed in New Jersey: Right to die is extended. Rulings in three cases give interests of individuals priority over states. *New York Times, 1*, 8–12.

SULLIVAN, M. W., LEWIS, M., & ALESSANDRI, S. M. (1993). Cross-age stability in emotional expressions during learning and extinction. *Developmental Psychology, 28*, 58–63.

SULLIVAN, R., & WILSON, N. F. (1995). New directions for research in prevention and treatment of delinquency: A review and proposal. *Adolescence, 30*, 1–17.

SUNDERLAND, A., WATTS, K., BADDELEY, A. D., & HARRIS, J. E. (1986). Subjective memory assessment and test performance in elderly adults. *Journal of Gerontology, 41*, 376–384.

SUSMAN, E. J. (1997). Modeling developmental complexity in adolescence: Hormones and behavior in context. *Journal of Research on Adolescence, 7*, 283–306.

SUSMAN, E. J., DORN, L. D., NOTTELMAN, E. D., INOFF-GERMAN, G., & CHROUSOS, D. P. (1997). Cortisol reactivity, distress behavior, and behavioral and psychological problems in young adolescents: A longitudinal perspective. *Journal of Research on Adolescence, 7*, 81–105.

SVEC, H. (1987). Anorexia nervosa: A misdiagnosis of the adolescent male. *Adolescence, 87*, 617–623.

SWAIN, I. U., ZELAZO, P. R., & CLIFTON, R. K. (1993). Newborn infants' memory for speech sounds retained over 24 hours. *Developmental Psychology, 29*, 312–323.

SWANBROW, D. (1989). The paradox of happiness. *Psychology Today, 23*, 37–39.

SWEET, A. Y. (1979). Classification of the low-birth-weight infant. In M. H. & A. A. Fanaroff (Eds.), *Care of the high-risk infant* (2nd ed.). New York: Saunders.

SZINOVACZ, M., & WASHO, C. (1992). Gender differences in exposure to life events and adaptation to retirement. *The Journals of Geronthology, 47*, S191–S196.

TAKEUCHI, D. T., WILLIAMS, D. R., & ADAIR, R. K. (1991). Economic stress in the family and children's emotional and behavior problems. *Journal of Marriage and the Family, 53*, 1031–1041.

TAMIS-LeMONDA, C. S., & BORNSTEIN, M. H. (1986). Habituation and maternal encouragement of attention in infancy as predictors as toddler language, play and representational competence. *Child Development, 56*, 738–751.

TAN, L. (1985). Laterality and motor skills in 4–year-olds. *Child Development, 56*, 119–124.

TANGNEY, J. P. (1988). Aspects of the family and children's television viewing control preferences. *Child Development, 59*, 1070–1079.

TANNER, J. M. (1962). *Growth of adolescence.* Springfield, IL: Charles C. Thomas.

TANNER, J. M. (1970). Physical growth. In P. H. Mussen (Ed.), *Carmichael's manual of child psychology* (3rd ed., Vol. 1). New York: Wiley.

TANNER, J. M. (1972). Sequence, tempo, and individual variation in growth and development of boys and girls aged twelve to sixteen. In J. Kegan & R. Coles (Eds.), *Twelve to sixteen: Early adolescence.* New York: W. W. Norton.

TANNER, J. M. (1973, September). *Scientific American.*

TAUB, D. E., & BLINDE, E. M. (1992). Eating disorders among adolescent female athletes: Influence of athletic participation and sport team membership. *Adolescence, 27*, 833–848.

TAUB, D. E., & BLINDE, E. M. (1994). Disordered eating and weight control among adolescent female athletes and performance squad members. *Journal of Adolescent Research, 9*, 483–497.

TAYLOR, J. L., MILLER, T. P., & TINKLENBERG, J. R. (1992). Correlates of memory decline: A four-year longitudinal study of older adults with memory complaints. *Psychology and Aging, 7*, 185–193.

TAYLOR, L. (1992). Relationship between affect and memory: Motivation-based selective generation. *Journal of Personality and Social Psychology, 62*, 876–882.

TAYLOR, M., CARTWRIGHT, B. S., & CARLSON, S. M. (1993). A developmental investigation of children's imaginary companions. *Developmental Psychology, 29*, 276–285.

TAYLOR, N. A. S., ALLSOPP, N. K., & PARKES, D. G. (1995). Preferred room temperature of young versus aged males: The influence of thermal sensation, thermal comforts, and affect. *Journal of Gerontology, 50A*, M216–M221.

TAYLOR, R. D., ROBERTS, D., & JACOBSON, L. (1997). Stressful life events, psychological well-being, and parenting in African-American mothers. *Journal of Family Psychology, 11*, 436–446.

TEACHMAN, J. D. (1991). Who pays? Receipt of child support in the United States. *Journal of Marriage and the Family, 53*, 759–772.

TEACHMAN, J. D., & POLONKO, K. A. (1990). Cohabitation and marital stability in the United States. *Social Forces, 69*, 207–220.

TEASDALE, N., STELMACH, G. E., & BREUNIG, A. (1991). Postural sway characteristics of the elderly under normal and altered visual and support surface conditions. *The Journals of Gerontology, 46*, B238–B244.

TEASLEY, S. D., (1995). The role of talk in children's peer collaborations. *Developmental Psychology, 31*, 207–220.

TEDESCO, L. A., & GAIER, E. L. (1988). Friendship bonds in adolescence. *Adolescence, 89*, 127–136.

TEEKEN, J. C., ADAM, J. J., PAAS, F. G. W. C., VAN BOXTEL, M. P. J., HOUX, P. J., & JOLLES, J. (1996). Effects of age and gender on discrete and reciprocal aiming movements. *Psychology and Aging, 11*, 195–198.

TELEVISION AND YOUR CHILDREN. (1985). Ontario, Canada: TV Ontario, Ontario Educational Communications Authority.

TENNSTEDT, S. L., DETTLING, U., & MCKINLAY, J. B. (1992). Refusal rates in a longitudinal study of older people: Implications for field methods. *Journal of Gerontology, 47*, S313– S318.

TENOVER, J. S., & BREMNER, W. J. (1991). Circadian rhythm of serum immunoreactive inhibin in young and elderly men. *The Journals of Gerontology, 46*, M181–M184.

TENTLER, T. N. (1977, October). Death and dying in many disciplines: A review article. *Comparative Studies in Society and History, 19*, 511–522.

TERAMOTO, S., FUKUCHI, Y., NAGASE, T., MATSUSE, T., & ORIMO, H. (1995). A comparison of ventilation components in young and elderly men during exercise. *Journal of Gerontology, 50A*, B34–B39.

TERMAN, L. (1925). *Genetic studies of genius: Vol. 1. Mental and physical traits of a thousand gifted children.* Stanford, CA: Stanford University Press.

TERMAN, L., & ODEN, M. H. (1959). *Genetic studies of genius: Vol. 4. The gifted group at midlife.* Stanford, CA: Stanford University Press.

TETI, D. M., & ABLARD, K. E. (1989). Security of attachment and infant-sibling relationships: A laboratory study. *Child Development, 60*, 1519–1528.

TETI, D. M., & GELFAND, D. M. (1991). Behavioral competence among mothers of infants in the first year: The mediational role of maternal self-efficacy. *Child Development, 62*, 918–929.

TETI, D. M., LAMB, M. E., & ELSTER, A. B. (1987). Long-range economic and marital consequences of adolescent marriage in three cohorts of adult males. *Journal of Marriage and the Family, 49*, 499–506.

TEVENDALE, L. H. D., DUBOIS, D. L., LOPEZ, C., & PRINDIVILLE, S. L. (1997). Self-esteem stability in early adolescent adjustment: An exploratory study. *Journal of Early Adolescence, 17*, 216–237.

TEYLER, T. J., & FOUNTAIN, S. B. (1987). Neuronal plasticity in the mammalian brain: Relevance to behavioral learning and memory. *Child Development, 58*, 698–712.

THE COURT EDGES AWAY FROM ROE V. WADE. (1989). *Family Planning Perspectives, 21*, 184–187.

THOMAS, A., & CHESS, S. (1977). *Temperament and development.* New York: Brunner/Mazel.

THOMAS, A., & CHESS, S. (1984). Genesis and evolution of behavioral disorders: From infancy to early adulthood. *American Journal of Psychiatry, 141*, 1–9.

THOMAS, A. & CHESS, S. (1987). Roundtable: What is temperament? *Child Development, 58*, 505–529.

THOMAS, A. M., FOREHAND, R., & NEIGHBORS, B. (1995). Change in maternal, depressive mood: Unique contributions to adolescent functioning over time. *Adolescence, 30*, 43–52.

THOMAS, K. R. (1991). Oedipal issues in counseling psychology. *Journal of Counseling and Development, 69*, 203–205.

THOMAS, V. G. (1990). Determinants of global life happiness and marital happiness in dual-career black couples. *Family Relations, 39*, 174–178.

THOMPSON, A. P. (1984). Emotional and sexual components of extramarital relations. *Journal of Marriage and the Family, 46*, 35–42.

THOMPSON, J. K. (1986). Larger than life. *Psychology Today, 20*, 39–44.

THOMPSON, L. (1992). Feminist methodology for family studies. *Journal of Marriage and the Family, 54*, 3–18.

THOMPSON, L., ACOCK, A. C., & CLARK, K. (1985). Do parents know their children? The ability of mothers and fathers to gauge the attitudes of their young adult children. *Family Relations, 34*, 315–320.

THOMPSON, L. W., BRECKENRIDGE, J. N., GALLAGHER, D., & PETERSON, J. (1984). Effects of bereavement on self-perceptions of physical health in elderly widows and widowers. *Journal of Gerontology, 39*, 309–314.

THOMPSON, M. P., NORRIS, F. H., & HANACEK, B. (1993). Age differences and the psychological consequences of Hurricane Hugo. *Psychology and Aging, 8*, 606–616.

THOMPSON, R. A., CONNELL, J. P., & BRIDGES, L. J. (1988). Temperament, emotion, and social interactive behavior in the strange situation: A component process analysis of attachment system functioning. *Child Development, 59*, 1102–1110.

THOMPSON, W. E., & DODDER, R. A. (1986). Containment theory and juvenile delinquency: A reevaluation through fact analysis. *Adolescence, 21*, 365–376.

THOMPSON, W. R., & GRUSEC, J. E. (1970). Studies of early experience. In P. H. Mussen (Ed.), *Carmichael's manual of child psychology* (Vol. 1). New York: Wiley.

THOMSON, E., & COLELLA, U. (1992). Cohabitation and marital stability: Quality or commitment? *Journal of Marriage and the Family, 54*, 259–267.

THORNDIKE, R. L., HAGEN, E. P., & SATTLER, J. M. (1985). *Stanford-Binet* (4th ed.). Chicago, IL: Riverside Publishing.

THORNE, A., & MICHAELIEU, Q. (1996). Situating adolescent gender and self-esteem with personal memories. *Child Development, 67*, 1374–1390.

THORNTON, A. (1989). Changing attitudes towards family issues in the United States. *Journal of Marriage and the Family, 1*, 873–893.

THORNTON, A., ORBUCH, T. L., & AXINN, W. G. (1995). Parent-child relationships during the transition to adulthood. *Journal of Family Issues, 16*, 538–564.

THORNTON, A., YOUNG-DEMARCO, L., & GOLDSCHEIDER, F. (1993). Leaving the parental nest: The experience of a young, white cohort in the 1980s. *Journal of Marriage and the Family, 55*, 216–229.

THORNTON, B., & RYCKMAN, R. M. (1991). Relationships between physical attractiveness, physical effectiveness, and self-esteem: A cross-sectional analysis among adolescents. *Journal of Adolescence, 14*, 85–98.

THORNTON, M. C., CHATTERS, L. M., TAYLOR, R. J., & ALLEN, W. R. (1990). Sociodemographic and environmental correlates of racial socialization by black parents. *Child Development, 61*, 401–409.

THREE YEARS AFTER ENACTMENT, CHILD SUPPORT LAWS APPEAR TO INCREASE PAYMENTS BY ABSENT FATHERS (1987). *Family Planning Perspectives, 19*, 272–273.

THURBER, C. A. (1995). The experience and expression of homesickness in preadolescent and adolescent boys. *Child Development, 66*, 1162–1178.

THURBER, C. A., & WEISZ, J. R. (1997). "You can try or you can just give up": The impact of perceived control and coping style on childhood homesickness. *Developmental Psychology, 33*, 508–517.

THURSTONE, L. L. (1938). *Primary mental abilities. Psychometric monographs.* No. 1. Chicago, IL: University of Chicago Press.

THURSTONE, L. L., & THURSTONE, T. B. (1949). *SRA primary and mental abilities.* Chicago, IL: Science Research Associates.

THURSTONE, L. L., & THURSTONE, T. B. (1953). *Examiner manual for the Primary Mental Abilities for Ages 5 to 7* (3rd ed.). Chicago, IL: Science Research Associates.

TIDWELL, R. (1988). Dropouts speak out: Qualitative data on early school departures. *Adolescence, 92*, 939–954.

TIEDJE, L. B., et al. (1990). Women with multiple roles: Role compatibility, perceptions, satisfaction, and mental health. *Journal of Marriage and the Family, 52*, 63–72.

TIERNO, M. J. (1991). Responding to the socially motivated behaviors of early adolescence: Recommendations from classroom management. *Adolescence, 26*, 567–577.

TIMNICK, L. (1982). How you can learn to be likable, confident, socially successful for only the cost of your present education. *Psychology Today, 26*, 42–49.

TINSLEY, B. J. (1992). Multiple influences on the acquisition and socialization of children's health attitudes and behavior: An integrative review. *Child Development, 63*, 1043–1069.

TOLAN, P. (1988). Socioeconomic, family, and social stress correlates of adolescent antisocial and delinquent behavior. *Journal of Abnormal Child Psychology, 16*, 317–331.

TOLSON, J. M., & URBERG, K. A. (1993). Similarilty between the adolescent and best friends. *Journal of Adolescent Research, 3*, 274–288.

TOLSON, T. F. J., & WILSON, M. N. (1990). The impact of two- and three-generational black family structure on perceived family climate. *Child Development, 61*, 416–428.

TOMPSON, R. (1997). Sensitivity and security: New questions to ponder. *Child Development, 68*, 595–597.

TOOTH, G. (1985, February 18). Why children's TV turns off so many parents. *U.S. News and World Report*, p. 65.

TOUFEXIS, A. (1992). When kids kill abusive parents. *Time, 140*, 60–61.

TOUT, K., DEHAAN, M., CAMPBELL, E. K., & GUNNAR, M. R. (1998). Social behavior correlates of cortisol activity in child care: Gender differences and time-of-day effects. *Child Development, 69*, 1247–1262.

TOWER, R. B., SINGER, D. G., SINGER, L. J., & BIGGS, A. (1979). Differential effects of television programming on preschooler's cognition, imagination, and social play. *American Journal of Orthopsychiatry, 49*, 265–281.

TRACHTENBERG, S., & BIKEN, R. J. (1994). Aggressive boys in the classroom: Biased attributions or shared perceptions? *Child Development, 65*, 829–835.

TRAPPED BY MUTILATOR TROY? NEED HELP FINDING DRACULA'S HEART? JUST CALL THE NINTENDO HOTLINE (1990, January 8). *People, 33*, 82.

TRAVER, N. (1992, October 26). Children without pity. *Time, 140*, 46–51.

TRAVILLION, K., & SNYDER, J. (1993). The role of maternal discipline and involvement in peer rejection and neglect. *Journal of Applied Developmental Psychology, 14*, 37–55.

TREICHEL, J. (1982). Anorexia nervosa: A brain shrinker? *Science News, 122*, 122–123.

TREIMAN, R., GOSWAMI, U., TINCOFF, R., & LEEVERS, H. (1997). Effects of dialect on American and British children's spelling. *Child Development, 68*, 229–245.

TROSTER, H., & BRAMBRING, M. (1993). Early motor development in blind infants. *Journal of Applied Developmental Psychology, 14*, 83–106.

TROTTER, R. J. (1986). Three heads are better than one. *Psychology Today, 20*, 56–62.

TROTTER, R. J. (1987a). Project day-care. *Psychology Today, 21*, 32–38.

TROTTER, R. J. (1987b, May). You've come a long way, baby. *Psychology Today, 21*, 34–45.

TRUSSELL, J. (1988). Teenage pregnancy in the United States. *Family Planning Perspectives, 20*, 262–272.

TRUSSELL, J., WARNER, D. L., & HATCHER, R. A. (1992). Condom slippage and breakage rates. *Family Planning Perspectives, 24*, 21–23.

TSCHANN, J. M., JOHNSTON, J. R., KLINE, M., & WALLERSTEIN, J. S. (1989). Family process and children's functioning during divorce. *Journal of Marriage and the Family, 51*, 431–444.

TUBMAN, J. G. (1993). Family risk factors, parental alcohol use, and problem behaviors among school-age children. *Family Relations, 42*, 81–86.

TUCKER, L. A. (1982). Relationship between perceived conatotype of body cathexis of college males. *Psychology Reports, 50*, 983–989.

TUCKER, L. A. (1983). Muscular strength and mental health. *Journal of Personality and Social Psychology, 45*, 1355–1360.

TUN, P. A. (1989). Age differences in processing expository and narrative text. *Journal of Gerontology, 44*, P9–P15.

TUN, P. A., WINGFIELD, A., STINE, E. A. L., & MECSAS, C. (1992). Rapid speech processing and divided attention: Processing rate vs. processing resources as an explanation of age effects. *Psychology and Aging, 7*, 536–550.

TURNER, P. J. (1991). Relations between attachment, gender, and behavior with peers in preschool. *Child Development, 62*, 1475–1488.

TURNER, R. (1991). One in seven 6th–12th graders had an unwanted sexual encounter, including one in five females. *Family Planning Perspectives, 23*, 286–287.

TURNER, R. (1992). First-trimester chorionic villus sampling may raise risk of spontaneous abortion and limb abnormality. *Family Planning Perspectives, 24*, 45–46.

TURNER, R. (March/April 1992). Underweight births are equally likely among poor blacks and whites. *Family Planning Perspectives, 24*, 95–96.

TURNER, R. (November/December 1992). Low birth weight linked to physical, behavioral problems at school age. *Family Planning Perspectives, 24*, 279–280.

TURNER, R. (1994). Receiving recommended prenatal health advice can increase birth weight. *Family Planning Perspectives, 26*, 187–189.

TYGART, C. (1988). Public school vandalism: Toward a synthesis of theories and transition to paradigm analysis. *Adolescence, 15*, 783–795.

TYGART, C. E. (1991). Juvenile delinquency and number of children in a family: Some empirical and theoretical updates. *Youth and Society, 22*, 525–536.

UBELL, E. (1990, January 14). You don't have to be childless. *Parade Magazine*, pp. 14, 15.

UCHINO, B. N., KIECOLT-GLASER, J. K., & CACIOPPO, J. T. (1992). Age-related changes in cardiovascular response as a function of a chronic stressor and social support. *Journal of Personality and Social Psychology, 63*, 839–846.

UHLENBERG, P., COONEY, T., & BOYD, R. (1990). Divorce for women after midlife. *Journal of Gerontology, 45*, S3–S11.

UHR, S., STAHL, S. M., & BERGER, P. A. (1984). Unmasking schizophrenia. *VA Practitioner*, 42–53.

ULBRICH, P. M., COYLE, A. T., & LLABRE, M. M. (1990). Involuntary childlessness and marital adjustment: His and hers. *Journal of Sex and Marital Therapy, 16*, 147–158.

UMBEL, V. M., PEARSON, B. Z., FERNANDES, M. C., & OILER, D. K. (1992). Measuring bilingual children's receptive vocabularies. *Child Development, 63*, 1012–1020.

UMBERSON, D. (1989). Relationships with children: Explaining parents' psychological well-being. *Journal of Marriage and the Family, 51*, 499–1012.

UMBERSON, G., & WILLIAMS, C. L. (1993). Divorced fathers, parental role strain and psychological distress. *Journal of Family Issues, 14*, 378–400.

UNGER, J. B., KIPKE, M. D., SIMON, T. R., JOHNSON, C. J., MONTGOMERY, S. B., & IVERSON, E. (1998). Stress, coping, and social support among homeless youth. *Journal of Adolescent Research, 13*, 134–157.

UNITED STATES PHARMACOPEIA, 1996. *Complete Drug Reference.* Consumers' Union: Consumer Report Books.

UPCHURCH, D. M., & McCARTHY, J. (1989). Adolescent childbearing and high school completion in the 1980s: Have things changed? *Family Planning Perspectives, 21*, 199–202.

URBERG, K. A., DEGIRMENCIOGLU, S. M., TOLSON, J. M., & HALLIDAY-SCHER, K. (1995). The structure of adolescent peer networks. *Developmental Psychology, 31*, 540–547.

U.S. BUREAU OF THE CENSUS. (1980). *Social indicators III.* Washington, DC: U.S. Government Printing Office.

U.S. BUREAU OF THE CENSUS. (1987). *Statistical abstract of the United States, 1987.* Washington, DC: U.S. Government Printing Office.

U.S. BUREAU OF THE CENSUS. (1988). *Statistical abstract of the U.S., 1988* (108th ed.). Washington, DC: U.S. Government Printing Office.

U.S. BUREAU OF THE CENSUS. (1989). *Statistical abstract of the United States, 1989* (109th ed.). Washington, DC: U.S. Government Printing Office.

U.S. BUREAU OF THE CENSUS. (1997). *Statistical abstract of the United States, 1995* (117th ed.). Washington, DC: U.S. Government Printing Office.

U.S. BUREAU OF THE CENSUS. (1998). *Statistical abstract of the United States, 1998* (116th ed.). Washington, DC: U.S. Government Printing Office.

U.S. DEPARTMENT OF AGRICULTURE AND U.S. DEPARTMENT OF HEALTH AND HUMAN SERVICES. (1985). *Dietary guidelines for Americans* (Home and Garden Bulletin, No. 232). Washington, DC: U.S. Government Printing Office.

U.S. DEPARTMENT OF HEALTH AND HUMAN SERVICES. (1979). *The Belmont Report: Ethical Principles and Guidelines for the Protection of Human*

Subjects of Research (Publication No. 1983, pp. 81–132, 1305). Department of Health, Education, and Welfare, Washington, DC: U.S. Government Printing Office.

U.S. DEPARTMENT OF HEALTH AND HUMAN SERVICES. (1980, June). *Marijuana research findings: 1980.* Rockville, MD: National Institute on Drug Abuse.

U.S. DEPARTMENT OF HEALTH AND HUMAN SERVICES (1981). *Statistics on incidence of depression.* Washington, DC: U.S. Government Printing Office.

U.S. DEPARTMENT OF HEALTH AND HUMAN SERVICES. Data from the 1995 National Survey of Family Growth, Series 23, No 19. Hattsville, Maryland, May 1997.

USEEM, E. L. (1991). Student selection into course sequences, in mathematics: The impact of parental involvement and school policies. *Journal of Research on Adolescence, 1,* 231–250.

USUI, W. M., KEIL, T. J., & DURIG, K. R. (1985). Socioeconomic comparisons and life satisfaction of elderly adults. *Journal of Gerontology, 40,* 110–114.

USUI, W. M., KEIL, T. J., & PHILLIPS, D. C. (1983). Determinants of life satisfaction: A note on race-interaction hypothesis. *Journal of Gerontology, 38,* 107–110.

UTTL, D., & GRAF, P. (1993). Episodic spatial memory in adulthood. *Psychology and Aging, 8,* 257–273.

VAILLANT, C. O., & VAILLANT, G. E. (1993). Is the U-curve of marital satisfaction an illusion? A 40-year study of marriage. *Journal of Marriage and the Family, 55,* 230–239.

VAILLANT, G. E. (1977a). *Adaptation to Life.* Boston, MA: Little, Brown.

VAILLANT, G. E. (1977b). The climb to maturity: How the best and brightest come of age. *Psychology Today, 11,* 34ff.

VAILLANT, G. E. (1991). The association of ancestral longevity with successful aging. *The Journals of Gerontology, 46,* P292–P298.

VALDEZ-MENCHACA, M. C., & WHITEHURST, G. J. (1992). Accelerating language development through picture book reading: A systematic extension to Mexican day care. *Developmental Psychology, 28,* 1106–1114.

VALENCIA, R. R. (1985). Predicting academic achievement in Mexican-American children using the Kaufman Assessment Battery for Children. *Education and Psychological Research, 5,* 11–17.

VALENZUELA, M. (1990). Attachment in chronically underweight young children. *Child Development, 61,* 1984–1996.

VANDELL, D. L., & WILSON, K. S. (1987). Infants' interactions with mother, sibling, peers: Contrasts and relations between interaction systems. *Child Development, 58,* 176–186.

VANDELL, D. L., OWEN, M. T., WILSON, K. S., & HENDERSON, V. K. (1988). Social development in infant twins: Peer and mother-child relationships. *Child Development,* 168–177.

VAN DEN BOOM, D. C. (1997). Sensitivity and attachment: Next steps for developmentalists. *Child Development, 64,* 592–594.

VAN DEN BROEK, P., LORCH, E. P., & THURLOW, R. (1996). Children's and adults' memory for television stories: The role of causal factors, story-grammar categories, and hierarchical levels. *Child Development, 67,* 3010–3028.

VAN DER BRANDE, P., VIJGEN, J., & DEMEDTS, M. (1991). Clinical spectrum of pulmonary tuberculosis in older patients: Comparison with younger patients. *The Journals of Gerontology, 46,* M204–M209.

VANDERVOORT, A. A., et al. (1992). Age and sex effects on mobility of the human ankle. *The Journals of Gerontology, 47,* M17–M21.

VANGELISTI, A. L. (1992). Older adolescents' perceptions of communication problems with their parents. *Journal of Adolescent Research, 7,* 382–402.

VAN IJZENDOORN, M. H., & DE WOLFF, M. S. (1997). In search of the absent father—meta-analysis of infant-father attachments: A rejoinder to our discussants. *Child Development, 68,* 604–609.

VAN IJZENDOORN, M. H., GOLDBERG, S., KROONENBERG, P. M., & FRENKEL, O. J. (1992). The relative effects of maternal and child problems on the quality of attachment: A meta-analysis of attachment in clinical samples. *Child Development, 63,* 840–858.

VANNOY, D. (1991). Social differentiation, contemporary marriage, and human development. *Journal of Family Issues, 12,* 251–267.

VAN ROOSMALEN, E. H., & MCDANIEL, S. A. (1992). Adolescent smoking intentions: Gender differences in peer context. *Adolescence, 27,* 87–105.

VAN THORRE, M. D. & VOGEL, F. X. (1985, Spring). The presence of bulimia in high school females. *Adolescence, 20,* 45–51.

VASEY, M. W., EL-HAG, N., & DALEIDEN, E. L. (1996). Anxiety and processing of emotionally threatening stimuli: Distinctive patterns of a selective attention among high- and low-anxious children. *Child Development, 67,* 773–1185.

VAUGHN, B. E., BLOCK, J. H., & BLOCK, J. (1988). Parents' agreement on child rearing during early childhood and the psychological characteristics of adolescents. *Child Development, 59,* 1020–1033.

VAUGHN, B. E., LEFEVER, G. B., SEIFER, R., & BARGLOW, P. (1989). Attachment behavior, attachment security, and temperament during infancy. *Child Development, 60,* 728–737.

VAUGHN, B. E., STEVENSON-HINDE, J., WATERS, E., KOTSAFTIS, A., LEFEVER, G. B., SHOULDICE, A., TRUDEL, M., & BELSKY, J. (1992). Attachment security and temperament in infancy and early childhood: Some conceptual clarifications. *Developmental Psychology, 28,* 463–473.

VAUGHN, B. E., & WATERS, E. (1990). Attachment behavior at home and in the laboratory: Q-short observations and strange situation classifications of one-year-olds. *Child Development, 61,* 1965–1973.

VERBRUGGE, L. M., KEPKOWSKI, J. M., & KONKOL, L. L. (1991). Levels of disability among U.S. adults with arthritis. *Journal of Gerontology, 46,* S71–S83.

VERDUYN, C. M., LORD, W., & FORREST, G. C. (1990). Social skills training in schools: An evaluation study. *Journal of Adolescence, 13,* 3–16.

VERHAEGHEN, P., MARCOEN, A., & GOOSSENS, L. (1992). Improving memory performance in the aged through mnemonic training: A meta-analytic study. *Psychology and Aging, 7,* 242–251.

VERNON-FEAGANS, L., EMANUEL, D. C., & BLOOD, I. (1997). The effects of Otitis Media and quality of day care on children's language development. *The Journal of Applied Developmental Psychology, 18,* 395–409.

VERNON-FEAGANS, L., MANLOVE, E. E., & VOLLING, B. L. (1996). Otitis Media and the social behavior of day-care-attending children. *Child Development, 67,* 1528–1539.

VICARY, J. R., & LERNER, J. V. (1986). Parental attributes and adolescent drug use. *Journal of Adolescence, 9,* 115–122.

VLAY, S. C., & FRICCHIONE, G. L. (1987). Ventricular tachyarrhythmia: Helping patients cope with stress. *Medical Aspects of Human Sexuality, 21,* 116–123.

VOTH, H. M., PERRY, J. A., MCCRANIE, J. E., & ROGERS, R. R. (1982). How can extramarital affairs be prevented? *Medical Aspects of Human Sexuality, 16,* 62–74.

VOYDANOFF, P., & DONNELLY, B. W. (1989a). Economic distress and mental health. *Lifestyles, 10,* 139–162.

VOYDANOFF, P., & DONNELLY, B. W. (1989b). Work and family roles and psychological stress. *Journal of Marriage and the Family, 51,* 923–932.

VUCHINICH, S., BANK, L., & PATTERSON, G. R. (1992). Parenting, peers and the stability of antisocial behavior in pre-adolescent boys. *Developmental Psychology, 28,* 510–521.

VYGOTSKY, L. S. (1978). *Mind in society: The development of higher psychological processes.* Cambridge, MA: Harvard University Press.

WADE, N. L. (1987). Suicide as a resolution of separation-individuation among adolescent girls. *Adolescence, 22,* 169–177.

WAEHRER, K., & CRYSTAL, S. (1995). The impact of coresidence on economic well-being of elderly widows. *Journal of Gerontology, 50B,* S250–S258.

WAGNER, B. M., & PHILLIPS, D. A. (1992). Beyond beliefs: Parent and child behaviors and children's perceived academic competence. *Child Development, 63,* 1380–1391.

WAGNER, R. K., TORGESEN, J. K., & RASHOTTE, C. A. (1994). Development of reading-related phonological processing abilities: New evidence of bidirectional causality from a latent variable longitudinal study. *Developmental Psychology, 30,* 73–87.

WAHLIN, A., et al. (1993). Prior knowledge and face recognition in a community-based sample of healthy, very old adults. *The Journals of Gerontology, 48,* P54–P61.

WAHLIN, A., HILL, R. D., WINBLAD, B., & BACKMAN, L. (1996). Effects of serum vitamin B_{12} and folic acid on episodic memory performance in very old age: A population-based study. *Psychology and Aging, 11,* 487–496.

WAKSMAN, S. A. (1984a, Spring). Assertion training with adolescents. *Adolescence, 19,* 123–130.

WAKSMAN, S. A. (1984b, Summer). A controlled evaluation of assertion training on performance in highly anxious adolescents. *Adolescence, 19,* 277–282.

WALD, M. S., CARLSMITH, J. M., & LEIDERMAN, P. H. (1988). *Protecting abused and neglected children.* Stanford, CA: Stanford University Press.

WALKER, E., DOWNEY, G., & BERGMAN, A. (1989). The effects of parental psychopathology and maltreatment on child behavior: A test of the diathesis-stress model. *Child Development, 60,* 15–24.

WALKER, L. J., & TAYLOR, J. H. (1991). Family interactions and the development of moral reasoning. *Child Development, 62,* 264–284.

WALLERSTEIN, J., & BLAKESLEE, S. (1990). *Second chances: Men, women, and children a decade after divorce.* London: Grant McIntyre.

WALLERSTEIN, J. S. (1989, January 23). Children after divorce: Wounds that don't heal. *New York Times Magazine,* pp. 19–21, 41–44.

WALLERSTEIN, J. S., & KELLY, J. B. (1980). *Surviving the breakup: How children and parents cope with divorce.* London: Grant McIntyre.

WALLINGA, C., PAGUIO, L, & SKEEN, P. (1987, August). When a brother or sister is ill. *Psychology Today, 21,* 42–43.

WALLIS, C. (1984, March 26). Hold the eggs and butter. *Time, 123,* 56–63.

WALLIS, C. (1987, February). You haven't heard anything yet. *Time.*

WALSH, A., & BEYER, J. A. (1987). Violent crime, sociopathy, and love deprivation among adolescent delinquents. *Adolescence, 22,* 705–717.

WALTERS, C. M., & MCKENRY, P. C. (1985). Predictors of life satsifaction among rural and urban umployed mothers: A research note. *Journal of Marriage and the Family, 47,* 1067–1071.

WANG, A. Y. (1994). Pride and prejudice in school gang members. *Adolescence, 29,* 279–291.

WANG, H., BASHORE, T. R., & FRIEDMAN, E. (1995). Exercise reduces age-dependent decrease in platelet protein kinase C activity and translocation (1995). *Journal of Gerontology, 50A,* M12–M16.

WANG, H. S., & BUSSE, E. W. (1974). Heart disease and brain impairment among aged persons. In E. Palmore (Ed.), *Normal aging II.* Durham, NC: Duke University Press.

WARAH, A. (1993). Overactive and boundary setting in anorexia nervosa: An existential perspective. *Journal of Adolescence, 16,* 93–100.

WARD, M., HUBERT, H. V., SHI, H., & BLOCH, D. A. (1995). Physical disability in older runners: Prevalence, risk factors, and progression with age. *Journal of Gerontology, 50A,* M70–M77.

WARD, R. A. (1980, May). Age and acceptance of euthanasia. *Journal of Gerontology, 35,* 421–431.

WARD, R. A., SHERMAN, S. R., & LAGORY, M. (1984). Subjective network assessments and subjective well-being. *Journal of Gerontology, 39,* 93–101.

WARRINGTON, E. K., & SILBERSTEIN, M. (1970). A questionnaire technique for investigating very long term memory. *Quarterly Journal of Experimental Psychology, 22,* 508–512.

WASIK, B. H., RAMEY, C. T., BRYANT, D. M., & SPARLING, J. J. (1990). A longitudinal study of two early intervention strategies: Project CARE. *Child Development, 61,* 1682–1696.

WASS, H., & CORR, C. A. (1984). *Childhood and death.* Washington, DC: Hemisphere Publishing Corp.

WASSERMAN, G. A., RAUGH, V. A., BRUNELLI, S. A., GARCIA-CASTRO, M., & NECOS, B. (1990). Psychosocial attributes and life experiences of disadvantaged minority mothers: Age and ethnic variations. *Child Development, 61,* 566–580.

WATERMAN, A. S. (1990). Curricula interventions for identity change: Substantive and ethical considerations. *Journal of Adolescence, 13,* 389–400.

WATERS, E., & SROUFE, L. A. (1983). Social competence as a developmental construct. *Developmental Review, 3,* 79–97.

WATSON, J. B., & RAYNOR, R. R. (1920). Conditional emotional reactions. *Journal of Experimental Psychology, 3,* 1–4.

WATSON, W. H., & MAXWELL, R. J. (1977). *Human aging and dying: A study in sociocultural gerontology.* New York: St. Martin's Press.

WATTS, W. D., & WRIGHT, L. S. (1990). The relationship of alcohol, tobacco, marijuana, and other illegal drug use to delinquency among Mexican-American, black, and white adolescent males. *Adolescence, 25,* 171–182.

WAUGH, N. C., & NORMAN, D. A. (1965). Primary memory. *Psychological Review, 72,* 89–104.

WAXMAN, S. R., & HALL, D. G. (1993). The development of a linkage between count nouns and object categories: Evidence from fifteen- to twenty-one-month-old infants. *Child Development, 64,* 1224–1241.

WAXMAN, S. R., & KOSOWSKI, T. D. (1990). Nouns mark category relations: Toddlers' and preschoolers' word-learning biases. *Child Development, 61,* 1461–1473.

WAXMAN, S. R., & SENGHAS, A. (1992). Relations among word meanings in early lexical development. *Developmental Psychology, 28,* 862–873.

WAXMAN, S. R., SHIPLEY, E. F., & SHEPPERSON, B. (1991). Establishing new subcategories: The role of category labels and existing knowledge. *Child Development, 62,* 127–138.

WEAVER, G. M., & WOOTTON, R. R. (1992). The use of the MMPI special scales in the assessment of delinquent personality. *Adolescence, 27,* 545–554.

WEBB, J. A., BAER, P. E., CAID, C. D., MCKELVEY, R. S., & CONVERSE, R. E. (1992). Development of an abbreviated form of the alcoholic expectancy questionnaire for adolescents. *Journal of Adolescence, 12,* 441–456.

WEBB, J. A., BAER, P. E., CAID, C. D., MCLAUGHLIN, R. J., & MCKELVEY, R. S. (1991). Concurrent and longitudinal assessment of risk for alcohol use among seventh graders. *Journal of Early Adolescence, 11,* 450–465.

WEBB, R. A. (1974). Concrete and formal operations in very bright 6- to 11–year-olds. *Human Development, 17,* 292–300.

WEBSTER V. REPRODUCTIVE HEALTH SERVICES, INC., 951 F. 2d., at 1079 (1988).

WECHSLER, D. (1981). *Manual for the Wechsler adult intelligence scale.* New York: Psychological Corporation.

WECHSLER, D. (1981). *Wechsler adult intelligence scale* (3rd ed.). New York: Psychological Corporation.

WECHSLER, D. (1989). *Wechsler preschool and primary scale for intelligence.* New York: Psychological Corporation.

WECHSLER, D. (1989). *Wechsler preschool and primary scale of intelligence—Revised.* San Antonio, TX: The Psychological Corporation.

WECHSLER, D. (1991). *Wechsler intelligence scale for children.* (3rd ed.). New York: Psychological Corporation.

WEHR, S. H., & KAUFMAN, M. E. (1987). The effects of assertive training on performance in highly anxious adolescents. *Adolescence, 85,* 195–205.

WEIFFENBACH, J. M., TYLENDA, C. A., & BAUM, B. J. (1990). Oral sensory changes in aging. *Journal of Gerontology, 45,* M121–M125.

WEIGEL, D. J., DEVEREUX, P., LEIGH, G. K., & BALLARD-REISCH, D. (1998). A longitudinal study of adolescents' perception of support and stress: Stability and change. *Journal of Adolescent Research, 13,* 158–177.

WEIGEL, R. R., WEIGEL, D. J., & BLUNDALL, J. (1987). Stress, coping, and satisfaction: Generational differences in farm families. *Family Relations, 36,* 45–48.

WEINSTEIN, E., & ROSEN, E. (1991). The development of adolescent sexual intimacy: Implications for counseling. *Adolescence, 26,* 331–340.

WEISNER, T. S., & WILSON-MITCHELL, J. E. (1990). Nonconventional family life-styles and sex typing in six-year-olds. *Child Development, 61,* 1915–1933.

WEISS, B., & DODGE, K. A. (1992). Some consequences of early harsh discipline: Child aggression and a maladaptive social information processing style. *Child Development, 63,* 1321–1335.

WEISS, M. J., ZELAZO, P. R., & SWAIN, I. U. (1988). Newborn response to auditory stimulus discrepancy. *Child Development, 59,* 1530–1541.

WELSH, M. C., PENNINGTON, B. F., OZONOFF, S., ROUSE, B., & MCCABE, E. R. B. (1990). Neuropsychology of early-treated phenylketonuria: Specific executive function deficits. *Child Development, 61,* 1697–1713.

WENTZEL, K. R. (1991). Relations between social competence and academic achievement in early adolescence. *Child Development, 62,* 1066–1078.

WENTZEL, K. R. (1994). Family functioning and academic achievement in middle school. A social-emotional perspective. *Journal of Early Adolescence, 14,* 268–291.

WERNER, E. E., & SMITH, R. R. (1982). *Vulnerable but invincible: A longitudinal study of resilient children and youth.* New York: McGraw-Hill.

WERNER, L. A., MAREAN, G. C., HALPIN, C. F., SPETNER, N. B., & GILLENWATER, J. M. (1992). Infant auditory temporal acuity. Gap detection. *Child Development, 63,* 260–272.

WERTSCH, J. V., & TULVISTE, P. (1992). L. S. Vygotsky and contemporary developmental psychology. *Developmental Psychology, 28,* 548–557.

WEST BERLIN HUMAN GENETICS INSTITUTE. (1987). *Studies on effect of nuclear radiation at Chernobyl on fetal development.* West Berlin: Human Genetics Institute.

WESTNEY, O. J., JENKINS, R. R., BUTTS, J. D., & WILLIAMS, I. (1984, Fall). Sexual development and behavior in black preadolescents. *Adolescence, 19,* 557–568.

WETHINGTON, E., & KESSLER, R. C. (1989). Employment, parental responsibility, and psychological distress. *Journal of Family Issues, 10,* 527–546.

WHALEN, C. K., HENKER, B., CASTRO, J., & GRANGER, D. (1987). Peer perceptions of hyperactivity and medication effects. *Child Development, 58,* 816–828.

WHITBECK, L. B., HOYT, D. R., MILLER, M., & KAO, M. (1992). Parental support, depressed affect, and sexual experience among adolescents. *Youth and Society, 24,* 166–177.

WHITBECK, L. B., HOYT, D. R., SIMONS, R. L., CONGER, R. D., ELDER, G. H., JR., LORENZ, F. O., & HUCK, S. (1992). Integenerational continuity of parental rejection and depressed affect. *Journal of Personality and Social Psychology, 63,* 1036–1049.

WHITBOURNE, S. K., ELLIOT, L. B., ZUSCHLAG, M. K., & WATERMAN, A. S. (1992). Psychosocial development in adulthood: A 22-year sequential study. *Journal of Personality and Social Psychology, 63,* 260–271.

WHITE, J., & ALLERS, C. T. (1994). Play therapy with abused children: A review of the literature. *Journal of Counseling and Development, 72,* 390–394.

WHITE, J. M. (1992). Marital status and well-being in Canada. *Journal of Family Issues, 13,* 390–409.

WHITE, K. J., & KISTNER, J. (1992). The influence of teacher feedback on young children's peer preferences and perceptions. *Developmental Psychology, 28,* 933–940.

WHITE, L. K., & BRINKERHOFF, D. B. (1981). Children's work in the family: Its significance and meaning. *Journal of Marriage and the Family, 43,* 789–798.

WHITE, S. H. (1992). G. Stanley Hall: From philosophy to developmental psychology. *Developmental Psychology, 28,* 25–34.

WHITEHEAD, I., & GRIGLIATTI, T. A. (1993). A correlation between DNA repaired capacity and longevity in adult Drosothili melanogaster. *Journal of Gerontology, 48,* B124–132.

WHITEHOUSE, J. (1981). The role of the initial attracting quality in marriage: Virtues and vices. *Journal of Marital and Family Therapy, 7,* 61–67.

WHITESELL, M. R., & HARTER, S. (1996). The interpersonal context of emotions: Anger with close friends and classmates. *Child Development, 67,* 1345–1359.

WHITESELL, M. R., ROBINSON, N. S., & HARTER, S. (1993). Coping with anger-provoking situations: Young adolescents' theories and effectiveness. *Journal of Applied Developmental Psychology, 14,* 521–554.

WHITTAKER, S., & BRY, B. H. (1991). Overt and covert parental conflict in adolescent problems: Observed marital interaction in clinic and nonclinic families. *Adolescence, 26,* 865–876.

WHITTEN, P., & WHITESIDE, E. J. (1989). Can exercise make you sexier? *Psychology Today, 23,* 42–44.

WIDMAYER, S. M., PETERSON, L. M., LARNER, M., CARNAHAN, S., CALDERON, A., WINGERD, J., & MARSHALL, R. (1990). Predictors of Haitian-American infant development at twelve months. *Child Development, 61,* 410–415.

WIERSON, M., LONG, P. J., & FOREHAND, R. L. (1993). Toward a new understanding of early menarche: The role of environmental stress in pubertal timing. *Adolescence, 28,* 913–924.

WIGFIELD, A., & ECCLES, J. S. (1994). Children's competence beliefs and general self-esteem change across elementary and middle school. *Journal of Adolescence, 14,* 107–138.

WILCOX, K. L., WOLCHIK, S. A., & BRAVER, S. L. (1998). Predictors of maternal preference for joint or sole legal custody. *Family Relations, 47,* 93–101.

WILCOXON, S. A. (1987). Grandparents and grandchildren. *Journal of Counseling and Development, 65,* 289–290.

WILLIAMS, C., & SPARK, A. (1988). Identifying and preventing coronary disease in families. *Medical Aspects of Human Sexuality, 22,* 92–98.

WILLIAMS, K. (1988). Parents reinforce feminine role in girls. *Medical Aspects of Human Sexuality, 22,* 106–107.

WILLIAMS, L. B. (1991). Determinants of unintended childbearing among never-married women in the United States: 1973–1988. *Family Planning Perspectives, 23,* 213–215.

WILLIAMS, L. S. (1992). Adoption actions and attitudes of couples seeking in vitro fertilization. *Journal of Family Issues, 13,* 19–113.

WILLIAMS, P., & LORD, S. R. (1995). Predictors of appearance to a structured exercise program for older women. *Psychology and Aging, 10,* 617–624.

WILLIAMS, R. (1989). The trusting heart. *Psychology Today, 23,* 36–42.

WILLIAMS, S. A., DENNEY, N. W., & SCHADLER, M. (1980). Elderly adults' perception of their own cognitive development during the adult years. *International Journal of Aging and Human Development,* 1980.

WILLIAMSON, J. A., & CAMPBELL, L. P. (1985). Parents and their children comment on adolescence. *Adolescence, 20,* 745–748.

WILLIS, L., THOMAS, P., GARY, P. J., & GOODWIN, J. S. (1987). A prospective study of response to stressful life events in intially healthy elders. *Journal of Gerontology, 42,* 627–630.

WILLITS, F. K., & CRIDER, D. M. (1988). Health rating and life satisfaction in the later middle years. *The Journal of Gerontology, 43,* S172–S176.

WILSON, M. D., KASTRINAKIS, M., D'ANGELO, L. J., & GETSON, M. (1994). Attitudes, knowledge, and behavior regarding condom use in urban Black adolescent males. *Adolescence, 29,* 13–26.

WILSON, P. T. (1985). *Amount of reading, reading instruction, and reading achievement.* Paper presented at the annual meeting of the National Reading Conference.

WILSON, R., & MATHENY, A. (1983). Assessment of temperament in infant twins. *Developmental Psychology, 19,* 172–183.

WILSON, S. M., LARSON, J. H., & STONE, K. L. (1993). Stress among job insecure workers and their spouses. *Family Relations, 42,* 74–80.

WILSON, S. M., & MEDORA, N. P. (1990). Gender comparisons of college students' attitudes toward sexual behavior. *Adolescence, 25,* 615–628.

WILTSE, S. E. (1984). A preliminary sketch of the history of child study in America. *Pedagogical Seminary, 3,* 189–212.

WINDLE, M., & MILLER-TUTZEUER, C. (1992). Confirmatory factor analysis and concurrent validity of the perceived social support-family measure among adolescents. *Journal of Marriage and the Family, 54,* 777–787.

WINEBERG, H. (1992). Childbearing and disillusion of the second marriage. *Journal of Marriage and the Family, 54,* 879–887.

WINEBERG, H. (1994). Marital reconciliation in the United States: Which couples are successful? *Journal of Marriage and the Family, 56,* 80–88.

WINFREE, L. T., JR., BACKSTROM, T. V., & MAYS, G. L. (1994). Social learning theory, self-reported delinquency, and youth gangs: A new twist on a general theory of crime and delinquency. *Youth and Society, 26,* 147–177.

WINGFIELD, A., ABERDEEN, J. S., & STINE, E. A. L. (1991). Word onset gating and linguistic context in spoken word recognition by young and elderly adults. *Journal of Gerontology, 46,* P127–P129.

WINGFIELD, A., LAHAR, C. J., & STINE, E. A. L. (1989). Age and decision strategies in running memory for speech: Effects of prosody and linguistic structure. *Journal of Gerontology, 44,* P106–P113.

WINTRE, M. G., POLIVY, J., & MURRAY, M. A. (1990). Self-predictions of emotional response patterns: Age, sex, and situational determinants. *Child Development, 61,* 1124–1133.

WISE, K. L., BUNDY, K. A., BUNDY, E. A., & WISE, L. A. (1991). Social skills training for young adolescents. *Adolescence, 26,* 233–242.

WISENSALE, S. K. (1992). Toward the 21st century: Family change and public policy. *Family Relations, 41,* 417–422.

WITELSON, S. F. (1987). Neurobiological aspects of language in children. *Child Development, 58,* 653–688.

WITMER, M. (1993). U.S. men and women now have highest mean age at marriage in this century, Census Bureau finds. *Family Planning Perspectives, 25,* 190–191.

WODARSKI, J. S. (1990). Adolescent substance abuse: Practical implications. *Adolescence, 25,* 667–688.

WOHL, A. J. (1988). Your heart and cholesterol. *Medical Aspects of Human Sexuality, 22,* 83–84.

WOLF, F. M. (1981, Summer). On why adolescent formal operators may not be critical thinkers. *Adolescence, 16,* 345–348.

WOLINSKY, F. D., & FITZGERALD, J. F. (1994). The risk of hip fracture among noninstitutionalized older adults. *Journal of Gerontology, 49,*

S165–S175. Virtually all hip fractures require hospitalization and result in considerable health care expenditures.

WOLSSON, L., WHIPPLE, R., DERBY, C. A., AMERMAN, P., & NASHNER, L. (1994). Gender differences in the balance of healthy elderly as demonstrated by dynamic posturography. *Journal of Gerontology, 49,* M160–M167.

WOOD, J., CHAPIN, K., & HANNAH, M. E. (1988). Family environment and its relationship to underachievement. *Adolescence, 23,* 283–290.

WOOD, K. C., BECKER, J. A., & THOMPSON, J. K. (1996). *Journal of Applied Developmental Psychology, 17,* 85–100.

WOOD, N. L., WOOD, R. A., & McDONALD, T. D. (1988). Integration of student development theory into the academic classroom. *Adolescence, 23,* 349–356.

WOODWARD, J. C., & KALYAN-MASIH, V. (1990). Loneliness, coping strategies and cognitive styles of the gifted rural adolescent. *Adolescence, 25,* 977–988.

WOODY-RAMSEY, J., & MILLER, P. H. (1988). The facilitation of selective attention in preschoolers. *Child Development, 59,* 1497–1503.

WOOLEY, J. D., & WELLMAN, H. M. (1990). Young children's understanding of realities, nonrealities, and appearances. *Child Development, 61,* 946–961.

WOOLLEY, J. D. (1997). Thinking about fantasy: Are children fundamentally different thinkers and believers from adults? *Child Development, 68,* 991–1011.

WOROBEY, J. L., & ANGEL, R. J. (1990). Functional capacity and living arrangements of unmarried elderly persons. *Journal of Gerontology, 45,* S95–S101.

WRIGHT, D. W., & YOUNG, R. (1998). The effects of family structure and maternal employment on the development of gender-related attitudes among men and women. *Journal of Family Issues, 19,* 300–314.

WRIGHT, L. K. (1991). The impact of Alzheimer's disease on the marital relationship. *The Gerontologist, 31,* 224–237.

WRIGHT, L. S. (1985). Suicidal thoughts and their relationships to family stress and personal problems among high school seniors and college undergraduates. *Adolescence, 20,* 575–580.

WU, V., & PENNING, M. J. (1997). Marital instability after mid life. *Journal of Family Issues, 18,* 459–478.

YANIV, I., & SHATZ, M. (1990). Heuristics of reasoning and analogy in children's visual perspective taking. *Child Development, 61,* 1491–1501.

YEE, M. D., & BROWN, R. (1992). Self-evaluations and intergroup attitudes in children aged three to nine. *Child Development, 63,* 619–629.

YEH, L. S., & HEDGESPETH, J. (1995). A multiple case study comparison of normal, private preparatory school and substance abusing/mood disordered adolescents and their families. *Adolescence, 30,* 412–428.

YONAS, A। & HARTMAN, B. (1993). Perceiving the affordance of contact in four- and five-month-old infants. *Child Development, 64,* 298–308.

YOUNG, G., & GATELY, T. (1988, June). Neighborhood impoverishment and child maltreatment. *Journal of Family Issues, 9,* 240–254.

YOUNG, K. T. (1990). American conceptions of infant development from 1955 to 1984: What the experts are telling parents. *Child Development, 61,* 17–28.

YOUNG, M. H., MILLER, B. C., NORTON, M. C., & HILL, E. J. (1995). The effect of parental supportive behavior on life satisfaction of adolescent offspring. *Journal of Marriage and the Family, 57,* 813–822.

YOUNG, T. J. (1993). Parricide rates and criminal street violence in the United States: Is there a correlation? *Adolescence, 28,* 171–172.

YOUNGBLADE, L. M., & BELSKY, J. (1992). Parent-child antecedents of five-year-olds' close friendships: A longitudinal analysis. *Development Psychology, 28,* 700–713.

YOUNGER, A. J., & DANIELS, T. N. (1992). Children's reasons for nominating their peers as withdrawn: Passive withdrawal versus active isolation. *Developmental Psychology, 28,* 955–960.

YOUNGER, A. J., & PICCININ, A. M. (1989). Children's recall of aggressive and withdrawn behavior: Recognition memory and likability judgments. *Child Development, 60,* 580–590.

YOUNGER, B. (1992). Developmental change in infant categorization: The perception of correlations among facial features. *Child Development, 63,* 1526–1535.

YOUNGS, G. A., JR., RATHGE, R., MULLIS, R., & MULLIS, A. (1990). Adolescent stress and self-esteem. *Adolescence, 25,* 333–342.

ZACKS, R. T., HASHER, L., DOREN, B., HAMM, V., & ATTIG, M. S. (1987). Encoding used memory of explicit and implicit information. *Journal of Gerontology, 42,* 418–422.

ZAHN-WAXLER, C., FRIEDMAN, R. J., COLE, C. M., MIZUTA, I., & HIRUMA, N. (1996). Japanese and United States preschool children's responses to conflict and distress. *Child Development, 67,* 2462–2477.

ZAHN-WAXLER, C., RADKE-YARROW, M., WAGNER, E., & CHAPMAN, M. (1992). Development of concern for others. *Developmental Psychology, 28,* 126–136.

ZAHN-WAXLER, C., ROBINSON, J. L., & EMDE, R. N. (1992). The development of empathy in twins. *Developmental Psychology, 28,* 1038–1047.

ZANI, B. (1991). Male and female patterns in the discovery of sexuality during adolescence. *Journal of Adolescence, 14,* 163–178.

ZAPATA, J. T., KATIMS, D. S., & YIN, Z. (1998). A two-year study of patterns and predictors of substance use among Mexican American youth. *Adolescence, 33,* 391–403.

ZARBATANY, L., HARTMANN, D. P., & RANKIN, D. B. (1990). The psychological functions of preadolescent peer activities. *Child Development, 61,* 1067–1080.

ZARIT, S. H., COLE, K. D., & GUIDER, R. L. (1981). Memory training strategies and subjective complaints of memory in the aged. *Gerontologist, 21,* 158–165.

ZARLING, C. L., HIRSCH, B. J., & LANDRY, S. (1988). Maternal social networks and mother-infant interactions in full-term and very low birthweight, preterm infants. *Child Development, 59,* 178–185.

ZARSKI, J. J., BUBENZER, D. L., & WEST, J. D. (1986). Social interest, stress, and the prediction of health status. *Journal of Counseling and Development, 64,* 386–388.

ZEBROWITZ, L. A., & MONTEPARE, J. M. (1992). Impressions of baby-faced individuals across the life span. *Developmental Psychology, 28,* 1143–1152.

ZELAZO, N. A., ZELAZO, P. R., COHEN, K. M., & ZELAZO, P. D. (1993). Specificity of practice effects on elementary neuromotor patterns. *Developmental Psychology, 29,* 686–691.

ZELKOWITZ, P. (1987). Social support and aggressive behavior in young children. *Family Relations, 36,* 129–134.

ZEMAN, J., & GARBER, J. (1996). Display rules for anger, sadness, and pain: It depends on who is watching. *Child Development, 67,* 957–973.

ZENTALL, S. A., & MEYER, M. J. (1987). Self-regulation of stimulation from ADD-H children during reading and vigilance task performance. *Journal of Abnormal Child Psychology, 15,* 519–536.

ZERBE, K. J. (1992). Why eating-disordered patients resist sex therapy: A response to Simpson and Ramberg. *Journal of Sex and Marital Therapy, 18,* 55–64.

ZERN, D. S. (1991). Stability and change in adolescents' positive attitudes toward guidance in moral development. *Adolescence, 26,* 261–272.

ZESKIND, P. S., KLEIN, L., & MARSHALL, T. R. (1992). Adults' perceptions of experimental modifications of durations of pauses and expiratory sounds in infant crying. *Developmental Psychology, 28,* 1153–1162.

ZIETLOW, P. H., & VAN LEAR, C. A., JR. (1991). Marriage duration and relational control: A study of developmental patterns. *Journal of Marriage and the Family, 53,* 773–785.

ZIMMERMAN, R. S., SPRECHER, S., LANGER, L. M., & HOLLOWAY, C. D. (1995). Adolescents' perceived ability to say "no" to unwanted sex. *Journal of Adolescent Research, 10,* 383–399.

ZIMMERMAN, S. L. (1992). Family trends: What implications for family policy? *Family Relations, 41,* 423–429.

ZOLLAR, A. C., & WILLIAMS, J. S. (1987). The contribution of marriage to the life satisfaction of black adults. *Journal of Marriage and the Family, 49,* 87–92.

ZUCAVIN, S. J. (1988). Fertility patterns: Their relationships to child physical abuse and child neglect. *Journal of Marriage and the Family, 50,* 983–993.

ZUCKER, R. A., & GOMBERG, E. S. L. (1986). Etiology of alcoholism reconsidered: The case for a biopsychosocial process. *American Psychologist, 41,* 783–793.

ZUCKERMAN, D. (1985, January). Too many sibs put our nation at risk? *Psychology Today, 19,* 5, 10.

ZUO, J. (1992). The reciprocal relationship between marital interaction and marital happiness: A three-wave study. *Journal of Marriage and the Family, 54,* 870–878.

ZURAVIN, S. J. (1991). Unplanned childbearing and family size: Their relationship to child neglect and abuse. *Family Planning Perspectives, 23,* 155–161.

ZUSMAN, J. (1966, January). Some explanations of the changing appearance of psychotic patients: Antecedents of the social breakdown syndrome concept. *Milband Memorial Fund Quarterly,* p. 64.

ZWEIBEL, N. R., & CASSEL, C. K. (1989). Treatment choices at the end of life: A comparison of decisions by older patients and their physicians—selected proxies. *Gerontologist, 29,* 615–621.

Photo Credits

The photos on the following pages are used courtesy of the photographer and © Lawrence Migdale/PIX: pp. 3, 4, 5 (top left), 6, 24 (top), 59 (bottom), 67, 78, 79 (top), 88, 90, 98 (top), 106 (bottom), 120, 123 (top), 128, 133, 137, 149, 152, 155, 158, 160, 178, 184, 193, 218, 227, 244, 256, 268, 284, 300, 322 (top and bottom), 326, 346, 355, 398, 403 (bottom), 405, 408, 412, 415, 432 (three photos), 433, 437 (bottom), 452, 483, 495 (top), 499, 501, 520, 526, 543, 549, 560.

Other photos: p. 2, Corbis Digital Stock; p. 5 (bottom), Bob Daemmrich/Stock Boston; p. 5 (top right), Billy Barnes/PhotoEdit; p. 8, Frank White/Liaison Agency, Inc.; p. 13 (left), Victor Englebert/Photo Researchers, Inc.; p. 13 (right), Paul W. Lieberhardt; p. 19 (left), Photo Researchers, Inc.; p. 19 (right), Bill Aron/Photo Researchers, Inc.; p. 22, Corbis Digital Stock; p. 24 (bottom), Photo Researchers, Inc.; p. 26, UPI/Corbis; p. 28, Sovfoto/Eastfoto; p. 29, UPI/Corbis; p. 30, Chuck Painter/Stanford University News Service; p. 33 (left), Corbis; p. 33 (right), Corbis; p. 35, Anderson/Monkmeyer Press; p. 37, Thomas McAvoy, Time–Life Picture Agency/Time Life Syndication; p. 38, Index Stock Imagery, Inc.; p. 42, Barbara Penoyar/PhotoDisc, Inc.; p. 44 (top left), D. W. Fawcett/Photo Researchers, Inc.; p. 44 (bottom left), Lennart Nilsson/Albert Bonniers Forlag AB; p. 44 (top right), Albert Bonniers Forlag AB; p. 44 (bottom right), Albert Bonniers Forlag AB; p. 46 (top), Albert Bonniers Forlag AB; p. 46 (bottom), Albert Bonniers Forlag AB; p. 52, Hank Morgan/Science/Photo Researchers, Inc.; p. 55, John Ficara/Woodfin Camp & Associates; p. 56, Runk/Schoenberger/Grant Heilman Photography, Inc.; p. 59 (top), Barbara Campbell/Liaison Agency, Inc.; p. 66, Jose Pelaez/The Stock Market; p. 71, Tom & Dee Ann McCarthy/The Stock Market; p. 76, Corbis Digital Stock; p. 79 (bottom), Margaret Miller/Photo Researchers, Inc.; p. 80, J. T. Miller/The Stock Market; p. 82, Craig Hammell/The Stock Market; p. 86, Lawrence Migdale/Pix; p. 96, Corbis Digital Stock; p. 98 (bottom), Erich Lessing/Art Resource, N.Y.; p. 99 (top), Culver Pictures, Inc.; p. 99 (bottom left), Lewis Hine/Corbis; p. 99 (bottom right), Lewis Hines/Corbis; p. 100 (bottom), Culver Pictures, Inc.; p. 100 (top), Culver Pictures, Inc.; p. 101, Culver Pictures, Inc.; p. 102, Corbis; p. 103 (left), Gesell Institute; p. 103 (right), Stanford University News Service; p. 105, Corbis; p. 106 (top), Penguin Books USA, Inc.; p. 110, Corbis Digital Stock; p. 111, Kathy Ferguson/PhotoEdit; p. 112, Jim Pickerell/The Image Works; p. 121, Bob Daemmrich/The Image Works; p. 123 (bottom), Nathan Benn/Stock Boston; p. 125 (top), Byron/Monkmeyer Press; p. 125 (bottom), Dollarhide/Monkmeyer Press; p. 129, Jeremy Horner/Tony Stone Images; p. 131, Kopstein/ Monkmeyer Press; p. 134, Alexis Duclos/Liaison Agency, Inc.; p. 135, Nancy Sheehan/PhotoEdit; p. 141, Cindy Charles/PhotoEdit; p. 146, Corbis Digital Stock; p. 148, David Wells/The Image Works; p. 153, Dorothy Littell/Stock Boston; p. 156, Billy E. Barnes/Stock Boston; p. 157, John Eastcott/The Image Works; p. 162, Will Faller; p. 164, David Young Wolff/PhotoEdit; p. 169, Carolyn Rovee-Collier; p. 173, Kopstein/Monkmeyer Press; p. 177, Charlyn Zlotnik/Woodfin Camp & Associates; p. 180, Conklin/Monkmeyer Press; p. 185, Ken Cavanagh/Photo Researchers, Inc.; p. 192, Corbis Digital Stock; p. 194, Kerbs/Monkmeyer Press; p. 197 (top), Bob Daemmrich/Stock Boston; p. 197 (bottom), Photofest; p. 198, Dorothy Littell Greco/The Image Works; p. 201, Das/Monkmeyer Press; p. 202, John Eastcott/The Image Works; p. 203, David W. Hamilton/The Image Bank; p. 204, Will & Deni McIntyre/Science Source/Photo Researchers, Inc.; p. 205, David Young Wolff/Picture Network International/Picture Quest; p. 206, J. Pickerell/The Image Works; p. 207 (3 photos), Carroll Izard; p. 207 (far right), Tiffany M. Field, Ph.D.; p. 209, E. Crews/The Image Works; p. 210, Susan Johns/Photo Researchers, Inc.; p. 211, Catherine Ursillo/Photo Researchers, Inc.; p. 212, Brady/Monkmeyer Press; p. 219, Collins/Monkmeyer Press; p. 224, Scott Cunningham/Merrill Education; p. 228, Mark Ludak/Impact Visuals Photo & Graphics, Inc.; p. 235, Grantpix/Monkmeyer Press; p. 236, James Marshall/The Stock Market; p. 238, Dorothy Littell/Stock Boston; p. 239, Walter Hodges/Tony Stone Images;

p. 242, J. Gerard Smith/Photo Researchers, Inc.; p. 245, Jim Whitmer Photography; p. 247, Michael Newman/PhotoEdit; p. 250, M. Bridwell/PhotoEdit; p. 251, Jim Pickerell/Stock Boston; p. 252, Esbin-Ansro/The Image Works; p. 255, Arthur Tilley/FPG International LLC; p. 261, AP/Wide World Photos; p. 264, Monkmeyer/Byron/Monkmeyer Press; p. 273, Richard Shock/Liaison Agency, Inc.; p. 282, Corbis Digital Stock; p. 287, Richard Hutchings/Photo Researchers, Inc.; p. 288, Bob Daemmrich/The Image Works; p. 290, Chuck Savage/The Stock Market; p. 292, Farrell Grehan/Photo Researchers, Inc.; p. 293, Richard Shock/Liaison Agency, Inc.; p. 298, Chuck Savage/The Stock Market; p. 305, Ron Chapple/Picture Network International/Picture Quest; p. 311, Frank Siteman/Stock Boston; p. 312, Schnepf/Liaison Agency, Inc.; p. 316, Susan Rosenberg/Science Photo Library/Photo Researchers, Inc.; p. 320, Will & Deni McIntyre/SuperStock, Inc.; p. 324, Bob Daemmrich/The Image Works; p. 327, Jim Harrison/Stock Boston; p. 330, L. Kolvoord/The Image Works; p. 331, Jim Bourg/Liaison Agency, Inc.; p. 333, Ken Lax/Photo Researchers, Inc.; p. 336, David Young Wolff/Tony Stone Images; p. 338, Rashid/Monkmeyer Press; p. 340, Rob Crandall/Stock Boston; p. 344, Corbis Digital Stock; p. 349, Mark Burnett/Stock Boston; p. 351, Tony Freeman/PhotoEdit; p. 352, Bob Daemmrich/Stock Boston; p. 356, Mark Anderson/Picture Network International/Picture Quest; p. 357, Paul Barton/The Stock Market; p. 359, LeDuc/Monkmeyer Press; p. 360, Richard T. Nowitz/Photo Researchers, Inc.; p. 365, Smith/Monkmeyer Press; p. 367, Kevin Cooper/AP/ Wide World Photos; p. 368, Andrew Lichtenstein/ Impact Visuals Photo & Graphics, Inc.; p. 372, Laima Druskis/Pearson Education/PH College; p. 374, Dunn/Monkmeyer Press; p. 377, PBJ Pictures/Liaison Agency, Inc.; p. 381, Paul Avis/Liaison Agency, Inc.; p. 384, Richard Steedman/The Stock Market; p. 390, Amy Etra/PhotoEdit; p. 394, Bob Daemmrich/ Stock Boston; p. 396, Jeff Isaac Greenberg/Photo Researchers, Inc.; p. 402, Michael Newman/PhotoEdit; p. 403 (top), Chuck Fishman/Woodfin Camp & Associates; p. 409, Bill Gillette/Stock Boston; p. 423, Grantpix/Monkmeyer Press; p. 428, Tom Stewart/The Stock Market; p. 430, David Stoeklein/The Stock Market; p. 435, John Henley/The Stock Market; p. 437 (top), AP/Wide World Photos; p. 439, Topham/The Image Works; p. 441, Dennis MacDonald/PhotoEdit; p. 443, Nathan Benn/Stock Boston; p. 446, David J. Sams/Stock Boston; p. 448, Dion Ogust/The Image Works; p. 449, James Wilson/Woodfin Camp & Associates; p. 453, Alan Carey/The Image Works; p. 457, AP/Wide World Photos; p. 462, Corbis Digital Stock; p. 465, P. Gontier/The Image Works; p. 466, Frank Siteman/Stock Boston; p. 473, Joe Carini/The Image Works; p. 480, Darren McCollester/Liaison Agency, Inc.; p. 488, Ariel Skelley/The Stock Market; p. 489, Vincent DeWitt/Stock Boston; p. 490, Catherine Lambermont/Liaison Agency, Inc.; p. 491, Bob Daemmrich/Stock Boston; p. 492, Orland Sentinel/Liaison Agency, Inc.; p. 493, Bob Daemmrich/The Image Works; p. 495 (bottom), Tony Freeman/PhotoEdit; p. 497, Elyse Lewin/The Image Bank; p. 500, Ed Wheeler/The Stock Market; p. 504, Nikola Solic/AP/Wide World Photos; p. 505, Stu Rosner/Stock Boston; p. 512, Dennis MacDonald/PhotoEdit; p. 515, Barbara Alper/Stock Boston; p. 517, Melanie Carr/Index Stock Photography; p. 522, Cindy Charles/PhotoEdit; p. 523, Roy Morsch/The Stock Market; p. 531, Nancy Brown/The Image Bank; p. 532, Ronnie Kaufman/The Stock Market; p. 536, Jon Feingersh/The Stock Market; p. 538, B. Bachmann/The Image Works; p. 544, Michael A. Keller Studios/The Stock Market; p. 545, Elyse Lewin/The Image Bank; p. 556, Corbis Digital Stock; p. 559, Bob Daemmrich/Stock Boston; p. 563, John Moss/Photo Researchers, Inc.; p. 565 (top), Jose L. Pelaez/The Stock Market; p. 565 (bottom), Sean O'Brien/Custom Medical Stock Photo, Inc.; p. 566, Ray Ellis/Photo Researchers, Inc.; p. 567, Rick Reinhard/Impact Visuals Photo & Graphics, Inc.; p. 570, Chris Takagi/Impact Visuals Photo & Graphics, Inc.; p. 573, Homer Sykes/Woodfin Camp & Associates; p. 574, Nathan Benn/Stock Boston.

Name Index

Subject Index